The Illustrated Bible

PART 3

Dino Mazzoli

London | New York

Published by Clink Street Publishing 2020

First edition.

ISBN:
978-1-913136-96-3 - paperback

HOW THE GOSPELS WERE WRITTEN

AT FIRST READING, SOMETHING IS IMMEDIATELY EVIDENT: THE FIRST THREE GOSPELS – MATTHEW, MARK AND LUKE – RESEMBLE ONE ANOTHER IN MANY PASSAGES, THEY RELATE THE SAME EVENTS, OFTEN IN THE SAME SEQUENCE. THIS IS WHY THEY ARE CALLED THE SYNOPTIC GOSPELS, WHICH MEANS THAT WE COULD PLACE THEM IN THREE COLUMNS TO COMPARE THE THREE WAYS OF RELATING THE SAME EVENT IN RATHER SIMILAR WORDS.
LITTLE BY LITTLE MODERN STUDIES HELP US TO FIND THE LINKS AND DEPENDENCES IN THE SYNOPTIC GOSPELS, BUT THE MORE RELIABLE SPECIALISTS ARE VERY MODEST IN THEIR CONCLUSIONS; WE WOULD NOT PRESUME TO REPLACE THEM IN SETTLING TRICKY QUESTIONS.

CONTRARIWISE, JOHN, BEGINNING WITH HIS PROLOGUE, AFFIRMS HIS ORIGINALITY AND ONLY FROM TIME TO TIME IS HE IN LINE WITH THE OTHERS.
IT WOULD BE A MISTAKE TO THINK THAT THE GOSPELS HAD BEEN WRITTEN IN ONE PIECE BY MEN LIKE MATTHEW, MARK OR LUKE WHO AT A GIVEN TIME DECIDED TO RECORD BY MEANS OF THE WRITTEN WORD THE ACTIVE MINISTRY AND THE TEACHING OF JESUS.
VERY GRADUALLY THERE EMERGES A NEED TO HAVE A WRITTEN RECORD OF THEIR TESTIMONY TO SAFEGUARD THE MEMORY OF IT; THIS IS WHAT WE DO DURING A REUNION, WE REGISTER A TESTIMONY IN ORDER TO SHARE IT WITH OTHERS.

THE GOSPEL IS AN EXCEPTIONAL AND UNIQUE WORK AMONG THE LITERARY WRITINGS OF ALL TIMES.
THE GOSPEL LEAVES US ITS PERFUME OF TRUTH EACH TIME WE ARE CAPABLE OF OPENING OURSELVES TO IT.

THE GOSPEL OF MATTHEW

WHO WAS MATTHEW, KNOWN ALSO AS LEVI? WE READ IN THE BIBLE THAT HE WAS A TAX COLLECTOR AND THAT JESUS CALLED HIM TO BE ONE OF HIS APOSTLES. AND YET WE KNOW FOR CERTAIN THAT THE GOSPEL UNDER HIS NAME WAS DRAWN UP IN ITS ACTUAL FORM TOWARDS THE YEAR 80 CE THAT IS AFTER HIS DEATH. COULD THE AUTHOR HAVE BEEN ONE OF HIS DISCIPLES AND USED A FIRST DRAFT COMPILED BY MATTHEW?
MOST PROBABLY THIS GOSPEL WAS WRITTEN IN A CHRISTIAN COMMUNITY OF BOTH JEWS AND GREEKS, POSSIBLY AT ANTIOCH, IT WAS A TIME DEEPLY MARKED BY CONFLICT BETWEEN JEWS AND CHRISTIANS, WHEN THE JEWISH COMMUNITY - SUFFERING TERRIBLY FROM THE WAR WITH ROME THAT DESTROYED THE NATION - WAS REORGANIZING ITSELF UNDER THE GUIDE OF THE PHARISEES. THESE LATTER HAD RECENTLY DECIDED TO EXCLUDE ALL JEWS WHO BELIEVED IN JESUS AND WERE MEMBERS OF THE CHRISTIAN COMMUNITY.

THIS GOSPEL INTENDS TO ASSURE CHRISTIAN THAT THEY HAVE NO REASON TO BE TROUBLED EVEN IF THEY ARE REJECTED BY THEIR OWN PEOPLE. THE VERY FACT THAT THE JEWISH COMMUNITY HAD NOT RECOGNIZED ITS MESSIAH RESULTED IN THE LOSS OF ITS RIGHTS TO GOD'S PROMISES, AND GOD HAD CREATED A NEW PEOPLE, WHICH IS THE CHURCH. MATTHEW REFERS TO NUMEROUS TEXTS OF THE OLD TESTAMENT TO PROVE THAT CHRISTIANS ARE THE TRUE HEIRS OF THE PEOPLE OF THE COVENANT.

MATTHEW WAS IMPRESSED BY THE FACT THAT JESUS DURING HIS TWO OR THREE YEARS OF MINISTRY PRESENTED HIMSELF MOST OFTEN AS A PREACHER, AS A TEACHER OF SCRIPTURE. HE INSISTS ON THE WORDS OF JESUS MORE THAN IN THE OTHER GOSPELS.

IT IS NOT A SURPRISE THAT MATTHEW BUILDS HIS GOSPEL AROUND FIVE "DISCOURSES" IN WHICH JESUS' WORDS ARE SPOKEN IN DIFFERENT OCCASIONS.

THE GOSPEL ACCORDING TO MATTHEW

THE ANCESTORS OF JESUS

1 1 THIS IS A DOCUMENT GIVING THE NAMES
OF THE ANCESTORS OF JESUS CHRIST, SON
OF DAVID, SON OF ABRAHAM. 2 ABRAHAM WAS
THE FATHER OF ISAAC,
ISAAC THE FATHER OF
JACOB THE FATHER OF
JUDAH AND HIS BRO-
THERS. 3 JUDAH WAS
THE FATHER OF PEREZ AND
ZARAH, THEIR MOTHER WAS
TAMAR, PEREZ WAS THE
FATHER OF HEZRON, AND
HEZRON OF RAM. 4
RAM WAS THE FATHER OF
AMMINABAD, AMMINABAD
OF NAHSHON, NAHSHON
OF SALMON. 5 SALMON
WAS THE FATHER OF BOAZ.
HIS MOTHER WAS RAHAB.
BOAZ WAS THE FATHER OF
OBED. HIS MOTHER WAS RUTH.
OBED WAS THE FATHER OF
JESSE. 6 JESSE WAS THE
FATHER OF DAVID, THE KING
DAVID WAS THE FATHER OF
SOLOMON. HIS MOTHER HAD
BEEN URIAH'S WIFE. 7
SOLOMON WAS THE FATHER
OF REHOBOAM. THEN CAME
THE KINGS: ABIJAH, ASA, 8 JEHOSHAPHAT, JORAM,
UZZIAH, 9 JOTHAN, AHAZ, HEZEKIAH 10 MANASSEH,
AMON, JOSIAH. 11 JOSIAH WAS THE FATHER OF JE-
CONIAH AND HIS BROTHERS AT THE TIME OF THE DE-
PORTATION TO BABYLON. 12 AFTER THE DEPORTATION
TO BABYLON JECONIAH WAS THE FATHER OF SHEALTIEL
THE FATHER OF ZERUBBABEL.
13 ZERUBBABEL WAS THE FATHER OF ABIUD, ABIUD OF
ELIAKIM, AND ELIAKIM OF AZOR. 14 AZOR WAS THE FA-
THER OF ZADOK, ZADOK THE FATHER OF ACKIM, AND ACKIM
THE FATHER OF ELIUD. 15 ELIUD WAS THE FATHER OF
ELEAZAR, ELEAZAR OF MATTHAN AND MATTHAN OF JACOB.

16 JACOB WAS THE FATHER OF JOSEPH, THE HUSBAND
OF MARY, AND FROM HER CAME JESUS WHO IS CALLED
THE CHRIST, THE ANOINTED.
17 THERE WERE THEN FOURTEEN GENERATIONS IN ALL
FROM ABRAHAM TO DAVID, AND FOURTEEN FROM DAVID
TO THE DEPORTATION TO BABYLON, AND AGAIN FO-
URTEEN FROM THE DEPORTATION TO BABYLON
TO THE BIRTH OF CHRIST.

JESUS BORN OF A VIRGIN MOTHER

18 THIS IS HOW JESUS CHRIST WAS BORN. MARY
HIS MOTHER HAD BEEN GIVEN TO JOSEPH IN MARRI-
AGE BUT BEFORE THEY LIVED TOGETHER, SHE
WAS FOUND TO BE PREGNANT THROUGH THE HO-
LY SPIRIT. 19 THEN JOSEPH, HER HUSBAND,
MADE PLANS TO DIVORCE HER IN ALL SECRECY.
HE WAS AN UPRIGHT MAN, AND IN NO WAY DID HE
WANT TO DISCREDIT HER. 20 WHILE HE WAS PON-
DERING OVER THIS, AN ANGEL OF THE LORD APPEARED
TO HIM IN A DREAM AND SAID, "JOSEPH, DESCENDANT OF
DAVID, DO NOT BE AFRAID TO TAKE MARY AS YOUR

WIFE. SHE HAS CONCEIVED BY THE HOLY SPIRIT,
21 AND WILL BEAR A SON, WHOM YOU ARE TO CALL
'JESUS' FOR HE WILL SAVE HIS PEOPLE FROM THEIR
SINS." 22 ALL THIS HAPPENED IN ORDER TO FULFILL WHAT
THE LORD HAD SAID THROUGH THE PROPHET: 23

> THE VIRGIN WILL CONCEIVE AND BEAR A
> SON, AND HE WILL BE CALLED EMMANUEL

WHICH MEANS: GOD-WITH-US. 24 WHEN JOSEPH WOKE UP,
HE DID WHAT THE ANGEL OF THE LORD TOLD HIM TO DO AND
HE TOOK HIS WIFE TO HIS HOME. 25 SO SHE GAVE BIRTH TO
A SON AND HE HAD NOT HAD RELATION WITH HER.
JOSEPH GAVE HIM THE NAME OF JESUS.

WISE MEN FROM THE EAST

2 1 WHEN JESUS WAS BORN IN BETHLEHEM, IN JUDEA,
DURING THE DAYS OF
KING HEROD, WISE
MEN FROM THE EAST ARRI-
VED IN JERUSALEM. 2
THEY ASKED, "WHERE IS
THE NEWBORN KING OF
THE JEWS? WE SAW THE
RISING OF HIS STAR IN
THE EAST AND HAVE CO-
ME TO HONOR HIM." 3
WHEN HEROD HEARD THIS
HE WAS GREATLY DIST-
URBED AND WITH HIM
ALL JERUSALEM. 4
HE IMMEDIATELY CAL-
LED A MEETING OF ALL
HIGH RANKING PRIESTS
AND THOSE LEARNED IN
THE LAW AND ASKED
THEM WHERE THE
MESSIAH WAS TO BE
BORN. 5 "IN THE
TOWN OF BETHLEHEM
IN JUDEA," THEY TOLD
HIM, "FOR THIS IS WHAT
THE PROPHET WROTE:

> 6 AND YOU, BETHLEHEM, LAND OF JUDAH,
> YOU ARE BY NO MEANS THE LEAST AMONG
> THE CLANS OF JUDAH, FOR FROM YOU
> WILL COME A LEADER, THE ONE WHO
> IS TO SHEPHERD MY PEOPLE ISRAEL."

7 THEN HEROD SECRETLY CALLED THE WISE MEN
AND GATHERED MORE PRECISE INFORMATION ON
THE APPEARANCE OF THE STAR. 8 THEN HE SENT
THEM TO BETHLEHEM WITH THE INSTRUCTION, "GO AND
PRECISE INFORMATION ABOUT THE CHILD. AS SOON
AS YOU HAVE FOUND HIM, REPORT TO ME, SO THAT
I TOO MAY GO AND HONOR HIM."
9 AFTER THE MEETING WITH THE KING, THEY
SET OUT. THE STAR THAT THEY HAD SEEN IN THE
SKY, IN THE EAST, WENT AHEAD OF THEM AND
STOPPED OVER THE PLACE WHERE THE CHILD
WAS. 10 THE WISE MEN WERE OVERJOYED ON
SEEING THE STAR AGAIN. 11 THEY WENT INTO THE

HOUSE AND WHEN THEY SAW THE CHILD WITH MARY
HIS MOTHER, THEY KNELT AND WORSHIPED HIM.
THEY OPENED THEIR BAGS AND OFFERED HIM
THEIR GIFTS OF GOLD, INCENCE AND MYRRH.
12 IN A DREAM THEY WERE WARNED NOT TO GO
BACK TO HEROD, SO THEY RETURNED TO THEIR
HOME COUNTRY BY ANOTHER WAY.

ESCAPE TO EGYPT

13 AFTER THE WISE MEN HAD LEFT, AN ANGEL OF
THE LORD APPEARED IN A DREAM TO JOSEPH AND
SAID, "GET UP, TAKE THE CHILD AND HIS MOTHER AND
FLEE TO EGYPT, AND STAY THERE UNTIL I TELL YOU.
HEROD WILL SOON BE LOOKING FOR THE CHILD IN
ORDER TO KILL HIM." 14 JOSEPH GOT UP, TOOK THE
CHILD AND HIS MOTHER, AND LEFT THAT NIGHT FOR EGYPT,
15 WHERE HE STAYED UNTIL THE DEATH OF HEROD. IN
THIS WAY, WHAT THE LORD HAD SAID THROUGH THE PROPHET
WAS FULFILLED:
I CALLED MY SON OUT OF EGYPT

16 WHEN HEROD FOUND OUT THAT HE HAD BEEN TRICKED BY THE
WISE MEN, HE WAS FURIOUS. HE GAVE ORDERS TO KILL ALL THE
BOYS IN BETHLEHEM AND ITS NEIGHBOURHOOD WHO WERE TWO
YEARS OLD OR UNDER. THIS WAS DONE IN LINE WITH WHAT
HE HAD LEARNED FROM THE WISE MEN ABOUT THE TIME
WHEN THE STAR APPEARED. 17 IN THIS WAY, WHAT THE
PROPHET JEREMIAH HAD SAID WAS FULFILLED

18 A CRY IS HEARD IN RAMAH, WAILING AND
LOUD LAMENTATION: RACHEL WEEPS FOR HER
CHILDREN. SHE REFUSES TO BE COMFORTED,
FOR THEY ARE NO MORE.

RETURN TO NAZARETH

19 AFTER HEROD'S DEATH,
AN ANGEL OF THE LORD
APPEARED IN A DREAM
TO JOSEPH AND SAID,
20 "GET UP, TAKE THE
CHILD AND HIS MOTHER
AND GO BACK TO THE
LAND OF ISRAEL, BE-
CAUSE THOSE WHO
TRIED TO KILL THE CHILD
ARE DEAD." 21 SO JO-
SEPH GOT UP, TOOK THE
CHILD AND HIS MOTHER
AND WENT TO THE
LAND OF ISRAEL. 22
BUT WHEN JOSEPH
HEARD THAT ARCHI-
LAUS HAD SUCCEED-
ED HIS FATHER HEROD
AS KING OF JUDEA, HE
WAS AFRAID TO GO
THERE. HE WAS GIVEN
FURTHER INSTRUCTIONS
IN A DREAM, AND WENT
TO THE REGION OF GALILEE.

23 THERE HE SETTLED IN A TOWN CALLED NAZARETH. IN
THIS WAY WHAT WAS SAID BY THE PROPHETS WERE FULFILLED:
HE SHALL BE CALLED A NAZOREAN

JOHN THE BAPTIST

3 1 IN THE COURSE OF TIME JOHN THE BAPTIST APPEARED IN
THE DESERT OF JUDEA AND PROCLAIMED HIS MESSAGE, 2
"CHANGE YOUR WAYS, THE KINGDOM OF HEAVEN IS NEAR!" 3 IT
WAS ABOUT HIM THAT THE PROPHET ISAIAH SAID: **I HEAR A VOICE
SHOUTING IN THE DESERT: PREPARE THE WAY FOR THE LORD; MAKE
HIS PATHS STRAIGHT.** 4 JOHN HAD A LEATHER GARMENT ON HIS
WAIST AND A CLOAK OF CAMEL'S HAIR; HIS FOOD WAS LOCUSTS AND
WILD HONEY. 5 PEOPLE CAME TO HIM FROM JERUSALEM, ALL JU-
DEA AND THE WHOLE JORDAN
VALLEY, 6 THEY WERE BAP-
TISED BY HIM IN THE JORDAN
AS THEY CONFESSED THEIR SINS.
7 WHEN HE SAW MANY PHA-
RISEES AND SADDUCEES CO-
MING TO WHERE HE BAPTIZED,
HE SAID TO THEM, "BROOD OF
VIPERS! WHO TOLD YOU COULD
ESCAPE THE PUNISHMENT THAT
IS TO COME? 8 LET IT BE SE-
EN YOU ARE SERIOUS IN YOUR
CONVERSION, 9 AND DO
NOT THINK: WE HAVE ABRA-
HAM FOR OUR FATHER; I
TELL YOU THAT GOD CAN
RAISE CHILDREN FOR ABRA-
HAM FROM THESE STONES!
10 THE AXE IS ALREADY LA-
ID TO THE ROOTS OF THE TREES;
ANY TREE THAT DOES NOT
PRODUCE GOOD FRUIT WILL BE
CUT DOWN AND THROWN IN-
TO THE FIRE. 11 I BAPTIZE
YOU IN WATER FOR CONVER-
SION, BUT THE ONE WHO IS
COMING AFTER ME IS MORE
POWERFUL THAN ME. INDEED I AM NOT WORTHY TO CARRY
HIS SANDALS. **HE WILL BAPTISE YOU IN THE HOLY
SPIRIT AND FIRE.**

12 HE HAS THE WINNOWING FAN IN HIS HAND
AND HE WILL CLEAR OUT HIS THRESHING
FLOOR. HE WILL GATHER HIS WHEAT
INTO THE BARN, BUT THE CHAFF HE WILL
BURN IN EVERLASTING FIRE."

314-CCCXIV ©.
DM
06

JESUS BAPTIZED BY JOHN

13 AT THAT TIME JESUS ARRIVED FROM GALI-
LE AND CAME TO JOHN AT THE JORDAN TO

BE BAPTIZED BY
HIM. 14 BUT JOHN
TRIED TO PREVENT
HIM, AND SAID, "HOW
IS IT YOU COME TO
ME: I SHOULD BE
BAPTIZED BY YOU!"
BUT JESUS ANSWE-
RED HIM, "LET IT
BE LIKE THAT FOR
NOW. WE MUST DO
JUSTICE TO GOD'S
PLAN." 15
JOHN AGREED.
16 AS SOON AS HE
WAS BAPTIZED,
JESUS CAME UP FROM
THE WATER. AT ONCE,
THE HEAVENS OPENED
TO HIM AND HE SAW THE
SPIRIT OF GOD COME
DOWN LIKE A DOVE AND
REST UPON HIM. 17 AT
THE SAME TIME A VOICE
FROM HEAVEN WAS HEARD,
"THIS IS MY SON,
THE BELOVED;
HE IS MY CHOSEN ONE."

JESUS TEMPTED IN THE DESERT

4 1 THEN THE SPIRIT LED JESUS INTO THE DES-
ERT TO BE TEMPTED BY THE DEVIL. 2 AFTER
SPENDING FORTY DAYS AND NIGHTS WITHOUT FOOD,
JESUS WAS HUNGRY. 3 THEN THE DEVIL CAME TO
HIM AND SAID, "IF YOU ARE SON OF GOD, ORDER THESE
STONES TO TURN INTO BREAD." 4 BUT JESUS REPLIED,

"SCRIPTURE SAYS, "PEOPLE CANNOT LIVE ON BREAD
ALONE, BUT ON EVERY WORD THAT COMES FROM
THE MOUTH OF GOD."

5 THEN THE DEVIL TOOK JESUS TO THE HOLY CITY, SET
HIM ON THE HIGHEST WALL OF THE TEMPLE AND SAID TO HIM,

6 "IF YOU ARE SON OF GOD, THROW YOURSELF DOWN, FOR
THE SCRIPTURE SAYS, GOD WILL CHARGE HIS ANGELS TO
RESCUE YOU. THEY WILL CARRY YOU LEST A STONE HURTS YOU."
JESUS ANSWERED, "BUT SCRIPTURE ALSO SAYS: 7

YOU SHALL NOT CHALLENGE THE LORD YOUR GOD."

8 THEN THE DEVIL TOOK JESUS TO A VERY HIGH MO-
UNTAIN AND SHOWED HIM ALL THE NATIONS OF THE
WORLD IN ALL THEIR GREATNESS AND SPLENDOR.
AND HE SAID, 9 "ALL THIS I WILL GIVE YOU, IF YOU KNE-
EL AND WORSHIP ME." 10 THEN JESUS ANSWERED,
"BE OFF, SATAN! THE SCRIPTURE SAYS:

WORSHIP THE LORD YOUR GOD AND SERVE
HIM ALONE."

11 THEN THE DEVIL LEFT HIM, AND ANGELS CAME
TO SERVE HIM.

12 WHEN JESUS HEARD THAT JOHN HAD BEEN ARRESTED,
HE WITHDREW INTO GALILEE. 13 HE LEFT NAZARETH, BUT
SETTLED DOWN IN CAPERNAUM, A TOWN BY THE LAKE OF GALI-
LEE, IN THE TERRITORY OF ZEBULUN AND NAPHTALI. 14

IN THIS WAY THE WORD OF THE PROPHET ISAIAH WAS FULFILLED:

15 LAND OF ZEBULUN AND LAND OF NAPHTALI CROSSED
BY THE ROAD OF THE SEA, AND YOU WHO LIVE BY THE JORDAN,
GALILEE, LAND OF PAGANS, LISTEN: 16 THE PEOPLE WHO
LIVED IN DARKNESS HAVE SEEN A GREAT LIGHT; ON THOSE
LIVING IN THE SHADOW LAND OF DEATH, A LIGHT HAS SHONE.

17 FROM THAT TIME ON JESUS BEGAN TO PROCLAIM HIS
MESSAGE, "CHANGE YOUR WAYS: THE KINGDOM OF
HEAVEN IS NEAR." 18 AS JESUS WALKED BY THE LAKE
OF GALILEE, HE SAW TWO BROTHERS, SIMON CALLED PETER,
AND ANDREW HIS BROTHER, CASTING A NET INTO THE LAKE,
FOR THEY WERE FISHERMEN. 19 HE SAID TO THEM, "COME,
FOLLOW ME, AND I WILL MAKE YOU FISHERS OF PEOPLE." 20
AT ONCE THEY LEFT THEIR NETS AND FOLLOWED HIM.
21 WENT ON FROM THERE HE SAW TWO OTHER BROTHERS,
JAMES SON OF ZEBEDEE, AND HIS BROTHER JOHN IN A

BOAT WITH THEIR FATHER ZEBEDEE, MENDING THEIR NETS.
JESUS CALLED THEM. 22 AT ONCE THEY LEFT THE BOAT
AND THEIR FATHER AND FOLLOWED HIM. 23 JESUS
WENT AROUND ALL GALILEE, TEACHING IN THEIR SYNAGO-
GUES, PROCLAIMING THE GOOD NEWS OF THE KINGDOM, AND
CURING ALL KINDS OF SICKNESS AND DISEASE AMONG
THE PEOPLE.
24 THE NEWS ABOUT HIM SPREAD THROUGH THE LAND
OF SYRIA, AND THE PEOPLE BROUGHT ALL THEIR SICK TO
HIM, AND ALL THOSE WHO SUFFERED: THE POSSESSED,
THE DERANGED, THE PARALYZED, HE HEALED THEM ALL.

25 LARGE CROWDS FOLLOWED HIM FROM
GALILEE AND THE TEN CITIES, FROM JERU-
SALEM, JUDEA, AND FROM ACROSS THE JORDAN.

THE BEATITUDES

5 1 WHEN JESUS SAW THE CROWDS, HE
WENT UP TO THE MOUNTAIN. HE SAT
DOWN AND HIS DISCIPLES GATHERED
AROUND HIM. 2 THEN HE SPOKE AND
BEGAN TO TEACH THEM:

3 FORTUNATE ARE THOSE WHO HAVE THE SPIRIT OF
THE POOR, FOR THEIRS IS THE KINGDOM OF HEAVEN.
4 FORTUNATE ARE THOSE WHO MOURN, THEY
SHALL BE COMFORTED.
5 FORTUNATE ARE THE GENTLE, THEY SHALL
POSSESS THE LAND.
6 FORTUNATE ARE THOSE WHO HUNGER AND THIRST
FOR JUSTICE, FOR THEY SHALL BE SATISFIED.
7 FORTUNATE ARE THE MERCIFUL, FOR THEY
SHALL FIND MERCY.
8 FORTUNATE ARE THOSE WITH A PURE
HEART, FOR THEY SHALL SEE GOD.
9 FORTUNATE ARE THOSE WHO WORK FOR PEACE, THEY
SHALL BE CALLED CHILDREN OF GOD.
10 FORTUNATE ARE THOSE WHO ARE PERSECUTED
FOR THE CAUSE OF JUSTICE, FOR THEIRS IS THE
KINGDOM OF HEAVEN.
11 FORTUNATE ARE YOU, WHEN PEOPLE INSULT YOU
AND PERSECUTE YOU AND SPEAK ALL KIND OF EVIL
AGAINST YOU BECAUSE YOU ARE MY FOLLOWERS.

12 BE GLAD AND JOYFUL, FOR A GREAT REWARD IS KEPT
FOR YOU IN GOD. THIS IS HOW THIS PEOPLE PERSECU-
TED THE PROPHETS WHO LIVED BEFORE YOU.

SALT AND LIGHT

13 YOU ARE THE SALT OF THE EARTH. BUT IF SALT HAS LOST
ITS TASTE, HOW CAN IT BE MADE SALTY AGAIN? IT HAS
BECOME USELESS. IT CAN ONLY BE THROWN AWAY AND
PEOPLE WILL TRAMPLE ON IT. 14 YOU ARE THE LIGHT
OF THE WORLD. A CITY BUILT ON A MOUNTAIN CANNOT
BE HIDDEN. 15 NO ONE LIGHTS A LAMP AND COVERS IT;
INSTEAD IT IS PUT ON A LAMPSTAND, WHERE IT GIVES
LIGHT TO EVERYONE IN THE HOUSE. 16 IN THE SAME
WAY YOUR LIGHT MUST SHINE BEFORE OTHERS, SO
THAT THEY MAY SEE THE GOOD YOU DO AND PRAISE
YOUR FATHER IN HEAVEN.

MORE PERFECT LAW

17 DO NOT THINK THAT I HAVE COME TO REMOVE THE LAW
AND THE PROPHETS. I HAVE NOT COME TO REMOVE BUT
TO FULFILL THEM. 18 I TELL YOU THIS: AS LONG AS
HEAVEN AND EARTH LAST NOT THE SMALLEST LET-
TER OR STROKE OF THE LAW WILL CHANGE UNTIL
ALL IS FULFILLED. 19
SO THEN, WHOEVER BRE-
AKS THE LEAST IMPORT-
ANT OF THESE COMMAND-
MENTS AND TEACHES
OTHERS TO DO THE SA-
ME WILL BE THE LEAST
IN THE KINGDOM OF HEA-
VEN. ON THE OTHER HAND,
WHOEVER OBEYS THEM AND
TEACHES OTHERS TO DO
THE SAME WILL BE GREAT
IN THE KINGDOM OF HEA-
VEN. 20 I TELL YOU, THEN,
THAT IF YOU ARE NOT
RIGHTEOUS IN A BETTER
WAY THAN THE TEACHERS
OF THE LAW AND THE PHA-
RISEES YOU WILL NEVER
ENTER THE KINGDOM OF
OF HEAVEN.

21 YOU HAVE HEARD THAT
IT WAS SAID TO OUR PE-
OPLE IN THE PAST: DO
NOT COMMIT MURDER;
ANYONE WHO DOES KILL
WILL HAVE TO FACE TRIAL.
22 BUT NOW I TELL YOU:
WHOEVER GETS ANGRY
WITH HIS BROTHER WILL HAVE TO FACE TRIAL. WHOEVER
INSULTS HIS BROTHER DESERVES TO BE BROUGHT BE-
FORE THE COUNCIL, WHOEVER HUMILIATES HIS BRO-
THER DESERVES TO BE THROWN INTO THE FIRE OF HELL.
23 SO, IF YOU ARE ABOUT TO OFFER YOUR GIFT AT THE
ALTAR AND YOU REMEMBER THAT YOUR BROTHER HAS
SOMETHING AGAINST YOU, 24 LEAVE YOUR GIFT
THERE IN FRONT OF THE ALTAR, GO AT ONCE AND MAKE
PEACE WITH YOUR BROTHER, AND THEN COME BACK AND
OFFER YOUR GIFT TO GOD.
25 DON'T FORGET
THIS: BE RECONCILED
WITH YOUR OPPONENT
QUICKLY WHEN YOU
ARE TOGETHER ON
THE WAY TO COURT.
OTHERWISE HE WILL
TURN YOU OVER TO
THE JUDGE, WHO WILL
HAND YOU OVER TO THE
POLICE, WHO WILL PUT
YOU TO JAIL. 26 THERE
YOU WILL STAY, UNTIL
YOU HAVE PAID THE LAST
PENNY.
27 YOU HAVE HEARD THAT
IT WAS SAID: DO NOT
COMMIT ADULTERY.
28 BUT I TELL YOU THIS:
ANYONE WHO LOOKS AT A
WOMAN TO SATISFY HIS
LUST HAS IN FACT ALREADY
COMMITTED ADULTERY
WITH HER IN HIS HEART.

29 SO, IF YOUR RIGHT
EYE CAUSES YOU TO SIN, PULL IT OUT AND THROW IT
AWAY! IT IS MUCH BETTER FOR YOU TO LOSE A PART
OF YOUR BODY THAN TO HAVE YOUR WHOLE BODY THROWN
INTO HELL. 30 IF YOUR RIGHT HAND CAUSES YOU TO
SIN, CUT IT OFF AND THROW IT AWAY! IT IS BETTER
FOR YOU TO LOSE A PART OF YOUR BODY THAN TO HAVE
YOUR WHOLE BODY THROWN INTO HELL.

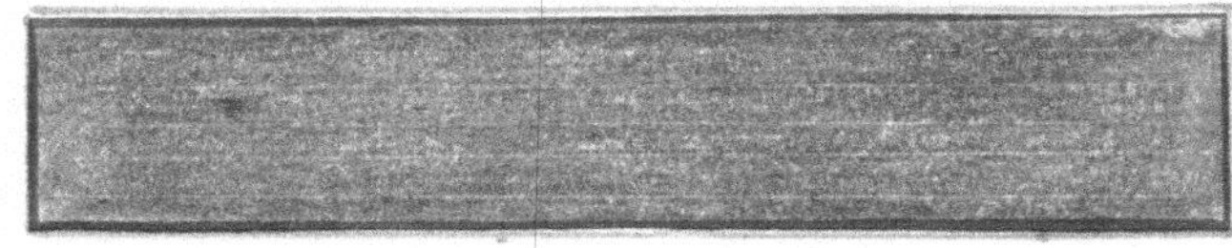

31 IT WAS ALSO SAID: ANYONE WHO DIVORCES HIS
WIFE MUST GIVE HER A WRITTEN NOTICE OF DIVORCE.
32 BUT I TELL YOU IS THIS: IF A MAN DIVORCES HIS
WIFE UNLESS IT BE FOR INFIDELITY, HE CAUSES HER
TO COMMIT ADULTERY. AND THE MAN WHO MARRIES
A DIVORCED WOMAN COMMITS ADULTERY.

OATHS

33 YOU HAVE ALSO HEARD THAT PEOPLE WERE TOLD IN
THE PAST: DO NOT BREAK

YOUR OATH; AN OATH SWORN
TO THE LORD MUST BE KEPT.
34 BUT I TELL YOU THIS:
DO NOT TAKE AN OATH
FOR ANY PROMISE, DO
NOT SWEAR BY THE HE-
AVENS, FOR THEY ARE
GOD'S THRONE, 35 NOR
BY THE EARTH, BECAUSE
IT IS HIS FOOTSTOOL, NOR
BY JERUSALEM BECA-
USE IT IS THE CITY OF
THE GREAT KING 36 DO
NOT EVEN SWEAR BY
YOUR HEAD, BECAUSE YOU
CANNOT MAKE A SINGLE
HAIR WHITE OR BLACK.
37 SAY YES WHEN YOU
MEAN YES AND SAY NO
WHEN YOU MEAN NO.
ANYTHING ELSE YOU SAY
COMES FROM THE DEVIL.
38 YOU HAVE HEARD IT WAS
SAID: AN EYE FOR AN EYE AND
A TOOTH FOR A TOOTH, 39 BUT I TELL YOU THIS; DON'T OPPOSE
EVIL WITH EVIL; IF SOMEONE SLAPS YOU ON YOUR RIGHT CHEEK,
OFFER HIM THE OTHER. 40 IF SOMEONE SUES YOU IN COURT,
FOR YOUR SHIRT, LET HIM HAVE YOUR COAT AS WELL. 41 IF
SOMEONE FORCES YOU TO GO ONE MILE, GO TWO MILES WITH
HIM. 42 GIVE WHEN ASKED AND DO NOT TURN YOUR BACK ON
ANYONE WHO WANTS TO BORROW FROM YOU. 43 YOU

HAVE HEARD IT WAS SAID: LOVE YOUR NEIGHBOR AND HATE YOUR
ENEMY. 44 BUT THIS I TELL YOU: LOVE YOUR ENEMIES AND PRAY
FOR THOSE WHO PERSECUTE YOU, 45 SO THAT YOU MAY BE
CHILDREN OF YOUR FATHER IN HEAVEN. FOR HE MAKES HIS SUN
RISE ON THE WICKED AND THE GOOD, AND GIVES RAIN TO THE
JUST AND THE UNJUST. 46 IF YOU LOVE THOSE WHO LOVE YOU,
WHAT IS SPECIAL ABOUT THAT? DO NOT EVEN TAX COLLECTORS DO
AS MUCH? 47 AND IF YOU ARE FRIENDLY ONLY TO YOUR FRIE-
NDS, WHAT IS SO EXCEPTIONAL ABOUT THAT? DO NOT EVEN
THE PAGANS DO AS MUCH? 48 FOR YOUR PART BE PERFECT,
AS YOUR HEAVENLY FATHER IS RIGHTEOUS AND PERFECT.

FOR GOD ALONE

6 1 BE CAREFUL NOT TO SHOW YOUR RIGHTEOUSNESS
BEFORE PEOPLE. IF YOU DO SO, YOU GAIN NOTHING
FROM YOUR FATHER IN HEAVEN. 2 WHEN YOU GIVE TO
THE POOR, DO NOT HAVE IT TRUMPETED BEFORE YOU, LIKE
THOSE WHO WANT TO BE SEEN IN THE SYNAGOGUES AND
IN THE STREETS SEEKING PEOPLE'S PRAISE. I ASSURE YOU
THEY HAVE BEEN PAID IN FULL. 3 IF YOU GIVE TO THE
POOR, DO NOT LET YOUR LEFT HAND KNOW WHAT
YOUR RIGHT HAND IS DOING, 4 SO THAT YOUR GIFT
REMAINS SECRET. YOUR FATHER WHO SEES WHAT IS KEPT
SECRET, WILL REWARD YOU.
5 WHEN YOU PRAY DO NOT BE LIKE THOSE WHO WANT
TO BE SEEN. THEY LOVE TO STAND AND PRAY IN THE
SYNAGOGUES OR ON STREET CORNERS TO BE SEEN
BY EVERYONE. I ASSURE YOU, THEY HAVE ALREADY BEEN
PAID IN FULL. 6 WHEN YOU PRAY, GO INTO YOUR RO-
OM, CLOSE THE DOOR AND PRAY TO YOUR FATHER WHO
IS WITH YOU IN SECRET; AND YOUR FATHER WHO
SEES WHAT IS KEPT SECRET WILL REWARD YOU.

OUR FATHER...

7 WHEN YOU PRAY, DO NOT USE A LOT OF WORDS,
AS THE PAGANS DO, FOR THEY HOLD THAT THE MORE

THEY SAY, THE MORE THEY WILL BE HEARD. 8 DO NOT BE
LIKE THEM. YOUR FATHER KNOWS WHAT YOU NEED, EVEN
BEFORE YOU ASK HIM. 9 THIS IS HOW YOU SHOULD PRAY:

OUR FATHER IN HEAVEN,
HOLY BE YOUR NAME,
10 YOUR KINGDOM COME
YOUR WILL BE DONE
ON EARTH AS IN HEAVEN
11 GIVE US TODAY THE
KIND OF BREAD WE NEED.
12 FORGIVE US OUR DEBTS
AS WE FORGIVE THOSE
WHO ARE IN DEBT TO US,
13 DO NOT BRING US TO THE
TEST. BUT DELIVER US
FROM THE EVIL ONE.

14 IF YOU FORGIVE OTHERS THEIR WRONGS, YOUR FATHER IN HE-
AVEN WILL FORGIVE YOURS. 15 IF YOU DO NOT FORGIVE OTHERS,
THEN YOUR FATHER WILL NOT FORGIVE YOU EITHER. 16 WHEN
YOU FAST, DO NOT PUT ON A MISERABLE FACE AS DO THE HYPO-
CRITES. THEY PUT ON A GLOOMY FACE, SO PEOPLE CAN SEE
THEY ARE FASTING. I TELL YOU THIS: THEY HAVE BEEN PAID IN
FULL ALREADY. 17 WHEN YOU FAST WASH YOUR FACE AND
MAKE YOURSELF LOOK CHEERFUL, 18 BECAUSE YOU ARE
NOT FASTING FOR APPEARANCES OR FOR PEOPLE, BUT
FOR YOUR FATHER WHO SEES BEYOND APPEARANCES.
AND YOUR FATHER, WHO SEES WHAT IS
KEPT SECRET WILL REWARD YOU.

PATER NOSTER QUI ES IN CÆLIS:
SANCTIFICETUR NOMEN TUUM;
ADVENIAT REGNUM TUUM;
FIAT VOLUNTAS
TUA
SICUT IN CÆLO, ET IN TERRA.
PANEM NOSTRUM QUOTIDIANUM
DA NOBIS HODIE;
ET DIMITTE NOBIS DEBITA NOSTRA,
SICUT ET NOS
DIMITTIMUS DEBITORIBUS NOSTRIS
ET NE NOS INDUCAS
IN TENTATIONEM
SED LIBERA
NOS
A MALO.
315 CCCXV
Amen
© DM 07

(19) DO NOT STORE UP TREASURE FOR YOURSELF HERE
ON EARTH WHERE MOTH AND RUST DESTROY IT, AND
WHERE THIEVES CAN STEAL IT. (20) STORE UP TREASURE
FOR YOURSELF WITH GOD, WHERE NO MOTH OR RUST CAN DES-
TROY NOR THIEF COME AND STEAL IT. (21) FOR WHERE YOUR
TREASURE IS, THERE ALSO YOUR HEART WILL BE.
(22) THE LAMP OF THE BODY IS THE EYE; IF YOUR EYES ARE
ARE SOUND, YOUR WHOLE BODY WILL BE IN THE LIGHT.

(23) IF YOUR EYES ARE DISEASED YOUR WHOLE BODY
WILL BE IN DARKNESS. THEN, IF YOUR LIGHT HAS BE-
COME DARKNESS, HOW DARK WILL BE THE DARKEST PART
OF YOU!

SET YOUR HEART ON THE KINGDOM

(24) NO ONE CAN SERVE TWO MASTERS; FOR HE WILL

EITHER HATE ONE AND LOVE THE OTHER, OR HE WILL BE LO-
YAL TO THE FIRST AND LOOK DOWN ON THE SECOND. YOU CAN-
NOT AT THE SAME TIME SERVE GOD AND MONEY.
(25) THIS IS WHY I TELL YOU NOT TO BE WORRIED ABOUT FO-
OD AND DRINK FOR YOURSELF, OR CLOTHES FOR YOUR BODY.
IS NOT LIFE MORE IMPORTANT THAN FOOD AND IS NOT THE
BODY MORE IMPORTANT THAN CLOTHES? (26) LOOK AT THE
BIRDS OF THE AIR; THEY DO NOT SOW, THEY DO NOT HARVEST
AND DO NOT STORE FOOD IN
BARNS, AND YOUR FATHER
IN HEAVEN FEEDS THEM.
ARE YOU NOT WORTH MUCH
MORE THAN BIRDS?
(27) WHICH OF YOU CAN ADD
A DAY TO HIS LIFE BY WORRY-
ING ABOUT IT? (28) WHY
ARE YOU SO WORRIED FOR
YOUR CLOTHES? LOOK AT
THE FLOWERS IN THE FI-
ELDS HOW THEY GROW.
THEY DO NOT TOIL OR SPIN.
(29) BUT I TELL YOU THAT
NOT EVEN SOLOMON IN
ALL HIS WEALTH WAS CLO-
THED LIKE ONE OF THESE.
(30) IF GOD SO CLOTHES
THE GRASS IN THE FIELD

WHICH BLOOMS TODAY AND
TO BE BURNED TOMORROW
IN A OVEN, HOW MUCH MORE
WILL HE CLOTHE YOU?
WHAT LITTLE FAITH YOU HAVE!
(31) DO NOT WORRY AND
SAY: WHAT ARE WE GOING
TO EAT? WHAT ARE WE GOING TO DRINK? OR; WHAT SHALL
WE WEAR? (32) THE PAGANS BUSY THEMSELVES WITH
SUCH THINGS; BUT YOUR HEAVENLY FATHER KNOWS THAT
YOU NEED THEM ALL. (33) SET YOUR HEART FIRST ON THE
KINGDOM AND JUSTICE OF GOD AND ALL THESE THINGS
WILL ALSO BE GIVEN TO YOU. (34) DO NOT WORRY ABOUT
TOMORROW FOR TOMORROW WILL WORRY ABOUT IT-
SELF. EACH DAY HAS ENOUGH TROUBLE OF ITS OWN.

DO NOT JUDGE AND YOU WILL NOT BE JUDGED

7 (1) DO NOT JUDGE AND YOU WILL NOT BE JUDGED.
(2) IN THE SAME WAY YOU JUDGE OTHERS,
YOU WILL BE JUDGED, AND THE MEASURE
YOU USE FOR OTHERS WILL BE USED FOR YOU.
(3) WHY DO YOU LOOK
AT THE SPECK IN YOUR
BROTHER'S EYE AND
NOT SEE THE PLANK IN
YOUR OWN EYE? (4) HOW
CAN YOU SAY TO YOUR
BROTHER: 'COME, LET
ME TAKE THE SPECK
FROM YOUR EYE,' AS
LONG AS THE PLANK IS
IN YOUR OWN? (5) HYPO-
CRITE, TAKE FIRST THE
PLANK OUT OF YOUR OWN
EYE, THEN YOU WILL SEE
CLEAR ENOUGH TO TAKE
THE SPECK OUT OF YOUR
BROTHER'S EYE.

(6) DO NOT GIVE WHAT IS
HOLY TO THE DOGS, OR
THROW YOUR PEARLS TO
PIGS; THEY MIGHT TRAMPLE
ON THEM AND EVEN
TURN ON YOU AND TEAR
YOU TO PIECES.

(7) ASK AND YOU WILL
RECEIVE; SEEK AND
YOU WILL FIND; KNOCK AND THE DOOR WILL BE
OPENED. (8) FOR EVERYONE WHO ASKS, RECE-
IVES; WHOEVER SEEKS, FINDS; AND THE DOOR
WILL BE OPENED TO HIM WHO KNOCKS.

(9) WOULD ANY OF YOU GIVE A STONE TO YOUR
SON WHEN HE ASKS FOR BREAD? (10) OR GIVE
HIM A SNAKE WHEN HE ASKS FOR A FISH?
(11) AS BAD AS YOU ARE, YOU KNOW HOW TO GIVE
GOOD THINGS TO YOUR CHILDREN. HOW MUCH MORE,
THEN, WILL YOUR FATHER IN HEAVEN GIVE GOOD
THINGS TO THOSE WHO ASK HIM! (12) SO, TO DO

OTHERS WHATEVER YOU WOULD THAT OTHERS DO TO YOU:
THERE YOU HAVE THE LAW AND THE PROPHETS.

(13) ENTER THROUGH THE NARROW GATE; FOR WIDE IS
THE GATE AND BROAD IS THE ROAD THAT LEADS TO
DESTRUCTION, AND MANY GO THAT WAY. (14) HOW
NARROW IS THE GATE THAT LEADS TO LIFE AND HOW
ROUGH THE ROAD; FEW THERE ARE WHO FIND IT.

THE TREE IS KNOWN BY ITS FRUITS

15 BEWARE OF FALSE PROPHETS:
THEY COME TO YOU IN SHEEP'S CLOTHING
BUT INSIDE THEY
ARE WILD WOLVES.

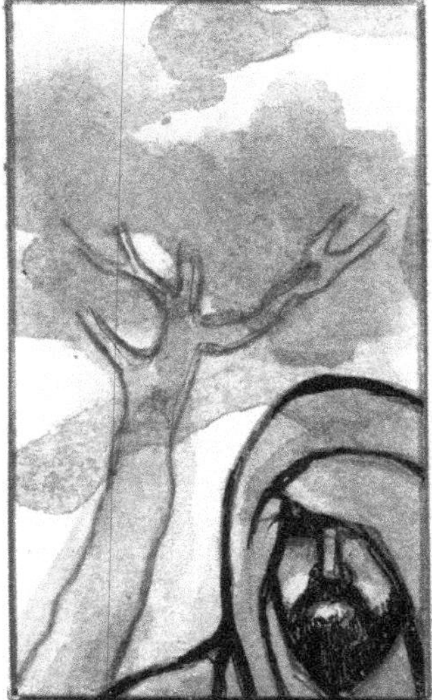

16 YOU WILL RECOG-
NIZE THEM BY THEIR
FRUITS. DO YOU EVER
PICK GRAPES FROM
THORNBUSHES, OR
FIGS FROM THISTLES?

17 A GOOD TREE AL-
WAYS PRODUCES
GOOD FRUITS, A ROT-
TEN TREE PRODUCES
BAD FRUITS. 18 A GO-
OD TREE CANNOT PRO-
DUCE BAD FRUIT AND A
ROTTEN TREE CANNOT
BEAR GOOD FRUIT. 19
ANY TREE THAT DOES NOT
BEAR GOOD FRUIT IS CUT
DOWN AND THROWN IN THE
FIRE. 20 SO YOU WILL
KNOW THEM BY THE
FRUIT.

WISE AND FOOLISH BUILDERS

21 NOT EVERYONE WHO SAYS TO ME: LORD! LORD! WILL
ENTER THE KINGDOM OF HEAVEN, BUT THE ONE WHO DOES
THE WILL OF MY FATHER IN HEAVEN. 22 MANY WILL SAY TO
ME ON THAT DAY, "LORD, LORD, DID WE NOT SPEAK IN YOUR NA-
ME? DID WE NOT CAST OUT DEVILS AND PERFORM MANY MI-
RACLES IN YOUR NAME?" 23 THEN I WILL TELL THEM OPEN-
LY: I HAVE NEVER KNOW YOU; AWAY FROM ME, YOU EVIL
PEOPLE!
24 "SO, THEN, ANYONE WHO HEARS THESE WORDS OF MINE
AND ACTS ACCORDINGLY IS LIKE A WISE MAN WHO BUILT HIS

HOUSE ON ROCK. 25 THE RAIN POURED, THE RIVERS FLO-
ODED, AND THE WIND BLEW AND STRUCK THAT HOUSE BUT
IT DID NOT COLLAPSE BECAUSE IT WAS BUILT ON ROCK. 26
BUT ANYONE WHO HEARS THESE WORDS OF MINE AND
DOES NOT ACT ACCORDINGLY, IS LIKE A FOOL WHO BUILT
HIS HOUSE ON SAND. 27 THE RAIN POURED, THE RIVERS
FLOODED AND THE WIND BLEW AND STRUCK THAT HOUSE,
IT COLLAPSED AND THE RUIN WAS COMPLETE."

28 WHEN JESUS HAD FINISHED THIS DISCOURSE,
THE CROWDS WERE AMAZED AT HIS TEACHING, 29
BECAUSE HE TAUGHT WITH AUTHORITY UNLIKE THE
REST OF THE TEACHERS OF THE LAW.

CURE OF A LEPER

8 1 WHEN JESUS CAME DOWN FROM THE
MOUNTAIN, LARGE CROWDS FOLLOWED
HIM, 2 THEN A LEPER CAME FORWARD.
HE KNELT BEFORE HIM AND SAID, "SIR, IF YOU
WANT TO, YOU CAN MAKE ME CLEAN." 3 JESUS
STRETCHED OUT HIS HAND, TOUCHED HIM AND SAID,
"I WANT TO, BE CLEAN AGAIN." AT THAT VERY MOMENT
THE MAN WAS CLEANSED FROM HIS LEPROSY. 4
THEN JESUS SAID TO HIM, "SEE THAT YOU DO NOT

TELL ANYONE, BUT GO TO THE PRIEST, HAVE YOUR-
SELF DECLARED CLEAN, AND OFFER THE GIFT
THAT MOSES ORDERED AS PROOF OF IT."

THE FAITH OF THE CENTURION

5 WHEN JESUS ENTERED CAPERNAUM, AN ARMY CAPTAIN
APPROACHED HIM TO ASK HIS HELP, 6 "SIR, MY SERVANT
LIES SICK AT HOME. HE IS PARALYZED AND SUFFERS TER-
RIBLY." 7 JESUS SAID TO HIM, "I WILL COME AND HEAL HIM."
8 THE CAPTAIN ANSWERED, "I AM NOT WORTHY TO HAVE YOU
UNDER MY ROOF. JUST GIVE AN ORDER AND MY BOY WILL BE
HEALED. 9 FOR I AM A MAN UNDER ORDERS AND I HAVE SOL-
DIERS UNDER ME. AND IF
I TELL MY SERVANT: 'GO,'
HE GOES, AND IF I SAY TO AN-
OTHER: 'COME,' HE COMES,
AND TO MY SERVANT: 'DO THIS,'
HE DOES IT." 10 WHEN JESUS
HEARD THIS HE WAS ASTO-
NISHED AND SAID TO HIS
FOLLOWERS, "I TELL YOU, I
HAVE NOT FOUND SUCH FAITH
IN ISRAEL. 11 I SAY TO YOU,
MANY WILL COME FROM
EAST AND WEST AND SIT WITH
ABRAHAM, ISAAC AND JACOB
AT THE FEAST IN THE KING-
DOM OF HEAVEN; 12 BUT
THOSE WHO EXPECTED THE
KINGDOM WILL BE THROWN
INTO THE DARKNESS; THERE
THEY WILL WAIL AND GRIND
THEIR TEETH". 13 THEN
JESUS SAID TO THE CAP-
TAIN, "GO HOME NOW. AS YOU
BELIEVED, SO LET IT BE." AND
AT THE MOMENT HIS SERVANT
WAS HEALED. 14 JESUS
WENT TO PETER'S HOUSE,
AND FOUND PETER'S MO-
THER-IN-LAW IN BED WITH FEVER. 15 HE TOOK HER BY THE
HAND AND THE FEVER LEFT HER; SHE GOT UP AND BEGAN
TO WAIT ON HIM.
16 TOWARDS EVENING THEY BROUGHT TO JESUS MANY POS-
SESSED BY EVIL SPIRITS, AND WITH A WORD HE DROVE OUT
THE SPIRITS. HE ALSO HEALED ALL WHO WERE SICK, 17
IN DOING THIS HE FULFILLED WHAT WAS SAID BY THE PRO-
PHET ISAIAH:

**HE BORE OUR INFIRMITIES AND TOOK
ON HIMSELF OUR DISEASES.**

JESUS CALMS THE STORM

18 WHEN HE SAW THE CROWD PRESS AROUD HIM
JESUS GAVE ORDERS TO CROSS TO THE OTHER SHORE.
19 A TEACHER OF THE LAW APPROACHED HIM AND SAID,
"MASTER, I WILL FOLLOW YOU WHEREVER YOU GO." 20
JESUS SAID TO HIM, "FOXES HAVE HOLES AND BIRDS HAVE
NESTS, BUT THE SON OF MAN HAS NOWHERE TO LAY HIS
HEAD." 21 ANOTHER DISCIPLE SAID TO HIM, "LORD, LET ME
GO AND BURY MY FATHER FIRST." 22 BUT JESUS ANSWERED
HIM, "FOLLOW ME, AND LET THE DEAD BURY THEIR OWN DEAD."

23 JESUS GOT INTO THE BOAT AND HIS DISCEPLES
FOLLOWED HIM. 24 WITHOUT WARNING A STORM HIT
THE LAKE, WITH WAVES SWEEPING THE BOAT. BUT JESUS
WAS ASLEEP. 25 THEY WOKE HIM AND CRIED, "LORD SAVE
US! WE ARE LOST!" 26 BUT JESUS ANSWERED, "WHY
ARE YOU SO AFRAID, YOU OF LITTLE FAITH?" THEN HE
STOOD UP AND ORDERED THE WIND AND SEA; AND IT BE-
CAME COMPLETELY CALM. 27 THE PEOPLE WERE ASTO-
NISHED. THEY SAID, "WHAT KIND OF MAN IS HE? EVEN
THE WINDS AND THE SEA OBEY HIM."

THE DEMONIACS AND THE PIGS

28 WHEN JESUS REACHED GADARA ON THE OTHER SIDE HE
WAS MET BY TWO DEMONIACS WHO CAME OUT FROM THE

TOMBS. THEY WERE SO
FIERCE THAT NO ONE
DARED TO PASS THAT
WAY. 29 SUDDENLY
THEY SHOUTED, "WHAT DO
YOU WANT WITH US, YOU,
SON OF GOD! HAVE YOU CO-
ME TO TORTURE US BEFO-
RE THE TIME?" 30 AT SO-
ME DISTANCE AWAY
THERE WAS A LARGE HERD
OF PIGS FEEDING. 31 SO
THE DEMONS BEGGED
HIM, "IF YOU DRIVE US
OUT, SEND US TO THAT
HERD OF PIGS."
32 JESUS ORDERED
THEM, "GO." SO THEY
LEFT AND WENT INTO
THE PIGS. THE WHOLE HERD
RUSHED DOWN THE CLIFF
INTO THE LAKE AND DROW-
NED. 33 THE MEN IN
CHARGE OF THEM RAN
OFF TO THE TOWN
WHERE THEY TOLD ME
THE WHOLE STORY,
ALSO WHAT HAPPENED
TO THE MEN POSSESSED WITH THE DEMONS.
34 THEN THE WHOLE TOWN WENT OUT TO MEET
JESUS, AND WHEN THEY SAW HIM, THEY BEGGED
HIM TO LEAVE THEIR TERRITORY.

JESUS CURES A PARALYTIC

1 9 JESUS GOT BACK INTO THE BOAT, CROSSED THE
LAKE AGAIN, AND CAME TO HIS HOMETOWN. 2
HERE THEY BROUGHT A PARALYZED MAN TO
HIM, LYING ON A BED.
JESUS SAW THEIR FAITH
AND SAID TO THE PARA-
LYTIC, "COURAGE MY
SON! YOUR SINS ARE
FORGIVEN." 3 THEN
SOME TEACHERS OF THE
LAW SAID TO THEMSEL-
VES, "THIS MAN INS-
ULTS GOD." 4 JESUS
WAS AWARE OF WHAT
THEY WERE THINKING
AND SAID, "WHY HAVE YOU
SUCH EVIL THOUGHTS?
5 WHICH IS EASIER TO
SAY: 'YOUR SINS ARE FOR-
GIVEN', OR 'STAND UP AND
WALK'? 6 YOU MUST
KNOW THAT THE SON OF
MAN HAS AUTHORITY ON
EARTH TO FORGIVE SINS."
HE THEN SAID TO THE PA-
RALYZED MAN, "STAND
UP! TAKE YOUR BED
AND GO HOME." 7
THE MAN GOT UP, AND
WENT HOME 8 WHEN
THE CROWDS SAW THIS,
THEY WERE FILLED
WITH AWE AND PRAISED GOD FOR GIVING SUCH PO-
WER TO PEOPLE.

JESUS CALLS MATTHEW

9 AS JESUS MOVED ON FROM THERE, HE SAW A MAN
NAMED MATTHEW AT HIS SIT IN THE CUSTOM HOUSE, AND
HE SAID TO HIM, "FOLLOW ME." AND MATTHEW GOT UP AND

FOLLOWED HIM. 10 NOW IT HAPPENED, WHILE JESUS WAS
AT TABLE IN MATTHEW'S HOUSE, MANY TAX COLLECT-
ORS AND OTHER SINNERS JOINED JESUS AND HIS DI-
SCIPLES. 11 WHEN THE PHARISEES SAW THIS THEY
SAID TO HIS DISCIPLES, "WHY IS IT THAT YOUR MASTER
EATS WITH THOSE SINNERS AND TAX COLLECTORS?"
12 WHEN JESUS HEARD THIS HE SAID, "HEALTHY PEOPLE
DO NOT NEED A DOCTOR, BUT SICK PEOPLE DO.

-316- CCCXVI
© IDM 06

13 GO AND FIND OUT WHAT THIS MEANS: WHAT
I WANT IS MERCY, NOT SACRIFICE. I DID NOT COME
TO CALL THE RIGHTEOUS BUT SINNERS."
14 THEN THE DISCIPLES OF JOHN CAME TO HIM WITH
A QUESTION, "HOW IS IT THAT WE AND THE PHARISEES
FAST ON MANY OCCASIONS, BUT NOT YOUR DISCIPLES?"
15 JESUS ANSWERED THEM, "HOW CAN YOU EXPECT
WEDDING GUESTS TO MOURN AS LONG AS THE
BRIDEGROOM IS WITH THEM? TIME WILL COME
WHEN THE BRIDEGROOM WILL BE TAKEN AWAY FROM
THEM, THEN THEY WILL FAST. 16 NO ONE PATCHES AN

OLD COAT WITH A PIECE OF UNSHRUNKEN CLOTH, FOR THE
PATCH WILL SHRINK AND TEAR AN EVEN BIGGER HOLE
IN THE COAT. 17 BESIDES YOU DON'T PUT NEW WINE IN
IN OLD WINESKINS. IF YOU DO SO, THE WINESKINS WILL
BURST AND THE WINE BE SPILT. NO, YOU PUT NEW WINE
IN FRESH SKINS; THEN BOTH ARE PRESERVED."

A WOMAN HEALED, A CHILD RAISED TO LIFE

18 WHILE JESUS WAS SPEAKING TO THEM, AN OFFICIAL
OF THE SYNAGOGUE CAME UP TO HIM, BOWED BEFORE
HIM AND SAID, "MY DAUGHTER HAS JUST DIED, BUT COME

AND PLACE YOUR HANDS
ON HER, AND SHE WILL LI-
VE." 19 JESUS STOOD
UP AND FOLLOWED HIM
WITH HIS DISCIPLES.
20 THEN A WOMAN
WHO HAD SUFFERED FROM
A SEVERE BLEEDING FOR
TWELVE YEARS CAME UP
FROM BEHIND AND TOU-
CHED THE EDGE OF HIS
CLOAK. 21 FOR SHE THO-
UGHT, "IF I ONLY TOUCH HIS
CLOAK, I WILL BE HEALED."
22 JESUS TURNED, SAW
HER AND SAID, "COURAGE,
MY DAUGHTER, YOUR FAITH
HAS SAVED YOU." AND FROM
THAT MOMENT THE WOMAN
WAS CURED. 23 WHEN
JESUS ARRIVED AT THE
OFFICIAL'S HOUSE AND
SAW THE FLUTE PLAYERS
AND THE EXCITED CROWD,
HE SAID, 24 "GET OUT OF
HERE! THE GIRL IS NOT
DEAD. SHE IS ONLY SLE-
EPING! AND THEY LAUGHED
AT HIM. 25 BUT ONCE THE
CROWD HAD BEEN TURNED
OUT, JESUS WENT IN AND
TOOK THE GIRL BY THE HAND, AND SHE STOOD UP. 26 THE
NEWS OF THIS SPREAD THROUGH THE WHOLE AREA.

27 AS JESUS MOVED ON FROM THERE, TWO BLIND
MEN FOLLOWED HIM, SHOUTING, "SON OF DAVID, HELP
US!" 28 WHEN HE WAS ABOUT TO ENTER THE HOUSE,
THE BLIND MEN CAUGHT UP WITH HIM, AND JESUS SAID
TO THEM, "DO YOU BELIEVE THAT I AM ABLE TO DO WHAT
YOU WANT?" THEY ANSWERED, "YES, SIR!" 29 THEN
JESUS TOUCHED THEIR EYES AND SAID,
"AS YOU HAVE BELIEVED, SO LET IT BE."

30 AND THEIR EYES WERE OPENED. THEN JESUS
GAVE THEM A STERN WARNING, "BE CAREFUL AND
LET NO ONE TO KNOW ABOUT THIS." 31 BUT AS
SOON AS THEY WENT AWAY, THEY SPREAD THE NEWS
ABOUT HIM THROUGH THE WHOLE AREA. 32 WHEN
THEY HAD JUST LEFT, SOME PEOPLE BROUGHT
TO JESUS A MAN WHO WAS DUMB BECAUSE HE
WAS POSSESSED BY A DEMON. 33 WHEN THE DEMON
WAS DRIVEN OUT, THE MAN WHO HAD BEEN DUMB
SPOKE. THE CROWDS WERE ASTONISHED AND SAID,
"NOTHING LIKE THIS
HAS EVER BEEN SEEN
IN ISRAEL." 34 BUT
THE PHARISEES SAID,
"HE DRIVES AWAY DE-
MONS WITH THE HELP
OF THE PRINCE OF DEMONS."

35 JESUS WENT AROUND
ALL THE TOWNS AND VIL-
LAGES, TEACHING IN
THEIR SYNAGOGUES
AND PROCLAIMING THE
GOOD NEWS OF THE
KINGDOM, AND HE CU-
RED EVERY SICKNESS
AND DISEASE.
36 WHEN HE SAW
THE CROWDS HE WAS
MOVED WITH PITY,
FOR THEY WERE
HARASSED AND
HELPLESS LIKE
SHEEP WITHOUT
A SHEPHERD. 37
THEN HE SAID TO HIS
DISCIPLES, "THE HARV-
EST IS HUGE BUT THE
WORKERS ARE FEW. 38 ASK THE MASTER OF THE
HARVEST TO SEND WORKERS TO GATHER HIS HARVEST."

THE TWELVE APOSTLES

10 1 THEN HE CALLED HIS TWELVE DISCEPLES TO
HIM AND GAVE THEM AUTHORITY OVER THE UN-
CLEAN SPIRITS TO DRIVE THEM OUT AND TO HEAL
EVERY DISEASE AND SICKNESS. 2 THESE ARE THE NAMES

OF THE TWELVE APOSTLES: FIRST SIMON, CALLED PETER,
AND HIS BROTHER ANDREW; 3 JAMES, THE SON OF ZEBE-
DEE, AND HIS BROTHER JOHN; PHILIP AND BARTHOLOMEW,
THOMAS AND MATTHEW, THE TAX COLLECTOR; JAMES, THE
SON OF ALPHAEUS, AND THADDAEUS; 4 SIMON THE
CANAANITE, AND JUDAS ISCARIOT, THE MAN
WHO WOULD BETRAY HIM.

THE FIRST MISSIONARIES

(5) JESUS SENT THIS TWELVE ON MISSION WITH THE WORDS,
"DO NOT VISIT PAGAN LANDS AND SAMARITANT TOWNS. (6)
GO INSTEAD TO THE LOST SHEEP OF THE PEOPLE OF ISRAEL.
(7) GO AND PROCLAIM THIS MESSAGE: THE KINGDOM OF
HEAVEN IS NEAR. (8) HEAL THE SICK, BRING THE DEAD BACK
TO LIFE, CLEANSE THE LEPERS, AND DRIVE OUT DEMONS.

YOU RECEIVED THIS AS A
GIFT, SO GIVE IT AS A GIFT.
(9) DO NOT CARRY GOLD,
SILVER OR COPPER IN
YOUR PURSES. (10) DO NOT
CARRY A TRAVELER'S BAG,
OR AN EXTRA SHIRT, OR
SANDALS, OR WALKING
STICK: A WORKER DE-
SERVES HIS LIVING. (11)
WHEN YOU COME TO A
TOWN OR A VILLAGE, LOOK
FOR A WORTHY PERSON
A STAY WITH HIM UNTIL
YOU LEAVE. (12) AS YOU
ENTER THE HOUSE, WISH
IT PEACE. (13) IF THE
PEOPLE IN THE HOUSE
DESERVE IT, YOUR PE-
ACE WILL BE ON THEM;
IF THEY DO NOT DESERVE
IT, YOUR BLESSING WILL
COME BACK TO YOU.
(14) AND IF SOME HOUSE
OR TOWN WILL NOT ACCEPT
YOU OR LISTEN TO YOUR
WORDS, LEAVE THAT HO-
USE AND THAT TOWN
AND SHAKE THE DUST OFF YOUR FEET. (15) I ASSURE YOU,
IT WILL GO EASIER FOR THE PEOPLE OF SODOM AND
GOMORRAH ON THE DAY OF JUDGMENT THAN IT WILL
FOR THE PEOPLE OF THAT TOWN.

YOU WILL BE PERSECUTED

(16) LOOK, I SEND YOU OUT LIKE SHEEP AMONG WOLVES. YOU
MUST BE CLEVER AS SNAKES AND INNOCENT AS DOVES. (17) BE
ON YOUR GUARD WITH RESPECT TO PEOPLE, FOR THEY WILL
HAND YOU OVER TO THEIR COURTS AND THEY WILL FLOG YOU
IN THEIR SYNAGOGUES. (18) YOU WILL BE BROUGHT TO TRIAL
BEFORE RULERS AND KINGS BECAUSE OF ME, AND YOU
WILL WITNESS TO THEM AND THE PAGANS. (19) BUT WHEN
YOU ARE ARRESTED, DO NOT WORRY ABOUT WHAT YOU ARE
TO SAY AND HOW YOU ARE TO SAY IT; WHEN THE HOUR COMES,

YOU WILL BE GIVEN WHAT YOU ARE TO SAY. (20) FOR IT IS NOT
YOU WHO WILL SPEAK, BUT THE SPIRIT OF YOUR FATHER IN YOU.
(21) BROTHER WILL HAND OVER BROTHER TO DEATH, AND A
FATHER HIS CHILD; CHILDREN AGAINST PARENTS TO HAVE
THEM PUT TO DEATH. (22) EVERYONE WILL HATE YOU BECAUSE
OF ME, BUT WHOEVER STANDS FIRM TO THE END WILL BE SA-
VED. (23) WHEN THEY PERSECUTE YOU IN ONE TOWN, GO
TO THE NEXT. FOR SURE, YOU WILL NOT HAVE GONE IN ALL
THE TOWNS OF ISRAEL BEFORE THE SON OF MAN COMES.
(24) A STUDENT IS NOT ABOVE HIS TEACHER, OR A SLAVE
ABOVE HIS MASTER. (25) A STUDENT SHOULD BE GLAD TO
BECOME LIKE HIS TEACHER, AND THE SLAVE LIKE HIS
MASTER. IF THE HEAD OF THE FAMILY WAS CALLED
BEELZEBUL, HOW MUCH MORE THE MEMBERS OF THE
FAMILY! SO, DO NOT BE AFRAID OF THEM. (26) THERE
IS NOTHING COVERED THAT WILL NOT BE UNCOVERED,
AND NOTHING HIDDEN THAT WILL NOT BE MADE KNOWN.
(27) WHAT I AM TELLING YOU IN THE DARK, YOU MUST
SPEAK IN THE LIGHT. WHAT YOU HEAR IN PRIVATE PRO-
CLAIM FROM THE HOUSETOPS. (28) DO NOT BE AFRAID
OF THOSE WHO KILL THE
BODY, BUT NOT THE PER-
SON. RATHER BE AFRAID
OF HIM WHO CAN DESTROY
BOTH BODY AND SOUL IN
HELL. (29) FOR ONLY A
FEW CENTS YOU CAN BUY
TWO SPARROWS, YET NOT
ONE SPARROW FALLS TO
THE GROUND WITHOUT
YOUR FATHER'S CONSENT.
(30) AS FOR YOU, EVERY
HAIR OF YOUR HEAD HAS
BEEN COUNTED. (31) SO
DO NOT BE AFRAID; YOU ARE
WORTH MUCH MORE
THAN MANY SPARROWS.
(32) WHOEVER ACKNOW-
LEDGES ME BEFORE OTH-
ERS I WILL ACKNOWLEDGE
BEFORE MY FATHER IN HE-
AVEN. (33) WHOEVER REJE-
CTS ME BEFORE OTHERS I
WILL REJECT BEFORE MY
FATHER IN HEAVEN.
(34) DO NOT THINK THAT
I HAVE COME TO BRING
PEACE ON EARTH. I HAVE
NOT COME TO BRING PE-

ACE, BUT A SWORD. (35) FOR I HAVE COME TO SET A MAN
AGAINST HIS FATHER AND A DAUGHTER AGAINST HER
MOTHER; A DAUGHTER-IN-LAW AGAINST HER MOTHER-
IN-LAW. (36) EACH ONE WILL HAVE AS ENEMIES THOSE
OF ONE'S OWN FAMILY. (37) WHOEVER LOVES FATHER
OR MOTHER MORE THAN ME IS NOT WORTHY OF ME.
AND WHOEVER LOVES SON OR DAUGHTER MORE THAN
ME IS NOT WORTHY OF ME.

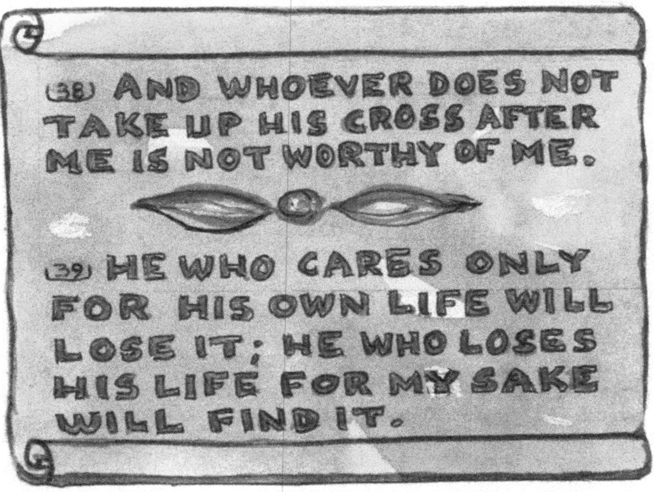

(40) HE WHO WELCOMES YOU WELCOMES ME, AND
HE WHO WELCOMES ME WELCOMES HIM WHO
SENT ME.
(41) THE ONE WHO WELCOMES A PROPHET AS A
PROPHET WILL RECEIVE THE REWARD OF A PRO-
PHET; THE ONE WHO WELCOMES A JUST MAN BE-
CAUSE HE IS A JUST MAN WILL RECEIVE THE
REWARD OF A JUST MAN.

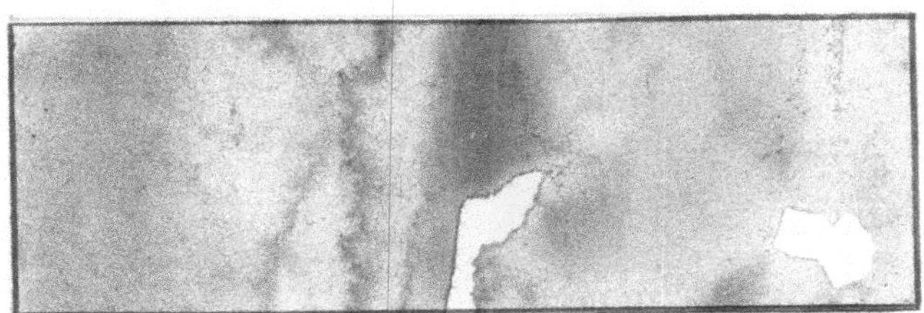

(42) AND I PROMISE YOU IF ANYONE GIVES EVEN A
CUP OF COLD WATER TO ONE OF THESE LITTLE ONES,
AS HE IS A DISCIPLE OF MINE, HE WILL NOT GO UNREWARDED."

JESUS AND JOHN THE BAPTIST

11 (1) WHEN JESUS HAD FINISHED GIVING HIS TWELVE
DISCIPLES THESE INSTRUCTIONS, HE WENT ON FROM
THERE TO TEACH AND TO PROCLAIM HIS MESSAGE
IN THEIR TOWNS. (2) WHEN JOHN THE BAPTIST
HEARD IN PRISON OF

THE ACTIVITIES OF (3)
CHRIST, HE SENT A MES-
SAGE BY HIS DISCEPLES
ASKING HIM: "ARE YOU THE
ONE WHO IS TO COME OR
SHOULD WE EXPECT SO-
MEONE ELSE?" JESUS
ANSWERED THEM, (4) "GO
BACK AND REPORT TO
JOHN WHAT YOU HEAR
AND SEE: (5) THE BLIND
SEE, THE LAME WALK,
THE LEPERS ARE MADE
CLEAN, THE DEAF HEAR,
THE DEAD ARE BROUGHT
BACK TO LIFE AND GOOD
NEWS IS REACHING THE
POOR. (6) AND HOW BLES-
SED IS WHO DOES NOT
TAKE OFFENSE AT ME."
(7) AS THE MESSENGERS
LEFT, JESUS BEGAN TO
SPEAK TO THE CROWDS
ABOUT JOHN, "WHEN YOU
WENT OUT TO THE DESERT,
WHAT DID YOU EXPECT TO
SEE? A REED SWEPT BY THE WIND? (8) WHAT DID YOU GO
OUT TO SEE? A MAN DRESSED IN FINE CLOTHES? PEOPLE
WHO WEAR FINE CLOTHES LIVE IN PALACES. (9) WHAT
DID YOU ACTUALLY GO OUT TO SEE? A PROPHET? YES, IN-
DEED, AND EVEN MORE THAN A PROPHET. (10) HE IS THE MAN
OF WHOM SCRIPTURE SAYS:

I SEND MY MESSENGER AHEAD OF YOU TO
PREPARE THE WAY BEFORE YOU.

(11) I TELL YOU THIS: NO ONE GREATER THAN JOHN THE
BAPTIST HAS OFFERED AMONG THE SONS OF WOMEN, AND
YET THE LEAST IN THE KINGDOM OF HEAVEN IS GREATER
THAN HE. (12) FROM THE DAYS OF JOHN THE BAPTIST UNTIL

NOW THE KINGDOM OF HEAVEN IS SOMETHING TO BE CON-
QUERED AND THOSE WHO ARE MOST DECISIVE SEIZE
IT. (13) UP TO THE TIME OF JOHN, THERE WAS ONLY
PROPHESY: ALL THE PROPHETS AND THE LAW; (14)
AND IF YOU BELIEVE ME, JOHN IS ELIJAH, WHOSE CO-
MING WAS PREDICTED. (15) IF ANYONE HAS EARS TO HE-
AR, LET HIM LISTEN. (16) NOW, TO WHAT CAN I COMPARE
THE PEOPLE OF THIS DAY? THEY ARE LIKE CHILDREN
SITTING IN THE MARKETPLACE, WITH SOME COM-
PLAINING TO OTHERS: (17) 'WE PLAYED THE FLUTE FOR
YOU BUT YOU WOULD NOT DANCE. WE SANG A FUNE-
RAL-SONG BUT YOU WOULD NOT CRY!' (18) FOR JOHN
CAME FASTING AND PEOPLE SAID: 'HE IS POSSESSED.'
(19) THEN THE SON OF MAN CAME, HE ATE AND DRANK,
AND PEOPLE SAID: 'LOOK AT THIS MAN! A GLUTTON AND
DRUNKARD, A FRIEND OF TAX COLLECTORS AND SINNERS!'
YET THEY WILL SEE THAT WISDOM DID EVERYTHING
WELL." (20) THEN JESUS BEGAN TO DENOUNCE THE CI-
TIES IN WHICH HE HAD PERFORMED MOST OF HIS MI-
RACLES, BECAUSE THE PEOPLE THERE DID NOT CHANGE

THEIR WAYS. (21) "ALAS FOR YOU CHORAZIN AND BEITHSA-
IDA! IF THE MIRACLES WORKED IN YOU HAD TAKEN PLACE
IN TYRE AND SIDON, THE PEOPLE THERE WOULD HAVE
REPENTED LONG AGO IN SACKCLOTH AND ASHES. (22)
BUT I ASSURE YOU, FOR TYRE AND SIDON IT WILL BE MORE
BEARABLE ON THE DAY OF JUDGEMENT THAN FOR YOU.
(23) AND YOU, CAPERNAUM, WILL YOU BE LIFTED UP TO HE-
AVEN? YOU WILL BE THROWN DOWN TO THE PLACE OF THE
DEAD! FOR IF THE MIRACLES WHICH WERE PERFORMED IN
YOU HAD TAKEN PLACE IN SODOM, IT WOULD BE STILL THERE
TODAY! (24) BUT I TELL YOU, IT WILL BE MORE BEARABLE
FOR SODOM ON THE DAY OF JUDGMENT THAN FOR YOU."

TAKE MY YOKE UPON YOU

(25) ON THAT OCCASION JESUS SAID, "FATHER,
LORD OF HEAVEN AND EARTH, I PRAISE YOU, BE-
CAUSE YOU HAVE HID-
DEN THESE THINGS
FROM THE WISE AND
LEARNED AND REVE-
ALED THEM TO SIMPLE
PEOPLE. (26) YES, FA-
THER, THIS IS WHAT
PLEASED YOU.
(27) EVERYTHING HAS
BEEN ENTRUSTED TO ME
BY MY FATHER. NO ONE
KNOWS THE SON EX-
CEPT THE FATHER,
AND NO ONE KNOWS THE
FATHER EXCEPT THE
SON AND THOSE TO
WHOM THE SON CHO-
OSES TO REVEAL HIM.
(28) COME TO ME ALL
YOU WHO WORK HARD
AND WHO CARRY HEAVY
BURDENS AND I WILL
REFRESH YOU. (29) TA-
KE MY YOKE UPON YOU
AND LEARN FROM ME

FOR I AM GENTLE AND HUMBLE OF HEART;
AND YOU WILL FIND REST. (30) FOR MY YOKE IS
GOOD AND MY BURDEN IS LIGHT."

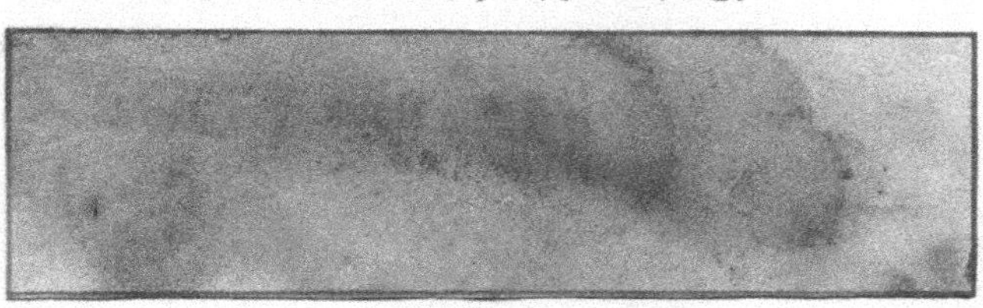

(2) These are the names
of the 12 Apostles: first Simon,
called Peter, and his brother
Andrew; (3) James, the son of Zebedee,
and his brother John; Philip and
Bartholomew, Thomas and Matthew,
the tax collector: James, the son of
Alphaeus, and Thaddaeus;
(4) Simon, the Canaanite, and
JUDAS ISCARIOT,
THE MAN WHO WOULD
BETRAY HIM.
(MATTHEW 10:2-4)
D Mazzoli 06
DM 06 ©

JESUS, LORD of the SABBATH

1 IT HAPPENED THAT JESUS WALKED THROUGH
THE WHEAT FIELDS ON A SABBATH. HIS DISCIPLES
WERE HUNGRY, AND BEGAN TO PICK SOME HEADS OF
WHEAT AND CRUSH THEM TO EAT THE GRAIN. 2 WHEN

THE PHARISEES NOTICED
THIS, THEY SAID TO JESUS,
"LOOK AT YOUR DISCIPLES,
THEY ARE DOING WHAT IS
PROHIBITED ON THE SAB-
BATH!" 3 JESUS ANSWE-
RED, "HAVE YOU NOT READ
WHAT DAVID DID WHEN HE
AND HIS MEN WERE HUNG-
RY? 4 HE WENT INTO
THE HOUSE OF GOD, AND
THEY ATE THE BREAD OF-
FERED TO GOD, ALTHOUGH
NEITHER HE NOR HIS MEN
HAD THE RIGHT TO EAT
IT, BUT ONLY THE PRIESTS.
5 AND HAVE YOU NOT
READ IN THE LAW THAT ON
THE SABBATH THE PRIESTS
IN THE TEMPLE BREAK THE
SABBATH REST, YET THEY
ARE NOT GUILTY? 6 I
TELL YOU THERE IS SO-
METHING GREATER THAN
THE TEMPLE HERE. 7
IF YOU REALLY KNEW THE
MEANING OF THE WORDS:
IT IS MERCY I WANT, NOT
SACRIFICE, YOU WOULD NOT HAVE CONDEMNED THE INNO-
CENT. 8 BESIDES THE SON OF MAN IS LORD OF THE
SABBATH." 9 JESUS LEFT THAT PLACE AND WENT IN-
TO ONE OF THEIR SYNAGOGUES. 10 A MAN WAS THERE
WITH A PARALIZED HAND, AND THEY ASKED JESUS, "IS
IT PERMITTED TO HEAL ON THE SABBATH?" THESE PE-
OPLE WANTED TO BRING A CHARGE AGAINST HIM. 11 BUT
HE SAID TO THEM, "WHAT IF ONE OF YOU HAS A SHEEP AND
IT FALLS INTO A PIT ON THE SABBATH? WILL YOU NOT HOLD
YOUR SHEEP AND LIFT IT OUT? 12 BUT A HUMAN PERSON IS
MUCH MORE VALUABLE THAN A SHEEP! IT IS THEN PERMITTED
TO DO GOOD ON THE SABBATH." 13 THEN JESUS SAID TO THE
MAN, "STRETCH OUT YOUR ARM." HE DID IT AND IT WAS COM-
PLETELY RESTORED, AS SOUND AS THE OTHER ONE.
14 THEN THE PHARISEES MADE PLANS TO KILL HIM. 15
AS JESUS WAS AWARE OF THE PLOT, HE LEFT THAT PLACE.

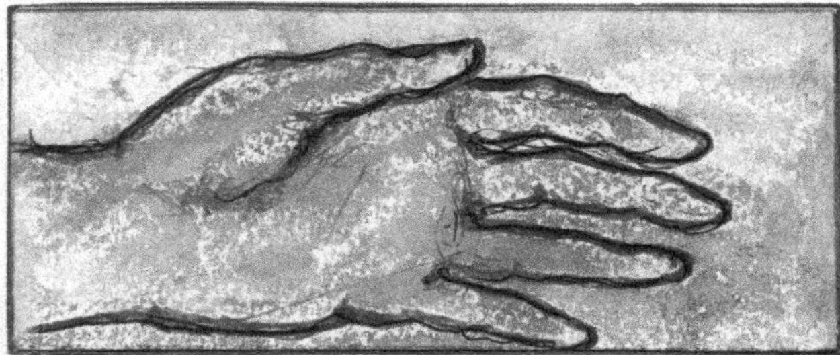

MANY PEOPLE FOLLOWED HIM. HE CURED ALL WHO WE-
RE SICK 16 AND GAVE THEM STRICT ORDERS NOT TO MAKE
HIM KNOWN. 17 IN THIS WAY ISAIAH'S PROPHECY WAS FULFILLED:

18 Here is my servant whom I have chosen, the
one I love, with whom I am pleased. I will put my
spirit upon him and he will announce to the
nations my judgment.
He will 19 not argue or shout, nor will his
voice be heard in the streets.
20 The bruised reed he will not crush;
nor snuff out the smoldering wick.
He will persist until justice is made
victorious.
21 And in him all the nations will
put their hope."

THE UNFORGIVABLE SIN

22 THEN SOME PEOPLE BROUGHT TO HIM A POSSES-
SED MAN WHO WAS BLIND AND COULD NOT TALK.
JESUS HEALED THAT MAN, WHO WAS THEN ABLE TO
SPEAK AND SEE. 23 ALL WERE AMAZED AND WON-
DERED, "COULD HE BE THE SON OF DAVID?" 24 WHEN
THE PHARISEES HEARD THIS, THEY SAID, "IT IS BY
BEELZEBUL, PRINCE OF THE DEVILS, THAT THIS MAN
DRIVES OUT DEVILS." 25 JESUS KNEW THEIR THINKING,
SO HE SAID TO THEM, "EVERY KINGDOM DIVIDED BY WAR
WILL FALL APART, AND DIVIDED TOWNS AND HOUSEHOLDS
CANNOT LAST. 26 SO IF SATAN DRIVES OUT SATAN, HE IS
DIVIDED; HOW THEN CAN HIS KINGDOM STAND? 27 AND IF

IT IS BY BEELZEBUL THAT I DRIVE OUT DEVILS, BY WHOM DO
YOUR OWN PEOPLE DRIVE THEM OUT? THEY WILL ANSWER YOU.
28 BUT IF IT IS BY THE SPIRIT OF GOD THAT I DRIVE OUT DEVILS,
THEN THE KINGDOM OF GOD IS ALREADY WITH YOU. 29 HOW
CAN ONE BREAK INTO THE STRONG MAN'S HOUSE AND MAKE
OFF WITH HIS BELONGING, UNLESS HE FIRST TIES HIM UP?
ONLY THEN HE CAN PLUNDER HIS HOUSE. 30 HE WHO IS NOT
WITH ME IS AGAINST ME, AND HE WHO DOES NOT GATHER WITH
ME SCATTERS. 31 AND SO I TELL YOU THIS: PEOPLE CAN BE
FORGIVEN ANY SIN, EVIL

THINGS AGAINST GOD, BUT
EVIL WORDS AGAINST THE
HOLY SPIRIT WILL NOT BE
FORGIVEN. 32 HE WHO
SPEAKS AGAINST THE SON
OF MAN, WILL BE FORGIVEN;
BUT HE WHO SPEAKS AGAINST
THE HOLY SPIRIT WILL NOT
BE FORGIVEN, IN THIS
AGE OR IN THE AGE TO CO-
ME. 33 MAKE A TREE
SOUND AND ITS FRUIT
WILL BE SOUND; LET A
TREE ROT AND ITS FRUIT
WILL BE ROTTEN; YOU
CAN KNOW A TREE BY ITS
FRUIT. 34 YOU BROOD OF
VIPERS, HOW CAN YOU SAY
ANYTHING GOOD AS YOU
ARE SO EVIL? FOR THE
MOUTH SPEAKS WORDS
FROM YOUR HEART. 35
A GOOD PERSON PRODUCES
WHAT IS GOOD WITHIN THE
STORE OF HIS OWN GOOD;
AN EVIL PERSON PRODUCES
EVIL FROM HIS EVIL STORE. 36 I TELL YOU THIS: ON THE
JUDGMENT DAY PEOPLE WILL HAVE TO GIVE AN ACCOUNT OF
ANY UNJUSTIFIED WORD THEY HAVE SPOKEN. 37 YOUR OWN
WORDS WILL DECLARE YOU EITHER INNOCENT OR GUILTY."

JESUS AND HIS OWN GENERATION

38 THEN SOME TEACHERS OF THE LAW AND SOME
PHARISEES SPOKE UP, "TEACHER, WE WANT TO
SEE A SIGN FROM YOU."

(39) JESUS ANSWERED THEM, "AN EVIL AND UNFAITHFUL
PEOPLE WANT A SIGN, BUT NO SIGN WILL BE GIVEN THEM
EXCEPT THE SIGN OF THE PROPHET JONAH. (40) IN THE SAME
WAY THAT JONAH SPENT THREE DAYS AND THREE NIGHTS
IN THE DEPTHS OF THE EARTH. (41) AT THE JUDGMENT, THE
PEOPLE OF NINIVEH WILL RISE WITH THIS GENERATION
AND CONDEMN IT, BECAUSE THEY REFORMED THEIR LIVES AT
THE PREACHING OF JONAH,
AND HERE THERE IS GRE-
ATER THAN JONAH. (42) AT
THE JUDGEMENT, THE
QUEEN OF THE SOUTH
WILL STAND UP AND CON-
DEMN YOU. SHE CAME
FROM THE ENDS OF THE
EARTH TO LISTEN TO THE
WISDOM OF SOLOMON, AND
HERE THERE IS GREATER
THAN SOLOMON.
(43) WHEN AN EVIL SPIRIT
GOES OUT OF A PERSON, IT
WANDERS OVER ARID WAS-
TELANDS LOOKING FOR A
PLACE TO REST BUT IT
CANNOT FIND ONE. (44) IT
SAYS TO ITSELF, 'I WILL
GO BACK TO MY HOUSE
WHICH I HAD TO LEAVE.'
SO IT GOES BACK AND FINDS
THE EMPTY HOUSE, CLEAN
AND IN ORDER. (45) OFF IT
GOES AGAIN TO BRING
BACK WITH IT, THIS TIME,
SEVEN SPIRITS, MORE EVIL
THAN ITSELF. THEY MOVE
IN AND SETTLE THERE, SO
THAT THIS PERSON IS FINALLY IN A WORSE STATE THAN HE
WAS AT THE BEGINNING. THIS IS WHAT WILL HAPPEN TO THIS
EVIL GENERATION." (46) WHILE JESUS WAS STILL TALKING
TO THE PEOPLE, HIS MOTHER AND HIS BROTHERS CAME
TO SPEAK TO HIM AND THEY WAITED OUTSIDE.
(47) SO SOMEONE SAID TO HIM, "YOUR MOTHER AND YOUR
BROTHERS ARE JUST OUTSIDE; THEY WANT TO SPEAK TO
YOU." (48) JESUS ANSWERED, "WHO IS MY MOTHER? WHO
ARE MY BROTHERS?" (49) THEN HE POINTED TO HIS

DISCIPLES AND SAID, "LOOK, HERE ARE MY MOTHER AND
MY BROTHERS. (50) WHOEVER DOES THE WILL OF MY FA-
THER IN HEAVEN IS FOR ME BROTHER, SISTER, OR MOTHER".

THE PARABLE OF THE SOWER

13 (1) THAT SAME DAY JESUS LEFT THE HOUSE AND
SAT DOWN BY THE LAKESIDE. (2) AS MANY PEOPLE
GATHERED AROUND HIM, HE GOT IN A BOAT. THERE
HE SAT WHILE THE WHOLE CROWD STOOD ON THE SHORE.
(3) AND HE SPOKE IN PARABLES ABOUT MANY THINGS.

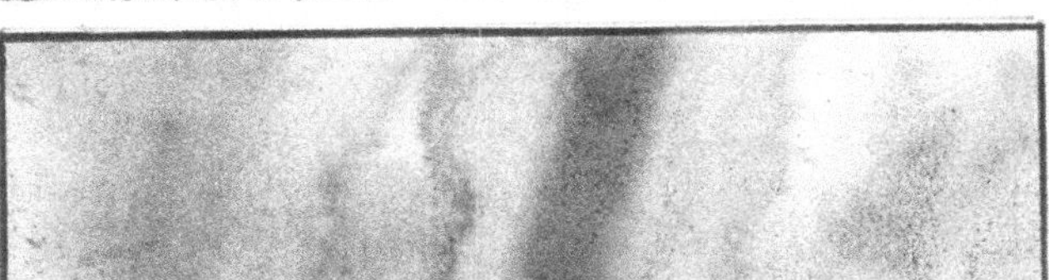

(4) JESUS SAID, "THE SOWER WENT OUT TO SOW AND,
AS HE SOWED, SOME SEEDS FELL ALONG THE PATH
AND THE BIRDS CAME AND ATE THEM UP. (5) OTHER
SEEDS FELL ON ROCKY GROUND WHERE THERE WAS
LITTLE SOIL, AND THE SEEDS SPROUTED QUICKLY BECA-
USE THE SOIL WAS NOT DEEP. (6) WHEN THE SUN ROSE
THE PLANTS WERE SCORCHED AND WITHERED BECAUSE
THEY HAD NO ROOTS. (7) AGAIN OTHER SEEDS FELL
AMONG THISTLES; AND THISTLES GREW AND CHOKED
THE PLANTS. (8) STILL OTHER SEEDS FELL ON GOOD
SOIL AND PRODUCED A CROP; SOME PRODUCED A HUN-
DREDFOLD, OTHER SIXTY AND OTHERS THIRTY. (9) IF

YOU HAVE EARS, THEN HEAR!" (10) THEN THE DISCIPLES
CAME TO HIM WITH THE QUESTION, "WHY DO YOU SPEAK
TO THEM IN PARABLES?" (11) JESUS ANSWERED, "TO YOU
IT HAS BEEN GIVEN TO KNOW THE SECRETS OF THE KING-
DOM OF HEAVEN, BUT NOT TO THESE PEOPLE. (12) FOR
THE ONE WHO HAS, WILL BE GIVEN MORE AND HE WILL
HAVE IN ABUNDANCE. BUT THE ONE WHO DOES NOT
HAVE WILL BE DEPRIVED OF EVEN WHAT HE HAS. (13) THAT
IS WHY I SPEAK IN PARABLES, BECAUSE THEY LOOK AND
DO NOT SEE; THEY HEAR, BUT THEY DO NOT LISTEN OR UN-
DERSTAND. (14) IN THEM THE WORDS OF THE PROPHET
ISAIAH ARE FULFILLED:

MUCH AS YOU HEAR, YOU DO NOT UNDERSTAND, MUCH
AS YOU SEE, YOU DO NOT PERCEIVE. (15) FOR THE HEART OF
THIS PEOPLE HAS GROWN DULL. THEY EARS HARDLY HEAR
AND THEIR EYES DARE NOT SEE. IF THEY WERE TO SEE WITH
THEIR EYES, HEAR WITH THEIR EARS AND UNDERSTAND WITH
THEIR HEART, THEY WOULD TURN BACK AND I WOULD HEAL THEM.

(16) BUT BLESSED ARE YOUR EYES BECAUSE THEY

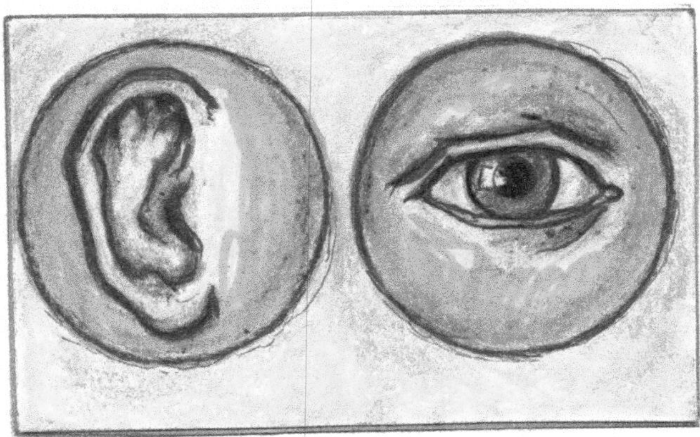

SEE AND YOUR EARS, BECAUSE THEY HEAR. (17) FOR I
TELL YOU THAT MANY PROPHETS AND UPRIGHT PEOPLE
WOULD HAVE LONGED TO SEE WHAT YOU SEE, BUT THEY
DID NOT, AND TO HEAR THE THINGS YOU HEAR, BUT THEY
DID NOT HEAR IT. (18) NOW LISTEN TO THE PARABLE OF
THE SOWER. (19) WHEN A PERSON HEARS THE MESSAGE
OF THE KINGDOM WITHOUT HIS HEART, THE DEVIL CO-
MES AND SNATCHES AWAY WHAT WAS SOWN IN HIS PER-
SON. THIS IS THE SEED THAT FELL ALONG THE FOOTPATH.

(20) THE SEED THAT FELL ON ROCKY GROUND STANDS
FOR THE ONE WHO HEARS THE WORD AND ACCEPTS IT AT
ONCE WITH JOY. (21) BUT HE IS FICKLE AND HAS NO
ROOTS. NO SOONER IS HE HARASSED OR PERSECUTED BE-
CAUSE OF THE WORD, THAN HE GIVES UP. (22) THE SEED
THAT FELL AMONG THE THISTLES IS THE ONE WHO HEARS
THE WORD, BUT THEN THE WORRIES OF THIS LIFE AND
THE LOVE OF MONEY CHOKE THE WORD, AND IT DOES NOT
BEAR FRUIT. (23) BUT THE SEED THAT FELL ON GOOD
SOIL IS THE ONE WHO HEARS THE WORD AND UNDER-
STANDS IT; HE BEARS FRUIT AND PRODUCES A HUN-
DRED, OR SIXTY, OR THIRTY TIMES MORE."

THE PARABLE OF THE WEEDS

(24) JESUS TOLD THEM ANOTHER PARABLE, "THE KINGDOM
OF HEAVEN CAN BE COMPARED TO A MAN WHO SOWED GOOD
SEED IN HIS FIELD. (25)
WHILE EVERYONE WAS
ASLEEP, HIS ENEMY CAME
AND SOWED WEEDS
AMONG THE WHEAT AND
LEFT. (26) WHEN THE
PLANTS SPROUTED AND
APPEARED PRODUCING
GRAIN, THE WEEDS ALSO AP-
PEARED. (27) THEN THE
SERVANTS OF THE OWNER
SAID TO HIM: 'SIR, WAS IT
NOT GOOD SEED THAT YOU
SOWED IN YOUR FIELD?
WHERE DID THE WEEDS CO-
ME FROM?' (28) HE ANS-
WERED THEM: 'THIS IS THE
WORK OF AN ENEMY.' THEY
ASKED HIM: DO YOU WANT
US TO GO AND PULL UP
THE WEEDS?' (29) HE
TOLD THEM: 'NO, WHEN YOU
PULL UP THE WEEDS, YOU
MIGHT UPROOT THE WHEAT
WITH THEM. (30) JUST LET
THEM GROW TOGETHER
UNTIL HARVEST; AND AT
HARVEST TIME I WILL SAY
TO THE WORKERS: PULL UP THE WEEDS FIRST, TIE THEM IN
BUNDLES AND BURN THEM; THEN GATHER THE WHEAT INTO MY
BARN.'"

• THE MUSTARD SEED AND THE YEAST •

(31) JESUS PUT ANOTHER PARABLE TO THEM, "THE KING-
DOM OF HEAVEN IS LIKE A MUSTARD SEED, WHICH A MAN

TOOK AND SOWED IN HIS FIELD. (32) IT IS SMALLER THAN ALL
OTHER SEEDS, BUT ONCE IT HAS FULLY GROWN, IT IS BIG-
GER THAN ANY GARDEN PLANT; LIKE A TREE, THE BIRDS
COME AND REST ON ITS BRANCHES." (33) HE TOLD THEM
ANOTHER PARABLE, "THE KINGDOM OF HEAVEN IS LIKE THE
YEAST WHICH A WOMAN TOOK AND BURIED IN THREE ME-
ASURES OF FLOUR UNTIL THE WHOLE MASS OF DOUGH
BEGAN TO RISE." (34) JESUS TAUGHT ALL THIS BY MEANS
OF PARABLES; HE DID NOT SAY ANYTHING TO THE
CROWDS WITHOUT USING A PARABLE.

(35) SO WHAT THE PROPHET HAD SAID WAS FULFILLED:

I WILL SPEAK IN PARABLES; I WILL PROCLAIM
THINGS KEPT SECRET SINCE THE BE-
GINNING OF THE WORLD.

(36) THEN HE SENT THE CROWDS AWAY AND WENT INTO
THE HOUSE, AND HIS DISCIPLES CAME TO HIM SAYING,
"EXPLAIN TO US THE PARABLE OF THE WEEDS IN THE
FIELD." (37) JESUS ANSWERED THEM, "THE ONE WHO
SOWS THE GOOD SEED IS THE SON OF MAN. (38) THE
FIELD IS THE WORLD; THE
GOOD SEED ARE THE PE-
OPLE OF THE KINGDOM;
THE WEEDS ARE THOSE
WHO BELONG TO THE EVIL
ONE. (39) THE ENEMY
WHO SOWS THEM IS THE
DEVIL; THE HARVEST IS
THE END OF TIME AND THE
WORKERS ARE THE AN-
GELS. (40) JUST AS THE
WEEDS ARE PULLED UP
AND BURNED IN THE FIRE,
SO WILL IT BE AT THE END
OF TIME. (41) THE SON OF
MAN WILL SEND HIS AN-
GELS, AND THEY WILL
WEED OUT OF HIS KING-
DOM ALL THAT IS SCAN-
DALOUS AND ALL WHO DO
EVIL. (42) AND THESE
WILL BE THROWN IN
THE BLAZING FURNA-
CE, WHERE THERE
WILL BE WEEPING
AND GNASHING OF
TEETH. (43) THEN THE
JUST WILL SHINE LIKE
THE SUN IN THE KINGDOM OF THEIR FATHER. IF
YOU HAVE EARS, THEN HEAR.

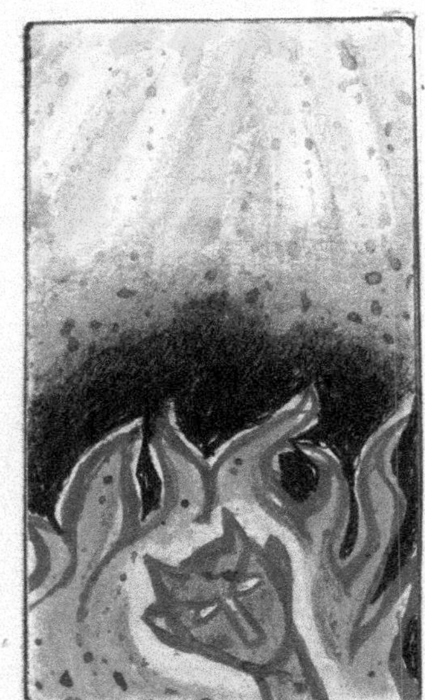

THE TREASURE, THE PEARL AND THE NET

(44) THE KINGDOM OF HEAVEN IS LIKE A TREASURE HIDDEN
IN A FIELD. THE MAN WHO FINDS IT BURIES IT AGAIN;
AND SO HAPPY IS HE, THAT HE GOES AND SELLS EVERY-
THING HE HAS, IN ORDER TO BUY THAT FIELD. AGAIN
(45) THE KINGDOM OF HEAVEN IS LIKE A TRADER WHO IS
LOOKING FOR FINE PEARLS. (46) ONCE HE HAS FOUND A
PEARL OF GREAT QUALITY, HE GOES AWAY, SELLS EVERY-
THING HE HAS AND BUYS IT. (47) AGAIN, THE KINGDOM OF

HEAVEN IS LIKE A BIG FISHING NET LET DOWN INTO THE
SEA, IN WHICH EVERY KIND OF FISH HAS BEEN CAUGHT.
(48) WHEN THE NET IS FULL, IT IS DRAGGED ASHORE.
THEN THEY SIT DOWN AND GATHER THE GOOD FISH IN
BUCKETS, BUT THROW THE WORTHLESS ONES AWAY.
(49) THAT IS HOW IT WILL BE AT THE END OF TIME; THE AN-
GELS WILL GO OUT TO SEPARATE THE WICKED FROM THE
JUST (50) AND THROW THEM INTO THE BLAZING FURNACE,
WHERE THEY WILL WEEP AND GNASH THEIR TEETH."

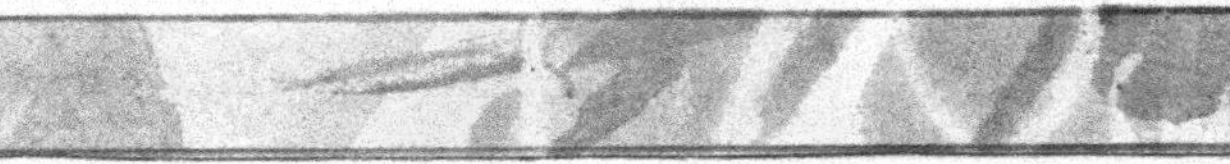

"I TELL YOU THIS: ON THE JUDGMENT DAY PEOPLE WILL HAVE TO GIVE..." (MATTHEW 12:36)
318
CCCXVIII
© DM 04

51 JESUS ASKED, "HAVE YOU UNDERSTOOD ALL
THESE THINGS?" "YES", THEY ANSWERED. 52
SO HE SAID TO THEM, "YOU WILL SEE THAT EVERY
TEACHER OF THE LAW WHO BECOMES A DISCI-
PLE OF THE KINGDOM IS LIKE A HOUSEHOLDER
WHO CAN PRODUCE FROM HIS STORE THINGS
BOTH NEW AND OLD."
53 WHEN JESUS HAD
FINISHED THESE PA-
RABLES, HE LEFT THE
PLACE. 54 HE WENT
TO HIS HOMETOWN
AND TAUGHT THE
PEOPLE IN THEIR
SYNAGOGUE. THEY
WERE AMAZED AND
SAID, "WHERE DID HE
GET THIS WISDOM AND
THESE SPECIAL PO-
WERS? 55 ISN'T HE
CARPENTER'S SON?
ISN'T MARY HIS MOTHER
AND AREN'T JAMES, JO-
SEPH, SIMON AND JUDAS
HIS BROTHERS? 56
AREN'T ALL HIS SIST-
ERS LIVING HERE?
HOW DID HE GET ALL
THIS?" 57 AND SO THEY
TOOK OFFENSE AT HIM.
JESUS SAID TO THEM, "THE
ONLY PLACE WHERE A
PROPHET IS NOT WELCOME
IN HIS HOMETOWN AND IN
HIS OWN FAMILY." 58 AND HE DID NOT PERFORM MANY
MIRACLES THERE BECAUSE OF THEIR LACK OF FAITH.

JOHN THE BAPTIST BEHEADED

14 1 AT THAT TIME THE NEWS ABOUT JESUS REACHED
KING HEROD. 2 AND HE SAID TO HIS SERVANTS,
"THIS MAN IS JOHN THE BAPTIST. JOHN HAS RISEN
FROM THE DEAD, AND THAT IS WHY MIRACULOUS POWERS
ARE AT WORK IN HIM." 3 HEROD HAD, IN FACT, ORDER-
ED THAT JOHN BE ARRESTED, BOUND IN CHAINS AND PUT IN
PRISON BECAUSE OF HERODIAS, THE WIFE OF HIS BROTHER
PHILIP. 4 FOR JOHN HAD SAID TO HIM, "IT IS NOT RIGHT
FOR YOU TO HAVE HER AS WIFE." 5 HEROD WANTED TO KILL

HIM BUT HE DID NOT DARE BECAUSE HE FEARED THE
PEOPLE WHO REGARDED JOHN AS A PROPHET. 6 ON
HEROD'S BIRTHDAY THE DAUGHTER OF HERODIAS DANCED
IN THE MIDST OF THE GUESTS; SO SHE DELIGHTED HEROD
7 THAT HE PROMISED UNDER OATH TO GIVE HER ANY-
THING SHE ASKED. 8 THE GIRL, FOLLOWING THE AD-
VICE OF HER MOTHER, SAID, "GIVE ME THE HEAD OF
JOHN THE BAPTIST HERE ON A DISH." 9 THE KING
WAS VERY DISPLEASED, BUT BECAUSE OF HIS PROMISE
UNDER OATH IN THE PRESENCE OF THE GUESTS, HE OR-
DERED IT TO BE GIVEN TO HER. 10 SO HE HAD JOHN BE-
HEADED IN PRISON 11 AND HIS HEAD BROUGHT
ON A DISH AND GIVEN TO THE GIRL. THE GIRL
THEN TOOK IT TO HER MOTHER.
12 THEN JOHN'S DISCIPLES CAME TO TAKE HIS BO-
DY AND BURY IT. AND THEY BROUGHT THE NEWS TO
JESUS.

FIRST MIRACLE OF THE LOAVES

13 ON HEARING THIS, JESUS SET OUT SECRETLY BY
BOAT FOR A SECLUDED PLACE. BUT THE PEOPLE HEARD
OF IT, AND THEY FOLLOWED HIM ON FOOT FROM THEIR
TOWNS. 14 WHEN JESUS WENT ASHORE, HE SAW THE
CROWD THERE AND HE HAD COMPASSION ON THEM. AND

HE HEALED THEIR SICK. 15 LATER ON, THE DISCIPLES CAME
TO HIM AND SAID, "WE ARE IN A LONELY PLACE AND IT IS NOW
LATE. YOU SHOULD SEND THESE PEOPLE AWAY TO THE VIL-
LAGES AND BUY FOOD FOR
THEMSELVES TO EAT."
BUT JESUS REPLIED, 16
"THEY DO NOT NEED TO
GO AWAY. YOU GIVE THEM
SOMETHING TO EAT." 17
THEY ANSWERED, "WE HA-
VE NOTHING HERE BUT
FIVE LOAVES AND TWO FI-
SHES." 18 JESUS SAID
TO THEM, "BRING THEM
HERE TO ME" 19 THEN
HE MADE EVERYONE SIT
DOWN ON THE GRASS.
HE TOOK THE FIVE LO-
AVES AND THE TWO
FISHES, RAISED HIS
EYES TO HEAVEN,
SAID THE BLESSING AND
BROKE THE LOAVES; GAVE
THEM TO THE DISCIPLES
TO DISTRIBUTE TO THE PE-
OPLE. 20 AND THEY ALL
ATE, AND EVERYONE HAD
ENOUGH; THEN THE DI-
SCIPLES GATHERED UP
THE LEFTOVERS, FILLING TWELVE BASKETS. 21 ABOUT
FIVE THOUSAND MEN HAD EATEN THERE WITHOUT
COUNTING WOMEN AND CHILDREN.

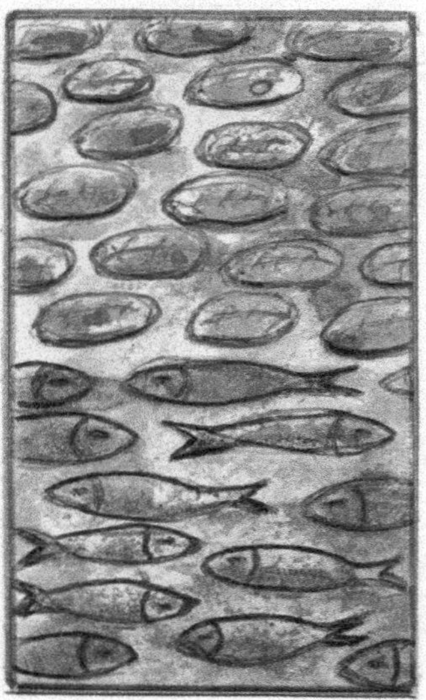

JESUS WALKS ON THE WATER

22 SOON JESUS MADE HIS DISCIPLES GET INTO THE BOAT
AND GO AHEAD OF HIM TO THE OTHER SIDE, WHILE HE SENT
THE CROWD AWAY. 23 HAVING SENT THE PEOPLE AWAY, HE
WENT UP THE MOUNTAIN BY HIMSELF TO PRAY; AT NIGHT-
FALL, HE WAS THERE ALONE. 24 MEANWHILE, THE BOAT
WAS VERY FAR FROM LAND, DANGEROUSLY ROCKED BY
WAVES FROM THE WIND WHICH WENT AGAINST IT.
25 AT DAYBREAK, JESUS CAME TO THEM
WALKING ON THE LAKE.

26 WHEN THEY SAW HIM WALKING ON THE SEA,
THEY WERE TERRIFIED, THINKING THAT IT WAS
A GHOST. AND THEY CRIED OUT IN FEAR. 27 BUT AT
ONCE JESUS SAID TO THEM, "COURAGE! DON'T BE
AFRAID. IT'S ME!" 28 PETER ANSWERED, "LORD, IF
IT IS YOU, COMMAND ME TO COME TO YOU WALKING ON
THE WATER." 29 JESUS SAID TO HIM, "COME." AND
PETER GOT OUT OF THE BOAT, WALKING ON THE WATER
TO GO TO JESUS. 30 BUT, IN FACE OF THE STRONG WIND,
HE WAS AFRAID AND BEGAN TO SINK. SO HE CRIED OUT,
"LORD, SAVE ME!" 31 JESUS STRETCHED OUT AT ONCE
HIS HAND, TOOK HOLD OF HIM, SAYING, "MAN OF LITTLE FAITH,
WHY DID YOU DOUBT?" 32 AS THEY GOT INTO THE BOAT, THE

WIND DROPPED. 33 THOSE IN THE BOAT BOWED DOWN BE-
FORE JESUS SAYING, "TRULY, YOU ARE THE SON OF GOD!"
34 THEY CAME ASHORE AT GENNESARETH. 35 THE LOCAL
PEOPLE RECOGNIZED JESUS, SO THEY SPREAD THE NEWS
THROUGHOUT THE REGION. THEY BROUGHT ALL THE SICK
TO HIM, 36 BEGGING HIM TO LET THEM TOUCH JUST THE
FRINGE OF HIS CLOAK. ALL WHO TOUCHED IT WERE HEALED.

GOD'S COMMAND AND HUMAN TRADITION

15 1 THEN SOME PHARISEES AND TEACHERS OF THE LAW
WHO HAD COME FROM JERUSALEM GATHERED AROUND
JESUS, AND THEY SAID TO HIM, 2 "WHY DON'T YOUR
DISCEPLES FOLLOW THE TRADITION OF THE ELDERS? IN
FACT, THEY DON'T WASH
THEIR HANDS BEFORE
EATING." 3 JESUS ANS-
WERED, "AND YOU, WHY DO
YOU BREAK GOD'S COM-
MAND FOR THE SAKE OF YO-
UR TRADITIONS? 4 FOR
GOD SAID: DO YOUR DUTY TO
YOUR FATHER AND MOTHER
AND: WHOEVER CURSES
HIS FATHER AND MOTHER
IS TO BE PUT TO DEATH.
5 BUT YOU SAY THAT
ANYONE MAY SAY TO
HIS FATHER OR MOTHER:
'WHAT YOU COULD HAVE
EXPECTED FROM ME, I
HAVE RESERVED FOR THE
TEMPLE.' 6 IN THIS
CASE, ACCORDING TO
YOU, A PERSON IS FREED
OF HIS DUTY TO HIS FA-
THER AND MOTHER.
AND SO, YOU HAVE ERASED
GOD'S COMMAND FOR
THE SAKE OF YOUR TRA-
DITIONS.
7 HYPOCRITES! ISAIAH
RIGHTLY PROPHESIED OF
YOU WHEN HE SAID:

8 THIS PEOPLE HONORS ME WITH
THEIR LIPS, BUT THEIR HEART IS
FAR FROM ME. 9 THE WORSHIP THEY
OFFER ME IS WORTHLESS, FOR THEY
ONLY TEACH HUMAN RULES."

WASHING HANDS AND CLEANNESS OF HEART

10 JESUS THEN CALLED THE PEOPLE NEAR HIM AND SAID
TO THEM, "LISTEN AND UNDERSTAND: 11 WHAT ENTERS IN-
TO THE MOUTH DOES NOT MAKE A PERSON UNCLEAN,
WHAT DEFILES HIM IS WHAT COMES OUT OF HIS MOUTH."
12 AFTER A WHILE THE DISCIPLES GATHERED AROUND
JESUS AND SAID, "DO YOU KNOW THAT THE PHARISEES
WERE OFFENDED BY
WHAT YOU SAID?" 13
JESUS ANSWERED, "EVE-
RY PLANT WHICH MY HE-
AVENLY FATHER HAS NOT
PLANTED SHALL BE UP-
ROOTED. 14 PAY NO AT-
TENTION TO THEM! THEY
ARE BLIND LEADING
THE BLIND. WHEN A
BLIND MAN LEADS AN-
OTHER THE TWO WILL
FALL INTO A PIT." 15
PETER SAID TO HIM, "EX-
PLAIN THIS SENTENCE
TO US." 16 JESUS REPLIED,
"SO EVEN YOU, TOO, ARE DULL?
17 DO YOU NOT SEE THAT
WHATEVER ENTERS THE
MOUTH GOES INTO THE
STOMACH AND THEN OUT
OF THE BODY? 18 BUT
WHAT COMES OUT OF THE
MOUTH COMES FROM THE
HEART, AND THAT IS WHAT
MAKES A PERSON UN-
CLEAN. 19 INDEED, IT
IS FROM THE HEART THAT
EVIL DESIRES COME —
MURDER, ADULTERY, IM-
MORALITY, THEFT, LIES, SLANDER. 20 THIS IS WHAT MA-
KES A PERSON UNCLEAN BUT EATING WITHOUT WASHING
THE HANDS DOES NOT MAKE A PERSON UNCLEAN."

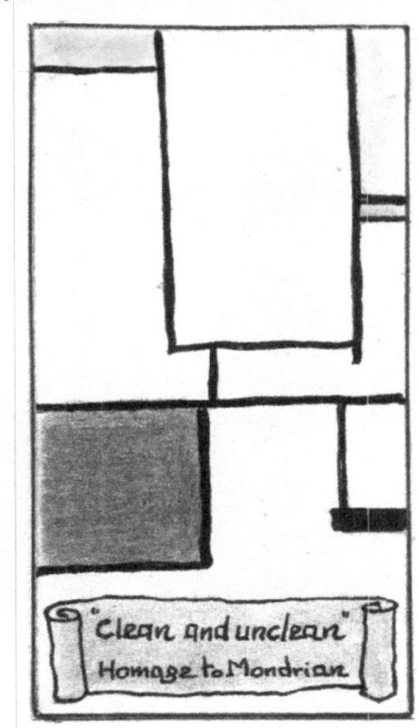

THE FAITH OF THE CANAANITE WOMAN

21 LEAVING THAT PLACE, JESUS WITHDREW TO THE REGION OF
TYRE AND SIDON. 22 NOW A CANAANITE WOMAN CAME FROM
THAT AREA AND BEGAN TO CRY OUT, "LORD, SON OF DAVID,
HAVE PITY ON ME! MY DAUGHTER IS TORMENTED BY A
DEMON." 23 BUT JESUS DID NOT ANSWER HER, NOT EVEN A
WORD. SO HIS DISCIPLES APPROACHED HIM AND SAID, "SEND
HER AWAY: SEE HOW SHE IS SHOUTING AFTER US." 24

THEN JESUS SAID TO HER, "I WAS SENT ONLY TO THE LOST
SHEEP OF THE NATION OF ISRAEL." 25 BUT THE WOMAN WAS
ALREADY KNEELING BEFORE JESUS AND SAID, "SIR, HELP ME!"
26 JESUS REPLIED, "IT IS NOT RIGHT TO TAKE THE BREAD
FROM THE CHILDREN AND THROW IT TO THE LITTLE DOGS." 27
THE WOMAN SAID, "IT IS TRUE, SIR, BUT EVEN THE LITTLE
DOGS EAT THE CRUMBS WHICH FALL FROM THEIR MASTER'S
TABLE." 28 THEN JESUS SAID, "WOMAN, HOW GREAT
IS YOUR FAITH! LET IT BE AS YOU WISH." AND HER
DAUGHTER WAS HEALED AT THAT MOMENT.

SECOND MIRACLE OF THE LOAVES

29 FROM THERE JESUS WENT TO THE SHORE OF LAKE
GALILEE, AND THEN WENT UP INTO THE HILLS WHERE HE
SAT DOWN. 30 GREAT CROWDS CAME TO HIM, BRINGING THE
DUMB, THE BLIND, THE LAME, THE CRIPPLED, AND MANY WITH
OTHER INFIRMITIES. THE PEOPLE CARRIED THEM TO HIM, AND
HE HEALED THEM. 31 ALL WERE ASTONISHED SEEING THE
DUMB SPEAKING, THE LAME WALKING, THE CRIPPLED HE-
ALED AND THE BLIND ABLE TO SEE; SO THEY GLORIFIED THE
GOD OF ISRAEL. JESUS

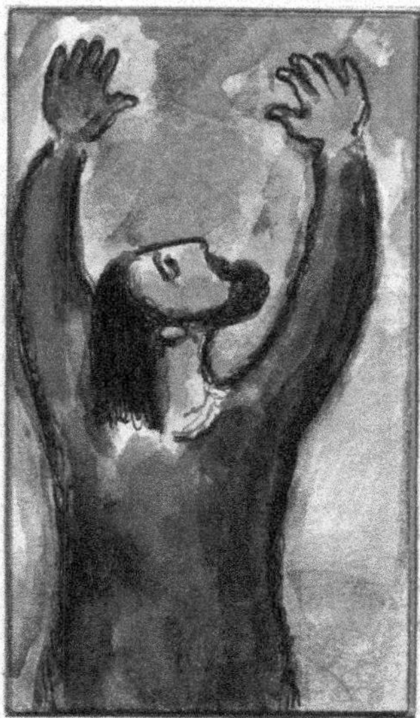

32 CALLED HIS DISCI-
PLES AND SAID TO THEM,
"I AM FILLED WITH COM-
PASSION FOR THESE PE-
OPLE; THEY HAVE BEEN
WITH ME FOR THREE
DAYS AND NOW HAVE NO-
THING TO EAT. I DO NOT
WANT TO SEND THEM
AWAY FASTING, OR THEY
MAY FAINT ON THE WAY."
33 HIS DISCIPLES SAID
TO HIM, "AND WHERE SHALL
WE FIND ENOUGH BREAD
IN THIS WILDERNESS TO
FEED THIS CROWD?" 34
JESUS SAID TO THEM,
"HOW MANY LOAVES DO YOU
HAVE?" THEY ANSWERED,
"SEVEN, AND A FEW SMALL
FISH." 35 SO JESUS OR-
DERED THE PEOPLE TO SIT
ON THE GROUND. THEN 36
HE TOOK THE SEVEN LOAVES
AND THE SMALL FISH AND
GAVE THANKS TO GOD. HE
BROKE THEM AND GAVE THEM TO HIS DISCIPLES, WHO DIS-
TRIBUTED THEM TO THE PEOPLE. 37 THEY ALL ATE AND
WERE SATISFIED, AND THE LEFTOVER PIECES FILLED SEVEN
WICKER BASKETS. 38 FOUR THOUSAND MEN HAD EATEN, NOT
COUNTING THE WOMEN AND CHILDREN. 39 THEN TAKING LE-
AVE OF THE CROWD, JESUS GOT INTO THE BOAT AND
CROSSED TO THE REGION OF MAGDALA.

THE PHARISEES ASK FOR A SIGN

16 1 THE PHARISEES AND SADDUCEES APPEARED.
THEY WANTED TO PUT JESUS TO THE TEST AND ASKED
HIM FOR SOME HEAVENLY SIGN. 2 JESUS REPLIED,
"WHEN EVENING COMES, YOU SAY: 'IT WILL BE A GOOD DAY AS
THE SKY IS RED.' 3 AND IN THE MORNING YOU SAY: 'THE
SKY IS RED IN THE EAST; TODAY WILL BE STORMY WEATHER.'
IF YOU KNOW HOW TO INTERPRET THE APPEARANCE OF THE
SKY, WHY CAN'T YOU INTERPRET THE SIGNS OF THE TIMES?"
4 AN EVIL AND UNBELIEVING PEOPLE WANT A SIGN, BUT

NO SIGN WILL BE GIVEN THEM EXCEPT THE SIGN OF JONAH."
SO JESUS LEFT THEM AND WENT AWAY.
5 WHEN THE DISCIPLES WENT TO THE OTHER SIDE, THEY
FORGOT TO TAKE BREAD. 6 IT WAS THEN THAT JESUS
SAID TO THEM, "BEWARE AND DO NOT TRUST THE YEAST
OF THE PHARISEES AND SADDUCEES." 7 AND THE
DISCIPLES SAID TO ONE ANOTHER,
"HE MEANS THE BREAD WE DID NOT BRING."

8 JESUS WAS AWARE OF THIS, SO HE SAID TO
THEM, "YOU OF LITTLE FAITH! WHY DO YOU SPEAK
ABOUT THE BREAD YOU HAVEN'T GOT? DO YOU STILL
NOT UNDERSTAND? DO YOU NOT REMEMBER THE FIVE
LOAVES FOR THE FIVE THOUSAND 9 AND HOW MANY BAS-
KETS YOU GATHERED? 10 OR THE SEVEN LOAVES
FOR THE FOUR THOUSAND AND HOW MANY
WICKER BASKETS YOU GATHERED?
11 HOW CAN YOU FAIL TO UNDERSTAND THAT

I WAS NOT TALKING OF BREAD WHEN I TOLD YOU: BEWARE
OF THE YEAST OF THE PHARISEES AND SADDUCEES?"
12 THEN THEY UNDERSTOOD THAT HE WAS NOT TALKING
OF YEAST FOR BREAD, BUT OF THE TEACHING OF THE
PHARISEES AND SADDUCEES.

13 AFTER JESUS CAME TO CAESAREA PHILIPPI, HE ASKED HIS
DISCIPLES, "WHAT DO PEOPLE SAY OF THE SON OF MAN? WHO DO
THEY SAY I AM?" 14 THEY SAID, "SOME SAY YOU ARE JOHN THE
BAPTIST, OTHERS ELIJAH OR
JEREMIAH OR ONE OF THE
PROPHETS." 15 JESUS AS-
KED THEM, "BUT YOU, WHO
DO YOU SAY I AM?" 16 PE-
TER ANSWERED, "YOU ARE
THE CHRIST, THE SON OF THE
LIVING GOD." 17 JESUS
REPLIED, "IT IS WELL FOR
YOU, SIMON SON OF JONA,
FOR IT IS NOT FLESH OR
BLOOD THAT HAS REVE-
ALED THIS TO YOU BUT MY
FATHER IN HEAVEN. 18
AND NOW I SAY TO YOU: YOU
ARE PETER AND ON THIS
ROCK I WILL BUILD MY
CHURCH AND THE POWERS OF
DEATH WILL NOT OVERCOME
IT. 19 I WILL GIVE YOU THE
KEYS OF THE KINGDOM OF
HEAVEN: WHATEVER YOU
BIND ON EARTH SHALL BE
BOUND IN HEAVEN; WHAT
YOU UNBIND ON EARTH
SHALL BE UNBOUND IN
HEAVEN." 20 THEN HE

ORDERED HIS DISCIPLES NOT TO TELL ANYONE THAT
HE WAS THE CHRIST.

JESUS PREDICTS HIS DEATH

21 FROM THAT DAY JESUS BEGAN TO MAKE IT CLEAR TO
HIS DISCIPLES THAT HE MUST GO TO JERUSALEM; JESUS
WOULD SUFFER MANY THINGS FROM THE JEWISH AUTHO-
RITIES, THE CHIEF PRIESTS AND THE TEACHERS OF
THE LAW. HE WOULD BE KILLED AND BE RAISED
ON THE THIRD DAY. 22 THEN PETER TOOK HIM
ASIDE AND BEGAN TO REPROACH HIM, "NEVER,
LORD! NO, THIS MUST NEVER HAPPEN TO YOU." 23 BUT
JESUS TURNED TO HIM AND SAID, "GET BEHIND ME,
SATAN! YOU WOULD HAVE ME STUMBLE. YOUR
THOUGHTS ARE NOT FROM GOD BUT FROM MAN."

"AND NOW I SAY TO YOU:
YOU ARE PETER AND
ON THIS ROCK I SHALL
BUILD MY CHURCH"
(MATTHEW 16:18)

(24) JESUS SAID TO HIS DISCIPLES, "IF ANYONE WANTS TO
FOLLOW ME, LET HIM DENY HIMSELF, TAKE UP HIS CROSS AND
FOLLOW ME. (25) FOR WHOEVER CHOOSES TO SAVE HIS
LIFE WILL LOSE IT, BUT THE ONE WHO LOSES HIS
LIFE FOR MY SAKE
WILL FIND IT.
(26) WHAT WILL ONE
GAIN BY WINNING
THE WHOLE WORLD
IF HE DESTROYS HIM-
SELF? THERE IS NO-
THING HE CAN GIVE
TO RECOVER HIS OWN
SELF.
(27) KNOW THAT THE
SON OF MAN WILL
COME IN THE GLORY
OF HIS FATHER WITH
THE HOLY ANGELS,
AND HE WILL REWARD
EACH ONE ACCORDING
TO HIS DEEDS.
(28) TRULY, I TELL YOU,
THERE ARE SOME
HERE WHO WILL NOT
DIE BEFORE THEY
SEE THE SON OF MAN
COMING AS A KING."

THE TRANSFIGURATION OF JESUS

17 (1) SIX DAYS LATER, JESUS TOOK WITH HIM PETER
AND JAMES AND HIS BROTHER JOHN AND LED THEM
UP A HIGH MOUNTAIN WHERE THEY WERE ALONE. (2)
JESUS'S APPEARANCE WAS CHANGED BEFORE THEM: HIS
FACE SHONE LIKE THE SUN AND HIS CLOTHES BECAME
BRIGHT AS LIGHT. (3) JUST THEN MOSES AND ELIJAH
APPEARED TO THEM, TALKING WITH JESUS.
(4) PETER SPOKE AND SAID TO JESUS, "MASTER, IT IS
GOOD THAT WE ARE HERE. IF YOU SO WISH, I WILL MA-
KE THREE TENTS: ONE FOR YOU, ONE FOR MOSES, AND
ONE FOR ELIJAH." (5) PETER WAS STILL SPEAKING

WHEN A BRIGHT CLOUD COVERED THEM IN ITS SHA-
DOW, AND A VOICE FROM THE CLOUD SAID, "THIS IS MY
SON, THE BELOVED, MY CHOSEN ONE. LISTEN TO HIM."
(6) ON HEARING THE VOICE, THE DISCIPLES FELL TO
THE GROUND, FULL OF FEAR. (7) BUT JESUS CAME,
TOUCHED THEM AND SAID, "STAND UP, DO NOT BE AFRAID."
(8) WHEN THEY RAISED THEIR EYES, THEY NO LONGER
SAW ANYONE EXCEPT JESUS. (9) AND AS THEY CAME
DOWN THE MOUNTAIN, JESUS COMMANDED THEM NOT
TO TELL ANYONE WHAT THEY HAD JUST SEEN, UNTIL
THE SON OF MAN BE RAISED FROM THE DEAD.
(10) THE DISCIPLES THEN ASKED HIM, "WHY DO THE TE-
ACHERS OF THE LAW SAY THAT ELIJAH MUST COME FIRST?"

(11) AND JESUS ANSWERED, "SO IT IS; FIRST COMES
ELIJAH TO SET EVERYTHING AS IT HAS TO BE. (12) BUT
I TELL YOU, ELIJAH HAS ALREADY COME AND THEY
DID NOT RECOGNIZE HIM, BUT TREATED HIM AS
THEY PLEASED. AND THEY WILL ALSO MAKE THE SON
OF MAN SUFFER." (13) THEN THE DISCIPLES UNDERSTOOD
THAT JESUS WAS REFERRING TO JOHN THE BAPTIST.

JESUS HEALS AN EPILEPTIC BOY

(14) WHEN THEY MET THE PEOPLE, A MAN APPROACHED
JESUS, KELK BEFORE HIM AND SAID, (15) "SIR, HAVE
PITY ON MY SON WHO IS AN EPILECTIC AND IS IN A
WRETCHED STATE. HE HAS OFTEN FALLEN INTO THE

FIRE OR INTO THE WATER. (16) I BROUGHT HIM TO YOUR
DISCIPLES BUT THEY COULD NOT HEAL HIM." (17) JESUS
REPLIED, "YOU, FAITHLESS AND EVIL PEOPLE! HOW LONG
MUST I BE WITH YOU? HOW LONG MUST I PUT UP WITH
YOU? BRING HIM HERE TO ME." (18) AND JESUS COM-
MANDED THE EVIL SPIRIT TO LEAVE THE BOY, AND THE
BOY WAS IMMEDIATELY HEALED. (19) THE DISCIPLES
THEN GATHERED AROUND JESUS AND ASKED HIM, "WHY
COULDN'T WE DRIVE OUT THE SPIRIT?" (20) JESUS
SAID, "BECAUSE YOU HAVE LITTLE FAITH. I SAY TO
YOU: IF ONLY YOU HAD THE FAITH THE SIZE OF A MUST-
ARD SEED YOU COULD TELL A MOUNTAIN TO MOVE, AND THE
MOUNTAIN WOULD OBEY. NOTHING WOULD BE IMPOSSIBLE

TO YOU. (21) ONLY PRAYER AND FASTING CAN DRIVE OUT THIS
KIND OF SPIRIT." (22) WHILE JESUS WAS IN GALILEE
WITH THE TWELVE, SAID TO THEM, "THE SON OF MAN WILL BE
DELIVERED INTO THE HANDS OF MEN, (23) AND THEY WILL
KILL HIM. BUT HE WILL RISE ON THE THIRD DAY."
THE TWELVE WERE DEEPLY GRIEVED.

THE TEMPLE TAX - (24) WHEN THEY RE-
TURNED TO CAPERNAUM, THE TEMPLE TAX COLLECT-
ORS CAME TO PETER AND ASKED HIM, "DOES YOUR MAS-
TER PAY THE TAX?" (25) HE ANSWERED, "CERTAINLY."
PETER THEN ENTERED THE HOUSE, AND JESUS ASKED
HIM, "WHAT DO YOU THINK, SIMON? WHO PAY TAXES
OR TRIBUTES TO THE KINGS OF THE EARTH: THEIR SONS
OR THE OTHER PEOPLE?" (26) PETER REPLIED, "THE
OTHERS." JESUS TOLD HIM, "THE SONS, THEN, ARE TAX-FREE."

27 BUT SO AS NOT TO OFFEND THIS PEOPLE, GO TO
THE SEA, THROW IN A HOOK AND OPEN THE MOUTH
OF THE FIRST FISH YOU CATCH. YOU WILL FIND A
COIN IN IT, TAKE IT AND PAY THEM FOR YOU AND ME."

WHO IS THE GREATEST? SCANDALS

18 1 AT THAT TIME THE DISCIPLES CAME TO JESUS
AND ASKED HIM, "WHO IS THE GREATEST IN THE
KINGDOM OF HEAVEN?" 2 THEN JESUS CALLED
A LITTLE CHILD, SET HIM IN THE MIDST OF THE DISCEPLES,

3 AND SAID, "I ASSURE YOU THAT UNLESS YOU CHANGE
AND BECOME LIKE LITTLE CHILDREN, YOU CANNOT
ENTER THE KINGDOM OF HEAVEN. 4 WHOEVER MAKES
HIMSELF LOWLY LIKE THIS CHILD IS THE GREATEST IN
THE KINGDOM OF HEAVEN, 5 AND WHOEVER RECEIVES
SUCH A CHILD IN MY NAME RECEIVES ME. 6 IF ANY OF
YOU SHOULD CAUSE ONE OF THESE LITTLE ONES WHO BE-
LIEVE IN ME TO STUMBLE AND FALL, IT WOULD BE BETTER
FOR YOU TO BE THROWN INTO THE DEPTHS OF THE SEA WITH
A GREAT MILLSTONE AROUND YOUR NECK.
7 WOE TO THE WORLD BECAUSE OF SO MANY SCANDALS!

SCANDALS NECESSARILY
COME, BUT WOE TO THE
ONE WHO HAS BROUGHT
IT ABOUT. 8 IF YOUR
HAND OR FOOT DRAGS
YOU INTO SIN, CUT IT OFF
AND THROW IT AWAY. IT IS
BETTER FOR YOU TO ENTER
LIFE WITHOUT A HAND OR
A FOOT THAN TO BE THROWN
INTO ETERNAL FIRE WITH
YOUR TWO HANDS AND
TWO FEET. 9 AND IF
YOUR EYE DRAGS YOU
INTO SIN, TEAR IT OUT
AND THROW IT AWAY. IT
IS BETTER FOR YOU TO
ENTER LIFE WITH ONE
EYE THAN TO BE THROWN
INTO THE FIRE OF HELL
WITH YOUR TWO EYES.
10 SEE THAT YOU DO NOT
DESPISE ANY OF THESE
LITTLE ONES, FOR I TELL
YOU: THEIR ANGELS IN
HEAVEN CONTINUALLY SEE THE FACE OF MY HEAVENLY
FATHER. 11 THE SON OF MAN HAS COME TO SAVE THE
LOST. 12 WHAT DO YOU THINK OF THIS? IF A MAN HAS
A HUNDRED SHEEP AND ONE OF THEM STRAYS, WON'T
HE LEAVE THE NINETY-NINE ON THE HILL SIDE AND GO
TO LOOK FOR THE STRAY ONE? 13 AND I TELL YOU:
WHEN HE FINALLY FINDS IT, HE IS MORE PLEASED FOR
IT THAN FOR THE NINETY-NINE THAT DIDN'T GET LOST.

14 IT IS THE SAME WITH YOUR FATHER IN HEAVEN:
THERE THEY DON'T WANT EVEN ONE OF THESE
LITTLE ONES TO BE LOST.

15 IF YOUR BROTHER HAS SINNED AGAINST YOU,
GO AND POINT OUT HIS FAULT TO HIM IN PRIVATE, AND
IF HE LISTEN TO YOU, YOU HAVE WON YOUR BROTHER.
16 IF HE DOESN'T LISTEN TO YOU, TAKE WITH YOU ONE OR
TWO OTHERS SO THAT THE
CASE MAY BE DECIDED BY
THE EVIDENCE OF TWO OR
THREE WITNESSES. 17 IF HE
STILL REFUSES TO LISTEN TO
THEM, INFORM THE ASSEM-
BLED CHURCH ABOUT HIM.
BUT IF HE DOES NOT LISTEN
TO THE CHURCH, THEN RE-
GARD HIM AS A PAGAN OR A
PUBLICAN. 18 I SAY TO YOU:
WHATEVER YOU BIND ON EARTH,
HEAVEN WILL KEEP UNBO-
UND. 19 IN LIKE MANNER,
I SAY TO YOU: IF ON EARTH
TWO OF YOU ARE UNITED IN
ASKING FOR ANYTHING,
IT WILL BE GRANTED TO
YOU BY MY HEAVENLY FA-
THER. 20 FOR WHERE
TWO OR THREE ARE GA-
THERED IN MY NAME, I AM
THERE AMONG THEM."

21 THEN PETER ASKED
HIM, "LORD, HOW MANY
TIMES MUST I FORGIVE
THE OFFENSES OF MY BROTHER? SEVEN TIMES?" 22
JESUS ANSWERED, "NO, NOT SEVEN TIMES, BUT
SEVENTY-SEVEN TIMES.

THE UNMERCIFUL SERVANT

23 THIS STORY THROWS LIGHT ON THE KINGDOM OF HE-
AVEN. A KING DECIDED TO SETTLE THE ACCOUNTS OF
HIS SERVANTS. 24 AMONG THE FIRST WAS ONE WHO
OWED HIM TEN THOUSAND PIECES OF GOLD. 25 AS THE
MAN COULD NOT REPAY THE DEBT, THE KING COM-
MANDED THAT HE BE SOLD AS A SLAVE WITH HIS

WIFE, CHILDREN AND ALL HIS GOODS IN PAYMENT. 26 THE OF-
FICIAL THREW HIMSELF AT THE KING'S FEET AND SAID, 'GIVE
ME TIME, AND I WILL PAY YOU BACK EVERYTHING.' 27 THE
KING TOOK PITY ON HIM AND NOT ONLY SET HIM FREE
BUT EVEN CANCELLED HIS DEBT." 28 THE OFFICIAL
THEN LEFT THE KING AND MET ONE OF HIS COMPANIONS
WHO OWED HIM A HUNDRED PIECES OF SILVER. HE GRABBED
HIM BY THE NECK ALMOST STRANGLING HIM, SHOUTING, 'PAY
ME WHAT YOU OWE!' 29 HIS COMPANION THREW HIMSELF
AT HIS FEET AND ASKED HIM, 'GIVE ME TIME AND I WILL
PAY EVERYTHING!' 30 THE OTHER DID NOT AGREE, BUT SENT
HIM TO PRISON UNTIL HE HAD PAID ALL HIS DEBT.

31 HIS COMPANIONS SAW WHAT HAPPENED. VERY INDIGNANT THEY REPORTED EVERYTHING TO THEIR LORD.

32 THEN THE LORD SUMMONED HIS OFFICIAL AND SAID, 'WICKED SERVANT, I FORGAVE YOU ALL THAT YOU OWED WHEN YOU BEGGED ME TO DO SO. 33 WEREN'T YOU BOUND TO HAVE PITY ON YOUR COMPANIONS AS I HAD PITY ON YOU?' 34 THE LORD WAS NOW ANGRY, SO HE HANDED HIS SERVANT OVER TO BE PUNISHED, UNTIL HE HAD PAID HIS WHOLE DEBT."

35 JESUS ADDED, "SO WILL MY HEAVENLY FATHER DO WITH YOU UNLESS EACH OF YOU SINCERELY FORGIVES HIS BROTHERS."

JESUS SPEAKS ABOUT DIVORCE

19 1 WHEN JESUS HAD FINISHED THE TEACHING, HE LEFT GALILEE AND ARRIVED AT THE BORDER OF JUDEA, ON THE OTHER SIDE OF THE JORDAN RIVER. 2 A GREAT CROWD WAS WITH HIM AND THERE, TOO, HE HEALED THEIR SICK. 3 SOME PHARISEES APPROACHED HIM. THEY WANTED TO TEST HIM AND ASKED, "IS A MAN ALLOWED TO DIVORCE HIS WIFE FOR ANY REASON HE WANTS?" 4 JESUS REPLIED, "HAVE YOU NOT READ THAT IN THE BEGINNING THE CREATOR MADE THEM MALE AND FEMALE, 5 AND HE SAID: MAN

HAS NOW TO LEAVE FATHER AND MOTHER, AND BE JOINED TO HIS WIFE, AND THE TWO SHALL BECOME ONE BODY? 6 SO THEY ARE NO LONGER TWO BUT ONE BODY: LET NO ONE SEPARATE WHAT GOD HAS JOINED."

7 THEY ASKED HIM, "THEN, WHY DID MOSES COMMAND US TO WRITE A BILL OF DISMISSAL IN ORDER TO DIVORCE?" 8 JESUS REPLIED, "MOSES KNEW YOUR STUBBORN HEART, SO HE ALLOWED YOU TO DIVORCE YOUR WIVES, BUT IT WAS NOT SO IN THE BEGINNING. 9 SO I SAY TO YOU: WHOEVER DIVORCES HIS WIFE, UNLESS IT BE FOR INFIDELITY, AND MARRIES ANOTHER, COMMITS ADULTERY."

10 THE DISCIPLES SAID, "IF THAT IS THE CONDITION OF A MARRIED MAN, IT IS BETTER NOT TO MARRY." 11 JESUS SAID, "NOT EVERYBODY CAN ACCEPT WHAT I HAVE SAID, BUT ONLY THOSE WHO HAVE RECEIVED THIS GIFT.

12 SOME ARE BORN INCAPABLE OF MARRIAGE. OTHERS HAVE BEEN MADE THAT WAY BY MEN. BUT THERE ARE OTHERS WHO HAVE GIVEN UP THE POSSIBILITY OF MARRIAGE FOR THE SAKE OF THE KINGDOM OF HEAVEN. HE WHO CAN ACCEPT THIS, SHOULD ACCEPT IT."

JESUS AND THE CHILDREN

13 THEN LITTLE CHILDREN WERE BROUGHT TO JESUS THAT HE MIGHT LAY HIS HANDS ON THEM WITH A PRAYER. BUT THE DISCIPLES SCOLDED THOSE WHO BROUGH THEM. 14 JESUS THEN SAID "LET THEM BE!

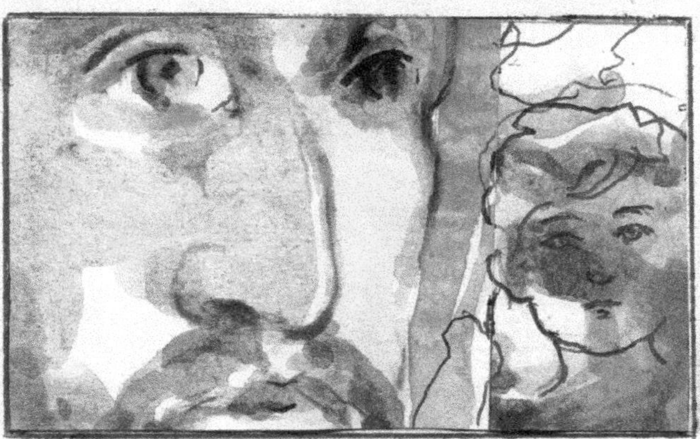

DO NOT STOP CHILDREN COMING TO ME, FOR THE KINGDOM OF HEAVEN BELONGS TO SUCH PEOPLE LIKE THEM. 15 JESUS THEN LAID HIS HANDS ON THEM AND WENT HIS WAY.

THE RICH YOUNG MAN

16 IT WAS THEN THAT A YOUNG MAN APPROACHED HIM AND ASKED, "MASTER, WHAT GOOD WORK MUST I DO TO RECEIVE ETERNAL LIFE?" 17 JESUS ANSWERED, "WHY DO YOU ASK ME OF WHAT IS GOOD? ONLY ONE IS GOOD. IF YOU WANT TO ENTER ETERNAL LIFE KEEP THE COMMANDMENTS." 18 THE YOUNG MAN SAID, "WHICH COMMANDMENTS?" JESUS REPLIED, "DO NOT KILL, DO NOT COMMIT ADULTERY, DO NOT STEAL, DO NOT BEAR FALSE WITNESS, 19 HONOR YOUR FATHER AND MOTHER, AND LOVE YOUR NEIGHBOR AS YOURSELF."

20 THE YOUNG MAN SAID TO HIM, "I HAVE KEPT ALL OF THESE, WHAT IS STILL LACKING?" 21 JESUS SAID, "IF YOU WISH TO BE PERFECT, GO AND SELL ALL THAT YOU POSSESS AND GIVE THE MONEY TO THE POOR AND YOU WILL BECOME THE OWNER OF A TREASURE IN HEAVEN. THEN COME BACK AND FOLLOW ME." 22 ON HEARING THIS, THE YOUNG MAN WENT AWAY SAD FOR HE HAD GREAT WEALTH. 23 JESUS SAID TO HIS DISCEPLES, "TRULY I SAY TO YOU: IT WILL BE HARD FOR ONE WHO IS RICH TO ENTER THE KINGDOM OF HEAVEN.

24 YES, BELIEVE ME: IT IS EASIER FOR A CAMEL TO ENTER THE EYE OF A NEEDLE THAN FOR THE ONE WHO IS RICH TO ENTER THE KINGDOM OF HEAVEN."

25 ON HEARING THIS THE DISCEPLES WERE ASTONISHED AND SAID, "WHO, THEN, CAN BE SAVED?" 26 JESUS LOOKED STEADILY AT THEM AND ANSWERED, "FOR HUMANS IT IS IMPOSSIBLE, BUT FOR GOD ALL THINGS ARE POSSIBLE."

DM © 11
320
CCCXX

27 THEN PETER SPOKE UP AND SAID, "YOU SEE WE HAVE
GIVEN UP EVERYTHING TO FOLLOW YOU: WHAT WILL BE
OUR LOT?" 28 JESUS ANSWERED, "YOU WHO HAVE
FOLLOWED ME, LISTEN TO MY WORDS: ON THE DAY
OF RENEWAL, WHEN THE SON OF MAN SITS ON HIS
THRONE IN GLORY, YOU, TOO, WILL SIT ON TWELVE
THRONES TO RULE THE TWELVE TRIBES OF ISRAEL.
29 AS FOR THOSE WHO HAVE LEFT HOUSES, BRO-
THERS, SISTERS, FATHER, MOTHER, CHILDREN OR
PROPERTY FOR MY NAME'S SAKE, THEY WILL

RECEIVE A HUNDREDFOLD AND BE GIVEN ETERNAL
LIFE. 30 MANY WHO ARE NOW FIRST WILL BE
LAST, AND MANY WHO ARE NOW LAST WILL BE FIRST.

THE WORKERS IN THE VINEYARD

20 1 THIS STORY THROWS LIGHT ON THE KINGDOM
OF HEAVEN. A LANDOWNER WENT OUT EARLY IN
THE MORNING TO HIRE WORKERS FOR HIS VINE-
YARD. 2 HE AGREED TO PAY THE WORKERS A SILVER COIN
PER DAY, AND SENT THEM TO HIS VINEYARD. 3 HE AGAIN WENT
OUT AT ABOUT NINE IN THE MORNING, AND SEEING MEN IDLE
IN THE SQUARE, 4 SAID TO THEM: "YOU, TOO, GO TO MY VINE-
YARD AND I WILL PAY YOU WHAT IS JUST." SO THEY WENT.

THE OWNER WENT OUT AT
MIDDAY AND AGAIN AT THREE
IN THE AFTERNOON, 5 AND
HE DID THE SAME. 6 FI-
NALLY HE WENT OUT AT
THE LAST WORKING HOUR
AND HE SAW OTHERS IDLE
STANDING THERE. HE SAID
TO THEM: 'WHY DO YOU
STAY IDLE THE WHOLE
DAY?' THEY ANSWERED:
'BECAUSE NO ONE HAS
HIRED US.' THE MASTER
SAID: 'GO AND WORK IN MY
VINEYARD.' 7-8 WHEN EVE-
NING CAME, THE OWNER
SAID TO HIS MANAGER,
'CALL THE WORKERS AND
PAY THEM BEGINNING
WITH THE LAST AND END-
ING WITH THE FIRST.' 9
THOSE WHO HAD COME AT
THE LAST HOUR TURNED
UP AND RECEIVED ONE DE-
NARIUS EACH. 10 WHEN
IT WAS THE TURN OF THE FIRST, THEY THOUGHT TO RECEIVE
MORE. 11 BUT THEY, TOO, RECEIVED A DENARIUS EACH. SO,
ON RECEIVING IT, THEY BEGAN TO GRUMBLE AGAINST THE
LANDOWNER. 12 THEY SAID: 'THESE HARDLY WORKED
AN HOUR, YET YOU HAVE TREATED THEM THE SAME AS US
WHO HAVE ENDURED THE DAY'S BURDEN AND HEAT.' 13
THE OWNER SAID TO ONE OF THEM, 'FRIEND, I HAVE NOT
BEEN UNJUST TO YOU. DID WE NOT AGREE ON A DENARIUS
A DAY? 14 SO TAKE WHAT IS YOURS AND GO. I WANT
TO GIVE TO THE LAST THE SAME AS I GIVE TO YOU. 15
DON'T I HAVE THE RIGHT TO DO AS I PLEASE WITH MY
MONEY? WHY ARE YOU ENVIOUS WHEN I AM KIND?'
16 SO WILL IT BE: THE LAST WILL
BE FIRST, THE FIRST WILL BE LAST."

THIRD PROPHECY OF THE PASSION

17 WHEN JESUS WAS GOING TO JERUSALEM, TOOK THE
TWELVE ASIDE AND SAID TO THEM, 18 "SEE, WE ARE GO-
ING TO JERUSALEM. THERE THE SON OF MAN WILL BE
GIVEN OVER TO THE CHIEF PRIESTS AND THE TEACHERS OF
THE LAW WHO WILL CONDEMN HIM TO DEATH. 19 THEY
WILL HAND HIM OVER TO THE FOREIGNERS WHO WILL
MOCK HIM, SCOURGE HIM AND CRUCIFY HIM. BUT HE
WILL BE RAISED TO LIFE ON THE THIRD DAY."

THE MOTHER OF JAMES AND JOHN ASKS FOR THE FIRST SEATS

20 THEN THE MOTHER OF JAMES AND JOHN CAME TO
JESUS WITH HER SONS,

AND SHE KNELT DOWN
TO ASK A FAVOR. JESUS
21 SAID TO HER, "WHAT
DO YOU WANT?" AND SHE
ANSWERED, "HERE YOU
HAVE MY TWO SONS.
GRANT THAT THEY
MAY SIT, ONE AT YOUR
RIGHT AND ONE AT
YOUR LEFT, WHEN YOU
ARE IN YOUR KINGDOM."
22 JESU SAID TO THE
BROTHERS, "YOU DO NOT
KNOW WHAT YOU ARE
ASKING. CAN YOU
DRINK THE CUP THAT
I AM ABOUT TO DRINK?"
THEY ANSWERED, "WE
CAN." 23 JESUS RE-
PLIED, "YOU WILL
INDEED DRINK MY
CUP, BUT TO SIT AT
MY RIGHT OR AT MY
LEFT IS NOT FOR ME
TO GRANT. THAT WILL
BE FOR THOSE FOR
WHOM THE FATHER
HAS PREPARED IT." 24 THE OTHER TEN HEARD
ALL THIS AND WERE ANGRY WITH THE TWO BRO-
THERS. 25 THEN JESUS CALLED THEM TO HIM
AND SAID, "YOU KNOW THAT THE RULERS OF THE NATIONS
ACT AS TYRANTS, AND THE POWERFULL OPPRESS THEM.
26 IT SHALL NOT BE SO AMONG YOU; WHOEVER DE-
CIDES TO BE MORE IMPORTANT IN YOUR GROUP SHALL

MAKE HIMSELF YOUR SERVANT. 27 AND WHOEVER
WANTS TO BE FIRST MUST MAKE HIMSELF THE SER-
VANT OF ALL. 28 BE LIKE THE SON OF MAN WHO HAS
COME, NOT TO BE SERVED BUT TO SERVE AND TO GIVE
HIS LIFE TO REDEEM MANY." 29 AS THEY LEFT JERI-
CHO, A GREAT CROWD FOLLOWED THEM ON THE WAY. 30
TWO BLIND MEN WERE SITTING BY THE ROADSIDE
AND WHEN THEY HEARD THAT JESUS WAS PAS-
SING BY, THEY BEGAN TO CALL OUT, "SON OF
DAVID, HAVE MERCY ON US!"

(31) THE PEOPLE TOLD THEM TO KEEP QUIET, BUT THEY
SHOUTED EVEN LOUDER, "LORD, SON OF DAVID, HAVE
MERCY ON US!" (32) JESUS STOPPED, CALLED OUT TO
THEM AND ASKED, "WHAT DO YOU WANT ME TO DO
FOR YOU?" (33) THEY SAID, "LORD, OPEN OUR EYES."
(34) JESUS WAS MOVED WITH COMPASSION AND
TOUCHED THEIR EYES. IMMEDIATELY THEY RECO-
VERED THEIR SIGHT AND BEGAN TO FOLLOW JESUS.

JESUS ENTERS JERUSALEM

21 (1) WHEN THEY DREW NEAR JERUSALEM AND
ARRIVED AT BETHPHAGE, ON THE MOUNT OF OLI-
VES, JESUS SENT TWO OF HIS DISCIPLES, (2)
SAYING, "GO TO THE VILLAGE IN FRONT OF YOU, AND

THERE YOU WILL FIND A DONKEY TIED UP WITH ITS COLT
BY HER. UNTIE THEM AND BRING THEM TO ME. (3) IF
ANYONE SAYS SOMETHING TO YOU, SAY: THE LORD NE-
EDS THEM BUT HE WILL SEND THEM BACK AT ONCE."
(4) THIS HAPPENED IN FULFILLMENT OF WHAT THE
PROPHET SAID:

(5) SAY TO THE DAUGHTER OF ZION: SEE, YOUR KING COMES
TO YOU IN ALL SIMPLICITY, RIDING ON A DONKEY,
A BEAST OF BURDEN, WITH ITS COLT.

(6) THE DISCIPLES WENT AS JESUS HAD INSTRUCTED
THEM, (7) AND THEY BROUGHT THE DONKEY WITH ITS
COLT. THEN THEY THREW THEIR CLOAKS ON ITS BACK,
AND JESUS SAT UPON THEM. (8) MANY PEOPLE ALSO
SPREAD THEIR CLOAKS ON THE ROAD, WHILE OTHERS CUT
LEAFY BRANCHES FROM THE TREES AND SPREAD THEM ON

THE ROAD. (9) THE PEOPLE WHO WALKED AHEAD OF JESUS AND
THOSE WHO FOLLOWED HIM BEGAN TO SHOUT

"HOSANNA TO THE SON OF DAVID! BLESSED IS HE WHO
COMES IN THE NAME OF THE LORD! HOSANNA,
GLORY IN THE HIGHEST!"

(10) WHEN JESUS ENTERED JERUSALEM, THE
WHOLE CITY WAS DISTURBED. THE PEOPLE
ASKED, "WHO IS THIS MAN?" (11) AND THE CROWD
ANSWERED, "THIS IS THE PROPHET JESUS
FROM NAZARETH OF GALILEE."

JESUS EXPELS THE DEALERS

(12) SO JESUS WENT INTO THE TEMPLE AND DROVE
OUT ALL WHO WERE BUYING AND SELLING IN THE
TEMPLE AREA. HE OVERTURNED THE TABLES
OF THE MONEY CHANGERS, AND THE STOOLS OF
THOSE WHO SOLD PI-
GEONS. (13) AND HE
SAID TO THEM, "IT IS
WRITTEN: MY HOUSE
SHALL BE CALLED A
HOUSE OF PRAYER.
BUT YOU HAVE NOW
TURNED IT INTO A
DEN OF THIEVES."
(14) THE BLIND AND
THE LAME ALSO
CAME TO HIM IN THE
TEMPLE AND JESUS
HEALED THEM. (15)
THE CHIEF PRIESTS
AND THE TEACHERS
OF THE LAW SAW THE
WONDERFUL THINGS
JESUS HAD JUST DO-
NE, AND THE CHIL-
DREN SHOUTING IN
THE TEMPLE AREA,
"HOSANNA TO THE SON
OF DAVID!" (16) THEY
BECAME INDIGNANT
AND SAID TO JESUS,
"DO YOU HEAR WHAT
THEY SAY?" JESUS ANSWERED, "YES; HAVE YOU NEVER
READ THIS: FROM THE MOUTHS OF CHILDREN AND IN-
FANTS YOU HAVE GOT PERFECT PRAISE?" (17) SO LE-
AVING THEM HE WENT OUT OF THE CITY AND CAME TO
BETHANY WHERE HE SPENT THE NIGHT.

JESUS CURSES THE FIG TREE

(18) WHILE RETURNING TO THE CITY EARLY IN THE MOR-
NING, JESUS FELT HUNGRY. (19) HE NOTICED A FIG TREE
BY THE ROAD, WENT UP TO
IT AND FOUND NOTHING ON
IT BUT LEAVES. THEN HE
SAID TO THE TREE, "NEVER
AGAIN BEAR FRUIT!" AND
IMMEDIATELY THE FIG
TREE WITHERED. WHEN
(20) THE DISCIPLES SAW
THIS, THEY WERE ASTO-
NISHED AND THEY SAID,
"HOW DID THE FIG TREE
SUDDENLY DRY UP?" (21)
JESUS TOLD THEM,
"TRULY, I SAY TO YOU: IF
YOU HAD FAITH AND DID
NOT DOUBT, NOT ONLY
COULD YOU DO WHAT I
HAVE DONE WITH THE
FIG TREE, BUT YOU
COULD EVEN SAY TO
THAT MOUNTAIN:
'GO AND THROW YOUR-
SELF INTO THE SEA!'
AND IT WOULD BE
DONE. (22) WHATEVER
YOU ASK FOR FULL OF
FAITH IN PRAYER, YOU
WILL RECEIVE."
(23) JESUS ENTERED THE TEMPLE AND WAS TEACHING
WHEN THE CHIEF PRIESTS, TEACHERS OF THE LAW AND JEWISH
AUTHORITIES ASKED HIM, "WHAT AUTHORITY HAVE YOU TO
ACT LIKE THIS? WHO GAVE YOU AUTHORITY TO DO ALL THIS?"
(24) JESUS ANSWERED THEM, "I WILL ALSO ASK YOU A
QUESTION, ONLY ONE. AND IF YOU GIVE MY AN ANSWER, I
THEN WILL TELL YOU BY WHAT AUTHORITY I DO THESE
THINGS. WAS JOHN'S BAPTISM A WORK OF GOD, OR WAS
SOMETHING HUMAN?" (25) THEY REASONED AMONG
THEMSELVES, "IF WE REPLY THAT IT WAS A WORK OF
GOD, HE WILL SAY: WHY, THEN, DID YOU NOT BELIEVE HIM?"

26 AND IF WE SAY: THE BAPTISM OF JOHN WAS HU-
MAN, BEWARE OF THE PEOPLE SINCE ALL HOLD JOHN
AS A PROPHET." 27 SO THEY ANSWERED JESUS, "WE
DO NOT KNOW." AND JESUS SAID, "NEITHER WILL I
TELL YOU BY WHAT RIGHT I DO THESE THINGS."

THE PARABLE OF THE TWO SONS

28 JESUS SAID, "WHAT DO YOU THINK OF THIS? A MAN
HAD TWO SONS. HE WENT TO THE FIRST AND SAID, "SON TO-
DAY GO AND WORK IN MY

VINEYARD.' 29 AND THE
SON ANSWERED: 'I DON'T
WANT TO.' BUT LATER HE
THOUGHT BETTER OF IT
AND WENT. 30 THEN THE
FATHER WENT TO THE
SECOND AND GAVE HIM
THE SAME COMMAND.
THIS SON REPLIED: 'I WILL
GO, SIR.' BUT HE DID NOT
GO. 31 WHICH OF THE
TWO DID WHAT THE FA-
THER WANTED?" THEY
ANSWERED, "THE FIRST."
AND JESUS SAID, "TRULY,
I SAY TO YOU: THE PUBLI-
CANS AND THE PROSTI-
TUTES ARE AHEAD OF YOU
ON THE WAY TO THE KING-
DOM OF HEAVEN. 32 FOR
JOHN CAME TO SHOW YOU
THE WAY OF GOODNESS
BUT YOU DID NOT BELIEVE
HIM, YET THE PUBLICANS
AND THE PROSTITUTES
DID. YOU WERE WITNESSES
OF THIS, BUT YOU NE-
ITHER REPENTED NOR BELIEVED HIM.

THE PARABLE OF THE TENANTS

33 LISTEN TO ANOTHER EXAMPLE: THERE WAS A
LANDOWNER WHO PLANTED A VINEYARD. HE PUT A FENCE
AROUND IT, DUG A HOLE FOR THE WINEPRESS, BUILT A TO-
WER, LEASED THE VINEYARD TO TENANTS AND WENT TO A
DISTANT COUNTRY. 34 AT HARVEST TIME, HE SENT HIS
SERVANTS TO THE TENANTS TO COLLECT HIS SHARE OF
THE HARVEST. 35 BUT THE TENANTS SEIZED HIS SERVANTS,
BEAT ONE, KILLED ANOTHER AND STONED ANOTHER. 36
HE AGAIN SENT MORE SERVANTS, BUT THEY WERE TREATED

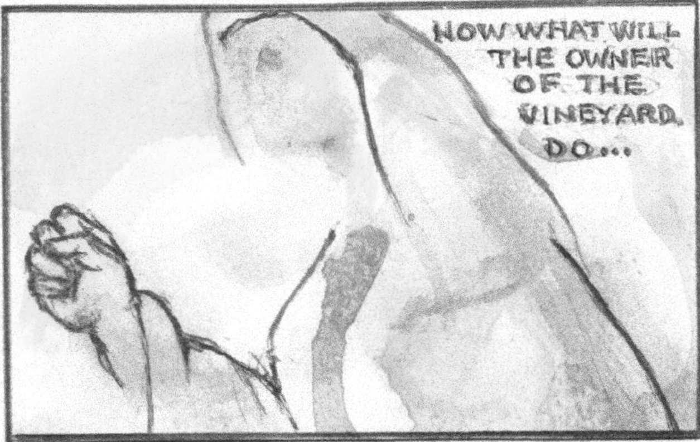

IN THE SAME WAY. 37 FINALLY HE SENT HIS SON, THINKING:
'THEY WILL RESPECT HIM.' 38 BUT WHEN THE TENANTS SAW
THE SON, THEY THOUGHT: 'HE IS THE ONE WHO IS TO INHERIT
THE VINEYARD. LET'S KILL HIM AND HIS INHERITANCE WILL
BE OURS.' 39 SO THEY SEIZED HIM, THREW HIM OUT OF
THE VINEYARD AND KILLED HIM. 40 NOW, WHAT WILL THE
OWNER OF THE VINEYARD DO WITH THE TENANTS WHEN HE
COMES?" 41 THEY SAID, "HE WILL BRING THOSE EVIL
MEN TO AN EVIL END, AND LEASE THE VINEYARD TO OTHERS
WHO WILL PAY HIM IN DUE TIME." 42 AND JESUS REPLIED,
"HAVE YOU NEVER READ WHAT THE SCRIPTURES SAY?

THE STONE REJECTED BY THE BUILDERS
HAS BECOME THE KEYSTONE. THIS WAS THE
LORD'S DOING; AND WE MARVEL AT IT.

43 THEREFORE I SAY TO YOU: THE KINGDOM OF HEAVEN WILL
BE TAKEN FROM YOU AND GIVEN TO A PEOPLE WHO WILL
YIELD A HARVEST. 44 "WHOEVER FALLS ON THIS STONE
WILL BE BROKEN TO PIECES, AND HE ON WHOM IT
FALLS WILL BE GROUND TO DUST."
45 WHEN THE CHIEF PRIESTS AND THE PHARISEES
HEARD THESE PARABLES, THEY REALIZED THAT JESUS

WAS REFERRING TO THEM. 46 THEY WOULD HAVE ARRESTED
HIM, BUT FEARED THE CROWD WHO LOOKED IN HIM A PROPHET.

THE WEDDING FEAST

22 1 JESUS WENT ON SPEAKING IN PARABLES:
2 "THIS STORY THROWS LIGHT ON THE KINGDOM
OF HEAVEN. A KING CELEBRATED THE WEDDING OF
HIS SON. 3 HE SENT HIS SERVANTS TO CALL THE INVITED
GUESTS TO THE WEDDING FEAST, BUT THE GUESTS REFUSED
TO COME. 4 AGAIN HE SENT OTHER SERVANTS TO SAY
TO THE INVITED GUESTS:

'I HAVE PREPARED A BAN-
QUET, SLAUGHTERED MY
FATTENED CALVES, EVERY-
THING IS READY, COME TO
THE FEAST.' 5 BUT THEY
PAID NO ATTENTION; SOME
WENT TO THEIR FIELDS
OR TO THEIR WORK. 6
THE REST SEIZED THE SER-
VANT, INSULTED AND KIL-
LED THEM. 7 THE KING
WAS ANGRY, SENT HIS TRO-
OPS THOSE MURDERERS
AND BURN THEIR CITY. 8
HE SAID TO HIS SERVANTS:
'THE BANQUET IS READY,
BUT THOSE INVITED GUESTS
WERE NOT WORTHY. 9 GO,
THEN, TO THE CROSSROADS
AND INVITE EVERYONE YOU
FIND TO THE WEDDING.' 10
THE SERVANTS WENT OUT
INTO THE STREETS AND GAT-
HERED EVERYONE THEY
FOUND, GOOD AND BAD
ALIKE, AND THE HALL WAS FILLED WITH GUESTS. 11 THE KING
CAME IN, LOOKED AT THE GUESTS, AND NOTICED A MAN NOT
WEARING THE FESTAL GARMENTS. 12 HE SAID TO HIM: 'FRIEND,
HOW DID YOU ENTER WITHOUT THE FESTAL GARMENT?' BUT
THE MAN WAS SILENT. 13 SO THE KING SAID TO HIS SERVANTS:
'BIND HIS HANDS AND FEET AND THROW HIM INTO THE DARK
WHERE THERE IS WEEPING AND GNASHING OF TEETH.' 14

'KNOW THAT MANY ARE CALLED, BUT FEW ARE CHOSEN."

PAYING TAXES TO CAESAR

15 THE PHARISEES WENT OUT AND TOOK COUNSEL ON HOW
THEY COULD TRAP JESUS WITH HIS OWN WORDS. 16
THEN SENT THEIR DISCIPLES WITH THE MEMBERS OF
HEROD'S PARTY FOR THIS PURPOSE. THEY SAID TO JESUS,
"MASTER, WE KNOW YOU ARE SINCERE AND TRULY TEACH GOD'S
WAY; YOU ARE NOT INFLUENCED BY OTHERS NOR ARE
YOU AFRAID OF ANYONE.

THE MOTHER OF JAMES AND JOHN ASKS FOR THE FIRST SEATS
Homage to Chagall
321
CCCXXI

17 TELL US, THEN, WHAT YOU THINK: IS IT AGAINST THE
LAW TO PAY TAXES TO CAESAR? SHOULD WE PAY 18
THEM OR NOT?" BUT JESUS UNDERSTOOD THEIR
EVIL INTENT, AND SAID TO THEM, "HYPOCRITES! WHY
ARE YOU TESTING ME? 19 SHOW ME THE COIN YOU PAY
THE TAXES WITH". THEY SHOWED HIM A DENARIUS,
20 AND JESUS SAID TO THEM, "WHOSE HEAD IS THIS
AND WHOSE NAME?" 21 THEY ANSWERED, "CAESAR'S"
THEN JESUS REPLIED, "THEREFORE, GIVE TO CAESAR

WHAT BELONGS TO CAESAR, AND TO GOD WHAT BELONGS TO
GOD." 22 ASTONISHED BY HIS ANSWER, THEY WENT AWAY.

THE RESURRECTION OF THE DEAD

23 THAT SAME DAY SOME SADDUCEES, WHO CLAIM THERE
IS NO RESURRECTION, QUESTIONED JESUS IN THIS WAY. 24
"MASTER, MOSES SAID THAT IF ANYONE DIES WITHOUT ANY
CHILDREN, HIS BROTHER MUST TAKE HIS WIFE AND HAVE
A CHILD WHO WILL BE OF THE DEAD MAN. 25 THERE WERE
SEVEN BROTHERS; THE FIRST MARRIED, AND HIS WIFE, AFTER
HIS DEATH, MARRIED HIS BROTHER, AS SHE HAD NO CHILDREN.
26 THE SAME THING HAPPENED TO THE SECOND AND THE THIRD
UNTIL THE SEVENTH. 27 THEN, LAST OF ALL, THE WOMAN ALSO
DIED. 28 NOW, IN THE RESURRECTION, TO WHICH OF THE SE-

VEN WILL SHE BE WIFE, FOR
ALL HAD HER AS WIFE?"
29 JESUS ANSWERED, "YOU
ARE WRONG BECAUSE YOU
UNDERSTAND NEITHER THE
THE SCRIPTURES NOR GOD'S
POWER. 30 IN THE RESUR-
RECTION, NEITHER MEN NOR
WOMEN WILL MARRY, FOR
THEY WILL BE LIKE ANGELS
IN HEAVEN. 31 AS FOR THE
RESURRECTION, HAVE YOU
NOT REFLECTED ON GOD'S
WORDS: 32 I AM THE GOD
OF ABRAHAM, OF ISAAC AND
OF JACOB? HE IS NOT THE
GOD OF THE DEAD, BUT OF
THE LIVING." 33 THE PEOPLE
WHO HEARD HIM WERE AS-
TONISHED AT HIS TEACHING.
34 WHEN THE PHARISEES
HEARD HOW JESUS HAD SI-
LENCED THE SADDUCEES,
THEY CAME TOGETHER. 35
ONE TEACHER OF THE LAW
TESTED HIM WITH THE QUES-
TION, 36 "TEACHER, IN
THE LAW, WHICH IS THE MOST
IMPORTANT COMMANDMENT?"
37 JESUS ANSWERED, "YOU SHALL THE LORD YOUR GOD,
LOVE WITH ALL YOUR HEART, WITH ALL YOUR SOUL
AND WITH ALL YOUR MIND. 38 THIS IS THE FIRST
AND THE MOST IMPORTANT OF ALL COMMANDMENT'S. 39
BUT THERE IS ANOTHER ONE SIMILAR TO IT: YOU SHALL LOVE
YOUR NEIGHBOR AS YOURSELF. 40 THE WHOLE LAW AND THE
PROPHETS ARE FOUNDED ON THESE TWO COMMANDMENTS."

THE MESSIAH, SON OF GOD

41 AS THE PHARISEES WERE GATHERED THERE, JESUS
ASKED THEM, 42 "WHAT DO YOU THINK OF THE CHRIST?"
WHOSE SON IS HE TO BE?" THEY ANSWERED, "DAVID'S".
43 JESUS THEN ASKED, "WHY DID DAVID, INSPIRED BY
GOD, CALL THE CHRIST LORD? FOR HE SAYS IN A PSALM:

44 THE LORD SAID TO MY LORD: SIT AT MY RIGHT UNTIL I
PUT YOUR ENEMIES UNDER YOUR FEET.

45 IF DAVID CALLS HIM LORD, HOW CAN HE BE HIS SON?"
46 NO ONE COULD ANSWER HIM, NOT A WORD. FROM
THAT DAY ON, NO ONE DARED QUESTION HIM ANYMORE.

DO NOT IMITATE THE TEACHERS OF THE LAW

23 1 THEN JESUS SAID TO THE CROWDS AND HIS DISCE-
PLES: 2 THE TEACHERS OF THE LAW AND THE PHARI-
SEES OCCUPY THE SEAT OF MOSES. 3 LISTEN AND DO
ALL THEY SAY, BUT DON'T ACT AS THEY DO, 4 FOR THEY FIRST
DON'T PRACTICE WHAT THEY TEACH. THEY GIVE HEAVY BUR-
DENS VERY DIFFICULT TO CARRY, ALL ON THE SHOULDERS OF
THE PEOPLE. BUT THEY DO
NOT RAISE A FINGER TO MO-
VE THEM. 5 THEY DO EVERY-
THING TO BE SEEN BY PE-
OPLE; THEY WEAR WIDE
BANDS OF THE LAW AND RO-
BES WITH LARGE TASSELS.
6 THEY OCCUPY THE FIRST
SEATS AT FEASTS AND SY-
NAGOGUES, 7 ENJOY
BEING GREETED IN THE
MARKETPLACE AND CAL-
LED 'MASTER' BY THE PE-
OPLE. 8 BUT YOU DON'T
LET YOURSELVES BE CAL-
LED MASTER AS YOU HAVE
ONLY ONE MASTER; YOU
ARE ALL BROTHERS. 9
DO NOT CALL ANYONE ON
EARTH FATHER, BECAUSE
YOU HAVE ONLY ONE FAT-
HER WHO IS IN HEAVEN.
10 NOR SHOULD YOU BE
CALLED 'LEADER', BECA-
USE CHRIST IS THE ONLY
LEADER FOR YOU. 11 LET
THE GREATEST OF YOU BE
THE SERVANT OF ALL.
12 FOR WHOEVER CONS-
IDER HIMSELF GREAT
SHALL BE HUMBLED, AND WHOEVER HUMBLES HIM-
SELF SHALL BE ESTEEMED.

SEVEN WOES FOR THE PHARISEES

13 THEREFORE, WOE TO YOU, TEACHERS OF THE LAW AND
PHARISEES, YOU HYPOCRITES! YOU SHUT THE DOOR TO
THE KINGDOM OF HEAVEN IN PEOPLE'S FACES. YOU DO
NOT ENTER, NEITHER ALLOW OTHERS TO DO SO.
14 WOE TO YOU, TEACHERS OF THE LAW AND PHARI-
SEES, YOU HYPOCRITS!

(15) YOU TRAVEL BY SEA AND LAND TO WIN A SINGLE
CONVERT, YET ONCE HE IS CONVERTED YOU TURN HIM
TWICE AS FIT FOR HELL AS YOURSELVES. (16) WOE TO
YOU BLIND GUIDES! YOU SAY: TO SWEAR BY THE TEMPLE
IS NOT BINDING, BUT TO SWEAR BY THE TREASURE OF
THE TEMPLE IS. (17) BLIND FOOLS! WHICH IS WORTH
MORE? THE GOLD IN THE TEMPLE OR THE TEMPLE
WHICH MAKES THE GOLD A SACRED TREASURE? YOU
SAY: (18) TO SWEAR BY THE ALTAR IS NOT BINDING, BUT
TO SWEAR BY THE OFFERING ON THE ALTAR IS. (19)

HOW BLIND YOU ARE!
WHICH IS OF MORE VALUE:
THE OFFERING OF THE
ALTAR OR THE ALTAR THAT
MAKES THE OFFERING SA-
CRED? (20) WHOEVER
SWEARS BY THE ALTAR
IS SWEARING BY THE ALTAR
AND EVERYTHING ON IT. (21)
WHOEVER SWEARS BY THE
TEMPLE IS SWEARING BY
IT AND BY GOD WHO DWELLS
IN THE TEMPLE. (22) WHO-
EVER SWEARS BY HEAVEN
IS SWEARING BY THE THRONE
OF GOD AND BY HIM WHO
IS SEATED ON IT. (23) WOE
TO YOU, TEACHERS OF THE
LAW AND PHARISEES, YOU
HYPOCRITES! YOU DO NOT
FORGET THE MINT, ANISE
AND CUMMIN SEEDS WHEN
YOU PAY THE TENTH OF EVERY-
THING, BUT THEN YOU FOR-
GET WHAT IS MORE FUNDA-
MENTAL IN THE LAW: JUST-
ICE, MERCY AND FAITH. YOU
MUST PRACTICE THESE,
WITHOUT NEGLECTING THE
OTHERS. (24) BLIND GUIDES! YOU STRAIN A MOSQUITO, BUT
SWALLOW A CAMEL. (25) WOE TO YOU, TEACHERS OF THE LAW
AND PHARISEES, YOU HYPOCRITES! YOU FILL THE PLATE AND
THE CUP WITH THEFT AND VIOLENCE, AND THEN SAY A BLES-
SING OVER THEM. (26) BLIND PHARISEES! PURIFY THE
INSIDE FIRST, THEN THE OUTSIDE TOO WILL BE PURIFIED.
(27) WOE TO YOU, TEACHERS OF THE LAW AND PHARISEES,
YOU HYPOCRITES! YOU ARE LIKE WHITEWASHED TOMBS
BEAUTIFUL OUTSIDE, BUT INSIDE THERE ARE ONLY DEAD BO-
NES AND FILTH. (28) IN THE SAME WAY YOU APPEAR AS RE-
LIGIOUS MEN BEFORE PEOPLE, BUT YOU ARE FULL OF HYPO-
CRISY AND WICKEDNESS. (29) WOE TO YOU, TEACHERS OF THE

LAW AND PHARISEES, YOU HYPOCRITES! YOU BUILD TOMBS FOR
THE PROPHETS AND DECORATE MONUMENTS OF HOLY MEN. (30)
YOU SAY: HAD WE LIVED IN THE TIME OF OUR FATHERS, WE
WOULD NOT HAVE JOINED THEM IN THE BLOOD OF PROPHETS.
(31) SO YOU CONFESS TO BE SONS OF THOSE WHO MURDE-
RED THE PROPHETS. (32) AND NOW, FINISH OFF WHAT
FATHERS BEGAN! (33) SERPENTS, RACE OF VIPERS! HOW
CAN YOU ESCAPE CONDAMNATION TO HELL?

(34) AND SO I AM SENDING YOU PROPHETS, WISE MEN
AND TEACHERS, BUT YOU WILL BEHEAD AND CRUCIFY
THEM, AND FLOG OTHERS IN THE SYNAGOGUES OR
DRIVE THEM FROM ONE CITY TO ANOTHER.
(35) BECAUSE OF THIS YOU WILL BE ACCOUNTABLE FOR ALL
THE INNOCENT BLOOD THAT HAS BEEN SHED ON THE
EARTH, FROM THE BLOOD OF ABEL TO THE BLOOD OF
ZECHARIAH, SON OF BARACHIAH, WHOM YOU MURDE-
RED BETWEEN THE ALTAR AND THE SANCTUARY.
(36) TRULY, I SAY TO YOU: THE PRESENT GENERA-
TION WILL PAY FOR ALL THIS.

(37) JERUSALEM, JERUSALEM! YOU MURDER THE

PROPHETS AND STONE THOSE SENT TO YOU BY GOD.
HOW OFTEN WOULD I HAVE GATHERED YOUR
CHILDREN TOGETHER, JUST AS A HEN GATHERS HER
CHICKS UNDER HER WINGS, BUT YOU REFUSED! (38)
NOW YOU WILL BE LEFT WITH AN EMPTY TEMPLE.
(39) I TELL YOU THAT YOU WILL NO LONGER SEE
ME UNTIL YOU SAY:

"BLESSED IS HE WHO COMES IN THE
NAME OF THE LORD!"

THE RUIN OF JERUSALEM AND THE END OF THE WORLD

24 (1) JESUS LEFT THE TEMPLE AND AS HE WAS WALK-
ING AWAY, HIS DISCIPLES CAME TO HIM AND POIN-
TED OUT THE GREAT
TEMPLE BUILDINGS. (2)
BUT HE SAID, "YOU SEE
ALL THIS? TRULY I SAY TO
YOU: NOT ONE STONE WILL
BE LEFT UPON ANOTHER
HERE, ALL WILL BE
THROWN DOWN." (3) LA-
TER WHEN JESUS WAS
SITTING ON THE MOUNT
OF OLIVES THE DISCIPLES
ASKED HIM PRIVATELY,
"TELL US WHEN THIS
WILL TAKE PLACE.
WHAT SIGN WILL BE GI-
VEN US BEFORE YOUR
COMING AND THE END
OF HISTORY?"
(4) JESUS ANSWERED,
"BE ON YOUR GUARD
AND LET NO ONE MIS-
LEAD YOU. (5) MANY
WILL COME, CLAIM-
ING MY TITLE AND SAY-
ING: 'I AM THE MESSIAH,'
AND THEY WILL MIS-
LEAD MANY PEOPLE.

(6) YOU WILL HEAR OF WARS AND THREATS OF WAR, BUT
DO NOT BE TROUBLED, FOR THESE THINGS MUST HAPPEN,
BUT IT IS NOT YET THE END. (7) NATIONS WILL FIGHT
ONE ANOTHER AND KINGDOM OPPOSE KINGDOM. THERE
WILL BE FAMINES AND EARTHQUAKES IN MANY PLACES,
(8) BUT ALL THESE ARE ONLY THE BEGINNING: THE FIRST
PAINS OF CHILDBIRTH. (9) THEN THEY WILL ARREST YOU,
TORTURE AND KILL YOU. ALL NATIONS WILL HATE YOU FOR
YOU BEAR MY NAME.

10 THEN MANY WILL STUMBLE AND FALL; WILL BETRAY
ONE ANOTHER AND BECOME ENEMIES. 11 FALSE PROPHETS
WILL COME AND MISLEAD CROWDS, 12 AND FOR THIS GREAT
WICKEDNESS, LOVE WILL GROW COLD IN MANY PEOPLE. 13
BUT HE WHO HOLDS OUT TO THE END WILL BE SAVED. 14
THE GOOD NEWS OF THE KINGDOM WILL BE PROCLAIMED
THROUGHOUT THE WORLD FOR ALL NATIONS, THEN THE END
WILL COME. 15 WHEN YOU SEE WHAT THE PROPHET DANIEL
FORETOLD: THE IDOL OF THE INVADER SET UP IN THE TEM-

PLE (MAY THE READER UN-
DERSTAND). 16 THEN LET
THOSE IN JUDEA FLEE TO
THE MOUNTAINS. 17 IF YOU
ARE ON THE HOUSETOP, DO
NOT COME DOWN TO TAKE
ANYTHING. 18 IF YOU ARE
IN THE FIELD, DO NOT TURN
BACK TO FETCH YOUR CLOAK.
19 HARD TIMES WILL
COME FOR PREGNANT WO-
MEN AND MOTHERS WITH
BABIES AT THE BREAST!
20 PRAY THAT YOU NOT
FLEE IN WINTER OR ON A
SABBATH. 21 FOR THERE
WILL BE GREAT PAIN NE-
VER KNOWN SINCE THE
BEGINNING OF THE WORLD
UNTIL NOW, AND NEVER TO
BE KNOWN AGAIN. 22 IF
THAT TIME WERE NOT TO
BE SHORTENED, NO ONE
WOULD SURVIVE. BUT GOD
WILL SHORTEN IT FOR THE
SAKE OF HIS CHOSEN ONES. 23 THEN, IF ANYONE SAYS TO
YOU: 'LOOK, THE MESSIAH IS HERE! HE IS THERE! DO
NOT BELIEVE IT. 24 FOR FALSE CHRISTS AND FALSE
PROPHETS WILL APPEAR, PERFORM SIGNS AND WONDERS SO
GREAT THAT WOULD DECEIVE EVEN GOD'S PEOPLE, IF THAT
WERE POSSIBLE. 25 SEE, I HAVE TOLD YOU EVERYTHING
AHEAD OF TIME. 26 SO, IF ANYONE TELLS YOU: 'HE IS IN
THE DESERT', DO NOT GO. IF THEY SAY: HE IS IN SUCH A

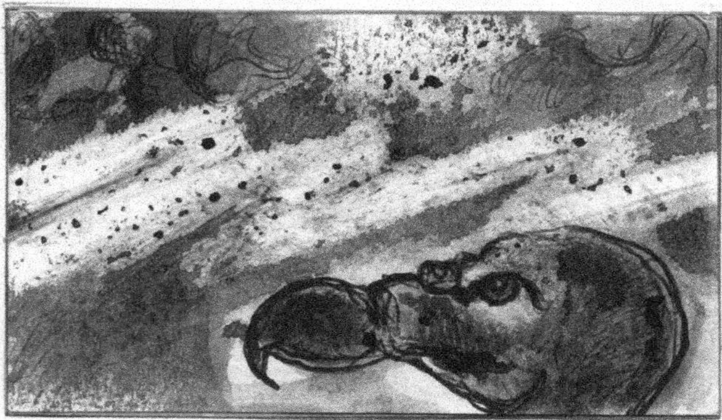

SECLUDED PLACE, DO NOT BELIEVE IT. 27 FOR THE COMING OF
THE SON OF MAN WILL BE LIKE FLASHING LIGHTNING FROM
THE EAST EVEN TO THE WEST. WHEREVER THE BODY
28 IS, THE VULTURES WILL GATHER.

THE COMING OF THE SON OF MAN

29 LATER, AFTER THE DISTRESS, THE SUN WILL GROW
DARK, THE MOON WILL NOT GIVE ITS LIGHT, THE STARS
WILL FALL FROM THE SKIES, AND THE UNIVERSE WILL BE
SHAKEN. 30 THEN THE SIGN OF THE SON OF MAN WILL
APPEAR IN THE HEAVEN: AS ALL THE NATIONS OF THE EARTH
BEAT THEIR BREASTS, THEY WILL SEE THE SON OF MAN
COMING IN THE CLOUDS OF HEAVEN WITH DIVINE POWER
AND THE FULLNESS OF GLORY. 31 HE WILL SEND HIS
ANGELS TO SOUND THE TRUMPET AND GATHER THE CHOSEN
ONES FROM THE FOUR WINDS, FROM ONE END OF THE EARTH TO
THE OTHER. 32 LEARN A LESSON FROM THE FIG TREE.
WHEN ITS BRANCES GROW TENDER AND ITS LEAVES BEGIN
TO SPROUT, YOU KNOW THAT SUMMER IS NEAR. 33 IN
THE SAME WAY, WHEN YOU SEE ALL THAT I TOLD YOU,
KNOW THAT THE TIME IS NEAR, BY THE DOOR. 34 TRULY,
I SAY TO YOU, THIS GENERATION WILL NOT PASS UNTIL
ALL THESE THINGS HAVE HAPPENED. 35 HEAVEN AND
EARTH WILL PASS AWAY, BUT MY WORDS WILL NOT PASS
AWAY. 36 BUT AS FAR AS THE DAY AND THAT HOUR, NO ONE
KNOWS WHEN IT WILL COME, NOT EVEN THE ANGELS OF
GOD NOR THE SON, BUT ONLY THE FATHER. 37 AT THE
COMING OF THE SON OF MAN IT WILL BE JUST AS IT WAS

IN THE TIME OF NOAH. 38 IN THOSE DAYS BEFORE THE
FLOOD, PEOPLE WERE EATING AND DRINKING, AND MAR-
RYING, UNTIL WHEN NOAH WENT INTO THE ARK. 39
YET THEY DID NOT KNOW WHAT WOULD HAPPEN UNTIL
THE FLOOD CAME AND SWEPT THEM AWAY. SO WILL IT BE
AT THE COMING OF THE SON OF MAN. 40 OF TWO MEN IN
THE FIELD, ONE WILL BE TAKEN AND THE OTHER LEFT.
41 OF TWO WOMEN GRINDING WHEAT TOGETHER AT THE
MILL, ONE WILL BE TAKEN AND THE OTHER LEFT.

BE ON THE ALERT

42 STAY AWAKE, THEN, AS YOU DO NOT KNOW ON WHAT
DAY YOUR LORD WILL COME. 43 JUST THINK: IF THE
OWNER OF THE HOUSE KNEW THAT THE THIEF WOULD
COME BY NIGHT AT A CERT-
AIN HOUR, WOULD STAY AW-
AKE TO PREVENT HIM FROM
BREAKING INTO HIS HOUSE.
44 SO BE ALERT, FOR THE
SON OF MAN WILL COME AT
THE HOUR YOU LEAST EXPECT.
45 AND A GOOD SERVANT
WHOM HIS MASTER HAS PUT
IN CHARGE OF HIS HOUSE-
HOLD TO FEED THEM AT
THE PROPER TIME. 46 FOR-
TUNATE IS THE SERVANT IF
HIS MASTER FINDS HIM
CARRYING OUT HIS DUTY.
47 TRULY, I SAY TO YOU,
HIS LORD WILL ENTRUST
HIM WITH EVERYTHING HE
HAS. 48 NOT SO WITH
THE BAD SERVANT WHO
WHO THINKS: MY MAS-
TER IS DELAYED. 49
AND HE BEGINS ILL-
TREATING HIS FELLOW
SERVANTS WHILE EAT-
ING AND DRINKING
WITH DRUNKARDS. 50

BUT HIS MASTER WILL COME ON THE DAY HE DOES
NOT KNOW AND AT THE HOUR HE LEAST EXPECTS. 51
HE WILL DISMISS THAT SERVANT AND TREATS HIM AS HYPOCRI-
TES ACT, WHERE THERE WILL BE WEEPING AND GNASHING OF TEETH.

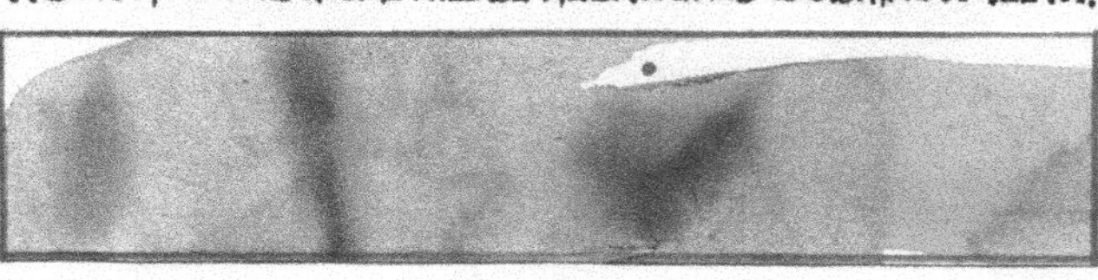

YOU SHALL LOVE YOUR NEIGHBOUR AS YOURSELF
Matthew 22:39
I HAVE A DREAM....
... THAT ALL MEN ARE CREATED EQUAL...
... THAT LITTLE BLACK BOYS AND BLACK GIRLS
WILL BE ABLE TO JOIN HANDS
WITH LITTLE WHITE BOYS
AND WHITE GIRLS
AS SISTERS and BROTHERS...
... And the glory of the Lord
will be revealed...
... I HAVE A DREAM!
CCCXXII
DM© 08

THE TEN BRIDESMAIDS

25 1 A STORY ON WHAT WILL BE THE KINGDOM OF HEAVEN.
TEN BRIDESMAIDS WENT WITH THEIR LAMPS TO MEET
THE BRIDEGROOM. 2 FIVE OF THEM WERE CARELESS
AND FIVE WERE SENSIBLE. 3 THE CARELESS ONES TOOK
THEIR LAMPS AND DID NOT BRING EXTRA OIL. 4 BUT THOSE
WHO WERE SENSIBLE, BROUGHT WITH THEIR LAMPS FLASKS
OF OIL. 5 AS THE BRIDEGROOM DELAYED, THEY GREW
DROWSY AND ALL FELL ASLEEP. 6 AT MIDNIGHT, A CRY RANG
OUT: 'THE BRIDEGROOM IS HERE, COME OUT AND MEET HIM!'
7 ALL THE MAIDENS WOKE UP AND TRIMMED THEIR LAMPS.
8 THE CARELESS ONES SAID TO THE SENSIBLE ONES: 'GIVE

US SOME OIL, FOR OUR LAMPS ARE GOING OUT.' 9 THEY ANS-
WERED: 'THERE MAY NOT BE ENOUGH FOR YOU AND US. YOU
BETTER GO TO THOSE WHO SELL AND BUY FOR YOURSELVES.'
10 THEY WERE OUT BUYING OIL WHEN THE BRIDEGROOM CAME
AND THOSE WHO WERE READY WENT WITH HIM TO THE WEDDING
FEAST, AND THE DOORS WERE SHUT. 11 LATER THE REST OF THE
BRIDESMAIDS ARRIVED AND CALLED OUT, 'LORD, LORD, OPEN TO
US!' 12 BUT HE ANSWERED, 'TRULY, I DON'T KNOW YOU.' 13 SO, STAY
AWAKE, FOR YOU DO NOT KNOW THE DAY NOR THE HOUR.'

THE PARABLE OF THE TALENTS

14 SOMEONE, BEFORE GOING ABROAD, CALLED HIS SERVANTS
TO ENTRUST HIS PROPERTY TO THEM. 15 HE GAVE FIVE TAL-
ENTS TO ONE, AND TWO TO ANOTHER AND ONE TO A THIRD, EACH
ONE ACCORDING TO HIS ABILITY; AND HE WENT AWAY. 16 HE WHO

RECEIVED FIVE TALENTS WENT
TO DO BUSINESS AND GAINED
FIVE MORE. 17 THE ONE WHO
RECEIVED TWO DID THE SAME
AND GAINED ANOTHER TWO.
18 BUT THE ONE WITH ONE
TALENT DUG A HOLE AND
HID HIS MASTER'S MONEY.
19 AFTER A LONG TIME THE
MASTER RETURNED AND AS-
KED FOR A RECKONING. 20
THE ONE WHO RECEIVED FIVE
TALENTS CAME WITH FIVE
MORE, SAYING: 'LORD, YOU
ENTRUSTED ME WITH FIVE
TALENTS: SEE, I HAVE GAI-
NED FIVE MORE.' 21 THE
MASTER SAID: 'VERY WELL
GOOD AND FAITHFUL SERVANT,
SINCE YOU HAVE BEEN FAITH-
FUL IN A FEW THINGS, I WILL
ENTRUST YOU WITH MUCH
MORE. COME AND SHARE
THE JOY OF YOUR MASTER.'
22 THE ONE WHO HAD TWO
TALENTS SAID: 'LORD, YOU
ENTRUSTED ME WITH TWO
TALENTS; I HAVE TWO MORE
I GAINED WITH THEM.' 23
THE MASTER SAID: 'WELL, GOOD AND FAITHFUL SERVANT, SINCE
YOU HAVE BEEN FAITHFUL IN LITTLE THINGS, I WILL ENTRUST
YOU WITH MUCH MORE. COME AND SHARE THE JOY OF YOUR MAS-
TER.' 24 FINALLY, THE ONE WHO RECEIVED A TALENT CAME AND
SAID: 'MASTER, I KNOW YOU ARE AN EXACTING MAN. YOU REAP
WHAT YOU HAVE NOT SOWN AND GATHER WHAT YOU HAVE
NOT INVESTED. 25 I WAS AFRAID, SO I HID YOUR MONEY
IN THE GROUND. HERE, TAKE WHAT IS YOURS.'

26 BUT THE MASTER REPLIED: 'WICKED AND WORTH-
LESS MAN, YOU KNOW THAT I REAP WHERE I HAVE NOT
SOWN AND GATHER WHERE I HAVE NOT INVESTED. 27
YOU SHOULD HAVE DEPOSITED MY MONEY IN THE BANK,
AND YOU WOULD HAVE GIVEN IT BACK TO ME WITH IN-
TEREST ON MY RETURN. 28 THEREFORE, TAKE THE TA-
LENT FROM HIM, AND GIVE IT TO THE ONE WHO HAS TEN. 29
FOR TO HIM WHO IS PRODUCTIVE, MORE WILL BE GIVEN,
AND HE WILL HAVE ABUNDANCE; BUT HE WHO DOES NOT
PRODUCE, EVEN WHAT HE HAS WILL BE TAKEN FROM HIM.
30 AS FOR THAT USELESS SERVANT, THROW HIM OUT
INTO THE DARK WHERE THERE WILL BE WEEPING
AND GNASHING OF TEETH.'

THE LAST JUDGMENT

31 "WHEN THE SON OF MAN COMES IN HIS GLORY WITH
ALL HIS ANGELS, HE WILL SIT ON THE THRONE OF HIS
GLORY. 32 ALL THE NA-
TIONS WILL BE BROUGHT
BEFORE HIM, AND AS A SHE-
PHERD SEPARATES SHE-
EP FROM GOATS, 33 SO
WILL HE DO WITH THEM,
PLACING THE SHEEP ON
HIS RIGHT AND THE GOATS
ON HIS LEFT. 34 THE KING
WILL SAY TO THOSE ON HIS
RIGHT: 'COME, BLESSED OF
MY FATHER! ACCEPT THE
KINGDOM PREPARED FOR
YOU FROM THE BEGINNING
OF THE WORLD. 35 FOR I
WAS HUNGRY AND YOU FED
ME, I WAS THIRSTY AND YOU
GAVE ME DRINK. 36 I WAS
A STRANGER AND YOU WEL-
COMED ME; I WAS NAKED
AND YOU CLOTHED ME. I WAS
SICK AND YOU VISITED ME.
I WAS IN PRISON AND YOU
CAME AND SEE ME.' 37 THE
UPRIGHT WILL ASK HIM:
'LORD, WHEN DID WE SEE
YOU HUNGRY AND GIVE

YOU FOOD; THIRSTY AND GIVE YOU DRINK, 38 OR A
STRANGER AND WELCOME YOU, OR NAKED AND CLOTHE
YOU? 39 WHEN DID WE SEE YOU SICK OR IN PRISON
AND GO TO SEE YOU?' 40 THE KING WILL ANSWER,
'TRULY, I SAY TO YOU: WHENEVER YOU DID THIS TO ONE
OF THE LEAST OF THESE BROTHERS, YOU DID IT TO ME.'
41 THEN HE WILL SAY TO THOSE ON HIS LEFT: 'GO, CUR-
SED PEOPLE, OUT OF MY SIGHT INTO THE ETERNAL FIRE
WHICH HAS BEEN PREPARED FOR THE DEVIL AND HIS AN-
GELS! 42 FOR I WAS HUNGRY AND YOU DID NOT GIVE ME

ANYTHING TO EAT, THIRSTY AND YOU GAVE ME NOTHING
TO DRINK; 43 I WAS A STRANGER AND YOU DIDN'T WEL-
COME ME; NAKED AND YOU DID NOT CLOTHE ME; I WAS SICK
AND IN PRISON AND YOU DID NOT VISIT ME.' 44 THEY, TOO,
WILL ASK: 'LORD, WHEN DID WE SEE YOU HUNGRY, THIRSTY,
NAKED OR A STRANGER, SICK OR IN PRISON, AND DID NOT
HELP YOU?' 45 THE KING WILL ANSWER THEM, 'TRULY,
I SAY TO YOU: WHATEVER YOU DID NOT FOR ONE OF THE LEAST
OF THESE, YOU DID NOT DO FOR ME.' 46 AND THESE WILL
GO INTO ETERNAL PUNISHMENT, BUT THE JUST TO ETERNAL LIFE."

26 (1) WHEN JESUS HAD FINISHED ALL HE WANTED TO SAY,
HE TOLD HIS DISCIPLES. (2) "YOU KNOW THAT IN TWO
DAYS IT WILL BE THE PASSOVER AND THE SON OF MAN
WILL BE HANDED OVER TO BE CRUCIFIED." (3) THE CHIEF PRI-
ESTS AND THE JEWISH AUTHORITIES MET AT THE PALACE
OF THE HIGH PRIEST WHOSE NAME WAS CAIAPHAS, (4)
AND THEY AGREED TO TRAP JESUS AND KILL HIM. (5) BUT
THEY SAID, "NOT DURING THE FEAST, LEST THERE
BE AN UPRISING AMONG THE PEOPLE."

THE ANOINTING AT BETHANY

(6) WHILE JESUS WAS IN BETHANY IN THE HOUSE OF
SIMON THE LEPER, (7) A WOMAN CAME TO HIM WITH A
PRECIOUS JAR OF EXPENSIVE PERFUME. SHE POURED IT
ON JESUS' HEAD AS HE WAS AT THE TABLE. (8) SEEING THIS
THE DISCIPLES WERE INDIGNANT AND SAID, "WHAT A BIG
WASTE!" (9) THE PERFUME COULD HAVE BEEN SOLD FOR
A LARGE SUM AND GIVEN TO THE POOR." (10) JESUS BECAME
AWARE OF THIS, SO HE SAID TO THEM, "WHY ARE YOU TROUBLING

THIS WOMAN? WHAT SHE
HAS DONE FOR ME IS A GO-
OD WORK. (11) YOU ALWAYS
HAVE THE POOR WITH YOU
BUT YOU WILL NOT HAVE
ME FOREVER. (12) SHE WAS
PREPARING FOR MY FU-
NERAL WHEN ANOINTING
MY BODY WITH THIS PER-
FUME. (13) TRULY, I SAY TO
YOU: WHEREVER THE GOS-
PEL IS PROCLAIMED, ALL
OVER THE WORLD, WHAT
SHE HAS DONE WILL BE
TOLD IN PRAISE OF HER."
(14) THEN ONE OF THE
TWELVE, WHO WAS CAL-
LED JUDAH ISCARIOT,
WENT TO THE CHIEF
PRIESTS AND SAID,
(15) "HOW MUCH WILL
YOU GIVE ME IF I HAND
HIM OVER TO YOU?"
THEY PROMISED TO
GIVE HIM THIRTY PI-
ECES OF SILVER. (16)
AND FROM THEN ON HE
KEPT LOOKING FOR
THE BEST WAY TO
HAND HIM OVER TO THEM.

THE LAST SUPPER

(17) ON THE FIRST DAY OF THE UNLEAVENED BREAD, THE
DISCIPLES CAME TO JESUS AND SAID TO HIM, "WHERE DO
YOU WANT US TO PREPARE THE PASSOVER MEAL FOR YOU?"
(18) JESUS ANSWERED, "GO INTO THE CITY, TO THE HOUSE OF
A CERTAIN MAN, AND TELL HIM: 'THE MASTER SAYS: MY HOUR
IS NEAR AND I WILL CELEBRATE THE PASSOVER WITH MY
DISCIPLES IN YOUR HOUSE.'" (19) THE DISCIPLES DID AS
JESUS HAD ORDERED AND PREPARED THE PASSOVER.
(20) IT WAS EVENING AND JESUS SAT AT TABLE WITH THE TWELVE.

(21) WHILE THEY WERE EATING, JESUS SAID, "TRULY,
I SAY TO YOU: ONE OF YOU WILL BETRAY ME." (22)
THEY WERE DEEPLY DISTRESSED AND ASKED
HIM IN TURN, "YOU DO NOT MEAN ME, DO YOU, LORD?"
(23) HE ANSWERED, "HE WHO WILL BETRAY ME IS THE
ONE WHO DIPS HIS BREAD IN THE DISH WITH ME. (24)
THE SON OF MAN IS GOING AS THE SCRIPTURE SAY HE
WILL. BUT ALAS FOR THAT
MAN WHO BETRAYS THE
SON OF MAN: BETTER FOR
HIM IF HE HAD NEVER BEEN
BORN." (25) JUDAS, WHO
WAS BETRAYING HIM, AL-
SO ASKED, "YOU DO NOT
MEAN ME, MASTER, DO
YOU?" JESUS REPLIED,
"YOU HAVE SAID IT."
(26) WHILE THEY WERE
EATING, JESUS TOOK
BREAD, SAID A BLES-
SING AND BROKE IT, GAVE
IT TO HIS DISCIPLES SAYING,
"TAKE AND EAT; THIS IS MY
BODY." (27) THEN HE TOOK
A CUP AND GAVE THANKS,
PASSED IT TO THEM SAYING,
"DRINK THIS, ALL OF YOU,
(28) FOR THIS IS MY BLO-
OD, THE BLOOD OF THE
COVENANT, POURED OUT
FOR MANY, FOR THE FOR-
GIVENESS OF SINS. (29) YES,
I SAY TO YOU, I WILL NOT

TASTE THE FRUIT OF THE VINE FROM NOW UNTIL THE DAY
I DRINK NEW WINE WITH YOU IN MY FATHER'S KINGDOM."
(30) AFTER SINGING PSLALMS OF PRAISE, THEY WENT OUT
TO THE MOUNT OF OLIVES. (31) JESUS SAID TO THEM,
"YOU WILL FALTER TONIGHT BECAUSE OF ME, AND ALL
WILL FALL. FOR THE SCRIPTURE SAYS: I WILL STRIKE
THE SHEPHERD AND THE SHEEP WILL BE SCATTERED.
(32) BUT AFTER MY RESURRECTION I WILL GO AHEAD
OF YOU TO GALILEE." (33) PETER SAID, "EVEN THOUGH
ALL DOUBT YOU AND FALL, I WILL NEVER FALL." (34)
JESUS REPLIED, "TRULY, I SAY TO YOU: THIS VERY NIGHT

BEFORE THE COCK CROWS, YOU WILL DENY ME THREE TI-
MES." (35) PETER SAID, "THOUGH I HAVE TO DIE WITH YOU, I WILL
NEVER DENY YOU." AND THE DISCIPLES SAID THE SAME.

GETHSEMANE

(36) JESUS CAME WITH THEM TO A PLACE CALLED GETHSE-
MANE, AND HE SAID TO HIS DISCEPLES, "SIT HERE WHILE
I GO OVER TO PRAY." (37) HE TOOK PETER AND THE TWO
SONS OF ZEBEDEE ALONG WITH HIM AND HE BEGAN
TO BE FILLED WITH ANGUISH AND DISTRESS.
(38) AND HE SAID TO THEM, "MY SOUL IS FILLED WITH
SORROW EVEN TO DEATH. REMAIN HERE AND STAY
AWAKE WITH ME." (39) HE WENT A LITTLE FARTHER
AND FELL TO THE GROUND, HIS FACE TOUCHING THE EARTH,
AND PRAYED, "FATHER, IF IT IS POSSIBLE, TAKE THIS CUP
AWAY FROM ME. YET NOT WHAT I WANT, BUT WHAT YOU WANT."

(40) HE WENT BACK TO HIS DISCIPLES AND FOUND THEM AS-
LEEP, AND HE SAID TO PETER, "COULD YOU NOT STAY AWAKE WITH
ME FOR EVEN AN HOUR? (41) STAY AWAKE AND PRAY, SO THAT
YOU MAY NOT SLIP INTO TEMPTATION. THE SPIRIT INDEED IS
EAGER, BUT HUMAN NATURE IS WEAK." (42) HE AGAIN WENT
AWAY AND PRAYED, "FATHER, IF THIS CUP CANNOT BE TAKEN A-
WAY FROM ME WITHOUT MY DRINKING IT, LET YOUR WILL BE
DONE." (43) WHEN HE CAME BACK TO HIS DISCIPLES, AGAIN
FOUND THEM ASLEEP, FOR THEY COULD NOT KEEP THEIR EYES
OPEN. (44) HE LEFT THEM AND AGAIN WENT TO PRAY THE
THIRD TIME, SAYING THE SAME WORDS. (45) THEN HE CA-
ME BACK TO HIS DISCIPLES AND SAID TO THEM,

"YOU CAN SLEEP ON NOW AND TAKE YOUR REST! THE HOUR HAS
COME AND THE SON OF MAN IS NOW GIVEN OVER INTO THE PO-
WER OF SINNERS. (46) GET UP, LET US GO. LOOK: THE
BETRAYER IS HERE."

JESUS ARRESTED

(47) HE WAS STILL SPEAKING WHEN JUDAS ARRIVED. WITH HIM
WAS A CROWD WITH SWORDS AND CLUBS, SENT BY THE CHIEF
PRIESTS AND THE JEWISH AUTHORITIES. (48) THE TRAITOR HAD

MADE A SIGNAL FOR THEM:
"THE ONE I KISS, HE IS THE
MAN; ARREST HIM." (49) HE
WENT TO JESUS AND SAID,
"GOOD EVENING, MASTER"
AND HE GAVE HIM A KISS.
(50) BUT JESUS SAID TO HIM,
"FRIEND, DO WHAT YOU CAME
FOR." THEN THEY SEIZED
AND ARRESTED JESUS. (51)
ONE OF THOSE WHO WERE
WITH JESUS DREW HIS SWORD
AND STRUCK AT THE SERVANT
OF THE HIGH PRIEST, CUT-
TING HIS EAR. (52) JESUS
SAID TO HIM, "PUT BACK YOUR
SWORD, FOR HE WHO USES
THE SWORD WILL PERISH BY
THE SWORD. (53) DO YOU NOT
KNOW THAT I COULD CALL ON
MY FATHER WHO AT ONCE HE
WOULD SEND ME MORE THAN
TWELVE LEGIONS OF ANGELS.
(54) IF SCRIPTURE SAYS THAT
THIS HAS TO BE, SHOULD IT
NOT BE FULFILLED?" (55)
AT THAT MOMENT, JESUS
SAID TO THE CROWD, "WHY DO
YOU COME TO ARREST ME WITH SWORDS AND CLUBS, AS IF I WERE
A ROBBER? DAY AFTER DAY I WAS SEATED AMONG YOU TEACH-
ING IN THE TEMPLE, YET YOU DID NOT ARREST ME. (56) BUT ALL
THIS HAS COME ABOUT IN FULFILLMENT OF WHAT THE PRO-
PHET SAID." THEN ALL HIS DISCIPLES DESERTED HIM AND FLED.

JESUS BEFORE THE SANHEDRIN

(57) THOSE WHO HAD ARRESTED JESUS BROUGHT HIM TO
THE HOUSE OF THE HIGH PRIEST CAIAPHAS, WHERE THE
TEACHERS OF THE LAW AND THE JEWISH AUTHORITIES WERE
ASSEMBLED. (58) PETER FOLLOWED HIM AT A DISTANCE AS
FAR AS THE COURTYARD OF THE HIGH PRIEST: HE ENTERED
AND SAT WITH THE GUARDS, WAITING TO SEE THE END.

(59) THE CHIEF PRIESTS AND THE WHOLE SUPREME COUN-
CIL NEEDED SOME FALSE EVIDENCE AGAINST JESUS SO THAT
THEY MIGHT PUT HIM TO DEATH. (60) BUT THEY WERE UN-
ABLE TO FIND ANY, EVEN THOUGH FALSE WITNESSES CAME
FORWARD. (61) AT LAST, TWO MEN CAME UP AND DECLARED,
"THIS MAN SAID: I AM ABLE TO DESTROY THE TEMPLE OF GOD
AND REBUILD IT IN THREE
DAYS." (62) THE HIGH PRI-
EST STOOD UP AND ASKED
JESUS, "HAVE YOU NO ANS-
WER AT ALL? WHAT IS THIS
EVIDENCE AGAINST YOU?"
(63) BUT JESUS KEPT SI-
LENT. SO THE HIGH PRIEST
SAID TO HIM, "IN THE NAME
OF THE LIVING GOD, I COM-
MAND YOU TO TELL US:
ARE YOU THE CHRIST, THE
SON OF GOD?" (64) JESUS
ANSWERED, "IT IS JUST AS
YOU SAY. I TELL YOU MORE:
FROM NOW ON, YOU WILL
SEE THE SON OF MAN SE-
ATED AT THE RIGHT HAND
OF THE MOST POWERFUL
GOD COMING ON THE CLOUDS
OF HEAVEN." (65) THEN THE
HIGH PRIEST TORE HIS
CLOTHES, SAYING, "HE HAS
BLASPHEMED. WHAT MORE
EVIDENCE DO WE NEED?
YOU HAVE JUST HEARD THE-
SE BLASPHEMOUS WORDS.
(66) WHAT IS YOUR DECISI-
ON?" THEY ANSWERED, "HE MUST DIE!" (67) THEY BEGAN TO
SPIT ON JESUS AND SLAP HIM WHILE OTHERS HIT HIM WITH
THEIR FISTS (68) SAYING, "CHRIST, PROPHESY! WHO HIT YOU?"

PETER DISOWNS JESUS

(69) MEANWHILE, AS PETER SAT OUT IN THE COURTYARD, A
YOUNG SERVANT-GIRL SAID TO HIM, "YOU ALSO WERE WITH
JESUS OF GALILEE." (70) BUT HE DENIED IT TO EVERYONE,
SAYING, "I DO NOT KNOW WHAT YOU ARE TALKING ABOUT."
(71) AS PETER WAS GOING OUT, ANOTHER SERVANT-GIRL SAW HIM
AND TOLD THE PEOPLE, "THIS MAN WAS WITH JESUS OF NAZARETH."
(72) PETER DENIED IT AGAIN WITH AN OATH, SWEARING, "I DO NOT
KNOW THAT MAN." (73) AFTER A WHILE, THOSE WHO WERE THERE

CAME AND SAID TO PETER, "YES, YOU ARE ONE OF THE GALILEANS;
YOUR ACCENT GIVES YOU AWAY." (74) HE BEGAN PROTESTING AND
SWEARING THAT HE DID NOT KNOW THE MAN. JUST THEN A COCK
CROWED. (75) AND PETER REMEMBERED THE WORDS OF JESUS,
"BEFORE THE COCK CROWS, YOU WILL DENY ME THREE TI-
MES." AND HE WENT AWAY WEEPING BITTERLY.

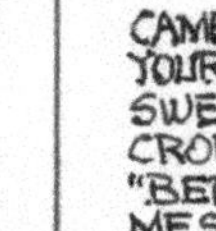

27 (1) EARLY IN THE MORNING ALL THE CHIEF PRIESTS
AND THE JEWISH AUTHORITIES MET TO LOOK FOR
WAYS OF PUTTING JESUS TO DEATH. (2) THEY HAD
HIM BOUND AND LED HIM AWAY TO BE HANDED
OVER TO PILATE, THE GOVERNOR.

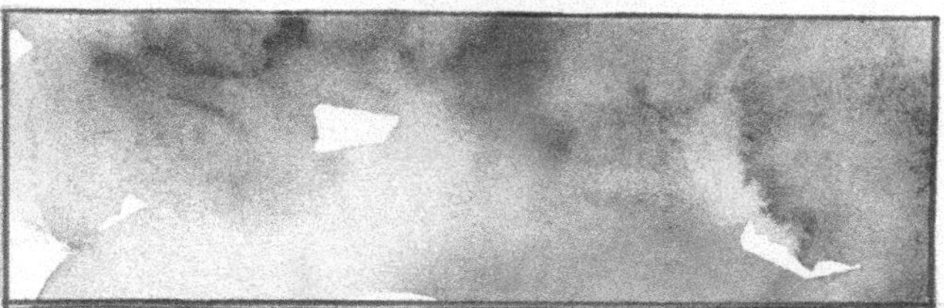

"LORD, WHEN DID WE SEE
U HUNGRY, THIRSTY,
NAKED OR A STRANGER.
SICK OR IN PRISON
AND DID WE NOT
HELP YOU?"
323
CCCXXIII
© DM 08

THE DEATH OF JUDAS

(3) WHEN JUDAS, THE TRAITOR, REALIZED THAT JESUS
HAD BEEN CONDEMNED, HE WAS FILLED WITH REMORSE
AND RETURNED THE THIRTY PIECES OF SILVER TO THE
CHIEF PRIESTS AND THE ELDERS, (4) SAYING, "I HAVE
SINNED BY BETRAYING AN
INNOCENT MAN TO DEATH".
THEY ANSWERED, "WHAT
DOES IT MATTER TO US?
THAT IS YOUR CONCERN."
(5) SO, THROWING THE MO-
NEY INTO THE TEMPLE, HE
WENT AWAY AND HANGED
HIMSELF. (6) THE PRIESTS
PICKED UP THE MONEY
AND SAID, "THIS MONEY
CANNOT BE PUT INTO THE
TEMPLE TREASURY, FOR
THIS IS THE PRICE OF BLOOD."
(7) SO THEY MET TOGE-
THER AND DECIDED TO BUY
THE POTTER'S FIELD
WITH THE MONEY AND
MAKE IT A CEMETERY FOR
FOREIGNERS. (8) THIS
IS WHY THAT PLACE HAS
HAS BEEN CALLED FI-
ELD OF BLOOD TO THIS
DAY. (9) SO WHAT THE
PROPHET JEREMIAH SA-
ID WAS FULFILLED; THEY
TOOK THE THIRTY PIECES
OF SILVER, THE PRICE THE
SONS OF ISRAEL SET ON
HIM. (10) AND THEY GAVE THEM FOR THE POTTER'S FI-
ELD, AS THE LORD COMMANDED ME.

JESUS BEFORE PILATE

(11) JESUS STOOD BEFORE THE GOVERNOR WHO QUESTIONED
HIM, "ARE YOU THE KING OF THE JEWS?" JESUS ANSWERED, "YOU
SAY SO." (12) THE CHIEF PRIESTS AND THE ELDERS ACCUSED HIM
BUT HE MADE NO ANSWER. (13) PILATE SAID TO HIM, "DO YOU
HEAR ALL THE CHARGES THEY BRING AGAINST YOU?" (14) BUT
HE DID NOT ANSWER A SINGLE QUESTION, SO THAT THE GO-
VERNOR WONDERED. (15) IT WAS CUSTOMARY FOR THE GO-
VERNOR TO RELEASE ANY PRISONER THE PEOPLE ASKED FOR
ON THE OCCASION OF THE PASSOVER. (16) NOW THERE WAS A
WELL-KNOWN PRISONER CALLED BARABBAS. (17) AS THE PE-
OPLE HAD GATHERED, PILATE ASKED THEM, "WHOM DO YOU WANT

ME TO SET FREE: BARABBAS, OR JESUS CALLED THE CHRIST?"
(18) FOR HE REALIZED THAT JESUS HAD BEEN HANDED OVER TO
HIM OUT OF ENVY. (19) AS PILATE WAS SITTING IN COURT,
HIS WIFE SENT HIM A MESSAGE, "HAVE NOTHING TO DO WITH
THAT HOLY MAN. BECAUSE OF HIM I HAD A DREAM LAST
NIGHT THAT DISTURBED ME GREATLY." (20) BUT THE
CHIEF PRIESTS AND THE ELDERS STIRRED THE CROWDS TO
ASK FOR THE RELEASE OF BARABBAS AND THE DEATH OF
JESUS. (21) WHEN THE GOVERNOR ASKED THEM AGAIN,
"WHICH OF THE TWO DO YOU WANT ME TO SET FREE?" THEY
ANSWERED, "BARABBAS."

(22) PILATE SAID TO THEM, "AND WHAT SHALL I DO WITH
JESUS CALLED THE CHRIST?" ALL ANSWERED, "CRUCIFY
HIM!" (23) PILATE INSISTED, "WHAT EVIL HAS HE DONE?"
BUT THEY SHOUTED LOUDER, "CRUCIFY HIM!"
(24) PILATE REALIZED THAT HE WAS GETTING NOWHERE
AND THAT INSTEAD THERE COULD BE A RIOT. HE THEN
ASKED FOR WATER AND WASHED HIS HANDS BEFORE
THE PEOPLE, SAYING, "I AM NOT RESPONSIBLE
FOR HIS BLOOD. IT IS YOUR DOING." (25) AND
ALL THE PEOPLE ANSWERED, "LET HIS BLOOD BE

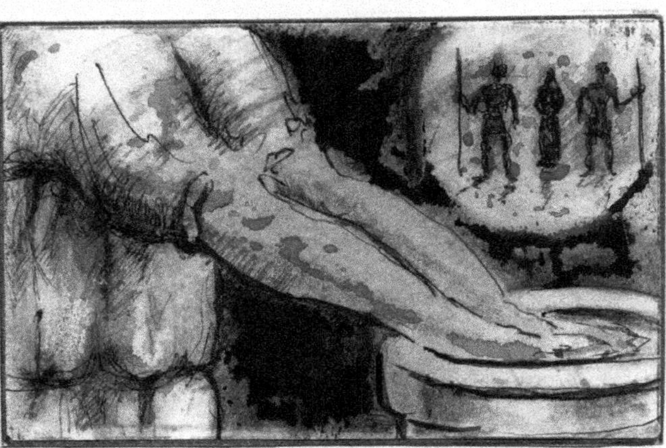

UPON US AND OUR CHILDREN." (26) THEN PILATE SET BA-
RABBAS FREE, BUT HAD JESUS SCOURGED, AND
HANDED HIM OVER TO BE CRUCIFIED.

THE WAY OF THE CROSS

(27) THE ROMAN SOLDIERS TOOK JESUS INTO THE PALACE OF
THE GOVERNOR AND THE TROOP GATHERED AROUND HIM. (28)
THEY STRIPPED HIM AND DRESSED HIM IN A PURPLE CLOAK.
(29) THEN, TWISTING A CROWN OF THORNS, THEY FOR-
CED IT ONTO HIS HEAD,
AND PLACED A REED IN
HIS RIGHT HAND. THEY
KNELT BEFORE JESUS
AND MOCKED HIM, SAY-
ING, "LONG LIFE TO THE
KING OF THE JEWS!"
(30) THEY SPAT ON HIM,
TOOK THE REED FROM
HIS HAND AND STRUCK
HIM ON THE HEAD WITH
IT. (31) WHEN THEY
HAD FINISHED MOCK-
ING HIM, THEY PULLED
OFF THE PURPLE
CLOAK AND DRESSED
HIM IN HIS OWN
CLOTHES AGAIN,
AND LED HIM OUT TO
BE CRUCIFIED. (32)
ON THE WAY THEY
MET A MAN FROM
CYRENE CALLED
SIMON, AND FOR-
CED HIM TO CARRY
THE CROSS OF JESUS.
(33) WHEN THEY RE-
ACHED THE PLACE
CALLED GOLGOTHA (OR CALVARY), MEANING
THE WORD "SKULL", (34) THEY OFFERED HIM
WINE MIXED WITH GALL. JESUS TASTED IT BUT
WOULD NOT TAKE IT. (35) THERE THEY CRUCIFIED HIM
AND DIVIDED HIS CLOTHES AMONG THEMSELVES, CASTING
LOTS TO DECIDE WHAT EACH SHOULD TAKE. THEN
THEY (36) SAT DOWN TO GUARD HIM.

37 HIS OFFENSE WAS DISPLAYED ABOVE HIS HEAD AND
IT READ, "THIS IS JESUS, THE KING OF THE JEWS." 38 THEY
ALSO CRUCIFIED TWO BANDITS WITH HIM, ONE ON HIS
RIGHT AND ONE ON HIS LEFT. 39 PEOPLE PASSING BY

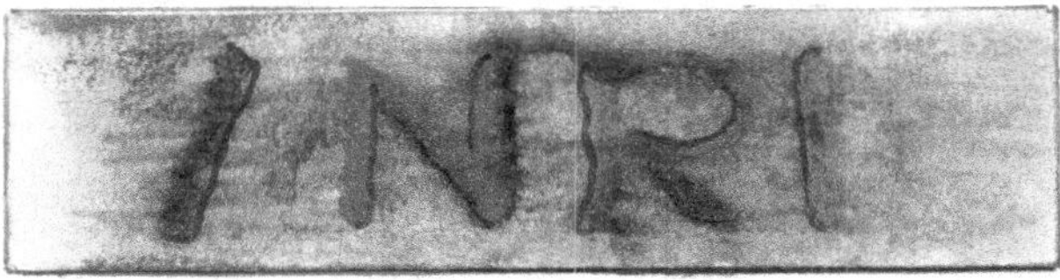

SHOOK THEIR HEADS AND INSULTED HIM, SAYING,
40 "AHA! SO YOU WILL DESTROY THE TEMPLE AND
AND BUILD IT UP AGAIN IN THREE DAYS. NOW SAVE
YOURSELF AND COME DOWN FROM THE CROSS, IF

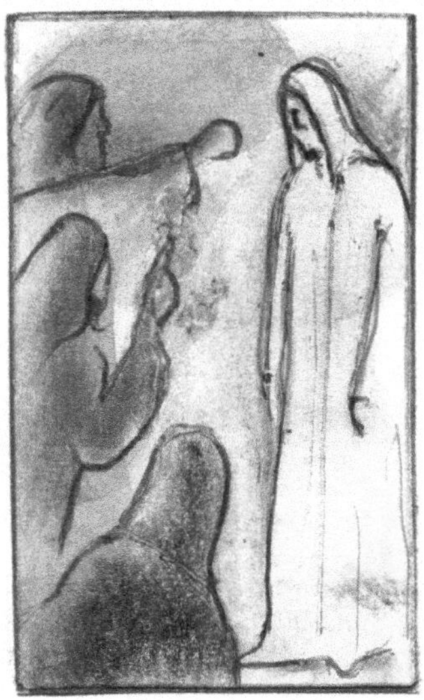

YOU ARE SON OF GOD."
41 IN THE SAME WAY
THE CHIEF PRIESTS, THE
ELDERS AND THE TE-
ACHERS OF THE LAW
MOCKED HIM. 42 THEY
SAID, "THE MAN WHO
SAVED OTHERS CANNOT
SAVE HIMSELF. LET THE
KING OF ISRAEL NOW
COME DOWN FROM HIS
CROSS AND WE WILL
BELIEVE IN HIM. 43 HE
TRUSTED IN GOD; LET GOD
RESCUE HIM IF GOD WANTS
TO, SINCE HE HIMSELF SA-
ID: I AM THE SON OF GOD."
44 EVEN THE ROBBERS
WHO WERE CRUCIFIED WITH
HIM INSULTED HIM. 45
FROM MIDDAY DARKNESS
FELL OVER THE WHOLE LAND
UNTIL MID-AFTERNOON."
46 AT ABOUT THREE O'
CLOCK, JESUS CRIED OUT
IN A LOUD VOICE. "ELOI, ELOI, LAMMA SABBACTH-
ANI?" WHICH MEANS: MY GOD, MY GOD, WHY HAVE
YOU FORSAKEN ME? 47 AS SOON AS THEY HEARD
THIS, SOME OF THE BYSTANDERS SAID, "HE IS
CALLING FOR ELIJAH." 48 AND ONE OF THEM
WENT QUICKLY, TOOK A SPONGE AND SOAKED

IT IN VINEGAR AND, PUTTING IT ON A REED, GAVE HIM
TO DRINK. 49 OTHER SAID, "LEAVE HIM ALONE, LET US SEE
WHETHER ELIJAH COMES TO HIS RESCUE." 50 BUT JESUS
CRIED OUT AGAIN IN A LOUD VOICE AND GAVE UP HIS SPIRIT.

AFTER THE DEATH OF JESUS

51 JUST THEN THE CURTAIN OF THE TEMPLE SANCTUARY WAS
TORN IN TWO FROM TOP TO BOTTOM, THE EARTH QUAKED, ROCKS
WERE SPLIT, 52 TOMBS WERE OPENED, AND SEVERAL
HOLY PEOPLE WHO HAD DIED WERE RAISED TO LIFE.
53 THEY CAME OUT OF THE TOMBS AFTER THE RESUR-
RECTION OF JESUS, ENTERED THE HOLY CITY AND AP-
PEARED TO MANY. 54 THE CAPTAIN OF THE SOLDIERS
WHO GUARDED JESUS WERE GREATLY TERRIFIED
WHEN THEY SAW THE EARTHQUAKE AND THAT HAD HAP-
PENED AND SAID, "TRULY, THIS MAN WAS A SON OF GOD."

55 THERE WERE ALSO SOME WOMEN THERE WHO WATCHED
FROM A DISTANCE; THEY HAD FOLLOWED JESUS FROM GALI-
LEE AND SAW TO HIS NEEDS. 56 AMONG THEM WERE MARY
MAGDALENE, MARY THE MOTHER OF JAMES AND JOSEPH,
AND THE MOTHER OF ZEBEDEE'S SONS.

THE BURIAL

57 IT WAS NOW EVENING AND A WEALTHY MAN ARRIVED
FROM ARIMATHEA, NAMED JOSEPH, WHO WAS ALSO A DISCI-
PLE OF JESUS. 58 HE WENT TO PILATE AND ASKED FOR
THE BODY OF JESUS, AND THE GOVERNOR ORDERED THAT

THE BODY BE GIVEN HIM. 59 SO JOSEPH TOOK THE BODY
OF JESUS, WRAPPED IT IN A CLEAN LINEN SHEET 60 AND
LAID IT IN HIS OWN NEW TOMB WHICH HAD BEEN CUT OUT OF
THE ROCK. THEN HE ROLLED A HUGE STONE ACROSS THE EN-
TRANCE OF THE TOMB AND LEFT. 61 MARY MAGDALENE AND
THE OTHER MARY REMAINED THERE IN FRONT OF THE TOMB.

THE GUARDS AT THE TOMB

62 ON THE NEXT DAY, THE DAY AFTER THE PASSOVER'S
PREPARATION, THE CHIEF PRIESTS AND THE PHARISE-
ES WENT TO PILATE 63 AND SAID TO HIM, "SIR, WE RE-
MEMBER THAT WHEN THAT
IMOSTOR WAS STILL A-
LIVE, HE SAID: I WILL
RISE AFTER THREE
DAYS. 64 THEREFORE,
HAVE HIS TOMB SECURED
UNTIL THE THIRD DAY,
LEST HIS DISCIPLES COME
AND STEAL THE BODY AND
SAY TO THE PEOPLE: HE WAS
RAISED FROM THE DEAD.
THIS WOULD BE A WORSE
LIE THAN THE FIRST." 65
PILATE ANSWERED THEM,
"YOU HAVE SOLDIERS, GO
AND TAKE ALL THE NE-
CESSARY PRECAUTIONS."
66 SO THEY WENT TO
THE TOMB AND SECURED
IT, SEALING THE STONE
AND PLACING IT UN-
DER GOOD GUARD.

28 1 AFTER THE SABBATH, AT DAWN OF THE FIRST DAY
OF THE WEEK, MARY MAGDALENE AND THE OTHER MARY

JESUS APPEARS TO THE WOMEN

WENT TO VISIT THE TOMB. 2 SUDDENLY THERE WAS A VIOLENT
EARTHQUAKE; THE ANGEL OF THE LORD DESCENDED FROM HE-
AVEN; HE CAME TO THE STONE, ROLLED IT FROM THE ENTRANCE
OF THE TOMB, AND SAT ON IT. 3 HIS APPEARANCE WAS LIKE
LIGHTNING AND HIS GARMENT WHITE AS SNOW. 4 THE GU-
ARDS TREMBLED IN FEAR AND BECAME LIKE DEAD MEN WHEN
THEY SAW THE ANGEL. 5 THE ANGEL SAID TO THE WOMEN,
"DO NOT BE AFRAID, FOR I KNOW THAT YOU ARE LOOKING

FOR JESUS WHO WAS CRUCIFIED. 6 HE IS NOT HERE,
FOR HE IS RISEN AS HE SAID. COME, SEE THE PLACE
WHERE THEY LAID HIM; 7 THEN GO AT ONCE AND TELL
HIS DISCIPLES THAT HE IS RISEN FROM THE DEAD AND IS
GOING AHEAD OF YOU TO GALILEE. YOU WILL SEE HIM THE-
RE. THIS IS MY MESSAGE FOR YOU." 8 THEY LEFT THE
TOMB AT ONCE IN HOLY FEAR, YET WITH GREAT JOY, AND SO
THEY RAN TO TELL THE NEWS TO THE DISCIPLES.
9 SUDDENLY, JESUS MET THEM ON THE WAY AND SAID,
"PEACE". THE WOMEN APPROACHED HIM, EMBRACED
HIS FEET AND WORSHIPED HIM.

10 BUT JESUS SAID TO THEM, "DO NOT BE AFRAID.
GO AND TELL MY BROTHERS TO SET OUT FOR GALILEE;
THERE THEY WILL SEE ME." 11 WHILE THE
WOMEN WERE ON THEIR WAY, THE GUARDS RETUR-
NED TO THE CITY AND SOME OF THEM REPORTED TO
THE CHIEF PRIESTS ALL THAT HAD HAPPENED. 12
THE CHIEF PRIESTS MET WITH THE JEWS AUTHORITIES
AND DECIDED TO GIVE THE SOLDIERS A GOOD SUM OF
MONEY, 13 WITH THIS INSTRUCTION, "SAY THAT
HIS DISCIPLES CAME BY NIGHT WHILE YOU WERE

ASLEEP, AND STOLE THE BODY OF JESUS. 14 IF PILATE CO-
MES TO KNOW OF THIS, WE WILL SATISFY HIM AND KEEP YOU
OUT OF TROUBLE." 15 THE SOLDIERS ACCEPTED THE MONEY
AND DID AS THEY WERE TOLD. THIS STORY HAS CIRCULA-
TED AMONG THE JEWS UNTIL THIS DAY.

JESUS SENDS THE APOSTLES

16 AS FOR THE ELEVEN DISCIPLES, THEY WENT TO
GALILEE, TO THE MOUNTAIN WHERE JESUS
HAD TOLD THEM TO GO. 17 WHEN THEY SAW JESUS,
THEY BOWED BEFORE HIM, ALTHOUGH SOME DOUBTED.

18 THEN JESUS APPROACHED THEM AND SAID, "I HAVE
BEEN GIVEN ALL AUTHORITY IN HEAVEN AND ON EARTH.
19 GO, THEREFORE, AND MAKE DISCIPLES FROM ALL

NATIONS, BAPTISE THEM IN THE NAME OF THE
FATHER AND OF THE SON AND OF THE HOLY SPI-
RIT, 20 AND TEACH THEM TO FULFILL ALL THAT I
HAVE COMMANDED YOU. I AM WITH YOU ALWAYS
UNTIL THE END OF THIS WORLD."

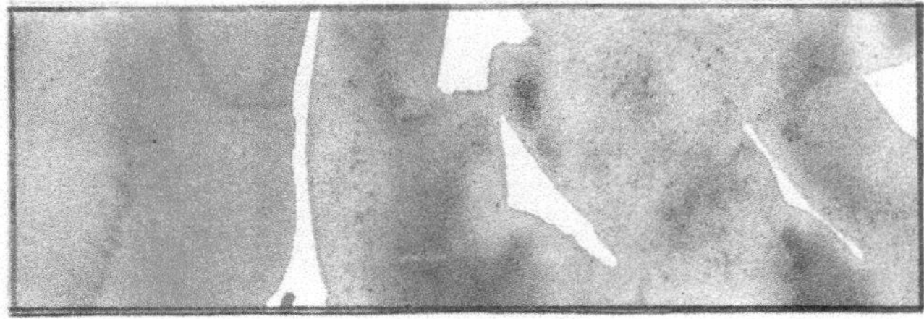

I.N.R.I.

HOMAGE TO MONDRIAN

THE GOSPEL OF MARK

FROM THE END OF THE FIRST CENTURY OR AT THE BEGINNING OF THE SECOND CENTURY A.D., THERE ARE TEXTS AFFIRMING THAT THE SECOND GOSPEL IS THE WORK OF MARK: HE ACCOMPANIED PETER TO ROME WHERE HE ALSO MET PAUL, AND FAITHFULLY PUT IN WRITING THE TEACHING OF PETER.

LIKE THE GOSPELS OF MATTHEW AND LUKE, THAT OF MARK IS BASED ON THE ORAL TRADITIONS CONCERNING JESUS OF NAZARETH, WHICH BY DEGREES WERE WRITTEN DOWN. THESE PARTIAL TEXTS THAT WERE PASSED ON FROM COMMUNITY TO COMMUNITY WERE COMPLETED BY THE ORAL WITNESS OF THOSE WHO HAD ACCOMPANIED JESUS DURING HIS EARTHLY LIFE. MARK WROTE HIS GOSPEL FOR A DEFINITE TYPE OF COMMUNITY: HE ADDRESSES CHRISTIANS OF PAGAN ORIGIN AND WISHES TO PROCLAIM THE MYSTERY OF JESUS, SON OF GOD, BY RELATING THE WORDS AND DEEDS BY WHICH HE REVEALED HIMSELF TO HUMANKIND.

MARK HOLDS THE PATTERN OF PRIMITIVE CATECHETICS. THE ACTS OF THE APOSTLES IN FACT TELLS US WHAT WAS THE BEGINNING AND THE END OF THIS PREACHING BY THE CHURCH OF JERUSALEM: AT THE TIME WHEN PETER WAS LOOKING FOR A REPLACEMENT OF JUDAS HE SAID: "SEE AMONG THOSE WHO HAVE BEEN DISCIPLES WITH US FROM THE MOMENT JESUS WAS BAPTIZED BY JOHN TO THE DAY HE WAS TAKEN UP" (ACTS 1:21-22).

THE GOSPEL ACCORDING TO

MARK

1 (1) THIS IS THE BEGINNING OF THE GOOD NEWS ABOUT
JESUS, THE SON OF GOD. (2) IT IS WRITTEN IN THE
BOOK OF ISAIAH, THE PROPHET, "I AM SENDING MY MES-
SENGER AHEAD OF YOU TO PREPARE YOUR WAY. (3) LET
THE PEOPLE HEAR THE VOICE CALLING IN THE DE-
SERT: PREPARE THE WAY OF THE LORD, LEVEL HIS
PATHS."

(4) SO JOHN BEGAN TO BAPTISE IN THE DESERT; HE

PREACHED A BAPTISM OF REPENTANCE FOR THE FOR-
GIVENESS OF SINS. (5) ALL JUDEA AND ALL THE PEOPLE
FROM THE CITY OF JERUSALEM WENT OUT TO JOHN TO CON-
FESS THEIR SINS AND BE BAPTISED BY HIM IN THE RI-
VER JORDAN. (6) JOHN WAS CLOTHED IN CAMEL'S HAIR
AND WORE A LEATHER GARMENT AROUND HIS
WAIST. HIS FOOD WAS LOCUSTS AND HONEY.

(7) HE PREACHED TO
THE PEOPLE, SAYING,
"AFTER ME COMES
ONE WHO IS MORE
POWERFUL THAN I AM.
(8) I HAVE BAPTIZED YOU
WITH WATER, BUT HE
WILL BAPTIZE YOU IN
THE HOLY SPIRIT. AS FOR
ME, I AM NOT WORTHY
TO BEND DOWN AND
UNTIE HIS SANDALS."
(9) AT THAT TIME JESUS
CAME FROM NAZARETH,
A TOWN OF GALILEE, AND
WAS BAPTIZED BY JOHN
IN THE JORDAN. (10)
AND THE MOMENT
HE CAME OUT OF THE
WATER, HEAVEN
OPENED BEFORE
HIM AND HE SAW
THE SPIRIT COMING
DOWN ON HIM LIKE
A DOVE.
(11) AND THESE WORDS
WERE HEARD FROM HEAVEN,

"YOU ARE MY SON, THE BELOVED,
THE ONE I HAVE CHOSEN."

(12) THEN THE SPIRIT DROVE HIM INTO THE
DESERT. (13) JESUS STAYED IN THE DESERT
FORTY DAYS AND WAS TEMPTED BY SATAN.
HE WAS WITH THE WILD ANIMALS, BUT AN-
GELS MINISTERED TO HIM.

JESUS CALLS HIS FIRST DISCIPLES

(14) AFTER JOHN WAS ARRESTED, JESUS WENT INTO GA-
LILEE AND BEGAN PREACHING THE GOOD NEWS OF GOD. (15)
HE SAID, "THE TIME HAS COME; THE KINGDOM OF GOD
IS AT HAND. CHANGE
YOUR WAYS AND BELI-
EVE THE GOOD NEWS."

(16) AS JESUS WAS WALK-
ING ALONG THE SHORE OF
LAKE GALILEE, HE SAW
SIMON AND HIS BROTHER
ANDREW CASTING A NET
IN THE LAKE, FOR THEY
WERE FISHERMEN. (17)
JESUS SAID TO THEM,
"FOLLOW ME, AND I WILL
MAKE YOU FISHERS OF
MEN." (18) AT ONCE, THEY
LEFT THEIR NETS AND
FOLLOWED HIM. JESUS
(19) WENT A LITTLE FAR-
THER ON AND SAW JAMES
AND JOHN, THE SONS OF
ZEBEDEE; THEY WERE
IN THEIR BOAT MENDING
THEIR NETS. (20) IM-
MEDIATELY, JESUS
CALLED THEM AND THEY
FOLLOWED HIM, LEA-
VING THEIR FATHER ZEBEDEE IN THE BOAT WITH THE MEN.

JESUS TEACHES AND DRIVES OUT AN EVIL SPIRIT

(21) THEY WENT INTO THE TOWN OF CAPERNAUM AND
JESUS BEGAN TO TEACH IN THE SYNAGOGUE DUR-
ING THE SABBATH ASSEMBLIES. (22) THE PEOPLE WERE
ASTONISHED AT HIS TEACHING, FOR HE SPOKE AS ONE
HAVING AUTHORITY AND NOT LIKE THE TEACHERS OF THE
LAW. (23) A MAN WITH AN EVIL SPIRIT WAS IN THEIR SYNA-
GOGUE (24) AND SHOUTED, "WHAT DO YOU WANT WITH US, JESUS
OF NAZARETH? HAVE YOU COME TO DESTROY US? I KNOW YOU

ARE THE HOLY ONE OF GOD." (25) JESUS FACED HIM AND SAID,
"BE SILENT AND COME OUT OF THIS MAN!" (26) THE EVIL SPIRIT
SHOOK THE MAN VIOLENTLY AND WITH A LOUD SHRIEK, CAME
OUT OF HIM. (27) ALL THE PEOPLE WERE ASTONISHED AND WON-
DERED, "WHAT IS THIS? WITH WHAT AUTHORITY HE PREACHES!
EVEN EVIL SPIRITS OBEY HIM!" AND JESUS' FAME SPREAD
THROUGHOUT ALL THE COUNTRY OF GALILEE (28).

JESUS HEALS MANY

(29) ON LEAVING THE SYNAGOGUE, JESUS WENT TO
THE HOME OF SIMON AND ANDREW WITH JAMES AND
JOHN. (30) AS SIMON'S MOTHER-IN-LAW WAS SICK
IN BED WITH FEVER, THEY TOLD HIM ABOUT HER AT ONCE.

(31) JESUS WENT TO HER AND TAKING HER BY THE HAND, RASED HER
UP. THE FEVER LEFT HER AND SHE BEGAN TO WAIT ON THEM. (32) THAT
EVENING AT SUNDOWN, THEY BROUGHT TO JESUS ALL THE SICK
AND THOSE WITH EVIL SPIRITS: (33) THE WHOLE TOWN WAS
PRESSING AROUND THE DOOR. (24) JESUS HEALED MANY
WHO HAD VARIOUS DISEASES, AND DROVE OUT MANY

DEMONS; BUT HE DID NOT LET THEM SPEAK,
FOR THEY KNEW WHO HE WAS.

JESUS' PRAYER AT NIGHT

(35) EARLY IN THE MORNING, BEFORE DAYLIGHT, JESUS WENT TO
A LONELY PLACE, WHERE HE PRAYED. (36) SIMON WENT OUT
WITH THE OTHERS TOO, SEARCHING FOR HIM; (37) WHEN
THEY FOUND HIM THEY SAID, "EVERYBODY IS LOOKING FOR
YOU." (38) JESUS ANSWERED, "LET'S GO TO THE NEARBY
VILLAGES SO THAT I MAY PREACH THERE TOO: FOR THAT
IS WHY I CAME." (39) SO JESUS SET OUT TO PREACH IN
ALL THE SYNAGOGUES THROUGHOUT GALILEE;
HE ALSO CAST OUT DEMONS.

JESUS CURES A LEPER

(40) A LEPER CAME AND BEGGED JESUS, "IF YOU SO WILL, YOU CAN

MAKE ME CLEAN." (41) MOVED
WITH PITY, JESUS STRETCHED
OUT HIS HAND AND TOUCHED
HIM, SAYING, "I WILL; BE CLE-
AN." (42) THE LEPROSY LEFT
THE MAN AT ONCE AND HE
WAS MADE CLEAN. (43) AS
JESUS SENT THE MAN AWAY,
HE WARNED HIM (44) DON'T
TELL ANYONE ABOUT THIS,
BUT GO TO THE PRIEST AND
FOR THE CLEANSING BRING
THE OFFERING ORDERED
BY MOSES; IN THE WAY
YOU WILL MAKE YOUR
DECLARATION. (45)
HOWEVER, AS SOON AS
THE MAN WENT OUT, HE BE-
GAN SPREADING THE NEWS
EVERYWHERE, SO THAT
JESUS COULD NO LONGER
ENTER ANY TOWN OPENLY.
BUT EVEN THOUGH JESUS
STAYED IN THE RURAL
AREAS, PEOPLE CAME TO
HIM FROM EVERYWHERE.

JESUS CURES A PARALYTIC

2 (1) AFTER SOME DAYS JESUS RETURNED TO CAPER-
NAUM. AS THE NEWS SPREAD THAT HE WAS AT HOME,
(2) SO MANY PEOPLE GATHERED THAT THERE WAS NO MORE
ROOM EVEN OUTSIDE THE DOOR. WHILE JESUS WAS PRE-
ACHING (3) SOME PEOPLE BROUGHT A PARALYZED MAN
TO HIM. (4) THE FOUR MEN WHO CARRIED HIM COULDN'T
GET NEAR JESUS BECAUSE OF THE CROWD, SO THEY
OPENED THE ROOF ABOVE THE ROOM WHERE JESUS
WAS AND, THROUGH THE HOLE, LOWERED THE MAN ON
HIS MAT. (5) WHEN JESUS SAW THE FAITH OF THESE
PEOPLE, HE SAID TO THE PARALYTIC, "MY SON, YOUR
SINS ARE FORGIVEN." (6) NOW SOME TEACHERS OF
THE LAW WHO WERE SITTING THERE WONDERED AND
SAID, (7) "HOW CAN HE SPEAK LIKE THIS INSULTING
GOD? WHO CAN FORGIVE
SINS EXCEPT GOD?" (8) AT

ONCE JESUS WAS AWARE
THROUGH HIS SPIRIT AS
WHAT THEY WERE THINK-
ING AND ASKED, "WHY DO
YOU WONDER? (9) IS IT
EASIER TO SAY TO THIS PA-
RALYZED MAN: 'YOUR SINS
ARE FORGIVEN,' OR TO SAY:
'RISE, TAKE UP YOUR MAT
AND WALK?' (10) BUT NOW
YOU SHALL KNOW THAT
THE SON OF MAN HAS
AUTHORITY ON EARTH TO
FORGIVE SINS." AND HE
SAID TO THE PARALYTIC,
(11) "STAND UP, TAKE
UP YOUR MAT AND GO
HOME." (12) THE MAN
ROSE. AND, IN THE
SIGHT OF ALL THOSE
PEOPLE, HE TOOK UP
HIS MAT AND WENT
OUT. ALL OF THEM
WERE ASTONISHED
AND PRAISED GOD
SAYING, "WE HAVE
NEVER SEEN ANYTHING LIKE THIS!"

THE CALL OF LEVI

(13) WHEN JESUS WENT OUT AGAIN BESIDE THE LAKE, A
CROWD CAME TO HIM AND HE TAUGHT THEM. (14) AS HE WALKED
ALONG, HE SAW A TAX COLLECTOR SITTING IN HIS OFFICE. THIS
WAS LEVI, THE SON OF ALPHEUS. JESUS SAID TO HIM, "FOLLOW
ME." AND LEVI GOT UP AND FOLLOWED HIM. (15) AND SO IT
HAPPENED THAT WHILE JESUS WAS EATING IN LEVI'S HO-
USE, TAX COLLECTORS AND SINNERS WERE SITTING WITH
HIM AND HIS DISCIPLES FOR THERE WERE INDEED MANY
OF THEM. (16) BUT THERE WERE ALSO TEACHERS OF THE

LAW OF THE PHARISEES' PARTY; WHEN THEY SAW HIM EAT-
ING WITH SINNERS AND TAX COLLECTORS, SAID TO HIS DISCIP-
LES, "WHY! HE EATS WITH TAX COLLECTORS AND SINNERS!"
(17) JESUS HEARD THEM AND ANSWERED, "HEALTHY PEOPLE
DON'T NEED A DOCTOR; BUT SICK PEOPLE DO. I DID NOT
COME TO CALL THE RIGHTEOUS BUT SINNERS."

NEW WINE, NEW SKIN

(18) ONE DAY, WHEN THE DISCIPLES OF JOHN THE BAPTIST
AND THE PHARISEES WERE FASTING, SOME PEOPLE ASKED
JESUS, "WHY THE DISCIPLES OF JOHN AND THE PHARISEES FAST
BUT YOURS DO NOT?" (19) JESUS ANSWERED, "HOW CAN THE
WEDDING GUESTS FAST WHILE THE BRIDEGROOM IS WITH
THEM? AS LONG AS THE BRIDEGROOM IS WITH THEM, THEY
CANNOT FAST.

JESUS CURES A LEPER (MARK 1)
HOMAGE TO VAN GOGH
326 CCCXXVI
© DM 09

20 BUT THE DAY WILL COME WHEN THE BRIDEGROOM WILL BE
TAKEN FROM THEM AND ON THAT DAY THEY WILL FAST. 21 NO ONE
SEWS A PIECE OF NEW CLOTH ON AN OLD COAT, FOR THE NEW PATCH
WILL SHRINK AND TEAR AWAY FROM THE OLD CLOTH, MAKING A
WORSE TEAR. 22 AND NO ONE PUTS NEW WINE INTO OLD WINE-
SKINS, FOR THE WINE WOULD BURST THE SKINS AND THEN BOTH
WINE AND SKINS WOULD BE LOST. BUT NEW WINE, NEW SKINS!"

23 ONE SABBATH JESUS WAS WALKING THROUGH GRAINFIELDS. AS
HIS DISCIPLES WALKED WITH HIM, BEGAN TO PICK THE HEADS OF
GRAIN CRUSHING THEM.

24 THE PHARISEES SAID TO
JESUS, "LOOK! THEY ARE DO-
ING WHAT IS FORBIDDEN ON
A SABBATH!" 25 HE SAID
TO THEM, "HAVE YOU NEVER
READ WHAT DAVID DID IN TI-
ME OF NEED, WHEN HE AND
HIS MEN WERE VERY HUN-
GRY? 26 HE WENT INTO THE
HOUSE OF GOD WHEN ABIA-
THAR WAS HIGH PRIEST AND
ATE THE BREAD OF OFFERING,
WHICH ONLY THE PRIESTS ARE
ALLOWED TO EAT, AND HE GA-
VE SOME TO HIS MEN WHO
WERE WITH HIM." 27 THEN
JESUS SAID, "THE SABBATH
WAS MADE FOR MAN, NOT
MAN FOR THE SABBATH.
28 SO THE SON OF MAN
IS MASTER EVEN ON
THE SABBATH."

CURE OF THE MAN WITH A WITHERED HAND

3 1 AGAIN JESUS ENTERED THE SYNAGOGUE. A MAN
WHO HAD A PARALYZED HAND WAS THERE 2 AND
SOME PEOPLE WATCHED JESUS: WOULD HE HEAL THE MAN
ON THE SABBATH? IF HE DID THEY COULD ACCUSE HIM. 3
JESUS SAID TO THE MAN WITH THE PARALYZED HAND,
"STAND HERE IN THE CENTER." 4 THEN HE ASKED THEM,
"WHAT DOES THE LAW ALLOW US TO DO ON THE SABBATH?
TO DO GOOD OR TO DO HARM? TO SAVE LIFE OR TO KILL?" BUT
THEY WERE SILENT. 5 THEN JESUS LOOKED AROUND AT
THEM WITH ANGER AND DEEP SADNESS BECAUSE THEY HAD
CLOSED THEIR MINDS. AND HE SAID TO THE MAN, "STRETCH

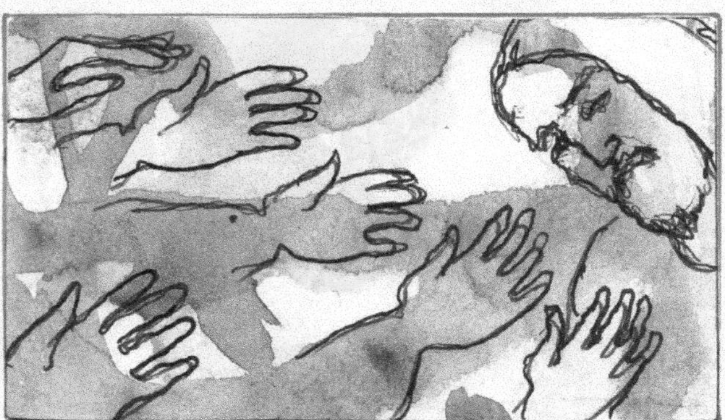

OUT YOUR HAND." HE DID IT AND HIS HAND WAS HEALED. 6
BUT WHEN THE PHARISEES LEFT, THEY MET HEROD'S MEN, LO-
OKING FOR A WAY TO DESTROY JESUS. 7 JESUS AND HIS DI-
SCIPLES WITHDREW TO THE LAKESIDE AND A LARGE CROWD FROM
GALILEE FOLLOWED HIM. MANY PEOPLE ALSO CAME FROM JUDEA,
8 JERUSALEM, IDUMEA, TRANSJORDAN AND THE REGION OF
TYRE AND SIDON, FOR THEY HAD HEARD ALL HE WAS DOING. 9
BECAUSE OF THE CROWD, JESUS TOLD HIS DISCIPLES TO HAVE A
BOAT READY, TO PREVENT THE PEOPLE CRUSHING HIM. 10 HE
HEALED SO MANY: ALL WHO HAD DISEASES KEPT PRESSING
TOWARDS HIM TO TOUCH HIM. 11 EVEN THE PEOPLE WITH
EVIL SPIRITS, WHEN THEY SAW HIM, WOULD FALL BEFORE
HIM AND CRY OUT, "YOU ARE THE SON OF GOD". 12
BUT HE WARNED THEM STERNLY NOT TO TELL ANY-
ONE WHO HE WAS.

THE TWELVE APOSTLES

13 THEN JESUS WENT UP INTO THE HILL COUNTRY AND
CALLED THOSE HE WANTED AND THEY CAME TO HIM. 14 SO
HE APPOINTED TWELVE TO BE WITH HIM; AND HE CALLED
THEM APOSTLES. HE WANTED TO SEND THEM OUT TO PRE-
ACH, 15 AND HE GAVE THEM AUTHORITY TO DRIVE OUT
DEMONS. 16 THESE ARE THE TWELVE: SIMON, TO
WHOM HE GAVE THE NAME PETER; 17 JAMES, SON
OF ZEBEDEE, AND JOHN HIS BROTHER, TO WHOM HE

GAVE THE NAME BOANERGES, MEANING "MEN OF THUNDER",
18 ANDREW, PHILIP, BARTHOLOMEW, MATTHEW, THOMAS,
JAMES SON OF ALPHEUS, THADDEUS, SIMON THE CANANEAN
19 AND JUDAS ISCARIOT, THE ONE WHO BETRAYED HIM.

THE SIN AGAINST THE SPIRIT

20 THEY WENT HOME. THE CROWD GATHERED AGAIN AND
THEY COULDN'T HAVE A MEAL. 21 KNOWING WHAT WAS HAP-
PENING HIS RELATIVES CAME TO HIM AND SAID, "HE IS OUT
OF HIS MIND," THEY SAID. 22 THE TEACHERS OF THE LAW WHO
CAME FROM JERUSALEM SAID, "HE IS IN THE POWER OF BE-
ELZEBUL: THE CHIEF OF
THE DEMONS HELPS HIM TO
DRIVE OUT DEMONS." JESUS
23 CALLED THEM, TEACHING
THROUGH STORIES AND PARA-
BLES, "HOW CAN SATAN DRIVE
OUT SATAN? 24 IF A NATION
IS DIVIDED BY CIVIL WAR, IT
CANNOT STAND. 25 IF A FAMI-
LY IS DIVIDED, IT WILL NOT
SURVIVE. 26 SO, IF SATAN
HAS RISEN AGAINST HIMSELF
AND IS DIVIDED, HE WILL NOT
STAND; HE IS FINISHED. 27
NO ONE CAN BREAK INTO THE
HOUSE OF THE STRONG ONE
TO PLUNDER HIS GOODS, UN-
LESS HE FIRST TIES UP THE
STRONG ONE. THEN HE CAN
PLUNDER HIS HOUSE. 28
TRULY, I SAY TO YOU, EVERY
HUMAN SIN WILL BE FORGI-
VEN, EVEN INSULTS TO GOD,
HOWEVER NUMEROUS. 29
BUT WHOEVER SLANDERS THE

HOLY SPIRIT WILL NEVER BE FORGIVEN: THE GUILT OF HIS SIN
IS FOREVER. 30 THIS WAS THEIR SIN WHEN THEY
SAID: 'HE HAS AN EVIL SPIRIT IN HIM.'"

JESUS' TRUE FAMILY

31 THEN HIS MOTHER AND HIS BROTHERS CAME. AS THEY
STOOD OUTSIDE, THE SENT SOMEONE TO CALL HIM. 32 THE
CROWD AROUND JESUS TOLD HIM, "YOUR MOTHER AND YOUR
BROTHERS AND SISTERS ARE OUTSIDE ASKING FOR YOU."
33 HE REPLIED, "WHO ARE MY MOTHER AND MY BROTHERS?"
34 AND LOOKING AROUND AT THOSE WHO SAT THERE
HE SAID, "HERE ARE MY MOTHER AND MY BROTHERS.
35 WHOEVER DOES THE WILL OF GOD IS BROTHER AND
SISTER AND MOTHER TO ME."

THE SOWER

4 (1) AGAIN JESUS BEGAN TO TEACH BY THE LAKE, BUT
SUCH A LARGE CROWD GATHERED ABOUT HIM THAT HE GOT
INTO THE BOAT, SAT IN IT ON THE LAKE WHILE THE CROWD
STOOD ON THE SHORE. (2) HE TAUGHT THEM THROUGH STORIES
OR PARABLES. IN HIS TEACHING HE SAID. (3) "LISTEN! THE
SOWER WENT OUT TO SOW. (4) AS HE SOWED, SOME OF THE
SEED FELL ALONG A PATH AND THE BIRDS CAME AND ATE
IT UP. (5) SOME OF THE SEED FELL ON ROCKY GROUND WITH
LITTLE SOIL IN IT; IT SPRANG UP QUICKLY AS IT HAD NO
DEPTH; (6) BUT WHEN THE SUN ROSE AND BURNED IT, IT

WITHERED BECAUSE IT HAD NO ROOTS. (7) OTHER SEED
FELL AMONG THORNBUSHES AND THE THORNS GREW AND
CHOKED IT, SO IT DIDN'T PRODUCE ANY GRAIN. (8) BUT SOME
SEED FELL ON GOOD SOIL, GREW, INCREASED AND YIELDED GRAIN;
SOME PRODUCED THIRTY TIMES AS MUCH, OTHERS SIXTY AND
OTHERS ONE HUNDRED TIMES AS MUCH." (9) AND JESUS
ADDED, "LISTEN THEN, IF YOU HAVE EARS."
(10) WENT THE CROWD LEFT, SOME WHO WERE AROUND HIM
WITH THE TWELVE ASKED ABOUT THE PARABLES. (11) HE ANS-
WERED THEM, "THE MYSTERY OF THE KINGDOM OF GOD HAS
BEEN GIVEN TO YOU. BUT FOR THOSE OUTSIDE, ALL COMES IN
PARABLES, (12) SO THAT

THE MORE THEY SEE, THEY DON'T PERCEIVE; THE
MORE THEY HEAR, THEY DON'T UNDERSTAND; IF NOT
THEY WOULD BE CONVERTED AND PARDONED."

(13) JESUS SAID TO THEM, "DON'T YOU UNDERSTAND THIS PA-
RABLE? HOW THEN WILL YOU UNDERSTAND ANY OF THE PA-
RABLES? (14) WHAT THE SO-
WER IS SOWING IS THE WORD.
(15) THOSE ALONG THE PATH
WHERE THE SEED FELL ARE
PEOPLE WHO HEAR THE
WORD, BUT AS SOON AS THEY
DO, SATAN COMES AND TAKES
AWAY THE WORD THAT WAS
SOWN IN THEM. (16) OTHER
PEOPLE RECEIVE THE WORD
LIKE ROCKY GROUND. AS SO-
ON AS THEY HEAR THE WORD,
THEY ACCEPT IT WITH JOY,
(17) BUT THEY HAVE NO RO-
OTS SO IT LASTS ONLY A
LITTLE WHILE. NO SOONER
DOES TROUBLE OR PERSECU-
TION COME BECAUSE OF THE
WORD, THAN THEY FALL.
(18) OTHERS RECEIVE THE
SEED AMONG THORNS.
AFTER THEY HEAR THE WORD,
(19) THEY ARE CAUGHT UP
IN THE WORRIES OF THIS LI-
FE, FALSE HOPES OF RI-
CHES AND OTHER DESIRES.
ALL THESE COME IN AND CHOKE THE WORD SO THAT
FINALLY IT PRODUCES NOTHING.
(20) AND THERE ARE OTHERS WHO RECEIVE THE
WORD AS GOOD SOIL. THEY HEAR THE WORD, TAKE
IT TO HEART AND PRODUCE: SOME THIRTY, SOME
SIXTY AND SOME ONE HUNDRED TIMES AS MUCH."

PARABLE OF THE LAMP

(21) JESUS SAID TO THEM, "WHEN THE LIGHT COMES, IS IT
TO BE PUT UNDER A TUB OR A BED? SURELY IT IS PUT ON
A LAMPSTAND. (22) WHATEVER IS HIDDEN WILL BE DIS-
CLOSED, AND WHATEVER IS KEPT SECRET WILL BE BROUGHT
TO LIGHT. (23) LISTEN THEN, IF YOU HAVE EARS!" (24) AND
HE ALSO SAID TO THEM, "PAY ATTENTION TO WHAT YOU HEAR.
IN THE MEASURE YOU GIVE, SO SHALL YOU RECEIVE AND
STILL MORE WILL BE GIVEN TO YOU. (25) FOR TO HIM WHO

PRODUCES SOMETHING, MORE WILL BE GIVEN, AND FROM
HIM WHO DOESN'T PRODUCE ANYTHING, EVEN WHAT HE
HAS WILL BE TAKEN AWAY FROM HIM."

THE SEED GROWING BY ITSELF

(26) HE ALSO SAID, "IN THE KINGDOM OF GOD IT IS LIKE
THIS. A MAN SCATTERS SEED ON THE SOIL. (27) WHETHER HE
IS ASLEEP OR AWAKE, BE IT DAY OR NIGHT, THE SEED SPROUTS
AND GROWS, HE KNOWS NOT HOW. (28) THE SOIL PRODUCES
OF ITSELF; FIRST THE BLADE, THEN THE EAR, THEN THE FULL
GRAIN IN THE EAR. (29) AND WHEN IT IS RIPE FOR HARVEST-
ING THEY TAKE THE SICKLE FOR THE CUTTING: THE TIME
FOR HARVEST HAS COME. BUT AS SOON AS THE GRAIN IS
RIPE, THE MAN STARTS CUTTING IT WITH A SICKLE,
BECAUSE HARVEST TIME HAS COME.

THE MUSTARD SEED

(30) JESUS ALSO SAID, "WHAT IS THE KINGDOM OF GOD
LIKE? TO WHAT SHALL WE COMPARE IT? (31) IT IS LIKE A MUS-
TARD SEED WHICH, WHEN SOWN, IS THE SMALLEST OF ALL SEEDS
SCATTERED ON THE SOIL. (32) BUT ONCE SOWN, IT GROWS UP

AND BECOMES THE LARGEST PLANT IN THE GARDEN AND GROWS
BRANCHES SO BIG THAT THE BIRDS OF THE AIR CAN TAKE SHEL-
TER IN ITS SHADE." (33) JESUS USED MANY SUCH STORIES
OR PARABLES, TO PROCLAIM THE WORD IN A WAY THEY
WOULD BE ABLE TO UNDERSTAND. (34) HE WOULD NOT TE-
ACH THEM WITHOUT PARABLES; BUT PRIVATELY TO HIS DI-
SCIPLES HE EXPLAINED EVERYTHING.

JESUS CALMS THE STORM

35 ON THE EVENING OF THE SAME DAY, JESUS SAID TO THEM
"LET'S GO ACROSS TO THE OTHER SIDE." 36 SO THEY LEFT THE
CROWD AND TOOK HIM AWAY IN THE BOAT HE WAS IN, AND
OTHER BOATS SET OUT WITH HIM. 37 THEN A STORM GA-

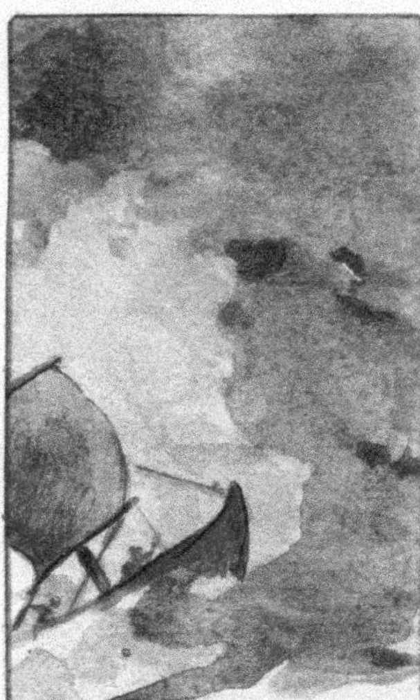

THERED AND BECAME A
BLOWING GALE. THE WAVES
SPILLED OVER INTO THE BO-
AT WHICH SOON IT FILLED
WITH WATER. 38 JESUS
WAS IN THE STERN, ASLEEP
ON THE CUSHION. THEY
WOKE HIM UP AND SAID,
"MASTER, DON'T YOU CA-
RE IF WE SINK?" 39
AS JESUS AWOKE, HE
REBUKED THE WIND
AND ORDERED THE SEA,
"QUIE NOW! BE STILL"
THE WIND DROPPED AND
THERE WAS A GREAT
CALM. 40 JESUS SAID
TO THEM "WHY ARE YOU
SO FRIGHTENED? DO YOU
STILL HAVE NO FAITH?"
41 BUT THEY WERE
TERRIFIED AND SAID
TO ONE ANOTHER, "WHO
CAN THIS BE? EVEN
THE WIND AND THE SEA
OBEY HIM!"

THE GERASENE DEMONIAC

5 1 THEY ARRIVED ON THE OTHER SIDE OF THE LAKE IN
THE GERASENES REGION. 2 LEAVING THE BOAT,
JESUS WAS MET BY A MAN WITH EVIL SPIRITS WHO HAD
COME FROM THE TOMBS. 3 HE LIVED AMONG THE TOMBS AND
COULDN'T BE RESTRAINED, EVEN WITH A CHAIN. 4 HE HAD
BEEN BOUND WITH FETTERS AND CHAINS BUT HE WOULD
PULL THE CHAINS APART AND SMASH THE FETTERS, AND
NO ONE COULD CONTROL HIM. 5 NIGHT AND DAY HE
STAYED AMONG THE TOMBS ON THE HILLS, SCREMING AND
BEATING HIMSELF WITH STONES. 6 WHEN HE SAW JESUS,

HE RAN AND FELL AT HIS FEET 7 AND CRIED WITH A LOUD
VOICE, "WHAT DO YOU WANT WITH ME, JESUS, SON OF THE MOST
HIGH GOD? FOR GOD'S SAKE I BEG YOU, DO NOT TORMENT
ME." 8 HE SAID THIS FOR JESUS HAD COMMANDED, "COME OUT
OF THIS MAN, EVIL SPIRIT." 9 JESUS ASKED HIM, "WHAT IS
YOUR NAME?" HE REPLIED, "LEGION IS OUR NAME, FOR WE
ARE MANY." 10 AND ALL OF THEM BEGGED JESUS NOT TO
SEND THEM OUT OF THAT REGION. 11 NOW, A GREAT HERD
OF PIGS WAS FEEDING ON THE HILLSIDE, 12 AND THE EVIL
SPIRITS BEGGED HIM, "SEND US TO THE PIGS AND LET US GO IN-
TO THEM." 13 SO JESUS LET THEM GO. THE EVIL SPIRITS CAME
OUT OF THE MAN AND WENT INTO THE PIGS, AND THE HERD RUSHED
DOWN THE CLIFF AND ALL WERE DROWNED IN THE LAKE. 14
THE HERDSMEN FLED AND REPORTED THIS IN THE TOWN AND
IN THE COUNTRYSIDE, SO ALL THE PEOPLE CAME TO SEE WHAT
HAD HAPPENED. 15 THEY CAME TO JESUS AND SAW THE
MAN FREED OF THE EVIL SPIRITS SITTING, CLOTHED AND
IN HIS RIGHT MIND, THE SAME MAN WHO HAD BEEN POSSES-
SED BY THE PIGS. THEY WERE AFRAID.

16 AND WHEN THOSE WHO HAD SEEN IT TOLD WHAT
HAD HAPPENED TO THE MAN AND TO THE PIGS 17 THE
PEOPLE BEGGED JESUS TO LEAVE THEIR NEIGH-
BORHOOD. 18 WHEN JESUS WAS GETTING INTO
THE BOAT THE MAN WHO HAD BEEN POSSESSED BEG-
GED TO STAY WITH HIM. 19 JESUS WOULD NOT LET
HIM AND SAID, "GO HOME TO YOUR PEOPLE AND TELL
THEM HOW MUCH THE LORD HAS DONE FOR YOU AND
HOW HE HAS HAD MERCY ON YOU." 20 SO THE MAN
WENT THROUGHOUT THE COUNTRY OF DECAPOLIS TEL-
LING EVERYONE HOW MUCH JESUS HAD DONE FOR HIM.
AND ALL THE PEOPLE WERE ASTONISHED.

JESUS AND THE DAUGHTER OF JAIRUS

21 JESUS CROSSED TO THE OTHER SIDE OF THE LAKE, AND ON THE
SHORE A LARGE CROWD GATHERED AROUND HIM. 22 JAIRUS, AN

OFFICIAL OF THE SYNAGOGUE SAW JESUS AND THREW HIMSELF AT
HIS FEET 23 AND ASKED HIM, "MY LITTLE DAUGHTER IS NE-
AR DEATH. COME AND LAY YOUR HANDS ON HER SO THAT SHE MAY
GET WELL AND LIVE." 24 JESUS WENT WITH HIM WITH MANY
FOLLOWERS, PRESSING FROM EVERY SIDE. 25 THERE WAS A WO-
MAN AMONG THEM WHO HAD BEEN BLEEDING FOR TWELVE YEARS.
26 SHE HAD SUFFERED A LOT AND SPENT ALL SHE HAD BECAUSE OF
MANY DOCTORS, BUT INSTEAD OF GETTING BETTER, SHE WAS WORSE.
27 AS SHE HEARD OF JESUS, SHE CAME UP BEHIND HIM AND TO-
UCHED HIS CLOAK 28 THINKING, "IF I JUST TOUCH HIS CLOTHING,
I SHALL GET WELL." 29 HER

FLOW OF BLOOD DRIED UP AT
ONCE AND SHE FELT THAT SHE
WAS HEALED OF HER ILLNESS.
30 BUT JESUS WAS AWARE
THAT HEALING POWER HAD
GONE OUT FROM HIM, SO HE
TURNED AROUND IN THE
CROWD AND ASKED, "WHO TO-
UCHED MY CLOTHES?" 31 HIS
DISCIPLES SAID, "YOU SEE HOW
MANY PEOPLE ARE AROUND
YOU. WHY DO YOU ASK WHO
TOUCHED YOU?" 32 BUT
HE KEPT LOOKING AROUND
TO SEE WHO HAD DONE IT.
33 THEN THE WOMAN AWA-
RE OF WHAT HAPPENED, CA-
ME FORWARD TREMBLING
AND AFRAID. SHE KNELT BE-
FORE HIM AND TOLD HIM
THE WHOLE TRUTH. 34
JESUS SAID TO HER, "DA-
UGHTER YOUR FAITH HAS
SAVED YOU; GO IN PEACE
AND BE FREE OF THIS IL-
LNESS." 35 WHILE
JESUS WAS STILL SPEAKING, SOME PEOPLE ARRI-
VED FROM THE OFFICIAL'S HOUSE TO INFORM HIM,
"YOUR DAUGHTER IS DEAD. WHY TROUBLE THE MAS-
TER ANY FURTHER?" 36 BUT JESUS IGNORED WHAT
THEY SAID AND TOLD THE OFFICIAL, DO NOT FEAR,
JUST BELIEVE."

327 CCCXXVII

37 HE ALLOWED NO ONE TO FOLLOW HIM EXCEPT PETER, JAMES
AND JOHN, JAMES' BROTHER. 38 WHEN THEY ARRIVED AT THE
HOUSE, JESUS SAW A GREAT COMMOTION, PEOPLE WEEPING
AND WAILING LOUDLY. 39 HE ENTERED AND SAID TO THEM,
"WHY ALL THIS COMMOTION AND WEEPING? THE CHILD IS NOT
DEAD BUT ASLEEP." 40 THEY LAUGHED AT HIM, BUT JESUS SENT
THEM OUTSIDE AND WENT WITH THE CHILD'S FATHER AND MO-
THER AND HIS COMPANIONS INTO THE ROOM WHERE THE
CHILD LAY. 41 TAKING HER BY THE HAND, HE SAID TO HER,
"TALITHA KUMI!" WHICH MEANS: "LITTLE GIRL, GET UP!"

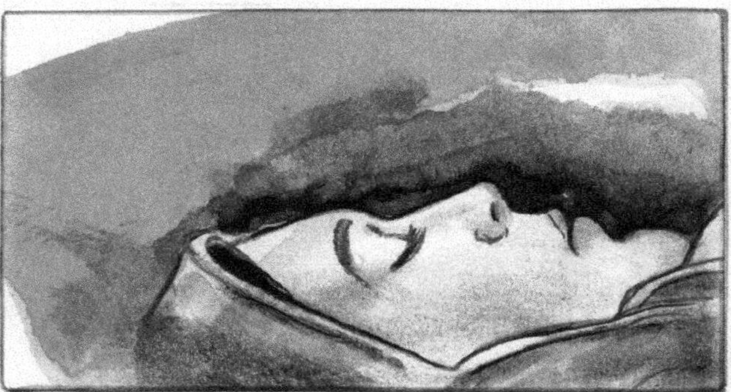

42 THE GIRL GOT UP AT ONCE AND WALKED AROUND; SHE WAS
TWELVE YEARS OLD. THE PARENTS WERE GREATLY ASTONISHED.
43 JESUS ORDERED TO SAY NOTHING ABOUT IT, AND TOLD
THEM TO GIVE HER SOMETHING TO EAT.

IS HE NOT THE CARPENTER?

6 1 LEAVING THAT PLACE, JESUS RETURNED TO HIS
OWN COUNTRY, AND HIS DISCIPLES FOLLOWED HIM. 2
ON THE NEXT SABBATH, HE BEGAN TEACHING IN THE SYNAGOGUE,
AND THOSE WHO HEARD HIM WERE ASTONISHED AND SAID, "HOW

THIS DID COME TO HIM? WHAT
KIND OF WISDOM HAS BEEN GI-
VEN TO HIM THAT HE PERFORMS
SUCH MIRACLES? 3 WHO IS
HE BUT THE CARPENTER, THE
SON OF MARY AND THE BRO-
THER OF JAMES AND JOSET
AND JUDAS AND SIMON?
HIS SISTERS, TOO, ARE THEY
NOT HERE AMONG US?" SO
THEY TOOK OFFENSE AT HIM.
4 JESUS SAID TO THEM, "A
PROPHET IS DESPISED ONLY
IN HIS OWN COUNTRY, AND
AMONG HIS RELATIVES
AND HIS OWN FAMILY." 5
AND HE COULD WORK NO
MIRACLES THERE, BUT
ONLY HEALED A FEW
SICK PEOPLE BY LAY-
ING HIS HANDS ON THEM.
6 JESUS HIMSELF
WAS ASTOUNDED AT
THEIR UNBELIEF.

JESUS SENDS OUT THE TWELVE

JESUS THEN WENT AROUND THE VILLAGES TEACHING. 7
HE CALLED THE TWELVE TO HIM AND SEND THEM OUT TWO BY
TWO, GIVING THEM AUTHORITY OVER EVIL SPIRITS. 8 AND
HE ORDERED THEM TO TAKE NOTHING FOR THE JOURNEY
EXCEPT A STAFF; NO FOOD, NO BAG, NO MONEY IN THEIR
BELTS. 9 THEY WERE TO WEAR SANDALS AND WERE
NOT TO TAKE AN EXTRA TUNIC. 10 AND HE ADDED, "IN
WHATEVER HOUSE YOU ARE WELCOMED, STAY THERE UNTIL
YOU LEAVE THE PLACE. 11 IF ANY PLACE DOESN'T RECEIVE
YOU AND THE PEOPLE REFUSE TO LISTEN TO YOU, LEAVE
AFTER SHAKING THE DUST OFF YOUR FEET. IT WILL BE
A TESTIMONY AGAINST THEM." 12 SO THEY SET OUT TO
PROCLAIM THAT THIS WAS THE TIME TO REPENT.
13 THEY DROVE OUT MANY DEMONS AND HEALED
MANY SICK PEOPLE BY ANOINTING THEM.

JOHN THE BAPTIST BEHEADED

14 KING HEROD ALSO HEARD ABOUT JESUS BECAUSE HIS
NAME HAD BECOME WELL-KNOWN. SOME PEOPLE SAID, "JOHN
THE BAPTIST HAS BEEN RAISED FROM THE DEAD AND THAT IS
WHY MIRACULOUS POWERS ARE AT WORK IN HIM." 15 OTHERS
THOUGHT, "HE IS ELIJAH," AND OTHERS, "HE IS A PROPHET
LIKE THE PROPHETS OF TIMES PAST." 16 WHEN HEROD
WAS TOLD OF THIS, HE THOUGHT: "I HAD JOHN BEHEADED,
YET HE HAS RISEN FROM THE DEAD!" 17 FOR THIS IS WHAT
HAD HAPPENED. HEROD HAD ORDERED JOHN'S ARREST
AND HAD HIM BOUND AND PUT IN PRISON BECAUSE OF HE-
RODIAS, THE WIFE OF HIS
BROTHER PHILIP. HEROD
HAD MARRIED HER 18
AND JOHN HAD TOLD HIM,
"IT IS NOT RIGHT FOR YOU
TO LIVE WITH YOUR BRO-
THER'S WIFE." 19 SO
HERODIAS HELD A GRUDGE
AGAINST JOHN AND WANTED
TO KILL HIM, BUT SHE COULD
NOT 20 BECAUSE HEROD
RESPECTED JOHN. HE KNEW
JOHN TO BE UPRIGHT AND HO-
LY MAN AND KEPT HIM SAFE.
HE LIKED LISTENING TO HIM,
SOMETIMES HOWEVER BECO-
MING DISTURBED BY HIM.
21 HERODIAS' CHANCE
CAME ON HEROD'S BIRTHDAY,
WHEN HE GAVE A DINNER
FOR ALL THE GOVERNMENT
OFFICIALS, MILITARY CHIEFS
AND LEADING MEN OF GALILEE.
22 ON THAT OCCASION
THE DAUGHTER OF HERODI-
AS CAME IN AND DANCED;
AND SHE DELIGHTED HE-
ROD AND HIS GUESTS. THE

KING SAID TO THE GIRL, "ASK ME FOR ANYTHING YOU WANT
AND I WILL GIVE IT TO YOU." 23 AND HE WENT SO FAR AS TO
SAY WITH MANY OATHS, "I WILL GIVE YOU ANYTHING YOU ASK,
EVEN HALF MY KINGDOM."
24 SHE WENT OUT TO CONSULT HER MOTHER, "WHAT
SHALL I ASK FOR?" THE MOTHER REPLIED, "THE HEAD
OF JOHN THE BAPTIST." 25 THE GIRL HURRIED TO THE KING
AND MADE HER REQUEST: I WANT YOU TO GIVE ME THE
HEAD OF JOHN THE BAPTIST, HERE AND NOW, ON A DISH."
26 THE KING WAS VERY DISPLEASED, BUT HE WOULD NOT

REFUSE IN FRONT OF HIS GUESTS BECAUSE OF HIS OATHS.
27 SO HE SENT ONE OF THE BODYGUARDS WITH ORDERS TO
BRING JOHN'S HEAD. THE MAN WENT AND BEHEADED JOHN
IN PRISON; 28 THEN HE BROUGHT THE HEAD ON A DISH
AND GAVE IT TO THE GIRL. AND THE GIRL GAVE IT TO HER
MOTHER. 29 WHEN JOHN'S DISCIPLES HEARD OF THIS, THEY
CAME AND TOOK HIS BODY AND BURIED IT.

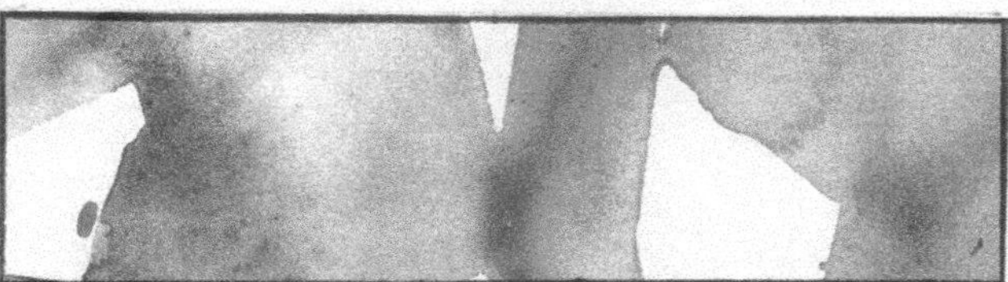

JESUS, SHEPHERD AND PROPHET

(30) THE APOSTLES RETURNED AND REPORTED TO JESUS ALL THEY HAD DONE AND TAUGHT. (31) HE SAID TO THEM, "GO OFF BY YOURSELVES TO A REMOTE PLACE AND HAVE SOME REST." FOR THERE WERE SO MANY PEOPLE THAT THE APOSTLES HAD NO TIME EVEN TO EAT. (32) AND THEY WENT AWAY IN THE BOAT TO A SECLUDED AREA BY THEMSELVES. (33) BUT PEOPLE SAW THEM LEAVING AND MANY COULD GUESS THEIR DESTINATION. SO THEY CAME ON FOOT FROM ALL THE TOWNS, ARRIVING AHEAD OF THEM. (34) JESUS SAW A LARGE CROWD AND HAD COMPASSION ON THEM FOR THEY WERE LIKE SHEEP WITHOUT A SHEPHERD. HE BEGAN A LONG TEACHING SESSION WITH THEM.

FIRST MIRACLES OF THE LOAVES

(35) IT WAS GETTING LATE, SO HIS DISCIPLES SAID TO HIM, THIS IS A LONELY PLACE AND IS NOW LATE. (36) YOU SHOULD SEND THE PEOPLE TO THE FARMS AND VILLAGES AROUND HERE TO BUY THEMSELVES SOMETHING TO EAT." JESUS SAID, "YOU GIVE THEM SOMETHING TO EAT." THEY REPLIED, "IF WE ARE TO FEED THEM, WE MUST BUY TWO HUNDRED SILVER COINS' OF BREAD." (37-38) BUT JESUS SAID, "YOU HAVE SOME LOAVES; GO AND SEE. THEY FOUND OUT AND SAID, "THERE ARE FIVE LOAVES AND TWO FISH." (39) HE TOLD THEM TO HAVE THE PEOPLE SIT DOWN IN GROUPS ON THE GREEN GRASS. (40) THIS THEY DID IN GROUPS OF HUNDREDS AND FIFTIES. (41) AND JESUS TOOK THE FIVE LOAVES AND THE TWO FISH AND, RAISING HIS EYES TO HEAVEN, SAID THE BLESSING, BROKE THE LOAVES, AND GAVE THEM TO HIS DISCIPLES TO DISTRIBUTE TO THE PEOPLE. HE ALSO DIVIDED THE TWO FISH AMONG THEM. (42) THEY ALL ATE AND EVERYONE HAD ENOUGH. (43) THE DISCIPLES GATHERED WHAT WAS LEFT AND FILLED TWELVE BASKETS WITH BITS OF BREAD AND FISH. (44) FIVE THOUSAND MEN HAD EATEN THERE.

JESUS WALKS ON THE WATER

(45) IMMEDIATELY, JESUS TOLD HIS DISCIPLES TO GET INTO THE BOAT AND GO AHEAD OF HIM TO THE OTHER SIDE, TOWARDS BETHSAIDA, WHILE HE SENT THE CROWD AWAY. (46) AS THEY HAD

GONE, HE WENT TO THE HILLSIDE TO PRAY. (47) WHEN EVENING CAME, HE WAS ALONE AND THE BOAT FAR OUT ON THE LAKE. (48) HE SAW HIS DISCIPLES STRAINING ON THE OARS, FOR THE WIND WAS AGAINST THEM, AND BEFORE DAYBREAK HE CAME TO THEM WALKING ON THE LAKE, AND HE WAS GOING TO PASS THEM BY. (49) WHEN THEY SAW HIM WALKING ON THE LAKE, THEY THOUGHT IT WAS A GHOST AND CRIED OUT; (50) FOR THEY ALL SAW HIM AND WERE TERRIFIED. BUT AT ONCE HE CALLED TO THEM, "COURAGE! IT'S ME; DON'T BE AFRAID."

(51) THEN JESUS GOT INTO THE BOAT WITH THEM AND THE WIND DIED DOWN. THEY WERE COMPLETELY ASTONISHED, (52) FOR THEY HAD NOT REALLY GRASPED THE FACT OF THE LOAVES: THEIR MINDS WERE DULL.
(53) HAVING CROSSED THE LAKE, THEY CAME ASHORE AT GENESARET WHERE THEY TIED UP THE BOAT. (54) AS THEY LANDED, PEOPLE RECOGNIZED JESUS (55) AND RAN TO SPREAD THE NEWS THROUGHOUT THE COUNTRYSIDE. WHEREVER HE WAS THEY BROUGHT TO HIM THE SICK LYING ON THEIR MATS. (56) AND WHEREVER HE WENT, TO VILLAGES, TOWNS OR FARMS, THEY LAID THE SICK IN THE

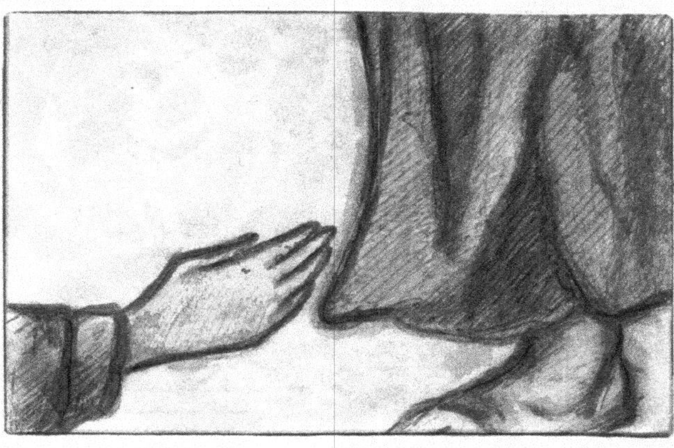

MARKETPLACE, BEGGING HIM TO LET THEM TOUCH THE FRINGE OF HIS CLOAK. ALL WHO TOUCHED HIM WERE CURED.

TRUE CLEANNESS

7 (1) THE PHARISEES AND SOME TEACHERS OF THE LAW GATHERED AROUND JESUS, AS THEY HAD JUST ARRIVED FROM JERUSALEM. (2) THEY SAW THAT SOME OF HIS DISCIPLES WERE EATING THEIR MEAL WITH UNCLEAN HANDS, THAT IS, WITHOUT WASHING THEM.
(3) NOW THE PHARISEES, AND ALL THE JEWS, NEVER EAT WITHOUT WASHING THEIR HANDS FOR THEY FOLLOW THE TRADITION OF THEIR ANCESTORS. NOR (4) DO THEY EAT ANYTHING COMING FROM THE MARKET WITHOUT FIRST WASHING THEMSELVES. THERE ARE MANY OTHER TRADITIONS THEY OBSERVE, LIKE THE RITUAL WASHING OF CUPS, POTS AND PLATES. (5) SO THE PHARISEES AND THE TEACHERS OF THE LAW ASKED HIM, "WHY YOUR DISCIPLES DON'T FOLLOW THE ELDERS' TRADITION, BUT EAT WITH UNCLEAN HANDS?" JESUS ANSWERED (6), "YOU GO NO FURTHER THAN APPEARANCES. HOW WELL ISAIAH PROPHESIED OF YOU WHEN HE WROTE: THIS PEOPLE HONORS ME WITH THEIR LIPS, BUT THEIR HEART IS FAR FROM ME. (7) THE WORSHIP THEY OFFER ME IS WORTHLESS, FOR WHAT THEY TEACH ARE ONLY HUMAN RULES. (8-9) YOU EVEN PUT ASIDE THE COMMANDMENT OF GOD TO HOLD FAST TO HUMAN TRADITION. (10) FOR EXAMPLE, MOSES SAID: DO YOUR DUTY TO YOUR FATHER AND YOUR MOTHER, AND: WHOEVER CURSES HIS FATHER OR HIS MOTHER IS TO BE PUT TO DEATH. (11) BUT, ACCORDING TO YOU SOMEONE COULD SAY TO HIS FATHER OR MOTHER: 'I ALREADY DECLARED CORBAN, WHICH MEANS, "OFFERED TO GOD", WHAT IS EXPECTED FROM ME.'

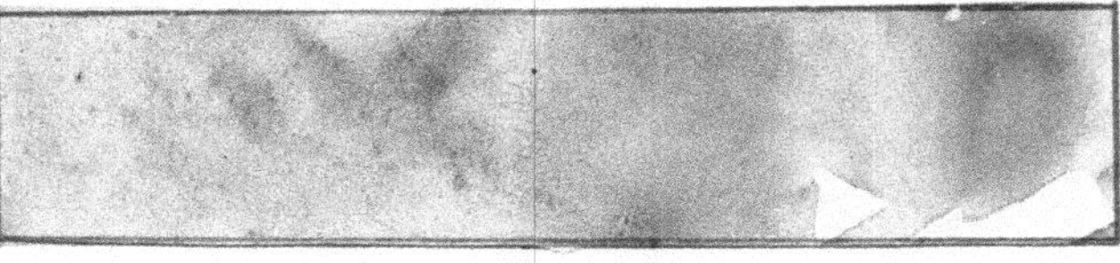

(12) IN THIS CASE, YOU NO LONGER PERMIT HIM TO HELP HIS
PARENTS (13) SO YOU NULLIFY THE WORD OF GOD THROUGH THE
TRADITION YOU HAVE HANDED ON. AND YOU DO MANY OTHER
THINGS LIKE THAT."
(14) JESUS THEN CALLED THE PEOPLE TO HIM AGAIN AND
SAID TO THEM "LISTEN TO ME, ALL OF YOU, AND TRY TO UNDER-
STAND. (15) NOTHING THAT ENTERS ANYONE FROM OUTSIDE
CAN MAKE HIM UNCLEAN. IT IS WHAT COMES OUT OF HIM
THAT MAKES HIM UNCLEAN. LISTEN, YOU WHO HAVE EARS! (16)

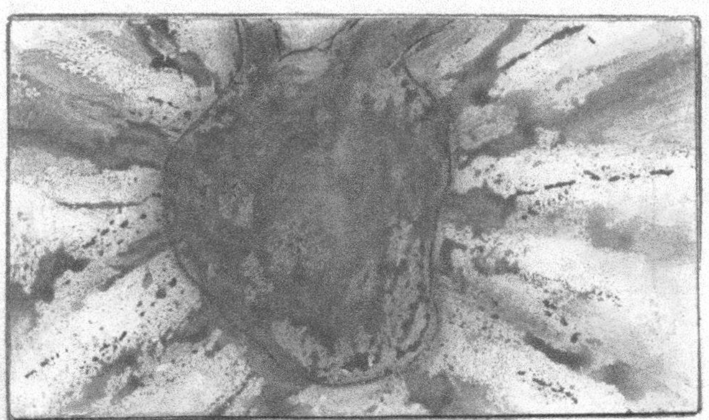

(17) WHEN JESUS GOT HOME, AWAY FROM THE CROWD, HIS DISCI-
PLES ASKED HIM ABOUT THIS SAYING (18) AND HE REPLIED,
"SO EVEN YOU ARE DULL ? DO YOU NOT SEE THAT WHATEVER
COMES FROM OUTSIDE CANNOT MAKE A PERSON UNCLEAN?
(19) SINCE IT ENTERS NOT THE HEART BUT THE STOMACH
AND IS FINALLY PASSED OUT." THUS JESUS DECLARED THAT
ALL FOODS ARE CLEAN. (20) AND HE WENT ON, "WHAT COMES
OUT OF A PERSON IS WHAT CAN MAKE HIM UNCLEAN (21) FOR
EVIL COMES OUT OF THE HEART: THEFT, MURDER, (22) ADUL-
TERY, JEALOUSY, GREED, MALICIOUSNESS, DECEIT, INDECENCY,
SLANDER, PRIDE AND FOLLY. (23) ALL THESE EVIL THINGS COME
FROM WITHIN AND MAKE A PERSON UNCLEAN."

THE FAITH OF THE SYROPHOENICIAN

(24) WHEN JESUS LEFT THAT PLACE HE WENT
TO THE BORDER OF THE TYRIAN COUNTRY. THERE
HE ENTERED A HOUSE AND DIDN'T WANT ANYONE TO
KNOW HE WAS THERE, BUT
HE COULD NOT REMAIN
HIDDEN. (25) A WOMAN
WHOSE SMALL DAUGHTER
HAD AN EVIL SPIRIT, CA-
ME TO HIM AND FELL AT
HIS FEET. (26) NOW THIS
WOMAN WAS A PAGAN,
A SYROPHOENICIAN BY
BIRTH, AND SHE BEGGED
HIM TO DRIVE THE DE-
MON OUT OF HER DA-
UGHTER. (27) JESUS TOLD
HER, "LET THE CHILDREN
BE FED FIRST, FOR IT
IS NOT RIGHT TO TAKE
THE CHILDREN'S BREAD
AND THROW IT TO THE
DOGS." (28) BUT SHE
REPLIED, "SIR, EVEN
THE DOGS UNDER THE
TABLE EAT THE CRUMBS
FROM THE CHILDREN'S
BREAD." (29) JESUS SAID
TO HER, "YOU MAY GO YO-
UR WAY, FOR SUCH A RE-
PLY THE DEMON HAS GONE
OUT OF YOUR DAUGHTER."

(30) AND WHEN THE WOMAN WENT HOME, SHE FOUND HER
CHILD LYING IN BED AND THE DEMON GONE.

HEALING OF A DEAF AND DUMB MAN

(31) AGAIN JESUS SET OUT: FROM THE COUNTRY
OF TYRE HE PASSED THROUGH SIDON AND SKIRTING
THE SEA OF GALILEE HE CAME TO THE TERRITORY OF
DECAPOLIS. (32) THERE A DEAF MAN WHO ALSO
HAD DIFFICULTY IN SPEAKING WAS BROUGHT TO
HIM. THEY ASKED JESUS TO LAY HIS HAND UPON HIM.
(33) JESUS TOOK HIM APART FROM THE CROWD, PUT
HIS FINGERS INTO THE
MAN'S EARS, TOUCHED
HIS TONGUE WITH SPIT-
TLE. (34) THEN, LOOK-
ING TO HEAVEN, HE
GROANED AND SAID
TO HIM: "EPHPHETHA,"
THAT IS, "BE OPENED."
(35) AND HIS EARS
WERE OPENED, HIS
TONGUE WAS LOOSE-
NED, AND HE BEGAN
TO SPEAK CLEARLY.
(36) JESUS ORDERED
THEM NOT TO TELL
ANYONE, BUT THE MORE
HE INSISTED ON THIS,
THE MORE THEY PRO-
CLAIMED IT. (37) THE
PEOPLE WERE COMPLE-
TELY ASTONISHED AND
SAID, "HE HAS DONE ALL
THINGS WELL; HE MA-
KES THE DEAF HEAR
AND THE DUMB SPEAK."

SECOND MIRACLE OF THE LOAVES

8 (1) SOON JESUS WAS AGAIN IN THE MIDST OF ANOT-
HER LARGE CROWD THAT HAD NOTHING TO EAT. SO HE
CALLED HIS DISCIPLES AND SAID, (2) "I FEEL SORRY FOR
THESE PEOPLE; THEY HAVE BEEN WITH ME FOR THREE DAYS
AND NOW HAVE NOTHING TO EAT. (3) IF I SEND THEM HOME
HUNGRY, THEY WILL FAINT ON THE WAY. SOME OF THEM HA-
VE COME A LONG WAY." (4) HIS DISCIPLES REPLIED, "WHERE IN
A DESERTED PLACE LIKE THIS COULD WE GET ENOUGH BREAD
TO FEED THESE PEOPLE?" (5) HE ASKED THEM, "HOW MANY
LOAVES HAVE YOU?" THEY ANSWERED, "SEVEN". (6) HE ORDE-
RED THE CROWD TO SIT DOWN ON THE GROUND. TAKING THE
SEVEN LOAVES AND GIVING THANKS, HE BROKE THEM AND

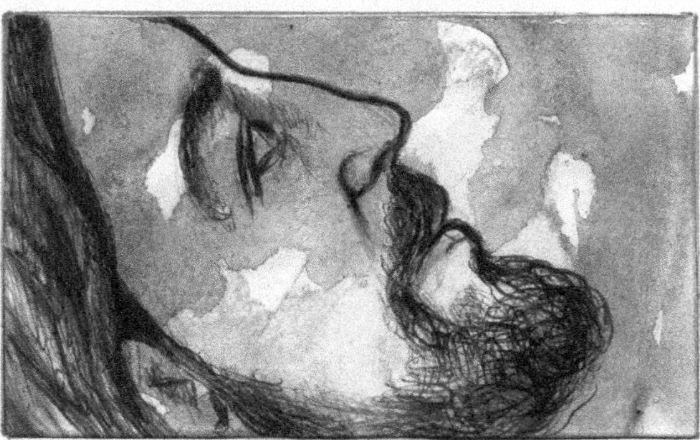

HANDED THEM TO HIS DISCIPLES TO DISTRIBUTE, WHICH THEY
DID AMONG THE PEOPLE. (7) THEY ALSO HAD SOME FISH; JESUS
SAID THE BLESSING AND ASKED THESE TO BE SHARED AS WELL.
(8) ALL ATE AND WERE SATISFIED. THE BROKEN PIECES WERE
COLLECTED IN SEVEN BASKETS OF LEFTOVERS. THERE WERE (9)
ABOUT FOUR THOUSAND PEOPLE. JESUS SENT THEM AWAY (10)
AND GOT INTO THE BOAT WITH HIS DISCIPLES AND WENT
TO THE REGION OF DALMANUTHA.

WHY DO THEY DEMAND A SIGN?

(11) THE PHARISEES CAME AND STARTED TO ARGUE
WITH JESUS. HOPING TO EMBARASS HIM, THEY ASKED
FOR SOME HEAVENLY SIGN. (12) THEN HIS SPIRIT WAS
MOVED. HE GAVE A DEEP SIGH AND SAID, "WHY DO THE PE-
OPLE OF THIS PRESENT TIME ASK FOR A SIGN? TRULY, I SAY
TO YOU, NO SIGN SHALL BE GIVEN TO THIS PEOPLE."

ON THAT OCCASION THE
DAUGHTER OF HERODIAS CAME
IN AND DANCED AND SHE DELIGHTED
HEROD AND HIS GUESTS.
(MARK 6:22)

13 THEN HE LEFT THEM, GOT INTO THE BOAT AND WENT TO THE OTHER SIDE OF THE LAKE. 14 THE DISCIPLES HAD FORGOTTEN TO BRING MORE BREAD AND HAD ONLY ONE LOAF WITH THEM. THEN 15 JESUS WARNED THEM, "KEEP YOUR EYES OPEN AND BEWARE OF THE YEAST OF THE PHARISEES AND OF HEROD." 16 AND THEY SAID TO ONE ANOTHER, "HE SAW THAT WE HAVE NO BREAD." 17 AWARE OF THIS, JESUS ASKED THEM, "WHY ARE YOU TALKING ABOUT THE LOAVES YOU ARE SHORT OF? DO YOU NOT SEE OR UNDERSTAND? ARE YOUR MINDS CLOSED? 18 HAVE YOU EYES THAT DON'T SEE AND EARS THAT DON'T HEAR? AND DO YOU NOT REMEMBER WHEN I 19 BROKE THE FIVE LOAVES AMONG FIVE THOUSAND? HOW MANY BASKETS FULL OF LEFTOVERS DID YOU COLLECT?" THEY ANSWERED, "TWELVE." 20 "AND HAVING SEVEN LOAVES FOR THE FOUR THOUSAND, HOW MANY WICKER BASKETS OF LEFTOVERS DID YOU COLLECT?" THEY ANSWERED, "SEVEN". JESUS 21 THEN SAID TO THEM, "DO YOU STILL NOT UNDERSTAND?"

CURE OF A BLIND MAN AT BETHSAIDA

22 WHEN THEY CAME TO BETHSAIDA, JESUS WAS ASKED TO TOUCH A BLIND MAN THEY BROUGHT TO HIM. 23 HE TOOK THE BLIND MAN BY THE HAND AND LED HIM OUTSIDE THE VILLAGE. HE PUT SPITTLE ON HIS EYES AND LAID HIS HANDS UPON HIM; THEN HE ASKED, "CAN YOU SEE ANYTHING?" 24 THE MAN, WHO WAS BEGINNING TO SEE, REPLIED, "I SEE PEOPLE LOOKING LIKE TREES, BUT MOVING AROUND." 25 THEN JESUS LAID HIS HANDS ON HIS EYES AGAIN AND THE MAN COULD SEE PERFECTLY. HIS SIGHT WAS RESTORED AND HE COULD SEE EVERYTHING CLEARLY. 26 JESUS SENT HIM HOME, SAYING, "DO NOT RETURN TO THE VILLAGE."

PETER'S DENIAL FORETOLD

27 JESUS SET OUT WITH HIS DISCIPLES FOR THE VILLAGES AROUND CESAREA PHILIPPI; ON THE WAY HE ASKED THEM, "WHO DO PEOPLE SAY I AM?" 28 THEY TOLD HIM, "SOME SAY YOU ARE JOHN THE BAPTIST; OTHERS SAY YOU ARE ELIJAH OR ONE

OF THE PROPHETS." THEN JESUS ASKED THEM, 29 "BUT YOU, WHO DO YOU SAY I AM?" PETER ANSWERED, "YOU ARE THE MESSIAH." 30 AND HE ORDERED THEM NOT TO TELL ANYONE ABOUT HIM. 31 JESUS BEGAN TO TEACH THAT THE SON OF MAN HAD TO SUFFER MANY THINGS AND BE REJECTED BY THE ELDERS, THE CHIEF PRIESTS AND THE TEACHERS OF THE LAW. HE WOULD BE KILLED AND AFTER THREE DAYS RISE AGAIN. 32 JESUS SAID THIS QUITE OPENLY, SO PETER TOOK HIM ASIDE AND PROTESTED STRONGLY. 33 TURNING AROUND, JESUS SAW HIS DISCIPLES VERY CLOSE. HE REBUKED PETER SAYING, "GET BEHIND ME, SATAN! YOUR THOUGHTS ARE NOT FROM GOD, BUT FROM MAN."

TAKE UP YOUR CROSS

34 THEN JESUS CALLED THE PEOPLE AND HIS DISCIPLES AND SAID, "IF YOU WANT TO FOLLOW ME, DENY YOURSELF, TAKE UP YOUR CROSS AND FOLLOW ME. 35 FOR IF YOU CHOOSE TO SAVE YOUR LIFE, YOU WILL LOSE IT; AND IF YOU LOSE YOUR LIFE FOR MY SAKE AND FOR THE SAKE OF THE GOSPEL, YOU

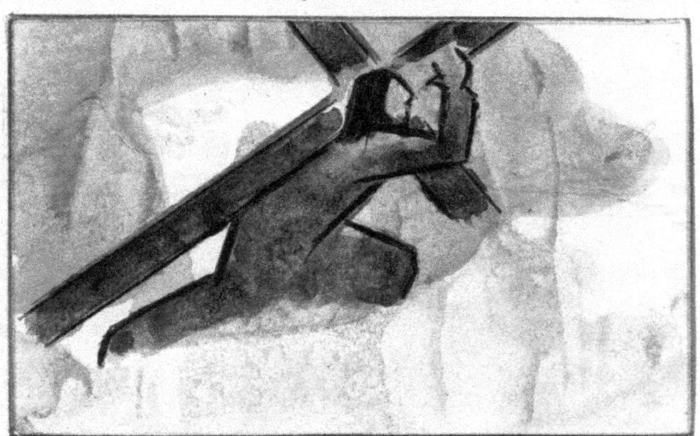

WILL SAVE IT. 36 WHAT GOOD IS IT TO GAIN THE WHOLE WORLD BUT DESTROY YOURSELF? 37 THERE IS NOTHING YOU CAN GIVE TO RECOVER YOUR LIFE. 38 I TELL YOU: IF ANYONE IS ASHAMED OF ME AND AND OF MY WORDS AMONG THIS ADULTEROUS AND SINFUL PEOPLE, THE SON OF MAN WILL ALSO BE ASHAMED OF HIM WHEN HE COMES IN THE GLORY OF HIS FATHER WITH THE HOLY ANGELS."

THE TRANSFIGURATION OF JESUS

9 1 AND HE WENT ON TO SAY, "TRULY I TELL YOU, THERE ARE SOME HERE WHO WILL NOT DIE BEFORE THEY SEE THE KINGDOM OF GOD COMING WITH POWER." 2 SIX DAYS LATER, JESUS, WITH PETER, JAMES AND JOHN, LED THEM UP A HIGH MOUNTAIN. THERE HIS APPEARANCE WAS CHANGED. 3 HIS CLOTHES SHONE TO A WHITE AS NO BLEACH OF THIS WORLD COULD MAKE THEM. 4 ELIJAH AND MOSES APPEARED TO THEM, AND WERE TALKING WITH JESUS. 5 PETER SAID TO JESUS, "MASTER, IT IS GOOD TO BE HERE; LET US MAKE THREE TENTS, ONE FOR YOU, ONE FOR MOSES AND ONE FOR ELIJAH." 6 FOR HE DID NOT KNOW WHAT TO SAY; THEY WERE OVERCOME WITH AWE. 7 BUT A CLOUD FORMED, COVERING IN A SHADOW EVERYONE, AND FROM THE CLOUD CAME THIS WORD, "THIS IS MY SON, THE BELOVED; LISTEN TO HIM." 8 AND SUDDENLY, AS THEY LOOKED AROUND, THEY NO LONGER SAW ANYONE EXCEPT JESUS WITH THEM. 9 AS THEY CAME DOWN THE MOUNTAIN, HE ORDERED THEM TO TELL NO ONE WHAT THEY HAD SEEN, UNTIL THE SON OF MAN BE RISEN FROM THE DEAD. 10 SO THEY KEPT THIS TO THEMSELVES, ALTHOUGH THEY DISCUSSED WITH ONE ANOTHER WHAT 'TO RISE FROM THE DEAD' COULD MEAN.

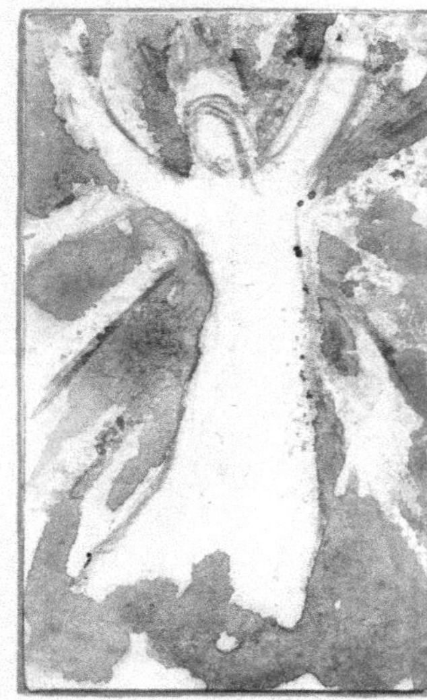

11 FINALLY THEY ASKED HIM, "WHY DO THE TEACHERS OF THE
LAW SAY THAT ELIJAH MUST COME FIRST?" 12 JESUS ANSWERED,
"OF COURSE, ELIJAH WILL COME FIRST SO THAT EVERYTHING MAY
BE AS IT SHOULD BE... BUT, WHY DO THE SCRIPTURES SAY THAT
THE SON OF MAN MUST SUFFER MANY THINGS AND BE DESPI-
SED? 13 I TELL YOU THAT ELIJAH HAS ALREADY COME AND
THEY HAVE TREATED HIM AS THEY PLEASED, AS THE
SCRIPTURES SAY OF HIM."

THE BOY WITH AN EVIL SPIRIT

14 WHEN THEY RETURNED WHERE THEY LEFT THE OTHER DI-
SCIPLES, THEY SAW MANY PEOPLE ARGUING WITH SOME TE-
ACHERS OF THE LAW. 15 WHEN THE PEOPLE SAW JESUS, THEY

WERE ASTONISHED AND RAN TO GREET HIM. 16 HE ASKED THEM,
"WHAT ARE YOU ARGUING ABOUT?" A MAN FROM THE CROWD
SAID, " 17 "MASTER, I BROUGHT MY SON TO YOU FOR HE HAS A
DUMB SPIRIT. 18 WHENEVER THE SPIRIT SEIZES HIM, IT
THROWS HIM DOWN AND HE FOAMS AT THE MOUTH, GRINDS
HIS TEETH AND GETS STIFF ALL OVER. I ASKED YOUR DISCI-
PLES TO DRIVE THE SPIRIT OUT, BUT THEY COULD NOT." 19
JESUS REPLIED, "YOU FAITHLESS PEOPLE, HOW LONG MUST I BE
WITH YOU? BRING HIM TO ME." 20 AND THEY BROUGHT THE BOY TO
HIM. AS THE SPIRIT SAW JESUS, IT CONVULSED THE BOY WHO FELL
AND ROLLED ON THE GROUND, FOAMING AT THE MOUTH. 21 JESUS

ASKED THE FATHER, "HOW LONG
HAS THIS BEEN HAPPENING
TO HIM?" HE REPLIED, "FROM
CHILDHOOD. 22 AND IT HAS
OFTEN THROWN HIM INTO THE
FIRE AND INTO THE WATER TO
DESTROY HIM. IF YOU CAN DO
ANYTHING, HAVE PITY ON US
AND HELP US." 23 JESUS
SAID, "WHY DO YOU SAY: 'IF
YOU CAN?' ALL THINGS ARE
POSSIBLE FOR ONE WHO BE-
LIEVES." 24 AT ONCE THE
FATHER OF THE BOY CRIED
OUT, "I DO BELIEVE, BUT
HELP THE LITTLE FAITH I
HAVE!" 25 JESUS SAW THE
INCREASING OF THE CROWD,
SO HE ORDERED THE EVIL
SPIRIT, I COMMAND YOU:
LEAVE THE BOY AND NEVER
ENTER HIM AGAIN." 26
THE EVIL SPIRIT SHOOK
AND CONVULSED THE BOY
AND WITH A TERRIBLE
SHRIEK CAME OUT. THE
BOY LAY LIKE A CORPSE
AND PEOPLE SAID, "HE IS DEAD." 27 BUT JESUS TOOK
HIM BY THE HAND AND LIFTED THE BOY AND HE STOOD
UP. 28 AFTER JESUS HAD GONE INDOORS, HIS DI-
SCIPLES ASKED HIM PRIVATELY, "WHY COULDN'T
WE DRIVE OUT THE SPIRIT?" 29 AND HE ANSWERED,
"ONLY PRAYER CAN DRIVE OUT THIS KIND,
NOTHING ELSE."

JESUS AGAIN SPEAKS OF HIS PASSION

30 AFTER LEAVING THAT PLACE, THEY MADE THEIR
WAY THROUGH GALILEE; BUT JESUS DID NOT WANT PE-
OPLE TO KNOW WHERE HE WAS 31 FOR HE WAS TEACH-
ING HIS DISCIPLES. AND HE TOLD THEM, "THE SON OF MAN
WILL BE DELIVERED INTO THE HANDS OF MEN. THEY WILL
KILL HIM, BUT THREE DAYS AFTER HE HAS BEEN KILLED,
HE WILL RISE." 32 THE DISCIPLES, HOWEVER, DID NOT UN-
DERSTAND THESE WORDS AND THEY WERE AFRAID
TO ASK HIM WHAT HE MEANT.

WHO IS THE GREATEST? 33 THEY CAME TO
CAPERNAUM AND, IN THE HOUSE, JESUS ASKED THEM, "ON
THE WAY, WHAT WERE YOU
DISCUSSING?" 34 BUT
THEY DID NOT ANSWER BE-
CAUSE THEY HAD BEEN AR-
GUING ON WHO WAS THE GRE-
ATEST. 35 THEN HE SAT
DOWN, CALLED THE TWELVE
AND SAID TO THEM, "IF ANY-
ONE WANTS TO BE FIRST, HE
MUST BE THE VERY LAST AND
MAKE HIMSELF THE SER-
VANT OF ALL." 36 THEN HE
TOOK A LITTLE CHILD, SET
HIM AMONG THEM, AND PUT-
TING HIS ARMS AROUND
HIM SAID TO THEM 37 "WHO-
EVER WELCOMES A CHILD,
WELCOMES ME; AND WHO-
EVER WELCOMES ME, WEL-
COMES NOT ME BUT THE ONE
WHO SENT ME." 38 JOHN
SAID TO HIM, "MASTER,
WE SAW A MAN WHO
DROVE OUT DEMONS
BY CALLING UPON
YOUR NAME, AND WE
TRIED TO STOP HIM BE-
CAUSE HE WAS NOT

FOLLOWING US." 39 JESUS ANSWERED, "DO NOT
FORBID HIM, FOR NO ONE WHO WORKS A MIRACLE IN
MY NAME CAN SOON AFTER SPEAK EVIL OF ME.
40 FOR WHOEVER IS NOT AGAINST US IS FOR US.
41 IF ANYONE GIVES YOU A DRINK OF WATER

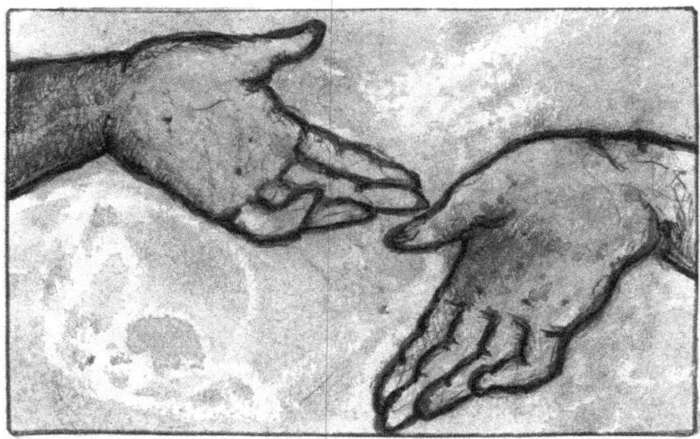

BECAUSE YOU BELONG TO CHRIST AND BEAR HIS NAME, TRULY,
I SAY TO YOU, HE WILL NOT GO WITHOUT REWARD.

IF YOUR EYE CAUSES YOU TO SIN

42 IF ANYONE SHOULD CAUSE ONE OF THESE LITTLE ONES WHO
BELIEVE IN ME TO STUMBLE AND SIN, IT WOULD BE BETTER FOR
HIM TO BE THROWN INTO THE SEA WITH A GREAT MILLSTONE
AROUND HIS NECK. 43 IF YOUR HAND MAKES YOU FALL INTO
SIN, CUT IT OFF! IT'S BETTER FOR YOU TO ENTER LIFE WITHOUT A
HAND THAN WITH TWO HANDS TO GO TO HELL, TO THE FIRE THAT
NEVER GOES OUT. 44-45 AND IF YOUR FOOT MAKES YOU FALL
INTO SIN, CUT IT OFF! IT IS BETTER FOR YOU TO ENTER
LIFE WITHOUT A FOOT THAN WITH BOTH FEET TO
BE THROWN INTO HELL.

46-47 AND IF YOUR EYE MAKES YOU FALL INTO SIN, TEAR IT
OUT! IT IS BETTER FOR YOU TO ENTER THE KINGDOM OF GOD
WITH ONE EYE THAN, KEEPING BOTH EYES, TO BE THROWN
INTO HELL. 48 WHERE THE WORMS THAT EAT THEM NE-
VER DIE, AND THE FIRE NEVER GOES OUT. 49 THE FIRE
ITSELF WILL PRESERVE THEM. 50 SALT IS A GOOD THING;
BUT IF IT LOSES ITS SALTINESS, HOW CAN YOU MAKE IT
SALTY AGAIN? HAVE SALT IN YOURSELVES AND BE AT
PEACE WITH ONE ANOTHER."

DIVORCE

10 1 JESUS LEFT THE PLACE AND WENT TO THE PRO-
VINCE OF JUDEA, BEYOND THE JORDAN RIVER. ONCE
MORE CROWDS GATHERED AROUND HIM AND ONCE
MORE HE TAUGHT THEM, AS HE ALWAYS DID. 2 SOME PHA-

RISEES ALSO CAME TO
TEST HIM, AND ASKED, "IT
IS RIGHT FOR A HUSBAND
TO DIVORCE HIS WIFE?" 3
HE REPLIED, "WHAT LAW
DID MOSES GIVE YOU?" 4
THEY SAID "MOSES ALLOWED
US TO WRITE A CERTIFICATE
OF DISMISSAL TO DIVORCE."
5 JESUS SAID TO THEM,
"MOSES WROTE THIS LAW BE-
CAUSE YOU ARE STUBBORN.
6 BUT AT THE BEGINNING OF
CREATION GOD MADE THEM
MALE AND FEMALE, 7 AND
MAN HAS TO LEAVE FATHER
AND MOTHER TO JOIN HIS
WIFE, 8 AND THE TWO OF
THEM SHALL BECOME ONE
BODY, NO LONGER TWO, JUST
ONE BODY. 9 LET NO ONE SE-
PARATE WHAT GOD HAS JO-
INED." 10 ONCE AT HOME,
THE DISCIPLES ASKED HIM
ABOUT THIS 11; HE TOLD
THEM, "WHOEVER DIVORCES
HIS WIFE AND MARRIES AN-
OTHER COMMITS ADULTERY AGAINST HER, 12 AND THE
WOMAN WHO DIVORCES HER HUSBAND AND MARRIES
ANOTHER ALSO COMMITS ADULTERY."

LET THE CHILDREN COME TO ME

13 PEOPLE WERE BRINGING THEIR LITTLE CHILDREN
TO HIM TO HAVE HIM TOUCH THEM, AND THE DISCIPLES RE-
BUKED THEM. 14 JESUS NOTICED IT, WAS VERY ANGRY
AND SAID, "LET THE CHILDREN COME TO ME AND DON'T

STOP THEM, FOR THE KINGDOM OF GOD BELONGS TO THEM.
15 TRULY, I SAY TO YOU, HE WHO DOESN'T RECEIVE THE KINGDOM
OF GOD LIKE A CHILD, WILL NOT ENTER IT." 16 HE THEN TOOK THE
CHILDREN IN HIS ARMS AND LAYING HIS HANDS ON THEM,
BLESSED THEM.

JESUS AND THE RICH MAN

17 JUST AS JESUS WAS SETTING OUT ON HIS JOURNEY,
A MAN RAN UP, KNELT BEFORE HIM AND ASKED, "GOOD
MASTER, WHAT MUST I DO TO HAVE ETERNAL LIFE?"
18 JESUS ANSWERED, "WHY DO YOU CALL ME GOOD? NO
ONE IS GOOD BUT GOD ALONE. 19 YOU KNOW THE COM-
MANDMENTS: DO NOT KILL, DO NOT COMMIT ADULTERY,
DO NOT STEAL, DO NOT BEAR FALSE WITNESS,
DO NOT CHEAT, HONOR YOUR FATHER AND MOTHER." 20
THE MAN REPLIED, "I HAVE OBEYED ALL THESE COMMAND-
MENTS SINCE MY CHILDHOOD." 21 THEN JESUS LOOKED
STEADILY AT HIM, LOVED HIM AND SAID, "FOR YOU, ONE
THING IS LACKING. GO, SELL WHAT YOU HAVE AND GIVE THE
MONEY TO THE POOR, AND YOU WILL HAVE RICHES IN HE-
AVEN. THEN COME AND FOLLOW ME." 22 ON HEAR-
ING THESE WORDS, HIS FACE FELL AND HE WENT
AWAY SORROWFUL FOR HE WAS A MAN OF GREAT WEALTH.

23 JESUS LOOKED AROUND AND SAID TO HIS DISCI-
PLES, "HOW HARD IS FOR THOSE WHO HAVE RICHES
TO ENTER THE KINGDOM OF GOD!" 24 THE DISCIP-
LES WERE SHOCKED AT THESE WORDS, BUT JESUS
INSISTED, "CHILDREN, HOW HARD IS TO ENTER THE
KINGDOM OF GOD! 25 IT IS EASIER FOR A CAMEL TO
GO THROUGH THE EYE OF A NEEDLE THAN FOR ONE WHO
IS RICH TO ENTER THE KINGDOM OF GOD." 26 THEY
WERE MORE ASTONISHED THAN EVER AND WONDERED,
"WHO, THEN, CAN BE SAVED?" 27 JESUS LOOKED STEADI-
LY AT THEM AND SAID, "FOR HUMANS IT IS IMPOSSIBLE, BUT
NOT FOR GOD; ALL THINGS ARE POSSIBLE WITH GOD."

THE REWARD FOR THOSE WHO FOLLOW JESUS

28 PETER SPOKE UP AND SAID, "WE HAVE GIVE UP EVERY-
THING TO FOLLOW YOU." 29 JESUS ANSWERED, "TRULY,
WHOEVER HAS LEFT HOUSE OR BROTHERS OR SISTERS,

OR FATHER OR MOTHER, OR CHILDREN, OR LANDS FOR MY
SAKE AND FOR THE GOSPEL, 30 WILL NOT LOSE HIS RE-
WARD. I SAY TO YOU: EVEN IN THE MIDST OF PERSECUTION
HE WILL RECEIVE A HUNDRED TIMES AS MANY HO-
USES, BROTHERS, SISTERS, MOTHERS, CHILDREN,
AND LANDS IN THE PRESENT TIME AND IN THE
WORLD TO COME HE WILL RECEIVE ETERNAL LIFE.
31 DO PAY ATTENTION: MANY WHO NOW ARE FIRST
WILL BE LAST, AND THE LAST, FIRST."
32 THEY WERE ON THE ROAD GOING UP TO JERUSALEM.
AND JESUS WAS WALKING AHEAD. THE TWELVE WERE ANXI-
OUS AND THE FOLLOWERS WERE AFRAID. ONCE MORE
JESUS TOOK THE TWELVE ASIDE TO TELL THEM WHAT
WAS TO HAPPEN TO HIM.

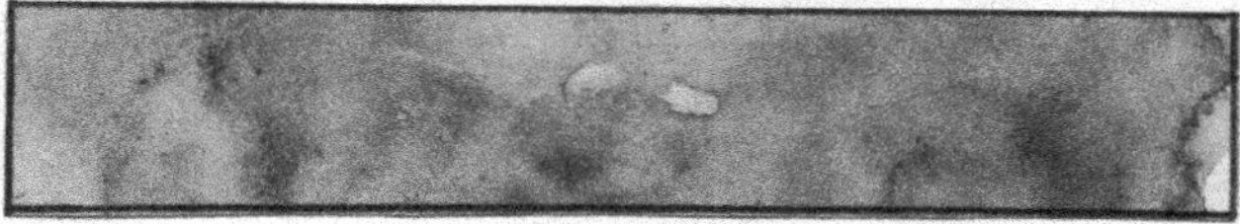

ON HEARING THESE WORDS, HIS FACE FELL AND HE WENT AWAY SAD AND SORROWFUL,
FOR HE WAS A MAN OF GREAT WEALTH. (MARK 10:22)

(33) WE ARE GOING UP TO JERUSALEM, AND THE SON OF MAN WILL
BE GIVEN OVER TO THE CHIEF PRIESTS AND THE TEACHERS OF THE LAW.
THEY WILL CONDEMN HIM TO DEATH AND HAND HIM OVER TO THE
FOREIGNERS (34) WHO WILL INSULT HIM, SPIT ON HIM, SCOURGE
HIM AND KILL HIM; BUT THREE DAYS LATER HE WILL RISE."

JAMES AND JOHN ASK FOR THE FIRST PLACES

(35) JAMES AND JOHN, ZEBEDEE'S SONS, CAME TO JESUS AND
SAID TO HIM, "MASTER, WE WANT TO GRANT US SOMETHING." (36)
HE SAID, "WHAT DO YOU WANT ME TO DO FOR YOU?" (37) THEY ANSWE-
RED, "GRANT US TO SIT AT YOUR RIGHT AND AT YOUR LEFT WHEN YOU
COME IN YOUR GLORY." (38) BUT JESUS SAID TO THEM, "YOU DON'T

KNOW WHAT YOU ARE ASKING. CAN YOU DRINK THE CUP THAT I DRINK
OR BE BAPTISED IN THE WAY I AM BAPTISED?" (39) THEY ANSWERED,
"WE CAN." JESUS TOLD THEM, "THE CUP THAT I DRINK YOU WILL
DRINK, AND YOU WILL BE BAPTIZED IN THE WAY I AM BAPTIZED,
(40) BUT TO SIT AT MY RIGHT OR AT MY LEFT IS NOT MINE TO GRANT.
IT HAS BEEN PREPARED FOR OTHERS."
(41) ON HEARING THIS, THE OTHER TEN WERE ANGRY WITH JAMES

AND JOHN; (42) JESUS THEN
CALLED THEM AND SAID, "AS
YOU KNOW, THE SO-CALLED
RULERS OF THE NATIONS
ACT AS TYRANTS AND THEIR
GREAT ONES OPPRESS THEM.
(43) BUT IT SHALL NOT BE
SO AMONG YOU; WHOEVER
WOULD BE GREAT AMONG
YOU MUST BE YOUR SER-
VANT, (44) AND WHOEVER
WOULD BE FIRST AMONG
YOU SHALL MAKE HIM-
SELF SLAVE OF ALL.
(45) THINK OF THE SON
OF MAN WHO HAS NOT
COME TO BE SERVED
BUT TO SERVE AND
TO GIVE HIS LIFE TO
REDEEM MANY."

JHS

THE BLIND MAN OF JERICHO

(46) THEY CAME TO JERICHO. AS JESUS WAS LEAVING
JERICHO WITH HIS DISCIPLES AND A LARGE CROWD, A BLIND
BEGGAR, BARTIMAEUS, THE SON OF TIMAEUS, WAS SIT-
TING BY THE ROADSIDE. (47) ON HEARING THAT IT WAS
JESUS OF NAZARETH PASSING BY, HE BEGAN TO
CALL OUT "SON OF DAVID, JESUS, HAVE MERCY ON ME!"
(48) MANY PEOPLE SCOLDED HIM AND TOLD HIM TO
KEEP QUIET, BUT HE SHOUTED ALL THE LOUDER, "SON
OF DAVID, HAVE MERCY ON ME!" (49) JESUS STOPPED
AND SAID, "CALL HIM." SO THEY CALLED THE BLIND MAN
SAYING, "TAKE HEART. GET UP, HE IS CALLING YOU."
(50) HE IMMEDIATELY THREW ASIDE HIS CLOAK, JUM-
PED UP AND WENT TO JESUS. (51) JESUS ASKED HIM,
"WHAT DO YOU WANT ME TO DO FOR YOU?" THE BLIND MAN
SAID, "MASTER, LET ME SEE AGAIN!"

(52) AND JESUS SAID TO HIM, "GO YOUR WAY, YOUR
FAITH HAS MADE YOU WELL." AND IMMEDIATELY HE COULD
SEE, AND HE FOLLOWED JESUS ALONG THE ROAD.

THE TRIUMPHANT ENTRY INTO JERUSALEM

11 (1) WHEN THEY ARRIVED—NEAR JERUSALEM—AT
BETHPHAGE AND BETHANY AND AT THE MOUNT OF
OLIVES, JESUS SENT TWO
OF HIS DISCIPLES SAYING,
(2) "GO TO THE VILLAGE ON
THE OTHER SIDE AND, AS YOU
ENTER IT, YOU WILL FIND
THERE A COLT TIED UP
THAT NO ONE HAS RIDDEN.
UNTIE IT AND BRING IT
HERE. (3) IF ANYONE SAYS
TO YOU: 'WHAT ARE YOU DO-
ING?' GIVE THIS ANSWER:
'THE LORD NEEDS IT, BUT
HE WILL SEND IT BACK
IMMEDIATELY.'" THEY
(4) WENT OFF AND FOUND
THE COLT OUT IN THE
STREET TIED AT THE DO-
OR. (5) AS THEY WERE
UNTYING IT, SOME OF
THE BYSTANDERS ASKED,
"WHY ARE YOU UNTYING
THAT COLT?" (6) THEY
ANSWERED AS JESUS HAD
TOLD THEM, AND THE PE-
OPLE ALLOWED THEM TO
CONTINUE. (7) THEY
BROUGHT THE COLT TO

JESUS, THREW THEIR CLOAKS ON ITS BACK, AND JESUS
SAT UPON IT. (8) MANY PEOPLE ALSO SPREAD THEIR CLOAKS
ON THE ROAD, WHILE OTHERS SPREAD LEAFY BRANCHES FROM
THE FIELDS. (9) THEN THOSE AHEAD AND THOSE WHO WALKED
BEHIND JESUS BEGAN TO SHOUT, "HOSANNAH! BLESSED IS HE
WHO COMES IN THE NAME OF THE LORD! (10) BLESSED IS THE
KINGDOM OF OUR FATHER DAVID WHICH COMES! HOSANNAH IN
THE HIGHEST! (11) JESUS ENTERED JERUSALEM AND WENT
INTO THE TEMPLE. AFTER LOOKING AROUND AND BEING LA-
TE, HE WENT OUT TO BETHANY WITH THE TWELVE.

JESUS CURSES THE BARREN FIG TREE

(12) THE NEXT DAY, AS THEY WERE LEAVING BETHANY, HE
FELT HUNGRY. (13) IN THE DISTANCE HE SAW A FIG TREE
COVERED WITH LEAVES, SO HE WENT TO SEE IF HE COULD

FIND ANYTHING ON IT. ONCE THERE, HE FOUND NOTHING BUT LE-
AVES, FOR IT WAS NOT THE SEASON FOR FIGS. (14) THEN HE SAID
TO THE FIG TREE, "MAY NO ONE EVER EAT YOUR FRUIT!"
AND HIS DISCIPLES HEARD THESE WORDS.

JESUS CLEARS THE TEMPLE

(15) WHEN IN JERUSALEM, JESUS WENT INTO THE TEMPLE
AND BEGAN TO DRIVE AWAY ALL THE PEOPLE HE SAW BUYING
AND SELLING THERE. HE OVERTURNED THE TABLES OF THE MONEY-
CHANGERS AND THE STOOLS OF THOSE WHO SOLD PIGEONS.

16 AND HE WOULD NOT LET ANYONE CARRY GOODS THROUGH
THE TEMPLE. 17 THEN JESUS TAUGHT THE PEOPLE, "DOES NOT
GOD'S SCRIPTURES SAY: MY HOUSE IS A HOUSE OF PRAYER FOR
ALL NATIONS? BUT YOU HAVE TURNED IT INTO A DEN OF THI-
EVES." 18 THE CHIEF PRIESTS AND THE TEACHERS OF THE LAW KNEW
OF THIS, AND THEY TRIED TO FIND A WAY TO DESTROY HIM. THEY
WERE AFRAID BECAUSE THE PEOPLE WERE CAPTIVATED BY HIS
TEACHING. 19 IN THE EVENING, JESUS LEFT THE CITY.

THE POWER OF FAITH

20 EARLY NEXT MORNING, AS THEY WALKED ALONG THE ROAD, THE DI-
SCIPLES SAW THE FIG TREE
WITHERED TO ITS ROOTS. 21
PETER THEN SAID TO HIM,
"MASTER, LOOK! THE FIG
TREE YOU CURSED HAS WI-
THERED." 22 AND JESUS
REPLIED, "HAVE FAITH IN
GOD. 23 TRULY, I SAY TO
YOU, IF YOU SAY TO THIS
MOUNTAIN, 'GET UP AND
THROW YOURSELF INTO
THE SEA', AND WITHOUT
ANY DOUBT BELIEVE THAT
WHAT YOU SAY WILL HAP-
PEN, IT WILL BE DONE FOR
YOU. 24 SO, I TELL YOU,
WHATEVER YOU ASK IN
PRAYER, BELIEVE YOU HAVE
RECEIVED IT, AND IT SHALL
BE DONE FOR YOU. 25 AND
AND WHEN YOU PRAY, FOR-
GIVE ALL YOU MAY HOLD
AGAINST ANYONE, 26 SO
THAT YOUR DIVINE
FATHER MAY ALSO
FORGIVE YOUR SINS."

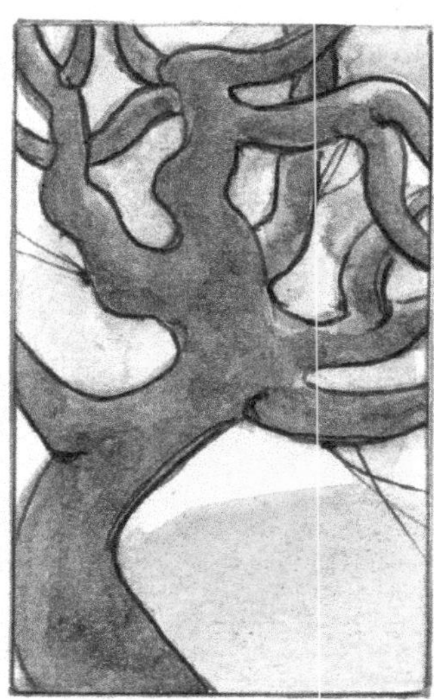

BY WHAT AUTHORITY DO YOU ACT?

27 AGAIN THEY WERE IN JERUSALEM. JESUS WAS WALKING IN THE
TEMPLE, AND THE CHIEF PRIESTS, THE TEACHERS OF THE LAW AND THE
ELDERS ASKED HIM, 28 "WHAT AUTHORITY YOU HAVE TO ACT LIKE
THIS? WHO GAVE YOU AUTHORITY TO DO THE THINGS YOU DO? 29
JESUS SAID, "I WILL ASK YOU A QUESTION, ONLY ONE. IF YOU ANSWER
ME, THEN I WILL TELL YOU WHAT AUTHORITY I HAVE TO ACT LIKE THIS.
30 WAS JOHN'S BAPTISM GOD'S WORK OR MERELY HUMAN? ANS-
WER ME." 31 THEY ARGUED AMONG THEMSELVES, "IF WE ANSWER

THAT IT WAS GOD'S WORK, HE WILL SAY: WHY THEN DID YOU NOT BELIEVE
HIM?" 32 BUT THEY COULDN'T ANSWER NEITHER THAT THE BAPTISM
OF JOHN WAS HUMAN, FOR THE PEOPLE SAW JOHN AS A PROPHET.
33 SO THEY ANSWERED JESUS, "WE DON'T KNOW", AND JESUS
SAID TO THEM, "NEITHER WILL I TELL YOU WHAT AUTHO-
RITY I HAVE TO ACT AS I DO."

PARABLE OF THE TENANTS

12 1 USING PARABLES, JESUS WENT ON TO SAY, "A MAN PLAN-
TED A VINEYARD, PUT A FENCE AROUND IT, DUG A HOLE FOR
THE WINE PRESS AND BUILT A WATCH TOWER. THEN HE LEASED
THE VINEYARD TO TENANTS AND WENT ABROAD.
2 IN DUE TIME HE SENT A SERVANT TO RECEIVE FROM THE
TENANTS HIS SHARE OF THE FRUIT. 3 BUT THEY SEIZED THE
SERVANT, STRUCK HIM AND SENT HIM BACK EMPTY-HANDED.
4 AGAIN THE MAN SENT ANOTHER SERVANT. THEY
ALSO STRUCK HIM IN THE HEAD AND TREATED HIM SHA-
MEFULLY. 5 HE SENT ANOTHER AND THEY KILLED HIM. IN
THE SAME WAY THEY TREATED MANY OTHERS; SOME THEY
STRUCK AND OTHERS THEY KILLED. 6 ONE WAS STILL
LEFT, HIS BELOVED SON. AN SO, LAST OF ALL, HE SENT HIM TO
THE TENANTS, FOR HE SAID, "THEY WILL RESPECT MY SON."
7 BUT THOSE TENANTS SAID TO ONE ANOTHER: 'THIS IS
THE ONE WHO IS TO INHERIT THE VINEYARD. LET'S KILL
HIM AND THE PROPERTY WILL BE OURS.' 8 SO THEY SEIZ-
ED HIM AND KILLED HIM, AND THREW HIM OUT OF THE

VINEYARD. 9 NOW, WHAT THE OWNER OF THE VINEYARD
DO? HE WILL COME AND DESTROY THOSE TENANTS AND GIVE
THE VINEYARD TO OTHERS." 10 AND JESUS ADDED, "HAVE YOU
NOT READ THE TEXT OF THE SCRIPTURES: THE STONE WHICH
THE BUILDERS REJECTED HAS BECOME THE KEYSTONE.
11 THIS WAS THE LORD'S DOING, AND WE MARVEL AT IT.
12 THEY WANTED TO ARREST HIM FOR THEY REALIZED THAT
JESUS MEANT THIS PARABLE FOR THEM, BUT THEY WERE AFRAID
OF THE CROWD. SO THEY LEFT HIM AND WENT AWAY.

PAYING TAXES TO CAESAR

13 THEY SENT TO JESUS SOME PHARISEES WITH MEMBERS OF
HEROD'S PARTY, AIMING TO TRAP HIM IN HIS OWN WORDS. 14
THEY SAID TO JESUS, "MAS-
TER, WE KNOW THAT YOU
ARE TRUE; YOU DO NOT
FEAR ANYONE, AND YOUR
ANSWERS ARE GIVEN AC-
CORDING TO GOD'S WAY.
TELL US, IS IT AGAINST THE
LAW TO PAY TAXES TO CA-
ESAR? SHOULD BE PAY
THEM OR NOT?" 15 BUT
JESUS SAW THROUGH THEIR
TRICK AND ANSWERED, "WHY
ARE YOU TESTING ME?"
BRING ME A COIN AND LET
ME SEE IT." 16 A COIN WAS
BROUGHT TO HIM. JESUS
ASKED, "WHOSE HEAD IS
THIS, AND WHOSE NAME?"
THEY ANSWERED, "CAESAR'S."
17 THEN JESUS SAID,
"GIVE BACK TO CAESAR
WHAT BELONGS TO CA-
ESAR, AND TO GOD
WHAT BELONGS TO
GOD." AND THEY WERE
GREATLY ASTONISHED.

THE RESURRECTION

18 THE SADDUCEES CAME TO JESUS. AS THEY CLAIM THAT
THERE IS NO RESURRECTION, QUESTIONED HIM ASKING,
19 "MASTER, IN THE SCRIPTURES MOSES' LAW SAYS: 'IF ANY-
ONE DIES LEAVING A WIFE BUT NO CHILDREN, HIS BROTHER
MUST TAKE THE WIFE, GIVE HER A CHILD OF HIS DECEASED
BROTHER.' 20 NOW, THERE WERE SEVEN BROTHERS. THE
FIRST MARRIED A WIFE, BUT HE DIED WITHOUT LE-
AVING ANY CHILDREN.

21 THE SECOND TOOK THE WIFE AND HE, TOO, DIED LEAVING
NO CHILDREN. THE SAME THING HAPPENED TO THE THIRD. 22
FINALLY THE SEVEN DIED LEAVING NO CHILDREN. LAST OF
ALL THE WOMAN DIED. 23 NOW, IN THE RESURRECTION, TO
WHICH OF THEM WILL SHE BE WIFE? FOR THE SEVEN HAD HER
AS WIFE." 24 JESUS REPLIED, "YOU COULD BE WRONG IN
THIS REGARD BECAUSE YOU UNDERSTAND NEITHER THE SCRIP-
TURES NOR THE POWER OF GOD. 25 WHEN THEY RISE FROM
THE DEAD, MEN AND WOMEN DO NOT MARRY BUT ARE LIKE
THE ANGELS IN HEAVEN. 26 NOW, ABOUT THE RESURRECTION

OF THE DEAD, HAVE YOU REFLECTED ON THE CHAPTER OF THE
BURNING BUSH IN THE BOOK OF MOSES? GOD SAID TO HIM: I
AM THE GOD OF ABRAHAM, THE GOD OF ISAAC AND THE GOD OF
JACOB. 27 NOW, HE IS THE GOD, NOT OF THE DEAD BUT OF
THE LIVING. YOU ARE TOTALLY WRONG.

THE GREATEST COMMANDMENT

28 A TEACHER OF THE LAW HAD BEEN LISTENING TO THAT
AND ADMIRED HOW JESUS ANSWERED THEM. SO HE CAME
UP AND ASKED HIM, "WHICH COMMANDMENT IS THE FIRST
OF ALL?" 29 JESUS ANSWERED, "THE FIRST IS: HEAR, IS-
RAEL! THE LORD, OUR GOD, IS ONE LORD; 30 AND YOU SHALL
LOVE THE LORD, YOUR GOD, WITH ALL YOUR HEART, WITH ALL
YOUR SOUL, WITH ALL YOUR MIND AND WITH ALL YOUR STRENGTH.

31 AND THE SECOND IS: YOU
SHALL LOVE YOUR NEIGHBOR
AS YOURSELF. THERE IS NO
COMMANDMENT GREATER
THAN THESE TWO." 32 THE
TEACHER OF THE LAW SAID
TO HIM, "WELL SPOKEN, MAS-
TER; YOU ARE RIGHT WHEN
YOU SAY THAT HE IS ONE AND
THERE IS NO OTHER. 33 TO
LOVE HIM WITH ALL OUR HE-
ART, WITH ALL OUR UNDER-
STANDING AND WITH ALL OUR
STRENGTH, AND TO LOVE OUR
NEIGHBOR AS OURSELVES
IS MORE IMPORTANT THAN
ANY BURN OFFERING OR SA-
CRIFICE." 34 JESUS
APPROVED THIS ANSWER
AND SAID, "YOU ARE
NOT FAR FROM THE KING-
DOM OF GOD."
BUT AFTER THAT, NO ONE
DARED TO ASK HIM ANY
MORE QUESTIONS.

WHOSE SON IS THE CHRIST?

35 AS JESUS WAS TEACHING IN THE TEMPLE, HE SAID, "THE
TEACHERS OF THE LAW SAY THAT THE MESSIAH IS THE SON
OF DAVID. HOW CAN THAT BE? 36 FOR DAVID, INSPIRED BY THE
HOLY SPIRIT, DECLARED: THE LORD SAID TO MY LORD: SIT AT
MY RIGHT UNTIL I PUT YOUR ENEMIES UNDER YOUR FEET.

37 IF DAVID HIMSELF CALLS HIM LORD, IN WHAT WAY CAN
HE BE HIS SON?" MANY PEOPLE CAME TO JESUS AND
LISTENED TO HIM GLADLY.

38 AS HE WAS TEACHING, HE ALSO SAID TO THEM,
"BEWARE OF THOSE TEACHERS OF THE LAW WHO EN-
JOY WALKING AROUND IN LONG ROBES AND BEING
GREETED IN THE MARKETPLACE, 39 AND WHO LIKE
TO OCCUPY RESERVED SEATS IN THE SYNAGOGUES
AND THE FIRST PLACES AT FEASTS. 40 THEY EVEN
DEVOUR THE WIDOW'S AND ORPHAN'S GOODS WHILE
MAKING A SHOW OF LONG PRAYERS. HOW SEVERE A
SENTENCE THEY WILL RECEIVE!"

THE WIDOW'S OFFERING

41 JESUS SAT DOWN OPPOSITE THE TEMPLE TREA-
SURY AND WATCHED THE
PEOPLE DROPPING MONEY
INTO THE TREASURY BOX;
AND MANY RICH PEOPLE
PUT IN LARGE OFFERINGS.
42 BUT A POOR WIDOW
ALSO CAME AND DROP-
PED IN TWO SMALL
COINS. 43 THEN
JESUS CALLED HIS
DISCIPLES AND SAID
TO THEM, "TRULY, I SAY
TO YOU, THIS POOR
WIDOW PUT IN MORE
THAN ALL THOSE
WHO GAVE OFFERINGS.
44 FOR ALL OF THEM
GAVE FROM THEIR
PLENTY, BUT SHE
GAVE FROM HER PO-
VERTY AND PUT IN
EVERYTHING SHE
HAD, HER VERY LIVING."

JESUS SPEAKS OF THE END

13 1 AS JESUS LEFT THE TEMPLE, ONE OF HIS
DISCIPLES SAID, "LOOK, MASTER, AT THE HUGE
STONES AND WONDERFUL BUILDINGS HERE!" 2 AND
JESUS SAID, "YOU SEE THESE GREAT BUILDINGS? NOT ONE
STONE WILL BE LEFT ON ANOTHER ONE, BUT ALL WILL BE
TORN DOWN." 3 LATER, WHEN JESUS WAS ON THE MOUNT OF
OLIVES, FACING THE TEMPLE, PETER, JAMES, JOHN AND ANDREW
APPROACHED HIM PRIVATELY AND ASKED, 4 "TELL US
WHEN THIS WILL BE. WHAT SIGN WILL BE GIVEN US
BEFORE ALL THIS HAPPENS?" 5 THEN JESUS BEGAN
TO TELL THEM, "DON'T LET ANYONE MISLEAD YOU.
6 MANY WILL COME, TAKING MY PLACE AND SAY: I AM THE
THE ONE YOU ARE WAITING FOR, AND THEY WILL DECEIVE

MANY PEOPLE. 7 WHEN YOU HEAR OF WAR AND THREATS OF
WAR, DON'T BE TROUBLED: THIS MUST OCCUR BUT THE END
IS NOT YET. 8 NATION WILL FIGHT NATION AND KING-
DOM WILL OPPOSE KINGDOM. THERE WILL BE EARTH-
QUAKES EVERYWHERE AND FAMINES, TOO. AND THESE
WILL BE LIKE THE FIRST PAINS OF CHILDBIRTH.

"TRULY I SAY TO YOU
THIS POOR WIDOW
PUT IN MORE THAN
ALL THOSE WHO GAVE
OFFERINGS. FOR ALL
OF THEM GAVE FROM
THEIR PLENTY, BUT
SHE GAVE FROM HER
POVERTY AND SHE PUT
EVERYTHING SHE
HAD, HER VERY
LIVING"
(MARK 12:43-44)
330 CCCXXX
DM 06 ©

(9) BE ON YOUR GUARD, FOR YOU WILL BE ARRESTED
AND TAKEN TO JEWISH COURTS. YOU WILL BE BEATEN
IN SYNAGOGUES; AND YOU WILL STAND BEFORE GO-
VERNORS AND KINGS FOR MY SAKE TO BEAR WIT-
NESS BEFORE THEM. (10) FOR THE PREACHING OF
THE GOSPEL TO ALL NATIONS HAS TO COME
FIRST. (11) SO WHEN
YOU ARE ARRESTED
AND BROUGHT TO TRIAL,
DON'T WORRY ABOUT
WHAT YOU ARE TO SAY;
BUT SAY WHATEVER
IS GIVEN YOU IN THAT
HOUR. FOR IT IS NOT
YOU WHO SPEAK, BUT
THE HOLY SPIRIT.

(12) BROTHER WILL
BETRAY BROTHER
EVEN TO DEATH, AND
THE FATHER HIS CHILD.
CHILDREN WILL TURN
AGAINST THEIR PARENTS
AND HAVE THEM PUT TO
DEATH.
(13) AND YOU WILL BE
HATED BY ALL FOR
MY NAME'S SAKE.

BUT WHOEVER HOLDS
OUT TO THE END
WILL BE SAVED.

LAST DAYS OF JERUSALEM

(14) WHEN YOU SEE THE IDOL OF THE OPPRESSOR SET WHERE IT
SHOULD NOT BE (MAY THE READER UNDERSTAND), SO LET THOSE IN
JUDEA FLEE TO THE MOUNTAINS. (15) IF YOU ARE ON THE HOUSETOP,
DON'T COME DOWN TO TAKE ANYTHING. (16) IF YOU ARE IN THE FIELD,
DON'T TURN BACK TO FETCH YOUR CLOAK. (17) HOW HARD IT WILL BE
FOR PREGNANT WOMEN AND MOTHERS WITH BABIES AT THE BREAST!
(18) PRAY THAT IT MAY NOT HAPPEN IN WINTER, (19) FOR THIS
WILL BE TIME OF DISTRESS, SUCH AS WAS NEVER KNOWN SINCE
GOD CREATED THE WORLD, UNTIL NOW AND IS NEVER AGAIN TO
BE KNOWN. (20) SO IF THE LORD HAD NOT SHORTENED THAT
TIME, NO ONE WOULD SURVIVE; BUT HE DECIDED TO SHORTEN
IT FOR THE SAKE OF HIS CHOSEN ONES. (21) IF ANYONE SAYS
TO YOU AT THAT TIME: 'LOOK, HERE IS THE MESSIAH! LOOK, HE
IS THERE!', DO NOT BELIEVE IT. (22) FOR FALSE MESSIAHS

AND FALSE PROPHETS WILL ARISE AND PERFORM SIGNS AND
WONDERS IN ORDER TO DECEIVE EVEN GOD'S CHOSEN PEOPLE, IF
THAT WERE POSSIBLE. (23) YOU MUST BE ON YOUR GUARD. I HAVE
TOLD YOU EVERYTHING AHEAD OF TIME.

THE COMING OF THE SON OF MAN

(24) LATER ON, IN THOSE DAYS, AFTER THAT DISASTROUS TIME,
THE SUN WILL GROW DARK, THE MOON WILL NOT GIVE ITS
LIGHT, (25) THE STARS WILL FALL OUT OF THE SKY AND
THE WHOLE UNIVERSE WILL BE SHAKEN. (26) THEN PE-
OPLE WILL SEE THE SON OF MAN COMING IN THE CLOUDS
WITH GREAT POWER AND GLORY.

(27) HE WILL SEND THE ANGELS TO GATHER HIS CHOSEN
PEOPLE FROM THE FOUR WINDS, FROM THE ENDS OF THE
EARTH TO THE ENDS OF THE SKY.
(28) LEARN A LESSON FROM THE FIG TREE. AS SOON AS
ITS BRANCHES BECOME TENDER AND IT BEGINS TO SPROUT
LEAVES, YOU KNOW THAT SUMMER IS NEAR. (29) IN THE
SAME WAY, WHEN YOU SEE THESE THINGS HAPPENING,
KNOW THAT THE TIME IS NEAR, EVEN AT THE DOOR.

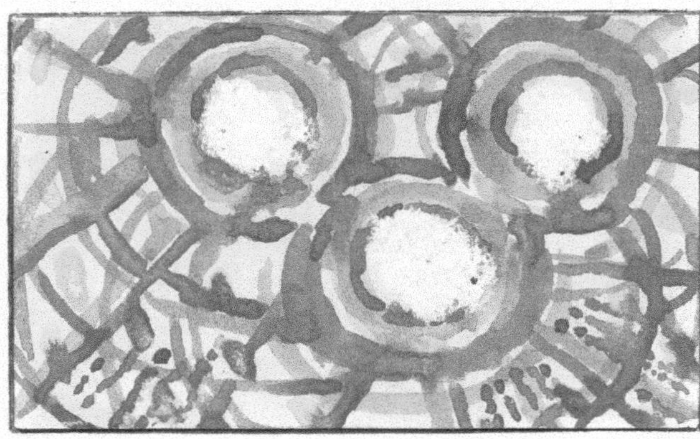

(30) TRULY, I SAY TO YOU, THIS GENERATION WILL NOT PASS
AWAY UNTIL ALL THIS HAS HAPPENED. (31) HEAVEN AND EARTH
WILL PASS AWAY, BUT MY WORD WILL NOT PASS AWAY.
(32) BUT, REGARDING THAT DAY AND THAT HOUR,
NO ONE KNOWS WHEN IT WILL COME, NOT EVEN
THE ANGELS OR THE SON, BUT ONLY THE FATHER.
(33) BE ALERT AND WATCH,
FOR YOU DON'T KNOW
WHEN THE TIME
WILL COME. (34) WHEN
A MAN GOES ABROAD
AND LEAVES HIS
HOME, HE PUTS HIS
SERVANTS IN CHARGE,
GIVING TO EACH ONE
SOME RESPONSIBILITY;
AND HE ORDERS THE
DOORKEEPER TO STAY
AWAKE. (35) SO STAY
AWAKE FOR YOU
DO NOT KNOW
WHEN THE LORD
OF THE HOUSE WILL
COME, IN THE EVE-
NING OR AT MID-
NIGHT, WHEN THE
COCK CROWS OR
BEFORE DAWN.

(36) IF HE COMES
SUDDENLY, DO NOT
LET HIM CATCH YOU
ASLEEP. (37) AND
WHAT I SAY TO YOU, I SAY TO ALL: WATCH."

CONSPIRACY AGAINST JESUS

14 (1) IT WAS NOW TWO DAYS TO THE FEAST OF THE PASSOVER
AND THE LEAVENED BREAD. THE CHIEF PRIESTS AND THE TEACHERS
OF THE LAW WERE LOOKING FOR A WAY TO ARREST JESUS AND PUT HIM
TO DEATH; (2) FOR THEY SAID, "NOT DURING THE FESTIVAL, OR
THERE MIGHT BE TROUBLE AMONG THE PEOPLE."

JESUS ANOINTED AT BETHANY

(3) JESUS WAS IN BETHANY IN THE HOUSE OF SIMON
THE LEPER, AS HE WAS RECLINING AT DINNER, A
WOMAN ENTERED CARRYING A PRECIOUS JAR OF
EXPENSIVE PERFUME MADE OF PURE NARD.
SHE BROKE THE JAR AND POURED THE PER-
FUMED OIL ON JESUS' HEAD.

4 SOME OF THEM BECAME ANGRY AND SAID, "WHAT A USELESS
WASTE OF PERFUME. 5 IT COULD HAVE BEEN SOLD FOR MORE
THAN THREE HUNDRED SILVER COINS AND THE MONEY GIVEN
TO THE POOR." AND THEY CRITICIZED HER. 6 BUT JESUS SAID,
"LET HER ALONE; WHY ARE YOU TROUBLING HER? WHAT SHE
HAS JUST DONE FOR ME IS A VERY CHARITABLE WORK.
7 AT ANY TIME YOU CAN HELP THE POOR, FOR YOU ALWAYS
HAVE THEM WITH YOU; BUT YOU WILL NOT HAVE ME FOR-
EVER. 8 THIS WOMAN HAS DONE WHAT WAS HERS TO
DO, SHE HAS ANOINTED MY BODY BEFORE-HAND FOR
MY BURIAL. 9 TRULY, I SAY TO YOU, WHEREVER IN THE
WORLD THE GOOD NEWS IS PROCLAIMED, WHAT SHE
HAS DONE WILL BE TOLD IN PRAISE OF HER." 10 THEN

JUDAS ISCARIOT, ONE OF THE TWELVE, WENT OFF TO THE CHIEF
PRIESTS IN ORDER TO BETRAY JESUS TO THEM. 11 EXITED ON HEAR-
ING HIM THEY PROMISED TO GIVE HIM MONEY. SO JUDAS STARTED
PLANNING THE BEST WAY TO HAND HIM OVER TO THEM.

THE LORD'S SUPPER

12 ON THE FIRST DAY OF THE FESTIVAL OF UNLEAVENED BREAD, THE
DAY WHEN THE PASSOVER LAMB WAS KILLED, THE DISCIPLES ASKED
HIM, "WHERE WOULD YOU HAVE US GO TO PREPARE THE PASSOVER
MEAL FOR YOU?" 13 SO JESUS SENT TWO OF HIS DISCIPLES WITH
THESE INSTRUCTIONS, "GO INTO THE CITY AND THERE A MAN

WILL COME TO YOU CARRY-
ING A JAR OF WATER. FOL-
LOW HIM TO THE HOUSE HE
ENTERS AND SAY TO THE
OWNER, 14 THE MASTER
SAYS: WHERE IS THE ROOM
WHERE I MAY EAT THE
PASSOVER MEAL WITH MY
DISCIPLES? 15 THEN HE
WILL SHOW YOU A LARGE RO-
OM UPSTAIRS, ALREADY
ARRANGED AND FURNISHED.
THERE YOU WILL PREPARE
FOR US." 16 THE DISCIPLES
WENT OFF. WHEN THEY RE-
ACHED THE CITY, THEY
FOUND EVERYTHING AS
JESUS HAD TOLD THEM;
AND THEY PREPARED THE
PASSOVER MEAL. 17 WHEN
IT WAS EVENING, JESUS AR-
RIVED WITH THE TWELVE.
18 WHILE THEY WERE AT
TABLE EATING, JESUS
SAID, "TRULY, I TELL YOU, ONE OF YOU WILL BETRAY ME, ONE
WHO SHARES MY MEAL." 19 THEY WERE DEEPLY DIS-
TRESSED AT HEARING THIS AND ASKED HIM, ONE AFTER
THE OTHER, "YOU DON'T MEAN ME, DO YOU?" 20 JESUS
ANSWERED, "IT IS ONE OF YOU TWELVE, ONE WHO DIPS
HIS BREAD IN THE DISH WITH ME. 21 THE SON OF MAN
IS GOING AS THE SCRIPTURES SAY HE WILL, BUT ALAS
FOR THAT MAN BY WHOM THE SON OF MAN IS BETRAYED;
BETTER FOR HIM IF HE HAD NEVER BEEN BORN."
22 WHILE THEY WERE EATING, JESUS TOOK BREAD,
BLESSED AND BROKE IT, AND GAVE IT TO THEM. AND
HE SAID, "TAKE THIS. IT IS MY BODY."

23 THEN HE TOOK A CUP AND AFTER HE HAD GIVEN
THANKS, PASSED IT TO THEM AND THEY ALL DRANK
FROM IT. 24 AND HE SAID, "THIS IS MY BLOOD, THE
BLOOD OF THE COVENANT, WHICH IS TO BE POURED
OUT FOR MANY. 25 TRULY, I SAY TO YOU, I WILL
NOT TASTE THE FRUIT OF THE VINE AGAIN UNTIL
THE DAY I DRINK THE NEW WINE IN THE KINGDOM OF GOD."

PETER'S DENIAL FORETOLD

26 AFTER SINGING PSALMS OF PRAISE, THEY WENT
OUT TO THE HILL OF OLIVES. 27 AND JESUS
SAID TO THEM, "ALL OF
YOU WILL BE CONFUSED
AND FALL AWAY. FOR THE
SCRIPTURE SAYS:
I WILL STRIKE THE SHE-
PHERD AND THE SHEEP
WILL BE SCATTERED.
28 BUT AFTER I AM
RAISED UP, I WILL GO
TO GALILEE AHEAD
OF YOU." 29 THEN
PETER SAID TO HIM,
"EVEN THOUGH ALL
THE OTHERS FALL AWAY,
I WILL NOT." 30 AND
JESUS REPLIED,
"TRULY, I SAY TO YOU,
TODAY, THIS VERY
NIGHT BEFORE THE
COCK CROWS TWICE,
YOU WILL DENY ME
THREE TIMES." 31
BUT PETER INSISTED,
"THOUGH I HAVE TO
DIE WITH YOU, I WILL
NEVER DENY YOU."
AND ALL SAID THE SAME.

GETHSEMANE

32 THEY CAME TO A PLACE CALLED GETHSEMANE AND
JESUS SAID TO HIS DISCIPLES, "SIT HERE WHILE I PRAY."
33 BUT HE TOOK PETER, JAMES AND JOHN ALONG
WITH HIM, AND BECOMING FILLED WITH FEAR AND DIS-
TRESS 34 HE SAID TO THEM, "MY SOUL IS FULL OF
SORROW, EVEN TO DEATH. REMAIN HERE AND STAY
AWAKE." 35 THEN HE WENT A LITTLE FURTHER ON AND FELL
TO THE GROUND, PRAYING THAT IF POSSIBLE THIS HOUR MIGHT
PASS HIM BY. JESUS SAID, 36 "ABBA" (DADDY), ALL THINGS
ARE POSSIBLE FOR YOU; TAKE THIS CUP AWAY FROM ME. YET

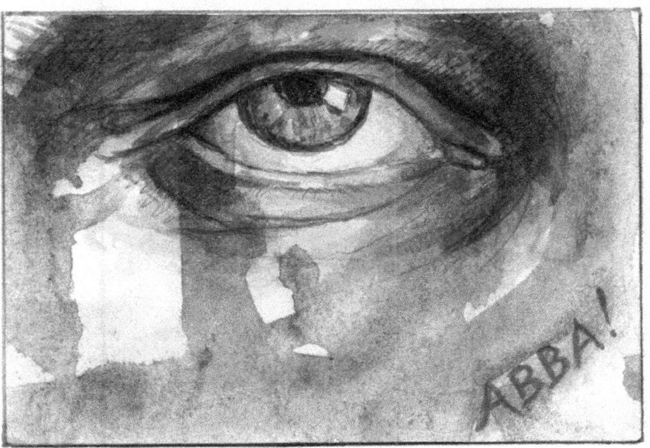

NOT WHAT I WANT, BUT WHAT YOU WANT." 37 THEN HE CA-
ME AND FOUND THEM ASLEEP AND SAID TO PETER, "SIMON,
ARE YOU SLEEPING? COULDN'T YOU STAY AWAKE FOR ONE
HOUR? 38 KEEP WATCH AND PRAY, ALL OF YOU, SO THAT
YOU MAY NOT SLIP INTO TEMPTATION. THE SPIRIT INDEED
IS EAGER BUT HUMAN NATURE IS WEAK. 39 HE WENT AND
SAID PRAYING THE SAME WORDS. 40 WHEN HE CAME BACK, HE
FOUND THEM ASLEEP AGAIN; THEY COULDN'T KEEP THEIR EYES
OPEN AND COULDN'T SAY ANYTHING TO HIM. 41 BACK FOR THE
THIRD TIME, HE SAID, "YOU CAN SLEEP AND REST NOW! IT'S ALL
OVER, THE TIME HAS COME. THE SON OF MAN IS NOW
GIVEN INTO THE HANDS OF SINNERS.

(42) GET UP, LET US GO. LOOK: THE ONE BETRAYING
ME IS RIGHT HERE."

THE ARREST

(43) WHILE JESUS WAS STILL SPEAKING JUDAS, ONE OF THE
TWELVE, CAME UP. WITH HIM WAS A CROWD ARMED WITH
SWORDS AND CLUBS, SENT BY THE CHIEF PRIESTS, THE TE-
ACHERS OF THE LAW AND THE ELDERS. (44) THE TRAITOR
HAD ARRANGED A SIGNAL FOR THEM, "THE ONE I KISS, HE IS
THE MAN. ARREST HIM AND TAKE HIM AWAY UNDER GUARD."

(45) SO, WHEN HE CAME, HE
WENT DIRECTLY TO JESUS
CALLING, "MASTER! MASTER!"
AND KISSED HIM. (46) THEN
THEY SEIZED JESUS AND
ARRESTED HIM. (47) ONE
OF THE BYSTANDERS DREW
HIS SWORD AND STRUCK
OUT AT THE HIGH PRIEST'S
SERVANT, CUTTING OFF HIS
EAR. (48) JESUS SAID TO THEM,
"YOU HAVE COME FOR A ROB-
BER, WITH SWORDS AND CLUBS
TO ARREST ME? DAY AFTER
DAY (49) I WAS AMONG YOU
TEACHING IN THE TEMPLE
AND YOU DIDN'T ARREST ME.
BUT LET THE SCRIPTURES BE
FULFILLED." (50) THEN THEY
ALL DESERTED HIM AND
FLED. (51) A YOUNG MAN CO-
VERED ONLY BY A LINEN
CLOTH FOLLOWED JESUS. AS
THEY SEIZED HIM (52) HE
LEFT THE CLOTH IN THEIR
HANDS AND FLED AWAY
NAKED. (53) THEY LED JESUS TO THE HIGH PRIEST AND ALL THE
CHIEF PRIESTS ASSEMBLED WITH THE ELDERS AND THE TE-
ACHERS OF THE LAW. (54) PETER HAD FOLLOWED HIM AT A
DISTANCE AND ENTERED THE COURTYARD OF THE HIGH PRIEST,
WHERE HE SAT WITH THE GUARDS, WARMING HIMSELF AT THE
FIRE. (55) NOW THE CHIEF PRIESTS AND THE WHOLE COUNCIL
TRIED TO FIND SOME EVIDENCE AGAINST JESUS IN ORDER TO PUT
HIM TO DEATH, BUT THEY WERE UNABLE TO FIND ANY. (56)
MANY CAME UP TO SPEAK FALSELY AGAINST HIM, BUT THEIR
EVIDENCE DID NOT AGREE. (57) FINALLY SOME GAVE THIS FALSE

WITNESS: (58) "WE HEARD HIM SAY: 'I WILL DESTROY THIS TEM-
PLE MADE BY HANDS AND IN THREE DAYS I WILL BUILD AN-
OTHER NOT MADE BY HUMAN HANDS.'" (59) BUT EVEN SO
THEIR EVIDENCE DID NOT AGREE.
(60) THE HIGH PRIEST THEN STOOD UP IN THE MIDST OF THEM
AND ASKED JESUS, "HAVE YOU NO ANSWER AT ALL? WHAT
OF THIS EVIDENCE AGAINST YOU?" BUT JESUS WAS SILENT
AND MADE NO REPLY (61). THE HIGH PRIEST PUT A SECOND
QUESTION TO HIM, "ARE YOU THE CHRIST, THE SON OF THE
BLESSED ONE?" THEN JESUS ANSWERED, "I AM, AND YOU
WILL SEE THE SON OF MAN SEATED AT THE RIGHT HAND OF
THE MOST POWERFUL AND COMING WITH THE CLOUDS OF
HEAVEN AROUND HIM". (62)

(63) THE HIGH PRIEST TORE HIS CLOTHES TO SHOW
HIS HORROR AND SAID, "WHAT MORE EVIDENCE DO
WE NEED?" (64) YOU HAVE JUST HEARD HIS BLAS-
PHEMOUS WORDS. WHAT IS YOUR DECISION? AND
THEY ALL CONDEMNED JESUS SAYING,

"HE MUST DIE."

(65) SOME OF THEM BEGAN TO SPIT ON JESUS, BLINDFOLDING HIM,
STRIKING HIM SAYING, "PLAY THE PROPHET!" AND THE GUARDS
SET UPON HIM WITH BLOWS.

PETER DISOWNS JESUS

(66) WHILE PETER
WAS BELOW IN THE COURTYARD, ONE OF THE HIGH PRIEST'S
SERVANT-GIRL CAME BY (67). SEEING PETER BY THE FIRE, SHE
LOOKED AT HIM AND SAID, "YOU ALSO WERE WITH JESUS, THE
NAZARENE." (68) BUT HE DENIED IT, "I DON'T KNOW OR UNDER-
STAND WHAT YOU ARE SAYING." AND HE WENT OUT THROUGH THE
GATEWAY. (69) THE SERVANT-
GIRL SAW HIM THERE AND
TOLD THE BYSTANDERS, "THIS
MAN IS ONE OF THEM" (70) BUT
PETER DENIED IT AGAIN. AF-
TER A LITTLE WHILE THOSE
STANDING BY SAID TO PETER,
"OF COURSE YOU ARE ONE
OF THEM; YOU ARE A GALI-
LEAN AREN'T YOU?" (71) AND
PETER BEGAN TO JUSTIFY
HIMSELF WITH CURSES AND
OATHS, "I DON'T KNOW THE
MAN YOU ARE TALKING
ABOUT." (72) JUST THEN
A COCK CROWED A SE-
COND TIME AND PETER
REMEMBERED WHAT
JESUS HAD SAID TO
HIM, "BEFORE THE
COCK CROWS TWICE
YOU WILL DENY ME
THREE TIMES." AND HE
BROKE DOWN AND WEPT.

15 JESUS BEFORE PILATE

(1) EARLY IN THE MORNING, THE CHIEF PRIESTS, THE ELDERS AND THE
TEACHERS OF THE LAW, THAT IS, THE SANHEDRIN, HAD THEIR PLAN
READY. THEY PUT JESUS IN CHAINS, LED HIM AWAY AND HANDED HIM
OVER TO PILATE. (2) PILATE ASKED HIM, "ARE YOU THE KING OF THE
JEWS?" JESUS ANSWERED, "YOU SAY SO". (3) AS THE CHIEF PRIESTS
ACCUSED HIM OF MANY THINGS, (4) PILATE ASKED HIM AGAIN, "HAVE
YOU NO ANSWER AT ALL? SEE HOW MANY CHARGES THEY BRING
AGAINST YOU!" (5) BUT JESUS GAVE NO FURTHER ANSWERS, SO
THAT PILATE WONDERED. (6) AT EVERY PASSOVER FESTIVAL, PI-
LATE USED TO FREE ANY PRISONER THE PEOPLE ASKED FOR. (7)
NOW THERE WAS A MAN CALLED BARABBAS, JAILED WITH THE RI-
OTERS WHO HAD COMMITTED MURDER IN THE UPRISING. (8)
WHEN THE CROWD WENT UP TO ASK PILATE THE USUAL
FAVOR, (9) HE SAID TO THEM, "DO YOU WANT ME
TO SET FREE THE KING OF THE JEWS?"

BEFORE THE COCK CROWS TWICE, YOU WILL DENY ME THREE TIMES. (MARK 14:30)
CCCXXXI
DMX6
331

10 FOR HE REALIZED THAT THE CHIEF PRIESTS HAD HANDED OVER
JESUS TO HIM OUT OF ENVY. 11 BUT THE CHIEF PRIESTS STIRRED
UP THE CROWD TO ASK INSTEAD FOR BARABBAS' RELEASE. 12
PILATE REPLIED, "AND WHAT SHALL I DO WITH THE MAN YOU
CALL KING OF THE JEWS?" 13 THE CROWD SHOUTED BACK,
"CRUCIFY HIM!" 14 PILATE ASKED, "WHAT EVIL HAS HE DONE?"
BUT THEY SHOUTED THE LOUDER, "CRUCIFY HIM!"

JESUS CROWNED WITH THORNS

15 AS PILATE WANTED TO PLEASE THE PEOPLE, HE FREED
BARABBAS AND AFTER FLOGGING JESUS HAD HIM HAN-
DED OVER TO BE CRU-

CIFIED. 16 THE SOLDIERS
TOOK HIM INSIDE THE COURT-
YARD KNOWN AS THE PRAE-
TORIUM AND CALLED THE
REST OF THEIR COMPA-
NIONS. 17 THEY CLOTHED
HIM IN A PURPLE CLOAK
AND TWISTING A CROWN OF
THORNS, THEY FORCED IT
ONTO HIS HEAD. 18 THEN
THEY BEGAN SALUTING
HIM, "LONG LIFE TO THE
KING OF THE JEWS!"
19 WITH A STICK THEY GAVE
HIM BLOWS ON THE HEAD
AND SPAT ON HIM; THEN
THEY KNELT BEFORE HIM
PRETENDING TO WOR-
SHIP HIM. 20 WHEN
THEY HAD FINISHED
MOCKING HIM, THEY PUL-
LED OFF THE PURPLE CLOAK
AND PUT HIS OWN CLOTHES ON HIM.

THE CRUCIFIXION

THE SOLDIERS LED HIM OUT OF THE CITY TO CRUCIFY HIM.
21 ON THE WAY THEY MET SIMON OF CYRENE, FATHER OF
ALEXANDER AND RUFUS, WHO WAS COMING IN FROM THE
COUNTRY, AND FORCED HIM TO CARRY THE CROSS OF JESUS.
22 WHEN THEY LED HIM TO A PLACE CALLED GOLGOTHA (WHICH
MEANS 'THE SKULL') THEY GAVE HIM WINE WITH MYRRH 23 BUT
HE WOULD NOT TAKE IT. 24 THEN THEY NAILED HIM TO THE
CROSS AND DIVIDED HIS CLOTHES AMONG THEMSELVES, CASTING

LOTS TO DECIDE WHAT EACH SHOULD TAKE. 25 AT ABOUT NINE
O'CLOCK IN THE MORNING THEY CRUCIFIED HIM. 26 HIS OFFENSE
WAS DISPLAYED ABOVE HIS HEAD; IT READ, "THE KING OF THE JEWS."
27 THEY ALSO CRUCIFIED TWO ROBBERS WITH HIM, ONE ON HIS
RIGHT AND ONE ON HIS LEFT. 28-29 PEOPLE PASSING BY LA-
UGHED AT HIM, SHOOK THEIR HEAD AND JEERED, "AHA! SO
YOU ARE ABLE TO TEAR DOWN THE TEMPLE AND BUILD IT UP
AGAIN IN THREE DAYS. 30 NOW SAVE YOURSELF AND COME
DOWN FROM THE CROSS!"
31 IN THE SAME WAY THE CHIEF PRIESTS AND THE TEACH-
ERS OF THE LAW MOCKED HIM SAYING TO ONE ANOTHER,
"THE MAN WHO SAVED OTHERS CANNOT SAVE HIMSELF.
32 LET'S SEE THE MESSIAH, THE KING OF ISRAEL, CO-
ME DOWN FROM HIS CROSS AND THEN WE WILL BELIEVE
IN HIM." EVEN THE MEN WHO WERE CRUCIFIED WITH
JESUS INSULTED HIM.

THE DEATH OF JESUS

33 WHEN NOON CAME, DARKNESS FELL OVER THE
WHOLE LAND AND LASTED UNTIL THREE O'CLOCK; 34
AND AT THREE O'CLOCK JESUS CRIED OUT IN A LOUD VOICE,
"ELOI, ELOI, LAMMA SABACHTHANI?" WHICH MEANS, "MY GOD,
MY GOD, WHY HAVE YOU DESERTED ME?" 35 AS SOON AS THEY
HEARD THESE WORDS, SOME OF THE BYSTANDERS SAID,
"LISTEN! HE IS CALLING FOR ELIJAH." 36 AND ONE OF THEM
FILLED A SPONGE WITH BITTER WINE, PUT IT ON A REED, GAVE
HIM TO DRINK, SAYING, "NOW LET'S SEE WHETHER ELIJAH
COMES TO TAKE HIM DOWN. 37 BUT JESUS UTTERED A LOUD
AND GAVE UP HIS SPIRIT. 38 AND IMMEDIATELY THE CURTAIN OF
THE TEMPLE SANCTUARY WAS TORN IN TWO FROM TOP TO BOT-
TOM. 39 THE CAPTAIN STANDING THERE SAW HOW JESUS

DIED AND HEARD THE CRY HE GAVE; AND HE SAID, "TRULY, THIS
MAN WAS THE SON OF GOD." 40 THERE WERE SOME WOMEN WATCH-
ING FROM A DISTANCE; AMONG THEM WERE MARY MAGDALENE,
MARY THE MOTHER OF JAMES THE YOUNGER AND JOSET AND SA-
LOME, 41 WHO HAD FOLLOWED JESUS WHEN HE WAS IN GALI-
LEE AND SAW TO HIS NEEDS. THERE WERE ALSO OTHERS WHO
HAD COME UP WITH HIM TO JERUSALEM.

THE BURIAL

42 IT WAS NOW EVENING AND AS IT WAS PREPARATION DAY,
THAT IS THE DAY BEFORE THE SABBATH, 43 JOSEPH OF ARI-
MATHEA BOLDLY WENT TO PILATE AND ASKED FOR THE BODY
OF JESUS. JOSEPH WAS A RESPECTED MEMBER OF THE COUNCIL
WHO WAS HIMSELF WAITING
FOR THE KINGDOM OF GOD.
44 PILATE WAS SURPRISED
THAT JESUS SHOULD
HAVE DIED SO SOON; SO
HE SUMMONED THE CAP-
TAIN AND INQUIRED IF
JESUS WAS ALREADY
DEAD. 45 AFTER HE-
ARING THE CAPTAIN,
HE LET JOSEPH HAVE
THE BODY.
46 JOSEPH TOOK IT
DOWN AND WRAPPED
IT IN THE LINEN SHEET
HE HAD BOUGHT. HE
LAID THE BODY IN A
TOMB WHICH HAD
BEEN CUT OUT OF THE
ROCK AND ROLLED
A STONE ACROSS
THE ENTRANCE OF
THE TOMB.

JOSEPH OF ARIMATHAEA

47 NOW MARY OF MAGDALA AND MARY
THE MOTHER OF JOSET TOOK NOTE OF
WHERE THE BODY HAD BEEN LAID.

HE HAS BEEN RAISED, HE IS NOT HERE

16 1 WHEN THE SABBATH WAS OVER, MARY OF MAGDALA, MA-
RY THE MOTHER OF JAMES AND SALOME BOUGHT SPICES SO
THAT THEY MIGHT GO AND ANOINT THE BODY. 2 AND VERY
EARLY IN THE MORNING ON THE FIRST DAY OF THE WEEK, JUST
AFTER SUNRISE, THEY CAME TO THE TOMB. 3 THEY WERE
SAYING TO ONE ANOTHER, "WHO WILL ROLL BACK THE STO-
NE FOR US FROM THE ENTRANCE OF THE TOMB?" BUT
4 AS THEY LOOKED UP, THEY NOTICED THAT THE STONE HAD
ALREADY BEEN ROLLED AWAY. IT WAS A VERY BIG STONE. 5
AS THEY ENTERED THE TOMB, THEY SAW A YOUNG MAN IN A
WHITE ROBE SEATED ON THE RIGHT, AND THEY WERE AMAZED,

6 BUT HE SAID TO THEM, "DON'T BE ALARMED; YOU ARE
LOOKING FOR JESUS OF NAZARETH WHO WAS CRUCIFIED;
HE HAS BEEN RAISED AND IS NOT HERE. THIS IS, HOWEV-
ER, THE PLACE WHERE THEY LAID HIM. 7 NOW GO AND TELL
HIS DISCIPLES AND PETER: JESUS IS GOING AHEAD OF YOU
TO GALILEE; YOU WILL SEE HIM THERE JUST AS HE TOLD YOU."
8 THE WOMEN WENT OUT OF THE TOMB AND FLED, BE-
SIDE THEMSELVES WITH FEAR. AND THEY SAID NOTHING
TO ANYONE BECAUSE THEY WERE AFRAID.

SHORT CONCLUSION OF MARK'S GOSPEL

9 AFTER JESUS ROSE EARLY ON THE FIRST DAY
OF THE WEEK, HE APPEARED FIRST TO MARY OF MAG-
DALA FROM WHOM HE HAD DRIVEN OUT SEVEN DE-
MONS. 10 SHE WENT AND REPORTED THE NEWS TO
HIS FOLLOWERS, WHO
WERE NOW MOURNING
AND WEEPING 11 BUT
WHEN THEY HEARD THAT
HE LIVED AND HAD BEEN
SEEN BY HER, THEY
WOULD NOT BELIEVE IT.
12 AFTER THIS HE
SHOWED HIMSELF IN
ANOTHER FORM TO TWO
OF THEM AS THEY WERE
WALKING INTO THE CO-
UNTRY. 13 THESE MEN
TOO WENT BACK AND TOLD
THE OTHERS, BUT THEY
DID NOT BELIEVE THEM.
14 LATER JESUS SHOWED
HIMSELF TO THE ELE-
VEN WHILE THEY
WERE AT TABLE.

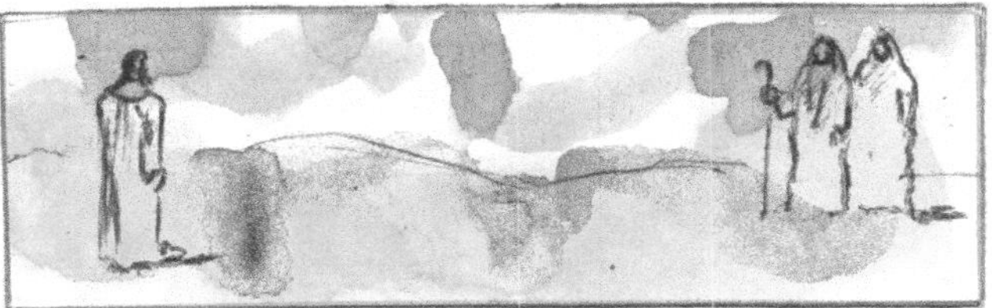

HE REPROACHED THEM FOR THEIR UNBELIEF
AND STUBBORNESS IN REFUSING TO BE-
LIEVE THOSE WHO HAD SEEN HIM AFTER
HE HAD RISEN.

15 THEN HE TOLD THEM, "GO OUT TO THE
WHOLE WORLD AND
PROCLAIM THE GOOD
NEWS TO ALL CRE-
ATION.

16 HE WHO BELIEVES
AND IS BAPTIZED
WILL BE SAVED; HE
WHO REFUSES TO
BELIEVE WILL BE
CONDEMNED.

17 SIGNS LIKE THESE
ACCOMPANY THOSE
WHO HAVE BELIEVED
IN MY NAME. THEY
WILL CAST OUT
DEMONS AND SPEAK
NEW LANGUAGES;

18 THEY WILL PICK
UP SNAKES AND,
IF THEY DRINK ANY-
THING POISONOUS,
THEY WILL BE UN-
HARMED.

THEY WILL LAY THEIR HANDS ON THE SICK
AND THEY WILL BE HEALED."

19 SO THEN, AFTER SPEAKING TO THEM,
THE LORD JESUS WAS TAKEN UP INTO
HEAVEN AND TOOK HIS PLACE AT THE
RIGHT HAND OF GOD.

20 THE ELEVEN WENT FORTH AND PREACHED
EVERYWHERE, WHILE THE LORD WORKED WITH
THEM AND CONFIRMED THE MESSAGE BY THE
SIGNS WHICH ACCOMPANIED THEM.

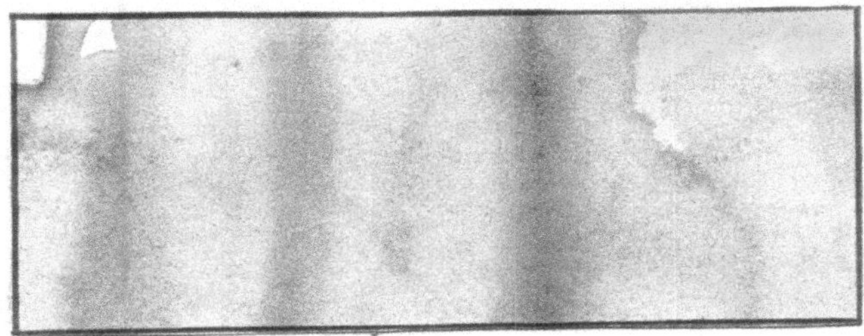

ELI LAMA SABACTANI!!
CCCXXXII
332
04
©

ELI
ELI LAMA SABACTANI
CCCXXXIII
333
DMazzoli 06 ©

THE GOSPEL OF LUKE

LUKE, A SYRIAN DOCTOR, WAS CONVERTED TO CHRISTIANITY WHEN THE FIRST MISSIONARIES LEFT THE JERUSALEM AND CAESAREA COMMUNITIES TO TAKE THE GOSPEL BEYOND THE BORDERS OF THE JEWISH COUNTRY. LUKE THEN LEFT HIS HOMELAND TO ACCOMPANY THE APOSTLE PAUL.

HE ARRIVED AT ROME, THE CAPITAL OF THE THEN KNOWN WORLD, WHERE HE STAYED FOR AT LEAST TWO YEARS. THERE HE MET PETER AND MARK WHO WERE PREACHING AMONG THE CHRISTIANS IN ROME.

WHEN HE WROTE HIS GOSPEL, AROUND THE YEAR 70 SOME TEXTS CONTAINING DEEDS AND MIRACLES OF JESUS WERE AVAILABLE TO HIM, THE SAME TEXTS WHICH MARK AND MATTHEW HAD USED. BUT IN HIS TRAVELS, HE HAD ALSO PICKED UP OTHER STORIES THAT CAME FROM JESUS' FIRST DISCIPLES. THESE STORIES WERE PRESERVED IN THE OLDEST CHURCHES OF JERUSALEM AND CAESAREA.
SUCH IS THE ORIGIN OF THE FIRST TWO CHAPTERS OF LUKE'S GOSPEL TELLING US ABOUT JESUS' INFANCY, BASED ON INFORMATION WHICH HIS MOTHER MARY MUST HAVE SUPPLIED.

LUKE'S CULTURAL BACKGROUND WAS GREEK AND HE WAS WRITING FOR GREEK PEOPLE. HE OMITTED SEVERAL MARCAN DETAILS, DEALING WITH JEWISH LAWS AND CUSTOMS WHICH WOULD HAVE BEEN HARD FOR HIS READERS TO UNDERSTAND.

THE GOSPEL ACCORDING TO LUKE

1 1 SEVERAL PEOPLE HAVE SET THEMSELVES TO RE-
LATE THE EVENTS THAT HAVE TAKEN PLACE AMONG US, 2
AS THEY WERE TOLD BY THE FIRST WITNESSES WHO
LATER BECAME MINISTERS OF THE WORD. 3 AFTER I
MYSELF HAD CAREFULLY GONE OVER THE WHOLE
STORY FROM THE BEGINNING, IT SEEMED RIGHT

FOR ME TO GIVE YOU, THEOPHILUS, AN ORDERLY AC-
COUNT, 4 SO THAT YOUR EXCELLENCY MAY KNOW
THE TRUTH OF ALL YOU HAVE BEEN TAUGHT.

THE BIRTH OF JOHN THE BAPTIST FORETOLD

5 IN THE DAYS OF HEROD, KING OF JUDEA, THERE LIVED
A PRIEST NAMED ZECHARIAH, BELONGING TO THE PRIESTLY
CLAN OF ABIAH. ELIZABETH, ZECHARIAH'S WIFE, ALSO BE-
LONGED TO A PRIESTLY FAMILY. 6 BOTH OF THEM WERE UP-
RIGHT IN THE EYES OF GOD
AND LIVED ACCORDING TO THE
LAWS AND COMMANDS OF THE
LORD. 7 BUT THEY HAD NO
CHILD. ELIZABETH COULDN'T
HAVE ANY AND THE WERE NOW
BOTH VERY OLD. 8 WHILE
ZECHARIAH WITH OTHERS
WERE FULFILLING THEIR OF-
FICE 9 IT FELL ON HIM BY
LOT, AS FOR THE CUSTOM OF
THE PRIESTS, TO ENTER THE
LORD SANCTUARY AND BURN
INCENSE. 10 AT THE TIME
OF OFFERING INCENSE ALL
THE PEOPLE WERE PRAYING
OUTSIDE. 11 IT WAS THEN
THAT AN ANGEL OF THE LORD
APPEAREAD TO HIM, AT THE
RIGHT SIDE OF THE ALTAR
OF INCENSE. 12 ON SEEING
THE ANGEL ZECHARIAH WAS
DEEPLY TROUBLED AND FEAR
TOOK HOLD OF HIM. 13
BUT THE ANGEL SAID TO
HIM, "DON'T BE AFRAID,
ZECHARIAH, BE ASSURED
THAT YOUR PRAYER HAS
BEEN HEARD. YOUR WI-

FE ELIZABETH WILL BEAR YOU A SON AND YOU SHALL
NAME HIM JOHN. 14 HE WILL BRING JOY AND GLADNESS
TO YOU AND MANY WILL REJOICE AT HIS BIRTH.
15 THIS SON OF YOURS WILL BE GREAT IN THE EYES
OF THE LORD. LISTEN: HE SHALL NEVER DRINK
WINE OR STRONG DRINK BUT HE WILL BE FILLED
WITH HOLY SPIRIT EVEN FROM HIS MOTHER'S WOMB.

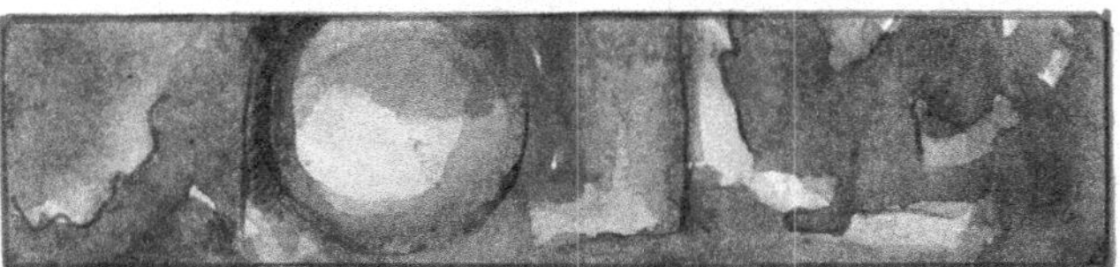

16 THROUGH HIM MANY OF THE PEOPLE OF ISRAEL WILL
TURN TO THE LORD THEIR GOD. 17 HE HIMSELF WILL OPEN
THE WAY TO THE LORD WITH THE SPIRIT AND POWER OF THE
PROPHET ELIJAH; HE WILL RECONCILE FATHERS AND CHIL-
DREN, AND LEAD THE DISOBEDIENT TO WISDOM AND RIGHT-
EOUSNESS, IN ORDER TO MAKE READY FOR THE LORD A
PEOPLE PREPARED." 18 ZECHARIAH SAID TO THE AN-
GEL: "HOW CAN I BELIEVE THIS? I AM AN OLD MAN AND MY WI-
FE IS ELDERY TOO." 19 THE ANGEL REPLIED, "I AM GABRIEL,
WHO STAND BEFORE GOD, AND I AM THE ONE SENT TO SPEAK
TO YOU AND BRING YOU THIS GOOD NEWS! MY WORDS WILL COME
TRUE IN THEIR TIME. BUT
20 YOU WOULD NOT BELI-
EVE AND YOU WILL BE SI-
LENT AND UNABLE TO SPEAK
UNTIL THIS HAS HAPPE-
NED." 21 MEANWHILE
THE PEOPLE WAITED FOR
ZECHARIAH AND WERE
SURPRISED THAT HE DE-
LAYED SO LONG IN THE
SANCTUARY. 22 WHEN
HE FINALLY APPEARED,
HE COULD NOT SPEAK
TO THEM AND THEY REA-
LIZED THAT HE HAD SE-
EN A VISION IN THE
SANCTUARY. HE RE-
MAINED DUMB AND
MADE SIGNS TO THEM.
23 WHEN HIS TIME
OF SERVICE WAS COM-
PLETED, ZECHARIAH
RETURNED HOME 24
AND SOME TIME LA-
TER ELIZABETH BE-
CAME PREGNANT. FOR
FIVE MONTHS SHE KEPT
TO HERSELF, REMAIN-
ING AT HOME, AND
THINKING, 25 "WHAT
IS THE LORD DOING FOR ME! THIS IS HIS TIME FOR
MERCY AND FOR TAKING AWAY MY PUBLIC DISGRACE."

THE ANNUNCIATION

26 IN THE SIXTH MONTH, THE ANGEL GABRIEL WAS SENT
FROM GOD TO A TOWN OF GALILEE CALLED NAZARETH. HE
WAS SENT 27 TO A YOUNG VIRGIN WHO WAS BETROTHED TO
A MAN NAMED JOSEPH, OF THE FAMILY OF DAVID; THE VIRGIN'S
NAME WAS MARY. 28 THE ANGEL CAME TO HER AND SAID,
"REJOICE, FULL OF GRACE, THE LORD IS WITH YOU." 29 MARY
WAS TROUBLED AT THESE WORDS, WONDERING WHAT THIS
GREETING COULD MEAN. 30 BUT THE ANGEL SAID, "DO NOT

FEAR, MARY, FOR GOD HAS LOOKED KINDLY ON YOU. YOU SHALL
31 CONCEIVE AND BEAR A SON AND YOU SHALL CALL HIM
JESUS. 32 HE WILL BE GREAT AND SHALL BE CALLED SON OF
THE MOST HIGH. THE LORD GOD WILL GIVE HIM THE KING-
DOM OF DAVID, HIS ANCESTOR; HE WILL RULE OVER THE PE-
OPLE OF JACOB FOREVER 33 AND HIS REIGN SHALL
HAVE NO END."
34 THEN MARY SAID TO THE ANGEL, "HOW THIS CAN BE IF I
AM A VERGIN?" 35 THE ANGEL SAID TO HER, "THE HOLY
SPIRIT WILL COME UPON YOU AND THE POWER OF THE
MOST HIGH WILL OVERSHADOW YOU; THEREFORE, THE HOLY
CHILD TO BE BORN SHALL BE CALLED SON OF GOD.

36 EVEN YOUR RELATIVE ELIZABETH IS EXPECTING A
SON IN HER OLD AGE ALTHOUGH SHE WAS UNABLE TO HAVE
A CHILD, AND SHE IS NOW IN HER SIXTH MONTH. 37 WITH
GOD NOTHING IS IMPOSSIBLE." 38 THEN MARY SAID, "I AM
THE HANDMAID OF THE LORD, LET IT BE DONE TO ME
AS YOU HAVE SAID." AND THE ANGEL LEFT HER.

MARY VISITS ELIZABETH

39 MARY THEN SET OUT FOR A TOWN IN THE HILLS
OF JUDEA. 40 SHE ENTERED THE HOUSE OF ZECHA-
RIAH AND GREETED

ELIZABETH. 41 WHEN
ELIZABETH HEARD
MARY'S GREETING, THE
BABY LEAPT IN HER
WOMB. ELIZABETH
WAS FILLED WITH
HOLY SPIRIT, AND
42 GIVING A LOUD
CRY, SAID, YOU ARE
MOST BLESSED AMONG
WOMEN AND BLESSED
IS THE FRUIT OF YOUR
WOMB! 43 HOW IS IT
THAT THE MOTHER OF MY
LORD COMES TO ME?
44 THE MOMENT
YOUR GREETING SO-
UNDED IN MY EARS, THE
BABY WITHIN ME
SUDDENLY LEAPT FOR
JOY.
45 BLESSED ARE YOU
WHO BELIEVED THAT
THAT THE LORD'S WORD
WOULD COME TRUE!"
46 AND MARY SAID:

"MY SOUL PROCLAIMS THE GREATNESS OF
THE LORD, 47 MY SPIRIT EXULTS IN GOD
MY SAVIOR! 48 HE HAS LOOKED UPON
HIS SERVANT IN HER LOWLINESS, AND PEOPLE
FOREVER WILL CALL ME BLESSED. 49 THE
MIGHTY ONE HAS DONE GREAT THINGS
FOR ME, HOLY IS HIS NAME! 50 FROM
AGE TO AGE HIS MERCY EXTENDS TO THOSE
WHO LIVE IN HIS PRESENCE.
51 HE HAS ACTED WITH POWER AND DONE
WONDERS, AND SCATTERED THE PROUD WITH

THEIR PLANS. 52 HE HAS PUT DOWN THE
MIGHTY FROM THEIR THRONES AND LIFTED
UP THOSE WHO ARE DOWNTRODDEN. 53 HE
HAS FILLED THE HUNGRY WITH GOOD THINGS
BUT HAS SENT THE RICH AWAY EMPTY. 54
HE HELD OUT HIS HAND TO ISRAEL, HIS SER-
VANT, FOR HE REMEMBERED HIS MERCY 55
EVEN AS HE PROMISED OUR FATHERS,
ABRAHAM AND HIS DESCENDANTS FOREVER."

56 AND MARY REMAINED WITH ELIZABETH ABOUT
THREE MONTHS AND THEN RETURNED HOME.

BIRTH OF JOHN THE BAPTIST

57 WHEN THE TIME CAME FOR ELIZABETH, SHE GAVE
BIRTH TO A SON. 58 HER NEIGHBORS AND RELATI-
VES HEARD THAT THE MERCIFUL LORD HAS DONE A WONDER-
FUL THING FOR HER AND THEY REJOICED WITH HER.

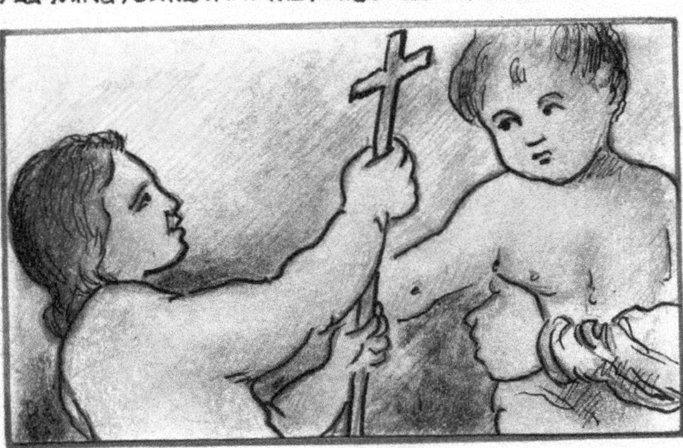

59 WHEN ON THE EIGHT DAY THEY CAME TO ATTEND THE CIRCUMCI-
SION OF THE CHILD, THEY WANTED TO NAME HIM ZECHARIAH AFTER
HIS FATHER. 60 BUT HIS MOTHER SAID, "NOT SO; HE SHALL BE
CALLED JOHN." 61 THEY SAID TO HER, "NO ONE IN YOUR FAMILY
HAS THAT NAME." 62 AND
THEY ASKED THE FATHER
BY MEANS OF SIGNS FOR
THE NAME HE WANTED TO
GIVE. 63 ZECHARIAH ASKED
FOR A WRITING TABLET
AND WROTE ON IT, "HIS NAME
IS JOHN," AND THEY WERE
VERY SURPRISED. 64 IM-
MEDIATELY ZECHARIAH
COULD SPEAK AGAIN
AND HIS FIRST WORDS
WERE IN PRAISE OF GOD.
65 A HOLY FEAR CA-
ME ON ALL IN THE NEIGH-
BOURHOOD, AND THROUGHOUT
THE HILLS OF JUDEA
THE PEOPLE TALKED
ABOUT THESE EVENTS.
66 ALL WHO HEARD OF
IT PONDERED IN THEIR
MINDS AND WONDERED
"WHAT WILL THE CHILD BE?"
FOR THEY UNDERSTOOD
THAT THE HAND OF THE
LORD WAS WITH HIM.

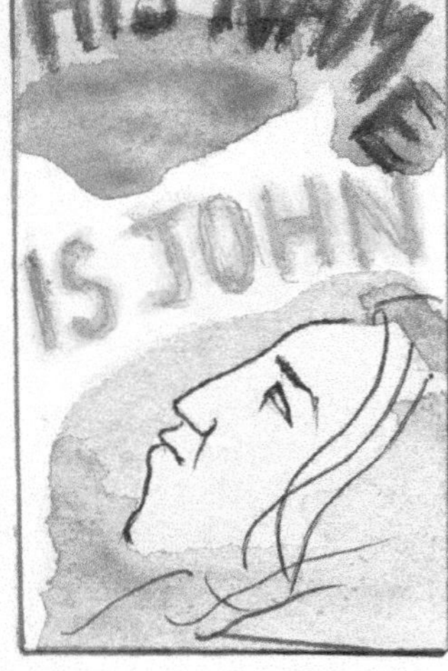

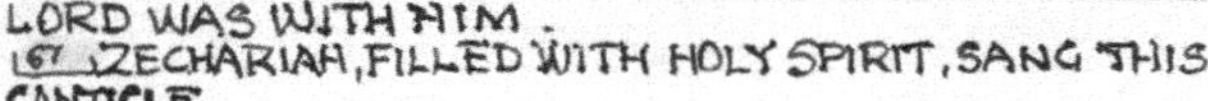

67 ZECHARIAH, FILLED WITH HOLY SPIRIT, SANG THIS
CANTICLE,

68 BLESSED BE THE LORD GOD OF ISRAEL,
FOR HE HAS COME AND REDEEMED HIS PE-
OPLE. 69 HE HAS RAISED UP FOR US A
VICTORIOUS SAVIOR IN THE HOUSE OF
DAVID HIS SERVANT, 70 AS HE PROMISED
THROUGH HIS PROPHETS OF OLD, 71
SALVATION FROM OUR ENEMIES AND
FROM THE HAND OF OUR FOES.
72 HE HAS SHOWN MERCY TO OUR FATHERS
AND REMEMBERED HIS HOLY COVENANT 73
THE OATH HE SWORE TO ABRAHAM, OUR
FATHER, 74 TO DELIVER US FROM THE ENEMY,

335 CCCXXXV
DM 06 ©

(75) THAT WE MIGHT SERVE HIM FEARLESSLY AS
A HOLY AND RIGHTEOUS PEOPLE ALL THE DAYS OF
OUR LIVES. (76) AND YOU, MY CHILD, SHALL BE
CALLED PROPHET OF THE MOST HIGH, FOR YOU
SHALL GO BEFORE THE LORD TO PREPARE THE
WAY FOR HIM (77) AND ENABLE HIS PEOPLE TO
KNOW OF THEIR SALVATION WHEN HE COMES
TO FORGIVE THEIR SINS. (78) THIS IS THE WORK
OF THE MERCY OF OUR GOD, WHO COMES FROM ON
HIGH AS A RISING SUN (79) SHINING ON THOSE
WHO LIVE IN DARKNESS AND IN THE SHADOW OF
DEATH, AND GUIDING OUR FEET INTO THE
WAY OF PEACE."

(80) AS THE CHILD GREW UP, HE WAS SEEN TO BE STRONG
IN THE SPIRIT; HE LIVED IN THE DESERT TILL THE DAY
WHEN HE APPEARED OPENLY IN ISRAEL.

THE BIRTH OF JESUS

2 (1) AT THAT TIME THE EMPEROR ISSUED A DECREE
FOR A CENSUS OF THE WHOLE EMPIRE TO BE TAKEN.
(2) THIS FIRST CENSUS WAS TAKEN WHILE
QUIRINUS WAS GOVERNOR OF SYRIA. (3) EVERYONE HAD
TO BE REGISTERED IN HIS OWN TOWN. SO EVERYONE
SET OUT FOR HIS OWN
CITY; (4) JOSEPH TOO
SET OUT FROM NAZA-
RETH OF GALILEE. AS
HE BELONGED TO THE
FAMILY OF DAVID, BEING
A DESCENDANT OF HIS,
HE WENT TO JUDEA TO
DAVID'S TOWN OF BETH-
LEHEM (5) TO BE RE-
GISTERED WITH MARY,
HIS WIFE, WHO WAS WITH
CHILD. (6) THEY WERE
IN BETHLEHEM WHEN
THE TIME CAME FOR
HER TO HAVE HER
CHILD, (7) AND SHE
GAVE BIRTH TO A
SON, HER FIRSTBORN.
SHE WRAPPED HIM IN
SWADDLING CLOTHES AND
LAID HIM IN THE MANGER
BECAUSE THERE WAS
NO PLACE FOR THEM IN
THE LIVING ROOM.

THE SHEPHERDS AND THE ANGELS

(8) THERE WERE SHEPHERDS CAMPING IN THE CO-
UNTRYSIDE, TAKING TURN TO WATCH OVER THEIR FLOCKS
BY NIGHT. (9) SUDDENLY AN ANGEL OF THE LORD APPEAR-
ED TO THEM, WITH THE GLORY OF THE LORD SHINING AROUND
THEM. AS THEY WERE TERRIFIED, (10) THE ANGEL SAID,
"DON'T BE AFRAID: I AM HERE TO GIVE YOU GOOD NEWS,
GREAT JOY FOR ALL THE PEOPLE. (11) TODAY A
SAVIOR HAS BEEN BORN TO YOU IN DAVID'S TOWN.
HE IS THE MESSIAH AND THE LORD. (12) LET THIS BE
A SIGN TO YOU: YOU WILL FIND A BABY WRAPPED IN
SWADDLING CLOTHES AND LYING IN A MANGER."

(13) SUDDENLY THE ANGEL WAS SURROUNDED BY
MANY MORE ANGELS, PRAISING GOD AND SAYING,
(14) "GLORY TO GOD IN THE HIGHEST; PEACE ON
EARTH FOR GOD IS BLESSING HUMANKIND."

(15) WHEN THE ANGELS HAD LEFT THEM AND GONE
BACK TO HEAVEN, THE SHEPHERDS SAID TO ONE ANOTHER,
"LET US GO AS FAR AS BETHLEHEM AND SEE WHAT
THE LORD HAS MADE KNOWN TO US." (16) SO THEY CAME
HURRIEDLY AND FOUND
MARY AND JOSEPH
WITH THE BABY LYING
IN THE MANGER. (17)
ON SEEING THIS THEY
RELATED WHAT THEY
HAD BEEN TOLD ABOUT
THE CHILD, (18) AND
ALL WERE ASTONISHED
ON HEARING THE SHE-
PHERDS. (19) AS FOR
MARY, SHE TREASURED
ALL THESE MESSAGES
AND CONTINUALLY PON-
DERED OVER THEM. (20)
THE SHEPHERDS THEN
RETURNED GIVING
GLORY AND PRAISE
TO GOD FOR ALL THEY
HAD HEARD AND SEEN,
JUST AS THE ANGELS
HAD TOLD THEM. (21)
ON THE EIGHT DAY THE
CIRCUMCISION OF THE
BABY HAD TO BE PER-
FORMED; HE WAS NAMED JESUS, THE NAME THE AN-
GEL HAD GIVEN HIM BEFORE HE WAS CONCEIVED.

JESUS IS PRESENTED IN THE TEMPLE

(22) WHEN THE DAY CAME FOR THE PURIFICATION AC-
CORDING TO THE LAW OF MOSES, THEY BROUGHT THE
BABY UP TO JERUSALEM TO PRESENT HIM TO THE
LORD (23) AS IT IS WRITTEN IN THE LAW OF THE LORD:
EVERY FIRSTBORN MALE SHALL BE CONSECRATED TO
GOD. (24) AND THEY OFFERED A SACRIFICE AS ORDERED
IN THE LAW OF THE LORD: A PAIR OF TURTLEDOVES OR TWO
YOUNG PIGEONS. (25) THERE LIVED IN JERUSALEM AT THIS

TIME A VERY UPRIGHT AND DEVOUT MAN NAMED SIMEON;
THE HOLY SPIRIT WAS IN HIM. HE LOOKED FORWARD
TO THE TIME WHEN THE LORD WOULD COMFORT ISRAEL
AND (26) HE HAD BEEN ASSURED BY THE HOLY SPIRIT
THAT HE WOULD NOT DIE BEFORE SEEING THE MESSIAH
OF THE LORD. (27) SO HE WAS LED INTO THE TEMPLE
BY THE HOLY SPIRIT AT THE TIME THE PARENTS
BROUGHT THE CHILD JESUS, TO DO FOR HIM AC-
CORDING TO THE CUSTOM OF THE LAW. (28) SIMEON TOOK
THE CHILD IN HIS ARMS AND BLESSED GOD, SAYING,

(29) "NOW, O LORD, YOU CAN DISMISS YOUR
SERVANT IN PEACE, FOR YOU HAVE FUL-
FILLED YOUR WORD (30) AND MY EYES HAVE
SEEN YOUR SALVATION, (31) WHICH YOU
DISPLAY FOR ALL THE PEOPLE TO SEE.
(32) HERE IS THE LIGHT YOU WILL RE-
VEAL TO THE NATIONS AND THE GLORY
OF YOUR PEOPLE ISRAEL."
(33) HIS FATHER AND MOTHER WONDERED AT WHAT
WAS SAID ABOUT THE CHILD. (34) SIMEON BLESSED
THEM AND SAID TO MARY
HIS MOTHER, "SEE HIM;
HE WILL BE FOR THE
RISE OR FALL OF THE
MULTITUDES OF ISRA-
EL. HE SHALL STAND
AS A SIGN OF CONT-
RADICTION, (35) WHI-
LE A SWORD WILL PI-
ERCE YOUR OWN SOUL.

THEN THE SECRET THOUGHTS OF MANY MAY BE BROUGHT TO LIGHT."

ANNA

(36) THERE WAS ALSO
A PROPHETESS NA-
MED ANNA, DAUGHTER
OF PHANUEL, OF THE
TRIBE OF ASHER.
AFTER LEAVING HER FATHER'S HOME SHE HAD
BEEN SEVEN YEARS WITH HER HUSBAND AND
SINCE THEN SHE HAD BEEN CONTINUALLY IN
THE TEMPLE, SERVING GOD AS A WIDOW
NIGHT AND NIGHT IN FASTING AND PRAYER.
(37) SHE WAS NOW EIGHTY-FOUR. (38) COMING UP
AT THAT TIME, SHE GAVE PRAISE TO GOD AND SPOKE
OF THE CHILD TO ALL WHO LOOKED FORWARD TO THE
DELIVERANCE OF JERUSALEM. (39) WHEN THE PA-
RENTS HAD FULFILLED ALL THAT WAS REQUIRED BY

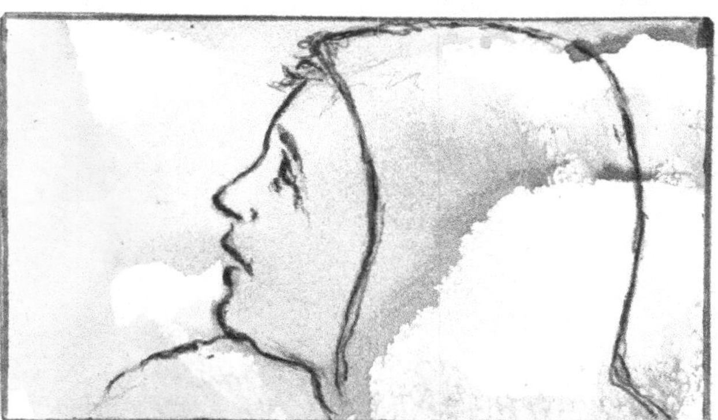

THE LAW OF THE LORD, THEY RETURNED TO THEIR
TOWN, NAZARETH IN GALILEE. (40) THERE THE CHILD
GREW IN STATURE AND STRENGTH AND WAS FILLED
WITH WISDOM: THE GRACE OF GOD WAS UPON HIM.

I MUST BE IN MY FATHER'S HOUSE

(41) EVERY YEAR THE PARENTS OF JESUS WENT TO
JERUSALEM TO THE FEAST OF THE PASSOVER, AS
WAS CUSTOMARY. (42) WHEN JESUS WAS TWELVE
YEARS OLD, HE WENT UP WITH THEM ACCORDING
TO THE CUSTOMS FOR THIS FEAST. (43) AFTER THE
FESTIVAL WAS OVER, THEY RETURNED, BUT THE
BOY JESUS REMAINED IN JERUSALEM AND HIS
PARENTS DID NOT KNOW IT. (44) ON THE FIRST DAY
OF THE JOURNEY THEY THOUGHT HE WAS IN THE COM-
PANY AND LOOKED FOR HIM AMONG THE RELATIVES
AND FRIENDS. (45) AS THEY DID NOT FIND HIM,
THEY WENT BACK TO JERUSALEM SEARCHING FOR HIM,
(46) AND AFTER THREE DAYS THEY FOUND HIM IN THE TEM-
PLE. SITTING AMONG THE TEACHERS, LISTENING TO
THEM AND ASKING QUESTIONS.
(47) AND ALL THE PEOPLE WERE AMAZED AT HIS
UNDERSTANDING AND HIS ANSWERS. (48) HIS PA-
RENTS WERE VERY SURPRISED WHEN THEY SAW
HIM AND HIS MOTHER SAID TO HIM, "SON, WHY
HAVE YOU DONE THIS TO US? YOUR FATHER
AND I WERE WORRIED WHILE SEARCHING FOR
YOU." (49) THEN HE SAID TO THEM, "WHY WERE
YOU LOOKING FOR ME? DO YOU NOT KNOW THAT
I MUST BE IN MY FATHER'S HOUSE?" (50) BUT
THEY DID NOT UNDERSTAND THIS ANSWER. (51)

JESUS WENT DOWN WITH THEM, RETURNING TO
NAZARETH, AND HE CONTINUED TO BE SUBJECT TO
THEM. AS FOR HIS MOTHER, SHE KEPT ALL THESE
THINGS IN HER HEART. (52) AND JESUS INCREASED
IN WISDOM AND AGE AND GRACE AND IN FA-
VOR WITH GOD AND MEN.

JOHN THE BAPTIST PREPARES THE WAY

3 (1) IT WAS THE FIFTEENTH YEAR OF THE
RULE OF THE EMPEROR TIBERIUS; PONTIUS
PILATUS WAS GOVERNOR OF JUDEA; HEROD
HAD AUTHORITY OVER GALILEE, HIS BROTHER
PHILIP RULED OVER
THE COUNTRY OF ITUREA
AND TRACHONITIS, AND LYS-
ANIAS OVER ABILENE. (2)
ANNAS AND CAIAPHAS WERE
THE HIGH PRIESTS WHEN
THE WORD OF GOD CAME
TO JOHN, THE SON OF ZE-
CHARIAH IN THE DESERT.
(3) JOHN PROCLAIMED
A BAPTISM FOR RE-
PENTANT PEOPLE TO
OBTAIN FORGIVENESS
OF SINS AND HE WENT
THROUGH THE WHOLE
COUNTRY BORDERING
THE JORDAN RIVER. (4)
IT WAS JUST AS IS
WRITTEN IN THE BO-
OK OF THE PROPHET
ISAIAH:

I HEAR A VOICE CRYING
OUT IN THE DESERT:
PREPARE THE WAY
OF THE LORD, MAKE
HIS PATH STRAIGHT.
(5) THE VALLEYS WILL BE FILLED AND THE
MOUNTAINS AND HILLS MADE LOW. EVERY-
THING CROOKED WILL BE MADE STRAIGHT AND
THE ROUGH PATHS SMOOTH; (6) AND EVERY
MORTAL WILL SEE THE SALVATION OF GOD.

(7) JOHN SAID TO THE CROWD WHO CAME OUT TO BE BAP-
TIZED BY HIM, "YOU BROOD OF VIPERS! HOW WILL YOU
ESCAPE WHEN DIVINE PUNISHMENT COMES? PRODU-
CE NOW (8) THE FRUITS OF A TRUE CHANGE OF HEART,
AND DO NOT DECEIVE YOURSELVES BY SAYING: 'WE ARE
SONS OF ABRAHAM,' FOR I TELL YOU, GOD CAN MAKE SONS
OF ABRAHAM FROM THESE STONES.

9 THE AXE IS ALREADY LAID TO THE ROOT OF THE TREE
AND EVERY TREE THAT FAILS TO PRODUCE GOOD FRUIT
WILL BE CUT DOWN AND THROWN INTO THE FIRE."
10 THE PEOPLE ASKED HIM, "WHAT ARE WE TO DO?"
11 AND JOHN ANSWERED, "IF YOU HAVE TWO COATS,
GIVE ONE TO THE PERSON WHO HAS NONE; AND IF
YOU HAVE FOOD, DO THE SAME. 12 EVEN TAX
COLLECTORS CAME TO BE BAPTIZED AND ASKED HIM,
"MASTER, WHAT MUST WE DO?" 13 JOHN SAID TO
THEM, "COLLECT NO MORE THAN YOUR FIXED RATE."
14 PEOPLE SERVING AS SOLDIERS ASKED JOHN,
"WHAT ABOUT US? WHAT ARE WE TO DO?" AND HE

ANSWERED, "DON'T TAKE ANYTHING BY FORCE OR
THREATEN THE PEOPLE BY DENOUNCING THEM
FALSELY. BE CONTENT WITH YOUR PAY."

15 THE PEOPLE WERE WONDERING ABOUT JOHN'S
IDENTITY. "COULD HE BE THE MESSIAH?" 16 THEN
JOHN ANSWERED THEM, "I BAPTIZE YOU WITH
WATER, BUT THE ONE WHO IS COMING WILL DO
MUCH MORE: HE WILL BAPTIZE YOU WITH HOLY

SPIRIT AND FIRE.
AS FOR ME, I AM NOT
WORTHY TO UNTIE
HIS SANDAL. 17 HE CO-
MES WITH A WINNO-
WING FAN TO CLEAR
HIS THRESHING FLOOR
AND GATHER THE GRAIN
INTO HIS BARN. BUT THE
CHAFF HE WILL BURN
WITH FIRE THAT NEVER
GOES OUT." 18 WITH
THESE AND MANY
OTHER WORDS JOHN
ANNOUNCED THE GO-
OD NEWS TO THE PE-
OPLE 19 UNTIL HE-
ROD HAD PUT HIM
IN PRISON, FOR JOHN
REPROACHED HEROD
FOR LIVING WITH
HERODIAS, THE
WIFE OF HIS BRO-
THER, AND FOR HIS
EVIL DEEDS.
20 THEN HEROD
ADDED ANOTHER
CRIME TO ALL THE REST HE HAD COMMITTED:
HE PUT JOHN IN PRISON.

JESUS IS BAPTISED BY JOHN

21 NOW, WITH ALL THE PEOPLE WHO CAME TO BE
BAPTIZED, JESUS TOO WAS BAPTIZED. THEN,
WHILE HE WAS PRAYING, THE HEAVENS OPENED:
22 THE HOLY SPIRIT CAME DOWN UPON HIM IN THE
BODILY FORM OF A DOVE AND A VOICE FROM
HEAVEN WAS HEARD,

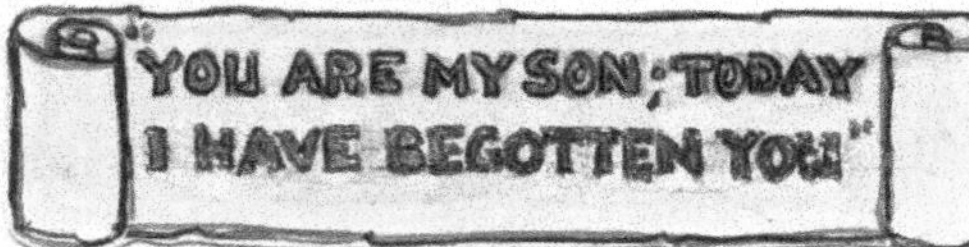

23 WHEN JESUS MADE HIS APPEARANCE, HE HAD
REACHED THE AGE OF THIRTY YEARS: HE WAS
KNOWN AS THE SON OF JOSEPH, WHOSE FATHER AND
FOREFATHERS WERE: HELI, 24 MATTHAT, LEVI, MEL-
KI, JANNAI, JOSEPH, 25 MATTATHIAS, AMOS, NA-
HUM, ESLI, NAGGAI, 26 MAATH, MATTATHIAS, SE-
MEIN, JOSECH, JODA, 27 JOANAN, RHESA,
ZERUBBABEL, SHEALTIEL, NERI, 28 MELKI,
ADDI, COSAM, ELMA-
DAM, ER, 29 JOSHUA,
ELIEZER, JORIM, MAT-
THAT, LEVI, 30 SI-
MEON, JUDAH, JO-
SEPH, JONAM, ELI-
AKIM, 31 MELEA,
MENNA, MATTHA-
THA, NATHAN, DA-
VID, 32 JESSE,
OBED, BOAZ, SAL-
MON, NAHSON,
33 AMMINADAB,
RAM, HEZRON, PE-
REZ, JUDAH, 34 JA-
COB, ISAAC, ABRA-
HAM, TERAH, NA-
HOR, 35 SERUG,
REU, PELEG, EBER,
SHELAH, 36 CAI-
NAN, ARPHAXAD, SHEM,
NOAH, LAMECH, 37
METHUSELAH, ENOCH,
JARED, MAHALEEL,
CAINAN, 38 ENOS,
SETH, AND ADAM,
WHO WAS FROM GOD.

JESUS TEMPTED IN THE WILDERNESS

4 1 JESUS WAS NOW FULL OF HOLY SPIRIT.
AS HE RETURNED FROM THE JORDAN, THE
SPIRIT LED HIM INTO THE DESERT WHERE
HE WAS 2 TEMPTED BY THE DEVIL FOR FOR-
TY DAYS. HE DID NOT EAT ANYTHING DURING THAT
TIME, AND IN THE END HE WAS HUNGRY. 3 THE DEVIL SAID
TO HIM, "IF YOU ARE SON OF GOD, TELL THIS STONE TO TURN
INTO BREAD." 4 BUT JESUS ANSWERED, "SCRIPTURE SAYS,
PEOPLE CANNOT LIVE ON BREAD ALONE." 5 THEN
THE DEVIL TOOK HIM UP TO A HIGH PLACE AND SHOWED

HIM IN A FLASH ALL THE NATIONS OF THE WORLD. 6
AND HE SAID TO JESUS, "I CAN GIVE YOU POWER OVER
ALL THE NATIONS AND THEIR WEALTH WILL BE YOURS,
FOR POWER AND WEALTH HAVE BEEN DELIVERED TO ME,
AND I GIVE THEM TO ANYONE I CHOOSE. 7 ALL THIS
WILL BE YOURS PROVIDED YOU WORSHIP ME."
8 BUT JESUS REPLIED, "SCRIPTURE SAYS:

YOU SHALL WORSHIP THE LORD YOUR
GOD AND SERVE HIM ALONE."

9 THEN THE DEVIL TOOK HIM UP TO JERUSALEM AND
AND SET HIM ON THE HIGHEST WALL OF THE TEMPLE;
AND HE SAID, "IF YOU ARE THE SON OF GOD, THROW YOUR-
SELF DOWN FROM HERE,

10 FOR IT IS WRITTEN:

GOD WILL ORDER HIS ANGELS TO TAKE CA-
RE OF YOU

11 AND AGAIN:

THEY WILL HOLD YOU IN THEIR HANDS,
LEST YOU HURT YOUR FOOT ON THE STONES."

12 BUT JESUS REPLIED," IT IS WRITTEN:

YOU SHALL NOT CHALLENGE THE LORD YOUR GOD."

13 WHEN THE DEVIL HAD EXHAUSTED EVERY WAY OF TEMPT-
ING JESUS, LEFT HIM, TO RETURN ANOTHER TIME.

JESUS PROCLAIMS HIS MISSION AT NAZARETH

14 JESUS ACTED WITH THE POWER OF THE SPIRIT, AND
ON HIS RETURN TO GALILEE THE NEWS ABOUT HIM SPREAD
THROUGHOUT ALL THAT TERRITORY. 15 HE TAUGHT IN
THE SYNAGOGUES OF THE JEWS AND EVERYONE PRAISED HIM.
16 WHEN JESUS CAME TO NAZARETH, WHERE HE HAD BEEN
BROUGHT UP, HE ENTERED THE SYNAGOGUE ON THE
SABBATH AS HE USUALLY DID. 17 HE STOOD UP AND
THEY HANDED HIM THE BOOK OF THE PROPHET ISAIAH.
JESUS THEN UNROLLED THE SCROLL AND FOUND
THE PLACE WHERE IT IS WRITTEN: 18

THE SPIRIT OF THE LORD IS UPON ME. HE HAS
ANOINTED ME TO BRING GOOD NEWS TO THE
POOR, TO PROCLAIM LIBERTY TO CAPTIVES
AND NEW SIGHT TO THE BLIND; TO FREE THE
OPPRESSED 19 AND ANNOUNCE THE
LORD'S YEAR OF MERCY."

20 JESUS THEN ROLLED UP THE SCROLL, GAVE IT TO THE
ATTENDANT AND SAT DOWN, WHILE THE EYES OF ALL IN
THE SYNAGOGUE WERE FIXED ON HIM. 21 THEN HE
SAID TO THEM, "TODAY THESE PROPHETIC WORDS COME
TRUE EVEN AS YOU LISTEN." 22 ALL AGREED WITH
HIM AND WERE LOST IN WONDER, WHILE HE KEPT ON
SPEAKING OF THE GRACE OF GOD. NEVERTHELESS
THEY ASKED, "WHO IS THIS BUT JOSEPH'S SON?"

23 SO HE SAID, "DOUBTLESS YOU WILL QUOTE
ME THE SAYING, "DOCTOR, HEAL YOURSELF! DO
HERE IN YOUR TOWN WHAT THEY SAY YOU DID IN
CAPERNAUM." 24 JESUS ADDED, "NO PROPHET
IS HONORED IN HIS OWN COUNTRY. 25 TRULY,
I SAY TO YOU, THERE WERE MANY WIDOWS IN
ISRAEL IN THE DAYS OF ELIJAH, WHEN THE HE-
AVENS WITHHELD RAIN FOR THREE YEARS AND
SIX MONTHS AND A
GREAT FAMINE CAME
OVER THE WHOLE LAND.
26 YET ELIJAH WAS NOT
SENT TO ANY OF THEM, BUT
TO A WIDOW OF ZARE-
PHATH, IN THE COUNTRY
OF SIDON. 27 THERE
WERE ALSO MANY
LEPERS IN ISRAEL
IN THE TIME OF EL-
ISHA, THE PROPHET,
AND NO ONE WAS
HEALED EXCEPT
NAAMAN, THE SYRIAN."
28 ON HEARING
THESE WORDS, THE
WHOLE ASSEMBLY
BECAME INDIGNANT.
29 THEY ROSE UP
AND BROUGHT HIM
OUT OF THE TOWN,
30 TO THE EDGE
OF THE HILL WHERE
NAZARETH IS BUILT,
INTENDING TO THROW
HIM DOWN THE CLIFF.
BUT HE PASSED
THROUGH THEIR MIDST AND WENT HIS WAY.

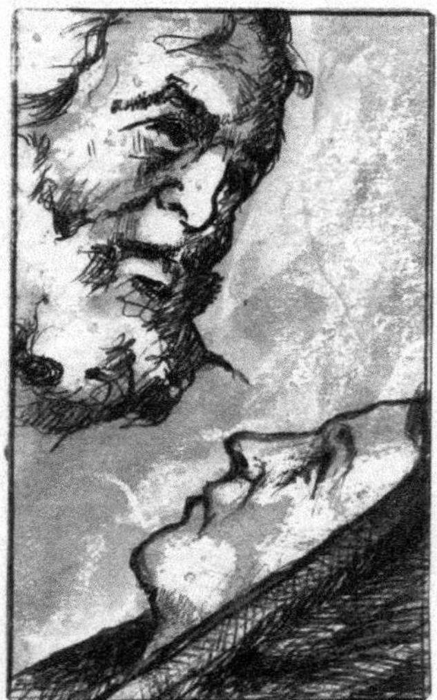

WITH THE POWER OF THE SPIRIT

31 JESUS WENT DOWN TO CAPERNAUM, A
TOWN OF GALILEE, AND BEGAN TEACHING THE
PEOPLE AT THE SABBATH MEETINGS. 32 THEY
WERE ASTONISHED AT THE WAY HE TAUGHT
THEM, FOR HIS WORD WAS SPOKEN WITH AUTHORITY.
33 IN THE SYNAGOGUE THERE WAS A MAN
POSSESSED BY A EVIL SPIRIT WHO SHOUTED IN
A LOUD VOICE, 34
"WHAT DO YOU WANT
WITH US, JESUS OF
NAZARETH? HAVE
YOU COME TO DESTROY
US? I RECOGNIZE YOU:
YOU ARE THE HOLY ONE
OF GOD." 35 THEN JESUS
SAID TO HIM SHARPLY,
"BE SILENT AND LEAVE
THIS MAN!" THE EVIL
SPIRIT THREW THE MAN
DOWN IN FRONT OF THEM
AND CAME OUT OF HIM
WITHOUT DOING HIM
HARM. 36 AMAZE-
MENT SEIZED ALL
THESE PEOPLE AND
THEY SAID TO ONE AN-
OTHER, "WHAT DOES
THIS MEAN? HE COM-
MANDS THE EVIL SPI-
RITS WITH AUTHORITY
AND POWER. HE ORDERS,
AND YOU SEE HOW THEY
COME OUT!" 37 AND
NEWS ABOUT JESUS
SPREAD THROUGH-
OUT THE SURROUND-
ING AREA.
38 LEAVING THE SYNAGOGUE, JESUS WENT TO THE
HOUSE OF SIMON. HIS MOTHER-IN-LAW WAS SUFFER-
ING FROM HIGH FEVER AND THEY ASKED HIM TO DO
SOMETHING FOR HER. 39 BENDING OVER HER, HE
REBUKED THE FEVER, AND IT LEFT HER. IMME-
DIATELY SHE GOT UP AND WAITED ON THEM.

(40) AT SUNSET, PEOPLE SUFFERING FROM MANY KINDS OF
SICKNESS WERE BROUGHT TO JESUS. LAYING HIS HANDS
ON EACH ONE, HE HEALED THEM. (41) DEMONS WERE
DRIVEN OUT, HOWLING AS THEY DEPARTED FROM THEIR
VICTIMS, "YOU ARE THE
SON OF GOD!" HE REBU-
KED THEM AND WOULD
NOT ALLOW THEM TO
SPEAK, FOR THEY KNEW
HE WAS THE MESSIAH.
(42) JESUS LEFT AT DAY-
BREAK AND LOOKED FOR
A SOLITARY PLACE. PE-
OPLE WENT OUT IN SE-
ARCH OF HIM AND, FIND-
ING HIM, THEY TRIED TO
DISSUADE HIM FROM
LEAVING. (43) BUT HE
SAID, "I HAVE TO GO TO
OTHER TOWNS TO ANNO-
UNCE THE GOOD NEWS

OF THE KINGDOM OF GOD. THAT IS WHAT I WAS SENT
TO DO." (44) SO JESUS CONTINUED TO PREACH IN THE
SYNAGOGUES OF THE JEWISH COUNTRY.

YOU WILL CATCH PEOPLE

5 (1) ONE DAY, AS JESUS STOOD BY THE LAKE OF
GENNESARET, WITH A CROWD GATHERED AROUND
HIM LISTENING TO THE WORD OF GOD, (2) HE CAUGHT
SIGHT OF TWO BOATS LEFT AT THE WATER'S EDGE BY
THE FISHERMEN NOW WASHING THEIR NETS. (3) HE
GOT INTO ONE OF THE BOATS, THE ONE OF SIMON, AND AS-
KED HIM TO PULL OUT A LITTLE FROM THE SHORE. THERE
HE SAT AND CONTINUED
TO TEACH THE CROWD.
(4) WHEN HE HAD FINI-
SHED SPEAKING HE SAID
TO SIMON, "PUT OUT INTO
DEEP WATER AND LOWER
YOUR NETS FOR A CATCH."
(5) SIMON REPLIED, "MAS-
TER, WE WORKED HARD
ALL NIGHT AND CAUGHT
NOTHING. BUT IF YOU SAY
SO, I WILL LOWER THE
NETS." (6) THIS THEY
DID AND CAUGHT SUCH A
LARGE NUMBER OF FISH
THAT THEIR NETS BEGAN
TO BREAK. (7) THEY SI-
GNALED THEIR PARTNERS
IN THE OTHER BOAT TO
COME AND HELP THEM.
THEY CAME AND FILLED
BOTH BOATS ALMOST TO
TO THE POINT OF SINK-
ING. (8) UPON SEEING
THIS, SIMON PETER FELL
AT JESUS' KNEES, SAYING,
"LEAVE ME, LORD, FOR I
AM A SINFUL MAN!" (9)

FOR HE AND HIS COMPANIONS WERE AMAZED AT THE
CATCH THEY HAD MADE (10) AND SO WERE SIMON'S
PARTNERS, JAMES AND JOHN, ZEBEDEE'S SONS.
JESUS SAID TO SIMON, "DO NOT BE AFRAID. YOU
WILL CATCH PEOPLE FROM NOW ON." (11) SO THEY BROUGHT
THE BOATS TO LAND AND FOLLOWED HIM, LEAVING EVERYTHING.

CURE OF A LEPER

(12) ONE DAY IN ANOTHER TOWN, A MAN CAME TO
JESUS COVERED WITH LEPROSY. ON SEEING HIM HE
BOWED DOWN TO THE GROUND, AND SAID, "LORD, IF
YOU WANT TO, YOU CAN MAKE ME CLEAN."

(13) STRETCHING OUT HIS HAND, JESUS TOUCHED
THE MAN SAYING, "YES, I WANT IT; BE CLEAN"
IN AN INSTANT THE LEPROSY LEFT HIM.
(14) THEN JESUS INSTRUCTED HIM, "TELL
THIS TO NO ONE. BUT GO AND SHOW YOURSELF
TO THE PRIEST. MAKE AN OFFERING FOR
YOUR HEALING, AS MOSES PRESCRIBED.
THAT

SHOULD BE A PROOF TO THE PEOPLE." (15) BUT
THE NEWS ABOUT JESUS SPREAD ALL THE MORE,
AND LARGE CROWDS CAME TO HIM TO LISTEN AND BE
HEALED OF THEIR SICKNESS. (16) AS FOR JESUS, HE
WOULD OFTEN WITHDRAW TO SOLITARY PLACES AND PRAY.

THE PARALYTIC SAVED

(17) ONE DAY JESUS WAS TEACHING AND MANY PHA-
RISEES AND TEACHERS OF THE LAW HAD COME
FROM EVERY TOWN IN GALILEE AND JUDEA AND
EVEN FROM JERUSALEM. THEY WERE SITTING THERE
WHILE THE POWER OF THE LORD WAS AT WORK TO HEAL THE
SICK. (18) THEN SOME MEN BROUGHT A PARALYZED MAN WHO
LAY ON HIS MAT. THEY TRIED TO ENTER THE HOUSE TO PLACE
HIM BEFORE JESUS, (19) BUT THEY COULDN'T FIND A WAY
THROUGH THE CROWD. SO THEY WENT UP ON THE ROOF
AND, REMOVING THE TILES, THEY LOWERED HIM ON HIS
MAT IN THE MIDDLE OF THE CROWD, IN FRONT OF JESUS.
(20) WHEN JESUS SAW THEIR FAITH, HE SAID TO THE
MAN, "MY FRIEND, YOUR SINS ARE FORGIVEN." (21) AT
ONCE THE TEACHERS OF THE LAW AND THE PHARISEES
BEGAN TO WONDER, "THIS MAN INSULTS GOD! WHO CAN
FORGIVE SINS BUT ONLY GOD?" (22) BUT JESUS KNEW
THEIR THOUGHTS AND ASKED THEM, "WHY ARE YOU

REACTING LIKE THIS?" (23) WHICH IS EASIER TO SAY: YOUR
SINS ARE FORGIVEN, OR: GET UP AND WALK? (24) NOW YOU
SHALL KNOW THAT THE SON OF MAN HAS AUTHORITY ON EARTH
TO FORGIVE SINS." AND HE SAID TO THE PARALYZED MAN, "GET UP,
TAKE YOUR MAT AND GO HOME." (25) AT ONCE THE MAN STOOD
BEFORE THEM. HE TOOK UP THE MAT HE HAD BEEN LYING ON AND
WENT HOME PRAISING GOD. (26) PEOPLE WERE AMAZED AND
PRAISED GOD, ALL FILLED WITH HOLY FEAR AND SAID, "WHAT
WONDERFUL THINGS WE HAVE SEEN TODAY!"

CALL OF LEVI

(27) AFTER THIS JESUS WENT OUT, AND AS HE NOTICED
A TAX COLLECTOR NAMED LEVI SITTING IN THE TAX-OF-
FICE HE SAID TO HIM, "FOLLOW ME." (28) SO LEVI, LEAVING
EVERYTHING, GOT UP AND FOLLOWED JESUS.

29 LEVI GAVE A GREAT FEAST FOR JESUS, AND MANY
TAX COLLECTORS CAME TO HIS HOUSE AND TOOK THEIR PLA-
CE AT TABLE WITH THE OTHER PEOPLE. 30 THEN THE PHA-
RISEES AND THEIR FELLOW TEACHERS COMPLAINED TO
JESUS' DISCIPLES, "HOW IS IT THAT YOU EAT AND DRINK
WITH TAX COLLECTORS AND OTHER SINNERS?" 31 BUT
JESUS SPOKE UP, "HEALTHY PEOPLE DON'T NEED A DOCTOR,
BUT SICK PEOPLE DO. 32 I HAVE COME TO CALL TO REPENT-
ANCE; I CALL SINNERS, NOT THE RIGHTEOUS". 33 SOME
PEOPLE ASKED HIM, "THE DISCIPLES OF JOHN FAST OFTEN
AND SAY PRAYERS, AND SO
DO THE DISCIPLES OF THE
PHARISEES. WHY IS IT
THAT YOUR DISCIPLES EAT
AND DRINK?" JESUS SAID,
34 "YOU CAN'T MAKE WED-
DING GUESTS FAST WHILE
THE BRIDEGROOM IS WITH
THEM. 35 BUT LATER THE
BRIDEGROOM WILL BE TA-
KEN FROM THEM AND THEY
WILL FAST IN THOSE DAYS."
36 JESUS ALSO TOLD THEM
THIS PARABLE, "NO ONE TEARS
A PIECE FROM A NEW COAT TO
PUT IT ON AN OLD ONE. IF HE
DOES, HE WILL HAVE TORN
THE NEW COAT AND THE PI-
ECE TAKEN FROM THE NEW
WILL NOT MATCH THE OLD.
37 NO ONE PUTS NEW WINE
INTO OLD WINESKINS; IF HE
DOES, THE NEW WINE WILL
BURST THE SKINS AND BE
SPILLED, AND THE SKINS
WILL BE DESTROYED AS
WELL. 38 BUT NEW WINE MUST BE PUT INTO FRESH SKINS.
39 YET NO ONE WHO HAS TASTED OLD WINE IS EAGER TO
GET NEW, FOR HE SAYS: THE OLD WINE IS GOOD."

JESUS, LORD OF THE SABBATH

6 1 ONE SABBATH JESUS WAS GOING THROUGH THE
CORNFIELDS AND HIS DISCIPLES BEGAN TO PICK HEADS
OF GRAIN CRUSHING THEM IN THEIR HANDS FOR FO-
OD. 2 SOME OF THE PHARISEES ASKED THEM, "WHY DO
YOU DO WHAT IS FORBIDDEN ON THE SABBATH?" 3 THEN
JESUS SPOKE, "HAVE YOU NEVER READ WHAT DAVID DID
WHEN HE AND HIS MEN WERE HUNGRY?" 4 HE ENTERED
THE HOUSE OF GOD, TOOK AND ATE THE BREAD OF THE
OFFERING AND EVEN GAVE SOME TO HIS MEN, THOUGH

ONLY PRIESTS ARE ALLOWED TO EAT THE BREAD." 5 AND
JESUS ADDED, "THE SON OF MAN IS LORD AND RULES
OVER THE SABBATH."
6 ON ANOTHER SABBATH JESUS ENTERED THE SYNA-
GOGUE AND BEGAN TEACHING. THERE WAS A MAN WITH A
PARALYZED HAND AND 7 THE TEACHERS OF THE LAW AND
THE PHARISEES WATCHED HIM: WOULD JESUS HEAL
THE MAN ON THE SABBATH? IF HE DID, THEY COULD AC-
CUSE HIM. 8 BUT JESUS KNEW THEIR THOUGHTS AND SAID
TO THE MAN, "GET UP AND STAND IN THE MIDDLE."
9 THEN HE SPOKE TO THEM, "I WANT TO ASK YOU:
WHAT IS ALLOWED BY THE LAW ON THE SABBATH, TO
DO GOOD OR TO DO HARM, TO SAVE LIFE OR DESTROY IT?"
10 AND JESUS LOOKED AROUND AT ALL OF THEM. THEN
HE SAID TO THE MAN, "STRETCH OUT YOUR HAND."

HE STRETCHED IT OUT AND HIS HAND WAS RESTORED,
BECOMING AS WHOLE AS THE OTHER. 11 BUT THEY

WERE FURIOUS AND BEGAN TO DISCUSS WITH ONE AN-
OTHER HOW THEY COULD DEAL WITH JESUS.

THE TWELVE

12 AT THIS TIME JESUS
WENT OUT INTO THE HILLS TO PRAY, SPENDING THE WHO-
LE NIGHT IN PRAYER WITH GOD. 13 WHEN DAY CAME, HE
CALLED HIS DISCIPLES TO HIM AND CHOSE TWELVE OF THEM
WHOM HE CALLED APOSTLES: 14 SIMON, WHOM HE NAMED
PETER, AND HIS BROTHER ANDREW, JAMES AND JOHN;
PHILIP AND BARTHOLOMEW; 15 MATTHEW AND THOMAS;
JAMES SON OF ALPHEUS AND SIMON CALLED THE ZEALOT;
16 JUDAS SON OF JAMES, AND JUDAS ISCARIOT, WHO WOULD
BE THE TRAITOR.

BLESSINGS AND WOES

17 COMING DOWN
THE HILL WITH THEM, JESUS STOOD ON A LEVEL PLACE. MANY
OF HIS DISCIPLES WERE THERE AND A LARGE CROWD OF
PEOPLE WHO HAD COME
FROM ALL PARTS OF JUDEA
AND JERUSALEM AND THE
COASTAL CITIES OF TYRE
AND SIDON. 18 THEY GA-
THERED TO HEAR HIM AND
BE HEALED OF THEIR DI-
SEASES; LIKEWISE PEOPLE
TROUBLED BY EVIL SPIRITS
WERE HEALED. 19 ALL THE
CROWD TRIED TO TOUCH
HIM BECAUSE OF THE PO-
WER WHICH WENT OUT FROM
HIM AND HEALED THEM ALL.
20 THEN LIFTING UP HIS
EYES TO HIS DISCIPLES,
JESUS SAID,

"FORTUNATE ARE YOU WHO
ARE THE POOR, THE KINGDOM
OF GOD IS YOURS."

21 FORTUNATE YOU WHO ARE
HUNGRY NOW, FOR YOU WILL
BE FILLED. FORTUNATE ARE
YOU WHO WEEP NOW, FOR
YOU WILL LAUGH.
22 FORTUNATE ARE YOU
WHEN PEOPLE HATE YOU, WHEN THEY REJECT YOU AND IN-
SULT YOU AND NUMBER YOU AMONG CRIMINALS, BECAUSE
OF THE SON OF MAN. 23 REJOICE IN THAT DAY AND LEAP
FOR JOY, FOR A GREAT REWARD IS KEPT FOR YOU IN HE-
AVEN. REMEMBER THAT IS HOW THE FATHERS OF
THIS PEOPLE TREATED THE PROPHETS.

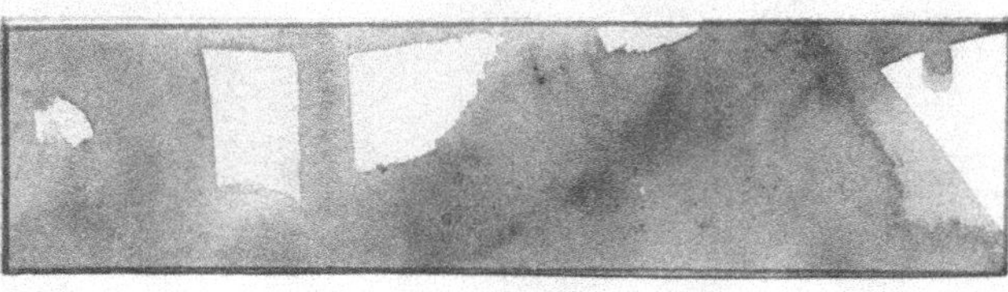

James
JOHN
Simon
Andrew
HOMAGE TO MODIGLIANI
337
CCCXXXVII
©
DM
09

24 BUT ALAS FOR YOU WHO HAVE WEALTH, FOR YOU
HAVE BEEN COMFORTED NOW. 25 ALAS FOR YOU WHO
ARE FULL, FOR YOU WILL GO HUNGRY. ALAS FOR YOU
WHO LAUGH NOW, FOR YOU WILL MOURN AND WEEP.
26 ALAS FOR YOU WHEN THE PEOPLE SPEAK
WELL OF YOU, FOR THAT IS HOW THE FATHERS OF
THESE PEOPLE TREATED THE FALSE PROPHETS.

LOVE OF ENEMIES

27 BUT I SAY TO YOU WHO HEAR ME: LOVE YOUR
ENEMIES, DO GOOD TO THOSE WHO HATE YOU.
28 BLESS THOSE WHO CURSE YOU AND PRAY

FOR THOSE WHO TREAT YOU BADLY. 29 TO THE ONE
WHO STRIKES YOU ON THE CHEEK, TURN THE OTHER
CHEEK; FROM THE ONE WHO TAKES YOUR COAT,
DO NOT KEEP BACK YOUR SHIRT. 30 GIVE TO
THE ONE WHO ASKS AND IF ANYONE HAS TAKEN
SOMETHING FROM YOU, DO NOT DEMAND IT BACK.
31 DO TO OTHERS AS YOU WOULD HAVE OTHERS DO TO
YOU. 32 IF YOU LOVE ONLY THOSE WHO LOVE YOU,
WHAT KIND OF GRACIOUSNESS IS YOURS? EVEN
SINNERS LOVE THOSE WHO LOVE THEM. 33 IF YOU
DO FAVORS TO THOSE WHO ARE GOOD TO YOU, WHAT
KIND OF GRACIOUSNESS IS YOURS? EVEN SINNERS DO
THE SAME. 34 IF YOU
LEND ONLY WHEN YOU
EXPECT TO RECEIVE, WHAT
KIND OF GRACIOUSNESS
IS YOURS? FOR SINNERS
ALSO LEND TO SINNERS,
EXPECTING TO RECEIVE
SOMETHING IN RETURN.
35 BUT LOVE YOUR ENE-
MIES AND DO GOOD TO
THEM, AND LEND WHEN
THERE IS NOTHING TO EX-
PECT IN RETURN. THEN
WILL YOU REWARD BE
GREAT AND YOU WILL
BE CHILDREN OF THE
MOST HIGH. FOR HE
IS KIND TOWARDS THE
UNGRATEFUL AND THE
WICKED. 36 BE MER-
CIFUL, JUST AS YOUR
FATHER IS MERCIFUL.
37 DON'T BE A JUD-
GE OF OTHERS AND YOU
WILL NOT BE JUDGED;
DO NOT CONDEMN
AND YOU WILL NOT

BE CONDEMNED; FORGIVE AND YOU WILL BE
FORGIVEN; 38 GIVE AND IT WILL BE GIVEN TO
YOU, AND YOU WILL RECEIVE IN YOUR SACK GOOD
MEASURE, PRESSED DOWN, FULL AND RUNNING
OVER. FOR THE MEASURE YOU GIVE WILL BE THE
MEASURE YOU RECEIVE BACK." 39 AND JESUS
OFFERED THIS EXAMPLE "CAN A BLIND PERSON
LEAD ANOTHER BLIND PERSON? SURELY BOTH
WILL FALL INTO A DITCH. 40 NO DISCIPLE IS
ABOVE HIS MASTER; IF HE LET HIMSELF BE FORMED,
HE WILL BE LIKE HIS MASTER.

41 SO WHY DO YOU PAY ATTENTION TO THE SPECK
IN YOUR BROTHER'S EYE WHILE YOU HAVE A LOG
IN YOUR EYE AND ARE NOT CONSCIOUS OF IT? 42
HOW CAN YOU SAY TO YOUR BROTHER: 'BROTHER,
LET ME TAKE THIS SPECK OUT OF YOUR EYE,' IF
AND WHEN YOU CAN'T REMOVE THE LOG IN YOUR
OWN? YOU HYPOCRITE! FIRST REMOVE THE
LOG FROM YOUR OWN
EYE AND THEN YOU
WILL SEE CLEARLY
ENOUGH TO REMOVE
THE SPECK FROM YOUR
BROTHER'S EYE. 43
NO HEALTHY TREE BE-
ARS BAD FRUIT, NO PO-
OR TREE BEARS GOOD
FRUIT. 44 AND EACH TREE
IS KNOWN BY THE FRUIT IT
BEARS. MOREOVER, YOU
DON'T GATHER FIGS FROM
THORNS, OR GRAPES FROM
BRAMBLES. 45 SIMILARLY,
A GOOD PERSON DRAWS GO-
OD THINGS FROM THE GOOD
OF HIS HEART, AND AN EVIL
PERSON DRAWS EVIL
THINGS FROM THE EVIL
OF HIS HEART. FOR THE
MOUTH SPEAKS FROM THE
FULLNESS OF THE HEART.
46 WHY DO YOU CALL
ME: 'LORD, LORD!' AND NOT
DO WHAT I SAY? 47 I
WILL SHOW YOU WHAT
THE ONE WHO COMES TO ME
AND LISTENS TO MY WORDS
AND ACTS ACCORDINGLY, IS
LIKE. 48 HE IS LIKE

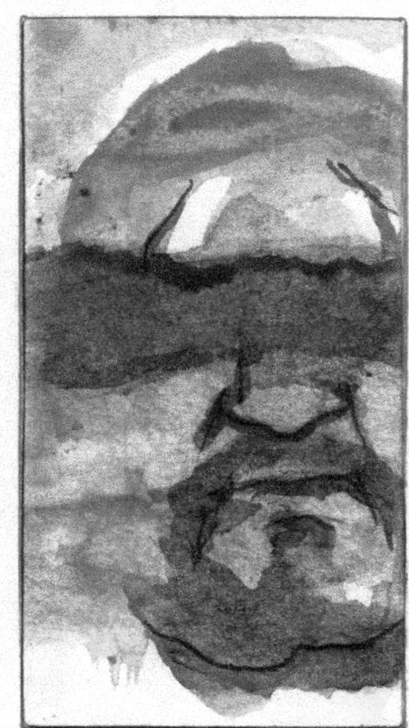

THE BUILDER WHO DUG DEEP AND LAID THE FOUNDATIONS
OF HIS HOUSE ON ROCK. THE RIVER OVERFLOWED AND THE
STREAM DASHED AGAINST THE HOUSE, BUT COULD NOT CAR-
RY IT OFF BECAUSE THE HOUSE HAD BEEN WELL BUILT.
49 BUT IF ANYONE LISTENS AND DOES NOT ACT, HE IS
LIKE A MAN WHO BUILT HIS HOUSE ON THE GROUND

WITHOUT A FOUNDATION. THE FLOOD BURST AGAINST IT, AND
THE HOUSE FELL AT ONCE; AND WHAT A DISASTER THAT WAS!"

THE FAITH OF A PAGAN

7 1 WHEN JESUS HAD FINISHED TEACHING IN THIS WAY
THE PEOPLE LISTENING TO HIM, HE WENT TO CAPERNAUM.
2 THERE WAS A CAPTAIN WHOSE SERVANT WAS VERY
SICK, NEAR TO DEATH, A MAN VERY DEAR TO HIM. 3 SO WHEN
HE HEARD OF JESUS, HE SENT SOME ELDERS OF THE JEWS TO
PERSUADE HIM TO COME AND SAVE HIS SERVANT'S LIFE. 4 THE
ELDERS CAME TO JESUS AND BEGGED HIM EARNESTLY, SAY-
ING, 5 "HE DESERVES THIS OF YOU, FOR HE LOVES OUR PE-
OPLE AND EVEN BUILT A SYNAGOGUE FOR US." 6 JESUS
WENT WITH THEM. HE WAS NOT FAR FROM THE HOUSE WHEN
THE CAPTAIN SENT FRIENDS TO GIVE THIS MESSAGE, "SIR,
DO NOT TROUBLE YOURSELF FOR I AM NOT WORTHY TO WEL-
COME YOU UNDER MY ROOF. 7 YOU SEE I DIDN'T AP-
PROACH YOU MYSELF. JUST GIVE THE ORDER AND
MY SERVANT WILL BE HEALED,

(8) FOR I MYSELF, A JUNIOR OFFICER, GIVE ORDERS TO MY SOLDIERS AND I SAY TO THIS ONE: 'GO', AND HE GOES, AND TO THE OTHER: 'COME', AND HE COMES; AND TO MY SERVANT: 'DO THIS,' AND HE DOES IT." (9) ON HEARING THESE WORDS, JESUS WAS FILLED WITH ADMIRATION. HE TURNED AND SAID TO THE PEOPLE WITH HIM, "I SAY TO YOU, NOT EVEN IN ISRAEL HAVE I FOUND SUCH GREAT FAITH." (10) THE PEOPLE SENT BY THE CAPTAIN WENT BACK TO HIS HOUSE AND THERE THEY FOUND THE SERVANT WELL.

THE SON OF A WIDOW RESTORED TO LIFE

(11) A LITTLE LATER JESUS WENT TO A TOWN CALLED NAIM AND MANY OF HIS DISCIPLES WENT WITH HIM, VERY MANY PEOPLES. (12) AS HE REACHED THE GATE OF THE TOWN, A DEAD MAN WAS CARRIED OUT. HE WAS THE ONLY SON OF HIS MOTHER AND SHE WAS A WIDOW; THERE FOLLOWED A LARGE CROWD OF TOWNSPEOPLE. (13) ON SEEING HER THE LORD HAD PITY ON HER AND SAID, "DON'T CRY". (14) THEN HE CAME UP AND TOUCHED THE STRETCHER AND THE MEN WHO CARRIED IT STOPPED. JESUS THEN SAID, "YOUNG MAN, AWAKE, I TELL YOU." (15) AND THE DEAD MAN GOT UP AND BEGAN TO SPEAK, AND JESUS GAVE HIM TO HIS MOTHER. (16) A HOLY FEAR CAME OVER THEM ALL AND THEY PRAISED GOD SAYING, "A GREAT PROPHET HAS APPEARED AMONG US; GOD HAS VISITED HIS PEOPLE." (17) AND THROUGHOUT JUDEA AND THE COUNTRY AREA PEOPLE TALKED OF JESUS' DEEDS.

THE MESSENGERS OF JOHN

(18) THE DISCIPLES OF JOHN GAVE HIM ALL THIS NEWS. SO HE CALLED TWO OF THEM AND (19) SENT THEM TO THE LORD WITH THIS MESSAGE, "ARE YOU THE ONE WE ARE EXPECTING, OR SHOULD WE WAIT FOR ANOTHER?" (20) THESE MEN CAME TO JESUS AND SAID,

"JOHN THE BAPTIST SENT US TO ASK YOU: ARE YOU THE ONE WE ARE TO EXPECT, OR SHOULD WE WAIT FOR ANOTHER? (21) AT THAT TIME JESUS HEALED MANY PEOPLE OF THEIR SICKNESS OR DISEASES: HE FREED THEM FROM EVIL SPIRITS AND HE GAVE SIGHT TO THE BLIND. (22) THEN HE ANSWERED THE MESSENGERS," GO BACK AND TELL JOHN WHAT YOU HAVE SEEN AND HEARD: THE BLIND SEE AGAIN, THE LAME WALK, LEPERS ARE MADE CLEAN, THE DEAF HEAR, THE DEAD ARE RAISED TO LIFE, AND THE POOR ARE GIVEN GOOD NEWS. NOW, LISTEN: (23) FORTUNATE ARE THOSE WHO ENCOUNTER ME, BUT NOT FOR THEIR DOWNFALL."

(24) WHEN JOHN'S MESSENGERS HAD GONE, JESUS BEGAN SPEAKING TO THE PEOPLE ABOUT JOHN. AND HE SAID, "WHAT DID YOU WANT TO SEE WHEN YOU WENT TO THE DESERT? A TALL REED BLOWING IN THE WIND? (25) WHAT WAS THERE TO SEE? A MAN DRESSED IN FINE CLOTHES? BUT PEOPLE WHO WEAR FINE CLOTHES AND ENJOY DELICATE FOOD ARE FOUND IN PALACES. (26) WHAT DID YOU GO OUT TO SEE? A PROPHET? YES, I TELL YOU, AND MORE THAN A PROPHET. (27) FOR JOHN IS THE ONE FORETOLD IN SCRIPTURE IN THESE WORDS:

I AM SENDING MY MESSENGER AHEAD OF YOU TO PREPARE YOUR WAYS.

(28) NO ONE MAY BE FOUND GREATER THAN JOHN FROM THE SONS OF WOMAN BUT, I TELL YOU, THE LEAST IN

THE KINGDOM OF GOD IS GREATER THAN HE. (29) ALL THE PEOPLE LISTENING TO HIM, EVEN THE TAX COLLECTORS, HAD ACKNOWLEDGED THE WILL OF GOD IN RECEIVING THE BAPTISM OF JOHN, (30) WHEREAS THE PHARISEES AND THE TEACHERS OF THE LAW IGNORED HIS BAPTISM AND THE WILL OF GOD. (31) WHAT COMPARISON CAN I USE FOR THIS PEOPLE? WHAT ARE THEY LIKE? (32) THEY ARE LIKE CHILDREN SITTING IN THE MARKETPLACE, COMPLAINING TO THEIR COMPANIONS: "WE PIPED YOU A TUNE AND YOU WOULDN'T DANCE; WE SANG FUNERAL SONGS AND YOU WOULDN'T CRY.'

(33) REMEMBER JOHN: HE DIDN'T EAT BREAD OR DRINK WINE, AND YOU SAID: 'HE HAS AN EVIL SPIRIT.' (34) NEXT CAME THE SON OF MAN, EATING AND DRINKING, AND YOU SAY: 'LOOK, A GLUTTON FOR FOOD AND WINE, A FRIEND OF TAX COLLECTORS AND SINNERS.' (35) BUT THE CHILDREN OF WISDOM ALWAYS RECOGNIZE HER WORK."

JESUS, THE WOMAN AND THE PHARISEE

(36) ONE OF THE PHARISEES ASKED JESUS TO SHARE HIS MEAL, SO HE WENT TO THE PHARISEE'S HOME AND AS USUAL RECLINED ON THE SOFA TO EAT. (37) AND IT HAPPENED THAT A WOMAN OF THIS TOWN, WHO WAS KNOWN AS A SINNER, HEARD THAT HE WAS IN THE PHARISEE'S HOUSE. SHE BROUGHT A PRECIOUS JAR OF PERFUME (38) AND STOOD BEHIND HIM AT HIS FEET, WEEPING. SHE WET HIS FEET WITH TEARS, SHE DRIED THEM WITH HER HAIR AND KISSED HIS FEET AND POURED THE PERFUME ON THEM. (39) THE PHARISEE WHO HAD INVITED JESUS WAS WATCHING AND THOUGHT, "IF THIS MAN WERE A PROPHET, HE WOULD KNOW WHAT SORT OF PERSON IS TOUCHING HIM: ISN'T THIS WOMAN A SINNER?" (40) THEN JESUS LOOKED AT THE PHARISEE AND SAID TO HIM, "SIMON, I HAVE SOMETHING TO ASK YOU." HE ANSWERED, "SPEAK, MASTER." AND JESUS SAID,

41 "TWO PEOPLE WERE IN DEBT TO THE SAME CREDITOR.
ONE OWED HIM FIVE HUNDRED SILVER COINS, AND THE OTHER
FIFTY. 42 AS THEY WERE UNABLE TO PAY HIM BACK, HE
GRACIOUSLY CANCELED THE DEBTS OF BOTH. NOW,
WHICH OF THEM WILL LOVE HIM MORE?" 43 SIMON AN-
SWERED, "THE ONE, I SUPPOSE, WHO WAS FORGIVEN MORE."
AND JESUS SAID, "YOU ARE RIGHT." 44 AND TURNING
TOWARD THE WOMAN, HE SAID TO SIMON, "DO YOU SEE
THIS WOMAN? 45 YOU GAVE ME NO WATER FOR MY
FEET WHEN I ENTERED YOUR HOUSE, BUT SHE HAS
WASHED MY FEET WITH HER TEARS AND DRIED THEM
WITH HER HAIR. YOU DIDN'T WELCOME ME WITH A KISS,
BUT SHE HAS NOT STOPPED KISSING MY FEET SINCE SHE

CAME IN. 46 YOU PROVIDED NO OIL FOR MY HEAD, BUT SHE
HAS POURED PERFUME ON MY FEET. 47 THIS IS WHY, I TELL
YOU, HER SINS, MANY SINS, ARE FORGIVEN, BECAUSE OF
HER GREAT LOVE. BUT THE ONE WHO IS FORGIVEN LITTLE, HAS
LITTLE LOVE." 48 JESUS SAID TO THE WOMAN, "YOUR SINS
ARE FORGIVEN." 49 THE OTHERS SITTING WITH HIM AT
THE TABLE BEGAN TO WONDER, "NOW THIS MAN CLAIMS
TO FORGIVE SINS!" 50 BUT JESUS AGAIN SPOKE TO THE WOMAN,
"YOUR FAITH HAS SAVED YOU: GO IN PEACE."

THE WOMEN WHO FOLLOWED JESUS

8 1 JESUS WALKED THROUGH TOWNS AND CO-
UNTRYSIDE, PREACHING AND GIVING THE
GOOD NEWS OF THE KINGDOM OF GOD. THE

TWELVE FOLLOWED
HIM. 2 AND ALSO
SOME WOMEN WHO
HAD BEEN HEALED
OF EVIL SPIRITS AND
DISEASES: MARY
CALLED MAGDALENE,
WHO HAD BEEN FREED
OF SEVEN DEMONS;
3 JOANNA, WIFE OF
CHUZA, HEROD'S
STEWARD; SUZANNA
AND OTHERS WHO
PROVIDED FOR
THEM OUT OF THEIR
OWN FUNDS.

PARABLE OF THE SOWER

4 AS A GREAT CROWD
GATHERED, PEOPLE CAME
TO HIM FROM EVERY TOWN,
JESUS BEGAN TEACHING
THEM THROUGH STORIES,
OR PARABLES. 5 "THE SOWER WENT OUT TO SOW THE
SEED. AND AS HE SOWED, SOME OF THE GRAIN FELL
ALONG THE WAY, WAS TRODDEN ON AND THE BIRDS OF THE
SKY ATE IT UP. 6 SOME FELL ON ROCKY GROUND, AND NO
SOONER HAD IT COME UP THAN IT WITHERED, BECAUSE IT
HAD NO WATER; 7 SOME FELL AMONG THORNS; THE
THORNS GREW UP WITH THE SEED AND CHOKED IT. 8
BUT SOME FELL AND GOOD SOIL AND GREW, PRODU-
CING FRUIT, A HUNDRED TIMES AS MUCH." AND JESUS
CRIED OUT, "LISTEN THEN, IF YOU HAVE EARS TO HEAR!"

9 THE DISCIPLES ASKED HIM, "WHAT DOES THIS STO-
RY MEANS?" 10 AND JESUS ANSWERED, "YOU HAVE
BEEN GRANTED TO KNOW THE MYSTERY OF THE KING-
DOM OF GOD. BUT TO OTHERS IT IS GIVEN IN THE FORM
OF STORIES, OR PARABLES, SO THAT SEEING THEY
MAY NOT PERCEIVE AND HEARING THEY MAY NOT
UNDERSTAND." 11 THE POINT OF THE PARABLE:

THE SEED IS THE WORD OF GOD. 12 THOSE ALONG THE
WAYSIDE ARE PEOPLE WHO HEAR IT, BUT IMMEDIATELY
THE DEVIL COMES AND TAKES

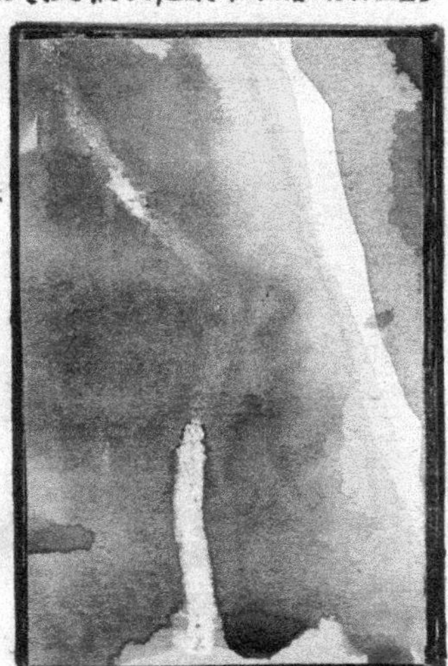

THE WORD FROM THEIR MINDS,
FOR HE DOESN'T WANT THEM
TO BELIEVE AND BE SAVED.
13 THOSE ON THE ROCKY GRO-
UND ARE PEOPLE WHO RECEIVE
THE WORD WITH JOY, BUT THEY
HAVE NO ROOT; THEY BELIEVE
FOR A WHILE AND GIVE WAY
IN TIME OF TRIAL. AMONG
14 THE THORNS ARE PE-
OPLE WHO HEAR THE WORD
BUT AS THEY GO THEIR WAY,
ARE CHOKED BY WORRIES,
RICHES, AND THE PLEASURES
OF LIFE; THEY BRING NO
FRUIT TO MATURITY. 15
THE GOOD SOIL, INSTEAD,
ARE PEOPLE WHO RECEIVE
THE WORD AND KEEP IT IN A
GENTLE AND GENEROUS MIND
AND PERSEVERING PATIENTLY
THEY BEAR FRUIT. 16 NO ONE,
AFTER LIGHTING A LAMP CO-
VERS IT WITH A BOWL OR
PUTS IT UNDER THE BED;
RATHER HE PUTS IT ON A LAMPSTAND SO THAT PEOPLE CO-
MING IN MAY SEE THE LIGHT. IN THE SAME WAY, 17 THERE
IS NOTHING HIDDEN THAT SHALL NOT BE UNCOVERED; NOTHING
KEPT SECRET THAT SHALL NOT BE KNOWN CLEARLY. 18
NOW, TAKE CARE HOW WELL YOU LISTEN, FOR WHOEVER PRO-
DUCES WILL BE GIVEN MORE, BUT HE WHO DOES NOT PRODUCE,
EVEN WHAT HE SEEMS TO HAVE WILL BE TAKEN AWAY FROM HIM."

JESUS' MOTHER AND BROTHERS

19 THEN HIS MOTHER AND HIS RELATIVES CAME TO HIM
BUT THEY COULD NOT GET TO HIM BECAUSE OF THE CROWD.
20 SOMEONE TOLD HIM, "YOUR MOTHER AND YOUR BROTHERS

ARE STANDING OUTSIDE AND WISH TO MEET YOU." 21 THEN
JESUS ANSWERED, "MY MOTHER AND MY BROTHERS ARE
THOSE WHO HEAR THE WORD OF GOD AND DO IT."

JESUS CALMS THE STORM

22 ONE DAY JESUS GOT INTO A BOAT WITH HIS DISCI-
PLES AND SAID TO THEM, "LET US GO ACROSS TO THE OTHER
SIDE OF THE LAKE." 23 SO THEY SET OUT, AND AS THEY SA-
ILED HE FELL ASLEEP. SUDDENLY A STORM CAME
DOWN ON THE LAKE AND THE BOAT BEGAN TO FILL
WITH WATER, AND THEY WERE IN DANGER.

SO THAT SEEING THEY MAY
NOT PERCEIVE AND
HEARING THEY MAY NOT
UNDERSTAND! (LUKE 8:10
338 CCCXXXVIII
© DM 07

(24) THE DISCIPLES WENT TO JESUS TO WAKE HIM, SAYING, "MASTER! MASTER! WE ARE SINKING!" JESUS WOKE UP HE REBUKED THE WIND AND THE ROLLING WAVES; THE STORM SUBSIDED, AND ALL WAS QUIET. (25) THEN JESUS SAID TO THEM, "WHERE IS YOUR FAITH?" THEY WERE AFRAID; THEY WERE ASTONISHED AS WELL AND SAID TO ONE ANOTHER, "WHO CAN THIS BE? SEE, HE COMMANDS EVEN THE WINDS AND THE SEA AND THEY OBEY HIM!"

THE POSSESSED MAN AND THE PIGS

(26) THE CROSSING ENDED IN THE COUNTRY OF GERASENES, ON THE SHORE FACING GALILEE. (27) AS JESUS STEPPED ASHORE, A MAN FROM THE TOWN APPROACHED HIM.

THIS MAN WAS POSSESSED BY DEMONS AND FOR A LONG TIME HE WAS WITHOUT CLOTHES, NOT LIVING IN A HOUSE, BUT AMONG TOMBS. (28) ONCE NEAR JESUS, HE YELLED, THREW HIMSELF ON THE GROUND AND SHOUTED, "WHAT DO YOU WANT WITH ME, JESUS, SON OF THE MOST HIGH GOD? I BEG YOU, DO NOT TORMENT ME." (29) FOR JESUS HAD ORDERED THE EVIL SPIRIT TO LEAVE THE MAN. THIS SPIRIT HAD SEIZED HIM MANY TIMES AS HE HAD BEEN BOUND WITH ROPES AND CHAINS AND KEPT UNDER CONTROL. HE WOULD SUDDENLY BREAK THE CHAINS AND BE DRIVEN BY THE EVIL SPIRIT INTO WILD PLACES. WHEN JESUS ASKED, (30) "WHAT IS YOUR NAME?", THE MAN SAID, "I AM LEGION", FOR MANY DEMONS HAD ENTERED INTO HIM. (31) AND THEY BEGGED JESUS NOT TO COMMAND THEM TO GO INTO THE PIT. (32) NEARBY A GREAT HERD OF PIGS WAS FEEDING SO THE DEMONS ASKED TO BE ALLOWED TO ENTER THE PIGS; AND JESUS LET THEM GO. (33) THE DEMONS THEN LEFT THE MAN AND ENTERED THE PIGS, AND THE HERD RUSHED DOWN INTO THE LAKE AND WAS DROWNED. (34) WHEN THE HERDSMEN SAW WHAT HAD HAPPENED, THEY FLED AND REPORTED IT IN THE TOWN AND COUNTRYSIDE. (35) THEN PEOPLE WENT OUT TO SEE WHAT HAD HAPPENED AND CAME TO JESUS. AND THERE THEY SAW THE MAN FROM WHOM THE DEMONS HAD

BEEN DRIVEN OUT. HE WAS CLOTHED AND IN HIS RIGHT MIND, AND WAS SITTING AT THE FEET OF JESUS. THEY WERE AFRAID. (36) THE PEOPLE WHO HAD SEEN IT TOLD THEM HOW THE MAN HAD BEEN HEALED, (37) AND ALL THIS CROWD FROM THE GERASENE COUNTRY ASKED JESUS TO DEPART FROM THEM, FOR A GREAT FEAR TOOK HOLD OF THEM. SO JESUS GOT INTO THE BOAT TO RETURN. (38) THEN THE MAN FREED OF THE DEMONS ASKED JESUS IF HE COULD STAY WITH HIM. (39) BUT JESUS SENT HIM ON HIS WAY, "GO BACK TO YOUR FAMILY AND TELL THEM HOW MUCH GOD HAS DONE FOR YOU." SO THE MAN WENT AWAY, PROCLAIMING THROUGH THE WHOLE TOWN HOW MUCH JESUS HAD DONE FOR HIM.

A WOMAN IS HEALED AND A CHILD RAISED TO LIFE

(40) WHEN JESUS RETURNED, THE PEOPLE WELCOMED HIM, FOR ALL HAD BEEN WAITING FOR HIM. (41) AT THAT TIME A MAN NAMED JAIRUS, AN OFFICIAL OF THE SYNAGOGUE, THREW HIMSELF AT JESUS FEET AND BEGGED HIM TO COME TO HIS HOUSE (42) BECAUSE HIS ONLY DAUGHTER, ABOUT TWELVE YEARS OLD, WAS DYING. AS JESUS WAS ON HIS WAY, THE CROWD PRESSED FROM EVERY SIDE. (43) THERE WAS A WOMAN WHO HAD SUFFERED FROM A BLEEDING FOR TWELVE YEARS. THIS WOMAN HAD SPENT EVERYTHING SHE HAD ON DOCTORS, BUT NONE OF THEM HAD BEEN ABLE TO CURE HER. (44) NOW SHE CAME UP BEHIND HIM AND TOUCHED THE FRINGE OF HIS CLOAK, AND HER

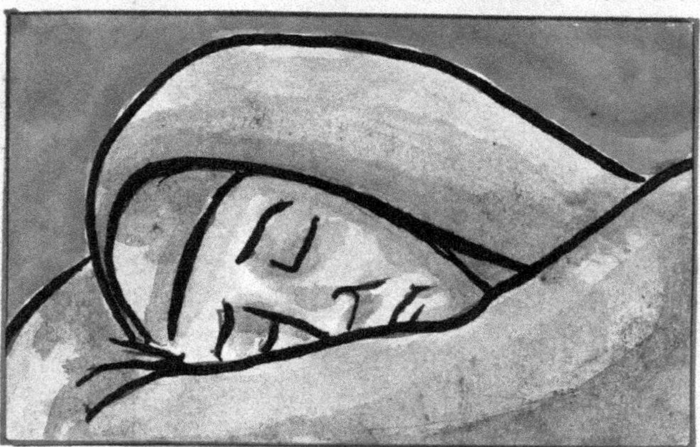

BLEEDING STOPPED AT ONCE. (45) JESUS ASKED, "WHO TOUCHED ME?" EVERYONE DENIED IT AND PETER SAID, "MASTER, THE CROWD IS PUSHING ALL AROUND YOU." (46) BUT JESUS SAID "SOMEONE TOUCHED ME, FOR I FELT POWER GO OUT FROM ME". (47) THE WOMAN KNEW SHE HAD BEEN DISCOVERED. SHE CAME TREMBLING AND KNELT BEFORE JESUS AND SHE OPENLY CONFESSED WHY SHE HAD TOUCHED HIM AND HOW SHE HAD BEEN INSTANTLY CURED. (48) JESUS SAID TO HER, "DAUGHTER, YOUR FAITH HAS SAVED YOU. GO IN PEACE."

(49) JESUS WAS SPEAKING WHEN A MAN ARRIVED FROM THE OFFICIAL'S HOME TO TELL HIM, "YOUR DAUGHTER HAS DIED; DON'T TROUBLE THE MASTER ANY MORE." BUT JESUS (50) HEARD THE NEWS AND SAID TO THE OFFICIAL, "DO NOT FEAR, ONLY BELIEVE." (51) JESUS ENTERED THE HOUSE AND HE WANTED ONLY PETER, JAMES AND JOHN TO FOLLOW HIM, WITH THE FATHER AND MOTHER OF THE CHILD. (52) AS ALL THE PEOPLE WERE WEEPING AND WAILING LOUDLY, JESUS SAID TO THEM, "DO NOT WEEP, SHE IS NOT DEAD BUT ASLEEP." (53) AND THEY LAUGHED AT HIM, KNOWING THAT SHE WAS DEAD (54) AS FOR JESUS, HE TOOK THE CHILD BY THE HAND AND SAID TO HER, "CHILD, WAKE UP!" (55) AND HER SPIRIT RETURNED AND SHE GOT UP AT ONCE; THEN JESUS TOLD THEM TO GIVE HER SOMETHING TO EAT. (56) THE PARENTS WERE AMAZED, BUT JESUS ORDERED THEM NOT TO LET ANYONE KNOW WHAT HAD HAPPENED.

JESUS AND THE MISSION

9 (1) JESUS CALLED HIS TWELVE DISCIPLES AND GAVE THEM POWER AND AUTHORITY TO DRIVE OUT ALL EVIL SPIRITS AND TO HEAL DISEASES. (2) HE SENT THEM TO PROCLAIM THE KINGDOM OF GOD AND TO HEAL THE SICK. (3) HE INSTRUCTED THEM, "DON'T TAKE ANYTHING FOR THE JOURNEY, NEITHER WALKING STICK, NOR BAG, NOR BREAD, NOR SILVER COINS OR EVEN A SPARE TUNIC.

4 WHATEVER HOUSE YOU ENTER, REMAIN THERE
UNTIL YOU LEAVE THAT PLACE. 5 AND WHER-
EVER THEY DON'T WELCOME YOU, LEAVE THE
TOWN AND SHAKE THE DUST FROM YOUR FEET:
IT WILL BE AS A TESTIMONY AGAINST THEM."
6 SO THEY SET OUT AND WENT THROUGH THE
VILLAGES, PROCLAIMING THE GOOD NEWS AND
HEALING PEOPLE EVERYWHERE.
7 KING HEROD HEARD OF ALL THIS AND DID
NOT KNOW WHAT TO THINK, FOR PEOPLE SAID,
"THIS IS JOHN, RAISED FROM THE DEAD."
8 OTHERS BELIEVED THAT ELIJAH OR ONE

OF THE ANCIENT PROPHETS HAD COME BACK TO
LIFE. 9 AS FOR HEROD, HE SAID, "I HAD JOHN
BEHEADED; WHO IS THE MAN ABOUT WHOM
I HEAR SUCH WONDERS?" AND HE WAS ANXIOUS
TO SEE HIM. 10 ON THEIR RETURN THE APOSTLES
TOLD JESUS EVERYTHING THEY HAD DONE. THEN HE
TOOK THEM ASIDE TO A LONELY PLACE, AND
THEY WENT AWAY TO A TOWN CALLED BETHSAIDA
TO BE BY THEMSELVES. 11 BUT THE CROWD HEARD
OF THIS AND CAUGHT UP WITH HIM. SO HE WELCOMED THEM
AND BEGAN SPEAKING OF THE KINGDOM OF GOD, CU-
RING THOSE WHO NEEDED HEALING.

MIRACLE OF THE LOAVES

12 THE DAY WAS DRAWING TO A CLOSE AND THE
TWELVE DREW NEAR TO TELL HIM, "SEND THE
CROWD AWAY AND LET THEM GO INTO THE VILLAGES

AND FARMS AROUND TO
FIND LODGING AND FOOD,
FOR WE ARE HERE IN A
LONELY PLACE." 13
BUT JESUS REPLIED,
"YOU YOURSELVES GIVE
THEM SOMETHING TO
EAT." THEY ANSWERED
"WE HAVE ONLY FIVE LO-
AVES AND TWO FISH: DO YOU
WANT US TO GO AND BUY FOOD
FOR ALL THIS CROWD?" 14
FOR THERE WERE ABOUT
FIVE THOUSAND MEN. THEN
JESUS SAID TO HIS DISCI-
PLES, "MAKE PEOPLE SIT
DOWN IN GROUPS OF FIF-
TIES." 15 SO THEY MA-
DE ALL OF THEM SETTLE
DOWN. 16 JESUS THEN
TOOK THE FIVE LOAVES
AND TWO FISH, AND RA-
ISING HIS EYES TO HE-
AVEN, PRONOUNCED A
BLESSING OVER THEM, HE BROKE THEM AND GAVE
THEM TO THE DISCIPLES TO DISTRIBUTE TO THE
CROWD. 17 THEY ATE AND EVERYONE HAD ENOUGH;
AND THEY THEN GATHERED UP WHAT WAS LEFT, AND
TWELVE BASKETS WERE FILLED WITH BROKEN PIECES.

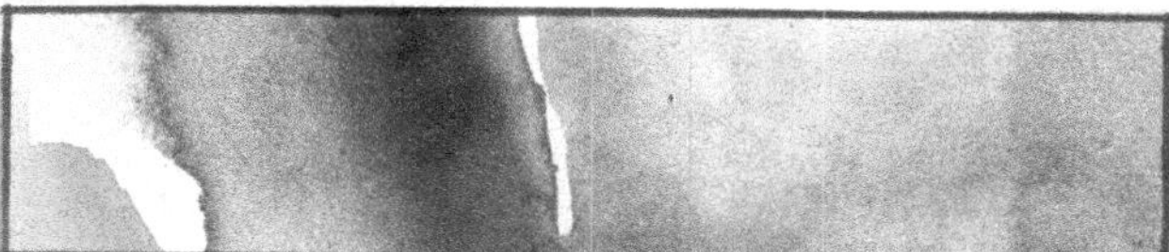

PETER'S PROFESSION OF FAITH

18 ONE DAY WHEN JESUS WAS PRAYING ALONE, NOT
FAR FROM HIS DISCIPLES, HE ASKED THEM, "WHAT
DO PEOPLE SAY ABOUT ME?" 19 THEY ANSWERED,
"SOME SAY THAT YOU ARE JOHN THE BAPTIST, OTHERS
SAY THAT YOU ARE ELIJAH, AND STILL OTHERS THAT YOU
ARE ONE OF THE FORMER PROPHETS RISEN FROM THE
DEAD." AGAIN JESUS ASKED THEM, 20 "WHO THEN
DO YOU SAY I AM?" PETER ANSWERED, "THE MESSIAH
OF GOD." 21 THEN JESUS SPOKE TO THEM, GIVING
THEM STRICT ORDERS
NOT TO TELL THIS TO
ANYONE. 22 AND HE
ADDED, "THE SON OF
MAN MUST SUFFER MA-
NY THINGS. HE WILL
BE REJECTED BY THE
ELDERS AND CHIEF PRI-
ESTS AND TEACHERS OF
THE LAW AND PUT TO DE-
ATH. THEN AFTER THREE
DAYS HE WILL BE RAISED
TO LIFE." 23 JESUS ALSO
SAID TO ALL THE PEOPLE,
"IF YOU WISH BE A FOLLO-
WER OF MINE, DENY YOUR-
SELF AND TAKE UP YOUR
CROSS EACH DAY, AND
FOLLOW ME. 24 FOR IF
YOU CHOOSE TO SAVE YOUR
LIFE, YOU WILL LOSE IT,
AND IF YOU LOSE YOUR LI-
FE FOR MY SAKE, YOU
WILL SAVE IT. 25 WHAT
WHAT DOES IT PROFIT YOU
TO GAIN THE WHOLE WORLD
WHILE YOU DESTROY AND

LOSE YOURSELF? 26 IF SOMEONE FEELS ASHAMED OF
ME AND OF MY WORDS, THE SON OF MAN WILL BE ASHA-
MED OF HIM WHEN HE COMES IN HIS GLORY AND IN
THE GLORY OF HIS FATHER WITH HIS HOLY ANGELS.
27 TRULY, I SAY TO YOU, THERE ARE SOME HERE WHO
WILL NOT EXPERIENCE DEATH BEFORE THEY SEE
THE KINGDOM OF GOD."

THE TRANSFIGURATION

28 ABOUT EIGHT DAYS AFTER JESUS HAD SAID ALL
THIS, HE TOOK PETER, JOHN AND JAMES AND WENT UP
THE MOUNTAIN TO PRAY. 29 AND WHILE HE WAS PRAYING,
THE ASPECT OF HIS FACE WAS CHANGED AND HIS CLOTHING
BECAME DAZZLING WHITE. 30 TWO MEN WERE TALKING

WITH JESUS: MOSES AND ELIJAH. 31 THEY HAD JUST APPE-
ARED IN HEAVENLY GLORY AND WERE TELLING HIM
ABOUT HIS DEPARTURE THAT HAD TO TAKE PLACE IN
JERUSALEM. 32 PETER AND HIS COMPANIONS HAD
FALLEN ASLEEP, BUT THEY AWOKE SUDDENLY AND SAW
JESUS' GLORY AND THE TWO MEN WITH HIM. 33 AS MOSES
AND ELIJAH WERE ABOUT TO LEAVE, PETER SAID TO HIM, "MASTER,
HOW GOOD IT IS FOR US TO BE HERE. FOR WE CAN MAKE THREE
TENTS, ONE FOR YOU, ONE FOR MOSES AND ONE FOR ELIJAH!"
FOR PETER DIDN'T KNOW WHAT TO SAY.

36 AND NO SOONER HAD HE SPOKEN THAN A CLOUD APPE-
ARED AND COVERED THEM; AND THE DISCIPLES WERE AFRAID
AS THEY ENTERED THE CLOUD. 35 THEN THESE WORDS CAME
FROM THE CLOUD, "THIS IS MY SON, MY CHOSEN ONE, LISTEN TO
HIM." 36 AND AFTER THE VOICE HAD SPOKEN, JESUS WAS
THERE ALONE. THE DISCIPLES KEPT THIS TO THEMSELVES
AT THE TIME, TELLING NO ONE OF ANYTHING THEY HAD SEEN.

THE EPILEPTIC DEMONIAC

37 THE NEXT DAY, WHEN THEY CAME DOWN FROM THE MOUNTAIN,
QUITE A GROUP MET JESUS. 38 A MAN AMONG THEM
CALLED OUT, "MASTER, I BEG YOU TO LOOK AT MY SON, MY ONLY
CHILD. WHEN THE EVIL SPI-
RIT SEIZES HIM, HE SUD-
DENLY SCREAMS. 39 THE
SPIRIT THROWS HIM INTO
A FIT AND HE FOAMS AT THE
MOUTH; IT SCARCELY EVER
LEAVES HIM AND IS WEAR-
ING HIM OUT. 40 I BEGGED
YOUR DISCIPLES TO DRIVE
IT OUT, BUT THEY COULD NOT."
41 JESUS ANSWERED, "YOU
FAITHLESS PEOPLE! HOW
WRONG YOU ARE! HOW LONG
MUST I BE WITH YOU AND PUT
UP WITH YOU? BRING YOUR
SON HERE." 42 AND WHILE
THE BOY WAS BEING
BROUGHT, THE DEMON
KNOCKED HIM TO THE GRO-
UND AND THREW HIM
INTO A FIT. BUT JESUS
SPOKE SHARPLY TO THE
EVIL SPIRIT, HEALED THE
BOY AND GAVE HIM BACK
TO HIS FATHER. 43 AND
ALL WHO SAW IT WERE
ASTONISHED AT GOD'S
WONDERFUL WORK.

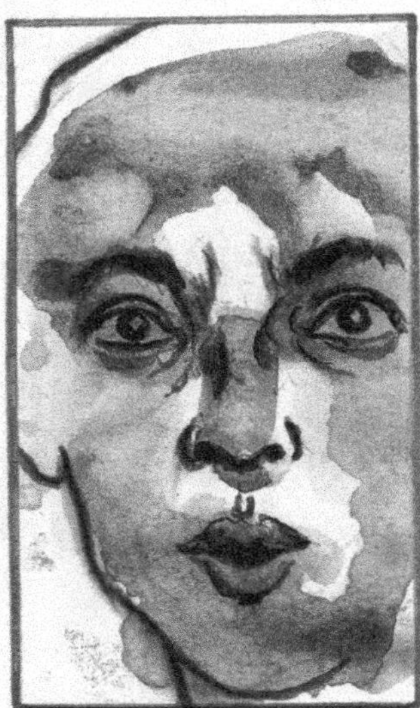

WHILE ALL WERE AMAZED AT EVERYTHING JESUS DID, HE
SAID TO HIS DISCIPLES, 44 "LISTEN AND REMEMBER WHAT
I TELL YOU NOW: THE SON OF MAN WILL BE DELIVERED
INTO THE HANDS OF MEN." 45 BUT THE DISCIPLES DID
NOT UNDERSTAND THIS SAYING: SOMETHING PREVEN-
TED THEM FROM GRASPING WHAT HE MEANT, AND
THEY WERE AFRAID TO ASK HIM ABOUT IT.

WHO IS THE GREATEST?

46 ONE DAY THE DISCIPLES WERE ARGUING ABOUT
WHICH OF THEM WAS THE MOST IMPORTANT. 47 BUT
JESUS KNEW THEIR THOUGHTS, SO HE TOOK A LITTLE
CHILD AND STOOD HIM BY HIS SIDE. 48 THEN HE SAID
TO THEM, "WHOEVER WELCOMES THIS LITTLE CHILD
IN MY NAME WELCOMES ME, AND WHOEVER WELCO-
MES ME, WELCOMES THE ONE WHO SENT ME. AND
LISTEN: HE WHO IS FOUND TO BE THE LEAST AMONG
YOU ALL, HE IS GREAT INDEED."
49 THEN JOHN SPOKE UP, "MASTER, WE SAW
SOMEONE WHO DROVE OUT DEMONS BY CALLING
UPON YOUR NAME, AND WE TRIED TO STOP HIM
BECAUSE HE DOESN'T FOLLOW YOU WITH US." 50 BUT
JESUS SAID, "DON'T STOP HIM. HE WHO IS NOT AGAINST
YOU IS FOR YOU."

JESUS UNWELCOME IN A SAMARITAN VILLAGE

51 AS THE TIME DREW NEAR WHEN JESUS WOULD
BE TAKEN UP TO HEAVEN, HE MADE UP HIS MIND
TO GO TO JERUSALEM. 52 HE HAD SENT AHEAD
OF HIM SOME MESSENGERS WHO ENTERED A SAMA-
RITAN VILLAGE TO PREPARE A LODGING FOR HIM.
53 BUT THE PEOPLE WOULD NOT RECEIVE HIM
BECAUSE HE WAS ON HIS WAY TO JERUSALEM.

54 SEEING THIS, JAMES AND JOHN, HIS DISCIPLES, SAID, "LORD,
DO YOU WANT US TO CALL DOWN FIRE FROM HEAVEN TO REDUCE
THEM TO ASHES?" 55 JESUS TURNED AND REBUKED THEM,
56 AND THEY WENT ON TO ANOTHER VILLAGE.

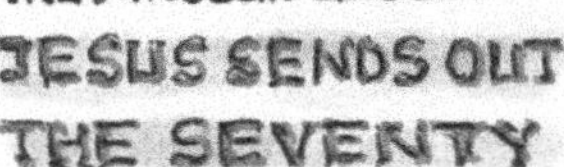

THE COST OF FOLLOWING JESUS

57 AS THEY WENT ON THEIR WAY, A MAN SAID
TO HIM, "I WILL FOLLOW
YOU WHEREVER YOU GO."
58 JESUS SAID TO HIM,
"FOXES HAVE HOLES
AND BIRDS OF THE AIR
HAVE NESTS; BUT THE
SON OF MAN HAS NO-
WHERE TO LAY HIS HE-
AD." 59 TO ANOTHER
JESUS SAID, "FOLLOW
ME." BUT HE ANSWERED,
"LET ME GO BACK NOW,
FOR FIRST I WANT TO
BURY MY FATHER."
60 AND JESUS SAID,
"LET THE DEAD BURY THEIR
DEAD; AS FOR YOU, LEAVE
THEM AND PROCLAIM THE
KINGDOM OF GOD." 61 AN-
OTHER SAID, "I WILL FOLLOW
YOU, LORD, BUT FIRST LET ME
SAY GOOD-BYE TO MY FAMI-
LY." 62 AND JESUS SAID,
"WHOEVER HAS PUT HIS
HAND TO THE PLOW AND LO-
OKS BACK IS NOT FIT FOR
THE KINGDOM OF GOD."

JESUS SENDS OUT THE SEVENTY

10 1 AFTER THIS THE LORD APPOINTED SEVENTY-
TWO OTHER DISCIPLES AND SENT THEM TWO BY TWO
AHEAD OF HIM TO EVERY TOWN AND PLACE, WHERE
HE HIMSELF WAS TO GO. 2 HE SAID TO THEM, "THE HARVEST
IS RICH, BUT THE WORKERS ARE FEW, SO ASK THE LORD OF THE
HARVEST TO SEND WORKERS TO HIS HARVEST. 3 COURAGE!
I AM SENDING YOU LIKE LAMBS AMONG WOLVES. 4 SET
OFF WITHOUT PURSE OR BAG OR SANDALS; AND DO NOT
STOP AT THE HOMES OF THOSE YOU KNOW

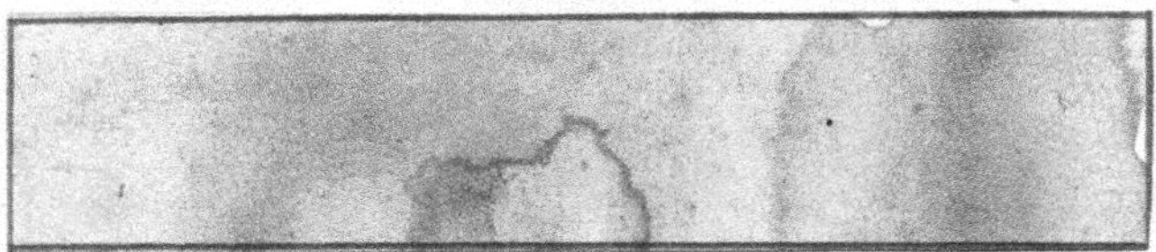

AS JESUS STEPPED ASHORE, A MAN FROM THE TOWN APPROACHED HIM. (LUKE 8:27)
DM 09 ©

(5) WHATEVER HOUSE YOU ENTER, FIRST BLESS THEM, SAY-
ING, "PEACE TO THIS HOUSE". (6) IF A PEACEFUL PERSON
LIVES THERE, THE PEACE SHALL REST UPON HIM. BUT
IF NOT, THE BLESSING WILL RETURN TO YOU. (7) STAY IN
THAT HOUSE EATING AND DRINKING AT THEIR TABLE,
FOR THE WORKER DESERVES HIS WAGES. DO NOT
MOVE FROM HOUSE TO HOUSE. (8) WHEN THEY WEL-
COME YOU IN ANY TOWN, EAT WHAT THEY OFFER YOU.
(9) HEAL THE SICK WHO ARE THERE AND SAY TO
THEM: 'THE KINGDOM OF GOD HAS DRAWN NEAR TO
YOU.' (10) BUT IN ANY TOWN WHERE YOU ARE NOT WEL-
COME, GO TO THE MARKETPLACE AND PROCLAIM: (11) 'EVEN
THE DUST OF YOUR TOWN THAT CLINGS TO OUR FEET, WE

WIPE OFF AND LEAVE WITH YOU. BUT KNOW AND BE SU-
RE THAT THE KINGDOM OF GOD HAD COME TO YOU.' (12) I TELL
YOU THAT ON THE JUDGMENT DAY IT WILL BE BETTER FOR
SODOM THAN FOR THIS TOWN. (13) ALAS FOR YOU CHORA-
ZIN! ALAS FOR YOU BETHSAIDA! SO MANY MIRACLES HAVE
BEEN WORKED IN YOU! IF THE SAME MIRACLES HAPPENED IN
TYRE AND SIDON, THEY WOULD ALREADY BE SITTING IN ASHES
AND WEARING THE SACKCLOTH OF REPENTANCE. (14) FOR TYRE
AND SIDON IT WILL SURELY BE BETTER THAN FOR YOU ON
THE JUDGMENT DAY. (15) AND WHAT OF YOU, CAPERNAUM? WILL
YOU BE LIFTED UP TO HEAVEN? YOU WILL BE THROWN DOWN
TO THE PLACE OF THE DEAD. (16) WHOEVER LISTEN TO YOU,
LISTEN TO ME, AND WHOEVER REJECTS YOU REJECTS
ME: AND HE WHO REJECTS ME, REJECTS THE ONE WHO SENT ME."

JESUS GIVES THANKS TO THE FATHER

(17) THE SEVENTY-TWO RETURNED FULL OF JOY. THEY
SAID, "LORD, EVEN THE DEMONS OBEYED US WHEN WE CAL-
LED ON YOUR NAME." (18)
JESUS REPLIED, "I SAW
SATAN FALL LIKE LIGHT-
NING FROM HEAVEN. (19)
YOU SEE, I HAVE GIVEN
YOU AUTHORITY TO TRAM-
PLE ON SNAKES AND
SCORPIONS AND TO OVER-
COME ALL THE POWER OF
THE ENEMY, SO THAT
NOTHING WILL HARM YOU.
(20) NEVERTHELESS,
DON'T REJOICE BECAUSE
THE EVIL SPIRITS SUBMIT
TO YOU; REJOICE RATHER
THAT YOUR NAMES ARE
WRITTEN IN HEAVEN."
(21) AT THAT TIME JESUS
WAS FILLED WITH THE JOY
OF THE HOLY SPIRIT AND
SAID, "I PRAISE YOU, FA-
THER, LORD OF HEAVEN
AND EARTH, FOR YOU HAVE
HIDDEN THESE THINGS
FROM THE WISE AND LE-
ARNED AND MADE THEM KNOWN TO LITTLE CHILDREN.

(22) YES, FATHER, SUCH HAS BEEN YOUR GRACIOUS
WILL. I HAVE BEEN GIVEN ALL THINGS BY MY FATHER,
SO THAT NO ONE KNOWS THE FATHER EXCEPT THE SON
AND HE TO WHOM THE SON CHOOSES TO REVEAL HIM.
(23) THEN JESUS TURNED TO HIS DISCIPLES AND
SAID TO THEM PRIVATELY, "FORTUNATE ARE YOU
TO SEE WHAT YOU SEE,
(24) FOR I TELL YOU THAT MANY PROPHETS AND KINGS
WOULD HAVE LIKED TO SEE WHAT YOU SEE BUT DIDN'T, AND
TO HEAR WHAT YOU HEAR BUT DID NOT HEAR IT."

THE GOOD SAMARITAN

(25) THEN A TEACHER OF THE LAW CAME AND BEGAN PUT-
TING JESUS TO THE TEXT. AND HE SAID, "MASTER, WHAT
SHALL I DO TO RECEIVE ETERNAL LIFE?" (26) JESUS RE-
PLIED, "WHAT IS WRITTEN
IN THE SCRIPTURE? HOW
DO YOU UNDERSTAND IT?"
(27) THE MAN ANSWERED.
"IT IS WRITTEN: YOU SHALL
LOVE THE LORD YOUR GOD
WITH ALL YOUR HEART,
WITH ALL YOUR SOUL, WITH
ALL YOUR STRENGTH AND
WILL ALL YOUR MIND. AND
YOU SHALL LOVE YOUR NE-
IGHBOR AS YOURSELF."
(28) JESUS REPLIED,
"WHAT A GOOD ANSWER!
DO THIS AND YOU SHALL
LIVE." (29) THE MAN WAN-
TED TO KEEP UP APPEAR-
ANCES, SO HE REPLIED,
"WHO IS MY NEIGHBOR?"
(30) JESUS THEN SAID,
"THERE WAS A MAN GOING
DOWN FROM JERUSALEM
TO JERICHO, AND HE FELL
INTO THE HANDS OF ROBBE-
RS. THEY STRIPPED HIM

BEAT HIM AND LEFT LEAVING HIM HALF DEAD. (31) IT HAP-
PENED THAT A PRIEST WAS GOING ALONG THE ROAD AND
SAW THE MAN, BUT PASSED BY ON THE OTHER SIDE. (32) LIKE-
WISE A LEVITE SAW THE MAN AND PASSED BY ON THE OTHER
SIDE. (33) BUT A SAMARITAN, TOO, WAS GOING THAT WAY, AND
WHEN HE SAW THE MAN HE WAS MOVED WITH COMPASSION.
(34) HE WENT TO HIM AND TREATED HIS WOUNDS WITH OIL
AND WINE AND WRAPPED THEM WITH BANDAGES. THEN HE

PUT HIM ON HIS OWN MOUNT AND BROUGHT HIM TO AN
INN WHERE HE TOOK CARE OF HIM. (35) THE NEXT DAY
HE HAD TO SET OFF, BUT HE GAVE TWO SILVER COINS TO THE
INNKEEPER AND TOLD HIM: 'TAKE CARE OF HIM AND WHAT-
EVER YOU SPEND ON HIM, I WILL REPAY WHEN I COME BACK.'"
(36) JESUS ASKED, "WHICH OF THESE THREE YOU THINK MADE
HIMSELF NEIGHBOR TO THE MAN WHO FELL INTO THE ROB-
BERS' HANDS?" (37) THE TEACHER OF THE LAW ANSWERED,
"THE ONE WHO HAD MERCY ON HIM.". AND JESUS
SAID, "GO THEN AND DO THE SAME."

MARTHA AND MARY

(38) AS JESUS AND HIS DISCIPLES WERE ON THEIR
WAY, HE ENTERED A VILLAGE AND A WOMAN CALLED
MARTHA WELCOMED HIM TO HER HOUSE. (39) SHE HAD A
SISTER NAMED MARY WHO SAT DOWN AT THE
LORD'S FEET TO LISTEN TO HIS WORDS.

(40) MARTHA, MEANWHILE, WAS BUSY WITH ALL THE
SERVING AND FINALLY SHE SAID, "LORD, DON'T YOU
CARE THAT MY SISTER HAS LEFT ME TO DO ALL
THE SERVING?" (41) BUT THE LORD ANSWERED,
"MARTHA, MARTHA, YOU WORRY AND ARE TROUBLED
ABOUT MANY THINGS, (42) WHEREAS ONLY ONE THING
IS NEEDED. MARY HAS CHOSEN THE BETTER PART,
AND IT WILL NOT BE TAKEN AWAY FROM HER."

LORD, TEACH US TO PRAY

11 (1) ONE DAY JESUS WAS PRAYING IN A CERTAIN PLACE
AND WHEN HE HAD FINISHED, ONE OF HIS DISCIPLES SAID
TO HIM, "LORD, TEACH US TO PRAY, JUST AS JOHN TAUGHT
HIS DISCIPLES." (2) HE SAID, "WHEN YOU PRAY, SAY THIS:

"FATHER, HALLOWED
BE YOUR NAME, MAY
YOUR KINGDOM COME,
(3) GIVE US EACH DAY
THE KIND OF BREAD WE
NEED, (4) AND FORGIVE
US OUR SINS, FOR WE
ALSO FORGIVE ALL WHO
DO US WRONG, AND DO NOT
LET US FALL INTO TEMPTATION"

(5) JESUS SAID TO THEM, "SUPPOSE ONE OF YOU HAS A
FRIEND AND GOES TO HIS HOUSE IN THE MIDDLE OF
THE NIGHT AND SAYS: 'FRIEND, LEND ME THREE LOAVES,
(6) FOR A FRIEND OF MINE WHO IS TRAVELING HAS
JUST ARRIVED AND I HAVE NOTHING TO OFFER HIM.'
(7) MAYBE YOUR FRIEND WILL ANSWER FROM IN-
SIDE: 'DON'T BOTHER ME NOW; THE DOOR IS LOCKED
AND MY CHILDREN AND I ARE IN BED, SO I CAN'T GET
UP AND GIVE YOU ANYTHING.' (8) BUT I TELL YOU, EVEN

THOUGH HE WILL NOT
GET UP AND ATTEND TO
HIM BECAUSE HE IS A FRI-
END, YET HE WILL GET UP
BECAUSE THE OTHER IS
A BOTHER TO HIM, AND HE
WILL GIVE HIM ALL HE
NEEDS. (9) AND SO I
SAY TO YOU, 'ASK AND IT WILL
BE GIVEN TO YOU; SEEK AND YOU
WILL FIND; KNOCK AND IT WILL
BE OPENED TO YOU. (10) FOR THE
ONE WHO ASKS RECEIVES, AND
THE ONE WHO SEARCHES FINDS
AND TO HIM WHO KNOCKS IT
WILL BE OPENED. (11) MANY
OF YOU ARE FATHERS; IF YOUR
SON ASKS FOR A FISH, WILL
YOU GIVE HIM A SNAKE IN-
STEAD? (12) AND IF YOUR SON
ASKS FOR AN EGG, WILL YOU
GIVE HIM A SCORPION?
(13) EVEN YOU EVIL PEOPLE
KNOW HOW TO GIVE GOOD GIFTS
TO YOUR CHILDREN, HOW MUCH
MORE WILL THE FATHER IN
HEAVEN GIVE HOLY SPIRIT TO THOSE WHO ASK HIM!"

JESUS AND BEELZEBUL

(14) ONE DAY JESUS WAS DRIVING OUT A DUMB DEMON.
WHEN THE DEMON HAD BEEN DRIVEN OUT AND THE MU-
TE PERSON COULD SPEAK, THE PEOPLE WERE AMAZED.
(15) YET SOME OF THEM SAID: 'HE DRIVES OUT DEMONS BY THE
POWER OF BEELZEBUL, THE CHIEF OF THE DEMONS."

(16) SO OTHERS WANTED TO PUT HIM TO THE TEXT BY
ASKING HIM FOR A HEAVENLY SIGN. (17) BUT JESUS
KNEW THEIR THOUGHTS AND SAID TO THEM, "EVERY
NATION DIVIDED BY CIVIL WAR IS ON THE ROAD TO RUIN,
AND WILL FALL. (18) IF SATAN ALSO IS DIVIDED, HIS EM-
PIRE IS COMING TO AN END. HOW CAN YOU SAY THAT I
DRIVE OUT DEMONS BY CALLING UPON BEELZEBUL?"

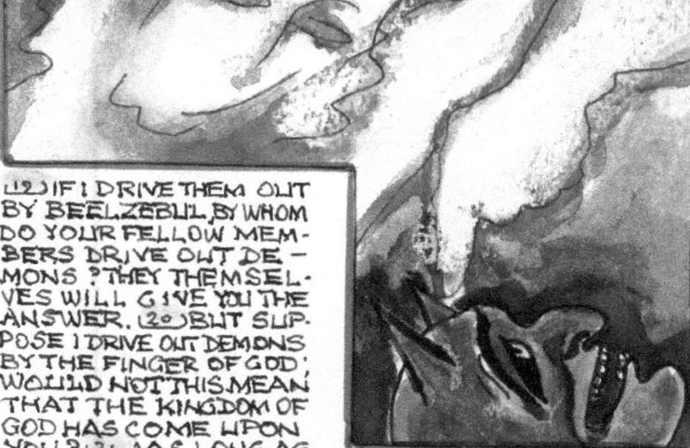

(19) IF I DRIVE THEM OUT
BY BEELZEBUL, BY WHOM
DO YOUR FELLOW MEM-
BERS DRIVE OUT DE-
MONS? THEY THEMSEL-
VES WILL GIVE YOU THE
ANSWER. (20) BUT SUP-
POSE I DRIVE OUT DEMONS
BY THE FINGER OF GOD;
WOULD NOT THIS MEAN
THAT THE KINGDOM OF
GOD HAS COME UPON
YOU? (21) AS LONG AS
THE STRONG AND AR-
MED MAN GUARDS THE HOUSE, HIS GOODS ARE
SAFE. (22) BUT WHEN A STRONGER ONE ATTACKS AND
OVERCOMES HIM, THE CHALLENGER TAKES AWAY
ALL THE WEAPONS HE RELIED ON AND DISPOSES OF HIS
SPOILS. (23) WHOEVER IS NOT WITH ME IS AGAINST ME,
AND WHOEVER DOES NOT GATHER WITH ME, SCATTERS.
(24) WHEN THE EVIL SPIRIT GOES OUT OF A MAN, HE WANDERS
THROUGH DRY LANDS LOOKING FOR A RESTING PLACE, AND
FINDING NONE, HE SAYS, 'I WILL RETURN TO MY HOUSE
FROM WHICH I CAME.' (25) SO HE RETURNS AND FINDS THE
HOUSE SWEPT AND EVERYTHING IN ORDER. (26) THEN HE
GOES TO FETCH SEVEN OTHER SPIRITS EVEN WORSE THAN
HIMSELF, TO ENTER THAT HOUSE AND SETTLE IN IT.
AND THE LAST STATE OF THAT PERSON IS WORSE THAN
THE FIRST."
(27) AS JESUS WAS SPEAKING, A WOMAN SPOKE FROM

THE CROWD AND SAID TO HIM, "BLESSED IS THE ONE WHO
BORE YOU AND NURSED YOU!" (28) JESUS REPLIED, "SU-
RELY BLESSED ARE THOSE WHO HEAR THE WORD OF GOD
AND KEEP IT AS WELL."
(29) AS THE CROWD INCREASED, JESUS BEGAN TO SPEAK IN
THIS WAY, "PEOPLE OF THE PRESENT TIME ARE EVIL PEOPLE.
THEY ASK FOR A SIGN, BUT NO SIGN WILL BE GIVEN TO THEM
EXCEPT THE SIGN OF JONAH. (30) AS JONAH BECAME A SIGN
FOR THE PEOPLE OF NINEVEH, SO WILL THE SON OF MAN
BE A SIGN FOR THIS GENERATION.
(31) THE QUEEN OF THE SOUTH WILL RISE UP ON JUDG-
MENT DAY WITH THE PEOPLE OF THESE TIMES AND
ACCUSE THEM, FOR SHE CAME FROM THE ENDS OF THE
EARTH TO HEAR THE WISDOM OF SOLOMON: AND
HERE THERE IS GREATER THAN SOLOMON."

(32) THE MEN OF NINEVEH WILL RAISE UP ON JUDGMENT DAY
WITH THE PEOPLE OF THESE TIMES AND ACCUSE THEM FOR
JONAH'S PREACHING MADE THEM TURN FROM THEIR SINS,
AND HERE THERE IS GREATER THAN JONAH. (33) YOU DO
NOT LIGHT A LAMP TO HIDE IT; RATHER YOU PUT IT ON A
LAMPSTAND SO THAT PEOPLE COMING IN MAY SEE THE
LIGHT. (34) YOUR EYE IS THE LAMP OF YOUR BODY.
IF YOUR EYE SEES CLE-
ARLY, YOUR WHOLE
PERSON BENEFITS FROM
THE LIGHT; BUT IF YOUR
EYESIGHT IS POOR, YOUR
WHOLE PERSON IS WITH-
OUT LIGHT. (35) SO BE
CAREFUL LEST THE
LIGHT INSIDE YOU BE-
COME DARKNESS. (36)
IF YOUR WHOLE PERSON
RECEIVES THE LIGHT,
HAVING NO PART THAT
IS DARK, YOU WILL BE-
COME LIGHT, AS WHEN
A LAMP SHINES ON YOU."

WOE TO YOU PHARISEES!

(37) AS JESUS WAS
SPEAKING, A PHARISEE
ASKED HIM TO HAVE A
MEAL WITH HIM. SO HE
WENT AND SAT AT THE TA-
BLE. (38) THE PHARI-
SEE THEN WONDERED
WHY JESUS DID NOT
FIRST WASH HIS HANDS BEFORE DINNER. (39) BUT THE
LORD SAID TO HIM, "SO THEN, YOU PHARISEES, YOU CLEAN THE
OUTSIDE OF THE CUP AND THE DISH, BUT INSIDE YOURSELVES
YOU ARE FULL OF GREED AND EVIL. (40) FOOLS! HE WHO MADE
THE OUTSIDE, ALSO MADE THE INSIDE. (41) BUT ACCORD-
ING TO YOU, BY THE MERE GIVING OF ALMS EVERYTHING
IS MADE CLEAN. (42) A CURSE IS ON YOU, PHARISEES;
FOR THE TEMPLE YOU GIVE A TENTH OF ALL, INCLUDING
MINT AND RUE AND THE OTHER HERBS, BUT YOU NEGLECT
JUSTICE AND THE LOVE OF GOD. THIS OUGHT TO BE PRACTI-
CED, WITHOUT NEGLECTING THE OTHER. (43) A CURSE IS

ON YOU, PHARISEES, FOR YOU LOVE THE BEST SEATS IN
THE SYNAGOGUES AND TO BE GREATED IN THE MARKET-
PLACE. (44) A CURSE IS ON YOU, PHARISEES, FOR YOU
ARE LIKE TOMBSTONES WHICH CAN HARDLY BE SEEN;
PEOPLE DON'T NOTICE THEM STEPPING ON THEM." (45) THEN
A TEACHER OF THE LAW SAID, "WHEN YOU SPEAK LIKE
THIS, MASTER, YOU INSULT US, TOO." (46) AND JESUS
ANSWERED, "A CURSE IS ON YOU ALSO, TEACHERS OF THE
LAW, FOR YOU PREPARE UNBEARABLE BURDENS AND LOAD
THEM ON THE PEOPLE, WHILE YOU DON'T MOVE A FINGER TO
HELP THEM. (47) A CURSE IS ON YOU, FOR YOU BUILD ME-
MORIALS TO THE PROPHETS YOUR FATHERS KILLED.

(48) SO YOU APPROVE AND AGREE WITH WHAT YOUR
FATHERS DID, IS IT NOT SO? THEY GOT RID OF THE
PROPHETS, AND NOW YOU CAN BUILD!"
(49) THE WISDOM OF GOD ALSO SAID: "I WILL SEND PRO-
PHETS AND APOSTLES AND THIS PEOPLE WILL KILL AND PER-
SECUTE SOME OF THEM. (50) BUT THE PRESENT GENE-
RATION WILL HAVE TO ANSWER FOR THE BLOOD OF ALL
THE PROPHETS THAT HAS BEEN SHED SINCE THE FO-
UNDATION OF THE WORLD, (51) FROM THE BLOOD OF
ABEL TO THE BLOOD OF ZECHARIAH, MURDERED BETWE-
EN THE ALTAR AND THE SANCTUARY. YES, I TELL YOU, THE
PEOPLE OF THIS TIME WILL HAVE TO ANSWER FOR THEM

ALL. (52) A CURSE ON YOU, TEACHERS OF THE LAW, FOR YOU HAVE
TAKEN THE KEY OF KNOWLEDGE. YOU YOURSELVES HAVE NOT EN-
TERED, AND YOU PREVENTED OTHERS FROM ENTERING." (53) AS
JESUS LEFT, THE TEACHERS OF THE LAW AND THE PHARISEES
BEGAN TO HARASS HIM, (54) ASKING HIM ENDLESS QUESTIONS
TRYING TO CATCH HIM IN SOMETHING HE MIGHT SAY.

OPEN AND FEARLESS SPEECH

12 (1) MEANWHILE A LARGE CROWD HAD GATHERED THAT
THEY CRUSHED ONE ANOTHER. THEN JESUS SPOKE TO
HIS DISCIPLES, "BEWARE OF THE YEAST OF THE PHA-
RISEES WHICH IS HYPOCRISY. (2) NOTHING IS COVERED
THAT WILL NOT BE UNCOVERED OR HIDDEN THAT WILL NOT
BE MADE KNOWN. (3) WHATEVER YOU HAVE SAID IN THE
DARKNESS WILL BE HEARD IN DAYLIGHT, AND WHAT YOU HA-
VE WHISPERED IN HIDDEN
PLACES, WILL BE PROCLAIMED
FROM THE HOUSETOPS.

(4) I TELL YOU, MY FRIENDS,
DO NOT FEAR WHO PUT TO
DEATH THE BODY AND
AFTER THAT CAN DO
NO MORE. (5) BUT I WILL
TELL YOU WHOM TO FEAR.
FEAR THE ONE WHO AFTER
KILLING YOU IS ABLE TO
THROW YOU INTO HELL.
THIS ONE YOU MUST FEAR.
(6) DON'T YOU GET FIVE
SPARROWS FOR TWO PEN-
NIES? YET NOT ONE OF
THEM HAS BEEN FORGOT-
TEN BY GOD. (7) EVEN
THE HAIRS OF YOUR
HEAD HAVE BEEN NUM-
BERED. SO DO NOT FEAR:
ARE YOU NOT WORTH MORE
THAN THOUSANDS OF SPAR-
ROWS? (8) I TELL YOU, WHO-
EVER ACKNOWLEDGES ME
BEFORE PEOPLE, THE
SON OF MAN WILL ALSO ACKNOWLEDGE BEFORE THE
ANGELS OF GOD. (9) BUT THE ONE WHO DENIES ME BE-
FORE OTHERS WILL BE DENIED BEFORE THE ANGELS
OF GOD. (10) THERE WILL BE PARDON FOR THE ONE
WHO CRITICIZES THE SON OF MAN, BUT THERE
WILL BE NO PARDON FOR THE ONE WHO
SLANDERS THE HOLY SPIRIT.

A curse on you,
Teachers of the Law...
Luke 11:52
DM 09 ©
CCCXL 340

11 WHEN YOU ARE BROUGHT BEFORE THE SYNAGOGUES,
GOVERNORS AND RULERS, DON'T WORRY ABOUT HOW YOU
WILL DEFEND YOURSELF OR WHAT TO SAY. 12 FOR
THE HOLY SPIRIT WILL TEACH YOU AT THAT TIME
ALL THAT YOU HAVE TO SAY."

THE RICH FOOL

13 SOMEONE IN THE CROWD SPOKE TO JESUS, "MASTER, TELL
MY BROTHER TO SHARE WITH ME OUR FATHER'S PROPERTY."
14 HE REPLIED, "MY FRIEND, WHO HAS APPOINTED ME AS
YOUR JUDGE OR YOUR ATTOREY?" 15 THEN JESUS SAID

TO THE PEOPLE, "BE ON YOUR GUARD AND AVOID EVERY
KIND OF GREED, FOR EVEN THOUGH YOU HAVE MANY POSSES-
SIONS, IT IS NOT THAT WHICH GIVES YOU LIFE." 16 AND JESUS
TOLD THEM THIS STORY, "THERE WAS A RICH MAN AND HIS
LAND HAD PRODUCED A GOOD HARVEST. 17 HE THOUGHT:
'WHAT SHALL I DO? I HAVE NO ROOM TO STORE MY HARVEST.'
18 SO THIS IS WHAT HE PLANNED: 'I WILL PULL DOWN MY
BARNS AND BUILD BIGGER ONES TO STORE ALL THIS GRAIN,
WHICH IS MY WEALTH. 19 THEN I MAY SAY TO MYSELF: MY
FRIEND, YOU HAVE MANY GOODS FOR MANY YEARS. REST,
EAT, DRINK, AND ENJOY YOURSELF.' 20 BUT GOD SAID TO
HIM: 'YOU ARE MISTAKEN! THIS VERY NIGHT YOUR LIFE
WILL BE TAKEN; WHO SHALL GET ALL YOU HAVE PUT A-
SIDE?' 21 THIS IS THE LOT OF THOSE WHO PILE UP
RICHES INSTEAD OF BECOMING RICH BEFORE GOD."

DO NOT WORRY!

22 THEN JESUS SAID TO HIS DISCIPLES, "I TELL YOU NOT TO
WORRY ABOUT YOUR LIFE: WHAT TO EAT? OR ABOUT YOUR

BODY: WHAT ARE WE TO
WEAR? 23 FOR YOUR LIFE
IS MORE THAN FOOD AND
THE BODY MORE THAN
CLOTHING. 24 LOOK AT
THE CROWS: THEY NEITHER
SOW OR REAP; THEY HAVE
NO STOREHOUSES AND NO
BARNS; YET GOD FEEDS
THEM. HOW MUCH MORE
IMPORTANT ARE YOU
THAN BIRDS! WHICH
25 OF YOU FOR ALL HIS
WORRYING CAN MAKE HIM-
SELF A LITTLE TALLER? 26
AND IF YOU ARE NOT ABLE
TO CONTROL SUCH A SMALL
THING, WHY DO YOU WORRY
ABOUT THE REST? 27 LO-
OK AT THE WILD FLOWERS:
THEY DO NOT SPIN OR WE-
AVE. BUT I TELL YOU,
EVEN SOLOMON WITH ALL
HIS WEALTH WAS NOT CLO-
THED AS ONE OF THESE.
28 IF GOD SO CLOTHES THE
GRASS IN THE FIELDS, WHICH
IS ALIVE TODAY AND TOMOR-
ROW IS THROWN INTO THE OVEN, HOW MUCH MORE WILL HE
CLOTHE YOU, PEOPLE OF LITTLE FAITH. 29 DO NOT SET
YOUR HEART ON WHAT YOU ARE TO EAT AND DRINK; STOP
WORRYING. 30 LET ALL THE NATIONS OF THE WORLD RUN
AFTER THESE THINGS: YOUR FATHER KNOWS YOU NEED THEM.
31 SEEK RATHER THE KINGDOM AND THESE THINGS WILL
BE GIVEN TO YOU AS WELL. 32 DO NOT BE AFRAID, LITTLE
FLOCK, FOR IT HAS PLEASED YOUR FATHER TO GIVE YOU THE
KINGDOM. 33 SELL WHAT YOU HAVE AND GIVE ALMS. GET
YOURSELVES PURSES THAT DO NOT WEAR OUT, AND MAKE
SAFE INVESTMENTS WITH GOD, WHERE NO THIEF COMES
AND NO MOTH DESTROYS. 34 FOR WHERE YOUR INVEST-
MENTS ARE, THERE WILL YOUR HEART BE ALSO.

BE READY

35 BE READY, DRESSED FOR SERVICE, AND KEEP
YOUR LAMP LIT, 36 LIKE PEOPLE WAITING FOR THEIR
MASTER TO RETURN FROM
THE WEDDING. AS SOON AS
HE COMES AND KNOCKS THEY
WILL OPEN TO HIM. 37 HAP-
PY ARE THOSE SERVANTS
WHOM THE MASTER FINDS
WIDE AWAKE WHEN HE CO-
MES. 38 TRULY, I TELL YOU
HE WILL PUT ON AN APRON
AND HAVE THEM SIT AT TAB-
LE AND HE WILL WAIT ON
THEM. HAPPY ARE THOSE
SERVANTS IF HE FINDS
THEM AWAKE WHEN HE
COMES AT MIDNIGHT OR
DAYBREAK! 39 PAY AT-
TENTION TO THIS: IF THE
MASTER OF THE HOUSE
HAD KNOWN AT WHAT TIME
THE THIEF WOULD COME HE
WOULD NOT HAVE LET HIM
BREAK INTO HIS HOUSE.
40 YOU ALSO MUST BE
READY, FOR THE SON OF
MAN WILL COME AT AN

HOUR YOU DO NOT EXPECT." 41 PETER SAID, "LORD, DID
YOU TELL THIS PARABLE ONLY FOR US OR FOR EVERYONE?"
42 THE LORD REPLIED, "IMAGINE, THEN, THE WISE AND FAITH-
FUL SERVANT WHOM THE MASTER SETS OVER HIS OTHER
SERVANTS TO GIVE THEM FOOD RATIONS AT THE PROPER
TIME. 43 FORTUNATE IS THE SERVANT IF HIS MASTER ON
COMING HOME FINDS HIM DOING HIS WORK. 44 TRULY, I
SAY TO YOU, THE MASTER WILL PUT HIM IN CHARGE OF ALL
HIS PROPERTY. 45 BUT IT MAY BE THAT THE SERVANT
THINKS: 'MY LORD DELAYS IN COMING,' AND HE BEGINS TO
ABUSE THE MENSERVANTS AND THE SERVANT GIRLS,
EATING, DRINKING AND GETTING DRUNK. 46 THEN THE

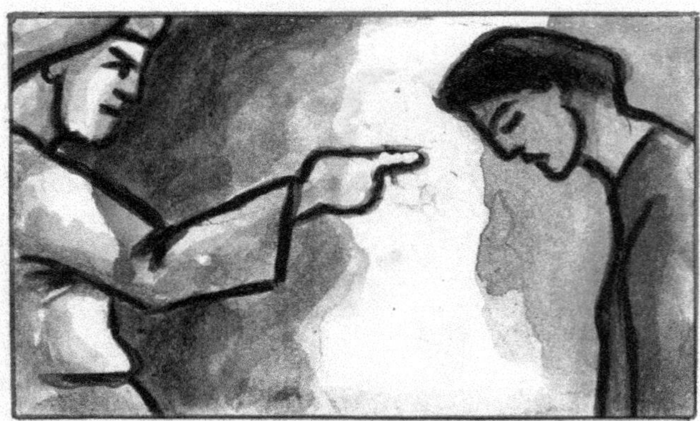

MASTER MAY COME ON A DAY HE DOES NOT EXPECT HIM
AND AT AN HOUR HE DOESN'T KNOW. HE WILL DISCHARGE
HIS SERVANT AND NUMBER HIM AMONG THE UNRELIABLE. 47
THE SERVANT WHO KNEW HIS MASTER'S WILL, BUT DID NOT
PREPARE TO DO WHAT HIS MASTER WANTED, WILL BE PU-
NISHED WITH SOUND BLOWS; BUT THE ONE WHO DID
WHAT DESERVED A PUNISHMENT 48 WITHOUT KNOW-
ING IT SHALL RECEIVE FEWER BLOWS. MUCH WILL BE
REQUIRED OF THE ONE WHO HAS BEEN GIVEN MUCH,
AND MORE WILL BE ASKED OF THE ONE WHO
HAD BEEN ENTRUSTED WITH MORE.

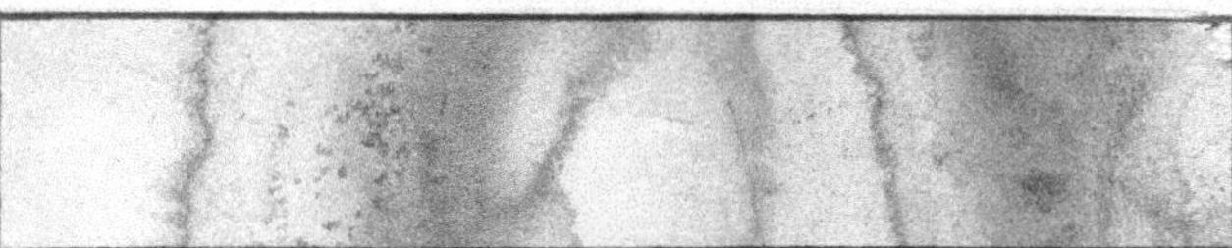

49 I HAVE COME TO BRING FIRE UPON THE EARTH AND
HOW I WISH IT WERE ALREADY KINDLED; 50 BUT I
HAVE A BAPTISM TO UNDERGO AND WHAT ANGUISH I
FEEL UNTIL IT IS OVER!
51 DO YOU THINK THAT I HAVE COME TO BRING
PEACE ON EARTH? NO, I TELL YOU, BUT RATHER
DIVISION. 52 FROM NOW ON, IN ONE HOUSE
FIVE WILL BE DIVIDED; THREE AGAINST TWO, AND TWO AGAINST
THREE. 53 THEY WILL
BE DIVIDED, FATHER AGAINST SON AND SON AGAINST FATHER; MOTHER AGAINST DAUGHTER AND DAUGHTER AGAINST MOTHER; MOTHER-IN-LAW AGAINST HER DAUGHTER-IN-LAW, AND DAUGHTER-IN-LAW AGAINST HER MOTHER-IN-LAW.

54 JESUS SAID TO THE CROWDS, "WHEN YOU SEE A CLOUD RISING IN THE WEST, YOU SAY AT ONCE: 'A SHOWER IS COMING,' AND SO IT
HAPPENS. 55 AND
WHEN THE WIND BLOWS FROM THE SOUTH, YOU SAY: 'IT WILL BE HOT', AND SO
IT IS. 56 YOU SUPERCIAL PEOPLE! YOU UNDERSTAND THE SIGNS OF THE EARTH AND THE SKY, BUT YOU DON'T UNDERSTAND THE PRESENT TIMES.

57 AND WHY DO YOU NOT JUDGE FOR YOUR-
SELVES WHEN IS FIT? 58 WHEN YOU GO
WITH YOUR ACCUSER BEFORE THE COURT, TRY TO SETTLE WITH HIM ON THE WAY, LEST

HE DRAG YOU TO THE JUDGE AND THE JUDGE DELIVER YOU
TO THE JAILER, AND THE JAILER THROW YOU IN PRISON. 59 I
TELL YOU, YOU WILL NOT GET OUT UNTIL YOU HAVE PAID THE VERY LAST PENNY."

THE FIGTREE WITHOUT FRUIT

13 1 ONE DAY SOME PERSONS TOLD JESUS WHAT HAD OCCURRED IN THE TEMPLE: PILATE HAD GALILEANS KILLED AND THEIR BLOOD MINGLED WITH THE BLOOD OF THEIR SA-
CRIFICES. 2 JESUS REPLIED, "DO YOU THINK THAT THESE GALILEANS WERE WORSE SINNERS OF ALL THE OTHER GALILEANS BECAUSE THEY SUFFERED THIS? 3 "NO. BUT UNLESS YOU CHANGE
YOUR WAYS, YOU WILL ALL PERISH AS THEY DID. 4 AND THOSE
EIGHTEEN PERSONS IN SILOAH WHO WERE CRUSHED WHEN THE TOWER FELL, DO YOU THINK THEY WERE MORE GUILTY THAN
ALL THE OTHERS IN JERUSALEM? 5 I TELL YOU: NO. BUT
UNLESS YOU CHANGE YOUR WAYS, YOU WILL ALL PERISH AS THEY DID."

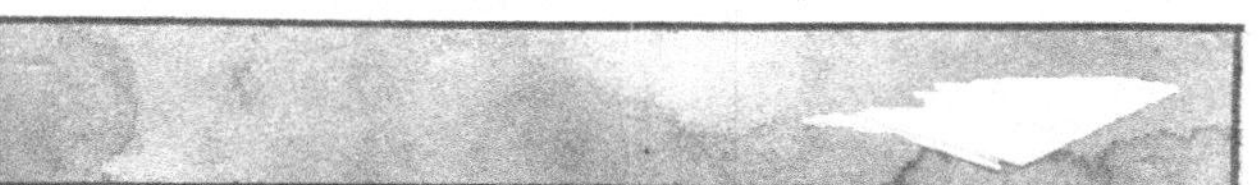

6 JESUS CONTINUED, "A MAN HAD A FIG TREE GROWING IN HIS VINEYARD. HE CAME LOOKING FOR FRUIT ON IT, BUT
FOUND NONE. 7 HE SAID TO THE GARDENER: 'LOOK HERE, FOR THREE YEARS I HAVE BEEN LOOKING FOR FIGS ON THIS TREE AND I HAVE FOUND NONE. CUT IT DOWN, WHY SHOULD
IT USE UP THE GROUND?' 8 THE GARDENER REPLIED: 'LEAVE IT
ONE MORE YEAR, SO THAT I MAY DIG AROUND IT AND ADD
SOME FERTILIZER; 9 PERHAPS IT WILL BEAR FRUIT FROM
NOW ON. BUT IF IT DOESN'T, YOU CAN CUT IT DOWN."

THE HEALING ON A SABBATH DAY

10 JESUS WAS TEACHING IN A SYNAGOGUE ON THE SAB-
BATH 11 AND A CRIPPLED WOMAN WAS THERE. AN EVIL

SPIRIT HAD KEPT HER BENT FOR EIGHTEEN YEARS SO THAT
SHE COULDN'T STRAIGHTEN UP AT ALL. 12 ON SEEING HER, JESUS
CALLED HER AND SAID, "WOMAN, YOU ARE FREED FROM YOUR INFIRMITY." 13 THEN HE LAID HIS HANDS UPON HER AND IMME-
DIATELY SHE WAS MADE STRAIGHT AND PRAISED GOD. 14 BUT
THE RULER OF THE SYNAGOGUE WAS INDIGNANT AS JESUS HAD
PERFORMED THIS HEALING ON THE SABBATH DAY AND HE SAID TO THE PEOPLE, "THERE ARE SIX WORKING DAYS: COME ON THOSE DAYS TO BE HEALED AND NOT ON
THE SABBATH." 15 BUT THE
LORD REPLIED, "YOU HYPOCRITES! EVERYONE OF YOU UNTIE HIS OX OR HIS DONKEY ON THE SABBATH AND LEADS IT OUT TO GIVE IT WATER. 16
HERE YOU HAVE A DAUGHTER OF ABRAHAM WHOM SATAN HAS BOUND FOR EIGHTEEN YEARS. SHOULD SHE NOT BE FREED FROM HER BONDS ON THE SABBATH?" 17 WHEN JESUS
SAID THIS, ALL HIS OPPONENTS FELT ASHAMED. BUT THE PEOPLE REJOICED AT THE MANY WONDERS THAT HAPPENED FROM HIM.

TWO PARABLES

18 JESUS CONTINUED, "WHAT IS THE KINGDOM OF GOD LIKE?
WHAT SHALL I COMPARE IT TO? 19 IMAGINE A PERSON WHO
HAS TAKEN A MUSTARD SEED AND PLANTED IT IN HIS GARDEN. THE SEED HAS GROWN AND BECOME LIKE A SMALL TREE, SO THAT THE BIRDS OF THE AIR SHELTER IN ITS BRAN-
CHES." 20 AND HE SAID AGAIN, "WHAT IS THE KINGDOM OF
GOD LIKE? 21 IMAGINE A WOMAN WHO HAS TAKEN YEAST AND HIDDEN IT IN THREE MEASURES OF FLOUR UNTIL IT IS ALL LEAVENED."

(22) JESUS WENT THROUGH TOWNS AND VILLAGES TE-
ACHING AND MAKING HIS WAY TO JERUSALEM. (23) SOME-
ONE ASKED HIM, "LORD, IS IT TRUE THAT FEW PEOPLE WILL
BE SAVED?" JESUS ANSWERED, (24) DO YOUR BEST TO EN-
TER BY THE NARROW DOOR, FOR MANY, I TELL YOU,
WILL TRY TO ENTER AND WILL NOT BE ABLE. WHEN
(25) ONCE THE MASTER OF THE HOUSE HAS
GOT UP AND LOCKED THE DOOR, YOU WILL STAND
OUTSIDE; THEN YOU WILL KNOCK AT THE DOOR CAL-
LING: 'LORD, OPEN TO US.' BUT HE WILL SAY TO YOU:
'I DO NOT KNOW WHERE YOU COME FROM.' (26) THEN

YOU WILL SAY: WE ATE AND DRANK WITH YOU AND YOU TAUGHT
IN OUR STREETS! (27) BUT HE WILL REPLY: 'I DON'T KNOW WHE-
RE YOU COME FROM. AWAY FROM ME ALL YOU WORKERS
OF EVIL.' (28) YOU WILL WEEP AND GRIND YOUR TEETH WHEN
YOU SEE ABRAHAM AND JACOB AND ALL THE PROPHETS
IN THE KINGDOM OF GOD, AND YOU YOURSELVES
LEFT OUTSIDE. (29) OTHERS WILL SIT AT TABLE IN THE
KINGDOM OF GOD, PEOPLE COMING FROM EAST AND
WEST, FROM NORTH AND SOUTH. (30) SOME WHO

ARE AMONG THE LAST
WILL BE THE FIRST, AND
OTHERS WHO WERE
FIRST WILL BE LAST!"
(31) AT THAT TIME SOME
PHARISEES CAME TO
JESUS AND GAVE HIM THIS
WARNING, "LEAVE THIS
PLACE AND GO ON YOUR
WAY, FOR HEROD WANTS
TO KILL YOU." JESUS
SAID, (32) GO AND GIVE
THE FOX MY ANSWER:
"I DRIVE OUT DEMONS
AND HEAL TODAY AND
TOMORROW, AND ON
THE THIRD DAY I FI-
NISH MY COURSE!"

(33) NEVERTHELESS, I
MUST GO ON MY WAY
TODAY AND TOMOR-
ROW AND FOR A LIT-
TLE LONGER, FOR
IT WOULD BE UNFITTING FOR A PROPHET TO
BE KILLED OUTSIDE JERUSALEM.

ALAS FOR YOU, JERUSALEM

(34) O JERUSALEM, JERUSALEM, YOU SLAY THE PROPHETS
AND STONE YOUR APOSTLES! HOW OFTEN HAVE I TRIED TO
BRING TOGETHER YOUR CHILDREN, AS A BIRD GATHERS
HER YOUNG UNDER HER WINGS, BUT YOU REFUSED!"
(35) FROM NOW ON YOUR TEMPLE WILL BE LEFT
EMPTY FOR YOU AND YOU WILL NO LONGER SEE ME
UNTIL THE TIME WHEN YOU WILL SAY:

BLESSED IS HE WHO COMES
IN THE NAME OF THE LORD."

14 (1) ON SABBATH, JESUS HAD GONE TO EAT A
MEAL IN THE HOUSE OF A LEADING PHARISEE,
AND HE WAS CAREFULLY WATCHED. (2) IN FRONT
OF HIM WAS A MAN SUFFERING FROM DROPSY;
(3) SO JESUS ASKED THE TEACHERS OF THE LAW
AND THE PHARISEES, "IS IT LAWFUL TO HEAL ON
ON THE SABBATH OR NOT?
(4) BUT NO ONE ANS-
WERED. JESUS THEN
TOOK THE MAN, HE-
ALED HIM AND SENT
HIM AWAY. (5) AND
HE ADDRESSED THEM,
"IF YOUR LAMB OR
YOUR OX FALLS INTO
A WELL ON A SAB-
BATH DAY, WHO
AMONG YOU DOES
NOT PULL HIM OUT?"

(6) AND THEY COULD
NOT ANSWER.

(17) JESUS THEN TOLD A PARABLE TO THE GUESTS, FOR HE HAD NOTI-
CED HOW THEY TRIED TO TAKE THE PLACES OF HONOR. HE SAID, (8)
"WHEN YOU ARE INVITED TO A WEDDING PARTY, DO NOT CHOOSE
THE BEST SEAT. IT MAY HAPPEN THAT A MORE IMORTANT GUEST
THAN YOU HAS BEEN INVITED, (9) AND YOUR HOST, WHO INVITED
BOTH OF YOU, WILL COME AND SAY TO YOU: 'GIVE HIM YOUR PLACE'.
WHAT SHAME IS YOURS WHEN YOU TAKE THE LOWEST PLA-
CE AND SEAT! (10) WHENEVER YOU ARE INVITED, GO RATHER
TO THE LOWEST SEAT, SO THAT YOUR HOST MAY COME AND
SAY TO YOU: 'FRIEND, YOU MUST COME UP HIGHER.' AND THIS
WILL BE A GREAT HONOR FOR YOU IN THE PRESENCE OF ALL
THE OTHER GUESTS. (11) FOR EVERYONE WHO MAKES MUCH OF
HIMSELF WILL BE HUMBLED, AND HE WHO HUMBLES HIMSELF
WILL BE ESTEEMED." (12) JESUS SAID TO THE MAN WHO HAD
INVITED HIM, "WHEN YOU GIVE A LUNCH OR A DINNER, DO NOT

INVITE YOUR FRIENDS, OR BROTHERS OR RELATIVES OR WEALTHY
NEIGHBORS, FOR SURELY THEY WILL ALSO INVITE YOU IN RE-
TURN AND YOU WILL BE REPAID. (13) WHEN YOU GIVE A FEAST,
INVITE INSTEAD THE POOR, THE CRIPPLED, THE LAME AND THE
BLIND. (14) FORTUNATE ARE YOU, FOR THEY CAN'T REPAY YOU; YOU
WILL BE REPAID AT THE RESURRECTION OF THE UPRIGHT."

A MAN ONCE GAVE A FEAST

(15) UPON HEARING THESE WORDS, ONE OF THOSE AT THE
TABLE SAID TO JESUS, "HAPPY ARE THOSE WHO EAT AT
THE BANQUET IN THE KINGDOM OF GOD!" (16) JESUS
REPLIED, "A MAN ONCE GAVE A FEAST AND
INVITED MANY GUESTS.

When you see a cloud rising in the west, you say at once: 'A shower is coming! And so it happens - (Luke 12:54)
©
DM
09

17 WHEN IT WAS TIME FOR THE FEAST HE SENT HIS SERVANT
TO TELL THOSE HE HAD INVITED TO COME, FOR EVERYTHING WAS
READY. 18 BUT ALL ALIKE BEGAN TO MAKE EXCUSES. THE
FIRST SAID: 'PLEASE EXCUSE ME. I MUST GO AND SEE THE PIECE
OF LAND I HAVE JUST BOUGHT.' 19 ANOTHER SAID: 'I AM SORRY,
BUT I AM ON MY WAY TO TRY OUT THE FIVE YOKE OF OXEN I HAVE
JUST BOUGHT.' 20 STILL ANOTHER SAID, 'HOW CAN I COME WHEN
I HAVE JUST MARRIED?' 21
THE SERVANT RETURNED
ALONE AND REPORTED THIS
TO HIS MASTER. UPON HEAR-
ING THE ACCOUNT, THE MAS-
TER OF THE HOUSE FLEW IN-
TO A RAGE AND SAID TO HIS
SERVANT: 'GO OUT QUICKLY
INTO THE STREETS AND AL-
LEYS OF THE TOWN AND BRING
IN THE POOR, THE CRIPPLED,
THE BLIND AND THE LAME.'
22 THE SERVANT REPOR-
TED AFTER A WHILE: 'SIR
YOUR ORDERS HAVE BEEN
CARRIED OUT, BUT THERE
IS STILL ROOM.' 23 THE
MASTER SAID: 'GO OUT
TO THE HIGHWAYS AND
COUNTRY LANES AND
FORCE PEOPLE TO COME
IN, TO MAKE SURE MY
HOUSE IS FULL.'
24 I TELL YOU, NONE
OF THOSE INVITED
WILL HAVE A MORSEL OF MY FEAST."

THE COST OF FOLLOWING JESUS

25 ONE DAY, WHEN LARGE CROWDS WERE WALKING ALONG
WITH JESUS, HE TURNED AND SAID TO THEM, 26 "IF YOU
COME TO ME, WITHOUT BEING READY TO GIVE UP YOUR
LOVE FOR YOUR FATHER AND MOTHER, YOUR SPOUSE AND
CHILDREN, YOUR BROTHERS AND SISTERS, AND YOURSELF,
YOU CANNOT BE MY DISCIPLES. 27 HE WHO DOESN'T FOLLOW
ME CARRYING HIS OWN CROSS CANNOT BE MY DISCIPLE.
28 DO YOU BUILD A HOUSE WITHOUT FIRST SITTING DOWN TO
COUNT THE COST TO SEE WHETHER YOU HAVE ENOUGH TO COM-
PLETE IT? 29 OTHERWISE, IF YOU HAVE LAID THE FOUNDATION
AND ARE NOT ABLE TO FINISH IT, EVERYONE WILL MAKE FUN
OF YOU: 30 'HE BEGAN TO BUILD AND WAS NOT ABLE TO FI-
NISH IT.' 31 AND WHEN A KING WAGES WAR AGAINST AN-

OTHER KING DOES HE GO TO FIGHT WITHOUT FIRST SIT-
TING DOWN TO CONSIDER WHETHER HIS TEN THOUSAND MEN
CAN STAND AGAINST THE TWENTY THOUSAND OF HIS ENEMY?
32 AND IF NOT, WHILE THE OTHER IS STILL A LONG
WAY OFF HE SENDS MESSENGERS FOR PEACE TALKS.
33 IN THE SAME WAY, NONE OF YOU MAY BECOME
MY DISCIPLE IF HE DOESN'T GIVE UP EVERYTHING HE HAS.
34 HOWEVER GOOD THE SALT MAY BE, IF IT HAS
LOST ITS TASTE, YOU CANNOT MAKE IT SALTY AGAIN.
35 IT IS FIT FOR NEITHER SOIL NOR MANURE. LET THEM
THROW IT AWAY. LISTEN THEN, IF YOU HAVE EARS!"

THE LOST SHEEP

15 1 MEANWHILE TAX COLLECTORS AND SINNERS WERE
SEEKING THE COMPANY OF JESUS, ALL OF THEM EA-
GER TO HEAR WHAT HE HAD TO SAY. 2 BUT THE PHARI-
SEES AND THE SCRIBES FROWNED AT THIS, MUTTERING, "THIS
MAN WELCOMES SINNERS AND EATS WITH THEM." 3 JESUS
THEN TOLD THEM THIS PARABLE:
4 "WHO AMONG YOU, IF HE HAS A HUNDRED SHEEP AND LO-
SES ONE OF THEM, WILL NOT LEAVE THE NINETY-NINE

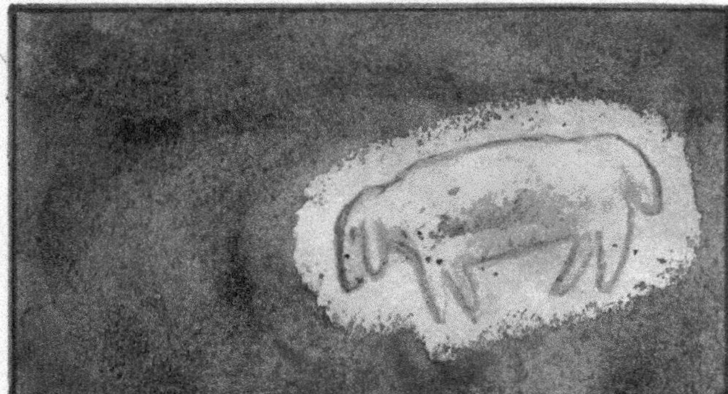

IN THE WILDERNESS AND SEEK OUT THE LOST ONE TILL HE
FINDS IT? 5 AND FINDING IT, WILL HE NOT JOYFULLY
CARRY IT HOME ON HIS SHOULDERS? 6 THEN HE WILL
CALL HIS FRIENDS AND NEIGHBORS TOGETHER AND
SAY: 'CELEBRATE WITH ME FOR I HAVE FOUND MY
LOST SHEEP.' 7 I TELL YOU, JUST SO, THERE WILL
BE MORE REJOICING IN HEAVEN OVER ONE REPEN-
TANT SINNER THAN OVER NINETY-NINE UPRIGHT
WHO DO NOT NEED TO REPENT.

8 WHAT WOMAN, IF SHE HAS TEN SILVER COINS AND
LOSES ONE, WILL NOT
LIGHT A LAMP AND SWE-
EP THE HOUSE IN A
THOROUGH SEARCH
TILL SHE FINDS THE
LOST COIN? 9 AND
FINDING IT, SHE WILL
CALL HER FRIENDS AND
NEIGHBORS AND SAY:
'CELEBRATE WITH ME
FOR I HAVE FOUND THE
SILVER COIN I LOST!'
10 I TELL YOU, IN
THE SAME WAY
THERE IS REJOI-
CING AMONG THE
ANGELS OF GOD
OVER ONE REPENTANT
SINNER.

THE PRODIGAL SON

11 JESUS CONTINUED: "THERE WAS A MAN WITH TWO
SONS. 12 THE YOUNGER SAID TO HIS FATHER: 'GIVE
ME MY SHARE OF THE ESTATE.' SO THE FATHER DIVIDED
HIS PROPERTY BETWEEN HIS TWO SONS. 13 SOME DAYS
LATER, THE YOUNGER SON GATHERED ALL HIS BELONGINGS
AND STARTED OFF FOR A DISTANT LAND WHERE HE
SQUANDERED HIS WEALTH IN LOOSE LIVING.
14 HAVING SPENT EVERYTHING, HE WAS HARD PRESSED
WHEN A SEVERE FAMINE BROKE OUT IN THAT LAND.

15 SO HE HIRED HIMSELF OUT TO A WELL-TO-DO
CITIZEN OF THAT PLACE AND WAS SENT TO
WORK ON A PIG FARM. 16 SO FAMISHED WAS
HE THAT HE LONGED TO FILL HIS STOMACH EVEN
WITH THE FOOD GIVEN TO THE PIGS, BUT NO
ONE OFFERED HIM ANYTHING.
17 FINALLY COMING TO HIS SENSES, HE SAID: 'HOW
MANY OF MY FATHER'S HIRED MEN HAVE FOOD TO
SPARE, AND HERE I AM STARVING TO DEATH! 18
I WILL GO BACK TO MY FATHER AND SAY TO HIM: FATHER,
I HAVE SINNED AGAINST GOD AND BEFORE YOU. 19 I NO LON-
GER DESERVE TO BE CALLED YOUR SON. TREAT ME AS ONE
OF YOUR HIRED SERVANTS.' WITH THAT THOUGHT IN MIND
HE SET OFF FOR HIS FATHER'S HOUSE. 20 HE WAS STILL

A LONG WAY OFF WHEN HIS FATHER SAW HIM. HE WAS SO DE-
EPLY MOVED WITH COMPASSION THAT HE RAN OUT TO MEET
HIM, THREW HIS ARMS AROUND HIS NECK AND KISSED HIM.
21 THE SON SAID, "FATHER, I HAVE SINNED AGAINST GOD AND BE-
FORE YOU. I NO LONGER DESERVE TO BE CALLED YOUR SON. 22 BUT
THE FATHER SAID TO HIS SERVANTS: 'QUICK! BRING OUT THE
FINES ROBE AND PUT IT ON HIM. PUT A RING ON HIS FINGER
AND SANDALS ON HIS FEET. 23 TAKE THE FATTENED CALF
AND KILL IT. WE SHALL CELEBRATE AND HAVE A FEAST. 24
FOR THIS SON OF MINE WAS DEAD AND HAS COME BACK TO
LIFE. HE WAS LOST AND IS FOUND.' AND THE FEAST BAGAN.

25 MEANWHILE, THE ELDER
SON HAD BEEN WORKING IN
THE FIELDS. AS HE RETUR-
NED AND WAS NEAR THE HO-
USE, HE HEARD MUSIC AND
DANCING. 26 HE CALLED
ONE OF HIS SERVANTS AND
ASKED WHAT IT WAS ALL
ABOUT. 27 THE SERVANT
ANSWERED, 'YOUR BROTHER
HAS COME HOME SAFE AND
SOUND, AND YOUR FATHER
HAS ORDERED THIS CELE-
BRATION AND KILLED THE
FATTENED CALF.' 28 THE
ELDER BECAME ANGRY
AND REFUSED TO GO IN. HIS
FATHER CAME OUT AND PLE-
ADED WITH HIM. 29 THE
INDIGNANT SON SAID: 'LOOK,
I HAVE SLAVED FOR YOU ALL
THESE YEARS. NEVER I
HAVE DISOBEYED YOUR
ORDERS. YET YOU HAVE
NEVER GIVEN ME A YOUNG
GOAT TO CELEBRATE WITH
MY FRIENDS. 30 THEN
WHEN THIS SON OF
YOURS RETURNS AFTER SQUANDERING YOUR PRO-
PERTY WITH LOOSE WOMEN, YOU KILL THE FATTENED
CALF FOR HIM.'
31 THE FATHER SAID:

**'MY SON, YOU ARE ALWAYS WITH ME,
AND EVERYTHING I HAVE IS YOURS. 32
BUT THIS BROTHER OF YOURS WAS DEAD
AND HAS COME BACK TO LIFE. HE WAS
LOST AND IS FOUND. AND FOR THAT
WE HAD TO CELEBRATE AND REJOICE.'"**

THE CRAFTY STEWARD

16 1 AT ANOTHER TIME, JESUS TOLD HIS DISCIPLES,
"THERE WAS A RICH MAN WHOSE STEWARD WAS RE-
PORTED TO HIM FOR FRAUDULENT SERVICE. 2 HE
SUMMONED THE STEWARD AND ASKED HIM: 'WHAT IS THIS I
HEAR ABOUT YOU? I WANT YOU TO RENDER AN ACCOUNT OF
YOUR SERVICE FOR IT IS ABOUT TO BE TERMINATED.' 3 THE
STEWARD THOUGHT TO HIMSELF: 'WHAT AM I TO DO NOW?
MY MASTER WILL DISMISS ME. I AM NOT STRONG ENOUGH
TO DO HARD WORK, AND I AM ASHAMED TO BEG. 4 I KNOW
WHAT I WILL DO: I MUST MAKE
SURE THAT WHEN I AM DIS-
MISSED, THERE WILL BE SOME
PEOPLE TO WELCOME ME INTO
THEIR HOUSE.' 5 SO HE CAL-
LED HIS MASTER'S DEBTORS
ONE BY ONE. HE ASKED THE
FIRST ONE: 'HOW MUCH DO
YOU OWE MY MASTER?' 6
THE REPLY WAS: 'A HUNDR-
ED JARS OF OIL.' THE STE-
WARD SAID: 'HERE IS YOUR
BILL. SIT DOWN AND WRITE
FIFTY.' 7 TO THE SE-
COND HE PUT THE SAME
QUESTION: 'HOW MUCH DO
YOU OWE?' THE ANSWER
WAS: 'A THOUSAND BUSHELS
OF WHEAT.' THEN HE SAID:
'TAKE YOUR BILL AND
WRITE EIGHT HUNDRED.'
8 THE MASTER COM-
MENDED THE DISHONEST
STEWARD FOR HIS ASTU-
TENESS, FOR THE PEOPLE
OF THIS WORLD ARE MORE

ASTUTE IN DEALING WITH THEIR OWN KIND THAN ARE
THE PEOPLE OF LIGHT. 9 AND SO I TELL YOU: USE MO-
NEY, TAINTED THOUGH IT BE, TO MAKE FRIENDS FOR YOUR-
SELVES, SO THAT WHEN IT FAILS, THESE PEOPLE MAY
WELCOME YOU INTO THE ETERNAL HOMES. 10 HE WHO
CAN BE TRUSTED IN LITTLE THINGS CAN ALSO BE TRUSTED
IN GREAT ONES: HE WHO IS DISHONEST IN SLIGHT MATTERS
WILL ALSO BE DISHONEST IN GREATER ONES. 11 SO IF YOU
HAVE NOT BEEN TRUSTWORTHY IN HANDLING MONEY, WHO
COULD ENTRUST YOU WITH TRUE WEALTH? 12 AND IF
YOU HAVE NOT BEEN TRUSTWORTHY WITH THINGS
WHICH ARE NOT REALLY YOURS, WHO WILL GIVE YOU
THE WEALTH WHICH IS YOUR OWN?

13 NO SERVANT CAN SERVE TWO MASTERS. EITHER
HE DOES NOT LIKE THE ONE AND IS FOND OF THE OTHER,

OR HE REGARDS ONE HIGHLY AND THE OTHER WITH
CONTEMPT. YOU CANNOT GIVE YOURSELF BOTH TO
GOD AND TO MONEY."
14 THE PHARISEES, WHO LOVED MONEY, HEARD ALL
THIS AND SNEERED AT JESUS. 15 HE SAID TO
THEM, "YOU DO YOUR BEST TO BE CONSIDERED
RIGHTEOUS MEN BY PEOPLE. BUT GOD KNOWS
THE HEART, AND WHAT IS HIGHEST AMONG
HUMANS IS LOATHED BY GOD.

16 THE TIME OF THE LAW AND THE PROPHETS HAS
ENDED WITH JOHN. THEN COMES THE PROCLAMATION OF
THE KINGDOM OF GOD AND THIS IS THE TIME FOR EVERYONE
TO CONQUER IT. 17 IT IS EASIER FOR HEAVEN AND
EARTH TO PASS AWAY THAN FOR A SINGLE LETTER OF
SCRIPTURE NOT TO BE FULFILLED.
18 THE MAN WHO DIVORCES HIS WIFE AND MAR-
RIES ANOTHER COMMITS ADULTERY; AND THE MAN
WHO MARRIES A WOMAN DIVORCED BY HER HUS-
BAND ALSO COMMITS ADULTERY.

THE RICH MAN AND LAZARUS

19 ONCE THERE WAS A RICH MAN WHO DRESSED IN
PURPLE AND FINE LINEN AND FEASTED EVERY DAY. 20
AT HIS GATE LAY LAZARUS,
A POOR MAN COVERED
WITH SORES. 21 WHO
LONGED TO EAT JUST THE
SCRAPS FALLING FROM
THE RICH MAN'S TABLE.
EVEN DOGS USED TO
COME AND LICK HIS
SORES. 22 IT HAPPENED
THAT THE POOR MAN DIED
AND ANGELS CARRIED HIM
TO HIS PLACE WITH ABRA-
HAM. THE RICH MAN ALSO
DIED AND WAS BURIED. 23
FROM HELL WHERE HE WAS
IN TORMENT, HE LOOKED UP
AND SAW ABRAHAM FAR OFF,
AND WITH HIM LAZARUS AT
REST. 24 HE CALLED OUT:
'FATHER ABRAHAM, HAVE
PITY ON ME AND SEND LAZA-
RUS WITH THE TIP OF HIS FIN-
GER DIPPED IN WATER TO
COOL MY TONGUE, FOR I
SUFFER SO MUCH IN THIS FIRE.' 25 ABRAHAM REPLIED: 'MY
SON, REMEMBER THAT IN YOUR LIFETIME YOU WERE WELL-
OFF WHILE THE LOT OF LAZARUS WAS MISFORTUNE. NOW HE IS
COMFORT AND YOU ARE IN AGONY. BUT THAT IS NOT ALL. 26 BET-
WEEN YOUR PLACE AND OURS A GREAT CHASM HAS BEEN FIXED,
SO THAT NO ONE CAN CROSS OVER FROM HERE TO YOU OR FROM
YOUR SIDE TO US.' 27 THE RICH MAN IMPLORED: 'THEN, I BEG
YOU, FATHER ABRAHAM, TO SEND LAZARUS TO MY FATHER'S
HOUSE 28 WHERE MY FIVE BROTHERS LIVE. LET HIM WARN
THEM SO THAT THEY MAY NOT END UP IN THIS PLACE OF TORMENT.'

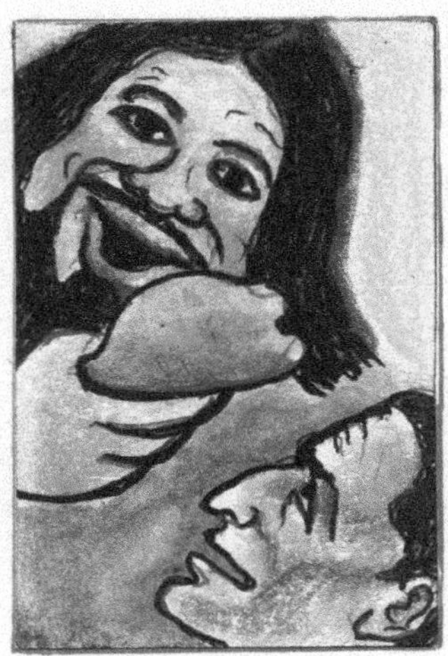

29 ABRAHAM REPLIED: 'THEY HAVE MOSES AND THE PROPHETS.
LET THEM LISTEN TO THEM.' 30 BUT THE RICH MAN SAID:
'NO, FATHER ABRAHAM, BUT IF SOMEONE FROM THE DEAD GOES
TO THEM, THEY WILL REPENT.' 31 ABRAHAM SAID: 'IF THEY
WILL NOT LISTEN TO MOSES AND THE PROPHETS, THEY WILL
NOT BE CONVINCED EVEN IF SOMEONE RISES FROM THE GRAVE.'

17 1 JESUS SAID TO HIS DISCIPLES, "SCANDALS WILL
NECESSARILY COME AND CAUSE PEOPLE TO FALL;
BUT WOE TO THE ONE WHO HAS BROUGHT IT ABOUT.
2 IT WOULD BE BETTER FOR HIM TO BE THROWN INTO THE
SEA WITH A MILLSTONE AROUND HIS NECK. TRULY THIS
WOULD BE BETTER FOR HIM THAN TO CAUSE ONE OF
THESE LITTLE ONES TO FALL. 3 BE CAREFUL, IF YOUR
BROTHER OFFENDS YOU, REBUKE HIM AND IF
HE IS SORRY, FORGIVE HIM.

4 AND IF HE OFFENDS YOU SEVEN TIMES IN A DAY
BUT SAYS TO YOU SEVEN TIMES: 'I AM SORRY,' FOR-
GIVE HIM."
5 THE APOSTLES SAID TO THE LORD, "INCREASE OUR
FAITH." AND THE LORD SAID, 6 "IF YOU HAVE FAITH
EVEN THE SIZE OF A MUSTARD SEED, YOU MAY SAY
TO THIS TREE: 'BE UPROOTED AND PLANT YOURSELF
IN THE SEA,' AND IT WILL OBEY YOU. 7 IF YOU

HAVE A SERVANT COMING IN FROM THE FIELDS AFTER
PLOWING OR TENDING SHEEP, DO YOU SAY TO HIM: 'CO-
ME AT ONCE AND SIT DOWN AT TABLE'? 8 NO, YOU TELL
HIM: 'PREPARE MY DINNER. PUT ON YOUR APRON AND WAIT
ON ME WHILE I EAT AND DRINK; YOU CAN EAT AND DRINK
AFTERWARDS.' 9 DO YOU THANK THIS SERVANT FOR DOING
WHAT YOU COMMANDED? 10 SO FOR YOU. WHEN YOU HAVE
DONE ALL THAT YOU HAVE BEEN TOLD TO DO, YOU MUST SAY:
'WE ARE NO MORE THAN SERVANTS; WE HAVE
ONLY DONE OUR DUTY.'"

THE TEN LEPERS

11 ON THE WAY TO JERUSALEM, JESUS WAS PASSING ALONG THE
BORDER BETWEEN SAMARIA AND GALILEE, AND 12 AS HE
ENTERED A VILLAGE, TEN
LEPERS CAME TO MEET
HIM. 13 KEEPING THEIR DIS-
TANCE, THEY CALLED TO HIM,
"JESUS, MASTER, HAVE PITY
ON US!" 14 JESUS SAID, "GO
AND SHOW YOURSELVES TO THE
PRIESTS." AS THEY WENT ON
THEIR WAY, THEY FOUND THEY
WERE CURED. 15 ONE OF
THEM, AS SOON AS HE SAW
HE WAS CLEANSED, TURN-
ED BACK PRAISING GOD IN
A LOUD VOICE, AND 16
THROWING HIMSELF ON
HIS FACE BEFORE JESUS,
HE GAVE HIM THANKS.
THIS MAN WAS A SAMA-
RITAN. 17 THEN JESUS
SAID, "WERE NOT ALL TEN
HEALED? WHERE ARE THE
OTHER NINE? 18 WAS NO
ONE FOUND TO RETURN AND
GIVE PRAISE TO GOD BUT
THIS ALIEN?" 19 AND
JESUS SAID TO HIM, "STAND UP AND GO YOUR WAY;
YOUR FAITH HAS SAVED YOU."

THE COMING OF THE KINGDOM OF GOD

20 THE PHARISEES ASKED JESUS WHEN THE KING-
DOM OF GOD WAS TO COME. HE ANSWERED, "THE
KINGDOM OF GOD IS NOT LIKE SOMETHING YOU CAN
OBSERVE 21 AND SAY OF IT: 'LOOK, HERE IT IS! THERE
IT IS!' SEE, THE KINGDOM OF GOD IS AMONG YOU."

"FATHER, I HAVE SINNED AGAINST GOD AND BEFORE YOU" (LUKE 15:21)
342
CCCXXXXII
© DM 08

22 AND JESUS SAID TO HIS DISCIPLES, "THE TIME IS
AT HAND WHEN YOU WILL LONG TO SEE ONE OF
THE GLORIOUS DAYS OF THE SON OF MAN, BUT YOU
WILL NOT SEE IT.
23 THEN PEOPLE WILL TELL YOU: 'LOOK THERE!
LOOK HERE!' DO NOT GO, DO NOT FOLLOW THEM.
24 FOR THE SON OF MAN WILL APPEAR LIKE
LIGHTNING THAT FLASHES FROM ONE END
OF THE SKY TO THE OTHER. 25 BUT FIRST HE

MUST SUFFER MANY THINGS AND BE REJECTED BY THIS
PEOPLE. 26 AS IT WAS IN THE DAYS OF NOAH, SO WILL
IT BE ON THE DAY THE SON OF MAN COMES. 27 THEN
PEOPLE ATE AND DRANK; THEY TOOK HUSBANDS AND
WIVES. BUT ON THE DAY NOAH ENTERED THE ARK, THE
FLOOD CAME AND DESTROYED THEM ALL. 28 JUST AS IT
WAS IN THE DAYS OF LOT: PEOPLE ATE AND DRANK, BOUGHT
AND SOLD, PLANTED AND BUILT. 29 BUT ON THE DAY LOT
LEFT SODOM, GOD MADE FIRE AND SULFUR RAIN DOWN FROM
HEAVEN WHICH DESTROYED THEM ALL. 30 SO WILL IT BE ON
THE DAY THE SON OF MAN IS REVEALED. 31 ON THAT DAY,

IF YOU ARE ON THE ROOF-
TOP, DON'T GO DOWN INTO
THE HOUSE TO GET YOUR
BELONGINGS, AND IF YOU
HAPPEN TO BE IN THE FIELDS,
DO NOT TURN BACK. 32 RE-
MEMBER LOT'S WIFE. 33
WHOEVER TRIES TO SAVE
HIS LIFE WILL LOSE HIM-
SELF, BUT WHOEVER GIVES
HIS LIFE WILL BE BORN
AGAIN. 34 I TELL YOU,
THOUGH TWO MEN ARE SHA-
RING THE SAME BED, IT MAY
BE THAT ONE WILL BE TA-
KEN AND THE OTHER LEFT."
35 THOUGH TWO WOMEN
ARE GRINDING CORN TOGE-
THER, ONE MAY BE TAKEN
AND THE OTHER LEFT."
37 THEN THEY ASKED
JESUS, "WHERE WILL THIS
TAKE PLACE, LORD?" AND HE
ANSWERED, "WHERE THE
BODY IS, THERE TOO WILL
THE VULTURES GATHER."

PRAY AND NEVER LOSE HEART

18 1 JESUS TOLD THEM A PARABLE TO SHOW THEM THAT
THEY SHOULD PRAY CONTINUALLY AND NOT LOSE HEART.
2 HE SAID, "IN A CERTAIN TOWN THERE WAS A JUDGE
WHO NEITHER FEARED GOD NOR PEOPLE. 3 IN THE SAME
TOWN WAS A WIDOW WHO KEPT COMING TO HIM, SAYING:
'DEFEND MY RIGHTS AGAINST MY OPPONENT'. 4 FOR A TIME
HE REFUSED, BUT FINALLY HE THOUGHT: 'EVEN THOUGH I
NEITHER FEAR GOD NOR CARE ABOUT PEOPLE, 5 THIS
WIDOW BOTHERS ME SO MUCH I WILL SEE THAT SHE
GETS JUSTICE; THEN SHE WILL STOP COMING AND WEAR-
ING ME OUT."
6 AND JESUS EXPLAINED, "LISTEN TO WHAT THE EVIL
JUDGE SAYS. 7 WILL GOD NOT DO JUSTICE FOR HIS
CHOSEN ONES WHO CRY TO HIM DAY AND NIGHT EVEN IF
HE DELAYS IN ANSWERING THEM? 8 I TELL YOU, HE WILL
SPEEDILY DO THEM JUSTICE. YET, WHEN THE SON OF MAN
COMES, WILL HE FIND FAITH ON EARTH?"

THE PHARISEE AND THE TAX COLLECTOR

9 JESUS TOLD ANOTHER PARABLE TO SOME PERSONS FULLY
CONVINCED OF THEIR OWN RIGHTEOUSNESS, WHO LOOKED
DOWN ON OTHERS. 10 "TWO MEN WENT UP TO THE TEMPLE
TO PRAY: ONE WAS A PHARISEE AND THE OTHER A TAX COL-
LECTOR. 11 THE PHARISEE STOOD BY HIMSELF AND SAID,
'I THANK YOU, GOD, THAT

I AM NOT LIKE OTHER PE-
OPLE, GRASPING, CROOKED,
ADULTEROUS, OR EVEN LIKE
THIS TAX COLLECTORS. 12
I FAST TWICE A WEEK AND GI-
VE THE TENTH OF ALL MY IN-
COME TO THE TEMPLE.' 13
IN THE MEANTIME THE TAX
COLLECTOR, STANDING FAR
OFF, WOULD NOT EVEN LIFT
HIS EYES TO HEAVEN, BUT
BEAT HIS BREAST SAYING:
'O GOD BE MERCIFUL TO ME,
A SINNER.' 14 I TELL YOU,
WHEN THIS MAN WENT DOWN
TO HIS HOUSE, HE WAS RE-
CONCILED WITH GOD, BUT
NOT THE OTHER. FOR WHO-
EVER MAKES HIMSELF OUT
TO BE GREAT WILL BE
HUMBLED, AND WHOEVER
HUMBLES HIMSELF WILL
BE RAISED HIGHER." 15
THEY EVEN BROUGHT LIT-
TLE CHILDREN TO JESUS
TO HAVE HIM TOUCH THEM;
BUT THEN THE DISCIPLES REBUKED THESE PEOPLE. 16 SO
JESUS CALLED THE CHILDREN TO HIM AND SAID, "LET
THE CHILDREN COME TO ME AND DON'T STOP THEM,
FOR THE KINGDOM OF GOD BELONGS TO SUCH AS THESE.
17 TRULY, I TELL YOU, WHOEVER DOES NOT RECE-
IVE THE KINGDOM OF GOD LIKE A CHILD, WILL NOT ENTER IT."

JESUS AND THE RICH RULER

18 A RULER ASKED JESUS,

"GOOD MASTER, WHAT SHALL I
DO TO INHERIT ETERNAL LIFE?"

19 JESUS SAID TO HIM, "WHY DO YOU CALL ME GOOD?

NO ONE IS GOOD BUT GOD ALONE. 20 YOU KNOW THE COM-
MANDMENTS. DO NOT COMMIT ADULTERY, DO NOT KILL, DO
NOT STEAL, DO NOT ACCUSE FALSELY, HONOR YOUR FATHER
AND YOUR MOTHER." 21 AND THE MAN SAID: I HAVE
KEPT ALL THESE COMMANDMENTS FROM MY YOUTH."

22 JESUS ANSWERED, "THERE IS STILL ONE THING YOU
ARE LACKING. SELL ALL YOU HAVE AND GIVE THE MONEY TO THE
POOR, AND YOU WILL HAVE RICHES IN GOD. AND THEN COME AND
FOLLOW ME." 23 WHEN HE HEARD THESE WORDS, THE MAN BE-
CAME SAD FOR HE WAS VERY RICH. 24 JESUS NOTICING THIS
SAID, "HOW HARD IT IS FOR PEOPLE WHO HAVE RICHES TO
ENTER THE KINGDOM OF GOD! 25 IT IS EASIER FOR A
CAMEL TO PASS THROUGH THE EYE OF A NEEDLE THAN FOR A
RICH PERSON TO ENTER THE
KINGDOM OF GOD." 26 THE

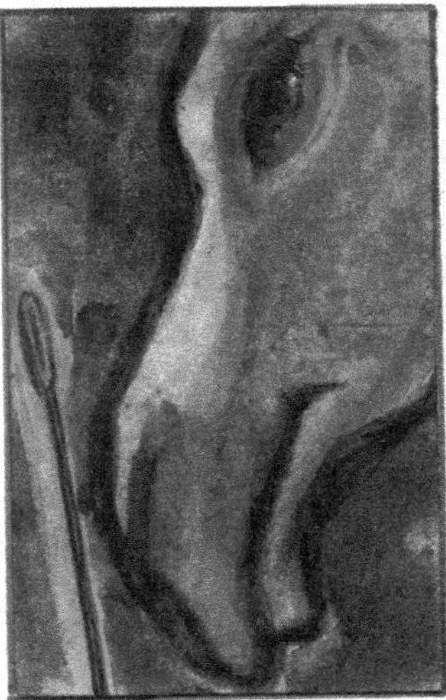

BYSTANDERS SAID, "WHO
THEN CAN BE SAVED?" AND
27 JESUS REPLIED, "WHAT
IS IMPOSSIBLE FOR HUMANS
IS POSSIBLE FOR GOD." 28
THEN PETER SAID, "WE LEFT
EVERYTHING WE HAD AND
FOLLOWED YOU." 29 JESUS
REPLIED, "TRULY, I TELL YOU,
WHOEVER HAS LEFT HOUSE
OR WIFE, OR BROTHERS OR
PARENTS OR CHILDREN FOR
THE SAKE OF THE KINGDOM
OF GOD, 30 WILL RECEIVE
MUCH MORE IN THIS PRE-
SENT TIME; AND IN THE
WORLD TO COME HE WILL
HAVE ETERNAL LIFE."
31 JESUS THEN TOOK
THE TWELVE ASIDE AND
TOLD THEM, "NOW, WE
ARE GOING UP TO JE-
RUSALEM AND EVERY-
THING THE PROPHETS
HAVE WRITTEN ABOUT THE SON OF MAN WILL BE
FULFILLED. 32 HE WILL BE DELIVERED UP TO THE
FOREIGN POWER. PEOPLE WILL MOCK HIM, INSULT
HIM AND SPIT ON HIM. 33 AFTER THEY HAVE
SCOURGED HIM, THEY WILL KILL HIM, BUT HE
RAISED ON THE THIRD DAY." 34 THE APOSTLES
COULD MAKE NOTHING OF THIS; THE MEANING

OF THESE WORDS REMAINED A MYSTERY TO THEM
AND THEY DID NOT UNDERSTAND WHAT HE SAID.

THE BLIND MAN OF JERICHO

35 WHEN JESUS DREW NEAR TO JERICHO, A BLIND
MAN SITTING BY THE ROAD, BEGGING. 36 AS HE HEARD
THE CROWD PASSING BY, HE INQUIRED WHAT IT WAS,
AND 37 THEY TOLD HIM THAT JESUS OF NAZARETH
WAS GOING BY. THEN HE CRIED OUT, 38 "JESUS, SON OF
DAVID, HAVE MERCY ON ME!" 39 THE PEOPLE IN FRONT
SCOLDED HIM, "BE QUIET!" BUT HE CRIED OUT ALL THE
MORE, "JESUS, SON OF DAVID, HAVE MERCY ON ME!"
40 JESUS STOPPED AND ORDERED THE BLIND MAN
TO BE BROUGHT TO HIM, AND WHEN HE CAME NEAR, HE
ASKED HIM, 41 "WHAT DO YOU WANT ME TO DO FOR YOU?"
AND THE MAN SAID, "LORD, THAT I MAY SEE!" 42 JESUS
SAID, "RECEIVE YOUR SIGHT, YOUR FAITH HAS SAVED YOU."
43 AT ONCE THE BLIND MAN WAS ABLE TO SEE, AND HE
FOLLOWED JESUS, GIVING PRAISE TO GOD. AND ALL THE
PEOPLE WHO WHERE THERE ALSO PRAISED GOD.

JESUS AND ZACCHEUS

19 1 WHEN JESUS ENTERED JERICHO AND WAS
GOING THROUGH THE CITY, 2 A MAN NAMED
ZACCHEUS WAS THERE. HE WAS A TAX COLLECT-
OR AND A WEALTHY MAN. 3 HE WANTED TO SEE WHAT
JESUS WAS LIKE, BUT HE WAS A SHORT MAN AND
COULD NOT SEE BECAUSE OF THE CROWD. 4 SO HE
RAN AHEAD AND CLIMBED UP A SYCOMORE TREE. FROM
THERE HE WOULD BE ABLE TO SEE JESUS WHO HAD TO
PASS THAT WAY. 5 WHEN JESUS CAME TO THE

PLACE, HE LOOKED UP AND SAID TO HIM, "ZACCHEUS,
COME DOWN QUICKLY FOR I MUST STAY AT YOUR HOUSE
TODAY." 6 SO ZACCHEUS HURRIED DOWN AND
RECEIVED HIM JOYFULLY. 7 ALL THE PEOPLE WHO SAW
IT BEGAN TO GRUMBLE AND SAID, "HE HAS GONE TO THE HOUSE
OF A SINNER AS A GUEST." 8 BUT ZACCHEUS SPOKE TO
JESUS, "THE HALF OF MY GOODS, LORD, I GIVE TO THE POOR, AND
IF I HAVE CHEATED ANYONE, I WILL PAY HIM BACK FOUR
TIMES AS MUCH." 9 LOOKING AT HIM JESUS SAID,
"SALVATION HAS COME TO THIS HOUSE TODAY, FOR
HE IS A TRUE SON OF ABRAHAM. 10 THE SON
OF MAN HAS COME TO SEEK AND TO
SAVE THE LOST."

THE TEN POUNDS

11 JESUS WAS NOW NEAR JERUSALEM AND THE PEOPLE WITH
HIM THOUGHT THAT GOD'S REIGN WAS ABOUT TO APPEAR.
SO AS THE WERE LISTEN-
ING TO HIM, HE WENT ON TO
TELL THEM A PARABLE.
12 HE SAID, "A MAN OF
NOBLE BIRTH WENT TO A
DISTANT PLACE TO HAVE
HIMSELF APPOINTED
KING OF HIS OWN PE-
OPLE, AFTER WHICH
HE WOULD RETURN. 13

THEN HE SUMMONED TEN
OF HIS SERVANTS AND GAVE
THEM TEN POUNDS. HE SAID,
"PUT THIS MONEY TO WORK
UNTIL I COME BACK. 14 BUT
HIS COMPRATIOTS WHO DIS-
LIKED HIM SENT A DELEGA-
TION AFTER HIM WITH THIS
MESSAGE: 'WE DO NOT WANT
THIS MAN TO BE OUR KING.'
15 HE RETURNED, HOW-
EVER, APPOINTED AS
KING. AT ONCE HE SENT
FOR THE SERVANTS
TO WHOM HE HAD GI-
VEN THE MONEY, TO
FIND OUT WHAT PRO-
FIT EACH HAD MADE.
16 THE FIRST CAME
IN AND REPORTED: 'SIR, YOUR TEN POUNDS HAS
EARNED TEN MORE.' 17 THE MASTER REPLIED: 'WELL
DONE, MY GOOD SERVANT. SINCE YOU HAVE PROVED
YOURSELF CAPABLE IN A SMALL MATTER, I CAN
TRUST YOU TO TAKE CHARGE OF TEN CITIES.'

(18) THE SECOND REPORTED: 'SIR, YOUR POUND EAR-
NED FIVE MORE POUNDS.' (19) THE MASTER REPLIED:
'RIGHT, TAKE CHARGE OF FIVE CITIES.' (20) THE
THIRD CAME IN AND SAID: 'SIR, HERE IS YOUR
MONEY WHICH I HID FOR SAFEKEEPING. (21) I WAS
AFRAID OF YOU FOR YOU ARE AN EXACTING PER-
SON: YOU TAKE UP WHAT YOU DID NOT LAY
DOWN AND REAP WHAT YOU DID NOT SOW.' (22)
THE MASTER REPLIED: 'YOU WORTHLESS SER-
VANT, I WILL JUDGE YOU BY YOUR OWN WORDS.
SO YOU KNEW I WAS AN EXACTING PERSON, TAKING
UP WHAT I DID NOT LAY DOWN AND REAPING

WHAT I DID NOT SOW! (23) WHY, THEN, DID YOU NOT PUT MY
MONEY ON LOAN SO THAT WHEN I GOT BACK I COULD HAVE
COLLECT IT WITH INTEREST?' (24) THEN THE MASTER SAID
TO THOSE STANDING BY: 'TAKE FROM HIM THE PO-
UND I HAVE GIVEN, AND GIVE IT TO THE ONE WITH
TEN POUNDS.' (25) THEY OBJECTED: 'BUT, SIR,
HE ALREADY HAS TEN!'
(26) 'I TELL YOU: EVERYONE WHO HAS WILL BE GIVEN MO-
RE; BUT FROM HIM WHO HAS NOT, EVEN WHAT HE
HAS WILL BE TAKEN AWAY. (27) AS FOR MY ENEMIES
WHO DID NOT WANT ME TO BE KING, BRING THEM IN AND
EXECUTE THEM RIGHT HERE IN MY PRESENCE.'"

JESUS ENTERS JERUSALEM

(28) SO JESUS SPOKE, AND HE WENT ON AHEAD OF
THEM, ON HIS WAY TO JERUSALEM. (29) WHEN HE DREW
NEAR TO BETHPHAGE AND BETHANY, CLOSE TO MOUNT OLI-
VET, HE SENT TWO OF HIS
DISCIPLES WITH THESE IN-
STRUCTIONS, (30) "GO TO
THE VILLAGE OPPOSITE AND
AS YOU ENTER IT YOU WILL
FIND A COLT TIED UP THAT
NO ONE HAS YET RIDDEN:
UNTIE IT AND BRING IT
HERE. (31) AND IF ANYONE
SAYS TO YOU: 'WHY ARE YOU
UNTYING THIS COLT?' YOU
SHALL GIVE THIS ANSWER:
'THE MASTER NEEDS IT.'"
(32) SO THE TWO DISCIPLES
WENT AND FOUND THINGS
JUST AS JESUS HAD SAID.
(33) AS THEY WERE UN-
TYING THE COLT, THE OWNER
SAID TO THEM, "WHY ARE YOU
UNTYING THE COLT?" (34)
AND THEY ANSWERED, "THE
MASTER NEEDS IT." (35)
SO THEY BROUGHT IT TO
JESUS AND THROWING
THEIR CLOAKS ON THE COLT,
THEY MOUNTED JESUS ON

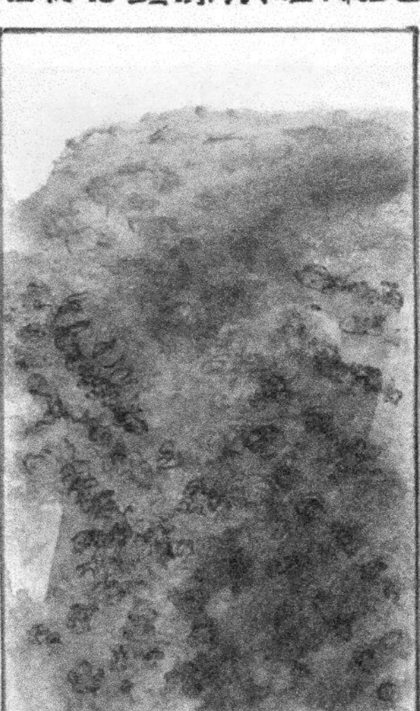

IT. (36) AND AS HE WENT DOWN, PEOPLE SPREAD THEIR
CLOAKS ON THE ROAD. (37) WHEN JESUS CAME NEAR
JERUSALEM, AT THE PLACE WHERE THE ROAD
SLOPES DOWN FROM THE MOUNT OF OLIVES, THE
WHOLE MULTITUDE OF HIS DISCIPLES BEGAN TO
REJOICE AND PRAISE GOD WITH A LOUD VOICE FOR
ALL THE MIRACLES THEY HAD SEEN. (38) AND THEY
CRIED OUT.

BLESSED IS HE WHO COMES AS KING IN THE NAME OF THE LORD.

IN HEAVEN AND GLORY IN THE HIGHEST HEAVENS."

(39) SOME PHARISEES IN THE CROWD SAID TO HIM, "MASTER,
REBUKE YOUR DISCIPLES." BUT JESUS ANSWERED, (40)
"I TELL YOU, IF THEY WERE TO REMAIN SILENT, THE
STONES WOULD CRY OUT." (41) WHEN JESUS HAD
COME IN SIGHT OF THE
CITY, HE WEPT OVER IT
(42) AND SAID, "IF ONLY
TODAY YOU KNEW THE
WAYS OF PEACE! BUT
NOW YOUR EYES ARE HELD
FROM SEEING. (43) YET
DAYS WILL COME UPON
YOU WHEN YOUR ENE-
MIES WILL SURROUND
YOU WITH BARRICADES
AND SHUT YOU IN AND
PRESS ON YOU FROM
EVERY SIDE. (44) AND
THEY WILL DASH YOU TO
THE GROUND AND YOUR
CHILDREN WITH YOU,
AND LEAVE NOT A STONE
WITHIN YOU, FOR YOU DID
NOT RECOGNIZE THE TI-
ME AND THE VISITATION
OF YOUR GOD."

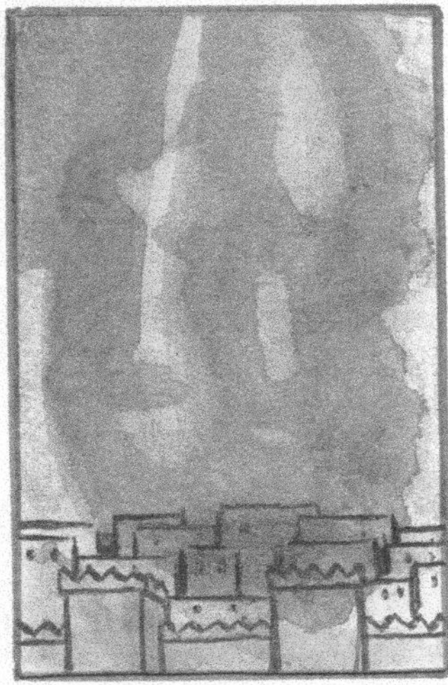

(45) THEN JESUS ENTERED THE TEMPLE AREA
AND BEGAN TO DRIVE OUT THE MERCHANTS. (46)
AND HE SAID TO THEM, "GOD SAYS IN THE SCRIPTURES:

MY HOUSE SHALL BE A HOUSE OF PRAYER

BUT YOU HAVE TURNED IT INTO A DEN OF ROBBERS."

(47) JESUS WAS TEACHING EVERY DAY IN THE TEMPLE.
THE CHIEF PRIESTS AND THE TEACHERS OF THE LAW WAN-
TED TO KILL HIM AND THE ELDERS OF THE JEWS AS WELL.
(48) BUT THEY WERE UNABLE TO DO ANYTHING, FOR
EVERYONE WAS LISTENING AND HANGING ON HIS WORDS.

20 (1) ONE DAY WHEN JESUS WAS TEACHING THE
PEOPLE IN THE TEMPLE AND PROCLAIMING
THE GOOD NEWS, THE CHIEF PRIESTS AND
THE TEACHERS OF THE LAW CAME WITH THE
ELDERS OF THE JEWS, (2) AND SAID TO
HIM, "TELL US, WHAT RIGHT HAVE YOU TO
ACT LIKE THIS? WHO GIVES YOU AUTHORITY
TO DO ALL THIS?"

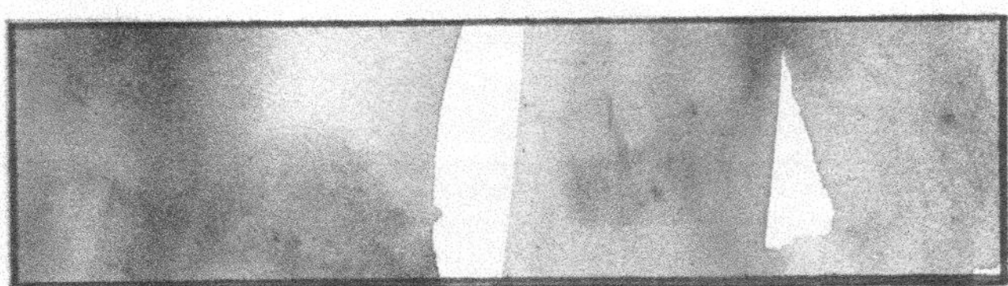

"WHEN HE HEARD THESE WORDS, THE MAN BECAME SAD FOR HE WAS VERY RICH"
(LUKE 18:23)
343
CCCXXXXIII
DM 08 ©

3 JESUS SAID TO THEM, "I ALSO WILL ASK YOU A QUESTION:
4 WAS JOHN'S BAPTISM A WORK OF GOD, OR WAS IT ME-
RELY SOMETHING HUMAN ?" 5 AND THEY ARGUED AMONG
THEMSELVES, "IF WE ANSWER THAT IT WAS A WORK OF
GOD, HE WILL SAY: 'WHY THEN DID YOU NOT BELIEVE HIM?'
6 BUT IF WE ANSWER THAT IT WAS SOMETHING HUMAN,
THE PEOPLE WILL STONE US, FOR THEY ALL REGARD JOHN
AS A PROPHET." 7 SO THEY ANSWERED JESUS, "WE
DON'T KNOW." 8 AND JESUS SAID TO THEM, "NE-
ITHER WILL I TELL YOU WHAT RIGHT I HAVE TO ACT
LIKE THIS."

THE MURDEROUS TENANTS

9 JESUS WENT ON TO TELL THE PEOPLE THIS PARABLE.
"A MAN PLANTED A VINEYARD AND LET IT OUT TO TENANTS

BEFORE GOING ABROAD FOR
A LONG TIME. 10 IN DUE
TIME HE SENT A SERVANT
TO THE TENANTS TO GET SO-
ME FRUIT FROM THE VINE-
YARD. BUT THE TENANTS BE-
AT HIM AND SENT HIM BACK
EMPTY-HANDED. 11 AGAIN
THE MAN SENT ANOTHER
SERVANT: THEY BEAT HIM
TOO AND TREATED HIM SHA-
MEFULLY AND SENT HIM
AWAY EMPTY-HANDED. 12
THE OWNER SENT A THIRD,
BUT HE WAS WOUNDED
AND THROWN OUT. 13
THE OWNER THEN THOUGHT,
'WHAT SHALL I DO? I WILL
SEND MY BELOVED SON;
SURELY THEY WILL RES-
PECT HIM.' 14 THE TENANTS,
HOWEVER, AS THEY SAW HIM,
SAID TO ONE ANOTHER:
'THIS IS THE ONE WHO WILL
INHERIT THE VINEYARD: LET
US KILL HIM AND THE PROPERTY WILL BE OURS.' 15 SO THEY
THREW HIM OUT OF THE VINEYARD AND KILLED HIM. 16 NOW,
WHAT WILL THE OWNER OF THE VINEYARD DO TO THEM? HE WILL
COME AND DESTROY THOSE TENANTS AND GIVE THE VINEYARD
TO OTHERS."
ON HEARING THIS, SOME OF THE RULERS SAID, "MAY IT NOT BE
SO!" 17 JESUS LOOKED DIRECTLY AT THEM AND SAID, "WHAT
DOES THIS TEXT OF THE SCRIPTURES MEAN:

**THE STONE WHICH THE BUILDERS REJECTED
HAS BECOME THE KEYSTONE.**

18 EVERYONE WHO FALLS ON THAT STONE WILL BE BROKEN TO

PIECES AND ANYONE THE STONE FALLS ON WILL BE CRUSHED."
19 THE TEACHERS OF THE LAW AND THE CHIEF PRIESTS WOULD HAVE
LIKED TO ARREST HIM, FOR THEY REALIZED THAT HE MEANT THIS
PARABLE FOR THEM, BUT THEY WERE AFRAID OF THE CROWD. 20
SO THEY LEFT, LOOKING FOR ANOTHER OPPORTUNITY.

PAYING TAXES TO CAESAR

THEY SENT SPIES WHO PRETENDED TO BE RIGHTEOUS
MEN, IN ORDER TO TRAP HIM IN HIS WORDS AND DELIVER HIM
TO THE AUTHORITY AND POWER OF THE ROMAN GOVERNOR.
21 THEY ASKED HIM, "MASTER, WE KNOW THAT YOU ARE
TRUE IN YOUR WORDS AND TEACHING, AND YOUR ANS-
WERS DO NOT VARY ACCORDING TO WHO IS LISTENING TO
YOU, FOR YOU TRULY TEACH THE WAY OF GOD. TELL US:
22 ARE ALLOWED TO PAY TAXES TO CAESAR OR NOT?"
23 BUT JESUS SAW THROUGH THEIR CUNNING AND SAID,
24 "SHOW ME A SILVER COIN. WHOSE HEAD IS THIS
AND WHOSE NAME?" THEY ANSWERED, "CAESAR'S." 25
AND JESUS SAID TO THEM, "RETURN TO CAESAR THE THINGS
THAT ARE CAESAR'S AND TO GOD WHAT BELONGS TO
GOD." 26 SO THEY WERE UNABLE TO TRAP HIM IN
WHAT HE SAID IN PUBLIC: THEY WERE SURPRISED
AT HIS ANSWER AND KEPT SILENT.

RESURRECTION OF THE DEAD

27 THEN SOME SADDUCEES ARRIVED. THESE PEOPLE SAY
THAT THERE IS NO RESURRECTION 28 AND THEY ASKED
JESUS THIS QUESTION, "MASTER, IN THE SCRIPTURE MO-
SES TOLD US: 'IF ANYONE DIES LEAVING A WIFE, BUT NO

CHILDREN, HIS BROTHER MUST TAKE THE WIFE, AND THE
CHILD TO BE BORN WILL BE REGARDED AS THE CHILD OF
THE DECEASED MAN'. 29 NOW, THERE WERE SEVEN BRO-
THERS, THE FIRST MARRIED A WIFE, BUT HE DIED WITHOUT
CHILDREN; 30 AND THE SECOND 31 AND THE THIRD
TOOK THE WIFE; IN FACT ALL SEVEN DIED LEAVING NO
CHILDREN. 32 LAST OF ALL THE WOMAN DIED. 33
ON THE DAY OF RESURRECTION, TO WHICH OF THEM WILL
THE WOMAN BE WIFE? FOR THE SEVEN HAD HER AS WIFE."
34 AND JESUS REPLIED,

"TAKING HUSBAND OR WI-
FE IS PROPER OF THE PE-
OPLE OF THIS WORLD, 35
BUT FOR THOSE WHO ARE
CONSIDERED WORTHY OF
THE WORLD TO COME AND
OF RESURRECTION FROM
THE DEAD, THERE IS NO
MORE MARRIAGE. 36
BESIDES, THEY CANNOT DIE
FOR THEY ARE LIKE THE
ANGELS. THEY TOO ARE
CHILDREN OF GOD BECAU-
SE THEY ARE BORN OF
THE RESURRECTION.
37 YES, THE DEAD
WILL BE RAISED, AND
EVEN MOSES SHOWED IT
TO BE TRUE IN THE PASSA-
GE OF THE BURNING BUSH,
WHERE HE CALLS THE
LORD THE GOD OF ABRAHAM,
THE GOD OF ISAAC AND THE
GOD OF JACOB. 38 FOR HE IS GOD OF THE LIVING AND NOT OF
THE DEAD, AND FOR HIM ALL ARE ALIVE." 39 SOME SCRI-
BES AGREED WITH JESUS, "MASTER, YOU HAVE SPO-
KEN WELL." 40 THEY DIDN'T DARE TO ASK HIM ANYTHING
ELSE. 41 THEN JESUS SAID TO THEM, "HOW CAN PE-
OPLE SAY THAT THE MESSIAH IS THE SON OF
DAVID? 42 FOR DAVID SAYS IN THE BOOK OF PSALMS:

**THE LORD SAID TO MY LORD: SIT
AT MY RIGHT 43 UNTIL I PUT
YOUR ENEMIES UNDER YOUR FEET.**

44 DAVID HERE CALLS HIM LORD: HOW
THEN CAN HE BE HIS SON?"

45 JESUS ALSO SAID TO HIS DISCIPLES BEFORE ALL
THE PEOPLE, 46 "BEWARE OF THESE TEACHERS OF THE
LAW WHO LIKE TO BE SEEN IN LONG ROBES AND
LOVE TO BE GREETED IN THE MARKETPLACES
AND TO TAKE THE RESERVED SEATS IN THE SYNA-
GOGUES AND PLACES OF HONOR AT FEASTS.
47 THEY EVEN DEVOUR THE PROPERTY OF WIDOWS
WHILE MAKING A SHOW OF LONG PRAYERS.

THEY WILL RECEIVE A VERY SEVERE SENTENCE!"

21 THE WIDOW'S MITE

1 JESUS LOOKED UP AND SAW RICH PEOPLE
PUTTING THEIR GIFTS INTO THE TREASURE BOX;
2 HE ALSO SAW A POOR WIDOW DROPPING INTO IT TWO
SMALL COINS. 3 AND HE SAID, "TRULY, I TELL YOU, THIS
POOR WIDOW PUT IN MORE THAN ALL OF THEM. 4 FOR
ALL GAVE AN OFFERING FROM THEIR PLENTY, BUT
SHE, OUT OF HER POVERTY, GAVE ALL SHE HAD TO LIVE ON."

SIGNS BEFORE THE DESTRUCTION OF JERUSALEM

5 WHILE SOME PEOPLE WERE TALKING ABOUT THE
TEMPLE, REMARKING THAT IT WAS ADORNED WITH FINE
STONEWORK AND RICH GIFTS, JESUS SAID TO THEM,

6 "THE DAYS WILL COME
WHEN THERE SHALL NOT
BE ONE STONE UPON AN-
OTHER OF ALL THAT YOU
NOW ADMIRE; ALL WILL
BE TORN DOWN." 7 AND
THEY ASKED HIM, "MASTER,
WHEN WILL THIS BE AND
WHAT WILL BE THE SIGN
THAT THIS IS ABOUT TO
TAKE PLACE?" JESUS
8 THEN SAID, "TAKE CARE
NOT TO BE DECEIVED, FOR
MANY WILL COME CLAIM-
ING MY TITLE AND SAYING:
'I AM HE THE MESSIAH:
THE TIME IS AT HAND.' DO
NOT FOLLOW THEM. WHEN
9 YOU HEAR OF WARS AND
TROUBLED TIMES, DON'T
BE FRIGHTENED: FOR ALL
THIS MUST HAPPEN FIRST,
EVEN THOUGH THE END
IS NOT SO SOON." 10
JESUS SAID, "NATIONS
WILL FIGHT EACH OTHER AND KINGDOM WILL OPPOSE
KINGDOM. 11 THERE WILL BE GREAT EARTHQUAKES,
FAMINES AND PLAGUES: IN MANY PLACES STRANGE AND
TERRIFYING SIGNS FROM HEAVEN WILL BE SEEN.
12 BEFORE ALL THIS HAPPENS, PEOPLE WILL LAY
THEIR HANDS ON YOU AND PERSECUTE YOU; YOU WILL
BE DELIVERED TO THE JEWISH COURTS AND PUT IN
PRISON, AND FOR MY SAKE YOU WILL BE BROUGHT
BEFORE KINGS AND GOVERNORS. 13 THIS WILL BE
YOUR OPPORTUNITY TO BEAR WITNESS. 14 SO
KEEP THIS IN MIND AND DON'T WORRY ABOUT THE ANSWERS,
FOR 15 I WILL GIVE YOU WORDS AND WISDOM THAT
NONE OF YOUR OPPONENTS WILL BE ABLE TO WITHSTAND
OR CONTRADICT. 16 YOU WILL BE BETRAYED EVEN BY
PARENTS, AND BROTHERS, BY RELATIVES AND FRI-
ENDS, AND SOME OF YOU WILL BE PUT TO DEATH. BUT
17 EVEN THOUGH YOU ARE HATED BY ALL FOR MY
NAME'S SAKE, 18 NOT A HAIR OF YOUR HEAD
WILL PERISH. 19 THROUGH PERSEVERANCE YOU WILL
POSSESS YOUR OWN SELVES. 20 WHEN YOU SEE JERU-

SALEM SURROUNDED BY
ARMIES, THEN YOU MUST
KNOW THAT THE TIME
HAS COME WHEN SHE
WILL BE REDUCED TO A
WASTELAND. 21 THEN, IF
YOU ARE IN JUDEA, FLEE TO
THE MOUNTAINS; IF YOU ARE
IN THE CITY, LEAVE IT AND LET
THOSE WHO ARE IN THE FI-
ELDS NOT RETURN TO THE
CITY. 22 FOR THESE
WILL BE THE DAYS
OF HER PUNISHMENT
AND ALL THAT WAS
ANNOUNCED IN THE
SCRIPTURE WILL BE
FULFILLED. 23 HOW
HARD WILL IT BE
FOR PREGNANT WO-
MEN AND FOR MO-
THERS WITH BABIES
AT THE BREAST!
FOR A GREAT CALAMI-
TY WILL COME UPON THE LAND, AND DIVINE JUSTICE
UPON THIS PEOPLE. 24 THEY WILL BE PUT TO DEATH
BY THE SWORD OR TAKEN AS SLAVES TO OTHER NATI-
ONS; AND JERUSALEM WILL BE TRAMPLED UPON
BY PAGANS UNTIL THE FULFILLMENT OF THEIR TIME.

THE COMING OF THE SON OF MAN

25 THERE WILL BE SIGNS IN SUN AND MOON AND STARS,
AND ON THE EARTH ANGUISH OF PERPLEXED NATIONS WHEN
THEY HEAR THE ROARING OF THE SEA AND ITS WAVES. PEOPLE

26 WILL FAINT WITH FEAR AT THE THOUGHT OF WHAT IS
TO COME UPON THE WORLD, FOR THE FORCES OF UNIVERSE
WILL BE SHAKEN. 27 AND AT THIS TIME THEY WILL SEE THE
SON OF MAN COMING IN A CLOUD WITH POWER AND GLORY.

THE SIGNS OF THE TIMES

28 WHEN YOU SEE THE FIRST EVENTS, STAND ERECT
AND LIFT UP YOUR HEADS, FOR YOUR DELIVERANCE IS
DRAWING NEAR." 29 AND JESUS ADDED THIS COMPARI-
SON, "LOOK AT THE FIG TREE AND ALL THE TREES.
30 AS SOON AS THEIR BUDS SPROUT, YOU KNOW
THE SUMMER IS ALREADY NEAR. 31 IN THE SAME
WAY, AS SOON AS YOU SEE THESE THINGS HAPPENING,
YOU KNOW THAT THE KINGDOM OF GOD IS NEAR. 32
TRULY, I TELL YOU, THIS GENERATION WILL NOT PASS
AWAY UNTIL ALL THIS HAS HAPPENED. 33 HEAVEN
AND EARTH WILL PASS AWAY, BUT MY
WORDS WILL NOT PASS AWAY.

34 BE ON YOUR GUARD: LET NOT YOUR HEARTS
BE WEIGHED DOWN WITH A LIFE OF PLEASURE,
DRUNKENNESS AND WORLDLY CARES LEST THAT DAY
CATCH YOU SUDDENLY AS A TRAP; 35 FOR IT WILL
COME UPON ALL THE INHABITANTS OF THE WHOLE
EARTH. 36 BUT WATCH AT ALL TIMES AND PRAY, THAT
YOU MAY BE ABLE TO ESCAPE ALL THAT IS BOUND TO
HAPPEN AND TO STAND BEFORE THE SON OF MAN."
37 IN THE DAY TIME
JESUS USED TO TEACH
IN THE TEMPLE, THEN
HE WOULD LEAVE THE
CITY AND PASS THE
NIGHT ON THE MOUNT
OF OLIVES.
38 AND EARLY IN
THE MORNING THE
PEOPLE WOULD COME
TO THE TEMPLE
TO HEAR HIM.

WATCH OUT !

THE CONSPIRACY AGAINST JESUS

22 1 THE FEAST OF UNLEAVENED BREAD WHICH IS
CALLED THE PASSOVER, WAS NOW DRAWING NE-
AR. 2 AND THE CHIEF PRIESTS AND THE TEACHERS
OF THE LAW WANTED TO KILL JESUS. THEY WERE LOOKING
FOR A WAY TO DO THIS BECAUSE THEY WERE AFRAID OF THE
PEOPLE. 3 THEN SATAN ENTERED INTO JUDAS, CAL-
LED ISCARIOT, ONE OF THE TWELVE. 4 AND HE WENT
OFF TO DISCUSS WITH THE CHIEF PRIESTS AND THE OF-
FICERS OF THE GUARD HOW TO DELIVER JESUS TO THEM.
5 THEY WERE DELIGHTED AND AGREED TO GIVE HIM MO-
NEY; 6 SO HE ACCEPTED, AND FROM THAT TIME HE WAITED
FOR AN OPPORTUNITY TO BETRAY HIM WITHOUT THE PEOPLE
KNOWING.

7 THEN CAME THE FEAST OF THE UNLEAVENED BREAD IN
WHICH THE PASSOVER LAMB HAD TO BE SACRIFICED. SO
8 JESUS SENT PETER AND JOHN SAYING, "GO AND GET

EVERYTHING READY FOR US TO EAT THE PASSOVER MEAL."
9 THEY ASKED HIM, "WHERE DO YOU WANT US TO PREPARE
IT?" 10 AND HE SAID, "WHEN YOU ENTER THE CITY, A MAN
WILL COME TO YOU CARRYING A JAR OF WATER. FOLLOW
HIM TO THE HOUSE HE ENTERS AND 11 SAY TO THE
OWNER: 'THE MASTER ASKS: WHERE IS THE ROOM WHERE
I MAY TAKE THE PASSOVER MEAL WITH MY DISCIPLES?'
12 HE WILL SHOW YOU A LARGE, FURNISHED ROOM
UPSTAIRS, AND THERE YOU WILL PREPARE FOR US."
13 THEY WENT OFF AND HAVING FOUND EVERYTHING JUST
AS JESUS HAD TOLD THEM, THEY PREPARED THE PASSOVER MEAL.

14 WHEN THE HOUR CAME, JESUS TOOK HIS PLACE AT
TABLE AND THE APOSTLES WITH HIM. 15 AND HE SAID TO
THEM, "I WAS EAGER TO EAT THIS PASSOVER WITH YOU
BEFORE I SUFFER; 16 FOR, I TELL YOU, I SHALL NOT EAT
IT AGAIN UNTIL IT IS FULFILLED IN THE KINGDOM OF GOD."
17 THEY PASSED HIM A CUP AND WHEN HE HAD GI-
VEN THANKS HE SAID, "TAKE IT AND SHARE IT AMONG
YOURSELVES: 18 FOR I TELL YOU THAT FROM NOW
ON I WILL NOT DRINK OF THE GRAPE OF THE VINE UN-
TIL THE KINGDOM OF GOD COMES." 19 JESUS ALSO

TOOK BREAD, AND AFTER GIVING THANKS, HE BROKE IT
AND GAVE IT TO THEM SAYING, "THIS IS MY BODY, WHICH IS
GIVEN FOR YOU. DO THIS IN REMEMBRANCE OF ME."
20 AND HE DID THE SAME WITH THE CUP AFTER EATING.
"THIS CUP IS THE NEW COVENANT, SEALED IN MY BLOOD
WHICH IS POURED OUT FOR YOU.
21 YET THE HAND OF THE TRAITOR IS WITH ME ON THE
TABLE. 22 KNOW THAT THE SON OF MAN IS GOING THE WAY
MARKED OUT FOR HIM, BUT ALAS FOR THAT MAN WHO
BETRAYS HIM!" 23 THEY BEGAN TO ASK ONE ANOTHER
WHICH OF THEM COULD DO SUCH A THING.

LAST CONVERSATION WITH JESUS

24 THEY ALSO BEGAN TO ARGUE AMONG THEMSEL-
VES WHICH OF THEM SHOULD BE CONSIDERED
THE MOST IMPORTANT.

25 AND JESUS SAID, "THE
KINGS OF THE PAGAN NATIONS
RULE OVER THEM AS LORDS,
AND THE MOST SEVERE OF
THEM IS CALLED 'GRACIOUS
LORD.' 26 BUT NOT SO
WITH YOU. LET THE GRE-
ATEST AMONG YOU BECOME
AS THE YOUNGEST, AND THE
LEADER AS THE SERVANT.
27 FOR WHO IS THE GRE-
ATEST, HE WHO SITS AT THE
TABLE OR HE WHO SER-
VES? HE WHO IS SEATED.
YET I AM AMONG YOU
AS THE ONE WHO SERVES.
28 BUT YOU HAVE
BEEN WITH ME, AND
STOOD BY ME THROUGH
MY TROUBLES; 29
BECAUSE OF THIS,
JUST AS THE KING-
SHIP HAS BEEN GI-
VEN TO ME BY MY FATHER, SO I GIVE IT TO YOU.
30 YOU WILL EAT AND DRINK AT MY TABLE IN
MY KINGDOM, AND YOU WILL SIT ON THRONES
AND GOVERN THE TWELVE TRIBES OF ISRAEL.

HOMAGE TO
NOLDE
LUKE 22:19-20
CCCXXXXIV
DM
09
©

31 SIMON, SIMON, SATAN HAS DEMANDED TO SIFT
YOU LIKE GRAIN, 32 BUT I HAVE PRAYED FOR YOU
THAT YOUR FAITH MAY NOT FAIL. AND WHEN YOU HAVE
RECOVERED YOU SHALL STRENGTHEN YOUR BROTHERS."
33 THEN PETER SAID, "LORD, WITH YOU I AM READY TO
GO TO PRISON AND DEATH." 34 BUT JESUS REPLIED,
"I TELL YOU, PETER, THE COCK WILL NOT CROW THIS
DAY BEFORE YOU HAVE DENIED THREE TIMES THAT
YOU KNOW ME." 35 JESUS ALSO SAID TO THEM,

"WHEN I SENT YOU WITHOUT PURSE OR BAGS OR
SANDALS, WERE YOU SHORT OF ANYTHING?"
THEY ANSWERED, "NO," 36 AND JESUS SAID TO
THEM, "BUT NOW, LET HIM WHO HAS A PURSE TAKE
TAKE IT AND A BAG AS WELL. AND IF ANYONE IS
WITHOUT A SWORD, LET HIM SELL HIS CLOAK TO BUY
ONE. 37 FOR SCRIPTURES SAYS: HE WAS NUM-
BERED AMONG CRIMINALS. THESE WORDS HAD
TO BE FULFILLED IN ME, AND NOW EVERYTHING WRIT-
TEN ABOUT ME IS TAKING PLACE.
38 THEN THEY SAID, "SEE, LORD, HERE ARE TWO SWORDS,
"BUT HE ANSWERED," THAT IS ENOUGH."

GETHSEMANE

39 AFTER THIS JESUS LEFT TO GO AS USUAL TO
MOUNT OLIVET AND THE DISCIPLES FOLLOWED HIM.
40 WHEN HE CAME TO THE PLACE, HE TOLD THEM, "PRAY
THAT YOU MAY NOT BE PUT TO THE TEST." 41 THEN

HE WENT A LITTLE FUR-
THER, ABOUT A STONE
THROW, AND KNEELING
DOWN HE PRAYED, 42
"FATHER, IF IT IS YOUR WILL,
REMOVE THIS CUP FROM ME;
STILL NOT MY WILL BUT
YOURS BE DONE." 43
AND AN ANGEL FROM
HEAVEN APPEARED TO
GIVE HIM STRENGTH. 44
AS HE WAS IN AGONY, HE
PRAYED EVEN MORE EARN-
ESTLY AND GREAT DROPS
OF BLOOD FORMED LIKE
SWEAT AND FELL TO THE
GROUND. 45 WHEN HE
ROSE FROM PRAYER, HE
WENT TO HIS DISCIPLES
BUT FOUND THEM WORN
OUT WITH GRIEF AND AS-
LEEP. 46 AND HE SAID
TO THEM "WHY DO YOU SLE-
EP? GET UP AND PRAY, SO
THAT YOU MAY NOT BE PUT
TO THE TEST." 47 JESUS
WAS STILL SPEAKING WHEN A GROUP OF MEN AP-
PEARED AND THE MAN NAMED JUDAS, ONE OF THE
TWELVE, WAS LEADING THEM. HE DREW NEAR
TO JESUS TO KISS HIM, 48 AND JESUS SAID
TO HIM, "DID YOU NEED THIS KISS TO BETRAY
THE SON OF MAN?" 49 THOSE WITH JESUS SE-
EING WHAT WOULD HAPPEN, SAID TO HIM, "MASTER,
SHALL WE USE THE SWORD?" 50 AND ONE OF THEM
STRUCK THE HIGH PRIEST'S SERVANT AND CUT OFF
HIS RIGHT EAR. 51 BUT JESUS STOPPED HIM,

"NO MORE OF THIS." HE TOUCHED THE MAN'S EAR
AND HEALED HIM. 52 THEN JESUS SPOKE TO THO-
SE COMING AGAINST HIM, THE CHIEF PRIESTS, OFFI-
CERS OF THE TEMPLE AND ELDERS AND HE SAID TO THEM,
"DID YOU REALLY SET OUT AGAINST A ROBBER? DO YOU
NEED SWORDS AND CLUBS TO ARREST ME? 53 DAY
AFTER DAY I WAS AMONG YOU TEACHING IN THE
TEMPLE AND YOU DID NOT ARREST ME. BUT
THIS IS THE HOUR OF POWER OF DARKNESS;
THIS IS YOUR HOUR."

THE TRIAL OF JESUS, PETER'S DENIAL

54 THEN THEY SEIZED HIM AND TOOK HIM AWAY, BRINGING
HIM TO THE HIGH PRIEST'S HOUSE. PETER FOLLOWED AT A
DISTANCE. 55 A FIRE WAS

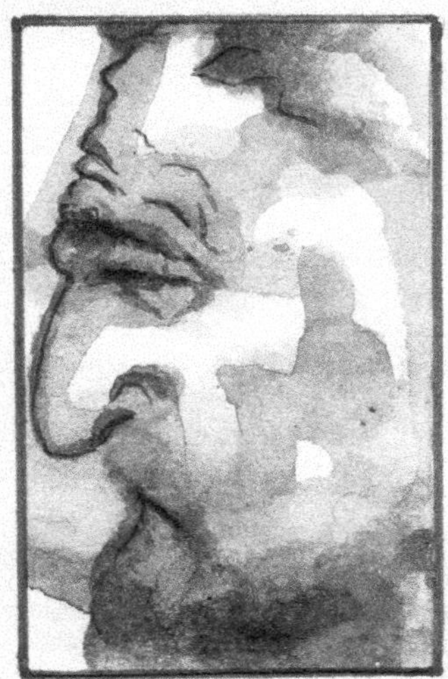

KINDLED IN THE MIDDLE OF
THE COURTYARD WHERE
PEOPLE GATHERED, AND
PETER SAT AMONG THEM.
56 A MAIDSERVANT NO-
TICED HIM. LOOKING AT
HIM INTENTLY IN THE
LIGHT OF THE FIRE
SHE EXCLAIMED, "THIS MAN
ALSO WAS WITH HIM!"
57 BUT HE DENIED IT,
SAYING, "WOMAN, I DON'T
KNOW HIM." 58 A LITTLE
LATER SOMEONE WHO SAW
HIM SAID, "YOU ARE ALSO
ONE OF THEM!" PETER RE-
PLIED, "MY FRIEND, I AM
NOT!" 59 AFTER ABOUT
ONE HOUR ANOTHER
ASSERTED, "SURELY
THIS MAN WAS WITH
HIM, FOR HE IS A
GALILEAN." AGAIN
60 PETER DENIED,
"MY FRIEND, I DON'T
KNOW WHAT YOU ARE TALKING ABOUT." HE HAD
NOT FINISHED SAYING THIS WHEN A COCK CROWED.
61 THE LORD TURNED AROUND AND LOOKED AT
PETER AND HE REMEMBERED THE WORD THAT THE
LORD HAD SPOKEN, "BEFORE THE COCK CROWS TO-
DAY YOU WILL HAVE DENIED ME THREE TIMES."
62 PETER WENT OUTSIDE, WEEPING BITTERLY.

63 MEANWHILE THE GUARDS WERE MOCKING AND BEATING
JESUS. 64 THEY BLINDFOLDED HIM, STRUCK HIM AND AS-
KED, "WHO HIT YOU? TELL US, PROPHET." 65 AND THEY

HURLED MANY OTHER INSULTING WORDS AT HIM. 66 AT DAY-
BREAK, THE COUNCIL OF THE ELDERS OF THE PEOPLE, AMONG
WHOM WERE THE PRIESTS AND THE SCRIBES, ASSEMBLED
AGAIN. THEN THEY HAD JESUS BROUGHT BEFORE THEM
AND THEY AGAIN QUESTIONED HIM: 67 "TELL US, ARE YOU
THE CHRIST?" JESUS REPLIED, "YOU WILL NOT BELIE-
VE IF I TELL YOU, 68 AND NEITHER WILL YOU ANSWER IF
I ASK YOU. 69 YET FROM NOW ON

"THE SON OF MAN WILL HAVE HIS SEAT AT THE
RIGHT HAND OF THE MIGHTY GOD."

(70) IN CHORUS THEY ASKED, "SO YOU ARE THE SON
OF GOD?" AND JESUS SAID TO THEM, "YOU ARE RIGHT,
I AM." (71) THEN THEY SAID, "WHAT NEED HAVE WE OF
WITNESSES? WE HAVE HEARD IT FROM HIS OWN LIPS."

JESUS BEFORE PILATE

23 (1) THE WHOLE COUNCIL ROSE AND BROUGHT JESUS
TO PILATE. (2) THEY GAVE THEIR ACCUSATION: WE FO-
UND THIS MAN SUBVERTING OUR NATION, OPPOSING
PAYMENT OF TAXES TO CAESAR, AND CLAIMING TO BE CHRIST
THE KING." (3) PILATE ASKED

JESUS, "ARE YOU THE KING
OF THE JEWS?" JESUS RE-
PLIED, "YOU SAID SO." (4)
TURNING TO THE CHIEF PRI-
ESTS AND THE CROWD, PILA-
TE SAID, "I FIND NO BASIS
FOR A CASE AGAINST THIS
MAN." (5) BUT THEY INSIS-
TED, "ALL THE COUNTRY OF
THE JEWS IS BEING STIRRED
UP WITH HIS TEACHING. HE
BEGAN IN GALILEE AND
NOW HE HAS COME ALL
THE WAY HERE." (6) WHEN
PILATE HEARD THIS, HE
ASKED IF THE MAN WAS A
GALILEAN. (7) FINDING
THE ACCUSED TO COME
UNDER HEROD'S JURIS-
DICTION, PILATE SENT
JESUS OVER TO HEROD
WHO HAPPENED TO BE IN
JERUSALEM AT THAT
TIME. (8) HEROD WAS
DELIGHTED TO HAVE
JESUS; FOR A LONG TIME
HE HAD WANTED TO SEE HIM BECAUSE OF HIS RENOWN, AND
WAS HOPING TO SEE JESUS WORK SOME MIRACLE. (9) HE
PILED UP MANY QUESTIONS, BUT GOT NO REPLY FROM
JESUS. (10) ALL THE WHILE THE CHIEF PRIESTS AND
THE SCRIBES REMAINED STANDING THERE, VEHEMEN-
TLY PRESSING THEIR ACCUSATIONS. (11) FINALLY, HEROD
RIDICULED HIM AND HIS GUARDS MOCKED HIM. AND
WHEN HE HAD PUT A RICH CLOAK ON HIM, HE SENT

HIM BACK TO PILATE. (12) PILATE AND HEROD WHO
WERE ENEMIES BEFORE, BECAME FRIENDS FROM
THAT DAY.
(13) PILATE THEN CALLED THE CHIEF PRIESTS AND
THE ELDERS BEFORE ALL THE PEOPLE, (14) AND SAID
TO THEM, "YOU HAVE BROUGHT THIS MAN BEFORE
ME AND ACCUSED HIM OF SUBVERSION. IN YOUR PRE-
SENCE I HAVE EXAMINED HIM AND FOUND NO BASIS
FOR YOUR CHARGHES, (15) AND NEITHER HAS
HEROD, FOR HE SENT HIM BACK TO ME. IT IS QUITE
CLEAR THAT THIS MAN HAS DONE NOTHING
THAT DESERVES A DEATH SENTENCE.

(16) I WILL THEREFORE HAVE HIM SCOURGED AND
THEN RELEASE HIM."
(17-18) HOWLING AS ONE MAN, THEY PROTESTED: "NO!
AWAY WITH THIS MAN! RELEASE BARABBAS INSTEAD."
(19) THIS MAN HAD BEEN THROWN INTO PRISON FOR AN
UPRISING IN THE CITY AND FOR MURDER, BUT ON THE
PASSOVER PILATE HAD TO RELEASE A PRISONER.
(20) SINCE PILATE WANTED TO RELELEASE JESUS, HE
APPEALED TO THE CROWD ONCE MORE, (21) BUT THEY
SHOUTED BACK, "TO THE CROSS WITH HIM! TO THE
CROSS!" (22) A THIRD TIME PILATE SAID TO THEM,
"WHY, WHAT EVIL HAS HE DONE? SINCE NO CRIME DES-
ERVING DEATH HAS BEEN PROVED, I SHALL HAVE

HIM SCOURGED AND LET HIM GO." (23) BUT THEY WENT
ON SHOUTING AND DEMANDING THAT JESUS BE CRUCI-
FIED, AND THEIR SHOUT GREW LOUDER. (24) SO PILATE
DECIDED TO PASS THE SENTENCE THEY DEMANDED. (25) HE
RELEASED THE MAN THEY ASKED FOR, THE ONE IN PRI-
SON FOR REBELLION AND MURDER, AND HE DELI-
VERED JESUS IN ACCORDANCE WITH THEIR WISHES.

THE WAY OF CALVARY

(26) WHEN THEY LED JESUS AWAY, THEY SEIZED SIMON OF
CYRENE, WHO WAS COMING IN FROM THE FIELDS, AND LAID
THE CROSS ON HIM, TO
CARRY IT BEHIND JESUS.
(27) A LARGE CROWD OF PE-
OPLE FOLLOWED HIM; AMONG
THEM WERE WOMEN BEAT-
ING THEIR BREAST AND WAI-
LING FOR HIM. (28) BUT
JESUS TURNED TO THEM
AND SAID, "WOMEN OF JE-
RUSALEM, DO NOT WEEP
FOR ME, WEEP RATHER
FOR YOURSELVES AND FOR
YOUR CHILDREN. (29) FOR
THE DAYS ARE COMING
WHEN PEOPLE WILL SAY:
HAPPY ARE THE WOMEN
WITHOUT CHILD! HAPPY
ARE THOSE WHO HAVE NOT
GIVEN BIRTH OR NURSED
A CHILD! (30) AND THEY
WILL SAY TO THE MOUNT-
AINS: **FALL ON US!
AND TO THE HILLS:
COVER US!**"
(31) FOR IF THIS IS THE
LOT OF THE GREEN WOOD, WHAT WILL HAPPEN
TO THE DRY?"

(32) ALONG WITH JESUS, TWO OTHER CRIMINALS WERE
LED OUT TO BE EXECUTED.

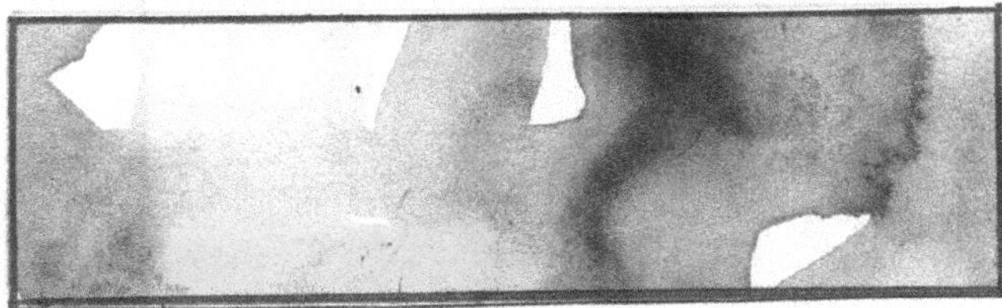

THE CROSS

(33) THERE AT THE PLACE CALLED THE SKULL HE
WAS CRUCIFIED TOGETHER WITH THE CRIMINALS,
ONE ON HIS RIGHT AND ANOTHER ON HIS LEFT.
(34) JESUS SAID, "FATHER, FORGIVE THEM FOR
THEY DO NOT KNOW WHAT THEY DO." AND THE
GUARDS
CAST LOTS TO DIVIDE HIS CLOTHES
AMONG THEMSELVES

(35) THE PEOPLE STOOD BY WATCHING. AS FOR THE
RULERS, THEY JEERED AT HIM, SAYING TO ONE AN-
OTHER, "LET THE MAN WHO SAVED OTHERS NOW SA-
VE HIMSELF, FOR HE IS THE MESSIAH, THE CHOSEN ONE
OF GOD!" (36) THE SOLDIERS ALSO MOCKED HIM
AND WHEN THEY DREW NEAR TO OFFER HIM BITTER
WINE, (37) THEY SAID, "SO YOU ARE THE KING OF
THE JEWS? FREE YOURSELF!" (38) FOR ABOVE HIM
WAS AN INSCRIPTION WHICH READ, I.N.R.I,
WHICH MEANS: 'THIS IS THE KING OF THE JEWS.'"

(39) ONE OF THE CRIMI-
NALS HANGING TO ONE
SIDE OF JESUS INSULTED
HIM, "SO YOU ARE THE
MESSIAH? SAVE YOUR-
SELF AND US AS WELL!"
(40) BUT THE OTHER
REBUKED HIM, SAYING,
"HAVE YOU NO FEAR
OF GOD, YOU WHO RE-
CEIVED THE SAME SEN-
TENCE AS HE DID?
(41) FOR US IT IS JUST:
THIS IS PAYMENT FOR
WHAT WE HAVE DONE.
BUT THIS MAN HAS DONE
NOTHING WRONG." TURN-
ING TO JESUS (42) HE
SAID, "JESUS REMEMBER
ME WHEN YOU COME INTO
YOUR KINGDOM." (43)
JESUS REPLIED, "TRU-
LY, YOU WILL BE WITH
ME TODAY IN PARADISE."
(44) IT WAS NOW ABOUT NOON. (45) THE SUN WAS HID-
DEN AND DARKNESS CAME OVER THE WHOLE LAND UN-
TIL MID-AFTERNOON. AND AT THAT TIME THE CURTAIN OF
THE SANCTUARY WAS TORN IN TWO. (46) THEN JESUS
GAVE A LOUD CRY, "FATHER, INTO YOUR HANDS, I COMMEND
MY SPIRIT." AND SAYING THAT, HE GAVE UP HIS SPIRIT.

(47) THE CAPTAIN ON SEEING THAT AND WHAT HAD
HAPPENED ACKNOWLEDGED THE HAND OF GOD. HE
SAID, "SURELY THIS WAS AN UPRIGHT MAN." (48) AND
ALL THE PEOPLE WHO HAD GATHERED TO WATCH
THE SPECTACLE, AS SOON AS THEY SAW WHAT
HAD HAPPENED WENT HOME BEATING THEIR BREASTS.

(49) ONLY THOSE WHO KNEW JESUS STOOD AT A
DISTANCE, ESPECIALLY THE WOMEN WHO HAD
FOLLOWED HIM FROM GALILEE; THEY WITNESSED
ALL THIS. (50) NOW A MEMBER OF THE JEWISH SUPRE-
ME COUNCIL, A GOOD AND RIGHTEOUS MAN NAMED
JOSEPH (51) FROM THE JUDEAN TOWN OF ARIMA-
THEA, DID NOT AGREE WITH THE DECISION AND
ACTION OF HIS FELLOW MEMBERS, FOR HE LI-
VED UPRIGHTLY IN THE
HOPE OF SEEING THE
KINGDOM OF GOD. (52)
HE WENT TO PILATE
AND ASKED FOR JESUS'
BODY. (53) HE THEN TOOK
IT DOWN, WRAPPED IT IN
A LINEN CLOTH AND LAID
IT IN A YET UNUSED TOMB
CUT OUT OF A ROCK.
(54) IT WAS PREPARATION
DAY AND THE STAR WHICH
MARKS THE BEGINNING
OF THE SABBATH WAS
SHINING. (55) SO THE
WOMEN WHO HAD
COME WITH JESUS
FROM GALILEE
FOLLOWED JOSEPH
TO SEE THE TOMB AND
HOW HIS BODY WAS
BEING PLACED. (56)
AND RETURNING
HOME, THEY PREPA-
RED PERFUMES AND
OINTMENTS.

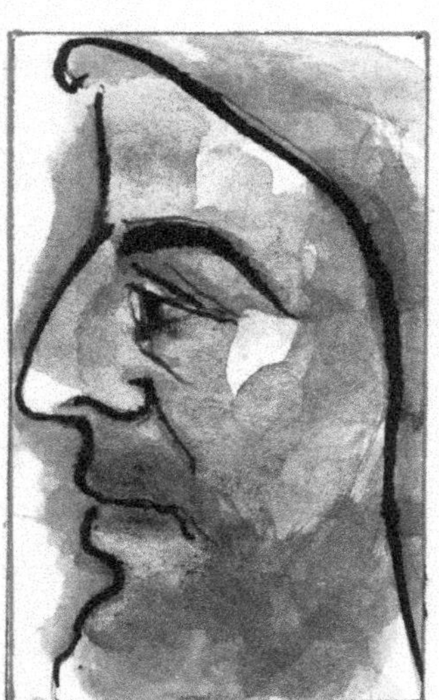

THE LORD HAS RISEN

24 (1) ON THE SABBATH THE WOMEN RESTED
ACCORDING TO THE COMMANDMENT, BUT
THE FIRST DAY OF THE WEEK, AT DAWN,
THEY WENT TO THE TOMB WITH THE PERFUMES
AND OINTMENTS THEY HAD PREPARED. (2) ON SEEING
THE STONE ROLLED AWAY FROM THE OPENING OF
THE TOMB, (3) THEY ENTERED AND WERE PUZZLED

TO FIND THAT THE BODY OF THE LORD JESUS WAS
NOT THERE.
(4) TWO MEN IN DAZZLING GARMENTS APPEAR-
ED BESIDE THEM. (5) IN FRIGHT THE WOMEN
BOWED TO THE GROUND. BUT THE MEN SAID, "WHY
LOOK FOR THE LIVING AMONG THE DEAD?"

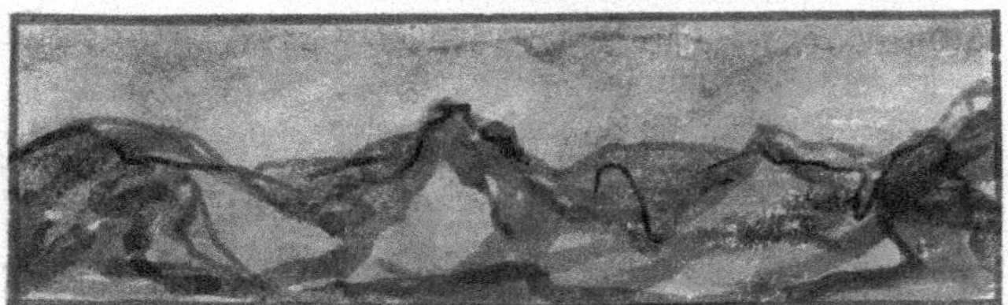

"TO THE CROSS WITH HIM.
TO THE CROSS!"
(LUKE 23:21) 345
DM C
07

6 YOU WON'T FIND HIM HERE. HE IS RISEN.
7 REMEMBER WHAT HE TOLD YOU IN GA-
LILEE, THAT THE SON OF MAN HAD TO BE GI-
VEN INTO THE HANDS OF SINNERS, BE CRU-
CIFIED, AND RISE ON THE THIRD DAY."
8 AND THEY RECALLED JESUS' WORDS.

9 RETURNING FROM
THE TOMB, THEY IN-
FORMED THE ELEVEN
AND THEIR COMPANI-
ONS. 10 AMONG THE
WOMEN WHO BROUGHT
THE NEWS WERE
MARY MAGDALENE,
JOANNA, AND MARY
THE MOTHER OF JA-
MES. 11 BUT HOW-
EVER MUCH THEY
INSISTED, THOSE
WHO HEARD DID
NOT BELIEVE THE
SEEMINGLY NON-
SENSICAL STORY.
12 THEN PETER
GOT UP AND RAN
TO THE TOMB. ALL HE SAW THERE ON BEND-
ING DOWN WERE THE LINEN CLOTHS. AND
THEN HE WENT HOME WONDERING.

13 THAT SAME DAY, TWO OF THEM WERE GOING
TO EMMAUS, A VILLAGE SEVEN MILES FROM
JERUSALEM, 14 AND THEY TALKED ABOUT
WHAT HAD HAPPENED. 15 WHILE THEY WERE
TALKING AND WONDERING, JESUS CAME UP AND
WALKED WITH THEM, 16 BUT THEIR EYES WERE HELD
AND THEY DID NOT RECOGNIZED HIM.

17 HE ASKED, "WHAT IS THIS YOU ARE TALKING
ABOUT?" THE TWO STOOD STILL, LOOKING SAD.

18 THEN ONE NAMED CLEOPHAS ANSWERED,
"WHY, IT SEEMS YOU ARE THE ONLY TRA-
VELLER IN JERUSALEM WHO DOESN'T
KNOW WHAT HAS HAPPENED THERE
THESE PAST FEW DAYS."
19 AND HE ASKED, "WHAT IS IT?"
THEY REPLIED, "IT IS ABOUT JESUS OF NAZA-
RETH. HE WAS A PROPHET, YOU KNOW. HE
WAS MIGHTY IN WORD AND DEED BEFORE
GOD AND THE PEOPLE. 20 BUT THE CHIEF

PRIESTS AND OUR RULERS SENTENCED HIM
TO DEATH. THEY HANDED HIM OVER TO BE
CRUCIFIED. 21 WE HAD HOPED THAT HE
WOULD REDEEM ISRAEL. IT IS NOW THE
THIRD DAY SINCE ALL THIS TOOK PLACE. 22 IT
IS TRUE THAT SOME WOMEN OF OUR GROUP
HAVE DISTURBED US.
WHEN THEY WENT TO
THE TOMB AT DAWN,
23 THEY DID NOT
FIND HIS BODY; THEY
CAME TO TELL US THAT
THEY HAD SEEN A VI-
SION OF ANGELS WHO
TOLD THEM THAT JESUS
WAS ALIVE. 24 SOME
FRIENDS OF OUR GRO-
UP WENT TO THE TOMB
AND FOUND EVERYTHING
JUST AS THE WOMEN
HAD SAID, BUT THEY
DID NOT SEE HIM."
25 HE SAID TO THEM,
"HOW DULL YOU ARE,
HOW SLOW OF UN-
DERSTANDING! YOU
FAIL TO BELIEVE THE
MESSAGE OF THE PRO-
PHETS. 26 IS IT NOT
WRITTEN THAT THE
CHRIST SHOULD SUF-
FER ALL THIS AND
THEN ENTER HIS GLORY?" 27 THEN STARTING
WITH MOSES AND GOING THROUGH THE PRO-
PHETS, HE EXPLAINED TO THEM EVERYTHING
IN SCRIPTURE CONCERNING HIMSELF.

28 AS THEY DREW NEAR THE VILLAGE THEY
WERE HEADING FOR, JESUS MADE AS IF TO
GO FARTHER.
29 BUT THEY PREVAILED UPON HIM,

"STAY WITH US, FOR NIGHT
COMES QUICKLY. THE DAY
IS NOW ALMOST OVER."

SO HE WENT IN TO STAY WITH THEM.

30 WHEN THEY WERE AT TABLE, HE TOOK THE
BREAD, SAID THE BLESSING, BROKE IT AND GAVE EACH
A PIECE. 31 THEN THEIR EYES WERE OPENED,
AND THEY RECOGNIZED HIM; BUT HE VANISHED OUT
OF THEIR SIGHT. 32 AND THEY SAID TO EACH OTHER,
"WERE NOT OUR HEARTS FILLED WITH ARDENT YEARNING
WHEN HE WAS TALKING TO US ON THE ROAD AND
AND EXPLAINING THE SCRIPTURES?"
33 THEY IMMEDIATELY SET OUT AND RETURNED
TO JERUSALEM. THERE THEY FOUND THE ELEVEN
AND THEIR COMPANIONS GATHERED TOGETHER. 34
THEY WERE GREETED BY THESE WORDS: "YES, IT

IS TRUE, THE LORD IS RISEN! HE HAS APPEARED TO SIMON!"
35 THEN THE TWO TOLD WHAT HAD HAPPENED ON THE
ROAD AND HOW JESUS MADE HIMSELF KNOWN WHEN
HE BROKE BREAD WITH THEM.

JESUS APPEARS TO THE APOSTLES

36 AS THEY WENT ON TALKING ABOUT THIS, JESUS
HIMSELF STOOD IN THE MIDST. AND HE SAID TO THEM,
"PEACE TO YOU!" 37 IN
THEIR PANIC AND FRIGHT
THEY THOUGHT THEY WE-
RE SEEING A GHOST, 38
BUT HE SAID TO THEM
"WHY ARE YOU UPSET AND
WHY DO SUCH IDEAS
CROSS YOUR MIND? 39
LOOK AT MY HANDS AND
FEET AND SEE THAT IT
IS I MYSELF. TOUCH ME
AND SEE FOR YOURSELVES
THAT A GHOST HAS NO
FLESH AND BONES AS
I HAVE." 40 AS HE
SAID THIS, HE SHO-
WED HIS HANDS
AND FEET.

41 IN THEIR JOY
THEY DIDN'T DARE

HOMAGE TO BLAKE

BELIEVE AND WERE STILL ASTONISHED. SO
HE SAID TO THEM, "HAVE YOU ANYTHING TO EAT?" 42
AND THEY GAVE HIM A PIECE OF BROILED FISH.
43 HE TOOK IT AND ATE IT BEFORE THEM.

LAST INSTRUCTIONS

44 THEN JESUS SAID TO THEM, "REMEMBER THE
WORDS I SPOKE TO YOU WHEN I WAS STILL WITH YOU:
EVERYTHING WRITTEN ABOUT ME IN THE LAW OF
MOSES, THE PROPHETS AND THE PSALMS HAD
TO BE FULFILLED."
45 THEN HE OPENED
THEIR MINDS TO UN-
DERSTAND THE SCRIP-
TURES. AND HE WENT
ON, 46 "YOU SEE
WHAT WAS WRITTEN:
THE MESSIAH HAD
TO SUFFER AND ON THE
THIRD DAY RISE FROM
THE DEAD. 47 THEN
REPENTANCE AND FOR-
GIVENESS IN HIS NAME
WOULD BE PROCLAIMED
TO ALL THE NATIONS,
BEGINNING FROM JE-
RUSALEM. 48 NOW
YOU SHALL BE WIT-
NESSES TO THIS.
49 AND THIS IS WHY
I WILL SEND YOU WHAT
MY FATHER PROMISED.
SO REMAIN IN THE CITY
UNTIL YOU ARE IN-

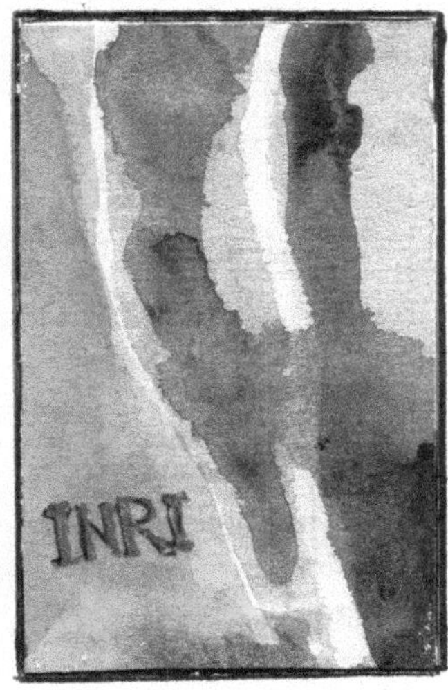

VESTED WITH POWER FROM ABOVE." 50 JESUS
LED THEM ALMOST AS FAR AS BETHANY; THEN HE
LIFTED UP HIS HANDS AND BLESSED THEM. 51
AND AS HE BLESSED THEM, HE WITHDREW AND WAS
TAKEN TO HEAVEN. THEY WORSHIPED HIM. 52
THEY RETURNED TO JERUSALEM FULL OF
JOY AND 53 WERE CONTINUALLY
IN THE TEMPLE PRAISING GOD.

THE GOSPEL ACCORDING TO JOHN

THE FIRST THREE GOSPELS PRESENTED THE WORKS AND WORDS OF JESUS WHICH WERE MOST APPROPRIATE FOR THE FOUNDATION OF THE CHURCH'S BASIC CATECHESIS. JOHN'S GOSPEL, ON THE OTHER HAND, HAS A MORE DEFINITE GOAL: "THIS HAS BEEN WRITTEN THAT YOU MAY BELIEVE THAT JESUS IS THE SON OF GOD..." (JN 20:31).

JOHN'S GOSPEL CLEARLY AFFIRMED, FOR THE FIRST TIME, JESUS' EXISTENCE IN GOD HIMSELF FOR ALL ETERNITY. THIS CLARITY REGARDING JESUS' ORIGIN ALSO MADE CLEARER THE VASTNESS OF HIS WORK. JESUS, BEING THE ETERNAL SON OF GOD BECOME HUMAN, DID NOT COME SOLELY TO TEACH US TO BE BETTER OR MORE RELIGIOUS, BUT TO TRANSFORM CREATION AND TO MAKE OF US TRUE SONS AND DAUGHTERS OF GOD.

THIS GOSPEL'S EMPHASIS ON JESUS' DIVINITY COULD MAKE LESS INTEREST IN HIS CONCRETE LIFE AMONG PEOPLE.

FROM THE BEGINNING, SOME CHRISTIANS USED JOHN'S GOSPEL TO JUSTIFY A FALSE CONCEPT OF JESUS AND HIS REDEMPTION, AS IF FORGETTING THAT HE REALLY DIED ON THE CROSS. POSSIBLY JOHN'S FIRST LETTER WRITTEN TO PRESENT THE GOSPEL REFERS TO THESE PERSONS.

IT IS CERTAIN THAT THE EVANGELIST COMPOSED, REARRANGED AND COMPLETED THESE WRITINGS OVER A LONG PERIOD OF TIME.

THE GOSPEL ACCORDING TO

JOHN

THE WORD BECAME A HUMAN

1
1 IN THE BEGINNING WAS THE WORD, AND
THE WORD WAS WITH GOD AND THE WORD
WAS GOD; 2 HE WAS IN THE BEGINNING
WITH GOD. 3 ALL THINGS WERE MADE
THROUGH HIM AND WITHOUT HIM NOTHING
CAME TO BE. 4 WHATEVER HAS COME TO
BE, FOUND LIFE IN HIM, LIFE WHICH FOR
HUMANS WAS ALSO LIGHT. 5 LIGHT
THAT SHINES IN THE DARK; LIGHT THAT
DARKNESS COULD NOT OVERCOME.

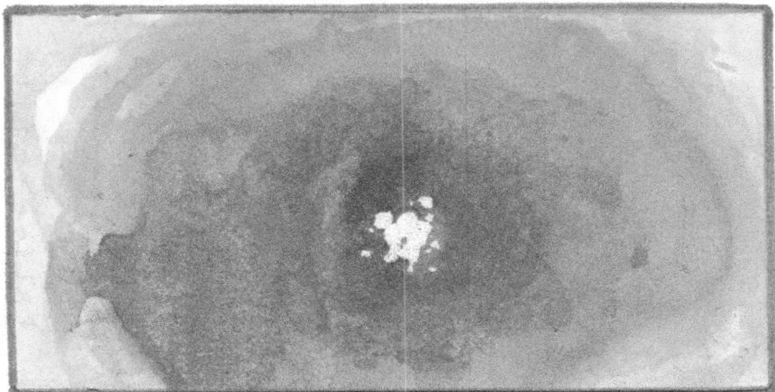

6 A MAN CAME, SENT BY GOD; HIS NAME
WAS JOHN. 7 HE CAME TO BEAR WIT-
NESS, AS A WITNESS TO INTRODUCE THE
LIGHT, SO THAT ALL MIGHT BELIEVE THRO-
UGH HIM. 8 HE WAS NOT THE LIGHT BUT
A WITNESS TO INTRODUCE THE LIGHT.
9 FOR THE LIGHT WAS COMING INTO THE
WORLD, THE TRUE LIGHT THAT ENLIGHTENS
EVERYONE. 10 HE WAS ALREADY IN THE
WORLD AND THROUGH HIM THE WORLD WAS
MADE, THE VERY WORLD THAT DID NOT KNOW
HIM 11 HE CAME TO HIS OWN, YET HIS OWN
PEOPLE DID NOT RECEIVE HIM; 12 BUT
ALL WHO HAVE RECEIVED HIM HE EM-
POWERS TO BECOME CHILDREN OF GOD
FOR THEY BELIEVE IN HIS NAME. 13
THESE ARE BORN, BUT WITHOUT SEED

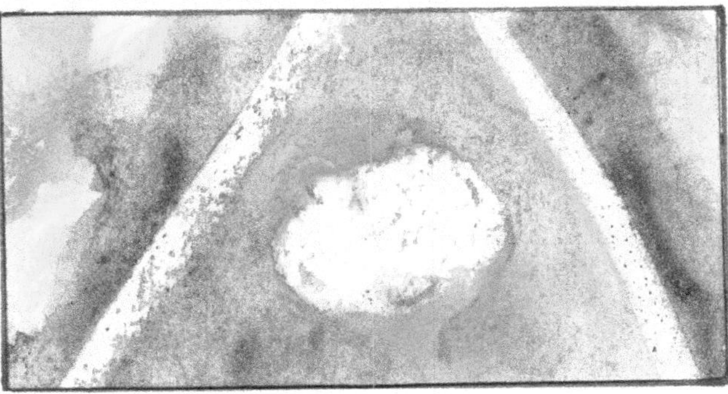

OR CARNAL DESIRE OR WILL OF MAN; THEY ARE
BORN OF GOD. 14 AND THE WORD WAS MADE
FLESH; HE HAD HIS TENT PITCHED AMONG US,
AND WE HAVE SEEN HIS GLORY, THE GLORY
OF THE ONLY SON COMING FROM THE FATHER:
FULLNESS OF TRUTH AND LOVING-KINDNESS.
15 JOHN BORE WITNESS TO HIM OPENLY,
SAYING: THIS IS THE ONE WHO COMES AF-
TER ME, BUT HE IS ALREADY AHEAD OF ME,
FOR HE WAS BEFORE ME. 16 FROM HIS
FULLNESS WE HAVE ALL RECEIVED, FAVOR
UPON FAVOR, 17 FOR GOD HAD GIVEN US
THE LAW THROUGH MOSES, BUT TRUTH AND
LOVING-KINDNESS CAME THROUGH JESUS
CHRIST. 18 NO ONE HAS EVER SEEN GOD,
BUT GOD-ONLY SON MADE HIM KNOWN:
THE ONE WHO IS IN AND WITH THE FATHER.

JOHN THE BAPTIST PRESENTS JESUS, THE LAMB OF GOD

19 THIS WAS THE TESTIMONY OF JOHN WHEN THE JEWS
SENT PRIESTS AND LEVITES TO ASK HIM, "WHO ARE YOU?"
20 JOHN RECOGNIZED THE TRUTH AND DID NOT DENY IT.

HE SAID, "I AM NOT THE MESSIAH." 21 AND THEY ASKED
HIM, "THEN WHO ARE YOU? ELIJAH?" HE ANSWERED, "I AM
NOT." THEY SAID, "ARE YOU A PROPHET?" HE ANSWERED,
"NO." 22 THEN THEY SAID TO HIM, "TELL US WHO YOU
ARE, SO THAT WE CAN GIVE SOME ANSWER TO THOSE
WHO SENT US. HOW DO YOU SEE YOURSELF?" 23 JOHN
SAID, QUOTING THE PROPHET ISAIAH, "I AM THE

VOICE CRYING OUT IN THE WILDERNESS:
MAKE STRAIGHT THE WAY OF THE LORD."

24 THESE PERSONS HAD BEEN SENT BY THE PHARISEES:
25 SO THEY PUT A FURTHER QUESTION TO JOHN: "THEN
WHY ARE YOU BAPTISING IF YOU ARE NOT THE MESSIAH,
OR ELIJAH, OR THE PROPHET?" 26 JOHN ANSWERED, "I
BAPTIZE YOU WITH WATER, BUT AMONG YOU STANDS
ONE WHOM YOU DO NOT
KNOW, 27 ALTHOUGH HE
COMES AFTER ME, I AM
NOT WORTHY TO UNTIE
THE STRAP OF HIS SAN-
DALS." 28 THIS HAPPE-
NED IN BETHANY BE-
YOND THE JORDAN, WHE-
RE JOHN WAS BAPTIZING.
29 THE NEXT DAY
JOHN SAW JESUS COM-
ING TOWARDS HIM AND
SAID: "THERE IS THE
LAMB OF GOD, WHO
TAKES AWAY THE SIN
OF THE WORLD. 30 IT
IS HE OF WHOM I SAID:
A MAN COMES AFTER
ME WHO IS ALREADY
AHEAD OF ME, FOR HE
WAS BEFORE ME. 31
I MYSELF DID NOT KNOW
HIM, BUT I CAME BAP-
TIZING TO PREPARE
FOR HIM, SO THAT HE
MIGHT BE REVEALED
IN ISRAEL." 32 AND

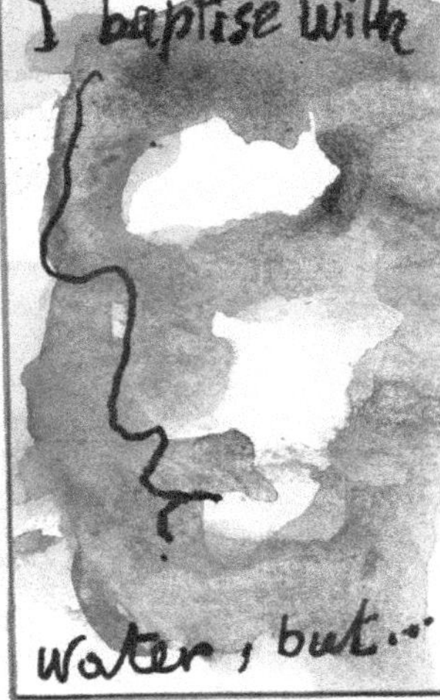

JOHN ALSO GAVE THIS TESTIMONY "I SAW
THE SPIRIT COMING DOWN ON HIM LIKE A DOVE
FROM HEAVEN AND RESTING ON HIM.
33 I MYSELF DID NOT KNOW HIM BUT GOD WHO
SENT ME TO BAPTISE TOLD ME: 'YOU WILL
SEE THE SPIRIT COMING DOWN AND RESTING
ON THE ONE WHO BAPTIZES WITH THE HOLY
SPIRIT.'
34 YES, I HAVE SEEN! AND I DECLARE THAT
THIS IS THE CHOSEN ONE OF GOD."

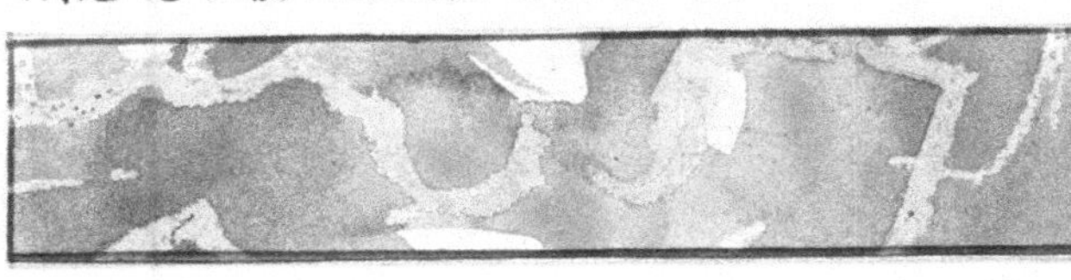

JESUS AND THE FIRST DISCIPLES

35 ON THE FOLLOWING DAY JOHN WAS STANDING THERE
AGAIN WITH TWO OF HIS DISCIPLES. 36 AS JESUS
WALKED BY, JOHN LOOKED AT HIM AND SAID, "THERE
IS THE LAMB OF GOD." 37 ON HEARING THIS, THE TWO
DISCIPLES FOLLOWED JESUS. 38 HE TURNED AND
SAW THEM FOLLOWING, AND HE SAID TO THEM,
"WHAT ARE YOU LOOKING FOR?" THEY ANSWERED,
"RABBI (WHICH MEANS MASTER), WHERE ARE YOU
STAYING?" 39 JESUS SAID, "COME AND SEE." SO
THEY WENT AND SAW
WHERE HE STAYED AND
AND SPENT THE REST
OF THAT DAY WITH HIM.
IT WAS ABOUT FOUR
O'CLOCK IN THE AFTER-
NOON. 40 ANDREW, THE
BROTHER OF SIMON PETER,
WAS ONE OF THE TWO WHO
HEARD WHAT JOHN HAD SAID
AND FOLLOWED JESUS. 41
EARLY THE NEXT MORNING
HE FOUND HIS BROTHER SI-
MON AND SAID TO HIM, "WE
HAVE FOUND THE MESSIAH,
WHICH MEANS THE CHRIST,
42 AND HE BROUGHT SIMON
TO JESUS. HE LOOKED AT HIM
AND SAID, "YOU ARE SIMON,
SON OF JOHN, BUT YOU SHALL
BE CALLED CEPHAS", WHICH
MEANS ROCK. 43 THE
NEXT DAY, JESUS DECIDED
TO SET OFF FOR GALILEE.
HE FOUND PHILIP AND SAID
TO HIM, "FOLLOW ME." 44
PHILIP WAS FROM BETH-
SAIDA, THE TOWN OF AN-
DREW AND PETER. 45

PHILIP FOUND NATHANAEL AND SAID TO HIM, "WE HAVE
FOUND THE ONE THAT MOSES WROTE ABOUT IN THE
LAW AND THE PROPHETS AS WELL: HE IS JESUS, SON OF
JOSEPH, FROM NAZARETH."
46 NATHANAEL REPLIED, "CAN ANYTHING GOOD COME
FROM NAZARETH?" PHILIP SAID, "COME AND SEE". WHEN 47
JESUS SAW NATHANAEL COMING, HE SAID TO HIM, "HERE COMES
AN ISRAELITE, A TRUE ONE; THERE IS NOTHING FALSE IN HIM."
48 NATHANAEL ASKED HIM, "HOW DO YOU KNOW ME?"
AND JESUS SAID TO HIM, "BEFORE PHILIP CALLED YOU,
YOU WERE UNDER THE FIG TREE AND I SAW YOU. 49
NATHANAEL ANSWERED, "MASTER, YOU ARE THE SON OF GOD!

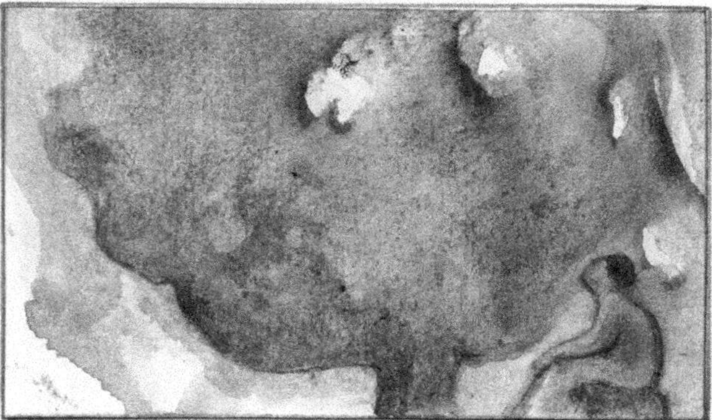

YOU ARE THE KING OF ISRAEL!" 50 BUT JESUS REPLIED,
"YOU BELIEVE BECAUSE I SAID: 'I SAW YOU UNDER THE FIG
TREE.' BUT YOU WILL SEE GREATER THINGS THAN THAT.
51 TRULY, I SAY TO YOU, YOU WILL SEE THE HEAVENS OPEN-
ED AND THE ANGELS OF GOD ASCENDING AND DES-
CENDING UPON THE SON OF MAN."

THE WEDDING AT CANA

2 1 THREE DAYS LATER THERE WAS A WEDDING
AT CANA IN GALILEE AND THE MOTHER OF JESUS
WAS THERE. 2 JESUS WAS ALSO INVITED TO
THE WEDDING WITH HIS DISCIPLES. 3 WHEN ALL
THE WINE PROVIDED FOR THE CELEBRATION HAD BEEN
SERVED AND THEY HAD RUN OUT OF WINE, THE MOTHER
OF JESUS SAID TO HIM, "THEY HAVE NO WINE." 4 JESUS
REPLIED, "WOMAN, YOUR THOUGHTS ARE NOT MINE! MY
HOUR HAS NOT YET COME." 5 HOWEVER HIS MOTHER SAID
TO THE SERVANTS, "DO WHATEVER HE TELLS YOU."
6 NEARBY WERE SIX STONE WATER JARS MEANT FOR
THE RITUAL WASHING AS PRACTICED BY THE JEWS;
EACH JAR COULD HOLD TWENTY OR THIRTY GALLONS.
7 JESUS SAID TO THE SERVANTS, "FILL THE JARS
WITH WATER." AND THEY FILLED THEM TO THE BRIM.
8 THEN JESUS SAID, "NOW DRAW SOME OUT AND

TAKE IT TO THE STEWARD." SO THEY DID. 9 THE STEWARD
TASTED THE WATER THAT HAD BECOME WINE, NOT KNOWING
FROM WHERE IT HAD COME, FOR ONLY THE SERVANTS WHO HAD
DRAWN THE WATER KNEW. SO HE CALLED THE BRIDEGROOM
10 TO TELL HIM, "EVERYONE SERVES THE BEST WINE
FIRST AND WHEN PEOPLE HAVE DRUNK ENOUGH, HE SERVES
THAT WHICH IS ORDINARY. INSTEAD YOU HAVE KEPT THE BEST
WINE UNTIL THE END." 11 THIS MIRACULOUS SIGN WAS THE
FIRST, AND JESUS PERFORMED IT AT CANA IN GALILEE. IN
THIS WAY HE LET HIS GLORY APPEAR AND HIS DISCIPLES
BELIEVED IN HIM. 12 AFTER THIS, JESUS WENT DOWN
TO CAPERNAUM WITH HIS MOTHER, HIS BROTHERS AND
HIS DISCIPLES; AND THEY STAYED THERE FOR A FEW DAYS.

JESUS CLEARS THE TEMPLE

13 AS THE PASSOVER OF THE JEWS WAS AT HAND
JESUS WENT UP TO JERUSALEM. 14 IN THE TEMPLE
COURT HE FOUND MERCHANTS SELLING OXEN, SHEEP
AND DOVES, AND MONEY-
CHANGERS SEATED AT
THEIR TABLES. MAKING
15 A WHIP OF CORDS, HE
DROVE THEM ALL OUT OF
THE TEMPLE COURT, TO-
GETHER WITH THE OXEN
AND SHEEP. HE KNOCKED
OVER THE TABLES OF THE
MONEY-CHANGERS, SCAT-
TERING THE COINS, 16 AND
ORDERED THE DOVE SEL-
LERS, "TAKE ALL THIS AWAY
AND STOP TURNING MY FA-
THER'S HOUSE INTO A MAR-
KET-PLACE!" 17 HIS DI-
SCIPLES RECALLED THE
WORDS OF SCRIPTURE:
ZEAL FOR YOUR HOUSE
DEVOURS ME AS A FIRE.
18 THE JEWS THEN ASK-
ED JESUS, "WHERE ARE
THE MIRACULOUS SIGNS
WHICH GIVE YOU THE
RIGHT TO DO THIS? 19
JESUS SAID, "DESTROY
THIS TEMPLE AND IN
THREE DAYS I WILL RAISE IT UP." 20 THE JEWS THEN
REPLIED, "TO BUILD THIS TEMPLE HAS TAKEN FORTY-SIX
YEARS, AND YOU WILL RAISE IT UP IN THREE DAYS?"
21 ACTUALLY, JESUS WAS REFERRING TO THE TEMPLE
OF HIS BODY. 22 ONLY WHEN HE HAD RISEN FROM THE
DEAD DID HIS DISCEPLES REMEMBER THESE WORDS;
THEN THEY BELIEVED BOTH THE SCRIPTURE
AND THE WORDS JESUS HAD SPOKEN.

John the Evangelist
347 CCCIIIL
DM 07 ©

23 JESUS STAYED IN JERUSALEM DURING THE
PASSOVER FESTIVAL AND MANY BELIEVED IN
HIS NAME WHEN THEY SAW THE MIRACULOUS
SIGNS HE PERFORMED. 24 BUT JESUS DID
NOT TRUST HIMSELF TO THEM, BECAUSE HE
KNEW ALL OF THEM. 25 HE HAD NO NEED OF
EVIDENCE ABOUT ANYONE FOR HE HIMSELF
KNEW WHAT THERE WAS IN EACH ONE.

JESUS AND NICODEMUS

3 1 AMONG THE PHARISEES THERE WAS
A RULER OF THE JEWS NAMED NICODEMUS.
2 HE CAME TO JESUS AT NIGHT AND
SAID, "RABBI, WE KNOW THAT YOU HAVE COME
FROM GOD TO TEACH US, FOR NO ONE CAN PER-
FORM MIRACULOUS SIGNS LIKE YOURS UNLESS
GOD IS WITH HIM." 3 JESUS REPLIED,

"TRULY, I SAY TO YOU, NO ONE CAN SEE THE KINGDOM OF
GOD UNLESS IS BORN AGAIN FROM ABOVE."

4 NICODEMUS SAID, "HOW CAN THERE BE REBIRTH FOR
A GROWN MAN? WHO COULD GO BACK TO HIS MOTHER'S
WOMB AND BE BORN AGAIN?" 5 JESUS REPLIED,

"TRULY, I SAY TO YOU: UNLESS ONE IS BORN AGAIN OF WATER
AND SPIRIT, HE CANNOT ENTER THE KINGDOM OF GOD.
6 WHAT IS BORN OF THE FLESH IS FLESH, AND WHAT
IS BORN OF THE SPIRIT IS SPIRIT. 7 BECAUSE OF THIS,
DON'T BE SURPRISED WHEN I SAY: YOU MUST BE BORN

AGAIN FROM ABOVE.' 8 THE WIND BLOWS WHERE IT
PLEASES AND YOU HEAR ITS SOUND, BUT YOU DON'T
KNOW WHERE IT COMES FROM OR WHERE IT IS GOING.
IT IS LIKE THAT WITH EVERYONE WHO IS BORN OF
THE SPIRIT."

9 NICODEMUS ASKED, "HOW CAN THIS BE? 10 JESUS ANS-
WERED, "YOU ARE A TEACHER IN ISRAEL, AND YOU DON'T
KNOW THESE THINGS!

11 TRULY, I SAY TO YOU, WE SPEAK OF WHAT WE KNOW AND
WE WITNESS TO THE THINGS WE HAVE SEEN, BUT YOU DON'T
ACCEPT OUR TESTIMONY. 12 IF YOU DON'T BELIEVE
WHEN I SPEAK OF EARTHLY THINGS, WHAT THEN, WHEN
I SPEAK TO YOU OF HEAVENLY THINGS? 13 NO ONE HAS
EVER GONE UP TO HEAVEN EXCEPT THE ONE WHO CAME
FROM HEAVEN, THE SON OF MAN. 14 AS MOSES
LIFTED UP THE SERPENT IN THE DESERT, SO MUST THE
SON OF MAN BE LIFTED UP, 15 SO THAT WHOEVER BELI-
EVES IN HIM MAY HAVE ETERNAL LIFE. 16 YES, GOD SO
LOVED THE WORLD THAT HE GAVE HIS ONLY SON THAT
WHOEVER BELIEVES IN HIM MAY NOT BE LOST, BUT
MAY HAVE ETERNAL LIFE. 17 GOD DID NOT SEND
THE SON INTO THE WORLD TO CONDEMN THE
WORLD, INSTEAD, THROUGH HIM THE WORLD IS TO
BE SAVED.
18 WHOEVER BELIEVES IN HIM WILL NOT BE CONDEM-
NED. HE WHO DOES NOT BELIEVE IS ALREADY

CONDEMNED, BECAUSE HE HAS NOT BELIEVED IN THE
NAME OF THE ONLY SON OF GOD. 19 THIS IS HOW
THE JUDGMENT IS MADE: LIGHT HAS COME INTO
THE WORLD AND PEOPLE LOVED DARKNESS RATHER
THAN LIGHT BECAUSE THEIR DEEDS WERE EVIL.
20 FOR WHOEVER DOES WRONG HATES THE LIGHT
AND DOESN'T COME TO THE LIGHT FOR FEAR
THAT HIS DEEDS WILL BE SHOWN AS EVIL.

21 BUT WHOEVER LIVES ACCORDING TO THE

TRUTH COMES INTO THE LIGHT SO THAT IT CAN BE
CLEARLY SEEN THAT HIS WORK HAS BEEN DONE IN GOD."

JOHN THE BAPTIST'S LAST TESTIMONY

22 AFTER THIS, JESUS WENT INTO THE TERRITORY
OF JUDEA WITH HIS DISCIPLES. HE STAYED THERE
WITH THEM AND BAPTIZED. 23 JOHN WAS BAPTIZING IN AE-
NON NEAR SALIM WHERE WATER WAS PLENTIFUL; PEOPLE
CAME AND WERE BAPTIZED. 24 THIS WAS BEFORE JOHN
WAS PUT IN PRISON. 25 NOW JOHN'S DISCIPLES HAD
BEEN QUESTIONED BY A JEW ABOUT SPIRITUAL CLEANSING,
26 SO THEY SAID, "RABBI, THE ONE WHO WAS WITH YOU
ACROSS THE RIVER JORDAN, AND ABOUT WHOM YOU
SPOKE FAVORABLY, IS NOW BAPTIZING AND ALL ARE
GOING TO HIM."
27 JOHN ANSWERED, "NO ONE CAN TAKE ON ANY-
THING IF IT HAS NOT BEEN GIVEN HIM FROM HE-
AVEN.
28 YOU YOURSELVES ARE MY WITNESSES THAT
I SAID: I AM NOT THE CHRIST; I HAVE BEEN SENT BEFORE HIM.'

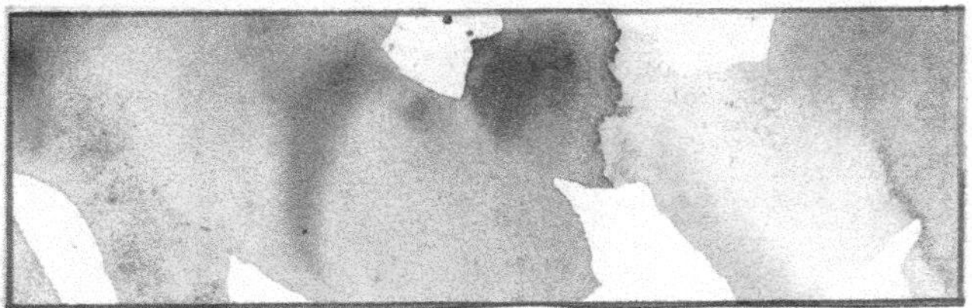

29 ONLY THE BRIDEGROOM HAS THE BRIDE;
BUT THE FRIEND OF THE BRIDEGROOM STANDS
BY AND LISTENS, AND REJOICES TO HEAR THE
BRIDEGROOM'S VOICE. MY JOY IS NOW FULL.
30 IT IS NECESSARY THAT HE INCREASE BUT
THAT I DECREASE.
31 HE WHO COMES FROM ABOVE IS ABOVE
ALL: HE WHO COMES FROM THE EARTH BE-
LONGS TO THE EARTH AND HIS WORDS, TOO,
ARE EARTHLY. THE ONE WHO COMES FROM
HEAVEN 32 SPEAKS OF THE THINGS HE HAS
SEEN AND HEARD; HE BEARS WITNESS TO THIS BUT
NO ONE ACCEPTS HIS TESTIMONY. 33 HE WHO RECEI-
VES HIS TESTIMONY ACKNOWLEDGES THE FAITHFULNESS OF
GOD; 34 FOR GOD SENT HIM AND HE SPEAKS GOD'S WORDS
AND GOD GIVES HIM THE SPIRIT WITHOUT MEASURE. 35 THE

FATHER LOVES THE SON AND HAS ENTRUSTED EVERYTHING
INTO HIS HANDS. 36 WHOEVER BELIEVES IN THE SON LIVES
WITH ETERNAL LIFE, BUT HE WHO WILL NOT BELIEVE IN THE
SON WILL NEVER KNOW LIFE AND FACES THE JUSTICE OF GOD."

JESUS AND THE SAMARITAN WOMAN

4 1 THE LORD KNEW THAT THE PHARISEES WERE INFOR-
MED ABOUT HIM; PEOPLE SAID THAT JESUS WAS AT-
TRACTING AND BAPTISING MORE DISCIPLES THAN JOHN,
2 IN FACT IT WAS NOT JESUS WHO WAS BAPTIZING BUT HIS
DISCIPLES. 3 SO JESUS LEFT JUDEA AND RETURNED TO

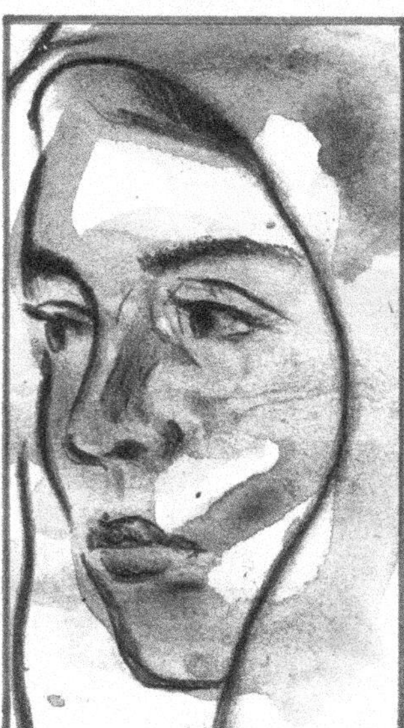

GALILEE. 4 HE HAD TO
CROSS SAMARIA. 5 HE
CAME TO A SAMARITAN
TOWN CALLED SYCHAR,
NEAR THE LAND THAT JA-
COB HAD GIVEN TO HIS
SON JOSEPH. 6 JACOB'S
WELL IS THERE. TIRED OF
HIS JOURNEY, JESUS SAT
DOWN BY THE WELL; IT
WAS ABOUT NOON. NOW A
7 SAMARITAN WOMAN
CAME TO DRAW WATER AND
JESUS SAID TO HER, "GIVE
ME A DRINK." 8 HIS DI-
SCIPLES HAD JUST GONE
INTO TOWN TO BUY SOME
FOOD. 9 THE SAMARITAN
WOMAN SAID TO HIM, "HOW
IS IT THAT YOU, A JEW, ASK
ME, A SAMARITAN FOR A
DRINK?" JEWS, IN FACT, HAVE
NO DEALINGS WITH SAMARI-
TANS. 10 JESUS REPLIED,
"IF YOU ONLY KNEW THE GIFT
OF GOD! IF YOU KNEW WHO
IT IS THAT ASKS YOU FOR A
DRINK, YOU WOULD HAVE
ASKED ME AND I WOULD
HAVE GIVEN YOU LIVING
WATER." 11 THE WOMAN ANSWERED, "SIR, YOU
HAVE NO BUCKET AND THIS WELL IS DEEP:
WERE IS YOUR LIVING WATER? 12 ARE YOU
GREATER THAN OUR ANCESTOR JACOB WHO GAVE US
THIS WELL AFTER HE DRANK FROM IT HIMSELF,
TOGETHER WITH HIS SONS AND HIS CATTLE?"

13 JESUS SAID TO HER,

"WHOEVER DRINKS OF THIS WATER
WILL BE THIRSTY AGAIN; 14 BUT WHO-
EVER DRINKS OF THE WATER THAT I
SHALL GIVE WILL NEVER BE THIRSTY;
FOR THE WATER THAT I SHALL GIVE
WILL BECOME IN HIM A SPRING OF WA-
TER WELLING UP TO ETERNAL LIFE."

15 THE WOMAN SAID TO HIM, "GIVE ME THIS WA-
TER, THAT I MAY NEVER BE THIRSTY AND NEVER

HAVE TO COME HERE TO DRAW WATER." JESUS
SAID, 16 "GO, CALL YOUR HUSBAND AND COME
BACK HERE." 17 THE WOMAN ANSWERED, "I HAVE
NO HUSBAND." AND JESUS REPLIED, "YOU ARE
RIGHT TO SAY: 'I HAVE NO HUSBAND'; 18 FOR
YOU HAVE HAD FIVE HUSBANDS AND THE ONE YOU
HAVE NOW IS NOT YOUR HUSBAND. WHAT YOU SAID IS TRUE."
19 THE WOMAN SAID TO HIM, "I SEE YOU ARE A PRO-
PHET; TELL ME: 20 OUR FATHERS USED TO COME TO
THIS MOUNTAIN TO WORSHIP GOD: BUT YOU JEWS, DO
YOU NOT CLAIM THAT JERUSALEM IS THE ONLY
PLACE TO WORSHIP GOD?" 21 JESUS SAID TO HER,

"BELIEVE ME, WOMAN, THE HOUR IS COMING WHEN
YOU SHALL WORSHIP THE FATHER, BUT THAT WILL
NOT BE ON THIS MOUNTAIN OR IN JERUSALEM.
22 YOU SAMARITANS WORSHIP WITHOUT KNOW-
LEDGE, WHILE WE JEWS WORSHIP WITH KNOW-
LEDGE, FOR SALVATION COMES FROM THE JEWS.

23 BUT THE HOUR IS COMING AND IS HERE, WHEN
THE WORSHIPERS WILL WORSHIP THE FATHER IN
SPIRIT AND TRUTH; FOR THAT IS THE WORSHIP THE
FATHER WANTS. 24 GOD IS SPIRIT AND THOSE WHO
WORSHIP GOD MUST WORSHIP IN SPIRIT AND TRUTH."

25 THE WOMAN SAID TO HIM, "I KNOW THAT THE MES-
SIAH, THAT IS THE CHRIST, IS COMING; WHEN HE COMES,
HE WILL TELL US EVERYTHING." 26 AND JESUS SAID:

"I WHO AM TALKING TO YOU, I AM HE."

27 AT THIS POINT THE DISCIPLES RETURNED AND WE-
RE SURPRISED THAT JESUS WAS SPEAKING WITH A
WOMAN. HOWEVER, NO ONE SAID, "WHAT DO YOU
WANT?" OR: "WHY ARE YOU TALKING WITH HER?"

28 SO THE WOMAN LEFT HER WATER JAR AND RAN
TO THE TOWN. THERE SHE SAID TO THE PEOPLE, 29
"COME AND SEE A MAN WHO TOLD ME EVERYTHING I DID!
COULD HE NOT BE THE CHRIST?" 30 SO THEY LEFT THE
TOWN AND WENT TO MEET HIM.
31 IN THE MEANTIME THE DISCIPLES URGED JESUS
"MASTER, EAT." 32 BUT HE SAID TO THEM, "I HAVE
FOOD TO EAT THAT YOU DON'T KNOW ABOUT." 33 AND
THE DISCIPLES WONDERED, "HAS ANYONE BROUGHT HIM
FOOD?" 34 JESUS SAID TO THEM,

"MY FOOD IS TO DO WITH THE WILL OF THE ONE WHO SENT
ME AND TO CARRY OUT HIS WORK. 35 YOU SAY THAT

IN FOUR MORE MONTHS IT WILL BE THE HARVEST; NOW,
I SAY TO YOU, LOOK UP AND SEE THE FIELDS WHITE AND
READY FOR HARVESTING. 36 PEOPLE WHO REAP
THE HARVEST ARE PAID FOR THEIR WORK, AND THE
FRUIT IS GATHERED FOR ETERNAL LIFE, SO THAT
SOWER AND REAPER MAY REJOICE TOGETHER.
37 INDEED THE SAYING HOLDS TRUE: 'ONE SOWS
AND ANOTHER REAPS.' 38 I SENT YOU TO REAP
WHERE YOU DIDN'T WORK OR SUFFER; OTHERS
HAVE WORKED AND YOU ARE NOW SHARING IN
THEIR LABORS."

39 IN THAT TOWN MANY SAMARITANS BELIEVED IN
HIM WHEN THEY HEARD THE WOMAN WHO DECLARED,
"HE TOLD ME EVERYTHING I DID." 40 SO, WHEN THEY

CAME TO HIM, THEY AS-
KED HIM TO STAY WITH
THEM AND JESUS STAY-
ED THERE TWO DAYS.
41 AFTER THAT MANY
MORE BELIEVED BECA-
USE OF HIS WORDS 42
AND THEY SAID TO THE
WOMAN, "WE NO LONGER
BELIEVE BECAUSE OF
WHAT YOU TOLD US;
FOR WE HAVE HEARD
FOR OURSELVES AND WE
KNOW THAT THIS IS THE
SAVIOR OF THE WORLD."

43 WHEN THE TWO DAYS
WERE OVER, JESUS LEFT
FOR GALILEE.
44 JESUS HIMSELF
SAID THAT NO PRO-
PHET IS RECOGNIZED
IN HIS OWN COUNTRY.

45 YET THE GALILEANS
WELCOMED HIM WHEN HE ARRIVED, BECA-
USE OF ALL THE THINGS HE HAD DONE IN JE-
RUSALEM DURING THE FESTIVAL WHICH
THEY HAD SEEN.
FOR THEY, TOO, HAD GONE TO THE FEAST.

JESUS CURES THE SON OF AN OFFICIAL

46 JESUS WENT BACK TO GALILEE WHERE HE HAD
CHANGED THE WATER INTO WINE. AT CAPERNAUM THERE
WAS AN OFFICIAL WHOSE SON WAS ILL. 47 AND WHEN
HE HEARD THAT JESUS HAD COME FROM JUDEA TO GALI-
LEE, HE ASKED HIM TO COME AND HEAL HIS SON, FOR HE
WAS AT THE POINT OF
DEATH. 48 JESUS SAID,

"UNLESS YOU SEE SIGNS
AND WONDERS, YOU WILL NOT
BELIEVE!" 49 THE OFFICIAL
SAID, "SIR, COME DOWN BEFO-
RE MY CHILD DIES." 50 AND
JESUS REPLIED, "GO, YOUR
SON IS LIVING." THE MAN HAD
FAITH IN THE WORD THAT
JESUS SPOKE TO HIM AND
WENT THIS WAY. 51 HE
WAS ALREADY GOING
DOWN THE HILLY ROAD
WHEN HIS SERVANTS
MET HIM WITH THIS
NEWS, "YOUR SON HAS
RECOVERED!" 52 SO HE
ASKED THEM AT WHAT HOUR
THE CHILD HAD BEGUN TO
RECOVER AND THEY SAID,
"THE FEVER LEFT HIM
YESTERDAY ABOUT ONE
O'CLOCK IN THE AFTER-
NOON." 53 THE FATHER
REALIZED THAT IT WAS
THE TIME WHEN JESUS
TOLD HIM, "YOUR SON IS LIVING." AND HE BECAME A
BELIEVER, HE AND ALL HIS FAMILY. 54 JESUS PER-
FORMED THIS SECOND MIRACULOUS SIGN WHEN
HE RETURNED FROM JUDEA TO GALILEE.

THE PARALYTIC AT THE POOL OF BETHZATHA

5 1 AFTER THIS THERE WAS A FEAST OF THE JEWS
AND JESUS WENT UP TO JERUSALEM. 2 NOW, BY THE
SHEEP GATE IN JERUSALEM, THERE IS A POOL CALLED
BETHZATHA IN HEBREW SURROUNDED BY FIVE GALLERIES.
3 HERE LAY A MULTITUDE OF SICK PEOPLE, LAME AND PARA-
LYZED. (4 ALL WERE WAITING FOR THE WATER TO MOVE, AS AT TIMES AN ANGEL
OF THE LORD WOULD DESCEND INTO THE POOL AND STIR UP THE WATER: THE FIRST PER-
SON TO ENTER AFTER THIS MOVEMENT OF THE WATER WOULD BE HEALED OF HIS
DISEASE) 5 THERE WAS A MAN WHO HAD BEEN SICK FOR THIRTY-

EIGHT YEARS. 6 JESUS SAW HIM, AND SINCE HE KNEW HOW
LONG HE HAD BEEN LYING THERE, HE SAID TO HIM, "DO YOU
WANT TO BE HEALED?" 7 THE SICK MAN REPLIED, "SIR, I HA-
VE NO ONE TO PUT ME INTO THE POOL WHEN THE WATER IS
DISTURBED; SO AS I AM ON MY WAY, ANOTHER STEPS DOWN
BEFORE ME." 8 JESUS SAID TO HIM, "STAND UP, TAKE YO-
UR MAT AND WALK." 9 AND AT ONCE THE MAN WAS HE-
ALED, AND HE TOOK UP HIS MAT AND WALKED. NOW THAT
DAY HAPPENED TO BE THE SABBATH. 10 SO THE JEWS
SAID TO THE MAN WHO HAD JUST BEEN HEALED, "IT IS THE
SABBATH AND THE LAW DOESN'T ALLOW YOU TO CARRY YOUR MAT."

'DO YOU WANT TO BE HEALED?' (JOHN 5:6)
348 CCCIIL
DM 09 ©

(11) HE ANSWERED THEM, "THE ONE WHO HEALED
ME SAID TO ME: 'TAKE UP YOUR MAT AND WALK'."
(12) THEY ASKED HIM, " WHO IS THE ONE WHO SAID
TO YOU: TAKE UP YOUR MAT AND WALK?" (13) BUT
THE SICK MAN HAD NO IDEA WHO IT WAS WHO HAD
CURED HIM, FOR JESUS HAD SLIPPED AWAY AMONG
THE CROWD THAT FILLED THE PLACE. (14) AFTERWARDS
JESUS MET HIM IN THE
TEMPLE COURT AND TOLD
HIM, "NOW YOU ARE WELL;
DON'T SIN AGAIN, LEST
SOMETHING WORSE
HAPPEN TO YOU." (15) AND
THE MAN WENT BACK
AND TOLD THE JEWS
THAT IT WAS JESUS WHO
HEALED HIM. (16) SO THE
JEWS PERSECUTED JESUS
BECAUSE HE PERFOR-
MED HEALINGS LIKE
THAT ON THE SABBATH.
(17) JESUS REPLIED,
"MY FATHER GOES ON
WORKING AND SO DO
I." (18) AND THE JEWS
TRIED ALL THE HARDER
TO KILL HIM, FOR JESUS
NOT ONLY BROKE THE
SABBATH OBSERVANCE,
BUT ALSO MADE HIM-
SELF EQUAL WITH
GOD, CALLING HIM
HIS OWN FATHER. (19) JESUS SAID TO THEM,

THE WORK OF THE SON

"TRULY, I ASSURE YOU, THE SON CANNOT DO ANYTHING BY
HIMSELF, BUT ONLY WHAT HE SEES THE FATHER DO. AND
WHATEVER HE DOES, THE SON ALSO DOES. (20) THE FATHER
LOVES THE SON AND SHOWS HIM EVERYTHING HE DOES; AND
HE WILL SHOW HIM EVEN GREATER THINGS THAN THESE,
SO THAT YOU WILL BE AMAZED. (21) AS THE FATHER RA-
ISES THE DEAD AND GIVES THEM LIFE, SO THE SON GIVES
TO WHOM HE WILLS. (22) IN THE SAME WAY THE FATHER
JUDGES NO ONE, FOR HE HAS ENTRUSTED ALL JUDGMENT
TO THE SON, (23) AND HE WANTS ALL TO HONOR THE SON
AS THEY HONOR THE FATHER. WHOEVER IGNORES THE SON,

IGNORES AS WELL THE FATHER WHO SENT HIM. (24) TRU-
LY, I SAY TO YOU, HE WHO HEARS MY WORD AND BELIEVES
HIM WHO SENT ME, HAS ENTERED ETERNAL LIFE; THERE
IS NO JUDGMENT FOR HIM BECAUSE HE HAS PASSED
FROM DEATH TO LIFE. (25) TRULY, THE HOUR IS COMING
AND HAS INDEED COME, WHEN THE DEAD WILL HEAR
THE VOICE OF THE SON OF GOD AND, ON HEARING IT, WILL
LIVE. (26) FOR THE FATHER HAS LIFE IN HIMSELF AND HE
HAS GIVEN TO THE SON ALSO TO HAVE LIFE IN HIMSELF. (27)
AND HE HAS EMPOWERED HIM AS WELL TO CARRY
OUT JUDGMENT, FOR HE IS A SON OF MAN. (28) DO
NOT BE SURPRISED AT THIS: THE HOUR IS COMING
WHEN ALL THOSE LYING IN TOMBS WILL HEAR MY VOICE

(29) AND COME OUT: THOSE WHO HAVE DONE GOOD
SHALL RISE TO LIVE, AND THOSE WHO HAVE DONE
EVIL WILL RISE TO BE CONDEMNED. (30) I CAN DO
NOTHING OF MYSELF, AND I NEED TO HEAR ANOTHER ONE TO
JUDGE; AND MY JUDGMENT IS JUST, BECAUSE I SEEK
NOT MY OWN WILL, BUT THE WILL OF HIM WHO SENT ME.
(31) IF I BORE WITNESS TO MYSELF, MY TESTIMONY WOULD
BE WORTHLESS. (32) BUT ANOTHER ONE IS BEARING
WITNESS TO ME AND I KNOW THAT HIS TESTIMONY IS
TRUE WHEN HE BEARS WITNESS TO ME. (33) JOHN ALSO
BORE WITNESS TO THE TRUTH WHEN YOU SENT MESSEN-
GERS TO HIM, (34) BUT I DO NOT SEEK SUCH HUMAN TESTI-
MONY; I RECALL THIS FOR YOU, SO THAT YOU MAY BE SAVED.

(35) JOHN WAS A BURNING AND SHINING LAMP
AND FOR A WHILE YOU WERE WILLING TO ENJOY
HIS LIGHT. (36) BUT I HAVE GREATER EVIDENCE
THAN THAT OF JOHN - THE WORKS WHICH THE FA-
THER ENTRUSTED TO ME TO CARRY OUT. THE VERY
WORKS I DO BEAR WITNESS: THE FATHER HAS
SENT ME.
(37) THUS HE WHO BEARS WITNESS TO ME IS
THE FATHER WHO SENT ME. YOU HAVE NEVER
HEARD HIS VOICE AND HAVE NEVER SEEN HIS
LIKENESS; (38) THEN, AS LONG AS YOU DO NOT
BELIEVE HIS MESSENGER, HIS WORD IS NOT IN
YOU.
(39) YOU SEARCH IN THE SCRIPTURES THINKING
THAT IN THEM YOU WILL FIND LIFE; YET SCRIPTU-
RES BEAR WITNESS TO ME, THAT YOU MAY LIVE,

(40) WHEN YOU REFUSE TO COME TO ME. (41) I AM NOT
SEEKING HUMAN PRAISE; (42) BUT I HAVE KNOWN THAT
LOVE OF GOD IS NOT WITHIN YOU. (43) EVEN THOUGH I
HAVE COME IN MY FATHER'S NAME, YOU DO NOT
ACCEPT ME; BUT IF ANOTHER COMES IN HIS
OWN NAME, YOU WILL ACCEPT HIM.

(44) AS LONG AS YOU SEEK PRAISE FROM ONE
ANOTHER INSTEAD OF SEEKING THE GLORY
COMING FROM THE ONLY GOD, HOW CAN YOU BELIEVE?

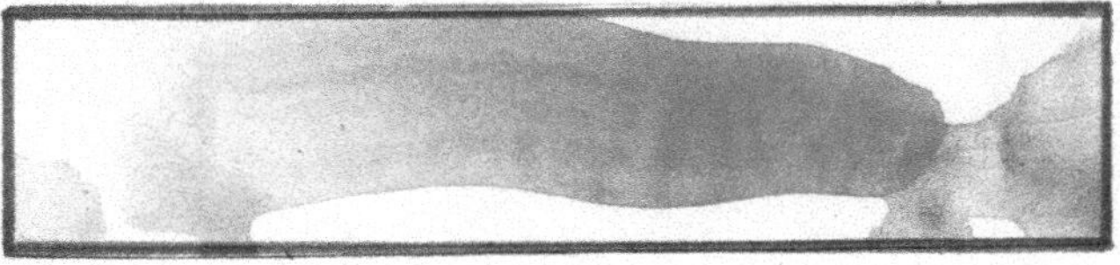

(45) DO NOT THINK THAT I SHALL ACCUSE YOU
TO THE FATHER. MOSES HIMSELF IN WHOM
YOU PLACED YOUR HOPE, ACCUSES YOU.
(46) IF YOU BELIEVED MOSES, YOU WOULD
BELIEVE ME, FOR HE WROTE OF ME.
(47) BUT IF YOU DO NOT BELIEVE WHAT HE
WROTE, HOW WILL YOU BELIEVE WHAT I SAY?

THE MULTIPLICATION OF THE LOAVES

6 (1) AFTER THIS JESUS WENT TO THE OTHER
SIDE OF THE SEA OF GALILEE, NEAR TIBERIAS.
(2) AND LARGE CROWDS FOLLOWED HIM BECAUSE OF
THE MIRACULOUS SIGNS THEY SAW WHEN HE HEALED THE

SICK. (3) SO HE WENT UP
INTO THE HILLS AND SAT
DOWN WITH HIS DISCIP-
LES. (4) NOW, THE JE-
WISH PASSOVER WAS AT
HAND. (5) LIFTING UP HIS
EYES, JESUS SAW THE
CROWDS COMING TO HIM
AND SAID TO PHILIP,
"WHERE SHALL WE BUY
BREAD SO THAT THIS PEOPLE
MAY EAT?" (6) HE SAID
THIS TO TEST PHILIP, FOR
HE KNEW WHAT WAS GOING
TO DO. (7) PHILIP ANS-
WERED HIM, "TWO HUN-
DRED SILVER COINS WO-
ULD NOT BUY ENOUGH
BREAD FOR EACH OF THEM
TO HAVE A PIECE." (8)
THEN ONE OF JESUS'
DISCIPLES, ANDREW,
SIMON PETER'S BRO-
THER, SAID, "THERE
(9) IS A BOY HERE WHO HAS FIVE BARLEY LOAVES
AND TWO FISH; BUT WHAT GOOD ARE THESE FOR SO
MANY?"
(10) JESUS SAID, "MAKE THE PEOPLE SIT DOWN." THERE WAS
PLENTY OF GRASS SO THE PEOPLE, ABOUT FIVE THOUSAND
MEN, SAT DOWN TO REST. (11) JESUS THEN TOOK THE LOAVES,
GAVE THANKS AND DISTRIBUTED THEM TO THOSE WHO
WERE SEATED. HE DID THE SAME WITH THE FISH AND
GAVE THEM AS MUCH AS THEY WANTED. (12) AND WHEN
THEY HAD EATEN ENOUGH, HE TOLD THE DISCIPLES,
"GATHER UP THE PIECES LEFT OVER, THAT NO-
THING MAY BE LOST." (13) SO THEY GATHERED

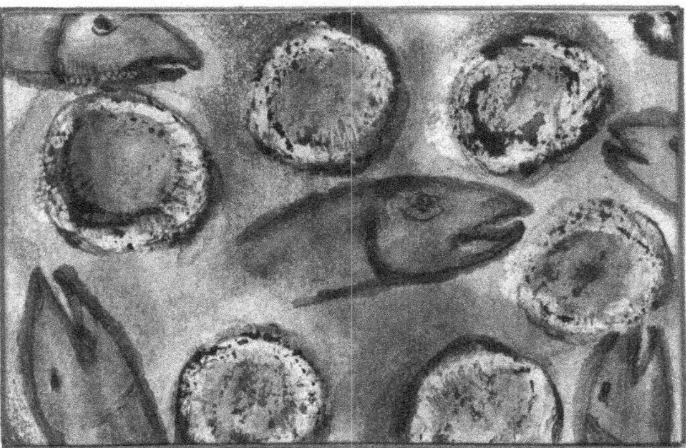

THEM UP AND FILLED TWELVE BASKETS WITH
BREAD, THAT IS WITH PIECES OF THE FIVE
BARLEY LOAVES LEFT BY THOSE WHO HAD EATEN.

(14) WHEN THE PEOPLE SAW THIS SIGN JESUS
HAD JUST GIVEN, THEY SAID, "THIS IS REALLY
THE PROPHET, HE WHO IS TO COME INTO THE WORLD."

(15) JESUS REALIZED THAT THEY WOULD COME
AND TAKE HIM BY FORCE TO MAKE HIM KING;
SO HE FLED TO THE HILLS BY HIMSELF.

(16) WHEN EVENING CAME, THE DISCIPLES
WENT DOWN TO THE SHORE. (17) AFTER A
WHILE THEY GOT INTO A BOAT TO MAKE
FOR CAPERNAUM ON THE OTHER SIDE OF
THE SEA, FOR IT WAS NOW DARK AND JESUS HAD
NOT YET COME TO THEM. (18) BUT THE SEA WAS
GETTING ROUGH BECAUSE A STRONG WIND WAS
BLOWING. (19) THEY HAD ROWED ABOUT THREE OR
FOUR MILES, WHEN THEY SAW JESUS WALKING

ON THE SEA, AND HE WAS DRAWING NEAR TO THE
BOAT, THEY WERE FRIGHTENED. (20) BUT HE SAID
TO THEM, "IT IS ME; DON'T BE AFRAID." (21) THEY
WANTED TO MAKE HIM GET INTO THE BOAT, BUT IM-
MEDIATELY THE BOAT WAS AT THE SHORE THEY AIMED TO.

(22) NEXT DAY THE PEOPLE WHO HAD STAYED
ON THE OTHER SIDE REALIZED THAT ONLY ONE
BOAT HAD BEEN THERE

AND THAT JESUS HAD
NOT ENTERED IT WITH
HIS DISCIPLES; BUT THE
DISCIPLES HAD GONE AWAY
ALONE. (23) BIGGER BOATS
FROM TIBERIAS CAME NE-
AR THE PLACE WHERE ALL
THESE PEOPLE HAD EATEN
THE BREAD. (24) WHEN THEY
SAW THAT NEITHER JESUS
NOR HIS DISCIPLES WERE
THERE, THEY GOT INTO THE
BOATS AND WENT TO CA-
PERNAUM LOOKING FOR
JESUS. (25) WHEN THEY
FOUND HIM ON THE OTHER
SIDE OF THE LAKE, THEY
ASKED, "MASTER, WHEN
DID YOU COME HERE?"
JESUS REPLIED (26), "TRU-
LY, I SAY TO YOU, YOU LOOK
FOR ME, NOT BECAUSE
YOU HAVE SEEN THE
SIGNS, BUT BECAUSE
YOU ATE BREAD AND WERE SATISFIED. (27) WORK
THEN, NOT FOR PERISHABLE FOOD, BUT FOR
THE LASTING FOOD WHICH GIVES ETERNAL
LIFE. THIS IS THE FOOD THAT THE SON OF MAN
GIVES TO YOU, WITH THE FATHER'S SEAL PUT ON HIM."

THE BREAD OF LIFE

(28) THEN THE JEWS ASKED HIM, "WHAT SHALL WE
DO? WHAT ARE THE WORKS THAT GOD WANTS US
TO DO?" (29) AND JESUS ANSWERED THEM, "THE
WORK GOD WANTS IS THIS: THAT YOU BELIEVE
IN THE ONE WHOM GOD HAS SENT." (30) THEN
THEY SAID, "SHOW US MIRACULOUS SIGNS, THAT WE
MAY SEE AND BELIEVE YOU. WHAT SIGN DO YOU PERFORM?
(31) OUR ANCESTORS ATE MANNA IN THE DESERT; AS THE
SCRIPTURE SAYS: THEY WERE GIVEN BREAD FROM
HEAVEN TO EAT." (32) JESUS THEN SAID TO THEM,

"TRULY, I SAY TO YOU, IT WAS NOT MOSES WHO GAVE YOU

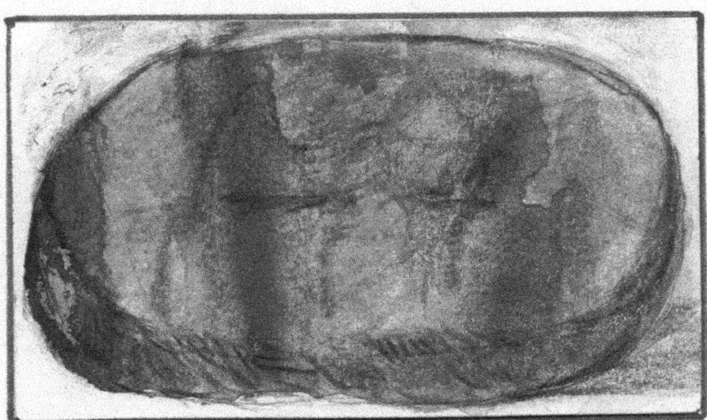

THE BREAD FROM HEAVEN. MY FATHER GIVES YOU THE TRUE
BREAD FROM HEAVEN. (33) THE BREAD GOD GIVES IS
THE ONE WHO COMES FROM HEAVEN AND GIVES LIFE TO
THE WORLD." (34) AND THEY SAID TO HIM, "GIVE US THIS
BREAD ALWAYS." (35) JESUS SAID TO THEM, "I AM THE
BREAD OF LIFE; HE WHO COMES TO ME SHALL NEVER
BE HUNGRY, AND HE WHO BELIEVES IN ME SHALL NE-
VER BE THIRSTY. (36) NEVERTHELESS, AS I SAID, YOU
REFUSE TO BELIEVE, EVEN WHEN YOU HAVE SEEN. (37) YET,
ALL THAT THE FATHER GIVES ME WILL COME TO ME,
AND WHOEVER COMES TO ME, I SHALL NOT TURN AWAY.
(38) FOR I HAVE COME FROM HEAVEN, NOT TO DO MY OWN
WILL, BUT THE WILL OF THE ONE WHO SENT ME.

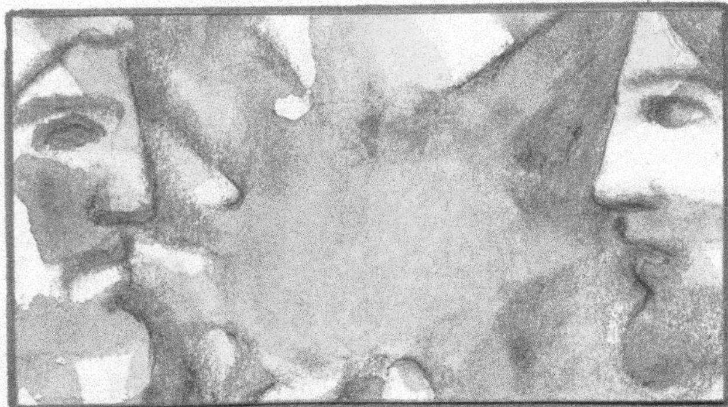

(39) AND THE WILL OF HIM WHO SENT ME IS THAT I LO-
SE NOTHING OF WHAT HE HAS GIVEN ME, BUT INSTEAD
THAT I RAISE IT UP ON THE LAST DAY. (40) THIS IS
THE WILL OF THE FATHER, THAT WHOEVER SEES
THE SON AND BELIEVES IN HIM SHALL LIVE
WITH ETERNAL LIFE; AND I WILL RAISE HIM UP ON
THE LAST DAY." (41) THE JEWS MURMURED BECAUSE
JESUS HAD SAID,

"I AM THE BREAD WHICH COMES FROM HEAVEN."

(42) AND THEY SAID, "THIS MAN IS THE SON
OF JOSEPH, ISN'T HE? WE KNOW HIS FATHER
AND MOTHER. HOW CAN HE SAY THAT HE HAS
COME FROM HEAVEN?" (43) JESUS ANSWERED THEM,
DO NOT MURMUR AMONG YOURSELVES. (44) NO ONE
CAN COME TO ME UNLESS HE IS DRAWN BY THE FATHER
WHO SENT ME; AND I WILL RAISE HIM UP ON THE LAST
DAY. (45) IT HAS BEEN WRITTEN IN THE PROPHETS: THEY
SHALL ALL BE TAUGHT BY GOD. SO WHOEVER LISTENS
AND LEARNS FROM THE FATHER COMES TO ME. (46)

FOR NO ONE HAS SEEN THE FATHER. THE ONE WHO COMES
FROM GOD HAS SEEN THE FATHER. (47) TRULY, I SAY TO YOU,
HE WHO BELIEVES HAS ETERNAL LIFE.

THE BODY OF CHRIST (48) I AM THE BREAD
OF LIFE. (49) THOUGH YOUR ANCESTORS ATE THE MANNA
IN THE DESERT, THEY DIED. (50) BUT HERE YOU HAVE THE
BREAD WHICH COMES FROM HEAVEN SO THAT YOU MAY
EAT OF IT AND NOT DIE. (51) I AM THE LIVING BREAD WHICH
HAS COME FROM HEAVEN; WHOEVER EATS OF THIS BREAD
WILL LIVE FOREVER. THE BREAD I SHALL GIVE IS MY
FLESH AND I WILL GIVE IT FOR THE LIFE OF THE
WORLD." (52) THE JEWS WERE ARGUING AMONG
THEMSELVES, "HOW CAN THIS MAN GIVE US HIS
FLESH TO EAT?" (53) SO JESUS REPLIED, "TRULY,

I SAY TO YOU, IF YOU DO NOT EAT THE FLESH OF THE
SON OF MAN AND DRINK HIS BLOOD, YOU HAVE
NO LIFE IN YOU. (54) HE WHO EATS MY FLESH
AND DRINKS MY BLOOD LIVES WITH ETERNAL
LIFE AND I WILL RAISE HIM UP ON THE LAST DAY.
(55) MY FLESH IS REALLY FOOD AND MY BLOOD IS DRINK.
(56) HE WHO EATS MY FLESH AND DRINKS MY BLO-
OD, LIVES IN ME AND I IN HIM. (57) JUST AS
THE FATHER, WHO IS LIFE, SENT ME AND I
HAVE LIFE FROM THE FATHER, SO HE WHO EATS
ME WILL HAVE LIFE FROM ME. (58) THIS IS THE
BREAD WHICH CAME FROM HEAVEN; UNLIKE THAT
OF YOUR ANCESTORS, WHO ATE AND LATER DIED.
HE WHO EATS THIS BREAD WILL LIVE FOREVER."

I AM THE BREAD OF LIFE
(JOHN 6 : 35)
349 CECIL
© DM 06

(59) JESUS SPOKE IN THIS WAY IN CAPERNAUM
WHEN HE TAUGHT THEM IN THE SYNAGOGUE.

WILL YOU ALSO GO AWAY?

(60) AFTER HEARING THIS, MANY OF JESUS' FOL-
LOWERS SAID, "THIS SORT OF TEACHING IS VERY
HARD! WHO CAN ACCEPT IT?"
(61) JESUS WAS AWARE THAT HIS DISCIPLES WERE MUR-
MURING ABOUT THIS AND SO HE SAID TO THEM, "DOES
THIS OFFEND YOU? (62) THEN HOW WILL YOU REACT
WHEN YOU SEE THE SON OF MAN ASCENDING TO WHERE HE
WAS BEFORE? (63) IT IS THE SPIRIT THAT GIVES LIFE; THE
FLESH CANNOT HELP. THE WORDS THAT I HAVE SPOKEN

TO YOU ARE SPIRIT AND THEY ARE LIFE. (64) BUT AMONG
YOU THERE ARE SOME WHO DO NOT BELIEVE."

FROM THE BEGINNING JESUS KNEW WHO WOULD
BETRAY HIM. (65) SO HE ADDED, "AS I HAVE TOLD
YOU, NO ONE CAN COME TO ME UNLES IT IS
GIVEN TO HIM BY MY FATHER."

(66) AFTER THIS MANY DISCIPLES WITHDREW

AND NO LONGER FOL-
LOWED HIM. JESUS
(67) ASKED THE TWELVE,
"WILL YOU ALSO GO
AWAY?" (68) PETER
ANSWERED HIM, "LORD,
TO WHOM SHALL WE
GO? ONLY YOU HAVE
THE WORDS OF ET-
ERNAL LIFE. (69) WE
NOW BELIEVE AND
KNOW THAT YOU ARE
THE HOLY ONE OF GOD."

(70) JESUS SAID TO
THEM, "I CHOSE YOU,
THE TWELVE, DID I NOT?
YET ONE OF YOU IS A
DEVIL." (71) JESUS
SPOKE OF JUDAS IS-
CARIOT, THE SON OF SI-
MON. HE, ONE OF THE TWEL-
VE, WAS TO BETRAY HIM.

JESUS GOES UP TO JERUSALEM

7 (1) AFTER THIS JESUS WENT AROUND GALILEE;
HE WOULD NOT GO ABOUT IN JUDEA BECAUSE THE
JEWS WANTED TO KILL HIM. (2) NOW THE
JEWISH FEAST OF THE TENTS WAS AT HAND. (3) SO
THE BROTHERS OF JESUS SAID TO HIM, "DON'T
STAY HERE; GO INSTEAD TO JUDEA AND LET YOUR
DISCIPLES SEE THE WORKS YOU ARE DOING.
(4) ANYONE WHO WANTS TO BE KNOWN DOESN'T WORK
SECRETLY. SINCE YOU ARE ABLE TO DO THESE THINGS,
SHOW YOURSELF TO THE WORLD."

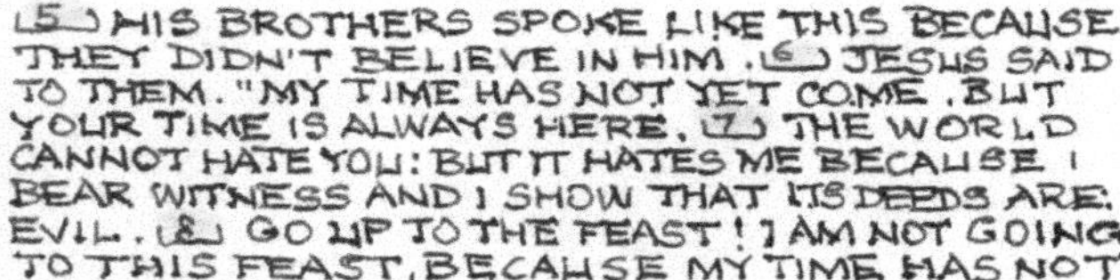

(5) HIS BROTHERS SPOKE LIKE THIS BECAUSE
THEY DIDN'T BELIEVE IN HIM. (6) JESUS SAID
TO THEM, "MY TIME HAS NOT YET COME, BUT
YOUR TIME IS ALWAYS HERE. (7) THE WORLD
CANNOT HATE YOU; BUT IT HATES ME BECAUSE I
BEAR WITNESS AND I SHOW THAT ITS DEEDS ARE
EVIL. (8) GO UP TO THE FEAST! I AM NOT GOING
TO THIS FEAST, BECAUSE MY TIME HAS NOT
YET COME." JESUS

(9) SPOKE LIKE THIS
AND REMAINED IN GA-
LILEE. (10) BUT AFTER
HIS BROTHERS HAD
GONE TO THE FESTI-
VAL, HE ALSO WENT UP
NOT PUBLICLY, BUT IN
SECRET. (11) THE JEWS
WERE LOOKING FOR
HIM AT THE FESTIVAL AND
ASKED, "WHERE IS HE?"
(12) THERE WAS A LOT
OF TALK ABOUT HIM
AMONG THE PEOPLE.
SOME SAID, "HE IS A
GOOD MAN," INSTEAD
OTHERS REPLIED, "NO,
HE IS MISLEADING THE
PEOPLE." (13) FOR FE-
AR OF THE JEWS NO
ONE SPOKE OPENLY
ABOUT HIM. (14) WHEN
THE FESTIVAL WAS
HALF OVER, JESUS
WENT TO THE TEMPLE
AND BEGAN TO TEACH. (15) THE JEWS MARVELED
AND SAID, "HOW IS IT THAT HE SPEAKS WITH SO
MUCH LEARNING WHEN HE HAS HAD NO TE-
ACHER?" (16) AND JESUS ANSWERED THEM,

"MY TEACHING IS NOT MINE, BUT IT COMES FROM THE
ONE WHO SENT ME. (17) ANYONE WHO DOES THE WILL
OF GOD SHALL KNOW WHETHER MY TEACHING IS FROM
GOD OR I SPEAK ON MY OWN AUTHORITY. (18) HE SPEAKS
(HE WHO) ON HIS AUTHORITY WISHES HONOR FOR
HIMSELF. BUT HE WHO WANTS TO GIVE GLORY TO HIM
WHO SENT HIM IS TRUTHFUL AND THERE IS NO
REASON TO DOUBT HIM." (19) MOSES GAVE YOU THE
LAW, DIDN'T HE? BUT NONE OF YOU KEEP THE LAW.
WHY, THEN, DO YOU WANT TO KILL ME?" THE PEOPLE
(20) REPLIED, "YOU HAVE A DEMON; WHO WANTS

TO KILL YOU?" (21) JESUS SAID, "I PERFORMED A SINGLE
DEED, AND YOU ARE ALL ASTOUNDED BY IT. (22) BUT REMEM-
BER THE CIRCUMCISION ORDERED BY MOSES-ACTUALLY IT WAS
NOT MOSES BUT THE ANCESTORS WHO BEGAN THIS PRACTICE. (23)
YOU CIRCUMCISE A MAN EVEN ON THE SABBATH. HOW IS IT THAT
YOU ARE INDIGNANT WITH ME BECAUSE I HEALED THE WHOLE
PERSON ON THE SABBATH? (24) DO NOT JUDGE BY APPEAR-
ANCES, BUT ACCORDING TO WHAT IS RIGHT."
(25) SOME OF THE PEOPLE OF JERUSALEM SAID, "IS
THIS NOT THE MAN THEY WANT TO KILL? (26) AND

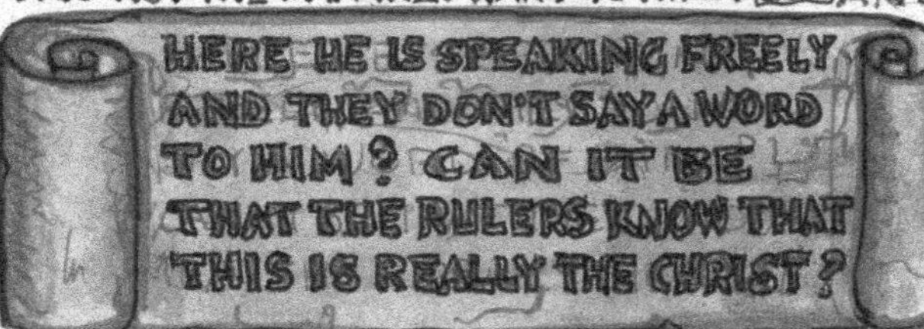

27 YET WE KNOW WHERE THIS MAN COMES
FROM; BUT WHEN THE CHRIST APPEARS, NO
ONE WILL KNOW WHERE HE COMES FROM."

28 SO JESUS ANNOUNCED IN A LOUD VOICE IN
THE TEMPLE COURT WHERE HE WAS TEACHING,
"YOU SAY THAT YOU KNOW ME AND KNOW WHERE
I COME FROM! I HAVE NOT COME OF MYSELF;
I WAS SENT BY THE ONE WHO IS TRUE, AND YOU
DON'T KNOW HIM. 29 I KNOW HIM FOR I CO-
ME FROM HIM AND HE SENT ME."

30 THEY WOULD HAVE ARRESTED HIM, BUT NO
ONE LAID HANDS ON HIM BECAUSE HIS TIME
HAD NOT YET COME. 31 MANY PEOPLE IN
THE CROWD, HOWEVER, BELIEVED IN HIM AND
SAID, "WHEN THE CHRIST COMES, WILL HE
GIVE MORE SIGNS THAN THIS MAN?"
32 THE PHARISEES HEARD ALL THESE RUMORS
AMONG THE PEOPLE; THEY AND THE CHIEF PRIESTS
SENT OFFICERS OF THE TEMPLE TO ARREST HIM.
33 JESUS THEN SAID, "I SHALL BE WITH YOU A LIT-
TLE LONGER; AFTER THAT I SHALL GO TO HIM
WHO SENT ME. 34 YOU WILL LOOK FOR ME AND
YOU WILL NOT FIND ME. WHERE I AM YOU CANNOT
COME." 35 THE JEWS SAID TO ONE ANOTHER,
"WHERE DOES THIS MAN INTEND TO GO WHERE WE
SHALL NOT FIND HIM? WILL HE GO ABROAD TO

THE JEWS DISPERSED AMONG THE GREEK NATIONS AND
TEACH THE GREEKS ALSO? 36 WHAT DOES HE MEAN
WHEN HE SAYS: 'YOU WILL LOOK FOR ME AND NOT FIND
ME,' AND: 'WHERE I AM GOING YOU CANNOT COME'?"

THE PROMISE OF LIVING WATER

37 ON THE LAST AND GREATEST DAY OF THE FEST-
IVAL, JESUS STOOD UP AND PROCLAIMED, "IF ANY-
ONE IS THIRSTY, LET HIM COME TO ME; 38 AND
LET HIM WHO BELIEVES IN ME DRINK, FOR
THE SCRIPTURE SAYS:

OUT OF HIM SHALL FLOW RIVERS OF LIVING WATER."

39 JESUS WAS REFERRING TO THE SPIRIT WHICH THOSE
WHO BELIEVE IN HIM WERE TO RECEIVE; THE SPIRIT
HAD NOT YET BEEN GIVEN BECAUSE JESUS HAD
NOT YET ENTERED INTO HIS GLORY.

DISPUTE ON THE ORIGIN OF CHRIST

40 MANY WHO HAD BEEN LISTENING TO THESE WORDS
BEGAN TO SAY, "THIS IS THE PROPHET." 41 OTHERS SAID,
"THIS IS THE CHRIST". BUT SOME WONDERED, "WOULD
THE CHRIST COME FROM GALILEE? 42 DOESN'T
SCRIPTURE SAY THAT THE CHRIST IS A DESCENDANT
OF DAVID AND FROM BETHLEHEM, THE CITY OF
DAVID?" 43 THE CROWD
WAS DIVIDED OVER HIM.
44 SOME WANTED TO
ARREST HIM, BUT NO ONE
LAID HANDS ON HIM. 45
THE OFFICERS OF THE
TEMPLE WENT BACK TO
THE CHIEF PRIESTS WHO
ASKED THEM, "WHY
DIDN'T YOU BRING HIM?"
46 THE OFFICER SAID,
"NO ONE EVER SPOKE
LIKE THIS MAN." 47 THE
PHARISEES THEN SAID,
"SO YOU, TOO, HAVE BEEN
LED ASTRAY! 48 HAVE
ANY OF THE RULERS OR
ANY OF THE PHARISEES BE-
LIEVED IN HIM? ONLY
49 THESE CURSED PEOPLE
WHO HAVE NO KNOWLEDGE
OF THE LAW!" 50 YET ONE
OF THEM, NICODEMUS,
WHO HAD GONE TO
JESUS EARLIER, SPOKE
OUT, 51 DOES OUR

LAW CONDEMN A PERSON WITHOUT FIRST HEAR-
ING HIM AND KNOWING THE FACTS?" THEY REPLIED,
52 "DO YOU, TOO, COME FROM GALILEE? LOOK IT
UP AND SEE FOR YOURSELF THAT NO PROPHET IS
TO COME FROM GALILEE." 53 AND THEY ALL WENT HOME.

THE ADULTERESS

8 1 AS FOR JESUS, HE WENT TO THE MOUNT OF
OLIVES, 2 AT DAYBREAK JESUS APPEARED
IN THE TEMPLE AGAIN. ALL THE PEOPLE CAME
TO HIM, AND HE SAT DOWN AND BEGAN TO TEACH THEM.
3 THEN THE TEACHERS OF THE LAW AND THE PHA-
RISEES BROUGHT A WOMAN WHO HAD BEEN CAUGHT
IN THE ACT OF ADULTERY.
THEY MADE HER STAND IN
FRONT OF EVERYONE. 4
"MASTER," THEY SAID,
"THIS WOMAN HAS BEEN
CAUGHT IN THE ACT OF
ADULTERY. 5 NOW THE
LAW OF MOSES ORDERS
THAT SUCH WOMEN BE
STONED TO DEATH; BUT YOU,
WHAT DO YOU SAY?" 6
THEY SAID THIS TO TEST
JESUS, IN ORDER TO
HAVE SOME CHARGE
AGAINST HIM. JESUS
BENT DOWN AND START-
ED WRITING ON THE
GROUND WITH HIS
FINGER. 7 AND AS
THEY CONTINUED TO
ASK HIM, HE STRAIGHT-
ENED UP AND SAID TO
THEM, "LET THE MAN
AMONG YOU WHO HAS NO

SIN BE THE FIRST TO THROW A STONE AT HER." AND
8 HE BENT DOWN AGAIN, WRITING ON THE GROUND.
9 AS A RESULT OF THESE WORDS, THEY WENT
AWAY, ONE BY ONE, STARTING WITH THE OLDEST,
AND JESUS WAS LEFT ALONE WITH THE WOMAN
STANDING BEFORE HIM. 10 THEN JESUS STOOD UP
AND SAID TO HER, "WOMAN, WHERE ARE THEY? HAS NO
ONE CONDEMNED YOU?" 11 SHE REPLIED, "NO ONE."
AND JESUS SAID, "NEITHER DO I CONDEMN YOU;
GO AWAY AND DON'T SIN AGAIN."

I AM THE LIGHT OF THE WORLD

(12) JESUS SPOKE TO THEM AGAIN,

"I AM THE LIGHT OF THE WORLD;
HE WHO FOLLOWS ME WILL NOT
WALK IN DARKNESS, BUT WILL
HAVE LIGHT AND LIFE."

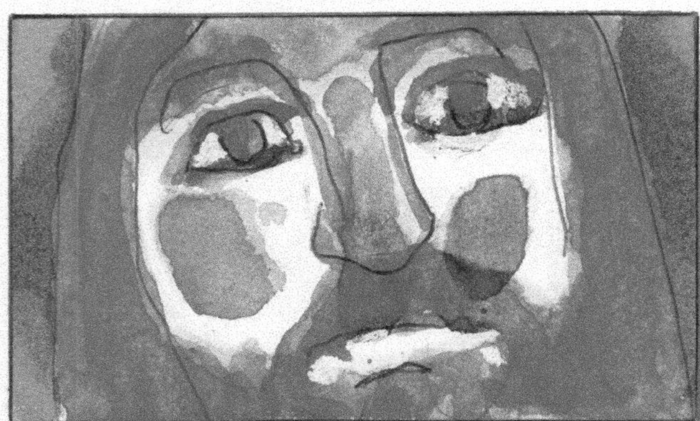

(13) THE PHARISEES REPLIED, "NOW YOU ARE
SPEAKING ON YOUR OWN BEHALF, YOUR TES-
TIMONY IS WORTHLESS." (14) JESUS SAID TO THEM,

"EVEN THOUGH I BEAR WITNESS TO MY-
SELF, MY TESTIMONY IS TRUE, FOR I
KNOW WHERE I HAVE COME FROM
AND WHERE I AM GOING. BUT YOU
DO NOT KNOW WHERE I COME
FROM OR WHERE I AM GOING. (15) YOU
JUDGE BY HUMAN STANDARDS; AS
FOR ME, I DON'T JUDGE ANYONE.
(16) BUT IF I HAD TO JUDGE, MY JUDG-
MENT WOULD BE VALID FOR I AM
NOT ALONE: THE FATHER WHO
SENT ME IS WITH ME. (17) IN YOUR
LAW IT IS WRITTEN THAT THE TESTIMO-
NY OF TWO MEN IS VALID; (18) SO I AM
BEARING WITNESS TO MYSELF, AND
THE FATHER WHO SENT ME BEARS
WITNESS TO ME."

(19) THEY ASKED HIM, "WHERE IS YOUR FATHER?"

JESUS ANSWERED,

"YOU DON'T KNOW ME OR MY FATHER; IF
YOU KNEW ME, YOU WOULD KNOW
MY FATHER AS WELL."

(20) JESUS SAID THESE THINGS WHEN HE WAS TEACH-
ING IN THE TEMPLE AREA, WHERE THEY RECEIVED
THE OFFERINGS. NO ONE ARRESTED HIM, BECAUSE HIS
HOUR HAD NOT YET COME. (21) AGAIN JESUS SAID TO THEM,

"I AM GOING AWAY, AND THOUGH YOU
LOOK FOR ME, YOU WILL DIE IN YOUR
SIN. WHERE I AM GOING YOU CANNOT COME."

(22) THE JEWS WONDERED, "WHY DOES HE
SAY THAT WE CAN'T COME WHERE HE IS GO-
ING? WILL HE KILL HIMSELF?" (23) JESUS SAID,

"YOU ARE FROM BELOW AND I AM FROM
ABOVE; YOU ARE OF THIS WORLD AND I
AM NOT OF THIS WORLD; (24) THAT IS WHY
I TOLD YOU WILL DIE IN YOUR SINS. AND
YOU SHALL DIE IN YOUR SINS UNLESS
YOU BELIEVE THAT I AM HE."

(25) THEY ASKED HIM, "WHO ARE YOU?"; AND JESUS SAID,

"JUST WHAT I HAVE TOLD YOU FROM THE

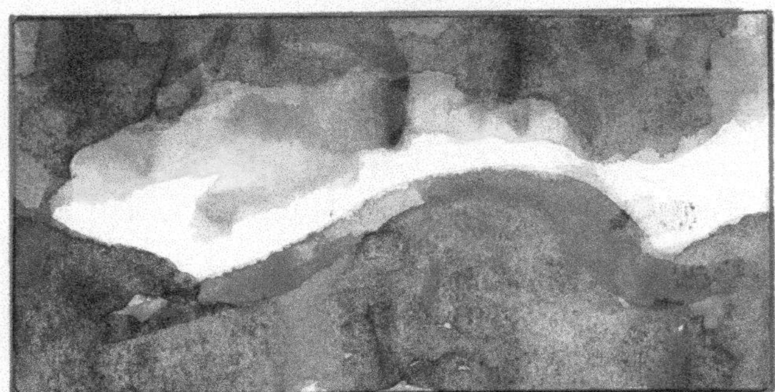

BEGINNING. (26) I HAVE MUCH TO SAY ABOUT
YOU AND MUCH TO CONDEMN; BUT THE ONE
WHO SENT ME IS TRUTHFUL AND EVERYTHING
I LEARNED FROM HIM, I PROCLAIM TO THE WORLD."

(27) THEY DIDN'T UNDERSTAND THAT JESUS WAS SPEAK-
ING TO THEM ABOUT THE FATHER. (28) SO JESUS SAID,

"WHEN YOU HAVE LIFTED UP THE SON OF
MAN, THEN YOU WILL KNOW THAT I AM
HE AND THAT I DO NOTHING OF
MYSELF, BUT I SAY JUST WHAT
THE FATHER TAUGHT ME. (29) HE WHO SENT

ME IS WITH ME AND HAS NOT LEFT ME ALONE;
BECAUSE I ALWAYS DO WHAT PLEASES HIM."

THE CHILDREN OF TRUTH

(30) AS JESUS SPOKE LIKE THIS, MANY BELIEVED IN HIM. (31)
JESUS WENT ON TO SAY TO THE JEWS WHO BELIEVED IN HIM:

"YOU WILL BE MY TRUE DISCIPLES IF YOU KEEP
MY WORD. (32) THEN YOU WILL KNOW THE
TRUTH AND THE TRUTH WILL MAKE YOU FREE."

(33) THEY ANSWERED HIM, "WE ARE THE DESCENDANTS OF
ABRAHAM AND HAVE NEVER BEEN SLAVES OF ANYONE.
WHAT DO YOU MEAN BY SAYING, "YOU WILL BE FREE?"
(34) JESUS ANSWERED THEM,

"TRULY, I SAY TO YOU, WHOEVER COMMITS
SIN IS A SLAVE. (35) BUT THE SLAVE
DOESN'T STAY IN THE HOUSE FOREVER;
THE SON STAYS FOREVER.

MARY OF
MAGDALA
LUCIAN FREUD
350
CCCL
©

(36) SO, IF THE SON MAKES YOU FREE,
YOU WILL BE REALLY FREE. (37) I KNOW
THAT YOU ARE THE DESCENDANTS OF ABRA-
HAM; YET YOU WANT TO KILL ME BECAUSE
MY WORD FINDS NO PLACE IN YOU. (38) FOR
MY PART I SPEAK OF WHAT I HAVE SEEN
IN THE FATHER'S PRESENCE, BUT YOU DO
WHAT YOU HAVE LEARNED FROM YOUR FATHER".

(39) THEY ANSWERED HIM, "OUR FATHER IS ABRAHAM".
THEN JESUS SAID,

"IF YOU WERE ABRAHAM'S CHILDREN,
YOU WOULD DO ABRAHAM DID. (40) BUT
NOW YOU WANT TO KILL ME, THE ONE

WHO TELLS YOU THE TRUTH, THE TRUTH I HAVE
LEARNED FROM GOD. THAT IS NOT WHAT AB-
RAHAM DID; (41) WHAT YOU ARE DOING ARE
THE WORKS OF YOUR FATHER."

THE JEWS SAID TO HIM, "WE ARE NOT ILLEGITIMATE
CHILDREN; WE HAVE ONE FATHER, GOD." JESUS
(42) REPLIED, "IF GOD WERE YOUR FATHER, YOU
WOULD LOVE ME, FOR I COME FROM GOD AND I AM
HERE. HE SENT ME, IT HAS NOT BEEN MY DECISION.
(43) WHY DON'T YOU FOLLOW MY TEACHING? IT IS
BECAUSE YOU CANNOT BEAR MY MESSAGE. YOUR
(44) FATHER IS THE DEVIL, AND YOU WILL CARRY
OUT HIS WISHES, A MURDERER FATHER FROM
THE BEGINNING. HE DIDN'T UPHOLD THE TRUTH FOR,
IN HIM, THERE IS NO TRUTH; AND NOW, WHEN HE
SPEAKS FOR HIMSELF, HE LIES. HE IS A LIAR AND
THE FATHER OF LIES. (45) NOW I SPEAK THE TRUTH

AND YOU DON'T BELIEVE ME. (46) WHICH OF YOU
COULD FIND ANYTHING FALSE IN ME? THEN, IF I
SPEAK THE TRUTH, WHY DO YOU NOT BELIEVE
ME? (47) HE WHO IS OF GOD HEARS THE WORDS
OF GOD; YOU DON'T HEAR BECAUSE YOU ARE
NOT OF GOD."

(48) THE JEWS RETORTED, "SO WE ARE RIGHT IN SAYING
THAT YOU ARE A SAMARITAN AND ARE POSSESSED BY
A DEMON." (49) JESUS SAID,

"I AM NOT POSSESSED, AND YOU TRY TO SHAME
ME WHEN I HONOR MY FATHER; (50) I DON'T
CARE ABOUT MY GLORY; THERE IS ONE WHO CARES
FOR ME AND HE WILL BE THE JUDGE.

(51) TRULY, I SAY TO YOU, IF ANYONE KEEPS MY
WORD, HE WILL NEVER EXPERIENCE DEATH."

(52) THE JEWS REPLIED, "NOW WE KNOW THAT YOU HAVE
A DEMON. ABRAHAM DIED AND THE PROPHETS AS WELL,
BUT YOU SAY: 'WHOEVER KEEPS MY WORD WILL NE-
VER EXPERIENCE DEATH.' WHO DO YOU CLAIM TO BE?
(53) DO YOU CLAIM TO BE GREATER THAN OUR FATHER

ABRAHAM, WHO DIED? AND THE PROPHETS ALSO DIED."
(54) THEN JESUS SAID,

"IF I WERE TO PRAISE MYSELF, IT WOULD COUNT FOR
NOTHING. THE FATHER GIVES GLORY TO ME, THE ONE
YOU CLAIM AS YOUR GOD, (55) ALTHOUGH YOU DO NOT
KNOW HIM. I KNOW HIM AND IF I WERE TO SAY THAT I
DON'T KNOW HIM, I WOULD BE A LIAR LIKE YOU.
BUT I KNOW HIM AND I KEEP HIS WORD. (56) AS
FOR ABRAHAM, YOUR ANCESTOR, HE LOOKED FOR-
WARD TO THE DAY WHEN I WOULD COME; AND HE
REJOICED WHEN HE SAW IT."

(57) THE JEWS THEN SAID TO HIM, "YOU ARE NOT YET FIFTY
YEARS OLD AND YOU HAVE SEEN ABRAHAM?" JESUS SAID,

(58) "TRULY, I SAY TO YOU, BEFORE ABRAHAM
WAS, I AM."

(59) THEY THEN PICKED UP STONES TO THROW AT HIM, BUT
JESUS HID HIMSELF AND LEFT THE TEMPLE.

JESUS HEALS THE MAN BORN BLIND

9 (1) AS JESUS WALKED ALONG, HE SAW A MAN
WHO HAD BEEN BLIND FROM BIRTH. (2) HIS
DISCIPLES ASKED HIM, "MASTER", "IF HE WAS
BORN BLIND BECAUSE OF SIN, WAS IT HIS SIN OR HIS
PARENTS?" (3) JESUS ANSWERED, "NEITHER THIS
MAN NOR HIS PARENTS SINNED; HE WAS BORN BLIND
SO THAT GOD'S POWER MIGHT BE SHOWN IN HIM. (4)

WHILE IT IS DAY WE MUST DO THE WORK
OF THE ONE WHO SENT ME, FOR THE NIGHT
WILL COME WHEN NO ONE CAN WORK.
(5) AS LONG AS I AM IN THE WORLD, I
AM THE LIGHT OF THE WORLD."

(6) AS JESUS SAID THIS, HE MADE PASTE WITH
SPITTLE AND CLAY AND RUBBED IT ON THE
EYES OF THE BLIND MAN.

(7) THEN HE SAID, "GO AND WASH IN THE POOL OF SI-
LOAM." (THIS NAME MEANS: SENT). SO HE WENT AND
AND WASHED AND CAME BACK ABLE TO SEE. (8) HIS
NEIGHBORS AND ALL THE PEOPLE WHO USED TO SEE
HIM BEGGING, WONDERED. THEY SAID, "ISN'T THIS THE
BEGGAR WHO USED TO SIT HERE?" (9) SOME SAID,
"IT'S THE ONE." OTHERS SAID, "NO, BUT HE LOOKS LIKE HIM."
BUT THE MAN SAID, "I AM THE ONE." (10) THEN THEY ASKED,
"HOW IS THAT YOUR EYES WERE OPENED?" (11) HE ANSWERED,
"THE MAN CALLED JESUS MADE A MUD PASTE, PUT

IT ON MY EYES AND
SAID TO ME: 'GO TO
SILOAM AND WASH.' SO
I WENT, AND WASHED AND
I COULD SEE." (12) THEY
ASKED, "WHERE IS HE?"
AND THE MAN ANSWERED,
"I DON'T KNOW." THE
(13) PEOPLE BROUGHT
THE MAN WHO HAD BE-
EN BLIND TO THE PHA-
RISEES. (14) NOW IT
WAS A SABBATH DAY
WHEN JESUS MADE
MUD PASTE AND
OPENED MY EYES. (15)
THE PHARISEES ASKED
HIM AGAIN, "HOW DID
YOU RECOVER YOUR
SIGHT?" AND HE SAID
ONCE MORE, "HE PUT
PASTE ON MY EYES AND
I WASHED, AND NOW I SEE."
(16) SOME OF THE PHARI-
SEES SAID, "THIS MAN IS
NOT FROM GOD, FOR HE
WORKS ON THE SABBATH";
BUT OTHERS WONDERED,
"HOW CAN A SINNER PERFORM SUCH MIRACULOUS SIGNS?"
THEY WERE DIVIDED (17) AND THEY QUESTIONED THE
BLIND MAN AGAIN, "WHAT DO YOU THINK OF THIS MAN
WHO OPENED YOUR EYES?" HE ANSWERED, "HE IS A
PROPHET."
(18) AFTER ALL THIS, THE JEWS BELIEVED NOTHING THAT THE
MAN HAD BEEN BLIND AND HAD RECOVERED HIS SIGHT; SO
THEY CALLED HIS PARENTS (19) AND ASKED THEM, "IS THIS
YOUR SON? YOU SAY THAT HE WAS BORN BLIND, HOW IS IT
THAT HE KNOW SEES?" (20) THE PARENTS ANSWERED, "HE
REALLY IS OUR SON AND HE WAS BORN BLIND; (21) BUT HOW
IT IS THAT HE NOW SEES, WE DON'T KNOW, NEITHER DO WE
KNOW WHO OPENED HIS EYES. ASK HIM, HE IS OLD ENOUGH.
LET HIM SPEAK FOR HIMSELF." (22) THE PARENTS SAID THIS

BECAUSE THEY FEARED THE JEWS WHO HAD ALREADY
AGREED THAT WHOEVER CONFESSED JESUS TO BE THE CHRIST
WAS TO BE PUT OUT OF THE JEWISH COMMUNITY. (23) BECAUSE
OF THIS HIS PARENTS SAID, "HE IS OLD ENOUGH, ASK HIM."
(24) SO A SECOND TIME THE PHARISEES CALLED THE MAN
WHO HAD BEEN BLIND, AND THEY SAID TO HIM, "TELL US THE
TRUTH; WE KNOW THAT THIS MAN IS A SINNER." (25) HE RE-
PLIED, "I DON'T KNOW WHETHER HE IS A SINNER OR NOT;
I ONLY KNOW THAT I WAS BLIND AND NOW I SEE." THEY
(26) SAID TO HIM, "WHAT DID HE DO TO YOU? HOW DID HE
OPEN YOUR EYES?" (27) HE REPLIED, "I HAVE TOLD YOU
ALREADY AND YOU WOULD NOT LISTEN. WHY DO YOU
WANT TO HEAR IT AGAIN? DO YOU ALSO WANT TO BE-
COME HIS DISCIPLES?" (28) THEN THEY STARTED TO
INSULT HIM. "BECOME HIS DISCIPLE YOURSELF! WE
ARE DISCIPLES OF MOSES.

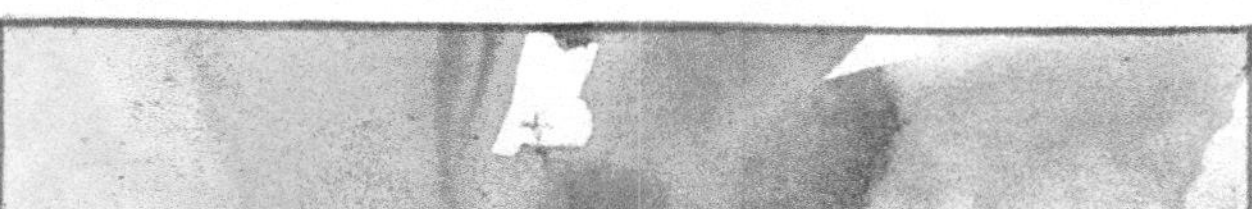

(29) WE KNOW THAT GOD HAS SPOKEN TO MOSES, BUT
AS FOR THIS MAN WE DON'T KNOW WHERE HE COMES
FROM." (30) THE MAN REPLIED, "IT IS AMAZING THAT YOU
DON'T KNOW WHERE THE MAN COMES FROM, AND YET HE
OPENED MY EYES! (31) WE KNOW THAT GOD DOESN'T LISTEN
TO SINNERS, BUT IF ANYONE HONORS GOD AND DOES HIS
WILL, GOD LISTENS TO HIM. (32) NEVER, SINCE THE WORLD
BEGAN, HAS IT BEEN HEARD THAT ANYONE OPENED THE
EYES OF A PERSON WHO WAS BORN BLIND. (33) IF THIS
MAN WERE NOT FROM GOD, HE COULD DO NOTHING."
(34) THEY ANSWERED HIM, "YOU WERE BORN A SI-
NNER AND NOW YOU TEACH US!" AND THEY DROVE
HIM AWAY. (35) JESUS HEARD THAT THEY HAD DRI-
VEN HIM AWAY. HE FOUND HIM AND SAID, "DO YOU

BELIEVE IN THE SON OF MAN?" (36) HE ANSWERED, "WHO IS
HE, THAT I MAY BELIEVE IN HIM?" (37) JESUS SAID, "YOU
HAVE SEEN HIM AND HE IS SPEAKING TO YOU." (38) HE
SAID, "LORD, I BELIEVE"; AND HE WORSHIPED HIM.
(39) JESUS SAID, "I CAME INTO THIS WORLD TO CAR-
RY OUT A JUDGMENT: THOSE WHO DO NOT SEE
SHALL SEE, AND THOSE WHO SEE SHALL BECOME
BLIND." (40) SOME PHARISEES STOOD BY AND ASKED
HIM, "SO WE ARE BLIND?" (41) AND JESUS ANSWERED,

"IF YOU WERE BLIND, YOU WOULDN'T BE GUILTY. NOW THAT
YOU SAY: 'WE SEE'; THAT IS THE PROOF OF YOUR SIN."

THE GOOD SHEPHERD

10 (1) TRULY, I SAY TO YOU, HE WHO DOES NOT EN-
TER THE SHEEPFOLD BY THE GATE, BUT CLIMBS
IN SOME OTHER
WAY, IS A THIEF AND A
ROBBER. (2) BUT THE
SHEPHERD OF THE SHEEP EN-
TERS BY THE GATE. (3) THE
KEEPERS OPENS THE GATE
TO HIM AND THE SHEEP HE-
AR HIS VOICE: HE CALLS
EACH OF THEM BY NAME
AND LEADS THEM OUT. (4)
WHEN HE HAS BROUGHT OUT
ALL HIS OWN, HE GOES BE-
FORE THEM AND THE SHEEP
FOLLOW HIM FOR THEY
KNOW HIS VOICE. (5)
A STRANGER THEY WILL
NOT FOLLOW, RATHER
THEY WILL RUN AWAY
FROM HIM BECAUSE
THEY DON'T RECOGNIZE
A STRANGER'S VOICE."
(6) JESUS USED THIS
COMPARISON, BUT THEY
DID NOT UNDERSTAND
WHAT HE WAS SAYING
TO THEM. (7) JESUS

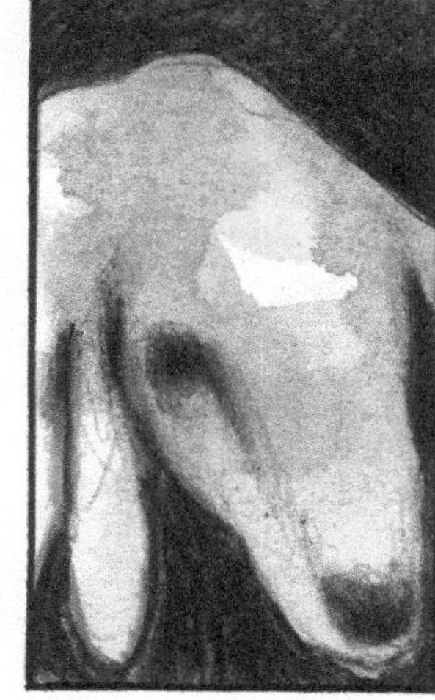

SAID, "TRULY, I SAY TO YOU, I AM THE GATE OF THE
SHEEPFOLD. (8) ALL WHO CAME WERE THIEVES
AND ROBBERS, AND THE SHEEP DID NOT HEAR
THEM. (9) I AM THE GATE. WHOEVER ENTERS BE-
CAUSE AND THROUGH ME WILL BE SAVED: HE WILL GO
IN AND OUT FREELY AND FIND FOOD.

10 THE THIEF COMES TO STEAL AND KILL
AND DESTROY, BUT I HAVE COME THAT THEY
MAY HAVE LIFE, LIFE IN ALL ITS FULLNESS.

11 I AM THE GOOD SHEPHERD. THE GOOD SHE-
PHERD GIVES HIS LIFE FOR THE SHEEP. 12 NOT SO
THE HIRED MAN OR ANY OTHER PERSON WHO
IS NOT THE SHEPHERD AND TO WHOM THE SHE-
EP DO NOT BELONG. HE ABANDONS THE SHE-
EP AS SOON AS HE SEES THE WOLF COMING;
THEN THE WOLF SNATCHES AND SCATTERS THE SHEEP.
13 HE IS ONLY A HIRED MAN AND HE CARES
NOTHING FOR THE SHEEP. 14 I AM THE GOOD

SHEPHERD. I KNOW MY OWN AND MY OWN KNOW
ME, 15 AS THE FATHER KNOWS ME AND I
KNOW THE FATHER. BECAUSE OF THIS I GIVE MY
LIFE FOR MY SHEEP. 16 I HAVE OTHER SHEEP THAT
ARE NOT OF THIS FOLD. THESE I HAVE TO LEAD AS
WELL, AND THEY SHALL LISTEN TO MY VOICE. THEN
THERE WILL BE ONE FLOCK SINCE THERE IS ONE
SHEPHERD. 17
THE FATHER LOVES ME BECAUSE I LAY DOWN
MY LIFE IN ORDER TO TAKE IT UP AGAIN. 18 NO
ONE TAKES IT FROM ME, BUT I LAY IT DOWN
FREELY. IT IS MINE TO LAY DOWN AND TO TAKE
UP AGAIN: THIS MISSION I RECEIVED FROM MY FATHER.
19 BECAUSE OF THESE WORDS, THE JEWS WERE

DIVIDED AGAIN. 20 MANY SAID, "HE HAS A DEMON AND HE IS
OUT OF HIS MIND. WHY LISTEN TO HIM?" 21 BUT OTHERS SAID,
"ONE POSSESSED DOESN'T SPEAK IN THIS WAY. CAN A
DEMON OPEN THE EYES OF THE BLIND?"

JESUS CLAIMS TO BE THE SON OF GOD

22 THE TIME CAME FOR THE FEAST OF THE DEDI-
CATION 23 AND JESUS WALKED BACK AND FORTH IN
THE PORTICO OF SOLOMON. 24 THE JEWS THEN GATHE-
RED AROUND HIM AND SAID TO HIM, "HOW LONG WILL YOU
KEEP US IN DOUBT? IF YOU ARE THE MESSIAH, TELL US
PLAINLY." 25 JESUS ANSWERED, "I HAVE ALREADY
TOLD YOU BUT YOU DO NOT BELIEVE.

26 THE WORKS I DO IN MY FATHER'S NAME
PROCLAIM WHO I AM. BUT YOU DON'T BELIEVE
BECAUSE, AS I SAID, YOU ARE NOT MY SHEEP.

27 MY SHEEP HEAR MY VOICE AND I KNOW THEM; THEY
FOLLOW ME 28 AND I GIVE THEM ETERNAL LIFE.
THEY SHALL NEVER PERISH AND NO ONE WILL EVER
STEAL THEM FROM ME. 29 WHAT THE FATHER
HAS GIVEN ME IS STRONGER THAN EVERYTHING AND
NO ONE CAN SNATCH IT FROM THE FATHER'S HAND.
30 "THE FATHER AND I ARE ONE"

31 THE JEWS THEN PICKED UP STONES TO THROW
AT HIM; 32 SO JESUS SAID, "I HAVE OPENLY DONE MANY
GOOD WORKS AMONG YOU WHICH THE FATHER GAVE ME
TO DO. FOR WHICH OF THESE DO YOU STONE ME?" 33
THE JEWS ANSWERED, "WE ARE NOT STONING YOU FOR
DOING A GOOD WORK BUT FOR INSULTING GOD; YOU
ARE ONLY A MAN AND YOU MAKE YOURSELF GOD."
34 THEN JESUS REPLIED, "IS THIS NOT WRITTEN IN
YOUR LAW: I SAID: YOU ARE GODS? 35 SO THOSE
WHO RECEIVED THIS WORD OF GOD WERE CALLED
GODS AND THE SCRIPTURE IS ALWAYS TRUE.
36 THEN WHAT SHOULD BE SAID OF THE ONE
ANOINTED AND SENT INTO THE WORLD BY MY
FATHER? AM I INSULTING GOD WHEN I SAY, "I AM
THE SON OF GOD"?

37 IF I AM NOT DOING THE WORKS OF MY FATHER,
DO NOT BELIEVE ME.
38 BUT IF I DO THEM, EVEN IF YOU HAVE NO
FAITH IN ME, BELIEVE ME BECAUSE OF THE

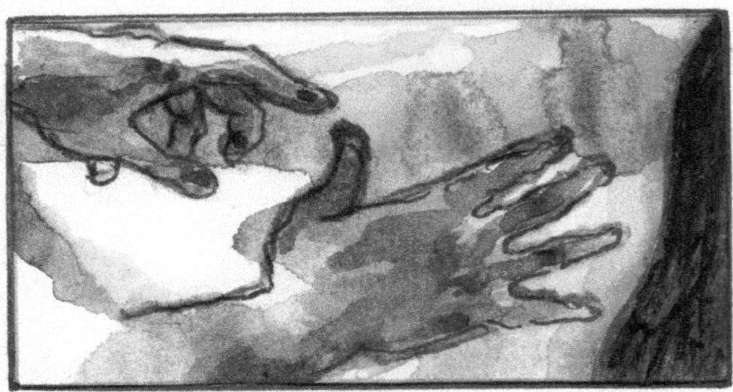

WORKS I DO, AND KNOW THAT THE FATHER IS
IN ME AND I IN THE FATHER."

39 AGAIN THEY TRIED TO ARREST HIM, BUT
JESUS ESCAPED FROM THEIR HANDS. 40 HE WENT
AWAY AGAIN TO THE OTHER SIDE OF THE JORDAN, TO
THE PLACE WHERE JOHN HAD BAPTIZED, AND THERE
HE STAYED.
41 MANY PEOPLE CAME TO HIM AND SAID, "JOHN SHOW-
ED NO MIRACULOUS SIGNS, BUT HE SPOKE OF THIS
MAN AND EVERYTHING HE SAID WAS TRUE." 42
AND MANY BECAME BELIEVERS IN THAT PLACE.

HOMAGE TO
PICASSO
"I AND THE FATHER
ARE ONE" (JOHN 10:30)
CCCLI
351
DM
07
©

THE RAISING OF LAZARUS

11 (1) THERE WAS A SICK MAN NAMED LAZARUS FROM BETHANY,
THE VILLAGE OF MARY AND HER SISTER MARTHA. (2) THE SAME
MARY WHO ANOINTED THE LORD WITH PERFUME AND WIP-
ED HIS FEET WITH HER HAIR. (3) SO THE SISTERS SENT THIS MES-
SAGE TO JESUS, "LORD, THE ONE YOU LOVE IS SICK." (4) ON HEARING
THIS JESUS SAID, "THIS ILLNESS WILL NOT END IN DEATH: RATHER

IT IS FOR GOD'S GLORY AND
THE SON OF GOD WILL BE GLO-
RIFIED THROUGH IT." (5) IT
IS A FACT THAT JESUS LOVED
MARTHA AND HER SISTER
AND LAZARUS; (6) YET, AF-
TER HE HEARD OF THE IL-
LNESS OF LAZARUS, HE
STAYED TWO MORE DAYS IN
THE PLACE WHERE HE WAS.
(7) ONLY THEN DID HE SAY
TO HIS DISCIPLES, "LET
US GO TO JUDEA AGAIN."
(8) THEY REPLIED, "MAS-
TER, RECENTLY THE JEWS
WANTED TO STONE YOU.
ARE YOU GOING THERE
AGAIN?"
(9) JESUS SAID TO THEM,
"ARE NOT TWELVE WORK-
ING HOURS NEEDED TO
COMPLETE A DAY? WHO-
EVER WALKS IN THE
DAYTIME SHALL NOT
STUMBLE, FOR HE SEES
WITH THE LIGHT OF THE
WORLD. (10) BUT IF ANY-
ONE WALKS BY NIGHT,
HE WILL STUMBLE FOR THERE IS NO LIGHT IN
HIM." (11) AFTER THAT JESUS SAID TO THEM, "OUR
FRIEND LAZARUS HAS FALLEN ASLEEP, BUT I AM
GOING TO WAKE HIM." (12) THE DISCIPLES REPLIED,
"LORD, A SICK MAN WHO SLEEPS WILL RECOVER."
(13) BUT JESUS HAD REFERRED TO LAZARUS'
DEATH, WHILE THEY THOUGHT THAT HE HAD MEANT
THE REPOSE OF SLEEP. (14) SO JESUS SAID PLAINLY,
"LAZARUS IS DEAD (15) AND FOR YOUR SAKE I AM
GLAD I WAS NOT THERE, FOR NOW YOU MAY BELIEVE.
BUT LET US GO THERE, WHERE HE IS." (16) THEN
THOMAS, CALLED THE TWIN, SAID TO HIS FELLOW
DISCIPLES, "LET US GO ALSO THAT WE MAY DIE
WITH HIM."
(17) WHEN JESUS CAME, HE FOUND THAT LAZARUS

HAD BEEN IN THE TOMB FOR FOUR DAYS. (18) AS BETHANY IS NE-
AR JERUSALEM, ABOUT TWO MILES AWAY, (19) MANY JEWS HAD CO-
ME TO MARTHA AND MARY TO OFFER CONSOLATION AT THEIR BRO-
THER'S DEATH. (20) WHEN MARTHA HEARD THAT JESUS WAS
COMING, SHE WENT TO MEET HIM WHILE MARY REMAINED
SITTING IN THE HOUSE. (21) AND SHE SAID TO JESUS, "IF
YOU HAD BEEN HERE, MY BROTHER WOULD NOT HAVE DIED.
(22) BUT I KNOW THAT WHATEVER YOU ASK FROM GOD,
GOD WILL GIVE YOU." (23) JESUS SAID, "YOUR BRO-
THER WILL RISE AGAIN." (24) MARTHA REPLIED,
"I KNOW THAT HE WILL RISE IN THE RESURREC-
TION, AT THE LAST DAY."

(25) BUT JESUS SAID TO HER, "I AM THE RESUR-
RECTION; WHOEVER BELIEVES IN ME, THOUGH HE
DIE, SHALL LIVE. (26) WHOEVER IS ALIVE BY BELIE-
VING IN ME WILL NEVER DIE. DO YOU BELIEVE THIS?"
(27) MARTHA ANSWERED, "YES, LORD, I HAVE COME TO
BELIEVE THAT YOU ARE THE CHRIST, THE SON OF GOD,
HE WHO IS COMING INTO THE WORLD."
(28) AFTER THAT MARTHA WENT AND CALLED HER SIS-
TER MARY SECRETLY, SAYING, "THE MASTER IS HERE
AND HE IS CALLING FOR YOU." (29) AS SOON AS MARY
HEARD THIS, SHE ROSE AND WENT TO HIM. (30)

JESUS HAD NOT YET COME INTO THE VILLAGE, BUT WAS STILL
IN THE PLACE WHERE MARTHA HAD MET HIM. THE JEWS
(31) WHO WERE WITH HER IN THE HOUSE CONSOLING HER,
ALSO CAME. WHEN THEY SAW HER GET UP AND GO OUT,
THEY FOLLOWED HER, THINKING THAT SHE WAS GOING
TO THE TOMB TO WEEP.
(32) AS FOR MARY, WHEN SHE CAME TO THE PLACE WHERE
JESUS WAS AND SAW HIM, SHE FELL AT HIS FEET AND SAID,
"LORD, IF YOU HAD BEEN HERE, MY BROTHER WOULD NOT HA-
VE DIED." (33) WHEN JESUS SAW HER WEEPING AND THE
JEWS ALSO WHO HAD COME WITH HER, HE WAS MOVED IN
THE DEPTHS OF HIS SPIRIT AND TROUBLED. (34) THEN HE
ASKED, "WHERE HAVE YOU LAID HIM?" THEY ANSWERED, "LORD,
COME AND SEE." (35) JESUS
WEPT. (36) THE JEWS SAID,
"SEE HOW THEY LOVED
HIM!" (37) BUT OTHERS
SAID, "IF HE COULD OPEN
THE EYES OF THE BLIND
MAN, COULD HE NOT HAVE
KEPT THIS MAN FROM DY-
ING?" (38) JESUS WAS
DEEPLY MOVED AGAIN AND
DREW NEAR TO THE TOMB.
IT WAS A CAVE WITH A
STONE LAID ACROSS IT.
(39) JESUS ORDERED, "TA-
KE THE STONE AWAY."
MARTHA SAID TO HIM, "LORD,
BY NOW HE WILL SMELL,
FOR THIS IS THE FOURTH
DAY." (40) JESUS REPLIED,
"HAVE I NOT TOLD YOU
THAT IF YOU BELIEVE
YOU WILL SEE THE GLO-
RY OF GOD?" SO THEY
(41) REMOVED THE STONE.
JESUS LIFTED UP HIS
EYES AND SAID, "FATHER,
I THANK YOU FOR YOU
HAVE HEARD ME. (42) I

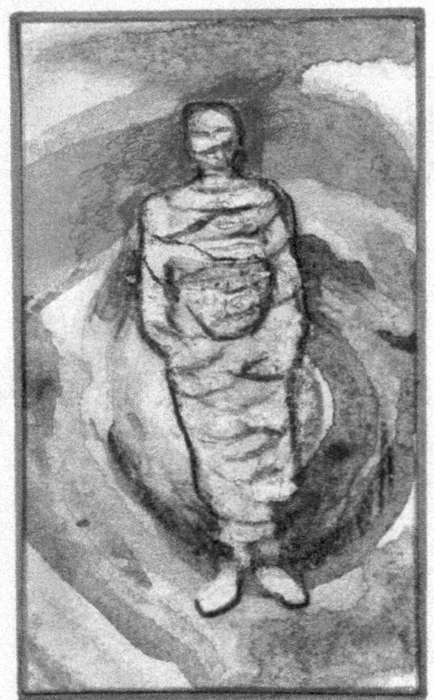

KNEW THAT YOU HEAR ME ALWAYS; BUT MY PRAYER
WAS THE SAKE OF THESE PEOPLE, THAT THEY MAY
BELIEVE THAT YOU SENT ME."
(43) WHEN JESUS HAD SAID THIS, HE CRIED OUT IN
A LOUD VOICE,

"LAZARUS, COME OUT!

(44) THE DEAD MAN CAME OUT, HIS HANDS AND
FEET BOUND WITH LINEN STRIPS AND HIS FACE
WRAPPED IN A CLOTH. SO JESUS SAID TO THEM,
"UNTIE HIM AND LET HIM GO."

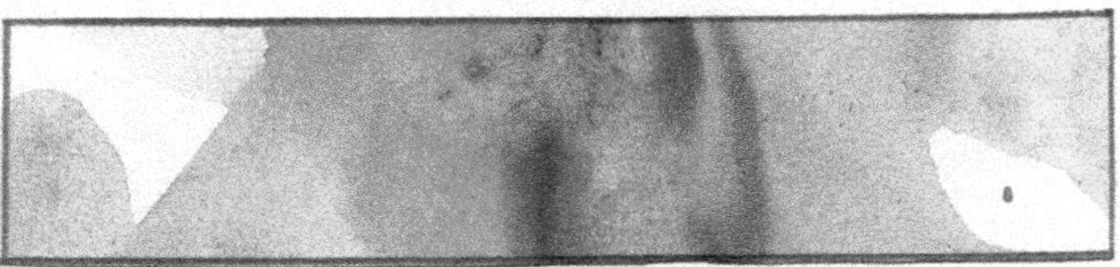

THE PLOT TO KILL JESUS

(45) MANY OF THE JEWS WHO HAD COME WITH MARY
BELIEVED IN JESUS WHEN THEY SAW WHAT HE DID; (46)
BUT SOME WENT TO THE PHARISEES AND TOLD THEM
WHAT JESUS HAD DONE. (47) SO THE CHIEF PRIESTS AND
THE PHARISEES CALLED THE SANHEDRIN COUNCIL.
THEY SAID, "WHAT ARE WE TO DO? FOR THIS MAN KEEPS ON
GIVING MIRACULOUS SIGNS. (48) IF WE LET HIM GO ON
LIKE THIS, ALL THE PEOPLE WILL BELIEVE IN HIM AND
AS A RESULT OF THIS, THE ROMANS WILL COME

AND SWEEP AWAY OUR
HOLY PLACE AND OUR
NATION." (49) THEN ONE
OF THEM, CAIAPHAS, WHO
WAS THE HIGH PRIEST
THAT YEAR, SPOKE UP,
"YOU KNOW NOTHING AT
ALL NOR DO YOU SEE THE
SITUATION. (50) IT IS BET-
TER TO HAVE ONE MAN
DIE FOR THE PEOPLE THAN
TO LET THE WHOLE NATION
BE DESTROYED." (51) IN SAY-
ING THIS CAIAPHAS DID NOT
SPEAK FOR HIMSELF, BUT
BEING HIGH PRIEST, HE
FORETOLD AS A PROPHET
THAT JESUS WOULD DIE
FOR THE NATION (52) AND
NOT FOR THE NATION ONLY,
BUT ALSO TO UNITE THE
SCATTERED CHILDREN OF
GOD. (53) SO, FROM THAT
DAY ON, THEY WERE DE-
TERMINED TO KILL HIM.
(54) BECAUSE OF THIS, JESUS
NO LONGER MOVED ABOUT FREELY AMONG THE JEWS. HE
WITHDREW INSTEAD TO THE COUNTRY NEAR THE WILD-
ERNESS AND STAYED WITH HIS DISCIPLES IN A TOWN
CALLED EPHRAIM. (55) THE JEWISH PASSOVER WAS AT
HAND AND PEOPLE FROM EVERYWHERE WERE COMING TO JERU-
SALEM TO PURIFY THEMSELVES BEFORE THE PASSOVER. (56)
THEY LOOKED FOR JESUS AND AS THEY STOOD IN THE TEM-
PLE, THEY TALKED WITH ONE ANOTHER, "WHAT DO YOU
THINK? WILL HE COME TO THE FESTIVAL?" (57)

MEANWHILE THE CHIEF PRIESTS AND THE ELDERS HAD ORDER-
ED THAT ANYONE WHO KNEW WHERE HE WAS SHOULD LET
THEM KNOW SO THAT THEY COULD ARREST HIM.

THE SUPPER AT BETHANY

12 (1) SIX DAYS BEFORE THE PASSOVER, JESUS CAME TO
BETHANY WHERE HE HAD RAISED LAZARUS, FROM
DEATH TO LIFE. (2) THEY GAVE A DINNER FOR HIM, AND
WHILE MARTHA WAITED ON THEM, LAZARUS SAT AT THE TABLE
WITH JESUS. (3) MARY TOOK A POUND OF COSTLY PERFUME
MADE FROM GENUINE NARD AND ANOINTED THE FEET OF JESUS,
WIPING THEM WITH HER HAIR. THE WHOLE HOUSE WAS FIL-
LED WITH THE FRAGRANCE OF THE PERFUME. (4) JUDAS,
SON OF SIMON ISCARIOT, THE DISCIPLE WHO WAS TO BE-
TRAY JESUS, REMARKED, (5) "THIS PERFUME COULD
HAVE BEEN SOLD FOR THREE HUNDRED SILVER COINS
AND THE MONEY TURNED OVER TO THE POOR."

(6) JUDAS, INDEED, HAD NO CONCERN FOR THE POOR; HE
WAS A THIEF AND AS HE HELD THE COMMON PURSE, HE
USED TO HELP HIMSELF TO THE FUNDS. (7) BUT JESUS
SPOKE UP, "LEAVE HER ALONE. WAS SHE NOT KEEPING IT
FOR THE DAY OF MY BURIAL? (8) THE POOR YOU AL-
WAYS HAVE WITH YOU, BUT YOU WILL NOT ALWAYS
HAVE ME."
(9) MANY JEWS HEARD THAT JESUS WAS THERE AND THEY
CAME, NOT ONLY BECAUSE OF JESUS, BUT ALSO TO SEE LAZARUS
WHOM HE HAD RAISED FROM THE DEAD. (10) SO THE CHIEF PRI-
ESTS THOUGHT ABOUT KILLING LAZARUS AS WELL, (11)
FOR MANY OF THE JEWS WERE DRIFTING AWAY
BECAUSE OF HIM AND BELIEVING IN JESUS.

THE MESSIAH ENTERS JERUSALEM

(12) THE NEXT DAY MANY PEOPLE WHO HAD COME FOR THE
FESTIVAL HEARD THAT JESUS WAS TO ENTER JERUSALEM.

(13) SO THEY TOOK BRANCHES OF PALM TREES AND WENT
OUT TO MEET HIM. AND THEY CRIED OUT,

"HOSANNA! BLESSED IS HE WHO COMES IN THE NAME OF THE
LORD! BLESSED IS THE KING OF ISRAEL!"

(14) JESUS FIND A DONKEY, SAT UPON IT, AS SCRIPTURE SAYS:

(15) DO NOT FEAR, CITY OF ZION, SEE YOUR KING IS COMING
SITTING ON THE COLT OF A DONKEY.

(16) THE DISCIPLES WERE NOT AWARE OF THIS AT FIRST,
BUT AFTER JESUS WAS
GLORIFIED, THEY REMEMB-
ERED THAT THIS HAD BEEN
WRITTEN OF HIM AND THAT
THEY HAD TAKEN PART OF
IT. (17) THE PEOPLE WHO CA-
ME WITH HIM BORE WITNESS
AND TOLD HOW HE HAD CAL-
LED LAZARUS OUT OF THE
TOMB AND RAISED HIM
FROM THE DEAD. (18) IT WAS
FOR THIS MIRACULOUS SIGN
GIVEN BY JESUS THAT SO MA-
NY PEOPLE WELCOMED HIM.
(19) IN THE MEANTIME
THE PHARISEES SAID TO
ONE ANOTHER, "WE ARE
GETTING NOWHERE;
THE WHOLE WORLD
HAS GONE AFTER
HIM."

UNLESS THE GRAIN DIES

(20) THERE WERE SOME GREEKS WHO HAD COME UP TO JE-
RUSALEM TO WORSHIP DURING THE FEAST. (21) THEY APPRO-
CHED PHILIP, WHO WAS FROM BETHSAIDA IN GALILEE, AND
ASKED HIM, "SIR, WE WISH TO SEE JESUS." (22) PHILIP WENT
TO ANDREW AND THE TWO OF THEM TOLD JESUS.

THEN JESUS SAID (23),

"THE HOUR HAS COME FOR THE SON OF MAN TO BE
GLORIFIED. (24) TRULY, I SAY TO YOU UNLESS THE
GRAIN OF WHEAT FALLS TO THE EARTH AND DIES, IT RE-
MAINS ALONE; BUT IF IT DIES, IT PRODUCES MUCH
FRUIT. (25) WHOEVER LOVES HIS LIFE DESTROYS IT,
AND WHOEVER DESPISES HIS LIFE IN THIS WORLD
KEEPS IT FOR EVERLASTING LIFE. (26) WHOEVER
WANTS TO SERVE ME, LET HIM FOLLOW ME AND
WHEREVER I AM, THERE SHALL MY SERVANT BE ALSO. IF
ANYONE SERVES ME, THE FATHER WILL HONOR HIM.

(27) NOW MY SOUL IS IN DISTRESS. SHALL I SAY:
'FATHER, SAVE ME FROM THIS HOUR'? BUT, I HAVE COME
TO THIS HOUR TO FACE ALL THIS. (28) FATHER, GLORIFY
YOUR NAME! THEN A VOICE CAME FROM HEAVEN, "I HAVE
GLORIFIED IT AND I WILL GLORIFY IT AGAIN."

(29) PEOPLE STANDING THERE HEARD SOMETHING AND
SAID IT WAS THUNDER; BUT OTHERS SAID, "AN ANGEL
WAS SPEAKING TO HIM." (30) THEN JESUS DECLARED,

"THIS VOICE DID NOT COME FOR MY SAKE BUT FOR YOURS;
(31) NOW SENTENCE HAS BEEN PASSED ON THIS WORLD;
NOW THE RULER OF THIS WORLD IS TO BE CAST DOWN.
(32) AND WHEN I AM LIFTED UP FROM THE EARTH, I
SHALL DRAW ALL TO MYSELF."

(33) WITH THESE WORDS JESUS REFERRED TO THE KIND
OF DEATH HE WAS TO DIE. (34) THE CROWD ANSWERED

HIM, "WE HAVE BEEN TOLD BY THE LAW THAT THE MESSIAH
STANDS FOREVER. HOW CAN YOU SAY THAT THE SON OF MAN
SHALL BE LIFTED UP? WHAT KIND OF SON OF MAN IS THIS?"

(35) JESUS SAID TO THEM, "THE LIGHT WILL BE WITH YOU
A LITTLE LONGER. WALK WHILE YOU HAVE THE LIGHT, LEST
THE DARKNESS OVERTAKE YOU. HE WHO WALKS IN THE DARK
DOESN'T KNOW WHERE HE GOES. (36) WHILE YOU HAVE THE
LIGHT, BELIEVE IN THE LIGHT AND BECOME SONS OF LIGHT."

AFTER JESUS HAD SAID THIS, HE WITHDREW
AND KEPT HIMSELF HIDDEN.

THE UNBELIEF OF THE JEWS

(37) EVEN THOUGH JESUS HAD DONE SO MANY MIRACULOUS
SIGNS AMONG THEM, THEY DIDN'T BELIEVE IN HIM. (38)
INDEED THE WORDS SPOKEN BY THE PROPHET ISAIAH
HAD TO BE FULFILLED:

LORD, WHO HAS BELIEVED WHAT WE PROCLAIMED? TO WHOM HAVE
GOD'S WAYS, THE SAVIOR, BEEN MADE KNOWN?

(39) THEY COULD NOT BELIEVE. ISAIAH HAD SAID ELSEWHERE:

(40) HE LET THEIR EYES BECOME BLIND AND THEIR HEARTS

HARD, SO THAT THEY COULD NEITHER SEE OR UNDERSTAND,
NOR BE CONVERTED, OTHERWISE I WOULD HAVE HEALED THEM.

(41) ISAIAH SAID THIS WHEN HE SAW HIS GLORY, AND HIS WORDS
REFER TO HIM. (42) MANY OF THEM, HOWEVER, BELIEVED IN
JESUS, EVEN AMONG THE RULERS, BUT THEY DID NOT ACKN-
OWLEDGED HIM BECAUSE OF THE PHARISEES, LEST THEY
BE PUT OUT OF THE JEWISH COMMUNITY. (43) THEY PREFER-
RED TO BE APPROVED BY PEOPLE RATHER THAN BY GOD. (44)
YET JESUS HAD SAID, AND EVEN CRIED OUT,

"HE WHO BELIEVES IN ME, BELIEVES NOT IN ME BUT IN HIM
WHO SENT ME. (45) AND HE WHO SEES ME, SEES HIM WHO
SENT ME. (46) I HAVE COME INTO THE WORLD AS LIGHT,
SO THAT WHOEVER BELIEVES IN ME MAY NOT REMAIN
IN DARKNESS. (47) IF ANYONE HEARS MY WORDS AND
DOES NOT KEEP THEM, I AM NOT THE ONE TO CON-
DEMN HIM; FOR I HAVE COME, NOT TO CONDEMN
THE WORLD, BUT TO SAVE THE WORLD. (48) HE WHO
REJECTS ME, AND DOES NOT RECEIVE MY WORD, AL-
READY HAS A JUDGE: THE VERY WORD I HAVE SPOKEN

WILL CONDEMN HIM ON THE LAST DAY. (49) FOR I HAVE
SPOKEN ON MY OWN AUTHORITY; THE FATHER WHO
SENT ME HAS INSTRUCTED ME IN WHAT TO SAY AND
HOW TO SPEAK. (50) I KNOW THAT HIS COMMANDMENT IS
ETERNAL LIFE, AND I GIVE MY MESSAGE AS
THE FATHER INSTRUCTED ME."

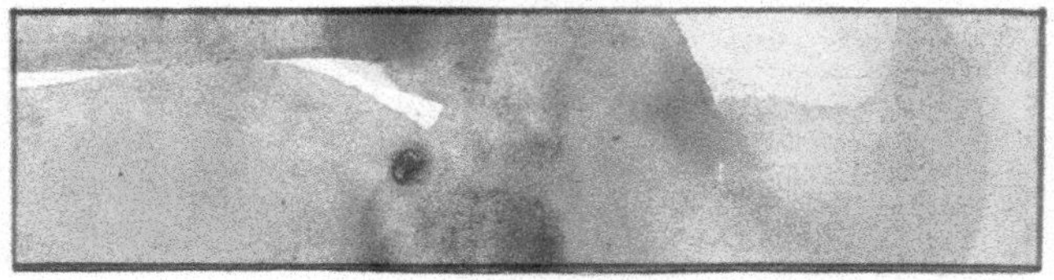

CCCLII
352
©
DM
09

SECOND PART
JESUS COMPLETES HIS WORK

13 (1) IT WAS BEFORE THE FEAST OF THE PASSOVER.
JESUS REALIZED THAT HIS HOUR HAD COME TO
PASS FROM THIS WORLD TO THE FATHER, AND AS
HE HAD LOVED THOSE WHO WERE HIS OWN IN THE WORLD,
HE WOULD LOVE THEM WITH PERFECT LOVE.

JESUS WASHES HIS DISCIPLES' FEET

(2) THEY WERE AT SUPPER; THE DEVIL HAD ALREADY PUT INTO
JUDAS' MIND, SON OF SIMON ISCARIOT, TO BETRAY HIM. (3)
BUT JESUS KNEW THAT THE FATHER HAD ENTRUSTED ALL
THINGS TO HIM, AS HE HAD COME FROM GOD, HE WAS GOING
TO GOD. (4) SO HE GOT UP

FROM TABLE, REMOVED HIS
GARMENT AND TAKING A
TOWEL, WRAPPED IT ARO-
UND HIS WAIST. (5) THEN
HE POURED WATER INTO A
BASIN AND BEGAN TO WASH
THE DISCIPLES' FEET AND
TO WIPE THEM WITH THE
TOWEL HE WAS WEARING.
(6) WHEN HE CAME TO SI-
MON PETER, SIMON SAID
TO HIM, "WHY, LORD, YOU
WANT TO WASH MY FEET!"
(7) JESUS SAID, "WHAT I
AM DOING YOU CANNOT UN-
DERSTAND NOW, BUT AF-
TERWARDS YOU WILL UNDER-
STAND IT." (8) PETER RE-
PLIED, "YOU SHALL NEVER
WASH MY FEET." JESUS
ANSWERED, "IF I DO NOT
WASH YOU, YOU CAN HAVE
NO PART WITH ME." (9)
THEN SIMON PETER SAID,
"LORD, WASH NOT ONLY MY
FEET, BUT ALSO MY HANDS
AND MY HEAD!" (10) JESUS
REPLIED, "WHOEVER HAS TAKEN A BATH DOES NOT NEED TO
WASH (EXCEPT THE FEET), FOR HE IS CLEAN ALL OVER. YOU
ARE CLEAN, THOUGH NOT ALL OF YOU." (11) JESUS KNEW WHO
WAS TO BETRAY HIM; BECAUSE OF THIS HE SAID, "NOT ALL
OF YOU ARE CLEAN." (12) WHEN JESUS HAD FINISHED
WASHING THEIR FEET, HE PUT ON HIS GARMENT AGAIN,
WENT BACK TO THE TABLE AND SAID TO THEM, "DO YOU
UNDERSTAND WHAT I HAVE DONE TO YOU? (13) YOU CALL
ME MASTER AND LORD, AND YOU ARE RIGHT, FOR SO I
AM. (14) IF I, THEN, YOUR LORD AND MASTER, HAVE WASH-
ED YOUR FEET, YOU ALSO MUST WASH ONE ANOTHER'S
FEET. (15) I HAVE JUST GIVEN YOU AN EXAMPLE THAT
AS I HAVE DONE, YOU ALSO MAY DO. (16) TRULY, I SAY TO

YOU, THE SERVANT IS NOT GREATER THAN HIS MASTER, NOR IS
THE MESSENGER GREATER THAN HE WHO SENT HIM. (17)
UNDERSTAND THIS, AND BLESSED ARE YOU IF YOU PUT IT INTO
PRACTICE. (18) I AM NOT SPEAKING OF YOU ALL, BECAUSE
I KNOW THE ONES I HAVE CHOSEN AND THE SCRIPTURE
HAS TO BE FULFILLED THAT SAYS, THE ONE WHO SHARED
MY TABLE HAS RISEN AGAINST ME. (19) I TELL YOU THIS
NOW BEFORE IT HAPPENS, SO THAT WHEN IT DOES HAPPEN,
YOU MAY KNOW THAT I AM HE. (20) TRULY, I SAY TO YOU, WHO-
EVER WELCOMES THE ONE I SEND, WELCOMES ME, AND WHOEVER
WELCOMES ME, WELCOMES THE ONE WHO SENT ME."

(21) AFTER SAYING THIS, JESUS WAS DISTRESSED IN
SPIRIT AND SAID PLAINLY, "TRULY, ONE OF YOU WILL
BETRAY ME." (22) THE DISCIPLES THEN LOOKED AT
ONE ANOTHER, WONDERING WHO HE MEANT. ONE OF
(23) THE DISCIPLES, THE ONE JESUS LOVED, WAS RE-
CLINING NEAR JESUS; (24) SIMON PETER SIGNALED
HIM TO ASK JESUS WHOM HE MEANT. (25) AND THE
DISCIPLE WHO WAS RECLINING NEAR JESUS ASKED
HIM, "LORD, WHO IS IT?" (26) JESUS ANSWERED,
"I SHALL DIP A PIECE OF BREAD IN THE DISH,
AND HE TO WHOM I GIVE IT, IS THE ONE." SO

JESUS DIPPED THE BREAD AND GAVE IT TO JUDAS ISCARI-
OT THE SON OF SIMON. (27) AND AS JUDAS TOOK THE
PIECE OF BREAD, SATAN ENTERED IN HIM. JESUS SAID
TO HIM, "WHAT ARE YOU GOING TO DO, DO QUICKLY."
(28) NONE OF THE OTHERS RECLINING AT TABLE UNDER-
STOOD WHY JESUS SAID THIS TO JUDAS. (29) AS HE HAD
THE COMMON PURSE, THEY THOUGHT THAT JESUS WAS
TELLING HIM, "BUY WHAT WE NEED FOR THE FEAST," OR,
"GIVE SOMETHING TO THE POOR." (30) JUDAS LEFT
AS SOON AS HE HAD EATEN THE BREAD. IT WAS NIGHT.
(31) WHEN JUDAS HAD GONE OUT, JESUS SAID, "NOW
IS THE SON OF MAN GLORIFIED AND GOD IS GLORIFI-
ED IN HIM. (32) GOD WILL GLORIFY HIM VERY SOON."

(33) MY CHILDREN, I AM WITH YOU FOR ONLY A LITTLE WHILE;
YOU WILL LOOK FOR ME, BUT, AS I ALREADY TOLD THE
JEWS, SO NOW I TELL YOU: WHERE I AM GOING YOU CAN-
NOT COME. (34)...

> "NOW I GIVE YOU A NEW
> COMMANDMENT: LOVE ONE
> ANOTHER. JUST AS I HAVE
> LOVED YOU, YOU ALSO MUST
> LOVE ONE ANOTHER. (35) BY THIS
> EVERYONE WILL KNOW THAT
> YOU ARE MY DISCIPLES, IF YOU
> HAVE LOVE FOR ONE ANOTHER"

(36) SIMON PETER SAID TO HIM, "LORD, WHERE
ARE YOU GOING?" JESUS ANSWERED, "WHERE I
AM GOING YOU CANNOT FOLLOW ME NOW, BUT
AFTERWARDS YOU WILL."
(37) PETER SAID, "LORD, WHY CAN'T I FOLLOW YOU
NOW? I AM READY TO GIVE MY LIFE FOR YOU."
(38) JESUS ANSWERED, "TO GIVE YOUR LIFE FOR ME!
**TRULY, I TELL YOU, THE COCK WILL
NOT CROW BEFORE YOU HAVE
DENIED ME THREE TIMES."**

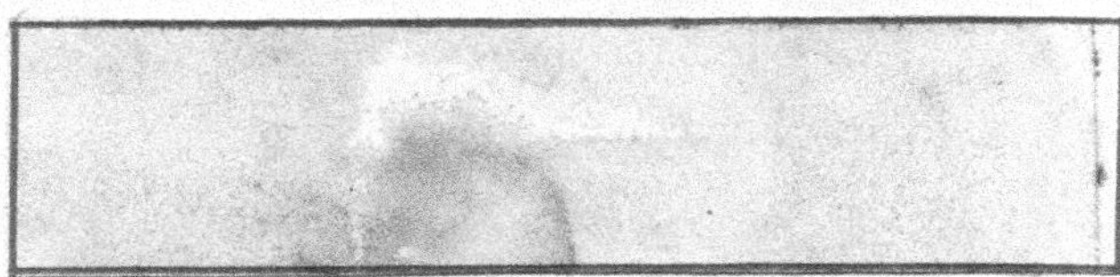

JOHN -14-15-

I AM GOING TO THE FATHER

14 1 DO NOT BE TROUBLED; TRUST IN GOD
AND TRUST IN ME. 2 IN MY FATHER'S HOUSE
THERE ARE MANY ROOMS. OTHERWISE I WOULD
NOT HAVE TOLD YOU THAT I GO TO PREPARE A PLACE
FOR YOU 3 AFTER I HAVE GONE AND PREPARED
A PLACE FOR YOU, I SHALL COME AGAIN AND TAKE
YOU TO ME, SO THAT WHERE I AM, YOU ALSO MAY
BE. 4 YOU KNOW THE WAY TO WHERE I AM GOING."

5 THOMAS SAID TO HIM, "LORD, WE DON'T KNOW
WHERE YOU ARE GOING; HOW CAN WE KNOW THE

THE WAY?" 6 JESUS SAID, "I AM THE WAY, THE TRUTH
AND THE LIFE; NO ONE COMES TO THE FATHER BUT
THROUGH ME. 7 IF YOU KNOW ME, YOU WILL KNOW
THE FATHER ALSO; INDEED YOU KNOW HIM AND YOU
HAVE SEEN HIM."
8 PHILIP ASKED HIM, "LORD, SHOW US THE FATHER
AND THAT IS ENOUGH. 9 JESUS SAID TO HIM.

"WHAT! I HAVE BEEN WITH YOU SO LONG AND YOU STILL DO
NOT KNOW ME, PHILIP? WHOEVER SEES ME SEES THE FA-
THER; HOW CAN YOU SAY: 'SHOW US THE FATHER'? 10 DO
YOU NOT BELIEVE, THAT I AM THE FATHER AND THE
FATHER IS IN ME? ALL THAT I SAY TO YOU, I DO NOT
SAY OF MYSELF. THE FATHER WHO DWELLS IN ME IS
DOING HIS WORK. 11 BELIEVE ME WHEN I SAY THAT I
AM IN THE FATHER AND THE FATHER IS IN ME; AT LEAST
BELIEVE IT ON THE EVIDENCE OF THESE WORKS THAT I DO.
12 TRULY, I SAY TO YOU, HE WHO BELIEVES IN ME WILL
DO THE SAME WORKS THAT I DO; HE WILL DO EVEN GRE-
ATER THAN THESE, FOR I AM GOING WHERE THE FATHER IS.

13 EVERYTHING YOU ASK IN MY NAME, I WILL DO, SO THAT
THE FATHER MAY BE GLORIFIED IN THE SON. 14 AND EVERY-
THING YOU ASK IN CALLING UPON MY NAME, I WILL DO. 15
IF YOU LOVE ME, YOU WILL KEEP MY COMMANDMENTS;
16 AND I WILL ASK THE FATHER AND HE WILL GIVE YOU AN-
OTHER HELPER TO BE WITH YOU FOREVER 17 THAT SPIRIT
OF TRUTH WHOM THE WORLD CANNOT RECEIVE BECAUSE
IT NEITHER SEES HIM NOR KNOWS HIM. BUT YOU
KNOW HIM FOR HE IS WITH YOU AND WILL BE IN YOU.
18 I WILL NOT LEAVE YOU ORPHANS, I AM COMING TO
YOU. 19 A LITTLE WHILE AND THE WORLD WILL SEE ME
NO MORE, BUT YOU WILL SEE ME BECAUSE I
LIVE AND YOU WILL ALSO LIVE.

20 ON THAT DAY YOU WILL KNOW THAT I AM
IN MY FATHER AND YOU IN ME, AND I IN YOU.
21 WHOEVER ACCEPTS AND KEEPS MY COMMANDMENTS
IS THE ONE WHO LOVES ME. IF HE LOVES ME, HE WILL
ALSO BE LOVED BY MY FATHER; I TOO SHALL LOVE
HIM AND SHOW MYSELF CLEARLY TO HIM."

22 JUDAS-NOT THE ISCARIOT-ASKED JESUS, "LORD,
HOW CAN IT BE THAT YOU WILL SHOW YOURSELF
CLEARLY TO US AND NOT TO THE WORLD?"

23 JESUS ANSWERED, "IF ANYONE LOVES ME, HE WILL KEEP
MY WORD AND MY FATHER WILL LOVE HIM; AND WE WILL COME TO

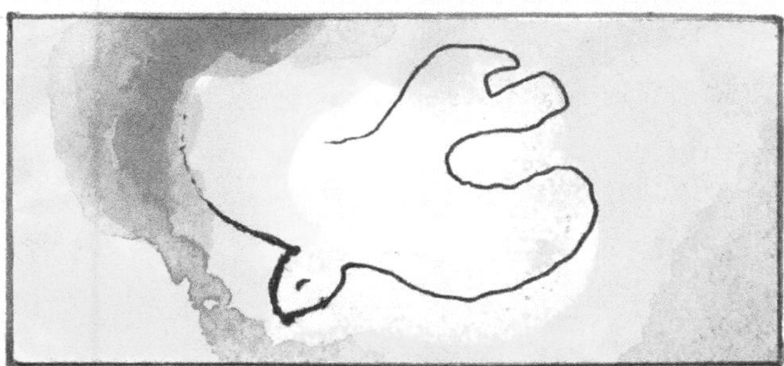

HIM AND MAKE OUR HOME WITH HIM. 24 I TOLD YOU ALL THIS,
BUT IF ONE DOESN'T LOVE ME, HE WILL NOT KEEP MY
WORDS. AND THESE WORDS THAT YOU HEAR ARE NOT MINE
BUT THE FATHER WHO SENT ME. 25 THAT IS WHILE I WAS
STILL WITH YOU 26 FROM NOW ON THE HELPER, THE HOLY
SPIRIT WHOM THE FATHER WILL SEND IN MY NAME, WILL
TEACH YOU ALL THINGS AND REMIND YOU OF ALL THAT I
HAVE TOLD YOU. 27 PEACE BE WITH YOU; I GIVE YOU MY
PEACE. NOT AS THE WORLD GIVES PEACE DO I GIVE IT TO YOU.
DO NOT BE TROUBLED; DO NOT BE AFRAID. 28 YOU
HEARD ME SAYING: 'I AM GOING AWAY, BUT I AM COMING
TO YOU.' IF YOU LOVED ME, YOU WOULD BE GLAD THAT I GO TO THE
FATHER, FOR THE FATHER IS GREATER THAN I. 29 I HAVE

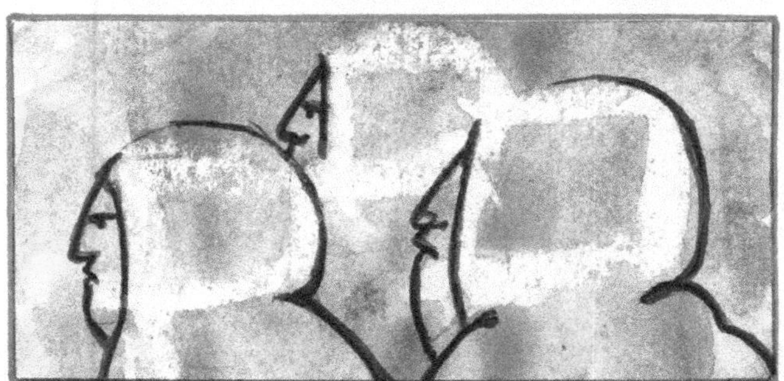

TOLD YOU THIS NOW BEFORE IT TAKES PLACE, SO THAT WHEN
IT DOES HAPPEN YOU MAY BELIEVE 30 FOR I WILL NO LONGER
SPEAK TO YOU. NOW THE RULER OF THIS WORLD IS AT HAND, AL-
THOUGH THERE IS NOTHING IN ME THAT HE CAN CLAIM.
31 BUT SEE, THE WORLD MUST KNOW THAT I LOVE THE
FATHER AND THAT I DO WHAT THE FATHER TAUGHT
ME TO DO. COME NOW, LET US GO.

THE VINE AND THE BRANCHES

15 1 I AM THE TRUE VINE AND MY FATHER IS THE VINE-
GROWER. 2 IF ANY OF MY BRANCHES DOESN'T BEAR FRUIT,
HE BREAKS IT OFF; AND HE PRUNES THE BRANCH THAT
DOES BEAR FRUIT AND BEAR EVEN MORE FRUIT. 3 YOU ARE
ALREADY MADE CLEAN BY THE WORD I HAVE SPOKEN TO YOU;
4 LIVE IN ME AS I LIVE IN YOU. THE BRANCH CANNOT
BEAR FRUIT BY ITSELF BUT HAS TO REMAIN PART OF
THE VINE; SO NEITHER CAN YOU IF YOU DO NOT
REMAIN IN ME. 5 I AM THE VINE AND YOU ARE THE
BRANCHES. AS LONG AS YOU REMAIN IN ME AND I IN YOU,
YOU BEAR MUCH FRUIT; BUT APART FROM ME YOU CAN
DO NOTHING. 6 WHOEVER DOES NOT REMAIN IN ME IS
LIKE A BRANCH THAT IS THROWN AWAY AND WITHERS;
AND THE WITHERED BRANCHES ARE GATHERED
AND THROWN INTO THE FIRE AND BURNED.

7 IF YOU REMAIN IN ME AND MY WORDS IN YOU,
YOU MAY ASK WHATEVER YOU WANT AT IT WILL
BE GIVEN TO YOU.
8 MY FATHER IS GLORIFIED WHEN YOU BECOME
MY DISCIPLES, THAT IS, WHEN YOU BEAR MUCH
FRUIT.
9 AS THE FATHER HAS LOVED ME, SO I HAVE LOVED
YOU; REMAIN IN MY LOVE. 10 YOU WILL REMAIN
IN MY LOVE IF YOU KEEP MY COMMANDMENTS JUST
AS I HAVE KEPT MY FATHER'S COMMANDMENTS AND
REMAIN IN HIS LOVE. 11 I HAVE TOLD YOU ALL THIS,
THAT MY OWN JOY MAY BE IN YOU AND YOUR JOY
MAY BE COMPLETE. 12 THIS IS MY COMMANDMENT:
LOVE ONE ANOTHER AS I HAVE LOVED YOU. 13

THERE IS NO GREATER LOVE THAN THIS, TO GIVE ONE'S LI-
FE FOR HIS FRIENDS; 14 AND YOU ARE MY FRIENDS IF
YOU DO WHAT I COMMAND YOU. 15 I SHALL NOT CALL
YOU SERVANTS ANY MORE, BECAUSE A SERVANT DOES NOT
KNOW WHAT HIS MASTER IS ABOUT. INSTEAD I CALL
YOU FRIENDS, SINCE I HAVE MADE KNOWN TO YOU EVERY-
THING I LEARNED FROM MY FATHER. 16 YOU DID NOT
CHOOSE ME; IT WAS I WHO CHOSE YOU AND SENT YOU
TO GO AND BEAR MUCH FRUIT, FRUIT THAT WILL LAST.
AND EVERYTHING YOU ASK THE FATHER IN MY NAME,
HE WILL GIVE YOU. 17 I COMMAND YOU TO LOVE ONE ANOTHER.

THE HOSTILE WORLD

18 IF THE WORLD HATES YOU, REMEMBER THAT THE
WORLD HATED ME BEFORE YOU. 19 THIS WOULD NOT
BE IF YOU BELONGED TO THE WORLD, BECAUSE THE WORLD
LOVES ITS OWN. BUT YOU ARE NOT OF THE WORLD SINCE
I HAVE CHOSEN YOU FROM THE WORLD: BECAUSE OF
THIS THE WORLD HATES YOU.
20 REMEMBER WHAT I TOLD YOU: THE SERVANT IS NOT
GREATER THAN HIS MASTER; IF THEY PERSECUTED
ME, THEY WILL PERSECUTE YOU, TOO. HAVE THEY KEPT
MY TEACHING? WILL THEY THEN KEEP YOURS? 21 ALL

THIS THEY WILL DO TO YOU FOR THE SAKE OF MY NAME BE-
CAUSE THEY DO NOT KNOW THE ONE WHO SENT ME.
22 IF I HAD NOT COME TO TELL THEM, THEY WOULD HA-
VE NO SIN, BUT NOW THEY HAVE NO EXCUSE FOR THEIR
SIN. 23 THOSE WHO HATE ME HATE MY FATHER.
24 IF I HAD NOT DONE AMONG THEM WHAT NO ONE
ELSE HAS EVER DONE, THEY WOULD HAVE NO SIN. BUT
AFTER THEY HAVE SEEN ALL THIS, THEY HATE

ME AND MY FATHER, 25 AND THE WORDS
WRITTEN IN THEIR LAW BECOME TRUE: THEY
HATED ME WITHOUT CAUSE.

THE SPIRIT WILL COME

26 FROM THE FATHER, I WILL SEND YOU THE SPIRIT
OF TRUTH WHO COMES FROM THE FATHER. WHEN
THIS HELPER COMES, HE WILL BE MY WITNESS, 27
AND YOU, TOO, WILL BE MY WITNESSES FOR YOU HAVE
BEEN WITH ME FROM THE BEGINNING.

16 1 I TELL YOU ALL THIS TO KEEP YOU FROM STUM-
BLING AND FALLING AWAY. 2 THEY WILL PUT
YOU OUT OF THE JEWISH COMMUNITIES. STILL
MORE, THE HOUR IS COMING WHEN ANYONE WHO

KILLS YOU WILL CLAIM TO BE SERVING GOD; 3 THEY WILL
DO THIS BECAUSE THEY HAVE NOT KNOWN THE FATHER
OR ME. 4 I TELL YOU ALL THESE THINGS NOW SO
THAT WHEN THE TIME COMES YOU MAY REMEMBER
THAT I TOLD YOU. I DID NOT TELL YOU ABOUT THIS IN THE
BEGINNING BECAUSE I WAS WITH YOU. 5 BUT NOW I AM
GOING TO THE ONE WHO SENT ME AND NONE OF YOU ASKS
ME WHERE I AM GOING, 6 FOR YOU ARE OVERCOME WITH
GRIEF BECAUSE OF WHAT I HAVE SAID. 7 INDEED BELI-
EVE ME: IT IS BETTER FOR YOU THAT I GO AWAY, FOR AS LONG AS
I DO NOT LEAVE, THE HELPER WILL NOT COME TO YOU; BUT IF
I GO AWAY, IT IS TO SEND HIM TO YOU. 8 WHEN HE COMES,
HE WILL VINDICATE THE TRUTH IN FACE OF THE WORLD
WITH REGARD TO SIN, TO THE WAY OF RIGHTEOUSNESS,

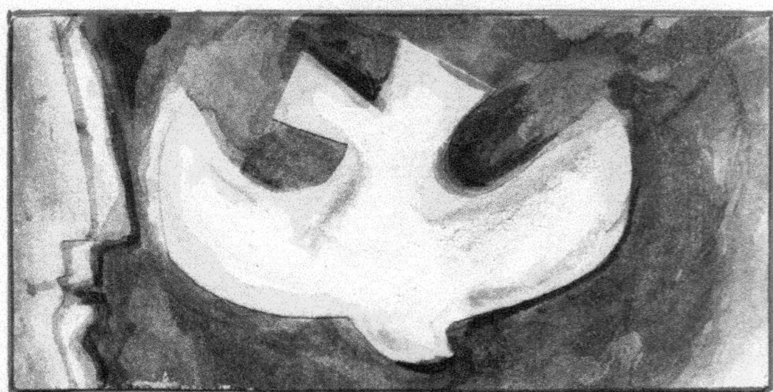

AND TO THE JUDGMENT. 9 WHAT WAS THE SIN? THEY DIDN'T
BELIEVE IN ME. 10 WHAT IS THE WAY OF RIGHTEOUSNESS? I AM
ON THE WAY TO THE FATHER, MEANWHILE YOU WILL NOT SEE
ME. 11 WHAT JUDGMENT? THE RULER OF THIS WORLD
HAS HIMSELF BEEN CONDEMNED. 12 I STILL HAVE MA-
NY THINGS TO TELL YOU, BUT YOU CANNOT BEAR THEM NOW.
13 WHEN HE, THE SPIRIT OF TRUTH COMES, HE WILL GU-
IDE YOU INTO THE WHOLE TRUTH.

HE HAS NOTHING TO SAY OF HIMSELF BUT HE WILL
SPEAK OF WHAT HE HEARS, AND HE WILL TELL
YOU OF THE THINGS TO COME. 14 HE WILL
TAKE WHAT IS MINE AND MAKE IT KNOWN TO YOU:
IN DOING THIS, HE WILL GLORIFY ME.

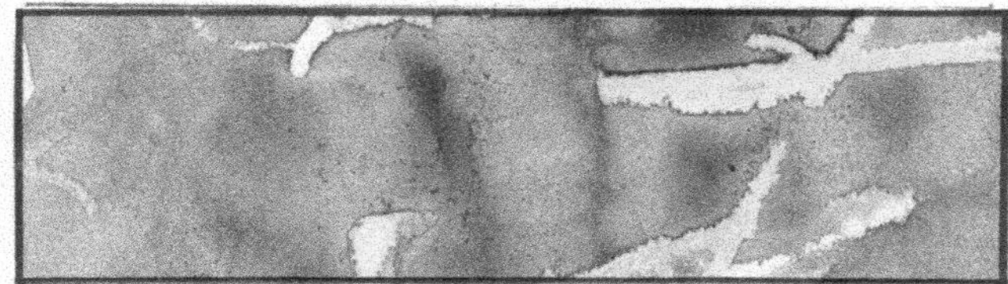

SAN PEDRO DEL BURGAL · ST. JOHN · 12 C. MURAL ·
CCCLIII
353
©
DM
09

15 ALL THAT THE FATHER HAS IS MINE; BECAUSE OF THIS
I HAVE JUST TOLD YOU, THAT THE SPIRIT WILL TAKE WHAT
IS MINE AND MAKE IT KNOWN TO YOU."

THE PROMISE OF A NEW PRESENCE

16 A LITTLE WHILE AND YOU WILL SEE ME NO MORE; AND
THEN A LITTLE WHILE, AND YOU WILL SEE ME." 17 SOME
OF THE DISCIPLES WONDERED, "WHAT DOES HE MEAN
BY: 'A LITTLE WHILE AND YOU WILL NOT SEE ME, AND
THEN A LITTLE WHILE AND YOU WILL SEE ME'? AND
WHY DID HE SAY: 'I GO TO THE FATHER'?" 18 THEY
SAID TO ONE ANOTHER,

"WHAT DOES HE MEAN BY
'A LITTLE WHILE'? WE
DON'T UNDERSTAND." 19
JESUS KNEW THAT THEY
WANTED TO QUESTION HIM;
SO HE SAID TO THEM, "YOU
ARE PUZZLED BECAUSE
I TOLD YOU THAT IN A LIT-
TLE WHILE YOU WILL SEE
ME NO MORE, AND THEN A
LITTLE WHILE LATER YOU
WILL SEE ME. 20 TRULY,
I SAY TO YOU, YOU WILL WE-
EP AND MOURN WHILE
THE WORLD REJOICES.
YOU WILL BE SORROWFUL,
BUT YOUR SORROW WILL
TURN TO JOY. 21 A WO-
MAN IN CHILDBIRTH IS
IN DISTRESS BECAUSE
HER TIME IS AT HAND.
BUT AFTER THE CHILD IS
BORN, SHE NO LONGER RE-
MEMBERS HER SUFFER-
ING BECAUSE OF SUCH
GREAT JOY; A HUMAN IS BORN INTO THE WORLD. 22 YOU
FEEL SORROWFUL NOW, BUT I WILL SEE YOU AGAIN;
AND YOUR HEARTS WILL REJOICE IN SUCH A WAY THAT NO
ONE WILL TAKE YOUR JOY FROM YOU. 23 WHEN THAT DAY
COMES YOU WILL NOT ASK ME ANYTHING. TRULY, I SAY
TO YOU, WHATEVER YOU ASK THE FATHER IN MY NAME, HE
WILL GIVE YOU. 24 SO FAR YOU HAVE NOT ASKED IN
MY NAME; ASK AND RECEIVE THAT YOUR JOY MAY BE
FULL. 25 I TAUGHT YOU ALL THIS IN VEILED LAN-
GUAGE, BUT THE TIME IS COMING WHEN I SHALL
NO LONGER SPEAK IN VEILED LANGUAGE, BUT WILL
TELL YOU PLAINLY OF THE FATHER. 26 WHEN THAT

DAY COMES, YOU WILL ASK IN MY NAME AND IT WILL
NOT BE FOR ME TO ASK THE FATHER FOR YOU,
27 FOR THE FATHER HIMSELF LOVES YOU BE-
CAUSE YOU HAVE LOVED ME AND YOU BELIEVE
THAT I COME FROM THE FATHER.

28 AS I COME FROM THE FATHER AND HAVE
COME INTO THE WORLD, SO I AM LEAVING THE
WORLD AND GOING TO THE FATHER."
29 THE DISCIPLES SAID TO HIM, "NOW YOU ARE SPEAK-
ING PLAINLY AND NOT IN VEILED LANGUAGE!"

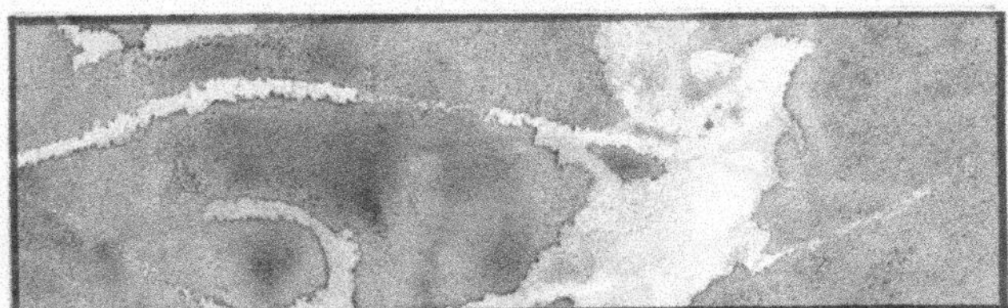

30 NOW WE SEE THAT YOU KNOW ALL THINGS, EVEN
BEFORE WE QUESTION YOU. BECAUSE OF THIS WE BE-
LIEVE THAT YOU CAME FROM GOD."

31 JESUS ANSWERED THEM, "YOU SAY THAT YOU BELIEVE!
32 THE HOUR IS COMING, INDEED IT HAS COME WHEN
YOU WILL BE SCATTERED, EACH ONE TO HIS HOME,
AND YOU WILL LEAVE ME ALONE. YET I AM NOT ALONE,
FOR THE FATHER IS WITH ME.

33 I HAVE TOLD YOU ALL THIS, SO THAT IN ME YOU MAY

HAVE PEACE, EVEN THOUGH YOU HAVE TROUBLE IN THE
WORLD. COURAGE! I HAVE OVERCOME THE WORLD."

PRAYER OF JESUS

17 1 AFTER SAYING THIS, JESUS LIFTED UP HIS
EYES TO HEAVEN AND SAID, "FATHER, THE HOUR
HAS COME; GIVE GLORY TO YOUR SON, THAT THE SON
MAY GIVE GLORY TO YOU. 2 YOU HAVE GIVEN HIM POWER
OVER ALL MORTALS, AND YOU WANT HIM TO BRING ETER-
NAL LIFE TO ALL YOU HAVE ENTRUSTED TO HIM. 3 FOR
THIS IS ETERNAL LIFE: TO KNOW YOU, THE ONLY
TRUE GOD, AND THE ONE YOU SENT, JESUS CHRIST.
4 I HAVE GLORIFIED YOU ON EARTH AND FINISHED
THE WORK THAT YOU GAVE ME TO DO. 5 NOW, FATHER,
GIVE ME IN YOUR PRESENCE THE SAME GLORY I HAD WITH
YOU BEFORE THE WORLD BEGAN. 6 I HAVE MADE
YOUR NAME KNOWN TO THOSE YOU GAVE ME FROM
THE WORLD. THEY WERE YOURS AND YOU GAVE THEM
TO ME, AND THEY KEPT YOUR WORD. 7 AND NOW THEY
KNOW THAT ALL YOU GIVEN ME COMES INDEED FROM YOU.
8 I HAVE GIVEN THEM THE TEACHING I RECEIVED FROM YOU,

AND THEY RECEIVED IT AND KNOW IN TRUTH THAT I CAME FROM
YOU; AND THEY BELIEVE THAT YOU HAVE SENT ME. 9 I
PRAY FOR THEM; I DO NOT PRAY FOR THE WORLD
BUT FOR THOSE WHO BELONG TO YOU AND WHOM
YOU HAVE GIVEN TO ME.
10 INDEED ALL I HAVE IS YOURS AND ALL YOU
HAVE IS MINE — AND NOW THEY ARE MY GLORY.

11 I AM NO LONGER IN THE WORLD, BUT THEY
ARE IN THE WORLD WHEREAS I AM GOING TO
YOU.
HOLY FATHER, KEEP THEM IN YOUR NAME THAT YOU
HAVE GIVEN ME, SO THAT THEY MAY BE ONE, JUST AS WE ARE.

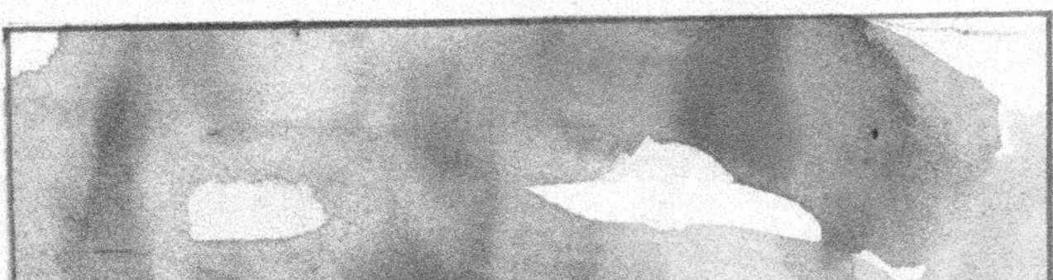

12 WHEN I WAS WITH THEM, I KEPT THEM SAFE IN YOUR
NAME, AND NOT ONE WAS LOST EXCEPT THE ONE WHO WAS
ALREADY LOST, AND IN THIS THE SCRIPTURE WAS FULFILLED.
13 BUT NOW I AM COMING TO YOU AND I LEAVE THESE WORDS
OF MINE IN THE WORLD THAT MY JOY MAY BE COMPLETE IN THEM.
14 I HAVE GIVEN THEM YOUR MESSAGE AND THE WORLD HAS
HATED THEM BECAUSE THEY ARE NOT OF THE WORLD; JUST AS
I AM NOT OF THE WORLD. 15 I DO NOT ASK YOU TO REMOVE
THEM FROM THE WORLD BUT TO KEEP THEM FROM THE EVIL
ONE. 16 THEY ARE NOT OF THE WORLD, JUST AS I AM NOT
OF THE WORLD. 17 CONSECRATE THEM IN THE TRUTH,
YOUR WORD IS TRUTH. 18 FOR I HAVE SENT THEM INTO

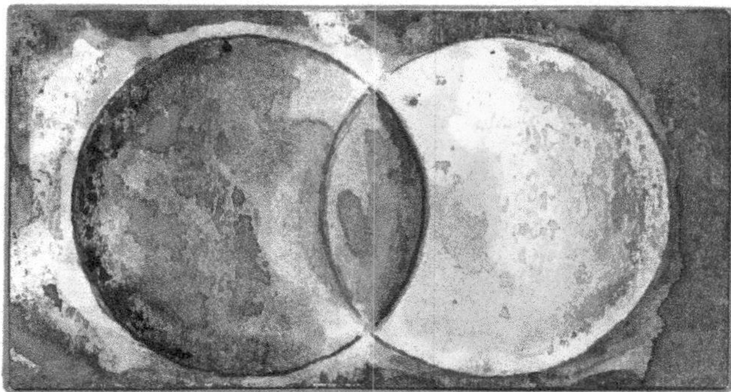

THE WORLD AS YOU SENT ME INTO THE WORLD. 19
FOR THEIR SAKE, I GO TO THE SACRIFICE BY
WHICH I AM CONSECRATED, SO THAT THEY TOO
MAY BE CONSECRATED IN TRUTH.

20 I PRAY NOT ONLY FOR THESE BUT ALSO FOR
THOSE WHO THROUGH THEIR WORD WILL BELI-
EVE IN ME. 21 MAY THEY ALL BE ONE AS YOU
FATHER ARE IN ME AND I AM IN YOU. MAY THEY
BE ONE IN US; SO THE WORLD MAY BELIEVE
THAT YOU HAVE SENT ME. 22 I HAVE GIVEN THEM
THE GLORY YOU HAVE GIVEN ME, THAT THEY MAY BE
ONE AS WE ARE ONE: 23 I IN THEM AND YOU IN ME.
THUS THEY SHALL REACH PERFECTION IN UNITY AND
THE WORLD SHALL KNOW THAT YOU HAVE SENT

ME AND THAT I HAVE LOVED THEM JUST AS YOU
LOVED ME. 24 FATHER, SINCE YOU HAVE GIVEN ME
THOSE PEOPLE, I WANT THEM TO BE WITH ME WHE-
RE I AM AND SEE THE GLORY YOU GAVE ME, FOR YOU
LOVED ME BEFORE THE FOUNDATION OF THE WORLD.

25 RIGHTEOUS FATHER, THE WORLD HAS NOT KNOWN
YOU BUT I HAVE KNOWN YOU, AND THESE HAVE
KNOWN THAT YOU HAVE SENT ME.

26 AS I REVEALED YOUR NAME TO THEM, SO WILL
I CONTINUE TO REVEAL IT, SO THAT THE LOVE WITH WHICH
YOU LOVED ME MAY BE IN THEM AND I ALSO MAY BE IN THEM."

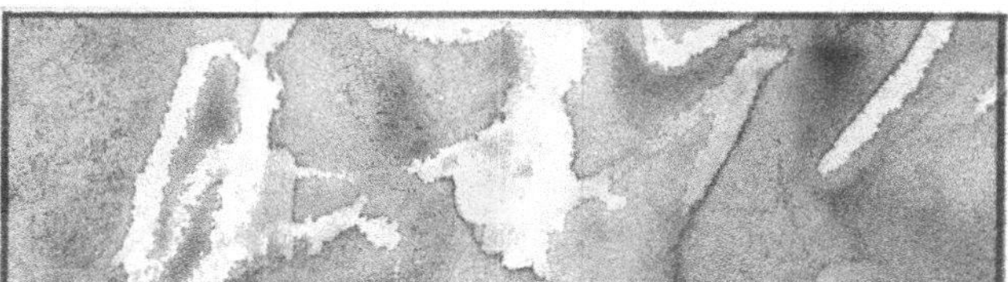

THE ARREST OF JESUS

18 1 WHEN JESUS HAD FINISHED SPEAKING, HE WENT
WITH HIS DISCIPLES TO THE OTHER SIDE OF THE KI-
DRON VALLEY. THERE WAS A GARDEN WHERE JESUS
ENTERED WITH HIS DISCIPLES. 2 NOW JUDAS, WHO BE-
TRAYED HIM, KNEW THE PLACE SINCE JESUS HAD OFTEN
MET THERE WITH HIS DISCIPLES. 3 HE LED SOLDIERS OF
THE ROMAN BATTALION AND GUARDS FROM THE CHIEF PRI-
ESTS AND PHARISEES, WHO WENT THERE WITH LANTERNS,
TORCHES AND WEAPONS. 4 JESUS KNEW ALL THAT WAS
GOING TO HAPPEN TO HIM; HE STEPPED FORWARD AND ASKED,
"WHO ARE YOU LOOKING FOR?"
5 THEY ANSWERED, "JESUS
THE NAZARENE." JESUS
SAID, "I AM HE." JUDAS, WHO
BETRAYED HIM, STOOD
THERE WITH THEM. WHEN
6 JESUS SAID, "I AM HE,"
THEY MOVED BACK AND
FELL TO THE GROUND. 7
HE ASKED A SECOND TIME,
"WHO ARE YOU LOOKING FOR?"
THEY ANSWERED, "JESUS THE
NAZARENE." 8 JESUS RE-
PLIED, "I TOLD YOU THAT I
AM HE. IF YOU ARE LOOKING
FOR ME, LET THE OTHERS
GO." 9 SO WHAT JESUS
HAD SAID CAME TRUE: "I
HAVE NOT LOST ONE OF THO-
SE YOU GAVE ME." 10 SI-
MON PETER HAD A SWORD;
HE DREW IT AND STRUCK
MALCHUS, THE HIGH PRI-
EST'S SERVANT, CUTTING
OFF HIS RIGHT EAR. 11
BUT JESUS SAID TO PETER,
"PUT YOUR SWORD INTO ITS SHEATH; SHALL I NOT DRINK
THE CUP WHICH THE FATHER HAS GIVEN ME?"

12 THE GUARDS AND SOLDIERS, WITH THEIR COMMANDER,
SEIZED AND BOUND JESUS; 13 THEY TOOK HIM FIRST TO
ANNAS, CAIAPHAS' FATHER-IN-LAW, THE HIGH PRIEST IN
THAT YEAR; 14 IT WAS CAIAPHAS WHO HAD TOLD THE JEWS:
"IT IS BETTER THAT ONE MAN SHOULD DIE FOR THE PEOPLE."
15 SIMON PETER WITH ANOTHER DISCIPLE FOLLOWED JESUS.
BECAUSE THIS DISCIPLE
WAS KNOWN TO THE HIGH
PRIEST, THEY LET HIM EN-
TER THE COURTYARD OF THE
HIGH PRIEST WITH JESUS,
16 BUT PETER HAD TO STAY
OUTSIDE THE DOOR. THE OT-
HER DISCIPLE KNOWN TO
THE HIGH PRIEST WENT OUT
AND SPOKE TO THE MAIDSER-
VANT AT THE GATE AND
BROUGHT PETER IN. THEN,
17 THIS SERVANT ON DUTY
AT THE DOOR SAID TO PETER,
"YOU ALSO ARE ONE OF HIS
DISCIPLES?" BUT HE ANS-
WERED, "I AM NOT." 18 THE
SERVANTS AND THE GU-
ARDS HAD MADE A CHAR-
COAL FIRE AND WERE
STANDING AND WARMING
THEMSELVES FOR IT WAS
COLD. PETER WAS ALSO
WITH THEM WARMING
HIMSELF. 19 THE HIGH
PRIEST QUESTIONED JESUS
ABOUT HIS DISCIPLES AND HIS TEACHING. 20 JESUS SAID,
"I HAVE SPOKEN OPENLY TO THE WORLD; I HAVE ALWAYS
TAUGHT WHERE THE JEWS MEET TOGETHER, ASSEMBLIES, SY-
NAGOGUES OR IN THE TEMPLE, I DIDN'T TEACH SECRETLY.
21 WHY THEN DO YOU ASK ME? ASK THOSE WHO HEARD
ME, THEY KNOW WHAT I SAID." 22 AT THIS REPLY ONE OF
THE GUARDS STANDING BY GAVE JESUS A BLOW ON THE FACE,
SAYING, "IS THAT THE WAY TO ANSWER THE HIGH PRIEST?"

(23) JESUS SAID TO HIM, "IF I HAVE SPOKEN WRONGLY, POINT
IT OUT; BUT IF I HAVE SPOKEN RIGHTLY, WHY DO YOU STRIKE
ME?" (24) THEN ANNAS SENT HIM, BOUND, TO CAIAPHAS, THE
HIGH PRIEST. (25) NOW SIMON PETER STOOD THERE WARMING
HIMSELF. THEY SAID TO HIM, "SURELY YOU ALSO ARE ONE
OF HIS DISCIPLES." HE DENIED IT AND ANSWERED, "I AM
NOT." (26) ONE OF THE HIGH PRIEST'S SERVANTS, A KINS-
MAN OF THE ONE WHOSE EAR PETER HAD CUT OFF, ASKED,
"DID I NOT SEE YOU WITH HIM IN THE GARDEN?" (27)
AGAIN PETER DENIED IT, AND AT ONCE THE COCK CROWED.

JESUS BEFORE PILATE

(28) THEN THEY LED JESUS FROM THE HOUSE OF CAIA-
PHAS TO THE COURT OF THE ROMAN GOVERNOR. IT WAS

NOW MORNING. THE JEWS
DIDN'T ENTER LEST THEY
BE MADE UNCLEAN BY COM-
ING INTO A HOUSE OF A
PAGAN AND BE UNABLE
TO EAT THE PASSOVER ME-
AL. (29) SO PILATE WENT
OUT AND ASKED, "WHAT
CHARGE DO YOU BRING
AGAINST THIS MAN?"
THEY ANSWERED, (30) "IF
HE WERE NOT A CRIMI-
NAL, WE WOULD NOT BE
HANDING HIM OVER TO
YOU." (31) PILATE SAID,
"TAKE HIM YOURSEL-
VES AND JUDGE HIM
ACCORDING TO YOUR
OWN LAW." BUT THEY
REPLIED, "WE ARE NOT
ALLOWED TO PUT ANY-
ONE TO DEATH." (32) IT
WAS CLEAR FROM THIS
WHAT KIND OF DEATH
JESUS WAS TO DIE,
ACCORDING TO WHAT
JESUS HIMSELF HAD
FORETOLD. (33) PILATE
THEN ENTERED THE CO-
URT AGAIN, CALLED JESUS AND ASKED HIM, "ARE YOU
THE KING OF THE JEWS?" (34) JESUS REPLIED, "DOES
THIS WORD COME FROM YOU, OR DID YOU HEAR IT FROM
OTHERS?" (35) PILATE ANSWERED, "AM I A JEW? YOUR
OWN NATION AND THE CHIEF PRIESTS HAVE HANDED YOU
OVER TO ME. WHAT HAVE YOU DONE?" (36) JESUS REPLIED,
"MY KINGSHIP DOES NOT COME FROM THIS WORLD. IF I

WERE KING LIKE THOSE IN THE WORLD, MY GUARDS WOULD
HAVE FOUGHT TO SAVE ME FROM BEING HANDED OVER TO
THE JEWS. BUT MY KINGSHIP IS NOT FROM HERE." (37) PI-
LATE ASKED HIM, "SO YOU ARE A KING?" AND JESUS AN-
SWERED, "JUST AS YOU SAY, I AM A KING. FOR THIS I WAS
BORN AND FOR THIS I HAVE COME INTO THE WORLD, TO
BEAR WITNESS TO THE TRUTH. EVERYONE WHO IS ON THE
SIDE OF TRUTH HEARS MY VOICE." (38) PILATE SAID,
"WHAT IS TRUTH?" PILATE THEN WENT OUT TO THE JEWS
AND SAID, "I FIND NO CRIME IN THIS MAN. (39) ACCORDING
TO A CUSTOM, I MUST RELEASE A PRISONER OF YOURS
AT THE PASSOVER. WITH YOUR AGREEMENT I WILL RELE-
ASE FOR YOU THE KING OF THE JEWS." (40) BUT THEY IN-
SISTED AND CRIED OUT, "NOT THIS MAN, BUT BARAB-
BAS!" NOW BARABBAS WAS A ROBBER.

19 (1) THEN PILATE HAD JESUS TAKEN AWAY AND
SCOURGED. (2) THE SOLDIERS ALSO TWISTED
THORNS INTO A CROWN AND PUT IT ON HIS HEAD.
THEY THREW A CLOACK OF ROYAL PURPLE AROUND HIS

SHOULDERS (3) AND BEGAN COMING UP TO HIM AND SALU-
TING HIM, "HAIL KING OF THE JEWS," AND THEY STRUCK
HIM ON THE FACE. (4) PILATE WENT OUTSIDE ANOTHER
TIME AND SAID TO THE JEWS, "LOOK, I AM BRINGING
HIM OUT AND I WANT YOU TO KNOW THAT I FIND NO
CRIME IN HIM." (5) JESUS THEN CAME OUT WEARING
THE CROWN OF THORNS AND THE PURPLE CLOAK AND
PILATE POINTED TO HIM SAYING, "HERE IS THE MAN!"

ECCE HOMO

(6) ON SEEING HIM, THE CHIEF PRIESTS AND THE GUARDS
CRIED OUT, "CRUCIFY HIM, CRUCIFY HIM!" PILATE RE-
PLIED, "TAKE HIM YOURSELVES AND HAVE HIM CRUCIFI-
ED, FOR I FIND NO CASE
AGAINST HIM." (7) THE
JEWS SAID, "WE HAVE A
LAW AND ACCORDING TO
IT THIS MAN MUST DIE
BECAUSE HE MADE HIM-
SELF SON OF GOD." WHEN
(8) PILATE HEARD THIS
HE WAS MORE AFRAID.
(9) AND COMING BACK
INTO THE COURT HE
ASKED JESUS,
"WHERE ARE YOU
FROM?" BUT JESUS
GAVE HIM NO ANS-
WER.
(10) THEN PILATE
SAID TO HIM, "YOU
WILL NOT SPEAK
TO ME? DO YOU
NOT KNOW THAT
I HAVE POWER
TO RELEASE YOU
JUST AS I HAVE
POWER TO CRUCIFY
YOU?"
(11) JESUS REPLIED,
"YOU WOULD HAVE
NO POWER OVER ME UNLESS IT HAD BEEN
GIVEN YOU FROM ABOVE, THEREFORE THE ONE
WHO HANDED ME OVER TO YOU IS EVEN MORE GUILTY."

You will have
no Power...

PILATE SAID,
"WHAT IS TRUTH?" (John 18:38)

(12) BECAUSE OF THIS PILATE TRIED TO RELEASE
HIM, BUT THE JEWS CRIED OUT, "IF YOU RELEASE THIS
MAN, YOU ARE NO FRIEND OF CAESAR. ANYONE WHO
MAKES HIMSELF KING IS DEFYING CAESAR." WHEN
(13) PILATE HEARD THIS, HE HAD JESUS BROUGHT
OUTSIDE OUTSIDE TO THE PLACE CALLED THE
STONE FLOOR - IN HEBREW GABBATHA - AND
THERE JESUS SAT IN THE TRIBUNE. (14) IT WAS THE PRE-
PARATION DAY FOR THE PASSOVER, ABOUT NOON. SO
PILATE SAID TO THE JEWS, "HERE IS YOUR KING." (15)
BUT THEY CRIED OUT, "AWAY! TAKE HIM AWAY! CRUCIFY
HIM! PILATE REPLIED, "SHALL I CRUCIFY YOUR KING?
THE CHIEF PRIEST ANSWERED, "WE HAVE NO KING BUT
CAESAR." (16) THE PILATE HANDED JESUS OVER
TO THEM TO BE CRUCIFIED.

JESUS IS CRUCIFIED

THEY TOOK CHARGE OF HIM. (17) BEARING HIS OWN CROSS, HE
WENT OUT OF THE CITY TO WHAT IS CALLED THE PLACE OF THE
SKULL, IN HEBREW GOL-
GOTHA. (18) THERE HE WAS
CRUCIFIED AND WITH HIM TWO
OTHERS ONE OF EITHER SI-
DE, AND. JESUS IN THE MID-
DLE. (19) PILATE HAD A
NOTICE FASTENED TO THE
CROSS THAT READ: JESUS
THE NAZAREAN, KING OF
THE JEWS. (20) MANY JE-
WISH PEOPLE SAW THIS
TITLE, BECAUSE WHERE,
JESUS WAS CRUCIFIED WAS
VERY CLOSE TO THE CITY.
IT WAS WRITTEN IN HEBREW,
LATIN AND GREEK (21) THE
CHIEF PRIESTS SAID TO
PILATE, "DO NOT WRITE:
'THE KING OF THE JEWS;
BUT: THIS MAN CLAIMED TO
BE KING OF THE JEWS." (22)
PILATE SAID, "WHAT I HAVE
WRITTEN, I HAVE WRITTEN."
(23) WHEN THE SOLDIERS
CRUCIFIED JESUS, THEY
TOOK HIS CLOTHES AND
DIVIDED THEM INTO FOUR
PARTS, ONE FOR EACH OF
THEM. BUT AS THE TUNIC
WAS WOVEN IN ONE PIECE FROM TOP TO BOTTOM (24) THEY
SAID, "LET US NOT TEAR IT, BUT CAST LOTS TO DECIDE WHO
WILL GET IT." THIS FULFILLED THE WORDS OF SCRIPTURE:
THEY DIVIDED MY CLOTHING AMONG THEM; THEY CAST
LOTS FOR MY GARMENT. THIS WAS WHAT THE SOLDIERS DID.

JESUS LAST WORDS

(25) NEAR THE CROSS OF JESUS STOOD HIS MOTHER, HIS

HIS MOTHER'S SISTER MARY, WHO WAS THE
WIFE OF CLEOPHAS, AND MARY OF MAGDALA.

(26) WHEN JESUS SAW THE MOTHER, AND THE DISCI-
PLE, HE SAID TO THE MOTHER, "WOMAN, THIS IS YOUR
SON." (27) THEN HE SAID TO THE DISCIPLE,
"THERE IS YOUR MOTHER." AND FROM THAT
MOMENT THE DISCIPLE TOOK HER TO HIS OWN
HOME.
(28) WITH WHAT JESUS KNEW ALL WAS NOW FIN-
ISHED AND HE SAID, I AM THIRSTY, TO FUL-
FIL WHAT WAS WRITTEN IN THE SCRIPTURE.
(29) A JAR FULL OF BITTER WINE STOOD THE-
RE; SO, PUTTING A SPONGE SOAKED IN THE
WINE ON A TWIG OF HYSSOP, THEY RAISED IT TO

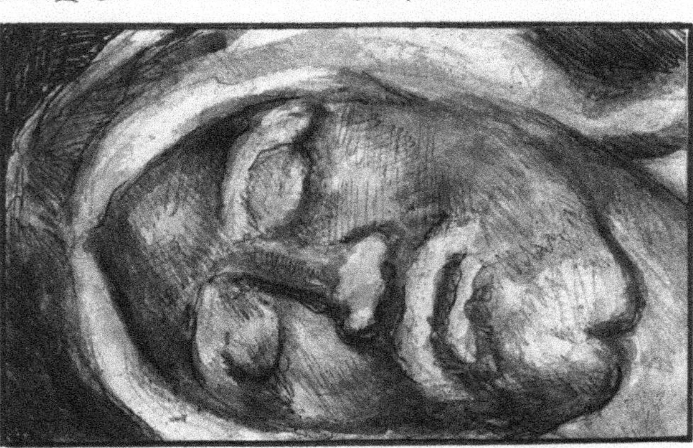

HIS LIPS. (30) JESUS TOOK THE WINE AND SAID, "IT
IS FINISHED.". THEN HE BOWED HIS HEAD AND
GAVE UP HIS SPIRIT.

THE PIERCED CHRIST

(31) AS IT WAS PREPARATION DAY, THE JEWS DID NOT
WANT THE BODIES TO REMAIN ON THE CROSS DUR-
ING THE SABBATH, FOR THIS SABBATH WAS A VERY
SOLEMN DAY. THEY
ASKED PILATE TO HA-
VE THE LEGS OF THE
CONDEMNED MEN BRO-
KEN, SO THEY MIGHT
TAKE AWAY THE BODIES.
(32) THE SOLDIERS CAME AND
BROKE THE LEGS OF THE
FIRST MAN AND OF THE
OTHER WHO HAD BEEN CRU-
CIFIED WITH JESUS. (33)
WHEN THEY CAME TO JESUS,
THEY SAW HE WAS ALRE-
ADY DEAD; SO THEY DID
NOT BREAK HIS LEGS.
(34) ONE OF THE SOL-
DIERS, HOWEVER, PIER-
CED HIS SIDE WITH A
LANCE AND IMMEDIA-
TELY THERE CAME
OUT BLOOD AND WATER.
(35) THE ONE WHO HAS
SEEN HERE GIVES HIS
WITNESS SO THAT YOU
MAY BELIEVE: HIS WIT-
NESS IS TRUE AND HE
KNOWS THAT HE SPEAKS
THE TRUTH. (36) ALL THIS
HAPPENED TO FULFIL THE WORDS OF SCRIPTURE,
NOT ONE OF HIS BONES SHALL BE BROKEN.

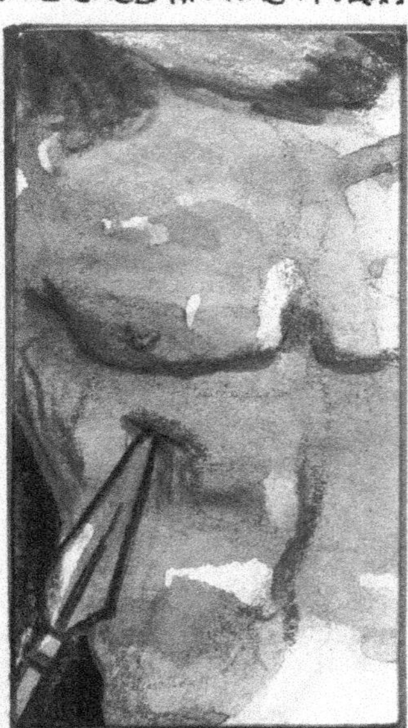

(37) ANOTHER TEXT SAYS: THEY SHALL LOOK
ON HIM WHOM THEY HAVE PIERCED.

(38) AFTER THIS, JOSEPH OF ARIMATHEA, APPROACHED
PILATE, FOR HE WAS A DISCIPLE OF JESUS, THOUGH
SECRETLY FOR FEAR OF THE JEWS. AND HE ASKED
PILATE TO LET HIM REMOVE THE BODY OF JESUS.
PILATE AGREED, SO HE CAME AND TOOK AWAY THE BODY.

(39) NICODEMUS, THE MAN WHO EARLIER HAD COME
TO JESUS BY NIGHT, ALSO CAME AND BROUGHT A
JAR OF MYRR MIXED WITH ALOES, ABOUT A HUND-
RED POUNDS. (40) THEY TOOK THE BODY OF JESUS
AND WRAPPED IT IN LINEN CLOTHS WITH THE SPICES,
FOLLOWING THE BURIAL CUSTOM OF THE JEWS.
(41) THERE WAS A GARDEN IN THE PLACE WHERE
JESUS HAD BEEN CRUCIFIED AND, IN THE GAR-
DEN, A NEW TOMB IN WHICH NO ONE HAD EVER
BEEN LAID. (42) AS THE TOMB WAS VERY NEAR,
THEY BURIED JESUS THERE BECAUSE THEY HAD
NO TIME LEFT FOR THE JEWISH PREPARATION DAY.

THE LORD IS RISEN

20 (1) NOW, ON THE FIRST DAY AFTER THE SABBATH,
MARY OF MAGDALA CAME TO THE TOMB EARLY
IN THE MORNING, WHILE IT WAS STILL DARK
AND SHE SAW THAT THE STONE BLOCKING THE

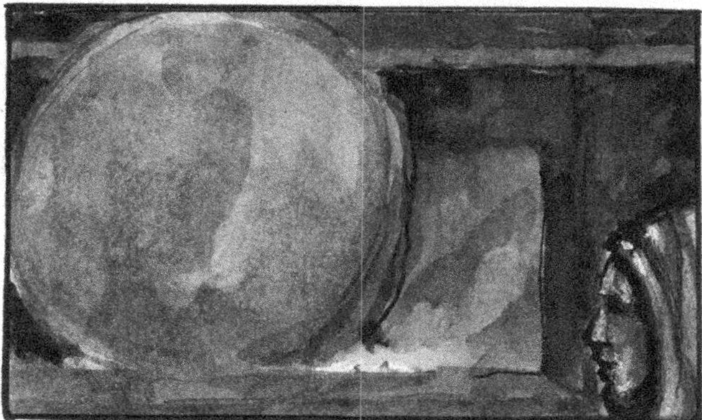

TOMB HAD BEEN MOVED AWAY. (2) SHE RAN TO
PETER AND THE OTHER DISCIPLE WHOM JESUS
LOVED. AND SHE SAID TO THEM, "THEY HAVE TA-
KEN THE LORD OUT OF THE TOMB AND WE DON'T
KNOW WHERE THEY HAVE LAID HIM."
(3) PETER THEN SET OUT WITH THE OTHER DISCIPLE
TO GO TO THE TOMB. (4) THEY RAN TOGETHER BUT

OTHER DISCIPLE OUT-
RAN PETER AND REACHED
THE TOMB FIRST. (5)
HE BENT DOWN AND
SAW THE LINEN CLOTHS
LYING FLAT, BUT HE
DID NOT ENTER. (6)
THEN SIMON PETER
CAME FOLLOWING HIM AND
ENTERED THE TOMB; HE,
TOO, SAW THE LINEN
CLOTHS LYING FLAT. (7)
THE NAPKIN, WHICH HAD
BEEN AROUND HIS HEAD
WAS NOT LYING FLAT LIKE
THE OTHER LINEN CLOTHS
BUT LAY ROLLED UP IN ITS
PLACE (8) THEN THE OTHER
DISCIPLE WHO HAD REACH-
ED THE TOMB FIRST ALSO
WENT IN; HE SAW AND BE-
LIEVED. (9) SCRIPTURE
CLEARLY SAID THAT HE
MUST RISE FROM THE
DEAD, BUT THEY HAD NOT
YET UNDERSTOOD THAT.
(10) THEN THE DISCIPLES WENT HOME. (11) MARY STOOD
WEEPING OUTSIDE THE TOMB, THEN SHE BENT DOWN AND LO-
OK INSIDE. (12) SHE SAW TWO ANGELS IN WHITE SITTING
WHERE JESUS' BODY HAD BEEN, ONE AT THE HEAD, AND THE
OTHER AT THE FEET. (13) THEY SAID, "WOMAN, WHY ARE YOU
WEEPING?" SHE ANSWERED, "THEY HAVE TAKEN MY LORD
AND I DON'T KNOW WHERE THEY HAVE PUT HIM." (14) AS
SHE SAID THIS, SHE TURNED AROUND AND SAW JESUS
STANDING THERE, BUT SHE DIDN'T RECOGNIZE HIM. (15)
JESUS SAID TO HER, "WOMAN, WHY ARE YOU WEEPING?
WHO ARE YOU LOOKING FOR?" SHE THOUGHT IT WAS THE
GARDENER AND ANSWERED, "LORD, IF YOU HAVE TAKEN
HIM AWAY, TELL ME WHERE YOU HAVE PUT HIM, AND I
WILL GO AND REMOVE HIM. (16) JESUS SAID TO HER,
"MARY." SHE TURNED AND SAID TO HIM, "RABBONI!" -
WHICH MEANS, MASTER. (17) JESUS SAID TO HER, "DO
NOT CLING TO ME; YOU SEE I HAVE NOT YET ASCENDED
TO THE FATHER. BUT GO TO MY BROTHERS AND SAY
TO THEM: I AM ASCENDING TO MY FATHER, WHO IS
YOUR FATHER, TO MY GOD, WHO IS YOUR GOD."
(18) SO MARY OF MAGDALA WENT AND ANNOUNCED TO
THE DISCIPLES, "I HAVE SEEN THE LORD, AND THIS IS
WHAT HE SAID TO ME."
(19) ON THE EVENING
OF THAT DAY, THE FIRST
DAY AFTER THE SAB-
BATH, THE DOORS WE-
RE LOCKED WHERE THE
DISCIPLES WERE, BE-
CAUSE OF THEIR FEAR
OF THE JEWS, BUT JESUS
CAME AND STOOD AMONG
THEM. HE SAID TO THEM,
"PEACE BE WITH YOU";
(20) THEN HE SHOWED
THEM HIS HANDS AND
HIS SIDE. THE DISCI-
PLES KEPT LOOKING
AT THE LORD AND
WERE FULL OF JOY.
(21) AGAIN JESUS
SAID TO THEM, "PE-
ACE BE WITH YOU!
AS THE FATHER HAS
SENT ME, SO I SEND

YOU." (22) AFTER SAYING THIS HE BREATHED ON
THEM AND SAID TO THEM "RECEIVE THE HOLY SPIRIT;
(23) FOR THOSE WHOSE SINS YOU FORGIVE,
THEY ARE FORGIVEN; FOR THOSE WHOSE
SINS YOU RETAIN, THEY ARE RETAINED."

(24) THOMAS, THE TWIN, ONE OF THE TWELVE,
WAS NOT WITH THEM WHEN JESUS CAME.

(25) THE OTHER DISCIPLES TOLD HIM, "WE HAVE
SEEN THE LORD." BUT HE REPLIED, "UNTIL I
HAVE SEEN IN HIS HANDS THE PRINT OF THE
NAILS AND PUT MY FINGER IN THE MARK OF THE
NAILS AND MY HAND IN HIS SIDE, I WILL NOT BELIEVE."

(26) EIGHT DAYS LATER, THE DISCIPLES WERE
IN THE HOUSE AGAIN AND THOMAS WAS WITH
THEM.

DESPITE THE LOCKED DOORS JESUS STOOD
IN THEIR MIDST AND SAID,

"PEACE BE WITH YOU!"

(27) THEN HE SAID TO THOMAS, "PUT YOUR FIN-
GER HERE AND SEE MY HANDS; STRETCH
OUT YOUR HAND AND PUT IT INTO MY SIDE.
DOUBT NO LONGER BUT BELIEVE."

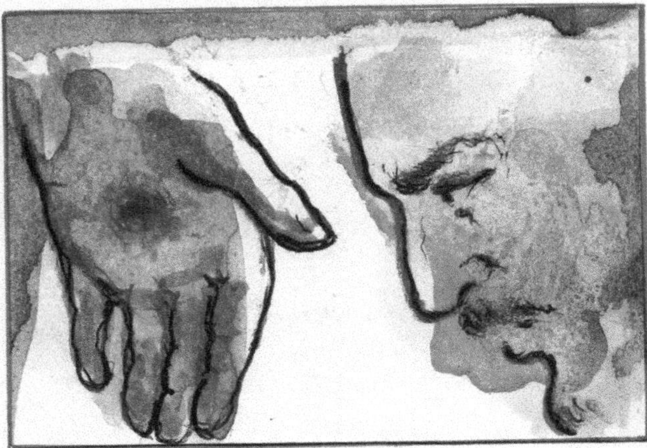

(28) THOMAS THEN SAID, "YOU ARE MY LORD AND
MY GOD!" (29) JESUS REPLIED, "YOU BELIEVE
BECAUSE YOU SEE ME, DON'T YOU? HAPPY ARE
THOSE WHO BELIEVE ALTHOUGH THEY DO NOT SEE"

CONCLUSION

(30) THERE WERE MANY OTHER SIGNS THAT
JESUS GAVE IN THE PRESENCE OF HIS DI-
SCIPLES, BUT THEY ARE NOT RECORDED IN

THIS BOOK (31) THESE ARE RECORDED SO THAT YOU MAY
BELIEVE THAT JESUS IS THE CHRIST, THE SON OF GOD;
BELIEVE AND YOU WILL HAVE LIFE THROUGH HIS NAME.

APPENDIX: THE APPEARANCE OF JESUS BY THE LAKE

21 (1) AFTER THIS JESUS REVEALED HIMSELF TO THE
DISCIPLES BY THE LAKE OF TIBERIAS. HE APPEARED
TO THEM IN THIS WAY. (2) SIMON PETER, THOMAS WHO
WAS CALLED THE TWIN, NATHANAEL OF CANA IN GALILEE,
THE SON OF ZEBEDEE AND TWO OTHER DISCIPLES WERE
TOGETHER; (3) AND SIMON PETER SAID TO THEM,
"I AM GOING FISHING." THEY REPLIED, "WE WILL
COME WITH YOU" AND THEY WENT OUT AND GOT
INTO THE BOAT. BUT THEY CAUGHT NOTHING
THAT NIGHT.

(4) WHEN DAY HAD ALREADY BROKEN, JESUS WAS
STANDING ON THE SHORE, BUT THE DISCIPLES
DID NOT KNOW THAT IT WAS JESUS. (5) JESUS
CALLED THEM, "CHILD-
REN, HAVE YOU ANY-
THING TO EAT?" THEY
ANSWERED "NOTHING."
(6) THEN HE SAID TO
THEM, "THROW THE NET
ON THE RIGHT SIDE
OF THE BOAT AND
YOU WILL FIND
SOME." WHEN THEY
HAD LOWERED THE
NET, THEY WERE NOT
ABLE TO PULL IT IN BE-
CAUSE OF THE GREAT
NUMBER OF FISH.

(7) THEN THE DISCI-
PLE JESUS LOVED
SAID TO PETER,
"IT'S THE LORD!"

AT THESE WORDS, "IT'S THE LORD," SIMON PETER PUT
ON HIS CLOTHES, FOR HE WAS STRIPPED FOR WORK,
AND JUMPED INTO THE WATER. THE (8) OTHER
DISCIPLES CAME IN THE BOAT DRAGGING
THE NET FULL OF FISH; THEY WERE NOT
FAR FROM LAND
ABOUT A HUNDRED
METERS.
(9) WHEN THEY LAND-
ED, THEY SAW A CHAR-
COAL FIRE WITH FISH
ON IT, AND SOME BREAD.

(10) JESUS SAID TO THEM,
"BRING SOME OF THE
FISH YOU HAVE JUST
CAUGHT."

(11) SO SIMON PETER
CLIMBED INTO THE
BOAT AND PULLED
THE NET TO SHORE.

IT WAS FULL OF
BIG FISH, ONE
HUNDRED AND
FIFTY THREE,
BUT, IN SPITE
OF THIS, THE NET
WAS NOT TORN. (12) JESUS SAID TO THEM,
"COME AND HAVE BREAKFAST", AND NOT
ONE OF THE DISCIPLES DARED ASK HIM,

"WHO ARE YOU?"

FOR THEY KNEW IT WAS THE LORD.

355
CCCLV

13 JESUS THEN CAME AND TOOK THE
BREAD AND GAVE IT TO THEM, AND HE DID
THE SAME WITH THE FISH.

14 THIS WAS THE THIRD TIME THAT JESUS
REVEALED HIMSELF TO THE DISCIPLES
AFTER RISING FROM THE DEAD. AFTER

Yes Lord, you Know that I love you

15 THEY HAD FINISHED BREAKFAST, JESUS SAID TO
SIMON PETER, "SIMON, SON OF JOHN, DO YOU LOVE ME
MORE THAN THESE?" HE ANSWERED, "YES LORD, YOU
KNOW THAT I LOVE YOU." AND JESUS SAID, "FEED MY
LAMBS." 16 A SECOND TIME JESUS ASKED HIM, "SIMON,
SON OF JOHN, DO YOU LOVE ME?" AND PETER ANSWERED,
"YES, LORD, YOU KNOW THAT I LOVE YOU." JESUS SAID TO
HIM, "LOOK AFTER MY SHEEP."
17 AND A THIRD TIME HE SAID TO HIM, "SIMON, SON OF
JOHN, DO YOU LOVE ME?" PETER WAS SADDENED BECAUSE
JESUS ASKED HIM A THIRD TIME, "DO YOU LOVE ME? AND
HE SAID, "LORD, YOU KNOW EVERYTHING; YOU
KNOW THAT I LOVE YOU." JESUS THEN SAID,

"FEED MY SHEEP

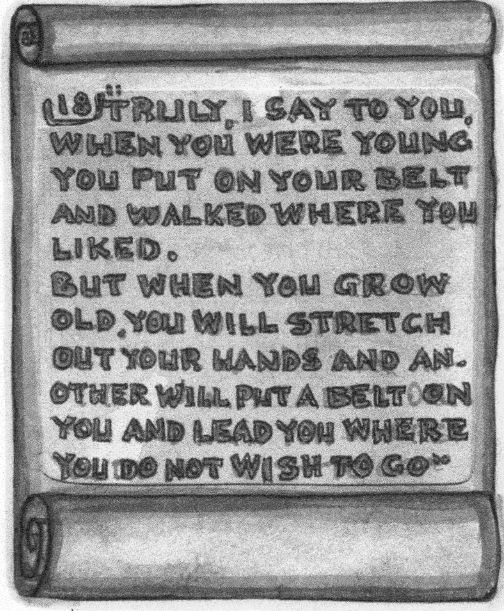

19 JESUS SAID THIS TO MAKE KNOWN THE
KIND OF DEATH BY WHICH PETER WAS TO
GLORIFY GOD. AND HE ADDED, "FOLLOW ME."

20 PETER LOOKED BACK AND SAW THAT THE
DISCIPLE JESUS LOVED WAS FOLLOWING AS
WELL, THE ONE WHO HAD RECLINED CLOSE TO
JESUS AT THE SUPPER AND HAD ASKED HIM,
"LORD, WHO IS TO BETRAY YOU?" 21 ON SEEING
HIM PETER ASKED JESUS, "LORD, WHAT
ABOUT HIM?" 22 JESUS ANSWERED, "IF YOU
WANT HIM TO REMAIN UNTIL I COME, DOES
THAT CONCERN YOU?" "FOLLOW ME."

23 BECAUSE OF THIS THE RUMOR SPREAD
AMONG THE BROTHERS THAT THIS DISCIPLE
WOULD NOT DIE. YET JESUS HAD NOT SAID TO
PETER, "HE WILL NOT DIE", BUT "SUPPOSE I
WANT HIM TO REMAIN UNTIL I COME."

HOMAGE TO NOLDE

24 IT IS THIS DISCIPLE WHO TESTIFIES
ABOUT THE THINGS HE HAD RECORDED IN
HERE AND WE KNOW THAT HIS TESTIMONY IS TRUE.

25 BUT JESUS DID MANY OTHER THINGS;
IF ALL WERE WRITTEN DOWN, THE WORLD
ITSELF WOULD NOT HOLD THE BOOKS
RECORDING THEM.

ACTS OF THE APOSTLES

DURING THE THREE YEARS OF PUBLIC LIFE, JESUS SET DOWN THE BASIS OF THE CHURCH: HE GATHERED HIS FIRST DISCIPLES AND ASSOCIATED THEM WITH HIS MISSION. HE PUT PETER IN CHARGE OF THE COMMUNITY AND MADE HIM THE GUARDIAN OF THE FAITH WITHIN THE NEW PEOPLE OF GOD. HE MADE OF THE TWELVE APOSTLES AND THE DISCIPLES A COMMUNITY OF WITNESSES AND PROMISED THEM THE GIFT OF THE SPIRIT WHO WOULD HELP THEM COME TO KNOW THE FULLNESS OF THE LIGHT WHICH HE CAME TO BRING INTO THE WORLD.

TWO GREAT GIANTS STAND OUT IN THE NEW ISRAEL WHICH IS THE CHURCH: PETER AND PAUL. PETER WILL DEVOTE HIMSELF IN PARTICULAR TO THE EVANGELIZATION OF THE JEWS, WHILE PAUL WILL BECOME THE APOSTLES TO THE GENTILES.

THE BOOK OF THE ACTS DOES NOT FOLLOW A RIGOROUS OUTLINE. ONE CAN, HOWEVER, PICK OUT SOME CLEAR-CUT DIVISIONS IN THE IN THE TEXT WHICH ALLOW US TO GLIMPSE LUKE'S PROJECT.

WITHOUT FOCUSING EXCLUSIVELY ON PETER AND PAUL, THE MAIN PART OF HIS WORK LUKE DEVOTED TO THEM. IN SPITE OF MANY EXCEPTIONS, PETER DOMINATES THE FIRST TWELVE CHAPTERS, WHILE IT IS PAUL'S TURN TO DOMINATE IN THE SECOND PART OF THE BOOK.
LUKE'S INTENTION IN THE ACTS IS TO HIGHLIGHT HOW THE MYSTERY OF CHRIST AND OF THE CHURCH FULFILLS THE OLD TESTAMENT.

ACTS OF THE APOSTLES

JESUS TAKEN UP TO HEAVEN

1
1 IN THE FIRST PART OF MY WORK, THEOPHILUS, I DID
WRITE OF ALL THAT JESUS DID AND TAUGHT FROM THE
BEGINNING 2 UNTIL THE DAY WHEN HE ASCENDED
TO HEAVEN. BUT FIRST HE HAD INSTRUCTED THE HOLY
SPIRIT THROUGH WHOM THE APOSTLES HE CHOSE. 3 AFTER
HIS PASSION, HE PRESENTED HIMSELF TO THEM, GIVING
MANY SIGNS THAT HE WAS ALIVE; OVER A PERIOD OF FORTY
DAYS HE APPEARED TO THEM AND TAUGHT THEM CONCERNING

THE KINGDOM OF GOD. 4 ONCE WHEN HE HAD BEEN EATING
WITH THEM, HE TOLD THEM, "DO NOT LEAVE JERUSALEM
BUT WAIT FOR THE FULFILLMENT OF THE FATHER'S PRO-
MISE ABOUT WHICH I HAVE SPOKEN TO YOU: 5 JOHN BAP-
TIZED WITH WATER, BUT YOU WILL BE BAPTIZED WITH
THE HOLY SPIRIT WITHIN A FEW DAYS."
6 WHEN THEY HAD COME TOGETHER, THEY ASKED HIM,
"IT IS NOW THAT YOU WILL RESTORE THE KINGDOM OF
ISRAEL?" 7 AND HE ANSWERED, "IT IS NOT FOR YOU
TO KNOW THE TIME OR
THE MOMENT WHICH
THE FATHER HAS FIXED
BY HIS OWN AUTHORITY.
8 BUT YOU WILL RECE-
IVE POWER WHEN THE
HOLY SPIRIT COMES
UPON YOU; AND YOU
WILL BE MY WITNESSES
IN JERUSALEM, THRO-
UGHOUT JUDEA AND
SAMARIA, EVEN TO THE
END OF THE EARTH."
9 AFTER JESUS SAID
THIS, HE WAS TAKEN UP
BEFORE THEIR EYES AND
A CLOUD HID HIM FROM
THEIR SIGHT. 10 WHILE
THEY WERE STILL LOOK-
ING UP TO HEAVEN WHE-
RE HE WENT, SUDDENLY,
TWO MEN DRESSED IN
WHITE STOOD BESIDE
THEM 11 AND SAID,
"MEN OF GALILEE, WHY
DO YOU STAND HERE LO-
OKING UP TO THE SKY?"

THIS JESUS WHO HAS BEEN TAKEN FROM YOU INTO
HEAVEN, WILL RETURN IN THE SAME WAY AS
YOU HAVE SEEN HIM GO THERE."

THE DISCIPLES AWAIT THE HOLY SPIRIT

12 THEN THEY RETURNED TO JERUSALEM FROM THE MO-
UNT CALLED OLIVES, WHICH IS A FIFTEEN-MINUTES WALK
AWAY. 13 ON ENTERING THE CITY THEY WENT TO THE
ROOM UPSTAIRS WHERE THEY WERE STAYING. PRESENT
THERE WERE PETER, JOHN, JAMES AND ANDREW; PHILIP
AND THOMAS, BARTHOLOMEW AND MATTHEW, JAMES,
SON OF ALPHEUS: SIMON THE ZEALOT AND JUDAS
SON OF JAMES. 14 ALL OF THESE TOGETHER GAVE
THEMSELVES TO CONSTANT PRAYER, WITH THEM
WERE SOME WOMEN AND ALSO MARY, THE MOTHER
OF JESUS, AND HIS BROTHERS.

– MATTHIAS ELECTED

15 IT WAS DURING THIS TIME THAT PETER STOOD UP
IN THE MIDST OF THE COMMUNITY - ABOUT ONE
HUNDRED AND TWENTY
IN ALL - 16 AND HE
SAID, "BROTHERS AND
SISTERS, IT WAS NE-
CESSARY THAT THE
SCRIPTURES REFER-
RING TO JUDAS BE FUL-
FILLED. THE HOLY SPIRIT
HAD SPOKEN THROUGH
DAVID ABOUT THE ONE
WHO WOULD LEAD THE
CROWD COMING TO AR-
REST JESUS. 17 HE WAS
ONE OF OUR NUMBER
AND HAD BEEN CALLED
TO SHARE OUR COMMON
MINISTRY. 18 WE KNOW
HE BOUGHT A FIELD
WITH THE REWARD OF
HIS SIN; YET HE THREW
HIMSELF HEAD-LONG TO
HIS DEATH, HIS BODY
BURST OPEN AND ALL
HIS BOWELS SPILLED
OUT. 19 THIS EVEN

BECAME KNOWN TO ALL THE PEOPLE LIVING IN JERU-
SALEM AND THEY NAMED THAT FIELD AKELDAMA IN
THEIR LANGUAGE, WHICH MEANS FIELD OF BLOOD. 20
IN THE BOOK OF PSALMS IT IS WRITTEN: LET HIS HOUSE
BECOME DESERTED AND MAY NO ONE LIVE IN IT. BUT IT
IS ALSO WRITTEN: MAY ANOTHER TAKE HIS OFFICE.
21 THEREFORE WE MUST CHOOSE SOMEONE FROM
AMONG THOSE WHO WERE WITH US DURING THE TIME
THAT THE LORD JESUS MOVED ABOUT WITH US, 22 BE-
GINNING WITH JOHN'S BAPTISM UNTIL THE DAY WHEN

JESUS WAS TAKEN AWAY FROM US. ONE HAS TO BECOME A
WITNESS TO HIS RESURRECTION. 23 THEY PROPOSED
TWO: JOSEPH, CALLED BARSABBAS, ALSO KNOWN AS JUSTUS,
AND MATTHIAS. 24 THEY PRAYED: "YOU KNOW, LORD, WHAT IS
THE HEARTS OF OURS. SHOW US, WHICH ONE YOU HAVE CHOSEN

25 TO REPLACE JUDAS IN THIS APOSTOLIC MINISTRY WHICH
HE DESERTED TO GO TO THE PLACE HE DESERVED." 26 THEN
THEY DREW LOTS BETWEEN THE TWO AND THE CHOICE FELL
ON MATTHIAS WHO WAS ADDED TO THE ELEVEN APOSTLES.

THE COMING OF THE HOLY SPIRIT

2 1 WHEN THE DAY OF PENTECOST CAME, THEY WERE
ALL TOGETHER IN ONE PLACE. 2 AND SUDDENLY
OUT OF THE SKY CAME A SOUND LIKE A STRONG
RUSHING WIND AND IT FILLED THE WHOLE HOUSE
WHERE THEY WERE SITTING. THERE APPEARED 3
TONGUES AS IF OF FIRE
WHICH PARTED AND CAME
TO REST UPON EACH ONE
OF THEM. 4 ALL WERE
FILLED WITH HOLY SPIRIT
AND BEGAN TO SPEAK
OTHER LANGUAGES, AS
THE SPIRIT ENABLED
THEM TO SPEAK. 5 STAY-
ING IN JERUSALEM WERE
RELIGIOUS JEWS FROM
EVERY NATION UNDER HE-
AVEN. 6 WHEN THEY
HEARD THIS SOUND, A LAR-
GE CROWD GATHERED, ALL EX-
CITED BECAUSE EACH HEARD
THEM SPEAKING IN HIS OWN
LANGUAGE. 7 BESIDE
THEMSELVES WITH AMA-
ZEMENT AND WONDER,
THEY SAID, "ARE NOT
ALL THESE WHO ARE
SPEAKING GALILEANS?
8 HOW IS IT THAT WE
HEAR THEM IN OUR OWN
NATIVE LANGUAGE? 9
HERE ARE PARTHIANS,
MEDES AND ELAMITES

AND RESIDENTS OF MESOPOTAMIA, JUDEA AND
CAPPADOCIA, PONTUS AND ASIA, 10 PHRYGIA,
PAMPHYLIA, EGYPT AND THE PARTS OF LYBIA BELONG-
ING TO CYRENE, AND VISITORS FROM ROME, 11
BOTH JEWS AND FOREIGNERS WHO ACCEPT JEWISH
BELIEF, CRETIANS AND ARABIANS; AND ALL OF US
HEAR THEM PROCLAIMING IN OUR OWN LANGUAGE
WHAT GOD, THE SAVIOR, DOES. 12 THEY WERE AMAZ-
ED AND GREATLY CONFUSED, AND THEY KEPT ASKING
ONE ANOTHER, "WHAT DOES THIS MEAN? 13 BUT
OTHERS LAUGHED AND SAID, "THESE PEOPLE ARE DRUNK."

PETER ADDRESSES THE CROWD

14 THEN PETER STOOD UP WITH THE ELEVEN AND, WITH A LO-
UD VOICE, ADDRESSED THEM, "FELLOW JEWS AND FOREIGNERS
IN JERUSALEM, LISTEN TO WHAT I HAVE TO SAY. 15 THESE

PEOPLE ARE NOT DRUNK AS YOU SUPPOSE, FOR IT IS ONLY
NINE O'CLOCK IN THE MORNING. 16 INDEED WHAT THE PRO-
PHET JOEL SPOKE ABOUT HAS HAPPENED: 17

IN THE LAST DAYS, GOD SAYS, I WILL POUR OUT MY SPIRIT ON
EVERY MORTAL. YOUR SONS AND DAUGHTERS THROUGH THE HO-
LY SPIRIT WILL SPEAK; YOUR YOUNG MEN WILL SEE VIS-
ION AND YOUR OLD MEN WILL HAVE DREAMS.

18 IN THOSE DAYS I WILL POUR OUT MY SPIRIT EVEN ON
MY SERVANTS, BOTH MEN AND WOMEN, AND THEY WILL BE
PROPHETS. 19 I WILL PERFORM MIRACLES IN THE SKY
ABOVE AND WONDERS ON THE EARTH BELOW. 20 THE
SUN WILL BE DARKENED AND THE MOON WILL TURN RED
AS BLOOD, BEFORE THE GREAT AND GLORIOUS DAY OF THE
LORD COMES. 21 THEN, WHOEVER CALLS UPON THE NAME
OF THE LORD WILL BE SAVED.

22 FELLOW ISRAELITES, LISTEN TO WHAT I AM GOING TO
TELL YOU ABOUT JESUS OF NAZARETH. GOD ACCREDITED
HIM AND THROUGH HIM DID POWERFUL DEEDS AND WONDERS
AND SIGNS IN YOUR MIDST, AS YOU WELL KNOW. 23 YOU

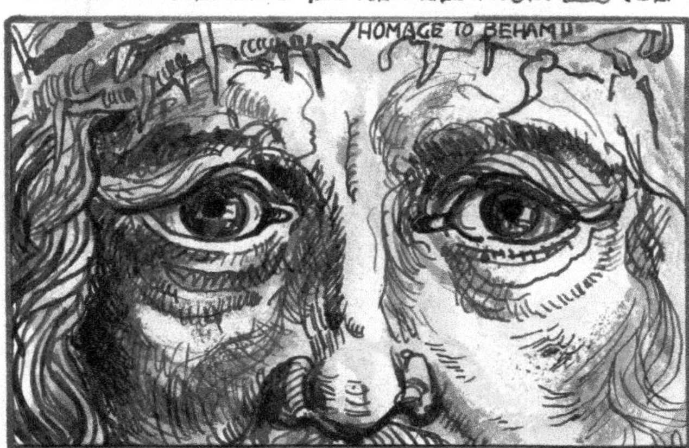

DELIVERED HIM TO SINNERS TO BE CRUCIFIED AND KILLED,
AND IN THIS WAY THE PURPOSE OF GOD FROM ALL TIMES
WAS FULFILLED. 24 BUT GOD RAISED HIM TO LIFE AND
RELEASED HIM FROM THE PAIN OF DEATH, BECAUSE IT WAS
IMPOSSIBLE FOR HIM TO BE HELD IN THE POWER OF DEATH.
25 DAVID SPOKE OF HIM WHEN HE SAID:

I SAW THE LORD BEFORE ME AT ALL TIMES; HE IS BY MY SIDE, THAT I
MAY NOT BE SHAKEN. 26 THEREFORE MY HEART WAS GLAD AND MY
TONGUE REJOICED; MY BODY TOO WILL LIVE IN HOPE. 27 BECAUSE
YOU WILL NOT FORSAKE ME IN THE ABODE OF THE DEAD, NOR ALLOW
YOUR HOLY ONE TO KNOW CORRUPTION. 28 YOU SHOW ME THE
PATHS OF LIFE, AND YOUR PRESENCE WILL FILL ME WITH JOY.

29 FRIENDS, THERE IS NO DOUBT THAT THE PATRIARCH DAVID
DIED AND WAS BURIED; HIS
TOMB IS WITH US TO THIS DAY.
30 BUT HE KNEW THAT GOD
HAD SWORN TO HIM THAT ONE
OF HIS DESCENDANTS WOULD
ONLY SIT UPON HIS THRONE
AND, 31 AS HE WAS A PRO-
PHET, HE FORESAW AND
SPOKE OF THE RESURREC-
TION OF THE MESSIAH. SO
HE SAID THAT HE WOULD
NOT BE LEFT IN THE RE-
GION OF THE DEAD, NOR
WOULD HIS BODY EXPE-
RIENCE CORRUPTION.
32 THE MESSIAH IS JESUS
AND WE ARE ALL WITNESS-
ES THAT GOD RAISED HIM TO
LIFE. 33 HE HAS BEEN
EXALTED AT GOD'S RIGHT
SIDE AND THE FATHER HAS
ENTRUSTED THE HOLY SPI-
RIT TO HIM; THIS SPIRIT
HE HAS JUST POURED ON

US AS YOU KNOW NOW YOU SEE AND HEAR. 34 DAVID DID
NOT ASCEND INTO HEAVEN, BUT HE HIMSELF SAID:

THE LORD SAID TO MY LORD; SIT AT MY RIGHT SIDE 35
UNTIL I MAKE YOUR ENEMIES AS STOOL FOR YOUR FEET. 36

LET ISRAEL THEN KNOW FOR SURE THAT GOD HAS MADE
LORD AND CHRIST THIS JESUS WHOM YOU CRUCIFIED."

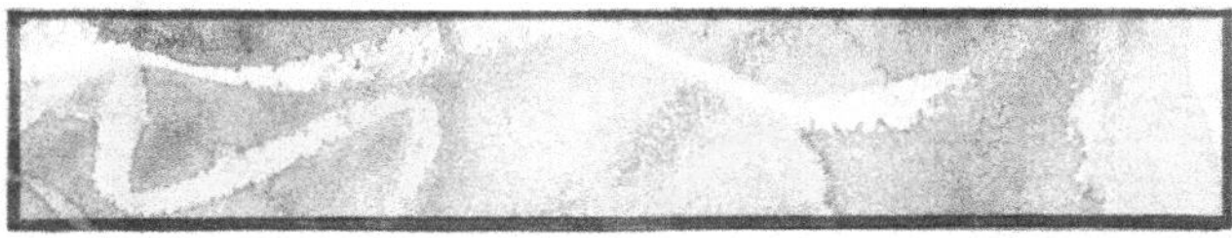

37 WHEN THEY HEARD THIS, THEY WERE DEEPLY TROUBLED, AND
ASKED PETER AND THE OTHER APOSTLES, "WHAT SHALL WE DO,
BROTHERS?" 38 PETER ANSWERED: "EACH OF YOU MUST RE-
PENT AND BE BAPTIZED IN THE NAME OF JESUS CHRIST, SO
THAT YOUR SINS MY BE FORGIVEN. THEN YOU WILL RECEIVE
THE GIFT OF THE HOLY SPIRIT. 39 FOR THE PROMISE OF GOD
WAS MADE TO YOU AND YOUR CHILDREN, AND TO ALL THE OTHER
NATIONS WHOM OUR GOD CALLS TO HIMSELF." 40 WITH MANY
OTHER WORDS PETER GAVE THE MESSAGE AND AP-
PEALED TO THEM SAYING, "SAVE YOURSELVES FROM

THIS CROOKED GENERATION." 41 SO THOSE WHO ACCEPT-
ED THIS WORD WERE BAPTIZED; SOME THREE THOUSAND
WERE ADDED TO THEIR NUMBER THAT DAY.

THE FIRST COMMUNITY

42 THEY WERE FAITHFUL TO THE TEACHING OF THE APOSTLES,
LIFE SHARING, BREAKING OF BREAD AND PRAYERS. 43 A
HOLY FEAR CAME, FOR MANY WONDERS AND MIRACLES WE-
RE DONE BY THE APOSTLES. 44 THE BELIEVERS LIVED TOGE-
THER AND SHARED ALL THEIR BELONGINGS. 45 THEY WOULD
SELL THEIR PROPERTY AND GOODS AND DISTRIBUTE THE
PROCEEDS TO OTHERS ACCORDING TO THEIR NEED. 46 EACH
DAY THEY MET IN THE TEMPLE AREA, BROKE BREAD IN THEIR
HOMES AND SHARING FOOD WITH JOY AND SIMPLICITY OF
HEART; 47 THEY PRAISED GOD AND WON THE PEOPLE FAVOR.
AND EVERY DAY THE LORD ADDED TO THEIR NUMBER
THOSE WHO WERE BEING SAVED.

PETER AND JOHN CURE A LAME MAN

3 1 ONCE WHEN PETER AND JOHN WERE GOING UP
TO THE TEMPLE AT THREE IN THE AFTERNOON, THE HOUR
FOR PRAYERS, 2 A MAN CRIPPLED FROM BIRTH WAS
BEING CARRIED IN. EVERY DAY THEY WOULD BRING HIM AND

PUT HIM AT THE TEMPLE
GATE CALLED "BEAUTIFUL";
THERE HE BEGGED FROM
THOSE WHO ENTERED THE
TEMPLE. 3 WHEN HE SAW
PETER AND JOHN GOING IN-
TO THE TEMPLE, HE ASKED
FOR ALMS. 4 THEY BOTH
LOOKED AT HIM AND PETER
SAID, "LOOK AT US." 5 SO
HE LOOKED AT THEM, EX-
PECTING TO RECEIVE
SOMETHING FROM THEM.
6 BUT PETER SAID, "I
HAVE NEITHER SILVER
NOR GOLD, BUT WHAT I
HAVE I GIVE YOU: IN THE
NAME OF JESUS CHRIST
THE NAZAREAN, WALK!"
7 THEN HE TOOK THE
BEGGAR BY HIS RIGHT
HAND AND HELPED HIM
UP. AT ONCE HIS FEET
AND ANKLES BECAME
FIRM, 8 AND JUMPING
UP HE STOOD ON HIS FEET AND BEGAN TO WALK. AND HE
WENT WITH THEM INTO THE TEMPLE WALKING AND LEAPING
AND PRAISING GOD.

9 ALL THE PEOPLE SAW HIM WALKING AND PRAISING
GOD; 10 THEY RECOGNIZED HIM AS THE ONE WHO USED TO
SIT BEGGING AT THE BEAUTIFUL GATE OF THE TEMPLE, AND
THEY WERE ASTONISHED AND AMAZED AT WHAT HAD HAPPENED
TO HIM. 11 WHILE HE CLUNG TO PETER AND JOHN, ALL THE PE-
OPLE ASTONISHED, CAME RUNNING TO THEM IN SOLO-
MON'S PORCH, AS IT WAS CALLED. 12 WHEN PETER SAW
THE PEOPLE, HE SAID TO THEM, "FELLOW ISRAELITES, WHY
ARE YOU AMAZED AT THIS? WHY DO YOU STARE AT US

AS IF IT WAS BY SOME PO-
WER OR HOLINESS OF OUR
OWN THAT WE MADE THIS
MAN WALK? 13 THE GOD OF
ABRAHAM, OF ISAAC AND OF
JACOB, THE GOD OF OUR
ANCESTORS HAS GLORIFI-
ED HIS SERVANT JESUS
WHOM YOU HANDED OVER
TO DEATH AND DENIED BE-
FORE PILATE, WHEN EVEN
PILATE HAD DECIDED TO
RELEASE HIM. 14 YOU
REJECTED THE HOLY AND
JUST ONE, AND YOU INSIS
TED THAT A MURDERER
BE RELEASED TO YOU. 15
YOU KILLED THE LORD OF
LIFE, BUT GOD RAISED HIM
FROM THE DEAD AND WE
ARE WITNESSES TO THIS.
16 IT IS HIS NAME, AND
FAITH IN HIS NAME, AND
THAT HAS HEALED THIS
MAN WHOM YOU SEE AND
RECOGNIZE. THE FAITH
WHICH COMES THROUGH JESUS HAS GIVEN HIM WHOLE-
NESS IN THE PRESENCE OF ALL OF YOU.
17 YET I KNOW THAT YOU ACTED OUT OF IGNORANCE,
AS DID YOUR LEADERS. 18 GOD HAS FULFILLED IN THIS
WAY WHAT WE HAD FORETOLD THROUGH ALL THE PRO-
PHETS, THAT HIS MESSIAH WOULD SUFFER. 19 REPENT,
THEN, AND TURN TO GOD SO THAT YOUR SINS MAY BE WIPED
OUT 20 AND THE TIME OF REFRESHMENT MAY COME BY THE
MERCY OF GOD, WHEN HE SENDS THE MESSIAH APPOINTED FOR
YOU, JESUS. 21 FOR HE MUST REMAIN IN HEAVEN UNTIL
THE TIME OF THE UNIVERSAL RESTORATION WHICH GOD

SPOKE LONG AGO THROUGH HIS HOLY PROPHETS. 22 WHEN
MOSES SAID: THE LORD GOD WILL RAISE UP FOR YOU A PRO-
PHET LIKE ME FROM AMONG YOUR OWN PEOPLE; YOU SHALL LISTEN
TO HIM IN ALL THAT HE SAYS TO YOU. 23 WHOEVER DOES NOT
LISTEN TO THAT PROPHET IS TO BE CUT OFF FROM AMONG HIS
PEOPLE. 24 IN FACT, ALL THE PROPHETS WHO HAVE SPOKEN
FROM SAMUEL ONWARD, HAVE ANNOUNCED THE EVENTS OF
THESE DAYS. 25 YOU ARE THE CHILDREN OF THE PROPHETS
AND HEIRS OF THE COVENANT WHICH GOD GAVE TO YOUR AN-
CESTORS WHEN HE SAID TO ABRAHAM: ALL THE NATIONS
WILL BE BLESSED THROUGH YOUR DESCENDANT.

357
CCCLVII
DM 09 ©

(26) IT IS TO YOU FIRST THAT GOD SENDS HIS SER-
VANT; HE RAISED HIM TO LIFE TO BLESS YOU BY
TURNING EACH OF YOU FROM YOUR WICKED WAYS."

PETER AND JOHN ARE ARRESTED

4 (1) WHILE PETER AND JOHN WERE STILL SPEAKING
TO THE PEOPLE, THE PRIESTS, THE CAPTAIN OF THE
TEMPLE GUARD AND THE SADDUCEES CAME UP TO
THEM. (2) THEY WERE GREATLY DISTURBED THE APOS-
TLES WERE TEACHING THE PEOPLE AND PROCLAIMING
THAT RESURRECTION FROM THE DEAD HAD BEEN PROVED
IN THE CASE OF JESUS. (3) THEY ARRESTED THEM IN THE
EVENING AND IN CUSTODY UNTIL THE FOLLOWING DAY. (4) BUT
DESPITE THIS, MANY OF THOSE WHO HEARD THE MESSAGE BE-
LIEVED AND THEIR NUMBER INCREASED TO ABOUT FIVE THOUSAND.

(5) THE NEXT DAY, THE JEWISH LEADERS, ELDERS, TEACHERS
OF THE LAW ASSEMBLED IN JERUSALEM. (6) ANNAS, THE HIGH
PRIEST, CAIAPHAS, JOHN, ALEXANDER AND ALL WHO WERE OF
THE HIGH PRIESTLY CLASS WERE THERE. (7) THEY BROUGHT
PETER AND JOHN BEFORE THEM AND BEGAN TO QUESTION
THEM, "HOW DID YOU DO THIS? WHOSE NAME DID YOU USE?"
(8) PETER, FILLED WITH THE HOLY SPIRIT, SPOKE UP, "LEAD-
ERS OF THE PEOPLE! ELDERS! (9) IT IS A FACT THAT WE ARE

BEING EXAMINED TODAY FOR
A GOOD DEED DONE TO A CRIP-
PLE. HOW WAS HE HEALED?
(10) YOU AND ALL THE PEOPLE
OF ISRAEL MUST KNOW THAT
THIS MAN STANDS BEFORE
YOU CURED THROUGH THE
NAME OF JESUS CHRIST THE
NAZAREAN. YOU HAD HIM
CRUCIFIED, BUT GOD RAISED
HIM FROM THE DEAD. (11)
JESUS IS THE "STONE RE-
JECTED BY THE BUILDERS
WHICH HAS BECOME THE
CORNERSTONE". (12) THERE IS
NO SALVATION IN ANYONE
ELSE, FOR THERE IS NO OTHER
NAME GIVEN TO HUMANKIND
ALL OVER THE WORLD BY WHICH
WE MAY BE SAVED."
(13) THEY WERE ASTONISHED
AT THE BOLDNESS OF PETER
AND JOHN, CONSIDERING
THAT THEY WERE UNEDUCA-
TED AND UNTRAINED MEN.
THEY ALSO RECOGNIZED THAT
THEY HAD BEEN WITH JESUS, (14) BUT, AS THE MAN WHO HAD
BEEN CURED STOOD BESIDE THEM, THEY COULD MAKE NO REPLY.
(15) SO THEY ORDERED THEM TO LEAVE THE COUNCIL ROOM
WHILE THEY CONSULTED WITH ONE ANOTHER. THEY ASKED
(16) "WHAT SHALL WE DO WITH THESE MEN? EVERYONE WHO
LIVES IN JERUSALEM KNOWS THAT A MIRACULOUS SIGN
HAS BEEN GIVEN THROUGH THEM, AND WE CANNOT DENY IT.
(17) BUT TO STOP THIS THING FROM SPREADING AMONG THE
PEOPLE, LET US WARN THEM NEVER AGAIN TO SPEAK TO
ANYONE IN THE NAME OF JESUS. (18) SO THEY
CALLED THEM BACK AND CHARGED THEM NOT TO SPEAK
OR TEACH AT ALL IN THE NAME OF JESUS. (19) BUT PETER
AND JOHN SAID, "JUDGE FOR YOURSELVES WHETHER IT IS
RIGHT IN GOD'S EYES FOR US TO OBEY YOU RATHER THAN
GOD. (20) WE CANNOT STOP SPEAKING ABOUT WHAT WE
HAVE SEEN AND HEARD." (21) THEN THE COUNCIL THREAT-
ENED THEM ONCE MORE AND LET THEM GO. THEY COULD
FIND NO WAY OF PUNISHING THEM BECAUSE OF THE PEOPLE
WHO GLORIFIED GOD FOR WHAT HAD HAPPENED, (22) FOR
THE MAN WHO HAD BEEN MIRACULOUSLY HEALED
WAS OVER FORTY YEARS OLD.

THE PRAYER OF THE COMMUNITY

(23) AS SOON AS PETER AND JOHN WERE SET FREE,
THEY WENT TO THEIR
FRIENDS AND REPORTED
WHAT THE CHIEF PRIESTS AND
ELDERS HAD SAID TO THEM.
(24) WHEN THEY HEARD IT,
THEY RAISED THEIR VOICES
AS ONE AND CALLED UPON
GOD. "SOVEREIGN LORD,
MAKER OF HEAVEN AND
EARTH, OF THE SEA AND
EVERYTHING IN THEM,
(25) YOU HAVE PUT THESE
WORDS IN THE MOUTH OF
DAVID, OUR FATHER AND
YOUR SERVANT, THROUGH
THE HOLY SPIRIT: WHY
DID THE PAGAN NATIONS
RAGE AND THE PEOPLE
CONSPIRE IN FOLLY?
(26)
THE KINGS OF THE EARTH
WERE ALIGNED AND
THE PRINCES GATHE-
RED TOGETHER AG-
AINST THE LORD AND
AGAINST HIS MESSIAH.

(27) FOR INDEED IN THIS VERY CITY
HEROD WITH PONTIUS PILATE, AND
THE PAGANS TOGETHER WITH THE
PEOPLE OF ISRAEL CONSPIRED AGAINST
YOUR HOLY SERVANT JESUS, WHOM
YOU ANOINTED.
(28) THUS, INDEED, THEY BROUGHT
ABOUT WHATEVER YOUR POWERFUL
WILL HAD DECIDED WOULD HAPPEN.
(29) BUT NOW, LORD, SEE THEIR THREATS
AGAINST US AND ENABLE SERVANTS
TO SPEAK YOUR WORD WITH ALL
BOLDNESS. (30) STRETCH OUT YOUR
HAND TO HEAL AND WORK SIGN FOR THE
NAME OF JESUS YOUR HOLY SERVANT.
(31) WHEN THEY HAD PRAYED, THE PLACE
WHERE THEY WERE GATHERED TOGETHER
SHOOK, AND THEY WERE ALL FILLED WITH HOLY
SPIRIT AND BEGAN TO SPEAK THE WORD
OF GOD BOLDLY.

AN ATTEMPT TO SHARE EVERYTHING

(32) THE WHOLE COMMUNITY OF BELIEVERS WERE ONE
IN HEART AND MIND. NO ONE CONSIDERED AS HIS OWN WHAT
OWNED, BUT RATHER THEY SHARED ALL THINGS IN COMMON.

33 WITH GREAT POWER, THE APOSTLES BORE WIT-
NESS TO THE RESURRECTION OF THE LORD JESUS AS THEY
WERE LIVING IN A TIME OF GRACE. 34 THERE WAS NO NE-
EDY PERSON AMONG THEM, FOR THOSE WHO OWNED LAND OR
HOUSES, SOLD THEM AND BROUGHT THE PROCEEDS OF THE
SALE. 35 AND THEY LAID IT AT THE FEET OF THE APOSTLES
WHO DISTRIBUTED IT ACCORDING TO EACH ONE'S NEED.
36 THIS IS WHAT A CERTAIN JOSEPH DID. HE WAS A
LEVITE FROM CYPRUS, WHOM THE APOSTLES CALLED
BARNABAS, MEANING: "THE ENCOURAGING ONE." 37
HE SOLD A FIELD WHICH HE OWNED AND HANDED
THE MONEY TO THE APOSTLES.

THE FRAUD OF ANANIAS AND SAPPHIRA

5 1 ANOTHER MAN NAMED ANANIAS, IN AGREEMENT
WITH HIS WIFE SAPPHIRA ALSO SOLD A PIECE OF
LAND, 2 BUT HE PUT ASIDE SOME OF THE PRO-
CEEDS FOR HIMSELF, AND THE REST HE TURNED OVER
TO THE APOSTLES. 3 PETER SAID TO HIM, "ANANIAS,
HOW IS IT THAT YOU LET SATAN FILL YOUR HEART AND
DO YOU INTEND TO DECEIVE THE HOLY SPIRIT BY KEEPING
SOME OF THE PROCEEDS OF YOUR LAND FOR YOURSELF? 4
WHO OBLIGED YOU TO SELL IT? AND AFTER IT WAS SOLD,
COULD YOU NOT HAVE KEPT ALL THE MONEY? HOW COULD
YOU THINK OF SUCH A THING? HOW HAVE YOU DECIDED

TO DECEIVE NOT MEN BUT
GOD?" 5 UPON HEARING
THESE WORDS, ANANIAS
FELL DOWN AND DIED.
GREAT FEAR CAME ON ALL
WHO HEARD OF IT; 6
THE YOUNG MEN STOOD UP,
WRAPPED HIS BODY AND CAR-
RIED IT OUT FOR BURIAL. 7
ABOUT THREE HOURS LATER
ANANIAS' WIFE CAME BUT
SHE WAS NOT AWARE OF
WHAT HAD HAPPENED. 8
PETER CHALLENGED HER,
"TELL ME WHETHER YOU
SOLD THAT PIECE OF LAND
FOR THIS PRICE!" 9 PETER
REPLIED, "HOW COULD YOU
TWO AGREE TO PUT THE
HOLY SPIRIT TO THE TEST?
THOSE WHO BURIED YOUR HUS-
BAND ARE AT THE DOOR AND
THEY WILL CARRY YOU OUT AS
WELL." 10 WITH THAT, SHE
FELL DEAD AT HIS FEET.
THE YOUNG MEN CAME IN,
FOUND HER DEAD AND CARRIED HER OUT FOR BURIAL BESIDE
HER HUSBAND. 11 AND GREAT FEAR CAME UPON THE WHOLE
CHURCH AND UPON ALL WHO HEARD OF IT.
12 MANY MIRACULOUS SIGNS AND WONDERS WERE
DONE AMONG THE PEOPLE THROUGH THE HANDS OF THE APOS-
TLES. THE BELIEVERS, OF ONE ACCORD, USED TO MEET IN
SOLOMON'S PORCH. 13 NONE OF THE OTHERS DARED
TO JOIN THEM, BUT THE PEOPLE HELD THEM IN HIGH ES-
TEEM. 14 SO AN EVER INCREASING NUMBER OF MEN AND
WOMEN BELIEVED IN THE LORD.

15 THE PEOPLE CARRIED THE SICK INTO THE STREETS
AND LAID THEM ON COTS AND ON MATS, SO THAT WHEN
PETER PASSED BY, AT LEAST HIS SHADOW MIGHT
FALL ON SOME OF THEM. 16 THE PEOPLE GATHERED
FROM THE TOWNS AROUND JERUSALEM, BRINGING
THEIR SICK AND THOSE WHO WERE TROUBLED BY
UNCLEAN SPIRITS, AND ALL OF THEM WERE HEALED.

THE APOSTLES ARRESTED AGAIN

17 THE HIGH PRIEST AND ALL HIS SUPPORTERS, THAT
IS THE PARTY OF THE SADDUCEES, BECAME VERY JE-
ALOUS OF THE APOSTLES; 18 SO THEY ARRESTED
THEM AND HAD THEM

THROWN INTO THE PU-
BLIC JAIL. 19 BUT AN
ANGEL OF THE LORD OP-
ENED THE DOOR OF THE
PRISON DURING THE
NIGHT, BROUGHT THEM
OUT, AND SAID TO THEM,
20 "GO AND STAND
IN THE TEMPLE COURT
AND TELL THE PEOPLE
THE FULL MESSAGE OF
THIS NEW LIFE." 21
ACCORDINGLY THEY
ENTERED THE TEMPLE
AT DAWN AND RESUMED
THEIR TEACHING.
WHEN THE HIGH PRIEST
AND HIS SUPPORTERS
ARRIVED, THEY CALLED
TOGETHER THE SANHE-
DRIN, THE FULL COUNCIL
OF THE ELDERS OF
ISRAEL. THEY SENT
WORD TO THE JAIL
TO HAVE THE PRISO-
NERS BROUGHT IN. 22
BUT WHEN THE TEMPLE
GUARDS ARRIVED AT THE JAIL, THEY DID NOT FIND
THEM INSIDE, SO THEY RETURNED WITH THE NEWS,
23 "WE FOUND THE PRISON SECURELY LOCKED
AND THE PRISON GUARDS AT THEIR POST OUTSIDE
THE GATE, BUT WHEN WE OPENED THE GATE,
WE FOUND NO ONE INSIDE."
24 UPON HEARING THESE WORDS, THE CAPTAIN OF
THE TEMPLE GUARDS AND THE HIGH PRIESTS WERE
BAFFLED, WONDERING WHERE ALL OF THIS WOULD END.

25 JUST THEN SOMEONE ARRIVED SAYING, "LOOK, THOSE MEN
YOU PUT IN PRISON ARE STANDING AND TEACHING IN THE
TEMPLE." 26 THE CAPTAIN WENT OFF WITH THE GU-
ARDS AND BROUGHT THEM BACK, BUT WITHOUT ANY FORCE,
FOR FEAR OF BEING STONED BY THE PEOPLE. 27 SO THEY
BROUGHT THEM IN AND MADE THEM STAND BEFORE THE
COUNCIL AND THE HIGH PRIEST QUESTIONED THEM,

28 "WE GAVE YOU STRICT ORDERS NOT TO PREACH SUCH
A SAVIOR; BUT YOU HAVE FILLED JERUSALEM WITH YOUR
TEACHING AND YOU INTEND CHARGING US WITH THIS MAN'S
KILLING." 29 PETER AND THE APOSTLES REPLIED, "BETTER
FOR US TO OBEY GOD THAN MEN! 30 THE GOD OF OUR AN-
CESTORS RAISED JESUS WHOM YOU KILLED BY HANGING
HIM ON A WOODEN POST. 31 GOD SET HIM AT HIS RIGHT
HAND AS LEADER AND SAVIOR, TO GRANT REPENTANCE AND
FORGIVENESS OF SINS IN ISRAEL. 32 WE ARE WITNESSES
TO ALL THESE THINGS AND THE HOLY SPIRIT WHOM GOD HAS
GIVEN TO THOSE WHO OBEY HIM."
33 WHEN THE COUNCIL HEARD THIS, THEY BECAME VERY
ANGRY AND WANTED TO KILL THEM. 34 BUT ONE OF THEM,
A PHARISEE NAMED GAMALIEL, A TEACHER OF THE LAW
HIGHLY RESPECTED BY
THE PEOPLE, STOOD UP IN
THE SANHEDRIN. HE OR-
DERED THE MEN TO BE
TAKEN OUTSIDE FOR A FEW
MINUTES 35 AND THEN
HE SPOKE TO THE ASSE-
MBLY, "FELLOW ISRA-
ELITES, CONSIDER
WELL WHAT YOU INTEND
TO DO TO THESE MEN. 36
FOR SOME TIME AGO
THEADUS CAME FORWARD
CLAIMING TO BE SOME-
BODY, AND ABOUT FOUR
HUNDRED MEN JOINED
HIM. BUT HE WAS KILLED
AND ALL HIS FOLLOWERS
WERE DISPERSED OR DIS-
APPEARED. 37 AFTER
HIM, JUDAS THE GA-
LILEAN APPEARED AT
THE TIME OF THE CENSUS
AND PERSUADED MANY
PEOPLE TO FOLLOW HIM.
BUT HE TOO PERISHED
AND HIS WHOLE FOL-
LOWING WAS SCATTERED.
38 SO, IN THIS PRESENT CASE, I ADVISE YOU TO HAVE
NOTHING TO DO WITH THESE MEN. LEAVE THEM ALONE.
IF THEIR PROJECT OR ACTIVITY IS OF HUMAN ORIGIN, IT
WILL DESTROY ITSELF. 39 IF, ON THE OTHER HAND, IT IS
FROM GOD, YOU WILL NOT BE ABLE TO DESTROY IT AND
YOU MAY INDEED FIND YOURSELVES FIGHTING AGAINST
GOD."

THE COUNCIL LET THEMSELVES BE PERSUADED. 40
THEY CALLED IN THE APOSTLES AND HAD THEM

WHIPPED, AND ORDERED THEM NOT TO SPEAK
AGAIN OF JESUS SAVIOR. THEN THEY SET THEM
FREE. 41 THE APOSTLES WENT OUT FROM THE
COUNCIL REJOICING THAT THEY WERE CONSIDERED
WORTHY TO SUFFER DISGRACE FOR THE SAKE OF THE
NAME. 42 DAY AFTER DAY, BOTH IN THE TEMPLE AND
IN PEOPLE'S HOMES, THEY CONTINUED TO TEACH AND
TO PROCLAIM THAT JESUS WAS THE MESSIAH.

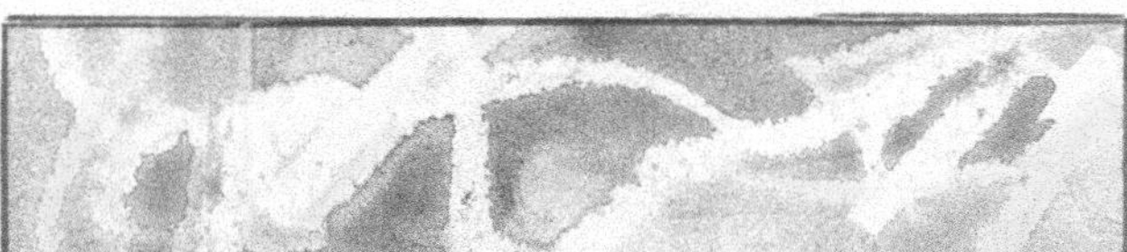

THE CHOOSING OF THE SEVEN

6 1 IN THOSE DAYS, AS THE NUMBER OF DISCIPLES
GREW, THE SO-CALLED HELLENISTS COMPLAINED
AGAINST THE SO-CALLED HEBREWS, BECAUSE
THEIR WIDOWS WERE BEING NEGLECTED IN THE
DAILY DISTRIBUTION. 2 SO THE TWELVE SUMMONED
THE DISCIPLES TOGETHER AND SAID, "IT IS NOT RIGHT THAT
WE SHOULD NEGLECT THE WORD OF GOD TO SERVE AT TABLES.
3 SO, BROTHERS, CHOOSE FROM AMONG YOURSELVES SE-
VEN RESPECTED MEN FULL OF SPIRIT AND WISDOM, THAT
WE MAY APPOINT THEM TO THIS TASK. 4 AS FOR US, WE
SHALL GIVE OURSELVES TO PRAYER AND TO THE MINISTRY

OF THE WORD." 5 THE WHOLE COMMUNITY AGREED AND
CHOSE STEPHEN, A MAN FULL OF FAITH AND HOLY SPIRIT;
PHILIP, PROCHORUS, NICANOR, TIMON, PARMENUS AND
NICOLAUS OF ANTIOCH WHO WAS A PROSELYTE. 6 THEY
PRESENTED THESE MEN TO THE APOSTLES WHO FIRST PRAY-
ED OVER THEM AND THEN LAID HANDS UPON THEM.
7 THE WORD OF GOD CONTINUED TO SPREAD; THE NUMBER OF
THE DISCIPLES IN JERUSALEM INCREASED GREATLY AND
EVEN MANY PRIESTS ACCEPTED THE FAITH.

THE STORY OF STEPHEN

8 STEPHEN, FULL OF GRACE AND POWER, DID GREAT WONDERS
AND MIRACULOUS SIGNS AMONG THE PEOPLE. 9 SOME PERSONS
THEN CAME FORWARD, WHO
BELONGED TO THE SYNAGO-
GUE OF FREEDMEN FROM
CYRENE, ALEXANDRIA, CI-
LICIA AND ASIA. 10 THEY
ARGUED WITH STEPHEN BUT
THEY COULD NOT MATCH
THE WISDOM AND THE SPI-
RIT WITH WHICH HE SPOKE.
11 AS THEY WERE UNABLE
TO FACE THE TRUTH, THEY
BRIBED SOME MEN TO
SAY, "WE HEARD HIM
SPEAK AGAINST MOSES
AND AGAINST GOD." 12
THEY STIRRED UP THE
PEOPLE, THE ELDERS AND
THE TEACHERS OF THE LAW;
THEY TOOK HIM BY SURPRI-
SE, SEIZED HIM AND
BROUGHT HIM BEFORE
THE COUNCIL. 13 THEN
THEY PRODUCED FALSE
WITNESSES WHO SAID,
"THIS MAN NEVER STOPS
SPEAKING AGAINST OUR
HOLY PLACE AND THE LAW. 14 WE HEARD HIM SAY THAT
JESUS THE NAZAREAN WILL DESTROY OUR HOLY PLACE
AND CHANGE THE CUSTOMS WHICH MOSES GAVE TO US."
15 ALL IN THE COUNCIL FIXED THEIR EYES ON HIM, AND HIS
FACE APPEARED TO THEM LIKE THE FACE OF AN ANGEL.

STEPHEN ©
CCCLVIII 358
DM 09

BROTHERS AND FATHERS

7 1 SO THE HIGH PRIEST ASKED HIM: "IS THIS TRUE?"
HE ANSWERED, "BROTHERS AND FATHERS, LISTEN TO
ME. 2 THE GOD OF GLORY APPEARED TO OUR FATHER
ABRAHAM IN MESOPOTAMIA, BEFORE HE WENT TO LIVE
IN HARAM. AND HE SAID TO HIM: 3 'LEAVE YOUR LAND
AND YOUR RELATIVES AND GO TO THE LAND WHICH I
WILL SHOW YOU.' 4 SO HE LEFT THE LAND OF THE
CHALDEANS AND SETTLED IN HARAN. AFTER THE
DEATH OF HIS FATHER, GOD MADE HIM MOVE TO THIS
IN WHICH LAND YOU NOW DWELL. 5 AND THERE HE DID
NOT GIVE HIM ANYTHING THAT WAS HIS OWN, NOT EVEN
THE SMALLEST PORTION OF LAND TO PUT HIS FOOT ON,

BUT PROMISED TO GIVE IT TO HIM IN POSSESSION AND TO
HIS DESCENDANTS, THOUGH HE HAD NO CHILD. 6 SO GOD
SPOKE: 'YOUR DESCENDANTS SHALL LIVE IN A STRANGE
LAND, THEY SHALL BE ENSLAVED AND MALTREATED FOR
FOUR HUNDRED YEARS. 7 SO I SHALL CALL THE NATION
WHICH THEY SERVE AS SLAVES TO RENDER THE ACCOUNT
FOR IT. THEY WILL COME AND WORSHIP ME HERE.' 8 WITH HIM
HE MADE THE COVENANT OF CIRCUMCISION. WHEN ISAAC WAS
BORN, ABRAHAM CIRCUMCISED HIM ON THE EIGHT DAY, ISAAC
DID THE SAME TO JACOB, AND JACOB TO THE TWELVE PATRIARCHS.
9 THE PATRIARCHS ENVIED JOSEPH SO THEY SOLD HIM TO EGYPT.

BUT GOD WAS WITH HIM. 10
HE RESCUED HIM FROM ALL HIS
AFFLICTIONS, GRANTED HIM
WISDOM AND MADE HIM PLE-
ASE PHARAOH KING OF EGYPT
AND HIS HOUSEHOLD. 11 THEN
THERE WAS FAMINE IN ALL THE
LAND OF EGYPT AND CANAAN;
IT WAS A GREAT MISERY AND
OUR ANCESTORS HAD NOTHING
TO EAT. 12 UPON LEARNING
THAT THERE WAS WHEAT IN
EGYPT, JACOB SENT OUR FA-
THERS THERE ON THEIR FIRST
VISIT. 13 ON THE SECOND
VISIT, JOSEPH MADE HIMSELF
KNOWN TO HIS BROTHERS,
AND PHARAOH CAME TO KNOW
THE FAMILY OF JOSEPH.
14 JOSEPH COMMANDED
THAT HIS FATHER JACOB BE
BROUGHT TO HIM WITH THE
WHOLE OF HIS FAMILY OF SE-
VENTY-FIVE PERSONS. 15
JACOB THEN WENT DOWN TO
EGYPT WHERE HE AND OUR ANCESTORS DIED. 16 THEY
WERE TRANSFERRED TO SHECHEM AND LAID IN THE TOMB THAT
ABRAHAM HAD BOUGHT FOR A SUM OF SILVER FROM THE
SONS OF HAMOR AT SHECHEM. 17 AS THE TIME OF PROMISE
DREW NEAR, WHICH GOD HAD MADE TO ABRAHAM, THE PEOPLE
INCREASED AND MULTIPLIED IN EGYPT 18 UNTIL CAME
ANOTHER KING WHO DID NOT KNOW JOSEPH.

19 DEALING CUNNINGLY WITH OUR RACE, HE FORCED OUR
ANCESTORS TO ABANDON THEIR NEWBORN INFANTS AND LET
THEM DIE. 20 AT THAT TIME MOSES WAS BORN AND GOD LOOK-
ED KINDLY ON HIM. FOR THREE MONTHS HE WAS NURSED IN
THE HOME OF HIS FATHER; 21 WHEN THEY ABANDONED HIM,
PHARAOH'S DAUGHTER TOOK HIM AND RAISED HIM AS HER
OWN SON. 22 SO MOSES WAS EDUCATED IN ALL THE WISDOM
OF THE EGYPTIANS. HE WAS MIGHTY IN WORD AND DEED.
23 AND WHEN HE WAS FORTY YEARS OLD, HE WANTED TO
VISIT HIS OWN PEOPLE,
THE ISRAELITES. WHEN
24 HE SAW ONE OF THEM
BEING WRONGED, HE DE-
FENDED THE OPPRESSED
MAN AND KILLED THE EGYP-
TIAN. 25 HE THOUGHT HIS
KINSFOLK WOULD UNDER-
STAND THAT GOD WAS
SENDING HIM TO THEM AS
A LIBERATOR, BUT THEY
DID NOT UNDERSTAND.
26 ON THE FOLLOWING
DAY, HE CAME TO THEM AS
THEY WERE FIGHTING
AND TRIED TO RECONCILE
THEM, SAYING: 'YOU ARE
BROTHERS, WHY DO YOU
HURT EACH OTHER?' 27
AT THAT MOMENT, THE
ONE WHO WAS INJUR-
ING HIS COMPANION RE-
BUFFED HIM SAYING:
'WHO APPOINTED YOU
AS OUR LEADER AND
JUDGE? 28 DO YOU
WANT TO KILL ME AS YOU

KILLED THE EGYPTIAN YESTERDAY?' 29 WHEN MOSES
HEARD THIS, HE FLED AND WENT TO LIVE AS A STRANGER
IN THE LAND OF MIDIAN WHERE HE HAD TWO SONS.
30 AFTER FORTY YEARS AN ANGEL APPEARED TO HIM IN THE
DESERT OF MOUNT SINAI IN THE FLAME OF A BURNING
BUSH. 31 MOSES WAS ASTONISHED AT THE VISION AND
AS HE LOOKED AT IT CLOSER, HE HEARD THE VOICE OF THE LORD:
32 'I AM THE GOD OF YOUR FATHERS, THE GOD OF ABRAHAM, ISA-
AC AND JACOB.' MOSES WAS FILLED WITH FEAR AND DID NOT
DARE LOOK AT IT. 33 BUT THE LORD SAID TO HIM: 'TAKE

OFF YOUR SANDALS FOR THE PLACE WHERE YOU STAND IS HOLY
GROUND. 34 I HAVE SEEN THE AFFLICTION OF MY PEOPLE IN
EGYPT AND HEARD THEM WEEPING, AND I HAVE COME DOWN TO
FREE THEM. AND NOW COME, I AM SENDING YOU TO EGYPT." 35
THIS MOSES WHOM THEY REJECTED SAYING: 'WHO APPOINTED
YOU LEADER AND JUDGE?' GOD SENT AS LEADER AND LIBERATOR
WITH THE ASSISTANCE OF THE ANGEL WHO APPEARED TO HIM
IN THE BUSH. 36 HE LED THEM OUT, PERFORMING SIGNS
AND WONDERS IN EGYPT, AT THE RED SEA AND IN THE DE-
SERT FOR FORTY YEARS. 37 THIS MOSES IS THE ONE
WHO SAID TO THE ISRAELITES: 'GOD WILL GIVE YOU A PRO-
PHET LIKE ME FROM AMONG YOUR BROTHERS.

38 THIS IS THE ONE WHO IN THE ASSEMBLY IN THE DESERT
BECAME THE MEDIATOR BETWEEN THE ANGEL WHO SPOKE
TO HIM ON MOUNT SINAI AND OUR ANCESTORS; HE RECE-
IVED THE WORDS OF LIFE THAT HE MIGHT COMMUNICATE
THEM TO US. 39 BUT HIM OUR FATHERS REFUSED TO OBEY,
THEY REJECTED HIM AND TURNED THEIR HEARTS TO EG-
YPT, SAYING TO AARON: 40 GIVE US GODS TO LEAD US SINCE
WE DO NOT KNOW WHAT HAS HAPPENED TO THAT MOSES
WHO BROUGHT US OUT OF
EGYPT.' 41 SO IN THOSE
DAYS THEY FASHIONED A
CALF, OFFERED SACRIFICES
TO THEIR IDOL AND REJOI-
CED IN THE WORK OF THEIR
HANDS. SO 42 GOD DE-
PARTED FROM THEM AND
LET THEM WORSHIP THE
STARS OF HEAVEN, AS IT IS
WRITTEN IN THE BOOK OF
THE PROPHETS: 'PEOPLE
OF ISRAEL, DID YOU OFFER
BURNT OFFERINGS AND
SACRIFICES FOR FORTY
YEARS IN THE DESERT?
43 NO YOU CARRIED IN-
STEAD THE TENT OF MOLOCH
AND THE STAR OF THE GOD
REHAN, IMAGES YOU MADE
TO WORSHIP, FOR THIS I WILL
BANISH YOU FARTHER THAN
BABYLON.' 44 OUR FA-
THERS HAD THE TENT OF
MEETING IN THE DESERT,
FOR GOD HAD DIRECTED
MOSES TO BUILD IT ACCORD-
ING TO THE PATTERN HE HAD
SEEN. 45 OUR FATHERS RECEIVED IT AND BROUGHT IT
UNDER THE COMMAND OF JOSHUA INTO THE LANDS OF THE
PAGANS THAT THEY CONQUERED AND WHOM GOD EXPEL-
LED BEFORE THEM. THEY KEPT IT UNTIL THE DAYS OF
DAVID 46 WHO FOUND FAVOR WITH GOD AND ASKED
HIM TO LET HIM BUILD A HOUSE FOR THE GOD OF JACOB.
47 HOWEVER, IT WAS SOLOMON WHO BUILT THAT TEMP-
LE. 48 IN REALITY, THE MOST HIGH DOES NOT DWELL
IN HOUSES MADE BY HUMAN HANDS AS THE PROPHET SAYS:

49 HEAVEN IS MY THRONE AND EARTH IS MY
FOOTSTOOL. WHAT HOUSE WILL YOU BUILD FOR
ME, SAYS THE LORD, HOW COULD YOU GIVE ME
A DWELLING PLACE? 50 WAS IT NOT I WHO
MADE ALL THESE THINGS?'

51 BUT YOU ARE A STUBBORN PEOPLE, YOU HAD
HARDENED YOUR HEARTS AND CLOSED YOUR
EARS. YOU HAVE ALWAYS RESISTED THE
HOLY SPIRIT JUST AS YOUR FATHER DID.
52 WAS THERE A PROPHET WHOM YOUR FATHERS
DID NOT PERSECUTE? THEY KILLED THOSE WHO ANNO-
UNCED THE COMING OF THE JUST ONE WHOM YOU
HAVE NOW BETRAYED AND MURDERED, 53 YOU WHO
RECEIVED THE LAW FROM THE ANGELS, BUT YOU WERE
NOT ABLE TO KEEP AND FULFILL IT."

54 WHEN THEY HEARD THIS REPROACH, THEY WERE
ENRAGED AND THEY GNASHED THEIR TEETH AGA-
INST STEPHEN. 55 BUT HE, FULL OF THE HOLY
SPIRIT, FIXED HIS EYES ON HEAVEN AND SAW
THE GLORY OF GOD AND JESUS AT GOD'S
RIGHT HAND, 56 SO HE DECLARED:

"I SEE THE HEAVENS OPEN AND THE SON OF
MAN AT THE RIGHT HAND OF GOD."

57 BUT THEY SHOUTED AND COVERED THEIR
EARS WITH THEIR
HANDS AND RUSHED
TOGETHER UPON HIM.
AND THE WITNESSES
LAID DOWN THEIR
CLOAKS AT THE FEET
OF A YOUNG MAN NA-
MED SAUL. 59 AS
THEY WERE STONING
HIM, STEPHEN PRAYED
SAYING: LORD JESUS,
RECEIVE MY SPIRIT."
60 THEN HE KNELT
DOWN AND SAID IN A
LOUD VOICE:

"LORD, DO NOT HOLD THIS SIN AGAINST THEM"

AND WHEN HE HAD
SAID THIS, HE DIED.

58 THEY BROUGHT HIM OUT OF THE CITY AND STONED HIM

Homage to Gultuso

• • •

8 1 SAUL WAS THERE, APPROVING HIS MURDER.
THIS WAS THE BEGINNING OF A GREAT PERSECUTION
AGAINST THE CHURCH IN JERUSALEM. ALL, EXCEPT THE
APOSTLES, WERE SCATTERED THROUGHOUT THE REGION OF JU-
DEA AND SAMARIA. 2 DEVOUT MEN BURIED STEPHEN AND
MOURNED DEEPLY FOR HIM. 3 SAUL MEANWHILE WAS TRYING
TO DESTROY THE CHURCH: HE ENTERED HOUSE AFTER HOUSE
AND DRAGGED OFF MEN AND WOMEN AND HAD THEM
PUT IN JAIL.

THE WORD IN SAMARIA

4 AT THE SAME TIME THOSE WHO WERE SCATTERED WENT
ABOUT PREACHING THE WORD. 5 PHILIP WENT TO A TOWN OF
SAMARIA PROCLAIMING THE CHRIST THERE. 6 ALL THE PE-
OPLE PAID CLOSE ATTENTION TO WHAT PHILIP SAID AS
THEY LISTENED TO HIM AND SAW THE MIRACULOUS SIGNS
WHICH HE DID. 7 FOR IN CASES OF POSSESSION, THE
UNCLEAN SPIRITS CAME OUT SHRIEKING LOUDLY. MANY
PEOPLE WHO WERE PARALYZED OR CRIPPLED WERE
HEALED. 8 SO THERE WAS GREAT JOY IN THAT TOWN.

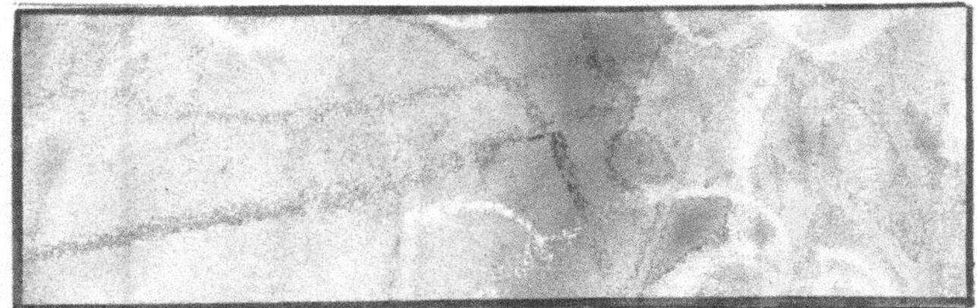

SIMON THE MAGICIAN

(9) A MAN NAMED SIMON HAD COME TO THIS TOWN, PRACTIC-
ING MAGIC. HE HELD THE SAMARITAN SPELLBOUND AND PAS-
SED HIMSELF OFF AS A VERY IMPORTANT PERSON. (10) ALL
THE PEOPLE, FROM THE LAST TO THE GREATEST, TRUSTED
HIM SAYING, "THIS IS THE POWER OF GOD, THE 'GREAT' ONE".
(11) THEY FOLLOWED HIM BECAUSE HE HAD HELD THEM UN-
DER THE SPELL OF HIS MAGIC FOR A LONG TIME. (12) BUT
WHEN THEY CAME TO BELIEVE PHILIP WHO ANNOUNCED
TO THEM THE KINGDOM OF GOD AND JESUS CHRIST AS SAVIOR,
BOTH MEN AND WOMEN WERE BAPTIZED. (13) SIMON
HIMSELF BELIEVED AND
WAS BAPTIZED, AND WO-
ULD NOT DEPART FROM
PHILIP. HE WAS ASTONISH-
ED WHEN HE SAW THE MI-
RACULOUS SIGNS AND
WONDERS THAT HAPPENED.
(14) NOW, WHEN THE AP-
OSTLES IN JERUSALEM
HEARD THAT THE SAMARI-
TANS HAD ACCEPTED THE
WORD OF GOD, THEY SENT
PETER AND JOHN TO THEM.
(15) THEY WENT DOWN AND
PRAYED FOR THEM THAT
THEY MIGHT RECEIVE THE
HOLY SPIRIT, (16) FOR HE
HAD NOT AS YET COME
DOWN ON ANY OF THEM
SINCE THEY HAD ONLY BE-
EN BAPTIZED IN THE NAME
OF THE LORD JESUS. (17)
SO PETER AND JOHN LAID
THEIR HANDS ON THEM
AND THEY RECEIVED THE
HOLY SPIRIT. (18) WHEN
SIMON SAW THAT THE SPI-
RIT WAS GIVEN THROUGH

THE LAYING ON OF THE APOSTLES' HANDS, HE OFFERED THEM
MONEY (19) SAYING, "GIVE ME ALSO THIS POWER SO THAT
ANYONE UPON WHOM I LAY MY HANDS MAY RECEIVE THE
HOLY SPIRIT."
(20) PETER REPLIED, "MAY YOU AND YOUR MONEY PE-
RISH FOR THINKING THAT THE GIFT OF GOD COULD BE
BOUGHT WITH MONEY! (21) YOU CANNOT SHARE IN THIS
SINCE YOU DO NOT UNDERSTAND THE THINGS OF GOD.
(22) REPENT, THEREFORE, OF THIS WICKEDNESS OF YOURS
AND PRAY TO THE LORD THAT YOU MAY BE FORGIVEN
SUCH A WRONG WAY OF THINKING; (23) I SEE YOU ARE

POISONED WITH BITTERNESS AND IN THE GRIP OF SIN." (24)
SIMON ANSWERED, "PRAY TO THE LORD FOR ME YOURSELVES,
SO THAT NONE OF THESE THINGS YOU SPOKE OF WILL HAPPEN
TO ME." (25) PETER AND JOHN GAVE THEIR TESTIMONY AND
SPOKE THE WORD OF THE LORD. AND THEY WENT BACK TO
JERUSALEM, BRINGING THE GOOD NEWS TO MANY SAMA-
RITAN VILLAGES ALONG THE WAY.

PHILIP BAPTIZES THE ETHIOPIAN

(26) AN ANGEL OF THE LORD SAID TO PHILIP, "GO SOUTH TOWARDS
THE ROAD THAT GOES FROM JERUSALEM TO GAZA, THE DE-
SERT ROAD." (27) SO HE SET OUT AND IT HAPPENED THAT AN
ETHIOPIAN WAS PASSING ALONG THAT WAY. HE WAS AN OF-
FICIAL IN CHARGE OF THE TREASURY OF THE QUEEN OF THE
ETHIOPIANS; HE HAD COME ON PILGRIMAGE TO JERUSALEM
(28) AND WAS ON HIS WAY HOME. HE WAS SITTING IN HIS
CARRIAGE AND READING THE PROPHET ISAIAH.
(29) THE SPIRIT SAID TO PHILIP, "GO AND CATCH UP WITH
THAT CARRIAGE." (30) SO PHILIP RAN UP AND HEARD
THE MAN READING THE PROPHET ISAIAH; AND HE ASKED, "DO
YOU UNDERSTAND WHAT YOU ARE READING?" THE ETHIOPIAN
REPLIED, (31) "HOW CAN I, UNLESS SOMEONE EXPLAINS IT

TO ME?" HE THEN INVITED PHILIP TO GET IN AND SIT BESIDE
HIM. (32) HE WAS READING THIS PASSAGE OF THE SCRIPTURE:

HE WAS LED LIKE A SHEEP TO BE SLAUGHTERED; LIKE A LAMB
THAT IS DUMB BEFORE THE SHEARER, HE DID NOT OPEN HIS MO-
UTH. (33) HE WAS HUMBLED AND DEPRIVED OF HIS RIGHTS.
WHO CAN SPEAK OF HIS DESCENDANTS? FOR HE WAS UP-
ROOTED FROM THE EARTH.

(34) THE OFFICIAL ASKED PHILIP, "TELL ME, PLEASE, DOES THE
PROPHET SPEAK FOR HIMSELF OR SOMEONE ELSE?" (35) PHILIP
TOLD HIM THE GOOD NEWS OF
JESUS, STARTING FROM THIS
TEXT OF SCRIPTURE. (36) AS
THEY TRAVELED THEY CAME
TO A PLACE WHERE THERE WAS
SOME WATER. THE ETHIOPIAN
SAID, "HERE IS WATER; WHAT
IS TO KEEP ME FROM BEING
BAPTIZED?" (37) PHILIP
ANSWERED, "YOU MAY BE
BAPTIZED IF YOU BELIEVE
WITH ALL YOUR HEART."
AND THE MAN REPLIED, "I
BELIEVE THAT JESUS
CHRIST IS THE SON OF GOD".
(38) HE ORDERED THE CAR-
RIAGE TO STOP; PHILIP AND
THE ETHIOPIAN WENT INTO
THE WATER AND PHILIP BAP-
TIZED HIM. (39) ONCE OUT
OF THE WATER, THE SPIRIT
OF THE LORD TOOK PHILIP
AWAY. THE ETHIOPIAN SAW
HIM NO MORE, BUT HE LEFT
FULL OF JOY ON HIS WAY. (40) PHILIP ARRIVED AT AZOTUS; HE
WENT ON ANNOUNCING THE GOOD NEWS IN ALL THE TOWNS
UNTIL HE REACHED CAESAREA.

SAUL MEETS JESUS

9 (1) MEANWHILE SAUL CONSIDERED NOTHING BUT VIOL-
ENCE AND DEATH FOR THE DISCIPLES OF THE LORD. (2) HE
WENT TO THE HIGH PRIEST AND ASKED HIM FOR LET-
TERS TO THE SYNAGOGUES OF DAMASCUS TO AUTHORIZE HIM
TO ARREST AND BRING TO JERUSALEM ANYONE HE MIGHT
FIND, MAN OR WOMAN, BELONGING TO THE WAY.

HOMAGE TO GUTTUSO
DM
09
CCCLIX - 359 ©

(3) AS HE TRAVELED ALONG AND APPROACHING DAMASCUS.
A LIGHT FROM THE SKY SUDDENLY FLUSHED AROUND HIM. (4)
HE FELL TO THE GROUND AND HEARD A VOICE SAYING TO HIM,
"SAUL, SAUL! WHY DO YOU PERSECUTE ME?" (5)
AND HE ASKED, "WHO ARE YOU, LORD?" THE VOICE
REPLIED, "I AM JESUS WHOM YOU ARE PERSE-
CUTING. (6) NOW GET UP AND GO INTO THE
CITY; THERE YOU WILL BE TOLD WHAT YOU
ARE TO DO."
(7) THE MEN WHO WERE TRAVELING WITH HIM STOOD
THERE SPEECHLESS; THEY HAD HEARD THE SOUND, BUT
COULD SEE NO ONE. (8) SAUL GOT UP FROM THE
GROUND AND, OPENING HIS EYES, HE COULD NOT SEE.

THEY TOOK HIM BY THE HAND AND BROUGHT HIM TO DAMAS-
CUS. (9) HE WAS BLIND AND HE DID NOT EAT OR DRINK FOR
THREE DAYS.
(10) THERE WAS A DISCIPLE IN DAMASCUS NAMED ANANIAS, TO
WHOM THE LORD CALLED IN A VISION, "ANANIAS!" HE ANSWERED,
"HERE I AM, LORD!" (11) THEN THE LORD SAID TO HIM, "GO AT ONCE
TO STRAIGHT STREET AND ASK, AT THE HOUSE OF JUDAS, FOR
A MAN OF TARSUS NAMED SAUL. YOU WILL FIND HIM PRAYING,
(12) FOR HE HAS JUST SEEN IN A VISION THAT A MAN NAMED ANA-
NIAS HAS COME IN AND PLACED HIS HANDS ON HIM, TO RESTORE
HIS SIGHT." (13) ANANIAS
ANSWERED, "LORD, I HAVE HE-
ARD FROM MANY SOURCES
ABOUT THIS MAN AND ALL THE
HARM HE HAS DONE TO YO-
UR SAINTS IN JERUSALEM,
(14) AND NOW HE IS HERE
WITH AUTHORITY FROM THE
HIGH PRIEST TO ARREST
ALL WHO CALL ON YOUR
NAME." (15) BUT THE
LORD SAID TO HIM, "GO!"
"THIS MAN IS MY CHOSEN
INSTRUMENT TO BRING
MY NAME TO THE PAGAN
NATIONS AND THEIR
KINGS, AND THE PEOPLE
OF ISRAEL AS WELL. (16)
I MYSELF WILL SHOW HIM
HOW MUCH HE WILL
HAVE TO SUFFER FOR MY
NAME." (17) SO ANANIAS
LEFT. WHEN HE ENTERED
THE HOUSE HE LAID HIS
HANDS UPON SAUL AND
SAID, "SAUL, MY BROTHER,
THE LORD JESUS, WHO AP-

PEARED TO YOU ON YOUR WAY HERE, HAS SENT ME TO YOU SO
THAT YOU MAY RECEIVE YOUR SIGHT AND BE FILLED WITH
THE HOLY SPIRIT." (18) IMMEDIATELY SOMETHING LIKE SCALES
FELL FROM HIS EYES AND HE COULD SEE. HE GOT UP AND
WAS BAPTIZED; (19) THEN HE TOOK FOOD AND WAS STRENGTHENED.

FOR SEVERAL DAYS SAUL STAYED WITH THE DISCIPLES IN DA-
MASCUS, (20) AND HE SOON BEGAN TO PROCLAIM IN THE
SYNAGOGUES THAT JESUS WAS THE SON OF GOD. (21) ALL
WHO HEARD WERE ASTONISHED AND SAID, "IS THIS NOT
THE ONE WHO CAST OUT IN JERUSALEM ALL THOSE CAL-
LING UPON HIS NAME? DID HE NOT COME HERE TO BRING
THEM BOUND BEFORE THE CHIEF PRIESTS?"

(22) BUT SAUL GREW MORE AND MORE POWERFUL,
AND HE CONFOUNDED ALL THE JEWS LIVING IN DA-
MASCUS WHEN HE PROVED THAT JESUS WAS THE MES-
SIAH. (23) AFTER A FAIRLY LONG TIME, THE JEWS
CONSPIRED TOGETHER TO KILL HIM. (24) BUT SAUL
BECAME AWARE OF THEIR PLAN: DAY AND NIGHT
THEY KEPT WATCH AT THE CITY GATE IN ORDER
TO KILL HIM. (25) SO HIS DISCIPLES TOOK HIM ONE
NIGHT AND LET HIM DOWN FROM THE TOP OF THE
WALL, LOWERING HIM IN A BASKET.
(26) WHEN SAUL CAME TO JERUSALEM, HE TRIED TO
JOIN THE DISCIPLES THERE, BUT THEY WERE AFRAID
OF HIM BECAUSE THEY COULD NOT BELIEVE THAT
HE WAS A DISCIPLE.
(27) BUT BARNABAS
TOOK HIM AND BROUGHT
HIM TO THE APOSTLES,
AND HE EXPLAINED TO
THEM HOW SAUL HAD
SEEN THE LORD ON HIS
WAY AND HOW THE LORD
HAD SPOKEN TO HIM,
AND HE EXPLAINED ALSO
HOW SAUL HAD PRE-
ACHED BOLDLY IN THE
NAME OF JESUS.
(28) THEN SAUL BEGAN
TO LIVE WITH THEM. HE
MOVED ABOUT FREELY
IN JERUSALEM AND
PREACHED OPENLY IN
THE NAME OF THE LORD.
(29) HE ALSO SPOKE TO THE
HELLENISTS AND ARGUED
WITH THEM, BUT THEY
WANTED TO KILL HIM.
(30) WHEN THE BRO-
THERS LEARNED OF
THIS, THEY TOOK HIM
DOWN TO CAESAREA
AND SENT HIM OFF TO
TARSUS. (31) MEAN-
WHILE, THE CHURCH

HAD PEACE AND WAS BUILT UP THROUGHOUT ALL
JUDEA AND GALILEE AND SAMARIA WITH EYES
TURNED TO THE LORD AND LIVED FILLED WITH
COMFORT FROM THE HOLY SPIRIT. (32)

PETER VISITS THE CHURCHES

AS PETER TRAVELED AROUND, HE WENT TO VISIT THE
SAINTS WHO LIVED IN LYDDA. (33) THERE HE FOUND
A MAN NAMED AENEAS WHO WAS PARALYZED, AND HAD BEEN
BEDRIDDEN FOR EIGHT YEARS. (34) PETER SAID TO HIM,
"AENEAS, JESUS CHRIST HEALS YOU; GET UP AND
MAKE YOUR BED!" AND THE MAN GOT UP AT ONCE. (35)

ALL THE PEOPLE LIVING IN LYDDA AND SHARON SAW HIM AND
TURNED TO THE LORD. (36) THERE WAS A DISCIPLE IN JOPPA
NAMED TABITHA, WHICH MEANS DORCAS OR GAZELLE. SHE
WAS ALWAYS DOING GOOD WORKS AND HELPING THE POOR.
(37) AT THAT TIME SHE FELL SICK AND DIED. THEY WASHED
HER BODY AND LAID HER IN THE UPSTAIRS ROOM.

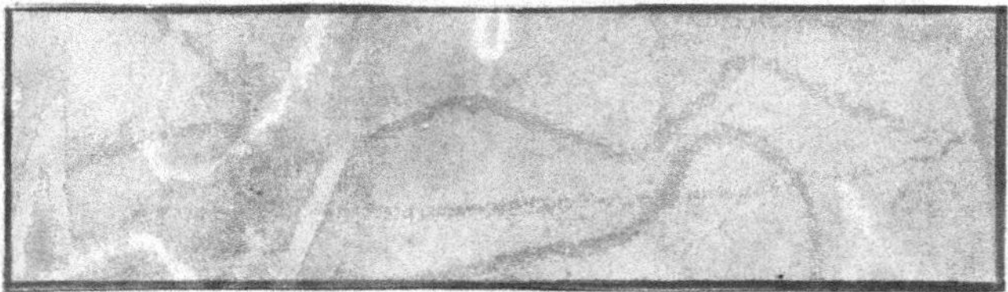

(38) AS LYDDA IS NEAR JOPPA, THE DISCIPLES, ON HEARING
THAT PETER WAS THERE, SENT TWO MEN TO HIM REQU-
ESTING, "PLEASE COME TO US WITHOUT DELAY." (39) SO
PETER WENT WITH THEM. ON HIS ARRIVAL THEY TOOK HIM UP-
STAIRS TO THE ROOM. ALL THE WIDOWS CROWDED AROUND HIM
IN TEARS, SHOWING HIM THE CLOTHES WHICH DORCAS HAD
MADE WHILE SHE WAS WITH THEM. (40) PETER MADE THEM
ALL LEAVE THE ROOM AND
THEN HE KNELT DOWN AND
PRAYED. TURNING TO THE
DEAD BODY HE SAID, "TA-
BITHA, STAND UP." SHE
OPENED HER EYES, LO-
OKED AT PETER AND
SAT UP. (41) PETER GAVE
HER HIS HAND AND
HELPED HER UP. THEN
HE CALLED IN THE SA-
INTS AND WIDOWS
AND PRESENTED HER
TO THEM ALIVE.
(42) THIS BECAME
KNOWN THROUGHOUT
ALL OF JOPPA AND
MANY PEOPLE BE-
LIEVED IN THE LORD
BECAUSE OF IT.

(43) AS FOR PETER, HE
REMAINED FOR SOME
TIME IN JOPPA AT
THE HOUSE OF SIMON,
A TANNER OF LEATHER.

THE BAPTISM OF CORNELIUS

10 (1) THERE WAS IN CAESAREA A MAN NAMED CORNELIUS,
CAPTAIN OF WHAT WAS CALLED THE ITALIAN BATTALION.
(2) HE WAS A RELIGIOUS AND GOD-FEARING MAN TO-
GETHER WITH HIS HOUSEHOLD. HE GAVE GENEROUSLY TO
THE PEOPLE AND CONSTANTLY PRAYED TO GOD.
(3) ONE AFTERNOON AT ABOUT THREE HE HAD A VISION IN
WHICH HE CLEARLY SAW AN ANGEL OF GOD COMING TO-
WARDS HIM AND CALLING HIM, "CORNELIUS!" (4) HE STA-
RED AT THE VISION IN TERROR AND SAID, "WHAT IS IT,
SIR?" AND THE ANGEL ANSWERED, "YOUR PRAYERS AND YOUR

ALMS HAVE ASCENDED BEFORE GOD. (5) SEND MEN TO JOPPA
AND SUMMON SIMON, ALSO KNOWN AS PETER; (6) HE IS GUEST
OF A TANNER, SIMON, WHO LIVES BY THE SEA. (7) AS THE ANGEL
LEFT, CORNELIUS CALLED TWO SERVANTS AND A DEVOUT SOL-
DIER FROM HIS BATTALION, (8) AND AFTER TELLING THEM
EVERYTHING, HE SENT THEM TO JOPPA. (9) THE NEX DAY, ON
APPROACHING THE CITY, PETER WENT UP TO THE ROOF AT
NOON TO PRAY. (10) HE BECAME HUNGRY AND WISHED TO
EAT, BUT WHILE THEY WERE PREPARING FOOD, HE FELL IN-
TO A TRANCE. (11) THE HEAVENS WERE OPENED AND
HE SAW AN OBJECT LIKE A LARGE SHEET COMING DOWN,
AND BEING LOWERED TO THE GROUND BY ITS FOUR COR-
NERS. (12) IN IT WERE ALL KINDS OF FOUR-LEGGED
ANIMALS OF THE EARTH, REPTILES AND BIRDS.

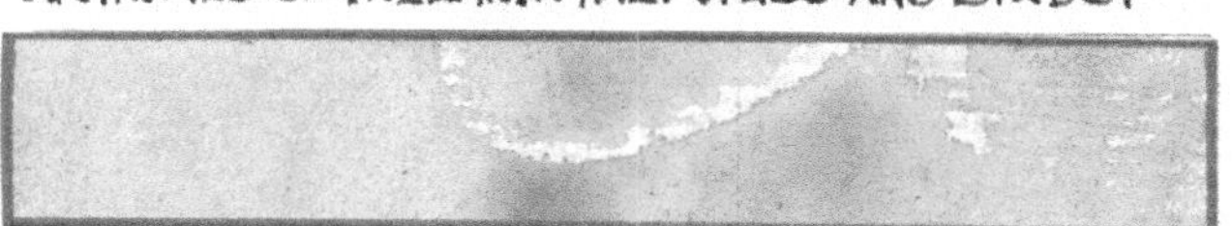

(13) THEN A VOICE SAID TO HIM, "GET UP, PETER,
KILL AND EAT!" (14) BUT PETER REPLIED, "CERTAINLY
NOT, LORD! I HAVE NEVER EATEN ANY COMMON OR UNCLEAN
CREATURE." (15) AGAIN A SECOND TIME THE VOICE SPOKE
"WHAT GOD HAS MADE CLEAN, YOU MUST NOT CALL UNCLEAN."
(16) THIS HAPPENED THREE TIMES; THEN THE SHEET WAS TAKEN
UP INTO THE SKY. (17) WHILE PETER'S MIND WAS STILL IN
THE VISION HE HAD SEEN, THE MESSENGERS OF CORNELIUS AR-
RIVED AT THE GATE ASKING FOR THE HOUSE OF SIMON. (18) THEY
INQUIRED WHETHER SIMON, ALSO KNOWN AS PETER, WAS
STAYING THERE. (19) THEN, AS PETER CONTINUED PONDERING
ON THE VISION, THE SPIRIT SPOKE TO HIM, "THERE ARE MEN
LOOKING FOR YOU; (20) GET UP AND GO DOWNSTAIRS AND

FOLLOW THEM WITHOUT HESITATION, FOR I HAVE SENT THEM."
(21) SO PETER SAID TO THE MEN, "I AM THE ONE YOU ARE LOOK-
ING FOR. WHAT BRINGS YOU HERE?" THEY ANSWERED, (22)
HE WHO SENT US IS CAPTAIN CORNELIUS. HE IS AN UPRIGHT
AND GOD-FEARING MAN, WELL RESPECTED BY ALL THE JEWISH
PEOPLE. HE HAS BEEN INSTRUCTED BY A HOLY ANGEL TO SUM-
MON YOU TO HIS HOUSE, SO THAT HE MAY LISTEN TO WHAT YOU
HAVE TO SAY." (23) SO PETER INVITED THEM IN AND PUT THEM
UP FOR THE NIGHT. THE NEXT DAY HE WENT OFF WITH THEM
TOGETHER WITH SOME OF THE BROTHERS FROM JOPPA. (24)
THE FOLLOWING DAY HE ARRIVED IN CAESAREA WHERE COR-
NELIUS WAS EXPECTING THEM; HE HAD CALLED TOGETHER
HIS RELATIVES AND CLOSE
FRIENDS. (25) AS PETER
WAS ABOUT TO ENTER,
CORNELIUS WENT TO HIM,
FELL ON HIS KNEES AND
BOWED LOW. (26) BUT PE-
TER LIFTED HIM UP SAYING,
"STAND UP, FOR I TOO AM A
HUMAN BEING." (27) AFTER
TALKING WITH HIM, PETER
ENTERED AND FOUND MANY
PEOPLE THERE. (28) THEN
HE SAID TO THEM, "YOU KNOW
THAT IS FORBIDDEN FOR
JEWS TO ASSOCIATE WITH
ANYONE FOREIGNER OR TO
ENTER HIS HOUSE, GOD
HAS MADE IT CLEAR TO ME
THAT NO ONE SHOULD CALL
ANY PERSON COMMON
OR CONSIDER HIM UNCLEAN;
(29) BECAUSE OF THIS I
CAME AT ONCE WHEN I
WAS SENT FOR. NOW I
SHOULD LIKE TO KNOW
WHY YOU SENT FOR ME."
(30) CORNELIUS SAID, "JUST

THREE DAYS AGO AT THIS TIME, ABOUT THREE IN THE AF-
TERNOON, I WAS PRAYING IN MY HOUSE WHEN A MAN IN
SHINING CLOTHES STOOD BEFORE ME (31) AND SAID TO ME,
"CORNELIUS, GOD HAS HEARD YOUR PRAYER AND YOUR
ALMS HAVE BEEN REMEMBERED BEFORE HIM. (32)
SEND SOMEONE, THEREFORE, TO JOPPA AND ASK FOR
SIMON, ALSO KNOWN AS PETER, WHO IS GUEST AT
THE HOUSE OF SIMON THE TANNER BY THE SEA."

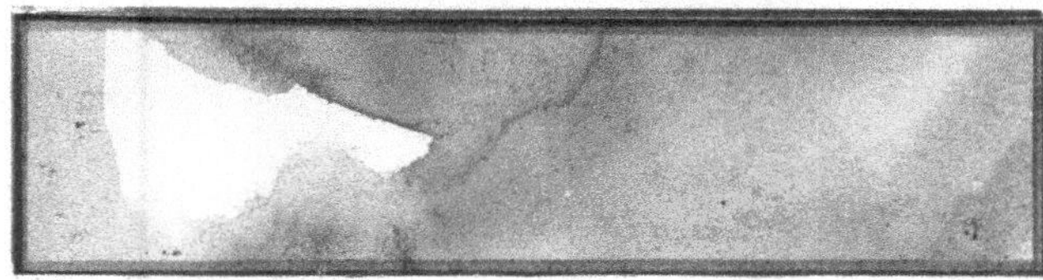

(33) SO I SENT FOR YOU AT ONCE AND YOU HAVE BEEN
KIND ENOUGH TO COME. NOW WE ARE ALL HERE IN GOD'S
PRESENCE, WAITING TO HEAR ALL THAT THE LORD HAS
COMMANDED YOU TO SAY."
(34) PETER SPOKE TO THEM, "TRULY, I REALIZE THAT GOD DOES
NOT SHOW PARTIALITY, (35) BUT IN ALL NATIONS HE LISTEN TO
EVERYONE WHO FEARS GOD AND DOES GOOD. (36) AND THIS
IS THE MESSAGE HE HAS SENT TO THE CHILDREN OF ISRAEL,
THE GOOD NEWS OF PEACE HE HAS PROCLAIMED THROUGH
JESUS CHRIST, WHO IS THE LORD OF ALL. (37) NO DOUBT YOU
HAVE HEARD OF THE EVENT THAT OCCURRED THROUGHOUT THE
WHOLE COUNTRY OF THE JEWS, BEGINNING FROM GALILEE,

AFTER THE BAPTISM JOHN PREACHED. (38) YOU KNOW HOW GOD
ANOINTED JESUS THE NAZAREAN WITH HOLY SPIRIT AND POWER.
HE WENT ABOUT DOING GOOD AND HEALING ALL WHO WERE UN-
DER THE DEVIL'S POWER, FOR GOD WAS WITH HIM. (39) WE ARE
WITNESSES OF ALL THAT HE DID THROUGHOUT THE COUNTRY OF
THE JEWS AND IN JERUSALEM ITSELF.
(40) FINALLY THEY PUT HIM TO DEATH BY HANGING HIM ON A
WOODEN CROSS. BUT GOD RAISED HIM TO LIFE ON THE THIRD
DAY AND LET HIM BE SEEN, (41) NOT BY ALL THE PEOPLE,
BUT BY THE WITNESSES THAT WERE CHOSEN BEFOREHAND
BY GOD-BY US WHO ATE AND DRANK WITH HIM AFTER HIS
RESURRECTION FROM DEATH. (42) AND HE COMMANDED US TO

PREACH TO THE PEOPLE
AND TO BEAR WITNESS THAT
HE IS THE ONE APPOINTED
BY GOD TO JUDGE THE LI-
VING AND THE DEAD. (43)
ALL THE PROPHETS SAY OF
HIM, THAT EVERYONE WHO
BELIEVES IN HIM HAS FOR-
GIVENESS OF SINS THROUGH
HIS NAME."
(44) PETER WAS STILL SPEAK-
ING WHEN THE HOLY SPI-
RIT CAME UPON ALL
WHO LISTENED TO THE
WORD. (45) AND THE BE-
LIEVERS OF JEWISH ORI-
GIN WHO HAD COME
WITH PETER WERE AMA-
ZED, "WHY! "GOD GI-
VES AND POURS THE
HOLY SPIRIT ON FO-
REIGNERS ALSO!"
(46) FOR INDEED THIS
HAPPENED: THEY HEARD
THEM SPEAKING IN
TONGUES AND PRAI-
SING GOD.

(47) THEN PETER DECLARED, "CAN WE REFUSE
TO BAPTIZE WITH WATER THESE PEOPLE WHO
HAVE RECEIVED THE HOLY SPIRIT, JUST AS WE HA-
VE?" (48) SO HE HAD THEM BAPTIZED IN THE NA-
ME OF JESUS CHRIST.
AFTER THAT THEY ASKED HIM TO REMAIN
WITH THEM FOR SOME DAYS.

PETER JUSTIFIES HIS CONDUCT

11 (1) NEWS CAME TO THE APOSTLES AND THE BRO-
THERS IN JUDEA THAT PAGANS HAD RECEIVED THE
WORD OF GOD. (2) SO, WHEN PETER WENT UP TO JE-
RUSALEM, THESE JEWISH BELIEVERS BEGAN TO ARGUE
WITH HIM, (3) "YOU WENT TO THE HOME OF UNCIRCUMCISED
PEOPLE AND ATE WITH THEM!" (4) SO PETER BEGAN TO GIVE
THEM THE FACTS AS THEY HAD HAPPENED. (5) "I WAS AT
PRAYER IN THE CITY OF JOPPA WHEN, IN A TRANCE, I SAW A
VISION. SOMETHING LIKE A LARGE SHEET CAME DOWN
FROM THE SKY AND DREW NEAR ME, LANDING ON THE
GROUND BY ITS FOUR CORNERS. (6) AS I STARED AT IT,

I SAW FOUR-LEGGED CREA-
TURES OF THE EARTH, REP-
TILES AND WILD BEASTS,
AND BIRDS OF THE SKY.'
(7) THEN I HEARD A
VOICE SAYING TO ME:
'GET UP, PETER, KILL
AND EAT!' (8) I REPLIED,
CERTAINLY NOT, LORD!
NO COMMON OR UN-
CLEAN CREATURE HAS
EVER ENTERED MY
MOUTH.' (9) A SECOND
TIME THE VOICE FROM
THE HEAVENS SPOKE,
"WHAT GOD HAS MADE
CLEAN, YOU MUST NOT
CALL UNCLEAN.' (10)
THIS HAPPENED FOR
THREE TIMES, AND THEN
IT WAS ALL DRAWN UP
INTO THE SKY. (11) AT
THAT MOMENT THREE
MEN, WHO HAD BEEN
SENT TO ME FROM
CAESAREA, ARRIVED
AT THE HOUSE WHERE
WE WERE STAYING.
(12) THE SPIRIT INSTRUC-
TED ME TO GO WITH THEM WITHOUT HESITATION: SO
THESE SIX BROTHERS CAME ALONG WITH ME AND
WE ENTERED INTO THE MAN'S HOUSE. (13) HE TOLD US
HOW HE HAD SEEN AN ANGEL STANDING IN HIS HO-
USE AND TELLING HIM: SEND SOMEONE TO JOPPA
AND FETCH SIMON, ALSO KNON AS PETER. (14) HE
WILL BRING YOU A MESSAGE BY WHICH YOU AND ALL
YOUR HOUSEHOLD WILL BE SAVED."
(15) I HAD BEGUN TO ADDRESS THEM WHEN SUDDENLY
THE HOLY SPIRIT CAME UPON THEM, JUST AS

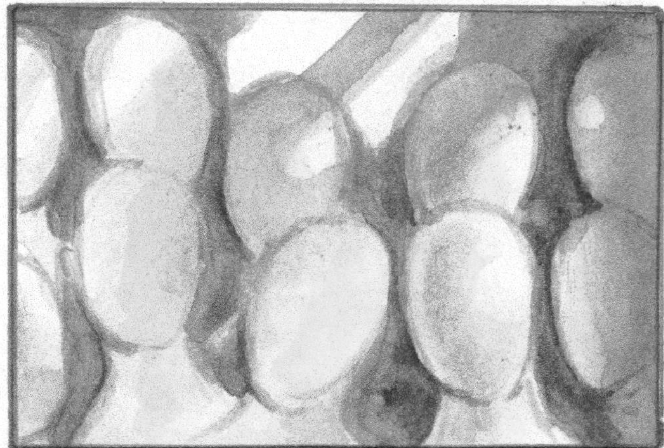

IT HAD COME ON US AT THE BEGINNING. (16) THEN I REMEM-
BERED WHAT THE LORD HAD SAID, 'JOHN BAPTIZED WITH
WATER, BUT YOU SHALL BE BAPTISED WITH THE HOLY
SPIRIT.' (17) IF, THEN, GOD HAD GIVEN THEM THE SAME
GIFT THAT HE HAD GIVEN US WHEN WE BELIEVED IN
THE LORD JESUS CHRIST, WHO WAS I TO RESIST GOD?"
(18) WHEN THEY HEARD THIS THEY SET THEIR MINDS AT
REST AND PRAISED GOD, SAYING, "THEN GOD HAS GI-
VEN LIFE-GIVING AND GRANTED REPENTANCE TO
THE PAGAN NATIONS AS WELL."

SAUL, SAUL, WHY DO YOU PERSECUTE ME? (9:4)
CCCLX
300
DM
09
©

THE FOUNDATION OF THE CHURCH AT ANTIOCH

(19) THOSE WHO HAVE BEEN SCATTERED BECAUSE OF THE
PERSECUTION OF STEPHEN TRAVELED AS FAR AS PHOENI-
CIA, CYPRUS AND ANTIOCH, TELLING THE MESSAGE, BUT
ONLY TO THE JEWS. (20) BUT THERE WERE SOME NATIVES OF
CYPRUS WHO, ON COMING TO ANTIOCH SPOKE ALSO TO THE
GREEKS, GIVING THEM THE GOOD NEWS OF THE LORD JESUS.
(21) THE HAND OF THE LORD WAS WITH THEM AS A GREAT
NUMBER BELIEVED AND TURNED TO THE LORD. (22) NEWS

OF THIS REACHED THE
EARS OF THE CHURCH IN
JERUSALEM, SO THEY
SENT BARNABAS TO ANTI-
OCH. (23) WHEN HE ARRIVED
AND SAW THE MANIFEST
SIGNS OF GOD'S FAVOR, HE
REJOICED AND URGED THEM
ALL TO REMAIN FIRMLY FA-
ITHFUL TO THE LORD; (24)
FOR HE WAS A GOOD MAN
FILLED WITH HOLY SPIRIT
AND FAITH. THUS LARGE
CROWDS CAME TO KNOW THE
LORD. (25) THEN BARNABAS
WENT OFF TO TARSUS TO
LOOK FOR SAUL (26) AND
WHEN HE FOUND HIM, HE
BROUGHT HIM TO ANTIOCH.
FOR A WHOLE YEAR THEY
HAD MEETINGS WITH THE
CHURCH AND INSTRUCTED
MANY PEOPLE. IT WAS IN
ANTIOCH THAT THE DI-
SCIPLES WERE FIRST
CALLED CHRISTIANS.

(27) AT THAT TIME SOME
PROPHETS WENT DOWN FROM JERUSALEM TO AN-
TIOCH (28) AND ONE OF THEM, NAMED AGABUS, IN-
SPIRED BY THE HOLY SPIRIT, FORETOLD THAT A
GREAT FAMINE WOULD SPREAD OVER THE WHOLE
WORLD.
THIS ACTUALLY HAPPENED IN THE DAYS OF THE
EMPEROR CLAUDIUS. (29) SO EACH OF THE DISCI-
PLES DECIDED, WITHIN HIS MEANS, TO SET SOME-
THING ASIDE AND TO SEND RELIEF TO THE BROTHERS

AND SISTERS WHO WERE LIVING IN JUDEA. (30) THEY SENT
THEIR DONATIONS TO THE ELDERS BY BARNABAS AND SAUL.

JAMES IS PUT TO DEATH: PETER MIRACULOUS ESCAPE

12 (1) ABOUT THAT TIME KING HEROD DECIDED
TO PERSECUTE SOME MEMBERS OF THE
CHURCH. (2) HE HAD JAMES, THE BROTHER OF JOHN,
KILLED WITH THE SWORD, (3) AND WHE HE SAW HOW
IT PLEASED THE JEWS, HE PROCEEDED TO ARREST
PETER ALSO. THIS HAPPENED DURING THE FESTIVAL
OF THE UNLEAVENED BREAD.

(4) HEROD HAD HIM SEIZED AND THROWN INTO PRISON
WITH FOUR SQUADS, EACH OF FOUR SOLDIERS, TO GUARD
HIM. HE WANTED TO BRING HIM TO TRIAL BEFORE THE
PEOPLE AFTER THE PASSOVER FEAST, (5) BUT WHILE
PETER WAS KEPT IN PRISON, THE WHOLE CHURCH
PRAYED EARNESTLY FOR HIM.
(6) ON THE VERY NIGHT BEFORE HEROD WAS TO BRING
HIM TO TRIAL, PETER WAS SLEEPING BETWEEN TWO SOL-
DIERS, BOUND BY A DOUBLE CHAIN, WHILE GUARDS KEPT
WATCH AT THE GATE OF THE PRISON. (7) SUDDENLY AN
ANGEL OF THE LORD STOOD THERE AND A LIGHT SHONE
IN THE PRISON CELL. THE ANGEL TAPPED PETER ON THE

SIDE AND WOKE HIM SAYING, "GET UP QUICKLY!" AT ONCE
THE CHAINS FELL FROM PETER'S WRISTS. THE ANGEL
SAID, "PUT ON YOUR BELT AND YOUR SANDALS." PETER
DID SO, (8) AND THE ANGEL ADDED, "NOW, PUT ON YOUR
CLOAK AND FOLLOW ME." (9) PETER FOLLOWED HIM OUT;
HE DID NOT REALIZE THAT WHAT WAS HAPPENING WITH THE
ANGEL WAS REAL; HE THOUGHT HE WAS SEEING A VISION.
(10) THEY PASSED THE FIRST GUARD AND THEN THE SECOND
AND THEY CAME TO THE IRON DOOR LEADING OUT TO THE
CITY, WHICH OPENED OF
ITSELF FOR THEM. THEY
WENT OUT AND MADE THEIR
WAY DOWN A NARROW AL-
LEY, WHEN SUDDENLY THE
ANGEL LEFT HIM. THEN
(11) PETER RECOVERED HIS
SENSES AND SAID, "NOW I
KNOW THAT THE LORD HAS
SENT HIS ANGEL AND HAS
RESCUED ME FROM HE-
ROD'S CLUTCHES AND
FROM ALL THAT THE JEWS
HAD IN STORE FOR ME."
(12) PETER THEN CAME TO
THE HOUSE OF MARY, THE
MOTHER OF JOHN ALSO KNOWN
AS MARK, WHERE MANY WE-
RE GATHERED TOGETHER
AND WERE PRAYING. (13)
WHEN HE KNOCKED AT THE
OUTSIDE DOOR, A MAID
NAMED RHODA CAME TO
ANSWER IT. (14) ON RECOG
NIZING THE VOICE OF PETER
SHE WAS SO OVERCOME
WITH JOY THAT, INSTEAD OF
OPENING THE DOOR, SHE
RAN IN TO ANNOUNCE THAT

PETER WAS AT THE DOOR. (15) THEY SAID TO HER, "YOU ARE
CRAZY!" AND AS SHE INSISTED, THEY SAID, "IT MUST
BE AN ANGEL."
(16) MEANWHILE, PETER CONTINUED KNOCKING AND, WHEN
THEY FINALLY OPENED THE DOOR, THEY WERE AMAZED
TO SEE HIM. (17) HE MOTIONED TO THEM WITH HIS HAND
TO BE QUIET AND TOLD THEM HOW THE LORD HAD
BROUGHT HIM OUT OF PRISON. AND HE SAID TO THEM,
"REPORT THIS TO JAMES AND TO THE BROTHERS."
THEN HE LEFT AND WENT TO ANOTHER PLACE.

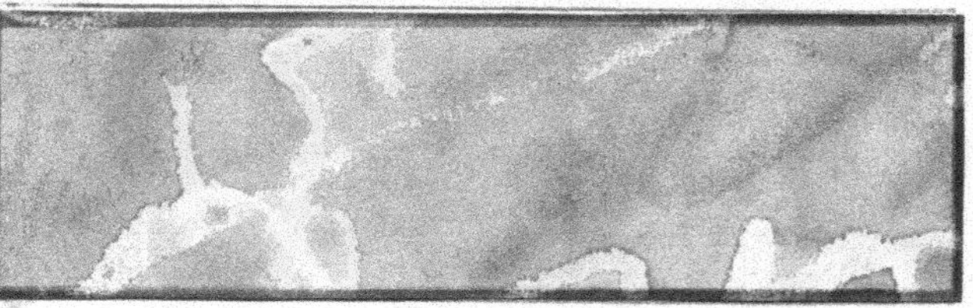

18 AT DAYBREAK THERE WAS A GREAT COMMOTION
AMONG THE SOLDIERS OVER WHAT HAD BECOME OF
PETER. 19 HEROD BEGAN A SEARCH FOR HIM AND,
NOT FINDING HIM, HAD THE GUARDS QUESTIONED
AND EXECUTED. AFTER THAT, HE CAME DOWN FROM
JUDEA TO CAESAREA AND STAYED THERE.

HEROD'S DEATH

20 AT THAT TIME HEROD WAS ANGRY WITH THE PEOPLE
OF TYRE AND SIDON. BY GENERAL AGREEMENT THEY APPEARED
BEFORE HIM AND, AFTER HAVING WON OVER BLASTUS, THE

KING'S TREASURER, THEY
ASKED FOR PEACE, FOR THEIR
COUNTRY WAS SUPPLIED WITH
FOOD FROM THE TERRITORY
OF HEROD. 21 ON THE AP-
POINTED DAY HEROD CLO-
THED IN ROYAL ROBES,
SAT ON HIS THRONE AND
ADDRESSED THEM. 22
SO THE ASSEMBLED PE-
OPLE SHOUTED BACK,
"A GOD IS SPEAKING,
NOT A MAN!"
23 THE ANGEL OF THE
LORD IMMEDIATELY
STRUCK HEROD FOR HE
DID NOT RETURN THE
HONOR TO GOD, AND HE
DIED EATEN BY WORMS.
24 MEANWHILE THE
WORD OF GOD WAS IN-
CREASING AND SPRE-
ADING. 25 BARNABAS
AND SAUL CARRIED OUT
THEIR MISSION AND
THEN CAME BACK
FROM JERUSALEM, TA-
KING WITH THEM JOHN ALSO CALLED MARK.

PAUL SENT BY THE CHURCH

13 1 THEY WERE AT ANTIOCH - IN THE CHURCH
WHICH WAS THERE - PROPHETS AND TEACHERS:
BARNABAS, SYMEON KNOWN AS NIGER, LUCIUS
OF CYRENE, MANAEN WHO HAD BEEN BROUGHT UP WITH
HEROD, AND SAUL. 2 ON ONE OCCASION WHILE THEY WERE
CELEBRATING THE LORD AND FASTING, THE HOLY SPIRIT SAID
TO THEM, "SET APART FOR ME BARNABAS AND SAUL AND
SEND THEM TO DO THE WORK FOR WHICH I HAVE CALLED
THEM."
3 SO, AFTER FASTING AND PRAYING, THEY LAID THEIR
HANDS ON THEM AND SENT THEM OFF,

PAUL FIRST MISSION

4 THESE MEN, SENT BY THE HOLY SPIRIT, WENT TO THE
PORT OF SELEUCIA AND FROM THERE SAILED TO CYPRUS.
5 ON THEIR ARRIVAL IN SALAMIS THEY PROCLAIMED THE
WORD OF GOD IN THE JEWISH SYNAGOGUE; JOHN WAS
WITH THEM AS AN ASSISTANT. 6 THEY TRAVELED
OVER THE WHOLE ISLAND AS FAR AS PAPHOS
WHERE THEY MET A CERTAIN MAGICIAN NAMED
BAR-JESUS, A JEWISH FALSE PROPHET 7 WHO LI-
VED WITH THE GOVERNOR SERGIUS PAULUS, AN

INTELLIGENT MAN. HE HAD SUMMONED BARNABAS AND SA-
UL AND WANTED TO HEAR THE WORD OF GOD. 8 BUT THEY
WERE OPPOSED BY THE ELYMAS (THAT IS, THE MAGICIAN)
WHO TRIED TO TURN THE GOVERNOR FROM THE FAITH.
THEN SAUL, ALSO KNOWN AS PAUL, FULL OF HOLY SPIRIT,
LOOKED INTENTLY AT
AT HIM 9-10 AND SAID,
"YOU SON OF THE DEVIL,
FULL OF ALL KINDS OF DE-
CEIT AND ENEMY OF ALL
THAT IS RIGHT! WILL
YOU NEVER STOP PERVER-
TING THE STRAIGHT PATHS
OF THE LORD? 11 NOW THE
LORD'S HAND IS ON YOU; YOU
WILL BECOME BLIND AND
FOR A TIME YOU WILL NOT
SEE THE LIGHT OF DAY."
AT ONCE A MISTY DARK-
NESS CAME UPON HIM,
AND HE GROPED ABOUT
FOR SOMEONE TO LEAD
HIM BY THE HAND. 12
THE GOVERNOR SAW
WHAT HAD HAPPENED;
HE BELIEVED, AND
WAS DEEPLY IMPRES-
SED BY THE TEACHING
ABOUT THE LORD.

PAUL IN THE CAPITAL OF PISIDIA

13 FROM PAPHOS, PAUL AND HIS COMPANIONS SET
SAIL AND CAME TO PERGA IN PAMPHYLIA, THERE
JOHN LEFT THEM AND RETURNED TO JERUSALEM.
14 WHILE THEY WENT ON FROM PERGA AND CAME
TO ANTIOCH IN PISIDIA. ON THE SABBATH DAY
THEY ENTERED THE SYNAGOGUE AND SAT DOWN.
15 AFTER THE READING OF THE LAW AND THE PROPHETS,
THE OFFICIAL OF THE SYNAGOGUE SENT THIS
MESSAGE TO THEM,

"BROTHERS, IF YOU HAVE ANY WORD
OF ENCOURAGEMENT FOR THE
ASSEMBLY, PLEASE SPEAK UP."

(16) SO PAUL AROSE, MOTIONED TO THEM FOR SILENCE AND
BEGAN, "FELLOW ISRAELITES AND ALL YOU WHO FEAR GOD,
LISTEN. (17) THE GOD OF OUR PEOPLE ISRAEL CHOSE OUR AN-
CESTORS AND AFTER HE HAD MADE THEM INCREASE DURING
THEIR STAY IN EGYPT, HE LED THEM OUT BY POWERFUL DE-
EDS. (18) FOR FORTY YEARS HE FED THEM IN THE DE-
SERT, AND (19) AFTER HE HAD DESTROYED SEVEN NATIONS
IN THE LAND OF CANAAN, HE GAVE THEM THEIR LAND AS AN
INHERITANCE. (20) ALL THIS TOOK FOUR HUNDRED AND
FIFTY YEARS. (21) AFTER THAT, HE GAVE THEM JUDGES
UNTIL SAMUEL THE PROPHET. THEN THEY ASKED FOR A

KING AND GOD GAVE THEM SAUL, SON OF KISH, OF THE TRIBE
OF BENJAMIN, AND HE WAS KING FOR FORTY YEARS.
(22) AFTER THAT TIME, GOD REMOVED HIM AND
RAISED UP DAVID AS KING, TO WHOM HE BORE WIT-
NESS SAYING: I HAVE FOUND DAVID, THE SON OF JESSE, A
MAN AFTER MY OWN HEART, WHO WILL DO ALL I WANT HIM
TO DO. (23) IT IS FROM THE DESCENDANTS OF DAVID THAT
GOD HAS NOW RAISED UP THE PROMISED SAVIOR OF ISRAEL,
JESUS. (24) BEFORE HE APPEARED, JOHN PROCLAIMED
A BAPTISM OF REPENTANCE FOR ALL THE PEOPLE OF IS-
RAEL. (25) AS JOHN WAS ENDING HIS LIFE'S WORK, HE
SAID: 'I AM NOT WHAT YOU THINK I AM, FOR AFTER ME AN-

OTHER ONE IS COMING
WHOSE SANDALS I AM NOT
WORTHY TO UNTIE.' (26)
BROTHERS, CHILDREN AND
DESCENDANTS OF ABRAHAM,
AND YOU ALSO WHO FEAR
GOD. TO YOU THIS MESSAGE OF
SALVATION HAS BEEN SENT.
(27) IT IS A FACT THAT
THE INHABITANTS OF
JERUSALEM AND THEIR
LEADERS DID NOT RE-
COGNIZE JESUS. YET IN
CONDEMNING HIM, THEY
FULFILLED THE WORDS OF
THE PROPHETS THAT ARE
READ EVERY SABBATH
BUT NOT UNDERSTOOD.
(28) EVEN THOUGH THEY
FOUND NO CHARGE AGA-
INST HIM THAT DESERVED
DEATH, THEY ASKED PILA-
TUS TO HAVE HIM EXECU-
TED. (29) AND AFTER THEY
HAD CARRIED OUT ALL
THAT WAS WRITTEN ABOUT
HIM, THEY TOOK HIM DOWN
FROM THE CROSS AND LAID HIM IN A TOMB. (30) BUT GOD
RAISED HIM FROM THE DEAD. (31) AND FOR MANY
DAYS THEREAFTER HE SHOWED HIMSELF TO THO-
SE WHO HAD COME UP WITH HIM FROM GALILEE TO
JERUSALEM. THEY HAVE NOW BECOME HIS WITNES-
SES BEFORE THE PEOPLE. (32) WE OURSELVES ANNO-
UNCE TO YOU THIS GOOD NEWS: ALL THAT GOD PROMISED
OUR ANCESTORS, (33) HE HAS FULFILLED FOR US, THEIR
DESCENDANTS, BY RAISING JESUS, ACCORDING TO WHAT
IS WRITTEN IN THE SECOND PSALM: YOU ARE MY SON,
TODAY I HAVE BEGOTTEN YOU.

(34) ON RAISING HIM FROM THE DEAD SO THAT HE
WOULD NEVER KNOW THE DECAY OF DEATH, GOD FUL-
FILLED HIS PROMISE: I WILL GIVE YOU THE HOLY BLES-
SINGS, THE SURE ONES, THAT I KEPT FOR DAVID.
(35) MOREOVER, IN ANOTHER PLACE IT IS SAID: YOU WILL NOT
ALLOW YOUR HOLY ONE TO SUFFER CORRUPTION. (36) NOW DA-
VID WAS SUBJECTED TO CORRUPTION, FOR HE DIED AND WAS LAID BE-
SIDE HIS ANCESTORS AFTER HAVING SERVED GOD IN HIS OWN
TIME. (37) BUT THE ONE GOD RAISED UP - JESUS - DIDN'T KNOW
CORRUPTION. (38) THROUGH HIM, FELLOW ISRAELITES, YOU
HAVE FORGIVENESS OF SINS AND ALL FROM WHICH YOU CO-
ULD NOT BE CLEANSED AND

FREED BY THE LAW OF MOSES:
THIS IS OUR GOOD NEWS. (39)
WHOEVER BELIEVES IN HIM
IS FREED OF ALL THIS. (40)
WATCH OUT LEST WHAT WAS
SAID BY THE PROPHET HAP-
PEN TO YOU: (41) TAKE CARE,
YOU CYNICS; BE AMAZED
AND DISAPPEAR! FOR I
AM ABOUT TO DO SOME-
THING IN YOUR DAYS THAT
YOU WOULD NEVER BELI-
EVE EVEN IF YOU HAD BEEN
TOLD." (42) AS THEY WITH-
DREW, THEY WERE INVIT-
ED TO SPEAK AGAIN ON
THE SAME SUBJECT THE
FOLLOWING SABBATH. (43)
AFTER THAT, WHEN THE
ASSEMBLY BROKE UP,
MANY JEWS AND DEVOUT
GOD-FEARING PEOPLE
FOLLOWED THEM AND
TO THESE THEY SPOKE,
URGING THEM TO HOLD
FAST TO THE GRACE OF GOD. (44) THE FOLLOWING

SABBATH ALMOST THE
ENTIRE CITY GATHERED
TO LISTEN TO PAUL, WHO
SPOKE A FAIRLY LONG
TIME ABOUT THE LORD.
(45) BUT THE PRESENCE
OF SUCH A CROWD MADE
THE JEWS JEALOUS. THEY
BEGAN TO OPPOSE WITH
INSULTS WHATEVER PAUL SAID. (46) THEN PAUL AND
BARNABAS SPOKE OUT FIRMLY, SAYING, "IT WAS
NECESSARY THAT GOD'S WORD BE FIRST PROCLAI-
MED TO YOU, BUT SINCE YOU NOW REJECT IT AND
JUDGE YOURSELVES TO BE UNWORTHY OF ETERNAL

LIFE, WE TURN TO NON-JEWISH PEOPLE. (47) FOR THIS WE
WERE COMMANDED BY THE LORD:
I HAVE SET YOU AS A LIGHT TO THE PA-
GAN NATIONS, SO THAT YOU MAY BRING
MY SALVATION TO THE ENDS OF THE EARTH."

Barnabas
DM 08

48 THOSE WHO WERE NOT JEWS REJOICED WHEN
THEY HEARD THIS AND PRAISED THE MESSAGE OF
THE LORD, AND ALL THOSE DESTINED FOR
EVERLASTING LIFE BELIEVED IN IT. THUS THE
WORD SPREAD THROUGHOUT THE WHOLE REGION.
49-50 SOME OF THE JEWS, HOWEVER, INCITED GOD-FEARING
WOMEN OF THE UPPER CLASS AND THE LEADING MEN OF THE CI-
TY AS WELL, AND STIRRED UP AN INTENSE PERSECUTION AGA-
INST PAUL AND BARNABAS. FINALLY, THEY HAD THEM EX-
PELLED FROM THEIR REGION. 51 THE APOSTLES SHOOK
THE DUST FROM THEIR FEET IN PROTEST AGAINST
THIS PEOPLE AND WENT TO ICONIUM, 52 LEAVING THE
DISCIPLES FILLED WITH JOY AND HOLY SPIRIT.

ICONIUM IS EVANGELIZED

14 1 ICONIUM WAS VISITED BY PAUL AND BARNABAS:
THEY WENT INTO THE JEWISH SYNAGOGUE AND PREACH-
ED IN SUCH A MANNER THAT A GREAT NUMBER OF JEWS
AND GREEKS BECAME BELIEVERS. 2 BUT THE JEWS WHO
WOULD NOT BELIEVE STIR-
RED UP THE PAGAN PEOPLE
AND POISONED THEIR MINDS
AGAINST THE BROTHERS. 3
IN SPITE OF THIS PAUL AND
BARNABAS SPENT A LONG
TIME THERE. THEY SPOKE
OF THE LORD, WHO CONFIR-
MED THE MESSAGE OF THE
GRACE OF GOD WITH THE
MIRACULOUS SIGNS AND
WONDERS HE GAVE THEM
POWER TO DO. 4 THERE,
TOO, ALL THE TOWN WAS
STIRRED BY THE TEACHING.
THEY WERE DIVIDED, SOME
SIDING WITH THE JEWS
AND SOME WITH THE APOS-
TLES.. 5 A MOVE WAS
MADE BY PAGANS AND
JEWS, TOGETHER WITH
THEIR LEADERS, TO HARM
THE APOSTLES AND STONE
THEM. 6 BUT PAUL AND
BARNABAS LEARNED OF
THIS AND FLED TO THE LY-
CAONIAN TOWNS OF LYSTRA AND DERBE AND TO THE CO-
UNTRYSIDE, 7 CONTINUING TO PREACH THE GOOD NEWS.

LYSTRA AND DERBE

PAUL AND BARNABAS SPENT A FAIRLY LONG TIME AT
LYSTRA. 8 THERE WAS A CRIPPLED MAN IN LYSTRA
WHO HAD NEVER BEEN ABLE TO STAND OR WALK. 9 ONE
DAY, AS HE WAS LISTENING TO THE PREACHING, PAUL LO-
OKED INTENTLY AT HIM AND SAW THAT HE HAD THE FAITH

TO BE SAVED. 10 SO HE SPOKE TO HIM LOUDLY, "IN THE
NAME OF THE LORD JESUS CHRIST, I COMMAND YOU TO
STAND UP ON YOUR FEET!" AND THE MAN STOOD UP
AND BEGAN TO WALK AROUND. 11 WHEN THE PEOPLE
SAW WHAT PAUL HAD DONE, THEY CRIED OUT IN THE LY-
CAONIA'S LANGUAGE, "THE GODS HAVE COME TO US IN HU-
MAN SHAPE!" 12 THEY NAMED BARNABAS ZEUS, AND PAUL
WAS CALLED HERMES, SINCE HE WAS THE CHIEF SPEAKER.

13 EVEN THE PRIEST OF THE TEMPLE OF ZEUS, WHICH STO-
OD OUTSIDE THE TOWN, BROUGHT OXEN AND GARLANDS TO THE
GATE; WITH THE PEOPLE, HE WANTED TO OFFER SACRIFICE TO
THEM. 14 WHEN BARNABAS AND PAUL HEARD THIS,
THEY TORE THEIR GARMENTS TO SHOW THEIR INDIGNATI-
ON AND RUSHED INTO THE CROWD SHOUTING 15 "FRIENDS,
WHY ARE YOU DOING THIS? WE ARE HUMAN BEINGS
WITH THE SAME WEAKNESS YOU HAVE AND WE ARE
NOW TELLING YOU TO TURN AWAY FROM THESE USE-
LESS THINGS TO THE LIVING GOD WHO MADE THE
HEAVENS, THE EARTH, THE SEA AND ALL THAT

PAUL AND BARNABAS • HOMAGE TO F. BACON •

IS IN THEM. 16 IN PAST GENERATIONS HE ALLOWED EACH
NATION TO GO ITS OWN WAY, 17 THOUGH HE NEVER DID
STOP MAKING HIMSELF KNOWN; FOR HE IS CONTINUALLY
DOING GOOD, GIVING YOU RAIN FROM HEAVEN AND FRUIT-
FUL SEASONS, PROVIDING YOU WITH FOOD AND FILLING
YOUR HEARTS WITH GLADNESS." 18 EVEN THESE WORDS
COULD HARDLY KEEP THE CROWD FROM OFFERING SACRI-
FICE TO THEM. 19 THEY WERE THERE TEACHING SOME
TIME. BUT SOME JEWS ARRIVED FROM ANTIOCH AND
ICONIUM TO ARGUE WITH PAUL AND BARNABAS. THEY

PERSUADED THE PEOPLE TO REJECT THEM, SAYING THAT ALL WAS
UNTRUE. THEY THEN STONED PAUL, DRAGGED HIM OUT OF THE
TOWN LEAVING HIM FOR DEAD. 20 BUT WHEN HIS DISCIPLES
GATHERED AROUND HIM, HE STOOD UP AND RETURNED TO THE
TOWN. THE NEXT DAY HE LEFT FOR DERBE WITH BARNABAS.

RETURN TO ANTIOCH

21 AFTER PROCLAIMING THE GOSPEL IN THAT
TOWN AND MAKING MANY DISCIPLES, THEY RE-
TURNED TO LYSTRA, ICONIUM AND ON TO ANTIOCH.

22 THEY WERE STRENGTHENING THE DISCEPLES AND
ENCOURAGING THEM TO REMAIN FIRM IN THE FAITH, AS THEY
SAID, "WE MUST GO THROUGH MANY TRIALS TO ENTER THE KING-
DOM OF GOD." 23 IN EACH CHURCH THEY APPOINTED ELDERS
AND, AFTER PRAYING AND FASTING, THEY COMMENDED THEM TO
THE LORD IN WHOM THEY HAD PLACED THEIR FAITH. THEN
24 THEY TRAVELED THROUGH PISIDIA, AND CAME TO
PAMPHYLIA. 25 THEY PREACHED THE WORD IN PERGA AND
WENT DOWN TO ATTALIA. 26 FROM THERE THEY SAILED
BACK TO ANTIOCH, WHERE THEY HAD FIRST BEEN COMMEN-
DED TO GOD'S GRACE FOR THE TASK THEY HAD NOW DONE.

27 ON THEY ARRIVAL THEY GATHERED THE CHURCH TOGE-
THER AND TOLD THEM ALL THAT GOD HAD DONE THROUGH
THEM AND HOW HE HAD OPENED THE DOOR OF FAITH TO
THE NON-JEWS. 28 THEY SPENT A FAIRLY LONG
TIME THERE WITH THE DISCIPLES.

THE COUNCIL AT JERUSALEM

15 1 SOME PERSONS WHO HAD COME FROM JUDEA TO
ANTIOCH WERE TEACHING THEIR FOLLOWERS IN THIS
WAY, "UNLESS YOU ARE CIRCUMCISED ACCORDING TO THE
LAW OF MOSES, YOU CANNOT BE SAVED." 2 BECAUSE OF THIS

THERE WAS TROUBLE, AND
PAUL AND BARNABAS HAD FI-
ERCE ARGUMENTS WITH THEM.
FOR PAUL TOLD THE PEOPLE TO
REMAIN AS THEY WERE WHEN
THEY BECAME BELIEVERS.
FINALLY THOSE WHO HAD CO-
ME FROM JERUSALEM SUG-
GESTED THAT PAUL AND BAR-
NABAS WITH OTHERS GO TO
JERUSALEM FOR DISCUS-
SIONS WITH THE APOSTLES
AND ELDERS. 3 THEY
WERE SENT ON THEIR
WAY BY THE CHURCH. AS
THEY PASSED THROUGH
PHOENICIA AND SAMARIA
THEY REPORTED HOW THE
NON-JEWS HAD TURNED
TO GOD, AND THERE WAS
GREAT JOY AMONG ALL
THE BROTHERS AND SIS-
TERS. 4 ON THEIR ARRI-
VAL IN JERUSALEM, THEY
WERE WELCOMED BY THE
CHURCH, THE APOSTLES AND THE ELDERS, TO WHOM THEY
TOLD ALL THAT GOD HAD DONE THROUGH THEM. 5 SOME
BELIEVERS, HOWEVER, WHO BELONGED TO THE PARTY OF THE
PHARISEES, STOOD UP AND SAID THAT NON-JEWISH MEN MUST
BE CIRCUMCISED AND INSTRUCTED TO KEEP THE LAW OF
MOSES. 6 SO THE APOSTLES AND ELDERS MET TO CON-
SIDER THIS MATTER. 7 AS THE DISCUSSIONS INCREASED,
PETER STOOD UP AND SAID, "BROTHERS, YOU KNOW WHAT
GOD DID AMONG US IN THE EARLY DAYS, SO THAT NON-
JEWS COULD HEAR THE GOOD NEWS FROM ME AND BELIEVE.

8 GOD, WHO CAN READ HEARTS, PUT HIMSELF ON THEIR
SIDE BY GIVING THE HOLY SPIRIT TO THEM JUST AS HE DID
TO US. 9 HE MADE NO DISTINCTION BETWEEN US AND
THEM AND CLEANSED THEIR HEARTS THROUGH FAITH.
10 SO WHY DO YOU WANT TO PUT GOD TO THE TEST? WHY DO
YOU LAY ON THE DISCIPLES A BURDEN THAT NEITHER OUR
ANCESTORS NOR WE OURSELVES WERE ABLE TO CARRY?
11 WE BELIEVE, INDEED, THAT WE ARE SAVED THROUGH
THE GRACE OF THE LORD
JESUS, JUST AS THEY
ARE." 12 THE WHOLE
ASSEMBLY KEPT SILENT
AS THEY LISTENED TO
PAUL AND BARNABAS
TELL OF ALL THE MIRACU-
LOUS SIGNS AND WOND-
ERS THAT GOD HAD DONE
THROUGH THEM AMONG
THE NON-JEWS.

13 AFTER THEY HAD
FINISHED, JAMES
SPOKE UP, "LISTEN TO
ME, BROTHERS. 14 SY-
MEON HAS JUST EXPLA-
INED HOW GOD FIRST
SHOWED HIS CARE BY
TAKING A PEOPLE FOR
HIMSELF FROM NON-
JEWISH NATIONS. 15
AND THE WORDS OF THE
PROPHETS AGREE WITH
THIS, FOR SCRIPTURE
SAYS,

16 AFTER THIS I WILL RETURN AND RE-
BUILD THE BOOTH OF DAVID WHICH HAS
FALLEN; I WILL REBUILD ITS RUINS AND SET
IT UP AGAIN. 17 THEN THE REST OF HUMANI-
TY WILL LOOK FOR THE LORD, AND ALL THE NAT-
IONS WILL BE CONSECRATED TO MY NAME. SO,
SAYS THE LORD, WHO DOES TODAY, 18 WHAT HE
DECIDED FROM THE BEGINNING.

19 BECAUSE OF THIS, I THINK THAT WE SHOULD NOT MAKE
DIFFICULTIES FOR THOSE NON-JEWS WHO ARE TURNING
TO GOD. 20 LET US JUST TELL THEM NOT TO EAT
FOOD THAT IS UNCLEAN FROM HAVING BEEN OFFERED
TO IDOLS; TO KEEP THEMSELVES FROM PROHIBI-
TED MARRIAGES; AND NOT TO EAT THE FLESH OF
ANIMALS THAT HAVE BEEN STRANGLED, OR ANY
BLOOD.
21 FOR FROM THE EARLIEST TIMES MOSES
HAS BEEN TAUGHT IN EVERY PLACE, AND EVE-
RY SABBATH HIS LAWS ARE RECALLED."

THE COUNCIL'S LETTERS

22 THEN THE APOSTLES AND ELDERS WITH THE WHOLE
CHURCH DECIDED TO CHOOSE REPRESENTATIVES FROM
AMONG THEM TO SEND TO ANTIOCH WITH PAUL AND
BARNABAS. THESE WERE JUDAS, KNOWN AS BAR-
SABBAS, AND SILAS, BOTH LEADING MEN AMONG THE
BROTHERS. 23 THEY TOOK WITH THEM THE FOLLOWING
LETTER: GREETINGS FROM THE APOSTLES AND ELDERS,
YOUR BROTHERS, TO THE BROTHERS OF NON-JEWISH BIRTH
IN ANTIOCH, SYRIA AND CILICIA. 24 WE HAVE HEARD
THAT SOME PERSONS

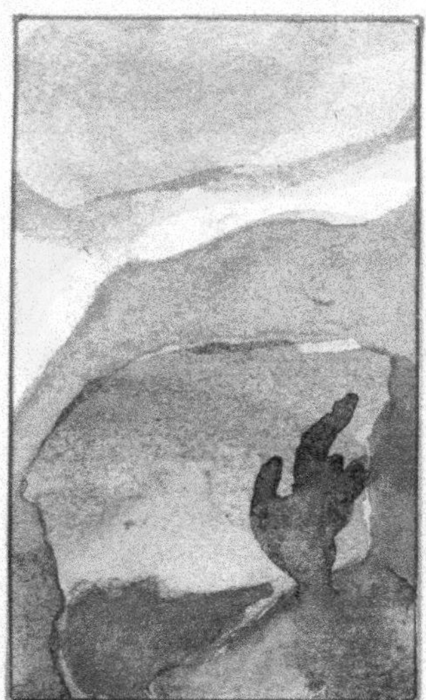

FROM US HAVE WORRIED
YOU WITH THEIR DISCUS-
SIONS AND TROUBLED YO-
UR PEACE OF MIND. THEY
WERE NOT APPOINTED BY
US. 25 BUT NOW, IT HAS
SEEMED RIGHT TO US IN
AN ASSEMBLY, TO CHOOSE
REPRESENTATIVES AND TO
SEND THEM TO YOU, WITH
OUR BELOVED BARNABAS
AND PAUL, 26 WHO HAVE
DEDICATED THEIR LIVES
TO THE SERVICE OF OUR
LORD JESUS CHRIST.
27 WE SEND YOU THEN
JUDAS AND SILAS WHO
THEMSELVES WILL GIVE
YOU THESE INSTRUCTIONS
BY WORD OF MOUTH. 28
WE, WITH THE HOLY
SPIRIT, HAVE DECIDED
NOT TO PUT ANY OTHER
BURDEN ON YOU EXCEPT
WHAT IS NECESSARY: YOU
29 ARE TO ABSTAIN
FROM BLOOD FROM THE MEAT OF STRANGLED ANIMALS
AND FROM PROHIBITED MARRIAGES. IF YOU KEEP YOUR-
SELVES FROM THESE, YOU WILL DO WELL. FAREWELL."

30 AFTER SAYING GOOD-BYE, THE MESSENGER WENT TO
ANTIOCH, WHERE THEY ASSEMBLED THE COMMUNITY AND HAN-
DED THEM THE LETTER. 31 WHEN THEY READ THE NEWS, ALL
WERE DELIGHTED WITH THE HELP IT GAVE THEM. JUDAS
32 AND SILAS, WHO WERE THEMSELVES PROPHETS,

SPOKE AT LENGTH TO ENCOURAGE AND GIVE
STRENGTH TO THEM. 33 AFTER THEY HAD
SPENT SOME TIME THERE, THE MESSENGERS
WERE SENT OFF IN PEACE BY THE BROTHERS;
34 SILAS, HOWEVER, PREFERRED TO STAY
WITH THEM AND ONLY JUDAS WENT OFF.

35 SO PAUL AND BARNABAS CONTINUED IN AN-
TIOCH, TEACHING AND PREACHING WITH MANY
OTHERS THE WORD OF GOD.

PAUL'S SECOND MISSION

36 AFTER SOME DAYS PAUL SAID TO BARNABAS, "LET US
RETURN AND VISIT THE BROTHERS IN EVERY TOWN WHERE
WE PROCLAIMED THE WORD OF THE LORD, TO SEE HOW THEY ARE
GETTING ON." 37 BARNABAS WANTED TO TAKE WITH THEM
JOHN ALSO CALLED MARK, 38 BUT PAUL DID NOT THINK IT
RIGHT TO TAKE HIM SINCE HE HAD NOT STAYED WITH THEM TO THE
END OF THEIR MISSION, BUT HAD TURNED BACK AND LEFT THEM
IN PAMPHYLIA. 39 SUCH A SHARP DISAGREEMENT RESULT-
ED THAT THE TWO FINALLY SEPARATED. BARNABAS TOOK

MARK ALONG AND SAILED FOR CYPRUS. 40 PAUL, FOR HIS
PART, CHOSE SILAS AND LEFT, COMMENDED BY THE BROTHERS
TO THE GRACE OF THE LORD. 41 HE TRAVELED THROUGH SYRIA
AND CILICIA, STRENGTHENING THE CHURCHES THERE.

PAUL RECRUITS TIMOTHY

16 1 PAUL TRAVELED ON TO DERBE AND THEN TO LYSTRA.
A DISCIPLE NAMED TIMOTHY LIVED THERE, WHOSE MO-
THER WAS A BELIEVER OF JEWISH ORIGIN, BUT
WHOSE FATHER WAS A GREEK. 2 AS THE BROTHERS AT
LYSTRA AND ICONIUM SPOKE WELL OF HIM, PAUL WANTED
TIMOTHY TO ACCOMPANY HIM.
3 SO HE TOOK HIM AND
BECAUSE OF THE JEWS OF
THAT PLACE WHO ALL
KNEW THAT HIS FATHER
WAS A GREEK, HE CIR-
CUMCISED HIM. 4 AS
THEY TRAVELED FROM
TOWN TO TOWN, THEY DE-
LIVERED THE DECISIONS
OF THE APOSTLES AND EL-
DERS IN JERUSALEM, FOR
THE PEOPLE TO OBEY. 5
MEANWHILE THE CHURCHES
GREW STRONGER IN FAITH
AND INCREASED IN NUM-
BER EVERY DAY. 6 THEY
TRAVELED THROUGH GA-
LATIA AND PHRYGIA BE-
CAUSE THEY HAD BEEN
PREVENTED BY THE
HOLY SPIRIT FROM
PREACHING THE MES-
SAGE IN THE PROVINCE
OF ASIA.

7 WHEN THEY CAME
TO MYSIA, THEY TRIED TO GO TO BITHYNIA, BUT
THE SPIRIT OF JESUS DID NOT ALLOW THEM
TO DO THIS. 8 SO, PASSING BY MYSIA, THEY
WENT DOWN TO TROAS.

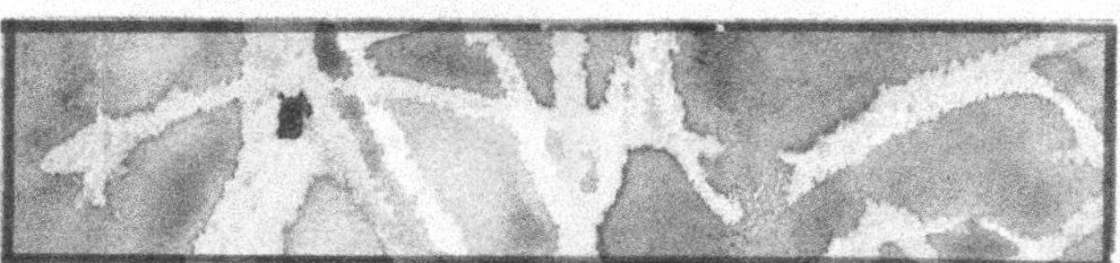

CCCLXII
362

PAUL GOES TO MACEDONIA

9 THERE ONE NIGHT PAUL HAD A VISION. A MACEDONIAN
STOOD BEFORE HIM AND BEGGED HIM, "COME TO MACEDONIA AND
HELP US!" 10 WHEN HE AWOKE, HE TOLD US OF THIS VI-
SION AND WE UNDERSTOOD THAT THE LORD WAS CALLING
US TO GIVE THE GOOD NEWS TO THE MACEDONIAN PEOPLE.
11 SO WE PUT OUT TO SEA FROM TROAS AND SAILED
STRAIGHT ACROSS TO SAMOTHRACE ISLAND, ON THE NEXT
DAY TO NEAPOLIS. FROM

12 THERE WE WENT TO
PHILIPPI, THE MAIN CITY
OF THE DISTRICT OF MA-
CEDONIA, AND A ROMAN
COLONY. WE SPENT SOME
DAYS IN THAT CITY. 13
ON THE SABBATH WE
WENT OUTSIDE THE CITY
GATE TO THE BANK OF THE
RIVER WHERE WE THOUGHT
THE JEWS WOULD GATHER
TO PRAY. WE SAT DOWN
AND BEGAN SPEAKING
TO THE WOMEN WHO WERE
GATHERING THERE. ONE
14 OF THEM WAS A
GOD-FEARING WOMAN
NAMED LYDIA FROM
THYATIRA CITY, A DE-
ALER IN PURPLE CLOTH.
AS SHE LISTENED THE
LORD OPENED HER
HEART TO RESPOND TO
WHAT PAUL WAS SAYING.
15 AFTER SHE HAD BEEN
BAPTIZED TOGETHER WITH
HER HOUSEHOLD, SHE IN-
VITED US TO HER HOUSE, "IF YOU THINK I AM FAITHFUL TO
THE LORD, COME AND STAY AT MY HOUSE." AND SHE PER-
SUADED US TO ACCEPT HER INVITATION.

PAUL AND SILAS IN PRISON

16 ONE DAY, AS WE WERE ON OUR WAY TO THE PLACE OF PRA-
YER, WE WERE MET BY A SLAVE GIRL WHO HAD A DIVINING
SPIRIT AND GAINED MUCH PROFIT FOR HER OWNERS BY
HER FORTUNE-TELLING. 17 SHE FOLLOWED PAUL AND
THE REST OF US SHOUTING, "THESE PEOPLE ARE SERVANTS
OF THE MOST HIGH GOD. THEY WILL MAKE KNOWN TO YOU A
WAY OF SALVATION." 18 THE GIRL DID THIS FOR SEVERAL

DAYS UNTIL PAUL WAS ANNOYED. THEN HE TURNED AROUND
AND SAID TO THE SPIRIT, "IN THE NAME OF JESUS CHRIST, I COM-
MAND YOU, COME OUT OF HER!" THE SPIRIT WENT OUT OF
HER THAT VERY MOMENT. 19 WHEN THE OWNERS RE-
ALIZED THAT ALL THE PROFITS THEY EXPECTED HAD GONE,
THEY SEIZED PAUL AND SILAS AND DRAGGED THEM IN-
TO THE MARKETPLACE BEFORE THE LOCAL AUTHORITIES.
20 AND WHEN THEY HAD TURNED THEM OVER TO THE OF-
FICIALS, THEY SAID. 21 "THESE PEOPLE ARE JEWS AND ARE
DISTURBING OUR CITY. THEY HAVE COME HERE TO INTRO-
DUCE CUSTOMS WHICH ARE NOT LAWFUL FOR US RO-
MANS TO ADOPT OR PRACTICE."

22 SO THEY SET THE CROWD AGAINST THEM
AND THE OFFICIALS TORE THE CLOTHES OFF
PAUL AND SILAS AND ORDERED THEM TO BE
FLOGGED.
23 AND AFTER INFLICTING MANY BLOWS ON
THEM, THEY THREW THEM INTO PRISON, CHAR-
GING THE JAILER TO GUARD THEM SAFELY. 24
UPON RECEIVING THESE INSTRUCTIONS, HE

THREW THEM INTO THE INNER CELL AND FASTENED
THEIR FEET BETWEEN HEAVY BLOCKS OF WOOD.

A MIRACULOUS DELIVERANCE

25 ABOUT MIDNIGHT, PAUL AND SILAS WERE PRAYING AND
SINGING HYMNS TO GOD, AND OTHER PRISONERS WERE LIST-
ENING. 26 SUDDENLY A SEVERE EARTHQUAKE SHOOK THE
PLACE, ROCKING THE PRISON TO ITS FOUNDATION. IMMEDIATELY
ALL THE DOORS FLEW OPEN AND THE CHAINS OF ALL THE PRI-
SONERS FELL OFF. 27 THE JAILER WOKE UP TO SEE THE PRI-
SON GATE WIDE OPEN. THINKING THAT THE PRISONERS HAD
ESCAPED, HE DREW HIS
SWORD TO KILL HIMSELF,

28 BUT PAUL SHOUTED
TO HIM, "DO NOT HARM YOUR-
SELF! WE ARE ALL STILL
HERE." 29 THE JAILER
ASKED FOR A LIGHT,
THEN RUSHED IN, AND
FELL AT THE FEET OF
PAUL AND SILAS. 30
AFTER HE HAD SECURED
THE OTHER PRISONERS, HE
LED THEM OUT AND ASKED,
"SIRS, WHAT MUST I DO TO
BE SAVED?" 31 THEY ANS-
WERED, "BELIEVE IN THE
LORD JESUS CHRIST AND
YOU AND YOUR HOUSEHOLD
WILL BE SAVED." 32 THEN
THEY SPOKE THE WORD OF
GOD TO HIM AND TO ALL
HIS HOUSEHOLD. 33 IT
WAS NIGHT BUT THE JAILER
WASHED THEIR WOUNDS;
HE AND HIS HOUSEHOLD
WERE BAPTIZED. 34 HE
LED THEM INTO HIS HOUSE,

MADE A MEAL FOR THEM AND CELEBRATED WITH HIS HOUSE-
HOLD HIS NEW FAITH IN GOD. 35 THE NEXT MORNING THE
OFFICIALS GAVE THE ORDER. "LET THOSE MEN GO." 36
THE JAILER SAID TO PAUL AND SILAS, "THE OFFICIALS HAVE
SENT AN ORDER FOR YOU AND SILAS TO BE RELEASED. GO
IN PEACE." 37 BUT PAUL SAID TO HIM, "THEY FLOG-
GED US PUBLICLY, AND JAILED US WITHOUT TRIAL,
MEN WHO ARE ROMAN CITIZENS; AND NOW
THEY WANT TO SMUGGLE US OUT SECRE-
TLY? OH NO! LET THEM COME THEMSELVES
AND LEAD US OUT."

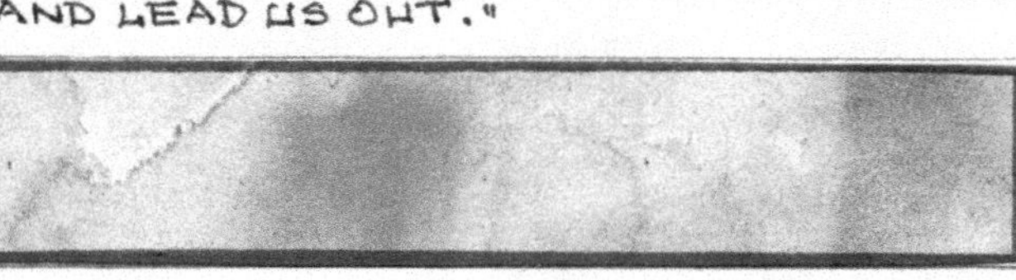

(38) THE POLICE OFFICERS REPORTED THIS TO THE OFFICIALS, WHO WERE AFRAID ON HEARING THAT PAUL AND SILAS WERE ROMAN CITIZENS. (39) SO THEY WENT TO THE PRISON WITH MANY OF THEIR FRIENDS AND INVITED THEM TO LEAVE, "WE DIDN'T KNOW THAT YOU WERE UPRIGHT MEN." AND AS PAUL AND SILAS WERE LEAVING, THEY ADDED, "WHEN YOU ARE OUT, PLEASE DON'T BRING TROUBLE ON US." (40) ONCE OUTSIDE, PAUL AND SILAS WENT TO LYDIA'S HOUSE TO ENCOURAGE THE BROTHERS; THEN THEY DEPARTED FROM THERE.

DIFFICULTIES IN THESSALONICA

17 (1) PAUL AND SILAS WENT THROUGH AMPHIPOLIS AND APOLLONIA AND CAME TO THESSALONICA, WHERE THERE WAS A JEWISH SYNAGOGUE. (2) AS HE USED TO DO, PAUL WENT TO THE SYNAGOGUE AND ON THREE SABBATHS HE HELD DISCUSSIONS ABOUT THE SCRIPTURES. (3) HE EXPLAINED AND PROVED THAT THE MESSIAH HAD TO SUFFER AND RISE FROM THE DEAD; HE SAID, "SUCH A MESSIAH IS THIS JESUS I AM PROCLAIMING TO YOU." (4) SOME OF THEM WERE CONVINCED AND JOINED PAUL AND SILAS. SO TOO DID VERY MANY GREEKS SYMPATHETIC TO JUDAISM AND MANY PROMINENT WOMEN. (5) THIS ONLY MADE THE JEWS JEALOUS, SO THEY GATHERED SOME OF THE GOOD-FOR-NOTHING STREET LOAFERS AND FORMED A MOB TO START A RIOT IN THE TOWN. THEY CAME TO THE HOUSE OF JASON, IN AN ATTEMPT TO BRING PAUL AND SILAS BEFORE THE PEOPLE'S ASSEMBLY. (6) NOT FINDING THEM THERE, THEY DRAGGED OFF JASON AND SOME OF THE BROTHERS TO THE CITY AUTHORITIES SHOUTING, "THESE PEOPLE WHO HAVE TURNED THE WORLD UPSIDE DOWN HAVE COME HERE ALSO, (7) AND JASON HAS GIVEN THEM HOSPITALITY. THEY ALL DISREGARD THE DECREES OF THE EMPEROR AND CLAIM THAT THERE IS ANOTHER KING, JESUS."

(8) IN THIS WAY THEY UPSET THE CROWD AND THE CITY OFFICIALS WHO HEARD THEM. (9) THE OFFICIALS RELEASED JASON AND THE OTHERS ON BAIL. (10) AS

SOON AS NIGHT FELL, THE BROTHERS SENT PAUL AND SILAS OFF TO BEROEA. ON THEIR ARRIVAL, THEY WENT TO THE JEWISH SYNAGOGUE. (11) ITS MEMBERS WERE MORE OPEN-MINDED THAN THOSE IN THESSALONICA AND WELCOMED THE MESSAGE WITH GREAT ENTHUSIASM. EACH DAY THEY EXAMINED THE SCRIPTURES TO SEE IF THESE THINGS WERE SO. (12) MANY OF THEM CAME TO BELIEVE, AS DID NUMEROUS INFLUENTIAL GREEK WOMEN, AND MANY MEN AS WELL.

(13) BUT WHEN THE JEWS OF THESSALONICA CAME TO KNOW THAT THE WORD OF GOD HAD BEEN PROCLAIMED BY PAUL IN BEROEA ALSO, THEY HURRIED THERE TO CAUSE A COMMOTION AND STIR UP THE CROWDS. (14) AT ONCE, THE BROTHERS SENT PAUL AWAY TO THE COAST, BUT BOTH SILAS AND TIMOTHY STAYED IN BEROEA. (15) PAUL WAS TAKEN TO ATHENS BY HIS ESCORT, WHO THEN RETURNED TO BEROEA WITH INSTRUCTIONS FOR SILAS AND TIMOTHY TO COME TO HIM AS SOON AS POSSIBLE.

PAUL IN ATHENS

(16) WHILE PAUL WAS WAITING FOR THEM IN ATHENS, HE FELT VERY UNEASY AT THE SIGHT OF A CITY FULL OF IDOLS. (17) HE HELD DISCUSSIONS IN THE SYNAGOGUE WITH

THE JEWS AND THE GOD-FEARING PEOPLE, AS WELL AS DAILY DEBATES IN THE PUBLIC SQUARE WITH ORDINARY PASSERSBY. (18) EPICUREANS AND STOIC PHILOSOPHERS DEBATED WITH HIM, SOME ASKING, "WHAT IS THIS BABBLER TRYING TO SAY?" OTHERS COMMENTED, "HE SOUNDS LIKE A PROMOTER OF FOREIGN GODS." BECAUSE HE WAS HEARD TO SPEAK OF JESUS AND THE RESURRECTION'.

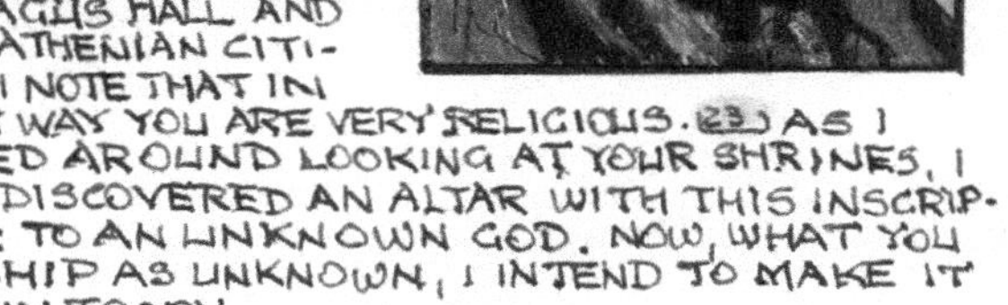

(19) SO THEY TOOK PAUL AND LED HIM OFF TO THE AREOPAGUS HALL AND SAID, "WE WOULD LIKE TO KNOW WHAT THIS NEW TEACHING IS THAT YOU ARE TALKING ABOUT. (20) SOME OF THE THINGS WE HEAR YOU SAY SOUND STRANGE TO US, AND WE WOULD LIKE TO KNOW WHAT THEY MEAN." (21) INDEED, ALL ATHENIAN CITIZENS, AS WELL AS THE FOREIGNERS WHO LIVED THERE, HAVE AS THEIR FAVORITE OCCUPATION TALKING OR LISTENING TO WHAT IS NEW. (22) THEN PAUL STOOD UP IN THE AREOPAGUS HALL AND SAID, "ATHENIAN CITIZENS, I NOTE THAT IN EVERY WAY YOU ARE VERY RELIGIOUS. (23) AS I WALKED AROUND LOOKING AT YOUR SHRINES, I EVEN DISCOVERED AN ALTAR WITH THIS INSCRIPTION: TO AN UNKNOWN GOD. NOW, WHAT YOU WORSHIP AS UNKNOWN, I INTEND TO MAKE IT KNOWN TO YOU. (24) GOD, WHO MADE THE WORLD AND ALL THAT IS IN IT, DOES NOT DWELL IN SANCTUARIES MADE BY HUMAN HANDS, BEING AS HE IS LORD OF HEAVEN AND EARTH.

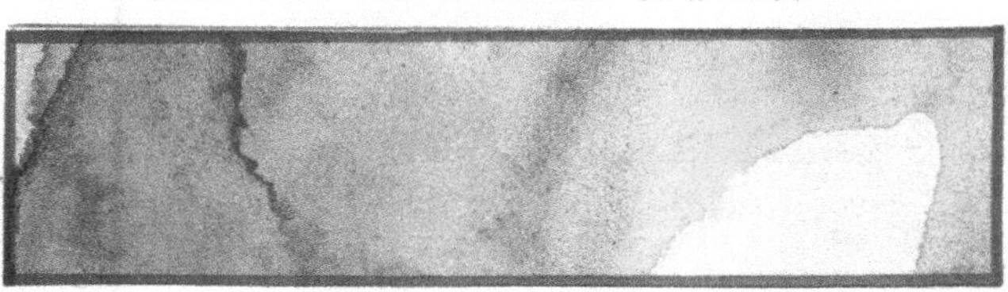

25 NOR DOES HIS WORSHIP DEPEND ON ANYTHING MADE
BY HUMAN HANDS, AS IF HE WERE IN NEED. RATHER IT IS
HE WHO GIVES LIFE AND BREATH AND EVERYTHING ELSE TO
EVERYONE. 26 FROM ONE STOCK HE CREATED THE WHOLE
HUMAN RACE TO LIVE THROUGHOUT ALL THE EARTH, AND HE
FIXED THE TIME AND THE BOUNDARIES OF EACH NATION.
27 HE WANTED THEM TO SEEK HIM BY THEMSELVES, EVEN
IF IT WERE ONLY BY GROPING FOR HIM. YET HE IS NOT FAR
FROM ANY ONE OF US. 28 FOR: IN HIM WE LIVE AND
HAVE OUR BEING, AS SOME OF YOUR POETS HAVE SAID:

FOR WE TOO ARE HIS OFFSPRING.

29 IF WE ARE INDEED GOD'S OFFSPRING, WE OUGHT NOT
TO THINK OF DIVINITY AS SOMETHING LIKE A STATUE OF
GOLD OR SILVER OR STONE, A PRODUCT OF HUMAN ART AND
IMAGINATION. 30 BUT NOW GOD PREFERS TO OVERLOOK
THIS TIME OF IGNORANCE AND HE CALLS ON ALL PE-
OPLE TO CHANGE THEIR WAYS. 31 HE HAS ALREADY
SET A DAY ON WHICH HE WILL JUDGE THE WORLD WITH
JUSTICE THROUGH A MAN HE HAS APPOINTED. AND,
HE HAS GIVEN A SIGN BY RA-
ISING THIS MAN FROM DEATH."
32 WHEN THEY HEARD 'RE-
SURRECTION', SOME MADE
FUN OF HIM, OTHERS SAID,
"WE MUST HEAR YOU ON
THIS TOPIC SOME OTHER
TIME." 33 AT THAT POINT
PAUL LEFT. 34 BUT A FEW
DID JOIN HIM, AND BE-
LIEVED. AMONG THEM
WERE DIONYSIUS, A
MEMBER OF THE
AREOPAGUS COURT
A WOMAN NAMED
DAMARIS, AND AL-
SO SOME OTHER
MEN AND WOMEN.

PAUL IN CORINTH

18 1 AFTER THIS, PAUL LEFT ATHENS AND WENT TO COR-
INTH. 2 THERE HE FOUND A JEW NAMED AQUILA, A
NATIVE OF PONTUS, WHO HAD COME FROM ITALY WITH
HIS WIFE PRISCILLA, AFTER A DECREE OF THE EMPEROR
CLAUDIUS WHICH ORDERED ALL JEWS TO LEAVE ROME.
3 PAUL WENT TO VISIT THEM, STAYED AND WORKED WITH
THEM BECAUSE THEY SHARED THE SAME TRADE OF TENTMA-
KING. EVERY SABBATH 4 HE HELD DISCUSSIONS IN THE
SYNAGOGUE, TRYING TO CONVINCE BOTH JEWS AND GRE-
EKS. 5 WHEN SILAS AND TIMOTHY CAME DOWN
FROM MACEDONIA, PAUL WAS ABLE TO GIVE HIMSELF
WHOLLY TO PREACHING AND PROVING TO THE
JEWS THAT JESUS WAS THE MESSIAH.

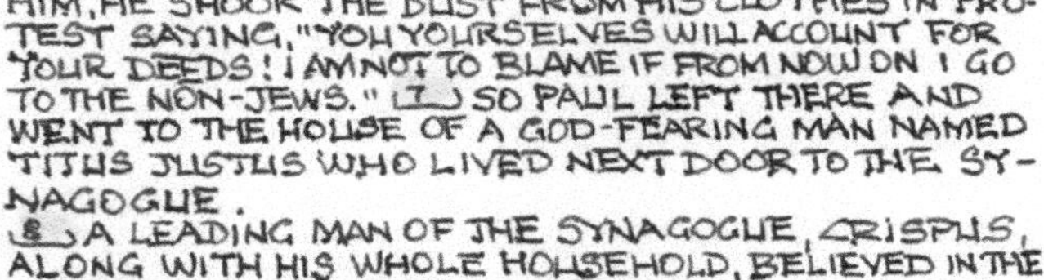

6 ONE DAY WHEN THEY OPPOSED HIM AND INSULTED
HIM, HE SHOOK THE DUST FROM HIS CLOTHES IN PRO-
TEST SAYING, "YOU YOURSELVES WILL ACCOUNT FOR
YOUR DEEDS! I AM NOT TO BLAME IF FROM NOW ON I GO
TO THE NON-JEWS." 7 SO PAUL LEFT THERE AND
WENT TO THE HOUSE OF A GOD-FEARING MAN NAMED
TITUS JUSTUS WHO LIVED NEXT DOOR TO THE SY-
NAGOGUE.
8 A LEADING MAN OF THE SYNAGOGUE, CRISPUS,
ALONG WITH HIS WHOLE HOUSEHOLD, BELIEVED IN THE

LORD. ON HEARING PAUL,
MANY MORE CORINTHIANS
BELIEVED AND WERE BAP-
TIZED. 9 ONE NIGHT, IN
A VISION, THE LORD SAID
TO PAUL, "DO NOT BE
AFRAID, BUT CONTINUE
SPEAKING AND DO NOT
BE SILENT, 10 FOR I
WILL HAVE A HARVEST
OF MANY PEOPLE IN THIS
CITY. SINCE I AM WITH
YOU, NO ONE WILL HARM
YOU." 11 SO PAUL
STAYED A YEAR AND A
HALF IN THAT PLACE,
TEACHING THE WORD
OF GOD AMONG THEM.

12 WHEN GALLIO WAS
GOVERNOR OF ACHAIA, THE
JEWS ROSE IN A BODY
AGAINST PAUL AND BROUGHT HIM BEFORE THE COURT. THEY
ACCUSED HIM, 13 "THIS MAN TRIES TO PERSUADE US TO
WORSHIP GOD IN WAYS THAT ARE AGAINST THE LAW." 14
PAUL WAS ABOUT TO SPEAK IN HIS OWN DEFENSE WHEN
GALLIO SAID TO THE JEWS, "IF IT WERE A MATTER OF A
MISDEED OR VICIOUS CRIME, I WOULD HAVE TO CON-
SIDER YOUR COMPLAINT. 15 BUT SINCE THIS IS A
QUARREL ABOUT TEACHINGS AND DIVINE NAMES
THAT ARE PROPER TO YOUR OWN LAW, SEE TO IT
YOURSELVES: I REFUSE TO JUDGE SUCH MATTERS."
16 AND HE SENT THEM OUT OF THE COURT. 17

THEN THEY ALL SEIZED SOSTHENES, A LEADING MAN
OF THE SYNAGOGUE, AND BEAT HIM IN FRONT OF THE
TRIBUNAL; BUT GALLIO PAID NO ATTENTION TO IT.
18 PAUL STAYED ON WITH THE DISCIPLES IN CO-
RINTH FOR MANY DAYS; HE THEN LEFT THEM AND
SAILED OFF WITH PRISCILLA AND AQUILA FOR
SYRIA. AND AS HE WAS NO LONGER UNDER
A VOW HE HAD TAKEN, HE SHAVED HIS HEAD
BEFORE SAILING FROM CENCHREAE.
19 WHEN THEY REACHED EPHESUS, HE LEFT
PRISCILLA AND AQUILA BEHIND AND ENTERED
THE SYNAGOGUE TO HOLD DISCUSSIONS WITH THE JEWS.

DMID ©
363 CCCLXIII

(20) BUT ALTHOUGH THEY ASKED HIM TO STAY LONGER,
HE DECLINED. (21) AND HE TOOK LEAVE OF THEM
SAYING, "GOD WILLING, I WILL COME BACK TO YOU
AGAIN." THEN HE SET SAIL FROM EPHESUS. (22)
ON LANDING AT CAESAREA, HE WENT UP TO
GREET THE CHURCH, AND THEN WENT DOWN TO
ANTIOCH.
(23) AFTER SPENDING SOME TIME THERE, HE LEFT AND
TRAVELED FROM PLACE TO PLACE THROUGH GALATIA
AND PHRYGIA, STRENGTHENING THE DISCIPLES.

(24) A CERTAIN JEW NAMED APOLLOS, A NATIVE OF ALEX-
ANDRIA, ARRIVED AT EPHESUS. HE WAS AN ELOQUENT

SPEAKER AND AN AUTHO-
RITY ON THE SCRIPTURES.
(25) AND HE HAD SOME
KNOWLEDGE OF THE WAY
OF THE LORD. WITH GREAT
ENTHUSIASM HE PRE-
ACHED AND TAUGHT COR-
RECTLY ABOUT JESUS,
ALTHOUGH HE KNEW
ONLY OF JOHN'S BAPTISM.
(26) AS HE BEGAN TO
SPEAK BOLDLY IN THE
SYNAGOGUE, PRISCILLA
AND AQUILA HEARD HIM;
SO THEY TOOK HIM HOME
WITH THEM AND EXPLA-
INED TO HIM THE WAY
OF GOD MORE ACCU-
RATELY. (27) AS AP-
OLLOS WISHED TO GO TO
ACHAIA, THE BROTHERS
ENCOURAGED HIM AND
WROTE TO THE DISCIPLES
THERE TO WELCOME HIM.
WHEN HE ARRIVED, HE
GREATLY STRENGTHENED
THOSE WHO, BY GOD'S
GRACE, HAD BECOME BELIEVERS, (28) FOR HE VIG-
OROUSLY REFUTED THE JEWS, PROVING FROM THE
SCRIPTURES THAT JESUS IS THE MESSIAH.

PAUL IN EPHESUS

19 (1) WHILE APOLLOS WAS IN CORINTH, PAUL
TRAVELED THROUGH THE INTERIOR OF THE
COUNTRY AND CAME TO EPHESUS. THERE HE
FOUND SOME DISCIPLES (2) WHOM HE ASKED, "DID
YOU RECEIVE THE HOLY SPIRIT WHEN YOU BECAME
BELIEVERS?" THEY ANSWERED, "WE HAVE NOT EVEN

HEARD THAT ANYONE MAY RECEIVE THE HOLY SPIRIT."
(3) PAUL THEN ASKED, "WHAT KIND OF BAPTISM HAVE
YOU RECEIVED?" AND THEY ANSWERED, "THE BAPTISM
OF JOHN."
(4) PAUL THEN EXPLAINED, "JOHN'S BAPTISM
WAS FOR CONVERSION, BUT HE HIMSELF SAID
THEY SHOULD BELIEVE IN THE ONE WHO WAS
TO COME, AND THAT ONE IS JESUS."

(5) UPON HEARING THIS, THEY WERE BAPTIZED
IN THE NAME OF THE LORD JESUS CHRIST.

(6) THEN PAUL LAID HIS HANDS ON THEM AND
THE HOLY SPIRIT CAME DOWN UPON THEM;
AND THEY BEGAN TO SPEAK IN TONGUES AND
TO PROPHESY. (7) THERE WERE ABOUT TWELVE
OF THEM IN ALL.

(8) PAUL WENT INTO THE SYNAGOGUE AND FOR THREE
MONTHS HE PREACHED AND DISCUSSED THERE
BOLDLY, TRYING TO CONVINCE THEM ABOUT THE
KINGDOM OF GOD. (9) SOME OF THEM, INSTEAD OF
BELIEVING, GREW OBSTINATE AND CRITICIZED

THE WAY PUBLICLY. SO PAUL DEPARTED FROM THEM
AND TOOK THE DISCIPLES WITH HIM. HE TAUGHT DAILY
IN THE LECTURE HALL OF A CERTAIN TYRANNUS,
FROM ELEVEN TO FOUR IN THE AFTERNOON. (10) HE
DID THIS FOR TWO YEARS, SO THAT ALL THOSE WHO
LIVED IN THE PROVINCE OF ASIA, BOTH JEWS
AND NON-JEWS, HEARD THE WORD OF THE LORD.

(11) GOD DID EXTRAORDINARY DEEDS OF POWER AT
THE HANDS OF PAUL. (12) EVEN HANDKERCHIEF
OR CLOTHS THAT HAD TOUCHED HIS SKIN WERE
LAID UPON THE SICK
AND THEIR ILLNESS
WERE CURED AND EVIL
SPIRITS ALSO DEPAR-
TED FROM THEM.
(13) SOME JEWS WHO
TRAVELED AROUND DRIV-
ING OUT EVIL SPIRITS,
ALSO TRIED TO USE
THE NAME OF THE LORD
JESUS OVER THOSE
POSSESSED BY EVIL
SPIRITS, SAYING, "I
COMMAND YOU BY THIS
JESUS WHOM PAUL
PREACHES."
(14) AMONG THEM WERE
THE SONS OF A JEWISH
PRIEST NAMED SCEVA.
(15) BUT ONE DAY, WHEN
THEY ENTERED A HO-
USE AND DARED TO
DO THIS, THE EVIL
SPIRIT SAID TO
THEM, "JESUS I
RECOGNIZE AND
PAUL I KNOW; BUT
WHO ARE YOU?" (16) THEN THE MAN WITH THE
EVIL SPIRIT SPRANG AT THEM AND OVERPOWERED
FIRST ONE AND THEN ANOTHER, AND HE HANDLED
THEM SO VIOLENTLY THAT THEY FLED FROM
THAT HOUSE NAKED AND MAULED. (17) THIS
BECAME KNOWN TO ALL THE JEWS AND GREEKS
LIVING IN EPHESUS; ALL OF THEM WERE VERY
IMPRESSED AND THE NAME OF THE LORD
JESUS CAME TO BE HELD IN GREAT HONOR.

(18) MANY OF THOSE WHO HAD BECOME BE-
LIEVERS CAME FORWARD AND OPENLY
ACKNOWLEDGED THEIR FORMER PRACTICES.

19 MANY WHO HAD PRACTICED MAGIC ARTS
COLLECTED THEIR BOOKS AND BURNED THEM
IN FRONT OF EVERYONE. WHEN THE VALUE OF
THESE WAS ASSESSED, IT CAME TO FIFTY THO-
USAND SILVER COINS.
20 IN THIS WAY, THE WORD OF THE LORD
SPREAD WIDELY AND WITH POWER.

THE SILVERSMITHS' RIOT

21 WHEN ALL THESE EVENTS WERE COMPLETED
PAUL, LED BY THE HOLY SPIRIT, DECIDED TO TRAVEL
THROUGH MACEDONIA AND ACHAIA AGAIN AND THEN GO

ON TO JERUSALEM. AND HE SAID, "AFTER I HAVE BEEN
THERE, I MUST VISIT ROME ALSO." 22 SO HE SENT
TWO OF HIS ASSISTANTS, TIMOTHY AND ERASTUS, TO
MACEDONIA AHEAD OF HIM, WHILE HE STAYED ON FOR
A TIME IN ASIA. 23 ABOUT THAT TIME THE CITY
WAS DEEPLY TROUBLED BECAUSE OF THE 'WAY'. 24
IT ALL BEGAN BECAUSE OF A SILVERSMITH NAMED DE-
METRIUS, WHO MADE SILVER MODELS OF THE TEM-
PLE OF THE GODDESS ARTEMIS AND WHOSE BU-
SINESS BROUGHT A GREAT DEAL OF PROFIT TO THE
WORKERS. 25 HE CALLED THEM AND OTHERS WHO DID
SIMILAR WORKS AND SAID,
"FRIENDS, YOU KNOW THAT
OUR PROSPERITY DEPENDS
ON THIS WORK. 26 BUT,
AS YOU CAN SEE AND HEAR
FOR YOURSELVES, THIS PAUL
HAS LED ASTRAY A GREAT
NUMBER OF PEOPLE, NOT
ONLY HERE IN EPHESUS
BUT ALSO THROUGHOUT
MOST OF THE PROVINCE
OF ASIA. AND HE HAS
CONVINCED THEM THAT
GODS MADE BY HUMAN
HANDS ARE NO GODS AT
ALL. 27 THE DANGER
GROWS THAT NOT ONLY
OUR TRADE WILL BE DIS-
CREDITED, BUT EVEN
THE TEMPLE OF THE GREAT
GODDESS ARTEMIS WILL
COUNT FOR NOTHING. SHE
WHOM ASIA AND ALL THE
WORLD WORSHIPS MAY
BE STRIPPED OF HER RE-
NOWN." 28 ON HEARING
THIS THEY BECAME ENRA-
GED AND BEGAN SHOUTING,
"GREAT IS ARTEMIS OF
THE EPHESIANS!" 29

THE UPROAR SPREAD THROUGHOUT THE WHOLE CITY.
THE MOB RUSHED TO THE THEATER, DRAGGING WITH
THEM GAIUS AND ARISTARCHUS, TWO MACEDONIANS
WHO WERE PAUL'S TRAVELING COMPANIONS.
30 PAUL WISHED TO FACE THIS CROWD, BUT THE DISCI-
PLES WOULD NOT LET HIM.
31 SOME OF THE COUNCELORS OF THE ASIAN PRO-
VINCE ALSO, WHO WERE FRIENDS OF PAUL, SENT
HIM A MESSAGE BEGGING HIM NOT TO SHOW
HIMSELF IN THE THEATER.

32 MEANWHILE THE WHOLE ASSEMBLY WAS IN
UPROAR. SOME SHOUTED ONE THING, AND SOME
SHOUTED ANOTHER AND MOST OF THEM DID NOT
KNOW WHY THEY WERE THERE. 33 SOME OF
THE CROWD WANTED A CERTAIN ALEXANDER TO SPEAK WHOM
THE JEWS PUT FORWARD. HE INTENDED TO MAKE A SPEECH OF
DEFENSE BEFORE THE CROWD, 34 BUT WHEN THEY RECOG-
NIZED THAT HE WAS A JEW, THEY ALL CHANTED FOR ABOUT
TWO HOURS, "GREAT IS ARTEMIS OF THE EPHESIANS!" 35
FINALLY THE TOWN CLERK WAS ABLE TO CALM THE MOB.
HE SAID, "CITIZENS OF
EPHESUS, WHO AMONG
YOU DOES NOT KNOW
THAT EPHESUS IS KEEP-
ER OF THE TEMPLE OF THE
GREAT ARTEMIS, AND OF
HER IMAGE WHICH FELL
FROM THE SKY? 36 SINCE
THESE THINGS ARE UN-
DENIABLE, YOU MUST
CALM YOURSELVES AND
DO NOTHING RASH. 37
THESE MEN WHOM YOU
BROUGHT HERE ARE NOT
TEMPLE-ROBBERS
NOR HAVE THEY SPO-
KEN ILL OF OUR GOD-
DESS. 38 IF DEMET-
RIUS AND HIS FEL-
LOW CRAFTSMEN IN-
TEND TO BRING CHAR-
GES AGAINST ANY-
ONE, THE COURTS ARE
OPEN AND THERE ARE
OFFICIALS. LET THEM
BRING CHARGES AG-
AINST EACH OTHER.

39 IF THERE IS ANY-
THING FURTHER THAT NEEDS TO BE INVESTIGATED,
LET IT BE DONE IN THE LAWFUL ASSEMBLY. 40
FOR AS IT IS TODAY, WE ARE IN DANGER OF BEING
CHARGED WITH RIOTING, SINCE THERE IS NO VALID
EXCUSE WE CAN GIVE FOR THIS WILD DEMONSTRATION."
41 AND THE TOWN CLERK DISMISSED THE ASSEMBLY.

PAUL RETURNS TO MACEDONIA

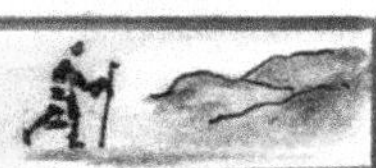

20 1 AFTER THE UPROAR DIED DOWN, PAUL CAL-
LED HIS DISCIPLES TOGETHER TO ENCOURAGE
THEM. THEN HE SAID GOOD-BYE AND SET
OUT ON HIS JOURNEY TO MACEDONIA. 2 HE TRA-
VELED THROUGHOUT THOSE REGIONS AND SPENT

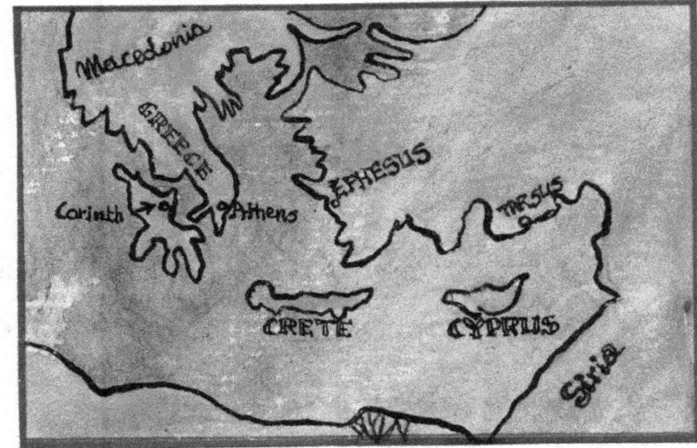

HIMSELF IN SPEAKING AND ENCOURAGING THEM. HE FIN-
ALLY ARRIVED IN GREECE. 3 WHEN HE HAD BEEN
THERE FOR THREE MONTHS, HE WANTED TO SET SAIL
FOR SYRIA BUT AS THE JEWS WERE PLOTTING AGAINST
HIM, HE DECIDED TO RETURN BY WAY OF MACEDONIA.

4 WHEN HE WAS ABOUT TO LEAVE FOR THE ASIAN PROVIN-
CES, SOME FRIENDS WENT WITH HIM, SOPATER, SON OF PYRRHUS,
FROM BEREA, ARISTARCHUS AND SECUNDUS FROM THESSALO-
NICA, GAIUS FROM DERBE, TIMOTHY, TYCHICUS AND TROPHIMUS
FROM ASIA. 5 THEY WENT AHEAD AND WAITED FOR US IN TRO-
AS, 6 WHILE WE SAILED FROM PHILIPPI AS SOON AS THE
FESTIVAL OF UNLEAVENED BREAD WAS OVER. FIVE DAYS LATER
WE JOINED THEM IN TROAS WHERE WE SPENT A WEEK.

THE EUCHARIST AT TROAS

7 ON THE FIRST DAY OF THE WEEK WE WERE TOGETHER FOR THE
BREAKING OF THE BREAD, AND PAUL, WHO INTENDED TO LEAVE
THE FOLLOWING DAY, SPOKE
AT LENGTH. THE DISCOURSE
WENT ON UNTIL MIDNIGHT,
8 WITH MANY LAMPS
BURNING IN THE UPSTAIRS
ROOM WHERE WE WERE GA-
THERED. 9 A YOUNG MAN
NAMED EUTYCHUS WAS
SITTING ON THE WINDOW
LEDGE, AND AS PAUL KEPT
ON TALKING, EUTYCHUS
GREW MORE AND MORE
SLEEPY, UNTIL HE FINAL-
LY WENT SOUND ASLEEP
AND FELL FROM THE THIRD
FLOOR TO THE GROUND.
THERE THEY FOUND HIM
DEAD. 10 PAUL WENT
DOWN, BENT OVER HIM
AND TOOK HIM IN HIS ARMS.
"DO NOT BE ALARMED," HE
SAID, "THERE IS LIFE IN
HIM." 11 THEN HE WENT
BACK UPSTAIRS, BROKE THE
BREAD AND ATE. AFTER
THAT HE KEPT ON TALK-
ING WITH THEM FOR A
LONG TIME UNTIL DAYBREAK AND THEN HE LEFT. 12
AS FOR THE YOUNG MAN, THEY LIFTED HIM UP ALIVE
AND WERE GREATLY COMFORTED.

13 WE WENT ON AHEAD TO THE SHIP AND SAILED
FOR ASSOS, WHERE WE WERE TO PICK UP PAUL. THIS
WAS THE ARRANGEMENT SINCE PAUL INTENDED
TO TRAVEL BY FOOT. 14 IN FACT, WE MET HIM

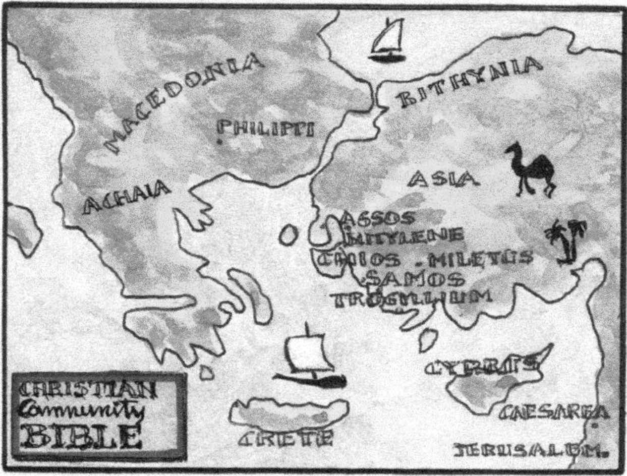

AT ASSOS AND TAKING HIM ABROAD, WE WENT
ON TO MITYLENE. 15 WE SAILED FROM THERE
AND ARRIVED OFF CHIOS THE NEXT DAY. A DAY
LATER WE CAME TO SAMOS AND THE FOLLOW-
ING DAY WE REACHED MILETUS.

16 PAUL HAD DECIDED TO SAIL PAST EPHESUS
SO AS NOT TO LOSE TIME IN ASIA, FOR HE WAS
EAGER TO REACH JERUSALEM BY THE DAY OF
PENTECOST, IF AT ALL POSSIBLE.

FAREWELL TO THE ELDERS

17 FROM MILETUS PAUL SENT WORD TO EPHESUS, SUMMON-
ING THE ELDERS OF THE CHURCH. 18 WHEN THEY CAME TO HIM,
HE SAID TO THEM, "YOU KNOW HOW I LIVED AMONG YOU FROM
THE FIRST DAY I SET FOOT IN ASIA, 19 HOW I SERVED THE
LORD IN HUMILITY THROUGH THE SORROWS AND TRIALS
THAT THE JEWS CAUSED ME. 20 YOU KNOW THAT I NEV-
ER HELD BACK FROM DOING ANYTHING THAT COULD BE
USEFUL FOR YOU; I SPOKE PUBLICLY AND IN YOUR
HOMES 21 AND I URGED JEWS AND NON-JEWS TO
TURN TO GOD AND BELIEVE IN OUR LORD JESUS.
22 BUT NOW I AM GOING TO JERUSALEM, IMPELLED

BY THE SPIRIT, WITHOUT KNOWING WHAT WILL HAPPEN TO
ME THERE. 23 YET IN EVERY CITY THE HOLY SPIRIT WARNS
ME THAT IMPRISONMENT AND TROUBLES AWAIT ME. INDEED
24 I PUT NO VALUE ON MY LIFE, IF ONLY I CAN FIN-
ISH MY RACE AND COMPLETE THE SERVICE TO WHICH
I HAVE BEEN ASSIGNED BY THE LORD JESUS, TO
ANNOUNCE THE GOOD NEWS OF GOD'S GRACE.
25 I NOW FEEL SURE THAT NONE OF YOU AMONG
WHOM I HAVE GONE ABOUT PROCLAIMING THE
KINGDOM OF GOD WILL EVER SEE ME AGAIN. 26
THEREFORE I DECLARE
TO YOU THIS DAY THAT
MY CONSCIENCE IS CLEAR
WITH REGARD TO ALL
OF YOU. 27 FOR I HAVE
SPARED NO EFFORT IN
FULLY DECLARING TO
YOU GOD'S WILL.
28 KEEP WATCH OVER
YOURSELVES AND OVER
THE WHOLE FLOCK THE
HOLY SPIRIT HAS PLACED
INTO YOUR CARE. SHE-
PHERD THE CHURCH OF THE
LORD WHICH HE HAS
WON AT THE PRICE OF HIS
OWN BLOOD. 29 I KNOW
THAT AFTER I LEAVE, WOL-
VES WILL COME AMONG
YOU AND NOT SPARE THE
FLOCK. 30 AND FROM
AMONG YOURSELVES
SOME WILL ARISE COR-
RUPTING THE TRUTH
AND INTRODUCING THE
DISCIPLES HOW TO IND-
UCE THEIR FOLLOWING.
31 BE ON THE WATCH,

REMEMBERING THAT FOR THREE YEARS, NIGHT AND DAY,
I DID NOT CEASE TO WARN EVERYONE EVEN WITH
TEARS. 32 NOW I COMMEND YOU TO GOD AND TO HIS
GRACE-FILLED WORD, WHICH IS ABLE TO MAKE
YOU GROW AND GAIN THE INHERITANCE THAT YOU
SHALL SHARE WITH ALL THE SAINTS.

33 I HAVE NOT LOOKED FOR ANYONE'S SILVER, GOLD
OR CLOTHING. 34 YOU YOURSELVES KNOW THAT
THESE HANDS OF MINE HAVE PROVIDED FOR BOTH
MY NEEDS AND THE NEEDS OF THOSE WHO WERE WITH ME.

ECCE HOMO
364- CCCLXIV
DM 09 ©

35 IN EVERY WAY I HAVE SHOWN YOU THAT BY SO
WORKING HARD ONE MUST HELP THE WEAK, RE-
MEMBERING THE WORDS THAT THE LORD JESUS
HIMSELF SAID, 'HAPPINESS LIES MORE IN GI-
VING THAN IN RECEIVING."

36 AFTER THIS DISCOURSE, PAUL KNELT
DOWN WITH THEM AND PRAYED. 37 THEN
THEY ALL BEGAN TO WEEP AND THREW THEIR
ARMS AROUND HIM AND KISSED HIM.
38 THEY WERE DEEPLY DISTRESSED BECAUSE

HE HAD SAID THAT THEY WOULD NEVER SEE
HIM AGAIN. AND THEY WENT WITH HIM TO THE SHIP.

ON TO JERUSALEM

21 1 WHEN WE HAD FINALLY TAKEN LEAVE OF
THEM, WE PUT OUT TO SEA AND SAILED STRAIGHT
TO COS, AND THE NEXT DAY TO RHODES, AND FROM
THERE TO PATARA. 2 THERE WE FOUND A SHIP
THAT MADE FOR PHOENICIA; WE WENT ABOARD
AND SET SAIL. 3 WE CAUGHT SIGHT OF CYPRUS
BUT PASSED IT BY ON OUR LEFT, AS WE CONTINUED
ON TOWARDS SYRIA. WE LANDED AT TYRE, WHERE
THE SHIP HAD TO UNLOAD CARGO. 4 THERE WE
FOUND THE DISCIPLES AND STAYED A WEEK.
WARNED BY THE SPIRIT, THEY TOLD PAUL NOT TO GO
TO JERUSALEM.

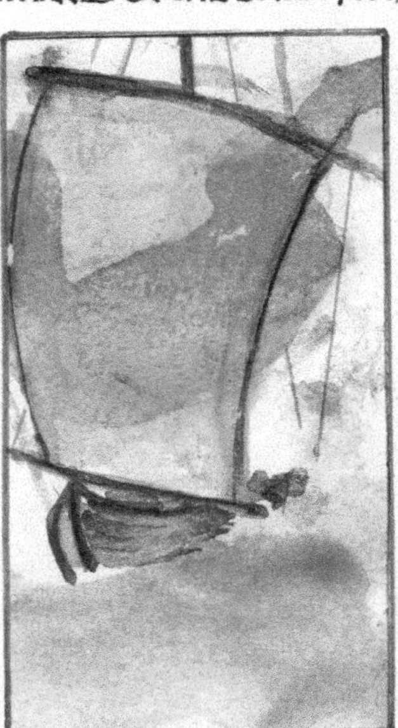

5 BUT WHEN IT WAS
TIME, WE DEPARTED
AND CONTINUED ON
OUR JOURNEY. ALL OF
THEM, WIVES AND
CHILDREN INCLUDED,
CAME OUT OF THE CITY
WITH US, AND ON THE
BEACH WE KNELT
DOWN AND PRAYED.
6 AFTER THAT WE SA-
ID GOOD-BYE TO ONE
ANOTHER; WE BOARDED
THE SHIP AND THEY RE-
TURNED HOME. 7 WE
CONTINUED OUR JOURNEY,
SAILING FROM TYRE TO
PTOLEMAIS, WHERE WE
GREETED THE BROTHERS
AND SISTERS AND SPENT
A DAY WITH THEM. 8
ON THE FOLLOWING DAY
WE LEFT AND CAME
TO CAESAREA. THERE
WE ENTERED THE HOUSE
OF PHILIP THE EVANGELIST
AND WE STAYED WITH HIM.
HE WAS ONE OF THE SEVEN
9 AND HAD FOUR UN-
MARRIED DAUGHTERS
WHO WERE GIFTED WITH PROPHECY. 10 WE WERE
THERE SOME DAYS WHEN A PROPHET NAMED
AGABUS CAME DOWN FROM JUDEA. COMING
TO US, HE TOOK PAUL'S BELT AND BOUND HIS
OWN FEET AND HANDS WITH IT, SAYING, 11
"THUS SPEAKS THE HOLY SPIRIT: THIS IS HOW THE
JEWS IN JERUSALEM WILL BIND THE OWNER
OF THIS BELT AND HAND HIM OVER TO FOREIGN POWER."

12 WHEN WE HEARD THIS, WE, TOGETHER WITH THESE
PEOPLE OF CAESAREA, BEGGED PAUL NOT TO GO UP
TO JERUSALEM. 13 THEN HE ANSWERED, "WHY ARE
YOU WEEPING AND BREAKING MY HEART? FOR I AM
READY NOT ONLY TO BE IMPRISONED BUT ALSO
TO DIE IN JERUSALEM FOR THE NAME OF THE LORD
JESUS." 14 WHEN HE WOULD NOT BE PERSU-
ADED, WE GAVE UP AND SAID, "THE LORD'S WILL
BE DONE."
15 AFTER THIS WE GOT READY AND WENT UP TO
JERUSALEM. 16 WITH US WERE SOME OF THE
DISCIPLES OF CAESAREA WHO BROUGHT US TO
THE HOUSE OF A CYPRIOT WHERE WE WERE TO
STAY. HE WAS CALLED MNASON AND WAS ONE
OF THE EARLY DISCIPLES.

THE CHURCH OF JERUSALEM

17 WHEN WE ARRIVED IN JERUSALEM THE
BROTHERS WELCOMED US WARMLY. 18 THE
NEXT DAY PAUL WENT WITH US TO JAMES'

HOUSE WHERE ALL
THE ELDERS HAD
GATHERED. AFTER
19 GREETING THEM
PAUL BEGAN TEL-
LING THEM IN DETAIL
EVERYTHING GOD
HAD DONE AMONG
THE NON-JEWS
THROUGH HIS MIN-
ISTRY. 20 AFTER
HEARING THIS, THEY
ALL PRAISED GOD,
BUT THEY SAID, "YOU
SEE, BROTHER, HOW
MANY THOUSANDS
OF JEWS OF JUDEA
HAVE NOW COME TO
BELIEVE, AND ALL
OF THEM ARE ZE-
ALOUS FOR THE LAW.
21 YET THEY HAVE
HEARD THAT YOU
TEACH THE JEWS
WHO LIVE IN PAGAN
NATIONS TO DEPART
FROM MOSES, TEL-
LING THEM NOT TO
HAVE THEIR SONS
CIRCUMCISED AND TO RENOUNCE JEWISH
CUSTOMS. 22 WE SHALL GATHER THE AS-
SEMBLY FOR, IN ANY CASE, THEY WILL HEAR
THAT YOU HAVE ARRIVED. 23 THEN DO AS WE
TELL YOU.
THERE ARE FOUR MEN AMONG US WHO HAVE
MADE A VOW. 24 TAKE THEM AND PURIFY YOUR-
SELF ALONG WITH THEM AND PAY THE SA-
CRIFICE FOR THEM TO SHAVE THEIR HEADS.

IN THAT WAY EVERYONE WILL KNOW THAT THERE IS NOTHING
TRUE ABOUT WHAT THEY SAY OF YOU, BUT THAT YOU KEEP
THE LAW. 25 AS FOR THE NON-JEWS WHO HAVE BECOME
BELIEVERS, WE SENT THEM A LETTER TO TELL THEM THAT
THEY ARE ONLY OBLIGED NOT TO EAT MEAT OFFE-
RED TO IDOLS, OR BLOOD, OR FLESH OF STRANGLED ANI-
MALS; AND TO AVOID PROHIBITED SEXUAL UNION."

26 SO THE NEXT DAY PAUL TOOK THE MEN; HE
PURIFIED HIMSELF WITH THEM AND ENTERED
THE TEMPLE TO GIVE NOTICE OF WHAT DAY THE
SACRIFICE WOULD BE OFFERED FOR EACH OF
THEM TO END HIS TIME OF PURIFICATION.

PAUL IS ARRESTED IN THE TEMPLE

27 WHEN THE SEVEN DAYS WERE ALMOST OVER, SOME
JEWS FROM ASIA, WHO SAW PAUL IN THE TEMPLE,
BEGAN TO STIR UP THE CROWD. THEY SEIZED HIM 28

SHOUTING, "FELLOW ISRAELITES, HELP! THIS IS THE MAN
WHO IS SPREADING HIS TEACHING EVERYWHERE AGAINST
OUR PEOPLE, OUR LAW AND THIS SANCTUARY. AND NOW HE
HAS EVEN BROUGHT NON-JEWS INTO THE TEMPLE AREA,
DEFILING THIS HOLY PLACE." 29 THEY SAID THIS BECA-
USE EARLIER THEY HAD SEEN TROPHIMUS, AN EPHES-
IAN, WITH PAUL IN THE CITY AND THEY THOUGHT THAT
PAUL HAD TAKEN HIM INTO THE TEMPLE.
30 THEN TURMOIL SPREAD THROUGH THE WHOLE
CITY. PEOPLE CAME RUNNING FROM ALL SIDES.
THEY SEIZED PAUL AND DRAGGED HIM OUTSIDE
THE TEMPLE. AT ONCE THE GATES WERE SHUT. 31
THEY WOULD HAVE KILLED HIM, HAD NOT A REPORT

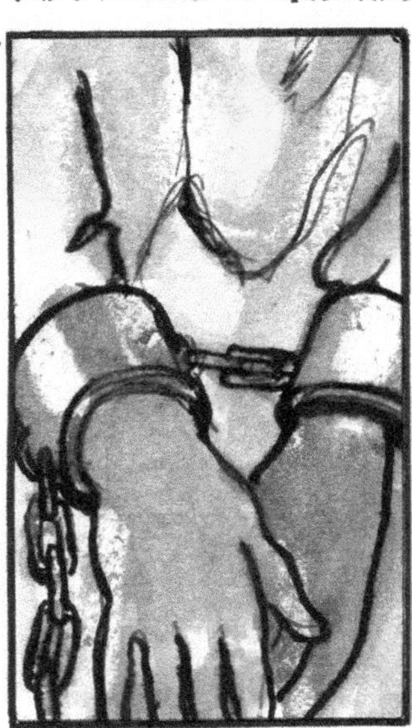

REACHED THE COMMAND-
ER OF THE ROMAN TRO-
OPS THAT ALL OF JERU-
SALEM WAS RIOTING.
32 AT ONCE THE COM-
MANDER TOOK SOME
OFFICERS AND SOLD-
IERS AND RUSHED
DOWN TO THE CROWD.
ON SEEING HIM WITH THE
SOLDIERS, THE CROWD
STOPPED BEATING PAUL.
33 THE COMMANDER
WENT OVER TO PAUL, ARRES-
TED HIM AND ORDERED
HIM TO BE BOUND WITH
TWO CHAINS; THEN HE IN-
QUIRED WHO HE WAS AND
WHAT HE HAD DONE. 34
BUT SOME IN THE CROWD
SHOUTED MANY THINGS,
AND AS THE COMMANDER
WAS UNABLE TO FIND OUT
THE FACTS, HE ORDERED
PAUL TO BE BROUGHT TO
HEADQUARTERS. WHEN
35 PAUL REACHED THE
STEPS, HE HAD TO BE CAR-
RIED UP BY THE SOLDIERS BECAUSE OF THE VIOLENCE
OF THE MOB. 36 FOR A MULTITUDE OF PEOPLE
FOLLOWED SHOUTING, "KILL HIM!"

37 JUST AS HE WAS ABOUT TO BE TAKEN INSIDE,
PAUL SAID TO THE COMMANDER, "MAY I SAY
SOMETHING TO YOU?" HE REPLIED, "SO YOU SPEAK GREEK!

ARE YOU NOT THE EGYPTIAN, THEN, WHO CAUSED
A RIOT SOME TIME AGO AND LET A BAND OF 38
FOUR THOUSAND TERRORISTS OUT INTO THE DE-
SERT?" PAUL ANSWERED, 39 "I AM A JEW, A
CITIZEN OF TARSUS, A WELL KNOW CITY IN CILICIA.
I BEG YOU, LET ME ADDRESS THESE PEOPLE."

THE COMMANDER AGREED. 40 SO PAUL STANDING ON
THE STEPS, MOTIONED TO THE PEOPLE WITH HIS
HAND AND, WHEN THEY WERE SILENT, HE
BEGAN TO SPEAK TO THEM IN HEBREW.

PAUL ADDRESSES THE JEWS

22 1 "BROTHERS AND FATHERS, LISTEN TO WHAT I HAVE
TO SAY IN MY DEFEN E." 2 WHEN THEY HEARD HIM
SPEAKING TO THEM

IN HEBREW, THEY BECAME
VERY QUIET, SO HE WENT
ON. 3 "I AM A JEW, BORN
IN TARSUS IN CILICIA, BUT
BROUGHT UP HERE IN THIS
CITY, WHERE I WAS EDU
CATED IN THE SCHOOL
OF GAMALIEL, ACCORD-
ING TO THE STRICT OB-
SERVANCE OF OUR LAW.
AND I WAS DEDICATED
TO GOD'S SERVICE AS
ARE ALL OF YOU TODAY.
4 AS FOR THIS 'WAY'
I PERSECUTED IT TO THE
POINT OF DEATH AND
ARRESTED ITS FOL-
LOWERS, BOTH MEN
AND WOMEN, THROW-
ING THEM INTO PRISON.
5 THE HIGH PRIEST
AND THE WHOLE CO-
UNCIL OF ELDERS CAN
BEAR WITNESS TO THIS.
FROM THEM I RECEIVED
LETTERS FOR THE JEWISH
BROTHERS IN DAMA-
SCUS AND I SET OUT TO ARREST THE CHRISTIANS
I WOULD FIND THERE AND BRING THEM BACK TO
JERUSALEM FOR PUNISHMENT. 6 BUT AS I
WAS TRAVELING NEARING DAMASCUS, AT ABOUT NOON A
GREAT LIGHT FROM THE SKY FLASHED ON ME. 7 I FELL
TO THE GROUND AND HEARD A VOICE SAYING TO ME: 'SA-
UL, SAUL, WHY DO YOU PERSECUTE ME?' 8 I ANSWERED:
'WHO ARE YOU, LORD?' AND HE SAID TO ME: 'I AM JESUS
THE NAZAREAN WHOM YOU ARE PERSECUTING.'

9 THE MEN WHO WERE WITH ME SAW THE LIGHT AND WERE
AFRAID, BUT DIDN'T UNDERSTAND THE VOICE WHO WAS
SPEAKING TO ME. 10 I ASKED: 'WHAT SHALL I DO, LORD?'
AND THE LORD REPLIED: 'GET UP AND GO TO DAMAS-
CUS; THERE YOU WILL BE TOLD ALL THAT YOU ARE
DESTINED TO DO.' 11 YET THE BRIGHTNESS
OF THAT LIGHT HAD BLINDED ME AND SO I
WAS LED BY HAND INTO DAMASCUS BY MY MEN.

12 THERE A CERTAIN ANANIAS CAME TO ME.
HE WAS A DEVOUT OBSERVER OF THE LAW AND
WELL SPOKEN OF BY ALL THE JEWS WHO
WERE LIVING THERE. 13 AS HE STOOD BY ME,
HE SAID: 'BROTHER SAUL, RECOVER YOUR
SIGHT.' AT THAT MOMENT I COULD SEE AND I
LOOKED AT HIM. 14 HE THEN SAID, 'THE GOD OF
OUR FATHERS HAS CHOSEN YOU TO KNOW HIS WILL,
TO SEE THE JUST ONE AND TO HEAR THE WORDS
FROM HIS MOUTH. 15 FROM NOW ON YOU SHALL

BE HIS WITNESS BEFO-
RE ALL THE PAGAN PE-
OPLES AND TELL THEM
ALL THAT YOU HAVE
SEEN AND HEARD. 16
AND NOW, WHY DELAY?
GET UP AND BE BAPTIZED
AND HAVE YOUR SINS
WASHED AWAY BY CALL-
ING UPON HIS NAME.'
17 ON MY RETURN TO
JERUSALEM I WAS PRAY-
ING IN THE TEMPLE
WHEN I FELL INTO A
TRANCE 18 AND I SAW
HIM. HE SPOKE TO ME:
'GET READY TO LEAVE
JERUSALEM WITHOUT
DELAY, BECAUSE THEY
WILL NOT ACCEPT YOUR
TESTIMONY ABOUT ME.'
19 I ANSWERED: 'LORD,
THEY KNOW WELL THAT I
IMPRISONED THOSE WHO
BELIEVED IN YOU AND HAD
THEM BEATEN IN EVERY
SYNAGOGUE. 20 AND
WHILE THE BLOOD OF
YOUR WITNESS STEPHEN
WAS BEING POURED OUT, I STOOD BY AND APPROVED IT
AND EVEN GUARDED THE CLOAKS OF HIS MURDERERS.'
21 AT THAT POINT HE SAID TO ME: 'GO, FOR I AM
SENDING YOU FAR AWAY TO THE PAGAN NATIONS.'"
22 UP TO THIS POINT THE CROWD LISTENED TO PA-
UL, BUT ON HEARING THE LAST WORDS, THEY BEGAN
TO SHOUT, "KILL HIM! HE DOES NOT DESERVE TO
LIVE!" 23 THEY WERE SCREAMING AND WAV-
ING THEIR CLOAKS AND THROWING DUST INTO
THE AIR. 24 SO THE COMMANDER ORDERED
PAUL TO BE BROUGHT INSIDE THE HEAD-QUARTERS
AND QUESTIONED AFTER FLOGGING, TO FIND OUT WHY

THEY MADE SUCH AN OUTCRY AGAINST HIM. 25
BUT WHEN THE SOLDIERS HAD STRAPPED HIM
DOWN, PAUL SAID TO THE OFFICER STANDING
THERE, "IS IT LEGAL TO FLOG A ROMAN CITI-
ZEN WITHOUT A TRIAL?"
26 ON HEARING THIS THE OFFICER WENT
TO THE COMMANDER AND SAID, "WHAT ARE
YOU DOING? THAT MAN IS A ROMAN CITIZEN."
27 SO THE COMMANDER CAME AND ASKED HIM,
"TELL ME, ARE YOU A ROMAN CITIZEN?"
"YES", ANSWERED PAUL.

28 THE COMMANDER THEN SAID, "IT COST ME
A LARGE SUM OF MONEY TO BECOME A ROMAN
CITIZEN." PAUL ANSWERED, "I AM ONE BY BIRTH."
29 THEN THOSE WHO WERE ABOUT TO QUESTION
HIM BACKED AWAY, AND THE COMMANDER HIMSELF
WAS ALARMED WHEN HE REALIZED THAT HE
HAD PUT A ROMAN CITIZEN IN CHAINS.

PAUL APPEARS BEFORE THE SANHEDRIN

30 THE NEXT DAY THE COMMANDER WANTED TO KNOW THE
CHARGES THE JEWS WERE MAKING AGAINST PAUL. SO
HE RELEASED HIM FROM PRISON AND CALLED THE HIGH

PRIEST AND THE WHOLE COUNCIL; AND THEY BROUGHT PA-
UL DOWN AND MADE HIM STAND BEFORE THEM.

23 1 PAUL LOOKED DIRECTLY AT THE COUNCIL AND SAID,
"BROTHERS, TO THIS DAY I HAVE LIVED WITH A CLEAR
CONSCIENCE BEFORE GOD." 2 AT THAT THE HIGH
PRIEST ANANIAS ORDERED HIS ATTENDANTS TO STRIKE
HIM ON THE MOUTH. 3 THEN PAUL SAID, "GOD WILL

STRIKE YOU, YOU WHITE-
WASHED WALL! YOU SIT TO
JUDGE ME ACCORDING TO
THE LAW, AND YOU BREAK
THE LAW BY ORDERING ME
TO BE STRUCK!" 4 AT THIS
THE ATTENDANTS SAID,
"HOW DARE YOU INSULT
GOD'S HIGH PRIEST?" 5
PAUL ANSWERED, "BRO-
THERS, I DIDN'T KNOW HE
WAS THE HIGH PRIEST. FOR
SCRIPTURE SAYS: 'YOU SHALL
NOT CURSE THE RULER OF
YOUR PEOPLE.'" 6 PAUL
KNEW THAT PART OF THE
COUNCIL WERE SADDUCEES
AND OTHERS PHARISEES;
SO HE SPOKE OUT IN THE
COUNCIL, "BROTHERS, I AM
A PHARISEE, SON OF A PHA-
RISEE. IT IS FOR THE HOPE
IN THE RESURRECTION OF
THE DEAD THAT I AM ON
TRIAL HERE." 7 AT
THESE WORDS, AN AR-
GUMENT BROKE OUT
BETWEEN THE PHARISE-
ES AND THE SADDUCEES AND THE WHOLE ASSEMBLY
WAS DIVIDED. 8 FOR THE SADDUCEES CLAIM THAT THERE
IS NEITHER RESURRECTION, NOR ANGELS NOR SPIRITS,
WHILE THE PHARISEES ACKNOWLEDGE ALL THESE
THINGS. 9 THEN THE SHOUTING GREW LOUDER,
AND SOME TEACHERS OF THE LAW OF THE PHA-
RISEE PARTY PROTESTED, "WE FIND NOTHING
WRONG WITH THIS MAN. MAY BE A SPIRIT OR
AN ANGEL HAS SPOKEN TO HIM."

IN RI
Homage to Eric Gill
365-CCCLXV
DM 09 ©

10 WITH THIS THE ARGUMENT BECAME SO VIOLENT
THAT THE COMMANDER FEARED THAT PAUL WOULD
BE TORN TO PIECES BY THEM. HE THEREFORE OR-
DERED THE SOLDIERS TO GO DOWN AND RESCUE
HIM FROM THEIR MIDST AND TAKE HIM BACK
TO HEADQUARTERS.
11 THAT NIGHT THE LORD STOOD BY PAUL AND SAID,
"COURAGE!" AS YOU HAVE BORNE WITNESS TO ME HERE
IN JERUSALEM, SO MUST YOU DO IN ROME."

THE PLOT TO KILL PAUL

12 WHEN IT WAS DAY, CERTAIN JEWS FORMED A CON-
SPIRACY: THEY BOUND THEMSELVES BY AN OATH NOT TO

EAT OR DRINK UNTIL THEY HAD KILLED PAUL. THERE
13 WERE MORE THAN FORTY OF THEM WHO JOINED IN THIS
CONSPIRACY. 14 THEY WENT TO THE HIGH PRIESTS AND
THE ELDERS AND SAID, "WE HAVE BOUND OURSELVES BY
OATH NOT TO TASTE FOOD UNTIL WE HAVE KILLED PAUL.
15 NOW THEN, IT IS UP TO YOU AND THE COUNCIL
TO CONVINCE THE ROMAN COMMANDER TO BRING
HIM DOWN TO YOU ON THE PRETEXT THAT YOU WANT
TO INVESTIGATE HIS CASE MORE THOROUGHLY. WE,
FOR OUR PART, ARE PREPARED TO KILL HIM BEFORE
HE GETS THERE." 16 BUT THE SON OF PAUL'S SISTER
HEARD ABOUT THE PLANNED AMBUSH, SO HE WENT

TO THE HEADQUARTERS
AND INFORMORMED PA-
UL. 17 PAUL SENT FOR
ONE OF THE OFFICERS
AND SAID, "TAKE THIS
YOUNG MAN TO THE COM-
MANDER FOR HE HAS
SOMETHING TO REPORT
TO HIM." 18 SO THE OF-
FICER TOOK HIM AND
BROUGHT HIM TO THE COM-
MANDER, SAYING, "THE
PRISONER PAUL CALLED
ME AND ASKED ME TO
BRING THIS BOY TO YOU
BECAUSE HE HAS SO-
METHING TO TELL YOU."
19 THE COMMANDER TO-
OK HIM BY THE HAND
AND DRAWING HIM ASIDE
ASKED HIM, "WHAT IS IT
THAT YOU HAVE TO REPORT
TO ME?" 20 THE BOY
REPLIED, "THE JEWS
HAVE AGREED AMONG
THEMSELVES TO ASK
YOU TOMORROW TO HAVE
PAUL BROUGHT TO THE
COUNCIL AS IF TO INQUIRE MORE THOROUGHLY
ABOUT HIM. 21 BUT DO NOT BE PERSUADED BY
THEM, FOR THERE ARE MORE THAN FORTY OF THEM
READY TO AMBUSH HIM, HAVING BOUND THEMSELVES
BY AN OATH NOT TO EAT OR DRINK UNTIL THEY HAVE
KILLED HIM. THEY ARE NOW READY TO DO IT
AND ARE AWAITING YOUR DECISION."

22 THE COMMANDER LET THE BOY GO WITH
THIS ADVICE. "DO NOT TELL ANYONE THAT YOU
GAVE ME THIS INFORMATION."

PAUL IS TRANSFERRED TO CAESAREA

23 THE COMMANDER SUMMONED TWO OF HIS OFFICERS AND
SAID TO THEM, "GET READY TO LEAVE FOR CAESAREA BY NINE
O'CLOCK TONIGHT, WITH TWO HUNDRED INFANTRYMEN, SEVENTY
HORSEMEN AND TWO HUNDRED SPEARMEN. 24 PROVIDE
HORSES ALSO FOR PAUL TO RIDE, SO THAT HE MAY BE
BROUGHT SAFELY TO FELIX THE GOVERNOR." 25 HE THEN
WROTE TO THE GOVERNOR A LETTER TO THIS EFFECT:

26 "CLAUDIUS LYSIAS GREETS THE EXCELLENT
GOVERNOR FELIX AND COMMUNICATES TO
HIM THE FOLLOWING: 27 THE JEWS HAD
ARRESTED THIS MAN TO KILL HIM WHEN I
INTERVENED WITH MY TROOPS AND TOOK
HIM OUT FROM THEM AS I KNEW HE WAS
A ROMAN CITIZEN. 28 AS I WANTED TO
KNOW WHAT CHARGE THEY HAD AGAINST
HIM, I PRESENTED HIM BEFORE THE
SANHEDRIN AND 29 I DISCOVERED
THAT THE ACCUSATION RELATED TO THEIR
LAW, BUT THERE WAS NOTHING WHICH
DESERVED DEATH OR IMPRISONMENT.
30 WHEN I WAS INFORMED THAT THE
JEWS HAD PREPARED A PLOT AGAINST
THIS MAN, I DECIDED
TO BEND HIM TO YOU
AND TOLD HIS
ACCUSERS TO
PRESENT THEIR
COMPLAINTS
BEFORE YOU.
FAREWELL."

31 THE SOLDIERS ACTED IN ACCORDANCE WITH THESE
INSTRUCTIONS. THEY TOOK PAUL AND BROUGHT HIM
TO ANTIPATRIS BY NIGHT. 32 ON THE FOLLOWING DAY,

THEY RETURNED TO THE FORTRESS BUT THE HORSEMEN WENT
WITH HIM. 33 ON ENTERING CAESAREA THEY HANDED THE
LETTER TO THE GOVERNOR AND PRESENTED PAUL TO HIM. 34
WHEN FELIX HAD READ THE LETTER, HE ASKED PAUL
FROM WHICH PROVINCE HE WAS, AND WHEN HE LEARNED
THAT PAUL WAS FROM CILICIA, 35 HE SAID TO HIM: "I
SHALL HEAR YOUR ACCUSERS WHEN THEY COME." AND
HE ORDERED THAT HE BE KEPT IN CUSTODY IN THE
PALACE OF HEROD.

ACTS -24-

THE CASE BEFORE FELIX

24 (1) AFTER FIVE DAYS ANANIAS THE HIGH PRIEST
CAME TO CAESAREA WITH SOME OF THE ELDERS
AND A LAWYER NAMED TERTULLUS. AND THEY PRE-
SENTED THEIR CASE AGAINST PAUL BEFORE THE GOVER-
NOR. (2) PAUL WAS CALLED IN AND TERTULLUS ACCU-
SED HIM IN THIS WAY: (3) "MOST EXCELLENT FELIX,
THANKS TO YOU, YOUR LABORS AND YOUR WISE RE
FORMS, OUR PEOPLE NOW ENJOY GREAT PEACE.

OIL ON CANVAS · 1997
92 x 66 cm.

WE ACCEPT ALL THIS
IN EVERY WAY AND IN
EVERY PLACE, AND WE
ARE TOTALLY GRATE-
FUL TO YOU. (4) SO AS
NOT TO TAKE MORE OF
YOUR TIME, I BEG YOU
TO LISTEN BRIEFLY TO
US WITH YOUR USUAL
KINDNESS. (5) WE HAVE
FOUND THAT THIS MAN
IS A PEST, HE CREATES
DIVISION AMONG THE
JEWS THROUGHOUT THE
WORLD AND IS A LEADER
OF THE NAZARENE SECT.
(6) HE EVEN TRIED TO
PROFANE THE TEMPLE,
SO WE SEIZED HIM. WE
WOULD HAVE JUDGED
HIM ACCORDING TO OUR
LAW, (7) BUT LYSIAS
THE COMMANDANT INTER-
VENED IN A VERY VIOLENT
WAY AND TOOK HIM FROM
US. (8) THEN HE DECLARED
THAT HIS ACCUSERS MUST
PRESENT THEMSELVES BE-
FORE YOU. BY EXAMINING HIM YOURSELF, YOU WILL LE-
ARN FROM HIM ABOUT ALL THAT WE ACCUSE HIM
OF." (9) THE JEWS CONFIRMED THIS, FIRMLY
MANTAINING THAT ALL THIS WAS SO.
(10) THEN THE GOVERNOR MOTIONED TO PAUL WHO
SAID:
"AS I KNOW THAT YOU HAVE ADMINISTERED THIS NA-
TION FOR MANY YEARS, I MAKE MY DEFENSE WITH
MUCH CONFIDENCE. (11) YOU YOURSELF CAN ASCERTAIN
THAT NO MORE THAN TWELVE DAYS AGO I WENT UP
TO JERUSALEM TO WORSHIP, (12) AND THAT THEY DID
NOT FIND ME DISPUTING WITH ANYONE OR INCITING
THE PEOPLE, EITHER IN THE TEMPLE OR IN THE

SYNAGOGUES OR IN THE CITY. (13) SO THEY
CANNOT PROVE THE THINGS OF WHICH THEY
NOW ACCUSE ME.
(14) BUT THIS I ADMIT BEFORE YOU, THAT I
SERVE THE GOD OF OUR FATHERS ACCORD-
ING TO THE WAY WHICH THEY CALL A SECT.
I BELIEVE EVERYTHING WRITTEN IN THE LAW
AND IN THE PROPHETS, (15) AND I HAVE THE
SAME HOPE IN GOD THAT THEY HAVE, THAT
THERE WILL BE A RESURRECTION OF THE DEAD,
BOTH THE GOOD AND THE SINNERS.

(16) SO I STRIVE ALWAYS TO HAVE A CLEAR
CONSCIENCE BEFORE GOD AND BEFORE PE-
OPLE.
(17) AFTER MANY YEARS, I CAME TO BRING
HELP TO THOSE OF MY NATION AND TO OFFER
SACRIFICES. (18) ON THAT OCCASION THEY
FOUND ME IN THE TEMPLE; I HAD BEEN PURI-
FIED ACCORDING TO THE LAW AND THERE
WAS NO CROWD OR COMMOTION. YET ALL
BEGAN WITH SOME JEWS FROM ASIA, (19)
WHO OUGHT TO BE HERE BEFORE YOU TO
ACCUSE ME, IF THEY HAVE ANYTHING AGAINST
ME. (20) LET THESE MEN SAY WHAT CRIME

HOMAGE TO LOWRY

THEY FOUND IN ME WHEN I STOOD BEFORE THE
SANHEDRIN, (21) UNLESS IT WAS FOR HAV-
ING DECLARED IN A LOUD VOICE WHEN I
WAS BEFORE THEM:

"TODAY I AM BEING JUDGED ON ACCOUNT OF
THE RESURRECTION OF THE DEAD."

(22) FELIX WHO WAS WELL INFORMED ABOUT THE
WAY, POSPONED THE CASE AND SAID TO THEM, "WHEN
THE COMMANDANT, LYSIAS
CAME DOWN, I WILL EXA-
MINE THE CASE THORO-
UGHLY." (23) SO HE ORDE
RED THE CAPTAIN TO KEEP
PAUL UNDER GUARD, GIV-
ING HIM SOME LIBERTY
AND WITHOUT PREVENT-
ING HIS FRIENDS FROM
ATTENDING TO HIM. (24)
AFTER SOME DAYS, FE-
LIX CAME WITH HIS WI-
FE DRUSILLA, WHO WAS A
JEW. HE SENT FOR PAUL
AND LET HIM SPEAK
ABOUT FAITH IN CHRIST.
(25) BUT WHEN PAUL
SPOKE ABOUT JUST-
ICE, SELF-CONTROL
AND THE FUTURE
JUDGEMENT, FELIX
WAS FRIGHTENED
AND HE SAID TO HIM:
"YOU MAY LEAVE
NOW; I SHALL SEND
FOR YOU SOME OT-
HER TIME."
(26) FELIX WAS HO-
PING THAT PAUL
WOULD GIVE HIM MONEY, SO HE SENT
FOR HIM OFTEN AND CONVERSED WITH HIM.

FELIX

(27) TWO YEARS PASSED, AND FELIX WAS
SUCCEEDED BY PORCIUS FESTUS; AND AS
FELIX WANTED TO REMAIN ON GOOD TERMS
WITH THE JEWS, HE LEFT PAUL IN PRISON.

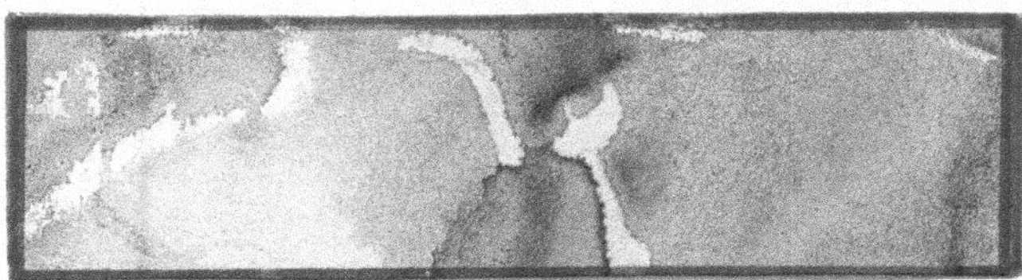

THE TRIAL BEFORE FESTUS

25 1 THREE DAYS AFTER FESTUS ARRIVED IN THE PRO-
VINCE, HE WENT FROM CAESAREA TO JERUSALEM.
2 THERE THE CHIEF PRIESTS AND THE ELDERS AC-
CUSED PAUL AGAIN 3 IN A HYPOCRITICAL WAY. THEY
ASKED AS A FAVOR FROM FESTUS THAT PAUL BE BROUGHT
TO JERUSALEM; BUT THEY WERE PLANNING TO KILL HIM
ON THE WAY. 4 FESTUS ANSWERED THAT PAUL WAS IN
CUSTODY IN CAESAREA AND, AS HE HIMSELF HAD TO GO
THERE SHORTLY, HE ADDED, 5 "LET THOSE OF YOU WHO
HAVE THE AUTHORITY GO DOWN WITH ME TO CAESAREA,

AND IF THIS MAN HAS DONE ANYTHING WRONG, LET
THEM ACCUSE HIM." 6 FESTUS DIDN'T STAY IN JERU-
SALEM FOR MORE THAN EIGHT OR TEN DAYS, AND THEN HE
WENT TO CAESAREA. THE NEXT DAY HE TOOK HIS SEAT ON
THE TRIBUNAL AND SENT FOR PAUL. 7 WHEN PAUL
ARRIVED, THE JEWS WHO CAME FROM JERUSALEM WITH
HIM PRESENTED MANY SERIOUS CHARGES WHICH THEY
COULD NOT PROVE. 8 PAUL DEFENDED HIMSELF FROM
ALL THESE SAYING, "I HAVE NOT COMMITTED ANY OFFEN-
SE AGAINST THE LAW OF THE JEWS, OR AGAINST THE
TEMPLE OR AGAINST CAESAR."
9 THEN FESTUS, WHO WANTED TO PLEASE THE JEWS,
ASKED PAUL: "DO YOU
WISH TO GO UP TO JERU-
SALEM TO BE TRIED BE-
FORE ME?" 10 PAUL ANS-
WERED, "I AM ON TRIAL BE-
FORE CAESAR'S TRIBU-
NAL: HERE I HAVE TO BE
TRIED. I HAVE DONE NO
WRONG TO THE JEWS:
YOU KNOW THIS VERY
WELL. 11 IF I HAVE COM
MITTED ANY CRIME TO
DESERVE DEATH, I AC-
CEPT DEATH. BUT IF I
HAVE NOT DONE ANY-
THING OF WHICH THEY
ACCUSE ME, NO ONE
CAN GIVE ME UP TO THEM.
I APPEAL TO CAESAR."
12 SO FESTUS, AFTER
CONFERRING WITH
HIS COUNCIL, ANS-
WERED, "YOU HAVE
APPEAL TO CAESAR.
TO CAESAR YOU SHALL
GO." 13 SOME DAYS
LATER KING AGRIPPA AND HIS SISTER BERNICE
ARRIVED IN CAESAREA TO GREET FESTUS. AS THEY
WERE TO STAY THERE SEVERAL DAYS, FESTUS TOLD THE
KING ABOUT PAUL'S CASE AND SAID TO HIM,
14 WE HAVE HERE A MAN WHOM FELIX LEFT
AS A PRISONER. 15 WHEN I WAS IN JERU-
SALEM, THE CHIEF PRIESTS AND THE ELDERS
OF THE JEWS ACCUSED HIM AND ASKED ME
TO SENTENCE HIM.

16 I TOLD THEM THAT IT IS NOT THE CUSTOM
OF THE ROMANS TO HAND OVER A MAN WITHOUT
GIVING HIM AN OPPORTUNITY TO DEFEND HIMSELF IN
FRONT OF HIS ACCUSERS. 17 SO THEY CAME AND
I TOOK MY SEAT WITHOUT DELAY ON THE TRIBUNAL
AND SENT FOR THE MAN.

18 WHEN THE ACCUSERS HAD THE FLOOR, THEY DID
NOT ACCUSE HIM OF ANY OF THE CRIMES THAT
I WAS LED TO THINK
HE HAD COMMITTED;
19 INSTEAD THEY
QUARRELED WITH
HIM ABOUT RELIGION
AND ABOUT A CERTAIN
JESUS WHO HAD DIED
BUT WHOM PAUL AS-
SERTED TO BE ALIVE.
20 I DID NOT KNOW
WHAT TO DO ABOUT THIS
CASE, SO I ASKED PAUL
IF HE WANTED TO GO TO
JERUSALEM TO BE TRIED
THERE. 21 BUT PAUL
APPEALED TO BE JUDGED
BY THE EMPEROR. SO I
ORDERED THAT HE BE
KEPT IN CUSTODY UN-
TIL I SEND HIM TO
CAESAR." 22 AGRIPPA
SAID TO FESTUS: "I
WOULD LIKE TO HEAR
THE MAN." FESTUS ANS-
WERED: "TOMORROW
YOU SHALL." 23 ON
THE FOLLOWING DAY,
AGRIPPA AND BERNICE ARRIVED WITH GREAT CERIMO-
NY INTO THE AUDIENCE HALL WITH THE COMMANDER AND
THE CITY ELDERS. FESTUS ORDERED PAUL TO BE BROUGHT
IN AND SAID: 24 KING AGRIPPA AND ALL HERE PRESENT,
HERE YOU SEE THIS MAN ABOUT WHOM THE WHOLE
COMMUNITY OF THE JEWS CAME TO SEE ME, IN JE-
RUSALEM AS WELL AS HERE, PROTESTING LOUDLY
THAT HE MUST NOT LIVE. 25 I, FOR MY PART, AM
CONVINCED THAT HE HAS NOT DONE ANYTHING
THAT DESERVES DEATH. BUT AFTER HE APPEALED
TO BE JUDGED BY THE EMPEROR, I DECIDED TO

SEND HIM ON. 26 WELL, IF I HAVE NO DEFINTE IN-
FORMATION, WHAT CAN I WRITE TO CAESAR ABOUT HIM?
THEREFORE I PRESENT HIM BEFORE ALL OF YOU, AND
ESPECIALLY BEFORE YOU, KING AGRIPPA, FOR YOU TO
EXAMINE HIM AND THAT HE MAY KNOW WHAT TO WRITE.
27 FOR IT SEEMS ABSURD TO ME TO SEND A PRISO-
NER WITHOUT INDICATING THE CHARGES AGAINST
HIM."

PAUL BEFORE KING AGRIPPA

26 1 AGRIPPA SAID TO PAUL: "YOU MAY SPEAK
IN YOUR OWN DEFENSE." SO PAUL STRET-
CHED OUT HIS HAND AND BEGAN IN THIS
WAY:

TODAY I AM BEING
JUDGED ON ACCOUNT
OF THE RESURRECTION
OF THE DEAD.
(ACTS 24:21)
366-CCCLXVI ©

2 "KING AGRIPPA, YOU HAVE JUST REFERRED TO THE
ACCUSATIONS OF THE JEWS. I CONSIDER MYSELF FORTUNATE
IN BEING ABLE TO DEFEND MYSELF AGAINST ALL THIS BE-
FORE YOU TODAY, 3 FOR YOU ARE AN EXPERT IN THE
CUSTOMS OF THE JEWS AND THEIR DISPUTES. THEREFORE
I BEG YOU TO LISTEN TO ME PATIENTLY.
4 ALL THE JEWS KNOW HOW I HAVE LIVED FROM MY
YOUTH, HOW I HAVE LIVED AMONG MY OWN PEOPLE
AND IN JERUSALEM. 5 THEY HAVE ALWAYS
KNOWN ME AND THEY CAN TELL YOU, IF THEY
WISH, THAT I HAVE LIVED AS A PHARISEE IN
THE MOST RIGOROUS SECT OF OUR RELIGION.
6 IF I AM NOW TRIED HERE, IT IS BECAUSE OF
THE HOPE I HAVE IN
THE PROMISE MADE BY
GOD TO OUR FATHERS.
7 THE PROMISE IS THE
GOAL WHICH OUR TWELVE
TRIBES HOPE TO ATTAIN
WITH THE FERVENT WOR-
SHIP THEY RENDER TO
GOD NIGHT AND DAY. FOR
THIS HOPE, O KING, THE
JEWS ACCUSE ME! 8
BUT WHY REFUSE TO BE-
LIEVE THAT GOD RAISES
THE DEAD? 9 I MY-
SELF IN THE BEGINNING
THOUGHT THAT I HAD
TO USE ALL POSSIBLE
MEANS TO CONTERACT
THE NAME OF JESUS
OF NAZARETH. THIS
10 I DID IN JERUSALEM
AND, WITH THE AUTHO-
RIZATION OF THE CHIEF
PRIESTS, I PUT IN PRI-
SON MANY WHO BELI-
EVED; AND I CAST MY
VOTE WHEN THEY WE-
RE CONDEMNED TO
DEATH. 11 I WENT RO-
UND THE SYNAGOGUES
AND MULTIPLIED PU-
NISHMENTS AGAINST
THEM TO FORCE THEM
TO RENOUNCE THEIR FAITH; SUCH WAS MY RAGE
AGAINST THEM THAT I PURSUED THEM EVEN TO
FOREIGN CITIES.

12 WITH THIS PURPOSE IN MIND I WENT TO DAMAS-
CUS WITH FULL AUTHORITY AND COMMISSIONED BY THE
CHIEF PRIESTS. ON THE WAY, 13 O KING, AT MIDDAY I SAW
A LIGHT FROM HEAVEN, MORE BRILLIANT THAN THE SUN,
THAT DAZZLED ME AND THOSE WHO ACCOMPANIED ME.
14 WE ALL FELL TO THE GROUND AND I HEARD A VO-
ICE SAYING TO ME IN HEBREW: 'SAUL, SAUL, WHY DO

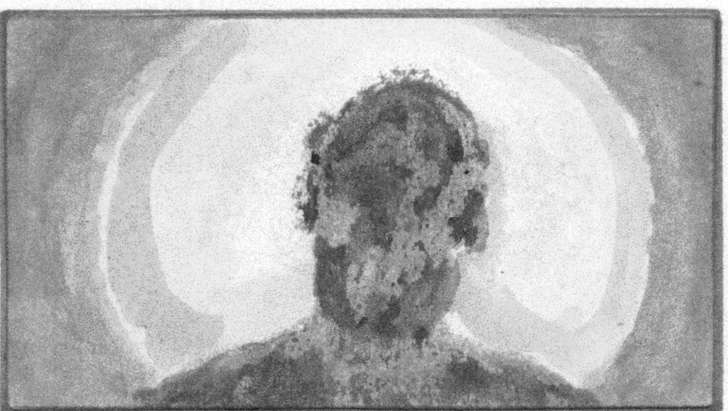

YOU PERSECUTE ME? IN VAIN DO YOU KICK AGAINST THE
GOAD.' 15 I ANSWERED, "WHO ARE YOU, LORD?" AND
THE LORD SAID: 'I AM JESUS, WHOM YOU PERSECUTE. 16
GET UP NOW AND STAND ON YOUR FEET. I HAVE REVEALED
MYSELF TO YOU TO MAKE YOU SERVANT AND WITNESS TO
WHAT I HAVE JUST SHOWN YOU AND TO WHAT I WILL SHOW
YOU LATER ON. 17 I WILL RESCUE YOU FROM ALL
EVIL THAT MAY COME FROM YOUR OWN PEOPLE OR
FROM THE PAGANS TO WHOM I AM SENDING YOU.
18 YOU SHALL OPEN THEIR EYES THAT THEY MAY TURN
FROM DARKNESS TO LIGHT, AND FROM THE POWER OF SATAN
TO GOD, AND, THROUGH FAITH IN ME, MAY OBTAIN FORGIVENESS
OF THEIR SINS AND A PLACE AMONG THE SANCTIFIED ONES.'

19 SINCE THAT TIME, KING AGRIPPA, I DIDN'T STRAY
FROM THIS HEAVENLY VISION; ON THE CONTRARY, 20 I BE-
GAN PREACHING FIRST TO THOSE IN DAMASCUS, THEN TO
THOSE IN JERUSALEM AND THROUGHOUT JUDEA, AND
THEN TO THE PAGAN NATIONS, THAT THEY SHOULD RE-
PENT AND TURN TO GOD, SHOWING THE FRUITS OF
TRUE CONVERSION. 21 I WAS CARRYING OUT THIS
MISSION WHEN THE JEWS ARRESTED ME IN THE
TEMPLE AND TRIED TO KILL ME. BUT WITH THE HELP
OF GOD, I STILL STAND HERE TODAY TO GIVE MY TES-
TIMONY BOTH TO THE GREAT AND THE SMALL.
22 I DO NOT TEACH ANYTHING OTHER THAN WHAT
MOSES AND THE PROPHETS ANNOUNCED BEFOREHAND:

23 THE MESSIAH HAD TO DIE, AND AFTER BEING THE
FIRST TO BE RAISED FROM THE DEAD, HE WOULD
PROCLAIM THE LIGHT TO HIS PEOPLE AS WELL AS
TO ALL NATIONS."
24 AS PAUL CAME TO THIS POINT OF HIS DEFENSE,
FESTUS SAID IN A LOUD VOICE: "PAUL YOU ARE MAD;
YOUR GREAT LEARNING HAS DERANGED YOUR MIND!"
25 BUT PAUL ANSWERED: "I AM NOT MAD, MOST EX-
ELLENT FESTUS, BUT EVERYTHING I HAVE SAID IS
RELIABLE AND TRUE.
26 THE KING IS ACQU-
AINTED WITH ALL THE-
SE THINGS, SO TO HIM
I SPEAK WITH SUCH CON-
FIDENCE. I AM CONVINCED
THAT HE KNOWS EVERY-
THING ABOUT THIS CA-
SE, FOR THESE THINGS
DID NOT HAPPEN IN A
DARK CORNER. 27 KING
AGRIPPA, DO YOU BELI-
EVE THE PROPHETS?
I KNOW THAT YOU DO."
28 AGRIPPA SAID TO
HIM: "A LITTLE MORE
AND YOU WOULD BELI-
EVE THAT YOU HAVE
ALREADY MADE ME A
CHRISTIAN!"
29 PAUL ANSWERED
HIM: "WHETHER LITTLE
OR MORE, I WOULD
THAT NOT ONLY YOU
BUT ALL WHO HEAR ME
THIS DAY MAY COME TO
BE AS I AM, EXCEPT
FOR THESE CHAINS."
30 THEN THE KING ROSE
AND, WITH HIM, THE GOVERNOR, BERNICE AND
ALL THE ATTENDANTS. 31 WHEN THEY WENT
OUT THEY TALKED AMONG THEMSELVES AND
SAID: "THIS MAN HAS DONE NOTHING TO DE-
SERVE DEATH OR IMPRISONMENT."
32 AND AGRIPPA SAID TO FESTUS: "HAD HE NOT APPEAL-
ED TO CAESAR, HE COULD HAVE BEEN SET FREE."

ACTS -27-

DEPARTURE FOR ROME

27 1 WHEN IT WAS DECIDED THAT WE SHOULD SAIL
FOR ITALY, THEY HANDED OVER PAUL AND THE
OTHER PRISONERS INTO THE CARE OF AN OF-
FICER OF THE AUGUSTAN BATTALION, NAMED JULIUS.
2 WE BOARDED A SHIP OF ADRAMYTTIUM BOUND FOR
THE ASIAN COASTS, AND WE LEFT ACCOMPANIED BY AR-
ISTARCHUS, A MACEDONIAN FROM THE CITY OF THESSA-
LONICA. 3 WE ARRIVED AT SIDON ON THE NEXT DAY.
JULIUS WAS VERY KIND TO PAUL, LETTING HIM
VISIT HIS FRIENDS AND BE CARED FOR BY THEM.
4 FROM THERE, WE SAILED ALONG THE SHELTER-
ED COAST OF CYPRUS, BECAUSE THE WINDS WERE
AGAINST US. 5 WE SAILED ACROSS THE SEAS OFF

CILICIA AND PAMPHYLIA AND ARRIVED AT MYRA IN
LYCIA. 6 THERE THE CAPTAIN FOUND A SHIP
FROM ALEXANDRIA SAILING FOR ITALY AND MADE
US BOARD IT.
7 WE SAILED SLOWLY FOR SEVERAL DAYS, AND
ARRIVED WITH GREAT DIFFICULTY AT CNIDUS.
AS THE WIND DID NOT ALLOW US TO ENTER THE
PORT, WE SAILED FOR THE SHELTER OF CRETE
WITH THE CAPE OF SALMONE WITHIN SIGHT. 8 WE
TURNED WITH DIFFICULTY AND ARRIVED AT A
PLACE CALLED GOOD
PORTS, NEAR THE CITY
OF LASEA. 9 TIME
PASSED AND WE HAD
CELEBRATED THE FEAST
OF THE FAST, WHEN THE
CROSSING BEGAN TO
BE DANGEROUS. 10
THEN PAUL SAID TO
THEM: "FRIENDS, I BE-
LIEVE THAT IT WOULD
NOT BE VERY WISE TO
PROCEED WITH OUR
CROSSING FOR WE
COULD LOSE NOT ONLY
THE CARGO AND THE
SHIP BUT ALSO OUR
LIVES." 11 BUT THE
ROMAN OFFICER RE-
LIED MORE ON THE
SHIP'S CAPTAIN AND
THE OWNER OF THE
SHIP THAN ON THE
WORDS OF PAUL.

12 AND AS THE PORT
WAS NOT SUITABLE FOR WINTERING, THE MA-
JORITY AGREED TO SET OUT FROM THERE IN
THE HOPE OF REACHING THE HARBOR OF CRETE
CALLED PHOENIX, OVERLOOKING AFRICA AND
CHOROS, WHERE THEY COULD SPEND THE WINTER.

STORM AND SHIPWRECK

13 THEN THE SOUTH WIND BEGAN TO BLOW AND
THEY THOUGHT THAT THEY HAD GAINED THEIR
PURPOSE; THEY WEIGHED ANCHOR AND SAILED
ALONG THE ISLAND OF CRETE. 14 BUT LATER, A
STRONG WIND, "THE NORTHEASTER" SWEPT ON THEM
FROM THE ISLAND. 15 THE SHIP WAS DRAGGED ALONG
AND COULDN'T FACE THE WIND, SO WE REMAINED ADRIFT.
16 AS WE WERE CROSSING UNDER THE LEE OF THE SMALL
ISLAND OF CAUDA, WITH EFFORT WE MANAGED TO SECURE
THE LIFEBOAT. 17 AFTER LIFTING IT ABOARD, THEY
USED CABLES TO UNDERGIRD THE HULL, AND SINCE WE
FEARED RUNNING AGROUND ON THE SANDS OF SYR-
TIS, THEY LOWERED THE SEA ANCHOR. SO WE CONTINUED
TO BE DRAGGED ALONG.
18 THE STORM LASHED
AT US SO STRONGLY THAT
ON THE NEXT DAY THEY
HAD TO THROW SOME OF
THE CARGO OVERBOARD.
19 ON THE THIRD DAY THE
SAILORS WITH THEIR OWN
HANDS THREW OUT THE GEAR
OF THE SHIP. 20 FOR SE-
VERAL DAYS NEITHER THE
SUN NOR THE STARS
COULD BE SEEN, AND THE
TEMPEST HAD NOT SUB-
SIDED; WE LOST ALL

HOPE. 21 AS WE HAD NOT EATEN FOR DAYS, PAUL STO-
OD UP AND SAID: "FRIENDS, IF YOU HAD FOLLOWED MY
ADVICE WHEN I TOLD YOU NOT TO SET SAIL FROM CRE-
TE, WE WOULD NOT BE IN SUCH DANGER NOW, AND WE COULD
HAVE AVOIDED THIS LOSS. 22 BUT NOW I WISH YOU TO RE-
GAIN COURAGE FOR NO ONE SHOULD DIE; ONLY THE SHIP SHALL
BE DESTROYED. 23 LAST NIGHT AN ANGEL OF GOD APPEARED
TO WHOM I BELONG AND WHOM I SERVE 24 AND HE SAID TO
ME: 'PAUL, DO NOT BE AFRAID, YOU MUST APPEAR BEFORE
CAESAR'S TRIBUNAL, AND GOD HAS GUARANTEED YOU
THE LIFE OF ALL THOSE WHO SAIL WITH YOU.' 25 HAVE

COURAGE, MY FRIENDS, FOR I TRUST IN GOD AND IT WILL BE
AS HE TOLD ME. 26 BUT WE HAVE TO RUN AGROUND ON
SOME ISLAND. 27 ON THE FOURTEENTH NIGHT, AS WE WE-
RE DRIFTING IN THE ADRIATIC SEA, THE SAILORS AT ABOUT
MIDNIGHT SUSPECTED THAT LAND WAS NEAR. 28 THEY
MEASURED THE WATER'S DEPTH AND IT WAS 37 METERS.
AFTER A WHILE, THEY MEASURED IT AGAIN AND IT WAS 27
METERS. 29 THEY FEARED WE MIGHT HIT SOME ROCKS,
SO THEY CAST OUT FOUR ANCHORS FROM THE STERN AND
WAITED FOR MORNING. 30 THEN THE CREW TRIED TO LEAVE
THE SHIP UNDER THE PRETEXT OF EXTENDING THE CABLES OF
THE ANCHORS FROM THE BOW, SO THEY LOWERED THE
LIFEBOAT INTO THE SEA.

31 BUT PAUL SAID TO THE CAPTAIN AND THE SOL-
DIERS: "IF THEY LEAVE THE SHIP, YOU CANNOT BE
SAVED. 32 SO THE SOLDIERS CUT THE MOORING
CABLES OF THE BOAT AND LET IT FALL.
33 AS THEY WAITED FOR DAWN, PAUL URGED
EVERYONE: "FOR FOURTEEN DAYS WE HAVE NOT
EATEN ANYTHING BECAUSE OF ANXIOUS WAIT-
ING. 34 I ASK YOU TO EAT NOW IF YOU WANT
TO LIVE; BE SURE THAT NOT EVEN A HAIR OF
YOUR HEAD WILL BE LOST." HAVING SAID
THIS, HE TOOK BREAD, GAVE THANKS TO
GOD IN EVERYBODY'S
PRESENCE, BROKE IT
AND BEGAN TO EAT.

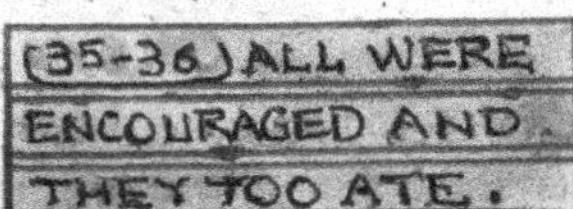

37 THEY WERE TWO
HUNDRED AND SEVENTY-
SIX PERSONS IN ALL.
38 WHEN THEY HAD
EATEN ENOUGH
THEY THREW ALL THE
WHEAT INTO THE SEA
TO LIGHTEN THE BOAT.

39 WHEN MORNING
CAME, THEY DID NOT
RECOGNIZE THE LAND
BUT NOTICED A BAY
WITH A BEACH, SO
THEY DECIDED TO RUN
THE SHIP AGROUND,
IF POSSIBLE.
40 THE CAST OFF THE
ANCHORS AND LEFT
THEM IN THE SEA;
AT THE SAME TIME,
THEY LOOSENED THE
ROPES OF THE RUD-
DERS, HOISTED THE FORESAIL TO THE WIND
AND HEADED FOR THE BEACH.

41 BUT THEY STRUCK A SANDBANK AND THE
SHIP RAN AGROUND. THE BOW STUCK AND WAS
IMMOVABLE, WHILE THE STERN WAS BROKEN
UP BY THE VIOLENT WAVES.

42 THE SOLDIERS THEN PLANNED TO KILL THE

THE PRISONERS FOR FEAR THAT SOME OF THEM
MIGHT ESCAPE BY SWIMMING. 43 BUT THE
CAPTAIN, WHO WISHED TO SAVE PAUL, DID NOT
ALLOW THEM TO DO THIS. HE ORDERED THOSE
WHO KNEW HOW TO SWIM, TO BE THE FIRST TO
JUMP INTO THE WATER AND HEAD FOR THE
SHORE, 44 AND THE REST TO HOLD ON TO
PLANKS OR PIECES OF THE SHIP. SO ALL OF
US REACHED LAND SAFE AND SOUND.

28 1 AFTER BEING SAVED, WE LEARNED THAT
THE ISLAND WAS CALLED MALTA. 2 THE
NATIVES WERE VERY CORDIAL. THEY LIT A
BIG BONFIRE AND TOOK GOOD CARE OF US ALL,
SINCE IT WAS RAINING AND COLD.
3 PAUL GATHERED A BUNDLE OF DRIED TWIGS
AND AS HE THREW THEM INTO THE FIRE, A VIPER

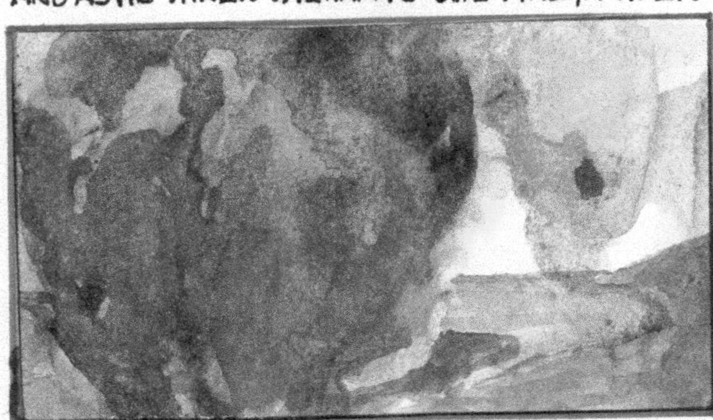

SUDDENLY CAME OUT BECAUSE OF THE HEAT AND
ENTWINED ITSELF AROUND HIS HAND. WHEN
4 THE NATIVES SAW THE VIPER HANGING FROM
HIS HAND, THEY SAID TO ONE ANOTHER: "SURELY
THIS MAN IS A MURDERER; HE HAS BARELY ESCA-
PED FROM THE RAGING SEA, YET DIVINE JUSTICE
WILL NOT ALLOW HIM TO LIVE." 5 BUT PAUL
SHOOK OFF THE VIPER INTO THE FIRE AND DID NOT
SUFFER ANY HARM. THEY WAITED TO SEE HIM TO
SWELL AND DIE; 6 BUT AFTER OBSERVING HIM
FOR A WHILE THEY SAW
THAT NOTHING HAPPE-
NED TO HIM, SO THEY
CHANGED THEIR MINDS
AND BEGAN TO SAY
THAT HE WAS A GOD.
7 NEAR THIS PLACE
WAS AN ESTATE OWNED
BY THE HEAD OF THE IS-
LAND, NAMED PUBLIUS.
FOR THREE DAYS THIS
MAN WELCOMED US
HOSPITABLY. 8 IT SO
HAPPENED THAT HIS
FATHER WAS IN BED
WITH FEVER AND DYSEN-
TERY. PAUL WENT TO
SEE HIM; HE PRAYED
AND LAID HIS HANDS
ON HIM AND HEALED
HIM. 9 BECAUSE OF
THIS, THE REST OF THE
SICK PEOPLE ON THE
ISLAND CAME TO SEE
HIM AND WERE CURED.
10 SO THEY SHOWERED
US WITH KINDNESS,
AND OUR DEPARTURE WAS PROVIDED BY THEM
WITH EVERYTHING WE NEEDED.

FROM MALTA TO ROME

11 AFTER THREE MONTHS, WE BOARDED A SHIP
WHICH HAD SPENT THE WINTER AT THE ISLAND.
IT BELONGED TO AN ALEXANDRIAN COMPANY AND
CARRIED THE FIGUREHEAD OF CASTOR AND POLLUX
AS INSIGNIA. 12 WE SAILED FOR SYRACUSE, STAY-
ING THERE FOR THREE DAYS 13 AND, AFTER CIRCLING
THE COAST, WE ARRIVED AT RHEGIUM. ON THE FOL-
LOWING DAY, A SOUTH WIND BEGAN TO BLOW, AND
AT THE END OF TWO DAYS WE ARRIVED AT PUTEOLI,

367 - CCCLXVII.

14 WHERE WE FOUND SOME OF OUR BROTHERS
WHO INVITED US TO STAY WITH THEM FOR A
WEEK. AND THAT WAS HOW WE CAME TO ROME.

15 THERE THE BROTHERS AND SISTERS HAD
BEEN INFORMED OF OUR ARRIVAL AND CAME
OUT TO MEET US AS FAR AS THE APPIAN FO-
RUM AND THE THREE TAVERNS. WHEN PAUL
SAW THEM, HE GAVE THANKS TO GOD AND
TOOK COURAGE.
16 UPON OUR ARRIVAL IN ROME, THE CAPTAIN

TURNED THE PRISONERS OVER TO THE MILITARY
GOVERNOR BUT PERMITTED PAUL TO LODGE IN A
PRIVATE HOUSE WITH A SOLDIER WHO GUARDED HIM.

PAUL MEETS THE JEWS IN ROME

17 AFTER THREE DAYS, PAUL CALLED TOGETHER
THE LEADER OF THE JEWS. WHEN THEY HAD GA-
THERED, HE SAID TO THEM: BROTHERS, THOUGH
I HAVE NOT DONE ANYTHING AGAINST OUR PE-
OPLE OR AGAINST THE TRADITIONS OF OUR FA-
THERS, I WAS ARRESTED IN JERUSALEM AND SO
HANDED OVER TO THE
ROMANS. 18 THEY
EXAMINED ME AND
WANTED TO SET ME
FREE, FOR THEY SAW NO-
THING IN MY CASE THAT
DESERVED DEATH. 19
BUT THE JEWS OBJEC-
TED, SO I WAS FORCED
TO APPEAL TO CAESAR
WITHOUT THE LEAST
INTENTION OF BRIN-
GING ANY CASE AGAINST
MY OWN PEOPLE.
20 THEREFORE I
HAVE ASKED TO SEE
YOU AND SPEAK
WITH YOU, SINCE
IT IS BECAUSE OF
THE HOPE OF IS-
RAEL THAT I BEAR
THESE CHAINS."
21 THEY ANSWERED:
"WE HAVE NOT RE-
CEIVED ANY LETTER
ABOUT YOU FROM
JUDEA, AND NONE
OF THE BROTHERS
WHO HAVE COME FROM

THERE HAVE BROUGHT ANY MESSAGE OR SAID
ANYTHING AGAINST YOU. 22 BUT WE WISH
TO HEAR FROM YOU WHAT YOU THINK, ALTHOUGH

WE KNOW ALREADY THAT EVERYWHERE PEOPLE
SPEAK AGAINST THIS SECT THAT YOU BELONG
TO."
23 THEY SET A DAY FOR HIM AND CAME IN GRE-
AT NUMBER TO HIS LODGING.
SO PAUL EXPLAINED EVERYTHING HE WANTED
TO TELL THEM REGARDING THE KINGDOM OF
GOD AND TRIED TO
CONVINCE THEM CON-
CERNING JESUS, TA-
KING THE LAW OF MO-
SES AND THE PROPHETS
AS HIS STARTING POINT.
THIS CONTINUED FROM
MORNING TILL NIGHT.
24 SOME WERE CON-
VINCED BY HIS WORDS,
OTHERS WERE NOT. 25
FINALLY THE JEWS
LEFT, STILL ARGUING
STRONGLY AMONG
THEMSELVES, AND
PAUL SENT THEM AWAY

WITH THIS STATEMENT: "WHAT THE HOLY SPIRIT
SAID HAS COME TRUE, WHEN HE SPOKE TO YO-
UR FATHERS THROUGH THE PROPHET ISAIAH:

> 26 GO TO THIS PEOPLE AND SAY TO THEM: HOW-
> EVER MUCH YOU HEAR, YOU WILL NOT UNDER-
> STAND; YOU WILL SEE AND SEE AGAIN BUT NOT
> PERCEIVE. 27 THE HEART OF THIS PEOPLE HAS
> GROWN HARD; THEY HAVE COVERED THEIR EARS
> AND CLOSED THEIR EYES AND HEAR WITH
> THEIR EARS, LEST THEIR SPIRIT UNDER-
> STAND, AND I SHOULD HEAL THEM.

28 LET IT BE KNOWN TO YOU, THEN, THAT
THIS SALVATION OF GOD HAS BEEN SENT
TO THE PAGANS: THEY WILL LISTEN." 29
30 PAUL STAYED FOR TWO WHOLE YEARS
IN A HOUSE HE HIMSELF RENTED, WHERE
HE RECEIVED WITHOUT ANY HINDRANCE
ALL THOSE WHO CAME TO SEE HIM. 31 HE

PROCLAIMED THE KINGDOM OF GOD AND TAUGHT
THE TRUTH ABOUT JESUS CHRIST QUITE
OPENLY AND WITHOUT ANY HINDRANCE.

PRESENTATION OF THE LETTERS OF PAUL

FROM THE BEGINNING THE CHURCH TOOK CARE TO PRESERVE THE LETTERS THEY RECEIVED FROM THE APOSTLES, SINCE IN THEM THEY HAD THE AUTHORITATIVE WITNESSES OF THE FAITH. IT WAS THEN MORE DIFFICULT THAT IT IS TODAY TO GATHER THESE DOCUMENTS, AND EVEN SAVE THE THE PERISHABLE MATERIAL OF THE PAPYRUS FROM DAMPNESS.
PAUL SAW HIMSELF AS "THE APOSTLES OF THE PAGAN NATIONS", SEEING THERE HIS PERSONAL VOCATION BESIDE PETER TO WHOM GOD HAD HAD CONFIDED THE CHARGE OF EVANGELIZING THE JEWISH WORLD, NOT ONLY IN PALESTINE, BUT ALSO THROUGHOUT THE ROMAN EMPIRE, WHEREVER THEY WERE ESTABLISHED.

PAUL HAD RECEIVED THIS MISSION FROM JESUS HIMSELF AT THE TIME OF HIS CONVERSION; SO HIGHLY FUNDAMENTAL WAS IT IN THE DIVINE PROJECT OF THE MISSION AND EXTENSION OF THE CHURCH THAT IT REMAINED UNFINISHED AT HIS DEATH. THE SPIRIT OF PAUL, ONE OF THE GREAT MANIFESTATIONS OF THE SPIRIT OF JESUS, THAT IS ALWAYS AT WORK IN OUR MIDST THROUGH HIS LETTERS.

JESUS HAD PRESENTED HIMSELF AS THE SAVIOR. AND FIRST OF ALL HE WANTED TO SAVE THE JEWISH PEOPLE. HE SPOKE TO THEM OF THE GREAT KINGDOM AND THEY UNDERSTOOD; GOD WOULD REIGN OVER THEM JUST AS HE WOULD REIGN IN THEIR LIVES.

LETTER TO THE ROMANS

IN THIS LETTER TO THE CHRISTIANS OF ROME, CAPITAL OF THE EMPIRE, PAUL WANTS TO RESPOND TO THE CONCERNS OF THE GREEKS BUT WITHOUT THEREBY NEGLECTING THE JEWS. FOR THEY WERE NUMEROUS WITH THE ROMAN COMMUNITY AS IN ALL THOSE OF THE ROMAN EMPIRE, AND FOR THOSE WHO HAD BELIEVED IN CHRIST IT WAS DIFFICULT TO REPOSITION ONESELF TOWARDS GOD AFTER THE GREAT MAJORITY OF THE PEOPLE HAD REJECTED CHRISTIAN FAITH. UP TO THEN THEY HAD SHARED THE HOPE OF THEIR PEOPLE THINKING THAT ALL ISRAEL WOULD RECOGNIZE THE COMING OF THE SAVIOR GOD, AND NOW THEY WERE NO MORE THAN A MINORITY APPARENTLY ON THE MARGIN OF A LONG BIBLICAL HISTORY.

THE LETTER TO THE ROMANS IS FOR THE MOST PART A LONG EXPOSITION ABOUT CHRISTIAN VOCATION. TO US IT WILL SEEM DIFFICULT, BECAUSE THAT IS WHAT IT IS.
WILL SHALL FIND THERE DISCUSSIONS AND A USE OF BIBLICAL TEXTS WHICH WILL OFTEN DISCONCERT US, FOR PAUL DISCUSSES AS HE HAD LEARNED TO DO IN THE RABBINICAL SCHOOLS OF JERUSALEM.

PAUL, MARKED BY HIS OWN HISTORY, PRESENTS THE BEGINNING OF FAITH AS A DRAMATIC CONVERSION.

PAUL SENT THIS LETTER IN 57 OR 58 PROBABLY FROM CORINTH. UP TILL THEN HE ADDRESSED HIMSELF TO THE COMMUNITIES HE KNEW AND WHOSE DIFFICULTIES HE WAS AWARE OF.

IN ROME AS ELSEWHERE IT WAS NOT EASY TO UNITE IN ONE COMMUNITY, JEWS AND CONVERTED PAGANS: ACCEPT THOSE WHO ARE DIFFERENT.

370
CCCLXX

LETTER TO THE ROMANS

1 1 FROM PAUL, A SERVANT OF JESUS CHRIST,
AN APOSTLE CALLED AND SET APART ON BE-
HALF OF THE GOOD NEWS, 2 THE VERY PROMI-
SES HE FORETOLD THROUGH HIS PROPHETS IN THE
HOLY SCRIPTURES RE-
GARDING HIS SON. 3

HE HAS BEEN BORN IN
THE FLESH, A DESCEN-
DANT OF DAVID, 4
AND HAS BEEN RECOGNI-
ZED AS THE SON OF GOD
ENDOWED WITH POWER,
UPON RISING FROM THE
DEAD THROUGH THE
HOLY SPIRIT.
THROUGH HIM, JESUS
CHRIST, OUR LORD, 5
AND FOR THE SAKE OF
HIS NAME, WE RECEIV-
ED GRACE AND MISSION
IN ALL THE NATIONS,
FOR THEM TO ACCEPT
THE FAITH: 6 ALL OF
YOU, THE ELECTED OF
CHRIST, ARE PART OF
THEM, YOU, THE BELO-
VED OF GOD IN ROME,
CALLED TO BE HOLY:
7 MAY GOD OUR
FATHER, AND THE
LORD JESUS CHRIST,
GIVE YOU GRACE AND PEACE.

PAUL LONGS TO VISIT THEM

8 FIRST OF ALL, I GIVE THANKS TO MY GOD
THROUGH JESUS CHRIST, FOR ALL OF YOU, BECAUSE
YOUR FAITH IS SPOKEN OF ALL OVER THE WORLD.
9 AND GOD, WHOM I SERVE IN SPIRIT BY ANNOUNCING
THE GOOD NEWS OF HIS SON, IS MY WITNESS
THAT I REMEMBER YOU IN MY PRAYERS AT ALL

TIMES. 10 I PRAY CONSTANTLY THAT, IF IT IS HIS
WILL, HE MAKES IT POSSIBLE FOR ME TO VI-
SIT YOU.
11 I LONG TO SEE YOU AND SHARE SOME SPI-
RITUAL BLESSINGS WITH YOU TO STRENGTHEN
YOU.
12 IN THAT WAY, WE WILL ENCOURAGE EACH
OTHER BY SHARING OUR COMMON FAITH.

13 YOU MUST KNOW, BROTHERS, THAT
MANY TIMES I HAVE MADE PLANS TO GO
TO YOU, BUT TILL NOW I HAVE BEEN PRE-
VENTED.
14 I WOULD LIKE TO HARVEST SOME FRU-
ITS AMONG YOU, AS I HAVE DONE AMONG
OTHER NATIONS.
WHETHER GREEKS OR FOREIGNERS, CULT-
URED OR IGNORANT, I FEEL UNDER OBLI-
GATION AT ALL.
15 HENCE MY EAGERNESS TO GIVE THE
MESSAGE ALSO TO YOU ROMANS.

16 FOR I AM NOT ASHAMED OF THIS GOOD NEWS;
IT IS GOD'S POWER SAVING THOSE WHO BE-
LIEVE, FIRST THE JEWS, AND THEN THE GREEKS.
17 THIS GOOD NEWS SHOWS US HOW GOD MAKES
PEOPLE UPRIGHT THROUGH FAITH, AS THE
SCRIPTURE SAYS:

"THE UPRIGHT ONE SHALL LIVE BY FAITH."

HUMANKIND UNDER GOD'S WRATH

18 GOD IS NOW READY TO CONDEMN THE WICKED-
NESS AND ANY KIND OF INJUSTICE OF THOSE WHO
HAVE SILENCED THE
TRUTH BY THEIR WICK-
ED WAYS. 19 FOR EVERY-
THING THAT COULD HAVE
BEEN KNOWN ABOUT
GOD WAS CLEAR TO THEM:
GOD HIMSELF MADE IT
PLAIN. 20 FOR, THOUGH
WE CANNOT SEE HIM, WE
CAN DISCOVER HIM BY
HIS WORKS: FOR HE CRE-
ATED THE WORLD AND
THROUGH HIS WORKS WE
UNDERSTAND HIM TO
BE ETERNAL AND
ALL-POWERFUL, AND
TO BE GOD. SO THEY
HAVE NO EXCUSE, 21
FOR THEY KNEW GOD
AND DID NOT GLORIFY
HIM AS WAS FITTING,
NOR DID THEY GIVE
THANKS TO HIM. ON
THE CONTRARY THEY
LOST THEMSELVES
IN THEIR REASONING
AND DARKNESS FIL-
LED THEIR MINDS.

22 BELIEVING THEMSELVES WISE, THEY
BECAME FOOLISH: 23 THEY EXCHANGED
THE GLORY OF THE IMMORTAL GOD FOR THE
LIKES OF MORTAL MEN, BIRDS, ANIMALS
AND REPTILES.

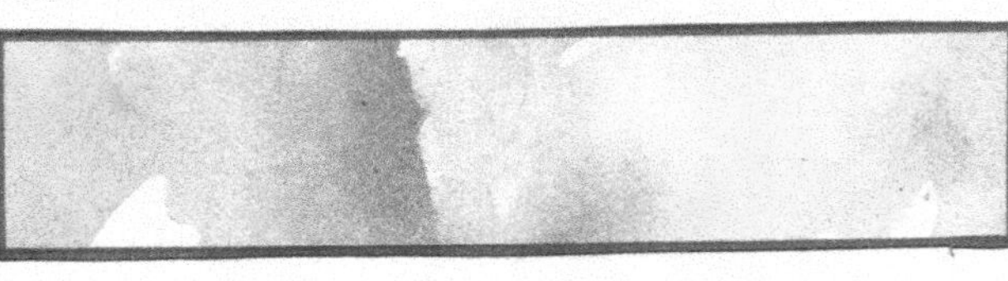

24 BECAUSE OF THIS GOD GAVE THEM UP TO THEIR
INNER CRAVINGS; THEY DID SHAMEFUL THINGS
AND DISHONORED THEIR BODIES.
25 THEY EXCHANGED GOD'S TRUTH FOR A LIE;
THEY HONORED AND WORSHIPED CREATED THINGS
INSTEAD OF THE CREATOR, TO WHOM BE PRAISE
FOR EVER, AMEN! 26 BECAUSE OF THAT, GOD
GAVE THEM UP TO SHAMEFUL PASSIONS: THEIR
WOMEN EXCHANGED NATURAL SEXUAL RELATI-
ONS FOR UNNATURAL ONES. 27 SIMILARLY,
THE MEN, GIVING UP NATURAL SEXUAL RE-
LATIONS WITH WOMEN, WERE LUSTFUL OF
EACH OTHER. THEY DID, MEN WITH MEN, SHA-
MEFUL THINGS, AND
BRINGING UPON
THEMSELVES THE PU-
NISHMENT THEY DE-
SERVE FOR THEIR
WICKEDNESS. 28 AND
SINCE THEY DID NOT
THINK THAT GOD WAS
WORTH KNOWING, HE
GAVE THEM UP TO THEIR
SENSELESS MINDS SO
THAT THEY COMMITTED
ALL KINDS OF OBSCE-
NITIES. 29 AND SO
THEY ARE FULL OF IN-
JUSTICE, PERVERSITY,
GREED, EVIL; THEY ARE
FULL OF JEALOUSY, MUR-
DER, STRIFE, DECEIT,
BAD WILL AND GOSSIP.
30 THEY COMMIT CA-
LUMNY, OFFEND GOD,
ARE HAUGHTY; THEY
ARE PROUD, LIARS,
CLEVER IN DOING EVIL.
THEY ARE REBELLIOUS
TOWARDS THEIR PA-
RENTS, 31 SENSE-
LESS, DISLOYAL, COLD-
HEARTED AND MERCILESS. 32 THEY KNOW OF
GOD'S JUDGEMENT WHICH DECLARES WORTHY OF
DEATH ANYONE LIVING IN THIS WAY; YET NOT ONLY
DO THEY DO ALL THESE THINGS, THEY EVEN
APPLAUD ANYONE WHO DOES THE SAME.

THE JEWS ALSO MUST FEAR JUDGMENT

2 1 THEREFORE, YOU HAVE NO EXCUSE, WHO-
EVER YOU ARE, IF YOU ARE ABLE TO JUDGE
OTHERS. FOR IN JUDGING YOUR NEIGHBOR
YOU CONDEMN YOURSELF, FOR YOU PRACTICE

WHAT YOU ARE JUDGING. 2 WE KNOW THAT GOD'S CON-
DEMNATION WILL JUSTLY REACH THOSE WHO COMMIT
THESE THINGS, 3 AND DO YOU THINK THAT BY CONDEM-
NING OTHERS YOU WILL ESCAPE FROM THE JUDG-
MENT OF GOD, YOU WHO ARE DOING THE SAME?
4 THIS WOULD BE TAKING ADVANTAGE OF GOD AND HIS
INFINITE GOODNESS, PATIENCE AND UNDERSTANDING,
AND NOT TO REALIZE THAT HIS GOODNESS IS IN ORDER
TO LEAD YOU TO CONVERSION.

5 IF YOUR HEART BECOMES HARD AND YOU RE-
FUSE TO CHANGE, THEN YOU ARE STORING FOR YO-
URSELF A GREAT PUNISHMENT ON THE DAY OF
JUDGMENT, WHEN GOD WILL APPEAR AS JUST
JUDGE. 6 HE WILL GIVE EACH ONE HIS DUE
ACCORDING TO HIS ACTIONS. 7 HE WILL GIVE
EVERLASTING LIFE TO THOSE WHO SEEK GLORY, HONOR
AND IMMORTALITY AND PERSEVERE IN DOING GOOD.
8 BUT ANGER AND VENGEANCE WILL BE THE LOT
TO THOSE WHO DO NOT SERVE TRUTH BUT INJUST-
ICE. 9 THERE WILL BE SUFFERING AND ANGUISH

FOR EVERYONE COMMITTING EVIL, FIRST THE JEW,
THEN THE GREEK. 10 BUT GOD WILL GIVE GLO-
RY, HONOR AND PEACE TO WHOEVER DOES GOOD, AND
FIRST THE JEW THEN THE GREEK, 11 BECAUSE ONE
IS NOT DIFFERENT FROM THE OTHER BEFORE GOD.

CONSCIENCE IS OUR JUDGE

12 THOSE WHO, WITHOUT KNOWING THE LAW, COMMITTED
SIN, WILL PERISH WITHOUT THE LAW, AND WHOEVER COMMIT-
TED SIN KNOWING THE LAW, WILL BE JUDGED BY THE LAW.
13 TO BE RIGHTEOUS BEFORE GOD IS NOT HEARING THE
LAW, BUT OBEYING IT. 14 WHEN THE NON-JEWS WHO DON'T
HAVE LAW, DO NATURALLY
WHAT THE LAW COMMANDS,
THEY ARE GIVING THEM-
SELVES A LAW, 15 SHOW-
ING THAT THE COMMAND-
MENTS OF THE LAW ARE
ENGRAVED IN THEIR MINDS.
THEIR CONSCIENCE, WILL
SPEAK TO THEM SHOWING
WHEN THEY CONDEMN OR
APPROVE THEIR ACTIONS.
16 THE SAME IS TO HAP-
PEN ON THE DAY WHEN
GOD, ACCORDING TO MY GOS-
PEL, WILL JUDGE PEOPLE'S
SECRET ACTIONS IN THE
PERSON OF JESUS CHRIST.
17 BUT I SUPPOSE YOU
CALL YOURSELF A JEW;
YOU HAVE THE LAW
AS FOUNDATION AND
FEEL PROUD OF YOUR
GOD. 18 YOU KNOW
THE WILL OF GOD AND
THE LAW TEACHES
YOU TO DISTINGUISH
WHAT IS BETTER.
19 AND SO YOU BE-
LIEVE YOU ARE THE
GUIDE FOR THE BLIND,
LIGHT IN DARKNESS,
20 TEACHER OF THOSE WHO DO NOT KNOW,
INSTRUCTOR OF CHILDREN, BECAUSE YOU
POSSESS IN THE LAW THE FORMULATION OF
TRUE KNOWLEDGE.

(21) WELL, THEN, YOU WHO TEACH OTHERS, WHY
DON'T YOU TEACH YOURSELF? IF YOU SAY THAT
ONE MUST NOT STEAL, WHY DO YOU STEAL?
(22) YOU SAY ONE MUST NOT COMMIT ADULT-
ERY, YET YOU COMMIT IT! YOU SAY YOU HATE
IDOLS, BUT YOU STEAL IN THEIR TEMPLES! (23)
YOU FEEL PROUD OF THE LAW, YET YOU DO NOT
OBEY IT, AND YOU DISHONOR YOUR GOD. (24)
IN FACT, AS THE SCRIPTURES SAY,

'THE OTHER NATIONS DESPISE THE NAME
OF GOD BECAUSE OF YOU.'

(25) CIRCUMCISION IS OF VALUE TO YOU IF YOU OBEY
THE LAW; BUT IF YOU DO NOT OBEY, IT IS AS IF YOU
WERE NOT CIRCUMCISED. (26) ON THE CONTRARY,
IF UNCIRCUMCISED MEN OBEY THE COMMANDMENTS
OF THE LAW, DO YOU NOT THINK THAT, IN SPITE OF
BEING PAGANS, THEY MAKE THEMSELVES LIKE
THE CIRCUMCISED? (27) THE ONE WHO OBEYS
THE LAW WITHOUT BEING MARKED IN HIS BODY WITH CIR-
CUMCISION, WILL JUDGE YOU WHO HAVE BEEN MARKED
WITH CIRCUMCISION AND WHO HAVE THE LAW WHICH YOU

DO NOT OBEY. (28) FOR EXTERNAL THINGS DO NOT
MAKE A TRUE JEW NOR IS REAL CIRCUMCISION THAT
WHICH IS MARKED ON THE BODY. (29) A JEW MUST BE SO
INTERIORLY; THE HEART'S CIRCUMCISION BELONGS TO SPI-
RIT AND NOT TO THE WRITTEN LAW; HE WHO LIVES IN THIS
WAY WILL BE PRAISED, NOT BY PEOPLE, BUT BY GOD.

WHAT ADVANTAGE IS IT TO BE A JEW?

3 (1) THEN, WHAT IS THE ADVANTAGE OF
BEING A JEW? AND WHAT IS THE USE
OF CIRCUMCISION? (2) IT IS IMPORTANT
FROM ANY POINT OF VIEW. IN THE FIRST PLA-
CE, IT WAS TO THE JEWS THAT GOD ENTRUSTED
HIS WORD.
(3) WELL NOW, IF SOME OF THEM WERE NOT
FAITHFUL, WILL THEIR UNFAITHFULNESS DO
AWAY WITH THE FAITHFULNESS OF GOD? OF COURSE NOT.

(4) RATHER, IT WILL BE PROVED THAT GOD IS TRUTH-
FUL, EVERY HUMAN A LIAR, AS THE SCRIPTURE SAYS:

'IT WILL BE PROVED THAT YOUR WORDS ARE TRUE AND YOU
WILL BE WINNER IF THEY WANT TO JUDGE YOU.'

(5) IF YOUR WICKEDNESS SHOWS GOD TO BE JUST, WOULD
IT BE RIGHT TO SAY THAT GOD IS UNJUST WHEN HE
GETS ANGRY AND PU-
NISHES US? (SOME PE-
OPLE MIGHT SPEAK LIKE
THIS.) (6) -NOT AT ALL
BECAUSE, OTHERWISE,
HOW COULD GOD JUDGE
THE WORLD? (7) -BUT
IF MY LIE MAKES THE
TRUTH OF GOD MORE
EVIDENT, THUS INCREAS-
ING HIS GLORY, IS IT COR-
RECT TO CALL ME A SIN-
NER? (8) -THEN, YOUR
ONLY CHOICE WOULD
BE A SIN, SO THAT
GOOD MAY COME
OF IT. SOME SLAND-
ERERS SAY THAT
THIS IS MY TEACHING,
BUT THEY WILL
HAVE TO ANSWER
FOR THOSE WORDS.
(9) DO WE HAVE, THEN,
ANY ADVANTAGE?
NOT REALLY.
FOR WE HAVE JUST
DEMONSTRATED
THAT ALL, JEWS AND
NON-JEWS, ARE
UNDER THE POWER OF SIN, AS THE SCRIPTURE
SAYS:

(10) AS THE SCRIPTURE SAYS:

Nobody is good, not even one, no
one understands, (11) no one
looks for God. (12) All have gone
astray and have become base.
There is no one doing what is
good, not even one.
(13) Their throats are open
tombs, their words deceit.
(14) Their lips hide poison of
vipers, from their mouth come
bitter curses.
(15) They run to where they
can shed blood, (16) they
leave behind ruin and misery.
(17) They do not know the way
of peace, (18) they have no
respect for God.

(19) NOW WE HAVE TO KNOW THAT WHATEVER
THE SCRIPTURE SAYS, IT IS SAID FOR THE
PEOPLE OF THE LAW, THAT IS FOR THE
JEWS.
LET ALL BE SILENT THEN AND RECOGNIZE THAT
THE WHOLE WORLD IS GUILTY BEFORE GOD.

(20) STILL MORE: NO MORTAL WILL BE WORTHY
BEFORE GOD BY PERFORMING THE DE-
MANDS OF THE LAW. WHAT COMES FROM
THE LAW IS THE CONSCIOUSNESS OF SIN.

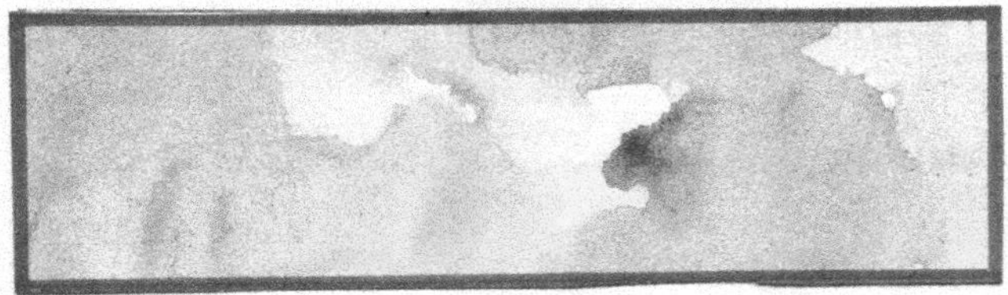

Memento Homo!
Tu es pulvis

et in pulvis
reverteris

FAITH, THE WAY TO SALVATION

21 YET, NOW WE ARE TOLD HOW GOD MAKES US
JUST AS HE WANTS US TO BE WITHOUT THE LAW.
THIS WAS ALREADY FORETOLD IN THE LAW AND THE
PROPHETS; 22 GOD MAKES US RIGHTEOUS BY ME-
ANS OF FAITH IN JESUS CHRIST, AND THIS IS AP-
PLIED TO ALL WHO BELIEVE, WITHOUT DISTINCTION
OF PERSONS. 23 BECAUSE ALL HAVE SINNED AND
ALL FALL SHORT OF THE GLORY OF GOD; 24 AND
ALL ARE FORGIVEN AND MADE HOLY THROUGH THE RE-
DEMPTION IN JESUS CHRIST. 25 FOR GOD HAS GIVEN

HIM TO BE THE VICTIM WHOSE BLOOD OBTAINS US
FORGIVENESS THROUGH FAITH.
SO GOD SHOWS US HOW HE MAKES US RIGHTEOUS.
PAST SINS ARE FORGIVEN 26 WHICH GOD OVERLO-
OKED TILL NOW. FOR NOW HE WANTS TO REVEAL HIS
WAY OF RIGHTEOUSNESS: HOW HE IS JUST AND HO-
LY AND HOW HE MAKES US RIGHTEOUS AND HOLY
THROUGH FAITH IN JESUS. 27 THEN WHAT BECOMES

OF OUR PRIDE? IT IS EX-
CLUDED. HOW? NOT BY
THE LAW AND ITS OBSER-
VANCES, BUT THROUGH AN-
OTHER LAW WHICH IS
FAITH. 28 FOR WE HOLD
THAT PEOPLE ARE IN
GOD'S GRACE BY FAITH
AND NOT BECAUSE OF
ALL THE THINGS ORDER-
ED BY THE LAW. 29 THEN
GOD WOULD BE THE GOD OF
THE JEWS; BUT IS HE NOT
GOD OF PAGAN NATIONS AS
WELL? 30 HE IS, FOR
THERE IS ONLY ONE GOD
AND HE WILL SAVE BY FA-
ITH THE CIRCUMCISED JEWS
AS WELL AS THE UNCIRCUM-
CISED NATIONS. 31 DO
WE, THEN, DENY THE VA-
LUE OF THE LAW BECA-
USE OF WHAT WE SAY OF
FAITH? OF COURSE NOT;
RATHER WE PLACE THE
LAW IN ITS PROPER PLACE.

ABRAHAM, FATHER OF THE JUST

4 1 LET US CONSIDER ABRAHAM, OUR FATHER IN THE
FLESH. WHAT HAS HE FOUND? 2 IF ABRAHAM
BECAME JUST BECAUSE OF HIS DEEDS, HE COULD
BE PROUD. BUT HE CANNOT BE THIS BEFORE GOD. 3
BECAUSE THE SCRIPTURE SAYS: ABRAHAM BELIEV-
ED GOD WHO, FOR THIS, HELD HIM TO BE A JUST MAN.

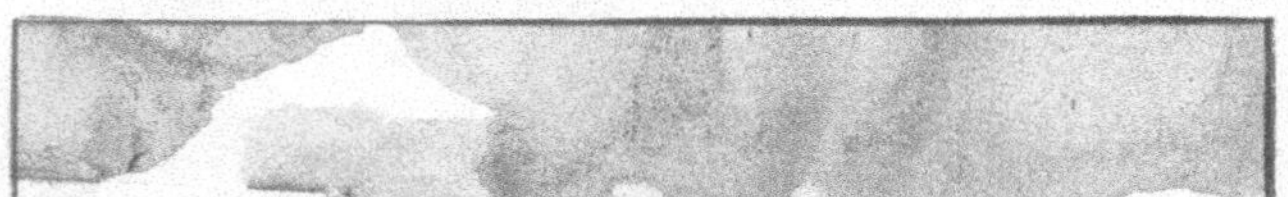

4 NOW, WHEN SOMEONE DOES A WORK, HIS SA-
LARY IS NOT GIVEN TO HIM AS A FAVOR, BUT AS
A DEBT THAT IS PAID. 5 ON THE CONTRARY,
FOR HE WHO HAS NO DEEDS TO SHOW BUT BELIE-
VES IN HIM WHO MAKES SINNERS RIGHTEOUS
BEFORE HIM, HIS FAITH IS TAKEN INTO ACCOUNT AND
HE IS HELD AS RIGHTEOUS. 6 DAVID CONGRATU-
LATES IN THIS WAY THOSE WHO BECOME HOLY BY THE
FAVOR OF GOD, AND NOT BY THEIR ACTIONS: 7

BLESSED ARE THOSE WHOSE SINS ARE FORGIVEN
AND WHOSE OFFENSE ARE FORGOTTEN; BLESSED
8 THE ONE WHOSE SIN GOD DOES NOT
TAKE INTO ACCOUNT!

9 IS THIS BLESSING
ONLY FOR THE CIRCUM-
CISED OR IS IT ALSO FOR
THE UNCIRCUMCISED?
WE HAVE JUST SAID THAT,
BECAUSE OF HIS FAITH,
ABRAHAM WAS MADE
A JUST MAN. 10 BUT
WHEN DID THIS HAP-
PEN? AFTER ABRAHAM
WAS CIRCUMCISED, OR
BEFORE? NOT AFTER,
BUT BEFORE. 11 HE
RECEIVED THE RITE OF
CIRCUMCISION AS A
SIGN OF THE RIGHT-
EOUSNESS GIVEN HIM
THROUGH FAITH WHEN
HE WAS STILL UNCIR-
CUMCISED, THAT HE MIGHT
BE THE FATHER OF ALL
THOSE UNCIRCUMCISED
WHO CAME TO FAITH
AND ARE MADE JUST.

12 AND HE WAS TO BE THE FATHER OF THE JEWS,
PROVIDED THAT BESIDES BEING CIRCUMCISED,
THEY ALSO IMITATE THE FAITH ABRAHAM
SHOWED BEFORE BEING CIRCUMCISED.

13 IF GOD PROMISED ABRAHAM, OR RATHER
HIS DESCENDANT, THAT THE WORLD WOULD
BELONG TO HIM, THIS WAS NOT BECAUSE OF
OF HIS OBEYING THE LAW, BUT BECAUSE

HE WAS JUST AND A FRIEND OF GOD THROUGH
FAITH. 14 IF NOW THE PROMISE IS KEPT
FOR THOSE WHO RELY ON THE LAW, THEN
FAITH HAS LOST ITS PLACE. AND THE PRO-
MISE WILL NEVER BE FULFILLED, 15 FOR
IT IS PROPER OF THE LAW TO BRING PUNISH-
MENT: LAW AND CONDEMNATION GO TOGETHER.

(16) FOR THAT REASON, FAITH IS THE WAY AND
ALL IS GIVEN BY GRACE; AND THE PROMISES OF ABRAHAM
ARE FULFILLED FOR ALL HIS DESCENDANTS, NOT ONLY FOR
HIS CHILDREN ACCORDING TO THE LAW, BUT ALSO FOR
ALL THE OTHERS WHO HAVE BELIEVED.
ABRAHAM IS THE FATHER OF ALL OF US, (17) AS IT
IS WRITTEN: I WILL MAKE YOU FATHER OF MANY
NATIONS. HE IS OUR FATHER IN THE EYES OF HIM
WHO GIVES LIFE TO THE DEAD, AND CALLS THE NON-
EXISTENT AS IF ALREADY EXISTENT, FOR THIS
IS THE GOD IN WHOM
HE BELIEVED.

(18) ABRAHAM BELIEVED
AND HOPED AGAINST
ALL EXPECTATION,
THUS BECOMING FA-
THER OF MANY NATI-
ONS, AS HE HAD BEEN
TOLD: SEE HOW MANY
WILL BE YOUR DESCEND-
ANTS. (19) HE DID NOT
DOUBT ALTHOUGH HIS
BODY COULD NO LONGER
GIVE LIFE - HE WAS
ABOUT A HUNDRED
YEARS OLD - AND IN SPI-
TE OF HIS WIFE SARAH
BEING UNABLE TO
HAVE CHILDREN. (20)
HE DID NOT DOUBT NOR
DID HE DISTRUST THE
PROMISE OF GOD, AND
BY BEING STRONG IN
FAITH, HE GAVE GLO-
RY TO GOD: (21) HE
WAS CONVINCED THAT
HE WHO HAD GIVEN THE PROMISE HAD POWER
TO FULFILL IT. (22) IT WAS BECAUSE OF THIS
FAITH THAT GOD HELD HIM TO BE A JUST MAN.
(23) BECAUSE OF THIS FAITH: THESE WORDS OF
SCRIPTURE ARE NOT ONLY FOR HIM, (24) BUT FOR US,
TOO, BECAUSE WE BELIEVE IN HIM WHO RAISED
JESUS, OUR LORD, FROM THE DEAD, (25) HE WHO WAS
DELIVERED FOR OUR SINS AND RAISED TO LIFE
FOR US TO RECEIVE TRUE RIGHTEOUSNESS.

NOW WE ARE AT PEACE WITH GOD

5 (1) BY FAITH WE HAVE RECEIVED TRUE RIGH-
TEOUSNESS, AND WE ARE AT PEACE WITH
GOD, TROUGH JESUS CHRIST, OUR LORD.
(2) THROUGH HIM WE OBTAIN THIS FAVOR IN WHICH

WE REMAIN AND WE EVEN BOAST TO EXPECT
THE GLORY OF GOD.
(3) NOT ONLY THAT, WE FEEL SECURE EVEN
IN TRIALS, KNOWING THAT TRIALS PRODUCE
PATIENCE.

(4) FROM PATIENCE COMES MERIT, MERIT IS
THE SOURCE OF HOPE, (5) AND HOPE DOES
NOT DISAPPOINT US BECAUSE THE HOLY SPI-
RIT HAS BEEN GIVEN TO US, POURING INTO OUR
HEARTS THE LOVE OF GOD.
(6) CONSIDER, MOREOVER, THE TIME THAT
CHRIST DIED FOR US: WHEN WE WERE STILL
SINNERS AND UNABLE TO DO ANYTHING.
(7) FEW WOULD ACCEPT TO DIE FOR AN UP-
RIGHT PERSON; ALTHOUGH, FOR A VERY GO-
OD PERSON, PERHAPS SOMEONE WOULD GIVE

HIS LIFE. (8) BUT SEE HOW GOD MANIFESTED
HIS LOVE FOR US: WHILE WE WERE STILL
SINNERS, CHRIST DIED FOR US (9) AND WE HAVE
BECOME JUST THROUGH HIS BLOOD. WITH MUCH
MORE REASON NOW HE WILL SAVE US FROM ANY
CONDEMNATION. (10) ONCE ENEMIES, WE HAVE
BEEN RECONCILED WITH GOD THROUGH THE DE-
ATH OF HIS SON; WITH MUCH MORE REASON NOW
WE MAY BE SAVED THROUGH HIS LIFE. (11) NOT ONLY
THAT; WE FEEL SECURE IN GOD BECAUSE OF CHRIST
JESUS, OUR LORD, THROUGH WHOME WE HAVE
BEEN RECONCILED.

(12) NOW, SIN ENTERED THE WORLD THROUGH
ONE MAN AND THROUGH
SIN, DEATH, AND LA-
TER ON DEATH SPREAD
TO ALL HUMANKIND,
BECAUSE ALL SINNED.
(13) AS LONG AS THERE
WAS NO LAW, THEY COULD
NOT SPEAK OF DISOBEDI-
ENCE, BUT SIN WAS AL-
READY IN THE WORLD.
(14) THIS IS WHY FROM
ADAM TO MOSES DE-
ATH REIGNED AMONG
THEM, ALTHOUGH
THEIR SIN WAS NOT
DISOBEDIENCE AS
IN ADAM'S CASE.
(15) SUCH HAS BEEN
THE FALL, BUT GOD'S
GIFT GOES FAR BE-
YOND. MULTITUDES
DIE BECAUSE OF THE
FAULT OF ONE MAN,

BUT HOW MUCH MORE DOES THE GRACE OF
GOD SPREAD WHEN THE GIFT HE GRANTED
REACHES THE MULTITUDES, FROM THIS UNI-
QUE MAN JESUS CHRIST.

16 THE GIFT OF GOD MORE THAN COMPENSATED
FOR SIN. THE DISOBEDIENCE THAT BROUGHT
CONDEMNATION WAS OF ONE SINNER, WHERE-
AS THE GRACE OF GOD BRINGS FORGIVENESS
TO A WORLD OF SINNERS. 17 IF DEATH REIGNED
THROUGH THE DISOBEDIENCE OF ONE AND ONLY
ONE PERSON, HOW MUCH MORE WILL THERE BE
A REIGN OF LIFE FOR THOSE WHO RECEIVE THE
GRACE AND THE GIFT OF TRUE RIGHTEOUSNESS
THROUGH THE ONE PERSON, JESUS CHRIST.
18 JUST AS ONE TRANSGRESSION BROUGHT

SENTENCE OF DEATH TO ALL, SO, TOO, ONE REHABILITA-
TION BROUGHT PARDON AND LIFE TO ALL; 19 AND
AS THE DISOBEDIENCE OF ONLY ONE MADE MANY SIN-
NERS, SO THE OBEDIENCE OF ONE PERSON ALLOWED A
MULTITUDE TO BE MADE JUST AND HOLY. 20 THE LAW
ITSELF, INTRODUCED LATER ON, CAUSED SIN TO IN-
CREASE; BUT WHERE SIN INCREASED, GRACE ABOUN-
DED ALL THE MORE. 21 AND AS SIN CAUSED DEATH
TO REIGN, SO GRACE WILL REIGN IN ITS OWN TIME,
AND AFTER MAKING US JUST AND FRIENDS OF GOD,
WILL BRING US TO ETERNAL LIFE THROUGH
JESUS CHRIST, OUR LORD.

THROUGH BAPTISM WE DIED WITH CHRIST

6 1 THEN, WHAT SHALL WE SAY? SHALL WE KEEP ON SIN-
NING SO THAT GRACE MAY COME ABUNDANTLY? 2
CAN WE LIVE AGAIN IN SIN? OF COURSE NOT: WE ARE
NOW DEAD REGARDING SIN.

3 YOU KNOW THAT IN BAP-
TISM WHICH UNITES US
TO CHRIST WE ARE ALL
BAPTIZED AND PLUNGED
INTO HIS DEATH. 4 BY
THIS BAPTISM IN HIS DE-
ATH, WE WERE BURIED WITH
CHRIST; AS CHRIST WAS RA-
ISED FROM AMONG THE DE-
AD BY THE GLORY OF THE
FATHER, SO WE BEGIN
WALKING IN A NEW LIFE.
5 IT WAS AN IMAGE OF
HIS DEATH WHEN WE WE-
RE GRAFTED IN HIM, AND
ALSO WE WILL SHARE IN
HIS RESURRECTION.
6 WE KNOW THAT OUR
OLD SELF WAS CRUCIFIED
WITH CHRIST, SO AS TO DES-
TROY WHAT OF US WAS
SIN, SO THAT WE MAY NO
LONGER SERVE SIN. 7
IF WE ARE DEAD, WE
ARE NO LONGER IN DEBT
TO HIM.
8 BUT IF WE HAVE
DIED WITH CHRIST,
WE BELIEVE WE WILL ALSO LIVE WITH HIM,

9 WE KNOW THAT CHRIST, ONCE RISEN FROM THE
DEAD, WILL NOT DIE AGAIN AND DEATH HAS NO MO-
RE DOMINATION OVER HIM. 10 THERE HAS BE-
EN DEATH: A DEATH TO SIN ONCE FOR ALL: THERE
IS LIFE: A LIFE IN GOD.
11 SO YOU, TOO, MUST CONSIDER YOURSELVES DEAD
TO SIN AND ALIVE TO GOD IN CHRIST JESUS. 12 DO
NOT ALLOW SIN ANY CONTROL OVER YOUR MOR-
TAL BEING; DO NOT SUBMIT YOURSELVES TO
ITS EVIL INCLINATIONS, 13 AND DO NOT
GIVE YOUR MEMBERS
OVER TO SIN, AS INS-
TRUMENTS TO DO
EVIL. ON THE CONT-
RARY, OFFER YOUR-
SELVES AS PERSONS
RETURNED FROM DE-
ATH TO LIFE AND LET
THE MEMBERS OF YO-
UR BODY BE A HOLY
INSTRUMENTS AT
THE SERVICE OF GOD.
14 SIN WILL NOT
LORD IT OVER YOU
AGAIN, FOR YOU ARE
NOT UNDER THE LAW,
BUT UNDER GRACE.

15 I ASK AGAIN: WE
ARE TO SIN BECAUSE
WE ARE NOT UNDER
THE LAW, BUT UNDER
GRACE? CERTAINLY NOT. 16 IF YOU HAVE GIVEN
YOURSELVES UP TO SOMEONE AS HIS SLAVE,
YOU ARE TO OBEY THE ONE WHO COMMANDS
YOU, AREN'T YOU? NOW WITH SIN YOU GO TO
DEATH, AND BY ACCEPTING FAITH YOU GO
THE RIGHT WAY. 17 LET US GIVE THANKS TO
GOD FOR, AFTER HAVING SIN AS YOUR MAS-
TER, YOU HAVE BEEN GIVEN TO ANOTHER, THAT
IS, TO THE DOCTRINE OF FAITH, TO WHICH YOU LIS-
TEN WILLINGLY. 18 AND BEING FREE FROM SIN,

YOU BEGAN TO SERVE TRUE RIGHTEOUSNESS. 19
YOU SEE THAT I USE SIMPLE WORDS, BECAUSE
PERHAPS IT IS DIFFICULT FOR YOU TO UNDER-
STAND.

THERE WAS A TIME WHEN YOU LET YOUR MEM-
BERS BE SLAVES OF IMPURITY AND DISOR-
DER, WALKING IN THE WAY OF SIN; CONVERT
THEM NOW INTO SERVANTS OF JUSTICE AND
HOLINESS, TO THE POINT OF BECOMING HOLY.

372 CCCLXXII

(20) WHEN YOU WERE SLAVES OF SIN, YOU DID NOT FEEL
UNDER OBLIGATION TO HOLINESS. (21) BUT WHAT WERE
THE FRUITS OF THOSE ACTIONS OF WHICH YOU ARE
NOT ASHAMED? SUCH THINGS BRING DEATH.

(22) NOW, HOWEVER, YOU HAVE BEEN FREED FROM
SIN AND SERVE GOD. YOU ARE BEARING FRUIT AND
GROWING IN HOLINESS, AND THE RESULT WILL
BE LIFE EVERLASTING. (23) SO ON ONE SIDE

IS SIN: ITS REWARD, DEATH; ON THE OTHER SIDE
IS GOD: HE GIVES US, BY GRACE, LIFE EVER-
LASTING IN CHRIST JESUS, OUR LORD.

THE CHRISTIAN IS NOT BOUND BY THE JEWISH RELIGION

7 (1) YOU, MY FRIENDS, UNDERSTAND LAW. THE LAW
HAS POWER ONLY WHILE A PERSON IS ALIVE.
(2) THE MARRIED WOMAN, FOR EXAMPLE, IS
BOUND BY LAW TO HER HUSBAND WHILE HE IS AL-
IVE; BUT IF HE DIES, SHE IS FREE FROM HER OB-
LIGATIONS AS A WIFE. (3) IF SHE GIVES HERSELF TO
ANOTHER WHILE HER HUSBAND IS ALIVE, SHE WILL BE

AN ADULTERESS; BUT
ONCE THE HUSBAND DIES,
SHE IS FREE AND IF SHE
GIVES HERSELF TO ANOTHER
MAN, SHE IS NOT AN ADUL-
TERESS. (4) IT WAS
THE SAME WITH YOU,
BROTHERS: YOU
HAVE DIED TO THE
LAW WITH THE PER-
SON OF CHRIST, AND
YOU BELONG TO AN-
OTHER, WHO HAS
RISEN FROM ALL
AMONG THE DEAD,
SO THAT WE MAY
PRODUCE FRUIT
FOR GOD.

(5) WHEN WE LIVED
AS HUMANS USED
TO DO, THE LAW
STIRRED UP THE
DESIRES FOR ALL
THAT IS SIN, AND
THEY WORKED IN
OUR BODIES WITH
FRUITS OF DEATH.
(6) BUT WE HAVE DIED TO WHAT WAS
HOLDING US; WE ARE FREED FROM THE
LAW AND NO LONGER SERVE A WRITTEN LAW,
WHICH WAS THE OLD; WITH THE SPIRIT WE ARE
IN THE NEW.

(7) THEN, SHALL WE SAY THAT THE LAW IS PART OF
SIN? OF COURSE NOT. HOWEVER, I WOULD NOT
KNOWN SIN, HAD IT NOT BEEN THROUGH THE LAW.
I WOULD NOT BE AWARE OF GREED IF THE LAW DID
NOT TELL ME: DO NOT COVET. (8) SIN TOOK AD-
VANTAGE OF THE COMMANDMENT TO STIR IN ME ALL
KINDS OF GREED; WHEREAS, WITHOUT A LAW, SIN
LIES DEAD. (9) FIRST THERE WAS NO LAW
AND I LIVED. THEN
THE COMMANDMENT
CAME AND GAVE LI-
FE TO SIN: (10) AND
I DIED. IT HAPPENED
THAT THE LAW OF LI-
FE HAD BROUGHT ME
DEATH. (11) SIN TOOK
ADVANTAGE OF THE
COMMANDMENT: IT
LURED ME AND KIL-
LED ME THROUGH
THE COMMANDMENT.
(12) BUT THE LAW
ITSELF IS HOLY,
JUST AND GOOD.
(13) IS IT POSSIBLE
THAT SOMETHING
GOOD BRINGS DEATH
TO ME? OF COURSE
NOT. THIS COMES
FROM SIN WHICH
MAY BE SEEN AS
SIN WHEN IT TAKES
ADVANTAGE OF SOME-
THING GOOD TO KILL: THE COMMANDMENT
LET SIN APPEAR FULLY SINFUL.

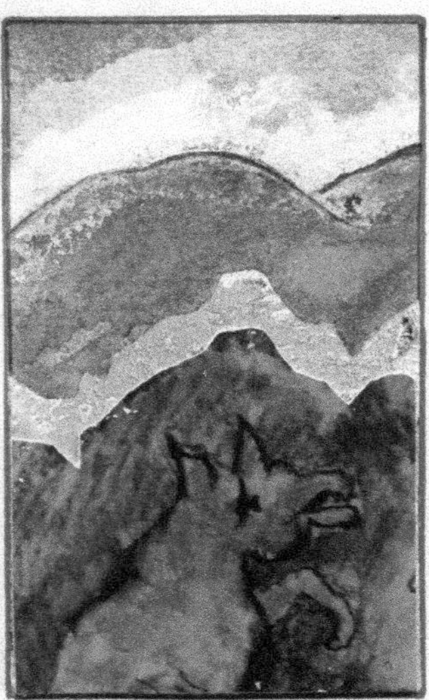

THE LAW WITHOUT CHRIST MAKES HUMANS DIVIDED

(14) WE KNOW THAT THE LAW IS SPIRITUAL; AS FOR
ME, I AM FLESH AND HAVE BEEN SOLD TO SIN. (15)
I CANNOT EXPLAIN WHAT IS HAPPENING TO ME, BECA-
USE I DO NOT DO WHAT I WANT, BUT ON THE CONT-
RARY, THE VERY THINGS I HATE. (16) WELL THEN,

IF I DO THE EVIL I DO NOT WANT TO DO, I AGREE
THAT THE LAW IS GOOD; (17) BUT I AM NOT THE ONE GO-
ING TOWARD EVIL, BUT IT'S SIN, LIVING IN ME. (18) I
KNOW THAT WHAT IS RIGHT DOES NOT ABIDE IN ME,
I MEAN, IN MY FLESH. I CAN WANT TO DO WHAT IS RIGHT,
BUT I AM UNABLE TO DO IT. (19) IN FACT, I DO NOT
DO THE GOOD I WANT, BUT THE EVIL I HATE.
(20) THEREFORE, IF I DO WHAT I DO NOT WANT TO DO,
I AM NOT THE ONE STRIVING TOWARDS EVIL,
BUT SIN WHICH IS IN ME.

(21) I DISCOVER, THEN, THIS REALITY: THOUGH I WISH
TO DO WHAT IS RIGHT, THE EVIL WITHIN ME ASSERTS
ITSELF FIRST.
(22) MY INMOST SELF AGREES AND REJOICES WITH
THE LAW OF GOD, (23) BUT I NOTICE IN MY BODY
ANOTHER LAW CHALLENGING THE LAW OF THE
SPIRIT, AND DELIVERING ME AS A SLAVE TO
THE LAW OF SIN WRITTEN IN MY MEMBERS.

(24) ALAS, FOR ME! WHO WILL FREE ME FROM
THIS BEING WHICH IS ONLY DEATH? (25) LET

US GIVE THANKS TO GOD THROUGH JESUS CHRIST,
OUR LORD. SO, MY CONSCIENCE SERVES GOD'S LAW, WHI-
LE MY MORTAL BEING SERVES THE LAW OF SIN.

WE HAVE RECEIVED THE SPIRIT

8 (1) THIS CONTRADICTION NO LONGER EXISTS
FOR THOSE WHO ARE IN JESUS CHRIST. (2)
FOR, IN JESUS CHRIST, THE LAW OF THE SPIRIT
OF LIFE HAS SET ME FREE FROM THE LAW OF SIN
AND DEATH. (3) THE LAW WAS WITHOUT EFFECT
BECAUSE FLESH WAS NOT RESPONDING. THEN
GOD, PLANNING TO DESTROY SIN, SENT HIS OWN SON, LIKE
THOSE SUBJECT TO THE SINFUL HUMAN CONDITION.
(4) SINCE THEN THE
PERFECTION INTENDED
BY THE LAW WOULD BE
FULFILLED IN THOSE
NOT WALKING IN THE
WAY OF THE FLESH, BUT
IN THE WAY OF THE SPIRIT.

LIFE-THE SPIRIT

(5) THOSE WALKING AC-
CORDING TO THE FLESH
TEND TOWARDS WHAT IS
FLESH; THOSE LED BY THE
SPIRIT, TO WHAT IS SPIRIT.
(6) FLESH TENDS TOWARD
DEATH, WHILE SPIRIT
AIMS AT LIFE AND PE-
ACE. (7) WHAT THE FLESH
SEEKS IS AGAINST GOD;
IT DOES NOT AGREE, IT
CANNOT EVEN SUBMIT
TO THE LAW OF GOD. (8)
SO, THOSE WALKING AC-
CORDING TO THE FLESH
CANNOT PLEASE GOD.

(9) YET YOUR EXIST-
ENCE IS NOT IN THE FLESH, BUT IN THE SPI-
RIT, BECAUSE THE SPIRIT OF GOD IS WITHIN
YOU. IF YOU DID HAVE THE SPIRIT OF CHRIST,
YOU WOULD NOT BELONG TO HIM.

(10) BUT CHRIST IS WITHIN YOU; THOUGH THE
BODY IS BRANDED BY DEATH AS A CONSEQUENCE
OF SIN, THE SPIRIT IS LIFE AND HOLINESS (11) AND
IF THE SPIRIT OF HIM WHO RAISED CHRIST FROM
THE DEAD IS WITHIN YOU, HE WHO RAISED CHRIST
FROM AMONG THE DEAD WILL ALSO GIVE YOU
LIFE TO YOUR MORTAL BODIES. YES HE WILL
DO IT THROUGH HIS SPIRIT WHO DWELLS
WITHIN YOU.
(12) THEN, BROTHERS, LET US LEAVE THE FLESH
AND NO LONGER LIVE
ACCORDING TO IT. (13)
IF NOT, WE WILL DIE.
RATHER, WALKING IN
THE SPIRIT, LET US PUT
TO DEATH THE BODY'S
DEEDS SO THAT WE
MAY LIVE. (14) ALL
THOSE WHO WALK IN
THE SPIRIT OF GOD
ARE SONS AND DAUGH-
TERS OF GOD. (15) THEN,
NO MORE FEAR; YOU
DID NOT RECEIVE A
SPIRIT OF SLAVERY,
BUT THE SPIRIT THAT
MAKES YOU ADOPTED
CHILDREN AND EVERY
TIME CRY, "ABBA! FA-
THER!" (16) THE SPI-
RIT ASSURES OUR SPI-
RIT THAT WE ARE
CHILDREN OF GOD
(17) IF WE ARE CHILD-
REN, WE ARE HEIRS,
TOO. OURS WILL BE
THE INHERITANCE OF
GOD AND WE WILL SHARE IT WITH CHRIST; FOR IF
WE NOW SUFFER WITH HIM, WE WILL ALSO SHARE
GLORY WITH HIM.

REDEMPTION

(18) I CONSIDER THAT THE SUFFERING OF OUR PRESENT
LIFE CANNOT BE COMPARED WITH THE GLORY THAT
WILL BE REVEALED AND GIVEN TO US. (19) ALL CREATION
IS EAGERLY EXPECTING THE BIRTH IN GLORY OF THE CHILDREN
OF GOD. (20) FOR IF NOW THE CREATED WORLD WAS UNABLE
TO ATTAIN ITS PURPOSE, THIS DID NOT COME FROM ITSELF
BUT FROM THE ONE WHO SUBJECTED IT. BUT IT IS
NOT WITHOUT HOPE; (21) FOR EVEN THE CREATED
WORLD WILL BE FREED FROM THIS FATE OF DEATH

AND SHARE THE FREEDOM AND GLORY OF THE CHILDREN
OF GOD. (22) WE KNOW THAT THE WHOLE CREATION GROANS
AND SUFFERS THE PANGS OF BIRTH. (23) NOT JUST CREATION
BUT EVEN US, ALTHOUGH THE SPIRIT WAS GIVEN TO
US AS A FORETASTE OF WHAT WE ARE TO RECEIVE, WE
GROAN IN OUR INNERMOST BEING, EAGERLY AWAIT-
ING THE DAY WHEN GOD WILL ADOPT US AND
TAKE TO HIMSELF OUR BODIES AS WELL.
(24) TO HOPE IS THE WAY WE ARE SAVED.
BUT IF WE SAW WHAT WE HOPED FOR, THERE
WOULD NO LONGER BE HOPE: HOW CAN WE
HOPE FOR WHAT IS ALREADY SEEN?

(25) SO WE HOPE FOR WHAT WE DO NOT SEE AND WE
WILL RECEIVE IT THROUGH PATIENT HOPE. (26) WE
ARE WEAK, BUT THE SPIRIT COMES TO HELP US. HOW
TO ASK? AND WHAT SHALL WE ASK FOR? WE DO NOT
KNOW, BUT THE SPIRIT INTERCEDES FOR US WITH-
OUT WORDS, AS IF WITH GROANS. (27) AND HE WHO
SEES INNER SECRETS KNOWS THE DESIRES OF
THE SPIRIT, FOR HE ASKS FOR THE HOLY ONES WHAT
IS PLEASING TO GOD.

WHO SHALL PART US FROM THE LOVE OF GOD?

(28) WE KNOW THAT IN EVERYTHING GOD WORKS FOR
THE GOOD OF THOSE WHO LOVE HIM, WHOM HE HAS
CALLED ACCORDING TO
HIS PLAN. (29) THOSE
WHOM HE KNEW BEFORE-
HAND, HE HAS ALSO PRED-
ESTINED TO BE LIKE HIS
SON, SIMILAR TO HIM, SO
THAT HE MAY BE THE
FIRSTBORN AMONG MA-
NY BROTHERS AND SIS-
TERS. (30) AND THOSE
WHOM GOD PREDESTI-
NED HE CALLED, AND
THOSE WHOM HE CAL-
LED HE MAKES RIGHT-
EOUS, AND TO THOSE
WHOM HE MAKES RIGHT-
EOUS HE WILL GIVE HIS
GLORY.
(31) WHAT SHALL WE
SAY AFTER THIS?
IF GOD IS WITH US
WHO SHALL BE THEN
AGAINST US?

THE APPIAN WAY

(32) IF HE HAD NOT SPARED HIS OWN SON, BUT
GAVE HIM UP FOR US ALL, HOW WILL HE NOT GI-
VE US ALL THINGS WITH HIM? (33) WHO SHALL
ACCUSE THOSE CHOSEN BY GOD: HE TAKES
AWAY THEIR GUILT.
(34) WHO WILL DARE TO CONDEMN THEM?
CHRIST WHO DIED, AND BETTER STILL, ROSE
AND IS SEATED AT THE RIGHT HAND OF GOD,

INTERCEDING FOR US? (35) WHO SHALL SEPA-
RATE US FROM THE LOVE OF CHRIST? WILL IT BE
TRIALS, OR ANGUISH, PERSECUTION OR HUNGER,
LACK OF CLOTHING, OR DANGERS OR SWORD?
AS THE SCRIPTURE SAYS: (36)

FOR YOUR SAKE WE ARE BEING KILLED
ALL DAY LONG; THEY TREAT US LIKE
SHEEP TO BE SLAUGHTERED.

(37) NO, IN ALL OF THIS WE ARE MORE THAN
CONQUERORS, THANKS TO HIM WHO HAS
LOVED US.
(38) I AM CERTAIN THAT NEITHER DEATH
NOR LIFE, NEITHER ANGELS NOR SPIRITUAL
POWER, NEITHER THE PRESENT (39) NOR THE
FUTURE, NOR COSMIC POWERS, WERE THEY
FROM HEAVEN OR FROM THE DEEP WORLD
BELOW, NOR ANY CREATURE WHATSOEVER

WILL SEPARATE US FROM THE LOVE OF GOD,
WHICH WE HAVE IN JESUS CHRIST, OUR LORD.

WHY HAVE THE JEWS NOT BELIEVED?

9 (1) I TELL YOU SINCERELY IN CHRIST, AND MY
CONSCIENCE ASSURES ME IN THE HOLY SPIRIT
THAT I AM NOT LYING: (2) I HAVE GREAT SADNESS
AND CONSTANT ANGUISH FOR THE JEWS. (3) I WOULD EVEN
DESIRE THAT I MYSELF SUFFER THE CURSE OF BEING CUT
OFF FROM CHRIST, INSTEAD OF MY BRETHERN: I MEAN MY
OWN PEOPLE, MY KIN.
(4) THEY ARE ISRAELI-
TES WHOM GOD ADOP-
TED AND ON THEM RESTS
HIS GLORY. THEIRS
ARE THE COVENANTS, THE
LAW, THE WORSHIP AND
GOD'S PROMISES. (5)
THEY ARE DESCENDANTS
OF THE PATRIARCHS AND
FROM THEM CHRIST WAS
BORN, HE ABOVE ALL.
BLESSED BE GOD FOR-
EVER AND EVER. AMEN!
(6) WE CANNOT SAY THAT
GOD'S PROMISE HAS FA-
ILED. NOT ALL ISRAELI-
TES BELONG TO ISRAEL.
(7) AND NOT BECAUSE
THEY ARE OF THE RACE
OF ABRAHAM ARE THEY
ALL HIS CHILDREN, FOR IT
WAS SAID TO HIM: 'THE
CHILDREN OF ISAAC WILL
BE CALLED YOUR DESCEN-

DANTS. (8) THIS MEANS THAT THE CHILDREN OF GOD
ARE NOT IDENTIFIED WITH THE RACE OF ABRAHAM,
BUT ONLY WITH THE CHILDREN BORN TO HIM
BECAUSE OF THE PROMISE OF GOD.

(9) TO SUCH A PROMISE THIS TEXT REFERS:
'I SHALL RETURN ABOUT THIS TIME AND
SARAH WILL HAVE A SON.'
(10) AND LISTEN: REBECCA, THE WIFE OF OUR
FATHER ISAAC, BECAME PREGNANT;

ECCE HOMO
HOMAGE TO GIACOMETTI
373 CCCLXXIII
DM 09 ©

11 AND BEFORE THE TWINS WERE BORN, WHEN
THEY HADN'T YET DONE RIGHT OR WRONG, ALL
FOR THEM DEPENDED ON THE CHOICE OF GOD.
12 IT WAS A MATTER NOT ON THE MERITS BUT
OF WHO IS CALLED. AND IT WAS THEN THAT REBECCA
WAS TOLD: THE ELDER WILL SERVE THE YOUNGER,
13 AS THE SCRIPTURE SAYS: I CHOSE JACOB
AND REJECTED ESAU.

GOD IS NOT UNJUST

14 SHALL WE SAY THAT GOD IS UNJUST? OF COURSE
NOT. 15 HOWEVER GOD SAID TO MOSES: I SHALL FORGI-
VE WHOM I FORGIVE AND HAVE PITY ON WHOM I HAVE

PITY, 16 SO WHAT IS IMPORTANT IS NOT THAT WE WOR-
RY OR HURRY, BUT THAT GOD HAS COMPASSION. 17 AND
HE SAYS IN SCRIPTURE TO PHARAOH: I MADE YOU PHAR
AOH TO SHOW MY POWER IN YOU, AND FOR THE WHOLE
WORLD TO KNOW MY NAME. 18 AND SO GOD TAKES
PITY ON WHOM HE WISHES, AND HARDENS THE HE-
ART OF WHOMSOEVER HE WISHES.
19 MAYBE YOU SAY: "WHY THEN DOES GOD COM-
PLAIN, IF IT IS IMPOSSIBLE TO EVADE HIS DECISI-
ON?" 20 BUT YOU, MY FRIEND, WHO ARE YOU TO

CALL GOD TO ACCOUNT?
SHOULD THE CLAY POT
SAY TO ITS MAKER:
WHY DID YOU MAKE
ME LIKE THIS? 21 IS
IT NOT UP TO THE POT-
TER TO MAKE FROM
THE SAME CLAY A
VESSEL FOR BEAUTY
AND A VESSEL FOR ME-
NIAL USE? 22 THUS
GOD ENDURES VERY
PATIENTLY VESSELS
THAT DESERVE HIS
WRATH, FIT TO BE BRO-
KEN, AND THROUGH
THEM HE WANTS TO
TO SHOW HIS WRATH
AND THE EXTENT OF HIS
POWER. 23 BUT HE
ALSO WANTS TO
SHOW THE RICHES OF
HIS GLORY IN OTHERS,
IN VESSELS OF MERCY
PREPARED FOR GLORY.
24 AND HE CALLED
US, NOT ONLY FROM
AMONG THE JEWS, BUT FROM AMONG THE PA-
GANS, TOO, 25 AS HE SAID THROUGH THE
PROPHET HOSEA:

I WILL CALL "MY PEOPLE" THOSE THAT
WERE NOT MY PEOPLE, AND "MY BELOVED",
THE ONE WHO WAS NOT BELOVED.

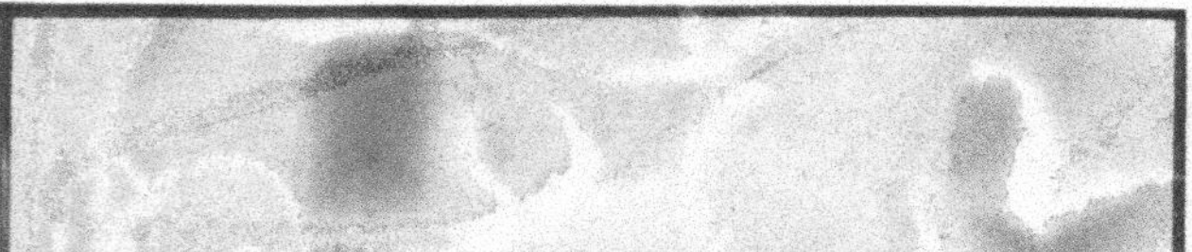

26 AND IN THE SAME PLACE WHERE
THEY WERE TOLD: "YOU ARE NOT MY
PEOPLE", THEY WILL BE CALLED
CHILDREN OF THE LIVING GOD.

27 WITH REGARD TO ISRAEL, ISAIAH PROCLAIMS:

EVEN IF THE ISRAELITES ARE AS NUMEROUS
AS THE SAND OF THE SEA, ONLY A FEW WILL BE SA-
VED. 28 THIS IS A MATTER THAT THE LORD WILL
SETTLE IN ISRAEL

WITHOUT FAIL OR DE-
LAY. 29 ISAIAH ALSO
ANNOUNCED: IF THE AL-
MIGHTY LORD HAD NOT
LEFT US SOME DESCEND-
ANTS, WE WOULD HAVE
BECOME LIKE SODOM
AND SIMILAR TO GOMOR-
RAH. 30 WHAT ARE WE
SAYING, THEN? THAT THE
PAGANS WHO WERE NOT
AIMING AT TRUE RIGHTEO-
USNESS FOUND IT (I SPEAK
OF RIGHTEOUSNESS THROUGH
FAITH); 31 WHILE ISRAEL,
STRIVING TO OBSERVE A
LAW OF RIGHTEOUSNESS,
LOST THE PURPOSE OF
THE LAW. 32 WHY? BE-
CAUSE THEY RELIED ON
THE OBSERVANCE OF
THE LAW, NOT ON
FAITH. AND THEY
STUMBLED OVER THE
STUMBLING STONE
(CHRIST), 33 AS IT WAS
SAID: LOOK, I AM LAYING
IN ZION A STONE THAT WILL MAKE PEOPLE STUMBLE, A
ROCK THAT WILL MAKE THEM FALL; BUT WHO-
EVER RELIES ON HIM WILL NOT BE DECEIVED.

THEY TRIED TO ACHIEVE THEIR OWN PERFECTION

10 1 MY BROTHERS, I WISH WITH ALL MY HEART THAT
THE JEWS BE SAVED AND I PRAY GOD FOR THEM.
2 I CAN TESTIFY THAT THEY ARE ZEALOUS FOR
GOD, ALTHOUGH IN THE WRONG WAY. 3 THEY DON'T

KNOW GOD'S WAY OF RIGHTEOUSNESS AND THEY TRY
TO ACHIEVE THEIR OWN RIGHTEOUSNESS; THIS IS
WHY THEY DID NOT ENTER GOD'S WAY OF RIGHT-
EOUSNESS. 4 FOR CHRIST IS THE AIM OF THE LAW
AND IT IS THEN THAT THE BELIEVER REACHES
THIS RIGHTEOUSNESS.
5 MOSES, INDEED, SPEAKS OF BECAMING JUST THROUGH
THE LAW; HE WRITES: THE ONE WHO OBEYS THE LAW
WILL FIND LIFE THROUGH IT, 6 BUT THE RIGHTEOU-
SNESS COMING FROM THE FAITH SAYS INSTEAD: DO NOT
SAY IN YOUR HEART: WHO WILL GO UP TO HEAVEN?
(BECAUSE IN FACT CHRIST CAME DOWN FROM THERE);

7 OR WHO WILL GO DOWN TO THE WORLD BE-
LOW? (BECAUSE IN FACT CHRIST CAME UP FROM
AMONG THE DEAD). 8 TRUE RIGHTEOUSNESS CO-
MING FROM FAITH ALSO SAYS: THE WORD OF
GOD IS NEAR YOU, ON YOUR LIPS AND IN YOUR
HEARTS. THIS IS THE MESSAGE THAT WE PRE-
ACH, AND THIS IS FAITH. 9 YOU ARE SAVED IF
YOU CONFESS WITH YOUR LIPS THAT JESUS IS
THE LORD AND IN YOUR HEART YOU BELIEVE
THAT GOD RAISED HIM FROM THE DEAD. 10 BY BE-
LIEVING FROM THE HEART, YOU OBTAIN TRUE RIGHT-
EOUSNESS; BY CONFESSING THE FAITH WITH YOUR
LIPS YOU ARE SAVED. 11 FOR SCRIPTURE SAYS: NO

ONE WHO BELIEVES IN HIM WILL BE ASHAMED. 12
HERE THERE IS NO DISTINCTION BETWEEN JEW AND
GREEK; ALL HAVE THE SAME LORD, WHO IS VERY GE-
NEROUS WITH WHOEVER CALLS ON HIM. 13 TRULY,
ALL WHO CALL UPON THE NAME OF THE LORD
WILL BE SAVED.
14 BUT HOW CAN THEY CALL UPON THE NAME OF
THE LORD WITHOUT HAVING BELIEVED IN HIM? AND HOW
CAN THEY BELIEVE IN HIM WITHOUT HAVING FIRST
HEARD ABOUT HIM? AND HOW WILL THEY HEAR ABOUT
HIM IF NO ONE PREACHES ABOUT HIM? 15 AND HOW

WILL THEY PREACH
ABOUT HIM IF NO ONE
SENDS THEM? AS SCRIP-
TURE SAYS: HOW BEAU-
TIFUL TO SEE THOSE CO-
MING TO BRING GOOD
NEWS. 16 ALTHOUGH
NOT EVERYONE OBEYED
THE GOOD NEWS, AS ISAIAH
SAID: LORD, WHO HAS BE-
LIEVED IN OUR PREACH-
ING? 17 SO, FAITH
COMES FROM PREACHING,
AND PREACHING IS RO-
OTED IN THE WORD OF
CHRIST. 18 I ASK: HAVE
THE JEWS NOT HEARD?
BUT OF COURSE THEY HAVE.
BECAUSE THE VOICE OF
THOSE PREACHING RES-
OUNDED ALL OVER THE
EARTH AND THEIR VOICE
WAS HEARD TO THE END
OF THE WORLD. 19 THEN
I MUST ASK: DID ISRAEL
NOT UNDERSTAND? MOSES
WAS THE FIRST TO SAY: I
WILL MAKE YOU JEALOUS
OF A NATION THAT IS NOT A NATION, I WILL EXITE YOUR
ANGER AGAINST A CRAZY NATION. 20 ISAIAH DARES
TO ADD MORE: I WAS FOUND BY THOSE NOT
LOOKING FOR ME, I HAVE SHOWN MYSELF TO
THOSE NOT ASKING FOR ME.
21 WHILE REFERRING TO ISRAEL, THE SA-
ME ISAIAH SAYS:

I HOLD OUT MY HANDS THE WHOLE DAY LONG
TO A DISOBEDIENT AND REBELLIOUS PEOPLE.

A REMNANT OF ISRAEL HAS BEEN SAVED

11 1 AND SO I ASK: HAS GOD REJECTED HIS PE-
OPLE? OF COURSE NOT. I MYSELF AM AN IS-
RAELITE, A DESCENDANT OF ABRAHAM, FROM
THE TRIBE OF BENJAMIN. 2 GOD HAS NOT REJECTED
THE PEOPLE HE KNEW. DON'T YOU KNOW WHAT THE
SCRIPTURE SAYS OF ELIJAH WHEN HE WAS ACCUSING IS-
RAEL BEFORE GOD? 3 HE SAID: "LORD, THEY HAVE
KILLED YOUR PROPHETS
DESTROYED YOUR ALTARS,
AND I ALONE REMAIN;
AND NOW THEY WANT TO
KILL ME." 4 WHAT WAS
GOD'S ANSWER? I KEPT
FOR MYSELF SEVEN
THOUSAND WHO DID NOT
WORSHIP BAAL. 5 IN
THE SAME WAY NOW
THERE IS A REMNANT
IN ISRAEL, THOSE WHO
WERE CHOSEN BY GRACE.
6 I SAY: BY GRACE,
NOT BECAUSE OF WHAT
THEY DID. OTHERWISE
GRACE WOULD NOT BE
GRACE. 7 WHAT
THEN? WHAT ISRAEL
WAS LOOKING FOR, IT
DID NOT FIND, BUT
THOSE WHOM GOD
ELECTED FOUND IT.
THE OTHERS HARD-
ENED THEIR HEARTS,
8 AS SCRIPTURE

SAYS: GOD MADE THEM DULL OF HEART AND
MIND; TO THIS DAY THEIR EYES CANNOT SEE
NOR THEIR EARS HEAR. 9 DAVID SAYS: MAY
THEY BE CAUGHT AND TRAPPED AT THEIR BAN-
QUETS: MAY THEY FALL, MAY THEY BE PUNISHED.
10 MAY THEIR EYES BE CLOSED SO THAT THEY
CANNOT SEE AND THEIR BACKS BE BENT FOREVER.

DO NOT DESPISE THOSE WHO STUMBLED

11 AGAIN I ASKED: DID THEY STUMBLE SO AS TO
FALL? OF COURSE NOT. THEIR STUMBLING ALLOWED
SALVATION TO COME TO THE PAGAN NATIONS
AND THIS, IN TURN, WILL STIR UP THE JEALOUSY

OF ISRAEL. 12 IF ISRAEL'S SHORTCOMING MADE THE WORLD
RICH, IF THE PAGAN NATIONS GREW RICH WITH WHAT THEY
LOST, WHAT WILL HAPPEN WHEN ISRAEL IS RESTORED?
13 LISTEN TO ME, YOU WHO ARE NOT JEWS: I AM
SPENDING MYSELF AS AN APOSTLE TO THE PAGAN
NATIONS, 14 BUT I HOPE MY MINISTRY WILL BE
SUCCESSFUL ENOUGH TO AWAKEN THE JEALOUSY
OF THOSE OF MY RACE, AND TO SAVE SOME OF THEM.

(15) IF THE WORLD MADE PEACE WITH GOD WHEN
THEY REMAINED APART, WHAT WILL IT BE WHEN
THEY ARE WELCOMED? NOTHING LESS THAN A
PASSING FROM DEATH TO LIFE.
(16) WHEN THE FIRST FRUITS ARE CONSECRATED
TO GOD, THE WHOLE IS CONSECRATED. IF THE RO-
OTS ARE HOLY, SO WILL BE THE BRANCHES.
(17) SOME BRANCHES HAVE BEEN CUT FROM THE
OLIVE TREE, WHILE YOU, AS A WILD OLIVE TREE,
HAVE BEEN GRAFTED IN THEIR STEAD, AND YOU ARE
BENEFITING FROM
THEIR ROOTS AND
SAP. (18) NOW, THERE-
FORE, DO NOT BE PRO-
UD AND DESPISE THE
BRANCHES, BECAUSE
YOU DO NOT SUPPORT
THE ROOTS, THE ROOTS
SUPPORT YOU. (19) YOU
MAY SAY, "THEY CUT
OFF THE BRANCHES
TO GRAFT ME." (20)
WELL AND GOOD, BUT
THEY WERE CUT OFF
BECAUSE THEY DID
NOT BELIEVE, WHILE
YOU STAND BY FAITH.
THEN DO NOT PRIDE
YOURSELF ON THIS
TOO MUCH, RATHER
BEWARE! (21) IF GOD
DID NOT SPARE THE
NATURAL BRANCHES,
EVEN LESS WILL HE
SPARE YOU.
(22) ADMIRE AT THE
SAME TIME BOTH
THE GOODNESS AND
SEVERITY OF GOD: HE
WAS SEVERE WITH THE FALLEN AND HE IS GENE-
ROUS WITH YOU, AS LONG AS YOU REMAIN FAITH-
FUL. OTHERWISE YOU WILL BE CUT OFF. (23) IF THEY
DO NOT KEEP ON REJECTING THE FAITH THEY WILL BE
GRAFTED IN, FOR GOD IS ABLE TO GRAFT THEM BACK
AGAIN. (24) IF YOU WERE TAKEN FROM THE WILD OLIVE
TREE TO WHICH YOU BELONGED AND, IN SPITE OF BEING A
DIFFERENT SPECIES, YOU WERE GRAFTED INTO THE GO-
OD OLIVE TREE, IT WILL BE MUCH EASIER AND NA-
TURAL FOR THEM TO BE GRAFTED INTO THEIR OWN TREE.

ISRAEL WILL BE SAVED

(25) I WANT YOU TO UNDERSTAND THE MYSTERIOUS
DECREE OF GOD, LEST YOU BE TOO CONFIDENT: A PART
OF ISRAEL WILL REMAIN HARDENED UNTIL THE

MAJORITY OF PAGANS HAVE ENTERED. (26) THEN THE
WHOLE OF ISRAEL WILL BE SAVED, AS SCRIPTURE
SAYS:

"FROM ZION WILL COME THE LIBERATOR WHO WILL
PURIFY THE SONS OF JACOB FROM ALL SIN. (27) AND
THIS IS THE COVENANT I WILL MAKE WITH THEM: I
WILL TAKE AWAY FROM THEM THEIR SINS."

(28) REGARDING THE GOSPEL, THE JEWS ARE OPPONENTS,
BUT IT IS FOR YOUR BENEFIT. REGARDING ELECTION,
THEY ARE STILL BELOVED BECAUSE OF THEIR FA-
THERS; (29) BECAUSE THE CALL OF GOD AND HIS
GIFTS CANNOT BE NULLIFIED.
(30) THROUGH THE REBELLION OF THE JEWS THE
MERCY OF GOD CAME TO YOU WHO DID NOT OBEY
GOD. (31) THEY IN TURN WILL RECEIVE MERCY
IN DUE TIME AFTER THIS REBELLION THAT
BROUGHT GOD'S MERCY TO YOU. (32) SO GOD
HAS SUBMITTED ALL TO DISOBEDIENCE, IN
ORDER TO SHOW HIS MERCY TO ALL. (33) HOW

DEEP ARE THE RICHES, THE WISDOM AND KNOWLEDGE
OF GOD! HIS DECISIONS CANNOT BE EXPLAINED, NOR HIS
WAYS UNDERSTOOD! (34) WHO HAS EVER KNOWN GOD'S
THOUGHTS? WHO HAS EVER BEEN HIS ADVISER? (35)
WHO HAS GIVEN HIM SOMETHING FIRST, SO THAT
GOD HAD TO REPAY HIM? (36) FOR EVERYTHING CO-
MES FROM HIM, HAS BEEN MADE BY HIM AND HAS TO
RETURN TO HIM. TO HIM BE THE GLORY FOR EVER! AMEN.

CHRISTIAN LIFE: BE CONCERNED FOR OTHERS

12 (1) I BEG YOU, DEARLY BELOVED, BY THE MER-
CY OF GOD, TO GIVE YOURSELVES AS A LIVING AND
HOLY SACRIFICE
PLEASING TO GOD: SUCH
IS THE WORSHIP OF A RA-
TIONAL BEING. (2) DON'T
LET YOURSELVES
BE SHAPED BY THE
WORLD WHERE YOU
LIVE, BUT RATHER
BY THE WILL OF
GOD: WHAT IS GOOD,
WHAT PLEASES,
WHAT IS PERFECT.

(3) THE GRACE THAT
GOD HAS GIVEN ME
ALLOWS ME TO TELL
EACH OF YOU: BE
ACTIVE, BUT NOT
INDISCREET.
LET EACH ONE EXER-
CISE WISELY THE
GIFTS OF FAITH
GRANTED BY GOD.

(4) SEE, THE BODY IS
ONE, EVEN IS FORMED
BY MANY MEMBERS, BUT NOT ALL OF THEM WITH
THE SAME FUNCTION.
(5) THE SAME WITH US; BEING MANY, WE ARE
ONE BODY IN CHRIST, DEPENDING ON ONE
ANOTHER. (6) LET EACH ONE OF US, THERE-
FORE, SERVE ACCORDING TO OUR DIFFE-
RENT GIFTS. DO YOU HAVE PROPHECY?

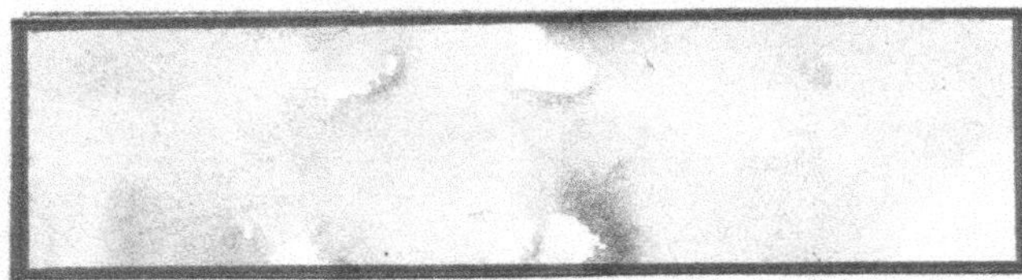

HOMAGE TO CARAVAGGIO
©
374-CCCLXXIV-
DM
69

7 LET THE DEACON FULFILL HIS OFFICE; LET
THE TEACHER TEACH, 8 THE ONE WHO ENCO-
URAGES, CONVINCE. YOU MUST, LIKEWISE
GIVE WITH AN OPEN HAND, PRESIDE WITH DE-
DICATION, AND BE CHEERFUL IN YOUR CHARITY.

9 LET LOVE BE SINCERE. HATE WHAT IS EVIL
AND HOLD TO WHATEVER IS GOOD.
10 REGARDING BROTHERLY LOVE, HAVE

LOVE FOR ONE ANOTHER; REGARDING RESPECT,
JUDGE OTHERS AS MORE WORTHY. 11 REGARD-
ING YOUR DUTIES DO NOT BE LAZY. BE FER-
VENT IN THE SPIRIT AND SERVE GOD. 12 HAVE HOPE AND
BE CHEERFUL. BE PATIENT IN TRIALS AND PRAY CONS-
TANTLY. 13 SHARE WITH OTHER CHRISTIANS IN NEED. WITH
THE PASSING BY, BE READY TO RECEIVE THEM.

14 BLESSED THOSE WHO PERSECUTE YOU; BLESS AND
DO NOT WISH EVIL ON
ANYONE. 15 REJOICE
WITH THOSE WHO ARE JOY-
FUL, AND WEEP WITH
THOSE WHO WEEP. 16
LIVE IN PEACE WITH
ONE ANOTHER. DO NOT
DREAM OF EXTRAORDINA-
RY THINGS; BE HUMBLE;
DO NOT HOLD YOU AS WISE.
17 DON'T RETURN EVIL
TO EVIL; LET EVERYONE SEE
YOUR GOOD WILL. 18 DO
YOUR BEST TO LIVE IN
PEACE WITH EVERYBODY. 19
BELOVED, DO NOT AVEN-
GE YOURSELVES, BUT
LET GOD BE THE ONE
WHO PUNISHES, AS
SCRIPTURE SAYS:
VENGEANCE IS MINE,
I WILL REPAY, SAYS
THE LORD. 20 AND
IT ADDS: IF YOUR
ENEMY IS HUNGRY,
FEED HIM; IF HE IS
THIRSTY, GIVE HIM
TO DRINK; BY DOING
THIS YOU WILL HEAP
BURNING COALS UPON
HIS HEAD. 21 DO NOT LET EVIL DEFEAT YOU, BUT
CONQUER EVIL WITH GOODNESS.

SUBMISSION TO AUTHORITY

13 1 LET EVERYONE BE SUBJECT TO THE
AUTHORITIES. FOR THERE IS NO AUTHORITY
THAT DOES NOT COME FROM GOD, AND THE
OFFICES HAVE BEEN ESTABLISHED BY GOD.
2 WHOEVER, THEREFORE, RESISTS AUTHORITY
GOES AGAINST A DECREE OF GOD, AND THOSE
WHO RESIST DESERVE TO BE CONDEMNED.

3 IN FACT, WHO FEARS AUTHORITY? NOT THO-
SE WHO DO GOOD, BUT THOSE WHO DO EVIL.
DO YOU WANT TO BE WITHOUT FEAR OF A
PERSON IN AUTHORITY? DO GOOD AND HE
WILL PRAISE YOU.
4 THEY ARE THE
STEWARDS OF GOD
FOR YOUR GOOD, BUT
IF YOU DO NOT BEHA-
VE, FEAR THEM FOR
THEY DO NOT CARRY
ARMS IN VAIN;
THEY ARE AT THE
SERVICE OF GOD
WHEN THEY JUDGE
AND PUNISH WRONG-
DOERS. 5 IT IS NE-
CESSARY TO OBEY,
NOT THROUGH FEAR
BUT AS A MATTER OF
CONSCIENCE. 6 IN
THE SAME WAY YOU
MUST PAY TAXES,
AND THE COLLECTORS
ARE GOD'S OFFICIALS.
7 GIVE EACH ONE
HIS DUE: TO WHOM-
EVER YOU OWE CONT-
RIBUTIONS, MAKE A
CONTRIBUTION; TO
WHOM TAXES ARE DUE
PAY TAXES; TO WHOM RESPECT IS DUE, GIVE RES-
PECT; TO WHOM HONOR IS DUE, GIVE HONOR.
8 DO NOT BE IN DEBT TO ANYONE. LET THIS
BE THE ONLY DEBT OF ONE TO ANOTHER: LOVE
BECAUSE HE WHO LOVES HIS NEIGHBOR HAS
FULFILLED THE WHOLE LAW.

9 YOU KNOW THE COMMANDMENTS: DO NOT

COMMIT ADULTERY, DO NOT KILL, DO NOT COVET;
AND WHATEVER ELSE ARE SUMMARIZED IN
THIS ONE: YOU WILL LOVE YOUR NEIGHBOR AS
YOURSELF. 10 LOVE CANNOT DO THE NEIGHBOR
ANY HARM; SO LOVE FULFILLS THE WHOLE LAW.

CHILDREN OF THE LIGHT

11 YOU KNOW WHAT HOUR IT IS. THIS IS THE TIME
TO AWAKE, FOR OUR SALVATION IS NOW NEAR-
ER THAN WHEN WE FIRST BELIEVED; 12 THE
NIGHT IS ALMOST OVER AND DAY IS AT HAND.
LET US DISCARD, THEREFORE, EVERYTHING
THAT BELONGS TO DARKNESS, AND LET
US PUT ON THE ARMOR OF LIGHT.

13 AS WE LIVE IN THE FULL LIGHT OF DAY, LET US
BEHAVE WITH DECENCY; NO BANQUETS WITH
DRUNKENNESS, NO PROSTITUTION, OR VICES, NO
FIGHTING OR JEALOUSY. 14 PUT ON, RATHER, THE LORD
JESUS CHRIST, AND DO NOT BE LED BY THE WILL OF THE
FLESH NOR FOLLOW ITS DESIRES.

THE WEAK AND THE STRONG

14 1 WELCOME THOSE WEAK IN FAITH AND DO NOT CRITI-
CIZE THEIR SCRUPLES. 2 SOME THINK THEY CAN
EAT ANY FOOD, WHILE OTHERS, LESS LIBERATED, EAT
ONLY VEGETABLES. 3 IF YOU EAT, DO NOT DESPISE THOSE

WHO ABSTAIN; IF YOU ABS-
TAIN, DO NOT CRITICIZE
THOSE WHO EAT, FOR GOD
HAS WELCOMED THEM.
4 WHO ARE YOU TO
PASS JUDGMENT ON THE
SERVANT OF ANOTHER? WHE-
THER HE STANDS OR FALLS,
THE ONE CONCERNED IS HIS
MASTER. BUT HE WILL NOT
FALL, FOR HIS MASTER IS
ABLE TO KEEP HIM STANDING.
5 FOR SOME, THERE
ARE GOOD AND BAD
DAYS; FOR OTHERS,
ALL DAYS ARE EQUAL.
LET EVERYONE ACT AC-
CORDING TO HIS OWN
OPINION.
6 HE WHO DISTIN-
GUISHES AMONG DAYS
DOES THAT FOR THE
LORD; AND HE WHO
EATS, EATS FOR THE
LORD AND IN EATING
HE GIVES THANKS TO
THE LORD. AND HE
WHO DOES NOT EAT
DOES IT FOR THE LORD AND GIVES HIM THANKS
AS WELL.
7 IN FACT, NONE OF US LIVES FOR HIMSELF, NOR
DIES FOR HIMSELF. 8 IF WE LIVE, WE LIVE FOR
THE LORD, AND IF WE DIE, WE DIE FOR THE
LORD. EITHER IN LIFE OR IN DEATH, WE
BELONG TO THE LORD.

9 CHRIST EXPERIENCED DEATH AND LIFE
TO BE LORD BOTH OF THE LIVING AND THE DEAD.

10 THEN YOU, WHY DO YOU CRITICIZE YOUR BRO-
THER? AND YOU, WHY DO YOU DESPISE HIM?
FOR WE WILL ALL APPEAR AT THE TRIBUNAL
OF GOD. 11 IT IS WRITTEN;

> I SWEAR BY MYSELF, WORD OF THE LORD, EVE-
> RY KNEE WILL BEND BEFORE ME, AND EVERY TON-
> GUE SHALL CONFESS TRUTH BEFORE GOD.

12 SO EACH OF US WILL ACCOUNT FOR HIMSELF
BEFORE GOD.
13 THEREFORE, LET US NOT CONTINUE CRITICIZ-
ING ONE ANOTHER; LET US TRY, RATHER, NEVER
TO PUT IN THE WAY OF OUR BROTHER ANYTHING
THAT WOULD MAKE HIM STUMBLE OR FALL.

14 I KNOW, I AM SURE OF THIS IN THE LORD
JESUS, THAT NOTHING IS UNCLEAN IN ITSELF,
IT IS RATHER ONLY UNCLEAN FOR THOSE
WHO CONSIDER IT TO BE UNCLEAN. 15

BUT IF YOU HURT YOUR BROTHER BECAUSE OF
A CERTAIN FOOD, YOU ARE NO LONGER WALK-
ING ACCORDING TO LOVE. LET NOT YOUR
16 EATING CAUSE THE LOSS OF ONE FOR WHOM
CHRIST DIED.
DON'T PUT YOURSELF IN THE WRONG WITH
SOMETHING GOOD. 17 THE KINGDOM OF GOD
IS NOT A MATTER OF FOOD OR DRINK; IT IS
JUSTICE, PEACE AND JOY IN THE HOLY SPIRIT.
18 AND IF YOU SERVE
CHRIST IN THIS WAY,
YOU WILL PLEASE
GOD AND BE PRAISED
BY PEOPLE. 19 LET
US LOOK, THEN, FOR

WHAT STRENGTHENS PEACE AND MAKES US
BETTER. 20 DO NOT DESTROY THE WORK OF
GOD BECAUSE OF FOOD. ALL FOOD IS CLEAN,
BUT IT BECOMES UNCLEAN FOR THE ONE WHO
EATS AGAINST HIS OWN BELIEF. 21 AND IT MAY
BE BETTER NOT TO EAT MEAT, OR DRINK WINE
OR ANYTHING ELSE THAT CAUSES YOUR BRO-
THER TO STUMBLE.
22 KEEP YOUR OWN BELIEF BEFORE GOD,
AND HAPPY ARE YOU IF YOU NEVER ACT
AGAINST YOUR OWN BELIEF.

23 INSTEAD, WHOEVER EATS SOMETHING IN
SPITE OF HIS DOUBT IS DOING WRONG, BECAUSE
HE DOES NOT ACT ACCORDING TO HIS BELIEF,
AND WHATEVER WE DO AGAINST OUR CONSCIENCE
IS SINFUL.

15 1 WE, THE STRONG AND LIBERATED, SHOULD
BEAR THE WEAKNESS OF THOSE WHO ARE NOT
STRONG, INSTEAD OF PLEASING OURSELVES.
2 LET EACH OF US BRING JOY TO OUR NEIGHBOR,
HELPING HIM TO GROW UP IN GOODNESS; 3
CHRIST HIMSELF DID NOT LOOK FOR HIS OWN

CONTENTMENT, AS SCRIPTURE SAYS: THE INSULTS
OF THOSE INSULTING YOU FELL UPON ME. 4 AND
WE KNOW THAT WHATEVER WAS WRITTEN IN THE PAST
WAS WRITTEN FOR OUR INSTRUCTION, FOR THE
COMFORT GIVEN US BY THE SCRIPTURE HELPS
US PERSEVERE AND SUSTAINS OUR HOPE.
5 MAY GOD, THE SOURCE OF ALL PERSEVERANCE
AND COMFORT, GIVE TO ALL OF YOU TO LIVE IN
PEACE IN CHRIST JESUS, 6 THAT YOU MAY
BE ABLE TO PRAISE IN ONE VOICE GOD, FATHER
OF CHRIST JESUS, OUR LORD.
7 WELCOME, THEN, ONE ANOTHER, AS CHRIST WEL-
COMED YOU FOR THE
GLORY OF GOD. 8 LOOK:
CHRIST PUT HIMSELF
AT THE SERVICE OF THE
JEWISH WORLD TO FUL-
FILL THE PROMISES
MADE BY GOD TO THEIR
FATHERS; HERE YOU
SEE GOD'S FAITHFUL-
NESS. 9 THE PAGANS
INSTEAD GIVE THANKS
TO GOD FOR HIS MERCY,
AS SCRIPTURE SAYS:
BECAUSE OF THAT, I WILL
SING AND PRAISE YOUR
NAME AMONG THE PA-
GANS. 10 AND IN AN-
OTHER PLACE: REJOICE,
PAGAN NATIONS, WITH
GOD'S PEOPLE. AND
11 AGAIN: PRAISE
THE LORD, ALL PEOPLE
AND LET ALL NATIONS
SPEAK OF HIS MAGNI-
FICENCE. 12 ISAIAH
SAYS: A DESCENDANT
OF JESSE WILL COME
WHO WILL RULE THE
PAGAN NATIONS
AND THEY WILL REST THEIR HOPE IN HIM.

13 MAY GOD, THE SOURCE OF HOPE,
FILL YOU WITH JOY AND PEACE IN
THE FAITH, SO THAT YOUR HOPE MAY
INCREASE BY THE POWER OF THE HOLY SPIRIT.

14 AS FOR ME, BROTHERS AND SISTERS, I AM CON-
VINCED THAT YOU HAVE GOODWILL, KNOWLEDGE AND
THE CAPACITY TO ADVISE EACH OTHER; 15 NEVER-
THELESS I HAVE WRITTEN BOLDLY IN SOME OF
THIS LETTER'S PARTS TO REMIND YOU OF
WHAT YOU ALREADY
KNOW. I DO THIS AC-
CORDING TO THE GRA-
CE GOD HAS GIVEN TO
ME 16 WHEN I WAS
SENT TO THE PAGAN
NATIONS. I DEDICATE
MYSELF TO THE SER-
VICE OF THE GOOD
NEWS OF GOD AS A
PRIEST OF CHRIST
JESUS, IN ORDER TO
PRESENT THE NON-
JEWS TO GOD AS
AN AGREEABLE
OFFERING CON-
SECRATED BY THE
HOLY SPIRIT.

17 THIS SERVICE OF GOD IS FOR ME A CAUSE
OF PRIDE IN CHRIST JESUS.
18 OF COURSE, I WOULD NOT DARE TO SPEAK
OF OTHER THINGS BUT WHAT CHRIST HIM-
SELF HAS DONE THROUGH ME, MY WORDS
AND MY WORKS, 19 WITH MIRACLES AND
SIGNS, BY THE POWER OF THE HOLY SPIRIT,
SO THAT THE NON-JEWS MAY OBEY THE

FAITH. IN THIS WAY I HAVE EXTENDED
THE GOOD NEWS TO ALL PARTS, FROM JE-
RUSALEM TO ILLIRICUM.
20 I HAVE BEEN VERY CAREFUL, HOWEVER,
AND I AM PROUD OF THIS, NOT TO PREACH IN
PLACES WHERE CHRIST IS ALREADY KNOWN,
AND NOT TO BUILD UPON FOUNDATIONS LAID BY
OTHERS. 21 LET IT BE AS SCRIPTURE SAYS:

THOSE NOT TOLD ABOUT HIM WILL SEE,
AND THOSE WHO HAVE NOT HEARD
WILL UNDERSTAND.

NERO
375 - CCCLXXV
DM 09 ©

HELP FOR THE CHRISTIANS IN JERUSALEM

22 THIS WORK HAS PREVENTED ME FROM
GOING TO YOU. 23 BUT NOW THERE IS NO
MORE PLACE FOR ME IN THESE REGIONS,
AND AS I HAVE WANTED FOR SO LONG
TO GO AND SEE YOU, 24 I HOPE TO VISIT
YOU WHEN I GO TO SPAIN. THEN YOU COULD
HELP ME TO GO TO
THAT NATION, ONCE
I HAVE FULLY ENJOY-
ED YOUR COMPANY.
25 RIGHT NOW I AM
GOING TO JERUSALEM
TO HELP THAT COMMU-
NITY. 26 KNOW THAT
THE CHURCHES OF MA-
CEDONIA AND ACHAIA
HAVE DECIDED TO MAKE
A CONTRIBUTION FOR
THE POOR AMONG THE
BELIEVERS OF JERUSA-
LEM. 27 THEY HAVE
DECIDED TO DO THAT
AND, IN FACT, THEY
WERE INDEBTED TO
THEM. FOR THE NON-
JEWS HAVE SHARED
THE SPIRITUAL GOODS
OF THE JEWS AND NOW
THEY MUST HELP THEM
MATERIALLY. 28 SO
I AM TO COMPLETE
THIS TASK AND GIVE
OVER THE AMOUNT THAT
HAS BEEN COLLECTED.
THEN I WILL GO TO
YOU AND FROM THERE TO SPAIN. 29 AND I AM SU-
RE THAT WHEN I GO TO YOU, I WILL GO WITH ALL
THE BLESSING OF GOD.

THE RIVER JORDAN
OIL ON CANVAS
47x28 cm. 1999

30 I BEG OF YOU, BROTHERS, BY CHRIST JESUS
OUR LORD AND BY THE LOVE OF THE SPIRIT,
TO JOIN ME IN THE FIGHT, PRAYING TO GOD

FOR ME; 31 PRAY THAT I MAY AVOID THE SNA-
RES OF THE ENEMIES OF FAITH IN JUDEA, AND
THAT THE COMMUNITY OF JERUSALEM MAY WEL-
COME THE HELP I BRING. 32 AND SO I WILL GO TO
YOU WITH JOY AND, GOD WILLING, BE REFRESHED
IN YOUR COMPANY. 33 THE GOD OF PEACE
BE WITH YOU. AMEN.

GREETINGS

16 1 I RECOMMEND TO YOU OUR SISTER
PHOEBE, DEACONESS OF THE CHURCH
OF CENCHRAE.
2 PLEASE RECEIVE HER IN THE NAME

OF THE LORD, AS IT SHOULD BE AMONG
BROTHERS AND SISTERS IN THE FAITH, AND
HELP HER IN WHATEVER IS NECESSARY,
BECAUSE SHE HELPED MANY, AMONG
THEM, MYSELF.

3 GREETINGS TO PRISCA AND AQUILAS
MY HELPERS IN CHRIST JESUS. 4 TO
SAVE MY LIFE,
THEY RISKED THE-
IRS: I AM VERY
GRATEFUL TO THEM,
AS ARE ALL THE
CHURCHES OF THE
PAGAN NATIONS.

5 GREETINGS
ALSO TO THE CHURCH
THAT MEETS IN
THEIR HOUSE.
GREETINGS TO MY
DEAR EPAENETUS,
THE FIRST IN THE
PROVINCE OF ASIA
TO BELIEVE IN CHRIST.

6 GREET MARY,
WHO WORKED
SO MUCH FOR YOU.

7 GREETINGS TO ANDRONICUS AND JUNIAS,
MY RELATIVES AND COMPANIONS IN PRISON;
THEY ARE WELL KNOWN APOSTLES AND
SERVED CHRIST BEFORE I DID. 8 GIVE GRE-
ETINGS TO AMPLIATUS, WHOM I LOVE SO MUCH
IN THE LORD. 9 GREETINGS TO URBANUS,
OUR FELLOW WORKER, AND TO MY DEAR STA-
CHYS. 10 GREETINGS TO APELLES, WHO SUF-
FERED FOR CHRIST,
AND THE FAMILY OF
ARISTOBULUS. 11
GREETINGS TO MY RE-
LATIVE HERODIAN AND
THOSE IN THE HOUSE-
HOLD OF NARCISSUS,
WHO WORKS IN THE
LORD'S SERVICE. 12
GREETINGS TO TRY-
PHAINA AND TRYP-
HOSA, WHO TOIL FOR
THE LORD'S SAKE.
13 GREETINGS TO
RUFUS, ELECTED
OF THE LORD, AND
HIS MOTHER WHO
WAS A SECOND MO-
THER TO ME. 14
GREETINGS TO SIN-
CRITUS, FLEGON,
HERMES, PATROBAS,
HERMAS AND THE
BROTHERS STAYING
WITH THEM. 15 GREET-
INGS TO PHILOLOGUS
AND JULIA, NEREUS
AND HIS SISTER, OLYMPAS AND ALL THE
BROTHERS IN CHRIST JESUS WITH THEM.
16 GREET ONE ANOTHER WITH A BROTHERLY
EMBRACE. ALL THE CHURCHES OF CHRIST
SEND THEIR GREETINGS.

A WARNING

17 BROTHERS AND SISTERS, I BEG OF YOU
TO BE CAREFUL OF THOSE WHO ARE CAUSING

DIVISIONS AND TROUBLES IN TEACHING YOU A
DIFFERENT TEACHING FROM THE ONE YOU
WERE TAUGHT. KEEP AWAY FROM THEM, 18

BECAUSE THOSE PERSONS DO NOT SERVE
CHRIST OUR LORD, BUT THEIR OWN INTE-
RESTS, DECEIVING WITH THEIR SOFT AND
ENTERTAINING LANGUAGE THOSE WHO ARE
SIMPLE OF HEART. 19 EVERYBODY KNOWS
THAT YOU ARE VERY OBEDIENT, AND BECAUSE
OF THAT I AM HAPPY, BUT I WISH TO WARN
YOU TO DO WHAT IS GOOD AND AVOID WHAT
IS EVIL. 20 THE GOD OF PEACE WILL SOON
CRUSH SATAN AND
PLACE HIM UNDER
YOUR FEET. MAY
CHRIST JESUS, OUR
LORD, BLESS YOU.
21 TIMOTHY, WHO
IS WITH ME, SENDS
YOU GREETINGS
AND SO DO LUCIUS,
JASON AND SOSI-
PATROS, MY RELA-
TIVES. 22 I, TER-
TIUS, THE WRITER
OF THIS LETTER,
SEND YOU GREET-
INGS IN THE LORD.
23 GREETINGS FROM
GAIUS, WHO HAS
GIVEN ME LODGING
AND IN WHOSE HO-
USE THE CHURCH
MEETS. GREETINGS
FROM ERASTUS,
TREASURER OF THE CITY, AND FROM OUR
BROTHER QUARTUS. GLORY BE TO GOD!

24-25 HE IS ABLE TO GIVE YOU STRENGTH,
ACCORDING TO THE GOOD NEWS I PROCLAIM,
ANNOUNCING CHRIST JESUS, NOW IS
REVEALED THE MYSTERIOUS PLAN KEPT HID-
DEN FOR LONG AGES IN THE PAST.

26 BY THE WILL OF THE ETERNAL GOD IT IS
BROUGHT TO LIGHT THROUGH THE PRO-
PHETIC BOOKS, AND ALL NATIONS SHALL
BELIEVE THE FAITH PROCLAIMED TO THEM.

THE ILLUSTRATOR IN THE ROMAN FORUMS

27 GLORY TO GOD, WHO ALONE IS WISE,
THROUGH CHRIST JESUS, FOREVER! AMEN.

1st to the CORINTHIANS

SOME PERSONS PRAISE THE FIRST CHRISTIANS AS IF THEY HAD BEEN MODELS OF ALL VIRTUES. IN FACT, THERE WERE NO MORE MIRACLES THEN THAN NOW. HERE AS ELSEWHERE, PAUL ADDRESSES MEN AND WOMEN LIVING IN A WORLD AS REAL AS OUR OWN. CORINTH HAD HIS OWN PARTICULAR CHARACTER AMONG THE MEDITERRANEAN CITIES.

THE CITY HAD A SANCTUARY DEDICATED TO THE GODDESS APHRODITE, THE GODDESS OF "LOVE" FOR THE GREEKS, AROUND WHICH HAD GROWN - WITH THE HELP OF MONEY - A PROSTITUTION THAT HAD NOTHING SACRED ABOUT IT OTHER THAN ITS NAME. QUITE NEAR CORINTH, THERE WAS A SPORTIVE CELEBRATION EVERY TWO YEARS. THIS DREW CROWDS OF PEOPLE. WE NOTICE IN THESE TWO LETTERS OF PAUL VERY CLEAR ALLUSIONS TO THESE DIFFERENT ASPECTS OF CORINTHIAN HISTORY: SLAVERY, PROSTITUTION, STADIUM SPORTS.

IN CORINTH, THERE EXISTED A DYNAMIC, THOUGH NOT VERY WELL ORDERED CHURCH, FORMED OF JEWS AND GREEKS CONVERTED BY PAUL. MANY OF THEM WERE IN DANGER OF RETURNING TO THE VICES OF THEIR FORMER LIVES, ONCE THE ENTHUSIASM OF THEIR FIRST YEARS AS GOOD CHRISTIANS HAD PASSED. THOSE RESPONSIBLE IN THE CHURCH WERE NOT CAPABLE OF DEALING WITH MANY PROBLEMS: INTERNAL DIVISIONS AND DOUBTS ABOUT FAITH.
THEY THEREFORE CALLED UPON PAUL, WHO WROTE THE PRESENT LETTER, BECAUSE HE COULD NOT INTERRUPT HIS WORK IN EPHESUS.

• • •

THE FIRST LETTER OF PAUL TO THE CORINTHIANS

1

1 FROM PAUL, CALLED TO BE AN APOSTLE OF
CHRIST JESUS BY THE WILL OF GOD, AND FROM
SOSTHENSES, OUR BROTHER, 2 TO GOD'S
CHURCH WHICH IS IN CORINTH; TO YOU WHOM GOD
HAS SANCTIFIED IN CHRIST JESUS AND CALLED TO
BE HOLY, TOGETHER WITH THOSE WHO EVERYWHERE
CALL UPON THE NAME OF OUR LORD CHRIST JESUS,
THEIR LORD AND OURS. 3 RECEIVE GRACE
AND PEACE FROM GOD
OUR FATHER, AND
CHRIST JESUS OUR
LORD. 4 I GIVE
THANKS CONSTANTLY
TO MY GOD FOR YOU
AND FOR THE GRACE
OF GOD GIVEN TO YOU
IN CHRIST JESUS. 5
FOR YOU HAVE BEEN
FULLY ENRICHED IN
HIM WITH WORDS AS
WELL AS WITH KNOW-
LEDGE, 6 EVEN AS
THE TESTIMONY CON-
CERNING CHRIST WAS
CONFIRMED IN YOU.
7 YOU DO NOT LACK
ANY SPIRITUAL GIFT
AND ONLY AWAIT
THE GLORIOUS CO-
MING OF CHRIST
JESUS, OUR LORD.
8 HE WILL KEEP
YOU STEADFAST TO
THE END, AND YOU
WILL BE WITHOUT
REPROACH ON THE DAY OF THE COMING OF
OUR LORD JESUS. 9 THE FAITHFUL GOD
WILL NOT FAIL YOU AFTER CALLING YOU
TO HIS FELLOWSHIP WITH HIS SON, JESUS CHRIST,
OUR LORD.

DIVISIONS AMONG THE FAITHFUL

10 I BEG YOU, BROTHERS, IN THE NAME OF
CHRIST JESUS, OUR LORD AND ONLY GOD,
TO AGREE AMONG YOURSELVES AND DO
AWAY WITH ALL DIVISIONS; PLEASE BE

ALWAYS PERFECTLY UNITED, WITH ONE
MIND AND ONE JUDGMENT. 11 FOR THE
FACT THAT I HEARD FROM PEOPLE OF CLOE'S
HOUSE ABOUT YOUR RIVALRIES.

12 WHAT I MEAN IS THIS: SOME SAY, "I AM FOR
PAUL," AND OTHERS: "I AM FOR APOLLO," OR, "I
AM FOR PETER," OR "I AM FOR CHRIST". 13
IS CHRIST DIVIDED OR HAVE I, PAUL, BEEN
CRUCIFIED FOR YOU? HAVE I BEEN BAPTIZED IN
THE NAME OF PAUL?
14 I THANK GOD THAT I DID NOT BAPTIZE ANY
OF YOU, EXCEPT CRISPUS AND GAIUS, 15
SO THAT NO ONE CAN SAY THAT HE WAS
BAPTIZED IN MY NAME. 16 WELL, I HAVE

ALSO BAPTIZED THE STEPHANAS FAMILY. AFTER THE-
SE, I DON'T RECALL HAVING BAPTIZED ANYONE ELSE.

THE FOLLY OF THE CROSS

17 FOR CHRIST DID NOT SEND ME TO BAPTIZE, BUT TO
PROCLAIM HIS GOSPEL. AND NOT WITH BEAUTIFUL
WORDS! THAT WOULD BE LIKE GETTING RID OF THE
CROSS OF CHRIST. 18 THE LANGUAGE OF THE CROSS RE-
MAINS NONSENSE FOR THE LOST ONES. YET FOR US
WHO ARE SAVED, IT IS
THE POWER OF GOD. 19
AS SCRIPTURE SAYS: I
WILL DESTROY THE WIS-
DOM OF THE WISE AND
MAKE FAIL THE FORE-
SIGHT OF THE FORE-
SIGHTED. 20 MASTERS
OF HUMAN WISDOM, MEN
OF LETTERS, PHILOSOPH-
ERS, THERE IS NO PLACE
FOR YOU! AND THE WIS-
DOM OF THIS WORLD? GOD
LET IT FAIL. 21 AT FIRST
GOD SPOKE THE LANGUA-
GE OF WISDOM, AND THE
WORLD DID NOT KNOW
GOD IN HIS WISDOM. GOD
THOUGHT OF SAVING THE
BELIEVERS THROUGH
THE FOOLISHNESS THAT
WE PREACH. 22 THE
JEWS ASK FOR MIRA-
CLES AND THE GRE-
EKS FOR A HIGHER
KNOWLEDGE, WHILE
23 WE PROCLAIM A
CRUCIFIED MESSIAH. FOR THE JEWS, WHAT A
GREAT SCANDAL! 24 AND FOR THE GREEKS,
WHAT NONSENSE! BUT HE IS CHRIST, THE PO-
WER OF GOD AND THE WISDOM OF GOD FOR
THOSE CALLED BY GOD AMONG BOTH JEWS AND
GREEKS.
25 IN REALITY, THE "FOOLISHNESS" OF GOD IS WISER
THAN HUMANS, AND THE "WEAKNESS" OF GOD
IS STRONGER THAN HUMANS.

26 BROTHERS AND SISTERS, LOOK AND SEE
WHOM GOD HAS CALLED. FEW AMONG YOU CAN
BE SAID TO BE CULTURED OR WEALTHY, AND
FEW BELONG TO NOBLE FAMILIES. 27 YET
GOD HAS CHOSEN WHAT THE WORLD CONSI-
DERS FOOLISH, TO SHAME THE WISE; HE HAS
CHOSEN WHAT THE WORLD CONSIDERS WEAK
TO SHAME THE STRONG. 28 GOD HAS CHO-
SEN COMMON AND UNIMPORTANT PEOPLE, MA-
KING USE OF WHAT IS NOTHING TO NULLIFY
THE THINGS THAT ARE. 29 SO THAT NO

MORTAL MAY BOAST BEFORE GOD. 30 BUT, BY
GOD'S GRACE YOU ARE IN CHRIST JESUS, WHO
HAS BECOME OUR WISDOM FROM GOD, AND WHO
MAKES US JUST AND HOLY AND FREE. 31 SCRIPTU-
RE SAYS: LET THE ONE WHO BOASTS
BOAST OF THE LORD.

2 1 WHEN I CAME TO REVEAL TO YOU THE
MYSTERY OF GOD'S PLAN I DID NOT COUNT
ON ELOQUENCE OR ON A SHOW OF LEARNING.
2 I WAS DETERMINED NOT TO KNOW ANYTHING OF
YOU BUT JESUS, THE MESSIAH, A CRUCIFIED MES-
SIAH. 3 I MYSELF CA-
ME WEAK, FEARFUL AND
TREMBLING; 4 MY
WORDS AND PREACHING
WERE NOT BRILLIANT
OR CLEVER TO WIN LIST-
ENERS. 5 IT WAS, RA-
THER, A SHOW OF SPIRIT
AND POWER, SO THAT YOUR
FAITH MIGHT BE A MAT-
TER, NOT OF HUMAN
WISDOM, BUT OF GOD'S
POWER.

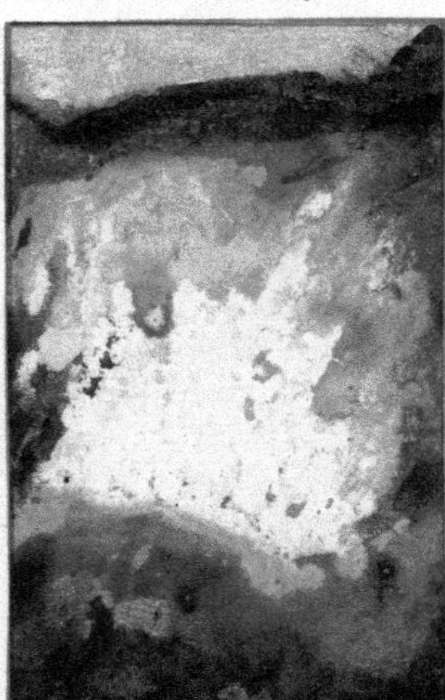

SPIRIT and WISDOM

6 IN FACT, WE DO SPEAK
OF WISDOM TO THE MATU-
RE IN FAITH, ALTHOUGH
IT IS NOT A WISDOM OF
THIS WORLD OR OF ITS
RULERS, WHO COME TO
NOTHING. 7 WE TEACH
THE MYSTERY AND SECRET
PLAN OF DIVINE WISDOM,
WHICH GOD DESTINED FROM THE BEGINNING TO BRING
US TO GLORY. 8 NO RULER OF THIS WORLD EVER
KNEW THIS; OTHERWISE THEY WOULD NOT HAVE
CRUCIFIED THE LORD OF GLORY.
9 BUT AS SCRIPTURE SAYS:

> EYE HAS NOT SEEN, EAR HAS NOT HEARD, NOR
> HAS IT DAWNED ON THE MIND WHAT GOD HAS
> PREPARED FOR THOSE WHO LOVE HIM.

10 GOD HAS REVEALED IT TO US, THROUGH HIS SPIRIT,
BECAUSE THE SPIRIT PROBES EVERYTHING,
EVEN THE DEPTH OF GOD.

11 WHO BUT HIS OWN SPIRIT KNOWS THE SE-
CRETS OF A PERSON? SIMILARLY, NO ONE BUT THE
SPIRIT OF GOD KNOWS THE SECRETS OF GOD. 12
WE HAVE NOT RECEIVED THE SPIRIT OF THE WORLD,
BUT THE SPIRIT WHO COMES FROM GOD AND,
THROUGH HIM, WE UNDERSTAND WHAT GOD
IN HIS GOODNESS
HAS GIVEN US. 13 SO
WE SPEAK OF THIS,
NOT IN TERMS INSPI-
RED BY HUMAN WIS-
DOM, BUT IN A LAN-
GUAGE TAUGHT BY
THE SPIRIT SHOWING
A SPIRITUAL WISDOM
TO SPIRITUAL PERSONS.
14 THE ONE WHO RE-
MAINS ON THE HUMAN
LEVEL DOES NOT UN-
DERSTAND THE THINGS
OF THE SPIRIT. THEY ARE
FOOLISHNESS FOR HIM
AND HE DOES NOT UN-
DERSTAND BECAUSE
THEY REQUIRE A
SPIRITUAL EXPERI-
ENCE. 15 ON THE
OTHER HAND, THE
SPIRITUAL PERSON
JUDGES EVERY-
THING BUT NO ONE
JUDGES HIM. 16
WHO HAS KNOWN
THE MIND OF GOD
THAT HE MAY
TEACH HIM? BUT WE HAVE THE MIND OF CHRIST.

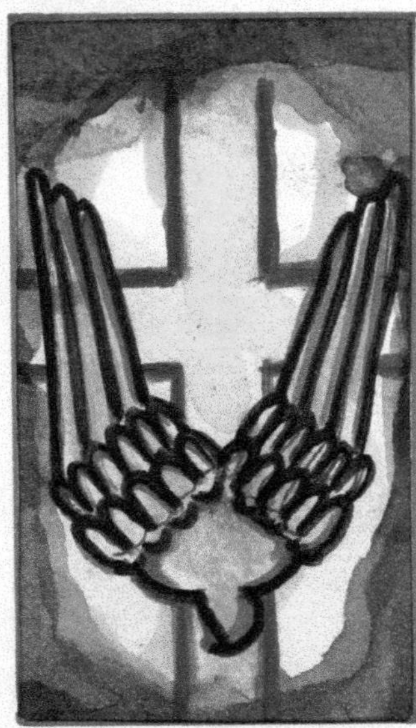

MANY WORKERS, ONE BUILDING.

3 1 I COULD NOT, FRIENDS, SPEAK TO YOU AS
SPIRITUAL PERSONS BUT AS FLESHLY PEOPLE,
FOR YOU ARE STILL INFANTS IN CHRIST. 2 I
GAVE YOU MILK AND NOT SOLID FOOD, FOR YOU WERE
NOT READY FOR IT AND UP TO NOW YOU CANNOT RECE-
IVE IT 3 FOR YOU ARE STILL FLESH. IF THERE IS JE-
ALOUSY AND STRIFE, WHAT CAN I SAY BUT THAT YOU
ARE AT THE LEVEL OF THE FLESH AND BEHAVE LIKE
ORDINARY PEOPLE. 4 WHILE ONE SAYS: "I FOL-
LOW PAUL," AND THE OTHER: "I FOLLOW APOLLOS,"

WHAT ARE YOU BUT PEOPLE STILL AT A HU-
MAN LEVEL?
5 FOR WHAT IS APOLLOS? WHAT IS PAUL?
THEY ARE MINISTERS AND THROUGH THEM
YOU BELIEVED, AS IT WAS GIVEN BY THE LORD
TO EACH OF THEM.

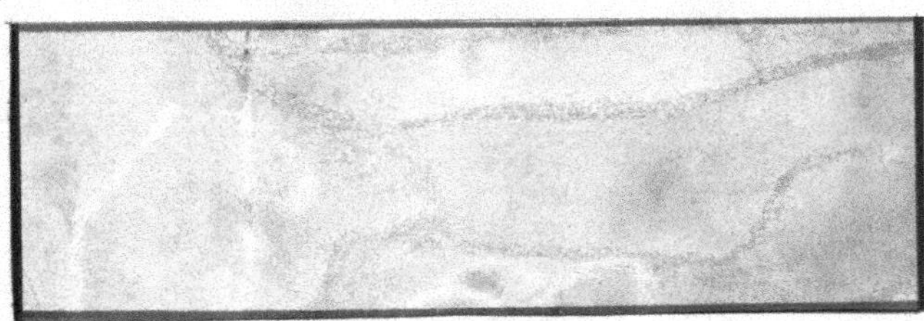

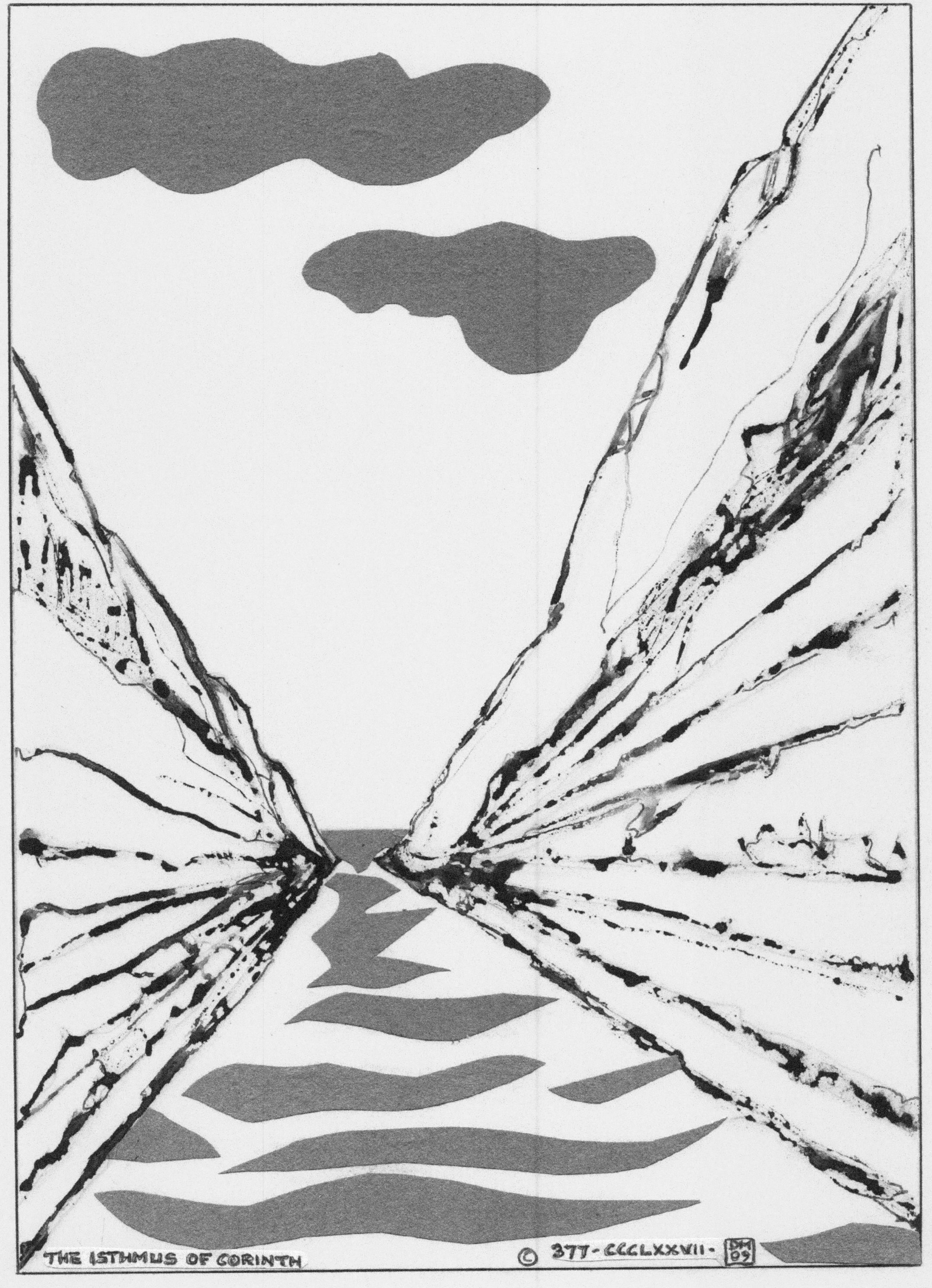
THE ISTHMUS OF CORINTH
© 377 - CCCLXXVII -
DM
09

6 I PLANTED, APOLLOS WATERED THE PLANT,
BUT GOD MADE IT GROW. 7 SO NEITHER THE
ONE WHO PLANTS NOR THE ONE WHO WATERS
IS ANYTHING, BUT GOD WHO MAKES THE PLANT
GROW.
8 THE ONE WHO PLANTS AND THE ONE WHO
WATERS WORK TO THE SAME END, AND THE
LORD WILL PAY EACH ACCORDING TO HIS WORK.
9 WE ARE FELLOW-WORKERS WITH GOD, BUT
YOU ARE GOD'S FI-
ELD AND BUILDING.

10 I, AS A GOOD AR-
CHITECT, ACCORDING
TO THE CAPACITY GIVEN
TO ME, I LAID THE FO-
UNDATION, AND ANOT-
HER IS TO BUILD ON
IT. LET EACH ONE BE
CAREFUL HOW HE
WORKS UPON IT.
11 NO ONE LAY A FO-
UNDATION OTHER THAN
THE ONE WHICH IS ALRE-
ADY LAID, WHICH IS
JESUS CHRIST. 12 THEN
IF SOMEONE BUILDS WITH
GOLD UPON THIS FOUN-
DATION, ANOTHER WITH
SILVER AND PRECIOUS
STONES, OR WITH WOOD,
BAMBOO OR STRAW, 13
THE WORK OF EACH ONE
WILL BE SHOWN FOR
WHAT IT IS. THE DAY
OF JUDGMENT WILL
REVEAL IT, BECAUSE
THE FIRE WILL MAKE
EVERYTHING KNOWN. THE FIRE WILL TEST THE
WORK OF EVERYONE. 14 IF YOUR WORK WITH-
STANDS THE FIRE, YOU WILL BE REWARDED; 15
BUT IF YOUR WORK BECOMES ASHES, YOU WILL
PAY FOR IT. YOU WILL BE SAVED, BUT IT WILL BE AS
IF PASSING THROUGH FIRE. 16 DO YOU KNOW THAT
YOU ARE GOD'S TEMPLE, AND THAT GOD'S SPIRIT ABI-
DES WITHIN YOU? 17 IF ANYONE DESTROYS THIS TEM-
PLE OF GOD, GOD WILL DESTROY HIM.
GOD'S TEMPLE IS HOLY, AND YOU ARE THIS TEMPLE.

DO NOT DIVIDE THE CHURCH

18 LET NO DECEIVE ANYONE HIMSELF. IF
ANYONE OF YOU CONSIDERS HIMSELF WI-
SE IN THE WAYS OF THE WORLD, LET HIM

BECOME A FOOL, SO THAT HE MAY BECOME
WISE. 19 FOR THE WISDOM OF THIS WORLD
IS FOOLISHNESS IN GOD'S EYES. TO THIS,
SCRIPTURE SAYS:

"GOD CATCHES THE WISE IN HIS OWN WISDOM."

20 IT ALSO SAYS: THE LORD KNOWS THE RE-
ASONING OF THE WISE, THAT IT IS USELESS.
21 BECAUSE OF THIS, LET NO ONE BECOME AN AD-
MIRER OF HUMANS, FOR EVERYTHING BELONGS TO
YOU, 22 PAUL, APOLLOS, CEPHAS, LIFE AND
DEATH, THE PRESENT AND THE FUTURE, EVE-
RYTHING IS YOURS, 23 AND YOU, YOU BELONG
TO CHRIST, AND CHRIST IS OF GOD.

4 1 LET EVERYONE THEN SEE US AS THE SER-
VANTS OF CHRIST AND STEWARDS OF THE SEC-
RET WORKS OF GOD. 2 BEING STEWARDS,
FAITHFULNESS SHALL BE DEMANDED OF US; 3

The AcroCorinth

BUT I DON'T MIND IF YOU OR ANY HUMAN COURT JUD-
GES ME. I DON'T EVEN JUDGE MYSELF, 4 MY CON-
SCIENCE DOES NOT ACCUSE ME OF ANYTHING
BUT THAT IS NOT ENOUGH FOR ME TO BE WITHOUT
REPROACH: THE LORD IS THE ONE WHO JUDGES ME.
5 THEREFORE, DO NOT JUDGE BEFORE THE TIME, UNTIL
THE COMING OF THE LORD. HE WILL BRING THE LIGHT
OF WHAT WAS HIDDEN IN
DARKNESS AND WILL
DISCLOSE THE SECRET
INTENTIONS OF MEN'S
HEARTS. THEN EACH
ONE WILL RECEIVE
FROM GOD THE PRAISE
HE DESERVES. 6 BRO-
THERS, YOU FORCED ME
TO APPLY THESE COMPA-
RISONS TO APOLLOS AND
MYSELF. LEARN BY THIS
EXAMPLE NOT TO BELI-
EVE YOURSEVES SU-
PERIOR BY SIDING
WITH ONE AGAINST
THE OTHER. 7 HOW
THEN ARE YOU DIF-
FERENT FROM THE
OTHERS? WHAT HAVE
YOU THAT YOU HAVE
NOT RECEIVED? AND
IF YOU RECEIVED IT,
WHY ARE YOU PROUD,
AS IF YOU DID NOT RE-
CEIVE IT?
8 SO YOU ARE ALREADY
RICH, SATISFIED, FEEL

LIKE KINGS WITHOUT US! I WISH YOU WERE KINGS,
SO THAT WE MIGHT ENJOY THE KINGSHIP WITH YOU!
9 IT SEEMS TO ME THAT GOD HAS PLACED US,
THE APOSTLES, IN THE LAST PLACE, AS IF
CONDEMNED TO DEATH, AND AS SPECTACLES
FOR THE WHOLE WORLD, FOR THE ANGELS AS
WELL AS FOR MORTALS.
10 WE ARE FOOLS FOR CHRIST, WHILE YOU
SHOW FORTH THE WISDOM OF CHRIST.
WE ARE WEAK, YOU ARE STRONG. YOU ARE
HONORED, WHILE WE ARE DESPISED.

11 UNTIL NOW WE HUNGER AND THIRST, WE
ARE POORLY CLOTHED AND BADLY TREATED, WHI-
LE MOVING FROM PLACE TO PLACE. 12 WE LABOR,
WORKING WITH OUR HANDS. PEOPLE INSULT US
AND WE BLESS THEM, THEY PERSECUTE US AND WE
ENDURE EVERYTHING; 13 THEY SPEAK EVIL
AGAINST ME AND THE REST OF US, AND OURS ARE
WORKS OF PEACE. WE HAVE BECOME LIKE THE
SCUM OF THE EARTH, LIKE THE GARBAGE OF
HUMANKIND UNTIL NOW.
14 I DO NOT WRITE THIS TO SHAME YOU, BUT
TO WARN YOU AS VERY
DEAR CHILDREN. 15
BECAUSE EVEN
THOUGH YOU MAY HAVE
TEN THOUSAND GUARD-
IANS IN THE CHRISTIAN
LIFE, YOU HAVE ONLY
ONE FATHER; AND IT
WAS I WHO GAVE YOU
LIFE IN CHRIST THROUGH
THE GOSPEL. 16 THE-
REFORE I PRAY YOU TO
FOLLOW MY EXAMPLE.
17 WITH THIS PURPO-
SE I SEND TO YOU TIMO-
THY, MY DEAR AND TRUST-
WORTHY SON IN THE SER-
VICE OF THE LORD. HE
WILL REMIND YOU OF MY
WAY OF CHRISTIAN LIFE,
AS I TEACH IT IN ALL
CHURCHES EVERYWHERE.
18 SOME OF YOU
THOUGHT THAT I COULD
NOT VISIT YOU AND BECOME VERY ARROGANT. 19
BUT I WILL VISIT YOU SOON, THE LORD WILLING,
AND I WILL SEE, NOT WHAT THOSE ARROGANT PEOPLE
SAY, BUT WHAT THEY CAN DO. 20 BECAUSE THE
KINGDOM OF GOD IS NOT A MATTER OF WORDS,
BUT OF POWER. 21 WHAT DO YOU PREFER, ME WITH
A STICK OR WITH LOVE AND GENTLENESS?

5 1 YOU HAVE BECOME NEWS WITH A CASE
OF IMMORALITY, AND SUCH A CASE THAT IS
NOT EVEN FOUND AMONG PAGANS. YES, ONE
OF YOU HAS TAKEN AS WIFE HIS OWN STEPMOTHER.
2 AND YOU FEEL PROUD! SHOULD YOU NOT BE

IN MOURNING INSTEAD AND EXPEL THE ONE WHO
DID SUCH A THING. 3 FOR MY PART, ALTHOUGH
I AM PHYSICALLY ABSENT, MY SPIRIT IS WITH YOU
AND, AS IF PRESENT, I HAVE ALREADY PASSED SENT-
ENCE ON THE MAN WHO COMMITTED SUCH A SIN.

4 LET US MEET TOGETHER, YOU AND MY SPIRIT,
AND IN THE NAME OF OUR LORD JESUS AND WITH
HIS POWER, 5 YOU SHALL DELIVER HIM TO SA-
TAN, SO THAT HE MAY LOSE EVERYTHING AND HIS
LIFE, BUT HIS SPIRIT BE SAVED IN THE DAY OF
JUDGMENT.

6 THIS IS NOT THE TIME TO PRAISE YOURSELVES.
DO YOU KNOW NOT THAT A LITTLE YEAST MAKES
THE WHOLE MASS OF DOUGH RISE? THROW
OUT 7, THEN, THE OLD YEAST AND BE NEW

DOUGH, IF CHRIST BECAME OUR PASSOVER, YOU
SHOULD BE UNLEAVENED BREAD. 8 LET US
CELEBRATE, THEREFORE, THE PASSOVER, NO
LONGER WITH OLD YEAST, WHICH IS SIN AND
PERVERSITY; LET US HAVE UNLEAVENED BREAD,
THAT IS PURITY AND SINCERITY.
9 IN MY LAST LETTER I INSTRUCTED YOU
NOT TO ASSOCIATE
WITH IMMORAL PE-
OPLE. 10 I DID NOT
MEAN, OF COURSE,
THOSE WHO DO NOT
BELONG TO THE
CHURCH AND WHO
ARE IMMORAL, EX-
PLOITERS, EMBEZ-
ZLERS OR WOR-
SHIPERS OF IDOLS.
OTHERWISE YOU
WOULD HAVE TO
LEAVE THIS WORLD.

11 WHAT I REALLY
MEANT WAS TO
AVOID AND NOT TO
MINGLE WITH ANY-
ONE WHO, CALLING
HIMSELF BROTHER,
BECOMES IMMORAL,
EXPLOITER, GOS-
SIP, DRUNKARD,
EMBEZZLER. IN WHICH CASE YOU SHOULD
NOT EVEN EAT WITH THEM.

12 WHY SHOULD I JUDGE OUTSIDERS? BUT
YOU, ARE YOU NOT TO JUDGE THOSE WHO
ARE INSIDE?
13 LET GOD JUDGE THOSE OUTSIDE, BUT
AS FOR YOU:
"DRIVE OUT THE WICKED PERSON FROM AMONG YOU."

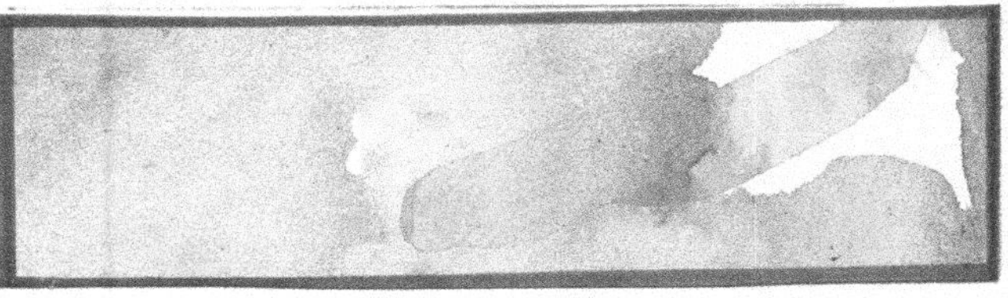

DO NOT BRING ANOTHER CHRISTIAN TO COURT

6 (1) WHEN YOU HAVE A COMPLAINT AGAINST A BROTHER, HOW
DARE YOU BRING HIM BEFORE PAGAN JUDGES INSTEAD OF
BRINGING HIS CASE BEFORE GOD'S PEOPLE? (2) DO YOU
KNOW THAT YOU SHALL ONE DAY JUDGE THE WORLD? AND IF
YOU ARE TO JUDGE THE WORLD, ARE YOU INCAPABLE OF JUDG-
ING SUCH SIMPLE PROBLEMS? (3) DO YOU NOT KNOW THAT
WE WILL EVEN JUDGE THE ANGELS? AND COULD YOU NOT DE-
CIDE EVERY DAY AFFAIRS? (4) YOU SHOULD ASK THOSE
WHO ARE THE LAST IN THE CHURCH TO DECIDE SUCH MAT-
TERS. (5) SHAME ON YOU! IS THERE NOT EVEN ONE

AMONG YOU WISE ENOUGH TO BE THE ARBITER AMONG
BROTHERS?
(6) BUT NO. A BROTHER BRINGS A SUIT AGAINST A BRO-
THER, AND HE FILES BEFORE UNBELIEVERS. (7) IF
IS ALREADY A FAILURE THAT YOU HAVE SUITS AGA-
INST EACH OTHER. WHY DO YOU NOT RATHER SUFFER
WRONG AND RECEIVE SOME DAMAGE? (8) BUT
NO. YOU WRONG AND
INJURE OTHERS, AND
THOSE ARE YOUR
BROTHERS AND SIS-
TERS.
(9) DO YOU NOT
KNOW THAT THE
WICKED WILL NOT
INHERIT THE KING-
DOM OF GOD? MAKE
NO MISTAKE ABOUT
IT: THOSE WHO LEAD
IMMORAL LIVES, OR
WORSHIP IDOLS, OR
WHO ARE ADULTERERS,
HOMOSEXUALS OF ANY
KIND, (10) OR THIEVES,
EXPLOITERS, DRUNK-
ARDS, GOSSIP OR EM-
BEZZLERS WILL NOT
INHERIT THE KINGDOM
OF HEAVEN. (11) SOME
OF YOU WERE LIKE
THAT, BUT YOU HAVE
BEEN CLEANSED
AND CONSECRATED TO GOD AND HAVE BE-
EN SET RIGHT WITH GOD BY THE NAME OF
THE LORD JESUS AND THE SPIRIT OF OUR GOD.

SEXUAL IMMORALITY

(12) EVERYTHING IS LAWFUL FOR ME, BUT NOT EVE-
RYTHING IS TO MY PROFIT. EVERYTHING IS LAWFUL
FOR ME, BUT I WILL NOT BECOME A SLAVE OF ANY-
THING. (13) FOOD IS FOR THE STOMACH, AND THE
STOMACH IS FOR FOOD, BUT GOD WILL DESTROY
THEM BOTH. YET THE BODY IS NOT FOR SEXUAL LICENT-
IOUSNESS, BUT FOR THE LORD; AND THE LORD IS FOR THE
BODY. (14) AND GOD WHO RAISED THE LORD, WILL AL-
SO RAISE US WITH HIS POWER. (15) DO YOU
NOT KNOW THAT YOUR
BODIES ARE MEMBERS
OF CHRIST? AND YOU
WOULD MAKE THAT
PART OF HIS BODY BE-
COME A PART OF A PRO-
STITUTE? NEVER?
(16) BUT YOU WELL
KNOW THAT WHEN YOU
JOIN YOURSELVES TO
A PROSTITUTE, YOU BE-
COME ONE FLESH WITH
HER. FOR SCRIPTURE
SAYS: THE TWO WILL
BECOME ONE FLESH.
(17) ON THE OTHER
HAND, HE WHO IS
UNITED TO THE LORD
BECOMES ONE SPIRIT
WITH HIM. (18) AVOID
UNLAWFUL SEX EN-
TIRELY. ANY OTHER
SIN A PERSON COM-
MITS DOES NOT AF-
FECTS HIS BODY BUT
HE WHO COMMITS
SEXUAL IMMORALITY SINS AGAINST HIS OWN
BODY. (19) DO YOU NOT KNOW THAT YOUR BODY IS
A TEMPLE OF THE HOLY SPIRIT WITHIN YOU, GI-
VEN BY GOD? YOU BELONG NO LONGER TO YOUR-
SELVES. (20) REMEMBER AT WHAT PRICE YOU
HAVE BEEN BOUGHT AND MAKE YOUR BODY
SERVE THE GLORY OF GOD.

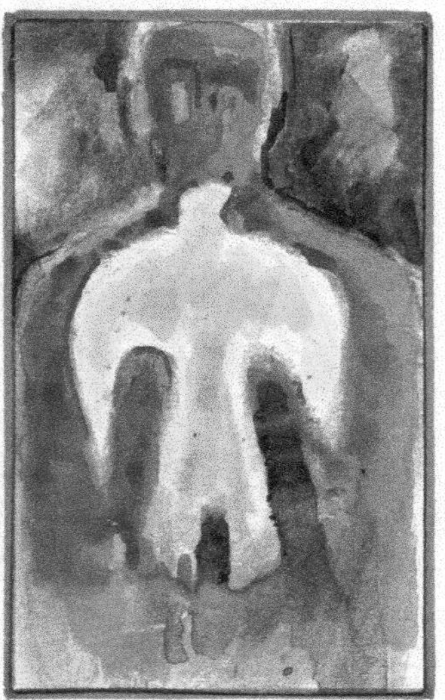

MARRIAGE AND ABSTINENCE

7 (1) NOW I WILL ANSWER THE QUESTIONS OF YOUR
LETTER. IT IS GOOD FOR A MAN NOT TO HAVE SEX
WITH A WOMAN. (2) BUT THE APPEAL OF SEX IS
THERE. LET EACH MAN HAVE HIS OWN WIFE AND EACH

WOMAN HER OWN HUSBAND. (3) LET THE HUSBAND FUL-
FILL HIS DUTY OF HUSBAND AND LIKEWISE THE WIFE.
(4) THE WIFE IS NOT THE OWNER OF HER OWN BO-
DY: THE HUSBAND IS. SIMILARLY, THE HUSBAND
IS NOT THE OWNER OF HIS BODY: THE WIFE IS.

HOMAGE TO
MATISSE
378- CCCLXXVIII ©
DM
09

5 DO NOT REFUSE EACH OTHER, EXEPT BY MUTU-
AL CONSENT AND ONLY FOR A TIME IN ORDER TO
DEDICATE YOURSELVES TO PRAYER, AND THEN
COME TOGETHER AGAIN, LEST YOU FALL INTO SA-
TAN'S TRAP BY LACK OF SELF-CONTROL. 6
I APPROVE OF THIS ABSTENTION, BUT I DO NOT OR-
DER IT. 7 I WOULD LIKE EVERYONE TO BE LIKE
ME, BUT EACH HAS FROM GOD HIS OWN GRACE, SO-
ME IN ONE WAY, OTHERS DIFFERENTLY. 8 TO THE
UNMARRIED AND THE WIDOWS I SAY THAT IT WOULD
BE GOOD FOR THEM TO REMAIN AS I AM. 9 BUT IF
THEY CANNOT CONTROL THEMSELVES, LET THEM
MARRY; IT IS BETTER TO MARRY THEN BURN OF PASSION.

MARRIAGE - DIVORCE

10 I COMMAND MARRIED COUPLES, NOT I BUT THE
THE LORD, THAT THE WIFE SHOULD NOT SEPARA-
TE FROM HER HUSBAND.

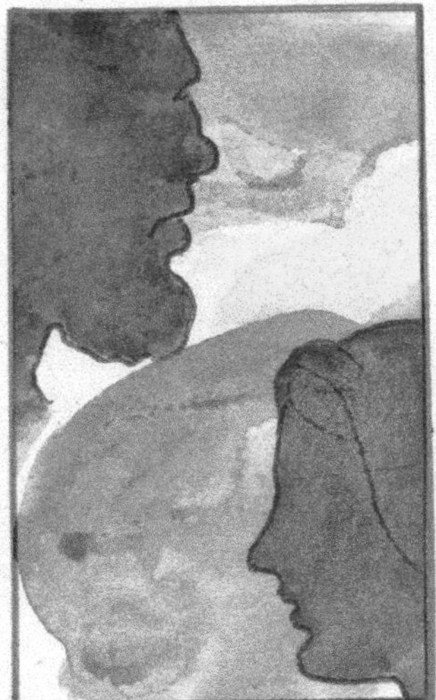

11 IF SHE SEPARATES
FROM HIM, LET HER
NOT MARRY AGAIN, OR
LET HER MAKE PEACE
WITH HER HUSBAND.
SIMILARLY THE HUS-
BAND SHOULD NOT
DIVORCE HIS WIFE.

12 TO THE OTHERS I
SAY, FROM ME AND
NOT FROM THE LORD,
IF A BROTHER HAS
A WIFE WHO IS NOT
A BELIEVER BUT
SHE AGREES TO
LIVE WITH HIM, LET
HIM NOT SEPARATE
FROM HER. 13 IN
THE SAME MANNER,
IF A WOMAN HAS A
HUSBAND WHO IS
NOT A BELIEVER
BUT HE AGREES TO
LIVE WITH HER, LET HER NOT SEPARATE FROM
HER HUSBAND. 14 BECAUSE THE UNBELIEVING
HUSBAND IS SANCTIFIED BY THE WIFE, AND THE UN-
BELIEVING WIFE IS SANCTIFIED BY THE HUS-
BAND WHO BELIEVES. OTHERWISE, YOUR CHIL-
DREN ALSO WOULD BE APART FROM GOD; BUT
AS IT IS, THEY ARE CONSECRATED TO GOD.

15 NOW, IF THE UNBELIEVING HUSBAND OR WIFE

WANTS TO SEPARATE, LET THEM DO SO. IN THIS CASE,
THE CHRISTIAN PARTNER IS NOT BOUND, FOR THE
LORD HAS CALLED US TO PEACE. 16 BESIDES ARE YOU
SURE, WIFE, THAT YOU COULD SAVE YOUR HUSBAND,
AND YOU, HUSBAND, THAT YOU COULD SAVE YOUR WIFE?
17 EXEPT FOR THIS, LET EACH ONE CONTINUE LIV-
ING AS HE WAS WHEN GOD CALLED HIM AS WAS
HIS LOT SET BY THE LORD. THIS IS WHAT
I ORDER IN ALL CHURCHES.

18 LET THE CIRCUMCISED JEW NOT REMOVE THE
MARKS OF THE CIRCUMCISION WHEN HE IS CALLED
BY GOD, AND LET THE NON-JEW NOT BE CIRCUMCI-
SED WHEN HE IS CALLED. 19 FOR IT IS OF NO IM-
PORTANCE TO BE CIRCUMCISED OR NOT, BUT ONLY
TO KEEP THE COMMANDMENTS OF GOD. 20 LET EACH
ONE, THEREFORE, REMAIN IN THE STATE IN WHICH HE
WAS WHEN HE WAS CALLED BY GOD. 21 IF YOU WE-
RE A SLAVE WHEN CALLED, DO NOT WORRY, YET
IF YOU CAN GAIN YOUR FREEDOM, TAKE THE OP-
PORTUNITY. 22 THE SLAVE CALLED TO BELIEVE

IN THE LORD IS A FREEDMAN IN THE LORD. AND HE
WHO HAS BEEN CALLED WHILE FREE, BECO-
MES A SLAVE OF CHRIST. 23 YOU HAVE BEEN
BOUGHT BY GOD AT A VERY HIGH PRICE; DO NOT
BECOME SLAVES OF A HUMAN BEING. 24 SO THEN,
BROTHERS AND SISTERS, CONTINUE LIVING IN
THE STATE YOU WERE BEFORE GOD AT THE TIME OF
HIS CALL.

MARRIAGE - VIRGINITY

25 WITH REGARD TO THOSE WHO REMAIN
VIRGINS, I HAVE NO SPECIAL COMMANDMENT
FROM THE LORD, BUT
I GIVE SOME ADVICE,
HOPING THAT I AM
WORTHY OF TRUST
BY THE MERCY OF
THE LORD.
26 I THINK THIS
IS GOOD IN THESE
HARD TIMES IN
WHICH WE LIVE. IT
IS GOOD FOR A MAN
TO REMAIN AS HE IS.
27 IF YOU ARE MAR-
RIED, DO NOT TRY
TO DIVORCE YOUR
WIFE; IF YOU ARE NOT
MARRIED, DO NOT
MARRY.
28 HE WHO MARRIES
DOES NOT SIN, NOR
DOES THE YOUNG
GIRL SIN WHO MAR-
RIES.
YET THEY WILL
FACE DISTURBING
EXPERIENCES
AND I WOULD LIKE TO SPARE YOU

29 I SAY THIS, BROTHERS AND SISTERS: TI-
ME IS RUNNING OUT, AND THOSE WHO ARE
MARRIED MUST LIVE AS IF NOT MARRIED.

30 THOSE WHO WEEP AS IF NOT WEEPING: THOSE
WHO ARE HAPPY AS IF THEY WERE NOT HAPPY; THOSE BUYING
SOMETHING AS IF THEY HAD NOT BOUGHT IT, AND THOSE
ENJOYING THE PRESENT LIFE AS IF THEY WERE NOT EN-
JOYING IT. 31 FOR THE ORDER OF THIS WORLD IS VANI-
SHING. 32 I WOULD LIKE YOU TO BE FREE ANXI-
ETIES. HE WHO IS NOT MARRIED IS CONCERNED OF
THE THINGS OF THE LORD AND HOW TO PLEASE THE LORD.
33 WHILE HE WHO IS MARRIED IS TAKEN UP WITH
THE THINGS OF THE WORLD AND HOW TO PLEASE
HIS WIFE, AND HE IS DIVIDED IN HIS INTERESTS.

34 LIKEWISE, THE UNMARRIED WOMAN AND THE
VIRGIN ARE CONCERNED WITH THE SERVICE OF
THE LORD, TO BE HOLY IN BODY AND SPIRIT. THE
MARRIED WOMAN, INSTEAD, WORRIES ABOUT THE
THINGS OF THE WORLD AND HOW TO PLEASE HER
HUSBAND. 35 I SAY THIS FOR YOUR OWN GOOD.
I DO NOT WISH TO LAY TRAPS FOR YOU BUT TO LEAD
YOU TO A BEAUTIFUL LIFE, ENTIRELY UNITED WITH
THE LORD.
36 IF ANYONE IS NOT SURE WHETHER HE IS BEHAV-
ING CORRECTLY WITH HIS FIANCEE BECAUSE OF
THE ARDOR OF HIS PAS-
SION, AND CONSIDERS IT
IS BETTER TO GET MARRI-
ED, LET HIM DO SO; HE
COMMITS NO SIN. 37
BUT IF ANOTHER, OR
FIRMER HEART, THINKS
THAT HE CAN CONTROL
HIS PASSION AND DE-
CIDES NOT TO MARRY
SO THAT HIS FIANCEE
MAY REMAIN A VIRGIN,
HE DOES BETTER. 38
SO THEN, HE WHO MAR-
RIES DOES WELL, AND
HE WHO DOES NOT
MARRY DOES BETTER.
39 THE WIFE IS BO-
UND AS LONG AS HER
HUSBAND LIVES.
IF HE DIES, SHE IS FREE
TO BE MARRIED TO
WHOMSOEVER SHE
WISHES, PROVIDED
THAT SHE DOES SO
IN THE CHRISTIAN WAY. 40 HOWEVER, SHE
WILL BE HAPPIER IF, FOLLOWING MY ADVICE,
SHE DOES NOT MARRY. AND I BELIEVE
THAT I ALSO HAVE THE SPIRIT OF GOD.

CAN WE SHARE IN PAGAN CUSTOMS?

8 1 REGARDING MEAT FROM THE OFFERINGS TO IDOLS,
WE KNOW THAT ALL OF US HAVE KNOWLEDGE BUT
KNOWLEDGE PUFFS UP, WHILE LOVE BUILDS. 2
IF ANYONE THINKS THAT HE HAS KNOWLEDGE, HE DOES
NOT YET KNOW AS HE SHOULD KNOW. 3 BUT IF
SOMEONE LOVES GOD, GOD KNOWS HIM. 4 CAN WE,
THEN, EAT MEAT FROM OFFERINGS TO THE IDOLS?
WE KNOW THAT AN IDOL HAS NO EXISTENCE AND THAT
THERE IS NO GOD BUT ONE. 5 PEOPLE SPEAK INDEED
OF OTHER GODS IN HE-
AVEN AND ON EARTH AND,
FOR THIS, THERE ARE
MANY GODS AND LORDS.
6 YET FOR US, THERE
IS BUT ONE GOD THE
FATHER, FROM WHOM
EVERYTHING COMES,
AND TO WHOM WE GO.
AND THERE IS ONE LORD,
CHRIST JESUS, THROUGH
WHOM EVERYTHING
COMES AND EXISTS AND
THROUGH HIM WE EX-
IST. 7 NOT EVERYONE,
HOWEVER, HAS THAT
KNOWLEDGE. FOR

SOME PERSONS, WHO UNTIL RECENTLY TOOK THE
IDOLS SERIOUSLY, THAT FOOD REMAINS LINKED TO
THE IDOL AND EATING OF IT STAINS THEIR CON-
SCIENCE WHICH IS UNFORMED.
8 IT IS NOT FOOD THAT BRING US CLOSER TO GOD. IF
WE EAT, WE GAIN NOTHING, IF WE DON'T EAT, WE DO
NOT LOSE ANYTHING. 9 WE ARE FREE, OF CO-
URSE, BUT LET NOT YOUR FREEDOM CAUSE OTHERS,
WHO ARE LESS PREPARED, TO FALL. 10 WHAT IF

In the Temple of some idols...

THIS PERSON WITH AN UNFORMED CONSCIENCE
SEES YOU, A PERSON OF KNOWLEDGE, SIT-
TING AT THE TABLE IN THE TEMPLE OF
IDOLS?
WILL NOT HIS WEAK CONSCIENCE, BECAUSE
OF YOUR EXAMPLE, MOVE HIM TO EAT ALSO?

11 THEN WITH YOUR KNOWLEDGE YOU WOULD HAVE
CAUSED YOUR WEAK BROTHER OR SISTER TO PER-
ISH, THE ONE FROM WHOM CHRIST DIED. 12 WHEN
YOU DISTURB THE WEAK CONSCIENCE OF YOUR
BROTHERS AND SIN AGAINST THEM, YOU SIN
AGAINST CHRIST HIMSELF. 13 THEREFORE,
IF ANY FOOD WILL BRING MY BROTHER TO SIN, I SHALL
NEVER EAT THIS FOOD LEST MY BROTHER OR SISTER FALL.

THE EXAMPLE OF PAUL

9 1 AS FOR ME, AM I NOT FREE? I AM AN APOSTLE AND I
HAVE SEEN JESUS, THE LORD, AND YOU ARE MY WORK
IN THE LORD. 2 ALTHOUGH I MAY NOT BE AN AP-
OSTLE FOR OTHERS, AT LEAST I AM ONE FOR YOU. YOU
ARE, IN THE LORD, EVI-
DENCE OF MY APOSTLE-
SHIP. 3 NOW THIS IS
WHAT I ANSWER TO THOSE
WHO CRITICIZE ME: 4

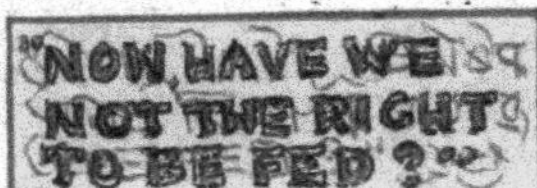

5 HAVE WE NOT THE
RIGHT TO BRING WITH
US A SISTER AS DO THE
OTHER APOSTLES AND THE
BROTHERS OF THE LORD,
AND CEPHAS? 6 AM I
THE ONLY ONE, WITH BAR-
NABAS, BOUND TO WORK?'
WHAT SOLDIER GOES TO WAR
AT HIS OWN EXPENSE?
7 WHAT FARMER DOES
NOT EAT FROM THE VINE-
YARD HE PLANTED? WHO
TENDS A FLOCK AND DOES
NOT DRINK FROM ITS
MILK? 8 ARE THESE RIGHTS ONLY ACCEPTED HUMAN
PRACTICE? NO, THE LAW SAYS THE SAME. IN THE LAW
OF MOSES IT IS WRITTEN: DO NOT MUZZLE THE OX
WHICH THRESHES GRAIN. 9 DOES THIS MEAN THAT
GOD IS CONCERNED WITH OXEN, 10 OR RATHER WITH
US? OF COURSE, IT APPLIES TO US. FOR OUR SAKE IT WAS
WRITTEN THAT NO ONE PLOWS WITHOUT EXPECTING
A REWARD FOR HIS PLOWING, AND NO ONE THRESHES

WITHOUT HOPING FOR A SHARE OF THE CROP. 11
THEN, IF WE HAVE SOWN SPIRITUAL RICHES
AMONG YOU, WOULD IT BE TOO MUCH FOR US TO
REAP SOME MATERIAL REWARD?

12 IF OTHERS HAVE HAD THIS RIGHT AMONG
YOU, SURELY WE HAVE IT ALL THE MORE. YET
WE MADE NO USE OF THIS RIGHT AND WE PRE-
FER TO ENDURE EVERYTHING RATHER THEN PUT
ANY OBSTACLE TO THE GOSPEL OF CHRIST.
13 DO YOU NOT KNOW THAT THOSE WORKING IN
THE SACRED SERVICE EAT FROM WHAT IS OF-
FERED FOR THE TEMPLE? AND THOSE SERV-
ING AT THE ALTAR RECEIVE THEIR PART FROM
THE ALTAR. 14 THE LORD ORDERED, LIKEWISE,
THAT THOSE ANNOUNCING THE GOSPEL LIVE FROM

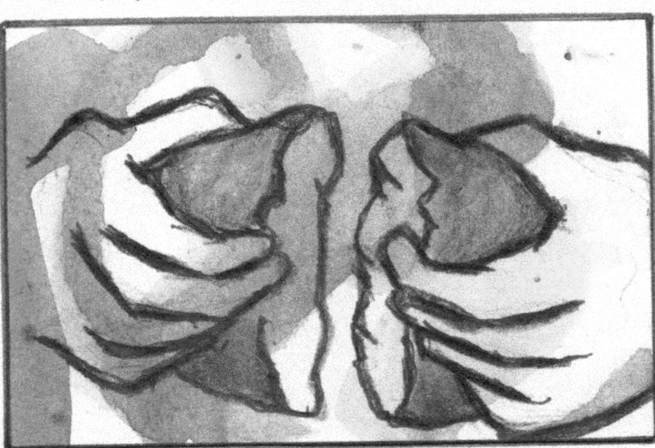

THE GOSPEL. 15 YET I HAVE NOT MADE USE OF MY
RIGHTS, AND NOW I DO NOT WRITE TO CLAIM THEM,
I WOULD RATHER DIE! FOR I AM PROUD OF THIS,
AND NO ONE WILL DEPRIVE ME OF IT. 16 LOOK, I
HAVE NO MERIT IN ANNOUNCING THE GOSPEL, FOR I
AM BOUND TO DO IT. WOE TO ME IF I DO NOT PREACH
THE GOSPEL. 17 IF I PREACHED VOLUNTARILY, I CO-
ULD EXPECT MY REWARD, BUT I AM BOUND TO DO IT
AND I AM ONLY FULFILL-
ING MY OFFICE. 18 HOW
CAN I, THEN, DESERVE A
REWARD? IN ANNOUNC-
ING THE GOSPEL, I WILL
DO IT FREELY WITHOUT
MAKING USE OF THE
RIGHTS GIVEN TO ME
BY THE GOSPEL. 19 SO,
FINALLY, FEELING FREE
WITH EVERYBODY, I BECA-
ME EVERYBODY'S SLA-
VE IN ORDER TO GAIN
A GREATER NUMBER.
20 TO SAVE THE JEWS
I BECAME A JEW WITH
THE JEWS, AND BECA-
USE THEY ARE UN-
DER THE LAW, I MY-
SELF CAME UNDER THE
LAW, ALTHOUGH I AM
FREE FROM IT. WITH
21 THE PAGANS, NOT SUB-
JECT TO THE LAW, I BE-
CAME ONE OF THEM, AL-
THOUGH I AM NOT
WITHOUT A LAW OF GOD, SINCE CHRIST IS MY LAW.
22 I SHARED, ALSO, THE SCRUPLES OF PE-
OPLE WITHOUT A LIBERATED CONSCIENCE,
IN ORDER TO GAIN THOSE WHO ARE STILL WEAK.

23 SO I MADE MYSELF ALL THINGS TO ALL PEOPLE
IN ORDER TO SAVE, BY ALL POSSIBLE MEANS,
SOME OF THEM. I DO IT FOR THE GOSPEL, AND
WITH THE HOPE OF SHARING ITS REWARD.

THE WIFE SHOULD NOT SEPARATE FROM HER HUSBAND
1 Corinthians 7:10
379
CCCLXXIX
© DM 04

FAITH DEMANDS SACRIFICE

(24) HAVE YOU NOT LEARNED ANYTHING FROM THE STADIUM? MANY RUN, BUT ONLY ONE GETS THE PRIZE. RUN, THEREFORE, INTENDING TO WIN IT, (25) AS ATHLETES WHO IMPOSE UPON THEMSELVES A RIGOROUS DISCIPLINE. YET FOR THEM THE WREATH IS OF LAURELS WHICH WITHER, WHILE FOR US, IT DOES NOT WITHER. (26) SO, THEN, I RUN KNOWING WHERE I GO. I BOX BUT NOT AIMLESSLY IN THE AIR. (27) I PUNISH MY BODY AND CONTROL IT, LEST AFTER PREACHING TO OTHERS, I MYSELF SHOULD BE REJECTED.

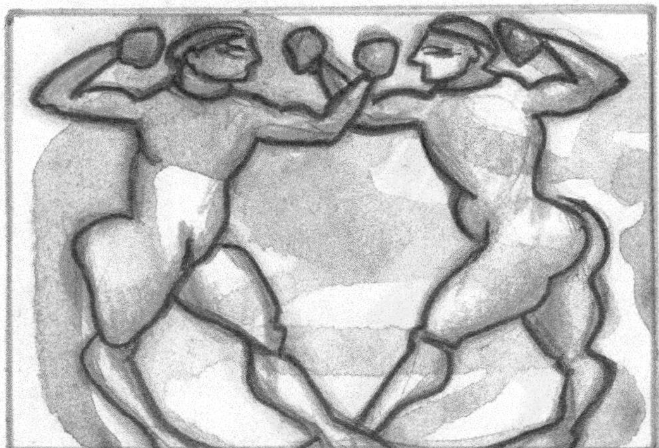

10 (1) LET ME REMIND YOU, BROTHERS AND SISTERS, ABOUT OUR ANCESTORS. ALL OF WERE UNDER THE CLOUD AND ALL CROSSED THE SEA. (2) THEY WERE IN A WAY BAPTIZED IN THE CLOUD AND IN THE SEA TO BE THE PEOPLE OF MOSES, (3) AND ALL OF THEM ATE FROM THE SPIRITUAL MANNA (4) AND ALL OF THEM DRANK FROM A SPIRITUAL DRINK. FOR YOU KNOW THAT THEY DRANK FROM A SPIRITUAL ROCK FOLLOWING THEM, AND THE ROCK WAS CHRIST, (5) HOWEVER, MOST OF THEM DID NOT PLEASE GOD, AND THE DESERT WAS ALL STREWN WITH THEIR BODIES. (6) ALL THIS WAS AN EXAMPLE FOR US, SO THAT WE MIGHT NOT BECOME PEOPLE OF EVIL DESIRES, AS THEY DID. (7) DO NOT FOLLOW IDOLS, AS SOME OF THEM DID, AND SCRIPTURE SAYS: THE PEOPLE SAT DOWN TO EAT AND DRINK AND STOOD UP FOR ORGY. (8) LET US NOT FALL INTO SEXUAL IMMORALITY AS SOME OF THEM DID, AND IN ONE DAY TWENTY-THREE THOUSAND OF THEM FELL DEAD. (9) AND LET US NOT TEMPT THE LORD AS SOME OF THEM DID, AND WERE KILLED BY SERPENTS; (10) NOR GRUMBLE AS SOME OF THEM DID AND WERE CUT DOWN BY THE DESTROYING ANGEL.

(11) THESE THINGS HAPPENED TO THEM AS AN EXAMPLE, AND THEY WERE WRITTEN AS A WARNING, AS THE LAST TIMES COME UPON US.

(12) THEREFORE, IF YOU THINK YOU STAND BEWARE, LEST YOU FALL. (13) NO TRIAL GREATER THAN HUMAN ENDURANCE HAS OVERCOME YOU. GOD IS FAITHFUL AND WILL NOT LET YOU BE TEMPTED BEYOND YOUR STRENGTH. HE WILL GIVE YOU, TOGETHER WITH THE TEMPTATION, THE STRENGTH TO ESCAPE AND TO RESIST. (14) SO, DEAR FRIENDS, SHUN THE CULT OF IDOLS.

(15) I ADDRESS YOU AS INTELLIGENT PERSONS; JUDGE WHAT I SAY. (16) THE CUP OF BLESSING THAT WE BLESS, IS IT NOT A COMMUNION WITH THE BLOOD OF CHRIST? AND THE BREAD THAT WE BREAK, IS IT NOT A COMMUNION WITH THE BODY OF CHRIST? (17) THE BREAD IS ONE, AND SO WE, THOUGH MANY, FORM ONE BODY, SHARING THE ONE BREAD.

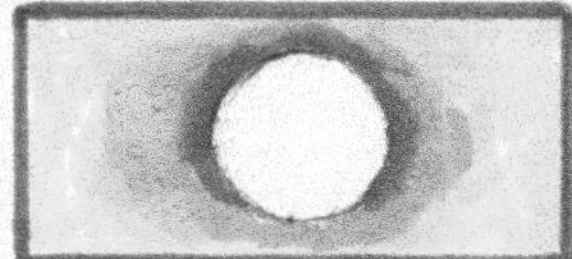

(18) CONSIDER THE ISRAELITES. FOR THEM, TO EAT OF THE VICTIM IS TO COME INTO COMMUNION WITH ITS ALTAR. (19) WHAT DOES ALL THAT MEAN? THAT THE MEAT IS REALLY CONSECRATED TO THE IDOL, OR THAT THE IDOL IS A BEING. (20) HOWEVER, WHEN THE PAGANS OFFER A SACRIFICE, THE SACRIFICE GOES TO THE DEMONS, NOT TO GOD. I DO NOT WANT YOU TO COME INTO FELLOWSHIP WITH DEMONS.

(21) YOU CANNOT DRINK AT THE SAME TIME FROM THE CUP OF THE LORD AND FROM THE CUP OF THE DEMONS. YOU CANNOT SHARE IN THE TABLE OF THE LORD AND IN THE TABLE OF THE DEMONS. (22) DO WE WANT PROVOKE THE JEALOUSY OF THE LORD? COULD WE BE STRONGER THAN HE?

PRACTICAL SOLUTIONS

(23) EVERYTHING IS LAWFUL FOR ME, BUT NOT EVERYTHING IS TO MY PROFIT. EVERYTHING IS LAWFUL FOR ME, BUT NOT EVERYTHING BUILDS UP.

(24) LET NO ONE PURSUE HIS OWN INTERESTS,
BUT THE INTERESTS OF THE OTHER.
(25) EAT, THEN, WHATEVER IS SOLD AT THE
MARKET, AND DO NOT RAISE QUESTIONS OF
CONSCIENCE ABOUT IT. (26) BECAUSE: THE
EARTH AND WHATEVER IS ON IT BELONGS
TO THE LORD. (27) IF SOMEONE WHO DOES
NOT SHARE YOUR FAITH INVITES YOU GO AND
EAT OF ANYTHING SERVED TO YOU WITHOUT PRO-
BLEMS OF CONSCIENCE. (28) HOWEVER, IF

SOMEBODY TELLS
YOU THAT THE MEAT
IS FROM THE OFFER-
INGS TO IDOLS, THEN
DO NOT EAT OUT OF
CONSIDERATION FOR
THOSE WARNING YOU
AND FOR THE SAKE OF
THEIR CONSCIENCE.
(29) I SAY: "IN CON-
SIDERATION OF THEIR
CONSCIENCE," NOT OF
YOURS, FOR IS IT CON-
VENIENT THAT MY
RIGHTS BE MISINTER-
PRETED BY THEM AND
THEIR CONSCIENCE?
(30) IS IT GOOD THAT
I BRING ON ME CRI-
TICS FOR SOME GOOD
THINGS I AM SHARING
AND FOR WHICH I WILL
GIVE THANKS?
(31) THEN, WHETHER
YOU EAT, OR DRINK,
OR WHATEVER YOU
DO, DO IT FOR THE
GLORY OF GOD. (32) GIVE NO OFFENSE TO THE
JEWS, OR TO THE GREEKS, OR TO THE CHURCH
OF GOD, (33) JUST AS I TRY TO PLEASE EVERY-
ONE IN EVERYTHING, I DO NOT SEEK MY OWN IN-
TEREST, BUT THAT OF MANY, FOR I WANT
THEM TO BE SAVED.

WOMEN'S DRESS AND MEDITERRANEAN CUSTOMS

11 (1) FOLLOW MY EXAMPLE AS I FOLLOW
THE EXAMPLE OF CHRIST. (2) I PRAISE
YOU BECAUSE YOU REMEMBER ME IN
EVERYTHING, AND YOU KEEP THE TRADITIONS
THAT I HAVE GIVEN YOU. (3) HOWEVER I WISH

TO REMIND YOU THAT EVERY MAN HAS CHRIST AS
HIS HEAD, WHILE WOMAN HAS HER HUSBAND AS
HER HEAD; AND GOD IS THE HEAD OF CHRIST. (4)
IF A MAN PRAYS OR PROPHESIES WITH HIS
HEAD COVERED, HE DISHONORS HIS HEAD.

(5) ON THE CONTRARY, THE WOMAN WHO PRAYS
OR PROPHESIES WITH HER HEAD UNCOVERED,
DOES NOT RESPECT HER HEAD. SHE MIGHT AS
WELL CUT HER HAIR. (6) IF A WOMAN DOES
NOT USE A VEIL, LET HER CUT HER HAIR; AND IF
IT IS A SHAME FOR A WOMAN TO HAVE HER
HAIR CUT OR SHAVED, THEN LET HER USE
A VEIL.
(7) MEN MUST NOT COVER THEIR HEAD, FOR
THEY ARE THE IMAGE OF GOD AND REFLECT

HIS GLORY, WHILE A WOMAN REFLECTS THE
GLORY OF MAN. (8) MAN WAS NOT FORMED
FROM WOMAN, BUT WOMAN FROM MAN. (9) NOR DID
GOD CREATE MAN FOR WOMAN, BUT WOMAN FOR
MAN. (10) THEREFORE, A WOMAN MUST RESPECT
THE ANGELS AND HAVE ON HER HEAD THE SIGN OF
HER DEPENDANCE.
(11) ANYWAY, THE CHRISTIAN ATTITUDE DOES
NOT SEPARATE MAN
FROM WOMAN, AND
WOMAN FROM MAN.
(12) AND IF GOD HAS
CREATED WOMAN FROM
MAN, MAN IS BORN FROM
WOMAN AND BOTH COME
FROM GOD. (13) JUDGE
FOR YOURSELVES: IS
IT PROPER FOR A
WOMAN TO PRAY
WITHOUT A VEIL?
(14) COMMON SENSE
TEACHES US THAT
IT IS SHAMEFUL
FOR A MAN TO
WEAR LONG HAIR,
(15) WHILE LONG
HAIR IS THE PRIDE
OF A WOMAN, AND
IT HAS BEEN GI-
VEN TO HER PRE-
CISELY AS A VEIL.

(16) IF SOME OF YOU
WANT TO ARGUE, LET IT BE KNOWN THAT IT IS
NOT OUR CUSTOM NOR THE CUSTOM IN THE
CHURCHES OF GOD.

THE LORD'S SUPPER

(17) TO CONTINUE WITH MY ADVICE, I CAN-
NOT PRAISE YOU, FOR YOUR GATHERINGS ARE
NOT FOR THE BETTER BUT FOR THE WORSE.

(18) FIRST, AS I HAVE HEARD, WHEN YOU GATHER
TOGETHER, THERE ARE DIVISIONS AMONG YOU
AND I PARTLY BELIEVE IT.

19 THERE MAY HAVE TO BE DIFFERENT
GROUPS AMONG YOU, SO THAT IT PLAINLY
APPEARS WHO ARE APPROVED AMONG YOU.

20 YOUR GATHERINGS ARE NO LONGER THE
SUPPER OF THE LORD, 21 FOR EACH ONE
EATS AT ONCE HIS OWN FOOD AND WHILE
ONE IS HUNGRY, THE OTHER IS GETTING
DRUNK. 22 DO YOU NOT HAVE HOUSES IN
WHICH TO EAT OR DRINK? OR PERHAPS YOU
DESPISE THE CHURCH OF GOD AND DESIRE
TO HUMILIATE THOSE WHO HAVE NOTHING?
WHAT SHALL I SAY? SHALL I PRAISE YOU?

FOR THIS I CANNOT PRAISE YOU. 23 THIS IS
THE TRADITION OF THE LORD THAT I RECEIVED
AND THAT IN MY TURN I HAVE HANDED ON TO
YOU: THE LORD JESUS, ON THE NIGHT THAT
HE WAS DELIVERED UP, TOOK BREAD AND,
24 AFTER GIVING THANKS, BROKE IT,
SAYING, "THIS IS MY BODY WHICH IS BRO-
KEN FOR YOU; DO THIS IN THE MEMORY
OF ME." 25 IN THE SAME MANNER, TAKING

THE CUP AFTER THE
SUPPER, HE SAID, "THIS
CUP IS THE NEW
COVENANT IN MY
BLOOD. WHEN-
EVER YOU DRINK
IT, DO IT IN THE
MEMORY OF ME."
26 SO, THEN, WHEN-
EVER YOU EAT OF
THIS BREAD AND
DRINK FROM THIS
CUP, YOU ARE PRO-
CLAIMING THE DEATH
OF THE LORD UNTIL
HE COMES. 27 THE-
REFORE, IF ANYONE
EATS OF THE BREAD
OR DRINKS FROM THE
CUP OF THE LORD UN-
WORTHILY, HE SINS
AGAINST THE BODY
AND BLOOD OF THE LORD.
28 LET EACH ONE EX-
AMINE HIMSELF BE-
FORE EATING OF THE
BREAD AND DRINKING
FROM THE CUP. 29 OTHERWISE, HE EATS AND
DRINKS HIS OWN CONDEMNATION IS NOT RECOG-
NIZING THE BODY.
30 THIS IS THE REASON WHY SO MANY OF
YOU ARE SICK AND WEAK AND SEVERAL HAVE
DIED. 31 IF WE EXAMINED AND CORRECTED
OURSELVES, THE LORD WOULD NOT HAVE TO
EXERCISE JUDGMENT AGAINST US.

32 THE LORD'S STROKES ARE TO CORRECT US,
SO THAT WE MAY NOT BE CONDEMNED WITH
THIS WORLD.
33 SO THEN, BROTHERS, WHEN YOU GATHER FOR A
MEAL, WAIT FOR ONE ANOTHER 34 AND, IF SOME-
ONE IS HUNGRY, LET HIM EAT IN HIS OWN HOUSE.
IN THIS WAY YOU WILL NOT GATHER FOR YOUR
COMMON CONDEMNATION. THE OTHER INSTRUCTIONS
I SHALL GIVE WHEN I GO THERE.

SPIRITUAL GIFTS AND HARMONY

12 1 WITH RESPECT TO SPIRITUAL
GIFTS, I WILL REMIND YOU OF THE
FOLLOWING.
2 WHEN YOU WERE
STILL PAGANS, YOU
WENT TO YOUR DUMB
IDOLS AS PEOPLE
POSSESSED. 3 I
TELL YOU THAT NO-
BODY INSPIRED BY
THE SPIRIT OF GOD
MAY SAY, "A CURSE
ON JESUS," AS NO
ONE CAN SAY, "JESUS
IS THE LORD," EX-
CEPT BY THE HOLY
SPIRIT.

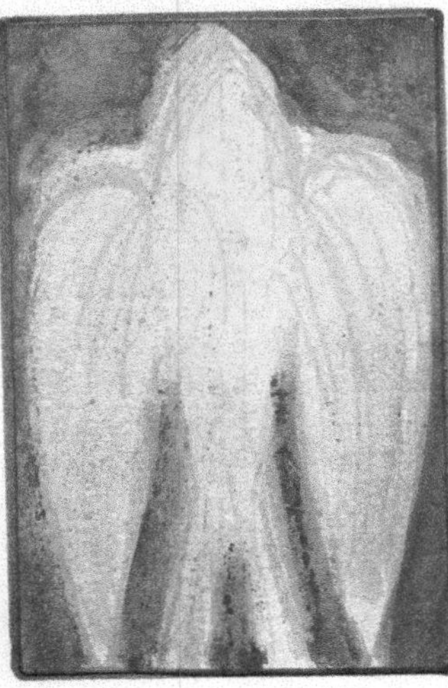

4 THERE IS DIVERSITY OF GIFTS, BUT
THE SPIRIT IS THE SAME.
5 THERE IS A DIVERSITY OF MINISTRIES,
BUT THE LORD IS THE SAME.
6 THERE IS A DIVERSITY OF WORKS,
BUT THE SAME GOD WORKS IN ALL.

7 THE SPIRIT REVEALS HIS PRESENCE IN EACH
ONE WITH A GIFT WHICH IS ALSO A SERVICE. 8
ONE IS TO SPEAK WITH WISDOM, THROUGH THE
SPIRIT. ANOTHER TEACHES ACCORDING TO
THE SAME SPIRIT. 10 ANOTHER WORKS MI-
RACLES, ANOTHER IS A PROPHET, ANOTHER
RECOGNIZES WHAT COMES FROM THE GOOD
OR EVIL SPIRIT; ANOTHER SPEAKS IN TONGUES,
AND STILL ANOTHER INTERPRETS WHAT
HAS BEEN SAID IN TONGUES.

9 To another is given faith, in which the
Spirit acts; to another the gift of healing,
and it is the same Spirit.

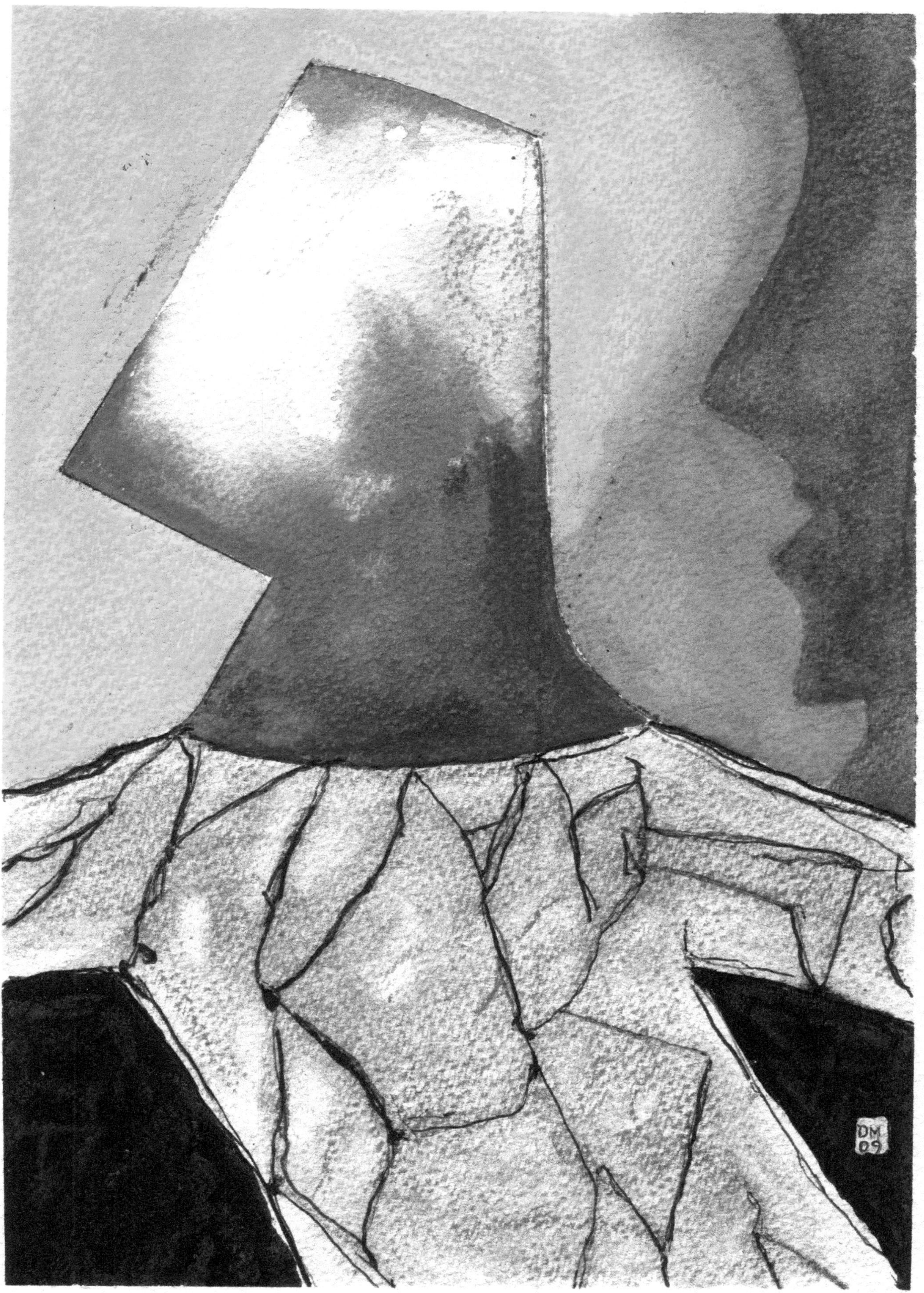

380 CCCLXXX ©

11 AND ALL OF THIS IS THE WORK OF THE
ONE AND HOLY SPIRIT, WHO GIVES TO EACH
ONE AS HE SO DESIRES.

COMPARISON WITH THE BODY

12 AS THE BODY IS ONE, HAVING MANY MEM-
BERS, AND ALL THE MEMBERS, WHILE BEING
MANY, FORM ONE BODY, SO IT IS WITH CHRIST.
13 ALL OF US, WHETHER JEWS OR GREEKS,
SLAVES OR FREE

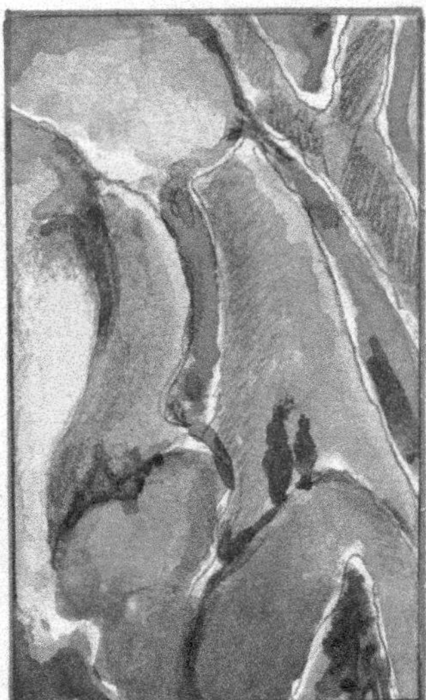

MEN, HAVE BEEN
BAPTIZED IN ONE
SPIRIT TO FORM
ONE BODY AND ALL
OF US HAVE BEEN
GIVEN TO DRINK
FROM THE ONE
SPIRIT.
14 THE BODY HAS
NOT JUST ONE
MEMBER, BUT MANY.
15 IF THE FOOT
SHOULD SAY, "I DO
NOT BELONG TO THE
BODY FOR I AM NOT A
HAND," IT WOULD BE
WRONG: IT IS PART OF
THE BODY! 16 EVEN
THOUGH THE EAR
SAYS, "I DO NOT
BELONG TO THE BO-
DY. 17 IF ALL THE
BODY WERE EYE,
WHO WOULD WE HE-
AR? AND IF ALL THE
BODY WERE EAR,
HOW WOULD WE SMELL?

18 GOD HAS ARRANGED ALL THE MEMBERS,
PLACING EACH PART OF THE BODY AS HE
PLEASED. 19 IF ALL WERE THE SAME
PART WHERE WOULD THE BODY BE?

20 BUT THERE ARE MANY MEMBERS AND ONE
BODY. 21 THE EYE CANNOT TELL THE HAND,
"I DO NOT NEED YOU," NOR THE HEAD TELL
THE FEET, "I DO NOT NEED YOU."

22 STILL MORE, THE PARTS OF OUR BODY
THAT WE MOST NEED ARE THOSE THAT
SEEM TO BE THE WEAKEST; 23 THE PARTS
THAT WE CONSIDER LOWER ARE TREATED
WITH MUCH CARE, 24 AND WE COVER
THEM WITH MORE MODESTY BECAUSE
THEY ARE LESS PRESENTABLE, WHE-
REAS THE OTHERS DO NOT NEED SUCH
ATTENTION.
25 GOD HIMSELF ARRANGED THE BODY
IN THIS WAY, GIVING MORE HONOR TO
THOSE PARTS THAT NEED IT, SO THAT
THE BODY MAY NOT BE DIVIDED, BUT RA-
THER EACH MEMBER MAY CARE FOR THE OTHERS.

26 WHEN ONE SUFFERS, ALL OF THEM
SUFFER, AND ONE RECEIVES HONOR, ALL
REJOICE TOGETHER.

27 NOW, YOU ARE THE BODY OF CHRIST
AND EACH OF YOU INDIVIDUALLY IS A
MEMBER OF IT. 28 SO GOD HAS AP-
POINTED US IN THE CHURCH. FIRST
APOSTLES, SECOND PROPHETS, THIRD
TEACHERS. THEN CAME MIRACLES, THEN
THE GIFT OF HEALING, MATERIAL HELP,
ADMINISTRATION IN THE CHURCH AND
THE GIFT OF TONGUES. 29 ARE ALL

APOSTLES? ARE ALL PROPHETS? ARE ALL TEACH-
ERS? CAN ALL PERFORM MIRACLES, 30 OR CU-
RE THE SICK, OR SPEAK IN TONGUES, OR EXPLA-
IN WHAT WAS SAID IN TONGUES? 31 SET YO-
UR HEARTS ON THE MOST PRECIOUS GIFTS.
BUT I WILL SHOW YOU A MUCH BETTER WAY.

NO GIFT HIGHER THAN LOVE

13 1 IF I COULD SPEAK ALL THE HUMAN
AND ANGELIC TONGUES, BUT HAD NO
LOVE, I WOULD ONLY BE SOUNDING
BRASS OR A CLANGING
CYMBAL. 2 IF I HAD

PROPHECY, KNOWING SE-
CRET THINGS WITH ALL
KINDS OF KNOWLEDGE, AND
HAD FAITH GREAT ENOUGH
TO REMOVE MOUNTAINS,
BUT HAD NO LOVE, I WO-
ULD BE NOTHING. 3 IF
I GAVE ALL I HAD TO THE
POOR, AND EVEN GAVE UP
MY OWN BODY, BUT
ONLY TO RECEIVE
PRAISE AND NOT
THROUGH LOVE, IT
WOULD BE OF NO VA-
LUE TO ME.
4 LOVE IS PATIENT,
KIND, WITHOUT
ENVY. IT IS NOT
BOASTFUL OR
ARROGANT. IT IS
NOT ILL-MANNERED
NOR DOES IT SEEK
ITS OWN INTEREST.

5 LOVE OVERCOMES
ANGER AND FORGETS OFFENSES. 6
IT DOES NOT TAKE DELIGHT IN WRONG,
BUT REJOICES IN TRUTH. 7 LOVE EXCU-
SES EVERYTHING, BELIEVES ALL THINGS,
HOPES ALL THINGS, ENDURES ALL THINGS.

8 LOVE WILL NEVER END. PROPHECIES MAY CE-
ASE, TONGUES BE SILENT AND KNOWLEDGE DISAP-
PEAR. 9 FOR KNOWLEDGE GRASPS SOMETHING OF
THE TRUTH AND PROPHECY AS WELL. 10 AND WHEN
WHAT IS PERFECT COMES, EVERYTHING IMPERFECT
WILL PASS AWAY. 11 WHEN I WAS A CHILD I RE-
ASONED AND THOUGHT LIKE A CHILD, BUT
WHEN I GREW UP, I GAVE UP CHILDISH WAYS.
12 LIKEWISE, AT PRESENT WE SEE DIMLY AS
IN A FAULTY MIRROR, BUT THEN WE SHALL SEE
FACE TO FACE. NOW WE KNOW IN PART, THEN
I WILL KNOW HIM AS HE KNOWS ME. 13 NOW
WE HAVE FAITH, HOPE AND LOVE, THESE

THREE, BUT THE GREATEST OF THESE IS LOVE.

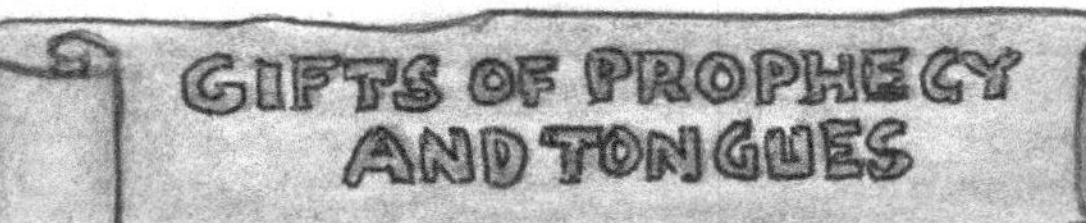

14 1 STRIVE, THEN, FOR LOVE AND SET
YOUR HEARTS AND SPIRITUAL GIFTS,
ESPECIALLY THAT YOU MAY PROPHESY.
2 HE WHO SPEAKS IN TONGUES DOES NOT
SPEAK TO PEOPLE, BUT TO GOD, FOR NO ONE
UNDERSTANDS HIM; THE SPIRIT MAKES HIM

SAY THINGS THAT ARE
NOT UNDERSTANDABLE.
3 THE PROPHET,
INSTEAD, ADDRES-
SES ALL PEOPLE TO
GIVE THEM STRENGTH,
ENCOURAGEMENT
AND CONSOLATION.
4 HE WHO SPEAKS
IN TONGUES STREN-
GTHENS HIMSELF,
BUT THE PROPHET
BUILDS THE CHURCH.
5 WOULD THAT
ALL OF YOU SPOKE
IN TONGUES! BUT
BETTER STILL IF
YOU WERE ALL PRO-
PHETS. THE PRO-
PHET HAS AN AD-
VANTAGE OVER THE
ONE SPEAKING IN
TONGUES, UNLESS SO-
MEONE EXPLAINS
WHAT WAS SPOKEN,
SO THAT THE COMMUNITY MAY PROFIT.
6 SUPPOSE, BROTHERS, I GO TO YOU AND
I SPEAK IN TONGUES, OF WHAT USE WILL
IT BE TO YOU IF I DO NOT BRING YOU SOME RE-
VELATION, KNOWLEDGE, PROPHECY OR TEACHING?

7 WHEN SOMEONE PLAYS THE FLUTE OR
HARP, OR ANY MUSICAL INSTRUMENT, IF THERE
ARE TONES AND NOTES, WHO WILL RECOGNIZE
THE TUNE? 8 AND IF THE BUGLE CALL IS
NOT CLEAR, WHO WILL GET READY FOR BAT-
TLE? 9 THE SAME WITH YOU, IF YOUR
WORDS ARE NOT UNDERSTOOD, WHO WILL
KNOW WHAT IS SAID?
YOU WILL BE TALK-
ING TO THE MOON.
10 THERE ARE MA-
NY LANGUAGES IN
THE WORLD, AND
EACH OF THEM HAS
MEANING. 11 BUT
IF I CANNOT FIND
ANY MEANING IN
WHAT IS SAID, I BE-
COME A FOREIGNER
TO THE SPEAKER,
AND THE SPEAKER
TO ME. 12 AS YOU
SET YOUR HEART
ON SPIRITUAL GIFTS,
BE EAGER TO BUILD
THE CHURCH AND
YOU WILL RECEIVE
ABUNDANTLY.
13 BECAUSE OF
THIS, HE WHO

SPEAKS IN TONGUES
SHOULD ASK GOD
FOR THE ABILITY TO EXPLAIN WHAT HE SAYS.
14 WHEN I AM PRAYING IN TONGUES, MY
SPIRIT PRAYS, BUT MY MIND REMAINS IDLE.
15 WHAT SHALL I DO, THEN? I WILL PRAY
WITH THE SPIRIT AND I WILL PRAY WITH
MY MIND. I WILL SING WITH THE SPIRIT AND I
WILL SING WITH MY MIND. 16 IF YOU PRAISE GOD
ONLY WITH YOUR SPIRIT, HOW WILL THE
ORDINARY PERSON ADD THE "AMEN" TO

YOUR THANKSGIVING, SINCE HE HAS NOT UN-
DERSTOOD WHAT YOU SAID? 17 YOUR THANKS-
GIVING WAS INDEED BEAUTIFUL, BUT IT WAS
USELESS FOR OTHERS.
18 I GIVE THANKS TO GOD BECAUSE I SPEAK
IN TONGUES MORE THAN ALL OF YOU, 19
BUT WHEN I AM IN THE ASSEMBLY, I PRE-
FER TO SAY FIVE WORDS FROM MY MIND,
WHICH MAY TEACH OTHERS, THAN TEN
THOUSAND WORDS IN TONGUES.

(20) BROTHERS AND SISTERS, DO NOT REMAIN AS
CHILDREN IN YOUR THINKING. BE LIKE INFANTS
IN DOING EVIL, BUT MATURE IN YOUR THINKING.
(21) GOD SAYS IN THE LAW: I WILL SPEAK TO THIS
PEOPLE THROUGH PEOPLE TALKING OTHER TON-
GUES AND THROUGH LIPS OF FOREIGNERS, BUT
EVEN SO MY PEOPLE WILL NOT LISTEN TO ME.
(22) SO, SPEAKING IN TONGUES IS FOR THOSE WHO BE-
LIEV FOR THOSE WHO REFUSE TO BELIEVE, NOT FOR THOSE
WHO BELIEVE, WHILE PROPHECY IS A SIGN FOR THOSE WHO
BELIEVE, NOT FOR THOSE WHO REFUSE TO BELIEVE.
(23) IMAGINE THAT THE WHOLE CHURCH IS GATHERED

TOGETHER AND ALL SPEAK IN TONGUES WHEN UNBELI-
EVERS AND UNINFORMED PEOPLE ENTER. WHAT WILL
THEY THINK? THAT YOU ARE CRAZY. (24) INSTEAD, SUP-
POSE THAT EACH OF YOU SPEAKS AS A PROPHET; AS
SOON AS AN UNBELIEVER OR AN UNINFORMED PER-
SON ENTERS, ALL OF YOU CALL HIM TO ACCOUNT AND
DISCLOSE HIS MOST SECRET THINKING. (25) THEN,
FALLING ON HIS FACE, HE WOULD BE URGED TO WOR-
SHIP GOD AND DECLARE THAT GOD IS TRULY AMONG
YOU.
(26) WHAT THEN SHALL WE CONCLUDE, BROTH-
ERS? WHEN YOU GATHER, EACH OF YOU CAN TAKE
PART WITH A SONG, A

TEACHING, OR A REVELA-
TION, BY SPEAKING IN
TONGUES OR INTER-
PRETING WHAT HAS
BEEN SAID IN TONGUES.
BUT LET ALL THIS
BUILD UP THE CHURCH.
(27) ARE YOU GOING TO
SPEAK IN TONGUES? LET
TWO OR THREE, AT MOST,
SPEAK, EACH IN TURN,
AND LET ONE INTER-
PRET WHAT HAS BEEN
SAID. (28) IF THERE IS
NO INTERPRETER, HOLD
YOUR TONGUE IN THE
ASSEMBLY AND SPEAK
TO GOD BY YOURSELF.
(29) AS FOR THE PROP-
HETS, LET TWO OR THREE
SPEAK, WITH THE OTHER
COMMENTING ON WHAT
HAS BEEN SAID. (30)
IF A REVELATION CO-
MES TO ONE OF THOSE
SITTING BY, LET THE
FIRST BE SILENT.
(31) EVEN ALL OF YOU COULD PROPHESY,
ONE BY ONE, FOR THE INSTRUCTION
AND ENCOURAGEMENT OF ALL.

(32) THE SPIRITS SPEAKING THROUGH PRO-
PHETS ARE SUBMITTED TO PROPHETS, (33)
BECAUSE GOD IS NOT A GOD OF CONFUSION,
BUT OF PEACE.
(34) LET WOMEN BE SILENT IN THE ASSEM-
BLIES, AS IN ALL THE CHURCHES OF THE
SAINTS. THEY ARE NOT ALLOWED TO
SPEAK. LET THEM BE SUBMISSIVE AS THE
LAW COMMANDS.
(35) IF THERE IS ANY-
THING THEY DESIRE
TO KNOW, LET THEM
CONSULT THEIR
HUSBANDS AT HO-
ME. FOR IT IS SHA-
MEFUL FOR A WO-
MAN TO SPEAK IN
CHURCH. (36) DID
THE WORD OF GOD,
PERHAPS, COME
FROM YOU? (37) IF
SOMEONE AMONG
YOU THINKS THAT
HE IS A PROPHET
OR A SPIRITUAL
PERSON, HE SHOULD
ACKNOWLEDGE THAT
WHAT I AM WRIT-
ING TO YOU IS THE
LORD'S COMMAND.

(38) IF HE DOES NOT
RECOGNIZE THAT,
GOD WILL NOT
RECOGNIZE HIM. (39) SO, THEN, BROTHERS,
SET YOUR HEARTS ON THE GIFT OF PRO-
PHECY, AND DO NOT FORBID SPEAKING IN
TONGUES. (40) HOWEVER, EVERYTHING SHOULD
BE DONE IN A FITTING AND ORDERLY WAY.

RESURRECTION IS A FACT

15 (1) LET ME REMIND YOU, BROTHERS AND SISTERS,
OF THE GOOD NEWS THAT I PREACHED TO YOU AND
WHICH YOU RECE-
IVED AND ON WHICH YOU
STAND FIRM. (2) BY THAT
GOSPEL YOU ARE SAVED,
PROVIDED THAT YOU HOLD
TO IT AS I PREACHED IT.
OTHERWISE, YOU WILL
HAVE BELIEVED IN VAIN.
(3) I HAVE FIRSTLY PAS-
SED TO YOU WHAT I MY-
SELF RECEIVED: CHRIST
DIED FOR OUR SINS, AS
SCRIPTURE SAYS; THAT
(4) HE WAS BURIED,
RAISED ON THE THIRD
DAY, ACCORDING TO THE
SCRIPTURES; (5) THAT
HE APPEARED TO CE-
PHAS AND THEN TO THE
TWELVE. (6) HE THEN
APPEARED TO MORE
THAN 500 BROTHERS;
MOST OF THEM ARE
STILL ALIVE AND
SOME GONE TO REST.
(7) THEN HE APPEA-
RED TO JAMES AND
AFTER THAT TO ALL THE APOSTLES. (8) AND
LAST OF ALL, AS TO ONE BORN ABNORMALLY
HE APPEARED TO ME ALSO. (9) FOR I AM THE LAST
OF THE APOSTLES, AND I DO NOT EVEN DESERVE
TO BE CALLED AN APOSTLE, BECAUSE I PER-
SECUTED THE CHURCH OF GOD.

381
CCCLXXXI
© DM 09

(10) NEVERTHELESS, BY THE GRACE OF GOD, I AM
WHAT I AM, AND HIS GRACE TOWARDS ME HAS NOT
BEEN WITHOUT FRUIT. FAR FROM IT, I HAVE TOILED
MORE THAN ALL OF THEM, ALTHOUGH NOT I, RA-
THER THE GRACE OF GOD IN ME.
(11) NOW, WHETHER IT WAS I OR THEY, THIS
WE PREACH AND THIS YOU HAVE BELIEVED. WELL,
(12) THEN, IF CHRIST IS PREACHED AS RISEN FROM
THE DEAD, HOW CAN SO-
ME OF YOU SAY THAT
THERE IS NO RESUR-
RECTION OF THE DEAD?

(13) IF THERE IS NO RE-
SURRECTION OF THE
DEAD, THEN CHRIST
HAS NOT BEEN RAISED.
(14) AND IF CHRIST HAS
NOT BEEN RAISED, OUR
PREACHING IS EMPTY
AND OUR BELIEF COMES
TO NOTHING. (15) AND
WE BECOME FALSE
WITNESSES OF GOD,
ATTESTING THAT HE
RAISED CHRIST, WHE-
REAS HE COULD NOT
RAISE HIM IF THE
DEAD ARE NOT RA-
ISED. (16) IF THE DEAD
ARE NOT RAISED, NE-
ITHER HAS CHRIST
BEEN RAISED. (17) AND
IF CHRIST HAS NOT
BEEN RAISED, YOUR FAITH GIVES YOU NOTHING,
AND YOU ARE STILL IN SIN. (18) ALSO THOSE
WHO FALL ASLEEP IN CHRIST ARE LOST. (19)
IF IT IS ONLY FOR THIS LIFE THAT WE HOPE IN
CHRIST, WE ARE THE MOST UNFORTUNATE OF ALL PEOPLE.

CHRIST GAVE US THE WAY

(20) BUT NO, CHRIST HAS BEEN RAISED FROM THE
DEAD. HE IS THE FIRST, AND THE FIRST FRUITS
OF THOSE WHO HAVE FALLEN ASLEEP. (21) A MAN
BROUGHT DEATH; A MAN ALSO BRINGS RESUR-
RECTION OF THE DEAD. (22) ALL DIE FOR BEING

ADAM'S, AND IN CHRIST ALL WILL RECEIVE LIFE.
(23) HOWEVER, EACH ONE IN HIS OWN TIME:
FIRST CHRIST, THEN CHRIST'S PEOPLE, WHEN HE
VISITS THEM. (24) THEN THE END WILL COME,
WHEN CHRIST DELIVERS THE KINGDOM TO GOD
THE FATHER, AFTER HAVING DESTROYED EVERY
RULE, AUTHORITY AND POWER.
(25) FOR HE MUST REIGN AND

'PUT ALL ENEMIES UNDER HIS FEET'

(26) THE LAST ENEMY TO BE DESTROYED
WILL BE DEATH.

(27) AS SCRIPTURE SAYS: GOD HAS SUB-
JECTED EVERYTHING UNDER HIS FEET.
WHEN WE SAY THAT EVERYTHING IS PUT UNDER
HIS FEET, WE EXCLUDE, OF COURSE, THE FATHER
WHO SUBJECTS EVERYTHING TO HIM. (28) WHEN
THE FATHER HAS SUBJECTED EVERYTHING TO HIM,
THE SON WILL PLACE HIMSELF UNDER HIM WHO SUB-
JECTS EVERYTHING. FROM THEN ON, GOD WILL BE
ALL IN ALL. (29) OTHERWISE, WHAT ARE THESE
PEOPLE DOING WHO ARE BAPTIZED ON BEHALF OF

OF THE DEAD? IF THE DEAD CANNOT BE RAISED, WHY DO
THEY WANT TO BE BAPTIZED FOR THE DEAD? (30) AS
FOR US, WHY DO WE CONSTANTLY RISK OUR LIFE? FOR
DEATH IS MY DAILY COMPANION. (31) I SAY THAT, BRO-
THERS AND SISTERS, BEFORE YOU WHO ARE MY PRIDE
IN CHRIST JESUS OUR LORD. (32) WAS IT FOR NOTHING
MORE THAN HUMAN GAIN THAT I FOUGHT IN EPHESUS LIKE
A LION TAMER? IF THE DEAD ARE NOT RAISED, LET US
EAT AND DRINK, FOR TOMORROW WE SHALL DIE! (33)
DO NOT BE DECEIVED; BAD THEORIES CORRUPT GO-
OD MORALS. WAKE UP, AND DO NOT SIN. (34) BECAUSE
SOME OF YOU ARE OUTSTANDINGLY IGNORANT
ABOUT GOD; I SAY THIS TO YOUR SHAME.

THE BODY AFTER THE RESURRECTION

(35) SOME OF YOU WILL ASK: HOW WILL THE DE-
AD BE RAISED? WITH WHAT KIND OF BODY
WILL THEY COME?

(36) YOU FOOLS! WHAT
YOU SOW CANNOT SPROUT
UNLESS IT DIES. (37) AND
WHAT YOU SOW IS NOT THE
BODY OF THE FUTURE PLANT
BUT A BARE GRAIN OF
WHEAT OR ANY OTHER
SEED, (38) AND GOD
WILL GIVE THE APPRO-
PRIATE BODY, AS HE
GIVES TO EACH SEED
IT'S OWN BODY. (39) NOW
LOOK: NOT ALL FLESH
IS THE SAME: ONE IS
THE FLESH OF HUMAN
BEINGS; ANOTHER THE
FLESH OF ANIMALS, AND
STILL OTHERS THE
FLESH OF BIRDS
AND OF FISH. (40)
THERE ARE, LIKE-
WISE, HEAVENLY BO-
DIES AND EARTHLY
BODIES DO NOT RE-
ALLY SHINE AS DO THE HEAVENLY ONES. (41) THE
BRIGHTNESS OF THE SUN DIFFERS FROM THE
BRIGHTNESS OF THE MOON AND THE STARS,
AND THE STARS HAVE DIFFERENT BRIGHTNESS.

42 IT IS THE SAME WITH THE RESURRECTION OF
THE DEAD. THE BODY IS SOWN IN DECOMPOSI-
TION; IT WILL BE RAISED NEVER MORE TO DIE.
43 IT IS SOWN IN HUMILIATION, AND IT WILL
BE RAISED FOR GLORY. IT IS BURIED IN WEAK-
NESS, BUT THE RESURRECTION SHALL BE WITH
POWER. WHEN BURIED
IT IS A NATURAL BODY,
BUT IT WILL BE RA-
ISED AS A SPIRITUAL
BODY. 44 FOR THERE
SHALL BE A SPIRITUAL
BODY AS THERE IS AT
PRESENT A LIVING
BODY. 45 SCRIPTURE
SAYS ABOUT THE FIRST
MAN: ADAM'S LIFE PRO-
CEEDED FROM A SOUL,
BUT THE LAST ADAM
HAS BECOME SPIRIT
THAT GIVES LIFE.
46 THE SPIRIT DOES
NOT APPEAR FIRST,
BUT THE NATURAL LI-
FE, AND AFTERWARDS
COMES THE SPIRIT.
47 THE FIRST MAN
COMES FROM THE EARTH
AND IS EARTHLY, WHI-
LE THE SECOND ONE
COMES FROM HEAVEN.
48 AS IT WAS WITH THE EARTHLY ONE, SO IS IT
WITH THE EARTHLY PEOPLE. AS IT IS WITH CHRIST, SO
WITH THE HEAVENLY. 49 JUST AS WE ARE BEARING
THE IMAGE OF THE EARTHLY ONE, WE SHALL ALSO
BEAR THE IMAGE OF THE HEAVENLY ONE.

THE DAY OF RESURRECTION

50 THIS I SAY, BROTHERS: FLESH AND BLOOD CANNOT SHA-
RE THE KINGDOM OF GOD; NOTHING OF US THAT IS TO
DECAY CAN REACH IMPERISHABLE LIFE. 51 I WANT
TO TEACH YOU THE MYSTERY; ALTHOUGH NOT ALL OF US
WILL DIE, ALL OF US HAVE TO BE TRANSFORMED, 52 IN
AN INSTANT, AT THE SOUND OF THE TRUMPET. YOU HAVE
HEARD OF THE LAST TRUMPET; THEN IN THE TWINKL-
ING OF AN EYE, THE DEAD WILL BE RAISED IMPERISH-
ABLE, WHILE WE SHALL BE TRANSFORMED. 53 FOR

IT IS NECESSARY THAT OUR MORTAL AND PERISHABLE
BEING PUT ON THE LIFE THAT KNOWS NEITHER DEATH
NOR DECAY. 54 WHEN OUR PERISHABLE BEING PUTS ON IM-
PERISHABLE LIFE, WHEN OUR MORTAL BEING PUTS ON IMMORT-
ALITY, THE SCRIPTURE WILL BE FULFILLED: DEATH HAS
BEEN SWALLOWED UP BY VICTORY. 55 DEATH, WHERE IS
YOUR VICTORY? DEATH, WHERE IS YOUR STING? 56 SIN IS
THE STING OF DEATH TO KILL, AND THE LAW IS WHAT
GIVES FORCE TO SIN. 57 BUT GIVE THANKS TO GOD
WHO GIVES US THE VICTORY THROUGH CHRIST
JESUS, OUR LORD.

58 SO THEN, MY DEAR BROTHERS AND SISTERS,
BE STEADFAST AND DO NOT BE MOVED. IMPROVE
CONSTANTLY IN THE WORK OF THE LORD, KNOW-
ING THAT WITH HIM YOUR LABOR IS NOT WITHOUT FRUIT.

COMMENDATIONS AND GREETINGS

16 1 WITH REGARD TO THE COLLECTION IN FAVOR OF
THE SAINTS, FOLLOW THE RULES THAT I GAVE TO
THE CHURCHES OF GALATIA. 2 EVERY SUNDAY,
LET EACH OF YOU PUT ASIDE WHAT HE IS ABLE TO SPA-
RE, SO THAT NO COLLECTION NEED BE MADE WHEN
I COME. 3 ONCE I AM WITH YOU, YOU WILL CHOOSE
THE PERSONS WHOM I MAY ACCREDIT WITH LET-
TERS TO TAKE YOUR GIFT TO JERUSALEM. 4 AND

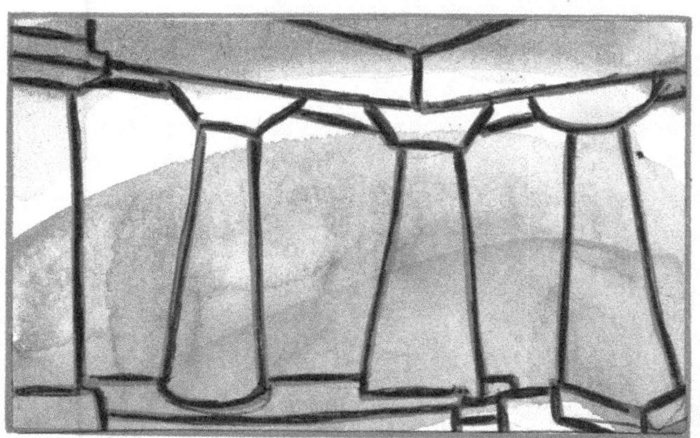

IF IT SEEMS BETTER FOR ME TO GO, THEY WILL GO
WITH ME. 5 I WILL VISIT YOU AFTER PASSING
THROUGH MACEDONIA, FOR I WANT TO GO ONLY
THROUGH MACEDONIA. 6 I WOULD LIKE TO STAY
WITH YOU FOR A WHILE, AND PERHAPS I WILL
SPEND THE WINTER SO THAT YOU MAY HELP ME
ON MY WAY WHEREVER I GO. 7 I DO NOT WANT
TO SEE YOU NOW JUST IN PASSING, FOR I RE-
ALLY HOPE TO STAY
WITH YOU, IF THE LORD
PERMITS. 8 BUT I
WILL STAY IN EPHESUS
UNTIL PENTECOST,
9 BECAUSE I HAVE GRE-
AT OPPORTUNITIES HERE,
EVEN THOUGH THERE ARE
MANY OPPONENTS. 10
WHEN TIMOTHY COMES,
MAKE HIM FEEL AT
EASE WITH YOU. CON-
SIDER THAT, LIKE ME,
HE IS WORKING FOR THE
LORD. 11 LET NO ONE
LOOK DOWN ON HIM.
HELP HIM CONTINUE
HIS JOURNEY SO THAT
HE MAY RETURN TO ME
WITHOUT DIFFICULTIES.
I AM EXPECTING HIM
WITH THE BROTHERS.

12 AS FOR APOLLOS, OUR
BROTHER, I HAVE STRON-
GLY URGED HIM TO VISIT YOU WITH THE BROTHERS, BUT
HE DID NOT WANT TO GO AT ALL; HE WILL VISIT YOU
AT HIS FIRST OPPORTUNITY. 13 BE ALERT, STAND
FIRM IN THE FAITH, ACT LIKE MEN, BE STRONG.
14 LET LOVE BE IN ALL. 15 NOW, BROTHERS AND
SISTERS, YOU KNOW THAT IN ACHAIA THERE IS
NONE BETTER THAN STEPHANAS AND HIS FA-
MILY AND THAT THEY HAVE DEVOTED THEM-
SELVES TO THE SERVICE OF THE BELIEVERS.

(16) I URGE YOU TO BE SUBJECT TO SUCH PERSONS AND TO ANYONE WHO WORKS AND TOILS WITH THEM.
(17) I AM GLAD OF THE COMING OF STEPHANAS, FORTUNATUS AND ACHAICUS WHO WERE ABLE TO REPRESENT YOU.
(18) IN FACT, THEY APPEASED MY SPIRIT AND YOURS. APPRECIATE PERSONS LIKE THEM. (19) THE CHURCHES OF ASIA GREET YOU.
AQUILA AND PRISCA GREET YOU IN THE LORD, AS DOES THE CHURCH THAT GATHERS IN THEIR HOUSE. (20) ALL THE BROTHERS AND SISTERS GREET YOU. GREET ONE ANOTHER WITH A HOLY KISS.
(21) THE GREETING IS FROM ME, PAUL, IN MY OWN HAND. (22) A CURSE ON ANYONE WHO DOES NOT LOVE THE LORD!
MARANATHA! COME, LORD!
(23) THE GRACE OF THE LORD JESUS BE WITH YOU.
(24) MY LOVE TO ALL IN CHRIST JESUS.

GREETINGS

INTRODUCTION TO 2nd CORINTHIANS

AT THE END OF HIS FIRST LETTER TO THE CORINTHIANS PAUL EXPRESSED THE DESIRE TO COME BACK AND SEE THEM SOON. HE WAS UNABLE TO RETURN, AND THEY TOOK THIS VERY BADLY. PAUL SENT A MESSENGER WHOM THE CORINTHIANS DEEPLY OFFENDED: SOME MEMBERS OF THE COMMUNITY WERE OPENLY REBELLING AGAINST THE APOSTLE. PAUL RESPONDED IN A LETTER "WRITTEN IN THE MIDST OF TEARS" WHEREBY HE DEMANDED SUBMISSION OF THE COMMUNITY. ONE OF PAUL'S BEST ASSISTANTS, TITUS, BROUGHT THE LETTER AND CONCLUDED WITH SUCCESS HIS MISSION. UPON TITUS' RETURN PAUL, REASSURED, SENT THIS SECOND LETTER (IN FACT IT WAS THE THIRD OR FOURTH) TO THE CORINTHIANS.
PAUL IS INCAPABLE OF SPEAKING ABOUT HIMSELF WITHOUT SPEAKING OF CHRIST, THROUGH BEAUTIFUL PAGES OF EVANGELIZATION.

ST. PAUL • 12th CENTURY
MOSAIC • CATHEDRAL OF
MONREALE • SICILY •
382 • CCCLXXXII •
© DM 09

THE SECOND LETTER OF PAUL TO THE CHURCH OF THE CORINTHIANS

1 (1) PAUL, AN APOSTLE OF CHRIST JESUS BY THE
WILL OF GOD, AND TIMOTHY, OUR BROTHER, TO THE
CHURCH OF GOD IN CORINTH AND TO ALL THE SA-
INTS IN THE WHOLE OF ACHAIA. (2) MAY YOU RECEIVE
GRACE AND PEACE FROM GOD OUR FATHER AND FROM
CHRIST JESUS, THE LORD.

BLESSED BE GOD, THE SOURCE OF ALL COMFORT

(3) BLESSED BE GOD, THE FATHER OF CHRIST JESUS,
OUR LORD, THE ALL-MERCIFUL FATHER AND THE GOD

OF ALL COMFORT! (4) HE
ENCOURAGES US IN ALL
OUR TRIALS, SO THAT
WE MAY ALSO ENCOURA-
GE THOSE IN ANY TRIAL
WITH THE SAME COM-
FORT THAT WE RECEIVE
FROM GOD. (5) JUST AS
THE SUFFERINGS OF
CHRIST OVERFLOW
TO US, SO, THROUGH
CHRIST, A GREAT COM-
FORT ALSO OVERFLOWS.
(6) IF WE ARE AFF-
LICTED FOR YOUR
SAKE, IT IS FOR YO-
UR COMFORT AND
SALVATION; AND WE
ALSO RECEIVE COM-
FORT FOR YOU, THAT
YOU MAY EXPERIEN-
CE THE SAME COM-
FORT THAT IS OURS
WHEN YOU COME
TO ENDURE THE
SAME SUFFERINGS WE ENDURE.

(7) OUR HOPE FOR YOU IS MOST FIRM; JUST
AS YOU SHARE IN OUR SUFFERINGS, SO SHALL
YOU ALSO SHARE IN OUR CONSOLATION.

(8) BROTHERS, WE WANT YOU TO KNOW SO-
ME OF THE TRIALS WE EXPERIENCED IN THE
PROVINCE OF ASIA.
WE WERE CRUSHED; IT WAS TOO MUCH;
IT WAS MORE THAN WE COULD BEAR.

(9) WE HAD ALREADY LOST ALL HOPE OF
COMING THROUGH ALIVE AND FELT BRAND-
ED FOR DEATH, BUT THIS HAPPENED THAT
WE MIGHT NO LONGER RELY ON OURSELVES
BUT ON GOD, WHO RAISES THE DEAD.
(10) HE FREED US FROM SUCH A DEADLY PERIL
AND WILL CONTINUE TO DO SO. WE TRUST HE
WILL CONTINUE PROTECTING US. (11) BUT
YOU MUST HELP US WITH YOUR PRAYERS.

WHEN SUCH A FAVOR IS OBTAINED BY THE IN-
TERCESSION OF MANY, SO WILL THERE BE MANY
TO GIVE THANKS TO GOD ON OUR BEHALF.

THE PLANS OF PAUL

(12) THERE IS SOMETHING WE ARE PROUD OF:
OUR CONSCIENCE TELLS US THAT WE HAVE LIVED
IN THIS WORLD WITH THE OPENNESS AND SINCERITY THAT
COMES FROM GOD. WE HAVE BEEN GUIDED NOT BY HUMAN MO-
TIVES, BUT BY THE GRACE OF GOD, MAINLY IN RELATION TO
YOU. (13) NO HIDDEN INTENTIONS IN MY LETTER, BUT
ONLY WHAT YOU CAN READ AND UNDERSTAND. (14) I TRUST
THAT WHAT YOU NOW ONLY PARTLY REALIZE, YOU
WILL COME TO UNDER-
STAND FULLY, AND SO BE
PROUD OF US, AS WE SHALL
ALSO BE PROUD OF YOU ON
THE DAY OF THE LORD JESUS.
(15) WITH THIS ASSURANCE
I WANTED TO GO AND VISIT
YOU FIRST, AND THIS WOULD
HAVE BEEN A DOUBLE
BLESSING FOR YOU. (16)
FROM THERE I THOUGHT
OF GOING TO MACEDONIA
AND FROM THERE COMING
BACK TO YOU, THAT YOU
MAY SEND ME ON MY
WAY TO JUDEA. (17) HAVE
I PLANNED THIS WITHOUT
THINKING AT ALL? OR DO
I CHANGE MY DECISIONS
ON THE SPUR OF THE MO-
MENT, SO THAT I AM
BETWEEN 'NO' AND 'YES?'
(18) GOD KNOWS THAT

OUR DEALING WITH YOU IS NOT YES AND NO, (19)
JUST AS THE SON OF GOD, CHRIST JESUS, WHOM
WE, SILVANUS, TIMOTHY AND I, PREACH TO YOU,
WAS NOT YES AND NO; WITH HIM IT WAS SIMPLY
YES. (20) IN HIM ALL THE PROMISES OF GOD
HAVE COME TO BE A 'YES', AND WE ALSO SAY
IN HIS NAME; **AMEN!**

GIVING THANKS TO GOD.

(21) GOD HIMSELF STRENGTHENS US AND YOU, TO
AIM AT CHRIST; HE HAS ANOINTED AND MARKED
US (22) WITH HIS OWN SEAL IN A FIRST OUTPOUR-
ING OF THE SPIRIT IN OUR HEARTS.

PAUL REFERS TO A SCANDAL

(23) GOD KNOWS, AND I SWEAR TO YOU BY MY OWN LI-
FE, THAT IF I DID NOT RETURN TO CORINTH, IT WAS BECA-
USE I WANTED TO SPARE YOU. (24) I DO NOT WISH TO
LORD IT OVER YOUR FAITH, BUT TO CONTRIBUTE TO
YOUR HAPPINESS; AS FOR FAITH, YOU ALREADY STAND FIRM.

2 (1) SO I GAVE UP A VISIT THAT WOULD AGAIN BE A
DISTRESSING ONE. (2) IF I MAKE YOU SAD, WHO
WILL MAKE ME HAPPY IF NOT YOU WHOM I HAVE
GRIEVED? (3) REMEMBER WHAT I WROTE YOU, "MAY
IT BE THAT WHEN I COME I DO NOT FEEL SAD BECAUSE
OF YOU, WHO SHOULD RATHER MAKE ME HAPPY."
I TRUST IN EVERYONE AND I AM SURE THAT MY JOY
WILL BE THE JOY OF YOU ALL.
(4) SO AFFLICTED AND WORRIED WAS I WHEN I WROTE
TO YOU, THAT I EVEN SHED TEARS. I DID NOT INTEND TO
CAUSE YOU PAIN, BUT RA-
THER TO LET YOU KNOW OF
THE IMMENSE LOVE THAT
I HAVE FOR YOU. (5) IF
ANYONE HAS CAUSED ME
PAIN, HE HAS HURT ME BUT
IN SOME MEASURE, ALL OF
YOU, AND I DO NOT WISH
TO EXAGGERATE. (6) THE
PUNISHMENT THAT HE RE-
CEIVED FROM THE MA-
JORITY IS ENOUGH FOR
HIM. (7) NOW YOU
SHOULD RATHER
FORGIVE AND COM-
FORT HIM, LEST EX-
CESSIVE SORROW
DISCOURAGE HIM.
(8) SO I BEG YOU TO
TREAT HIM WITH
LOVE.

• • •

(9) THIS IS WHY I WRO-
TE TO YOU, TO TEST
YOU AND TO KNOW IF YOU WOULD OBEY IN EVERY-
THING. (10) THE ONE YOU FORGIVE, I ALSO
FORGIVE. AND WHAT I FORGAVE, IF INDEED
I HAD ANYTHING TO FORGIVE, I FORGAVE
FOR YOUR SAKE IN THE PRESENCE OF
CHRIST, (11) LEST SATAN TAKE ADVANT-
AGE OF US: FOR WE KNOW HIS DESIGNS.

WE ARE THE FRAGRANCE OF CHRIST

(12) SO I CAME TO TROAS TO PREACH THE GOSPEL OF
CHRIST, AND THE LORD OPENED DOORS FOR ME.
(13) HOWEVER I COULD NOT BE AT PEACE BE-
CAUSE I DID NOT FIND MY BROTHER TITUS
THERE, SO I TOOK LEAVE OF THEM AND WENT
TO MACEDONIA. (14)
THANKS BE TO GOD,
WHO ALWAYS LEADS US
IN THE TRIUMPHANT FOL-
LOWING OF CHRIST AND,
THROUGH US, SPREADS
THE KNOWLEDGE OF HIM
EVERYWHERE, LIKE AN
AROMA. (15) WE ARE
CHRIST'S FRAGRANCE
RISING UP TO GOD,
AND PERCEIVED BY
THOSE WHO ARE SA-
VED AS WELL AS BY
THOSE WHO ARE LOST.
(16) TO THE LATTER,
IT SMELLS OF DEATH
AND LEADS THEM TO DE-
ATH. TO OTHERS IT IS
THE FRAGRANCE OF LIFE
AND LEADS TO LIFE.
(17) BUT WHO IS
WORTHY OF SUCH A
MISSION? UNLIKE
SO MANY WHO MAKE
MONEY OUT OF THE
WORD OF GOD, WE SPEAK WITH SINCERITY
AND PROCLAIM CHRIST SENT BY GOD, THE FATHER.

3 (1) AM I AGAIN COMMENDING MYSELF? OR DO I
NEED TO PRESENT TO YOU LETTERS OF RECOM-
MENDATION AS SOME HAVE DONE, OR SHOULD
I ASK YOU FOR THOSE LETTERS? (2) YOU ARE THE
LETTER. WE BEAR IT IN OUR HEART, YET ALL CAN READ
AND UNDERSTAND IT. (3) YES, WHO COULD DE-
NY THAT YOU ARE CHRIST'S LETTER WRITTEN

BY US, A LETTER WRITTEN NOT WITH INK BUT
WITH THE SPIRIT OF THE LIVING GOD, CARVED
NOT IN SLABS OF STONES, BUT IN HEARTS OF
FLESH. (4) THIS IS OUR CONFIDENCE BEFORE GOD,
THANKS BE TO CHRIST! (5) WE DO NOT DARE
CONSIDER THAT OUR WORK IS DUE TO ANY
MERIT OF OURS; WE KNOW THAT OUR ABILI-
TY COMES FROM GOD. (6) HE HAS ENABLED US
TO BE MINISTERS OF A NEW COVENANT NO
LONGER DEPENDING ON A WRITTEN LAW
BUT ON THE SPIRIT. THE WRITTEN LAW KILLS,
BUT THE SPIRIT GIVES LIFE.

(7) THE MINISTRY OF THE LAW CARVED ON STONES
BROUGHT DEATH; IT WAS NEVERTHELESS SUR-
ROUNDED BY GLORY AND WE KNOW THAT THE IS-
RAELITES COULD NOT FIX THEIR EYES ON THE
FACE OF MOSES, SUCH WAS HIS RADIANCE (8)
THOUGH FLEETING. HOW MUCH MORE GLORIO-
US WILL THE MINISTRY OF THE SPIRIT BE! (9)
IF THERE WAS GREATNESS IN A MINISTRY WHICH
USED TO CONDEMN, HOW MUCH MORE WILL THERE BE
IN THE MINISTRY THAT BRINGS HOLINESS? (10)
THE MINISTRY OF THE
LAW WAS HELD AS
GLORIOUS, AN IMPER-
FECT GLORY; YET IT
WILL NO LONGER BE
SO WHEN A GLORY
FAR MORE SUPERIOR
APPEARS. (11) THE MI-
NISTRY OF THE LAW
WAS PROVISORY AND
HAD ONLY MOMENTS OF
GLORY; BUT OURS EN-
DURES WITH A LAST-
ING GLORY. (12) SINCE
WE HAVE GREAT AMBI-
TION, WE ARE CONFIDENT,
(13) UNLIKE MOSES, WHO
COVERED HIS FACE WITH A
VEIL. OTHERWISE THE IS-
RAELITES WOULD HAVE
SEEN HIS PASSING RA-
DIANCE FADE. (14) THEY
BECAME BLIND, HOW-
EVER, UNTIL THIS DAY,
THE SAME VEIL PREVENTS
THEM FROM UNDERSTANDING THE OLD COVENANT AND
THEY DO NOT REALIZE THAT FOR THOSE IN CHRIST
IT IS NULLIFIED. (15) UP TO THIS VERY DAY, OFTEN
THEY READ MOSES, THE VEIL REMAINS OVER
THEIR UNDERSTANDING (16) BUT, FOR WHOEVER
TURNS TO THE LORD THE VEIL SHALL BE REMO-
VED. (17) THE LORD IS SPIRIT, AND WHERE THE
SPIRIT OF THE LORD IS, THERE IS FREEDOM.

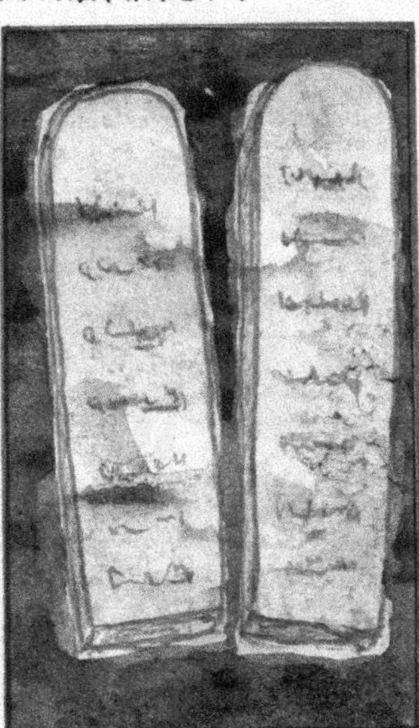

(18) SO, WITH UNVEILED FACES, WE ALL MUST REFLECT THE
GLORY OF THE LORD, WHILE WE ARE TRANSFORMED INTO HIS
LIKENESS AND EXPERIENCE HIS GLORY MORE AND MO-
RE BY THE ACTION OF THE LORD WHO IS SPIRIT.

TREASURE IN VESSELS OF CLAY

4 (1) THIS IS WHY WE DO NOT FEEL DISCOURA-
GED AS WE FULFILL THIS MINISTRY MECIFUL-
LY GIVEN TO US. (2) WE REFUSE TO STAY WITH
HALF-TRUTHS THROUGH FEAR; WE DO NOT BEHAVE
WITH CUNNING OR FALSIFY THE MESSAGE OF GOD
BUT, SHOWING THE TRUTH, WE DESERVE THE RESPECT OF
EVERYONE BEFORE GOD. (3) IN FACT IF THE GOSPEL WE
PROCLAIM REMAINS OBSCURE, IT IS OBSCURE ONLY FOR
THOSE WHO GO TO THEIR OWN DESTRUCTION.

(4) THE GOD OF THIS WORLD HAS BLINDED THE
MINDS OF THESE UNBELIEVERS LEST THEY SEE
THE RADIANCE OF THE GLORIOUS GOSPEL OF CHRIST,
WHO IS GOD'S IMAGE. (5) IT IS NOT OURSELVES
WE PREACH, BUT CHRIST JESUS AS LORD; AND
FOR JESUS' SAKE WE BECOME YOUR SERVANTS.
(6) GOD WHO SAID,
"LET THE LIGHT SHINE OUT OF DARKNESS"
HAS ALSO MADE THE LIGHT SHINE IN OUR HEARTS TO
RADIATE AND TO MAKE KNOWN THE GLORY OF GOD, AS

IT SHINES IN THE FACE OF CHRIST. (7) HOWEVER,
WE CARRY THIS TREASURE IN VESSELS OF CLAY,
SO THAT THIS ALL-SURPASSING POWER MAY
NOT BE SEEN AS OURS BUT AS GOD'S.
(8) TRIALS OF EVERY SORT COME TO US, BUT WE
ARE NOT DISCOURAGED. (9) WE ARE LEFT WITH-
OUT ANSWER, BUT DO NOT DESPAIR; PERSECUTED
BUT NOT ABANDONED, KNOCKED DOWN BUT NOT
CRUSHED. (10) WE CARRY EVERYWHERE IN OUR
PERSON THE DEATH OF
JESUS, SO THAT THE
LIFE OF JESUS MAY
ALSO BE MANIFESTED
IN US. (11) FOR WE, THE
LIVING, ARE GIVEN UP
TO DEATH FOR JESUS'
SAKE, SO THAT THE LIFE
OF JESUS MAY APPEAR
IN OUR MORTAL EXIST-
ENCE. (12) AND AS DE-
ATH IS AT WORK IN US,
LIFE COMES TO YOU.
(13) WE HAVE RECE-
IVED THE SAME SPIRIT
OF FAITH REFERRED
TO IN SCRIPTURE THAT
SAYS: 'I BELIEVED
AND SO I SPOKE.'
WE ALSO BELIEVE
AND SO WE SPEAK.

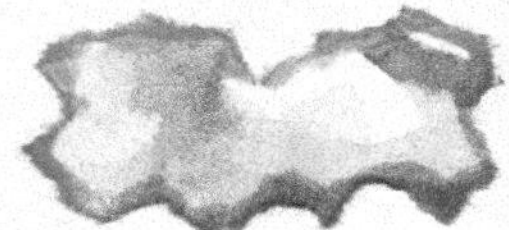

(14) WE KNOW THAT HE WHO RAISED THE LORD
JESUS WILL ALSO RAISE US WITH JESUS
AND BRING US, WITH YOU, INTO HIS PRESENCE.

(15) FINALLY, EVERYTHING IS FOR YOUR OWN GOOD,
SO THAT GRACE WILL COME MORE ABUNDAN-
TLY UPON YOU AND GREAT WILL BE THE
THANKSGIVING FOR THE GLORY OF GOD.

SAINT BARNABAS · FRA ANGELICO ·
DOMINICAN PRIORY - SAN MARCO · FLORENCE ·
383 CCCLXXXIII

OUR HEAVENLY DWELLING

16 SO WE ARE NOT DISCOURAGED. ON THE CONTRARY, AS
OUR OUTER BEING WASTES AWAY, THE INNER SELF IS RE-
NEWED EVERY DAY. 17 THE SLIGHT AFFLICTION WHICH
QUICKLY PASSES AWAY PREPARES US FOR AN ETER-
NAL WEALTH OF GLORY SO GREAT AND BEYOND ALL
COMPARISON. 18 SO WE NO LONGER PAY ATTENT-
ION TO THE THINGS THAT ARE SEEN, BUT TO THOSE THAT
ARE UNSEEN, FOR THE THINGS THAT WE SEE LAST FOR
A MOMENT, BUT THAT WHICH CANNOT BE SEEN IS ETERNAL.

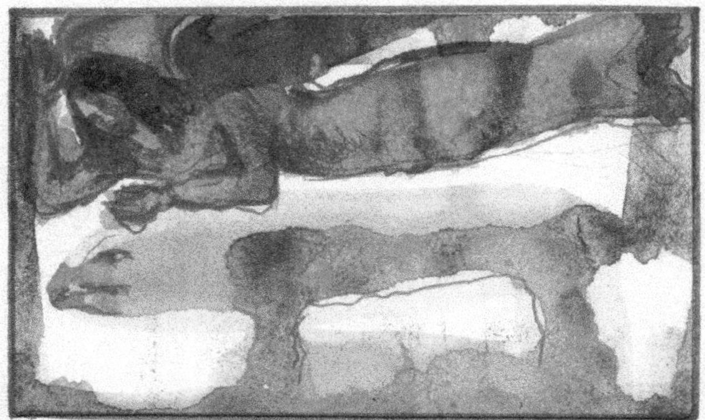

5 1 WE KNOW THAT WHEN OUR EARTHLY DWEL-
LING, OR RATHER OUR TENT, IS DESTROYED, WE
MAY COUNT ON A BUILDING FROM GOD, A HEAVEN-
LY DWELLING NOT BUILT BY HUMAN HANDS, THAT LASTS
FOREVER. 2 THEREFORE WE LONG AND GROAN: WHY
MAY WE NOT PUT ON THIS HEAVENLY DWELLING OVER
THAT WHICH WE HAVE? 3 ARE WE SURE THAT WE
SHALL STILL BE WEARING OUR EARTHLY DWELLING
AND NOT BE UNCLOTHED? 4 AS LONG AS WE ARE
IN THE FIELD-TENT, WE INDEED MOAN OUR UN-
BEARABLE FATE FOR

WE DO NOT WANT THIS
CLOTHING TO BE REMO-
VED FROM US; WE
WOULD RATHER PUT
THE OTHER OVER IT
THAT THE MORTAL BO-
DY MAY BE ABSORBED
BY TRUE LIFE. 5
THIS IS GOD'S PURPOSE
FOR US, AND HE HAS GIV-
EN US THE SPIRIT AS A
PLEDGE OF WHAT WE ARE
TO RECEIVE. 6 SO WE
FEEL CONFIDENT ALWAYS.
WE KNOW THAT WHILE
LIVING IN THE BODY, WE
WANDER AWAY FROM THE
LORD, 7 LIVING BY
FAITH, WITHOUT SEEING;
8 BUT WE DARE TO
THINK THAT HE WOULD
BE AWAY FROM THE BODY
TO GO AND LIVE WITH THE
LORD. 9 SO, TO KEEP
THIS HOUSE OR LOSE IT,
WE ONLY WISH TO PLEASE THE LORD. 10 FOR WE HAVE
TO BE BROUGHT TO LIGHT BEFORE THE TRIBUNAL OF CHRIST
FOR EACH ONE TO RECEIVE WHAT HE DESERVES FOR HIS GO-
OD OR EVIL DEEDS IN THE PRESENT LIFE.

MESSAGE OF RECONCILIATION ~

11 SO WE KNOW THE FEAR OF THE LORD AND WE
TRY TO CONVINCE PEOPLE WHILE WE LIVE OPEN-
LY BEFORE GOD. AND I TRUST THAT YOU KNOW IN YOUR
CONSCIENCE WHAT WE TRULY ARE.
12 WE DO NOT TRY TO WIN YOUR ESTEEM AGAIN;
WE WANT TO GIVE YOU A REASON TO FEEL PROUD
OF US, THAT YOU MAY RESPOND TO THOSE WHO
HEED APPEARANCES AND NOT THE REALITY. 13
NOW, IF I HAVE SPOKEN FOOLISHLY, LET GOD
ALONE HEAR; IF WHAT I HAVE SAID MAKES
SENSE, TAKE IT FOR YOURSELVES.
14 INDEED THE LOVE OF CHRIST HOLDS US AND
WE REALIZE THAT IF HE DIED FOR ALL, ALL HAVE DIED.
15 HE DIED FOR ALL

SO THAT THOSE WHO LI-
VE MAY LIVE NO LON-
GER FOR THEMSELVES,
BUT FOR HIM WHO DIED
AND ROSE AGAIN FOR
THEM. 16 AND SO
FROM NOW ON, WE DO
NOT REGARD ANYONE
FROM A HUMAN POINT
OF VIEW; AND EVEN IF
WE ONCE KNEW CHRIST
PERSONALLY, WE SHOULD
NOW REGARD HIM IN AN-
OTHER WAY. 17 FOR THAT
SAME REASON, HE WHO
IS IN CHRIST IS A NEW
CREATURE. FOR HIM
THE OLD THINGS
HAVE PASSED AWAY;
A NEW WORLD HAS
COME. 18 ALL THIS
IS THE WORK OF GOD
WHO IN CHRIST RE-
CONCILED US TO
HIMSELF, AND WHO ENTRUSTED TO US THE MINIS-
TRY OF RECONCILIATION, 19 BECAUSE IN CHRIST
GOD RECONCILED THE WORLD WITH HIMSELF, NO
LONGER TAKING INTO ACCOUNT THEIR TRESPAS-
SES AND ENTRUSTING TO US THE MESSAGE OF
RECONCILATION.
20 SO WE PRESENT OURSELVES AS AMBASSADORS IN
THE NAME OF CHRIST, AS IF GOD HIMSELF MAKES AN

APPEAL TO YOU THROUGH US. LET GOD RECONCILE YOU;
THIS WE ASK YOU IN THE NAME OF CHRIST. 21 HE HAD
NO SIN, BUT GOD MADE HIM BEAR OUR SIN, SO THAT IN
HIM WE MIGHT SHARE THE HOLINESS OF GOD.

THE TRIALS OF AN APOSTLE

6 1 BEING GOD'S HELPERS WE BEG YOU: LET IT
NOT BE IN VAIN THAT YOU RECEIVED THIS
GRACE OF GOD. 2 SCRIPTURE SAYS: AT THE
FAVORABLE TIME I LISTEN TO YOU, ON THE DAY OF SAL-
VATION I HELP YOU. THIS IS THE FAVORABLE TIME,
THIS IS THE DAY OF SALVATION. 3 WE ARE CONCER-
NED NOT TO GIVE ANYONE AN OCCASION TO STUMBLE
OR CRITICIZE OUR MISSION.

4 INSTEAD WE PROVE WE ARE TRUE MINISTERS OF
GOD IN EVERY WAY BY OUR ENDURANCE IN SO MANY
TRIALS, IN HARDSHIPS, AFFLICTIONS, FLOGGINGS,
5 IMPRISONMENT, RIOTS, FATIGUE, SLEEPLESS
NIGHTS AND DAYS OF HUNGER. 6 PEOPLE CAN NO-
TICE IN OUR UPRIGHT LIFE, KNOWLEDGE, PATIENCE
AND KINDNESS, ACTION OF THE HOLY SPIRIT, 7
SINCERE LOVE, WORDS OF TRUTH AND POWER OF
GOD. SO WE FIGHT WITH THE WEAPONS OF JUSTICE,
TO ATTACK AS WELL AS TO DEFEND. 8 SOMETIMES

WE ARE HONORED, OTHER TIMES INSULTED; WE RECE-
IVE CRITICISM AS WELL AS PRAISE. WE ARE REGARD-
ED AS LIARS ALTHOUGH WE SPEAK THE TRUTH; 9 AS
UNKNOWN THOUGH WE ARE WELL KNOWN; AS DEAD
AND YET WE LIVE. PUNISHMENTS COME UPON US
BUT WE HAVE NOT, AS YET, BEEN PUT TO DEATH. 10
WE APPEAR TO BE AFFLICTED, BUT WE REMAIN HAP-
PY; WE SEEM TO BE POOR, BUT WE ENRICH MANY; AP-
PARENTLY WE HAVE NOTHING, BUT WE POSSESS EVERY-
THING! 11 CORINTHIANS! I HAVE SPOKEN TO YOU AND
I HAVE UNCOVERED MY IN-
NER THOUGHT. 12 MY
HEART IS WIDE OPEN TO YOU,
BUT YOU FEEL UNEASY BE-
CAUSE OF YOUR CLOSED
HEART; 13 REPAY US
WITH THE SAME MEASU-
RE, I SPEAK TO YOU AS TO
MY CHILDREN, OPEN YOUR
HEARTS WIDE ALSO.

HAVE NOTHING TO DO WITH EVIL

14 DON'T MAKE COVEN-
ANTS WITH THE UNBELIE-
VERS: CAN JUSTICE WALK
WITH WICKEDNESS? CAN
LIGHT COEXIST WITH DARK-
NESS 15 AND CAN BE HAR-
MONY BETWEEN CHRIST AND
SATAN? WHAT UNION CAN BE
BETWEEN ONE WHO BELIE-
VES AND ONE WHO DOES
NOT BELIEVE? 16 GOD'S
TEMPLE MUST NOT HAVE IDOLS, AND WE ARE THE TEMPLE OF
THE LIVING GOD, AS SCRIPTURE SAYS; I WILL DWELL AND
LIVE IN THEIR MIDST, I WILL BE THEIR GOD AND THEY
SHALL BE MY PEOPLE. 17 THEREFORE: COME OUT
FROM THEIR MIDST AND SEPARATE FROM THEM, SAYS THE
LORD. DO NOT TOUCH ANYTHING UNCLEAN 18 AND I WILL
BE GRACIOUS TO YOU. I WILL BE A FATHER TO YOU, THAT YOU
MAY BECOME MY SONS AND DAUGHTERS, SAYS THE POWERFUL GOD.

7 1 SINCE WE HAVE SUCH PROMISES, DEAR FRIENDS,
LET US PURIFY OURSELVES FROM ALL DEFILEMENT OF
BODY AND SPIRIT, AND COMLETE THE WORK OF
SANCTIFICATION IN THE FEAR OF GOD.

WELCOME US IN YOUR HEARTS ~

2 WELCOME US IN YOUR HEARTS. WE HAVE INJURED
NO ONE, WE HAVE HARMED NO ONE, WE HAVE CHEATED
NO ONE. 3 I DO NOT SAY THIS TO CONDEMN YOU; I HA-
VE JUST SAID THAT YOU ARE IN OUR HEART TO LIVE TO-
GETHER AND DIE AS ONE. 4 I HAVE GREAT CONFIDENCE
IN YOU AND I AM INDEED PROUD OF YOU. I FEEL VERY MU-
CH ENCOURAGED AND MY JOY OVERFLOWS IN SPITE
OF ALL THIS BITTERNESS. 5 KNOW THAT WHEN I
CAME TO MACEDONIA,
I HAD NO REST AT ALL
BUT I WAS AFFLICTED BY
ALL KINDS OF DIFFICUL-
TIES: CONFLICT OUTSI-
DE AND FEAR WITHIN.
6 BUT GOD WHO ENCO-
URAGES THE HUMBLE GA-
VE ME COMFORT WITH
THE ARRIVAL OF TITUS,
7 NOT ONLY BECAUSE
OF HIS ARRIVAL, BUT AL-
SO BECAUSE YOU HAD
RECEIVED HIM VERY
WELL. HE TOLD ME OF
YOUR DEEP AFFECTION
FOR ME: YOU WERE AF-
FECTED BY WHAT HAPPE-
NED, YOU WORRIED AB-
OUT ME, AND THIS MA-
DE ME REJOICE ALL
THE MORE. 8 IF MY
LETTER CAUSED YOU

PAIN, I DO NOT REGRET IT. PERHAPS I DID REGRET
IT, FOR I SAW THAT THE LETTER CAUSED YOU SADNESS
FOR A MOMENT BUT NOW I REJOICE, 9 NOT BE-
CAUSE OF YOUR SADNESS BROUGHT YOU TO RE-
PENTANCE.

THIS IS A SADNESS FROM GOD, SO THAT NO
EVIL CAME TO YOU BECAUSE OF ME.
10 SADNESS FROM GOD BRINGS FIRM

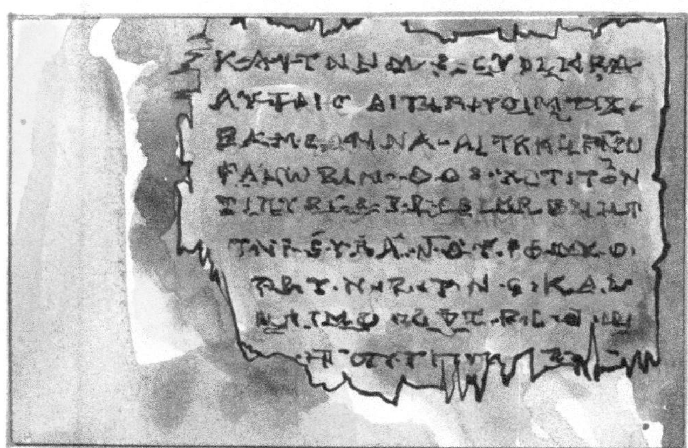

REPENTANCE THAT LEADS TO SALVATION
AND BRINGS NO REGRET, BUT WORDLY
GRIEF PRODUCES DEATH.
11 SEE WHAT THIS SADNESS FROM GOD
HAS PRODUCED IN YOU: WHAT CONCERN
FOR ME! WHAT APOLOGIES! WHAT IND-
IGNATION AND FEAR! WHAT A LONGING
TO SEE ME, TO MAKE AMENDS AND DO ME
JUSTICE!
YOU HAVE FULLY PROVED THAT YOU WE-
RE INNOCENT IN THIS MATTER.

12 IN REALITY, I WROTE TO YOU NOT ON
ACCOUNT OF THE OFFENDER OR OF THE OF
FENDED, BUT THAT YOU MAY BE CONSCIOUS
OF THE CONCERN YOU HAVE FOR ME BEFORE
GOD. 13 I WAS ENCO-
URAGED BY THIS.
IN ADDITION TO THIS
CONSOLATION OF
MINE, I REJOICE ES-
PECIALLY TO SEE TITUS
VERY PLEASED WITH
THE WAY YOU ALL
REASSURED HIM.
14 I HAD NO CAUSE
TO REGRET MY PRA-
ISE OF YOU TO HIM.
YOU KNOW THAT I AM
ALWAYS SINCERE
WITH YOU; LIKEWISE
MY PRAISE OF YOU TO
TITUS HAS BEEN JUS-
TIFIED. 15 HE NOW
FEELS MUCH MORE AF-
FECTION FOR YOU AS
HE REMEMBERS THE
OBEDIENCE OF ALL
AND THE RESPECT AND
HUMILITY WITH WHICH
YOU RECEIVED HIM.

16 REALLY I REJOICE
FOR I CAN BE TRULY PROUD OF YOU.

THE COLLECTION FOR THOSE IN JERUSALEM

8 1 THEN, NOW I WANT TO KNOW ABOUT A
GIFT OF DIVINE GRACE AMONG THE CHURCHES
OF MACEDONIA. 2 WHILE THEY WERE SO
AFFLICTED AND PERSECUTED, THEIR JOY OVER-
FLOWED AND THEIR EXTREME POVERTY TURNED IN-
TO A WEALTH OF GENEROSITY. 3-4 ACCORDING
TO THEIR MEANS, EVEN BEYOND THEIR MEANS,
THEY WANTED TO SHARE IN HELPING THE SAINTS.
THEY ASKED US FOR THIS FAVOR SPONTANEOUSLY

AND WITH MUCH INSISTENCE 5 AND, FAR
BEYOND ANYTHING WE EXPECTED, THEY
PUT THEMSELVES AT THE DISPOSAL OF
THE LORD AND OF US BY THE WILL OF GOD.

6 ACCORDINGLY, I URGED TITUS TO COMPLE-
TE AMONG YOU THIS WORK OF GRACE
SINCE HE BEGAN IT WITH YOU.

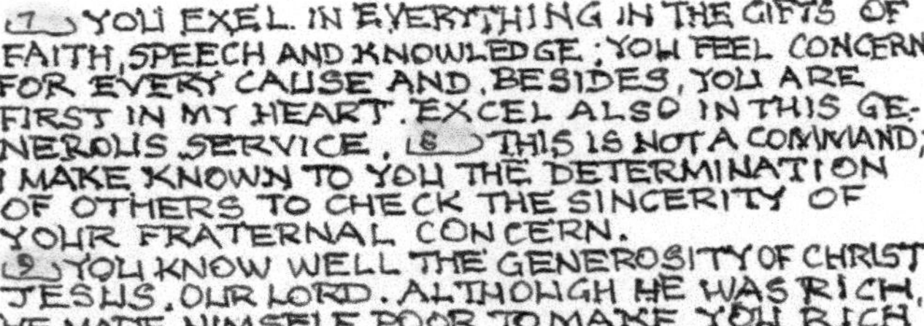
7 YOU EXEL IN EVERYTHING IN THE GIFTS OF
FAITH, SPEECH AND KNOWLEDGE; YOU FEEL CONCERN
FOR EVERY CAUSE AND, BESIDES, YOU ARE
FIRST IN MY HEART. EXCEL ALSO IN THIS GE-
NEROUS SERVICE. 8 THIS IS NOT A COMMAND;
I MAKE KNOWN TO YOU THE DETERMINATION
OF OTHERS TO CHECK THE SINCERITY OF
YOUR FRATERNAL CONCERN.
9 YOU KNOW WELL THE GENEROSITY OF CHRIST
JESUS, OUR LORD. ALTHOUGH HE WAS RICH,
HE MADE HIMSELF POOR TO MAKE YOU RICH

THROUGH HIS POVERTY. 10 I ONLY MAKE A
SUGGESTION, BECAUSE YOU WERE THE FIRST
NOT ONLY IN COOPERATING, BUT IN BEGIN-
NING THIS PROJECT A YEAR AGO.
11 SO COMPLETE THIS WORK AND, ACCORDING
TO YOUR MEANS, CARRY OUT WHAT YOU DE-
CIDED WITH MUCH ENTHUSIASM.

12 WHEN THERE IS A GOOD DISPOSITION,
EVERYTHING YOU GIVE IS WELCOMED AND
NO ONE LONGS FOR
WHAT YOU DO NOT
HAVE. 13 I DO NOT
MEAN THAT OTHERS
SHOULD BE AT EASE
AND YOU BURDENED.
STRIVE FOR EQUA-
LITY; 14 AT PRES-
ENT GIVE FROM YOUR
ABUNDANCE WHAT
THEY ARE SHORT OF,
AND IN SOME WAY
THEY ALSO WILL GI-
VE FROM THEIR AB-
UNDANCE WHAT YOU
LACK. THEN YOU
WILL BE EQUAL.
15 AND WHAT
SCRIPTURE SAYS
SHALL COME TRUE:
TO HIM WHO HAD
MUCH, NOTHING WAS
IN EXCESS; TO HIM
WHO HAD LITTLE,

NOTHING WAS LACKING. 16 BLESSED BE
GOD WHO INSPIRES TITUS WITH SUCH CA-
RE FOR YOU!
17 HE NOT ONLY LISTENED TO MY APPEAL
BUT HE WANTED TO GO AND SEE YOU ON
HIS OWN INITIATIVE.
18 I AM SENDING WITH HIM THE BROTHER
WHO HAS GAINED THE ESTEEM OF THE CHUR-
CHES IN THE WORK OF THE GOSPEL.

384- CCCLXXXIV
DM 09 ©

19 MOREOVER THEY APPOINTED HIM TO TRAVEL
WITH US IN THIS BLESSED WORK WE ARE CARRY-
ING ON FOR THE GLORY OF THE LORD BUT ALSO BE-
CAUSE OF OUR PERSONAL ENTHUSIASM.
20 WE DECIDED ON THIS SO THAT NO ONE CO-
ULD SUSPECT US WITH REGARD TO THIS GE-
NEROUS FUND THAT WE ARE ADMINISTERING.
21 LET US SEE TO IT THAT ALL MAY
APPEAR CLEAN NOT ONLY BEFORE GOD
BUT ALSO BEFORE
PEOPLE. 22 WE
ALSO SEND WITH
THEM ANOTHER
BROTHER WHO ON
SEVERAL OCCA-
SIONS HAS SHOWN
US HIS ZEAL AND,
NOW, IS MORE EN-
THUSIASTIC BECA-
USE OF HIS CONFI-
DENCE IN YOU.

23 YOU THEN HAVE
TITUS, OUR COM-
PANION AND MIN-
ISTER, TO SERVE
YOU AND, WITH HIM,
YOU HAVE OUR BRO-
THERS, REPRESE-
NTATIVES OF THE
CHURCHES AND A
GLORY OF CHRIST.
24 SHOW THEM
HOW YOU LOVE,
AND PROVE BEFORE
THE CHURCHES ALL THE GOOD THINGS I SAID
TO THEM ABOUT YOU.

MORE ABOUT THE COLLECTION

9 1 IT IS NOT NECESSARY FOR ME TO WRITE
TO YOU ABOUT ASSISTANCE TO THE SAINTS.
2 I KNOW YOUR READINESS AND I PRAIS-
ED YOU BEFORE THE MACEDONIANS. I SAID, "IN
ACHAIA THEY HAVE BEEN READY FOR THE COL-
LECTION SINCE LAST YEAR." AND YOUR EN-
THUSIASM CARRIED MOST OF THEM ALONG.
3 SO I SEND YOU THESE BROTHERS OF
OURS. MAY ALL MY PRAISE OF YOU NOT

FALL FLAT IN THIS CASE! MAY YOU BE
READY, AS I SAID 4 IF SOME MACEDONI-
ANS COME WITH ME; LET THEM NOT FIND
YOU UNPREPARED. WHAT A SHAME FOR ME,
AND PERHAPS FOR YOU, AFTER SO MUCH CONFI-
DENCE! 5 SO I THOUGHT IT NECESSARY TO ASK
OUR BROTHERS TO GO AHEAD OF US AND SEE YOU
TO ORGANIZE THIS BLESSED WORK YOU HAVE
PROMISED.

IT SHALL COME FROM YOUR GENEROSITY AND
NOT BE AN IMPOSED TASK.

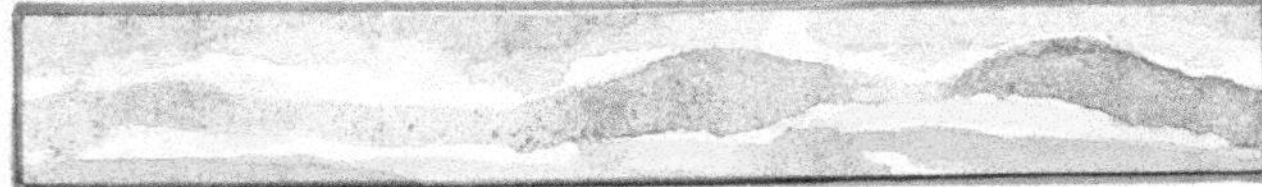

6 REMEMBER: HE WHO SOWS MEAGERLY WILL
REAP MEAGERLY, AND THERE SHALL BE GENERO-
US HARVESTS FOR HIM WHO SOWS GENEROUS-
LY. 7 LET EACH ONE GIVE WHAT HE DECIDED
UPON PERSONALLY, AND NOT RELUCTANTLY

AS IF OBLIGED. GOD LOVES A CHEERFUL GIVER. 8 AND
GOD IS ABLE TO FILL YOU WITH EVERY GOOD THING,
SO THAT YOU HAVE ENOUGH OF EVERYTHING AT
ALL TIMES, AND MAY GIVE ABUNDANTLY
FOR ANY GOOD WORK.
9 SCRIPTURE SAYS: HE DISTRIBUTED, HE GA-
VE TO THE POOR, HIS GOOD WORKS LAST FOR-
EVER. 10 GOD WHO
PROVIDES THE SOWER
WITH SEED WILL AL-
SO PROVIDE HIM THE
BREAD HE EATS. HE
WILL MULTIPLY THE
SEED FOR YOU AND
ALSO INCREASE THE
INTERESTS OF YOUR
GOOD WORKS. 11
BECOME RICH IN
EVERY WAY, AND
GIVE ABUNDANTLY.
WHAT YOU GIVE WILL
BECOME, THROUGH
US, A THANKSGIVING
TO GOD.

12 FOR THIS SA-
CRED RELIEF, AF-
TER PROVIDING
THE SAINTS WITH
WHAT THEY NEED,
WILL RESULT IN
MUCH THANKSGIVING TO GOD. 13 THIS WILL
BE A TEST FOR THEM: THEY WILL GIVE
THANKS BECAUSE YOU OBEY THE RE-
QUIREMENTS OF CHRIST'S GOSPEL AND
SHARE GENEROUSLY WITH THEM AND
WITH ALL.

14 THEY SHALL PRAY TO GOD FOR YOU
AND FEEL AFFECTION FOR YOU BECAUSE
THE GRACE OF GOD OVERFLOWS IN YOU.

15 YES, THANKS BE TO GOD FOR HIS
INDESCRIBABLE GIFT!

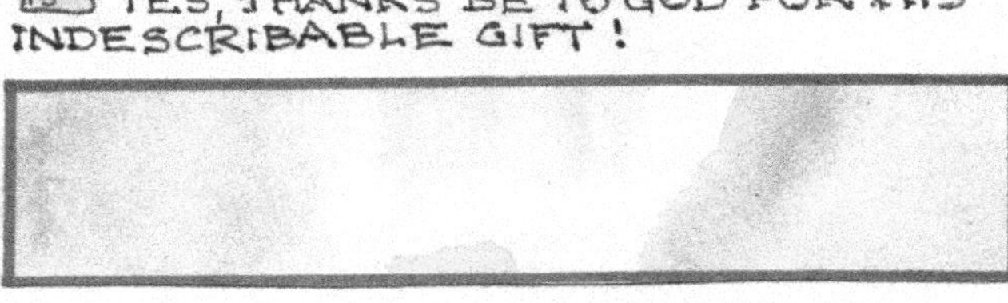

PAUL'S DEFENSE AND ADMONITION

10 (1) IT IS I, PAUL, WHO BY THE HUMILITY AND
KINDNESS OF CHRIST APPEAL TO YOU. THE PAUL
"WHO IS TIMID AMONG YOU AND BOLD WHEN FAR
AWAY FROM YOU!" (2) DO NOT FORCE ME TO ACT BOLD-
LY WHEN I COME, AS I AM DETERMINED AND WILL DARE
TO ACT AGAINST SOME PEOPLE WHO THINK THAT I ACT
FROM HUMAN MOTIVES.
(3) ALTHOUGH I LIVE IN THIS WORLD, I DO NOT

FIGHT IN A HUMAN WAY. (4) OUR WEAPONS ARE
NOT HUMAN WEAPONS BUT THEY HAVE DIVINE
POWER TO DESTROY STRONGHOLDS. WE DESTROY
ARGUMENTS AND HAUGHTY THOUGHTS WHICH
(5) OPPOSE THE KNOWLEDGE OF GOD.
WE COMPEL ALL UNDERSTANDING TO OBEY CHRIST,
(6) AND I AM PREPARED TO PUNISH ANY DIS-
OBEDIENCE WHEN YOU SHOULD SHOW PER-
FECT OBEDIENCE.
(7) SEE THINGS AS THEY REALLY ARE; IF ANY-

ONE IS CONVINCED
THAT HE BELONGS
TO CHRIST, LET HIM
CONSIDER THAT JUST
AS HE IS CHRIST'S,
SO AM I.
(8) ALTHOUGH I MAY
SEEM TOO CONFIDENT
IN THE AUTHORITY
THAT THE LORD GA-
VE ME FOR BUILD-
ING YOU UP AND NOT
FOR PULLING YOU
DOWN, I WILL NOT
BE PUT TO SHAME
FOR SAYING THIS.
(9) DO NOT THINK
THAT I CAN ONLY
FRIGHTEN YOU
WITH LETTERS.

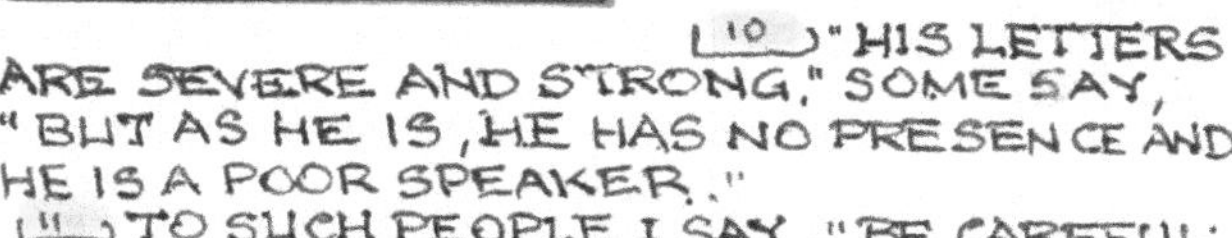

(10) "HIS LETTERS
ARE SEVERE AND STRONG," SOME SAY,
"BUT AS HE IS, HE HAS NO PRESENCE AND
HE IS A POOR SPEAKER."
(11) TO SUCH PEOPLE I SAY, "BE CAREFUL:
WHAT MY LETTERS SAY FROM AFAR, IS
WHAT I WILL DO WHEN I COME."

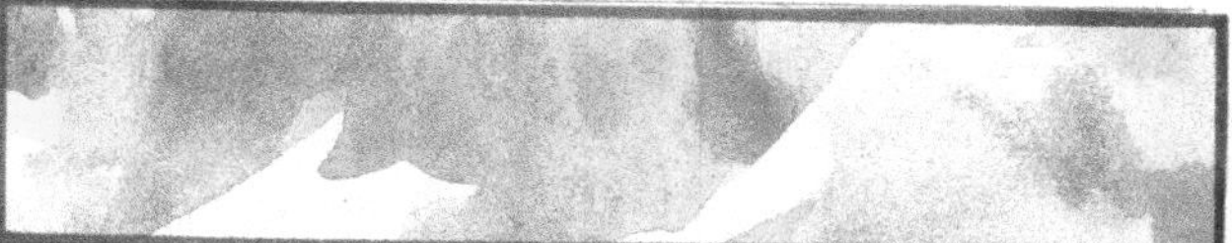

(12) HOW COULD I VENTURE TO EQUATE, OR
COMPARE MYSELF WITH PEOPLE WHO PRO-
CLAIM THEIR OWN MERITS?
FOOLS! THEY MEASURE THEMSELVES WITH
THEIR OWN MEASURE AND COMPARE THEM-
SELVES WITH THEMSELVES.

(13) AS FOR ME, I WILL NOT BOAST BEYOND
MEASURE, FOR I WILL NOT GO PAST THE
LIMITS THAT THE
GOD OF TRUE ME-
ASURE HAS SET
FOR ME: HE GAVE
THE MEASURING
STICK WHEN HE
MADE ME SET
FOOT IN YOUR
PLACE.
(14) IT IS NOT THE
SAME WHEN SOME-
ONE GOES BEYOND
HIS FIELD TO A
PLACE WHERE HE
HAS NOT BEEN
ABLE TO SET FO-
OT. BUT I AM HE
WHO FIRST RE-
ACHED YOU WITH
THE GOSPEL OF
CHRIST. (15) I AM
NOT MAKING MY-
SELF IMPORTANT
WHERE OTHERS

HAVE WORKED. ON THE CONTRARY, WE
HOPE THAT AS YOUR FAITH INCREASES,
SO TOO OUR AREA OF MINISTRY AMONG
YOU WILL BE ENLARGED WITHOUT GOING
BEYOND OUR LIMIT. (16) SO WE SHALL BRING
THE GOSPEL TO PLACES BEYOND YOURS WITHOUT
ENTERING INTO THE FIELD OF OTHERS, OR BOAST-
ING AND MAKING OURSELVES IMPORTANT WHERE
THE WORK IS ALREADY DONE. (17) HE WHO BOASTS,
LET HIM BOAST IN THE LORD. (18) IT IS NOT THE
ONE WHO COMMENDS HIMSELF WHO IS APPRO-
VED, BUT HE WHOM THE LORD COMMENDS.

11 (1) MAY YOU BEAR WITH ME IN LITTLE FOOLISH-
NESS! BUT YOU WILL. (2) I CONFESS THAT I SHARE
THE JEALOUSY OF GOD FOR YOU, FOR I HAVE PRO-
MISED YOU IN MARRIAGE TO CHRIST, THE ONLY SPOUSE, TO

PRESENT YOU TO HIM AS A PURE VIRGIN. (3) AND THIS
IS MY FEAR: THE SERPENT THAT SEDUCED EVE WITH
CUNNING COULD ALSO CORRUPT YOUR MINDS AND DI-
VERT YOU FROM THE CHRISTIAN SINCERITY. (4)
SOMEONE NOW COMES AND PREACHES ANOTHER
JESUS DIFFERENT FROM THE ONE WE PREACH,
OR YOU ARE OFFERED A DIFFERENT SPIRIT FROM
THE ONE YOU HAVE RECEIVED, WITH A DIFFERENT
GOSPEL FROM THE ONE YOU HAVE ACCEPTED, AND YOU AGREE!

5 I DO NOT SEE HOW I AM INFERIOR TO THOSE
SUPER-APOSTLES. 6 DOES MY SPEAKING LE-
AVE MUCH TO BE DESIRED? PERHAPS, BUT NOT
MY KNOWLEDGE, AS I HAVE ABUNDANTLY TO
YOU SHOWN IN EVERY WAY.

PAUL COMMENDS THE APOSTLE PAUL

7 PERHAPS MY SIN WAS THAT I HUMBLED MYSELF
IN ORDER TO UPLIFT YOU, OR THAT I GAVE YOU THE

GOSPEL FREE OF CHARGE. 8 I CALLED UPON THE SER-
VICES OF OTHER CHURCHES AND SERVED YOU WITH THE
SUPPORT I RECEIVED FROM THEM. 9 WHEN I WAS
WITH YOU, ALTHOUGH I WAS IN NEED, I DID NOT BE-
COME A BURDEN TO ANYONE. THE BROTHERS FROM
MACEDONIA GAVE ME WHAT I NEEDED. I HAVE TA-
KEN CARE NOT TO BE A BURDEN TO YOU IN
ANYTHING AND I WILL CONTINUE TO DO SO. 10 BY
THE TRUTH OF CHRIST WITHIN ME, I WILL
LET NO ONE IN THE LAND OF ACHAIA STOP
THIS BOASTING OF MINE. 11 WHY? BECA-
USE I DID NOT LOVE YOU? GOD KNOWS THAT

I DO! 12 AND I WILL
CONTINUE TO DO SO
TO SILENCE ANY PE-
OPLE ANXIOUS TO
COMPLETE WITH ME
AND APPEAR AS EQU-
AL TO ME. 13 IN RE-
ALITY, THEY ARE FALSE
APOSTLES, DECEIVERS
DISGUISED AS APOS-
TLES OF CHRIST. 14 IT
IS NOT SURPRISING:
IF SATAN DISGUISES
HIMSELF HIMSELF AS
AN ANGEL OF LIGHT,
15 HIS SERVANTS
CAN EASILY DISGUISE
THEMSELVES AS MI-
NISTERS OF SALVATI-
ON, UNTIL THEY RE-
CEIVE WHAT THEIR
DEEDS DESERVE.
16 I SAY AGAIN:
DO NOT TAKE ME
FOR A FOOL, BUT
IF YOU DO TAKE ME
AS SUCH, BEAR WITH
ME THAT I MAY SING MY OWN PRAISE A
LITTLE.
17 I WILL NOT SPEAK IN THE LANGUAGE
OF CHRIST, BUT IN THAT OF A FOOL, BRINGING
MY OWN MERITS TO PROMINENCE.

18 AS SOME PEOPLE BOAST OF HUMAN ADVAN-
TAGES, I WILL DO THE SAME. 19 FORTUNATELY
YOU BEAR RATHER WELL WITH FOOLS, YOU WHO
ARE SO WISE! 20 YOU TOLERATE BEING EN-
SLAVED AND EXPLOITED, ROBBED, TREATED WITH
CONTEMPT AND SLAPPED IN THE FACE. WHAT
21 A SHAME THAT I ACTED SO WEAKLY WITH
YOU! BUT IF OTHERS ARE SO BOLD, I SHALL
ALSO DARE, ALTHOUGH I MAY SPEAK LIKE A
FOOL. 22 ARE THEY HEBREWS? SO AM I.
ARE THEY ISRAELITES? SO AM I. ARE THEY
DESCENDANTS OF
ABRAHAM? SO AM I.
23 ARE THEY MI-
NISTERS OF CHRIST?
(I BEGIN TO TALK
LIKE A MADMAN) I AM
BETTER THAN THEY.
BETTER THAN THEY
WITH MY NUMEROUS
LABORS. BETTER THAN
THEY WITH THE TIME
SPENT IN PRISON. THE
BEATINGS I RECEIVED
ARE BEYOND COMPA-
RISON. HOW MANY
TIMES HAVE I FOUND
MYSELF IN DANGER OF
DEATH! 24 FIVE TI-
MES THE JEWS SEN-
TENCED ME TO THIRTY-
NINE LASHES. 25
THREE TIMES I WAS
BEATEN WITH A ROD,
ONCE I WAS STONED.
THREE TIMES I WAS

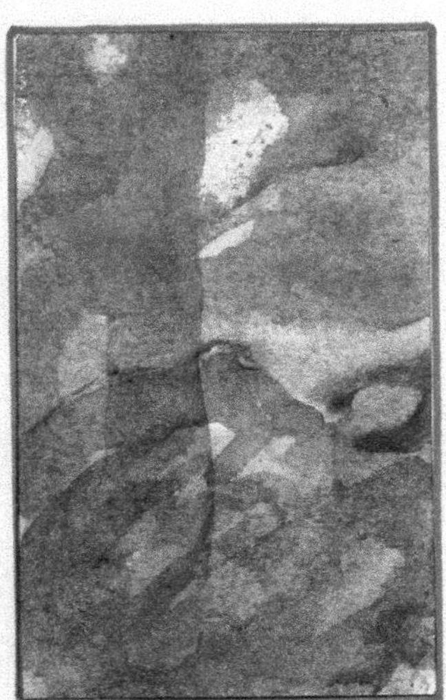

SHIPWRECKED, AND ONCE I SPENT A NIGHT AND
A DAY ADRIFT ON THE HIGH SEAS. 26 I HAVE
BEEN IN HAZARDS OF TRAVELING BECAUSE OF RIVERS,
OF BANDITS, OF MY FELLOW JEWS, OR OF THE PAGANS;
IN DANGER IN THE CITY, OPEN COUNTRY, SEA, AND FALSE
BROTHERS. 27 I HAVE OFTEN WORKED WITHOUT
SLEEP, I HAVE BEEN HUNGRY AND THIRSTY AND STAR-
VING, COLD AND WITHOUT SHELTER. 28 BESIDES
THESE AND OTHER THINGS, THERE WAS MY DAILY CON-
CERN FOR ALL THE CHURCHES. 29 WHOEVER WAVERS, DO

I NOT WAVER WITH HIM? WHOEVER STUMBLES, AM I NOT
ON HOT BRICKS? 30 IF WE BOAST, LET ME TELL YOU
WHEN I WAS FOUND WEAK. 31 THE GOD FATHER OF LORD
JESUS-MAY HE BE BLESSED FOREVER-KNOWS I SPEAK THE
TRUTH. 32 AT DAMASCUS, KING ARETAS' GOVERNOR PLA-
CED THE CITY UNDER GUARD TO ARREST ME. 33 AND I
HAD TO BE LET DOWN IN A BASKET THROUGH A WINDOW IN THE
WALL. IN THAT WAY I SLIPPED THROUGH HIS HANDS.

EXTRAORDINARY GRACES

12 1 IT IS USELESS TO BOAST; BUT IF I HAVE
TO, I WILL GO ON TO SOME VISIONS AND RE-
VELATIONS OF THE LORD. 2 I KNOW A
CERTAIN CHRISTIAN: FOURTEEN YEARS AGO HE
WAS TAKEN UP TO THE THIRD HEAVEN.

HOW MANY TIMES HAVE I FOUND MYSELF IN DANGER OF DEATH! FIVE TIMES THE JEWS SENTENCED ME TO THIRTY-NINE LASHES. THREE TIMES I WAS BEATEN WITH A ROD...
(2 Corinthians 11-25)
385
CCCLXXXV
© DM 09

3 WHETHER THE BODY, IN OR OUT OF IT, I DO
NOT KNOW, GOD KNOWS. BUT I KNOW THAT THIS
MAN, WHETHER IN THE BODY OR OUT OF THE BO-
DY - I DO NOT KNOW, GOD KNOWS - 4 WAS TA-
KEN UP TO PARADISE WHERE HE HEARD WORDS
THAT CANNOT BE TOLD: THINGS WHICH HUMANS
CANNOT EXPRESS. 5 OF THAT MAN I CAN INDEED
BOAST, BUT OF MYSELF I WILL NOT BOAST EX-
CEPT OF MY WEAKNESSES. 6 IF I WANTED TO
BOAST, IT WOULD NOT BE FOOLISH OF ME, FOR I
WOULD SPEAK THE

TRUTH. 7 HOWEVER, I
BETTER GIVE UP LEST
SOMEBODY THINK MO-
RE OF ME THAN HE AC-
TUALLY SEES IN ME OR
HEARS OF ME. LEST I
BECOME PROUD AFTER
SO MANY AND EXTRA-
ORDINARY REVELATIONS,
I WAS GIVEN A THORN
IN MY FLESH, A TRUE
MESSENGER OF SATAN,
TO SLAP ME IN THE FA-
CE. 8 THREE TIMES I
PRAYED TO THE LORD
THAT IT LEAVE ME, 9
BUT HE ANSWERED,
"MY GRACE IS ENOUGH
FOR YOU; MY GREAT
STRENGTH IS REVE-
ALED IN WEAKNESS."
GLADLY, THEN, WILL I
BOAST OF MY WEAK-
NESS THAT THE STRENGTH
OF CHRIST MAY BE MINE.
10 SO I REJOICE
WHEN I SUFFER IN-
FIRMITIES, HUMILIATIONS, WANT, PERSECUTIONS;
ALL FOR CHRIST! FOR WHEN I AM WEAK, THEN I AM
STRONG. 11 I HAVE ACTED AS A FOOL BUT YOU FOR-
CED ME. YOU SHOULD HAVE BEEN THE ONES PRAIS-
ING ME. YET I DO NOT FEEL OUTDONE BY THOSE SUPER-
APOSTLES, 12 EVEN THOUGH I AM NOTHING. ALL
THE SIGNS OF A TRUE APOSTLE ARE FOUND IN ME:
PATIENCE IN ALL TRIALS, SIGNS, MIRACLES AND
WONDERS. 13 NOW, IN WHAT WAY WERE YOU NOT TREATED

LIKE THE REST OF THE CHURCHES? ONLY: I WAS NO BUR-
DEN TO YOU - FORGIVE ME FOR THIS OFFENSE!

THIS IS MY THIRD VISIT TO YOU

14 FOR THE THIRD TIME I PLAN TO VISIT YOU, AND I WILL
NOT BE A BURDEN TO YOU FOR I AM NOT INTERESTED IN
WHAT YOU HAVE BUT ONLY IN YOU. CHILDREN SHOULD
NOT HAVE TO COLLECT MONEY FOR THEIR PARENTS,
BUT THE PARENTS FOR THEIR CHILDREN.

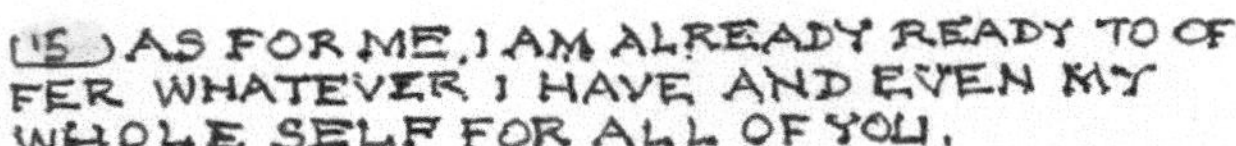

15 AS FOR ME, I AM ALREADY READY TO OF-
FER WHATEVER I HAVE AND EVEN MY
WHOLE SELF FOR ALL OF YOU.

IF I LOVE YOU SO MUCH, AM I TO BE LOVED LESS?

16 WELL, I WAS NOT A BURDEN TO YOU? HAVE
WE NOT PERFORMED A TRICK TO DECEIVE YOU?
TELL ME: 17 DID I TAKE MONEY FROM YOU

THROUGH ANY OF MY MESSENGERS? 18
I ASKED TITUS TO GO TO YOU AND I SENT
ANOTHER BROTHER WITH HIM.

BUT DID TITUS TAKE MONEY FROM
YOU? HAVE WE
BOTH ACTED
IN THE SAME SPI-
RIT? 19 PERHAPS
YOU THINK THAT
WE ARE AGAIN
APOLOGIZING;
BUT NO: WE SPEAK
IN CHRIST AND BE-
FORE GOD, AND I DO
THIS FOR YOU, DEAR

FRIENDS, TO BUILD YOU UP. 20 I FEAR THAT
IF I GO AND SEE YOU, I MIGHT NOT FIND
YOU AS I WOULD WISH, AND YOU IN
TURN, MIGHT NOT FIND ME TO YOUR LIKING.

I MIGHT SEE RIVALRIES,
ENVY, GRUDGES, DISPUTES,
SLANDERS, GOSSIP, CON-
CEIT, DISORDER.

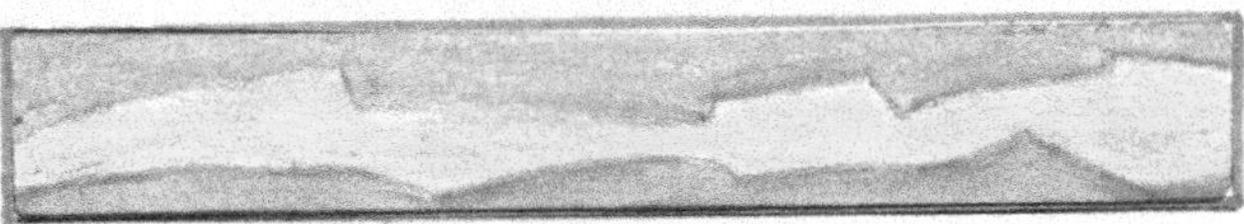

(21) LET IT NOT BE THAT IN COMING AGA-
IN TO YOU, GOD HUMBLE ME BECAUSE
OF YOU AND I HAVE TO GRIEVE OVER
MANY OF THOSE WHO LIVE IN SIN, ON
SEEING THAT THEY HAVE NOT YET GI-
VEN UP AN IMPURE WAY OF LIVING
THEIR WICKED CONDUCT AND THE
VICES THEY FORMERLY PRACTICED.

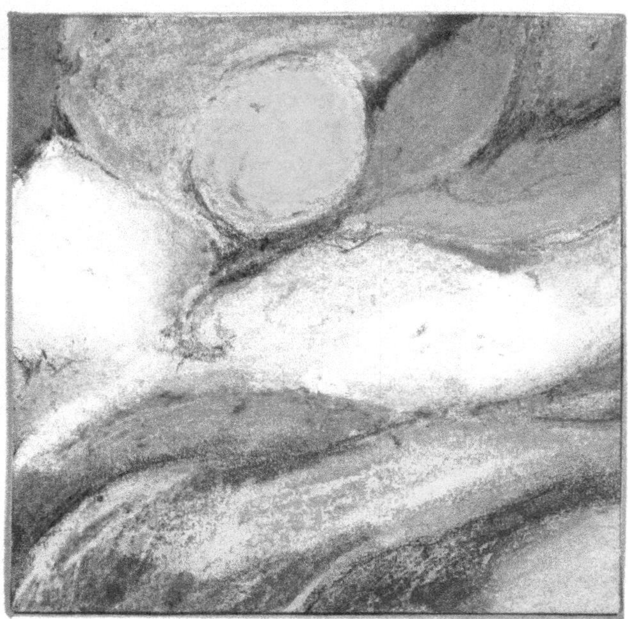

13 (1) THIS WILL BE MY THIRD VISIT TO YOU.
ANY CHARGE MUST BE DECIDED
UPON BY THE DECLARATION OF
TWO OR THREE WITNESSES.

(2) I HAVE SAID THIS AND I SAY IT AGAIN,
JUST AS I DID ON MY SECOND VISIT. BE-
ING STILL FAR AWAY, I SAY TO YOU WHO
LIVED IN SIN AS
WELL AS TO THE
REST: WHEN I
RETURN TO YOU,
I WILL NOT HAVE
PITY.

(3) YOU WANT TO
KNOW IF CHRIST
IS SPEAKING
THROUGH ME?
SO YOU WILL.
HE IS NOT USED
TO DEALING WE-
AKLY WITH YOU,
BUT RATHER HE
ACTS WITH POWER.

(4) IF HE WAS CRU-
CIFIED IN HIS
WEAKNESS,
NOW HE LIVES
BY THE STRENGTH
OF GOD; AND SO
WE ARE WEAK
WITH HIM, BUT HE WILL BE WELL
ALIVE WITH HIM, ESPECIALLY BE-
CAUSE GOD ACTS POWERFULLY WITH
YOU THROUGH HIS HOLINESS.

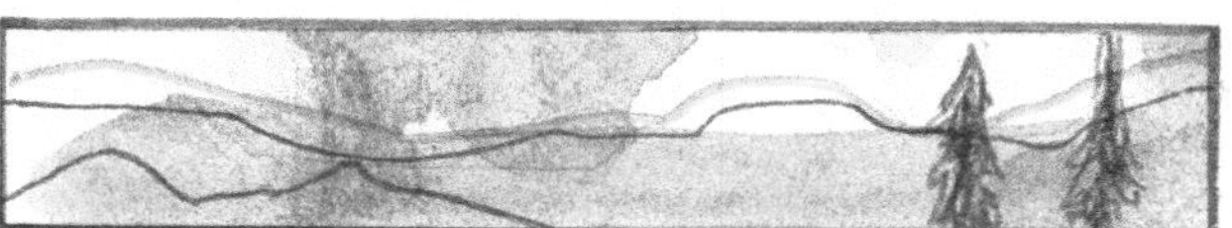

(5) EXAMINE YOURSELVES: ARE YOU
ACTING ACCORDING TO FAITH?
TEST YOURSELVES. CAN YOU ASSERT
THAT CHRIST JESUS IS IN YOU?

(6) IF NOT, YOU HAVE FAILED THE
TEST. I HOPE YOU
RECOGNIZE
THAT WE OUR-
SELVES HAVE
NOT FAILED IT.

(7) WE PRAY GOD
THAT YOU MAY
DO NO WRONG,
NOT THAT WE
WISH TO BE AC-
KNOWLEDGED
BUT WE WANT
YOU TO DO RIGHT,
EVEN IF IN THIS
WE APPEAR TO
HAVE FAILED.

(8) FOR WE DO
NOT HAVE POWER
AGAINST THE
TRUTH, BUT ONLY
FOR THE TRUTH.

(9) WE REJOICE
IF WE ARE WEAK
WHILE YOU ARE STRONG. FOR ALL WE
HOPE IS THAT YOU BECOME PERFECT.

(10) THIS IS WHY I AM WRITING NOW, SO
THAT WHEN I COME I MAY NOT HAVE TO
ACT STRICTLY AND MAKE USE OF THE
AUTHORITY THE LORD HAS GIVEN ME
FOR BUILDING UP AND NOT FOR DESTROYING.

(11) FINALLY, BROTHERS AND SISTERS,
BE HAPPY, STRIVE TO BE PERFECT,
HAVE COURAGE, BE OF ONE MIND
AND LEAVE IN PEACE, AND THE GOD OF

LOVE AND PEACE WILL BE WITH YOU. (12)
GREET ONE ANOTHER WITH A HOLY
KISS. ALL THE SAINTS GREET YOU.

(13) THE GRACE OF CHRIST JESUS THE
LORD, THE LOVE OF GOD AND THE FELLOW-
SHIP OF THE HOLY SPIRIT BE WITH YOU ALL.

THE LETTER TO THE GALATIANS

PAUL WRITES BECAUSE THE COMMUNITY IS IN DANGER. THERE ARE TENSIONS AND DOUBTS: CERTAIN PEOPLE WOULD LIKE TO RESTORE JEWISH PRACTICES, BECAUSE THEY HAVE FORGOTTEN THAT TO BE A CHRISTIAN IT IS NOT FIRST A RELIGION BUT A FAITH.
THE DISCOVERY OF THE GOSPEL HAD BEEN FOR THE GALATIANS A BATH IN FREEDOM. FAITH IS TO GIVE ONESELF TO GOD AND TO HIS MYSTERY, AS AWESOME AS THE CROSS WHICH IS ITS SYMBOL.

THERE IS NO OTHER GOSPEL

1 1 FROM PAUL, AN APOSTLE SENT NOT BY HU-
MANS NOR BY HUMAN MEDIATION BUT BY
CHRIST JESUS AND BY
GOD, THE FATHER, WHO
RAISED HIM FROM THE
DEAD; 2 I AND ALL
THE BROTHERS WHO
ARE WITH ME GRE-
ET THE CHURCHES
IN GALATIA:
3 MAY YOU RECEIVE
GRACE AND PEACE
FROM GOD OUR
FATHER AND FROM
CHRIST JESUS OUR
LORD.
4 HE GAVE HIMSELF
FOR OUR SINS TO
RESCUE US FROM
THIS EVIL WORLD,
IN FULFILLMENT
OF THE WILL OF GOD
THE FATHER:
5 GLORY TO HIM
FOR EVER AND
EVER. 6 I AM SUR-
PRISED AT HOW QUICKLY YOU HAVE ABANDONED
GOD WHO CALLED YOU FOR THE GRACE OF CHRIST,
AND HAVE GONE TO ANOTHER GOSPEL.

7 INDEED, THERE IS NO OTHER GOSPEL, BUT SOME
PEOPLE ARE SOWING CONFUSION AMONG YOU WANT TO
CHANGE THE GOSPEL OF CHRIST. 8 BUT EVEN IF WE
OURSELVES WERE GIVING YOU ANOTHER GOSPEL DIF-
FERENT FROM THE ONE WE PREACHED TO YOU, OR IF IT
WERE AN ANGEL FROM HEAVEN, I WOULD SAY, FIRE
HIM! 9 AS I HAVE SAID I NOW SAY AGAIN: IF AN-
OTHER PREACHES THE GOSPEL IN A WAY OTHER THAN

YOU RECEIVED IT, FIRE HIM. 10 ARE YOU TO PLEASE
HUMANS OR OBEY GOD? DO YOU THINK THAT I TRY TO
PLEASE PEOPLE? IF I WERE STILL TRYING TO PLEASE PE-
OPLE, I WOULD NOT BE A SERVANT OF CHRIST.

PAUL TEACHES WHAT HE RECEIVED FROM GOD

11 LET ME REMIND YOU, BROTHERS, THAT THE GOSPEL
WE PREACHED IS NOT A HUMAN MESSAGE, 12 NOR DID I RE-
CEIVE IT FROM ANYONE, I WAS NOT NOT TAUGHT OF IT BUT IT
CAME TO ME AS A REVELATION FROM CHRIST JESUS.

ECCE
HOMO

386

CCCLXXXVI

©

13 YOU HAVE HEARD OF MY PREVIOUS ACTIVITY
IN THE JEWISH COMMUNITY; I FURIOUSLY PER-
SECUTED THE CHURCH OF GOD AND TRIED TO DES-
TROY IT. 14 FOR I WAS DEVOTED TO THE JEWISH
RELIGION THAN MANY FELLOW JEWS OF MY
AGE, AND I DEFENDED THE TRADITIONS OF MY
FATHER MORE FANATICALLY.
15 BUT YOU KNOW THAT GOD CALLED ME

OUT OF HIS GREAT
LOVE, HE WHO HAD
CHOSEN ME FROM
MY MOTHER'S
WOMB; AND HE WAS
PLEASED 16 TO
REVEAL IN ME HIS
SON, THAT I MIGHT
MAKE HIM KNOWN
AMONG THE PAGAN
NATIONS. THEN I
DID NOT SEEK HU-
MAN ADVICE 17
NOR DID I GO UP TO
JERUSALEM TO
THOSE WHO WERE
APOSTLES BEFORE ME.
I IMMEDIATELY WENT
TO ARABIA, AND FROM
THERE I RETURNED
AGAIN TO DAMASCUS;
18 LATER, AFTER
THREE YEARS, I WENT
UP TO JERUSALEM
TO MEET CEPHAS
AND I STAYED FOR
FIFTEEN DAYS WITH HIM. 19 BUT I DID
NOT SEE ANY OTHER APOSTLE EXCEPT
JAMES, THE LORD'S BROTHER. 20 I SAY ALL THIS
BEFORE GOD, HE KNOWS THAT THIS IS TRUE. 21
AFTER THAT I WENT TO SYRIA AND CILICIA. 22
THE CHURCHES OF CHRIST IN JUDEA DID NOT
KNOW ME PERSONALLY; 23 THEY HAD ONLY

HEARD OF ME: "HE WHO ONCE PERSECUTED US IS NOW
PREACHING THE FAITH HE TRIED TO DESTROY."
24 AND THEY PRAISED GOD BECAUSE OF ME.

PAUL WITH THE APOSTLES

2 1 AFTER FOURTEEN YEARS I AGAIN WENT UP TO JE-
RUSALEM WITH BARNABAS AND TITUS 2 FOLLOW-
ING A REVELATION, I WENT TO LAY BEFORE THEM
THE GOSPEL I WAS PREACHING TO THE PAGANS. I
HAD A PRIVATE MEETING WITH THE LEADERS, LEST
I SHOULD BE WORKING OR HAVE WORKED IN WRONG
WAYS. 3 BUT THEY DIDN'T IMPOSE CIRCUMCISION,
NOT EVEN ON TITUS WHO IS GREEK AND WHO
WAS WITH ME.

4 THERE WERE SOME INTRUDERS AND FALSE
BROTHERS WHO HAD GAINED ACCESS TO WATCH
OVER THE WAY WE LIVE THE FREEDOM CHRIST HAS
GIVEN US. THEY WOULD HAVE US ENSLAVED BY
THE LAW, 5 BUT WE REFUSED TO YIELD EV-
EN FOR A MOMENT; SO THAT THE TRUTH
OF THE GOSPEL REMAIN INTACT IN YOU.

6 THE OTHERS, THE MORE RESPECTABLE
LEADERS - IT DOES NOT MATTER WHAT THEY

WERE BEFORE; GOD PAYS NO ATTENTION TO THE STA-
TUS OF A PERSON - GAVE ME NO NEW INSTRUCTIONS.
7 THEY RECOGNIZED THAT I HAVE BEEN
ENTRUSTED TO GIVE THE GOOD NEWS TO
THE PAGAN NATIONS, JUST AS PETER
HAS BEEN ENTRUSTED TO GIVE IT TO
THE JEWS. 8 IN
THE SAME WAY
THAT GOD MADE
PETER THE APOSTLE
OF THE JEWS, HE MADE
ME THE APOSTLE OF
THE PAGANS. JAMES,
9 PETER AND JOHN
ACKNOWLEDGED THE
GRACE GOD GAVE ME.
THOSE MEN WHO WERE
REGARDED AS THE PIL-
LARS OF THE CHURCH
STRETCHED OUT THEIR
HAND TO ME AND BAR-
NABAS AS A SIGN OF
FELLOWSHIP -; WE
WOULD GO TO THE
PAGANS AND THEY
TO THE JEWS. 10
WE SHOULD ONLY
KEEP IN MIND THE
POVERTY OF OUR
BROTHERS IN JERU-
SALEM: I HAVE TAKEN
CARE TO DO THIS.

THE CONFLICT WITH PETER

11 WHEN CEPHAS CAME TO ANTIOCH, I CONFRONTED
HIM SINCE HE WAS TO BE BLAMED. 12 BEFORE SOME
OF JAMES' KINSMEN ARRIVED, HE USED TO EAT WITH NON-
JEWISH PEOPLE, BUT WHEN THEY ARRIVED AND DIDN'T MIN-
GLE ANYMORE WITH THEM, FOR FEAR OF THESE CIRCUM-
CISED PEOPLE. 13 THE REST OF THE JEWS FOLLOWED
HIM IN THIS PRETENCE, AND EVEN BARNABAS WAS PART
OF THIS DOUBLE-DEALING. 14 WHEN I SAW THAT THEY
WERE NOT ACTING IN LINE WITH THE TRUTH OF THE
GOSPEL, I SAID TO CEPHAS PUBLICLY: IF YOU WHO
ARE JEWISH AGREED TO LIVE LIKE THE NON-JEWS,
SETTING ASIDE THE JEWISH CUSTOMS, WHY DO YOU
NOW COMPEL THE NON-JEWS TO LIVE LIKE JEWS?

15 WE ARE JEWS BY BIRTH; WE ARE NOT PA-
GAN SINNERS. 16 YET WE KNOW THAT NO
ONE IS MADE JUST AND HOLY BY THE OBSER-
VANCE OF THE LAW BUT BY FAITH IN CHRIST
JESUS. SO WE HAVE BELIEVED IN CHRIST JESUS
THAT WE MAY RECEIVE TRUE RIGHTEOUSNESS
FROM FAITH IN CHRIST JESUS, AND NOT FROM
THE PRACTICES OF THE LAW BECAUSE THE
OBSERVANCE OF THE LAW DOES NOT MAKE
ANY MORTAL A JUST PERSON. 17 WE THOUGHT
WE WOULD FIND IN CHRIST THE WAY OF RIGHT-
EOUSNESS; IF IN DO-
ING THIS WE WERE IN
THE WRONG, THEN
CHRIST WOULD BE
WORKING FOR SIN.
NOT SO! 18 BUT LOOK:
IF WE DO AWAY WITH
SOMETHING AND THEN
RESTORE IT, WE AD-
MIT WE DID WRONG.
19 AS FOR ME, THE
VERY LAW BROUGHT
ME TO DIE TO THE LAW
THAT I MAY LIVE FOR
GOD. I AM CRUCIFIED
WITH CHRIST, AND IT
IS NO LONGER I WHO
LIVE, BUT CHRIST IN
ME. I NOW LIVE MY
MORTAL LIFE WITH
FAITH IN THE SON OF
GOD WHO LOVED ME
AND GAVE HIMSELF FOR
ME. 20 BY DOING SO I
DIDN'T IGNORE THE
GIFT OF GOD. 21 FOR,
IF HOLINESS WERE THROUGH THE PRACTICE OF THE
LAW, CHRIST WOULD HAVE DIED FOR NOTHING.

WE ARE SAVED BY FAITH

3 1 HOW FOOLISH YOU ARE, GALATIANS! HOW
COULD THEY BEWITCH YOU AFTER JESUS CHRIST
HAS BEEN PRESENTED TO YOU AS CRUCIFIED?
2 I SHALL ASK YOU ONLY THIS: DID YOU RECEIVE

THE SPIRIT BY THE PRACTICE OF THE LAW, OR BY BE-
LIEVING THE MESSAGE? 3 HOW CAN YOU BE SUCH
FOOLS: YOU BEGIN WITH THE SPIRIT AND END
UP WITH THE FLESH! 4 SO YOU HAVE EXPERI-
ENCED ALL THIS IN VAIN! WOULD THAT IT WE-
RE NOT SO! 5 DID GOD GIVE YOU THE SPIRIT
AND WORK MIRACLES AMONG YOU, BECAUSE OF
YOUR OBSERVANCE OF THE LAW OR BECA-
USE YOU BELIEVED IN HIS MESSAGE?

6 REMEMBER ABRAHAM: HE BELIEVED GOD
WHO, BECAUSE OF THIS, HELD HIM TO BE A
JUST MAN. 7 UNDERSTAND THEN THAT
THOSE WHO FOLLOW THE WAY OF FAITH
ARE CHILDREN OF ABRAHAM.

8 THE SCRIPTURES FORESAW THAT BY THE
WAY OF FAITH, GOD WOULD GIVE TRUE
RIGHTEOUSNESS TO THE NON-JEWISH NATI-
ONS. FOR GOD'S PROMISE TO ABRAHAM WAS

THIS: IN YOU SHALL ALL THE NATIONS BE BLES-
SED. 9 SO NOW THOSE WHO TAKE THE
WAY OF FAITH RECEIVE THE SAME BLESSING
AS ABRAHAM WHO BELIEVED; 10 BUT THOSE
WHO RELY ON THE PRACTICE OF THE LAW ARE UNDER A
CURSE, FOR IT IS WRITTEN: CURSED BE HE WHO DOES
NOT ALWAYS FULFILL EVERYTHING WRITTEN IN THE
LAW. 11 IT IS PLAINLY WRITTEN THAT NO ONE BECOMES
RIGHTEOUS, IN GOD'S WAY,
BY THE LAW: BY FAITH
THE RIGHTEOUS SHALL
LIVE. 12 YET THE LAW GI-
VES NO PLACE TO FAITH,
FOR IT SAYS: HE WHO
FULFILLS THE COMMAN-
DMENTS SHALL HAVE
LIFE THROUGH THEM.
13 NOW CHRIST RES-
CUED US FROM THE
CURSE OF THE LAW,
BY BECOMING CURSED
HIMSELF FOR OUR
SAKE, AS IT IS WRIT-
TEN: THERE IS A
CURSE ON EVERYONE
WHO IS HANGED ON
A TREE. 14 SO THE
BLESSING GRANTED
TO ABRAHAM REACH-
ED THE PAGAN NATIONS
IN AND WITH CHRIST,
AND WE RECEIVED
THE PROMISED
SPIRIT THROUGH THE GIFT OF FAITH.

THE PROMISE, NOT THE LAW, WAS THE GIFT OF GOD

15 BROTHERS, LISTEN: WHEN ANYONE HAS MADE HIS
WILL IN THE PRESCRIBED FORM, NO ONE CAN ANNUL
IT OR ADD ANYTHING TO IT. 16 WELL NOW, WHAT GOD
PROMISED ABRAHAM WAS FOR HIS DESCENDANT.
SCRIPTURE DOES NOT SAY: FOR THE DESCEN-
DANTS, AS IF THERE WERE MANY. IT MEANS
ONLY ONE: THIS WILL BE FOR YOUR DES-
CENDANT, AND THIS IS CHRIST.

17 NOW I SAY THIS: IF GOD HAS MADE A TESTAMENT
IN DUE FORM, IT CANNOT BE ANNULLED BY THE LAW
WHICH CAME FOUR HUNDRED AND THIRTY YEARS LA-
TER: GOD'S PROMISE CANNOT BE CANCELLED.
18 BUT IF WE NOW INHERIT FOR KEEPING THE LAW,
IT IS NOT BECAUSE OF THE PROMISE. GOD HOWEVER HAD
PROMISED AND GIVEN THE INHERITANCE TO ABRAHAM.

GOD'S PEDAGOGY

19 WHY THEN THE LAW? IT CAME BECAUSE OF
SIN. BUT NOTICE THAT IT WAS SOMETHING
ADDED; THAT IT WAS
ONLY VALID UNTIL
THE DESCENDANT TO
WHOM THE PROMISE
WAS ADDRESSED SHO-
ULD COME; AND THAT
IT WAS PUT INTO EF-
FECT BY THE ANGELS
WITH MOSES AS A
MEDIATOR 20 BET-
WEEN THEM: IF IT WERE
GIVEN BY GOD HIMSELF,
HE IS ONE. 21 DOES
THE LAW THEN COMPETE
WITH THE PROMISES OF
GOD? NOT AT ALL. ONLY
IF WE HAD BEEN GIVEN
A LAW CAPABLE OF
GIVING LIFE, COULD
RIGHTEOUSNESS BE THE
FRUIT OF THE LAW. 22
BUT THE WRITTEN LAW
ACTUALLY CLOSED OUT
EVERY VIEWPOINT OTHER
THAN THAT OF SIN. SO THE BELIEVERS RECEIVE THE
PROMISE AS THE FRUIT OF CHRISTIAN FAITH.

GOD'S SONS AND DAUGHTERS

23 BEFORE THE TIME OF FAITH HAD COME, THE LAW
CONFINED US AND KEPT US IN CUSTODY UNTIL THE TIME
OF FAITH SHOULD COME. 24 THE LAW THEN BROUGHT
US TO CHRIST AS A CHILD TO HIS MASTER, SO THAT WE
RECEIVE TRUE RIGHTEOUSNESS THROUGH FAITH. 25 WITH
THE COMING OF FAITH, THAT SERVANT HAS ENDED HIS

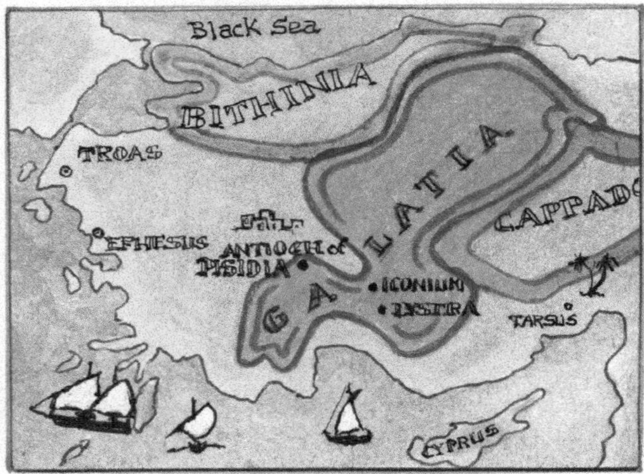

COMMAND. 26 NOW, IN CHRIST JESUS, ALL OF YOU ARE
SONS AND DAUGHTERS OF GOD THROUGH FAITH. 27 ALL
OF YOU WHO WERE GIVEN TO CHRIST THROUGH BAPTISM,
HAVE PUT ON CHRIST. 28 HERE THERE IS NO LON-
GER GREEK, OR SLAVE AND FREEDMAN, MAN AND
WOMAN: BUT ALL OF YOU ARE ONE IN CHRIST JESUS.
29 AND BECAUSE YOU BELONG TO CHRIST, YOU
ARE OF ABRAHAM'S RACE AND YOU ARE TO IN-
HERIT GOD'S PROMISE.

4 1 BUT LISTEN, AS LONG AS THE HEIR OF THE
HOST IS A CHILD, HE HAS NO ADVANTAGE ON
THE SLAVES, ALTHOUGH HE IS THE MASTER
OF THEM ALL. 2 HE IS SUBJECT TO THOSE WHO
CARE FOR HIM AND WHO ARE ENTRUSTED WITH HIS
AFFAIRS UNTIL THE TIME SET BY HIS FATHER COMES.
3 IN THE SAME WAY WE AS CHILDREN WERE
FIRST SUBJECTED TO THE CREATED FORCES
THAT GOVERN THE WORLD. 4 BUT WHEN THE
FULLNESS OF TIME CAME, GOD SENT HIS SON.
HE CAME BORN OF WOMAN AND SUBJECT OF THE LAW,

5 IN ORDER TO REDEEM THE SUBJECTS OF THE LAW,
THAT WE MAY BE GIVEN OUR FULL RIGHTS OF SONS'
AND DAUGHTERS OF GOD. 6 AND BECAUSE YOU ARE
SONS, GOD HAS SENT INTO YOUR HEARTS THE SPI-
RIT OF HIS SON WHICH
CRIES OUT: ABBA! THAT
IS, FATHER! 7 YOU
YOURSELF ARE NO LON-
GER A SLAVE BUT A
SON OR DAUGHTER,
AND YOURS IS THE IN-
HERITANCE BY GOD'S
GRACE. 8 WHEN YOU
DID NOT KNOW GOD, YOU
SERVED THOSE WHO ARE
NOT GODS. 9 BUT NOW
THAT YOU HAVE KNOWN
GOD – OR RATHER HE HAS
KNOWN YOU – HOW CAN
YOU TURN BACK TO WE-
AK AND IMPOVERISHED
CREATED THINGS? DO
YOU WANT TO BE ENS-
LAVED AGAIN? WILL
10 YOU AGAIN OBSER-
VE THIS AND THAT DAY,
AND THE NEW MOON,
AND THIS PERIOD
THAT YEAR...? 11 I FEAR I MAY HAVE WAST-
ED MY TIME WITH YOU.

I STILL SUFFER FOR YOU

12 I IMPLORE YOU, DEARLY BELOVED, DO AS I DO,
JUST AS I BECAME LIKE YOU. YOU HAVE NOT
OFFENDED ME IN ANYTHING.
13 REMEMBER THAT I WAS SICK WHEN
I FIRST ANNOUNCED THE GOSPEL TO YOU.

ALTHOUGH 14 I WAS A TRIAL TO YOU, YOU
DID NOT DESPISE OR REJECT ME,
BUT RECEIVED ME AS AN ANGEL OF
GOD, AS CHRIST JESUS.

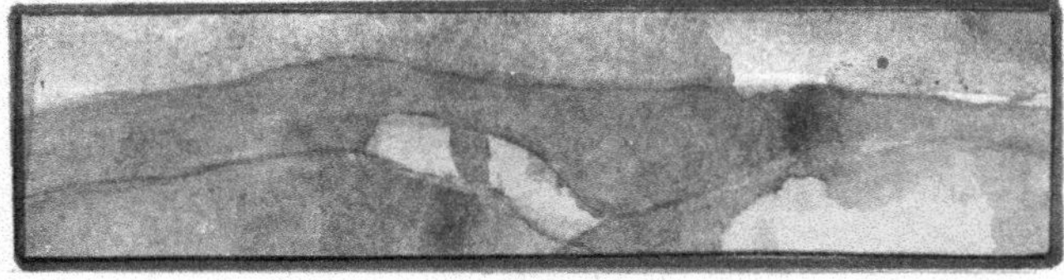

RAPHAEL URBINAS
MADONNA DEL GRANDUCA
CCCLXXXVII
©
IDM
08

15 WHERE IS THE BLISS? FOR I CAN TESTIFY THAT
YOU WOULD HAVE EVEN PLUCKED OUT YOUR EYES
TO GIVE THEM TO ME. 16 BUT NOW, HAVE I BE-
COME YOUR ENEMY FOR TELLING YOU THE TRUTH?

17 THOSE WHO SHOW CONSIDERATION TO YOU ARE
NOT SINCERE; THEY WANT TO SEPARATE YOU
FROM ME, SO THAT YOU MAY SHOW INTEREST
IN THEM. 18 WOULD THAT YOU WERE SUR-
ROUNDED WITH SINCERE CARE AT ALL TI-
MES, AND NOT ONLY FROM ME WHEN I AM

WITH YOU! 19 MY CHILDREN I STILL SUFFER
THE PAINS OF CHILDBIRTH UNTIL CHRIST IS
FORMED IN YOU. 20 HOW I WOULD LIKE TO
BE WITH YOU NOW AND SPEAK TO YOU PERSO-
NALLY, FOR I DON'T KNOW WHAT TO SAY FOR THE BEST.

SARAH AND HAGAR

21 TELL ME, YOU WHO DESIRE TO SUBMIT YOUR-
SELVES TO THE LAW, DID YOU LISTEN TO IT? 22
IT SAYS THAT ABRAHAM HAD TWO SONS, ONE
BY A SLAVE WOMAN,

THE OTHER BY THE
FREE WOMAN, HIS
WIFE. 23 THE SON
OF THE SLAVE WO-
MAN WAS BORN IN
THE ORDINARY WAY;
BUT THE SON OF THE
FREE WOMAN WAS
BORN IN FULFILLMENT
OF GOD'S PROMISE.
24 HERE WE HAVE AN
ALLEGORY: IT MEANS
THERE ARE TWO COVE-
NANTS. THE FIRST IS
THE ONE FROM MOUNT
SINAI REPRESENTED
THROUGH HAGAR: HER
CHILDREN HAVE SLA-
VERY FOR THEIR LOT.
25 WE KNOW THAT
HAGAR WAS FROM
MOUNT SINAI IN ARA-
BIA: SHE STANDS FOR
THE PRESENT CITY OF
JERUSALEM, WHICH IS
IN SLAVERY WITH HER
CHILDREN. 26 BUT JERUSALEM, OUR MOTHER, IS
FREE. 27 AND SCRIPTURE SAYS ON HER:
'REJOICE, BARREN WOMAN WITHOUT CHILDREN,
BREAK FORTH IN SHOUTS OF JOY, YOU WHO
DO NOT KNOW THE PAINS OF CHILDBIRTH,
FOR MANY SHALL BE THE CHILDREN OF THE FOR-
SAKEN MOTHER, MORE THAN OF THE MARRIED WOMAN.

28 YOU, DEARLY BELOVED, ARE CHILDREN OF
THE PROMISE, LIKE ISAAC. 29 BUT AS AT
THAT TIME THE CHILD BORN ACCORDING TO THE
FLESH PERSECUTED ISAAC, WHO WAS BORN AC-
CORDING TO THE SPIRIT, SO IS IT NOW. 30 AND
WHAT DOES SCRIPTURE SAY? CAST OUT THE SLA-
VE WOMAN AND HER SON, FOR THE SON OF THE
SLAVE CANNOT SHARE THE INHERITANCE WITH
THE SON OF THE FREE WOMAN.
31 BRETHREN, WE ARE NOT CHILDREN OF
THE SLAVE WOMAN, BUT OF THE FREE WOMAN.

5

1 CHRIST FREED US TO MAKE US
REALLY FREE.
SO REMAIN
FIRM AND DO NOT
SUBMIT AGAIN
TO THE YOKE OF
SLAVERY.

2 I, PAUL, SAY THIS
TO YOU: IF YOU RE-
CEIVE CIRCUMCI-
SION, CHRIST CAN
NO LONGER HELP
YOU. 3 ONCE MO-
RE I SAY TO WHO-
EVER RECEIVES
CIRCUMCISION: YOU
ARE NOW BOUND TO
KEEP THE WHOLE
LAW. 4 ALL YOU WHO
PRETEND TO BECOME
RIGHTEOUS THROUGH
THE OBSERVANCE
OF THE LAW HAVE
SEPARATED YOUR-
SELVES FROM CHRIST AND HAVE FALLEN AWAY
FROM GRACE. 5 AS FOR US, THE SPIRIT IM-
PARTS TO US THIS HOPE THAT THROUGH FAITH
WE SHALL BE JUST AS GOD WANTS US TO BE. 6
IN CHRIST JESUS, IT IS IRRELEVANT WHE-
THER WE BE CIRCUMCISED OR NOT; WHAT MAT-
TERS IS FAITH WORKING THROUGH LOVE. YOU

7 HAD BEGUN YOUR RACE WELL, WHO
THEN HINDERED YOU ON THE WAY? WHY DID
YOU STOP OBEYING THE TRUTH? 8 THIS
WAS NOT IN OBEDIENCE TO GOD WHO CALLS
YOU; 9 IN FACT, A LITTLE LEAVEN IS AF-
FECTING THE WHOLE OF YOU.

10 I AM PERSONALLY CONVINCED THAT
YOU WILL GO ASTRAY, BUT HE WHO CON-
FUSES YOU, WHOEVER HE MAY BE, SHALL
RECEIVE PUNISHMENT.
11 I MYSELF, BRETHREN, COULD I NOT
PREACH CIRCUMCISION? THEN I WOULD
NO LONGER BE PERSECUTED. BUT WHERE
WOULD BE THE SCANDAL OF THE CROSS?

12 WOULD THAT THOSE WHO CONFUSE YOU
MIGHT GO AS FAR AS MUTILATING THEMSELVES!

13 YOU, BROTHERS AND SISTERS, WERE CALLED
TO ENJOY FREEDOM; I AM NOT SPEAKING OF THAT
FREEDOM WHICH GIVES FREE REIN TO THE DE-
SIRES, BUT OF THAT WHICH MAKES YOU SLAVES
OF ONE ANOTHER
THROUGH LOVE. 14
FOR THE WHOLE LAW
IS SUMMONED UP IN
THIS SENTENCE:
YOU SHALL LOVE YOUR NE-
IGHBOR AS YOURSELF. 15
BUT IF YOU BITE AND TEAR
EACH OTHER TO PIECES, BE
CAREFUL LEST YOU ALL DIE.
16 SO I SAY TO YOU: WALK
WITH THE SPIRIT AND DO
NOT GIVE AWAY TO THE DE-
SIRES OF THE FLESH. 17
THE DESIRES OF THE FLESH
WAR AGAINST THE SPIRIT,
AND THE SPIRIT'S ARE
OPPOSED TO THE FLESH.
BOTH ARE IN CONFLICT ON
EACH OTHER, SO THAT YOU
CANNOT DO ALL YOU WOULD
LIKE. 18 BUT LET THE
SPIRIT LEAD YOU: THIS
HAS NOTHING TO DO
WITH SUBMITTING TO THE
LAW.
19 YOU WELL KNOW
WHAT COMES FROM THE FLESH:
IMMORALITY, IMPURITY AND SHAMELESSNESS,

LOVE YOUR NEIGHBOUR. W.WU-OIL ON CANVAS-1990

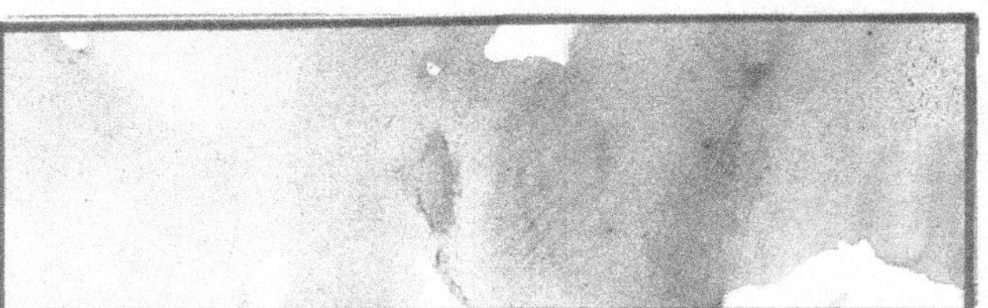

20 IDOL WORSHIP AND MAGIC, HATRED,
JEALOUSY AND VIOLENCE, ANGER,
AMBITION, DIVISIONS, FACTIONS,
21 AND ENVY,
DRUNKENNESS,
ORGIES AND THE
LIKE.
I AGAIN SAY TO YOU
WHAT I HAVE AL-
READY SAID:
THOSE WHO DO
THESE THINGS
SHALL NOT IN-
HERIT THE KING-
DOM OF GOD.

22 BUT THE FRUIT
OF THE SPIRIT IS
CHARITY, JOY AND
PEACE, PATIENCE,
UNDERSTANDING
OF OTHERS, KIND-
NESS AND FIDE-
LITY, 23 GENTLE-
NESS AND SELF-CONTROL.

FOR SUCH THINGS THERE IS NO LAW OR PU-
NISHMENT. 24 THOSE WHO BELONG TO
CHRIST HAVE CRUCIFIED THE FLESH WITH ITS VI-
CES AND DESIRES. 25 IF WE LIVE BY THE SPIRIT,
LET US LIVE IN A SPIRITUAL WAY. 26 LET'S NOT BE
CONCEITED: NO RIVALRY OR ENVY TO ONE ANOTHER.

VARIOUS COUNSELS

6 1 BRETHREN, IN THE EVENT OF SOME-
ONE FALLING INTO A SIN, YOU WHO ARE
SPIRITUAL SHALL SET HIM ARIGHT WITH THE

SPIRIT OF KINDNESS, TAKE CARE FOR YOU,
TOO, MAY BE TEMPTED.

2 CARRY EACH OTHER'S BURDENS AND
SO FULFILL THE LAW OF CHRIST.

3 IF ANYONE THINKS HE IS SOMETHING,
WHEN IN FACT HE IS NOTHING, HE DECEIVES
HIMSELF.

4 LET EACH OTHER EXAMINE HIS OWN CON-
DUCT AND BOAST FOR HIMSELF, IF HE
WANTS TO DO SO BUT NOT BEFORE OTH-
ERS.
5 IN THIS, LET EACH ONE CARRY HIS
OWN THINGS.

6 HE WHO RECE-
IVES THE TEACHING
OF THE WORD
OUGHT TO SHARE
THE GOOD THINGS HE
HAS WITH THE ONE
WHO INSTRUCTS HIM.

7 DO NOT BE FOOL-
ED. GOD CANNOT
BE DECEIVED.
YOU REAP WHAT
YOU SOW.

8 THE PERSON
WHO SOWS FOR THE
BENEFIT OF HIS
OWN FLESH SHALL
REAP CORRUPTION
AND DEATH FROM
THE FLESH. HE
WHO SOWS IN THE
SPIRIT SHALL
REAP ETERNAL LIFE FROM THE SPI-
RIT.
9 LET US DO GOOD WITHOUT BEING
DISCOURAGED; IN DUE TIME WE SHALL
REAP THE REWARD OF OUR CONSTANCY. 10
SO WHILE THERE IS TIME, LET US DO GOOD TO
ALL AND ESPECIALLY TO OUR FAMILY IN THE FAITH.

I AM CRUCIFIED WITH CHRIST

11 SEE THESE LARGE LETTERS I USE
WHEN I WRITE TO YOU IN MY OWN HAND.
WHO OBLIGES YOU TO BE CIRCUMCISED?
12 THOSE WHO ARE MOST ANXIOUS TO PUT
UP A GOOD SHOW IN LIFE: WHAT IF THE
CROSS OF CHRIST SHOULD BRING THEM
SOME TROUBLE! 13 NOT FOR BEING CIR-
CUMCISED DO THEY OBSERVE THE LAW;
WHAT INTERESTS THEM IS THE EXTERNAL RITE.
WHAT A BOAST FOR THEM IF THEY HAD YOU

CIRCUMCISED! 14 FOR ME, I DON'T WISH TO TAKE PRI-
DE IN ANYTHING EXCEPT IN THE CROSS OF CHRIST JESUS
OUR LORD. THROUGH HIM THE WORLD HAS BEEN CRUCI-
FIED TO ME AND I TO THE WORLD. 15 LET US NO
LONGER SPEAK OF THE CIRCUMCISED AND OF NON-
JEWS, BUT OF A NEW CREATION.
16 LET THOSE WHO LIVE ACCORDING TO THIS
RULE RECEIVE PEACE AND MERCY; THEY
ARE THE ISRAEL OF GOD! 17 LET NO ONE
TROUBLE ME ANY LONGER: FOR MY PART,
I BEAR IN MY BODY THE MARKS OF JESUS.
18 BRETHREN, MAY THE GRACE OF CHRIST JESUS
OUR LORD BE WITH YOUR SPIRIT. AMEN.

388 - CCCLXXXVIII

THE LETTER TO THE EPHESIANS

THIS LETTER TO THE EPHESIANS SEEMS TO HAVE BEEN WRITTEN AFTER THE ONE TO THE COLOSSIANS. PAUL AGAIN TAKES UP AND DEVELOPS GOD'S PLAN WHICH HE MUST HAVE UNDERSTOOD THROUGH A REVELATION. THE WORLD HAS BEEN CREATED FOR HUMANKIND TO ENABLE IT TO EMERGE AS THE NEW HUMAN, ONE FAMILY IN CHRIST. ALL WILL FIND THEMSELVES, EACH ONE IN PLACE, AROUND A PERSON CAPABLE OF WELCOMING ALL, EACH IN HIS OWN FULLNESS.

JUST AS OTHER RELIGIONS CLAIMED TO OFFER A UNIVERSAL WAY OF SALVATION, THEY OFFERED CHRIST, AS THE ONLY SAVIOR OF THE HUMANITY.

1 1 PAUL, AN APOSTLE OF CHRIST JESUS BY THE WILL OF
GOD, TO THE SAINTS IN EPHESUS. TO YOU WHO BELIEVE IN

CHRIST: 2 RECEIVE GRACE AND PEACE FROM GOD OUR
FATHER AND FROM JESUS THE LORD. 3 BLESSED BE
GOD, THE FATHER OF CHRIST JESUS OUR LORD WHO IN
CHRIST HAS BLESSED US FROM HEAVEN WITH EVERY SPIRITU-
AL BLESSING. 4 GOD CHOSE US IN HIM BEFORE THE
CREATION OF THE WORLD TO BE HOLY AND WITHOUT SIN

IN HIS PRESENCE. 5 FROM ETERNITY HE DESTINED US
IN LOVE TO BE HIS ADOPTED SONS THROUGH CHRIST
JESUS, THUS FULFILLING HIS FREE AND GENEROUS
WILL. THIS WAS HIS PURPOSE:

6 THAT HIS LOVING-KINDNESS WHICH
HE GRANTED US IN HIS BELOVED MIGHT
FINALLY RECEIVE ALL GLORY AND PRAISE.
7 FOR IN CHRIST WE OBTAIN FREEDOM,
SEALED BY HIS BLOOD, AND HAVE THE
FORGIVENESS OF SINS. IN THIS APPEARS
THE GREATNESS OF HIS GRACE, 8 WHICH
HE LAVISHED ON US. IN ALL WISDOM AND
UNDERSTANDING, 9 GOD HAS MADE
KNOWN TO US HIS MYSTERIOUS DESIGN,

IN ACCORDANCE WITH HIS LOVING-KIND-
NESS IN CHRIST. 10 IN HIM AND UNDER
HIM GOD WANTED TO UNITE, WHEN THE
FULLNESS OF TIME HAD COME, EVERY-
THING IN HEAVEN AND ON EARTH.
11 BY A DECREE OF HIM WHO DIS-
POSES ALL THINGS ACCORDING TO HIS
OWN PLAN AND DECISION WE, THE JEWS,
HAVE BEEN CHOSEN AND CALLED 12
AND WE WERE AWAITING THE MES-
SIAH, FOR THE PRAISE OF HIS GLORY.
13 YOU, ON HEARING THE WORD OF TRUTH
THE GOSPEL THAT SAVES YOU, HAVE BE-
LIEVED IN HIM. AND, AS PROMISED, YOU

WERE SEALED WITH THE HOLY SPIRIT 14
THE FIRST PLEDGE OF WHAT WE SHALL RE-
CEIVE ON THE WAY OF OUR DELIVERANCE AS
A PEOPLE OF GOD, FOR THE PRAISE OF HIS GLORY.

GOD HAS PUT ALL THINGS UNDER THE FEET OF CHRIST

15 I HAVE BEEN TOLD OF YOUR FAITH, OF YOUR AF-
FECTION TOWARDS ALL THE BELIEVERS, 16 SO
I ALWAYS GIVE THANKS TO GOD, REMEMBERING
YOU IN MY PRAYERS. 17 MAY THE GOD OF
CHRIST JESUS OUR LORD, THE FATHER OF
GLORY, REVEAL HIMSELF TO YOU AND GIVE
YOU SPIRIT OF WISDOM, THAT YOU MAY KNOW HIM.

18 MAY HE ENLIGHTEN YOUR INNER VISION,
THAT YOU MAY APPRECIATE THE THINGS WE
HOPE FOR, SINCE WE WERE CALLED BY GOD. MAY
YOU KNOW HOW GREAT IS THE INHERITANCE, THE
GLORY, GOD SETS APART FOR HIS SAINTS; 19 MAY
YOU UNDERSTAND WITH
WHAT EXTRAORDINARY
POWER HE ACTS IN FA-
VOR OF US WHO BELI-
EVE. 20 HE REVEALED
HIS POWER IN CHRIST
WHEN HE RAISED HIM
FROM THE DEAD AND
HAD HIM SIT AT HIS
RIGHT HAND IN HE-
AVEN, 21 FAR ABOVE
ALL RULE, POWER,
AUTHORITY, DOMINION,
OR ANY OTHER SU-
PERNATURAL FORCE
THAT COULD BE NA-
MED, NOT ONLY IN
THIS WORLD BUT IN
THE WORLD TO CO-
ME AS WELL. THUS
22 HAS GOD PUT
ALL THINGS UNDER
THE FEET OF CHRIST
AND SET HIM ABOVE
ALL THINGS, AS HEAD
OF THE CHURCH 23

WHICH IS HIS BODY. HE WHO FILLS ALL IN ALL UN-
FOLDS HIS FULLNESS IN THE CHURCH.

BY GRACE YOU HAVE BEEN SAVED

2 1 YOU WERE DEAD THROUGH THE FAULTS AND
SINS 2 IN WHICH YOU ONCE LIVED. YOU CON-
FORMED TO THIS WORLD AND FOLLOWED THE
SOVEREIGN RULER WHO REIGNS BETWEEN HEAVEN
AND EARTH AND WHO GOES ON WORKING IN THOSE
WHO RESIST THE FAITH. 3 ALL OF US BELONGED

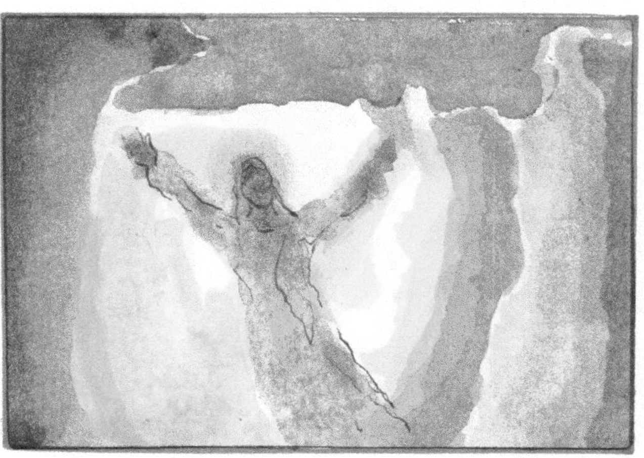

TO THEM AT ONE TIME AND WE FOLLOWED HUMAN
GREED; WE OBEYED THE URGES OF OUR HUMAN
NATURE AND CONSENTED TO ITS DESIRES. BY
OURSELVES, WE WENT STRAIGHT TO THE JUDG-
MENT LIKE THE REST OF HUMANKIND.

4 BUT GOD, WHO IS RICH IN MERCY, REVEALED HIS
IMMENSE LOVE AND 5 GAVE US LIFE WITH
CHRIST AFTER BEING DEAD THROUGH OUR SINS.
BY GRACE YOU HAVE BEEN SAVED! 6 AND HE
RAISED US TO LIFE WITH CHRIST, GIVING
US A PLACE WITH HIM IN HEAVEN.

7 IN SHOWING US SUCH KINDNESS IN CHRIST
JESUS, GOD WILLED TO REVEAL AND UNFOLD
IN THE COMING AGES THE EXTRAORDINARY
RICHES OF HIS GRACE.
8 BY THE GRACE OF GOD YOU HAVE BEEN
SAVED THROUGH GRACE OF FAITH. THIS
HAS NOT COME FROM YOU: IT IS GOD'S
GIFT. 9 THIS WAS NOT THE RESULT
OF YOUR WORKS, SO YOU ARE NOT TO FEEL
PROUD.
10 WHAT WE ALL ARE IS THE WORK OF GOD.

HE HAS CREATED US IN CHRIST JESUS FOR THE GOOD
WORKS HE HAS PREPARED THAT WE SHOULD DE-
VOTE OURSELVES TO THEM.

CHRIST IS OUR PEACE

11 REMEMBER THAT YOU WERE PAGANS IN YOUR FLESH
AND THE JEWS WHO CALL THEMSELVES CIRCUMCISED BECA-
USE OF A SURGICAL CIRCUMCISION, CALLED YOU UNCIRCUM-
CISED. 12 AT THAT TIME YOU WERE WITHOUT CHRIST,
YOU DIDN'T BELONG TO COMMUNITY OF ISRAEL. GOD'S
COVENANTS AND PROMISES WERE NOT FOR YOU; YOU
HAD NO HOPE AND WITH-
OUT GOD IN THIS WORLD.
13 BUT NOW, IN CHRIST
JESUS AND BY HIS BLO-
OD, YOU WHO ONCE WERE
FAR HAVE COME NEAR. 14
CHRIST IS OUR PEACE, HE
WHO HAS MADE THE TWO
PEOPLES ONE, 15 DESTROY-
ING IN HIS OWN FLESH THE
WALL, THE HATRED WHICH
SEPARATED US. HE ABOL-
ISHED THE LAW, ITS COM-
MANDS AND PRECEPTS.
HE MADE PEACE UNITING
TWO PEOPLE IN HIM, CRE-
ATING OUT OF THE TWO
ONE NEW MAN. 16 HE DE-
STROYED HATRED AND RE-
CONCILED US BOTH TO
GOD THROUGH THE
CROSS, MAKING THE
TWO ONE BODY. 17 HE
CAME TO PROCLAIM PE-
ACE TO YOU WHO WERE
FAR OFF, PEACE TO THE
JEWS WHO WERE NEAR.
18 THROUGH HIM, WE
THE TWO PEOPLES, APPRO-
ACH THE FATHER IN ONE
SPIRIT. 19 NOW YOU ARE NO LONGER STRANGERS
OR GUESTS, BUT FELLOW CITIZENS OF THE HOLY PE-
OPLE: YOU ARE OF THE HOUSEHOLD OF GOD, YOU ARE
THE HOUSE 20 WHOSE FOUNDATIONS ARE THE
APOSTLES AND PROPHETS, AND WHOSE CORN-
ERSTONE IS CHRIST JESUS.

21 IN HIM THE WHOLE STRUCTURE IS JOINED
TOGETHER AND RISES TO BE A HOLY TEMPLE
IN THE LORD. 22 IN HIM YOU TOO ARE BEING
BUILT TO BECOME THE SPIRITUAL SANCTUARY OF GOD.

GOD'S INHERITANCE IS FOR ALL

3 1 FOR THIS REASON I, PAUL, CAME TO BE THE
PRISONER OF CHRIST FOR YOU, THE NON-JEWS.
2 YOU MAY HAVE HEARD OF THE GRACE OF
GOD HE BESTOWED ON ME FOR YOUR SAKE. 3
BY A REVELATION HE
GAVE ME THE KNOW-
LEDGE OF HIS MYST-
ERIOUS DESIGN, AS I
HAVE EXPLAINED IN A
FEW WORDS, 4 ON
READING THEM YOU
WILL HAVE SOME
IDEA OF HOW I UNDER-
STAND THE MYSTERY
OF CHRIST. 5 THE
MYSTERY WAS NOT
MADE KNOWN TO
PAST GENERATIONS
BUT ONLY NOW, AND
THROUGH REVELA-
TIONS GIVEN TO HO-
LY APOSTLES AND
PROPHETS. 6 NOW
THE NON-JEWISH
PEOPLE SHARE THE
INHERITANCE; IN
CHRIST JESUS THE
NON-JEWS ARE IN-
CORPORATED AND
ARE TO ENJOY THE
PROMISE. THIS IS
THE GOOD NEWS
7 OF WHICH I HAVE
BECOME MINISTER BY A GIFT OF GOD, A GRACE
HE GAVE ME, A POWER THAT WORKS IN ME.

8 THIS GRACE WAS GIVEN TO ME, THE LEAST
AMONG ALL THE BELIEVERS: TO ANNOUNCE TO
THE PAGAN NATIONS THE IMMEASURABLE RI-
CHES OF CHRIST AND 9 TO MAKE CLEAR
TO ALL HOW THE MYSTERY, HIDDEN FROM
THE BEGINNING IN GOD, THE CREATOR

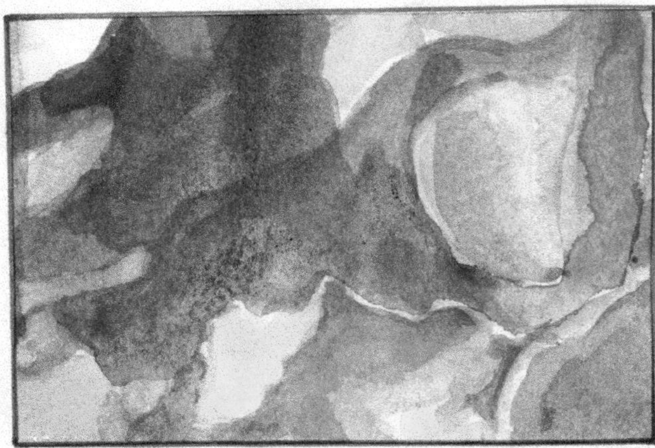

OF ALL THINGS, IS TO BE FULFILLED. 10 EVEN THE
HEAVENLY FORCES AND POWERS WILL NOW
DISCOVER THROUGH THE CHURCH THE WIS-
DOM OF GOD IN ITS MANIFOLD EXPRESSION, AS
THE PLAN IS BEING FULFILLED 11 WHICH GOD
DESIGNED FROM THE BEGINNING IN CHRIST
JESUS, OUR LORD. 12 IN HIM WE RECEIVE
BOLDNESS AND CONFIDENCE TO APPROACH
GOD. 13 SO I ASK YOU NOT TO BE DISCOURAGED
AT SEEING THE TRIALS I ENDURE FOR YOU, BUT
RATHER TO FEEL PROUD BECAUSE OF THEM.

Remember that you were pagans...
Ephesians 2:11
389 · CCCLXXXIX
©
DW
09

14 AND NOW I KNEEL IN THE PRESENCE OF
THE FATHER 15 FROM WHOM EVERY FAMILY
IN HEAVEN AND ON EARTH HAS RECEIVED ITS NAME.

16 MAY HE STRENGTHEN IN YOU THE INNER SELF
THROUGH HIS SPIRIT, ACCORDING TO THE RICHES
OF HIS GLORY; 17 MAY CHRIST DWELL IN YOUR
HEARTS THROUGH FAITH; MAY YOU BE ROOTED
AND FOUNDED IN LOVE.

18 ALL OF THIS SO
THAT YOU MAY UN-
DERSTAND WITH ALL
THE BELIEVERS THE
WIDTH, THE LENGTH,
THE HEIGHT AND THE
DEPTH - IN A WORD,
19 THAT YOU MAY
KNOW THE LOVE OF
CHRIST WHICH SUR-
PASSES ALL KNOW-
LEDGE, THAT YOU
MAY BE FILLED
AND REACH THE
FULLNESS OF GOD.

20 GLORY TO GOD
WHO SHOWS HIS
POWER IN US
AND CAN DO MUCH
MORE THAN WE
COULD ASK OR
IMAGINE; GLORY
21 TO HIM IN THE
CHURCH AND IN
CHRIST JESUS
THROUGH ALL
GENERATIONS FOR EVER AND EVER. AMEN.

WE SHALL BECOME THE PERFECT CREATION

4 1 THEREFORE I, THE PRISONER OF CHRIST,
INVITE YOU TO LIVE THE VOCATION YOU
HAVE RECEIVED. 2 BE HUMBLE, KIND,
PATIENT, AND BEAR WITH ONE ANOTHER IN
LOVE. 3 MAKE EVERY EFFORT TO KEEP A-
MONG YOU THE UNIT OF SPIRIT THROUGH
BONDS OF PEACE. 4 LET THERE BE ONE
BODY AND ONE SPIRIT, FOR GOD, IN CALLING

YOU, GAVE THE SAME SPIRIT TO ALL. 5 ONE LORD,
ONE FAITH, ONE BAPTISM. 6 ONE GOD, THE FATHER
OF ALL, WHO IS ABOVE ALL AND WORKS THROUGH
ALL AND IS IN ALL. 7 BUT TO EACH OF US DIVINE
GRACE IS GIVEN ACCORDING TO THE MEASURE OF
CHRIST'S GIFT. 8 THEREFORE IT IS SAID: WHEN
HE ASCENDED TO THE HEIGHTS, HE BROUGHT CAP-
TIVES AND GAVE HIS GIFTS TO MEN.
9 HE ASCENDED; THIS REFERS TO THE ONE
WHO FIRST DESCENDED TO THE DEAD IN
THE LOWER PARTS OF THE WORLD.

10 HE HIMSELF WHO WENT DOWN, THEN AS-
CENDED FAR ABOVE ALL THE HEAVENS TO
FILL ALL THINGS. 11 AS FOR HIS GIFTS, TO SO-
ME HE GAVE TO BE APOSTLES, TO OTHER PROPHETS,
OR EVEN EVANGELISTS, OR PASTORS AND TEACHERS.
12 SO HE PREPARED THOSE WHO BELONG TO
HIM FOR THE MINISTRY, IN ORDER TO BUILD UP
THE BODY OF CHRIST, 13 UNTIL WE ARE ALL
UNITED IN THE SAME FAITH AND KNOWLEDGE OF THE
SON OF GOD. THUS WE SHALL BECOME THE
PERFECT MAN, UPON REACHING MATURITY
AND SHARING THE FULLNESS OF CHRIST. 14

THEN NO LONGER SHALL WE BE LIKE CHILDREN
TOSSED ABOUT BY ANY WAVE OR WIND OF DOC-
TRINE, AND DECEIVED BY THE CUNNING OF MEN
WHO DRAG THEM ALONG INTO ERROR. 15 RATHER,
WITH SINCERE LOVE, WE SHALL GROW IN EVERY WAY
TOWARDS HIM WHO IS THE HEAD, CHRIST.
16 FROM HIM COMES THE GROWTH OF THE
WHOLE BODY TO WHICH A NETWORK OF JOINTS
GIVES ORDER AND COHESION, TAKING INTO
ACCOUNT AND MAKING USE OF THE FUNCTION
OF EACH ONE. SO THE BODY BUILDS ITSELF IN LOVE.

PUT ON THE NEW SELF

I SAY TO YOU AND WITH INSISTENCE I ADVISE YOU IN THE
LORD 17: DO NOT IMITATE THE PAGANS WHO LIVE
AN AIMLESS LIFE. 18

THEIR UNDERSTANDING
IS IN DARKNESS AND THEY
REMAIN IN IGNORANCE
BECAUSE OF THEIR CON-
SCIENCE, BLIND AND
VERY FAR FROM THE LI-
FE OF GOD. 19 AS A RE-
SULT OF THEIR CORRUP-
TION, THEY HAVE INDUL-
GED INTO SENSUALITY
AND HAVE GIVEN THEM-
SELVES TO EVERY KIND
OF IMMORALITY. BUT IT
20 IS NOT FOR THIS
THAT YOU HAVE FOLLOW-
ED CHRIST. 21 BUT THAT
YOU HEARD OF HIM AND
RECEIVED HIS TEACHING
SEEN IN JESUS HIMSELF.
22 YOU MUST GIVE UP
YOUR FORMER WAY OF
LIVING, THE OLD SELF,
WHOSE DECEITFUL
DESIRES BRINGS
SELF-DESTRUCTION.
23 RENEW YOURSELVES SPIRITUALLY, FROM
INSIDE. 24 AND PUT ON THE NEW SELF, OR SELF AC-
CORDING TO GOD, WHICH IS CREATED IN TRUE
RIGHTEOUSNESS AND HOLINESS. 25 THEREFO-
RE, GIVE UP LYING: LET EVERYONE SPEAK
THE TRUTH TO HIS NEIGHBOR FOR WE ARE
MEMBERS OF ONE ANOTHER.

26 BE ANGRY BUT DO NOT SIN: DO NOT LET
YOUR ANGER LAST UNTIL THE END OF THE DAY,
27 LEST YOU GIVE THE DEVIL A FOOTHOLD.
28 LET THE ONE WHO USED TO STEAL, STE-
AL NO MORE, BUT BUSY HIMSELF WORKING US-
EFULLY WITH HIS HANDS SO THAT HE MAY HAVE
SOMETHING TO SHARE WITH THE NEEDY.
29 DO NOT LET EVEN ONE BAD WORD COME
FROM YOUR MOUTH, BUT ONLY GOOD WORDS

THAT WILL ENCOURAGE WHEN NECESSARY AND
BE HELPFUL TO THOSE WHO HEAR. 30 DO NOT
SADDEN THE HOLY SPIRIT OF GOD WHICH YOU
WERE MARKED WITH. IT WILL BE YOUR DISTINC-
TIVE MARK ON THE DAY OF SALVATION. 31 DO
AWAY WITH ALL QUARRELING, RAGE, ANGER,
INSULTS AND EVERY KIND OF MALICE: 32 BE
GOOD AND UNDERSTANDING, MUTUALLY FOR-
GIVING ONE ANOTHER AS GOD FORGAVE YOU
IN CHRIST.

IMITATE GOD

5 1 AS MOST BELOVED CHILDREN OF GOD, STRI-
VE TO IMITATE HIM. 2 FOLLOW THE WAY OF LOVE,
THE EXAMPLE OF CHRIST WHO LOVED YOU.
HE GAVE HIMSELF UP FOR US AND BECAME THE
OFFERING AND SAC-

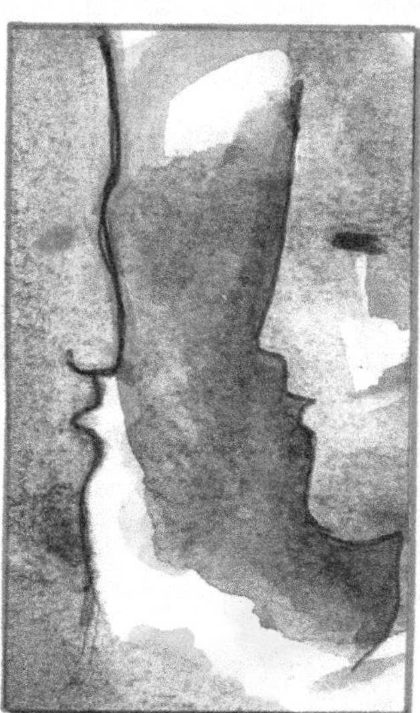

RIFICAL VICTIM WHOSE
FRAGRANCE RISES TO
GOD. 3 AND SINCE YOU
ARE HOLY, THERE MUST
BE AMONG YOU EVEN A
HINT OF IMPURITY, GREED
AND SEXUAL IMMORALITY:
THESE SHOULD BE NAMED
AMONG YOU. 4 SO TOO
FOR SCANDALOUS NON-
SENSE, WORDS AND
FOOLISHNESS, WHICH
ARE NOT FITTING; INS-
TEAD OFFER THANKSGIV-
ING TO GOD. 5 KNOW
THIS: NO DEPRAVED, IM-
PURE OR COVETOUS PER-
SON WHO SERVES THE
GOD 'MONEY' SHALL
HAVE PART IN THE KING-
DOM OF GOD. 6 LET NO
ONE DECEIVE YOU WITH
EMPTY ARGUMENTS, FOR
THESE ARE THE SINS
WHICH GOD IS ABOUT TO
CONDEMN IN PEOPLE WHO
DO NOT OBEY. 7 DO NOT ASSOCIATE WITH SUCH PE-
OPLE. 8 YOU WERE ONCE DARKNESS, BUT NOW
YOU ARE LIGHT IN THE LORD. BEHAVE AS CHIL-
DREN OF LIGHT: 9 THE FRUITS OF LIGHT ARE
KINDNESS, JUSTICE AND TRUTH IN EVERY FORM.

10 YOU YOURSELVES SEARCH OUT WHAT PLE-
ASES THE LORD, 11 AND TAKE NO PART IN WORKS
OF DARKNESS THAT ARE OF NO BENEFIT; EXPOSE
THEM INSTEAD. 12 INDEED IT IS A SHAME EVEN TO
SPEAK OF WHAT THOSE PEOPLE DO IN SECRET,
13 BUT AS SOON AS IT IS EXPOSED TO THE
LIGHT, EVERYTHING BECOMES CLEAR. 14
AND WHAT HAS BE-

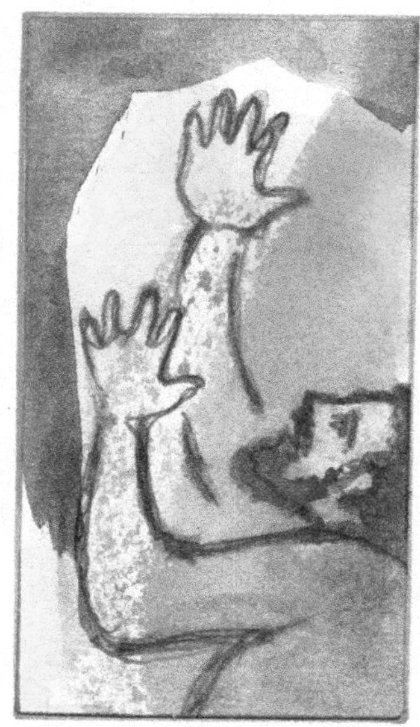

COME CLEAR BECO-
MES LIGHT. THERE-
FORE IT IS SAID:
"AWAKE, YOU WHO SLE-
EP, ARISE FROM THE
DEAD, THAT THE
LIGHT OF CHRIST
MAY SHINE ON YOU."
15 PAY ATTENTION
TO HOW YOU BEHAVE.
DO NOT LIVE AS THE
UNWISE DO, BUT AS
RESPONSIBLE PER-
SONS, 16 TRY TO MA-
KE GOOD USE OF THE
PRESENT TIME, BE-
CAUSE THESE DAYS
ARE EVIL. 17 SO DO
NOT BE FOOLISH BUT
UNDERSTAND WHAT
THE WILL OF THE LORD
IS. 18 DO NOT GET
DRUNK: WINE LEADS
TO LEVITY; BUT BE FIL-
LED WITH THE HOLY
SPIRIT. 19 GATHER
TOGETHER TO PRAY
WITH PSALMS, HYMNS AND SPIRITUAL SONGS.
SING AND CELEBRATE THE LORD IN YOUR HEART,
20 GIVING THANKS TO GOD THE FATHER IN THE
NAME OF CHRIST JESUS, OUR LORD, ALWAYS
AND FOR EVERYTHING.

HUSBANDS, LOVE YOUR WIVES

21 LET ALL KIND OF SUBMISSION TO ONE ANOTHER BECO-
ME OBEDIENCE TO CHRIST. 22 SO WIVES TO THEIR HUS-
BANDS: AS TO THE LORD. 23 THE HUSBAND IS THE HEAD
OF HIS WIFE, AS CHRIST IS THE HEAD OF THE CHURCH, HIS BO-
DY AND THE SAVIOR. 24 AS THE CHURCH SUBMITS TO CHRIST
SO THE WIFE TO HER HUSBAND. 25 AS FOR YOU, HUSBANDS,
LOVE YOUR WIVES AS CHRIST LOVED THE CHURCH AND GAVE HIM-
SELF FOR HER. 26 HE WASHED HER AND MADE HER HOLY BY
BAPTISM IN THE WORLD. 27 AS HE WANTED A CHURCH

WITHOUT STAIN OR WRINKLE OR BLEMISH, BUT HOLY AND
BLAMELESS, HE HIMSELF HAD TO PREPARE AND PRESENT
HER TO HIMSELF. 28 IN THE SAME WAY, HUSBANDS SHOULD
LOVE THEIR WIVES AS THEY LOVE THEIR OWN BODIES. HE
WHO LOVES HIS WIFE LOVES HIMSELF. 29 NO ONE HATES
HIS BODY; HE FEEDS AND TAKES CARE OF IT. THAT IS WHAT
CHRIST DOES WITH THE CHURCH. 30 BECAUSE WE ARE A
PART OF HIS BODY. 31 SCRIPTURE SAYS: BECAUSE OF
THIS A MAN SHALL LEAVE HIS FATHER AND MOTHER TO BE
UNITED WITH HIS WIFE, AND THE TWO SHALL BECOME
ONE FLESH.
32 THIS IS A GREAT MYSTERY, AND I REFER TO CHRIST
AND THE CHURCH. 33 AS FOR YOU, LET EACH ONE LOVE
HIS WIFE AS HIMSELF, AND LET THE WIFE
RESPECT HER HUSBAND.

CHILDREN, PARENTS, SERVANTS AND MASTERS

6 1 CHILDREN OBEY YOUR PARENTS FOR THIS IS
RIGHT: 2 HONOR YOUR FATHER AND YOUR MO-
THER. AND THIS IS THE FIRST COMMANDMENT THAT
HAS PROMISE: 3 THAT YOU MAY BE HAPPY AND EN-
JOY LONG LIFE IN THE LAND. 4 AND YOU, FA-
THERS, DO NOT MAKE REBELS OF YOUR CHILDREN,
BUT EDUCATE THEM BY CORRECTION AND INSTR-
UCTION WHICH THE LORD MAY INSPIRE.
5 SERVANTS, OBEY YOUR MASTERS OF THIS
WORLD WITH FEAR AND RESPECT, WITH SIM-
PLICITY OF HEART, AS IF OBEYING CHRIST. 6

DO NOT SERVE ONLY WHEN YOU ARE WATCHED
OR IN ORDER TO PLEASE OTHERS, BUT BECOME
SERVANTS OF CHRIST WHO DO GOD'S WILL WITH
ALL YOUR HEART. 7 WORK WILLINGLY, FOR
THE LORD AND NOT FOR HUMANS, MINDFUL
THAT THE GOOD EACH ONE HAS DONE, 8 WHE-
THER SERVANT OR FREE, WILL BE REWARDED
BY THE LORD. 9 AND YOU, MASTERS, DEAL WITH
YOUR SERVANTS IN THE SAME WAY, AND DO NOT
THREATEN THEM, SINCE YOU KNOW THAT THEY AND
YOU HAVE THE SAME LORD WHO IS IN HEAVEN AND
HE TREATS ALL FAIRLY.

BE STRONG IN THE LORD

10 FINALLY, BE STRONG IN THE LORD WITH HIS
ENERGY AND STRENGTH. 11 PUT ON THE WHOLE AR-

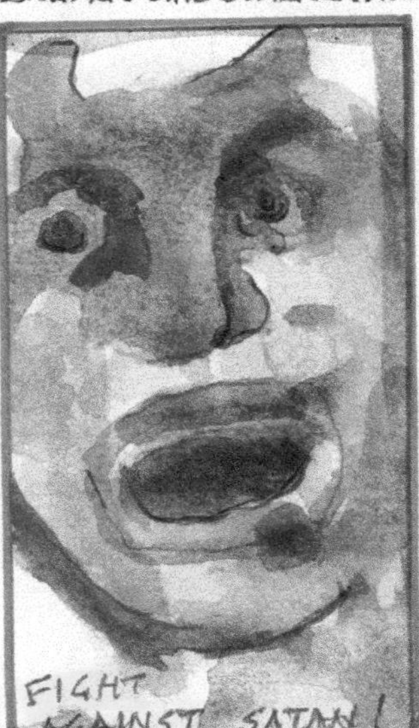

MOR OF GOD TO BE ABLE
TO RESIST THE CUNNING
OF THE DEVIL. 12 OUR
BATTLE IS NOT AGAINST
HUMAN FORCES BUT
AGAINST THE RULERS
AND AUTHORITIES AND
THEIR DARK POWERS
THAT GOVERN THE WORLD.
WE ARE STRUGGLING
AGAINST THE SPIRITS
AND SUPERNATURAL
FORCES OF EVIL.
13 THEREFORE PUT
ON THE WHOLE ARMOR
OF GOD, THAT IN THE DAY
OF EVIL, YOU MAY RE-
SIST AND STAND
YOUR GROUND,
MAKING USE OF ALL
YOUR WEAPONS,
14 TAKE TRUTH AS YOUR BELT, JUSTICE
AS YOUR BREASTPLATE, 15 AND ZEAL
AS YOUR SHOES TO PROPAGATE THE GOSPEL
OF PEACE.

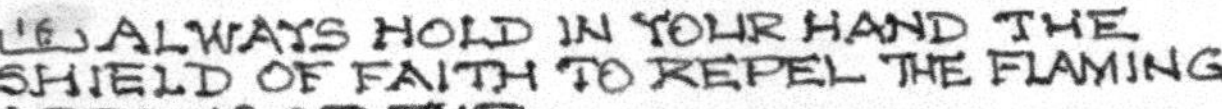

16 ALWAYS HOLD IN YOUR HAND THE
SHIELD OF FAITH TO REPEL THE FLAMING
ARROWS OF THE
DEVIL. 17 FINAL-
LY, USE THE HEL-
MET OF SALVATI-
ON AND THE SWORD
OF THE SPIRIT,
THAT IS, THE WORD
OF GOD.

18 PRAY AT ALL
TIMES AS THE SPI-
RIT INSPIRES YOU.
KEEP WATCH TOGE-
THER WITH SUSTA-
INED PRAYER AND
SUPPLICATION FOR
ALL THE BROTHERS.
19 PRAY ALSO FOR
ME, SO THAT WHEN
I SPEAK, I MAY BE
GIVEN WORDS TO
PROCLAIM BRAVELY
THE MYSTERY OF
THE GOSPEL. EVEN
20 WHEN IN CHAINS
I AM AN AMBASSADOR
OF GOD; MAY HE
GIVE ME THAT
STRENGTH TO SPEAK AS I SHOULD. I ALSO
21 WANT YOU TO KNOW HOW I AM AND WHAT
I AM DOING. TYCHICUS, OUR BELOVED BRO-
THER AND FAITHFUL MINISTER IN THE LORD,
WILL TELL YOU EVERYTHING. 22 I AM SEND-
ING HIM PRECISELY TO GIVE YOU NEWS
OF US AND COMFORT YOU ALL. 23 MAY

PEACE AND LOVE WITH FAITH FROM GOD
THE FATHER AND FROM CHRIST JESUS
THE LORD, BE WITH THE BROTHERS AND
SISTERS.

24 AND MAY HIS BLESSING BE WITH ALL
WHO LOVE CHRIST JESUS, OUR LORD,
WITH UNDYING LOVE.

LET ALL KIND OF SUBMISSION
TO ONE ANOTHER BECOME
OBEDIENCE TO CHRIST
(Ephesians 5:21)
© DM 04

LETTER TO THE PHILIPPIANS

HERE AGAIN A REAL LETTER FROM PAUL PERSONAL, WARM, FULL OF ATTENTION AND TENDERNESS THAT PAUL SENT FROM PRISON TO THE COMMUNITY THAT HAD ALWAYS BEEN THE MOST CONCERNED FOR HIS WELL-BEING.

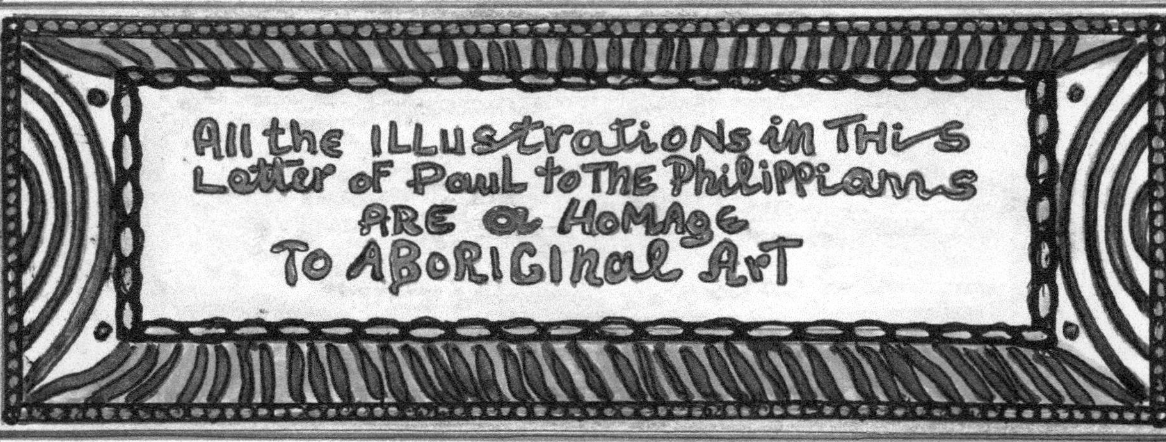

1 1 FROM PAUL AND TIMOTHY, SERVANTS
OF CHRIST JESUS, TO THE SAINTS IN PHI-
LIPPI, WITH THEIR BISHOPS AND DEACONS;

TO YOU ALL IN CHRIST JESUS:

2 MAY GRACE AND PEACE BE YOURS FROM
GOD, OUR FATHER, AND CHRIST JESUS, THE LORD.

3 I GIVE THANKS TO MY GOD EACH TIME I RE-
MEMBER YOU, 4 AND WHEN I PRAY FOR YOU,

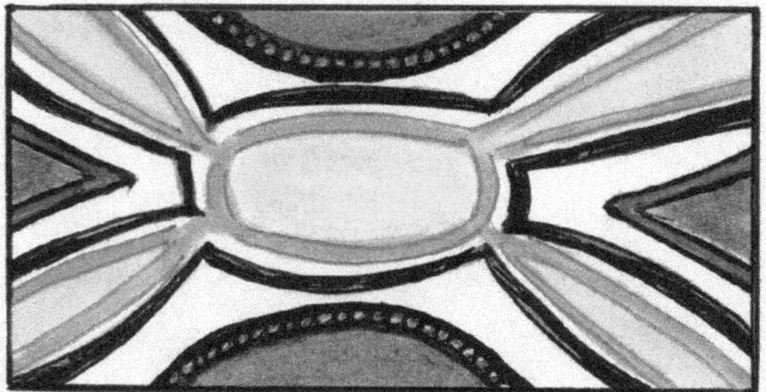

I PRAY WITH JOY. 5 I CANNOT FORGET ALL YOU SHA-
RED WITH ME IN THE SERVICE OF THE GOSPEL FROM THE
FIRST DAY UNTIL NOW. 6 SINCE GOD BEGAN SUCH
A GOOD WORK, I AM CERTAIN THAT HE WILL COMPLETE
IT IN THE DAY OF CHRIST JESUS. 7 THIS IS MY HOPE
FOR YOU, FOR I CARRY YOU ALL IN MY HEART: WHETHER I AM
IN PRISON OR DEFENDING AND CONFIRMING THE GOSPEL, YOU
ARE WITH ME AND SHARE
THE SAME GRACE. GOD
8 KNOWS THAT I LOVE
YOU DEARLY WITH THE
LOVE OF CHRIST JESUS,
9 AND IN MY PRAY-
ERS I ASK YOU THAT
YOUR LOVE MAY
LEAD YOU EACH DAY
TO A DEEPER KNOW-
LEDGE AND CLEARER
DISCERNMENT, 10
THAT YOU MAY HAVE
GOOD CRITERIA FOR
EVERYTHING.
SO YOU MAY BE PU-
RE OF HEART AND
COME BLAMELESS
TO THE DAY OF CHRIST,
11 FILLED WITH
THE FRUIT OF HOLI-
NESS WHICH COMES
THROUGH CHRIST
JESUS, FOR THE
GLORY AND PRA-
ISE OF GOD.

CHRIST IS MY LIFE

12 I WANT TO KNOW, BROTHERS AND SIS-
TERS, THAT YOU ARE AWARE THAT WHAT
HAS HAPPENED TO ME HAS SERVED THE
CAUSE TO ADVANCE THE GOSPEL.

13 ACTUALLY THE WHOLE PRAETORIAN GUARD,
AND EVEN THOSE OUTSIDE THE PALACE, KNOW THAT
I AM IN CHAINS FOR CHRIST. 14 AND WHAT IS MORE,
MY CONDITION AS PRISONER HAS ENCOURAGED
MOST OF OUR BROTHERS WHO ARE NOW EMBOLD-
ENED TO PROCLAIM THE WORD OF GOD MORE
OPENLY AND WITHOUT FEAR.
15 SOME, IT IS TRUE, ARE MOVED BY ENVY AND WANT
TO CHALLENGE ME, BUT OTHERS PREACH CHRIST WITH
A GOOD INTENTION. 16 THESE LATTER ARE MOVED

BY LOVE AND REALIZE
THAT I AM HERE FOR THE
GOSPEL. 17 THE OTHERS
ANNOUNCE CHRIST TO
CHALLENGE ME. THEY DO
NOT ACT WITH A PURE
INTENTION BUT THINK
THEY ARE MAKING MY
PRISON MORE UNBEAR-
ABLE. 18 BUT IN ANY
CASE, WHETHER THEY
ARE SINCERE OR NOT,
CHRIST IS PROCLAIMED
AND BECAUSE OF THIS I
REJOICE AND HAVE NO
REGRETS.
19 I KNOW THAT ALL
THIS WILL BE A GRA-
CE FOR ME BECAUSE
OF YOUR PRAYERS
AND THE HELP GI-
VEN BY THE SPIRIT
OF CHRIST.
20 I AM HOPEFUL,
EVEN CERTAIN,
THAT I SHALL NOT
BE ASHAMED.
I FEEL AS ASSURED
NOW, AS BEFORE,
THAT CHRIST WILL BE EXALTED THROUGH
MY PERSON, WHETHER I LIVE OR DIE.

21 FOR ME, TO LIVE IS CHRIST, AND EVEN
DEATH IS PROFITABLE FOR ME.
22 BUT IF I AM NOT TO GO ON LIVING, I
SHALL BE ABLE TO ENJOY FRUITFUL LA-
BOR. WHICH SHALL I CHOOSE?

SO I FEEL TORN 23 BETWEEN THE TWO. I
DESIRE GREATLY TO LEAVE THIS LIFE

AND TO BE WITH CHRIST, WHICH WILL BE BET-
TER BY FAR, 24 BUT IT IS NECESSARY
FOR YOU THAT I REMAIN IN THIS LIFE.
25 AND BECAUSE I AM CONVINCED OF THIS, I
KNOW THAT I WILL STAY AND REMAIN WITH
YOU FOR YOUR PROGRESS AND HAPPINESS IN THE
FAITH. 26 I WILL COME TO YOU AGAIN, WITH MORE RE-
ASON FOR BEING PROUD OF BELONGING TO CHRIST JESUS.

STAND FIRM IN FAITH —

27 TRY, THEN, TO ADJUST YOUR LIVES AS FOR THE
GOSPEL OF CHRIST. MAY I SEE IT WHEN I COME TO YOU,
AND IF I CANNOT COME, MAY I AT LEAST HEAR THAT YOU
STAND FIRM IN THE SAME SPIRIT, STRIVING TO
UPHOLD THE FAITH OF THE GOSPEL WITH ONE
HEART.
28 DO NOT BE AFRAID OF YOUR OPPONENTS. THIS
WILL BE A SIGN THAT THEY ARE DEFEATED AND YOU
ARE SAVED, SAVED BY GOD. 29 FOR THROUGH CHRIST

YOU HAVE BEEN GRANTED NOT ONLY TO BELIEVE IN
CHRIST BUT ALSO TO SUFFER FOR HIM. 30 AND YOU
NOW SHARE THE SAME STRUGGLE THAT YOU SAW
I HAD AND THAT CONTINUE TO HAVE, AS YOU KNOW.

IMITATE THE HUMILITY OF JESUS

2 1 IF I MAY ADVISE YOU IN THE NAME OF
CHRIST AND IF YOU CAN HEAR IT AS THE VO-
ICE OF LOVE; IF WE SHARE THE SAME
SPIRIT AND ARE CA-

PABLE OF MERCY
AND COMPASSION,
THEN I BEG OF YOU
2 MAKE ME VERY
HAPPY: HAVE ONE
LOVE, ONE SPIRIT,
ONE FEELING, 3
DO NOTHING THROUGH
RIVALRY OR VAIN
CONCEIT. ON THE CON-
TRARY LET EACH OF
YOU GENTLY CON-
SIDER THE OTHERS
AS MORE IMPORTANT
THAN YOURSELVES.

4 DO NOT SEEK YO-
UR OWN INTEREST,
BUT RATHER THAT
OF OTHERS. 5 LET
WHAT WAS SEEN
IN CHRIST JESUS
BE SEEN IN YOU:
6 THOUGH BEING
DIVINE IN NATURE,
HE DID NOT CLAIM
IN FACT EQUALITY WITH GOD, 7 BUT EM-
PTIED HIMSELF, TAKING ON THE NATURE OF A
SERVANT, MADE IN HUMAN LIKENESS, AND IN
HIS APPEARANCE FOUND AS A MAN.
8 HE HUMBLED HIMSELF BY BEING OBE-
DIENT TO DEATH, DEATH ON THE CROSS.
9 THAT IS WHY GOD EXALTED HIM AND GA-
VE HIM THE NAME WHICH OUTSHINES ALL NAMES,

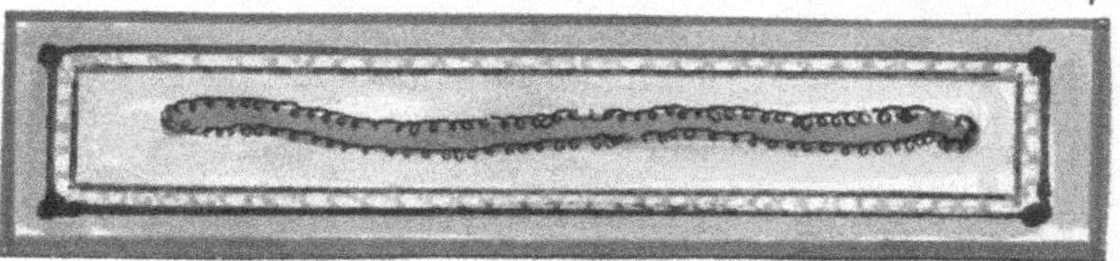

10 SO THAT AT THE NAME OF
JESUS ALL KNEES SHOULD BEND
IN HEAVEN, ON EARTH AND
AMONG THE DEAD, 11 AND ALL
TONGUES PROCLAIM THAT
CHRIST JESUS IS THE LORD TO
THE GLORY OF GOD THE FATHER.

12 THEREFORE, MY DEAREST FRIENDS, AS YOU ALWAYS
OBEYED ME WHILE I WAS WITH YOU, EVEN MORE NOW
THAT I AM FAR FROM YOU, CONTINUE WORKING

OUT YOUR SALVATION "WITH FEAR AND
TREMBLING."
13 IT IS GOD WHO MAKES YOU NOT ONLY
WISH BUT ALSO CARRY OUT WHAT PLEASES
HIM. 14 DO EVERYTHING WITHOUT GRUM-

BLING, 15 SO THAT
WITHOUT FAULT OR
BLAME, YOU WILL
BE CHILDREN OF
GOD WITHOUT RE-
PROACH AMONG A
CROOKED AND PER-
VERSE GENERATI-
ON. YOU ARE A
LIGHT AMONG
THEM LIKE STARS
IN THE UNIVERSE,
16 HOLDING TO THE
WORD OF LIFE. I SHALL
FEEL PROUD OF YOU ON
THE DAY OF CHRIST ON SE-
EING THAT MY EFFORT AND
LABOR HAVE NOT BEEN
IN VAIN. 17 AND IF I
HAVE TO POUR OUT MY
BLOOD AS AN OFFERING
TO CELEBRATE YOUR
FAITH, I REJOICE AND
CONTINUE TO SHARE
YOUR JOY; 18 AND YOU LIKEWISE SHOULD
REJOICE AND SHARE MY JOY.

PAUL'S MESSENGERS

19 THE LORD JESUS LETS ME HOPE THAT I MAY SO-
ON SEND YOU TIMOTHY, AND HAVE NEWS OF YOU. WITH
THIS I WILL FEEL ENCOURAGED. 20 FOR I HAVE
NO ONE SO CONCERNED FOR YOU AS HE IS.
21 MOST FOLLOW THEIR OWN INTEREST, NOT
THOSE OF CHRIST JESUS. 22 BUT TIMOTHY
HAS PROVED HIMSELF, AS YOU KNOW, LIKE A SON AT
THE SIDE OF HIS FATHER, HE HAS BEEN
WITH ME AT THE SERVICE OF THE GOSPEL.

23 BECAUSE OF THAT I HOPE TO SEND HIM
TO YOU AS SOON AS I SEE HOW THINGS WORK
OUT FOR ME.
24 NEVERTHELESS THE LORD LETS ME
THINK THAT I MYSELF SHALL BE COMING
SOON. 25 I JUDGED IT NECESSARY TO SEND
BACK TO YOU EPAPHRODITUS, WHO WORKED
AND FOUGHT AT MY
SIDE AND WHOM YOU
SENT TO HELP ME IN
MY GREAT NEED. 26
IN FACT, HE MISSED
YOU VERY MUCH AND
WAS STILL MORE
WORRIED BECAUSE
YOU HAD HEARD OF
HIS SICKNESS. 27
HE WAS INDEED SICK
AND ALMOST DIED, BUT
GOD TOOK PITY ON HIM
AND ON ME, SPARING
ME GREATER SORROW.
28 AND SO I AM EA-
GER TO SEND HIM
TO YOU, SO THAT ON
SEEING HIM YOU
WILL BE GLAD AND
I WILL BE AT PEACE.
29 RECEIVE HIM
THEN WITH JOY, AS
IS FITTING IN THE
LORD. CONSIDER
HIGHLY PERSONS
LIKE HIM, 30 WHO ALMOST DIED FOR THE WORK
OF CHRIST; HE RISKED HIS LIFE TO SERVE ME ON YOUR
BEHALF WHEN YOU COULD NOT HELP ME.

3 FINALLY, MY BROTHERS AND SISTERS, REJOICE IN THE LORD.

DO NOT TURN BACK TO THE JEWISH LAW

1 FINALLY, MY BROTHERS AND SISTERS,
REJOICE IN THE LORD.

IT IS NOT A BURDEN FOR ME TO WRITE

AGAIN THE SAME THINGS, AND FOR YOU IT
IS SAFER. 2 BEWARE OF THE DOGS, BE-
WARE OF THE BAD WORKERS;
BEWARE OF THE CIRCUMCISED.

THE HOLY SPIRIT
391
CCCIXC
DM
09
©

3 WE ARE THE TRUE CIRCUMCISED PEOPLE
SINCE WE SERVE ACCORDING TO THE SPIRIT
OF GOD, AND OUR CONFIDENCE IS IN CHRIST
JESUS RATHER THAN IN OUR MERITS.
4 I MYSELF DO NOT LACK THOSE HUMAN
QUALITIES IN WHICH PEOPLE HAVE CON-
FIDENCE, IF SOME OF THEM SEEM TO BE AC-
CREDITED WITH SUCH QUALITIES, HOW
MUCH MORE AM I!
5 I WAS CIRCUM-
CISED WHEN EIGHT
DAYS OLD. I WAS BORN
OF THE RACE OF IS-
RAEL, OF THE TRIBE
OF BENJAMIN; I AM A
HEBREW, BORN OF
HEBREWS. WITH RE-
GARD TO THE LAW, I
AM A PHARISEE.
6 AND SUCH WAS
MY ZEAL FOR THE LAW
THAT I PERSECUTED
THE CHURCH. AS FOR
BEING RIGHTEOUS AC-
CORDING TO THE LAW,
I WAS BLAMELESS.
7 BUT ONCE I FO-
UND CHRIST, ALL THO-
SE THINGS THAT I
MIGHT HAVE CONSI-
DERED AS PROFIT, I
RECKONED AS LOSS.
8 STILL MORE,
EVERYTHING SEEMS
TO ME AS NOTHING
COMPARED WITH THE
KNOWLEDGE OF CHRIST JESUS, MY LORD. FOR
HIS SAKE I HAVE LET EVERYTHING FALL AWAY
AND I NOW CONSIDER ALL AS GARBAGE, IF IN-
STEAD I MAY GAIN CHRIST.
9 MAY I BE FOUND IN HIM, WITHOUT MERIT OR HO-
LINESS OF MY OWN FOR HAVING FULFILLED THE LAW,
BUT WITH THE HOLINESS GIVEN BY GOD, COMING FROM
THE FAITH OF CHRIST AND THROUGH HIM, WHICH
DEPENDS ON FAITH IN CHRIST JESUS. 10 I WANT
TO KNOW HIM; I WANT TO EXPERIENCE THE POWER
OF HIS RESURRECTION AND SHARE IN HIS SUFFER-
ING AND BECOME LIKE HIM IN HIS DEATH. 11

MAY I ATTAIN THE RESURRECTION FROM THE
DEAD! 12 I DO NOT BELIEVE I HAVE ALREADY RE-
ACHED THE GOAL, NOR DO I CONSIDER MYSELF PER-
FECT, BUT I PRESS ON TILL I POSSESS CHRIST JESUS,
SINCE I HAVE BEEN PURSUED BY HIM. 13 NO,
BROTHERS AND SISTERS, I DO NOT CLAIM TO HAVE
CLAIMED THE PRIZE YET. I SAY ONLY THIS:
FORGETTING WHAT IS BEHIND ME, I RACE
FORWARD AND RUN TOWARDS THE GOAL, 14
MY EYES ON THE PRIZE TO WHICH GOD HAS
CALLED US FROM ABOVE IN CHRIST JESUS.

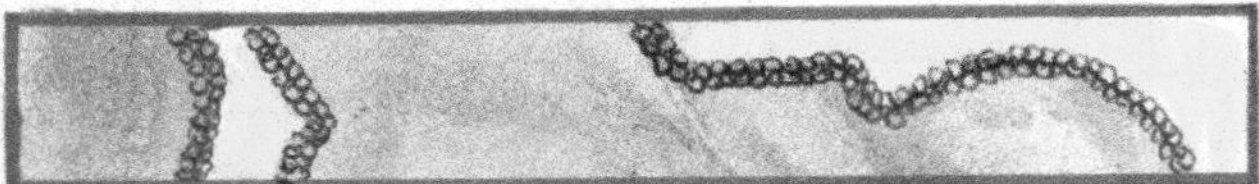

15 LET ALL OF US WHO CLAIM TO BE PERFECT
HAVE THE SAME WAY OF THINKING, BUT IF THERE
IS SOMETHING OF WHICH YOU DIFFER, GOD WILL
MAKE IT CLEAR TO YOU. 16 IN THE MEANTIME,
LET US HOLD ON TO WHAT WE HAVE ATTAINED.

17 UNITE IN IMITATING ME, BROTHERS AND SISTERS,
AND LOOK AT THOSE WHO WALK IN OUR WAY OF
LIFE. 18 FOR MANY LIVE AS ENEMIES OF THE
CROSS OF CHRIST. I HAVE SAID IT TO YOU MANY
TIMES, AND NOW I REPEAT IT WITH TEARS: 19

THEY ARE HEADING FOR RUIN; THEIR BELLY IS THEIR
GOD AND THEY FEEL PROUD OF WHAT SHOULD BE THE-
IR SHAME. THEY ONLY THINK OF EARTHLY THINGS.
20 FOR US, OUR PLACE IS IN HEAVEN, FROM WHERE WE
AWAIT THE COMING OF OUR SAVIOR, JESUS CHRIST THE
LORD. 21 HE WILL TRANSFIGURE OUR LOWLY BODY,
MAKING IT LIKE HIS OWN BODY, RADIANT IN GLORY,
THROUGH THE POWER
WHICH IS HIS TO SUBMIT
EVERYTHING TO HIMSELF.

AGREE WITH ONE ANOTHER - BE HAPPY

4 1 THEREFORE,
MY BROTHERS —
WHOM I LOVE AND LONG
FOR, YOU MY GLORY
AND CROWN, BE
STEADFAST IN THE
LORD.

2 I BEG EVODIA AND
SYNTYCHE TO AGREE
WITH EACH OTHER
IN THE LORD.

3 AND YOU, SY-
CYCUS, MY TRUE
COMPANION, I BEG
YOU TO HELP THEM.

DO NOT FORGET THAT
THEY HAVE LABO-
RED WITH ME IN
THE SERVICE OF
THE LORD AND HIS
GOSPEL, TOGE-
THER WITH CLEMENT AND MY OTHER
FELLOW-WORKERS WHOSE NAMES
ARE WRITTEN IN THE:

(4) REJOICE IN THE LORD ALWAYS, I SAY
IT AGAIN: REJOICE (5) AND MAY EVERYONE
EXPERIENCE YOUR GENTLE AND UNDER-
STANDING HEART. THE LORD IS NEAR: (6) DO
NOT BE ANXIOUS ABOUT ANYTHING.
IN EVERYTHING RESORT TO PRAYER AND SUP-
PLICATION TOGETHER WITH THANKSGIVING
AND BRING YOUR REQUESTS BEFORE GOD.
(7) THEN THE PEACE OF GOD, WHICH SURPAS-
SES ALL UNDERSTANDING, WILL KEEP YOUR

HEARTS AND MINDS IN CHRIST JESUS. (8) FIN-
ALLY, BROTHERS AND SISTERS, FILL YOUR MINDS
WITH WHATEVER IS TRUTHFUL, HOLY, JUST, PU-
RE, LOVELY AND NOBLE. BE MINDFUL OF WHAT-
EVER DESERVES PRAISE AND ADMIRATION.
(9) PUT INTO PRACTICE WHAT YOU HAVE LE-
ARNED FROM ME, WHAT I PASSED ON TO YOU, WHAT
YOU HEARD FROM ME OR SAW ME DOING, AND
THE GOD OF PEACE WILL BE WITH YOU.

PAUL'S THANKFULNESS

(10) I REJOICE IN THE LORD BECAUSE OF YOUR CON-
CERN FOR ME. YOU WE-
RE INDEED CONCERNED
FOR ME BEFORE, BUT
YOU HAD NO OPPORTUNI-
TY TO SHOW IT. (11) I
DO NOT SAY THIS BE-
CAUSE OF BEING IN
WANT: I HAVE LE-
ARNED TO MANAGE
WITH WHAT I HAVE.

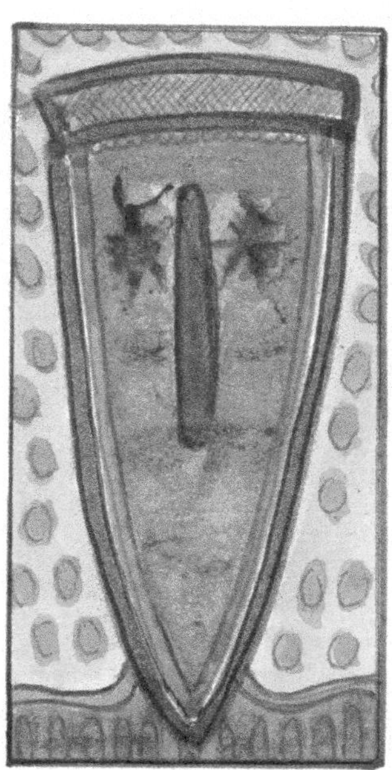

**(12) I KNOW WHAT
IT IS TO BE IN
WANT AND
WHAT IS TO
HAVE IN
PLENTY. I AM
TRAINED FOR
BOTH: TO BE
HUNGRY OR SATISFIED: TO
HAVE MUCH OR LITTLE.**

(13) I CAN DO ALL THINGS IN HIM WHO
STRENGTHENS ME.

(14) HOWEVER YOU DID RIGHT IN SHARING
MY TRIALS. (15) YOU PHILIPPIANS, REMEM-
BER THAT IN THE
BEGINNING, WHEN
WE FIRST PRE-
ACHED THE GOS-
PEL, AFTER I LEFT
MACEDONIA YOU
ALONE OPENED
FOR ME A DEBIT
AND CREDIT AC-
COUNT, (16) AND
WHEN I WAS IN
THESSALONICA,
TWICE YOU SENT
ME WHAT I NEEDED.

(17) IT IS NOT YOUR
GIFT THAT I VALUE
BUT RATHER THE
INTEREST INCREAS-
ING IN YOUR OWN
ACCOUNT. (18) NOW
I HAVE ENOUGH AND
MORE THAN ENOUGH
WITH EVERYTHING
EPAPHRODITUS DID
BRING ME ON YOUR
BEHALF AND WHICH
I RECEIVED AS "FRAGRANT OFFERINGS
PLEASING TO GOD."

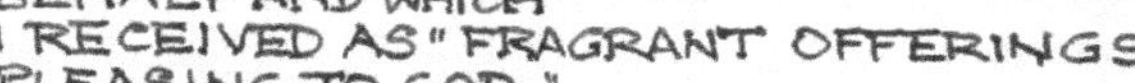

(19) GOD HIMSELF WILL PROVIDE YOU WITH
EVERYTHING YOU NEED, ACCORDING TO
HIS RICHES, AND SHOW YOU HIS GENE-
ROSITY IN CHRIST JESUS.

(20) GLORY TO GOD, OUR FATHER, FOR

EVER AND EVER: AMEN. (21) GREET ALL
WHO BELIEVE IN CHRIST JESUS. THE BRO-
THERS WITH ME GREET YOU.
(22) ALL THE BELIEVERS HERE GREET YOU,
ESPECIALLY THOSE FROM CAESAR'S HOUSE-
HOLD.

(23) THE GRACE OF CHRIST JESUS, THE
LORD, BE WITH YOUR SPIRIT.

LETTER TO THE COLOSSIANS

TOWARDS THE YEAR 62, PAUL, A PRISONER IN ROME, WRITES TO THE FAITHFULS OF COLOSSAE, WHO, WITHOUT BEING AWARE OF IT, BELITTLE CHRIST. THEY DIDN'T FEEL ASSURED WITH ONLY FAITH IN CHRIST AND THEY WANT TO ADD SOME PRACTICES FROM THE OLD TESTAMENT. OR THEY TRY TO INCLUDE CHRIST IN A BOARD OF CELESTIAL PERSONS, OR "ANGELS" WHO ARE SUPPOSED TO HAVE IN HAND THE KEY OF OUR DESTINY.
CAUGHT IN FINE DISCOURSES, THE COLOSSIANS GO THE WAY OF CERTAIN CHRISTIANS WHO BELIEVE IN SPIRITUALISM, ALSO ASTROLOGY AND HOROSCOPES.

LETTER TO THE COLOSSIANS

1 (1 PAUL, APOSTLE OF CHRIST JESUS
BY THE WILL OF GOD AND TIMOTHY
OUR BROTHER, (2 TO THE SAINTS OF

COLOSSAE, OUR FAITHFUL BROTHERS AND SISTERS
IN CHRIST: RECEIVE GRACE AND PEACE FROM
GOD OUR FATHER, AND CHRIST JESUS OUR LORD.

(3 THANKS BE TO GOD, THE FATHER OF CHRIST JESUS,
OUR LORD! WE CONSTANTLY PRAY FOR YOU, (4 FOR WE
HAVE KNOWN OF YOUR
FAITH IN CHRIST JESUS
AND YOUR LOVE FOR ALL THE
SAINTS. YOU AWAIT IN
HOPE THE INHERITANCE
RESERVED FOR YOU IN
HEAVEN, (5 OF WHICH
YOU HAVE HEARD BY THE
WORD OF TRUTH. THIS
GOSPEL, (6 ALREADY
PRESENT AMONG
YOU, IS BEARING
FRUIT AND GROWING
THROUGHOUT THE WORLD,
AS IT DID AMONG
YOU FROM THE DAY
YOU ACCEPTED IT
AND UNDERSTOOD
THE GIFT OF GOD
IN ALL ITS TRUTH.

(7 HE WHO TAUGHT
YOU, EPAPHRAS,
OUR DEAR COMPANION IN THE SERVICE OF
CHRIST, FOR US FAITHFUL MINISTER OF CHRIST;

8 HAS REMINDED ME OF THE LOVE YOU HAVE
FOR ME IN THE SPIRIT. 9 BECAUSE OF THIS,
FROM THE DAY WE RECEIVED NEWS OF YOU, WE
HAVE NOT CEASED PRAYING TO GOD FOR YOU, THAT
YOU MAY ATTAIN THE FULL KNOWLEDGE OF
HIS WILL THROUGH THE GIFTS OF WISDOM AND
SPIRITUAL UNDERSTANDING. 10 MAY YOUR
LIFESTYLE BE WOR-
THY OF THE LORD
AND COMPLETELY
PLEASING TO HIM,
MAY YOU BEAR FRUIT
IN EVERY GOOD WORK
AND GROW IN THE
KNOWLEDGE OF GOD.
11 MAY YOU BECOME
STRONG IN EVERY-
THING BY A SHAR-
ING OF THE GLORY
OF GOD, SO THAT
YOU MAY HAVE
GREAT ENDURANCE
AND PERSEVERE
IN JOY. 12 CONST-
ANTLY GIVE THANKS
TO THE FATHER
WHO HAS EMPO-
WERED US TO RE-
CEIVE OUR SHARE
IN THE INHERITANCE
OF THE SAINTS IN
HIS KINGDOM OF
LIGHT.
13 HE RESCUED US
FROM THE POWER
OF DARKNESS AND
TRANSFERRED US TO THE KINGDOM OF HIS
BELOVED SON.
14 IN HIM WE ARE REDEEMED AND FORGIVEN.

CHRIST IS THE BEGINNING OF EVERYTHING

15 HE IS THE IMAGE OF THE UNSEEN
GOD, AND FOR ALL CREATION HE IS
THE FIRSTBORN, 16 FOR IN HIM ALL
THINGS WERE CREATED, IN HEAVEN AND

ON EARTH, VISIBLE AND INVISIBLE:
THRONES, RULERS, AUTHORITIES,
POWERS ... ALL WAS MADE THROUGH
HIM AND FOR HIM.
17 HE IS BEFORE ALL AND ALL
THINGS HOLD TOGETHER IN HIM.

18 AND HE IS THE HEAD OF HIS BODY,
THE CHURCH, FOR HE IS THE FIRST,
THE FIRST RAISED FROM THE DEAD
THAT HE MAY BE THE FIRST IN
EVERYTHING,

19 FOR GOD WAS PLEASED TO
LET FULLNESS DWELL IN HIM.
20 THROUGH HIM GOD WILLED TO RE-
CONCILE ALL THINGS TO HIMSELF, AND
THROUGH HIM, THROUGH HIS BLOOD
SHED ON THE CROSS, GOD ESTABLI-
SHES PEACE ON EARTH AS IN HEAVEN.

21 YOU YOURSELVES WERE ONCE ESTRANGED
AND OPPOSED TO GOD BECAUSE OF YOUR EVIL
DEEDS, 22 BUT NOW YOU HAVE BEEN RECONCI-
LED. GOD RECONCILED YOU BY GIVING UP TO DE-
ATH THE BODY OF CHRIST, SO THAT YOU MAY BE
WITHOUT FAULT, HOLY AND BLAMELESS BE-
FORE HIM. 23 STAND FIRM ON THE FOUNDATION
OF YOUR FAITH, AND BE STEADFAST IN HOPE.
KEEP IN MIND THE GOSPEL YOU HAVE HEARD,
WHICH HAS BEEN PREACHED TO EVERY
CREATURE UNDER HEAVEN, AND OF WHICH
I, PAUL, BECAME A MINISTER.
24 AT PRESENT I REJOICE WHEN I SUFFER
FOR YOU; I COMPLETE
IN MY OWN FLESH IN
WHAT IS LACKING IN
THE SUFFERINGS OF
CHRIST FOR THE SAKE
OF HIS BODY, WHICH IS
THE CHURCH. 25 FOR
I AM SERVING THE CHURCH
SINCE GOD ENTRUSTED TO
ME THE MINISTRY OF
BRINGING INTO EFFECT
HIS DESIGN FOR YOU.
26 I MEAN THAT MYS-
TERIOUS PLAN THAT
FOR CENTURIES AND
GENERATIONS REMA-
INED SECRET, AND
WHICH GOD HAS
NOW REVEALED TO
HIS HOLY ONES.

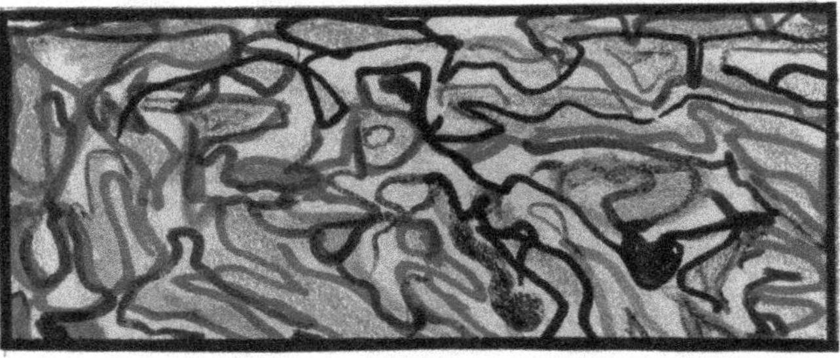

27 GOD WILLED TO
MAKE KNOWN TO
THEM THE RICHES
AND EVEN THE GLO-
RY THAT HIS MYS-
TERIOUS PLAN RE-
SERVED FOR THE PA-
GAN NATIONS: CHRIST
IS IN YOU AND YOU MAY HOPE GOD'S GLORY.

28 THIS CHRIST WE PREACH. WE WARN AND
TEACH EVERYONE TRUE WISDOM, AIMING
TO MAKE EVERYONE PERFECT IN CHRIST.

29 FOR THIS CAUSE I LABOR AND GREA-
TLY STRUGGLE WITH THE ENERGY OF
CHRIST WORKING POWERFULLY IN ME.

CCCVIIIC · 392 ·
©

LOURDES
© CCCVMC - 393 - DM03

LET CHRIST JESUS, THE LORD, BE YOUR DOCTRINE

2 1 I WANT YOU TO KNOW HOW I STRIVE FOR
YOU, FOR THOSE OF LAODICEA AND FOR SO
MANY WHO HAVE NOT MET ME PERSONALLY.
2 I PRAY THAT ALL MAY BE ENCOURAGED.
MAY YOU BE ESTABLISHED IN LOVE, THAT YOU MAY
OBTAIN ALL THE RI-
CHES OF A FULL UN
DERSTANDING AND
KNOW THE MYSTERY OF
GOD, CHRIST HIMSELF.
3 FOR IN HIM ARE
HIDDEN ALL THE TRE-
ASURES OF WISDOM AND
KNOWLEDGE. 4 SO LET
NO ONE DECEIVE YOU
WITH PERSUASIVE AR-
GUMENTS. ALTHOUGH
5 I AM FAR FROM
YOU, MY SPIRIT IS
WITH YOU AND I RE-
JOICE IN RECALLING
HOW WELL-DISCIPLIN-
ED YOU ARE AND HOW
FIRM IN THE FAITH
OF CHRIST. 6 IF YOU
HAVE ACCEPTED AS
LORD CHRIST JESUS,
LET HIM BE YOUR DOC-
TRINE. 7 BE ROOTED
AND BUILT UP IN HIM;
LET FAITH BE YOUR
PRINCIPLE, AS YOU

WERE TAUGHT, AND YOUR THANKSGIVING
OVERFLOWING. 8 SEE THAT NO ONE DECE-
IVES YOU WITH PHILOSOPHY OR ANY HOLLOW
DISCOURSE: THESE ARE MERELY HUMAN
DOCTRINES NOT INSPIRED BY CHRIST BUT BY
THE WISDOM OF THIS WORLD. 9 FOR IN HIM
DWELLS THE FULLNESS OF GOD IN BODILY FORM.
10 HE IS THE HEAD OF ALL COSMIC POWER AND AU-
THORITY, AND IN HIM YOU HAVE EVERYTHING.

11 IN CHRIST JESUS YOU WERE GIVEN
A CIRCUMCISION BUT NOT BY HUMAN

Beware of False Prophets...

HANDS, WHICH REMOVED YOU COMPLETE-
LY FROM THE CARNAL BODY: I REFER

12 TO BAPTISM. ON RECEIVING IT YOU
WERE BURIED WITH CHRIST; AND YOU
ALSO ROSE WITH HIM FOR HAVING BELI-
EVED IN THE POWER OF GOD WHO RAISED
HIM FROM THE DEAD.

13 YOU WERE DEAD. YOU WERE IN SIN AND
UNCIRCUMCISED AT THE SAME TIME. BUT

GOD GAVE YOU LIFE WITH CHRIST. HE FORGAVE ALL
YOUR SINS. 14 HE CANCELED THE RECORD OF OUR DEBTS,
THOSE REGULATIONS AGAINST US. HE DID AWAY WITH
ALL THAT AND NAILED IT TO THE CROSS. VICTORIOUS
15 THROUGH THE CROSS, HE STRIPPED THE RUL-
ERS AND AUTHORITIES OF THEIR POWER, HUMBLED
THEM BEFORE THE EYES OF THE WHOLE WORLD AND
DRAGGED THEM BEHIND HIM AS PRISONERS.

USELESS DOCTRINES

16 LET NO ONE CRITICIZE YOU IN MATTERS OF FOOD
OR DRINK OR FOR NOT OBSERVING FESTIVALS,
NEW MOONS AND SAB-
BATH. 17 THESE THINGS
WERE ONLY SHADOWS
OF WHAT WAS TO COME,
WHEREAS THE REALI-
TY IS THE PERSON OF
CHRIST. 18 DO NOT LET
BE ROBBED OF HIM BY
THOSE WHO OFFER YOU
A RELIGION OF FEAR
AND THE ANGEL'S
WORSHIP. IN FACT,
THEY ONLY APPRECIA-
TE THEIR OWN VISIONS
AND ARE PUFFED UP
WITH THEIR IDLE NO-
TIONS, 19 INSTEAD
OF HOLDING FIRMLY
TO THE HEAD, CHRIST.
HE NOURISHES AND GI-
VES UNITY TO THE BO-
DY BY A COMPLEX
SYSTEM OF NERVES AND
LIGAMENTS, MAKING
IT GROW ACCORDING
TO THE PLAN OF GOD. 20 IF YOU HAVE REALLY DI-
ED WITH CHRIST, AND RID OF THE PRINCIPLES OF THE
WORLD, WHY DO YOU NOW LET YOURSELVES BE
TAUGHT AS IF YOU BELONGED TO THE WORLD?
21 "DO NOT EAT THIS, DO NOT TASTE THAT, DO
NOT TOUCH THAT..."

22 THESE ARE HUMAN RULES AND TEACH-
INGS, REFERRING TO THINGS THAT ARE PERI-
SHABLE, THAT WEAR OUT AND DISAPPEAR.

23 These doctrines may seem to be profound because they speak of religious observance and humility and of disregarding the body. In fact, they are useless as soon as the flesh rebels.

SEEK THE THINGS THAT ARE ABOVE

3 1 So then, if you are risen with Christ, seek the things that are above, where Christ is seated at the right hand of God. 2 Set your mind

on the things that are above, not on earthly things. 3 For you have died and and your life is now hidden with Christ in God. 4 When Christ, who is our life, reveal himself, you also will be revealed with him in glory. 5 Therefore, put to death what is earthly in your life,

that is immorality, impurity, inordinate passions, wicked desires and greed which is a way of worshiping idols. 6 These are the things that arouse the wrath of God. 7 For a time you followed this way and lived in such disorders. 8 Well then, reject all that: anger, evil intentions, malice; and let no abusive words be heard from your lips.

PUT ON THE NEW SELF

9 Do not lie to one another. You have been stripped of the old self and its way of thinking 10 to put on the new, which is being renewed and is to reach perfect knowledge and the likeness of its creator.

11 There is no distinction between Jew and Greek, between circumcised and uncircumcised. There are no strangers, barbaricans, slaves or free men, but Christ is all and is in all.

12 Clothe yourselves, then, as is fitting for God's chosen people, holy and beloved of him. Put on compassion, kindness, humility, meekness and patience 13 to bear with one another and forgive whenever there is any occasion to do so. As the Lord has forgiven you, forgive one another. 14 Let all this be done with love; through it everything is united and made perfect. 15 May the peace of Christ overflow in your hearts; for this end you were called to be one body. And be thankful. 16 Let the word of God dwell in you in all its richness. Teach and admonish one another with words of wisdom, with thankful hearts sing to God psalms, hymns and spontaneous praise. 17 And whatever you do or say, do it in the name of Jesus, the Lord, giving thanks to God the Father through him.

ON OBEDIENCE

18 Wives, submit yourselves to your husbands, as you should do in the Lord. 19 Husbands, love your wives and do not get angry with

them. 20 Children, obey your parents in everything, for that pleases the Lord. 21 Parents, don't be too demanding of your children, lest they become discouraged. 22 Servants, obey your masters in everything; not only while they are present to gain favor with them, but sincerely, because you fear the Lord.

23 WHATEVER YOU DO, DO IT WHOLE-
HEARTEDLY, WORKING FOR THE LORD,
AND NOT FOR HUMANS.

24 YOU WELL KNOW THAT THE LORD WILL
REWARD YOU WITH THE INHERITANCE.
YOU ARE SERVANTS, BUT YOUR LORD IS CHRIST.

25 EVERY EVILDOER WILL RECEIVE HIS DUE,

BECAUSE GOD DOES NOT MAKE EXCEPTIONS
IN FAVOR OF ANYONE.

4 1 AS FOR YOU, MASTERS, GIVE YOUR SERVANTS
WHAT IS FAIR AND REASONABLE, KNOWING
THAT YOU ALSO HAVE A MASTER IN HEAVEN.

FURTHER INSTRUCTIONS

2 BE STEADFAST IN PRAYER AND EVEN SPEND
THE NIGHT PRAYING AND GIVING THANKS. 3
PRAY ESPECIALLY FOR
US AND OUR PREACH-
ING: MAY THE LORD GI-
VE US WORDS TO ANNO-
UNCE THE MYSTERY OF
CHRIST. BECAUSE OF THIS
I AM IN CHAINS; PRAY
4 THAT I MAY BE ABLE
TO REVEAL THIS MYS-
TERY AS I SHOULD.
5 DEAL WISELY
WITH THOSE WHO DO
NOT BELONG TO THE
CHURCH: TAKE AD-
VANTAGE OF EVERY
OPPORTUNITY. 6 LET
YOUR CONVERSATION
BE PLEASING WITH
A TOUCH OF WIT.
KNOW HOW TO
SPEAK TO EVERY-
ONE IN THE BEST
WAY.

7 TYCHICUS WILL GIVE NEWS OF ME.
HE IS OUR DEAR BROTHER AND FOR ME A
FAITHFUL ASSISTANT AND FELLOW-WO-
RKER FOR THE LORD.
8 I AM PURPOSELY SENDING HIM TO GIVE
YOU NEWS OF ME AND TO ENCOURAGE YOU.

9 WITH HIM I AM SENDING ONESIMUS,
OUR FAITHFUL AND DEAR BROTHER, WHO
IS ONE OF YOURS.
THEY WILL TELL YOU ABOUT EVERYTHING
THAT IS HAPPENING HERE.

10 MY COMPANION IN PRISON, ARISTARCHUS,
GREETS YOU, AS DOES MARK, THE COUS-
IN OF BARNABAS,
ABOUT WHOM YOU
HAVE ALREADY RE-
CEIVED INSTRUC-
TIONS. IF HE CALLS
ON YOU, RECEIVE
HIM WARMLY. JESUS
11 CALLED JUSTUS,
ALSO GREETS YOU.
THEY ARE THE ONLY
JEWS PEOPLE WORK-
ING WITH ME FOR
THE KINGDOM OF
GOD, AND BECAUSE
OF THAT THEY HAVE
BEEN A COMFORT
TO ME.
12 GREETINGS ALSO
FROM YOUR COUN-
TRYMAN EPAPHRAS,
A GOOD SERVANT
OF CHRIST JESUS.
HE CONSTANTLY
BATTLES FOR YOU
THROUGH HIS PRA-
YER THAT YOU BE PERFECT AND FIRM IN
WHATEVER GOD ASKS OF YOU. 13 I ASSU-
RE YOU THAT HE IS DEEPLY CONCERNED ABOUT
YOU, AS HE IS FOR THE LAODICEANS AND
THOSE OF HIERAPOLIS. 14 GREETINGS FROM
LUKE, OUR DEAR DOCTOR AND FROM DEMAS. 15
GREET THE BROTHERS AND SISTERS OF LAO-
DICEA, AND DON'T FORGET NYMPHA AND THE
CHURCH THAT GATHERS IN HER HOUSE.
16 AFTER READING THIS LETTER, SEE THAT
IT IS READ IN THE CHURCH OF THE LAODICEANS,

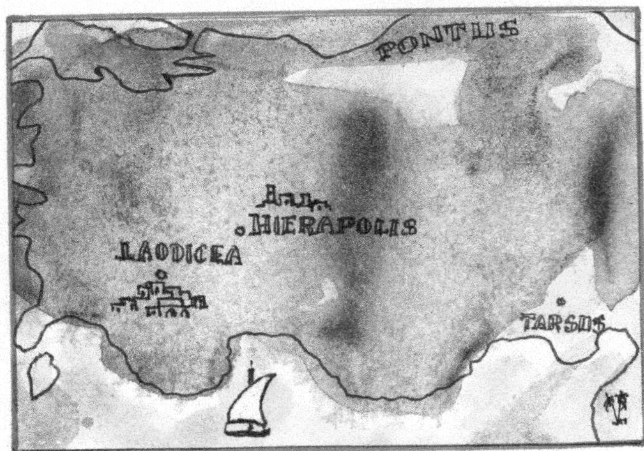

AND HAVE THE LETTER THEY RECEIVED READ
IN YOURS. 17 AND SAY TO ARCHIPUS, "DO
NOT FORGET THE MINISTRY GIVEN TO YOU
IN THE LORD."

18 GREETINGS IN MY OWN HAND, PAUL. REMEMBER
THAT I AM IN CHAINS. GRACE BE WITH YOU.

TYCHICUS AND
ONESIMUS
394 - CCCVIC
© DM 09

LETTERS TO THE THESSALONIANS

IN THE YEAR 50, PAUL ARRIVES IN THESSALONICA, A MAJOR CITY AND THE CAPITAL OF THE PROVINCE OF MACEDONIA. HERE, AFTER BEING REJECTED BY THE JEWS, HE ADDRESSES HIS PREACHING TO THE PAGANS AND SUCCEEDS IN FORMING A COMMUNITY.

THE FIRST LETTER OF PAUL TO THE CHURCH IN THESSALONICA

1 (1) FROM PAUL, SYLVANUS AND TIMOTHY
TO THE CHURCH OF THESSALONICA
WHICH IS IN GOD THE FATHER AND IN
CHRIST JESUS, THE LORD.
MAY THE PEACE AND GRACE OF GOD BE
WITH YOU. (2) WE GIVE THANKS TO GOD

AT ALL TIMES FOR YOU AND REMEMBER YOU
IN OUR PRAYERS. (3) WE CONSTANTLY RE-
CALL BEFORE GOD OUR FATHER THE WORK
OF YOUR FAITH, THE LABORS OF YOUR LOVE
AND ENDURANCE IN WAITING FOR CHRIST JESUS OUR LORD.

(4) WE REMEMBER, BROTHERS, THE CIRCUM-
STANCES OF YOUR BEING CALLED.
(5) THE GOSPEL WE BROUGHT YOU WAS
SUCH NOT ONLY IN
WORDS. MIRACLES,
HOLY SPIRIT AND
PLENTY OF EVERY-
THING WERE GIVEN
TO YOU. YOU ALSO
KNOW HOW WE DEALT
WITH YOU FOR YOUR
SAKE. (6) IN RETURN
YOU ARE NOW FOLLOWERS
OF US AND THE LORD THE
JOY OF THE HOLY SPI-
RIT IN THE MIDST OF
GREAT OPPOSITION.
(7) AND YOU BECAME
A MODEL FOR THE
FAITHFUL OF MACEDO-
NIA AND ACHAIA, (8)
SINCE FROM YOU
THE WORD OF THE
LORD SPREAD TO
MACEDONIA AND
ACHAIA, AND STILL
FURTHER. THE FAITH
YOU HAVE IN GOD
HAS BECOME NEWS
IN SO MANY PLACES THAT WE NEED SAY NO
MORE ABOUT IT. (9) OTHERS TELL OF HOW
YOU RESPONDED TO US AND TURNED FROM
IDOLS TO THE LORD.
FOR YOU SERVE THE LIVING AND TRUE GOD.

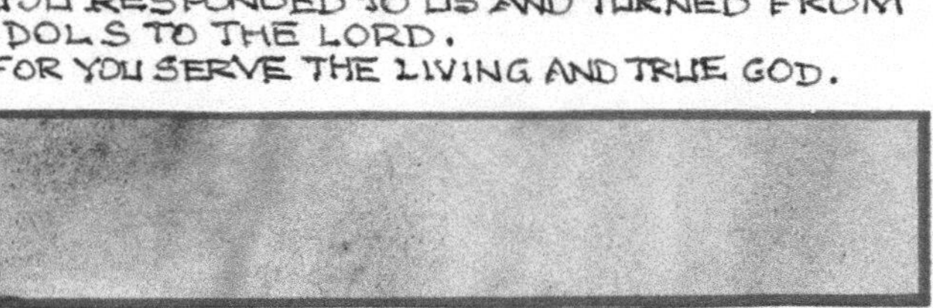

10 AND YOU WAIT FOR HIS SON FROM HEAVEN
WHOM HE RAISED FROM THE DEAD, JESUS,
WHO FREES US FROM IMPENDING PUNISHMENT.

THE BEGINNING OF THE CHURCH

2 1 YOU WELL KNOW, BROTHERS, THAT OUR
VISIT TO YOU WAS NOT IN VAIN. 2 WE
HAD BEEN ILL-TREATED AND INSULTED
IN PHILIPPI, BUT, TRUSTING IN OUR GOD, WE DARED

ANNOUNCE TO YOU THE MESSAGE OF GOD, AND FACE
FRESH OPPOSITION. 3 OUR WARNINGS DID NOT
CONCEAL ANY ERROR OR IMPURE MOTIVE, NOR DID
WE DECEIVE ANYONE. 4 BUT AS GOD HAS EN-
TRUSTED HIS GOSPEL TO US AS TO FAITHFUL MI-
NISTERS, WE WERE ANXIOUS TO PLEASE GOD WHO
SEES THE HEART, RATHER THAN MEN. 5 WE
NEVER PLEASED YOU WITH FLATTERY, AS YOU
KNOW, NOR DID WE TRY TO EARN MONEY, AS GOD
KNOWS. 6 WE DID NOT TRY TO MAKE A NAME

FOR OURSELVES 7
AMONG PEOPLE, EI-
THER WITH YOU OR
ANYBODY ELSE, AL-
THOUGH WE WERE
MESSENGERS OF CHRIST
AND COULD HAVE MADE
OUR WEIGHT FELT.
ON THE CONTRARY, WE
WERE GENTLE WITH
YOU, AS A NURSING MO-
THER WHO FEEDS AND
CUDDLES HER BABY.
8 AND SO GREAT IS
OUR CONCERN THAT WE
ARE READY TO GIVE YOU,
AS WELL AS THE GOSPEL,
EVEN OUR LIVES, FOR
YOU HAVE BECOME
OUR BELOVED BROTH-
ERS. 9 REMEMBER
OUR LABOR AND TOIL:
WHEN WE PREACHED
THE GOSPEL, WE WORK-
ED DAY AND NIGHT SO AS NOT TO BE A BURDEN TO
YOU. 10 YOU ARE WITNESSES WITH GOD THAT WE
WERE HOLY, JUST AND BLAMELESS TOWARD ALL OF
YOU WHO NOW BELIEVE. 11 WE WARNED EACH
OF YOU AS A FATHER WARNS HIS SON; 12 WE
ENCOURAGED AND URGED YOU TO ADOPT A
WAY OF LIFE WORTHY OF GOD WHO CALLS
YOU TO SHARE HIS OWN GLORY AND KINGDOM.

13 THIS IS WHY WE NEVER CEASE GIVING
THANKS TO GOD FOR, ON RECEIVING OUR
MESSAGE, YOU ACCEPTED IT, NOT AS A
HUMAN TEACHING BUT AS THE WORD OF
GOD. THAT IS WHAT IT REALLY IS, AND AS
SUCH IT IS AT WORK IN YOU WHO BELIEVE.

14 BROTHERS AND SISTERS, YOU FOLLOW-
ED THE EXAMPLE
OF THE CHURCHES
OF GOD IN JUDEA,
CHURCHES OF
CHRIST JESUS.

FOR YOU SUFFERED
FROM YOUR COM-
PATRIOTS THE
SAME TRIALS THEY
SUFFERED FROM
THE JEWS, 15
WHO KILLED THE
LORD JESUS AND THE
PROPHETS, AND WHO
PERSECUTED US.
THEY DISPLEASE GOD
AND HARM ALL PE-
OPLE 16 WHEN THEY
PREVENT US FROM
SPEAKING TO THE PA-
GANS AND TRYING
TO SAVE THEM. BY
DOING SO THEY ARE
HEAPING UP THEIR
SINS, BUT NOW
JUDGMENT IS CO-
MING UPON THEM. 17 WE ARE FOR A TIME
DEPRIVED OF YOUR PRESENCE, BUT NOT
IN OUR HEART, AND WE EAGERLY LONG TO
SEE YOU.
18 FOR WE HAVE WANTED TO VISIT YOU,
AND I, PAUL, MORE THAN ONCE; BUT SA-
TAN PREVENTED US. 19 IN FACT, WHO

BUT YOU ARE OUR HOPE AND JOY? WHO BUT YOU WILL
BE OUR GLORIOUS CROWN IN CHRIST, OUR LORD, WHEN
HE RETURNS? 20 YES, YOU ARE OUR GLORY AND JOY.

PAUL'S CONCERN

3 1 AS I COULD NO LONGER BEAR IT, I DECIDED
TO GO ALONE TO ATHENS, 2 AND SEND
YOU TIMOTHY, OUR BROTHER AND SERV-
ANT OF GOD IN THE GOSPEL OF CHRIST. I WANTED HIM
TO ENCOURAGE AND STRENGTHEN YOU IN THE FAITH,
3 SO THAT NONE OF YOU MIGHT TURN BACK
BECAUSE OF THE TRIALS YOU ARE NOW ENDUR-
ING. YOU KNOW THAT SUCH IS OUR DESTINY.

(4) I WARNED YOU OF THIS WHEN I WAS THERE:
"WE SHALL HAVE TO FACE PERSECUTION".
AND SO IT WAS, AS YOU HAVE SEEN. THEREFORE
(5) I COULD NOT STAND IT ANY LONGER AND
SENT TIMOTHY TO APPRAISE YOUR FAITH AND
SEE IF THE TEMPTER HAS TEMPTED YOU AND
MADE OUR WORK USELESS.
(6) BUT NOW TIMOTHY HAS JUST RETURNED
WITH GOOD NEWS OF
YOUR FAITH AND LOVE.
HE TOLD US THAT YOU
REMEMBER US KIND-
LY AND THAT YOU
LONG TO SEE US AS
MUCH AS WE LONG TO
SEE YOU. (7) WHAT
A CONSOLATION FOR
US, BROTHERS, IN
THE MIDST OF OUR
TROUBLES AND TRIALS,
THIS FAITH OF YOURS!
(8) IT IS A BREATH OF
LIFE FOR US WHEN
YOU STAND FIRM IN
THE LORD. (9) HOW
CAN WE THANK GOD
ENOUGH FOR ALL THE
JOY THAT WE FEEL
BEFORE GOD BECAUSE
OF YOU? (10) DAY AND
NIGHT WE BEG OF
HIM TO LET US SEE
YOU AGAIN, THAT WE
MAY COMPLETE THE
INSTRUCTION OF THE
BELIEVERS. (11) MAY GOD OUR FATHER AND
JESUS OUR LORD PREPARE THE WAY FOR US TO
VISIT YOU. (12) MAY THE LORD INCREASE MORE
AND MORE YOUR LOVE FOR EACH OTHER AND
FOR ALL PEOPLE, AS HE INCREASES OUR LOVE
FOR YOU. (13) MAY HE STRENGTHEN YOU INTER-
IORLY TO BE HOLY AND BLAMELESS BEFORE
GOD, OUR FATHER, ON THE DAY THAT JESUS,
OUR LORD, WILL COME WITH ALL HIS SAINTS.

A CALL TO A LIFE OF PURITY AND WORK

4 (1) FOR THE REST, BROTHERS, WE
ASK YOU IN THE NAME OF JESUS, THE
LORD, AND WE URGE YOU TO LIVE IN
A WAY THAT PLEASES GOD, JUST AS

YOU HAVE LEARNED FROM US. THIS YOU DO,
BUT TRY TO DO STILL MORE. (2) YOU KNOW
THE INSTRUCTIONS WE GAVE YOU ON BE-
HALF OF THE LORD JESUS: (3) THE WILL
OF GOD FOR YOU IS TO BECOME HOLY AND
NOT TO HAVE UNLAWFUL SEX.

(4) LET EACH OF YOU BEHAVE TOWARDS HIS
WIFE AS A HOLY AND RESPECTFUL HUSBAND,
(5) RATHER THAN BEING LED BY LUST, AS
ARE PAGANS WHO DO NOT KNOW GOD.
(6) IN THIS MATTER, LET NO ONE OFFEND OR
WRONG HIS BROTHER. THE LORD WILL DO
JUSTICE IN ALL THESE THINGS, AS WE HAVE WARNED
AND SHOWN YOU. (7) GOD HAS CALLED US TO
LIVE, NOT IN IMPURITY BUT IN HOLINESS, (8)
AND THOSE WHO DO NOT HEED THIS INSTRUCTION
DISOBEY, NOT A HUMAN, BUT GOD HIMSELF

WHO GIVES YOU HIS HOLY SPIRIT. (9) REGARDING BRO-
THERLY LOVE, YOU DON'T NEED ANYONE TO WRITE
TO YOU, FOR GOD HIMSELF TAUGHT YOU HOW TO LOVE
ONE ANOTHER. (10) YOU ALREADY PRACTICE IT WITH
WITH ALL THE BROTHERS AND SISTERS OF MACEDONIA,
BUT I INVITE YOU TO DO MORE. (11) CONSIDER HOW
IMPORTANT IT IS TO LIVE QUIETLY WITHOUT BOTH-
ERING OTHERS, TO MIND YOUR OWN BUSINESS
AND WORK WITH YOUR HANDS, AS WE HAVE CHAR-
GED YOU. (12) IN OBEYING THESE RULES YOU
WILL WIN THE RESPECT OF OUTSIDERS AND
BE DEPENDENT ON NO ONE.

DO NOT GRIEVE AS OTHERS DO

(13) BROTHERS, WE WANT YOU NOT TO BE MISTAKEN
ABOUT THOSE WHO ARE ALREADY ASLEEP, LEST YOU
GRIEVE AS DO THOSE
WHO HAVE NO HOPE.
(14) WE BELIEVE THAT
JESUS DIED AND ROSE;
IT WILL BE THE SAME
FOR THOSE WHO HAVE
DIED IN JESUS. GOD
WILL BRING THEM TOGE-
THER WITH JESUS AND
FOR HIS SAKE. (15) BY
THE SAME WORD OF
THE LORD WE ASSERT
THIS: THOSE OF US
WHO ARE TO BE ALIVE
AT THE LORD'S COMING
WILL NOT GO AHEAD
OF THOSE WHO ARE AL-
READY ASLEEP. WHEN
(16) THE COMMAND
BY THE ARCHANGE'S
VOICE IS GIVEN, THE
LORD HIMSELF WILL
COME DOWN FROM
HEAVEN WHILE THE
DIVINE TRUMPET CALL
IS SOUNDING. THEN

THOSE WHO HAVE DIED IN THE LORD WILL RISE
FIRST. (17) AS FOR US WHO ARE STILL ALIVE, WE
WILL BE BROUGHT ALONG WITH THEM IN THE
CLOUDS TO MEET THE LORD IN THE CELESTIAL
WORLD. WE WILL BE WITH THE LORD FOREVER.

395
CCCVC
©
DM
09

18 SO, THEN COMFORT ONE ANOTHER
WITH THESE WORDS.

YOU ARE CITIZENS OF THE LIGHT

5 1 YOU DO NOT NEED ANYONE TO WRITE
TO YOU ABOUT THE DELAY AND THE APPOIN-
TED TIME FOR THESE EVENTS. 2 YOU KNOW
THAT THE DAY OF THE LORD WILL COME LIKE A
THIEF IN THE NIGHT.

3 WHEN PEOPLE FEEL
SECURE AND AT PEACE
THE DISASTER WILL SUD-
DENLY COME ON THEM
AS THE BIRTH PANGS OF
A WOMAN IN LABOR, AND
THEY WILL NOT ESCAPE.
4 BUT YOU BROTHERS,
ARE NOT IN DARKNESS;
SO THAT DAY WILL NOT
SURPRISE YOU LIKE A
THIEF. 5 ALL OF YOU
ARE CITIZENS OF THE
LIGHT AND THE DAY.
6 LET US NOT, THE-
REFORE, SLEEP AS OT-
HERS DO, BUT REMAIN
ALERT AND SOBER. 7
NIGHT IS THE TIME FOR
THOSE WHO SLEEP TO
SLEEP, AND FOR THOSE
WHO GET DRUNK TO
DRINK. 8 SINCE WE
BELONG TO THE DAY,
LET US BE SOBER, LET US PUT ON THE BREAST-
PLATE OF FAITH AND LOVE, AND LET THE HOPE OF SAL-
VATION BE OUR HELMET. 9 FOR GOD HAS NOT
WILLED US TO BE CONDEMNED BUT TO WIN SAL-
VATION THROUGH CHRIST JESUS OUR LORD. 10
HE DIED FOR US SO THAT WE MIGHT ENTER
INTO LIFE WITH HIM, WHETHER WE ARE
STILL AWAKE OR ALREADY ASLEEP. 11 THERE-
FORE ENCOURAGE ONE ANOTHER AND BUILD UP
ONE ANOTHER, AS YOU ARE DOING NOW. BROTHERS,
12 AND SISTERS, I WANT YOU TO BE THANKFUL TO THOSE

OF YOU WHO LABOR, WHO LEAD YOU IN THE WAY OF THE
LORD AND REPRIMAND YOU. 13 ESTEEM AND LOVE
THEM HIGHLY FOR WHAT THEY ARE DOING. LIVE AT
PEACE AMONG YOURSELVES. 14 WE URGE YOU TO WARN THE
IDLE, ENCOURAGE THOSE WHO FEEL DISCOURAGED, SUSTAIN
THE WEAK, BE PATIENT WITH EVERYONE. 15 SEE THAT
NO ONE REPAYS EVIL FOR EVIL, BUT TRY TO DO GOOD,
WHETHER AMONG YOURSELVES OR TOWARDS
OTHERS. 16 REJOICE ALWAYS, 17 PRAY
WITHOUT CEASING 18 AND GIVE THANKS TO
GOD AT EVERY MOMENT. THIS IS THE WILL
OF GOD, YOUR VOCATION AS CHRISTIANS.

19 DO NOT QUENCH THE SPIRIT, 20 DO
NOT DESPISE THE PROPHETS' WARNINGS.

21 PUT EVERYTHING TO THE TEST AND HOLD
FAST TO WHAT IS GOOD. 22 AVOID EVIL,
WHEREVER IT MAY BE. 23 MAY THE GOD OF
PEACE MAKE YOU HOLY AND BRING YOU TO
PERFECTION. MAY YOU BE COMPLETELY BLA-
MELESS, IN SPIRIT, SOUL AND BODY, TILL

THE COMING OF CHRIST JESUS, OUR LORD;
24 HE WHO CALLED YOU IS FAITHFUL AND WILL
DO IT. 25 BROTHERS AND SISTERS, PRAY FOR
US. 26 GREET ALL THE BROTHERS AND SIS-
TERS WITH A HOLY KISS. 27 I ORDER YOU
IN THE NAME OF THE LORD THAT THIS LETTER
BE READ TO ALL THE BROTHERS. 28 MAY THE
GRACE OF CHRIST JESUS OUR LORD BE WITH YOU.

THE SECOND LETTER OF PAUL TO THE THESSALONIANS

1 1 FROM PAUL, SYLVANUS AND TIMOTHY,
TO THE CHURCH OF THE THESSALONIANS
WHICH IS IN GOD OUR FATHER AND IN
CHRIST JESUS, THE LORD. 2 MAY GRACE
AND PEACE BE YOURS FROM GOD THE FATHER

AND CHRIST JESUS, THE LORD. 3 BROTHERS AND
SISTERS, WE SHOULD GIVE THANKS TO GOD
AT ALL TIMES FOR YOU. IT IS FITTING TO DO SO
FOR YOUR FAITH IS GROWING AND YOUR LOVE
FOR ONE ANOTHER INCREASING.
4 WE TAKE PRIDE IN YOU AMONG THE
CHURCHES OF GOD BECAUSE OF YOUR EN-
DURANCE AND YOUR FAITH IN THE MIDST
OF PERSECUTION AND SUFFERINGS.

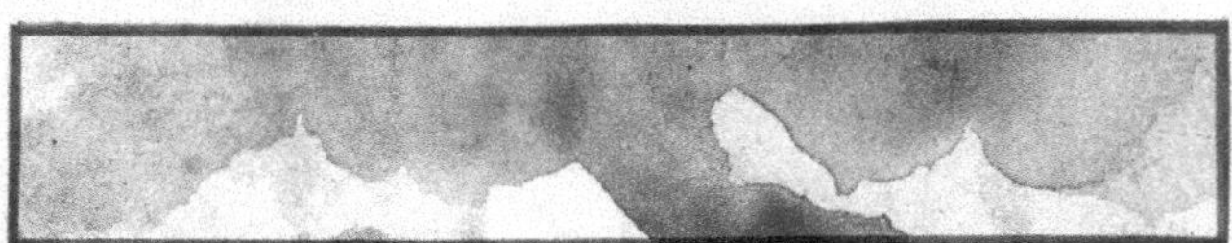

5 IN THIS THE JUST JUDGMENT OF GOD MAY
BE SEEN; FOR YOU MUST SHOW YOURSELVES
WORTHY OF THE KINGDOM OF GOD FOR WHICH
YOU ARE NOW SUFFERING.

THE COMING OF CHRIST

6 INDEED, IT IS JUST THAT GOD REPAYS WITH
AFFLICTION THOSE WHO PERSECUTE YOU, 7

BUT TO YOU WHO SUF-
FER, HE WILL GRANT
REST WITH US WHEN
THE LORD JESUS
WILL BE SHOWN IN HIS
GLORY, COMING FROM
HEAVEN AND SURRO-
UNDED BY HIS COURT
OF ANGELS. 8 THEN
WITH FLAMING FIRE
WILL BE PUNISHED
THOSE WHO DO NOT
RECOGNIZE GOD AND
DO NOT OBEY THE
GOSPEL OF JESUS, OUR
LORD. 9 THEY WILL
BE SENT TO ETERNAL
DAMNATION FAR AWAY
FROM THE FACE OF THE
LORD AND HIS MIGHTY
GLORY. 10 ON THAT
DAY THE LORD WILL
BE GLORIFIED IN THE
MIDST OF HIS SAINTS,
AND REVEAL HIS WON-
DERS THROUGH THOSE
WHO BELIEVE IN HIM,
THAT IS THROUGH
YOU WHO HAVE RECEIVED OUR TESTIMONY.
11 THIS IS WHY WE CONSTANTLY PRAY FOR YOU:
MAY OUR GOD MAKE YOU WORTHY OF HIS CALLING.
MAY HE, BY HIS POWER, FULFILL YOUR GOOD PUR-
POSES AND YOUR WORK PROMPTED BY FAITH. 12
IN THAT WAY, THE NAME OF JESUS OUR LORD WILL
BE GLORIFIED THROUGH YOU, AND YOU THROUGH
HIM, ACCORDING TO THE LOVING PLAN OF GOD
AND OF CHRIST JESUS THE LORD.

2 1 BROTHERS, LET US SPEAK ABOUT THE
COMING OF CHRIST JESUS, OUR LORD, AND
OUR GATHERING TO MEET HIM. 2 DO
NOT BE EASILY UNSETTLED. DO NOT BE

ALARMED BY WHAT A PROPHET SAYS OR BY ANY
REPORT, OR BY SOME LETTER SAID TO BE OURS,
SAYING THE DAY OF THE LORD IS AT HAND.
3 DO NOT LET YOURSELVES BE DECEIVED
IN ANY WAY. APOSTASY MUST COME FIRST, WHEN
THE MAN OF SIN WILL APPEAR;

4 THAT INSTRUMENT OF EVIL WHO OPPOSES
AND DEFILES WHATEVER IS CONSIDERED DI-
VINE AND HOLY, EVEN TO THE POINT OF SITTING
IN THE TEMPLE OF GOD AND CLAIMING TO BE GOD.
5 DO YOU REMEMBER I SPOKE OF IT WHEN I
WAS STILL WITH YOU?
BUT YOU 6 ALSO KNOW WHAT PREVENTS
HIM FROM APPEARING UNTIL HIS DUE
TIME.

7 THE MYSTERY OF SIN IS ALREADY AT

WORK, BUT HE WHO RESTRAINS IT AT PRE-
SENT HAS TO BE TAKEN AWAY.

8 THEN THE WICKED ONE WILL APPEAR,
WHOM THE LORD IS TO SWEEP AWAY

WITH THE BREATH
OF HIS MOUTH
AND DESTROY IN
THE SPLENDOR OF
HIS COMING. 9
THIS LAWLESS ONE
WILL APPEAR WITH
THE POWER OF SA-
TAN, PERFORMING
MIRACLES AND
WONDERFUL SIGNS
AT THE SERVICE OF
OF DECEPTION.
10 ALL THE DEC-
EITS OF EVIL
WILL THEN BE
USED FOR THE RU-
IN OF THOSE WHO
REFUSED TO LOVE
TRUTH AND BE SA-
VED. 11 THIS IS
WHY GOD WILL
SEND THEM THE
POWER OF DELU-
SION, THAT THEY
MAY BELIEVE WHAT
IS FALSE.

12 SO ALL THOSE WHO CHOSE WICKED-
NESS INSTEAD OF BELIEVING THE
TRUTH WILL BE CONDEMNED.

PERSEVERE IN FAITH

13 BUT WE HAVE TO GIVE THANKS FOR YOU
AT ALL TIMES, DEAR BROTHERS AND SIS-
TERS IN THE LORD. FOR GOD CHOSE
YOU FROM THE BEGINNING TO BE SAVED

THROUGH TRUE
FAITH AND TO BE
MADE HOLY BY THE
SPIRIT. 14 TO THIS
END HE CALLED YOU
THROUGH THE GOS-
PEL WE PREACH,
FOR HE WILLED
YOU TO SHARE THE
GLORY OF CHRIST
JESUS OUR LORD.
15 BECAUSE OF THAT,
BROTHERS, STAND
FIRM AND HOLD
TO THE TRADITIONS
THAT WE TAUGHT
YOU BY WORD OR BY
LETTER. 16 MAY
CHRIST JESUS OUR
LORD WHO HAS LO-
VED US, MAY GOD
OUR FATHER, WHO
IN HIS MERCY GI-
VES US EVERLAS-
TING COMFORT
AND TRUE HOPE,
STRENGTHEN YOU.
17 MAY HE ENCOU-
RAGE YOUR HEARTS
AND MAKE YOU STEADFAST IN EVERY GOOD
WORK AND WORD.

3 1 FINALLY, BROTHERS AND SISTERS,
PRAY FOR US THAT THE WORD OF GOD MAY
FINISH THE RACE AND BE CROWNED AS
IT WAS WITH YOU. 2 MAY GOD GUARD US
FROM WICKED AND EVIL PEOPLE, SINCE
NOT EVERYONE HAS FAITH. 3 THE LORD
IS FAITHFUL; HE WILL STRENGTHEN YOU
AND KEEP YOU SAFE FROM THE EVIL ONE.

4 BESIDES, WE HAVE IN THE LORD THIS
CONFIDENCE THAT YOU ARE DOING AND
WILL CONTINUE TO DO WHAT WE ORD-
ER YOU.
5 MAY THE LORD DIRECT YOUR HEARTS
TO THE LOVE OF GOD AND TO PERSE-
VERANCE FOR THE SAKE OF CHRIST.

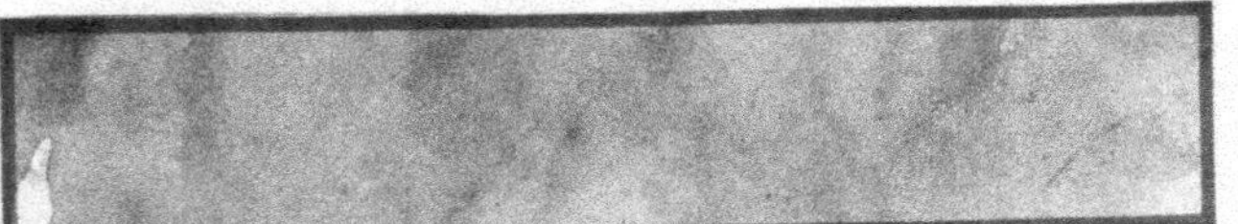

LET EVERYONE WORK

6 BROTHERS, WE COMMAND YOU TO STAY
AWAY FROM ANY BROTHER WHO IS LIVING
IN IDLENESS CONTRARY TO THE TRADITI-
ONS WE PASSED ON TO YOU.
7 YOU KNOW HOW YOU OUGHT TO FOLLOW
OUR EXAMPLE; WE WORKED WHILE WE
WERE WITH YOU.
8 DAY AND NIGHT WE LABORED AND

TOILED SO AS NOT TO BE A BURDEN TO
ANY OF YOU. 9 WE HAD THE RIGHT TO
ACT OTHERWISE, BUT WE WANTED TO
GIVE YOU AN EXAMPLE.

10 BESIDES, WHILE WE WERE WITH YOU,
WE SAID CLEARLY: IF ANYONE IS NOT WILL-
ING TO WORK, LET HIM NOT EAT.
11 HOWEVER WE HEARD THAT SOME
AMONG YOU LIVE IN IDLENESS - BUSY-
BODIES, DOING
NO WORK. 12 IN
THE NAME OF
CHRIST JESUS OUR
LORD WE COMMAND
THESE PEOPLE TO
WORK AND EARN
THEIR OWN LIVING.

13 AND YOU, BRO-
THERS, DO NOT
WEARY IN DOING
WHAT IS RIGHT.

14 IF SOMEONE DOES
NOT OBEY OUR IN-
STRUCTION IN
THIS LETTER,
TAKE NOTE AND DO NOT HAVE ANY-
THING TO DO WITH HIM, SO THAT HE
MAY BE ASHAMED.
15 HOWEVER, DO NOT TREAT HIM AS
AN ENEMY, BUT WARN HIM AS A BRO-
THER.
16 MAY THE LORD OF PEACE GIVE YOU
HIS PEACE AT ALL TIMES AND IN EVE-
RY WAY.
MAY THE LORD BE WITH YOU ALL.

17 I, PAUL, WRITE THIS GREETING
WITH MY OWN HAND. THIS IS MY SIGN-
ATURE IN ALL MY LETTERS. THIS IS
HOW I WRITE.
18 MAY THE GRACE OF CHRIST JESUS
OUR LORD BE WITH YOU.

HOMAGE TO MAGRITTE
CCCIVE
396
©

THE PASTORAL LETTERS

THESE LETTERS OF SIMILAR ORIGIN ARE ENTITLED IN THE GROUP OF PAUL'S LETTERS. BUT BOTH THE FORM AND CONTENT OF THESE LETTERS SHOW THAT THEY ARE NOT FROM HIM. THEY MUST HAVE BEEN WRITTEN IN THE PRESSURE OF CIRCUMSTANCES WE HAVE MENTIONED ABOUT 90-100 A.D.
THESE LETTERS ARE CALLED PASTORAL BECAUSE ARE ADDRESSED TO "PASTORS OF SOULS".

THE FIRST LETTER TO TIMOTHY

1 (1) FROM PAUL, APOSTLE OF CHRIST
JESUS BY A COMMAND OF GOD OUR
SAVIOUR AND OF CHRIST JESUS

OUR HOPE, (2) TO TIMOTHY, MY TRUE
SON IN THE FAITH, MAY GOD THE FAT-
HER AND CHRIST JESUS OUR LORD GIVE
YOU GRACE, MERCY AND PEACE.

FALSE TEACHERS

(3) WHEN I LEFT FOR MACEDONIA I URGED TO RE-
MAIN IN EPHESUS. I URGED YOU TO WARN SOME
PERSONS NOT TO TEA-
CH FALSE DOCTRINE
(4) OR TO CONCERN
THEMSELVES WITH FA-
BLES AND ENDLESS
GENEALOGIES. THESE
GIVE RISE TO DISCUS-
SIONS RATHER THAN
PROMOTING A BETTER
SERVICE OF GOD THROUGH
FAITH. (5) THE AIM OF
OUR WARNING IS LOVE
WHICH COMES FROM
A PURE MIND, A GO-
OD CONSCIENCE AND
SINCERE FAITH. (6)
SOME HAVE TURNED
AWAY FROM SUCH A
MOTIVATION AND
HAVE STRAYED INTO
USELESS DISCUSSIONS.

(7) THEY CLAIM TO
BE TEACHERS OF
THE LAW WHEN, IN
FACT, THEY UNDER-
STAND NEITHER WHAT THEY SAY NOR
THE THINGS THEY SPEAK ABOUT.

8 WE KNOW THAT THE LAW IS GOOD AS LONG
AS IT SERVES ITS PURPOSE. 9 THE LAW IS NOT
FOR THE RIGHTEOUS, BUT FOR THE LAWLESS AND FOR
THE WICKED AND SINFUL, FOR THOSE WHO DO
NOT RESPECT GOD AND RELIGION, FOR THOSE
WHO KILL THEIR PARENTS, FOR MURDERERS,
10 FOR THOSE WHO INDULGE IN UNLAWFUL
SEX OR, AND, HOMOSEXUALITY, FOR KIDNAP-
PERS AND EXPLOITERS, FOR LIARS AND
PERJURERS AND FOR ALL THAT IS CONTRARY

TO SOUND DOCTRINE, 11 TO THE GOSPEL
OF THE GOD OF GLORY AND HAPPINESS,
WHICH WAS ENTRUSTED TO ME.

12 I GIVE THANKS TO CHRIST JESUS, OUR
LORD, WHO IS MY STRENGTH, WHO HAS CONSIDE-
RED ME TRUSTWORTHY AND APPOINTED ME
TO HIS SERVICE, 13 ALTHOUGH I HAD BEEN
A BLASPHEMER, A PERSECUTER AND A

RABID ENEMY.
HOWEVER HE TOOK
MERCY ON ME BE-
CAUSE I DID NOT
KNOW WHAT I WAS
DOING WHEN I OP-
POSED THE FAITH;
14 AND THE GRACE
OF OUR LORD WAS MORE
THAN ABUNDANT, TO-
GETHER WITH FAITH
AND CHRISTIAN LOVE.
15 THIS SAYING IS
TRUE AND WORTHY OF
BELIEF: CHRIST JESUS
CAME INTO THE WORLD
TO SAVE SINNERS, OF
WHOM I AM THE FIRST.
16 BECAUSE OF
THAT I WAS FOR-
GIVEN; CHRIST
JESUS WANTED
TO DISPLAY HIS
GREATNESS IN
ME SO THAT I
MIGHT BE AN EXAMPLE FOR ALL WHO
ARE TO BELIEVE AND OBTAIN ETERNAL
LIFE.

17 TO THE KING OF AGES, THE ONLY GOD
WHO LIVES BEYOND EVERY PERISHABLE
AND VISIBLE CREATION - TO HIM BE
HONOR AND GLORY FOREVER. AMEN!

18 TIMOTHY, MY SON, I COMMAND YOU
TO FIGHT THE GOOD FIGHT, FULFILLING
THE PROPHETIC WORDS PRONOUNCED
OVER YOU.
19 HOLD ONTO FAITH AND GOOD CON-
SCIENCE, UNLIKE THOSE WHO, IGNORING
CONSCIENCE, HAVE FINALLY WRECKED
THEIR FAITH. 20 AMONG THEM ARE
HYMENEUS AND ALEXANDER WHOM I HAVE
DELIVERED TO SATAN TO BE TAUGHT NOT
TO BLASPHEME.

2

1 FIRST OF ALL I URGE THAT PETITI-
ONS, PRAYERS,
INTERCESSIONS
AND THANKSGIVING
BE MADE FOR EVE-
RYONE, 2 FOR RU-
LERS OF STATES AND
ALL IN AUTHORITY,
THAT WE MAY ENJOY
A QUIET AND PE-
ACEFUL LIFE IN
GODLINESS AND
RESPECT. 3 THIS
IS GOOD AND PLE-
ASES GOD. 4 FOR
HE WANTS ALL TO
BE SAVED AND CO-
ME TO THE KNOW-
LEDGE OF TRUTH.
5 AS THERE IS
ONE GOD, THERE
IS ONE MEDIATOR
BETWEEN GOD
AND MEN, CHRIST
JESUS, 6 TRUE

MAN, WHO GAVE HIS LIFE FOR THE RED-
EMPTION OF ALL. THIS IS THE TESTIMONY,
GIVEN IN ITS PROPER TIME AND, 7 OF
THIS, GOD HAS MADE ME APOSTLE AND HE-
RALD. I AM NOT LYING, I AM TELLING THE
TRUTH: HE MADE ME TEACHER OF THE
NATIONS REGARDING FAITH AND TRUTH.
8 I WANT MEN IN EVERY PLACE TO LIFT PURE

HANDS IN PRAYER TO HEAVEN WITHOUT ANGER
AND DISSENSION. 9 LET WOMEN DRESS WITH
SIMPLICITY AND MODESTY, NOT ADORNED WITH
FANCY HAIRSTYLES, GOLD, JEWELS AND
EXPENSIVE CLOTHES, 10 BUT WITH GOOD
WORKS, AS IS FITTING TO WOMEN SERVING
GOD. 11 LET A WOMAN QUIETLY RECEIVE INST-
RUCTION AND BE SUBMISSIVE. 12 I ALLOW NO
WOMAN TO TEACH OR TO HAVE AUTHORITY OVER
MEN. LET THEM BE QUIET. 13 FOR ADAM WAS
CREATED FIRST AND THEN EVE.

14 ADAM WAS NOT DECEIVED; IT WAS THE WO-
MAN WHO WAS DECEIVED AND FELL INTO SIN.
15 BUT WOMAN WILL BE SAVED THROUGH
MATERNITY, PROVIDED THAT HER LIFE BE
ORDERLY AND HOLY, IN FAITH AND LOVE.

REGARDING OVERSEERS AND DEACONS

3 1 IF SOMEONE ASPIRES TO THE OVERSEER'S
MINISTRY, HE IS WITHOUT A DOUBT LOOK-
ING FOR A NOBLE TASK. 2 IT IS NEC-
ESSARY THAT THE OVERSEER (OR BISHOP)
BE BEYOND REPROACH,

THE HUSBAND OF
ONE WIFE, RESPON-
SIBLE, JUDICIOUS,
OF GOOD MANNERS,
HOSPITABLE AND
SKILLFUL IN TE-
ACHING. 3 HE MUST
NOT BE ADDICTED TO
WINE OR QUARRELSO-
ME, BUT GENTLE AND
PEACEFUL AND NOT A
LOVER OF MONEY, 4
BUT A MAN WHOSE
HOUSEHOLD IS WELL
MANAGED, WITH OBE-
DIENT AND WELL-MAN-
NERED CHILDREN. 5
IF HE CANNOT GOVERN
HIS OWN HOUSE, HOW
CAN HE LEAD THE AS-
SEMBLY OF GOD?
6 HE MUST NOT BE
A RECENT CONVERT, LEST HE BECOME CON-
CEITED AND FALL INTO THE SAME CONDEMN-
ATION AS THE DEVIL. 7 MOREOVER HE MUST
ENJOY A GOOD REPUTATION AMONG THE OUTSID-
ERS, LEST PEOPLE SPEAK EVIL ABOUT HIM AND HE
FALL INTO SNARE, THE SNARE OF THE DEVIL. 8 THE
DEACONS, LIKEWISE, MUST BE SERIOUS AND SINCERE MEN
AND MODERATE IN DRINKING WINE, NOT GREEDY FOR
MONEY, 9 MEN WHO KEEP THE MYSTERY OF FAITH
WITH A CLEAR CONSCIENCE. 10 LET THEM BE FIRST
TRIED AND, IF FOUND BLAMELESS, BE ACCEPTED AS

DEACONS. 11 IN THE SAME WAY THE THE WOMEN
MUST BE CONSCIENTIOUS, NOT GIVEN TO GOSSIP,
BUT RESERVED AND TRUSTWORTHY. 12 A DE-
ACON MUST BE HUSBAND OF ONE WIFE, AND MUST
KNOW HOW TO GUIDE HIS CHILDREN AND MANAGE HIS
HOUSEHOLD. 13 THOSE WHO SERVE WELL
AS DEACONS WILL WIN HONORABLE RANK,
WITH AUTHORITY TO SPEAK OF CHRISTIAN FAITH.

14 I GIVE YOU THESE INSTRUCTIONS, AL-
THOUGH I HOPE I WILL SEE YOU SOON. 15 IF I
DELAY, YOU WILL KNOW HOW YOU OUGHT TO
CONDUCT YOURSELF IN THE HOUSEHOLD OF
GOD, THAT IS, THE CHURCH OF THE LIVING
GOD, WHICH IS THE PILLAR AND FOUNDATION
OF THE TRUTH. 16 HOW GREAT INDEED IS
THE MYSTERY OF DIVINE BLESSING!

HE WAS SHOWN IN THE FLESH AND
SANCTIFIED BY THE SPIRIT; PRESENTED
TO THE ANGELS AND PROCLAIMED TO ALL
NATIONS. THE WORLD BELIEVED IN HIM: HE
WAS TAKEN UP IN GLORY!

4 1 THE SPIRIT TELLS US THAT IN THE LAST DAYS
SOME WILL DEFECT FROM THE FAITH AND FOLLOW
DECEITFUL SPIRITS AND DEVILISH DOCTRINES,
2 LED BY LYING HYPOCRITES WHOSE CONSCIENCE
HAS BEEN BRANDED WITH THE STAMP OF INFAMY. 3
THESE PERSONS FORBID MARRIAGE AND CONDEMN
THE USE OF CERTAIN

FOOD WHICH GOD CRE-
ATED FOR THOSE WHO
KNOW THE TRUTH, AND
WHICH THE BELIEVERS
RECEIVE WITH THANKS-
GIVING. 4 EVERYTHING
CREATED BY GOD IS GOOD,
ALL FOOD IS LAWFUL; NO-
THING IS TO BE REJECTED
IF THERE IS THANKSGI-
VING, 5 FOR IT IS BLES-
SED WITH GOD'S WORD
AND PRAYER, AND MADE
HOLY. 6 IF YOU EXPLAIN
THIS TO THE BROTHERS,
YOU'LL BE A GOOD SER-
VANT OF CHRIST JESUS,
NOURISHED BY THE TE-
ACHING OF FAITH AND THE
SOUND DOCTRINE WHICH
YOU HAVE FOLLOWED.
7 REJECT IRRELIGIOUS
FABLES AND OLD WIVES'
TALES. TRAIN YOURSELF IN GODLINESS. 8 PHYSICAL
TRAINING IS OF LIMITED VALUE; GODLINESS, INSTEAD, IS
VERY USEFUL, HOLDING PROMISE FOR THE PRESENT LIFE
AND THE ONE TO COME. 9 HERE YOU HAVE A DOCTRINE
YOU CAN TRUST. 10 WE TOIL AND ENDURE BECAUSE
WE TRUST IN THE LIVING GOD, THE SAVIOR OF ALL,
ESPECIALLY OF THOSE WHO BELIEVE.

ADVICE TO TIMOTHY 11 COMMAND AND TEACH
THESE THINGS. 12 LET NO ONE REPROACH YOU ON AC-
COUNT OF YOUR YOUTH. BE A MODEL TO THE BELIE-
VERS IN THE WAY YOU SPEAK AND ACT, IN YOUR
LOVE, YOUR FAITH AND PURITY OF LIFE.

HOMAGE TO VANESSA BELL
397
CCCIIIC
©
DM
09

13 DEVOTE YOURSELF TO READING, PREACHING
AND TEACHING, UNTIL I COME.
14 DO NOT NEGLECT THE SPIRITUAL GIFT
CONFERRED ON YOU WITH PROPHETIC WORDS
WHEN THE ELDERS LAID THEIR HANDS UPON
YOU. 15 THINK ABOUT IT AND PRACTICE IT
SO THAT YOUR PROGRESS MAY BE SEEN BY ALL.

16 TAKE CARE OF YOURSELF AND ATTEND TO

YOUR TEACHING. BE STEADFAST IN DOING THIS AND
YOU WILL SAVE BOTH YOURSELF AND YOUR HEARERS.

THE WIDOWS IN THE CHURCH

5 1 DO NOT REBUKE THE OLDER MAN; ON
THE CONTRARY, ADVISE HIM AS IF HE WERE YOUR
FATHER. TREAT THE YOUNG AS YOUR BROTHERS,
2 THE ELDER WOMEN AS MOTHERS AND THE YOUNG
GIRLS AS YOUR SISTERS, WITH GREAT PURITY. 3
TAKE CARE OF WIDOWS WHO ARE REALLY WIDOWS.
4 IF A WIDOW HAS CHILDREN OR GRANDCHILDREN
THEY SHOULD FIRST LEARN THEIR FAMILY DUTIES

AND GIVE THEIR PA-
RENTS FINANCIAL HELP.
THIS IS CORRECT AND
PLEASES GOD. 5 A
TRUE WIDOW IS ONE WHO,
IN BEING LEFT ALONE, HAS
SET HER HOPE IN GOD, DAY
AND NIGHT PRAYING TO HIM
AND ASKING HIM FOR HELP.
6 ON THE CONTRARY, A
WIDOW WHO LIVES AS
SHE PLEASES IS DEAD
EVEN WHILE SHE LI-
VES. 7 WARN THEM
ABOUT THIS THAT THEY
MAY BE BLAMELESS.
8 THOSE WHO DO
NOT TAKE CARE OF
THEIR OWN, ESPECIAL-
LY THOSE OF THEIR
HOUSEHOLD, HAVE DE-
NIED THE FAITH AND
ARE WORSE THAN UN-
BELIEVERS. 9 LET
NO ONE BE PUT ON THE
LIST OF WIDOWS UNLESS SHE IS SIXTY YEARS OLD AND
HAS BEEN MARRIED ONLY ONCE. 10 SHE MUST BE
COMMENDED FOR HER GOOD WORKS AND THE EDUCA-
TION OF HER CHILDREN. HAS SHE OFFERED HOSPITA-
LITY TO AND HUMBLY SERVED THE SAINTS, HELPED
THE SUFFERING AND PRACTICED OTHER GOOD DEEDS?

11 DO NOT ACCEPT YOUNGER WIDOWS. THEY MAY HAVE
OTHER DESIRES THAN FOR CHRIST AND WANT TO MARRY;

12 THEN THEY DESERVE CONDEMNATION FOR
BREAKING THEIR FIRST COMMITMENT. 13 BE-
SIDES THEY FORM THE HABIT OF BEING IDLE,
GOING FROM HOUSE TO HOUSE. AND IT IS NOT
JUST IDLENESS! THEY BECOME GOSSIPS
AND BUSYBODIES, SAYING WHAT THEY
SHOULD NOT.
14 SO I WANT YOUNG WIDOWS TO MARRY AND
HAVE CHILDREN, TO RULE THEIR HOUSEHOLD
AND GIVE ADVERSARIES NO GROUNDS FOR
CRITICISM. 15 SOME
HAVE ALREADY ON
THE WAY TO FOLLOW
SATAN. 16 IF ANY
CHRISTIAN WOMAN
HAS WIDOWS IN HER
FAMILY, LET HER
ASSIST THEM: IN
THIS WAY THE CHU-
RCH WILL NOT BE
BURDENED AND MAY
ASSIST THOSE WHO
ARE TRULY WIDOWS.

PRESBYTERS

17 LET THE ELDERS
WHO RULE WELL RECE-
IVE DOUBLE COMPENSA-
TION, MAINLY THOSE
WHO PREACH AND TE-
ACH. 18 SCRIPTURE
SAYS: DO NOT MUZZLE
THE OX WHILE IT
THRESHES GRAIN, AND:
THE WORKER DESERVES HIS WAGES. 19 DO NOT AC-
CEPT ACCUSATIONS AGAINST AN ELDER EXCEPT ON THE
EVIDENCE OF TWO OR THREE WITNESSES. 20 IF HE
CONTINUES TO SIN, REBUKE HIM IN THE PRESENCE
OF THE COMMUNITY, AS A WARNING TO THE REST.
21 I URGE YOU, IN THE PRESENCE OF GOD AND
CHRIST JESUS AND OF THE HOLY ANGELS, TO
OBEY THESE RULES WITH IMPARTIALITY, WITH-
OUT MAKING DISTINCTIONS. 22 DON'T BE HASTY
IN THE LAYING ON OF HANDS, THUS BECOMING AN ACCOMP-
LICE IN THE SINS OF OTHERS. KEEP YOURSELF FREE FROM

BLAME. 24 THE SINS OF SOME PEOPLE ARE PLAIN TO
SEE, EVEN BEFORE THEY ARE EXAMINED; THE SINS OF
OTHERS ARE KNOWN ONLY LATER ON. 25 LIKEWISE
GOOD DEEDS ARE CONSPICUOUS; EVEN WHEN THEY
ARE NOT, THEY CAN'T REMAIN HIDDEN. 23 DO NOT
DRINK ONLY WATER BUT TAKE A LITTLE WINE TO
HELP YOUR DIGESTION, FOR YOUR MANY ILLNESS.

6 1 LET THOSE WHO ARE SLAVES AL-
WAYS SHOW RESPECT TO THEIR
MASTERS, SO THAT NO ONE MAY
SPEAK ILL OF GOD AND HIS TEACHING.

(2) AND THOSE WHOSE MASTERS ARE
CHRISTIANS SHOULD NOT SHOW LESS
RESPECT UNDER THE PRETEXT THAT
THEY ARE BROTHERS. ON THE CONTRARY,
THEY MUST GIVE A BETTER SERVICE SINCE
THEY ARE DOING GOOD WORKS ON BE-
HALF OF BELIEVERS AND DEAR FRIENDS.

LOVE OF MONEY

TEACH AND STRESS THESE THINGS. (3) WHOE-
VER TEACHES IN SOME OTHER WAY, NOT

FOLLOWING THE SO-
UND TEACHING OF
OUR LORD CHRIST
JESUS AND TRUE RE-
LIGIOUS INSTRUCTION,
(4) IS CONCEITED AND
UNDERSTANDS NOTHING.
HE IS CRAZY ABOUT
CONTROVERSIES AND
DISCUSSIONS WHICH
RESULT IN ENVY, INSU-
LTS, (5) BLOWS AND
CONSTANT ARGUMENTS
BETWEEN PEOPLE OF DE-
PRAVED MINDS FAR FROM
THE TRUTH. FOR THEM, RE-
LIGION IS FOR FINANCIAL
GAIN. (6) RELIGION IS
A TREASURE IF WE ARE
CONTENT WITH WHAT
WE HAVE. WE BROUGHT
(7) NOTHING INTO
THE WORLD AND
WE WILL LEAVE IT
WITH NOTHING.
(8) LET US THEN BE
CONTENT WITH HAV-
ING FOOD AND CLO-
THING. (9) THOSE WHO STRIVE TO BE RICH
FALL INTO TEMPTATIONS AND TRAPS.

A LOT OF FOOLISH AND HARMFUL AND
HARMFUL AMBITIONS PLUNGE THEM INTO
RUIN AND DESTRUCTION. (10) INDEED, THE
LOVE OF MONEY IS THE ROOT OF EVERY EVIL.
BECAUSE OF THIS GREED, SOME HAVE WANDERED
AWAY FROM THE FAITH, BRINGING ON THEMSELVES

AFFLICTION OF EVERY KIND. (11) BUT YOU, MAN OF
GOD, SHUN ALL THIS. STRIVE TO BE HOLY AND GODLY.
LIVE IN FAITH AND LOVE, WITH ENDURANCE AND
GENTLENESS. (12) FIGHT THE GOOD FIGHT OF FA-
ITH AND WIN EVERLASTING LIFE TO WHICH WE WERE
CALLED WHEN YOU MADE THE GOOD PROFES-
SION OF FAITH IN THE PRESENCE OF SO MANY
WITNESSES. (13) NOW, IN THE PRESENCE OF
GOD WHO GIVES LIFE TO ALL THINGS, AND OF
CHRIST JESUS WHO GAVE THE GOOD TESTI-
MONY BEFORE PONTIUS PILATE,
(14) I COMMAND YOU TO KEEP THE COMMAND-
MENT.
KEEP YOURSELF PURE AND BLAMELESS
UNTIL THE GLORIOUS COMING OF CHRIST
JESUS, OUR LORD, (15) WHICH GOD WILL

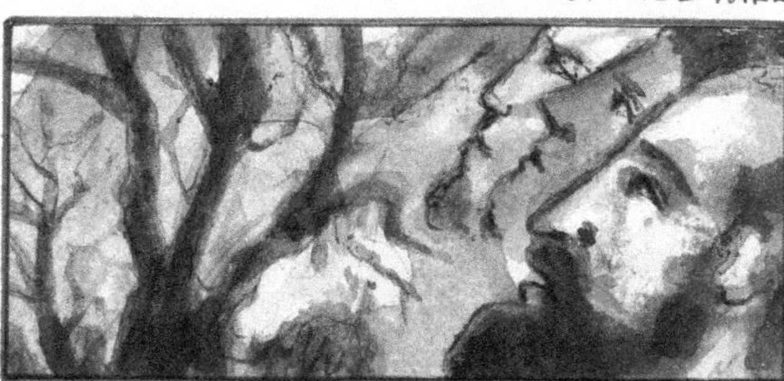

BRING ABOUT AT THE PROPER TIME, HE, THE
MAGNIFICENT SOVEREIGN, KING OF KINGS
AND LORD OF LORDS.
(16) TO HIM, ALONE IMMORTAL, WHO LIVES IN
UNAPPROACHABLE LIGHT AND WHOM NO MAN
HAS EVER SEEN OR
CAN SEE, TO HIM BE
HONOR AND POWER
FOR EVER AND EVER.
AMEN! (17) COMMAND
THE RICH OF THIS
WORLD NOT TO BE AR-
ROGANT OR TO PUT
THEIR TRUST IN
THE UNCERTAINTY OF
WEALTH. LET THEM RA-
THER TRUST IN GOD
WHO GENEROUSLY GI-
VES US ALL WE NEED
FOR OUR HAPPINESS.
(18) LET THEM DO
GOOD, BE RICH IN
GOOD DEEDS AND
BE GENEROUS;
LET THEM SHARE
WITH OTHERS. (19)
IN THIS WAY, THEY SHALL HEAP UP A
SOUND CAPITAL FOR THE FUTURE AND
GAIN TRUE LIFE.
(20) TIMOTHY, GUARD WHAT HAS BEEN EN-
TRUSTED TO YOU; AVOID USELESS AND

PROFANE WORDS, AS WELL AS DISCUSSIONS
ARISING FROM FALSE KNOWLEDGE.
(21) SOME HAVE LOST THEIR FAITH IN
ACCEPTING SUCH KNOWLEDGE.

THE GRACE OF GOD BE WITH YOU ALL.

THE SECOND LETTER TO TIMOTHY

1 (1) FROM PAUL, APOSTLE OF CHRIST JESUS
BY THE WILL OF GOD, FOR THE SAKE OF
HIS PROMISE OF ETERNAL LIFE IN
CHRIST JESUS, (2) TO MY DEAR SON TIMOTHY.
MAY GRACE, MERCY AND PEACE BE WITH YOU
FROM GOD THE FATHER AND CHRIST JESUS OUR LORD.

A SPIRIT OF BASHFULNESS?

(3) I GIVE THANKS TO GOD WHOM I SERVE WITH A

CLEAR CONSCIENCE THE WAY MY FATHERS DID, AS
I REMEMBER YOU CONSTANTLY, DAY AND NIGHT, IN
MY PRAYERS. (4) I RECALL YOUR TEARS AND I
LONG TO SEE YOU THAT I MAY BE FILLED WITH JOY.
I AM REMINDED OF YOUR SINCERE FAITH, (5) SO
LIKE THE FAITH OF YOUR GRANDMOTHER LOIS
AND OF YOUR MOTHER EUNICE, WHICH I AM SU-
RE YOU HAVE INHERITED. (6) FOR THIS REASON I
INVITE YOU TO FAN INTO A FLAME THE GIFT OF GOD

YOU RECEIVED THROUGH
THE LAYING ON OF MY
HANDS. (7) FOR GOD DID
NOT CONFER ON US A
SPIRIT OF BASHFULNESS,
BUT OF STRENGTH, LOVE
AND GOOD JUDGMENT.
(8) DON'T BE ASHAMED
OF TESTIFYING TO OUR LORD,
NOR OF SEEING ME IN CHA-
INS. INSTEAD, DO YOUR
SHARE FOR THE GOSPEL
WITH THE STRENGTH OF GOD.
(9) HE SAVED AND CAL-
LED US, A CALLING WHICH
PROCEEDS FROM HIS HO-
LINESS. THIS IS NOT
FOR OUR MERITS, BUT ON
HIS GENEROSITY AND
HIS INITIATIVE. THIS
CALLING GIVEN TO US
FROM ALL TIME IN CHRIST
JESUS (10) HAS JUST
BEEN MANIFESTED WITH
THE GLORIOUS APPEAR-
ANCE OF CHRIST JESUS,
OUR LORD, WHO DESTROYED DEATH AND BROUGHT LI-
FE AND IMMORTALITY TO LIGHT IN HIS GOSPEL.
(11) OF THIS MESSAGE I WAS MADE HERALD, APOS-
TLE AND TEACHER. (12) FOR ITS SAKE I NOW SUF-
FER THIS TRIAL, BUT I AM NOT ASHAMED, FOR I
KNOW IN WHOM I HAVE BELIEVED AND I AM CON-
VINCED THAT HE IS CAPABLE OF TAKING CARE
OF ALL I HAVE ENTRUSTED TO HIM UNTIL THAT DAY.

(13) FOLLOW THE PATTERN OF THE SOUND DOC-
TRINE WHICH YOU HAVE HEARD FROM ME, CON-
CERNING FAITH AND LOVE IN CHRIST JESUS.
(14) KEEP THIS PRE-
CIOUS DEPOSIT WITH
THE HELP OF THE HO-
LY SPIRIT WHO LI-
VES WITHIN US. (15)
YOU KNOW THAT ALL
FROM THE PROVINCE
OF ASIA HAVE DESER-
TED ME, ESPECIALLY
PHYGELUS AND HERMO-
GENES. (16) MAY GOD
BLESS THE HOUSEHOLD
OF ONESIPHORAS,
FOR HE OFTEN CAME
TO VISIT ME AND WAS
NOT ASHAMED OF MY
CHAINS. (17) ON THE
CONTRARY, ON AR-
RIVING IN ROME HE
SEARCHED FOR ME
UNTIL HE FOUND ME.
(18) MAY THE LORD
GRANT THAT HE
FIND MERCY FROM
THE LORD ON THAT
DAY. YOU WELL KNOW
ALL THE SERVICES
HE RENDERED AT EPHESUS.

A GOOD SOLDIER OF CHRIST

2 (1) YOU, MY SON, BE STRONG WITH THE GRA-
CE YOU HAVE IN CHRIST JESUS. (2) ENTRUST
TO RELIABLE PEOPLE EVERYTHING YOU HAVE
LEARNED FROM ME IN THE PRESENCE OF MANY WIT-
NESSES, THAT THEY MAY INSTRUCT OTHERS. (3) LA-
BOR LIKE A GOOD SOLDIER OF CHRIST JESUS. (4)
NO SOLDIER LETS HIMSELF BE INVOLVED IN
CIVILIAN TRADE: IT IS ENOUGH FOR HIM TO
PLEASE HIS COMMANDING OFFICER. NO ATHLETE

(5) IS CROWNED UNLESS HE COMPETES ACCORDING TO
THE RULES. (6) AND AGAIN, HE WHO TILLS THE LAND
IS THE FIRST TO ENJOY THE FRUITS OF THE HARVEST. (7)
THINK OVER WHAT I AM TELLING YOU: THE LORD WILL
GIVE YOU UNDERSTANDING IN EVERYTHING.
(8) REMEMBER CHRIST JESUS, RISEN FROM THE DEAD,
JESUS SON OF DAVID, AS PREACHED IN MY GOSPEL. (9)
FOR THIS GOSPEL I LABOR AND WEAR CHAINS LIKE AN
EVILDOER, BUT THE WORD OF GOD IS NOT CHAINED.
(10) SO I BEAR EVERYTHING FOR THE SAKE OF THE
CHOSEN PEOPLE, THAT THEY, TOO, MAY OBTAIN
THE SALVATION GIVEN TO US IN CHRIST
JESUS AND SHARE ETERNAL GLORY.

PAUL and TIMOTHY
398
CCCIIC
© DM 09

11 THIS STATEMENT IS TRUE:
IF WE HAVE DIED WITH HIM, WE SHALL ALSO
LIVE WITH HIM; 12 IF WE ENDURE WITH HIM,
WE SHALL REIGN WITH HIM; IF WE DENY
HIM, HE WILL ALSO DENY US; 13 IF WE
ARE UNFAITHFUL, HE REMAINS FAITHFUL
FOR HE CANNOT DENY HIMSELF.

DO NOT FIGHT OVER WORDS

14 REMIND YOUR PEOPLE OF THESE THINGS AND
URGE THEM IN THE PRESENCE OF GOD NOT TO

FIGHT OVER WORDS,
WHICH DOES NO GOOD,
BUT ONLY RUINS THOSE
WHO LISTEN. 15 BE
FOR GOD AN ACTIVE
AND PROVED MINISTER,
A BLAMELESS WORKER
CORRECTLY HANDLING
THE WORD OF TRUTH.
16 DO NOT TAKE
PART IN USELESS
CONVERSATIONS, ALIEN
TO THE FAITH. THIS
LEADS TO A GREATER
LACK OF FAITH. SUCH
17 TEACHING SPRE-
ADS LIKE GANGRENE:
I AM THINKING OF
HYMENEUS AND
PHILETUS. 18 THEY
STRAYED FROM THE
TRUTH, HOLDING THAT
RESURRECTION HAS
ALREADY TAKEN PLA-
CE; AND WITH THIS
THEY UPSET THE FAITH
OF SOME. 19 BUT THE SOLID FOUNDATIONS LAID
BY GOD ARE NOT SHAKEN; ON THEM IT IS WRITTEN:
THE LORD KNOWS THOSE WHO ARE HIS, AND: LET
HIM WHO CONFESS THE NAME OF THE LORD TURN
AWAY FROM EVIL.
20 IN A GREAT HOUSE WE FIND NOT ONLY
VESSELS OF GOLD AND SILVER, BUT ALSO OF
WOOD AND CLAY. SOME ARE RESERVED FOR
SPECIAL USES, OTHERS, FOR ORDINARY ONES.

21 IF ANYONE CLEANSES HIMSELF OF WHAT I AM
SPEAKING OF, HE WILL BECOME A NOBLE VESSEL,
USEFUL TO THE LORD, PREPARED FOR ANY HOLY
PURPOSE. 22 SHUN PASSIONS OF YOUTH AND SE-
EK RIGHTEOUSNESS, FAITH, LOVE AND PEACE, TOGE-
THER WITH THOSE WHO CALL ON THE LORD WITH A PURE
HEART. 23 AVOID STUPID AND SENSELESS DISCUS-
SIONS, SINCE THEY CAUSE MISUNDERSTANDING.
24 GOD'S SERVANT MUST NOT BE QUARRELSO-
ME, BUT KIND TO ALL, ALWAYS TEACHING AND PA-
TIENT WITH THOSE WHO DO NOT UNDERSTAND.
25 LET HIM GENTLY CORRECT HIS OPPONENTS;
PERHAPS GOD MAY GRANT THEM TO REPENT AND
DISCOVER THE TRUTH, 26 WITHDRAWING THEM
FROM THE SNARE OF THE DEVIL WHO HELD
THEM CAPTIVE TO HIS OWN WILL.

3 1 BE QUITE SURE THAT THERE WILL BE
DIFFICULT TIMES IN THE LAST DAYS. 2 PE-
OPLE WILL BECOME SELFISH, LOVERS OF MO-
NEY, BOASTFUL, CONCEITED, GOSSIPS, DISOBEDIENT
TO THEIR PARENTS, UNGRATEFUL, UNHOLY. THEY
3 WILL BE UNABLE TO LOVE AND TO FORGIVE;
THEY WILL BE SLANDERERS, WITHOUT SELF-CONTROL,
CRUEL, ENEMIES OF GOOD, 4 TRAITORS, SHAMELESS,

FULL OF PRIDE, MORE IN LOVE WITH PLEASURE THAN
WITH GOD. 5 THEY WILL KEEP THE APPEARANCE
OF PIETY, WHILE REJECTING ITS DEMANDS. KE-
EP AWAY FROM SUCH PEOPLE.
6 OF THE SAME KIND ARE THOSE WHO EN-
TER HOUSES AND CAPTIVATE WEAK WOMEN,
FULL OF SINS, SWAYED BY ALL KINDS OF PAS-
SIONS, 7 WHO ARE ALWAYS LEARNING BUT
NEVER GRASPING KNOWLEDGE OF THE TRUTH.
8 THESE PEOPLE OF CORRUPT MIND AND FALSE
FAITH OPPOSE THE TRUTH JUST AS JANNES AND
JAMBRES OPPOSED

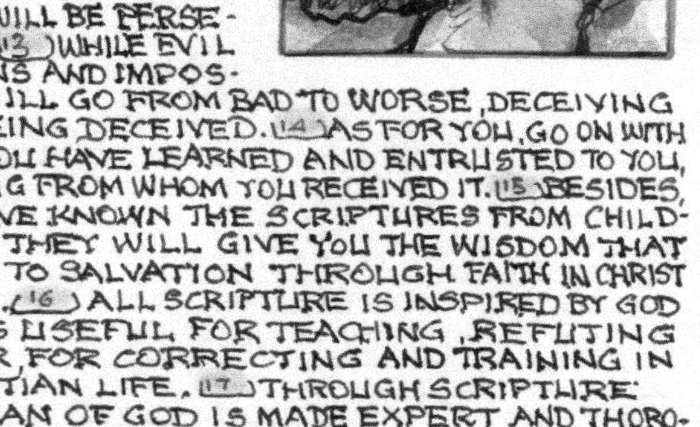

MOSES. 9 YET THEY
MAY NOT GO VERY FAR,
FOR THEIR FOLLY WILL
BE CLEAR TO ALL, AS
IN THE CASE OF THO-
SE TWO. 10 YOU, IN-
STEAD, HAVE CLOSELY
FOLLOWED MY TEACHING,
MY WAY OF LIFE, FAITH,
PROJECTS, PATIENCE, LO-
VE, ENDURANCE, 11 PER-
SECUTIONS AND SUFFE-
RINGS. YOU KNOW WHAT
HAPPENED TO ME AT
ANTIOCH, ICONIUM
AND LYSTRA. HOW MA-
NY TRIALS I HAD TO
BEAR! YET THE LORD
RESCUED ME FROM THEM
ALL. 12 ALL WHO WANT
TO SERVE GOD IN CHRIST
JESUS WILL BE PERSE-
CUTED, 13 WHILE EVIL
PERSONS AND IMPOS-
TORS WILL GO FROM BAD TO WORSE, DECEIVING
AND BEING DECEIVED. 14 AS FOR YOU, GO ON WITH
WHAT YOU HAVE LEARNED AND ENTRUSTED TO YOU,
KNOWING FROM WHOM YOU RECEIVED IT. 15 BESIDES,
YOU HAVE KNOWN THE SCRIPTURES FROM CHILD-
HOOD; THEY WILL GIVE YOU THE WISDOM THAT
LEADS TO SALVATION THROUGH FAITH IN CHRIST
JESUS. 16 ALL SCRIPTURE IS INSPIRED BY GOD
AND IS USEFUL FOR TEACHING, REFUTING
ERROR, FOR CORRECTING AND TRAINING IN
CHRISTIAN LIFE. 17 THROUGH SCRIPTURE
THE MAN OF GOD IS MADE EXPERT AND THORO-
UGHLY EQUIPPED FOR EVERY GOOD WORK.

PREACH THE WORD

4 1 IN THE PRESENCE OF GOD AND CHRIST JESUS,
WHO IS TO JUDGE THE LIVING AND THE DEAD, AND
BY THE HOPE I HAVE OF HIS COMING AND
HIS KINGDOM, I URGE YOU 2 TO PREACH THE
WORD, IN SEASON AND OUT OF SEASON, RE-
PROVING, REBUKING
OR ADVISING, ALWAYS
WITH PATIENCE AND
PROVIDING INSTRUCTION.
3 FOR THE TIME IS
COMING WHEN PEOPLE
WILL NO LONGER EN-
DURE SOUND DOCTRINE
BUT WILL BE SO EAGER
TO HEAR WHAT IS NEW,
THAT THEY WILL NE-
VER HAVE ENOUGH
TEACHERS AFTER
THEIR OWN LIKING.
4 AND THEY WILL
ABANDON THE TRUTH
TO HEAR FABLES. 5
SO BE PRUDENT, DO
NOT MIND YOUR LABOR,
GIVE YOURSELF TO YO-
UR WORK AS AN EVAN-
GELIST, FULFILL YOUR
MINISTRY. 6 AS FOR
ME THE TIME OF SACRIFICE HAS ARRIVED, AND
AT THE MOMENT MY DEPARTURE'S TIME HAS
COME. 7 I HAVE FOUGHT THE GOOD FIGHT, I
HAVE FINISHED THE RACE, I HAVE KEPT THE
FAITH.
8 NOW THERE IS LAID UP FOR ME THE
CROWN OF RIGHTEOUSNESS WITH WHICH

THE LORD, THE JUST JUDGE, WILL REWARD ME
ON THAT DAY; AND NOT ONLY ME, BUT ALL THO-
SE WHO HAVE LONGED FOR HIS GLORIOUS COMING.

FINAL GREETINGS

9 DO YOUR BEST TO COME TO ME AS
SOON AS POSSIBLE. 10 YOU MUST KNOW

THAT DEMAS HAS DESERTED ME, FOR
THE LOVE OF THIS WORLD: HE RETURN-
ED TO THESSALONICA.
CRESCENS HAS GONE TO GALATIA AND TI-
TUS TO DALMATIA. 11 ONLY LUKE REMA-
INS WITH ME. GET MARK AND BRING HIM
WITH YOU, FOR HE IS A USEFUL HELPER IN MY
WORK. 12 I SENT TYCHICUS TO EPHESUS.
13 BRING WITH YOU THE CLOAK I LEFT AT TROAS,
IN CARPO'S HOUSE AND ALSO THE SCROLLS,

ESPECIALLY THE PARCHMENTS. 14 ALEXANDER
THE METALWORKER HAS CAUSED ME GREAT HARM.
THE LORD WILL REPAY HIM FOR WHAT HE HAS
DONE. 15 DISTRUST HIM FOR HE HAS BE-
EN VERY MUCH OPPOSED TO OUR PREACH-
ING. 16 DURING
MY FIRST HEARING
IN COURT NO ONE
SUPPORTED ME;
ALL DESERTED ME.
MAY THE LORD NOT
HOLD IT AGAINST
THEM. 17 BUT THE
LORD WAS AT MY
SIDE, GIVING ME
STRENGTH TO PRO-
CLAIM THE WORD
FULLY, AND LET ALL
THE PAGANS HEAR
IT. SO I WAS RESCUED
FROM THE LION'S
MOUTH. 18 THE
LORD WILL SAVE
ME FROM ALL EVIL,
BRINGING ME TO HIS
HEAVENLY KINGDOM.
GLORY TO HIM FOR
EVER AND EVER.
AMEN! 19 GREETINGS TO PRISCA AND
AQUILA AND TO THE FAMILY OF ONESI-
PHORUS. 20 ERASTUS REMAINED IN COR-
INTH. I LEFT TROPHIMUS SICK IN MILETUS.
21 TRY TO COME HERE BEFORE THE WINTER.

EUBULUS, PUDENS, LINUS, CLAUDIA AND
ALL THE BROTHERS AND SISTERS SEND YOU
GREETINGS. 22 THE LORD BE WITH
YOUR SPIRIT.
MAY GRACE BE WITH YOU ALL.

LETTER TO TITUS

1 1 FROM PAUL, SERVANT OF GOD, APOSTLE OF
CHRIST JESUS, AT THE SERVICE OF GOD'S CHOSEN
PEOPLE, SO THAT THEY MAY BELIEVE AND REACH
THE KNOWLEDGE OF TRUTH AND GODLINESS. 2 THE
ETERNAL LIFE WE ARE WAITING FOR WAS PROMISED

FROM THE BEGINNING BY GOD WHO NEVER LIES, 3
AND AS THE APPOINTED TIME HAD COME, HE MADE IT
KNOWN THROUGH THE MESSAGE ENTRUSTED TO ME
BY A COMMAND OF GOD OUR SAVIOR. 4 GREETINGS
TO YOU, TITUS, MY TRUE SON IN THE FAITH WE SHA-
RE. MAY GRACE AND PEACE BE WITH YOU FROM
GOD THE FATHER AND CHRIST JESUS OUR LORD.

ON THE ELDERS OF THE CHURCH

5 I LEFT YOU IN CRETE BECAUSE I WANTED YOU
TO PUT RIGHT WHAT WAS DEFECTIVE AND APPO-
INT ELDERS IN EVERY TOWN FOLLOWING MY INSTRUC-

TIONS. 6 THEY MUST BE
BLAMELESS, MARRIED
ONLY ONCE, WHOSE CHIL-
DREN ARE BELIEVERS
AND NOT OPEN TO THE
CHARGE OF BEING IMMO-
RAL AND REBELLIOUS.
7 SINCE THE OVERSE-
ER (OR BISHOP) IS THE
STEWARD OF GOD'S HO-
USE, HE MUST BE BE-
YOND REPROACH: NOT
PROUD, HOT-HEADED,
OVERFOND OF WINE,
QUARRELSOME OR GRE-
EDY FOR GAIN. 8 ON
THE CONTRARY HE MUST
BE HOSPITABLE, A LO-
VER OF WHAT IS GOOD,
WISE, UPRIGHT, DEVO-
UT AND SELF-CONTROL-
LED. 9 HE MUST HOLD
TO THE MESSAGE OF
FAITH JUST AS IT WAS TAUGHT, SO THAT, IN HIS
TURN, HE MAY TEACH SOUND DOCTRINE AND RE-
FUTE THOSE WHO OPPOSE IT. 10 YOU KNOW THAT
THERE ARE MANY REBELLIOUS MINDS, TALKERS OF
NONSENSE, DECEIVERS, ESPECIALLY THE PARTY OF
THE CIRCUMCISED. 11 THEY HAVE TO BE SILENCED
WHEN THEY DISTURB WHOLE FAMILIES, TEACHING
FOR LOW GAIN WHAT SHOULD NOT BE TAUGHT.
12 A CRETAN, ONE OF THEIR OWN PROPHET, HAS
SAID, "CRETANS: ALWAYS LIARS, WICKED
BEASTS AND LAZY GLUTTONS."

13 THIS IS TRUE. FOR THIS REASON REBUKE THEM
SHARPLY IF YOU WANT THEM TO HAVE A SOUND FAITH,
14 INSTEAD OF HEEDING JEWISH FABLES AND
PRACTICES OF PEOPLE WHO REJECT THE TRUTH.
15 TO THE PURE EVERYTHING IS PURE: TO THE
CORRUPT AND UNBELIEVING NOTHING IS PURE;
THEIR MINDS AND CONSCIENCES HAVE BEEN DE-
FILED. 16 THEY PRETEND TO KNOW GOD BUT
DENY HIM WITH THEIR DEEDS. THEY ARE DE-
TESTABLE, DISOBEDIENT AND UNFIT FOR DOING
ANYTHING GOOD.

LIVE AS RESPONSIBLE PERSONS

2 1 LET YOUR WORDS STRENGTHEN SOUND
DOCTRINE. 2 TELL THE OLDER MEN TO BE
SOBER, WISE, SO-
UND IN FAITH, LOVE AND
PERSEVERANCE. 3

THE OLDER WOMEN
IN LIKE MANNER MUST
BEHAVE AS BEFITS HO-
LY WOMEN, NOT GIVEN
TO GOSSIPING OR
DRINKING WINE, 4
BUT AS GOOD COUN-
SELORS, ABLE TO TE-
ACH YOUNGER WOMEN
TO LOVE THEIR HUSB-
ANDS AND CHILDREN,
5 TO BE JUDICIOUS
AND PURE, TO TAKE
CARE OF THEIR HO-
USEHOLDS, TO BE
KIND AND SUBMIS-
SIVE TO THEIR HUS-
BANDS, LEST OUR
FAITH BE ATTACKED.
6 ENCOURAGE THE
YOUNG MEN TO BE
SELF-CONTROLLED.
7 SET THEM AN
EXAMPLE BY YOUR ON WAY OF DOING.

LET YOUR TEACHING BE EARNEST AND
SINCERE, 8 AND YOUR PREACHING BE-
YOND REPROACH. THEN YOUR OPPONENTS

WILL FEEL ASHAMED AND WILL HAVE NOTHING
TO CRITICIZE.
9 TEACH SLAVES TO BE SUBJECT TO THEIR
MASTERS, AND TO GIVE SATISFACTION IN
EVERY RESPECT, INSTEAD OF ARGUING.

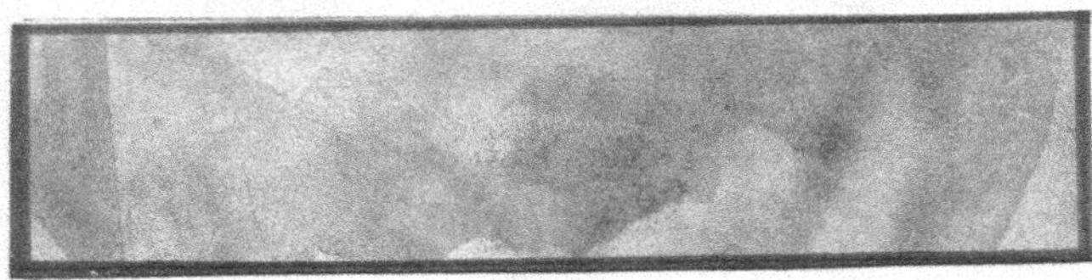

TITUS
399
CCCIC
© DM 09

10 THEY MUST NOT STEAL FROM THEM BUT
BE TRUSTWORTHY. IN THIS WAY THEY WILL
DRAW EVERYONE TO ADMIRE THE DOCTRINE
OF GOD OUR SAVIOR.

11 FOR GOD SAVIOR HAS REVEALED HIS LOVING PLAN
TO ALL, 12 TEACHING US TO REJECT AN IR-
RELIGIOUS WAY OF LIFE AND WORDLY GREED,
AND TO LIVE IN THIS WORLD AS RESPONSIBLE
PERSONS, UPRIGHT AND SERVING GOD, WHILE
13 WE AWAIT OUR BLESSED HOPE, THE GLO-
RIOUS MANIFESTATION OF OUR GREAT GOD

AND SAVIOR CHRIST JESUS. 14 HE GAVE HIMSELF
FOR US, TO REDEEM US FROM EVERY EVIL AND TO
PURIFY A PEOPLE HE WANTED TO BE HIS OWN AND
DEDICATED TO WHAT IS GOOD. 15 TEACH THESE
THINGS, ENCOURAGE AND REPROVE WITH ALL AU-
THORITY. LET NO ONE DESPISE YOU.

REMIND THE BELIEVERS

3 1 REMIND THE BELIEVERS TO BE SUBMIS-
SIVE TO RULERS AND AUTHORITIES, TO BE
OBEDIENT AND TO TAKE INITIATIVE IN DO-
ING GOOD. 2 TELL THEM TO INSULT NO ONE;
THEY MUST NOT
BE QARRELSOME
BUT GENTLE AND
UNDERSTANDING WITH
EVERYONE. 3 WE
OURSELVES WERE
ONCE FOOLISH,
DISOBEDIENT AND
MISLED. WE WERE
SLAVES OF OUR DE-
SIRES, SEEKING
PLEASURE OF
EVERY KIND. WE
LIVED IN MALICE
AND ENVY, HATE-
FUL AND HATING
EACH OTHER.
4 BUT GOD OUR
SAVIOR REVEAL-
ED HIS EMINENT
GOODNESS AND
LOVE FOR HUMAN-
KIND 5 AND SA-
VED US, NOT BE-
CAUSE OF GOOD
DEEDS WE MAY HAVE DONE, BUT FOR THE
SAKE OF HIS OWN MERCY.
HE GAVE US REBIRTH IN BAPTISM AND
RENEWED US BY THE HOLY SPIRIT 6
POURED OVER US THROUGH CHRIST JESUS OUR SAVIOR.

7 BY THE GRACE OF GOD WE WERE MA-
DE HOLY AND NOW WE HOPE FOR EVER-
LASTING LIFE, OUR INHERITANCE.

THIS IS THE TRUTH

8 THIS IS THE TRUTH. I WANT YOU TO
INSIST ON THESE THINGS, FOR THOSE
WHO BELIEVE IN
GOD MUST EXCEL
IN GOOD DEEDS;
THAT IS WHAT
MATTERS AND IS
PROFITABLE TO US.
9 AVOID STUPID
ARGUMENTS, DIS-
CUSSIONS ABOUT
GENEALOGIES
AND QUARRELS AB-
OUT THE LAW, FOR
THEY ARE USELESS
AND UNIMPORTANT.
10 IF ANYONE PROMO-
TES SECTS IN THE
CHURCH, WARN HIM
ONCE AND THEN A
SECOND TIME. IF
HE STILL CONTINUES,
BREAK WITH HIM
11 KNOWING THAT
SUCH A PERSON IS
MISLEAD AND SIN-
FUL; HE IS A SELF-CONDEMNED MAN.

12 WHEN I SEND ARTEMAS OR TYCHICUS TO
YOU, TRY TO COME TO ME AT NICOPOLIS AS SOON
AS POSSIBLE, FOR I HAVE DECIDED TO SPEND
THE WINTER THERE. 13 DO YOUR BEST TO SEND
ZENAS THE LAWYER AND APOLLOS ON THEIR WAY
SOON, AND SEE TO IT THAT THEY HAVE EVE-
RYTHING THEY NEED. 14 OUR PEOPLE MUST

LEARN TO BE OUTSTANDING IN GOOD WORKS
AND TO FACE URGENT NEEDS, INSTEAD OF
REMAINING IDLE AND USELESS.

15 ALL WHO ARE WITH ME SEND GREETINGS.
GREET THOSE WHO LOVE US IN THE FAITH.

GRACE BE WITH YOU ALL.

LETTER TO PHILEMON

PHILEMON FROM COLOSSAE HAS A SLAVE NAMED ONESIMUS: A TYPICAL
NAME FOR A SLAVE SINCE ONESIMUS MEANS "USEFUL". PAUL ASKS
THE SLAVE TO BE SEEN AS A BROTHER AND SUGGESTS TO LET HIM GO FREE.

PAUL'S LETTER TO PHILEMON

1 FROM PAUL, A PRISONER OF CHRIST JESUS, AND
FROM OUR BROTHER TIMOTHY TO PHILEMON, OUR
FRIEND AND FELLOW WORKER, 2 TO OUR DEAR SIS-
TER APPHIA, TO ARCHIPPUS FAITHFUL COMPANION
IN OUR SOLDIERING,
AND TO ALL THE CHU-
RCH GATHERED IN
YOUR HOUSE. 3 GRACE
AND PEACE BE WITH YOU
FROM GOD THE FATHER
AND JESUS CHRIST THE
LORD. 4 I NEVER CEASE
TO GIVE THANKS TO MY
GOD WHEN I REMEMBER
YOU IN MY PRAYERS, 5
FOR I HEAR OF YOUR LO-
VE AND FAITH TOWARDS
THE LORD AND ALL THE
HOLY ONES. 6 AND I
PRAY THAT THE SHAR-
ING OF YOUR FAITH MAY
MAKE KNOWN ALL THE
GOOD THAT IS OURS IN
CHRIST. 7 I HAD GREAT
SATISFACTION AND COM-
FORT ON HEARING OF YOUR

CHARITY, FOR YOU HAVE CHEERED THE HEARTS OF OUR BRO-
THERS. 8 BECAUSE OF THIS, ALTHOUGH IN CHRIST I HAVE
THE FREEDOM TO SAY WHAT YOU SHOULD DO, 9 YET I
PREFER TO REQUEST YOU IN LOVE. THE ONE TALKING

IS PAUL, THE OLD MAN, NOW PRISONER OF CHRIST. 10
AND MY REQUEST IS ON BEHALF OF ONESIMUS,
WHOSE FATHER I HAVE BECOME WHILE I WAS IN
PRISON. 11 THIS ONESIMUS HAS NOT BEEN HELP-
FUL TO YOU, BUT NOW HE WILL BE HELPFUL TO
YOU AND TO ME BOTH. 12 IN RETURNING HIM TO YOU,
I AM SENDING YOU MY OWN HEART.

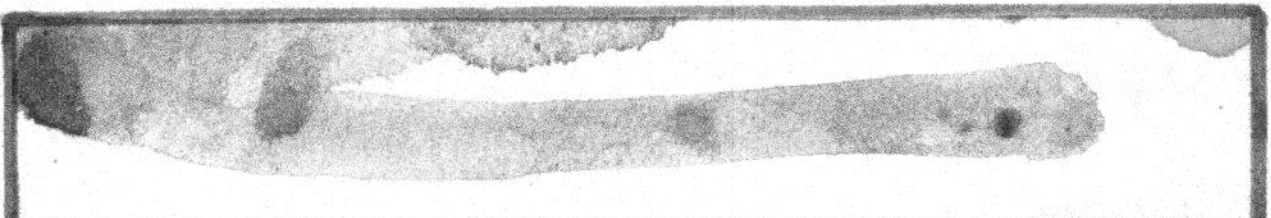

13 I WOULD HAVE LIKED TO KEEP HIM AT MY
SIDE, TO SERVE ME ON YOUR BEHALF WHILE I
AM IN PRISON FOR THE GOSPEL, 14 BUT I DID
NOT WANT TO DO ANYTHING WITHOUT YOUR AGREEM-
ENT, NOR IMPOSE A GOOD DEED ON YOU WITHOUT YOUR
FREE CONSENT. 15 PERHAPS ONESIMUS HAS BEEN

PARTED FROM YOU FOR A WHILE SO THAT YOU
MAY HAVE HIM BACK FOREVER, 16 A SLAVE,
YET NOT A SLAVE. HE IS A VERY DEAR BROTHER
TO ME, AND HE WILL BE EVEN DEARER TO YOU.
17 AND SO, BECAUSE OF OUR FRIENDSHIP, RE-
CEIVE HIM AS IF HE WERE I MYSELF.
18 AND IF HE HAS CAUSED ANY HARM, OR OWES
YOU ANYTHING, CHARGE IT TO ME. 19 I, PAUL,
WRITE THIS AND SIGN IT WITH MY OWN HAND:
I WILL PAY IT... WITHOUT FURTHER MENTION

OF YOUR DEBT TO ME, WHICH IS YOURSELF. 20 SO, MY
BROTHER, PLEASE DO ME THIS FAVOR FOR THE LORD'S
SAKE. GIVE ME THIS COMFORT IN CHRIST. 21 CON-
FIDENT OF YOUR OBEDIENCE I WRITE TO YOU, KNOW-
ING YOU WILL DO EVEN MORE THAN I ASK.
22 AND ONE MORE THING, GET A LODGING READY
FOR ME BECAUSE, THANKS TO ALL YOUR PRA-
YERS, I HOPE TO RETURN TO YOU.
23 EPAPHRAS, MY FELLOW PRISONER IN CHRIST
JESUS, SENDS GREETINGS, 24 SO DO MARK,
ARISTARCHUS, DEMAS AND LUKE, MY ASSIS-
TANTS. 25 MAY THE GRACE OF THE LORD
CHRIST JESUS BE WITH YOU. AMEN!

LETTER TO THE HEBREWS

"HEBREWS" WAS THE NAME GIVEN TO THE JEWS LIVING IN PALESTINE, UNLIKE THE MAJORITY OF THEM WHO HAD EMIGRATED TO OTHER COUNTRIES.

THIS LETTER IS ADDRESSED TO THE FIRST CHRISTIANS COMMUNITIES IN PALESTINE, FORMED BY JEWS - BY RACE - WHO HAD BEEN PERSECUTED AND PUNISHED AND WHOSE POSSESSIONS HAD EVEN BEEN CONFISCATED, ALL BECAUSE THEY HAD BECOME FOLLOWERS OF CHRIST.
THIS LETTER IS ADDRESSED TO MEN FAMILIAR WITH THE OLD TESTAMENT: THEY MAY WELL BEEN JEWISH PRIESTS CONVERTED TO CHRIST, WHO WERE GOING THROUGH A SERIOUS CRISIS.

TO CONFIRM THEIR FAITH, THIS LETTER SHOWS THAT THE JEWISH RELIGION WITH ITS IMPOSING CERIMONIES IN THE TEMPLE, WAS BUT THE IMAGE OF SOMETHING GREATER.
THE PARDON OF SIN AND THE SPIRIT OF RELIGION - THE ASPIRATION OF THE ENTIRE OLD TESTAMENT - WAS TO BE THE WORK OF THE AUTHENTIC PRIEST OF ALL HUMANITY, JESUS, THE SON OF GOD.

THERE IS NO OTHER SACRIFICE BUT HIS, WHICH BEGINS ON THE CROSS AND ENDS IN GLORY.

LETTER TO THE HEBREWS

GOD HAS SPOKEN

1 (1) GOD HAS SPOKEN IN THE PAST TO
OUR FATHERS THROUGH THE PROPH-
ETS, IN MANY DIFFERENT WAYS, AL-
THOUGH NEVER COMPLETELY; (2) BUT IN OUR

TIMES HE HAS SPO-
KEN DEFINITIVELY
TO US THROUGH
HIS SON. HE IS THE
ONE GOD APPOINTED
HEIR OF ALL THINGS,
SINCE THROUGH HIM HE
HE UNFOLDED THE STA-
GES OF THE WORLD. (3)
HE IS THE RADIANCE
OF GOD'S GLORY AND
BEARS THE STAMP OF
GOD'S HIDDEN BEING,
SO THAT HIS POWERFUL
WORD UPHOLDS THE
UNIVERSE. AND AFTER
TAKING AWAY SIN, HE
TOOK HIS PLACE AT THE
RIGHT HAND OF THE DI-
VINE MAJESTY IN HE-
AVEN. (4) SO HE IS
NOW FAR SUPERIOR TO
ANGELS JUST AS THE NAME HE RECEIVED SETS
HIM APART FROM THEM. (5) TO WHAT ANGEL DID GOD
SAY: YOU ARE MY SON, I HAVE BEGOTTEN YOU
TODAY?
AND WHAT THE ANGEL DID PROMISE: I SHALL BE
A FATHER TO HIM AND HE WILL BE A SON TO ME?
(6) ON SENDING HIS FIRSTBORN TO THE WORLD, GOD
SAYS: LET THE ANGELS ADORE HIM.
(7) WHEREAS ABOUT ANGELS WE FIND WORDS LIKE

THESE: GOD SENDS THE ANGELS LIKE WIND,
MAKES HIS SERVANTS FLAMES OF FIRE.
(8) BUT OF THE SON WE READ THIS:
YOUR THRONE, O GOD, WILL LAST FOREVER
AND EVER; A RULE OF JUSTICE IS YOUR RULE.
(9) YOU LOVED RIGHTEOUSNESS AND
HATED WICKEDNESS; THEREFORE GOD,
YOUR GOD, HAS ANOINTED YOU WITH
THE OIL OF GLADNESS, ABOVE YOUR
FELLOW KINGS.

(10) AND ALSO THESE WORDS:
LORD, IN THE BEGINNING YOU PLA-
CED THE EARTH ON ITS FOUNDATION AND
THE HEAVENS ARE THE WORK OF YOUR
HANDS. (11) THEY WILL DISAPPEAR, BUT
YOU REMAIN. THEY WILL BE FOR YOU LIKE
AN OLD GARMENT; (12) YOU WILL FOLD
THEM LIKE A CLOAK AND CHARGE THEM.
YOU, ON THE CONTRARY, ARE ALWAYS THE SA-
ME AND YOUR YEARS WILL NEVER END.
(13) GOD NEVER SAID TO ANY OF HIS ANGELS:

SIT HERE AT MY RIGHT SIDE UNTIL I PUT
YOUR ENEMIES AS A FOOTSTOOL UNDER
YOUR FEET.
(14) FOR ALL THESE SPIRITS ARE ONLY SERVANTS, AND GOD
SENDS THEM TO HELP THOSE WHO SHALL BE SAVED.

2 (1) SO WE MUST PAY THE CLOSEST ATTENT-
ION TO THE PREACH-
ING WE HEARD,

LEST WE DRIFT AWAY.
(2) IF WORDS SPOKEN
THROUGH ANGELS BE-
COME LAW AND ALL DI-
SOBEDIENCE OR NEG-
LET RECEIVED ITS DUE
REWARD, (3) HOW CO-
ULD WE NOW ESCAPE
IF WE NEGLECT SUCH
POWERFUL SALVA-
TION? FOR THE LORD
HIMSELF ANNOUN-
CED IT FIRST AND
IT WAS LATER CON-
FIRMED BY THOSE
WHO HEARD IT. (4) GOD
CONFIRMED THEIR
TESTIMONY BY SIGNS,
WONDERS AND MIRA-
CLES OF EVERY KIND -
ESPECIALLY BY THE
GIFTS OF THE HOLY
SPIRIT WHICH HE
DISTRIBUTED ACCORDING TO HIS WILL. (5) THE
ANGELS WERE NOT GIVEN DOMINION OVER THE
NEW WORLD OF WHICH WE ARE SPEAKING. (6) IN-
STEAD SOMEONE DECLARED IN SCRIPTURE:
WHAT IS MAN, THAT YOU SHOULD BE
MINDFUL OF HIM? (7) FOR A WHILE
YOU PLACED HIM A LITTLE LOWER
THAN THE ANGELS, BUT YOU CROWN-
ED HIM WITH GLORY AND HONOR.

8 YOU HAVE GIVEN HIM DOMI-
NATION OVER ALL THINGS.
WHEN IT IS SAID THAT GOD GAVE HIM POWER
OVER ALL THINGS, NOTHING IS EXCLUDED. AS
IT IS, WE DO NOT YET SEE HIS DOMINION OVER
ALL THINGS. 9 BUT JESUS WHO SUFFERED DEATH
AND "FOR A LITTLE WHILE WAS PLACED LOWER
THAN THE ANGELS" HAD BEEN "CROWNED WITH HO-
NOR AND GLORY." FOR THE MERCIFUL PLAN OF
GOD DEMANDED THAT HE EXPERIENCE DEATH
ON BEHALF OF EVERYONE.
10 GOD, FROM WHOM ALL COMES AND BY WHOM

ALL THINGS EXIST, WANTED TO BRING TO GLORY A
GREAT NUMBER OF SONS, AND HE THOUGHT IT FITTING
TO MAKE PERFECT THROUGH SUFFERING THE INITI-
ATOR OF THEIR SALVATION. 11 SO HE WHO GIVES AND
THOSE WHO RECEIVE HOLINESS ARE ONE. HE HIMSELF
IS NOT ASHAMED OF CALLING US BROTHERS, 12 AS
WE READ: "LORD, I WILL PROCLAIM YOUR NAME TO
MY BROTHERS; I WILL PRAISE YOU IN THE CON-
GREGATION." 13 HE ALSO SAYS: I WILL TRUST
IN GOD; HERE I AM AND THE CHILDREN GOD HAS
GIVEN ME. 14 AND BECAUSE ALL THOSE CHIL-
DREN SHARE ONE SAME NATURE OF FLESH

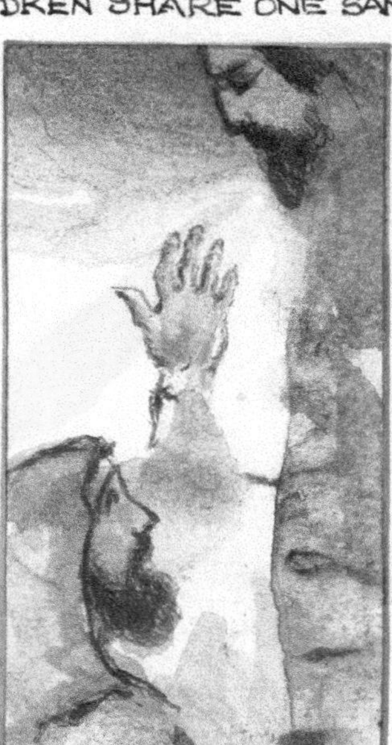

AND BLOOD, JESUS
LIKEWISE HAD TO
SHARE THIS NATURE.
THIS IS WHY HIS DE-
ATH DESTROYED THE
ONE HOLDING THE
POWER OF DEATH, THAT
IS THE DEVIL, 15 AND
FREED THOSE WHO RE-
MAINED IN BONDAGE
ALL THEIR LIFETIME
BECAUSE OF THE FEAR
OF DEATH. JESUS
16 CAME TO TAKE
BY THE HAND NOT
THE ANGELS BUT
THE HUMAN RACE.
17 SO HE HAD TO
BE LIKE HIS BRO-
THERS IN EVERY
RESPECT, IN ORD-
ER TO BE THE HIGH
PRIEST FAITHFUL
TO GOD AND MER-
CIFUL TO THEM,
A PRIEST ABLE
TO ASK PARDON
AND ATONE FOR THEIR SINS.
18 HAVING BEEN TESTED THROUGH
SUFFERING, HE IS ABLE TO HELP THO-
SE WHO ARE TESTED.

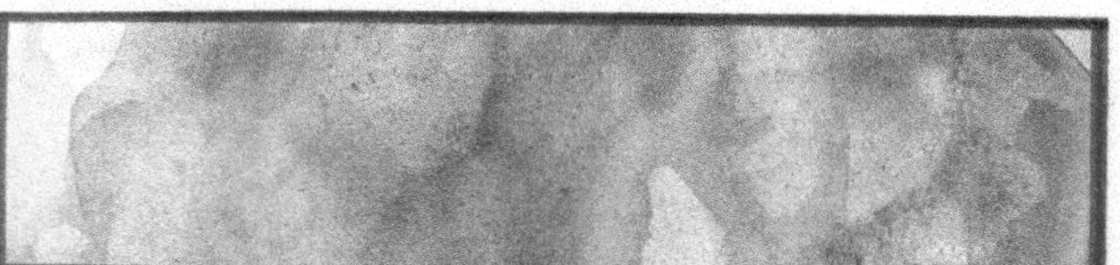

CHRIST CAME AS THE NEW MOSES

3 1 HOLY BROTHERS, CALLED TO A SUPER-
NATURAL VOCATION, CONSIDER JESUS, THE
APOSTLE AND HIGH PRIEST OF OUR FAITH.
2 HE IS FAITHFUL TO GOD WHO APPOINTED
HIM, JUST AS MOSES WAS A FAITHFUL STEWARD
OVER GOD'S HOUSEHOLD 3 BUT JESUS DESER-
VES MUCH GREATER
HONOR THAN MOSES,
SINCE HE WHO BUILDS
THE HOUSE IS GREAT-
ER THAN THE HOUSE.
4 AS EVERY HOUSE
HAS A BUILDER, GOD
IS THE BUILDER OF
ALL. 5 IT IS SAID
THAT MOSES WAS
FOUND FAITHFUL AS
A SERVANT OF GOD
OVER ALL HIS HOUSE-
HOLD, AND AS WITNESS
OF A FORMER REVELA-
TION FROM GOD. 6
CHRIST CAME AS THE
SON, TO WHOM THE
HOUSE BELONGS; AND
WE ARE HIS HOUSE-
HOLD, PROVIDED
THAT WE STAND FIRM
IN HOPE AND COURAGE.

7 LISTEN TO WHAT
THE HOLY SPIRIT SAYS:
IF ONLY YOU WOULD HEAR GOD'S
VOICE TODAY! 8 DO NOT BE STUB-
BORN, AS THEY WERE IN THE PLACE
CALLED REBELLION, 9 WHEN YOUR
FATHERS CHALLENGED ME IN THE DESERT,
ALTHOUGH THEY HAD SEEN MY DEEDS
10 FOR FORTY YEARS. THAT IS WHY

I WAS ANGRY WITH THESE PEOPLE AND SAID:
THEY HEARTS ARE ALWAYS GOING ASTRAY AND THEY
DO NOT UNDERSTAND MY WAYS. 11 I WAS ANGRY AND
MADE A SOLEMN VOW: THEY WILL NEVER ENTER MY REST.

12 SO, BROTHERS, BE CAREFUL LEST SOME OF YOU COME
TO HAVE AN EVIL AND UNBELIEVING HEART THAT FALLS
AWAY FROM THE LIVING GOD. 13 ENCOURAGE ONE
ANOTHER, DAY BY DAY, AS LONG AS IT IS CALLED
TODAY. LET NO ONE BECOME HARDENED IN THE
DECEITFUL WAY OF SIN. 14 WE ARE ASSOCIATED
WITH CHRIST PROVIDED WE HOLD STEAD-
FASTLY TO OUR INITIAL HOPE UNTIL THE END,

401
CCCCI
©
DM
09

15 SCRIPTURE SAYS: IF YOU HEAR GOD'S VOICE, DO
NOT BE STUBBORN AS THEY WERE IN THE PLACE CAL-
LED REBELLION. 16 WHO ARE THOSE WHO HAD
HEARD AND STILL REBELLED? THEY WERE ALL
THOSE WHO CAME OUT OF EGYPT WITH MOSES.
17 WITH WHOM WAS GOD ANGRY FOR FORTY YEARS?
WITH THOSE WHO SINNED AND WHOSE BODIES IN
THE DESERT FELL. 18 TO WHOM DID GOD SWEAR
THAT THEY WOULD ENTER INTO HIS REST? TO
THOSE WHO HAD DISOBEYED. 19 WE SEE THEN
THAT UNBELIEF PREVENTED THEM FROM RE-
ACHING THEIR REST.

4 1 THEREFORE LET US FEAR WHILE WE ARE INVIT-
ED TO ENTER THE REST OF GOD, LEST ANY OF YOU
BE LEFT BEHIND. 2 WE HAVE BEEN INVITED LIKE

THEM. BUT THE MESSAGE
THEY HEARD DID NOT BE-
NEFIT THEM FOR THEY
DID NOT HOLD TO THIS BE-
LIEF. 3 WE ARE NOW TO
ENTER THIS REST BECA-
USE WE BELIEVED, AS IT
WAS SAID: I WAS ANGRY
AND MADE A SOLEMN
VOW: THEY WILL NEVER
ENTER MY REST — THAT
IS THE REST OF GOD AFT-
ER HE CREATED THE
WORLD. 4 IN ANOTHER
PART IT WAS SAID ABOUT
THE SEVENTH DAY: AND
GOD RESTED ON THE SE-
VENTH DAY FROM ALL
HIS WORKS. 5 BUT NOW
IT IS SAID: THEY WILL NOT
ENTER MY REST. 6
WE MUST CONCLUDE
THAT SOME WILL ENTER
THE REST OF GOD AND
THAT THOSE WHO FIRST RECEIVED THE GOOD NEWS
DID NOT, BECAUSE OF THEIR DISOBEDIENCE. 7 YET
GOD AGAIN ASSIGNS A DAY WHEN HE SAYS:
TODAY, AND DECLARES THROUGH DAVID MANY
YEARS LATER: IF YOU HEAR GOD'S VOICE TO-
DAY, DO NOT BE STUBBORN.
8 SO IT WAS NOT JOSHUA WHO LET THEM EN-
TER THE LAND OF REST; OTHERWISE GOD WOULD
NOT HAVE ASSIGNED ANOTHER DAY LATER ON. 9

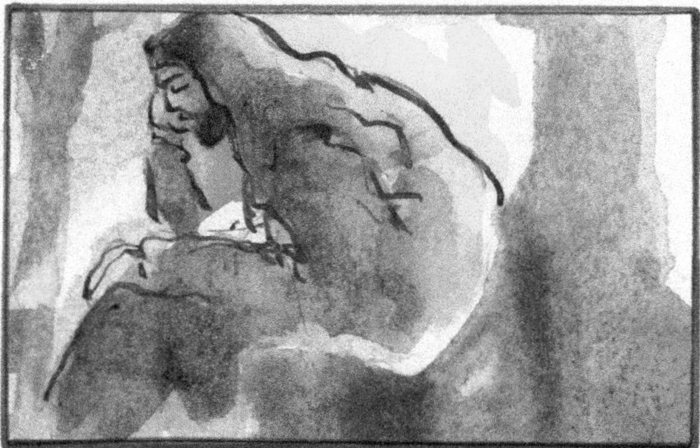

THEN SOME OTHER REST, OR SABBATH, IS RESER-
VED FOR THE PEOPLE OF GOD. 10 HE WHO ENTERS
THIS REST OF GOD RESTS FROM ALL HIS WORKS AS GOD
RESTS FROM HIS WORK. 11 LET US STRIVE, THEN, TO
ENTER THE REST AND NOT TO SHARE THE MISFORTUNE
OF THOSE WHO DISOBEYED. 12 FOR THE WORD OF
GOD IS LIVING AND EFFECTIVE, SHARPER THAN ANY
TWO-EDGED SWORD. IT PIERCES TO THE DIVISION
OF SOUL AND SPIRIT, OF JOINTS AND MARROW, AND
JUDGES THE INTENTIONS AND THOUGHTS OF THE HEART.

13 ALL CREATION IS TRANSPARENT TO HIM;
EVERYTHING IS UNCOVERED AND LAID BARE TO
THE EYES OF HIM TO WHOM WE
RENDER ACCOUNT.

CHRIST IS OUR HIGH PRIEST

14 WE HAVE A GREAT HIGH PRIEST, JESUS, THE SON OF
GOD, WHO HAS ENTERED HEAVEN. LET US, THEN, HOLD
FAST TO THE FAITH WE PROFESS. 15 OUR HIGH

PRIEST IS NOT INDIFFERENT TO OUR WEAKNESSES, FOR
HE WAS TEMPTED IN EVERY WAY JUST AS WE ARE, YET
WITHOUT SINNING. 16 LET US, THEN, WITH CONFIDENCE
APPROACH GOD, THE GIVER OF GRACE; WE WILL
OBTAIN MERCY AND HELP THROUGH HIS FAVOR.

5 1 EVERY HIGH PRIEST IS TAKEN FROM AMONG MEN
AND APPOINTED TO BE THEIR REPRESENTATIVE BE-
FORE GOD. IT FALLS TO HIM TO OFFER GIFTS AND SA-
CRIFICES FOR SIN. 2
HE IS ABLE TO UNDER-
STAND THE IGNORANT
AND ERRING FOR HE
HIMSELF IS SUBJECT
TO WEAKNESS. 3 THIS
IS WHY HE MUST OFFER
SACRIFICES FOR HIS SINS
AND PEOPLE'S SINS. ONE
4 DOES NOT TAKE ON
HIMSELF THIS DIGNITY,
BUT, AS AARON, HE HAS TO
BE CALLED BY GOD. 5
CHRIST DIDN'T BECOME
HIGH PRIEST IN TAKING
ON HIMSELF THIS DIGNITY,
BUT IT WAS GIVEN TO HIM
BY THE ONE WHO SAYS:
"YOU ARE MY SON, I HAVE
BEGOTTEN YOU TODAY. 6
AND AGAIN: YOU ARE A
PRIEST FOREVER IN
THE PRIESTLY ORDER
OF MELCHIZEDEK. IN THE

7 DAYS OF HIS LIFE, CHRIST OFFERED HIS SACRIFICE
WITH TEARS AND CRIES. HE PRAYED TO HIM WHO COULD
SAVE HIM FROM DEATH, AND HE WAS HEARD FOR HIS HUM-
BLE SUBMISSION. 8 ALTHOUGH HE WAS A SON, HE
LEARNED OBEDIENCE THROUGH SUFFERING, 9 AND
ONCE MADE PERFECT, HE BECAME THE SOURCE OF ETER-
NAL SALVATION FOR THOSE WHO OBEY HIM. THIS
IS HOW 10 GOD PROCLAIMED HIM PRIEST IN
THE ORDER OF MELCHIZEDEK.

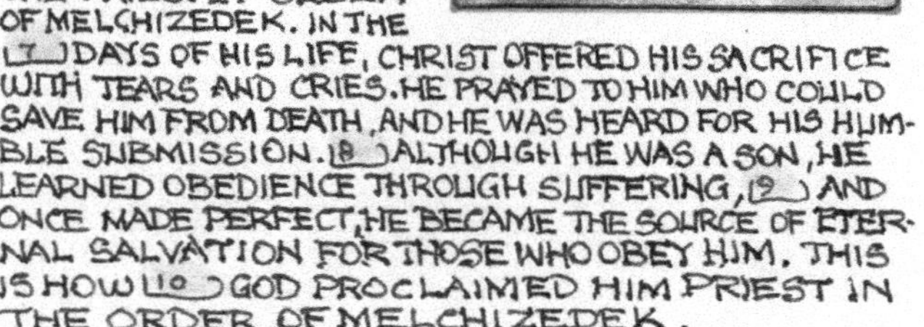

YOU SHOULD BE TEACHERS

11 ABOUT THIS WE HAVE MUCH TO SAY, BUT IT IS DIF-
FICULT TO EXPLAIN, FOR YOU HAVE BECOME DULL IN
UNDERSTANDING. 12 YOU SHOULD BE TEACHERS
BY THIS TIME, BUT IN FACT YOU NEED TO BE TAUGHT
AGAIN THE BASIC ELEMENTS OF GOD'S TEACHING.
YOU NEED MILK, NOT SOLID FOOD. 13 THOSE FED
WITH MILK ARE STILL INFANTS: THIS REFERS TO

THOSE WHO HAVE NOT BEEN TESTED IN THE WAY
OF RIGHTEOUSNESS. 14 SOLID FOOD IS FOR ADULTS
WHO HAVE TRAINED TO DISTINGUISH GOOD FROM EVIL.

LET US MOVE FORWARD

6 1 THEREFORE LET US LEAVE THE ELEMENTARY
TEACHING ABOUT CHRIST AND MOVE FORWARD
TO A MORE ADVANCED KNOWLEDGE WITHOUT LAY-
ING AGAIN THE FOUNDATION, THAT IS: TURNING
AWAY FROM DEAD WORKS, FAITH IN GOD, 2 THE
TEACHING ABOUT BAP-
TISMS AND LAYING ON
OF HANDS, THE RESUR-
RECTION OF THE DEAD
AND THE FINAL JUDG-
MENT. 3 THIS IS WHAT
WE SHALL DO, GOD PERMIT-
TING. 4 AS IT WOULD BE
IMPOSSIBLE TO RENEW BY
PENANCE THOSE WHO HA-
VE ONCE TASTED AND RE-
CEIVED THE HOLY SPIRIT,
5 TASTED THE BEAUTY
OF THE WORD OF GOD AND
THE WONDERS OF THE SU-
PERNATURAL WORLD. 6
IF IN SPITE OF THIS THEY
HAVE CEASED TO BELIE-
VE AND FALLEN AWAY, IT
IS IMPOSSIBLE TO MOVE
THEM A SECOND TIME TO
REPENTANCE WHEN THEY
ARE CRUCIFYING, ON
THEIR OWN ACCOUNT, THE
SON OF GOD, SPURNING
HIM PUBLICLY. 7 SOIL
THAT DRINKS THE RAIN

FALLING ON IT AND PRODUCES PROFITABLE GRASS
FOR THOSE WHO TILL IT, RECEIVES THE BLES-
SING OF GOD, 8 BUT THE SOIL THAT PRODU-
CES THORNS AND BUSHES IS POOR SOIL AND
IN DANGER OF BEING CURSED.
IN THE END IT WILL BE BURNED.

REMAIN FIRM IN OUR HOPE

9 YET EVEN THOUGH WE SPEAK LIKE THIS, WE ARE
MORE OPTIMISTIC, DEAR FRIENDS, REGARDING YOU
AND YOUR SALVATION. 10 GOD IS NOT UNJUST AND
WILL NOT FORGET WHAT YOU HAVE DONE FOR LOVE OF
HIS NAME: YOU HAVE AND STILL HELPED THE BELI-
EVERS. 11 WE DESIRE EACH OF YOU TO HAVE THE
SAME ZEAL FOR RE-
ACHING WHAT YOU HAVE
HOPED FOR. 12 DO NOT
GROW CARELESS BUT
IMITATE THOSE WHO,
BY THEIR FAITH AND DE-
TERMINATION, INHERIT
THE PROMISE. 13 RE-
MEMBER GOD'S PROMISE
TO ABRAHAM. GOD WANTED
TO CONFIRM IT WITH AN
OATH AS NO ONE IS HIGH-
ER THAN GOD. 14 HE
SWORE BY HIMSELF.
I SHALL BLESS YOU AND
GIVE YOU MANY DESCEN-
DANTS. 15 BY PATIENT-
LY WAITING, ABRAHAM
OBTAINED THE PROMISE.
16 PEOPLE ARE USED
TO SWEARING TO
SOMEONE HIGHER
THAN THEMSELVES
AND THEIR OATH AF-
FIRMS EVERYTHING
THAT COULD BE DE-
NIED. 17 SO GOD COMMITTED HIMSELF WITH
AN OATH IN ORDER TO CONVINCE THOSE WHO WE-
RE TO WAIT FOR HIS PROMISE THAT HE WOULD
NEVER CHANGE HIS MIND. 18 THUS WE HAVE
TWO CERTAINTIES IN WHICH IT IS IMPOSSI-
BLE THAT GOD BE PROVED FALSE: PROMISE
AND OATH. THAT IS ENOUGH TO ENCOURAGE
US STRONGLY WHEN WE LEAVE EVERYTHING TO

HOLD TO THE HOPE SET FOR US. 19 THIS HOPE IS LIKE
A SPIRITUAL ANCHOR, SECURE AND FIRM, THRUST BE-
YOND THE CURTAIN OF THE TEMPLE INTO THE SANCTU-
ARY, 20 WHERE JESUS HAS ENTERED AHEAD OF US, JESUS,
HIGH PRIEST FOR EVER IN THE ORDER OF MELCHIZEDEK.

MELCHIZEDEK A FIGURE OF CHRIST

7 1 SCRIPTURE SAYS THAT MELCHIZEDEK, KING
OF SALEM, PRIEST OF THE MOST HIGH GOD,
CAME OUT TO MEET ABRAHAM WHO RETUR-
NED FROM DEFEATING THE KINGS. HE BLESSED
ABRAHAM AND ABRAHAM GAVE HIM A TENTH OF
EVERYTHING. 2 LET US NOTE THAT THE NAME
MELCHIZEDEK MEANS KING OF JUSTICE, AND
THAT KING OF SALEM MEANS KING OF PEACE.

3 THERE IS NO MENTION OF FATHER, MOTHER
OR GENEALOGY; NOTHING IS SAID ABOUT THE BE-
GINNING OR THE END OF HIS LIFE. IN THIS HE IS THE
FIGURE OF THE SON OF GOD, THE PRIEST WHO REMA-
INS FOREVER.
4 SEE THEN HOW GREAT MELCHIZEDEK WAS.
EVEN ABRAHAM GAVE HIM A TENTH OF THE SPOILS!
5 WHEN THE DESCENDANTS OF LEVI ARE CONSE-

CRATED PRIESTS, THEY
ARE COMMANDED TO
COLLECT TITHES FROM
THEIR PEOPLE, THAT IS
FROM THEIR BROTHERS,
ALTHOUGH THEY, TOO, ARE
DESCENDANTS OF AB-
RAHAM. 6 HERE,
HOWEVER, MELCHIZE-
DEK, WHO DOES NOT BE-
LONG TO THE FAMILY OF
THE LEVITES, IS GIVEN
TITHES FROM ABRAHAM.
STILL MORE, HE BLES-
SED HIM, THE MAN OF
GOD'S PROMISE. 7
THERE IS NO DOUBT
THAT HE WHO BLESSES
IS HIGHER THAN THE
ONE WHO IS BLESSED.
8 IN THE FIRST CASE
WE SEE MORTAL MEN
RECEIVING TITHS;
HERE INSTEAD, MEL-
CHIZEDEK IS MENTIO-
NED AS ONE WHO LIVES ON. 9 WHEN ABRAHAM
PAYS THE TENTH, IT IS, SO TO SPEAK, THE LEVITES,
RECEIVERS OF THE TITHES, WHO PAY THE TITHES,
10 BECAUSE, IN A WAY, LEVI WAS STILL IN THE
BODY OF ABRAHAM, HIS ANCESTOR, WHEN MEL-
CHIZEDEK MET HIM.

11 THE INSITUTIONS OF THE CHOSEN PEOPLE
ARE FOUNDED UPON THE LEVITICAL PRIEST-
HOOD, BUT WITH IT THEY COULD NOT ATTAIN
WHAT IS PERFECT AND PERMANENT. IF THAT
WERE POSSIBLE, WHY WOULD THERE BE NEED
OF ANOTHER PRIEST AFTER MELCHIZEDEK'S OR-
DER INSTEAD OF AARON'S? 12 IF THERE IS A

CHANGE IN THE PRIESTHOOD, THE LAW ALSO HAS
TO BE CHANGED. 13 JESUS, TO WHOM ALL THIS
HAS REFERENCE, WAS FROM A TRIBE THAT NEVER
SERVED AT THE ALTAR. 14 ALL KNOW THAT HE
BELONGED TO THE TRIBE OF JUDAH THAT MOSES
DOESN'T MENTION WHEN HE SPEAKS OF PRIESTHOOD.

15 ALL THIS, HOWEVER, BECOMES CLEAR IF
THIS PRIEST AFTER THE LIKENESS OF MELCHIZEDEK
16 HAS IN FACT RECEIVED HIS MISSION, NOT ON
THE BASIS OF HUMAN LAW, BUT BY THE POWER OF
AN IMMORTAL LIFE. 17 BECAUSE SCRIPTURE SA-
YS: YOU ARE A PRIEST FOREVER IN THE PRIESTLY
ORDER OF MELCHIZEDEK. 18 WITH THIS THE
FORMER DISPOSITION IS REMOVED AS INSUF-
FICIENT AND USELESS 19 (FOR THE LAW DID
NOT BRING ANYTHING TO PERFECTION). AT THE

SAME TIME A BETTER HOPE IS GIVEN TO US: THAT
OF DRAWING NEAR TO GOD. 20 THIS CHANGE IS CON-
FIRMED BY GOD'S OATH. WHEN THE OTHERS BECA-
ME PRIESTS, GOD DID NOT COMPROMISE HIMSELF
WITH AN OATH, 21 BUT JESUS IS CONFIRMED WITH
AN OATH, AS IT IS SAID: THE LORD HAS SWORN -
AND WILL NOT CHANGE HIS MIND: YOU ARE A
PRIEST FOREVER 22
THEREFORE, JESUS
IS OUR ASSURANCE
OF A BETTER COVEN-
ANT. 23 THE FOR-
MER PRIESTS WERE
MANY SINCE, AS
MORTAL MEN, THEY
COULD NOT REMAIN
IN OFFICE. 24 BUT
JESUS REMAINS FOR-
EVER AND THE PRIEST-
HOOD SHALL NOT BE
TAKEN AWAY FROM
HIM, 25 CONSEQU-
ENTLY HE IS ABLE TO
SAVE FOR ALL TIME
THOSE WHO APPRO-
ACH GOD THROUGH
HIM. HE ALWAYS LIVES
TO INTERCEDE ON THE-
IR BEHALF. 26 IT WAS
FITTING THAT OUR
HIGH PRIEST BE HO-

LY, UNDEFILED, SET APART FROM SINNERS AND
EXALTED ABOVE THE HEAVENS; 27 A PRIEST
WHO DOES NOT FIRST NEED TO OFFER SACRI-
FICE FOR HIMSELF BEFORE OFFERING FOR
THE SINS OF THE PEOPLE, AS HIGH PRI-
ESTS DO.
HE OFFERED HIMSELF IN SACRIFICE ONCE
AND FOR ALL.

28 AND WHEREAS THE LAW ELECTED
WEAK MEN AS HIGH PRIESTS, NOW, AFTER
THE LAW, THE WORD OF GOD WITH AN OATH
APPOINTED THE SON, ...

...MADE PERFECT FOREVER.

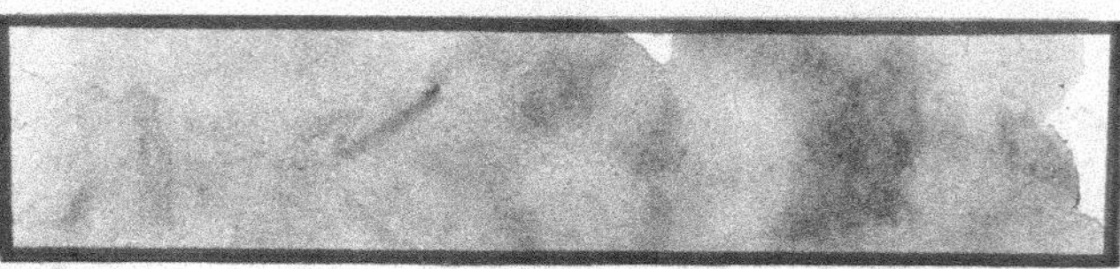

MELCHIZEDEK
402. CCCCII
© DM 05

A NEW SANCTUARY AND A NEW COVENANT

8 (1) THE MAIN POINT OF WHAT WE ARE SAY-
ING IS THAT WE HAVE A HIGH PRIEST. HE IS
SEATED AT THE RIGHT HAND OF THE DIVINE
MAJESTY IN HEAVEN, (2) WHERE HE SERVES AS
MINISTER OF THE TRUE TEMPLE AND SANCTUARY,
SET UP NOT BY MEN
BUT BY THE LORD.

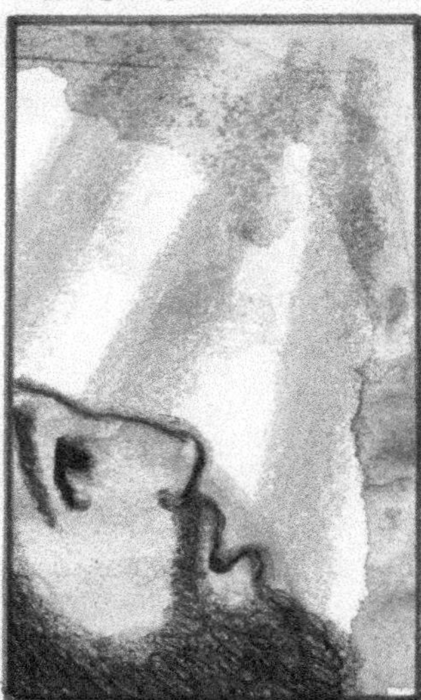

(3) A HIGH PRIEST IS
APPOINTED TO OFFER
TO GOD GIFTS AND SA-
CRIFICES, AND JESUS
ALSO HAS TO OFFER SO-
ME SACRIFICE. (4) HAD
HE REMAINED ON EARTH,
HE WOULD NOT BE A
PRIEST, SINCE OTHERS
OFFER THE GIFTS AC-
CORDING TO THE LAW.
(5) IN FACT, THE RITU-
AL CELEBRATED BY
THOSE PRIESTS IS ON-
LY AN IMITATION AND
SHADOW OF THE SUPER-
NATURAL RITUAL. WE
KNOW THE WORD OF
GOD TO MOSES WITH
REGARD TO THE CONST-
RUCTION OF THE HOLY
TENT. HE SAID: YOU
ARE TO MAKE EVERYTHING ACCORDING TO THE
PATTERN SHOWN TO YOU ON THE MOUNTAIN.

(6) NOW, HOWEVER, JESUS ENJOYS A MUCH HI-
GHER MINISTRY IN BEING THE MEDIATOR OF
A BETTER COVENANT, FOUNDED ON BETTER PRO-
MISES. (7) IF ALL HAD BEEN PERFECT IN

THE FIRST COVENANT, THERE WOULD HAVE BE-
EN NO NEED FOR ANOTHER ONE. (8) YET GOD
SEES DEFECTS WHEN HE SAYS:

THE DAYS ARE COMING - IT IS THE WORD OF
THE LORD - WHEN I WILL DRAW UP A NEW COVENANT
WITH THE PEOPLE OF ISRAEL AND WITH THE PE-
OPLE OF JUDAH. (9) IT WILL NOT BE LIKE THE CO-
VENANT THAT I MADE WITH THEIR FATHERS ON
THE DAY I TOOK THEM BY THE HAND AND LED
THEM OUT OF EGYPT. THEY DID NOT KEEP
MY COVENANT, AND SO I MYSELF HAVE FOR-
SAKEN THEM, SAYS THE LORD.

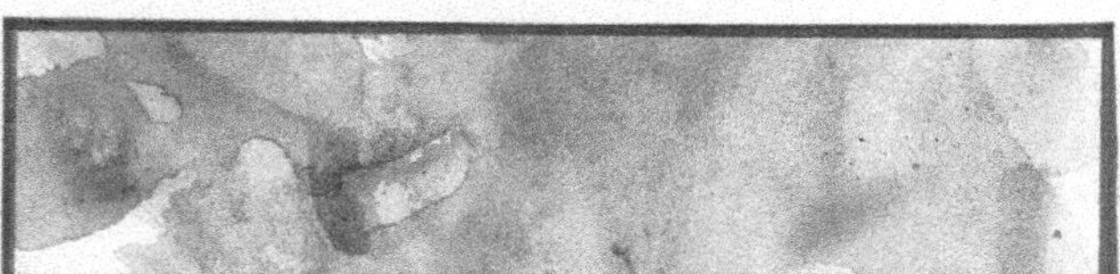

(10) BUT THIS IS THE COVENANT THAT I
WILL MAKE WITH THE PEOPLE OF ISRAEL
IN THE DAYS TO COME: I WILL PUT MY LAWS
INTO THEIR MINDS AND WRITE THEM ON
THEIR HEARTS: I WILL BE THEIR GOD
AND THEY WILL BE MY PEOPLE.
(11) NONE OF THEM WILL HAVE TO TEACH HIS
NEIGHBOR OR TO TELL HIS BROTHER: KNOW

THE LORD, FOR THEY WILL KNOW ME FROM THE
LEAST TO THE GREATEST. (12) I WILL FORGIVE
THEIR SINS AND NO LONGER REMEMBER ALL
THEIR WRONGS.
(13) HERE WE ARE BEEN TOLD OF A NEW
COVENANT; WHICH MEANS THAT THE FIRST
ONE HAD BECOME OBSOLETE, AND WHAT IS
OBSOLETE AND AGING IS SOON TO DISAPPEAR.

THE TEMPLE IN JERUSALEM

9 (1) THE FIRST COVENANT HAD RITES AND RE-
GULATIONS. THERE WAS ALSO A SANCTUARY,
AN EARTHLY ONE.
(2) A FIRST ROOM HAD
THE LAMPSTAND, THE
TABLE AND THE BREAD
OF THE PRESENCE. THIS
ROOM IS CALLED THE HO-
LY PLACE. (3) BEHIND
THE SECOND CURTAIN, A
SECOND SANCTUARY -
CALLED THE MOST HOLY
PLACE, (4) WITH THE
GOLD ALTAR FOR THE
BURNING OF THE INCEN-
SE, AND THE ARK OF THE
COVENANT, FULLY CO-
VERED WITH GOLD. IN
THE ARK WAS A GOLDEN
JAR HOLDING THE MAN-
NA, AARON'S ROD THAT
SPROUTED LEAVES AND
THE TWO SLABS OF THE CO-
VENANT, (5) ABOVE THE
TWO CHERUBIM OF GLO-
RY OVERSHADOWED THE

SEAT OF MERCY. BUT WE CANNOT GO HERE INTO DETAIL.
(6) WITH EVERYTHING AS DESCRIBED, THE PRIESTS
CONTINUALLY ENTER THE FIRST ROOM TO FULFILL
THEIR MINISTRY; (7) BUT THE HIGH PRIEST ENTERS
ONLY ONCE A YEAR THE SECOND ONE, AND BRINGING THE
BLOOD TO OFFER FOR HIMSELF AND FOR THE SINS OF
THE PEOPLE. (8) BY THIS, THE HOLY SPIRIT
TEACHES US THAT THE WAY INTO THE INNER
SANCTUARY IS NOT OPEN AS LONG AS
THE FIRST ROOM STILL STANDS.

(9) HERE IS A TEACHING BY MEANS OF FIGURES
FOR THE PRESENT AGE; THE GIFTS AND SACRI-
FICES PRESENTED TO GOD CANNOT BRING THE
PEOPLE OFFERING THEM THE INTERIOR
PERFECTION.
(10) THESE ARE NO MORE THAN FOOD, DRINK
AND DIFFERENT KINDS OF CLEANSING BY WA-
TER; ALL THESE ARE HUMAN REGULATIONS
AWAITING A REFORMATION.

JESUS ENTERED WITH HIS OWN BLOOD

(11) BUT NOW CHRIST HAS APPEARED AS THE HIGH
PRIEST WITH REGARD TO THE GOOD THINGS OF
THESE NEW TIMES. HE
PASSED THROUGH A
SANCTUARY MORE NOBLE
AND PERFECT, NOT MA-
DE BY HANDS, THAT IS,
NOT CREATED. (12) HE
DID NOT TAKE WITH HIM-
SELF THE BLOOD OF GO-
ATS AND BULLS BUT HIS
OWN BLOOD, WHEN HE
ENTERED ONCE AND
FOR ALL INTO THIS SANC-
TUARY AFTER OBTA-
INING DEFINITIVE RE-
DEMPTION. (13) IF THE
SPRINKLING OF PE-
OPLE DEFILED BY SIN
WITH THE BLOOD OF
GOATS AND BULLS
OR WITH THE ASHES
OF A HEIFER PROVI-
DES THEM WITH EX-
TERIOR CLEANNESS
AND HOLINESS, (14)
HOW MUCH MORE
WILL IT BE WITH THE
BLOOD OF CHRIST?

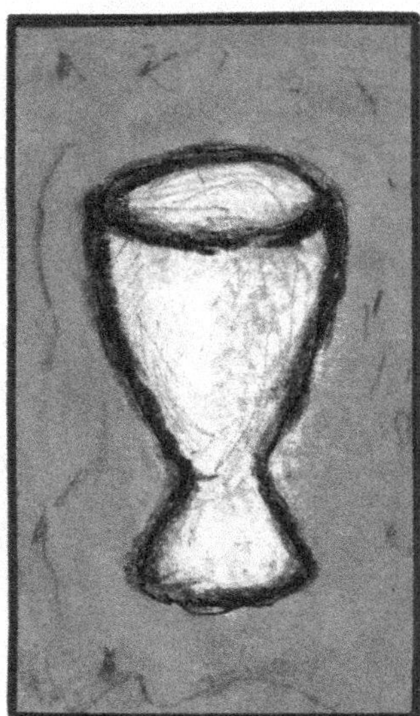

HE, MOVED BY ETERNAL SPIRIT, OFFERED HIM-
SELF AS AN UNBLEMISHED VICTIM TO GOD
AND HIS BLOOD CLEANSES US FROM DEAD
WORKS, SO THAT WE MAY SERVE THE LIVING
GOD. (15) SO CHRIST IS THE MEDIATOR OF A NEW
COVENANT OR TESTAMENT. HIS DEATH MADE
ATONEMENT FOR THE SINS COMMITTED UNDER
THE OLD TESTAMENT, AND THE PROMISE IS HAN-
DED OVER TO ALL WHO ARE CALLED TO THE

EVERLASTING INHERITANCE. (16) WITH EVERY TES-
TAMENT ONE MUST WAIT UNTIL ITS AUTHOR HAS
DIED. (17) FOR A TESTAMENT INFERS DEATH AND HAS
NO VALUE WHILE THE MAKER OF IT IS STILL ALIVE.
(18) THAT IS WHY THE FIRST COVENANT WAS NOT RA-
TIFIED WITHOUT BLOOD. (19) MOSES PROCLAIMED TO
THE PEOPLE ALL THE COMMANDMENTS OF THE LAW; THEN
HE TOOK THE BLOOD OF BULLS AND GOATS AND MIX-
ED IT WITH WATER, HYSSOP AND RED WOOL, AND
SPRINKLED THE BOOK OF THE COVENANT AND THE
PEOPLE (20) SAYING:
THIS IS THE BLOOD OF THE COVENANT
THAT GOD COMMANDED YOU.
(21) IN THE SAME WAY HE SPRINKLED WITH BLOOD
THE SANCTUARY AND ALL THE OBJECTS OF THE RITUAL.

(22) ACCORDING TO THE LAW, ALMOST ALL CLEANSINGS
HAVE TO BE PERFORMED WITH BLOOD; THERE IS NO FOR-
GIVENESS WITHOUT THE SHEDDING OF BLOOD. (23) IT
WAS NECESSARY THAT MERE COPIES OF SUPERNATU-
RAL REALITIES NEED BE PURIFIED, BUT NOW THESE
REALITIES NEED BETTER SACRIFICES. (24) CHRIST
DID NOT ENTER SOME
SANCTUARY MADE BY
HANDS, A COPY OF THE
TRUE ONE, BUT HEAVEN
ITSELF. HE IS NOW IN
THE PRESENCE OF GOD
ON OUR BEHALF. (25) HE
HAD NOT TO OFFER HIMSELF
MANY TIMES, AS THE HIGH
PRIEST DOES: HE WHO MAY
RETURN EVERY YEAR, FOR
THE BLOOD IS NOT HIS
OWN. (26) OTHERWISE
HE WOULD HAVE SUFFER-
ED MANY TIMES FROM
THE CREATION OF THE
WORLD. BUT NO, HE
MANIFESTED HIMSELF
ONLY NOW AT THE END
OF THE AGES TO TAKE
AWAY SIN BY SACRIFI-
CE, (27) AND AS HUMANS
DIE ONLY ONCE AND
AFTERWARDS ARE JUDGED, (28) IN THE SAME WAY
CHRIST SACRIFICED HIMSELF ONCE TO TAKE AWAY
THE SINS OF THE MULTITUDE. THERE WILL BE NO
FURTHER QUESTION OF SIN WHEN HE COMES AGAIN
TO SAVE THOSE WAITING FOR HIM.

10 (1) THE RELIGION OF THE LAW IS ONLY A SHADOW
OF THE GOOD THINGS TO COME; IT HAS THE PAT-
TERNS BUT NOT THE REALITIES. SO, YEAR AF-
TER YEAR, THE SAME SACRIFICES ARE OFFERED WITHOUT
BRINGING THE WORSHIPERS TO WHAT IS THE END.
(2) IF THEY HAD BEEN CLEANSED ONCE AND
FOR ALL, THEY WOULD NO LONGER HAVE FELT
GUILT AND WOULD HAVE STOPPED OFFER-
ING THE SAME SACRIFICES.

3 BUT NO, YEAR AFTER YEAR THEIR SACRIFI-
CES WITNESS TO THEIR SINS 4 AND NEVER
WILL THE BLOOD OF BULLS AND GOATS TAKE
AWAY THEIR SINS. 5 THIS IS WHY, ON ENTER-
ING THE WORLD, CHRIST SAYS:

> YOU DID NOT DESIRE SACRIFICE AND OF-
> FERING; 6 YOU WERE NOT PLEASED WITH
> BURNT OFFERINGS AND SIN OFFERINGS. 7
> THEN I SAID: "HERE I AM. IT WAS WRITTEN OF
> ME IN THE SCROLL. I WILL DO YOUR WILL, O GOD."

8 FIRST HE SAYS: SACRIFICE, OFFERINGS, BURNT
OFFERINGS AND SIN OFFERINGS YOU DID NOT DESIRE

NOR WERE YOU PLEASED
WITH THEM, ALTHOUGH
THEY WERE REQUIRED
BY THE LAW. 9 THEN
HE SAYS: HERE I AM TO
DO YOUR WILL.
THIS IS ENOUGH TO
NULLIFY THE FIRST
WILL AND ESTABLISH
THE NEW. 10 NOW,
BY THIS WILL OF GOD,
WE ARE SANCTIFIED
AT ONCE BY THE SA-
CRIFICE OF THE BODY
OF CHRIST JESUS.
11 SO, WHEREAS
EVERY PRIEST
STANDS DAILY BY THE
ALTAR OFFERING
REPEATEDLY THE
SAME SACRIFICES
THAT CAN NEVER
TAKE AWAY SINS
12 CHRIST HAS
OFFERED FOR ALL
TIMES A SINGLE SACRIFICE FOR SINS AND
HAS TAKEN HIS SEAT AT THE RIGHT HAND OF
GOD, 13 WAITING UNTIL GOD PUTS HIS
ENEMIES AS A FOOTSTOOL UNDER HIS FEET.

14 BY A SINGLE SACRIFICE HE HAS BROUGHT
THOSE WHO ARE SANCTIFIED TO WHAT IS
PERFECT FOREVER.

15 THIS ALSO WAS TESTIFIED BY THE HOLY

SPIRIT. FOR AFTER HAVING DECLARED: 16

> THIS IS THE COVENANT THAT I WILL
> MAKE WITH THEM IN THE DAYS TO
> COME – SAYS THE LORD – I WILL PUT
> MY LAWS IN THEIR HEARTS AND
> WRITE THEM ON THEIR MINDS.

17 HE SAYS: THEIR SINS AND EVIL DEEDS
I WILL REMEMBER NO MORE.

18 SO, IF SINS ARE FORGIVEN, THERE IS
NO LONGER NEED OF ANY SACRIFICE FOR SIN.

BE CONFIDENT IN GOD

19 SO, MY BROTHERS, WE ARE ASSURED OF ENTER-
ING THE SANCTUARY BY THE BLOOD OF JESUS
20 WHO OPENED FOR US THIS NEW AND LIVING
WAY PASSING "THROUGH" THE CURTAIN, "THAT

IS, HIS BODY. 21 BECAUSE WE HAVE A HIGH
PRIEST IN CHARGE OF THE HOUSE OF GOD,
22 LET US APPROACH WITH A SINCERE
HEART, WITH FULL FAITH, INTERIORLY
CLEANSED FROM A BAD CONSCIENCE AND
OUR BODIES WASHED WITH PURE WATER.

23 LET US HOLD FAST TO OUR HOPE WITH-
OUT WAVERING, BECAUSE HE WHO PROMISED
IS FAITHFUL. 24 LET US CONSIDER HOW WE MAY
SPUR ONE ANOTHER TO
LOVE AND GOOD WORKS.

25 DO NOT ABANDON
THE ASSEMBLIES AS
SOME OF YOU DO, BUT
ENCOURAGE ONE AN-
OTHER, AND ALL THE
MORE SINCE THE DAY
IS DRAWING NEAR.
26 IF WE SIN WILLFULLY
AFTER ACKNOWLEDGING
THE TRUTH, THERE IS NO
LONGER SACRIFICE FOR
SIN, 27 BUT ONLY THE
FEAR OF JUDGMENT AND
OF FIRE WHICH DEVOURS
THE REBELLIOUS. 28 FOR
WHOEVER VIOLATED MO-
SES' LAW HAS NO MERCY.
HE IS PUT TO DEATH BY
THE TESTIMONY OF TWO
OR THREE PERSONS. 29
WHAT, THEN, DO YOU THINK
IT WILL BE FOR THE
PERSON WHO HAS DESPISED THE SON OF GOD?
HOW SEVERELY SHALL HE BE PUNISHED FOR
HAVING DEFILED THE BLOOD OF THE COVE-
NANT THAT SANCTIFIED HIM AND FOR HAVING
INSULTED THE SPIRIT GIVEN TO HIM?
30 FOR WE HAVE THE **ONE** WHO SAYS:

> REVENGE IS MINE, I WILL REPAY.

AND ALSO:

> THE LORD WILL JUDGE HIS PEOPLE.

31 WHAT A DREADFUL THING TO FALL IN-
TO THE HANDS OF THE LIVING GOD.

THE RISEN CHRIST.
MICHELANGELO · 1519
Church of St. Maria
sopra Minerva. Rome.
A SCULPTURE.
403 CCCCIII
DM
09 ©

32 REMEMBER THE FIRST DAYS WHEN YOU WERE
ENLIGHTENED. YOU HAD TO UNDERGO A HARD 33
STRUGGLE IN THE FACE OF SUFFERING. PUBLI-
CLY YOU WERE EXPOSED TO HUMILIATIONS
AND TRIALS, AND HAD TO SHARE THE SUF-
FERINGS OF OTHERS WHO WERE SIMILAR-
LY TREATED. 34 YOU SHOWED SOLIDARITY
WITH THOSE IN PRISON; YOU WERE DISPOS-
SESSED OF YOUR GOODS AND ACCEPTED IT
GLADLY FOR YOU KNEW YOU WERE ACQUIRING
A MUCH BETTER AND MORE DURABLE POSSES-
SION. 35 DO NOT NOW THROW AWAY YOUR

CONFIDENCE WHICH WILL BE HANDSOMELY REWARD-
ED. 36 BE PATIENT IN DOING THE WILL OF GOD,
AND THE PROMISE WILL BE YOURS; SAYS SCRIPTURE:
37 A LITTLE, A LITTLE LONGER, AND HE
WHO IS COMING WILL COME: HE WILL NOT
DELAY. 38 MY RIGHTEOUS ONE WILL LI-
VE IF HE BELIEVES; BUT IF HE DISTRUSTS,
I WILL NOT LOOK KINDLY ON HIM.
39 WE ARE NOT AMONG THOSE WHO WITHDRAW
AND PERISH, BUT AMONG THOSE WHO BELI-
EVE AND WIN PERSONAL SALVATION.

THE HEROES OF FAITH

11 1 FAITH IS THE WAY OF HOLDING ONTO WHAT
WE HOPE FOR, BEING CERTAIN OF WHAT WE
CANNOT SEE. 2 BECAUSE OF THEIR FAITH OUR AN
CESTORS WERE APPROVED. 3 BY FAITH WE UNDERSTAND
THAT THE STAGES OF CRE-
ATION WERE DISPOSED BY
GOD'S WORD, AND WHAT IS
VISIBLE IS FROM WHAT
CANNOT BE SEEN. 4 BE-
CAUSE OF ABEL'S FAITH
HIS OFFERING WAS
MORE ACCEPTABLE
THAN THAT OF HIS
BROTHER CAIN, WHICH
MEANT HE WAS UP-
RIGHT, AND GOD HIM-
SELF APPROVED HIS
OFFERING. BECAUSE
OF THIS FAITH HE
CRIED TO GOD, AS
SAID IN SCRIPTURE,
EVEN AFTER HE DIED.

5 BY FAITH ENOCH
WAS TAKEN TO HEAVEN
INSTEAD OF EXPER-
IENCING DEATH: HE
COULD NOT BE FOUND
BECAUSE GOD HAD
TAKEN HIM. IN FACT,
IT IS SAID THAT BE-
FORE BEING TAKEN UP HE HAD PLEASED GOD.
6 YET WITHOUT FAITH IT IS IMPOSSIBLE TO PLE-
ASE HIM: NO ONE DRAWS NEAR TO GOD WITHOUT
FIRST BELIEVING THAT HE EXISTS AND THAT HE RE-
WARDS THOSE WHO SEEK HIM EARNESTLY.

7 BY FAITH NOAH WAS INSTRUCTED OF EVENTS
WHICH COULD NOT YET BE SEEN AND, HEEDING
WHAT HE HEARD, HE BUILT A BOAT IN WHICH
TO SAVE HIS FAMILY. THE FAITH OF NOAH
CONDEMNED THE WORLD AND HE REACHED
HOLINESS BORN OF FAITH.
8 IT WAS BY FAITH THAT ABRAHAM, CAL-
LED BY GOD, SET OUT FOR A COUNTRY THAT
WOULD BE GIVEN TO HIM AS AN INHERITANCE;
FOR HE PARTED WITH-
OUT KNOWING WHERE
HE WAS GOING. 9 BY
FAITH HE LIVED AS A
STRANGER IN THAT
PROMISED LAND.
THERE HE LIVED IN
TENTS, AS DID ISAAC
AND JACOB, BENE-
FICIARIES OF THE
SAME PROMISE. 10
INDEED, HE LOOKED
FORWARD TO THAT CI-
TY OF SOLID FOUND-
ATION OF WHICH GOD
IS THE ARCHITECT AND
BUILDER. 11 BY FA-
ITH SARAH HERSELF
RECEIVED POWER TO
BECOME A MOTHER
IN SPITE OF HER ADVAN-
CED AGE; SINCE SHE
BELIEVED THAT HE
WHO HAD MADE THE
PROMISE WOULD BE
FAITHFUL. 12 THERE-
FORE, FROM AN AL-
MOST IMPOTENT MAN
WERE BORN DESCEND-
ANTS AS NUMEROUS AS THE STARS OF HEAVENS,
AS MANY AS THE GRAINS OF SAND ON THE
SEASHORE.

13 DEATH FOUND ALL THESE PEOPLE STRONG
IN THEIR FAITH. THEY HAD NOT RECEIVED WHAT
WAS PROMISED, BUT THEY HAD LOOKED A-
HEAD AND HAD REJOICED IN IT FROM AFAR,
SAYING THAT THEY WERE FOREIGNERS AND
TRAVELERS ON EARTH. 14 THOSE WHO SPEAK
IN THIS WAY PROVE THAT THEY ARE LOOKING

FOR THEIR OWN COUNTRY. 15 FOR IF THEY HAD LONGED
FOR THE LAND THEY HAD LEFT, IT WOULD HAVE BEEN
EASY FOR THEM TO RETURN. 16 BUT NO, THEY AS-
PIRED TO A BETTER CITY, THAT IS, A SUPERNA-
TURAL ONE; SO GOD, WHO PREPARED THE
CITY FOR THEM IS NOT ASHAMED OF BEING
CALLED THEIR GOD.
17 BY FAITH ABRAHAM WENT TO OFFER ISAAC
WHEN GOD TESTED HIM. AND SO HE WHO HAD RECEI-
VED THE PROMISE OF GOD OFFERED HIS ONLY
SON 18 ALTHOUGH GOD HAD TOLD HIM:
"ISAAC'S DESCENDANTS WILL BEAR YOUR NAME."

19 ABRAHAM REASONED THAT GOD IS CAPA-
BLE EVEN OF RAISING THE DEAD, AND HE REC-
EIVED BACK HIS SON, WHICH HAS A FIGURATIVE
MEANING.
20 BY FAITH ALSO ISAAC BLESSED JACOB AND
ESAU, DETERMINING THEIR FUTURE. 21 BY FA-
ITH JACOB, BEFORE HE DIED, BLESSED BOTH
CHILDREN OF JOSEPH AND WORSHIPED AS
HE LEANED ON HIS STAFF.
22 BY FAITH JOSEPH, WHEN ABOUT TO DIE,

WARNED THE CHILD-
REN OF ISRAEL OF
THEIR EXODUS AND
GAVE ORDERS ABOUT
HIS REMAINS. 23 BY
FAITH THE PARENTS
OF THE NEWLYBORN MO-
SES HID HIM FOR THREE
MONTHS, FOR THEY SAW
THE BABY WAS VERY
BEAUTIFUL AND THEY
DID NOT FEAR THE OR-
DER OF PHARAOH. 24
BY FAITH MOSES, AL-
READY AN ADULT, RE-
FUSED TO BE CALLED
SON OF PHARAOH'S DA-
UGHTER. 25 HE PRE-
FERRE TO SHARE ILL
TREATMENT WITH THE
PEOPLE OF GOD, RATHER
THAN ENJOY THE PLE-
ASURES OF SIN. 26
MOSES CONSIDERED
HUMILIATION FOR THE
SAKE OF CHRIST GRE-
ATER RICHER THAN THE WEALTH OF EGYPT, AND
HE LOOKED AHEAD TO HIS REWARD. 27 BY FA-
ITH HE LEFT EGYPT WITHOUT FEARING THE
KING'S ANGER, AND HE PERSEVERED AS IF
HE COULD SEE ANOTHER INVISIBLE WRATH.

28 BY FAITH MOSES HAD THE PASSOVER CELE-
BRATED, SPRINKLING THE DOORS WITH BLOOD SO
THAT THE "DESTROYER WOULD NOT KILL THEIR
FIRSTBORN SONS. 29 BY FAITH THEY CROSSED
THE RED SEA, AS IF ON DRY LAND, WITH THE EG-
YPTIANS WHO TRIED TO CROSS IT WERE SWAL-
LOWED BY THE WATERS AND DROWNED. 30 BY

FAITH THE WALLS OF JERICHO CRUMBLED AND FELL, AF-
TER ISRAEL HAD MARCHED ROUND THEM FOR SEVEN DAYS.
31 BY FAITH, THE PROSTITUTE RAHAB ESCAPED DEATH
WHICH BEFELL THE UNBELIEVERS FOR HAVING WELCO-
MED THE SPIES. 32 DO I NEED TO SAY MORE? THERE
IS NO TIME TO SPEAK OF GIDEON, BARAK, JEPHTHAH,
SAMSON, DAVID, SAMUEL AND THE PROPHETS. 33
THROUGH FAITH THEY FOUGHT AND CONQUERED NA-
TIONS, ESTABLISHED JUSTICE, SAW THE FULFILL-
MENT OF GOD'S PROMISES, SHUT THE LIONS' MOUTHS,
34 QUENCED RAGING FIRE, ESCAPED THE SWORD,
HEALED OF SICKNESS, WERE VALIANT IN BATTLE,
REPULSED FOREIGN INVADERS. 35 SOME WOMEN
RECOVERED THEIR DEAD BY RESURRECTION BUT
THERE WERE OTHERS, PERSECUTED AND TORTURED
BELIEVERS, WHO, FOR THE SAKE OF A BETTER
RESURRECTION, REFUSED TO DO WHAT WOULD
HAVE SAVED THEM. 36 OTHERS SUFFERED
CHAINS AND PRISON. 37 THEY WERE STO-
NED, SAWN IN TWO, KILLED BY THE SWORD.
THEY FLED FROM PLACE TO PLACE WITH NO
OTHER CLOTHING THAN THE SKINS OF SHEEP AND
GOATS, LACKING EVERYTHING, AFFLICTED, ILL-TREATED.

38 THESE MEN OF WHOM THE WORLD WAS NOT WORTHY
HAD TO WANDER THROUGH WASTELANDS AND MOUNT-
AINS, AND TAKE REFUGE IN THE DENS OF THE LAND. 39
HOWEVER, ALTHOUGH ALL OF THEM WERE PRAISED BE-
CAUSE OF THEIR FAITH, THEY DIDN'T ENJOY THE PRO-
MISE 40 BECAUSE GOD HAD US IN MIND AND SAW BE-
YOND. HE DIDN'T WANT THEM TO REACH THIS AHEAD OF US.

THE CORRECTION OF THE LORD

12 1 WHAT A CLOUD OF INNUMERABLE
WITNESSES
SURROUND US!
SO LET US BE RID
OF EVERY ENCUM-
BRANCE, ESPECIAL-
LY OF SIN, TO PER-
SEVERE IN RUNNING
THE RACE MARKED
OUT BEFORE US. 2
LET US LOOK TO
JESUS THE FOUNDER
OF OUR FAITH, WHO
WILL BRING IT TO
COMPLETION. FOR
THE SAKE OF THE
JOY RESERVED FOR
HIM, HE ENDURED THE
CROSS, SCORNING
IT'S SHAME, AND THEN
SAT AT THE RIGHT
OF THE THRONE OF
GOD. 3 THINK
OF JESUS WHO SUF-
FERED SO MANY
CONTRADICTIONS
FROM EVIL PE-
OPLE, AND YOU WILL NOT BE DISCOU-
RAGED OR GROW WEARY.

4 **HAVE YOU ALREADY SHED YOUR
BLOOD IN THE BATTLE AGAINST SIN?**

5 DO NOT FORGET THE COMFORTING WORDS
THAT WISDOM ADDRESSES TO YOU AS CHILD-
REN: MY SON, PAY ATTENTION WHEN THE LORD
CORRECTS YOU AND DO NOT BE DISCOURAGED
WHEN HE PUNISHES YOU. 6 FOR THE LORD
CORRECTS THOSE HE LOVES AND CHASTISES
EVERYONE HE ACCEPTS AS A SON.
7 WHAT YOU ENDURE IS IN ORDER TO COR-
RECT YOU. GOD TREATS YOU LIKE SONS AND
WHAT SON IS NOT CORRECTED BY HIS FATHER?

8 IF YOU WERE
WITHOUT CORRECTION
WHICH HAS BEEN RE-
CEIVED BY ALL, (AS IS
FITTING FOR SONS)
YOU WOULD NOT BE
SONS BUT BASTARDS.
9 BESIDES, WHEN
OUR PARENTS ACCORD-
ING TO THE FLESH COR-
RECTED US, WE RESPEC-
TED THEM. HOW MUCH
MORE SHOULD WE BE
SUBJECT TO THE FA-
THER OF THE SPIRITS
TO HAVE LIFE? 10
OUR PARENTS COR-
RECTED US AS THEY
SAW FIT, WITH A VIEW
TO THIS VERY SHORT
LIFE; BUT GOD CORRECTS
US FOR OUR OWN GOOD
THAT WE MAY SHARE
HIS HOLINESS. 11 ALL
CORRECTION IS PAINFUL
AT THE MOMENT, RA-
THER THAN PLEASANT; LATER IT BRINGS THE
FRUIT OF PEACE, THAT IS, HOLINESS TO THOSE
WHO HAVE BEEN TRAINED BY IT. 12 LIFT UP
THEN, YOUR DROPPING HANDS, AND STRENGTHEN
YOUR TREMBLING KNEES; 13 MAKE LEVEL
THE WAYS FOR YOUR FEET, SO THAT THE LA-
ME MAY NOT BE DISABLED, BUT HEALED.

STRIVE TO BE HOLY

14 STRIVE FOR PEACE WITH ALL AND
STRIVE TO BE HOLY, FOR WITHOUT HOLINESS NO
ONE WILL SEE THE LORD. 15 SEE THAT NO ONE
FALLS FROM THE GRACE OF GOD, LEST A BITTER

PLANT SPRING UP AND ITS POISON CORRUPT MANY
AMONG YOU. 16 LET NO ONE BE IMMORAL OR IR-
RELIGIOUS LIKE ESAU, WHO SOLD HIS BIRTHRIGHT
FOR A SINGLE MEAL.
17 YOU KNOW THAT LATER, WHEN HE WISHED
TO GET THE BLESSING, HE WAS REJECTED
ALTHOUGH HE PLEADED WITH TEARS.

18 REMEMBER YOUR INITIATION. THERE WAS
NO MATERIAL PRESENCE NOR HEAT OF A
BLAZING FIRE, DARKNESS AND GLOOM AND
STORMS... 19 BLASTS OF TRUMPETS OR SUCH A
VOICE THAT THE PEOPLE PLEADED THAT NO FUR-
THER WORD BE SPOKEN. 20 BECAUSE OF THIS
THEY RESPECTED THE ORDER NOT TO APPROACH:
EVERY MAN OR BEAST REACHING THE MOUNTAIN
SHALL BE STONED. 21 THE SIGHT WAS NO TER-
RIFYING THAT MOSES SAID: I TREMBLE WITH FEAR.
22 BUT YOU CAME NEAR THE MOUNT ZION, TO THE
CITY OF THE LIVING GOD, TO THE HEAVENLY JERUSALEM,

WITH ITS INNUMERABLE ANGELS. YOU HAVE COME TO
THE SOLEMN FEAST, 23 THE ASSEMBLY OF THE
FIRSTBORN OF GOD, WHOSE NAMES ARE WRITTEN IN
HEAVEN. THERE IS GOD, JUDGE OF ALL, WITH THE
SPIRITS OF THE UPRIGHT BROUGHT TO PERFECT-
ION. 24 THERE IS JESUS, THE MEDIATOR OF THE
NEW COVENANT, WITH THE
SPRINKLED BLOOD THAT
CRIES OUT MORE EFFEC-
TIVELY THAN ABEL'S. 25
BE CAREFUL NOT TO RE-
JECT GOD WHEN HE
SPEAKS. IF THOSE WHO
DID NOT HEED THE PRO-
PHET'S WARNINGS
WERE NOT SPARED ON
EARTH, HOW MUCH MO-
RE SHALL WE BE PUNI-
SHED IF WE DO NOT HEED
THE 'ONE' WARNING US
FROM HEAVEN? 26 HIS
VOICE SHOOK THE EARTH. HE
SAYS: IN THIS LAST TIME I
WILL SHAKE EARTH AND
ALSO HEAVENS. 27 THE
WORDS INDICATE THE
REMOVAL OF ALL THAT
CAN BE SHAKEN, CREAT-
ING THINGS, AND ONLY THOSE THAT CANNOT BE SHAKEN
WILL REMAIN. 28 SUCH IS THE KINGDOM WE RECEIVE.
LET'S BE GRATEFUL AND OFFER TO GOD WORSHIP WITH
REVERENCE AND AWE. 29 OUR GOD IS A CONSUMING FIRE.

WORDS OF ENCOURAGEMENT

13 1 PRESERVE BROTHERLY LOVE. 2 DON'T NEGLECT
TO OFFER HOSPITALITY; SOME PEOPLE HAVE ENTER-
TAINED ANGELS WITHOUT KNOWING IT. 3 REMEMBER
PRISONERS AS IF YOU WERE WITH THEM IN CHAINS, AND FOR
THOSE WHO ARE SUFFERING. YOU ALSO HAVE A BODY.
4 MARRIAGE MUST BE RESPECTED BY ALL AND
HUSBAND AND WIFE FAITHFUL TO EACH OTHER. GOD
WILL PUNISH THE IMMORAL AND THE ADULTEROUS.

MY SON, PAY ATTENTION
WHEN THE LORD CORRECTS
YOU... (Hebrews 12:5)
404 - CCCCIV
© DM 09

5 DO NOT DEPEND ON MONEY. BE CONTENT
WITH HAVING ENOUGH FOR TODAY FOR
GOD HAS SAID:
I WILL NEVER FORSAKE YOU
OR ABANDON YOU.
6 AND WE SHALL CONFIDENTLY ANSWER:
THE LORD IS MY HELPER, I WILL
NOT FEAR; WHAT CAN MAN DO TO ME?

7 REMEMBER YOUR LEADERS WHEN THEY

TAUGHT YOU THE
WORD OF GOD.
CONSIDER THEIR
END AND IMITATE
THEIR FAITH. CHRIST
JESUS 8 IS THE SAME
TODAY AS YESTERDAY
AND FOREVER. 9 DO
NOT BE LED ASTRAY
BY ALL KINDS OF
STRANGE TEACHINGS.
YOUR HEART WILL BE
STRENGTHENED BY
THE GRACE OF GOD
RATHER THAN BY FO-
ODS OF NO USE TO
ANYONE. 10 WE
HAVE AN ALTAR
FROM WHICH THOSE
STILL SERVING IN
THE TEMPLE CAN-
NOT EAT.
11 AFTER THE HIGH
PRIEST HAS OFFERED
THE BLOOD IN THE
SANCTUARY FOR THE
SINS OF THE PEOPLE,
THE CARCASSES OF THE ANIMALS ARE BURNT
OUTSIDE THE CAMP. 12 FOR THE SAME RE-
ASON JESUS, TO PURIFY THE PEOPLE WITH
WITH HIS OWN BLOOD, SUFFERED THE PAS-
SION OUTSIDE THE HOLY CITY.
13 LET US, THEREFORE, GO TO HIM OUTSIDE
THE SACRED AREA, SHARING HIS SHAME.
14 FOR WE HAVE HERE NO LASTING CITY
AND WE ARE LOOKING FOR THE ONE TO COME.
15 LET US, THEN, CONTINUALLY THROUGH
JESUS OFFER A SACRIFICE OF PRAISE TO

GOD THAT IS THE FRUIT OF LIPS CELEBRATING
HIS NAME. 16 DO NOT NEGLECT GOOD WORKS
AND COMMON LIFE, FOR THESE ARE SACRIFI-
CES PLEASING TO GOD. 17 OBEY YOUR LEADERS
AND SUBMIT TO THEM, FOR THEY ARE CONCERNED
FOR YOUR SOULS AND ARE ACCOUNTABLE FOR THEM.
LET THIS BE A JOY FOR THEM RATHER THAN
A BURDEN, WHICH WOULD BE OF NO ADVANTAGE FOR YOU.

18 PRAY FOR US, FOR WE BELIEVE OUR
INTENTIONS ARE PURE AND THAT WE ONLY
WANT TO ACT HONORABLY IN ALL THINGS.

19 NOW I URGE YOU ALL THE MORE TO PRAY FOR
ME THAT I MAY BE GIVEN BACK TO YOU THE
SOONER.
20 MAY GOD GIVE YOU PEACE, HE WHO

BROUGHT BACK FROM AMONG THE DEAD
JESUS THE LORD, THE GREAT SHEPH-
ERD OF THE SHEEP, WHOSE BLOOD SEALS
THE ETERNAL COVENANT.

21 HE WILL TRAIN YOU IN EVERY GOOD
WORK, THAT YOU
MAY DO HIS WILL,
FOR IT IS HE WHO
WORKS IN US WHAT
PLEASES HIM
THROUGH JESUS
CHRIST, TO WHOM
ALL GLORY BE
FOR EVER AND
EVER, AMEN!

22 BROTHERS, I
BEG YOU TO TAKE
THESE WORDS
OF ENCOURAGE-
MENT. FOR MY
PART, I HAVE WRITTEN TO YOU TOO BRI-
EFLY. 23 KNOW THAT OUR BROTHER
TIMOTHY HAS BEEN RELEASED. IF HE
COMES SOON I WILL VISIT YOU WITH HIM.

24 GREETINGS TO ALL YOUR LEADERS AND TO THE
SAINTS. GREETINGS FROM THOSE IN ITALY.

25 GRACE BE WITH YOU ALL.

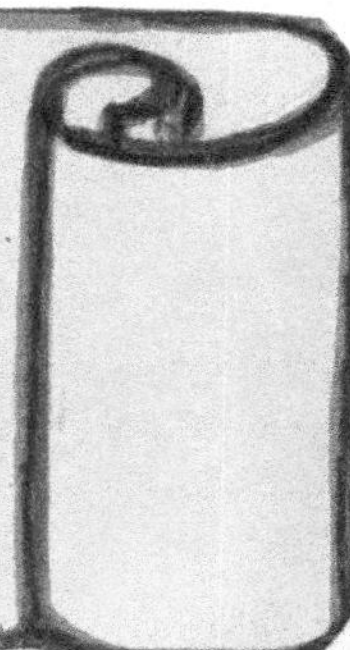

LETTERS TO ALL CHRISTIANS

LETTER OF JAMES

OF ALL THE APOSTLES, JAMES, "THE BROTHER OF THE LORD", WAS THE MOST ATTACHED TO JEWISH TRADITIONS. IN SPEAKING TO THE FAITHFUL IN JERUSALEM, HE TAUGHT THEM SIMPLE, PRATICAL THINGS, INSPIRED BY THE WISDOM OF THE OLD TESTAMENT. THE LETTER WAS PROBABLY WRITTEN BETWEEN THE YEARS 50 AND 60 AFTER CHRIST.

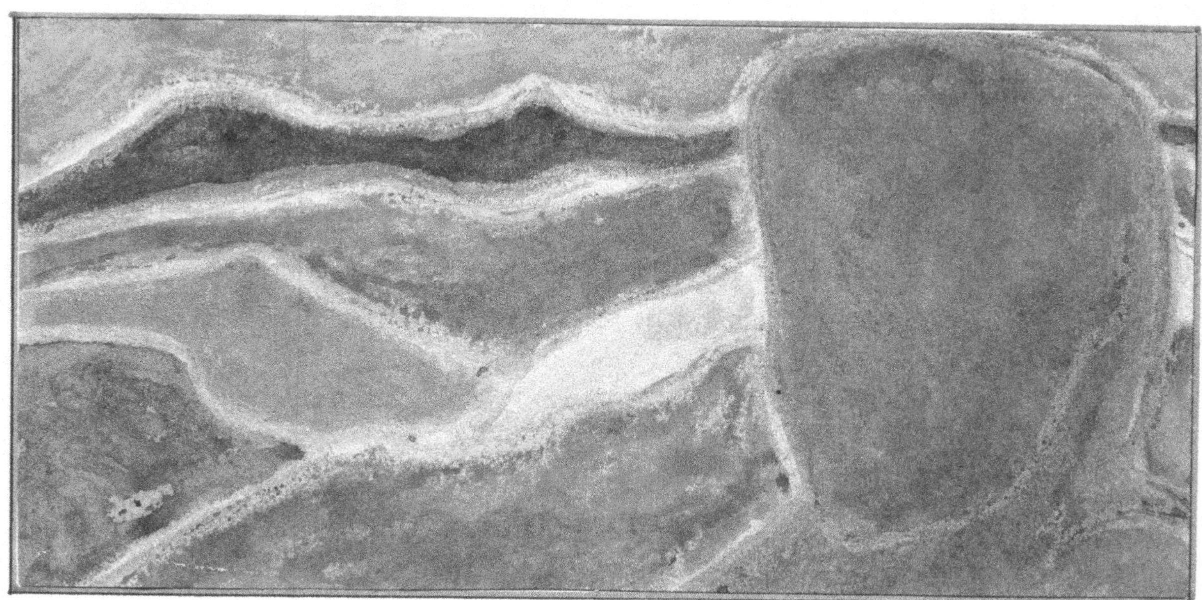

LETTER OF JAMES

1 [1] JAMES, A SERVANT OF GOD AND OF THE
LORD JESUS CHRIST, SENDS GREETINGS TO THE
TWELVE TRIBES SCATTERED AMONG THE NATIONS.

ENDURE TRIALS PATIENTLY

2 CONSIDER YOURSELVES FORTUNATE, MY BROTHERS,
WHEN YOU MEET WITH EVERY KIND OF TRIAL. 3 FOR
YOU KNOW THAT THE TESTING OF YOUR FAITH MAKES

YOU STEADFAST. 4 LET YOUR STEADFASTNESS BE-
COME PERFECT WITH DEEDS, THAT YOU YOURSELVES
MAY BE PERFECT AND BLAMELESS, WITHOUT ANY DE-
FECT. 5 IF ANY ONE OF YOU LACKS WISDOM, LET
HIM ASK GOD FOR IT, AND GOD WILL GIVE IT TO HIM. BE-
CAUSE HE GIVES TO EVERYONE EASILY AND UNCON-
DITIONALLY. 6 BUT HE SHOULD ASK WITH FAITH,

NO DOUBTING, FOR HE
WHO DOUBTS IS LIKE A
WAVE DRIVEN AND TOSSED
ON THE SEA BY THE WIND.
7 SUCH A PERSON
SHOULD NOT EXPECT
ANYTHING FROM
THE LORD. 8 HE IS
A DIVIDED MAN AND
HIS CONDUCT WILL
ALWAYS BE INSE-
CURE. 9 LET THE
POOR MAN BOAST,
BECAUSE HE HAS
BEEN UPLIFTED 10
AND LET THE RICH
ONE BOAST WHEN HE IS HUMBLED, BECAUSE HE
WILL PASS AWAY LIKE THE FLOWER OF THE FIELD.
11 THE SUN RISES AND ITS HEAT DRIES
THE GRASS; THE FLOWER WITHERS AND
ITS BEAUTY VANISHES. SO, TOO, WILL THE
RICH PERSON FADE AWAY EVEN IN THE
MIDST OF HIS PURSUITS.

12 HAPPY THE ONE WHO PATIENTLY ENDU-
RES TRIALS, BECAUSE AFTERWARDS HE
WILL RECEIVE THE CROWN OF LIFE WHICH
THE LORD PROMISED TO THOSE WHO LOVE
HIM.
13 LET NO ONE SAY WHEN HE IS TEMPTED,
"THIS TEMPTATION COMES FROM GOD."
GOD IS NEVER TEMPTED AND HE CAN NEVER
TEMPT ANYONE. 14 INSTEAD, EACH OF US IS
LURED AND ENTICED BY HIS OWN EVIL DE-
SIRE.
15 ONCE THIS DESIRE HAS CONCEIVED, IT GIVES
BIRTH TO SIN; WHEN
FULLY GROWN, GIVES
BIRTH TO DEATH.

16 DO NOT BE DE-
CEIVED, DEAR BRO-
THERS. 17 EVERY
GOOD AND PERFECT
GIFT COMES FROM
ABOVE, FROM THE
FATHER OF LIGHT
IN WHOM THERE
IS NO CHANGE OR
SHADOW OF CHANGE.
18 BY HIS OWN
WILL HE GAVE US
LIFE THROUGH THE
WORD OF TRUTH,
THAT WE MIGHT
BE A KIND OF OF-
FERING TO HIM
AMONG HIS CRE-
ATURES. 19 MY
DEAR BROTHERS, BE QUICK TO HEAR BUT SLOW
TO SPEAK AND SLOW TO ANGER, 20 FOR HUMAN
ANGER DOES NOT FULFILL THE JUSTICE OF
GOD. 21 SO GET RID OF ANY FILTH AND REJECT
THE PREVAILING EVIL, AND WELCOME THE WORD
WHICH HAS BEEN PLANTED IN YOU AND HAS THE
POWER TO SAVE YOU.
22 BE DOERS OF THE WORD AND NOT JUST HEARERS,
LEST YOU DECEIVE YOURSELVES. 23 THE HEARER
WHO DOES NOT BECOME A DOER IS LIKE A MAN WHO

LOOKS AT HIMSELF IN THE MIRROR. 24 HE LOOKS AND
THEN PROMPTLY FORGETS WHAT HE LOOKS LIKE.
25 BUT HE WHO FIXES HIS GAZE ON THE PERFECT
LAW OF FREEDOM AND HOLDS ONTO IT, NOT LIS-
TENING AND THEN FORGETTING, BUT ACTING
ON IT, WILL FIND BLESSING ON HIS DEEDS.
26 IF ANYONE CONSIDERS HIMSELF A RELIGIOUS
PERSON BUT DOES NOT RESTRAIN HIS TONGUE,
HE DECEIVES HIMSELF AND HIS RELIGION IS
IN VAIN. 27 IN THE SIGHT OF GOD, OUR FATHER,
PURE AND BLAMELESS RELIGION LIES IN
HELPING THE ORPHANS AND WIDOWS IN
THEIR NEED AND KEEPING ONESELF
FROM THE WORLD'S CORRUPTION.

The rich and the poor

2 (1) My brothers, if you truly believe in our
glorified Lord, Jesus Christ, you will not
discriminate between persons. (2) Suppose a
man enters the synagogue where you are assembled and he is dressed magnificently and wears a
gold ring; at the same time, a poor man enters
dressed in rags. (3) If you focus your attention on

the well-dressed man,
and say to him, "Come and
sit in the best seat,"
while to the poor man
you say, "Stay standing
or else sit down at
my feet," (4) have
you not, in fact, ma-
de a distinction bet-
ween the two? Have
you not judged, using
a double standard?
(5) Look, brothers,
did God not choose
the poor of this world
to receive the ri-
ches of faith and
to inherit the king-
dom which he has
promised to those
who love him?
(6) Yet you despi-
se them! Is it not
the rich who are aga-
inst you and drag you
to court? (7) Do they
not insult the holy
name of Christ by which you are called?
(8) If you keep the law of the kingdom, according to scripture: Love your neighbor as yourself, you do well; (9) but if you make
distinctions between persons, you break
the law and are condemned by the same
law. (10) If anyone keeps the whole law but
fails in one aspect, he is guilty of breaking it
all. (11) For he who said: Do not commit adultery also
said, Do not kill. If then, you do not commit adultery
but you do commit murder, you have broken the law.

(12) Therefore, speak and behave like people who
are going to be judged by the law of freedom. (13)
There will be justice without mercy for those who
have not shown mercy, **for mercy is
greater than judgment.**

Faith is shown in action

(14) Brothers, what good is it to profess faith without showing works? Such faith has no power to save you. (15) If a brother or sister is in need of food
or clothes (16) and one of you says, "May things
go well for you; be satisfied and warm," without attending to their material needs,
what good is that? (17) So it is for faith
without deeds: it is totally dead.

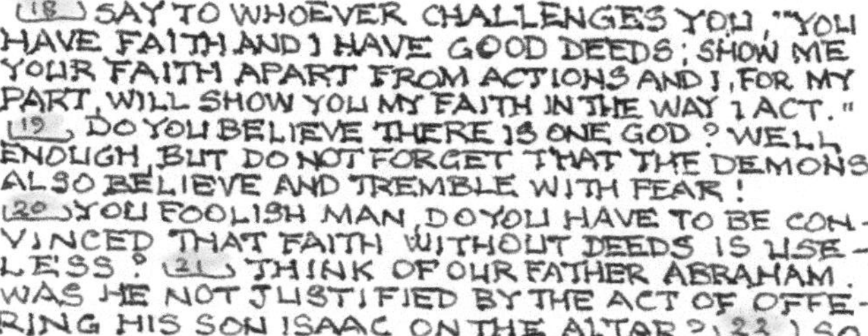
(18) Say to whoever challenges you, "You
have faith and I have good deeds; show me
your faith apart from actions and I, for my
part, will show you my faith in the way I act."
(19) Do you believe there is one God? Well
enough, but do not forget that the demons
also believe and tremble with fear!
(20) You foolish man, do you have to be convinced that faith without deeds is useless? (21) Think of our father Abraham.
Was he not justified by the act of offering his son Isaac on the altar? (22) So

you see, his faith was active along with his deeds
and became perfect by what he did. (23) The
word of scripture was thus fulfilled.
Abraham believed in God so he was considered a
righteous man and he was called the friend
of God. (24) So you see, a person obtains holiness by his deeds and not by faith alone. (25)
Likewise, we read of Rahab the prostitute
that she was acknowledged and saved because she welcomed the spies and showed
them another way to leave. (26) So, just as
the body is dead without its spirit, so
faith, without deeds, is also dead.

Sins of the tongue

3 (1) Brothers, don't all be teachers!
You know that, as teachers, we will be
judged strictly;
(2) in fact, we make mis-
takes, like everybody
else. A person who com-
mits no offense in spe-
ech is perfect and capa-
ble of ruling the whole
self. (3) We put a bit
into the horse's mo-
uth to master it and,
with this, we con-
trol its whole body.
(4) The same is true of
ships: however big
they are and driven by
strong winds, the hel-
msman steers them
with a tiny rudder.
(5) In the same way,
the tongue is a ti-
ny part of the body
but it is capable
of great things.
A small flame is en-
ough to set a huge

forest on fire. (6) The tongue is a similar fla-
me; it is in itself a whole world of evil, it in-
fects the whole being and sets fire to our
world with the very fire of hell. (7) Wild
animals, birds, reptiles and sea creatures of every
kind are and have been ruled by the human species.

8 NOBODY, HOWEVER, CAN CONTROL THE
TONGUE; IT IS AN UNTIRING WHIP, FULL OF
DEADLY POISON.
9 WE USE IT TO BLESS GOD, OUR FATHER, AND
ALSO TO CURSE THOSE MADE IN GOD'S
LIKENESS. 10 FROM THE SAME MOUTH
COME BOTH BLESSING AND CURSE.

BROTHERS, THIS SHOULD NOT BE THE CA-
SE. 11 CAN BOTH FRESH AND SALT WA-
TER GUSH FROM THE SAME SOURCE?

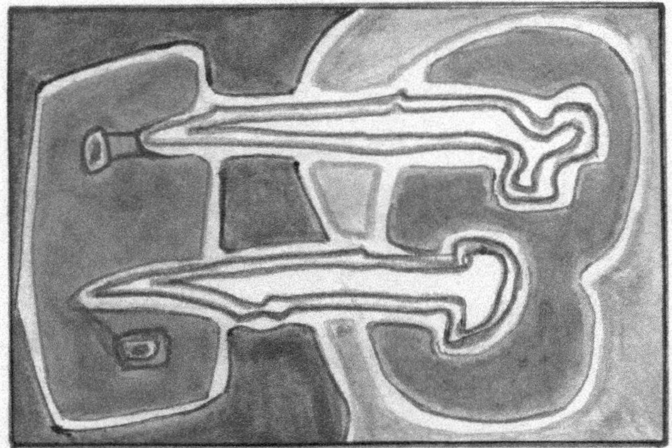

12 CAN A FIG TREE PRODUCE OLIVES OR
A GRAPEVINE GIVE FIGS? NEITHER IS THE
SEA ABLE TO GIVE FRESH WATER.

TRUE WISDOM - 13 IF YOU CONSIDER TO BE
WISE AND LEARNED, SHOW IT BY YOUR GOOD LIFE AND
ACTIONS, IN ALL HUMILITY, BE AN EXAMPLE FOR OTHERS.

14 BUT IF YOUR HEART IS
FULL OF BITTER JEALOUSY
AND AMBITION, DO NOT
TRY TO SHOW OFF; THAT
WOULD BE COVERING UP
THE TRUTH; 15 THIS
KIND OF WISDOM DOES
NOT COME FROM ABOVE
BUT FROM THE WORLD: IT
IS EARTHLY AND DEVILISH.
16 WITH JEALOUSY AND
AMBITION, YOU WILL
ALSO FIND DISCORD AND
ALL THAT IS EVIL. 17 IN-
STEAD, THE WISDOM WHICH
COMES FROM ABOVE IS
PURE AND PEACE-LOV-
ING. PERSONS WITH
THIS WISDOM SHOW UN-
DERSTANDING AND LIS-
TEN TO ADVICE; THEY
ARE FULL OF COMPAS-
SION AND GOOD WORKS.
THEY ARE IMPARTIAL AND
SINCERE. 18 PEACE-MA-
KERS WHO SOW PEACE
THEY WILL REAP A HARVEST OF JUSTICE.

WICKED AMBITIONS

4 1 WHAT CAUSES FIGHTS AND QUARRELS AMONG
YOU? IS IT NOT YOUR INNER LONGINGS WHICH MAKE WAR
WITHIN YOUR OWN SELVES? 2 WHEN YOU LONG FOR SO-
METHING YOU CANNOT HAVE, YOU KILL FOR IT AND WHEN YOU
DON'T GET WHAT YOU DESIRE, YOU SQUABBLE AND FIGHT.
THE FACT IS, YOU DO NOT HAVE WHAT YOU WANT BECA-
USE YOU DO NOT PRAY FOR IT. 3 YOU PRAY FOR
SOMETHING AND YOU DO NOT GET IT BECAUSE YOU
PRAY WITH THE WRONG MOTIVE OF INDULGING YOUR
PLEASURES. 4 YOU ADULTERERS! DON'T YOU
KNOW THAT MAKING FRIENDS WITH THE WORLD
MAKES YOU ENEMIES OF GOD? THEN, HE WHO CHO-
OSES TO BE THE WORLD'S FRIEND HAS MA-
DE HIMSELF GOD'S ENEMY.

5 SURELY, SCRIPTURE IS NOT WRONG WHEN IT
SAYS THAT OUR SPIRIT TENDS TOWARDS EXCESS.
6 BUT GOD'S GRACE OVERCOMES IT. SCRIPTURE
ALSO SAYS, GOD OPPOSES THE PROUD BUT HE GIVES
HIS FAVOR TO THE HUMBLE. 7 GIVE, THEN, TO GOD,
GIVE IN TO HIM; RESIST THE DEVIL AND HE WILL FLEE
from you. 8 Draw
close to God and
he will come close
to you. Clean your
hands, you sinners,

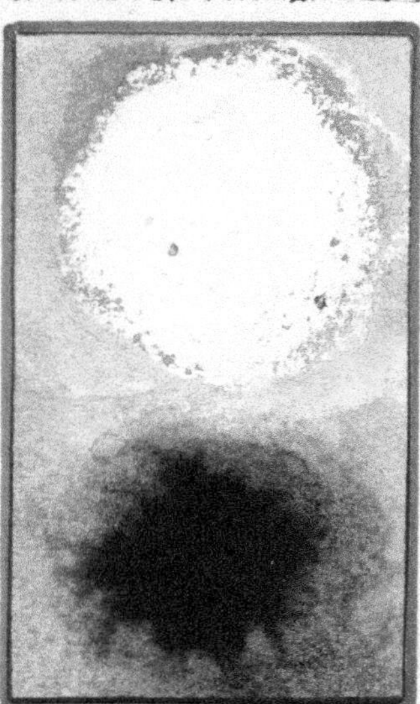

AND PURIFY YOUR HEARTS,
YOU DOUBTERS. 9
RECOGNIZE YOUR
DISTRESS, BE MISERA-
BLE AND WEEP. TURN
YOUR LAUGHTER INTO
TEARS AND YOUR JOY
INTO SADNESS. HUMBLE
10 YOURSELVES BEFO-
RE THE LORD AND HE
WILL RAISE YOU UP.
11 BROTHERS, DO NOT
CRITICIZE ONE ANOT-
HER. ANYONE WHO
SPEAKS AGAINST A BRO-
THER OR CONDEMN HIM,
SPEAKS AGAINST THE
LAW AND CONDEMNS
THE LAW. IF, HOWEVER
YOU CONDEMN THE
LAW, YOU ARE NO LONGER AN OBSERVER OF
THE LAW BUT A JUDGE OF IT. 12 THERE IS ONLY
ONE LAWGIVER AND ONE JUDGE: HE WHO HAS
THE POWER TO SAVE OR CONDEMN. SO YOU, WHO
ARE YOU TO JUDGE YOUR NEIGHBOR?

13 LISTEN NOW, YOU WHO SPEAK LIKE THIS,
"TODAY OR TOMORROW WE WILL GO OFF TO
THIS CITY AND SPEND A YEAR THERE; WE WILL
DO BUSINESS AND MAKE MONEY." 14 YOU

HAVE NO IDEA WHAT TOMORROW WILL BRING. WHAT
IS YOUR LIFE? NO MORE THAN A MIST WHICH AP-
PEARS FOR A MOMENT AND THEN DISAPPEARS.

15 INSTEAD OF THIS, YOU SHOULD SAY, "GOD WILLING,
WE WILL LIVE AND DO THIS OR THAT." 16 BUT NO!
YOU BOAST OF YOUR PLANS; THIS BRAZEN
PRIDE IS WICKED.
17 ANYONE WHO KNOWS WHAT IS GOOD
AND DOES NOT DO IT, SINS.

ST. JAMES
406 CCCCVI
© DM 09

THE MISFORTUNES OF THE RICH

5 1 SO, NOW FOR WHAT CONCERNS THE RICH! CRY
AND WEEP FOR THE MISFORTUNES WHICH ARE COMING
UPON YOU. 2 YOUR RICHES ARE ROTTING AND YOUR
CLOTHES EATEN UP BY THE MOTHS. 3 YOUR SILVER AND
GOLD HAVE RUSTED AND THEIR RUST GROWS INTO A WITNESS
AGAINST YOU. IT WILL CONSUME YOUR FLESH LIKE FIRE, FOR
HAVING PILED UP RICHES IN THESE THE LAST DAYS. 4 YOU
DECEIVED THE WORKERS WHO HARVESTED YOUR FI-
ELDS BUT NOW THEIR WAGES CRY OUT TO THE HEAVENS.

THE REAPERS' COMPLAINTS HAVE REACHED THE EARS OF
THE LORD OF HOSTS. 5 YOU LIVED IN LUXURY AND PLEASURE
IN THIS WORLD AND FELT HAPPY WHILE OTHERS WERE
MURDERED. 6 YOU HAVE EASILY CONDEMNED AND KIL-
LED THE INNOCENT SINCE THEY OFFERED NO RESISTANCE.

FORWARD WITH THE LORD

7 BE PATIENT THEN, MY BROTHERS, UNTIL THE COMING OF
THE LORD. SEE HOW THE SOWER WAITS FOR THE PRECIOUS
FRUITS OF THE EARTH, LOOKING FORWARD TO THE AUT-
UMN AND SPRING RAINS.

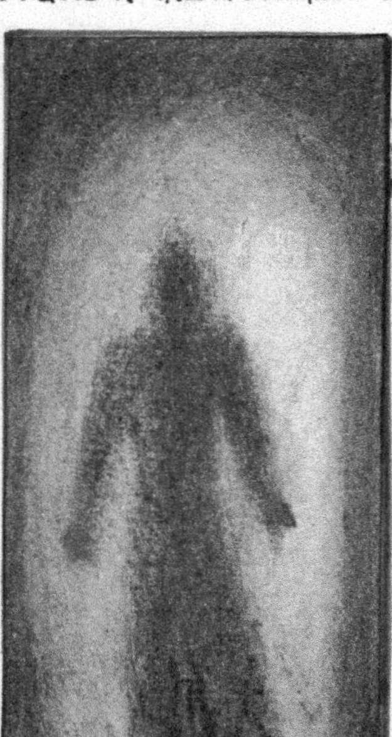

8 YOU ALSO BE PATIENT
AND DO NOT LOSE HEART,
BECAUSE THE LORD'S
COMING IS NEAR. 9
BROTHERS, DO NOT
FIGHT AMONG YOUR-
SELVES AND YOU WILL
NOT BE JUDGED. SEE,
THE JUDGE IS ALREADY
AT THE DOOR. 10 TAKE
FOR YOURSELVES AS AN
EXAMPLE OF PATIENCE
THE SUFFERING OF THE
PROPHETS WHO SPOKE IN
THE LORD'S NAME. 11
SEE HOW THOSE WHO
WERE PATIENT ARE
CALLED BLESSED.
YOU HAVE HEARD OF
THE PATIENCE OF JOB
AND KNOW HOW THE
LORD DEALT WITH
HIM IN THE END.
"FOR THE LORD IS
MERCIFUL AND
SHOWS COMPASSION".
12 ABOVE ALL,
BROTHERS, DO NOT SWEAR EITHER BY HE-
AVEN OR BY EARTH, OR MAKE A HABIT OF
SWEARING. LET YOUR "YES" BE YES AND YOUR "NO"
BE NO, LEST YOU BECOME LIABLE FOR JUDGMENT.

THE SICK -

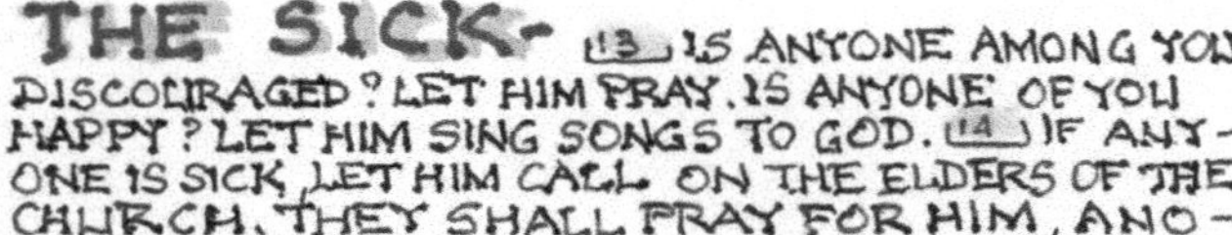

13 IS ANYONE AMONG YOU
DISCOURAGED? LET HIM PRAY. IS ANYONE OF YOU
HAPPY? LET HIM SING SONGS TO GOD. 14 IF ANY-
ONE IS SICK, LET HIM CALL ON THE ELDERS OF THE
CHURCH. THEY SHALL PRAY FOR HIM, ANO-
INTING HIM WITH OIL
IN THE NAME OF THE
LORD. 15 THE PRAYER
SAID IN FAITH WILL SA-
VE THE SICK PERSON;
THE LORD WILL RAISE
HIM UP AND IF HE HAS
COMMITTED ANY SINS,
HE WILL BE FORGIVEN.

16 THERE WILL BE HE-
ALING IF YOU CONFESS
YOUR SINS TO ONE AN-
OTHER AND PRAY FOR
EACH OTHER. THE PRA-
YER OF THE UPRIGHT
MAN HAS GREAT PO-
WER, PROVIDED HE
PERSEVERES. ELIJAH
17 WAS A HUMAN
BEING LIKE OURSEL-
VES AND WHEN HE PRA-
YED EARNESTLY FOR
IT NOT TO RAIN, NO RAIN
FELL FOR THREE AND
A HALF YEARS. THEN
18 HE PRAYED AGAIN: THE SKY YIELDED RAIN
AND THE EARTH PRODUCED ITS FRUIT.

19 BROTHERS, IF ANY ONE OF YOU STRAYS
FAR AWAY FROM THE TRUTH AND ANOTHER
PERSON BRINGS HIM BACK TO IT, 20

BE SURE OF THIS: HE WHO BRINGS BACK A
SINNER FROM THE WRONG WAY WILL SAVE
HIS SOUL FROM DEATH AND WIN FORGIVE-
NESS FOR MANY SINS.

FIRST LETTER OF PETER

PETER HAD NEITHER THE GENIUS NOR THE LITERARY TALENT OF PAUL. INSTEAD, WITH SIMPLE WORDS, HE ADDRESSED THE CHRISTIANS OF THE ASIAN PROVINCE, WERE THE FIRST PERSECUTIONS WERE BEGINNING.

1 1 FROM PETER, APOSTLE OF JESUS
CHRIST, TO THE JEWS WHO LIVE
OUTSIDE THEIR HOMELAND, SCAT-
TERED IN PONTUS, GALATIA, CAP-
PADOCIA, ASIA AND BITHYNIA. 2
TO THOSE WHOM GOD THE FATHER HAS CAL-
LED, ACCORDING TO HIS PLAN, AND MADE HOLY

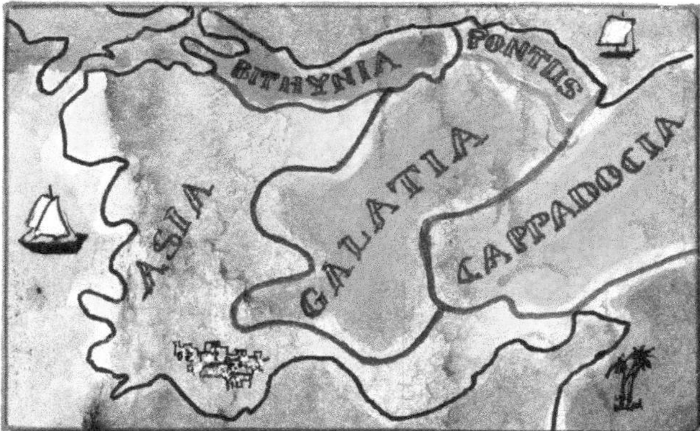

BY THE SPIRIT, TO OBEY JESUS CHRIST AND BE
PURIFIED BY HIS BLOOD; MAY GRACE AND
PEACE INCREASE AMONG YOU.

YOU HAVE BEEN SAVED

3 LET US PRAISE GOD, THE FATHER OF OUR LORD
JESUS CHRIST, FOR HIS GREAT MERCY. IN RA-
ISING JESUS CHRIST FROM THE DEAD HAS GIVEN
US NEW LIFE AND THE HOPE OF SHARING
LIFE BEYOND DEATH, 4 WITHOUT SIN
AND ALL FLEETING THINGS. THIS INHERI-
TANCE IS KEPT IN THE HEAVENS FOR YOU, 5
SINCE GOD'S POWER SHALL KEEP YOU FA-
ITHFUL UNTIL SALVATION IS REVEALED IN
THE LAST DAYS. 6
THERE IS CAUSE FOR
JOY, THEN, EVEN
THOUGH YOU MAY,
FOR A TIME, HAVE
TO SUFFER MANY TRI-
ALS. 7 THUS WILL YOUR
FAITH BE TESTED, LIKE
GOLD IN A FURNACE.
GOLD, HOWEVER, PASSES
AWAY BUT FAITH, WORTH
SO MUCH MORE, WILL
BRING YOU IN THE END
PRAISE, GLORY AND HO-
NOR WHEN JESUS
CHRIST APPEARS. 8
YOU HAVE NOT YET SE-
EN HIM AND YET YOU
LOVE HIM; EVEN WITH-
OUT SEEING HIM, YOU
BELIEVE IN HIM AND
EXPERIENCE A HEAVEN-
LY JOY BEYOND ALL
WORDS, 9 FOR YOU
ARE REACHING THE

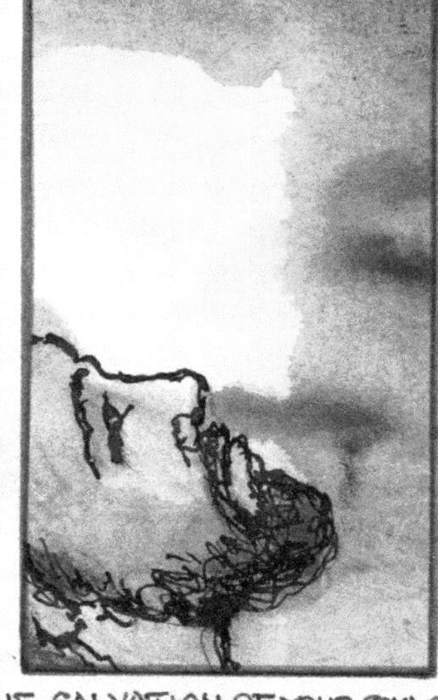

GOAL OF YOUR FAITH: THE SALVATION OF YOUR SOULS.
10 THIS WAS THE SALVATION FOR WHICH THE
PROPHETS SO EAGERLY LOOKED WHEN, IN DAYS
PAST, THEY FORETOLD THE FAVOR OF GOD WITH
REGARD TO YOU.
11 BUT THEY COULD ONLY INVESTIGATE AS
WHEN THE SPIRIT OF CHRIST PRESENT
WITHIN THEM POINTED OUT THE TIME
AND THE CIRCUMSTANCES OF THIS—
THE SUFFERINGS OF CHRIST AND
THE GLORIES WHICH WOULD FOLLOW.

12 IT WAS REVEALED TO THEM THAT THEY
WERE NOT WORKING FOR THEMSELVES
BUT FOR YOU.
THUS, IN THESE DAYS, AFTER THE HOLY
SPIRIT HAS BEEN SENT FROM HEAVEN,
THE GOSPEL'S PREACHERS HAVE TAUGHT
YOU THESE MYSTERIES WHICH EVEN THE
ANGELS LONG TO SEE.

13 SO, THEN, LET YOUR SPIRIT BE READY.
BE ALERT, WITH CONFIDENT TRUST IN THE GRA-
CE YOU WILL RECEIVE

WHEN JESUS CHRIST
APPEARS. 14 LIKE
OBEDIENT CHILDREN,
DO NOT RETURN TO
YOUR FORMER LIFE
GIVEN OVER TO IGNOR-
ANCE AND PASSIONS.
15 IMITATE THE ONE
WHO CALLED YOU. AS
HE IS HOLY SO YOU,
TOO, BE HOLY IN ALL
YOUR CONDUCT, SINCE
16 SCRIPTURE SAYS:
BE HOLY FOR I AM
HOLY. 17 YOU CALL
UPON A FATHER WHO
MAKES NO DISTINCTION
BETWEEN PERSONS
BUT JUDGES EACH ONE
ACCORDING TO HIS DE-
EDS; TAKE SERIOUSLY,
THEN, THESE YEARS
WHICH YOU SPEND IN
A STRANGE LAND. 18
REMEMBER THAT YOU
WERE FREED FROM
THE USELESS WAY OF LIFE OF YOUR FATHERS, NOT
WITH GOLD AND SILVER 19 BUT WITH THE PRE-
CIOUS BLOOD OF THE LAMB WITHOUT SPOT OR BLE-
MISH. 20 GOD, WHO HAS KNOWN CHRIST BEFORE
THE WORLD BEGAN, REVEALED HIM TO YOU IN THE
LAST DAYS.
21 THROUGH HIM, YOU HAVE FAITH IN GOD WHO

RAISED HIM FROM THE DEAD AND GLORIFIED
HIM IN ORDER THAT YOU MIGHT PUT ALL
YOUR FAITH AND HOPE IN GOD.

22 IN OBEYING THE TRUTH, YOU HAVE GAINED
INTERIOR PURIFICATION FROM WHICH CO-
MES SINCERE LOVE FOR OUR BROTHERS. LOVE
ONE ANOTHER, THEN, WITH ALL YOUR HEART,
23 SINCE YOU ARE BORN AGAIN, NOT FROM MOR-
TAL BEINGS, BUT WITH ENDURING LIFE, THROUGH
THE WORD OF GOD WHO LIVES AND REMAINS FOREVER.

24 IT IS WRITTEN: ALL FLESH IS GRASS AND
ITS GLORY LIKE THE FLOWERS OF THE FIELD. THE
GRASS WITHERS AND THE FLOWER FALLS, BUT THE
WORD OF THE LORD ENDURES FOREVER. THE WORD
IS THE GOSPEL WHICH HAS BEEN BROUGHT TO YOU.

CHRIST IS THE CORNERSTONE

2 1 SO, GIVE UP ALL EVIL AND DECEIT, HYPOCRI-
SY, ENVY AND EVERY KIND OF GOSSIP. LIKE
2 NEWBORN CHILDREN, EAGERLY LONG-
ING FOR THE PURE MILK OF THE WORD WHICH

WILL HELP YOU GROW AND REACH SALVATION.
3 DID YOU NOT TASTE THE GOODNESS OF THE
LORD? 4 HE IS THE LIVING STONE REJEC-
TED BY PEOPLE BUT CHOSEN BY GOD AND PRE-
CIOUS TO HIM. 5 ON DRAWING CLOSE TO
HIM, YOU ALSO BECOME LIVING STONES BUILT IN-
TO A SPIRITUAL TEMPLE, A HOLY COMMUNI-
TY OF PRIESTS OFFERING SPIRITUAL SACRI-
FICES WHICH PLEASE GOD THROUGH JESUS
CHRIST. 6 SCRIPTURE
SAYS: SEE, I LAY IN
ZION A CHOSEN AND
PRECIOUS CORNER-
STONE; WHOEVER
BELIEVES IN HIM WILL
NOT BE DISAPPOINTED.
7 THIS MEANS HONOR
FOR YOU WHO BELIEV-
ED, BUT FOR UNBELI-
EVERS ALSO THE
STONE WHICH THE
BUILDERS REJECTED
HAS BECOME THE COR-
NERSTONE 8 AND IT
IS A STONE TO STUMBLE
OVER, A ROCK WHICH LAYS
PEOPLE LOW. THEY
STUMBLE OVER IT IN RE-
JECTING THE WORD,
BUT THE PLAN OF
GOD IS FULFILLED IN
THIS. 9 YOU ARE A
CHOSEN RACE,
A COMMUNITY OF PRI-
EST-KINGS, A CON-
SACRATED NATION,
A PEOPLE GOD HAS
MADE HIS OWN TO PROCLAIM HIS WONDERS.
FOR HE CALLED YOU FROM YOUR DARKNESS
TO HIS OWN WONDERFUL LIGHT.
10 AT ONE STAGE YOU WERE NO PEOPLE,
BUT NOW YOU ARE GOD'S PEOPLE. YOU HAD
NOT RECEIVED HIS MERCY, BUT NOW
YOU HAVE BEEN GIVEN MERCY.

407 - CCCCVII

LIVE A BLAMELESS LIFE

11 MY DEAR BROTHERS, WHILE YOU STAND
STRANGERS AND EXILES, I URGE YOU NOT TO IN-
DULGE IN SELFISH PASSIONS WHICH WAGE WAR
ON THE SOUL. 12 LIVE A BLAMELESS LIFE
AMONG THE PAGANS; SO WHEN THEY ACCUSE
YOU FALSELY OF ANY WRONG, THEY MAY SEE
YOUR GOOD WORKS AND GIVE GLORY TO GOD
ON THE DAY HE COMES TO THEM. 13 FOR THE

LORD'S SAKE, RESPECT ALL HUMAN AUTHORI-
TY: THE KING AS CHIEF AUTHORITY, 14 THE
GOVERNORS AS SENT BY HIM TO PUNISH EVILDO-
ERS AND TO ENCOURAGE THOSE WHO DO GOOD.
15 AND GOD WANTS YOU TO DO GOOD SO THAT
YOU MAY SILENCE THOSE FOOLS WHO IGNORANT-
LY CRITICIZE YOU. 16 BEHAVE AS FREE MEN
BUT DO NOT SPEAK OF FREEDOM AS A LICENSE
FOR VICE; YOU ARE FREE MEN AND GOD'S SER-
VANTS. 17 REVERENCE EACH PERSON, LOVE
YOUR BROTHERS AND SISTERS, FEAR GOD AND
SHOW RESPECT TO THE EMPEROR.

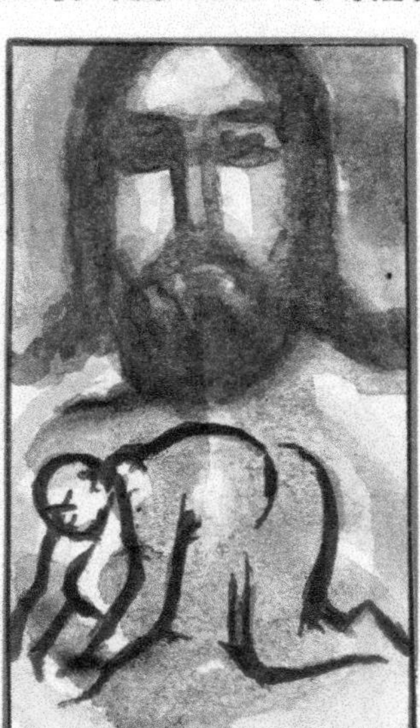

18 SERVANTS MUST
RESPECT THEIR MAS-
TERS, NOT ONLY THOSE
WHO ARE GOOD AND
UNDERSTANDING, BUT
ALSO THOSE WHO ARE
DIFFICULT. 19 FOR
THERE IS A MERIT IN
PUTTING UP WITH UN-
PROVOKED SUFFERING,
FOR THE SAKE OF GOD.
20 WHAT MERIT WOULD
THERE BE IN TAKING A
BEATING WHE YOU HAVE
DONE WRONG? BUT IF
YOU ENDURE PUNISH-
MENT WHEN YOU HAVE
DONE WELL, THAT IS A
GRACE BEFORE GOD. 21
THIS IS YOUR CALLING:
REMEMBER CHRIST
WHO SUFFERED FOR
YOU, LEAVING YOU AN
EXAMPLE SO THAT YOU
MAY FOLLOW IN HIS
WAY. 22 HE DID NO
WRONG AND THERE WAS NO DECEIT IN HIS MO-
UTH. 23 HE DID NOT RETURN INSULT FOR
INSULT AND, WHEN SUFFERING, HE DID NOT
CURSE BUT PUT HIMSELF IN THE HANDS
OF GOD WHO JUDGES JUSTLY. 24 HE WENT TO THE
CROSS BURDENED WITH OUR SINS SO THAT WE
MIGHT DIE TO SIN AND LIVE AN UPRIGHT LIFE. FOR
BY HIS WOUNDS YOU HAVE BEEN HEALED.

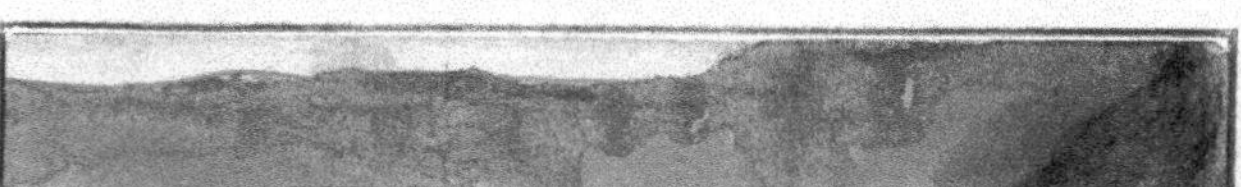

25 YOU WERE LIKE STRAY SHEEP, BUT
YOU HAVE COME BACK TO THE SHEPHERD
AND GUARDIAN OF YOUR SOULS.

HUSBANDS AND WIVES

3 1 IN THE SAME WAY, WIVES MUST BE SUB-
MISSIVE TO THEIR HUSBANDS. IF ANY
OF THEM RESISTS THE WORD, THEY WILL
BE WON OVER WITHOUT WORDS BY THE CONDUCT
OF THEIR WIVES. 2

IT WILL BE ENOUGH
FOR THEM TO SEE YO-
UR RESPONSIBLE
AND BLAMELESS CON-
DUCT. 3 DO NOT BE
TAKEN UP WITH OUT-
WARD APPEARANCES:
HAIRSTYLES, GOLD
NECKLACES AND CLO-
THES. 4 THERE IS
SOMETHING MORE PER-
MANENT THAT SHINES
FROM WITHIN A PER-
SON: A GENTLE AND
PEACEFUL DISPOSI-
TION. THIS IS REALLY
PRECIOUS IN GOD'S
EYES. 5 THIS WAS
THE WAY THE HOLY
WOMEN OF THE PAST
DRESSED. THEY PUT
THEIR TRUST IN GOD
AND WERE OBEDIENT
TO THEIR HUSBANDS,
6 NAMELY SARAH
WHO HAD SUCH RES-
PECT FOR ABRAHAM THAT SHE CALLED HIM
HER LORD. YOU ARE HER CHILDREN IF YOU
DO WHAT IS RIGHT AND ARE NOT AFRAID.

7 HUSBANDS, IN YOUR TURN, BE SENSIBLE IN YOUR
LIFE TOGETHER. BE CONSIDERATE, REALIZING
THAT THE WOMAN IS OF A MORE FRAIL DISPOSI-
TION AND THAT YOU BOTH SHARE IN THE GIFT
OF LIFE. IF YOU DO THIS, GOD WILL READI-
LY ANSWER YOUR PRAYERS. 8 FINALLY, YOU

SHOULD ALL BE OF ONE MIND: SHARE EACH
OTHER'S TROUBLES WITH MUTUAL AFFECT-
ION, BE COMPASSIONATE AND HUMBLE.

9 DO NOT REPAY EVIL FOR EVIL OR ANSWER
ONE INSULT WITH ANOTHER. GIVE A BLESSING
INSTEAD, SINCE THIS IS WHAT YOU HAVE
BEEN CALLED TO DO, AND SO YOU WILL
RECEIVE THE BLESSING.

10 FOR YOU, IF YOU SEEK LIFE AND WANT TO
SEE HAPPINESS, KEEP YOUR TONGUE FROM EVIL
AND YOUR MOUTH FROM SPEAKING DECEIT.
11 TURN AWAY FROM EVIL AND DO GOOD; SEEK
PEACE AND PURSUE IT. 12 BECAUSE THE LORD'S
EYES ARE TURNED TO THE JUST AND HIS EARS
LISTEN TO THEIR APPEAL.
BUT THE LORD FROWNS ON EVILDOERS.

DO NOT FEAR OR BE DISTURBED

13 WHO CAN HARM YOU IF YOU DEVOTE YOUR-

SELVES TO DOING GO-
OD? 14 IF YOU SUFFER
FOR THE SAKE OF RIGHT-
EOUSNESS, HAPPY ARE
YOU. DO NOT FEAR WHAT
THEY FEAR OR BE DIS-
TURBED AS THEY ARE,
15 BUT BLESS THE
LORD CHRIST IN YOUR
HEARTS. ALWAYS HAVE
AN ANSWER READY WHEN
YOU ARE CALLED UPON
TO ACCOUNT FOR YOUR
HOPE, BUT GIVE IT SIM-
PLY AND WITH RESPECT.
16 KEEP YOUR CON-
SCIENCE CLEAR SO THAT
THOSE WHO SLANDER
YOU MAY BE PUT TO
SHAME BY YOUR UP-
RIGHT, CHRISTIAN LI-
VING. 17 BETTER TO
SUFFER FOR DOING
GOOD, IF IT IS GOD'S
WILL, THAN FOR DOING EVIL AND WRONG.

ENDURE SUFFERING AS CHRIST DID

18 REMEMBER HOW CHRIST DIED, ONCE AND FOR ALL,
FOR OUR SINS. HE, THE JUST ONE, DIED FOR THE UN-
JUST IN ORDER TO LEAD US TO GOD. HE DIED AS HUM-
ANS DO, BUT WAS RAISED TO LIFE BY THE SPIRIT,
19 AND IT WAS THEN THAT HE WENT TO PREACH
TO THE IMPRISONED SPIRITS. 20 THEY WERE THE
GENERATION WHO DIDN'T BELIEVE WHEN GOD, IN HIS

GREAT PATIENCE, DID NOT PUNISH THE WORLD AS NOAH
WAS BUILDING THE ARK WITH ONLY EIGHT PERSONS
ESCAPING THROUGH WATER. 21 THAT WAS A TYPE OF
THE BAPTISM WHICH NOW SAVES YOU; THIS BAPTISM
IS NOT A PHYSICAL CLEANSING BUT ASKING GOD TO RE-
CONCILE US THROUGH THE RESURRECTION OF JESUS
CHRIST. 22 HE HAS ASCENDED TO HEAVEN AND IS AT
THE RIGHT HAND OF GOD, HAVING SUBJECTED
THE ANGELS, DOMINATIONS AND POWERS.

4 1 GIVEN THAT CHRIST SUFFERED IN HIS HU-
MAN LIFE, ARM YOURSELVES WITH THIS CERTA-
INTY: HE WHO SUFFERS IN HIS BODY HAS BRO-
KEN WITH SIN 2 AND WILL SPEND THE REST OF
HIS LIFE FOLLOWING THE WILL OF GOD AND
NOT HUMAN PASSIONS. 3 YOU HAVE GIVEN
ENOUGH TIME, IN THE PAST, TO LIVING AS THE
PAGANS DO: A LIFE OF EXCESS, EVIL PAS-
SIONS, DRUNKENNESS, ORGIES AND WOR-
SHIP OF IDOLS.
4 THEY NOW FIND IT STRANGE THAT YOU ARE
NO LONGER SWEPT ALONG WITH THEM IN
THIS RUINOUS FLOOD, AND THEY MISIN-
TERPRET IT. 5 BUT THEY WILL BE AC-
COUNTABLE TO THE ONE WHO IS READY TO

JUDGE THE LIVING AND THE DEAD. 6 THE GOSPEL
HAS BEEN PREACHED TO MANY WHO ARE NOW
DEAD. AS HUMANS THEY RECEIVED A DEADLY SEN-
TENCE, BUT THROUGH THE SPIRIT THEY SHALL
LIVE FOR GOD. 7 THE END OF ALL THINGS IS
NEAR; LIVE WISELY AND SPEND EVENING TIME
PRAYING 8 ABOVE ALL,

LET YOUR LOVE FOR ONE
ANOTHER BE SINCERE,
FOR LOVE COVERS A
MULTITUDE OF SINS. 9
WELCOME ONE ANOTHER
INTO YOUR HOUSES
WITHOUT COMPLAIN-
ING. 10 SERVE ONE
ANOTHER WITH THE
GIFTS EACH OF YOU RE-
CEIVED, THUS BECOM-
ING GOOD MANAGERS OF
THE VARIED GRACES
OF GOD. 11 IF YOU
SPEAK, DELIVER THE
WORD OF GOD; IF
YOU HAVE A SPECIAL
MINISTRY, LET IT BE
SEEN AS GOD'S POW-
ER SO THAT, IN EVERY-
THING, GOD MAY BE
GLORIFIED IN JESUS
CHRIST. TO HIM BE-
LONG GLORY AND
POWER FOREVER
AND EVER. AMEN.

BE GLAD TO SHARE IN THE SUFFERINGS OF CHRIST

12 MY DEAR PEOPLE, DO NOT BE SUR-
PRISED THAT YOU ARE BEING TESTED
BY FIRE. IT IS NOT AN UNUSUAL OCCURRENCE.

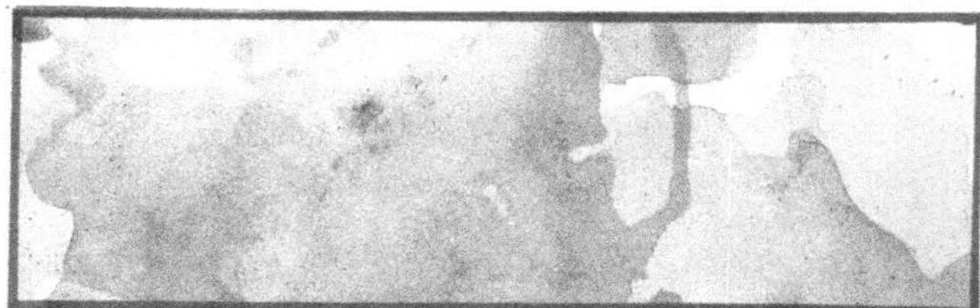

13 INSTEAD, YOU SHOULD BE GLAD TO SHARE IN THE
SUFFERING OF CHRIST BECAUSE, ON THE DAY HIS
GLORY IS REVEALED, YOU WILL ALSO FULLY REJO-
ICE. 14 YOU ARE FORTUNATE IF YOU ARE INS-
ULTED BECAUSE OF THE NAME OF CHRIST, FOR
THE SPIRIT OF GLORY RESTS IN YOU. 15 I SUPPOSE
THAT NONE OF YOU SHOULD SUFFER FOR BEING A
MURDERER, A THIEF, A CRIMINAL OR AN INFORMER;
16 BUT IF ANYONE SUFFERS ON ACCOUNT OF BEING
A CHRISTIAN, LET HIM NOT BE ASHAMED; RATHER
LET THIS NAME BRING GLORY TO GOD. 17 THE

TIME OF JUDGMENT HAS COME AND IT BEGINS WITH
GOD'S HOUSEHOLD. IF ITS BEGINNING SO AFFECTS
US, WHAT WILL BE THE END OF THOSE WHO REFUSE
TO BELIEVE IN THE GOSPEL? 18 IF THE JUST
ONE IS BARELY SAVED, WHAT WILL HAPPEN TO
THE SINNER AND UNBELIEVER? 19 SO, THEN,
IF YOU SUFFER ACCORDING TO GOD'S WILL, EN-
TRUST YOURSELF TO THE FAITHFUL CREATOR
AND CONTINUE TO DO GOOD.

FURTHER ADMONITIONS

5 1 I NOW ADDRESS MYSELF TO THOSE EL-
DERS AMONG YOU; I, TOO, AM AN ELDER
AND A WITNESS TO THE SUFFERING OF
CHRIST, HOPING TO SHARE THE GLORY WHICH IS TO BE RE-
VEALED. 2 SHE-
PHERD THE FLOCK WHICH GOD HAS ENTRUSTED TO YOU, GUARDING IT NOT OUT OF OBLIGATION BUT WILLINGLY FOR GOD'S SAKE; NOT AS ONE LOOKING FOR A REWARD BUT WITH A GENEROUS HEART;
3 DO NOT LORD IT OVER THOSE IN YOUR CARE, RATHER BE AN EXAMPLE TO YOUR FLOCK.

4 THEN, WHEN THE CHIEF SHEPHERD
APPEARS, YOU WILL BE GIVEN A CROWN
OF UNFADING GLORY.

5 IN THE SAME WAY, LET THE YOUNGER
ONES AMONG YOU RESPECT THE AUTHORI-
TY OF THE ELDERS.
ALL OF YOU, BE HUMBLE IN YOUR DEALINGS
WITH EACH OTHER, BECAUSE GOD OPPOSES
THE PROUD BUT GIVES HIS GRACE TO THE
HUMBLE.
6 BOW DOWN, THEN BEFORE THE POWER OF
GOD SO THAT HE WILL RAISE UP AT THE APPO-
INTED TIME. 7 PLACE
ALL YOUR WORRIES ON HIM SINCE HE TAKES CARE OF
YOU. 8 BE SOBER AND ALERT BECAUSE YOUR ENEMY THE DEVIL PROWLS ABOUT LIKE A ROARING LION SEEKING SOMEONE TO DE-
VOUR. 9 STAND
YOUR GROUND, FIRM IN YOUR FAITH, AND KNOWING THAT OUR BROTHERS, SCATTERED THROUGHOUT THE WORLD, ARE CONFRONTING SIMILAR PERSECUTIONS.
10 GOD, THE GIVER OF GRACE, HAS CALLED YOU TO SHARE IN CHRIST'S ETERNAL GLORY AND AFTER YOU HAVE SUFFE-

RED A LITTLE HE WILL BRING YOU TO
PERFECTION; HE WILL CONFIRM, STRENG-
THEN AND ESTABLISH YOU FOREVER.
11 GLORY BE TO HIM FOREVER AND EVER. AMEN.

12 I HAVE HAD THESE FEW LINES OF ENCO-
URAGEMENT WRITTEN TO YOU BY SILVANUS,
OUR BROTHER, WHOM I KNOW TO BE TRUST-
WORTHY. FOR I WANTED TO REMIND YOU

OF THE KINDNESS OF GOD REALLY PRESENT
IN ALL THIS. HOLD ON TO IT.
13 GREETINGS FROM THE COMMUNITY
IN BABYLON, GATHERED BY GOD, AND FROM
MY SON, MARK.
14 GREET ONE ANOTHER WITH A FRIENDLY
EMBRACE.
PEACE TO YOU ALL WHO ARE IN CHRIST.

QUO VADIS,
DOMINE?

EO ROMAM, QUE TIBI
RELINQUENDA FUIT

408 - CCCCVIII DM-08 ©

SECOND LETTER OF PETER

THIS IS THE LATEST BOOK IN THE WHOLE BIBLE, PROBABLY WAS WRITTEN AROUND THE YEAR 100, AND IT IS PRESENTED AS THE 2nd LETTER BY PETER, IT DEALS WITH THE CHURCH OF THAT TIME.

1 1 SYMEON PETER, A SERVANT AND APOSTLE
OF JESUS CHRIST, TO THOSE WHO HAVE
BEEN SANCTIFIED BY OUR GOD AND SA-
VIOR JESUS CHRIST AND HAVE RECEIVED A FAITH

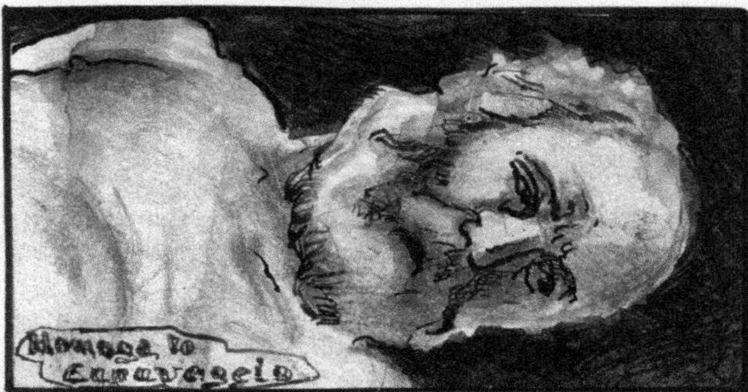

AS PRECIOUS AS OURS: 2 MAY GRACE AND PEACE
ABOUND IN YOU THROUGH THE KNOWLEDGE OF
GOD AND OF JESUS OUR LORD.

WE SHARE IN THE DIVINE NATURE

3 HIS DIVINE POWER HAS GIVEN US EVERYTHING WE
NEED FOR LIFE AND PIETY, FIRST THE KNOWLEDGE
OF THE ONE WHO CALLED US THROUGH HIS OWN GLO-
RY AND MIGHT, BY WHICH WE ARE GIVEN THE MOST
EXTRAORDINARY AND PRECIOUS PROMISES.
4 THROUGH THEM YOU SHARE IN THE DIVINE
NATURE, AFTER REPELLING THE CORRUPTION
AND EVIL DESIRES OF THIS WORLD.

5 SO STRIVE WITH THE GREATEST DETERMINATION
AND INCREASE YOUR FAITH WITH STRENGTH, STRENGTH
WITH KNOWLEDGE, 6 KNOWLEDGE WITH MODERA-
TION, MODERATION WITH CONSTANCY, CONSTANCY WITH
PIETY, 7 PIETY WITH
FRATERNAL LOVE, FRATER-
NAL LOVE WITH CHARITY.
8 IF ALL THESE RICHES
ARE IN YOU SO AS TO ABO-
UND IN YOU YOU WILL NOT
BE IDLE AND USELESS:
YOU WILL BE ROOTED IN THE
KNOWLEDGE OF JESUS
CHRIST OUR LORD. 9
WHOEVER IS NOT AWARE
OF THIS IS BLIND AND
SHORTSIGHTED AND
HAS FORGOTTEN THAT
HE WAS PURIFIED
FROM HIS FORMER
SINS. 10 THEREFORE,
BROTHERS AND SISTERS
STRIVE MORE TO RES-
POND TO THE CALL
OF GOD WHO CHOSE
YOU. IF YOU DO SO,
YOU WILL NEVER
STUMBLE. 11 MORE-
OVER YOU WILL BE
GENEROUSLY GRANTED

ENTRY TO THE ETERNAL KINGDOM OF OUR LORD
AND SAVIOR JESUS CHRIST.
12 SO I SHALL ALWAYS REMIND YOU OF THESE
THINGS, THOUGH YOU KNOW THEM AND REMAIN
FIRM IN THE TRUTH THAT YOU HAVE. IT SEEMS
13 FITTING THAT AS LONG AS I LIVE IN THE
TENT OF THIS BODY, I REFRESH YOUR MEMORY
OF THEM, 14 KNOWING THAT MY TENT MAY
SOON BE FOLDED UP, AS OUR LORD JESUS
CHRIST HAS SHOWN ME.

(15) I WILL, NONETHELESS, ENDEAVOR TO SEE THAT AFTER MY DEPARTURE YOU WILL BE CONSTANTLY REMINDED OF ALL THIS.

THE FOUNDATION OF FAITH

(16) INDEED, WHAT WE TAUGHT YOU ABOUT THE POWER AND THE RETURN OF CHRIST JESUS OUR LORD WAS NOT DRAWN FROM MYTHS OR FORMULATED THEORIES. WE OURSELVES WERE EYEWITNESSES OF HIS MAJESTY, (17) WHEN HE RECEIVED GLORY AND HONOR FROM GOD THE FATHER, WHEN FROM THE MAGNIFICENT GLORY THIS MOST EXTRAORDINARY WORD

CAME UPON HIM: "THIS IS MY BELOVED SON, THIS IS MY CHOSEN ONE." (18) WE OURSELVES HEARD THIS VOICE FROM HEAVEN WHEN WE WERE WITH HIM ON THE HOLY MOUNTAIN. (19) WE BELIEVE MOST FIRMLY IN THE MESSAGE OF THE PROPHETS WHICH YOU SHOULD CONSIDER RIGHTLY AS A LAMP SHINING IN A DARK PLACE, UNTIL THE BREAK OF DAY, WHEN THE MORNING STAR SHINES IN YOUR HEARTS. (20) KNOW THIS WELL: NO PROPHECY OF SCRIPTURE CAN BE HANDED OVER TO PRIVATE INTERPRETATION, (21) SINCE NO PROPHECY COMES FROM HUMAN DECISION, FOR IT WAS MEN OF GOD, MOVED BY THE HOLY SPIRIT, WHO SPOKE.

FALSE TEACHERS

2 (1) JUST AS THERE HAVE BEEN FALSE PROPHETS IN THE MIDST OF THE PEOPLE OF ISRAEL, SO WILL THERE BE FALSE TEACHERS AMONG YOU. THEY WILL INTRODUCE HARMFUL SECTS AND, BY DENYING THE MASTER WHO SAVED THEM, THEY WILL BRING UPON THEMSELVES SUDDEN PERDITION. (2) MANY, NONETHELESS, WILL IMITATE THEIR VICES AND BECAUSE OF THEM THE WAY OF TRUTH WILL BE DISCREDITED. (3) THEY WILL TAKE ADVANTAGE OF YOU WITH DECEITFUL WORDS FOR THE SAKE OF MONEY. BUT THEIR CONDEMNATION HAS ALREADY BEGUN AND THEIR DESTRUCTION AWAITS THEM.

...FALSE TEACHERS...

(4) IN FACT, GOD DID NOT PARDON THE ANGELS WHO SINNED BUT CAST THEM INTO HELL, CONFINING THEM IN DARK PITS, KEEPING THERE TILL THE DAY OF JUDGMENT.

(5) NEITHER DID HE PARDON THE ANCIENT WORLD WHEN HE UNLEASHED THE WATERS OF THE FLOOD UPON THE WORLD OF WICKED PEOPLE BUT PROTECTED ONLY NOAH, THE EIGHTH PROPHET OF RIGHTEOUSNESS. (6) GOLD ALSO CONDEMNED THE CITIES OF SODOM AND GOMORRAH, REDUCING THEM TO ASHES, TO SERVE AS A WARNING TO THE WICKED IN THE FUTURE. (7) BUT HE SAVED LOT, A GOOD MAN DEEPLY AFFLICTED BY THE UNBRIDLED CONDUCT OF THOSE VICIOUS PEOPLE. (8) FOR LOT, A RIGHTEOUS MAN WHO LIVED IN THEIR MIDST, SUFFERED DAY AFTER DAY IN THE GOODNESS OF HIS HEART AS HE SAW AND HEARD OF THEIR CRIMES. (9) SO, THEN, THE LORD KNOWS HOW TO FREE FROM TRIAL THOSE WHO SERVE HIM AND KEEP THE WICKED FOR PUNISHMENT ON THE DAY OF JUDGMENT. (10) HE WILL DO THIS ESPECIALLY FOR CERTAIN PEOPLE WHO FOLLOW THE BASER DESIRES OF THEIR NATURE AND DESPISE THE LORD'S MAJESTY.

St. Peter (after Mantegna)

PROUD AND DARING THEY ARE NOT AFRAID OF INSULTING FALLEN SPIRITS (11) WHILE THE ANGELS, SUPERIOR TO THEM IN STRENGTH AND POWER, DO NOT PERMIT THEMSELVES ANY INJURIOUS ACCUSATION IN THE PRESENCE OF THE LORD. THOSE

(12) PEOPLE ARE LIKE IRRATIONAL ANIMALS BORN TO BE CAUGHT AND KILLED; AFTER THEY HAVE SLANDERED WHAT THEY CANNOT UNDERSTAND, THEY WILL END LIKE ANIMALS (13) AND THEY WILL SUFFER THE REPAYMENT OF THEIR WICKEDNESS.

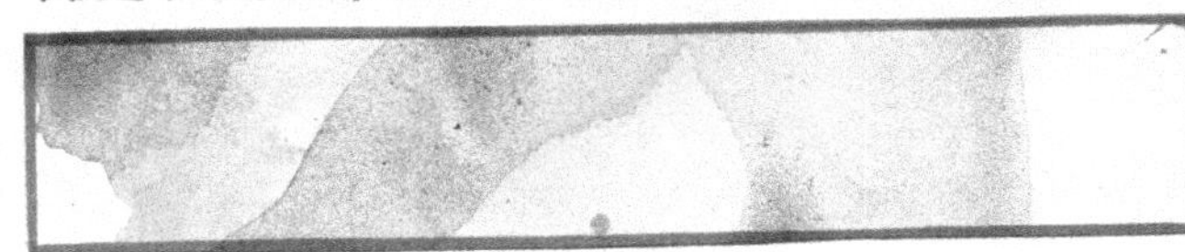

THEY ENJOY FLEETING PLEASURES; THEY ARE
OBSCENE AND VICIOUS WHO DELIGHT IN DECEIV-
ING YOU WHEN THEY SHARE IN YOUR FRATERNAL MEALS.
14 THEY CANNOT LOOK AT A WOMAN WITHOUT DESIR-
ING HER, THEY DO NOT TIRE OF SINNING AND SEDUCING
WEAK SOULS. THEY ARE FULL OF GREED, AN ACCUR-
SE PEOPLE. 15 THEY ABANDONED THE RIGHT WAY
AND FOLLOWED BALAAM, SON OF BEOR WHO WAS AT-
TACHED TO WHAT HE GAINED FROM HIS WRONG-
DOING. 16 BUT HE WAS REBUKED FOR HIS SIN:

HIS SHE-ASS BEGAN TO SPEAK WITH A HU-
MAN VOICE, STOPPING THE PROPHET IN HIS
MADNESS.
17 THESE PEOPLE ARE LIKE WATERLESS
SPRINGS, CLOUDS DRIVEN BY A STORM
WHICH MOVE SWIFTLY INTO THE BLACKEST
DARKNESS.

18 WITH THEIR BOASTFUL AND EMPTY

DISCOURSES, THEY
ENCOURAGE THE
LUST AND IMPURE
DESIRE OF THOSE
WHO HAVE JUST
FREED THEMSELVES
FROM THE COMMON
ERRORS.
19 THEY PROMISE
FREEDOM WHEN
THEY THEMSELVES
ARE SLAVES OF
CORRUPTION: FOR
ANYONE IS A SLA-
VE OF WHAT DOMI-
NATES HIM.

20 INDEED, AFTER
BEING FREED
FROM WORLDLY
VICES THROUGH
THE KNOWLEDGE
OF THE LORD AND
SAVIOR JESUS
CHRIST, THEY RE-
TURNED TO THOSE
VICES AND SURRENDERED TO THEM;
AND THE PRESENT STATE HAS BE-
COME WORSE THAN THE FIRST.

21 IT WOULD HAVE BEEN BETTER FOR
THEM NOT TO HAVE KNOWN THE WAY OF
HOLINESS THAN, KNOWING IT, TO TURN

AWAY FROM THE SACRED DOCTRINE THAT
THEY HAD BEEN TAUGHT. 22 IN THEIR
CASE THESE PROVERBS ARE RELEVANT:

"THE DOG TURNS BACK TO ITS OWN VOMIT."

AND: "HARDLY HAS THE PIG BEEN WASHED
THAN IT AGAIN WALLOWS IN THE MUD."

WHY IS THE SECOND COMING OF CHRIST DELAYED?

3 1 DEARLY BELOVED BROTHERS AND
SISTERS, THIS
IS THE SECOND
LETTER I WRITE
TO YOU, IN BOTH
I HAVE INTENDED
TO REMIND YOU OF
SOUND DOCTRINE.
2 DO NOT FORGET
THE WORDS OF THE
HOLY PROPHETS AND
THE TEACHING OF OUR
LORD AND SAVIOR,
AS YOU HEARD IT
THROUGH HIS APOS-
TLES. 3 REMEMBER,
FIRST OF ALL, THAT
IN THE LAST DAYS

SCOFFERS WILL APPEAR, THEIR MOCKERY
SERVING THEIR EVIL DESIRES.
4 AND THEY WILL SAY, "WHAT HAS BE-
COME OF HIS PROMISED COMING?

SINCE OUR FATHERS IN FAITH DIED,
EVERYTHING STILL GOES ON AS IT WAS
FROM THE BEGINNING OF THE WORLD.

ST. PETER
HOMAGE TO
CÉZANNE
409
CCCCIX
© DM 09

5 INDEED, THEY DELIBERATELY IGNORE
THAT IN THE BEGINNING THE HEAVENS
EXISTED FIRST AND EARTH APPEARED
FROM THE WATER, TAKING ITS FORM
BY THE WORD OF GOD.

6 BY THE SAME WORD OF GOD, THIS
WORLD PERISHED IN THE FLOOD. 7

LIKEWISE, THE
WORD OF GOD MAIN-
TAINS THE PRESENT
HEAVENS AND EARTH
UNTIL THEIR DES-
TRUCTION BY FIRE;
THEY ARE KEPT
FOR THE DAY OF
JUDGMENT, WHEN
THE GODLESS WILL
BE DESTROYED.
8 DO NOT FORGET,
BROTHERS, THAT
WITH THE LORD
ONE DAY IS LIKE
A THOUSAND YEARS,
AND A THOUSAND
IS LIKE ONE DAY.

9 THE LORD DOES NOT DELAY IN FUL-
FILLING HIS PROMISE, THOUGH SOME PE-
OPLE SPEAK OF DELAY; RATHER HE GI-
VES YOU TIME BECAUSE HE DOES NOT
WANT ANYONE TO PERISH, BUT THAT ALL
MAY COME TO CONVERSION.

10 THE DAY THE LORD IS TO COME LIKE
THE DAY OF A THIEF, AND THEN THE

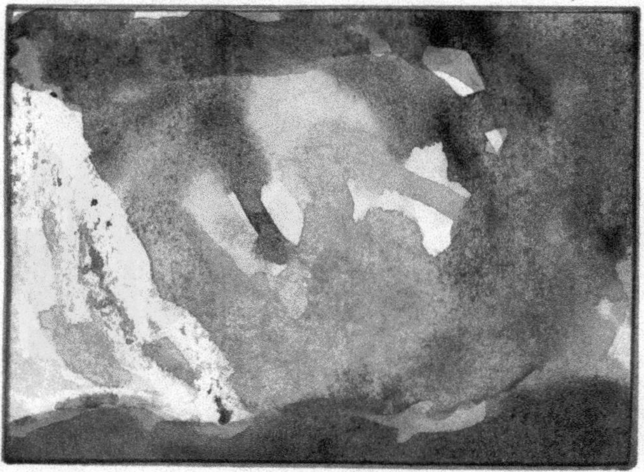

HEAVENS WILL DISSOLVE WITH A GREAT
NOISE; THE ELEMENTS WILL MELT
AWAY BY FIRE, AND THE EARTH WITH
ALL THAT IS ON IT WILL BE BURNED UP.

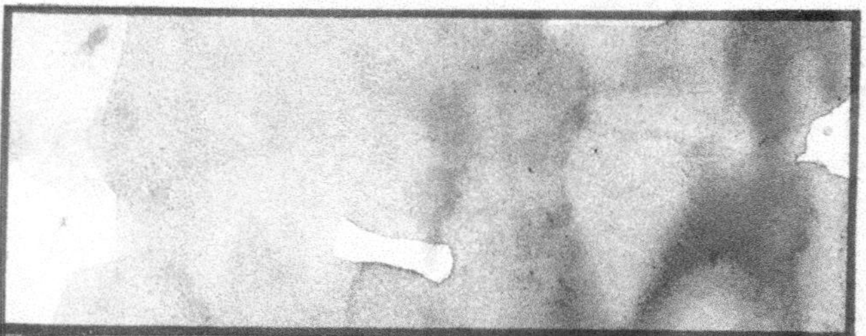

11 SINCE ALL THINGS ARE TO VANISH,
HOW HOLY AND RELIGIOUS YOUR
WAY OF LIFE MUST BE, 12 AS YOU
WAIT FOR THE DAY OF GOD AND LONG
FOR ITS COMING, WHEN THE HEAVENS
WILL DISSOLVE IN FIRE AND THE ELE-
MENTS MELT AWAY IN THE HEAT.

13 WE WAIT FOR A NEW HEAVEN AND A

NEW EARTH IN WHICH JUSTICE REIGNS,
ACCORDING TO GOD'S PROMISE.
14 THEREFORE, BELOVED BROTHERS,
AS YOU WAIT IN EXPECTATION OF THIS,
STRIVE THAT GOD MAY FIND YOU ROOTED
IN PEACE, WITHOUT BLEMISH OR FAULT.
15 AND CONSIDER
THAT GOD'S PATI-
ENCE IS FOR OUR
SALVATION, AS OUR
BELOVED BROTHER
PAUL WROTE TO
YOU, WITH THE WIS-
DOM GIVEN HIM.
16 HE SPEAKS OF
THESE THINGS IN
ALL HIS LETTERS.
THERE ARE, HOW-
EVER, SOME POINTS
IN THEM THAT ARE
DIFFICULT TO UNDER-
STAND, WHICH PE-
OPLE WHO ARE IG-
NORANT AND IM-
MATURE IN THEIR
FAITH TWIST, AS
THEY DO WITH THE
REST OF THE SCRIP-
TURES, TO THEIR
OWN DESTRUCTION.

17 SO THEN, DEARLY BELOVED, AS YOU
HAVE BEEN WARNED, BE CAREFUL LEST
THOSE PEOPLE WHO HAVE GONE ASTRAY
DECEIVE YOU IN TURN AND DRAG YOU A-
LONG, MAKING YOU STUMBLE AND FI-
NALLY FALL AWAY.

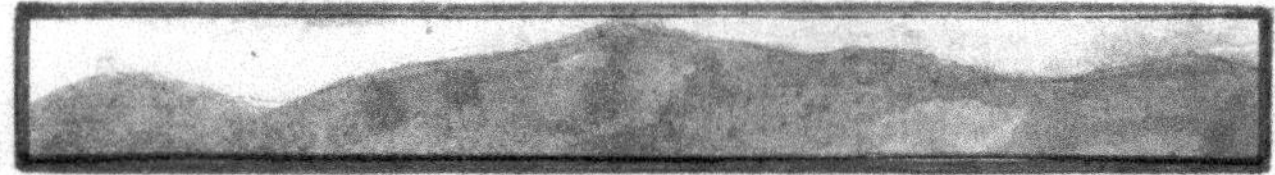

18 GROW IN THE GRACE AND KNOWLEDGE
OF OUR LORD AND SAVIOR JESUS CHRIST:
TO HIM THE GLORY, NOW AND TO
THE DAY OF ETERNITY. AMEN.

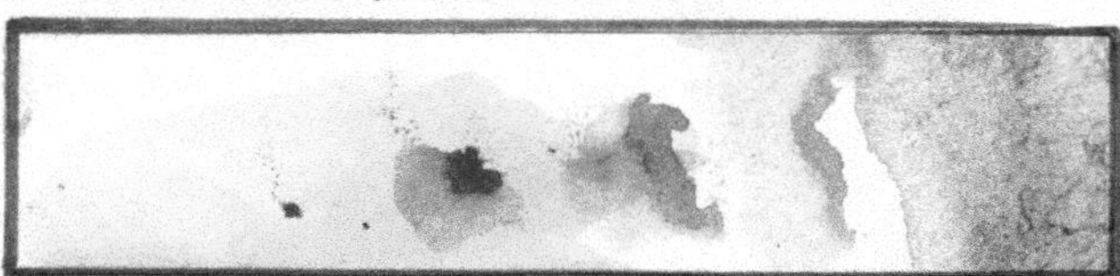

LETTERS OF JOHN

FROM ALL TIME THE CHRISTIAN IDEAL HAS SEEMED TOO PALE OR TOO NARROW FOR MANY PEOPLE. WE THINK OF THOSE WHO TODAY RELY ON SCIENCE TO WIDEN THE POSSIBILITIES OF LIFE. JESUS IS GOD HIMSELF WE WANT TO REACH, WE ARE SEEKERS OF TRUTH AND WE WANT TO MERGE INTO THIS TRUTH FROM WHICH WE HAVE COME.
JOHN AFFIRMS IN THIS FIRST LETTER: IF YOU HAVE THE SON OF GOD, YOU HAVE TOTAL TRUTH, YOU ARE ON THE WAY OF AUTHENTIC LOVE AND YOU ARE IN COMMUNION WITH GOD HIMSELF.

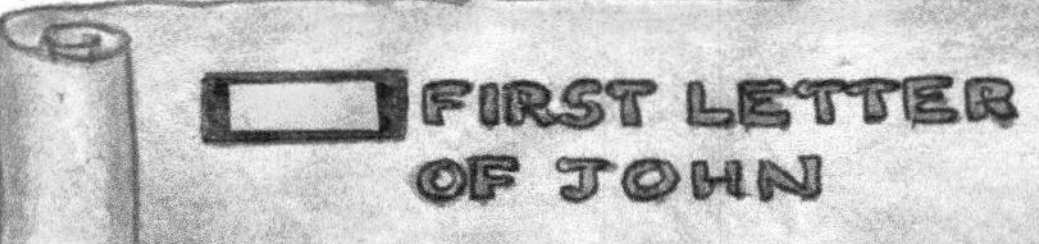

1 1 THIS IS WHAT HAS BEEN FROM THE BE-
GINNING, AND WHAT WE HAVE HEARD
AND HAVE SEEN WITH OUR OWN EYES,
WHAT WE HAVE LOOKED AT AND TOUCHED WITH OUR
HANDS, I MEAN THE WORD IS LIFE... 2 THE LIFE
MADE HIMSELF KNOWN, WE HAVE SEEN ETERNAL

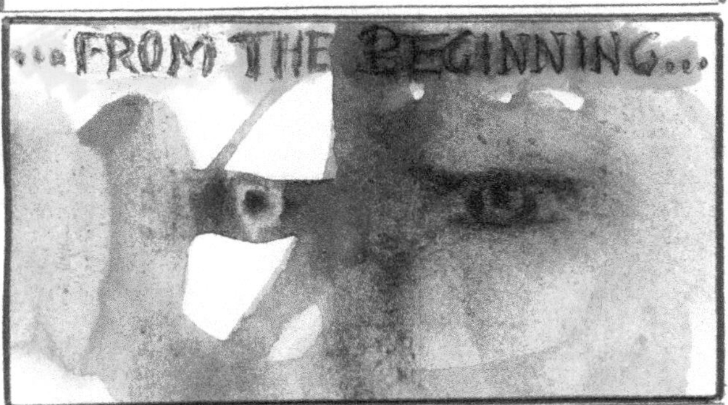

LIFE AND WE ARE HIS WITNESSES, AND WE ARE
YOU OF HIM. HE WAS WITH THE FATHER AND HE
MADE HIMSELF KNOWN TO US. 3 WE TELL YOU
WHAT WE HAVE SEEN AND HEARD, THAT YOU MAY
BE IN FELLOWSHIP WITH US, AND US, WITH THE

FATHER AND WITH HIS SON, JESUS CHRIST.
4 WE WRITE THIS FOR YOU TO HAVE PERFECT JOY.
WALK IN THE LIGHT 5 WE HEARD HIS MESSAGE
FROM HIM AND ANNOUNCE IT TO YOU: GOD IS LIGHT AND
THERE IS NO DARKNESS IN HIM.

(6) IF WE SAY WE ARE IN FELLOW-
SHIP WITH HIM, WHILE WE WALK
IN DARKNESS, WE LIE INSTEAD
OF BEING IN TRUTH.

(7) BUT IF WE WALK IN THE
LIGHT, AS HE IS IN THE LIGHT,
WE ARE IN FELLOWSHIP WITH
ONE ANOTHER, AND THE BLOOD
OF JESUS, THE SON OF GOD, PU-
RIFIES US FROM ALL SIN.

(8) IF WE SAY, "WE HAVE NO SIN",
WE DECEIVE OURSELVES AND THE
TRUTH IS NOT IN US. (9) IF WE CON-
FESS OUR SINS, HE WHO IS FAITHFUL
AND JUST WILL FORGIVE US OUR
SINS AND CLEANSE US FROM ALL
WICKEDNESS. (10) IF WE SAY THAT WE
DO NOT SIN WE MAKE GOD A LIAR,
HIS WORD IS NOT IN US.

FULFILL THE COMMANDMENT OF LOVE

2 (1) MY LITTLE CHILDREN, I WRITE
TO YOU THAT YOU MAY NOT SIN. BUT
IF ANYONE SINS, WE HAVE AN IN-
TERCESSOR WITH THE FATHER, JESUS
CHRIST, THE JUST ONE. (2) HE IS
THE SACRIFICIAL VICTIM FOR OUR SINS
AND THE SINS OF THE WHOLE WORLD.

(3) HOW CAN WE KNOW THAT WE KNOW
HIM? IF WE FULFILL HIS COMMANDS. (4)
IF ANYONE SAYS, "I KNOW HIM", BUT
DOES NOT FULFILLS HIS COMMANDS, HE
IS A LIAR AND THE TRUTH IS
NOT IN HIM.

(5) BUT IF ANYONE KEEPS HIS WORD,
GOD'S LOVE IS MADE COMPLETE
IN HIM. THIS IS HOW WE KNOW THAT
WE ARE IN HIM: (6) HE WHO CLAIMS
TO LIVE IN HIM MUST LIVE AS HE
LIVED. (7) MY DEAR FRIENDS, I AM
NOT WRITING YOU A NEW COMMAN-
DMENT, BUT REMINDING YOU OF
AN OLD ONE, ONE YOU HAD FROM

THE BEGINNING. THIS OLD COMMAND-
MENT IS THE WORD YOU HAVE HEARD.
(8) BUT, IN A WAY, I GIVE IT AS A NEW
COMMANDMENT FOR IT WAS INDEED
NEW IN JESUS CHRIST AND MUST BE SO
IN YOU AS WELL, BECAUSE THE DARKNESS
IS PASSING AWAY AND THE TRUE LIGHT AL-
READY SHINES. (9) IF ANYONE CLAIMS TO BE
IN THE LIGHT BUT HATES HIS BROTHER, HE
IS IN DARKNESS. (10) HE WHO LOVES HIS
BROTHER IS IN THE LIGHT AND NOTHING IN
HIM WILL MAKE HIM FALL. (11) BUT HE WHO
HATES HIS BROTHER IS IN THE DARK AND
WALKS IN DARKNESS WITHOUT KNOWING

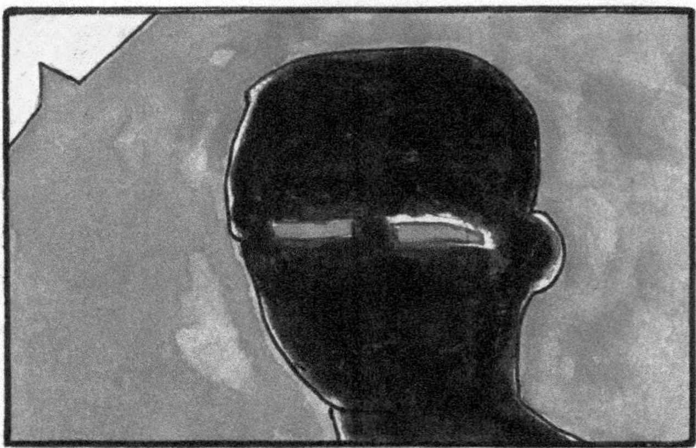

WHERE HE GOES, FOR THE DARKNESS HAS
BLINDED HIM. (12) MY DEAR CHILDREN, I
WRITE THIS TO YOU: YOU HAVE ALREADY
RECEIVED THE FORGIVENESS OF YOUR SINS THROUGH
THE NAME OF JESUS CHRIST. (13) FATHERS, I WRITE
THIS TO YOU: YOU KNOW HIM WHO IS FROM THE
BEGINNING. YOUNG MEN, I WRITE THIS TO YOU:
YOU HAVE OVERCOME THE EVIL ONE. MY DEAR
CHILDREN, I WRITE TO YOU BECAUSE YOU AL-
READY KNOW THE FATHER. (14) FATHERS, I
WRITE TO YOU BECAUSE YOU KNOW HIM WHO IS
FROM THE BEGINNING. YOUNG MEN, I WRITE TO
YOU BECAUSE YOU ARE STRONG AND THE
WORD OF GOD LIVES IN YOU WHO HAVE
INDEED OVERCOME THE EVIL ONE.

DM 09 ©
410 - CCCCX

15 DO NOT LOVE THE WORLD
OR WHAT IS IN IT.

IF ANYONE LOVES THE WORLD,
THE LOVE OF THE FATHER IS
NOT IN HIM.
16 FOR EVERYTHING IN THE
WORLD — THE CRAVING OF THE
FLESH, THE GREED OF EYES
AND PEOPLE BOASTING OF THEIR

SUPERIORITY — ALL THIS BELONGS
TO THE WORLD, NOT TO THE FATHER.
17 THE WORLD PASSES AWAY WITH
ALL HIS CRAVING BUT THOSE WHO DO
GOD'S WILL REMAIN FOREVER.

REJECT THE ANTICHRIST

18 MY DEAR CHILDREN, IT IS THE
LAST HOUR. YOU WERE TOLD THAT AN AN-
TICHRIST WOULD COME; BUT SEVERAL
ANTICHRISTS HAVE ALREADY COME, BY
WHICH WE KNOW THAT IT IS NOW THE LAST
HOUR. 19 THEY WENT OUT FROM US,
THOUGH THEY DIDN'T REALLY BELONG

TO US. HAD THEY BELONGED TO US, THEY
WOULD HAVE REMAINED WITH US. SO IT
IS CLEAR THAT NOT ALL OF US WERE RE-
ALLY OURS. 20 BUT YOU HAVE THE
ANOINTING FROM THE HOLY ONE SO THAT ALL OF YOU
HAVE TRUE WISDOM. 21 I WRITE TO YOU, NOT BE-
CAUSE YOU LACK KNOWLEDGE OF THE TRUTH, BUT
BECAUSE YOU ALREADY KNOW IT, AND LIES DON'T KNOW
THE TRUTH. 22 WHO IS THE LIAR? HE WHO DENIES
THAT JESUS IS THE CHRIST. HE IS THE ANTI-
CHRIST, HE WHO DENIES BOTH THE
FATHER AND THE SON.

23 HE WHO DENIES THE SON IS WITH-
OUT THE FATHER, AND HE WHO ACKNOW-
LEDGES THE SON ALSO HAS THE FATHER.
24 LET WHAT YOU HEARD FROM THE BE-
GINNING REMAIN IN YOU. IF WHAT YOU
HEARD FROM THE BEGINNING REMAINS
IN YOU, YOU, TOO, WILL REMAIN IN THE SON
AND IN THE FATHER. 25 AND THIS IS THE
PROMISE HE HIMSELF GAVE US: ETER-
NAL LIFE. 26 I WRITE THIS TO YOU FOR
THOSE WHO TRY TO LEAD YOU ASTRAY.

27 YOU RECEIVED FROM HIM AN ANOINTING,
AND IT REMAINS IN YOU, SO YOU DO NOT NE-
ED SOMEONE TO TEACH YOU. HIS ANOINTING
TEACHES YOU ALL THINGS, IT SPEAKS THE
TRUTH AND DOES NOT LIE TO YOU; SO RE-
MAIN IN HIM, AND KEEP WHAT HE HAS
TAUGHT YOU. 28 AND NOW, MY CHILDREN,
LIVE IN HIM, SO THAT WHEN HE APPEARS IN
HIS GLORY, WE MAY BE CONFIDENT AND NOT
ASHAMED BEFORE HIM WHEN HE CO-
MES. 29 YOU KNOW THAT HE IS THE
JUST ONE: KNOW THEN THAT ANYONE
LIVING JUSTLY IS BORN OF GOD.

3 1 SEE WHAT SINGULAR LOVE THE
FATHER HAS FOR US: WE ARE CALLED THE
CHILDREN OF GOD, AND WE REALLY ARE.

THIS IS WHY THE WORLD DOES NOT KNOW
US, FOR IT DID NOT KNOW HIM. 2 BE-
LOVED, WE ARE GOD'S CHILDREN
AND WHAT WE SHALL BE HAS NOT
YET BEEN SWOWN. YET WHEN
HE APPEARS IN HIS GLORY, WE
KNOW THAT WE SHALL BE LIKE
HIM, FOR THEN WE SHALL SEE
HIM AS HE IS.

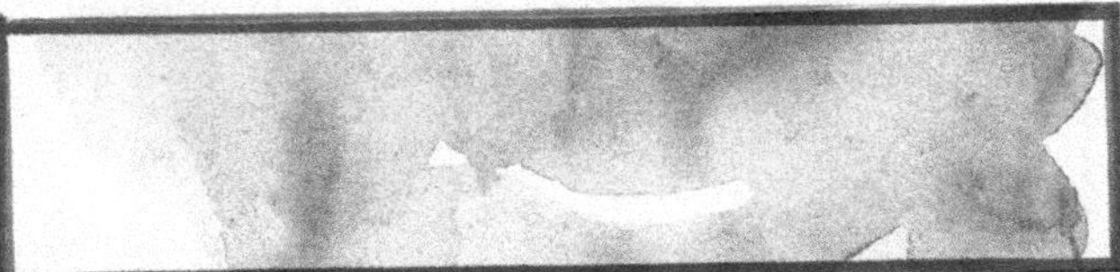

(3) ALL WHO HAVE SUCH A HOPE TRY
TO BE PURE AS HE IS PURE. (4) ANYONE WHO
COMMITS A SIN ACTS AS AN ENEMY OF THE LAW
OF GOD; ANY SIN IS A REJECTION OF HIS LAW.
(5) YOU KNOW THAT HE CAME TO TAKE AWAY
OUR SINS, AND THAT THERE IS NO SIN IN HIM.
(6) WHOEVER REMAINS IN HIM HAS NO
SIN, WHOEVER SINS HAS NOT SEEN OR
KNOWN HIM. (7) MY LITTLE CHILDREN, DO
NOT BE LED ASTRAY; THOSE WHO DO WHAT
IS RIGHT ARE UPRIGHT, JUST AS JESUS

CHRIST IS UPRIGHT. (8) BUT THOSE WHO
SIN BELONG TO THE DEVIL, FOR THE DEVIL
SINS FROM THE BEGINNING. THIS IS THE
WAY AND REASON WHY THE SON OF GOD WAS
SHOWN TO US, HE WAS TO UNDO THE WORKS
OF THE DEVIL. (9) THOSE BORN OF GOD DO
NOT SIN, FOR THE SEED OF GOD REMAINS IN
THEM; THEY CANNOT SIN BECAUSE THEY
ARE BORN OF GOD. (10) WHAT IS THE WAY
TO RECOGNIZE THE CHILDREN OF GOD
AND THOSE OF THE DEVIL? HE WHO DOES
NOT DO WHAT IS RIGHT IS NOT OF GOD; SO,
TOO, HE WHO DOES NOT LOVE HIS BROTHER.

(11) FOR THIS IS THE MESSAGE TAUGHT TO
YOU FROM THE BEGINNING: WE MUST LOVE
ONE ANOTHER. (12) DO NOT IMITATE CAIN
WHO KILLED HIS BROTHER, FOR HE BELONG-
ED TO THE EVIL ONE. WHY DID HE KILL HIM?
BECAUSE HE HIMSELF DID EVIL AND HIS
BROTHER DID GOOD. (13) LIKEWISE THE
WORLD HATES US, SO, BE NOT SURPRI-
SED, BROTHERS; (14) WE LOVE OUR
BROTHERS AND SISTERS, AND
WITH THIS WE KNOW THAT WE
HAVE PASSED FROM DEATH TO
LIFE. HE WHO DOES NOT LOVE
REMAINS IN DEATH.

(15) HE WHO HATES HIS BROTHER
IS A MURDERER; AND, AS YOU KNOW,
ETERNAL LIFE DOES NOT REMAIN IN
THE MURDERER. (16) THIS IS HOW WE
HAVE KNOWN WHAT LOVE IS: HE GAVE
HIS LIFE FOR US. WE, TOO, OUGHT TO GIVE
OUR LIFE FOR OUR BROTHERS. (17) IF ANY-
ONE ENJOYS THE RICHES OF THIS WORLD,
BUT CLOSES HIS HEART WHEN HE SEES
HIS BROTHER OR SISTER IN NEED, HOW
WILL THE LOVE OF GOD REMAIN IN HIM?
(18) MY DEAR CHILDREN, LET US LOVE NOT
ONLY WITH WORDS AND WITH OUR LIPS,
BUT IN TRUTH AND IN DEED. (19) WE SHALL

KNOW THAT WE ARE OF THE TRUTH AND WE
MAY CALM OUR CONSCIENCE IN HIS PRESEN-
CE. (20) EVERY TIME IT REPROACHES US LET
US SAY: GOD IS GREATER THAN OUR CON-
SCIENCE, AND HE KNOWS EVERYTHING. (21)
WHEN OUR CONSCIENCE DOESN'T CONDEMN US, DEAR
FRIENDS, WE MAY HAVE COMPLETE CONFIDENCE IN GOD.
(22) THEN WHATEVER WE ASK WE SHALL RECEIVE,
SINCE WE KEEP HIS COMMANDS AND DO WHAT PLEASES
HIM. (23) HIS COMMAND IS THAT WE BELIEVE IN THE
NAME OF HIS SON JESUS CHRIST AND THAT WE LOVE
ONE ANOTHER, AS HE HAS COMMANDED US. WHOEVER

(24) KEEPS HIS COMMANDS REMAINS IN GOD AND GOD
IN HIM. IT IS BY THE SPIRIT GOD HAS GIVEN US
THAT WE KNOW HE LIVES IN US.

DO NOT TRUST EVERY INSPIRATION

4 (1) MY BELOVED, DO NOT TRUST EVERY INSPI-
RATION. TEST THE SPIRITS TO SEE WHETHER THEY
COME FROM GOD, FOR MANY FALSE PROPHETS ARE
NOW IN THE WORLD. (2) HOW WILL YOU RECOG-
NIZE THE SPIRIT OF GOD? ANY SPIRIT RECOGNIZ-
ING JESUS AS THE CHRIST WHO HAS TAKEN
OUR FLESH IS OF GOD. (3) BUT ANY SPIRIT WHICH
DOES NOT RECOGNIZE JESUS IS NOT FROM GOD,
IT IS THE SPIRIT OF THE ANTICHRIST. YOU HAVE
HEARD OF HIS COMING AND NOW HE IS IN THE WORLD.

(4) YOU, MY DEAR CHILDREN, ARE OF GOD
AND YOU HAVE ALREADY OVERCOME THESE
PEOPLE, FOR THE ONE WHO IS IN YOU IS MO-
RE POWERFUL THAN HE WHO IS IN THE WORLD.
(5) THEY ARE OF THE WORLD AND THE WORLD
INSPIRES THEM AND THOSE OF THE WORLD
LISTEN TO THEM. (6) WE ARE OF GOD AND THO-
SE WHO KNOW GOD LISTEN TO US, BUT THOSE
WHO ARE NOT OF GOD IGNORE US. THIS IS
HOW WE KNOW THE SPIRIT OF TRUTH

AND THE SPIRIT OF ERROR AS WELL.

GOD-LOVE IS THE SOURCE OF LOVE

(7) MY DEAR FRIENDS, LET US LOVE ONE AN-
OTHER FOR LOVE COMES FROM GOD. EVERY-
ONE WHO LOVES IS BORN OF GOD AND KNOWS GOD, FOR
GOD IS LOVE AND HE KNOWS GOD. (8) HE WHO DOES NOT
LOVE HAS NOT KNOWN GOD, FOR GOD IS LOVE. (9) HOW
DID THE LOVE OF GOD APPEAR AMONG US? GOD SENT
HIS ONLY SON INTO THIS WORLD THAT WE MIGHT HAVE
LIFE THROUGH HIM. (10) THIS IS LOVE: NOT THAT WE LO-
VED GOD BUT THAT HE FIRST LOVED US AND SENT HIS
SON AS AN ATONING SACRIFICE FOR OUR SINS. (11)
DEAR FRIENDS, IF SUCH HAS BEEN THE
LOVE OF GOD, WE, TOO, MUST LOVE

A good family
Homage to Chagall

ONE ANOTHER. (12) NO ONE HAS EVER
SEEN GOD, BUT IF WE LOVE ONE ANOTHER
GOD LIVES IN US, AND HIS LOVE SPREADS
FREELY AMONG US. (13) HOW MAY WE
KNOW THAT WE LIVE IN GOD AND HE IN US? BECA-
USE GOD HAS GIVEN US HIS SPIRIT. (14) WE OUR-
SELVES HAVE SEEN AND DECLARE THAT THE FATHER
SENT HIS SON TO SAVE THE WORLD.

(15) WHEN SOMEONE ACKNOWLEDGES
THAT JESUS IS THE SON OF GOD, GOD RE-
MAINS IN HIM AND HE IN GOD. (16) WE HAVE
KNOWN THE LOVE OF GOD AND HAVE BELIEV-
ED IN IT. GOD IS LOVE. HE WHO LIVES IN LOVE,
LIVES IN GOD AND GOD IN HIM. (17) WHEN
DO WE KNOW THAT WE HAVE REACHED A PER-
FECT LOVE? WHEN THIS WORLD WE LIVE
IN, WE ARE LIKE HIM IN EVERYTHING,

AND EXPECT WITH CONFIDENCE THE DAY OF
JUDGMENT. (18) THERE IS NO FEAR IN LOVE.
PERFECT LOVE DRIVES AWAY FEAR, FOR
FEAR HAS TO DO WITH PUNISHMENT; HE
WHO FEARS DOESN'T KNOW PERFECT LOVE.
(19) SO LET US LOVE ONE ANOTHER, SINCE HE
LOVED US FIRST. (20) IF ANYONE SAYS, "I
LOVE GOD," WHILE HE HATES HIS BROTHER,
HE IS A LIAR. HOW CAN HE LOVE GOD WHOM
HE DOES NOT SEE, IF HE DOES NOT LOVE HIS

BROTHER WHOM HE SEES? WE RECEIVED
FROM HIM THIS COMMANDMENT: LET HIM
WHO LOVES GOD ALSO LOVE HIS BROTHER.

FAITH COMES FROM GOD

5 (1) ALL THOSE WHO BELIEVE THAT THE
ANOINTED IS JESUS, ARE BORN OF GOD. IF
YOU LOVE THE FATHER YOU ALSO LOVE ALL
THOSE BORN OF HIM. (2) HOW MANY WE
KNOW THAT WE LOVE THE CHILDREN OF GOD?
IF WE LOVE GOD AND FULFILL HIS COMMANDS,
(3) FOR GOD'S LOVE REQUIRES TO KEEP
HIS COMMANDS. IN FACT, HIS COMMAND-
MENTS ARE NOT A BURDEN (4) BECA-
USE ALL THOSE BORN OF GOD OVER-
COME THE WORLD, AND THE VICTORY
WHICH OVERCOMES THE WORLD IS OUR
FAITH. (5) WHO HAS OVERCOME THE
WORLD? THE ONE WHO BELIEVES
THAT JESUS IS THE SON OF GOD.

HOMAGE TO ANDREA DEL CASTAGNO
411 - cccex

6 JESUS CHRIST WAS ACKNOWLEDGED
THROUGH WATER, BUT ALSO THROUGH BLO-
OD. NOT ONLY WATER BUT WATER AND BLOOD.
AND THE SPIRIT, TOO, WITNESSES TO HIM
FOR THE SPIRIT IS TRUTH. 7 THERE ARE
THEN THREE TESTIMONIES: 8 THE SPIRIT,
THE WATER AND THE BLOOD, AND THESE
THREE WITNESSES AGREE. 9 IF WE AC-
CEPT HUMAN TESTIMONY, WITH GREATER
REASON MUST WE ACCEPT THAT OF GOD,
GIVEN IN FAVOR OF HIS SON. IF ANYONE BE-
LIEVES 10 IN THE SON OF GOD, HE HAS

GOD'S TESTIMONY IN HIM. BUT HE WHO
DOES NOT BELIEVE MAKES GOD A LIAR, SINCE HE
DOES NOT BELIEVE HIS WORDS WHEN HE WIT-
NESSES TO HIS SON. 11 WHAT HAS GOD SAID? THAT
HE HAS GRANTED US ETERNAL LIFE. HE WHO DOES
HAVE THIS LIFE IN HIS SON. 12 HE WHO HAS THE SON
HAS LIFE. HE WHO DOES NOT HAVE THE SON OF GOD
DOES NOT HAVE LIFE.

KEEP YOURSELVES FROM IDOLS

13 I WRITE YOU, THEN, ALL THESE THINGS
THAT YOU MAY KNOW THAT YOU HAVE ETERNAL LIFE,
ALL YOU WHO BELIEVE IN THE NAME OF THE SON OF
GOD. 14 THROUGH HIM WE ARE FULLY CONFIDENT
THAT WHATEVER WE ASK, ACCORDING TO HIS WILL, HE
WILL GRANT US. 15 IF WE KNOW THAT HE HEARS US
WHENEVER WE ASK, WE KNOW THAT WE ALREADY HAVE

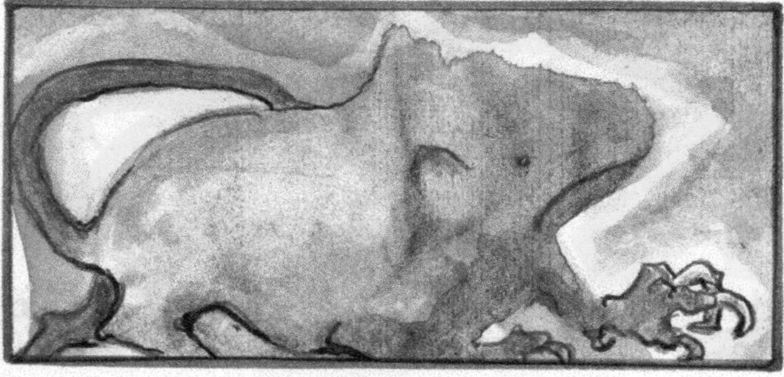

WHAT WE ASKED OF HIM. 16 IF YOU SEE YOUR BROTHER
SINNING, A SIN NOT LEADING TO DEATH, PRAY FOR HIM, AND
GOD WILL GIVE HIM LIFE. I SPEAK OF THE SIN WHICH
DOESN'T LEAD TO DEATH. THERE IS ALSO A SIN THAT
LEADS TO DEATH; I DON'T ASK TO PRAY ABOUT THIS. 17
EVERY KIND OF WRONGDOING IS SIN, BUT NOT ALL
SIN LEADS TO DEATH. 18 WE KNOW THAT THOSE
BORN OF GOD DO NOT SIN, FOR WHAT HAS BEEN
BORN OF GOD TAKES CARE OF THEM, AND THE EVIL
ONE CAN DO NOTHING AGAINST THEM. 19 WE KNOW THAT
WE BELONG TO GOD, WHILE THE WHOLE
WORLD LIES IN EVIL. 20 WE KNOW THAT
THE SON OF GOD HAS COME AND HAS GIVEN US PO-
WER TO KNOW THE WHOLE TRUTH.
WE ARE IN HIM WHO IS TRUE, HIS SON JESUS CHRIST.
HE IS THE TRUE GOD AND ETERNAL LIFE. 21 MY DEAR
CHILDREN, KEEP YOURSELVES FROM IDOLS.

1 I, THE ELDER, TO THE CHOSEN LADY AND HER CHILDREN,
WHOM I LOVE SINCERELY, AND WITH ME ALL WHO KNOW
THE TRUTH, 2 FOR OF THIS TRUTH WHICH IS AND
WILL BE IN US FOREVER. 3 GRACE, MERCY AND PEACE

BE WITH YOU IN THE NAME OF GOD THE FATHER AND
OF HIS SON, CHRIST JESUS, IN TRUTH AND LOVE. 4
I REJOICED GREATLY ON MEETING SOME OF YOUR
CHILDREN WHO LIVE IN ACCORDANCE WITH THE TRUTH,
ACCORDING TO THE COMMAND WE RECEIVED FROM THE
FATHER. 5 AND NOW, I ASK YOU, LADY, I WRITE TO
YOU NOT A NEW COMMANDMENT BUT THAT WHICH
WE HAD FROM THE BEGINNING, I ASK YOU: LET US
LOVE ONE ANOTHER. 6

THIS IS LOVE: TO WALK
ACCORDING TO HIS COM-
MANDMENTS. AND THIS
IS THE COMMANDMENT:
THAT YOU WALK IN LO-
VE AS YOU HAVE LE-
ARNED FROM THE BE-
GINNING. 7 MANY
DECEIVERS HAVE
GONE OUT INTO THE
WORLD, PEOPLE WHO
DO NOT ACKNOWLEDGE
THAT JESUS IS THE
CHRIST WHO CAME
IN THE FLESH. THEY
ARE IMPOSTORS
AND ANTICHRISTS.
8 TAKE CARE OF
YOURSELVES THAT
YOU DO NOT LOSE THE
FRUIT OF YOUR LA-
BORS, BUT RECEIVE A PERFECT REWARD. EVERY-
9 ONE WHO GOES BEYOND AND DOES NOT RE-
MAIN WITHIN THE TEACHING OF CHRIST DOES
NOT HAVE GOD. HE WHO REMAINS IN THE
TEACHING HAS BOTH THE FATHER AND THE
SON.
10 IF ANYONE COMES TO YOU AND DOES
NOT BRING THIS TEACHING, DO NOT RE-
CEIVE HIM INTO YOUR HOUSES OR EVEN
GREET HIM. 11 IN GREETING HIM YOU WOULD
BECOME AN ACCOMPLICE IN HIS WICKED DEEDS.
12 I HAVE MANY THINGS TO WRITE TO
YOU, BUT I PREFER NOT TO USE PAPER
AND INK. I HOPE TO MEET YOU AND SPEAK TO
YOU PERSONALLY, THAT OUR JOY MAY BE
FULL. 13 THE CHILDREN OF YOUR
CHOSEN SISTER GREET YOU.

THIRD LETTER OF JOHN

1 I, THE ELDER, TO MY DEAR FRIEND
GAIUS, WHOM I LOVE SINCERELY.

2 DEAR FRIEND, MAY EVERYTHING GO
WELL WITH YOU AND MAY YOU ENJOY
HEALTH OF BODY

AND SOUL. 3 I
GREATLY REJO-
ICED WITH THE
BROTHERS WHO
ARRIVED AND PRA-
ISED YOUR TRUTH,
AND HOW YOU LI-
VE THE TRUTH.
4 NOTHING
GIVES ME GRE-
ATER JOY THAN
TO KNOW THAT
MY CHILDREN
LIVE IN THE
TRUTH.
5 BROTHER,
YOU DO WELL
TO CARE FOR THE
BROTHERS AND
SISTERS AS YOU
DO. I MEAN THOSE
COMING FROM
OTHER PLACES.

6 THEY SPOKE
OF YOUR CHARITY BEFORE THE ASSEM-
BLED CHURCH. IT WILL BE WELL TO PRO-
VIDE THEM WITH THAT AND WHAT THEY
NEED TO CONTINUE THEIR JOURNEY,
AS IF YOU DID IT FOR GOD.
7 IN REALITY THEY HAVE SET
OUT ON THE ROAD FOR HIS NAME

WITHOUT ACCEPTING ANYTHING
FROM THE PAGANS.

8 WE SHOULD RECEIVE SUCH
PERSONS, MAKING OURSELVES
THEIR COOPERATORS IN THE
WORK OF THE TRUTH.

9 I HAVE WRITTEN THESE WORDS
TO THE CHURCH, BUT DIOTREPHES,
WHO IS ANXIOUS TO PRESIDE
OVER IT, DOES NOT ACKNOWLEDGE
OUR AUTHORITY.

10 SO WHEN I COME, I WILL NOT
CEASE REPROACHING HIS MAN-
NER OF ACTING, SINCE HE DIS-
CREDITED US WITH WORDS OF

EVIL INTENT. AND NOT CONTENT
WITH THAT, HE DOES NOT RECEIVE
THE BROTHERS AND EVEN RESTRA-
INS THOSE WHO WANT TO RECEIVE
THEM, AND EXPELS THEM FROM
THE CHURCH. 11 DEAR FRIEND, DO
NOT IMITATE EVIL, BUT ONLY THE
GOOD. HE WHO DOES GOOD IS OF
GOD. HE WHO DOES EVIL DOES NOT
KNOW GOD. 12 NOW ABOUT DE-
METRIUS: EVERYONE PRAISES HIM,
EVEN THE TRUTH ITSELF. WE, TOO,

PRAISE HIM, AND YOU KNOW THAT
WHEN WE RECOMMEND ANYONE,
WE DO IT ACCORDING TO THE TRUTH.
13 I HAVE MANY THINGS TO TELL
YOU, BUT I DO NOT WANT TO DO IT IN
WRITING. 14 I HOPE TO SEE YOU
SOON, AND WE WILL TALK FACE TO FACE.

PEACE BE WITH YOU. YOUR FRI-
ENDS GREET YOU. GREET THE
FRIENDS FOR ME, EACH ONE BY NAME.

LETTER OF JUDE

THE HOLY SPIRIT MAY HAVE WANTED TO LEAVE US THE LETTER OF JUDE SO THAT WE MAY APPRECIATE THE GOSPELS AND OTHER WRITINGS OF THE APOSTLES BETTER. WRITTEN CIRCA THE END OF THE FIRST CENTURY.

1 JUDE, SERVANT OF JESUS CHRIST AND BRO-
THER OF JAMES. TO THOSE CALLED TO FAITH, BELO-
VED BY GOD THE FATHER AND KEPT IN CHRIST JESUS.
2 MAY MERCY, PEACE AND LOVE ABOUND IN YOU.
3 MOST BELOVED, I HAD WANTED TO WRITE TO
YOU ABOUT THE SALVA-
TION WE ALL SHARE,
BUT NOW I FEEL I MUST
URGE YOU TO FIGHT FOR
THE FAITH GOD HAS GI-
VEN ONCE FOR ALL TO
THE SAINTS. 4 SOME
INDIVIDUALS HAVE
SLIPPED INTO YOUR
MIDST, GODLESS
PEOPLE ALREADY
CONDEMNED. THEY
MAKE USE OF
THE GRACE OF
OUR GOD AS A
LICENSE FOR IM-
MORALITY AND
DENY OUR ONLY
MASTER AND LORD
JESUS
CHRIST

St. Jude

5 ALTHOUGH YOU MAY BE AWARE
OF IT, I WISH TO REMIND YOU THAT

THE LORD SAVED HIS PEOPLE FROM THE
LAND OF EGYPT, BUT LATER DELIVERED
TO DEATH THOSE WHO DID NOT BELIEVE.

6 HE DID THE SAME WITH THE ANGELS WHO
DID NOT KEEP THEIR RANK BUT ABANDONED
THEIR DWELLING PLACES. GOD ENCLOSED
THEM IN ETERNAL PRISONS, IN THE PIT OF
DARKNESS UNTIL THE GREAT DAY OF JUDGE-
MENT. 7 SODOM AND GOMORRAH AND THE

SURROUNDING CITIES WHO PROSTITUTED
THEMSELVES AND WERE LURED INTO UN-
NATURAL UNIONS ARE ALSO A WARNING
OF THE PUNISHMENT OF ETERNAL FIRE. 8 IN SPI-
TE OF ALL THIS, THESE PEOPLE NOW DO THE SAME:
IN THEIR RAVINGS, THEY DEBASE THEIR BODIES
SCORN THE CELESTIAL AUTHORITIES, BLAS-
PHEME AGAINST THE ANGELS.

9 WHEN THE ARCHANGEL MICHAEL
FOUGHT AGAINST THE DEVIL AND DIS-
PUTED ABOUT THE BODY OF MOSES,
HE DID NOT DARE INSULT HIM, BUT
SIMPLY SAID,
"MAY THE LORD REBUKE YOU!"

REMAIN FIRM IN
THE LOVE OF GOD...
(Jude 21)
412 CCCCXII
© DM 09

10 NOT SO THESE PEOPLE, THEY IN-
SULT AND SCORN WHAT THEY CANNOT
UNDERSTAND; WHAT THEY KNOW BY IN-
STINCT LIKE ANIMALS, THEY USE FOR
THEIR CORRUPTION.

11 WOE TO THEM!
THEY FOLLOW THE FOOTSTEPS OF CAIN
AND LIKE BALAAM GO ASTRAY BECAUSE
OF MONEY: THEY WILL FINALLY PER-
ISH LIKE THE REBELLIOUS KORAH.

12 WHEN YOU CELEBRATE YOUR FRA-
TERNAL MEALS, THEY SPOIL EVERY-
THING, COMING ONLY FOR THE FOOD AND
SHAMELESSLY SEEING TO THEIR OWN
NEEDS.

THEY ARE LIKE CLOUDS CARRIED AL-

ONG BY THE WIND
WHICH NEVER BRINGS
RAIN, LIKE TREES
WITHOUT FRUITS
AT THE END OF
AUTUMN, TWICE
DEAD WITHOUT UP-
ROOTED. 13 THE
SCUM OF THEIR VI-
CES ARE SPLASHED
LIKE FOAM ON THE
ROUGH WAVES OF
THE SEA, THEY ARE
LIKE SHOOTING
STARS WHICH THE
THICK DARKNESS
ENGULFS FOR EVER.
14 THE PATRIARCH
ENOCH, THE SEVENTH
AFTER ADAM, SAID
THESE WORDS AB-
OUT THEM: THE LORD
COMES WITH THO-
USANDS OF ANGELS
15 TO JUDGE EVE-
RYONE AND CALL
THE WICKED TO ACCOUNT FOR ALL THE
EVIL DEEDS THEY COMMITTED; HE
WILL PUNISH ALL THE INJURIOUS
WORDS THE IMPIOUS SINNERS UT-
TERED AGAINST HIM.

16 ALL THESE ARE DISCONTENTED WHO
CURSE THEIR LOT AND FOLLOW THEIR
PASSIONS. THEIR MOUTH IS FULL OF AR-
ROGANT WORDS, AND THEY FLATTER
PEOPLE FOR THEIR OWN INTEREST.

17 BUT, MOST BELOVED, REMEMBER
WHAT THE APOSTLES OF CHRIST JESUS,
OUR LORD, ANNOUNCED TO YOU.

18 THEY SAID TO YOU, "AT THE END OF
TIME, THERE WILL BE SCOFFERS LED
BY THEIR DESIRES

WHICH ARE THOSE
OF GODLESS PE-
OPLE." 19 AC-
TUALLY, THESE
PEOPLE ARE THOSE
WHO CAUSE DIVI-
SIONS, THEY ARE
WORLDLY MEN AND
DO NOT HAVE THE
HOLY SPIRIT.

20 BUT, DEARLY
BELOVED, BUILD
YOUR LIFE ON THE
FOUNDATION OF
YOUR MOST HOLY
FAITH, PRAYING
IN THE HOLY SPI-
RIT.

21 REMAIN FIRM IN THE LOVE OF GOD,
WELCOMING THE MERCY OF CHRIST
JESUS, OUR LORD, WHICH LEADS TO
ETERNAL LIFE.
22 TRY TO CONVINCE THOSE WHO DOUBT
23 AND SAVE THEM BY SNATCHING
THEM FROM CONDEMNATION. TREAT
'THE OTHERS WITH COMPASSION'
BUT ALSO WITH PRUDENCE, SHUNNING EVEN

THE CLOTHES WHICH TOUCHED THEIR BODY.
24 TO THE ONE GOD WHO IS ABLE TO
KEEP YOU FROM ALL SIN AND BRING
YOU HAPPY AND WITHOUT BLEMISH BE-
FORE HIS OWN GLORY, 25 TO THE ONE
GOD WHO SAVES US THROUGH JESUS
CHRIST, OUR LORD, TO HIM BE GLORY
HONOR, MIGHT, AND POWER, FROM
PAST AGES, NOW AND FOREVER. AMEN.

REVELATION

CAUGHT UP IN AN ECSTASY, JOHN SAW THE GLORY OF THE RISEN CHRIST AND THUS HE UNDERSTOOD THE DESTINY OF THE CHURCH THREATENED BY THE FIRST PERSECUTIONS. SUCH IS THE ORIGIN OF HIS BOOK: REVELATION OF JESUS CHRIST.

IN WRITING THIS "REVELATION OF JESUS CHRIST", JOHN WAS EXPRESSING WHAT THE LORD TAUGHT HIM IN MANY WAYS BY MEANS OF HIS GIFT AS A PROPHET, BUT HE ALSO ADOPTED THE USUAL THEME OF APOCALYPTIC BOOKS. WHEN HE DEALT WITH CONTEMPORARY EVENTS, HE PLACED THEM IN HIS VISIONS AND FANTASTIC ILLUSTRATIONS.
HE DID THE SAME IN THE SECOND PART OF HIS BOOK, TEACHING US WHAT WOULD BE HISTORY.
WE WILL BETTER UNDERSTAND THIS REVELATION IF WE INTERPRET THE VISION, NUMBERS AND SYMBOLS ACCORDING TO THE RULES OF THE APOCALYPTIC LITERATURE.

THE RISEN CHURCH IS THE CENTER OF HISTORY; THE WORLD IS THE PLACE OF THE STRUGGLE BETWEEN THE CHURCH, HEADED BY CHRIST, AND SATAN'S FORCES; CHRISTIANS ARE CALLED TO GIVE THEIR WITNESS WITH COURAGE.

1 1 THE REVELATION OF JESUS CHRIST.
GOD GAVE HIM THE REVELATION TO LET
HIS SERVANTS KNOW WHAT IS SOON
TO TAKE PLACE. HE SENT HIS ANGEL TO
MAKE IT KNOWN TO HIS SERVANT, JOHN, 2
WHO REPORTS EVERYTHING HE SAW, FOR THIS

IS THE WORD OF GOD AND THE DECLARATION
OF JESUS CHRIST.
3 HAPPY IS THE ONE WHO READS ALOUD
THESE PROPHETIC WORDS, AND HAPPY THOSE
WHO HEAR THEM AND TREASURE EVERYTHING
WRITTEN HERE, FOR THE TIME IS NEAR.

4 FROM JOHN TO THE SEVEN CHURCHES
OF ASIA: RECEIVE GRACE AND PEACE FROM

HIM WHO IS, WHO WAS
AND WHO IS TO COME,
AND FROM THE SEVEN
SPIRITS OF GOD WHICH
ARE BEFORE HIS THRONE,
5 AND FROM JESUS
CHRIST, THE FAITH-
FUL WITNESS, THE
FIRSTBORN OF
THE DEAD, THE RU-
LER OF THE KINGS
OF THE EARTH.
TO HIM WHO LOVES US
AND HAS WASHED AWAY
OUR SINS WITH HIS OWN
BLOOD, 6 MAKING US A
KINGDOM OF PRIESTS FOR
GOD HIS FATHER, TO HIM
BE THE GLORY AND POW-
ER FOR EVER AND EVER.
AMEN. 7 SEE HE COMES
WITH THE CLOUDS AND
EVERYONE WILL SEE
HIM, EVEN THOSE WHO
PIERCED HIM AND ALL
THE NATIONS OF THE EARTH WILL MOURN HIS DEATH.
YES, IT WILL BE SO.
8 "I AM THE ALPHA AND THE OMEGA," SAYS
THE LORD GOD, HE WHO IS, WHO WAS AND
WHO IS TO COME: THE MASTER OF THE UNIVERSE.

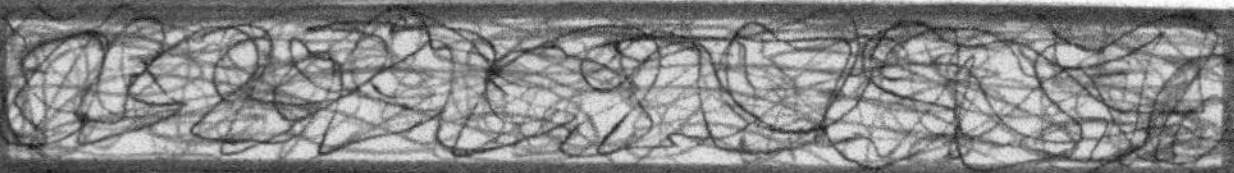

9 I, JOHN, YOUR BROTHER, WHO SHARE WITH
YOU, IN JESUS, THE SUFFERINGS, THE KINGDOM AND
THE PATIENT ENDURANCE, WAS ON THE ISLAND OF
PATMOS, BECAUSE OF THE WORD OF GOD AND WITNES-
SING TO JESUS. 10 ON THE LORD'S DAY, THE SPIRIT
TOOK POSSESSION OF ME AND I HEARD A VOICE BE-
HIND ME WHICH SOUNDED LIKE A TRUMPET, 11
"WRITE DOWN ALL THAT YOU SEE, IN A BOOK, AND SEND
IT TO THE SEVEN CHURCHES OF EPHESUS, SMYRNA, PER-
GAMUM, THYATIRA, SARDIS, PHILADELPHIA AND LAODICEA".
12 I TURNED TO SEE WHO
WAS SPEAKING TO ME;
BEHIND ME WERE SE-
VEN GOLDEN LAMPS-
TANDS, 13 AND, IN THE
MIDDLE OF THESE, I
SAW SOMEONE LIKE A
SON OF MAN, DRESSED
IN A LONG ROBE TIED
WITH A GOLDEN GIRDLE.
14 HIS HEAD AND HIS
HAIR ARE WHITE AS WOOL
OR AS SNOW AND HIS EYES
ARE LIKE FLAMES OF FI-
RE. 15 HIS FEET LIKE
BURNISHED BRONZE
WHEN IT HAS BEEN RE-
FINED IN A FURNACE.
HIS VOICE IS LIKE THE
ROARING OF THE WAVES.
16 I SAW SEVEN STARS
IN THE RIGHT HAND
AND A SHARP, DOUB-
LE-EDGED SWORD
COMING OUT OF HIS
MOUTH; HIS FACE
SHONE LIKE THE

SUN IN ALL ITS BRILLIANCE. 17 SEEING
HIM, I FELL AT HIS FEET LIKE ONE DEAD
BUT HE TOUCHED ME WITH HIS RIGHT HAND
AND SAID, "DO NOT BE AFRAID. IT IS I, THE FIRST
AND THE LAST. 18 I AM THE LIVING ONE; I WAS
DEAD AND NOW I AM ALIVE FOR EVER AND EVER;
AND MINE ARE THE KEYS OF DEATH AND THE
NETHERWORLD. 19 NOW WRITE WHAT YOU
HAVE SEEN, BOTH WHAT IS AND WHAT IS YET TO

COME. 20 KNOW THE SECRET OF THE SEVEN
GOLDEN LAMPSTANDS; THE SEVEN STARS
ALSO THAT YOU SAW IN MY RIGHT HAND:
**THE SEVEN STARS ARE THE ANGELS
OF THE SEVEN CHURCHES AND THE SEVEN
LAMPSTANDS ARE THE SEVEN CHURCHES.**

THE 7 MESSAGES TO THE CHURCHES

2 (1) WRITE THIS TO THE ANGEL OF THE CHURCH IN
EPHESUS, "THUS SAYS THE ONE WHO HOLDS THE
SEVEN STARS IN HIS RIGHT HAND AND WHO WALKS
AMONG THE SEVEN GOLDEN LAMPSTANDS: (2) I KNOW
YOUR WORKS, YOUR DIFFICULTIES AND SUFFERING.
I KNOW YOU CANNOT TOLERATE EVILDOERS BUT HAVE
TESTED THOSE WHO CALL THEMSELVES APOSTLES AND
HAVE PROVED THEM TO

BE LIARS. (3) YOU HAVE
PERSEVERED AND HAVE
SUFFERED FOR MY NAME
WITHOUT LOSING HEART.
(4) NEVERTHELESS, I HA-
VE THIS COMPLAINT AGA-
INST YOU: YOU HAVE LOST
YOUR FIRST LOVE. (5)
REMEMBER FROM WHERE
YOU HAVE FALLEN AND
REPENT, AND DO WHAT
YOU USED TO DO BEFORE.
IF NOT, I WILL COME TO
YOU AND REMOVE YOUR
LAMPSTAND FROM ITS
PLACE; THIS I WILL DO,
UNLESS YOU REPENT.
(6) YET IT IS IN YOUR
FAVOR THAT YOU HATE
THE DOING OF THE NI-
COLAITANS, WHICH I
ALSO HATE. (7) IF ANY-
ONE HAS EARS LET
HIM LISTEN TO WHAT
THE SPIRIT SAYS TO
THE CHURCHES: TO
THE VICTOR I WILL GIVE TO EAT OF THE TREE OF
LIFE WHICH IS IN GOD'S PARADISE."

(8) WRITE THIS TO THE ANGEL OF THE CHURCH IN
SMYRNA, "THUS SAYS THE FIRST AND THE LAST, HE
WHO WAS DEAD AND RETURNED TO LIFE: (9) I KNOW
YOUR TRIALS AND YOUR POVERTY: YOU ARE
RICH INDEED. I KNOW HOW YOU ARE SLANDERED BY
THOSE WHO PRETEND TO BE JEWS BUT WHO ARE,
IN FACT, OF THE SYNAGOGUE OF SATAN. (10) DO
NOT BE AFRAID OF WHAT WILL HAPPEN TO

YOU. THE DEVIL WILL THROW SOME OF YOU INTO PRI-
SON TO TEST YOU AND THERE WILL BE TEN DAYS OF
TRIALS. REMAIN FAITHFUL EVEN TO DEATH AND I
WILL GIVE YOU THE CROWN OF LIFE.
(11) IF ANYONE HAS EARS, LET HIM LISTEN
TO WHAT THE SPIRIT SAYS TO THE CHUR-
CHES: THE VICTOR HAS NOTHING TO
FEAR FROM THE SECOND DEATH."

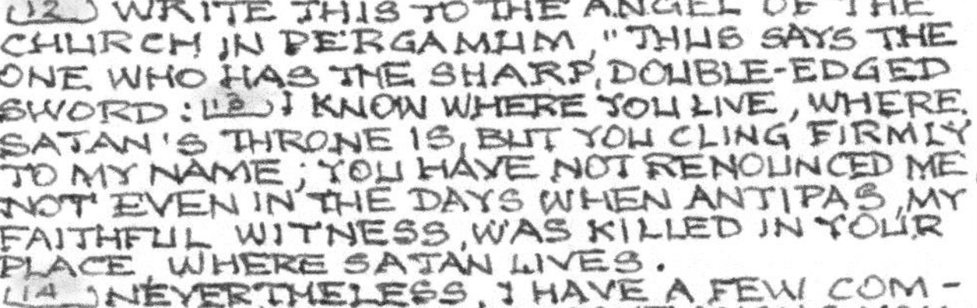

(12) WRITE THIS TO THE ANGEL OF THE
CHURCH IN PERGAMUM, "THUS SAYS THE
ONE WHO HAS THE SHARP, DOUBLE-EDGED
SWORD: (13) I KNOW WHERE YOU LIVE, WHERE
SATAN'S THRONE IS, BUT YOU CLING FIRMLY
TO MY NAME; YOU HAVE NOT RENOUNCED ME,
NOT EVEN IN THE DAYS WHEN ANTIPAS, MY
FAITHFUL WITNESS, WAS KILLED IN YOUR
PLACE, WHERE SATAN LIVES.
(14) NEVERTHELESS, I HAVE A FEW COM-
PLAINTS AGAINST YOU: SOME AMONG YOU

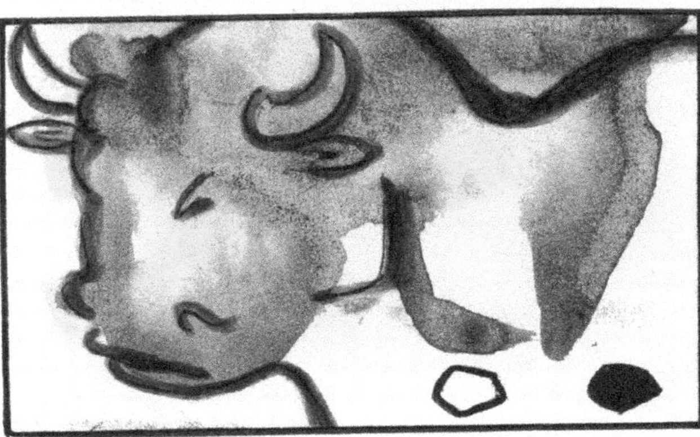

HOLD THE TEACHING OF BALAAM, WHO TAUGHT
BALAK HOW TO MAKE THE ISRAELITES STUM-
BLE BY EATING FOOD SACRIFICED TO IDOLS
AND COMMITTING ADULTERY. (15) ALSO, AMONG
YOU SOME FOLLOW THE TEACHING OF THE NICOLA-
ITANS. (16) REPENT, THEN; IF NOT, I WILL COME TO YOU
SOON TO ATTACK THESE PEOPLE WITH THE SWORD OF
MY MOUTH. (17) IF ONE HEARS, LET HIM LISTEN TO WHAT
THE SPIRIT SAYS TO THE CHURCHES: TO THE VICTOR THE
HIDDEN MANNA. I WILL GIVE HIM A WHITE STONE WITH
A NEW NAME WRITTEN

ON IT WHICH NO ONE (EX-
CEPT THE RECEIVER),
DOES KNOW. (18) WRITE
THIS TO THE ANGEL OF
THE CHURCH IN THYATIRA,
"THUS SAYS THE SON OF
GOD WITH EYES LIKE
FLAMES OF FIRE AND
WHOSE FEET ARE LIKE
BURNISHED BRONZE.
(19) I KNOW ALL YOUR
WORKS: LOVE, SERVICE,
FAITH, ENDURANCE AND
YOUR LATER WORKS
GREATER THAN THE FIRST.
(20) BUT I HAVE A COM-
PLAINT AGAINST YOU: YOU
TOLERATE YOUR JEZEBEL,
THIS WOMAN WHO CALLS
HERSELF A PROPHETESS
WHO DECEIVES MY SER-
VANTS, TEACHING THEM
PROSTITUTION AND THE
EATING OF FOOD SACRIFI-
CED TO IDOLS. (21) I GAVE
HER TIME TO REPENT BUT SHE IS UNWILLING TO LEAVE
HER PROSTITUTION. (22) SO I AM GOING TO THROW HER ON-
TO A BED AND INFLICT MANY TRIALS ON HER PARTNERS
IN ADULTERY UNLESS THEY REPENT OF THEIR EVIL.
(23) I WILL STRIKE HER FOLLOWERS DEAD AND ALL THE
CHURCHES WILL KNOW THAT I AM HE WHO PROBES
THE HEART AND MIND; I WILL GIVE EACH OF YOU
WHAT YOUR CONDUCT DESERVES.
(24) LISTEN TO ME NOW, THE REST OF YOU IN THY-
ATIRA, YOU WHO DO NOT HOLD WITH THIS
TEACHING AND HAVE NOT LEARNED
"THE SECRETS OF SATAN", AS THEY ARE
CALLED. I HAVE NO CAUSE TO REPROACH YOU;

25 ONLY HOLD ON TO WHAT YOU HAVE, UNTIL I
COME. 26 TO HIM WHO IS VICTOR AND KEEPS
TO MY WAYS TO THE END, I WILL GIVE POWER
OVER THE NATIONS; 27 HE WILL RULE THEM
WITH AN IRON ROD AND SHATTER THEM LIKE
EARTHEN POTS; HE WILL BE LIKE ME, WHO RE-
CEIVED THIS POWER FROM MY FATHER. 28 MO-
REOVER, I WILL GIVE HIM THE 'MORNING STAR.'
29 IF ANYONE HAS EARS TO HEAR, LET HIM

LISTEN TO WHAT THE SPIRIT SAYS TO THE CHURCHES."

3 1 WRITE THIS TO THE ANGEL OF THE CHURCH IN
SARDIS. "THUS SAYS HE WHO HOLDS THE SEVEN
SPIRITS OF GOD AND THE SEVEN STARS: I KNOW YOUR
WORTH. YOU THINK YOU LIVE BUT YOU ARE DEAD. WAKE
UP 2 AND STRENGTHEN THAT WHICH IS NOT ALREADY
DEAD. FOR I HAVE FOUND YOUR WORKS TO BE IMPER-
FECT IN THE SIGHT OF MY
GOD. 3 REMEMBER WHAT
YOU WERE TAUGHT; KEEP
IT AND CHANGE YOUR WAYS.
IF YOU DO NOT REPENT I
WILL COME UPON YOU AS
A THIEF AT AN HOUR YOU
LEAST EXPECT. 4 THERE
ARE SOME LEFT IN SARDIS
WHO HAVEN'T SOILED THE-
IR ROBES; THESE WILL CO-
ME WITH ME DRESSED IN
WHITE, SINCE THEY DE-
SERVE IT. 5 THE VICTOR
WILL BE DRESSED IN WHITE
AND I WILL NEVER ERASE
HIS NAME FROM THE BOOK
OF LIFE: INSTEAD, I WILL
ACKNOWLEDGE IT BEFORE
MY FATHER AND HIS ANGELS.
6 IF ANYONE HAS EARS
TO HEAR, LET HIM LISTEN
TO WHAT THE SPIRIT SAYS
TO THE CHURCHES." WRITE

7 THIS TO THE ANGEL OF THE CHURCH IN PHILADELPHIA,
"THUS SAYS HE WHO IS HOLY AND TRUE, WHO HOLDS DAVID'S
KEY; IF HE OPENS, NOBODY SHUTS AND IF HE SHUTS NO-
BODY OPENS. 8 I KNOW YOU WORTH; I HAVE OPENED
A DOOR BEFORE YOU, WHICH NOBODY CAN CLOSE, FOR
YOU HAVE KEPT MY WORD AND NOT RENOUNCED ME, IN
SPITE OF YOUR LACK OF POWER.
9 I AM GIVING YOU SOME OF THE SYNAGOGUE OF
SATAN WHO CALL THEMSELVES JEWS BUT
THEY ARE ONLY LIARS. I WILL MAKE THEM
FALL AT YOUR FEET AND RECOGNIZE THAT
I HAVE LOVED YOU.

10 BECAUSE YOU HAVE KEPT MY WORDS WITH MUCH
ENDURANCE, I, FOR MY PART, WILL KEEP YOU SAFE IN
THE HOUR OF TRIAL WHICH IS COMING UPON THE WHOLE
WORLD, TO TEST THE PEOPLE OF THE EARTH. 11 I AM
COMING SOON; HOLD FAST TO WHAT YOU HAVE, LEST
ANYONE TAKE YOUR CROWN. 12 I WILL MAKE THE
VICTOR INTO A COLUMN IN THE SANCTUARY OF MY
GOD AND THE NAME OF THE CITY WHERE HE WILL
STAY FOREVER. I WILL WRITE ON HIM THE NAME OF
MY GOD AND THE NAME OF THE CITY OF MY GOD, THE
NEW JERUSALEM, WHICH COMES DOWN FROM MY
GOD IN HEAVEN, AND MY OWN NEW NAME. 13 IF ANY-
ONE HAS EARS TO HEAR, LET HIM LISTEN TO WHAT THE
SPIRIT SAYS TO THE
CHURCHES." 14 WRITE
TO THE ANGELS OF THE
CHURCH IN LAODICEA."
THUS SAYS THE AMEN,
THE FAITHFUL AND TRUE
WITNESS, THE BEGINNING
OF GOD'S CREATION: I KNOW
15 YOUR WORKS: YOU ARE
NEITHER COLD NOR HOT!
WOULD THAT YOU WERE
COLD OR HOT! 16 YOU ARE
LUKEWARM, NEITHER HOT
NOR COLD SO I WILL SPIT
YOU OUT OF MY MOUTH.
17 YOU THINK YOU ARE
SO RICH THAT YOU NEED
NOTHING, AND DON'T RE-
ALIZE YOU ARE TO BE
PITIED, POOR, BLIND AND
NAKED. 18 I ADVISE YOU
TO BUY FROM ME GOLD BE-
EN TESTED BY FIRE, SO THAT YOU MAY BE RICH; WHITE
CLOTHES TO WEAR SO THAT YOUR NAKEDNESS MAY NOT
SHAME YOU, AND OINTMENT FOR YOUR EYES THAT YOU
MAY SEE. 19 I REPRIMAND AND CORRECT ALL THOSE I
LOVE. BE EARNEST AND CHANGE YOUR WAYS. 20 LOOK,
I STAND AT THE DOOR AND KNOCK. IF ANYONE HEARS
MY CALL AND OPENS THE DOOR, I WILL COME IN TO HIM
AND HAVE SUPPER WITH HIM, AND HE WITH ME.
21 I WILL LET THE VICTOR SIT WITH ME ON MY

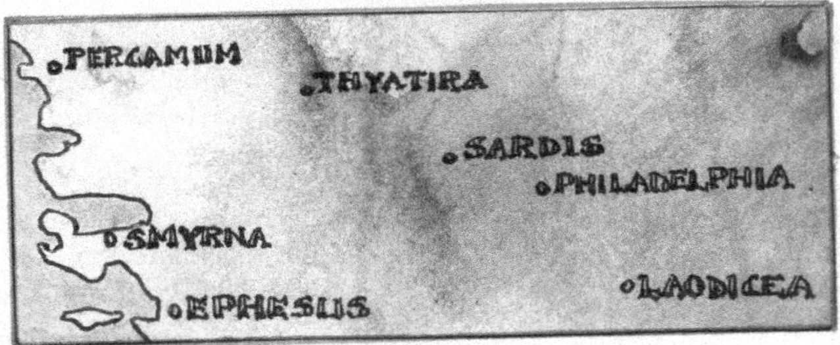

THRONE AS I WAS VICTORIOUS AND TOOK MY PLACE WITH
MY FATHER ON HIS THRONE. 22 IF ANYONE HAS EARS TO HEAR
LET HIM HEAR WHAT THE SPIRIT SAYS TO THE CHURCHES."

A LOOK AT THE PAST: CHRIST AND ISRAEL

THE THRONE IN HEAVEN

4 1 THEN I LOOKED UP TO THE WALL OF THE SKY AND
SAW AN OPEN DOOR. THE VOICE I FIRST HEARD LIKE
A TRUMPET SAID, "COME UP HERE, I WILL SHOW YOU
WHAT WILL COME IN THE FUTURE." 2 IMMEDIATELY I
WAS SEIZED BY THE SPIRIT. THERE, IN HEAVEN, WAS A
THRONE AND ONE SITTING ON IT. 3 HE WHO SAT THERE
LOOKED LIKE JASPER AND CARNELIAN AND ROUND THE
THRONE WAS A RAINBOW RESEMBLING AN EMERALD. 4
IN A CIRCLE AROUND THE THRONE ARE TWENTY-FOUR THRO-
NES AND SEATED ON THESE ARE TWENTY-FOUR ELDERS,
DRESSED IN WHITE CLOTHES, AND WITH
GOLDEN CROWNS ON THEIR HEADS.

TO THE VICTOR I WILL GIVE TO EAT OF THE TREE OF LIFE, WHICH IS IN GOD'S PARADISE

(REVELATION 2:7)

Z

The Deportations Continue

On 20 January 1943 Himmler wrote to th
Reich Minister of Transport about 'the
removal of Jews' from every area to which
German rule or authority then extended. To
complete this task, Himmler explained, 'I need
our help and support. If I am to wind things up
uickly, I must have more trains for transport.'
'I must have more trains....' In his letter
immler went on to express his understanding of
Minister's problems, at a time when the
man army, just defeated at Stalingrad, was
to rush extra troops and munitions to the
to prevent the Soviet forc

5 FLASHES OF LIGHTNING COME FORTH FROM
THE THRONE, WITH VOICES AND THUNDERCLAPS.
SEVEN FLAMING TORCHES BURN BEFORE THE
THRONE; THESE ARE THE SEVEN SPIRITS OF GOD.
6 BEFORE THE THRONE THERE IS A PLATFORM,
TRANSPARENT LIKE CRYSTAL. AROUND AND BESIDE
THE THRONE STAND FOUR LIVING CREATURES, FULL
OF EYES, BOTH IN FRONT AND BEHIND. 7 THE FIRST
LIVING CREATURE IS LIKE A LION, THE SECOND LIKE
A BULL, THE THIRD HAS THE FACE OF A MAN AND
THE FOURTH LOOKS LIKE A FLYING EAGLE. EACH
8 OF THE FOUR LIVING CREATURES HAS SIX

WINGS FULL OF EYES, ALL AROUND AS WELL AS WITH-
IN; DAY AND NIGHT THEY SING WITHOUT CEASING,
HOLY, HOLY, HOLY IS THE LORD GOD, MASTER OF
THE UNIVERSE, HE WAS, HE IS AND HE IS TO COME.
9 WHENEVER THE LIVING CREATURES GIVE GLORY,
HONOR AND THANKS TO THE ONE ON THE THRONE, HE
WHO LIVES FOR EVER AND EVER, 10 THE TWENTY-FOUR
ELDERS FALL DOWN BEFORE HIM AND WORSHIP THE
ONE WHO LIVES FOR EVER AND EVER. THEY LAY THEIR
CROWNS IN FRONT OF THE THRONE AND SAY,
11 OUR LORD AND GOD, WORTHY ARE YOU TO RE-
CEIVE GLORY, HONOR AND POWER! FOR YOU HAVE
CREATED ALL THINGS; BY YOUR WILL THEY
CAME TO BE AND WERE MADE.

5 THE COMING OF THE LAMB

1 THEN I SAW
IN THE RIGHT HAND OF HIM WHO WAS SEATED ON THE
THRONE A SCROLL WRITTEN
ON BOTH SIDES, SEALED WITH
SEVEN SEALS. 2 A MIGHTY
ANGEL EXCLAIMED IN A
LOUD VOICE, "WHO IS
WORTHY TO OPEN THIS
AND BREAK THE SEALS?"
3 BUT NO ONE IN HEA-
VEN OR ON EARTH OR UN-
DER THE EARTH (AMONG
THE DEAD) WAS FOUND
ABLE TO OPEN THE BOOK
AND READ IT. 4 I WEPT
MUCH WHEN I SAW THAT
NO ONE WAS FOUND
WORTHY TO OPEN THE
BOOK AND READ IT. 5
THEN ONE OF THE EL-
DERS SAID TO ME, "DO
NOT WEEP. LOOK, THE
LION OF THE TRIBE OF
JUDAH, THE SHOOT OF
DAVID, HAS CONQUERED:
HE WILL OPEN THE BOOK OF THE SEVEN SEALS."

6 AND I SAW NEXT TO THE THRONE WITH ITS FOUR
LIVING CREATURES AND THE TWENTY-FOUR ELDERS A
LAMB STANDING, ALTHOUGH IT HAD BEEN SLAIN. I SAW
HIM WITH SEVEN HORNS AND SEVEN EYES, WHICH ARE
THE SEVEN SPIRITS OF GOD SENT OUT TO ALL THE
EARTH. 7 THE LAMB MOVED FORWARD AND TO-
OK THE BOOK FROM
THE RIGHT HAND OF
HIM WHO WAS SEA-
TED ON THE THRONE.
8 WHEN HE TOOK IT,
THE FOUR LIVING CRE-
ATURES AND THE
TWENTY-FOUR ELDERS
BOWED BEFORE THE
LAMB. THEY ALL HELD
IN THEIR HANDS HARPS
AND GOLDEN CUPS FULL
OF INCENSE WHICH
ARE THE PRAYERS
OF THE HOLY ONES.
• • •
9 THIS IS THE NEW
SONG THEY SANG:

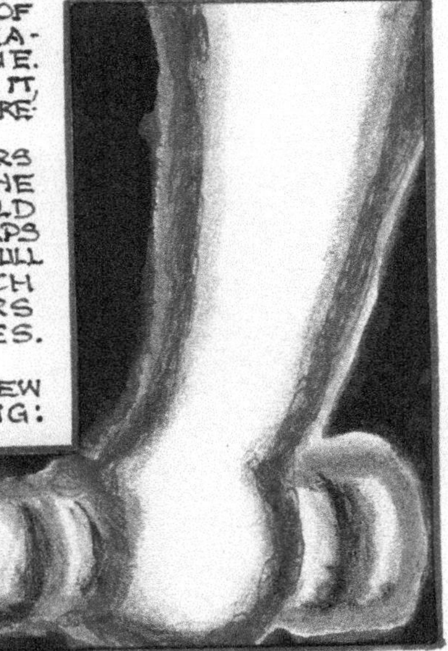

YOU ARE WORTHY TO TAKE THE BOOK AND
OPEN ITS SEALS, FOR YOU WERE SLAIN AND
BY YOUR BLOOD YOU PURCHASED FOR GOD PE-
OPLE OF EVERY RACE, LANGUAGE AND NATION;
10 AND YOU MADE THEM A KINGDOM AND PRI-
ESTS FOR OUR GOD TO REIGN OVER THE LAND.
11 I WENT ON LOOKING; I HEARD THE NOISE OF A MULTITU-
DE OF ANGELS GATHERED AROUND THE THRONE, THE LIVING
CREATURES AND THE ELDERS, MILLIONS AND MILLIONS OF
THEM, 12 CRYING OUT WITH A LOUD VOICE:
WORTHY IS THE LAMB WHO WAS SLAIN TO RECE-
IVE POWER AND RICHES, WISDOM AND STRENGTH,
HONOR, GLORY AND PRAISE.

13 THEN I HEARD THE VOICE OF THE WHOLE UNIVERSE,
HEAVEN, EARTH, SEA AND THE PLACE OF THE DEAD: EVERY
CREATURE CRIED OUT:
TO HIM WHO SITS UPON THE THRONE AND TO
THE LAMB BE PRAISE, HONOR, GLORY AND
POWER FOR EVER AND EVER.
14 AND THE FOUR LIVING CREATURES SAID, AMEN, WHILE
THE ELDERS BOWED DOWN AND WORSHIPED.

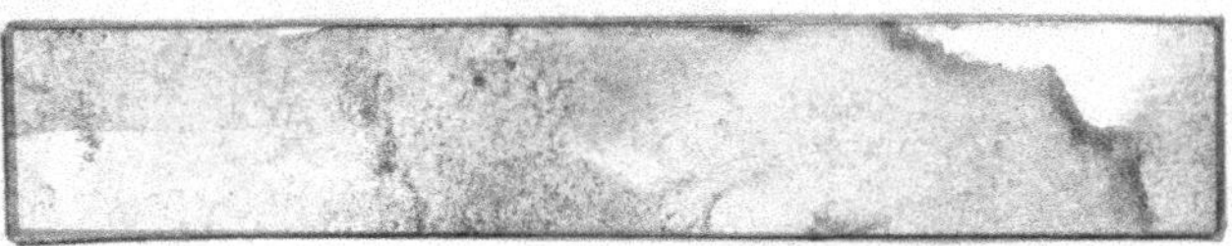

THE SEVEN SEALS

6 1 I SAW THE LAMB OPENING THE FIRST OF THE SEVEN
SEALS AND I HEARD ONE OF THE FOUR LIVING CREATURES
CRY OUT WITH A VOICE LIKE A THUNDER "COME AND
SEE!" 2 A WHITE HORSE APPEARED, AND ITS RIDER HAD
A BOW. HE WAS CROWNED, AND HE WENT OUT AS A CON-
QUEROR TO CONTINUE HIS CONQUEST.
3 WHEN HE OPENED THE SECOND SEAL, I HEARD THE SE-
COND LIVING CREATURE CRY OUT, "COME!" 4 THEN ONE
HORSE THE COLOR OF FI-
RE CAME OUT. ITS RIDER
WAS ORDERED TO TAKE PEA-
CE AWAY FROM THE EARTH,
THAT PEOPLE MIGHT
KILL ONE ANOTHER; SO
HE WAS GIVEN A GREAT
SWORD. 5 WHEN HE
OPENED THE THIRD SEAL,
I HEARD THE THIRD CRE-
ATURE CRY OUT, "COME!"
THIS TIME IT WAS A
BLACK HORSE, AND ITS
RIDER HELD A BALAN-
CE IN HIS HAND. THEN
6 FROM THE MIDST OF
THE FOUR LIVING CRE-
ATURES A VOICE WAS
HEARD: "A MEASURE
OF WHEAT FOR A PIECE
OF SILVER, AND THREE
MEASURES OF BARLEY
FOR A PIECE AS WELL!
DO NOT SPOIL THE OIL OR
THE WINE." 7 WHEN HE
OPENED THE FOURTH SE-
AL, I HEARD A CRY FROM
THE FOURTH LIVING CRE-
ATURE, "COME!" 8 A
GREENISH HORSE APPE-

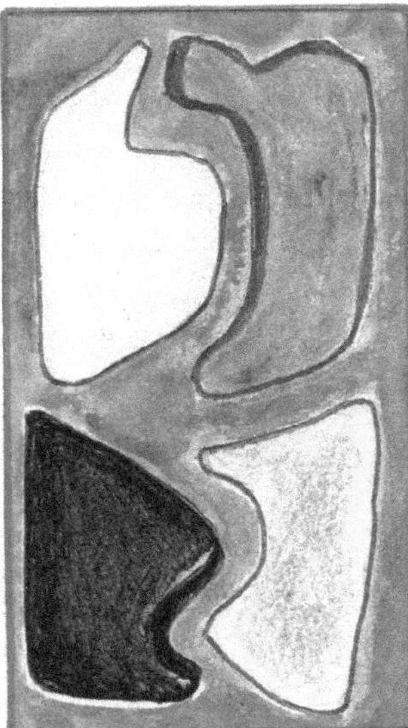

ARED, ITS RIDER WAS CALLED DEATH, AND THE NE-
THERWORLD RODE BEHIND HIM. HE WAS ALLOWED TO
UTTERLY DESTROY BY SWORD, FAMINE, PESTILENCE
AND WILD BEASTS A FOURTH OF THE INHABITANTS OF
OF THE EARTH. 9 WHEN HE OPENED THE FIFTH
SEAL, I SAW UNDER THE ALTAR THE SPIRITS OF THOSE
WHO PROCLAIMED THE WORD OF GOD AND WERE SLAIN
FOR ITS SAKE. 10 THEY BEGAN TO CRY ALOUD, "HOLY
AND RIGHTEOUS LORD, HOW LONG WILL IT BE BEFORE
YOU RENDER JUSTICE AND AVENGE OUR BLOOD ON THE IN-
HABITANTS OF THE EARTH?" 11 THEN EACH ONE OF THEM

WAS GIVEN A WHITE GARMENT, AND THEY WERE TOLD TO
WAIT A LITTLE WHILE, UNTIL THE NUMBER OF THEIR BRO-
THERS AND FELLOW SERVANTS WHO WOULD BE KILLED
AS THEY HAD BEEN WOULD BE COMPLETED. 12 AND
MY VISION CONTINUED. WHEN THE LAMB OPENED THE
SIXTH SEAL, CAME A VIOLENT EARTHQUAKE, THE SUN BE-
CAME BLACK AS A MOURNING DRESS, AND THE MOON TURNED
BLOOD-RED, 13 AND THE STARS IN THE SKY FELL TO THE
EARTH LIKE DRY FIGS FALLING FROM A FIG TREE SHAK-
EN BY A HURRICANE. 14 THE SKY WAS FOLDED UP LIKE
ROLLED PARCHMENT; THERE WAS NO MOUNTAIN OR CON-
TINENT THAT WAS NOT REMOVED FROM ITS PLACE.
15 THE KINGS OF THE EARTH AND THEIR MINISTERS,
THE GENERALS, THE RICH AND POWERFUL, AND ALL THE
PEOPLE, SLAVES AS WELL AS FREE PERSONS, HID IN CA-
VES OR AMONG ROCKS ON THE MOUNTAINS. 16 SAYING,
"FALL ON US MOUNTAINS AND ROCKS, AND HIDE US FOR
WE ARE AFRAID OF HIM WHO SITS ON THE THRONE, AND OF
THE WRATH OF THE LAMB. 17 THE GREAT DAY OF HIS
WRATH HAS COME, AND WHO CAN ENDURE IT?"

144,000 FROM ISRAEL AND THE GREAT CROWD FROM EVERY NATION

7 1 AFTER THIS, THERE WERE FOUR ANGELS STANDING
AT THE FOUR CORNERS OF THE EARTH, HOLDING
BACK THE FOUR WINDS
TO PREVENT THEIR BLOW-
ING AGAINST THE EARTH,
THE SEA AND THE TREES.
2 I SAW ANOTHER ANGEL
ASCENDING FROM THE SUN-
RISE, CARRYING THE SEAL
OF THE LIVING GOD, AND
HE CRIED OUT WITH A LO-
UD VOICE TO THE FOUR
ANGELS EMPOWERED
TO HARM THE EARTH AND
THE SEA, 3 "DO NOT
HARM THE EARTH OR
THE SEA OR THE TRE-
ES UNTIL WE HAVE
SEALED THE SERVANTS
OF OUR GOD UPON THEIR
FOREHEADS." 4 THEN
I HEARD THE NUMBER
OF THOSE MARKED WITH
THE SEAL: A HUNDRED
AND FORTY-FOUR THOU-
SAND FROM ALL THE TRI-
BES OF THE SONS OF
ISRAEL: 5 FROM THE
TRIBE OF JUDAH, TWELVE THOUSAND WERE SEALED;

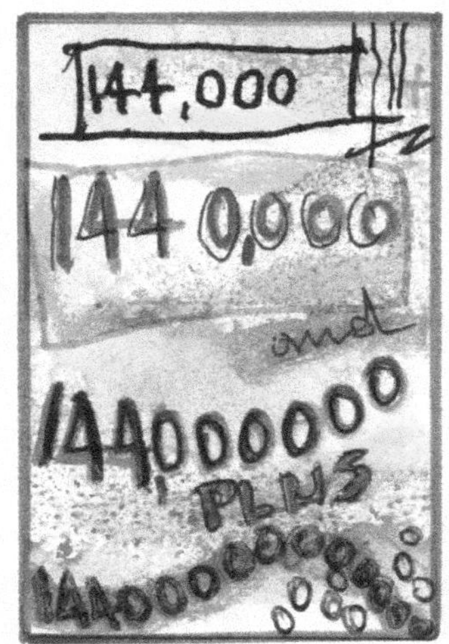

FROM THE TRIBE OF REUBEN, TWELVE THOUSAND; FROM
THE TRIBE OF GAD, TWELVE THOUSAND, 6 FROM THE
TRIBE OF ASHER, TWELVE THOUSAND; FROM THE TRI-
BE OF NAPHTALI, TWELVE THOUSAND; FROM THE
TRIBE OF MANASSEH, TWELVE THOUSAND; FROM
7 THE TRIBE OF SIMEON, TWELVE THOUSAND;
FROM THE TRIBE OF LEVI, TWELVE THOUSAND;
FROM THE TRIBE OF ISSACHAR, TWELVE THOUSAND;
8 FROM THE TRIBE OF ZEBULUN, TWELVE THOUSAND;
FROM THE TRIBE OF JOSEPH, TWELVE THOUSAND,
FROM THE TRIBE OF BENJAMIN, TWELVE THOUSAND.

9 AFTER THIS I SAW A GREAT CROWD, IMPOSSIBLE

TO COUNT, FROM EVERY NATION, RACE, PEOPLE
AND TONGUE, STANDING BEFORE THE THRONE
OF THE LAMB, CLOTHED IN WHITE, WITH PALM
BRANCHES ON THEIR HANDS, 10 AND THEY
CRIED OUT WITH A LOUD VOICE, "WHO SAVES
BUT OUR GOD WHO SITS ON THE THRONE AND THE LAMB?"

11 ALL THE ANGELS WERE AROUND THE THRONE,
THE ELDERS AND THE FOUR LIVING CREATURES;
THEY BOWED BEFORE THE THRONE WITH THEIR FA-
CES TO THE GROUND TO WORSHIP GOD. 12 THEY SAID:
AMEN. PRAISE, GLORY, WISDOM,
THANKS, HONOR, POWER, STRENGTH TO
OUR GOD FOREVER AND EVER. AMEN!

13 AT THAT MOMENT, ONE OF THE ELDERS SPOKE UP AND
SAID TO ME. "WHO ARE THESE PEOPLE CLOTHED IN
WHITE, AND WHERE DID
THEY COME FROM?" 14

I ANSWERED, "SIR, IT IS
YOU WHO KNOW THIS."
THE ELDER REPLIED
"THEY ARE THOSE WHO HA-
VE COME OUT OF THE GRE-
AT PERSECUTION; THEY
HAVE WASHED AND MADE
THEIR CLOTHES WHITE IN
THE BLOOD OF THE LAMB.
15 THIS IS WHY THEY
STAND BEFORE THE THRO-
NE OF GOD AND SERVE HIM
DAY AND NIGHT IN HIS SAN-
CTUARY. HE WHO SITS ON
THE THRONE WILL SPREAD
HIS TENT OVER THEM.
16 NEVER AGAIN WILL
THEY SUFFER HUNGER
OR THIRST OR BE BUR-
NED BY THE SUN OR ANY
SCORCHING WIND, 17
FOR THE LAMB NEAR THE
THRONE WILL BE THEIR
SHEPHERD, AND HE WILL
BRING THEM TO SPRINGS
OF LIFE-GIVING WATER
AND GOD WILL WIPE
AWAY THEIR MANY TEARS."

8 1 WHEN THE LAMB OPENED THE SEVENTH SE-
AL THERE WAS SILENCE IN HEAVEN FOR ABOUT
HALF AN HOUR. 2 THEN I LOOKED AT THE SE-
VEN ANGELS STANDING BEFORE GOD WHO WERE GIVEN
SEVEN TRUMPETS.
3 ANOTHER ANGEL CAME AND STOOD BEFORE THE
ALTAR OF INCENSE WITH A GOLDEN CENSER.

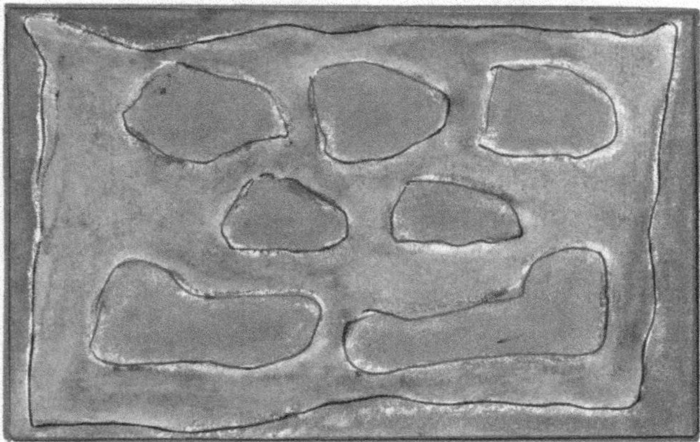

HE WAS GIVEN MUCH INCENSE TO BE OFFERED
WITH THE PRAYERS OF ALL THE HOLY ONES,
ON THE GOLDEN ALTAR BEFORE THE THRONE;
4 AND THE CLOUD OF INCENSE ROSE WITH THE
PRAYERS OF THE HOLY ONES FROM THE HANDS OF
THE ANGEL TO THE PRESENCE OF GOD.

5 THEN THE ANGEL TOOK THE CENSER AND
FILLED IT WITH BURNING COALS FROM
THE ALTAR, AND THREW THEM ON THE EARTH.
AND THERE CAME THUNDER, LIGHTNING AND
EARTHQUAKES.

THE SEVEN TRUMPETS

6 THE SEVEN ANGELS WITH THE SEVEN TRUMPETS
PREPARED TO SOUND THEM. 7 WHEN THE FIRST
BLEW HIS TRUMPET, THERE CAME HAIL AND FI-
RE, MIXED WITH BLOOD, WHICH FELL ON THE
EARTH. AND A THIRD OF THE EARTH WAS BUR-
NED UP WITH A THIRD OF THE TREES AND THE
GREEN GRASS.
8 WHEN THE SECOND ANGEL BLEW HIS TRUMPET,

SOMETHING LIKE A GREAT MOUNTAIN WAS THROWN IN-
TO THE SEA, A THIRD OF THE SEA WAS TURNED INTO BLO-
OD. 9 AT ONCE, A THIRD OF THE LIVING CREATURES IN
THE SEA DIED AND A THIRD OF THE SHIPS PERISHED.
10 WHEN THE THIRD ANGEL SOUNDED HIS TRUMPET A GREAT
STAR FELL FROM HEAVEN, LIKE A BALL OF FIRE, ON A THIRD
OF RIVERS AND SPRINGS. 11 THE STAR CALLED "WORM-
WOOD", AND A THIRD OF
THE WATERS WAS TURN-
ED INTO WORMWOOD AND
MANY PEOPLE DIED BE-
CAUSE OF THE WATER
WHICH HAD TURNED
BITTER. 12 THE FO-
URTH ANGEL BLEW HIS
TRUMPET, AND A THIRD
OF THE SUN, THE MOON
AND THE STARS WAS AF-
FECTED. DAYLIGHT DE-
CREASED ONE THIRD,
AND THE LIGHT AT
NIGHT AS WELL. 13
AND MY VISION
CONTINUED: I NO-
TICED AN EAGLE
FLYING THROUGH
THE HIGHEST HE-
AVEN AND CRYING
WITH A LOUD VO-
ICE, "WOE, WOE
WOE TO THE IN-
HABITANTS OF
THE LAND WHEN
THE LAST THREE
ANGELS SOUND
THEIR TRUMPETS."

9 1 AND THE FIFTH ANGEL BLEW HIS TRUMPET. A STAR 2
FELL FROM HEAVEN TO EARTH. THE STAR WAS GIVEN THE KEY
TO THE DEPTHS OF THE ABYSS; A CLOUD OF SMOKE ROSE AS IF
FROM A GREAT FURNACE WHICH DARKENED THE SUN AND AIR.
3 LOCUSTS CAME FROM THIS SMOKE AND SPRE-
AD THROUGHOUT THE EARTH. THEY WERE GI-
VEN THE SAME HARMFUL POWER AS THE
SCORPIONS OF THE EARTH.

4 THEN THEY WERE TOLD NOT TO HARM
THE MEADOWS, THE GREEN GRASS OR
THE TREES, BUT ONLY THE PEOPLE WHO
DO NOT BEAR GOD'S SEAL UPON THEIR FOREHEADS.

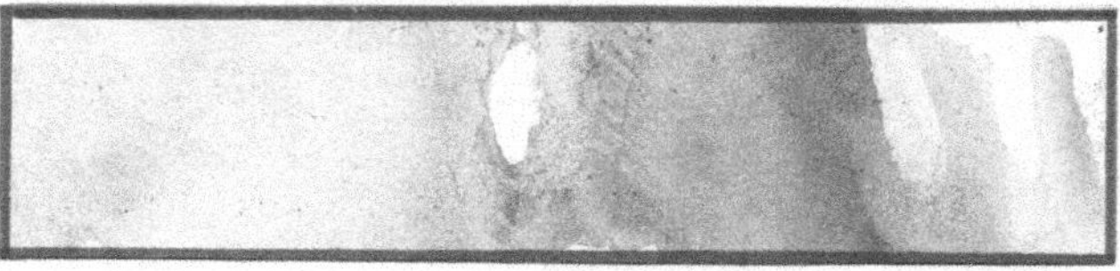

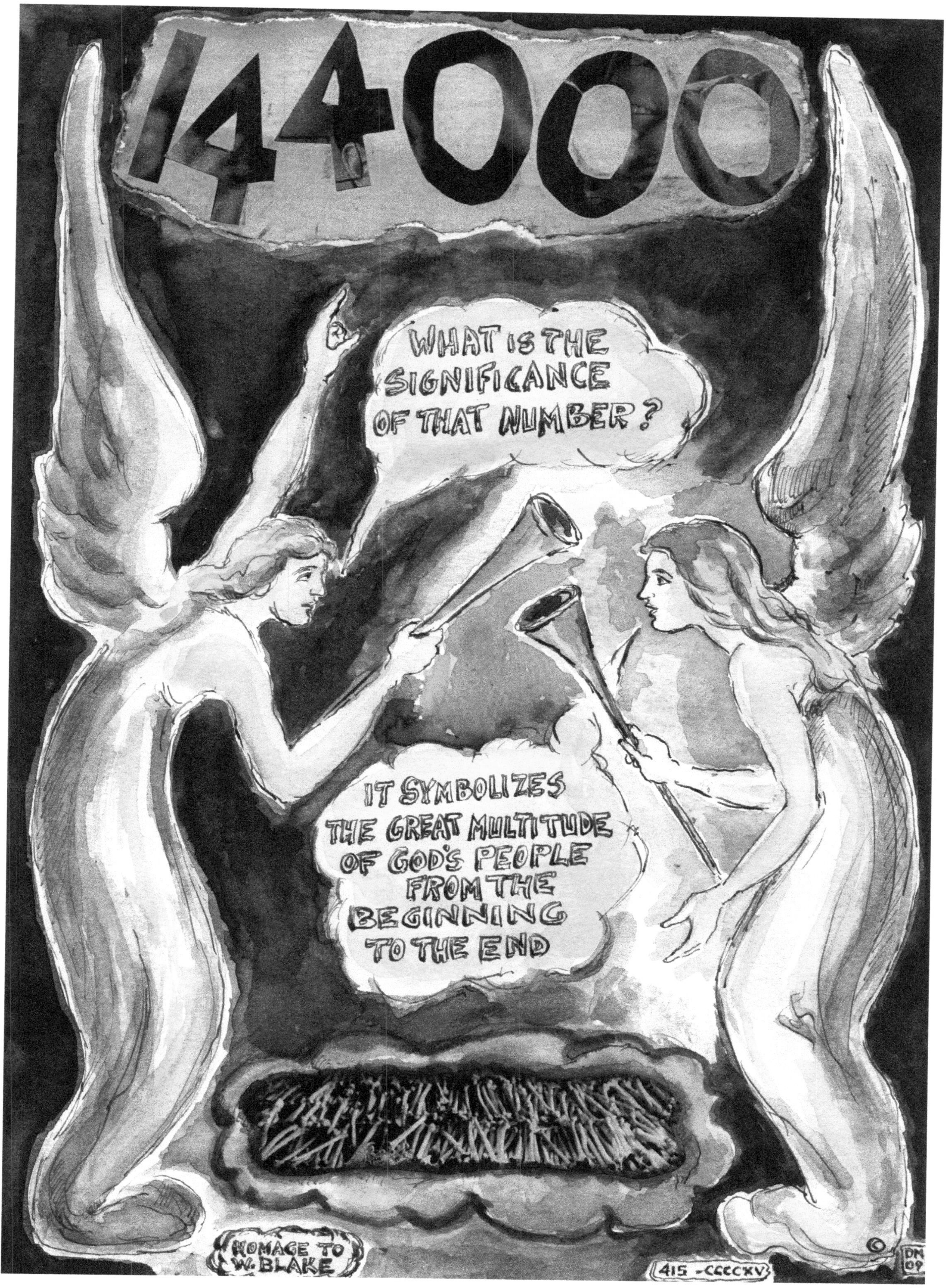

144000

WHAT IS THE SIGNIFICANCE OF THAT NUMBER?

IT SYMBOLIZES THE GREAT MULTITUDE OF GOD'S PEOPLE FROM THE BEGINNING TO THE END

HOMAGE TO W. BLAKE

5 THEY WERE NOT TO KILL THEM, BUT ONLY TOR-
TURE THEM FOR FIVE MONTHS. THIS PAIN IS LIKE THE
STING OF SCORPIONS. 6 IN THOSE DAYS, PEOPLE WILL
FOR DEATH BUT WILL NOT FIND IT; THEY WILL LONG TO
DIE, BUT DEATH WILL ELUDE THEM. 7 THESE LOCUSTS
LOOK LIKE HORSES EQUIPPED FOR BATTLE; THEY WEAR
GOLDEN CROWNS ON THEIR HEADS, AND THEIR FACES
ARE LIKE THOSE OF HUMAN BEINGS. 8 THEIR HAIR
IS LIKE WOMEN'S HAIR, AND THEIR TEETH LIKE LION'S
TEETH; 9 THEIR CHESTS ARE LIKE IRON BREAST-
PLATES; AND THE NOISE OF THEIR WINGS LIKE A

ROAR OF AN ARMY OF CHARIOTS AND HORSES RUSHING
FOR BATTLE. 10 THEIR TAILS ARE LIKE THOSE OF
SCORPIONS AND HAVE STINGS; THE POWER
THEY HAVE TO TORTURE PEOPLE FOR FIVE MONTHS
IS IN THEIR TAILS. 11 THESE LOCUSTS HAVE A KING,
WHO IS THE ANGEL OF THE ABYSS WHOSE NAME IN
HEBREW IS ABADDON OR APOLLYON IN GREEK (DES-
TRUCTION IN ENGLISH).
12 THE FIRST WOE HAS PASSED. TWO OTHERS ARE TO
COME.
13 THE SIXTH ANGEL BLEW HIS TRUMPET: THEN I HEARD

A VOICE CALLING FROM
THE CORNERS OF THE
GOLDEN ALTAR BEFORE
GOD. 14 IT SAID TO THE
SIXTH ANGEL WHO HAD
JUST SOUNDED THE TRUM-
PET, "RELEASE THE FOUR
ANGELS CHAINED AT THE
BANKS OF THE GREAT RI-
VER EUPHRATES." 15
AND THE FOUR ANGELS
WERE RELEASED WHO
HAD BEEN WAITING FOR
THIS YEAR, THIS MONTH,
THIS DAY AND THIS
HOUR, READY TO UT-
TERLY DESTROY A
THIRD OF HUMAN-
KIND. 16 THE NUMBER
OF THE SOLDIERS ON
HORSES WAS TWO
HUNDRED MILLION;
THIS IS THE NUMBER I
HEARD. 17 I SAW IN MY
VISION HORSES AND RI-
DERS; THEY WEAR BREAST-
PLATES THE COLOR OF FIRE,
HYACINTH AND SULFUR.
THE HORSES' HEADS LOOK
LIKE LIONS' HEADS, AND FIRE, SMOKE AND SULFUR COME
OUT OF THEIR MOUTHS. 18 THEN A THIRD OF HUMAN-
KIND WAS KILLED BY THESE THREE PLAGUES: FIRE,
SMOKE AND SULFUR WHICH THE HORSES RELEASED
THROUGH THEIR MOUTHS, 19 FOR THE POWER OF THE
HORSES WAS BOTH IN THEIR MOUTHS AND THEIR TAILS,
TAILS LOOKING LIKE SERPENTS, AND THEIR HEADS ARE
ABLE TO INFLICT INJURY AS WELL. 20 HOWEVER, THE REST
OF HUMANKIND WHO WERE NOT KILLED BY THESE PLAGUES DID
NOT RENOUNCE THEIR WAY OF LIFE: THEY WENT ON WORSHIP-
ING THE DEMONS, KEEPING IDOLS OF GOLD, SILVER, BRONZE,
STONE, WOOD THAT CANNOT SEE, HEAR OR WALK.
21 NO, THEY DID NOT REPENT OF THEIR CRIMES, OR
THEIR SEXUAL IMMORALITY OR THEIR THEFT.

WHAT HAS BEEN PROCLAIMED BY THE PROPHETS IS FULFILLED

10 1 THEN I SAW ANOTHER MIGHTY ANGEL COMING
DOWN FROM HEAVEN WRAPPED IN A CLOUD. A RAIN-
BOW WAS AROUND HIS HEAD, HIS FACE WAS LIKE THE
SUN AND HIS LEGS LIKE PILLARS OF FIRE. 2 I COULD
SEE A SMALL BOOK OPEN IN HIS HAND. HE STOOD, HIS
RIGHT FOOT PLANTED ON
THE SEA AND HIS LEFT ON
THE LAND, 3 CALLED
IN A LOUD VOICE LIKE THE
ROARING OF A LION. THEN
4 THE SEVEN THUNDERS
SOUNDED THEIR OWN MES-
SAGE. I WAS ABOUT TO
WRITE WHAT THE SEVEN
THUNDERS HAD SOUNDED,
WHEN A VOICE FROM HE-
AVEN SAID TO ME, "KEEP
THE WORDS OF THE SEVEN
THUNDERS SECRET AND DO
NOT WRITE THEM DOWN."
5 THE ANGEL I SAW STAN-
DING ON THE SEA AND
LAND, RAISED HIS RIGHT
HAND TO HEAVEN, SWEAR-
ING 6 BY HIM WHO LIVES
FOR EVER AND EVER, AND
WHO CREATED THE HE-
AVENS, THE EARTH, THE
SEA AND EVERYTHING
IN THEM. HE SAID, "THE-
RE IS NO MORE DELAY;
7 AS SOON AS THE
TRUMPET CALL OF THE
SEVENTH ANGEL IS HEARD,
THE MYSTERIOUS PLAN

OF GOD WILL BE FULFILLED ACCORDING TO THE GO-
OD NEWS HE PROCLAIMED THROUGH HIS SERVANTS
THE PROPHETS." 8 AND THE VOICE I HAD HEARD FROM
HEAVEN SPOKE AGAIN, SAYING, "GO NEAR THE ANGEL
WHO STANDS ON THE SEA AND ON THE LAND, AND TAKE
THE SMALL BOOK OPEN IN HIS HAND." 9 SO I AP-
PROACHED THE ANGEL AND ASKED HIM FOR THE
SMALL BOOK; HE SAID TO ME, "TAKE IT AND EAT; AL-
THOUGH IT BE SWEET AS HONEY IN YOUR MOUTH,

IT WILL BE BITTER TO YOUR STOMACH." 10 I TOOK
THE SMALL BOOK FROM THE HAND OF THE
ANGEL, AND ATE IT. IT WAS AS SWEET AS HO-
NEY IN MY MOUTH, BUT WHEN I HAD EATEN IT,
IT TURNED BITTER IN MY STOMACH.

11 I WAS TOLD, "YOU MUST AGAIN PROCLAIM GOD'S WORDS
ABOUT MANY PEOPLES, NATIONS, TONGUES AND KINGS."

REVELATION - 11 - 12 -

THE TWO WITNESSES

11 (1) THEN I WAS GIVEN A STAFF LIKE A MEASURING STICK,
AND I WAS TOLD, "GO AND MEASURE THE TEMPLE AND THE
ALTAR OF GOD, AND COUNT THOSE WHO WORSHIP THERE.
(2) DON'T MEASURE THE OUTER COURTYARD, FOR THIS HAS
BEEN GIVEN TO THE PAGANS WHO WILL TRAMPLE OVER THE
HOLY CITY FOR FORTY-TWO MONTHS. (3) I WILL NOW EN-
TRUST MY WORD TO MY TWO WITNESSES TO PROCLAIM IT FOR
ONE THOUSAND TWO HUNDRED AND SIXTY DAYS, DRESSED IN
SACKCLOTH." (4) THESE ARE

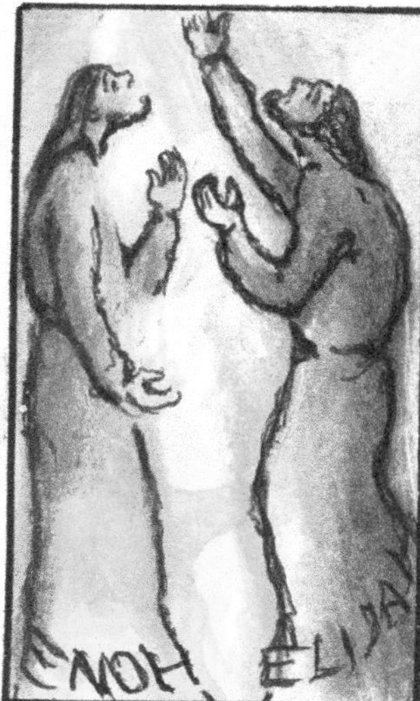

THE TWO OLIVE TREES AND
THE TWO LAMPS WHICH ARE
BEFORE THE LORD OF THE
EARTH. (5) IF ANYONE INT-
ENDS TO HARM THEM, FIRE
WILL EXIT THEIR MOUTHS
TO DEVOUR THEIR ENEMI-
ES: THIS IS HOW WHOEVER
INTENDS TO HARM THEM WILL
PERISH. (6) THEY HAVE THE
POWER TO CLOSE THE SKY
AND HOLD BACK THE RAIN
DURING THE TIME OF THEIR
PROPHETIC MISSION; THEY
ALSO HAVE THE POWER TO
CHANGE WATER INTO BLOOD
AND PUNISH THE EARTH WITH
A THOUSAND PLAGUES, ANY
TIME THEY WISH. (7) BUT
WHEN MY WITNESSES HA-
VE FULFILLED THEIR MIS-
SION, THE BEAST COMING UP
FROM THE ABYSS WILL MAKE
WAR UPON THEM, AND WILL
CONQUER AND KILL THEM.
(8) THEIR DEAD BODIES
WILL LIE IN THE SQUARE OF THE GREAT CITY WHICH THE
BELIEVERS CALL SODOM OR EGYPT, WHERE THEIR
LORD WAS CRUCIFIED. (9) AND THEIR DEAD BODIES
WILL BE EXPOSED FOR THREE DAYS AND A HALF TO PEOPLE
OF ALL TRIBES, RACES, LANGUAGES AND NATIONS WHO
WILL BE ORDERED NOT TO HAVE THEM BURIED. (10) THEN
THE INHABITANTS OF THE EARTH WILL REJOICE, CONGRA-
TULATE ONE ANOTHER, AND EXCHANGE GIFTS BECAUSE
THESE TWO PROPHETS WERE A TORMENT TO THEM. (11)
BUT AFTER THOSE THREE AND A HALF DAYS, A SPIRIT OF
LIFE COMING FROM GOD ENTERED THEM. THEY STOOD UP,
AND THOSE WHO LOOKED AT THEM WERE SEIZED WITH
GREAT FEAR. (12) A LOUD VOICE FROM HEAVEN CALLED

THEM, "COME UP HERE." SO THEY WENT UP TO HE-
AVEN IN THE MIDST OF THE CLOUDS IN THE SIGHT OF
THEIR ENEMIES. (13) AT THAT MOMENT, THERE WAS A
VIOLENT EARTHQUAKE WHICH DESTROYED A TENTH
OF THE CITY AND CLAIMED SEVEN THOUSAND VIC-
TIMS. THE REST WERE OVERCOME WITH FEAR,
AND ACKNOWLEDGED THE GOD OF HEAVEN. (14) THE
SECOND WOE HAS PASSED. THE THIRD IS COMING.

◆ (15) THE SEVENTH ANGEL BLEW HIS TRUMPET,
THEN LOUD VOICES RESOUNDED IN HEAVEN: "THE
WORLD HAS NOW BECOME THE KINGDOM OF OUR GOD
AND OF HIS CHRIST. HE WILL REIGN FOR EVER AND EVER."

(16) THE TWENTY-FOUR ELDERS WHO SIT ON THEIR
THRONES BEFORE GOD BOWED DOWN TO WORSHIP
GOD, (17) SAYING,

WE THANK YOU, LORD GOD, MASTER OF THE UNIVERSE,
WHO ARE AND WHO WERE, FOR YOU HAVE BEGUN YOUR
REIGN, MAKING USE OF YOUR INVINCIBLE POWER. (18)
THE NATIONS RAGED BUT YOUR WRATH HAS COME, THE
TIME TO JUDGE THE DEAD AND REWARD YOUR SER-
VANTS THE PROPHETS, THE SAINTS AND THOSE WHO
HONOR YOUR NAME, WHETHER GREAT OR SMALL, AND
DESTROY THOSE WHO DESTROY THE EARTH. (19)

THEN THE SANCTUARY OF GOD IN THE HEAVENS WAS
OPENED, AND THE ARK OF THE COVENANT OF GOD COULD
BE SEEN INSIDE THE SANCTUARY. THERE WERE FLASHES
OF LIGHTNING, PEALS OF THUNDER, AN EARTHQU-
AKE AND A VIOLENT HAILSTORM.

THE WOMAN AND THE DRAGON

12 (1) A GREAT SIGN APPEARED IN HEAVEN; A WOMAN,
CLOTHED WITH THE SUN, WITH THE MOON UNDER
HER FEET AND A CROWN OF TWELVE STARS ON HER
HEAD. (2) SHE WAS PREGNANT AND CRIED OUT IN PAIN,

LOOKING FOR HER TIME
OF DELIVERY. (3) THEN AN-
OTHER SIGN APPEARED: A
HUGE, RED DRAGON WITH
SEVEN HEADS AND TEN
HORNS AND WEARING SE-
VEN CROWNS ON ITS HE-
ADS. (4) IT HAD JUST
SWEPT ALONG A THIRD
OF THE STARS OF HEAVEN
WITH ITS TAIL, THROWING
THEM DOWN TO EARTH. THE
DRAGON STOOD IN FRONT OF
THE WOMAN WHO WAS AB-
OUT TO GIVE BIRTH SO THAT
IT MIGHT DEVOUR THE CHILD
AS SOON AS IT WAS BORN.
(5) SHE GAVE BIRTH TO A
BOY, HE WHO IS TO RULE
ALL THE NATIONS WITH AN
IRON SCEPTER; THEN HER
CHILD WAS TAKEN UP TO
GOD AND TO HIS THRONE (6)
WHILE THE WOMAN FLED TO
THE DESERT WHERE GOD
HAD A PLACE FOR HER AND
SHE WOULD BE LOOKED AF-
TER FOR ONE THOUSAND
TWO HUNDRED AND SIXTY DAYS. (7) WAR BROKE OUT IN HE-
AVEN WITH MICHAEL AND HIS ANGELS BATTLING WITH THE DRA-
GON WHO FOUGHT BACK WITH HIS ANGELS, (8) BUT THEY WE-
RE DEFEATED AND LOST THEIR PLACE IN HEAVEN. (9) THE
GREAT DRAGON, THE ANCIENT SERPENT KNOWN AS THE DE-
VIL OR SATAN, SEDUCER OF THE WHOLE WORLD, WAS
THROWN OUT. HE WAS HURLED DOWN TO EARTH,
TOGETHER WITH HIS ANGELS.

10 THEN I HEARD A LOUD VOICE FROM HEAVEN: NOW
HAS SALVATION COME, WITH THE POWER AND THE KING-
DOM OF OUR GOD, AND THE RULE OF HIS ANOINTED. FOR
OUR BROTHER'S ACCUSER HAS BEEN CAST OUT, WHO
ACCUSED THEM NIGHT AND DAY, BEFORE GOD! 11
THEY CONQUERED HIM BY THE BLOOD OF THE LAMB
AND BY THE WORD OF THEIR TESTIMONY, FOR THEY
GAVE UP THEIR LIVES GOING TO DEATH.
12 REJOICE, THEREFORE, O YOU HEAVENS AND
YOU WHO DWELL IN
THEM; BUT WOE TO YOU,
EARTH AND SEA, FOR THE
DEVIL HAS COME TO YOU
IN ANGER KNOWING THAT
HE HAS BUT A LITTLE
TIME.
13 WHEN THE DRAGON
SAW THAT HE HAD BEEN
THROWN DOWN TO THE
EARTH, HE PURSUED THE
WOMAN WHO HAD BEEN
GIVEN BIRTH TO THE
MALE CHILD. 14 THEN
THE WOMAN WAS GIVEN
THE TWO WINGS OF THE
GREAT EAGLE SO THAT
SHE MIGHT FLY INTO
THE DESERT WHERE SHE
WOULD BE LOOKED AFTER
FOR THREE AND A HALF
YEARS. 15 THE SERPENT
POURED WATER OUT ON
HIS MOUTH AFTER THE
WOMAN, TO CARRY HER
AWAY IN THE FLOOD. 16
BUT THE EARTH CAME TO
HER RESCUE; IT OPENED
ITS MOUTH AND SWALLO-
WED THE FLOOD WHICH THE DRAGON HAD POURED
FROM ITS MOUTH. 17 THEN THE DRAGON WAS FURI-
OUS WITH THE WOMAN AND WENT OFF TO WAGE WAR ON
THE REST OF HER CHILDREN, THOSE WHO KEEP GOD'S
COMMANDMENTS AND BEAR WITNESS TO JESUS.
18 AND HE STOOD ON THE SEASHORE.

THE BEAST AND THE FALSE PROPHET

13 1 THEN, I SAW A BEAST RISING OUT OF THE SEA,
WITH TEN HORNES AND SEVEN HEADS, WITH TEN CRO-
WNS ON ITS HORNS. ON EACH HEAD WAS A BLASPHE-
MOUS TITLE CHALLENGING GOD. 2 THE BEAST I SAW

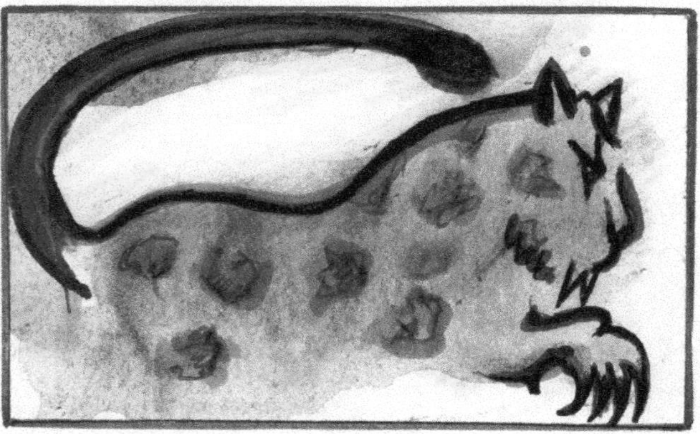

LOOKED LIKE A LEOPARD, WITH PAWS LIKE A BEAR AND A
MOUTH LIKE A LION. THE DRAGON PASSED ON HIS POWER,
HIS THRONE AND HIS GREAT AUTHORITY TO THE BEAST.
3 ONE OF ITS HEADS SEEMED TO BE FATALLY WOUNDED
BUT THIS WOUND HEALED. THE WHOLE EARTH WONDER-
ED AND THEY FOLLOWED THE BEAST. 4 PEOPLE PROS-
TRATED THEMSELVES BEFORE THE DRAGON WHO
HAD GIVEN SUCH AUTHORITY TO THE BEAST AND
THEY PROSTRATED THEMSELVES BEFORE THE BE-
AST, SAYING, "WHO IS LIKE THE BEAST? WHO CAN
OPPOSE IT?" 5 THE BEAST WAS GIVEN SPEECH AND IT
SPOKE BOASTFUL AND BLASPHEMOUS WORDS AGAINST GOD;
IT WAS ALLOWED TO WIELD ITS POWER FOR FORTY-TWO MONTHS.

6 IT SPOKE BLASPHEMIES AGAINST GOD, HIS NAME AND
HIS SANCTUARY, THAT IS, THOSE WHO ALREADY DWELL IN
HEAVEN. 7 IT WAS ALLOWED TO MAKE WAR ON THE
SAINTS AND TO CONQUER THEM. IT WAS GIVEN AUTHO-
RITY OVER PEOPLE OF EVERY TRIBE, LANGUAGE AND
NATION; 8 THIS IS WHY ALL THE INHABITANTS OF
THE EARTH WILL WORSHIP BEFORE IT, THOSE WHOSE
NAMES HAVE NOT BEEN WRITTEN IN THE BOOK OF
LIFE OF THE SLAIN LAMB, SINCE THE FOUNDATION
OF THE WORLD.
9 IF ANYONE HAS EARS TO HEAR, LET HIM LISTEN: 10

IF YOUR LOT IS THE PRISON, TO PRISON YOU WILL GO; IF YOUR
LOT IS TO BE KILLED BY THE SWORD, BY THE SWORD WILL
YOU BE SLAIN. THIS IS, FOR THE SAINTS, THE TIME OF ENDU-
RANCE AND FAITH. 11 THEN I SAW ANOTHER BEAST
RISE OUT OF THE EARTH, WITH TWO HORNS LIKE THE LAMB
BUT SPEAKING LIKE THE DRAGON. 12 THE SECOND BE-
AST IS TOTALLY AT THE SERVICE OF THE FIRST ONE AND
ENJOYS ITS AUTHORITY. SO IT MAKES THE WORLD AND ITS
INHABITANTS WORSHIP THE FIRST BEAST WHOSE FATAL
WOUND HAS BEEN HEELED. 13 IT WORKS GREAT
WONDERS, EVEN MAK-
ING FIRE DESCEND
FROM HEAVEN TO
EARTH, IN THE SIGHT
OF ALL. 14 THROUGH
THESE GREAT WON-
DERS WHICH IT'S ABLE
TO DO ON BEHALF OF THE
BEAST, IT DECEIVES THE
INHABITANTS OF THE
EARTH, PERSUADING
THEM TO MAKE A STA-
TUE OF THE BEAST WHICH,
ALTHOUGH WOUNDED
BY THE SWORD, IS STILL
ALIVE. 15 IT HAS BE-
EN ALLOWED TO GIVE
A SPIRIT TO THIS STA-
TUE: THE STATUE OF
THE BEAST SPEAKS
AND THOSE WHO REFU-
SE TO WORSHIP IT ARE
KILLED. 16 SO THIS
SECOND BEAST MA-
KES EVERYONE, GREAT
AND SMALL, RICH
AND POOR, FREE
AND ENSLAVED, BE
BRANDED ON THE

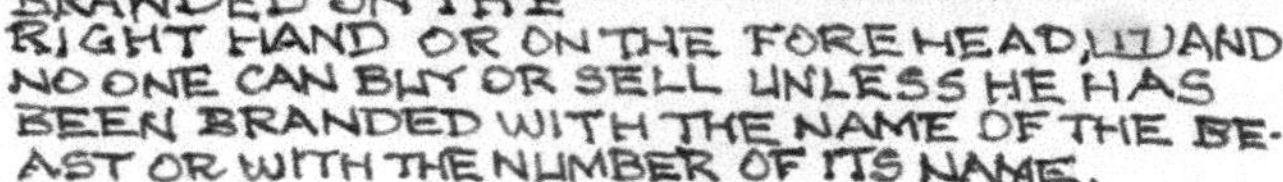

RIGHT HAND OR ON THE FOREHEAD. 17 AND
NO ONE CAN BUY OR SELL UNLESS HE HAS
BEEN BRANDED WITH THE NAME OF THE BE-
AST OR WITH THE NUMBER OF ITS NAME.

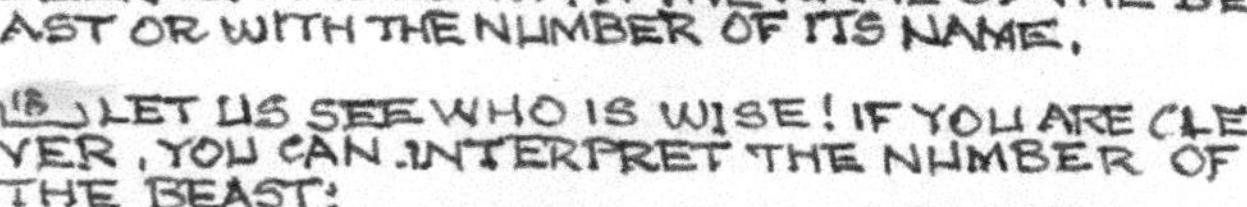

18 LET US SEE WHO IS WISE! IF YOU ARE CLE-
VER, YOU CAN INTERPRET THE NUMBER OF
THE BEAST:
IT IS A HUMAN NUMBER. THE NUMBER 666.

A GREAT SIGN
APPEARED IN
HEAVEN : A WOMAN,
CLOTHED WITH THE
SUN, WITH THE MOON
UNDER HER FEET
AND A CROWN OF
TWELVE STARS ON
HER HEAD (REV. 12-1)
A16 - CCCCXVI -
© DM 09

144,000 ON MOUNT ZION

14 1 I WAS GIVEN ANOTHER VISION: THE LAMB
WAS STANDING ON MOUNT ZION, SURROUNDED BY
ONE HUNDRED AND FORTY-FOUR THOUSAND PEOPLE
WHO HAD HIS NAME AND HIS FATHER'S NAME WRITTEN
ON THEIR FOREHEADS. 2 A SOUND REVERBERATED IN
HEAVEN LIKE THE SOUND OF THE ROARING OF WAVES OR DE-
AFENING THUNDER; IT WAS LIKE A CHORUS OF SINGERS,
ACCOMPANIED BY THEIR HARPS. 3 THEY SING A NEW
SONG BEFORE THE THRONE, WITH THE FOUR LIVING CRE-
ATURES AND THE ELDERS, A SONG WHICH NO ONE CAN

LEARN EXCEPT THE 144,000 WHO HAVE BEEN TAKEN
FROM THE EARTH. 4 THEY ARE THOSE WHO WERE
NOT DEFILED WITH WOMEN BUT WERE CHASTE; THESE
ARE GIVEN TO FOLLOW THE LAMB WHEREVER HE GO-
ES. THEY ARE THE FIRST TAKEN FROM HUMANKIND
WHO ARE ALREADY OF GOD AND THE LAMB. 5 NO
DECEIT HAS BEEN FOUND IN THEM; THEY ARE FA-
ULTLESS. 6 THEN I SAW ANOTHER ANGEL FLYING HIGH
IN THE SKY, SENT TO PROCLAIM THE DEFINITIVE GOOD
NEWS TO THE INHABITANTS OF THE EARTH, TO EVERY
NATION, RACE, LANGUAGE AND PEOPLE. 7 HE CRIED OUT
WITH A LOUD VOICE,

"GIVE GOD GLORY AND
HONOR, FOR THE HOUR
OF HIS JUDGMENT HAS
COME. WORSHIP HIM WHO
MADE THE HEAVENS, THE
EARTH, THE SEA AND
ALL THE WATERS" 8
ANOTHER ANGEL FOL-
LOWED HIM, CRYING OUT,
"FALLEN IS BABYLON
THE GREAT, FALLEN THE
PROSTITUTE WHO HAS
MADE ALL THE NATIONS
DRUNK WITH HER UNLE-
ASHED PROSTITUTION!"
9 A THIRD ANGEL THEN
FOLLOWED, SHOUTING AL-
OUD, "IF ANYONE WOR-
SHIPS THE BEAST OR ITS
IMAGE OR HAS HIS FORE-
HEAD OR HAND BRANDED,
10 HE WILL DRINK THE
WINE OF GOD'S ANGER
WHICH HAS BEEN PRE-
PARED, UNDILUTED, IN
THE CUP OF HIS FURY:
HE WILL BE TORTURED BY FIRE AND BRIMSTONE,
IN THE PRESENCE OF THE HOLY ANGELS AND THE
LAMB." 11 THE SMOKE OF THEIR TORMENT GOES UP
FOR EVER AND EVER; THERE WILL BE NO REST, DAY OR
NIGHT, FOR THOSE WHO WORSHIPED THE BEAST AND
ITS IMAGE, AND FOR THOSE WHO WERE BRANDED
WITH THE MARK OF ITS NAME.

12 THIS IS THE TIME FOR PATIENT ENDURANCE FOR
THE SAINTS, FOR THOSE WHO KEEP THE COMMAND-
MENTS OF GOD AND FAITH IN JESUS.

13 I HEARD SOMEONE FROM HEAVEN SAY,
"WRITE THIS: HAPPY FROM NOW ARE THE DEAD
WHO HAVE DIED IN THE LORD. THE SPIRIT SAYS:
LET THEM REST FROM THEIR LABORS; THEIR GO-
OD DEEDS GO WITH THEM."

14 THEN I HAD THIS VISION: I SAW A WHITE CLOUD
AND THE ONE SITTING ON IT LIKE A SON OF MAN,
WEARING A GOLDEN CROWN ON HIS HEAD AND A
SHARP SICKLE IN HIS HAND. 15 AN ANGEL
CAME OUT OF THE SANCTUARY, CALLING LOUDLY
TO THE ONE SITTING
ON THE CLOUD, "PUT
IN YOUR SICKLE AND
REAP, FOR HARVEST
TIME HAS COME AND
THE HARVEST OF THE
EARTH IS RIPE." 16
HE WHO WAS SITTING
ON THE CLOUD SWUNG
HIS SICKLE AT THE
EARTH AND REAPED
THE HARVEST. THEN
17 ANOTHER ANGEL,
WHO ALSO HAD A SHARP
SICKLE, CAME OUT OF THE
HEAVENLY SANCTUARY.
18 STILL ANOTHER AN-
GEL, THE ONE WHO HAS
CHARGE OF THE ALTAR
FIRE, EMERGED AND
SHOUTED TO THE
FIRST WHO HELD THE
SHARP SICKLE,
"SWING YOUR SHARP
SICKLE AND REAP
THE BUNCHES OF THE
VINE OF THE EARTH FOR

THEY ARE FULLY RIPE." 19 SO THE ANGEL DID
SWING HIS SICKLE AND GATHERED IN THE VINT-
AGE, THROWING ALL THE GRAPES INTO THE GREAT
WINEPRESS OF THE ANGER OF GOD. 20 THE GRA-
PES WERE TRODDEN OUTSIDE THE CITY AND
BLOOD FLOWED FROM THE WINEPRESS, TO THE
HEIGHT OF THE HORSES' BRIDLES AND OVER AN
AREA OF SIXTEEN HUNDRED FURLONGS.

15 1 THEN I SAW ANOTHER GREAT AND MARVE-
LOUS SIGN IN THE HEAVENS: SEVEN ANGELS
BROUGHT SEVEN PLAGUES WHICH ARE THE
LAST, FOR WITH THESE THE WRATH OF GOD WILL END.

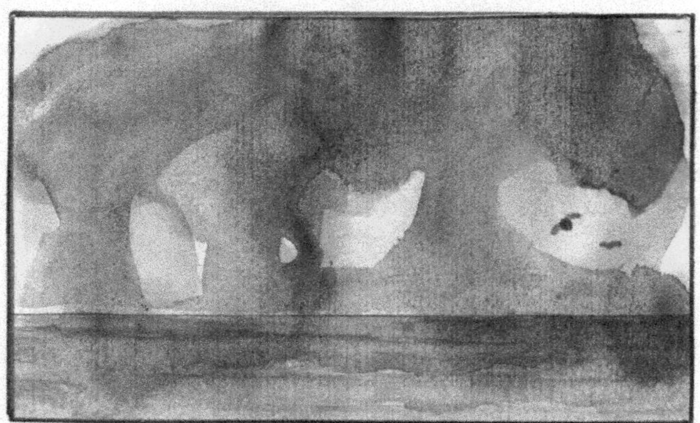

2 THERE WAS A SEA OF CRYSTAL MINGLED WITH
FIRE, AND THE CONQUERORS OF THE BEAST, OF ITS NAME
AND THE MARK OF ITS NAME STOOD BY IT. THE HAD BE-
EN GIVEN THE CELESTIAL HARPS 3 AND THEY SANG
THE SONG OF MOSES THE SERVANT OF GOD AND THE
SONG OF THE LAMB:

GREAT AND MARVELOUS ARE YOUR WORKS,
O LORD GOD, AND MASTER OF THE UNIVERSE,
JUSTICE AND TRUTH GUIDE YOUR STEPS,
O KING OF THE NATIONS.

(4) LORD, WHO WILL NOT GIVEN HONOR AND
GLORY TO YOUR NAME? FOR YOU ALONE ARE
HOLY. ALL THE NATIONS WILL COME AND
BOW BEFORE YOU, FOR THEY HAVE NOW
SEEN YOUR JUDGMENTS.

THE SEVEN CUPS

(5) THEN THE SANCTUARY OF THE TENT OF DIVINE DECLA-
RATION WAS OPENED, (6) AND THE SEVEN ANGELS
BRINGING THE SEVEN PLAGUES CAME OUT OF THE
SANCTUARY, CLOTHED IN PURE AND BRIGHT LINEN, WITH
THEIR WAISTS GIRDED WITH GOLDEN BELTS. (7) ONE OF THE
FOUR LIVING CREATURES GAVE THE SEVEN ANGELS SEVEN

GOLDEN CUPS WITH GOD'S WRATH, GOD FOR EVER AND
EVER. (8) THEN SMOKE FILLED THE SANCTUARY OF GOD'S
GLORY AND POWER, AND NO ONE COULD ENTER UNTIL THE
SEVEN PLAGUES OF THE SEVEN ANGELS WERE COMPLETED.

16 (1) I HEARD A LOUD VOICE CALLING FROM THE SANC-
TUARY TO THE SEVEN ANGELS, "GO AND EMPTY ON
THE EARTH THE SEVEN CUPS OF GOD'S WRATH."
(2) THE FIRST ANGEL EMPTIED HIS CUP ON THE EARTH
AND MALIGNANT AND PAINFUL SORES APPEARED ON THOSE
WITH THE BEAST'S MARK AND HAD BOWED BEFORE ITS
IMAGE. (3) THE SECOND ANGEL EMPTIED HIS CUP INTO THE

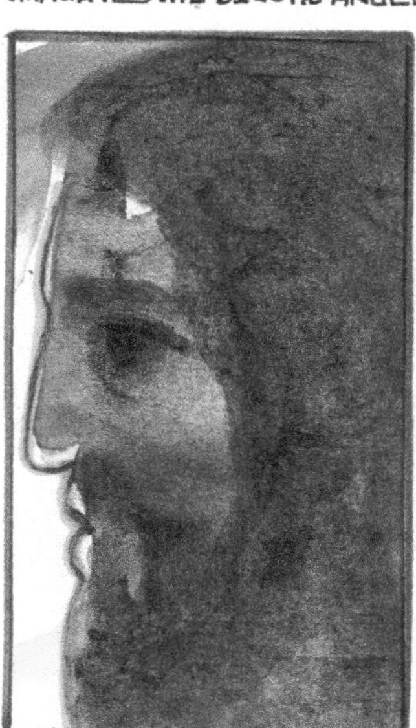

SEA WHICH TURNED INTO
BLOOD LIKE THAT OF THE
DEAD, AND EVERY LIVING
THING IN THE SEA DIED.
(4) THE THIRD ANGEL EMP-
TIED HIS CUP INTO THE RI-
VERS AND SPRINGS WHICH
TURNED INTO BLOOD. (5)
AND I HEARD THE ANGEL OF
THE WATERS SAY, "YOU WHO
ARE AND WHO WERE, O HOLY
ONE, YOU ARE JUST IN PU-
NISHING THEM IN THIS
WAY; (6) AS THEY HAVE SHED
THE BLOOD OF YOUR HOLY
ONES AND THE PROPHETS,
YOU HAVE MADE THEM
DRINK BLOOD; THEY
RIGHTLY DESERVED IT."
(7) I HEARD ANOTHER
CRY FROM THE ALTAR,
"YES, LORD AND GOD, MAS-
TER OF THE UNIVERSE, YO-
UR JUDGMENTS ARE
TRUE AND JUST." (8)
THE FOURTH ANGEL POURED
OUT HIS CUP ON THE SUN
AND ITS HEAT BEGAN TO
SCORCH PEOPLE. THEY
(9) WERE SEVERELY BUR-
NED AND BEGAN TO INSULT GOD WHO HAS POWER ON
THOSE PLAGUES, INSTEAD OF ACKNOWLEDGING HIM.
(10) THE FIFTH ANGEL EMPTIED HIS CUP ON THE THRONE
OF THE BEAST, AND SUDDENLY HIS KINGDOM WAS IN DARK-
NESS AND THE PEOPLE BIT THEIR TONGUES IN AGONY.
(11) THEY INSULTED THE MOST HIGH GOD FOR THEIR
PAIN AND WOUNDS, BUT THEY DID NOT REPENT.
(12) THE SIXTH ANGEL POURED OUT HIS CUP ON THE
GREAT RIVER EUPHRATES; ITS WATER WAS DRIED UP,
LEAVING A FREE PASSAGEWAY FOR THE KINGS OF THE EAST.

(13) I SAW COMING FROM THE MOUTHS OF THE
MONSTER, THE BEAST AND THE FALSE PROPHET,
THREE UNCLEAN SPIRITS WHICH LOOKED LIKE
FROGS. (14) THEY ARE, IN FACT, SPIRITS OF DEMONS
THAT PERFORM MARVELOUS THINGS AND GO TO
THE KINGS OF THE WHOLE WORLD TO GATHER
THEM FOR BATTLE ON THE GREAT DAY OF GOD,
THE MASTER OF THE UNIVERSE. (15) "BEWARE! I CO-
ME LIKE A THIEF; HAPPY IS THE ONE WHO STAYS AWAKE
AND DOESN'T TAKE OFF HIS CLOTHES; HE WILL NOT HA-
VE TO GO NAKED AND HIS BODY BE EXPOSED FOR ALL TO SEE."
(16) THEY ASSEMBLED AT
A PLACE CALLED ARMAG-
EDDON IN HEBREW (OR
THE HILLS OF MEGIDDO). (17)
THE SEVENTH ANGEL EMP-
TIED HIS CUP INTO THE
AIR. A VOICE CAME FORTH
FROM THE THRONE AND
WAS HEARD OUTSIDE THE
SANCTUARY SAYING, "IT
IS DONE." (18) AND THERE
WERE FLASHES OF LIGHT-
NING, PEALS OF THUNDER
AND A VIOLENT EARTH-
QUAKE. NO, NEVER HAS
THERE BEEN AN EARTH-
QUAKE SO VIOLENT SINCE
PEOPLE EXISTED. (19) THE
GREAT CITY WAS SPLIT
INTO THREE, WHILE
THE CITIES OF THE
NATIONS COLLAPSED.
FOR THE TIME HAD CO-
ME FOR BABYLON THE
GREAT TO BE REMEM-
BERED BEFORE GOD AND
TO BE GIVEN THE CUP
OF THE FOAMING WINE

OF HIS ANGER. (20) THEN THE CONTINENTS WITHDREW
AND THE MOUNTAIN RANGES HID. (21) GREAT HAIL-
STONES FROM HEAVEN, HEAVY AS STONES, DROPPED ON
THE PEOPLE WHO INSULTED GOD BECAUSE OF THIS DISA-
STROUS HAILSTORM, FOR IT WAS A TERRIBLE PLAGUE.

THE JUDGMENT OF BABYLON

17 (1) THEN ONE OF THE SEVEN ANGELS OF THE
SEVEN CUPS CAME TO ME AND SAID, "NOW I WILL
SHOW YOU THE JUDGMENT OF THE SOVEREIGN
PROSTITUTE WHO DWELLS ON THE GREAT WATERS.
(2) SHE IT IS WHO LET THE KINGS OF THE EARTH SIN
WITH HER; WITH THE WINE OF HER IDOLATRY THE PEOPLE

OF THE EARTH HAVE BECOME DRUNK." (3) THE ANGEL TO-
OK ME TO THE DESERT: IT WAS A NEW VISION. A WOMAN
WAS SEATED ON A RED BEAST. THE BEAST, WHICH
HAD SEVEN HEADS AND TEN HORNS, COVERED
ITSELF WITH TITLES AND STATEMENTS THAT OF-
FEND GOD. (4) THE WOMAN WAS CLOTHED IN PUR-
PLE AND SCARLET, WITH ORNAMENTS OF GOLD,
PRECIOUS STONES AND PEARLS. SHE HELD IN
HER HANDS A GOLDEN CUP FULL OF LOATHSOME
IDOLATRY AND IMPURE PROSTITUTION.

5 HER NAME COULD BE READ - IN A MYSTERIOUS WAY -
ON HER FOREHEAD: BABYLON THE GREAT, MOTHER OF PROSTI-
TUTES AND OF THE LOATHSOME IDOLS OF THE WORLD. 6 AND
I SAW THE WOMAN DRUNK WITH THE BLOOD OF THE HOLY
ONES AND THE MARTYRS OF JESUS. WHAT I SAW GREATLY
SURPRISED ME, 7 BUT THE ANGEL SAID TO ME, "WHY
ARE YOU SURPRISED? I WILL REVEAL TO YOU THIS WOMAN'S
SECRET AND OF THE BEAST WITH SEVEN HEADS AND TEN
HORNS THAT SHE MOUNTS. 8 THE BEAST YOU SAW HAS
BEEN, THOUGH IT IS NOT. IT WILL COME UP FROM THE

ABYSS AND THEN GO TO PERDITION. WHAT A SURPRISE
FOR THE INHABITANTS OF THE EARTH WHOSE NAMES ARE
NOT WRITTEN IN THE BOOK OF LIFE FROM THE CREATION
OF THE WORLD! THEY WILL MARVEL ON DISCOVERING THAT
THE BEAST WHO HAS BEEN IS NOT AND PASSES AWAY. 9
LET US SEE IF YOU GUESS: THE SEVEN HEADS ARE SEVEN
HILLS ON WHICH THE WOMAN SITS. AND THEY ARE ALSO SE-
VEN KINGS, 10 FIVE OF WHICH HAVE FALLEN, ONE IS IN PO-
WER, AND THE SEVENTH HAS NOT YET COME BUT WILL RE-
MAIN ONLY A SHORT WHILE.
11 THE BEAST THAT HAS BEEN BUT IS NOT CAN BE
CONSIDERED AS THE EIGHTH THOUGH IT TAKES PLA-
CE AMONG THE SEVEN;
AND HE GOES TO PERDITI-
ON. 12 THE TEN HORNS
ARE TEN KINGS WHO HA-
VE NOT YET RECEIVED PO-
WER BUT WILL HAVE AU-
THORITY FOR AN HOUR
WITH THE BEAST. 13 THEY
ALL HAVE ONE AIM AND
THEY PLACE AUTHORITY
AND POWER AT THE SER-
VICE OF THE BEAST. THEY
14 WILL FIGHT AGAINST
THE LAMB, BUT THE LAMB
WILL CONQUER THEM,
FOR HE IS LORD OF LORDS
AND KING OF KINGS; AND
WITH HIM WILL BE HIS
FOLLOWERS WHO HAVE
BEEN CALLED AND CHO-
SEN AND ARE FAITHFUL.
15 THE ANGEL WENT
ON, "THOSE WATERS ARE
THE ONES YOU SAW ON
WHICH THE PROSTITUTE
IS SEATED, ARE PEOPLES,
MULTITUDE AND NATIONS
OF EVERY LANGUAGE. 16
THE TEN HORNS AND THE
BEAST WILL PLAN EVIL

AGAINST THE PROSTITUTE. THEY WILL DESTROY HER
AND LEAVE HER NAKED; THEY WILL EAT HER FLESH
AND SET HER ON FIRE.
17 GOD MAKES USE OF THEM TO CARRY OUT HIS
PLAN, SO HE HAS INSPIRED THEM WITH THEIR
COMMON PURPOSE AND THEY WILL PLACE THEIR
POWER AT THE SERVICE OF THE BEAST UNTIL
THE WORDS OF GOD ARE FULFILLED.

A LAST WORD: 18 THE WOMAN YOU SAW IS THE
GREAT CITY WHICH REIGNS OVER THE KINGS
OF THE WHOLE WORLD."

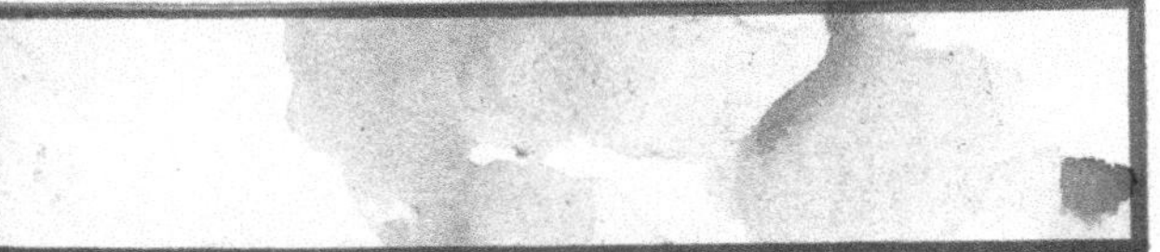

FALLEN IS BABYLON THE GREAT!!

1 AFTER THIS I SAW ANOTHER ANGEL COMING
DOWN FROM HEAVEN.
SO GREAT WAS HIS AUTHORITY THAT THE WHOLE
EARTH WAS LIT UP WITH HIS GLORY.
2 IN A STRONG VOICE HE CRIED OUT:

18 "FALLEN IS BABYLON THE GREAT! FAL-
LEN. SHE HAS
BECOME A
HAUNT OF DE-
MONS, A LODGE
FOR EVERY
UNCLEAN SPI-
RIT, A NEST FOR
ANY FILTHY AND
DISGUSTING
BIRD. 3 SHE
HAS MADE ALL
NATIONS DRUNK
WITH THE WINE
OF HER LEWD-
NESS. FORNICA-
TED WITH KINGS
OF THE EARTH,
AND GLUTTED
THE WORLD'S
MERCHANTS
WITH HER WANT-
ONNESS AND
WEALTH."
4 THEN I HEARD
ANOTHER VO-
ICE FROM HEAVEN:
DEPART FROM
HER, MY PEOPLE,

LEST YOU SHARE IN HER EVIL AND
SO SHARE IN HER PUNISHMENTS;
5 FOR HER SINS ARE PILED UP TO
HEAVEN, AND GOD KEEPS COUNT
OF HER CRIMES. 6 GIVE BACK TO
HER AS SHE HAS GIVEN, PAY HER
TWICE FOR WHAT SHE HAS DONE.
LET HER DRINK A DOUBLE PORTION
OF WHAT SHE MADE OTHERS DO.

7 GIVE HER AS MUCH TORMENT AND

GRIEF AS THE WANTONNESS SHE ENJO-
YED HERSELF. FOR SHE SAID TO HER-
SELF, 'I SIT AS QUEEN, I AM NOT A
WIDOW, NEVER WILL I GO INTO MO-
URNING!' 8 AND SO, SUDDENLY,
HER PLAGUES WILL COME, DEATH,
MOURING AND FAMINE.

SHE WILL BE CONSUMED BY FIRE,
FOR MIGHTY IS THE LORD, THE JUDGE,
WHO HAS PASSED SENTENCE ON HER."

THEN THE SANCTUARY WAS FILLED WITH SMOKE. (REV. 15:8)
419-CCCCXVII - DM09 ©

9 THE KINGS WHO SHARED HER LUXURY AND COM-
MITTED ADULTERY WITH HER WILL SEE THE SMOKE AS
SHE BURNS, AND THEY WILL WEEP AND LAMENT. THEY
WILL 10 KEEP THEIR DISTANCE, TERRIFIED AT HER PU-
NISHMENT, AND EXCLAIM:
"ALAS, ALAS! GREAT CITY THAT YOU ARE, O
BABYLON, SEAT OF POWER! YOUR DOOM HAS
COME IN A SINGLE HOUR!"
11 THE MERCHANTS OF THE WORLD WILL MOURN OVER
HER, FOR THEY WILL LOSE A MARKET FOR THEIR GO-
ODS. 12 THEIR CARGOES

OF GOLD AND SILVER, PRE-
CIOUS STONES AND PEARLS,
FINE LINEN AND PURPLE
GARMENTS, SILK AND
SCARLET CLOTH, FRA
GRANT WOOD, IVORY
PIECES AND EXPENSIVE
FURNITURE, BRONZE,
IRON AND MARBLE. 13
CINNAMON AND SPICES,
PERFUME, MYRRH AND
FRANKINCENSE, WINE
AND OLIVE OIL, FINE
FLOUR AND GRAIN, CAT-
TLE AND SHEEP, HOR-
SES AND CARRIAGES,
SLAVES AND HUMAN LI-
VES. 14 THEY WILL SAY:
"GONE IS THE FRUIT YOU
LONGED FOR, GONE ARE
YOUR LUXURY AND SPLEN-
DOR. NEVER WILL YOU RE-
COVER THEM, NEVER!" 15
THE MERCHANTS WHO
DEALT IN THESE GOODS
WHO GREW RICH FROM
BUSINESS WITH THE CITY,
WILL STAND AT A SAFE
DISTANCE FOR FEAR
OF HER PUNISHMENT. WEEPING AND MOURNING, 16
THEY WILL CRY OUT:
"WOE, WOE TO THE GREAT CITY, TO THE LINEN
AND PURPLE AND SCARLET YOU WORE, TO YO-
UR GOLD AND PEARLS, YOUR FINERY, 17 YO-
UR GREAT WEALTH DESTROYED IN AN HOUR!"

EVERY CAPTAIN AND NAVIGATOR, EVERY SAILOR
AND SEAFARER, WILL STAND AFAR 18 CRYING
OUT ON SEEING THE SMOKE GOING UP AS THE CI-
TY BURNS TO THE GROUND. "WHAT CITY COULD

HAVE COMPARED WITH THIS ONE?" 19 THEY WILL POUR
DUST ON THEIR HEADS AND CRY OUT IN MOURNING:
"ALAS, ALAS, GREAT CITY, WHERE ALL WHO
HAD SHIPS AT SEA GREW RICH WITH
HER TRADE! IN AN HOUR SHE HAS BE-
EN DEVASTATED." 20 REJOICE OVER
HER, O HEAVENS! REJOICE, PROPHETS,
SAINTS AND APOSTLES!! GOD HAS
RENDERED JUSTICE TO YOU.

21 A POWERFUL ANGEL PICKED UP A BOUL-
DER THE SIZE OF A LARGE MILLSTONE AND
THREW IT INTO THE SEA, SAYING: "WITH
SUCH VIOLENCE WILL BABYLON, THE GREAT CITY,
BE THROWN DOWN, NEVER AGAIN TO BE SEEN.

22 NEVER AGAIN WILL TUNES OF HARPISTS,
MINSTRELS, TRUMPETERS AND FLUTISTS BE
HEARD IN YOU. NEVER AGAIN WILL WORK-
MEN OF ANY TRADE BE FOUND IN YOU. NE-
VER AGAIN WILL THE NOISE OF THE MILL
BE HEARD. 23 NEVER AGAIN WILL THE
LIGHT OF A LAMP SHINE IN YOU. THE VO-
ICE OF BRIDEGROOM AND BRIDE WILL
NEVER AGAIN BE HEARD IN YOU.

BECAUSE YOUR TRADERS WERE THE WORLD'S
GREAT AND YOU LED THE NATIONS ASTRAY BY
YOUR MAGIC SPELL. 24 IN THIS CITY WAS FOUND
BLOOD OF PROPHETS AND SAINTS, YES-THE
BLOOD OF ALL WHO HAVE BEEN SLAIN ON THE EARTH."

SONGS IN HEAVEN

19 1 AFTER THIS I HEARD WHAT SOUNDED LIKE THE
LOUD SINGING OF A GREAT ASSEMBLY IN HEAVEN:
ALLELUIA! SALVATION, GLORY AND MIGHT BELONG TO
OUR GOD, 2 FOR HIS JUDGMENTS ARE TRUE AND JUST.
HE HAS CONDEMNED THE GREAT HARLOT WHO CORRUPTED
THE WORLD WITH HER ADULTERY. HE HAS AVENGED HIS
SERVANTS' BLOOD SHED BY HER HAND IN HARLOTRY. 3
ONCE MORE THEY SANG:
ALLELUIA! THE SMOKE
FROM HER GOES UP FOR
EVER AND EVER! 4
THE TWENTY-FOUR
ELDERS AND THE FOUR
LIVING CREATURES
FELL AND WORSHIPED GOD
SEATED ON THE THRONE AND
THEY CRIED: AMEN! ALLE-
LUIA! 5 A VOICE CAME
FROM THE THRONE: "PRA-
ISE YOUR GOD, ALL YOU
HIS SERVANTS, ALL YOU
WHO REVERE HIM, BOTH
SMALL AND GREAT!"
6 THEN I HEARD WHAT
SOUNDED LIKE A GRE
AT CROWD, LIKE THE
ROARING OF THE WA-
VES, LIKE PEALS OF THUN-
DER, ANSWERING: ALLE-
LUIA! THE LORD NOW RE-
IGNS, OUR LORD, THE MAS-
TER OF THE UNIVERSE! 7
LET US REJOICE AND GIVE
HIM GLORY! THIS IS THE TIME TO CELEBRATE THE WED-
DING OF THE LAMB, HIS BRIDE IS READY. 8 FINE LINEN,
BRIGHT AND CLEAN, IS GIVEN HER TO WEAR. THIS LI-
NEN STANDS FOR THE GOOD WORKS OF THE HOLY ONES.
9 THE ANGEL TOLD ME, "WRITE: HAPPY ARE THOSE IN-
VITED TO THE WEDDING OF THE LAMB." AND HE WENT
ON, "THESE ARE TRUE WORDS OF GOD."
10 AS I FELL DOWN AT HIS FEET TO WORSHIP HIM, HE
SAID TO ME, "BEWARE, I AM BUT A SERVANT LIKE YOU
AND YOUR BROTHERS WHO UTTER THE TESTIMONIES OF
JESUS (THESE TESTIMONIES OF JESUS ARE
PROCLAIMED THROUGH THE SPIRIT OF THE PRO-
PHETS). WORSHIP GOD ALONE."

THE TRIUMPH OF THE WORD OF GOD

11 THEN I SAW HEAVEN OPENED AND A WHITE HORSE
APPEARED. ITS RIDER IS THE 'FAITHFUL AND TRUE'. HE
JUDGES AND WAGES JUST WARS. 12 HIS EYES ARE
FLAMES OF FIRE; HE WEARS MANY CROWNS AND
WRITTEN ON HIM IS HIS OWN NAME, WHICH NO ONE

CAN UNDERSTAND EX-
CEPT HIMSELF. 13
HE IS CLOTHED IN
A CLOAK DRENCHED
IN BLOOD. HIS NAME
IS 'THE WORD OF GOD'.
14 THE ARMIES OF
HEAVEN CLOTHED
IN PURE WHITE LI-
NEN FOLLOW HIM ON
WHITE HORSES. 15
A SHARP SWORD
COMES OUT OF HIS
MOUTH. WITH IT HE
WILL STRIKE THE
NATIONS FOR HE
MUST 'RULE THEM
WITH AN IRON ROD'.
HE TREADS THE WI-
NEPRESS OF THE BUR-
NING WRATH OF GOD
THE MASTER OF THE
UNIVERSE. 16 THIS
IS WHY THIS TITLE
IS WRITTEN ON HIS
CLOAK AND ON HIS
THIGH: KING OF KINGS
AND LORD OF LORDS.

17 I ALSO SAW AN ANGEL STANDING IN THE
SUN. HE CRIED OUT WITH A LOUD VOICE TO
ALL THE BIRDS OF THE AIR, "COME HERE TO
THE GREAT FEAST OF GOD."

18 "COME AND EAT THE FLESH OF KINGS OF THE
EARTH, OF GENERALS AND VALIANT MEN: COME
AND DEVOUR THE SOLDIER AND HIS HORSE,
FREE MEN AND SLAVES, BOTH SMALL AND
GREAT."
19 THEN I SAW THE BEAST WITH THE KINGS

OF THE EARTH AND THEIR ARMIES GATHERED
TOGETHER TO FIGHT AGAINST HIM WHO RIDES
ON THE HORSE AND HIS ARMY.
20 BUT THE BEAST WAS CAPTURED WITH
THE FALSE PROPHET WHO SERVED IT AND
PERFORMED SIGNS BY WHICH HE DECEIVED
THOSE WHO HAD RECEIVED THE MARK OF
THE BEAST AND WORSHIPED ITS STATUE.

THE TWO WERE THROWN ALIVE INTO THE FIERY
LAKE OF BURNING SULFUR, AND ALL 21 THE REST
WERE KILLED BY THE SWORD WHICH COMES FROM
THE MOUTH OF THE RIDER WHO MOUNTS THE
HORSE. ALL THE BIRDS WERE FED WITH THEIR FLESH.

THE 1000 YEARS

20 1 THEN AN ANGEL CAME DOWN FROM HEAVEN,
HOLDING IN HIS HAND THE KEY TO THE
ABYSS AND THE HUGE CHAIN. 2 HE SE-
IZED THE MONSTER, THE ANCIENT SERPENT,

NAMELY SATAN OR THE DEVIL, AND CHAINED
HIM FOR A THOUSAND YEARS.
3 HE THREW HIM INTO THE ABYSS AND CLO-
SED ITS GATE WITH THE KEY, THEN SECUR-
ED IT WITH LOCKS, THAT HE MIGHT NOT DE-
CEIVE THE NATIONS IN THE FUTURE UNTIL
THE THOUSAND YEARS
HAVE PASSED. THEN
HE WILL BE RELEASED
FOR A LITTLE WHILE.
4 THERE WERE THRO-
NES AND SEATED ON
THEM WERE THOSE
WITH THE POWER TO
JUDGE. I THEN SAW THE
SPIRITS OF THOSE
WHO HAD BEEN BE-
HEADED FOR HAVING
HELD THE TEACHINGS
OF JESUS AND ON AC-
COUNT OF THE WORD
OF GOD. I SAW ALL
THOSE WHO HAD
REFUSED TO WOR-
SHIP THE BEAST
OR ITS IMAGE, OR
RECEIVE THEN ITS
MARK ON THE FORE-
HEAD OR ON THE
HAND.

THEY RETURNED TO LIFE AND REIGNED WITH
THE MESSIAH FOR A THOUSAND YEARS.

THIS IS THE FIRST RESURRECTION.

5 THE REST OF THE DEAD WILL NOT RETURN TO LI-
FE BEFORE THE END OF THE THOUSAND YEARS.

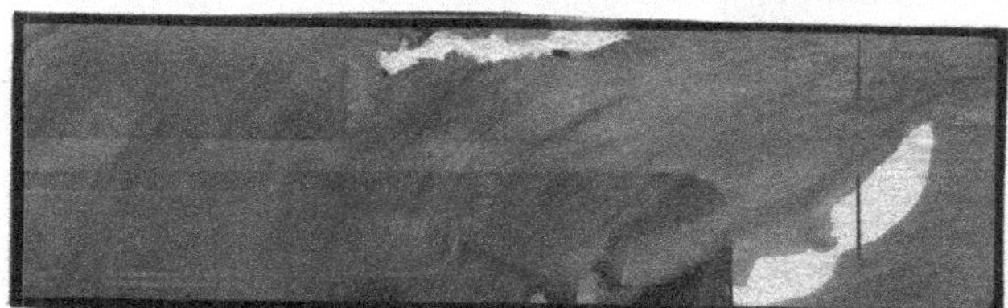

(6) HAPPY AND HOLY IS THE ONE WHO SHA-
RES IN THE FIRST RESURRECTION, FOR THE
SECOND DEATH HAS NO POWER OVER THEM;
THEY WILL BE PRIESTS OF GOD AND OF HIS
MESSIAH AND REIGN WITH HIM A THOUSAND
YEARS.
(7) AT THE END OF THESE THOUSAND YEARS, SA-
TAN WILL BE RELEASED FROM HIS PRISON;
(8) THEN HE WILL SET OUT TO DECEIVE THE
NATIONS OF THE FOUR CORNERS OF THE WORLD,

GOG and MAGOG ~ HOMAGE TO P. HERON

NAMELY GOG AND MAGOG, AND GATHER THEM FOR
WAR. WHAT AN ARMY, SO NUMEROUS LIKE THE
SAND OF THE SEASHORE! (9) THEY INVADED THE
LAND AND SURROUNDED THE CAMP OF THE HOLY
ONES, THE MOST BELOVED CITY, BUT FIRE
CAME DOWN FROM HEAVEN AND DEVOURED THEM.
(10) THEN THE DEVIL, THE SEDUCER, WAS THROWN
INTO THE LAKE OF FIRE AND SULFUR, WHERE
THE BEAST AND THE FALSE PROPHET ALREADY
WERE. THEIR TORMENT WILL LAST DAY AND
NIGHT FOR EVER AND EVER.

THE LAST JUDGMENT

(11) AFTER THAT I SAW A GREAT AND SPLENDID

THRONE AND THE ONE
SEATED UPON IT. AT
ONCE HEAVEN AND
EARTH DISAPPEARED,
LEAVING NO TRACE.
(12) I SAW THE DEAD
BOTH GREAT AND SMALL,
STANDING BEFORE
THE THRONE WHILE
BOOKS WERE OPENED.
ANOTHER BOOK, THE
BOOK OF LIFE, WAS AL-
SO OPENED. THEN
THE DEAD WERE JUD-
GED ACCORDING TO
THE RECORDS OF
THESE BOOKS, THAT
IS, EACH ONE ACCOR-
DING TO HIS WORKS.

(13) THE SEA GAVE UP
THE DEAD IT HAD
KEPT, AS DID DEATH
AND THE NETHER-
WORLD, SO THAT
EVERYONE MIGHT
BE JUDGED AC-
CORDING TO HIS
WORKS.
(14) THEN DEATH AND THE NETHERWORLD
WERE THROWN INTO THE LAKE OF FIRE.
THIS LAKE OF FIRE IS THE SECOND DE-
ATH. (15) ALL WHO WERE NOT RECORDED
IN THE BOOK OF LIFE WERE THROWN IN-
TO THE LAKE OF FIRE.

THE NEW HEAVEN AND THE NEW EARTH

21 THEN I SAW A NEW HEAVEN AND A NEW
EARTH. THE FIRST HEAVEN AND THE
FIRST EARTH AND PASSED AWAY AND
NO LONGER WAS THE
RE ANY SEA. (2) I
SAW THE NEW JERU-
SALEM, THE HOLY CI-
TY COMING DOWN
FROM GOD, OUT OF
HEAVEN, ADORNED
AS A BRIDE PREPARED
FOR HER HUSBAND.
(3) A LOUD VOICE
CAME FROM THE
THRONE, "HERE IS
THE DWELLING OF
GOD AMONG MEN:
HE WILL PITCH HIS
TENT AMONG THEM
AND THEY WILL BE
HIS PEOPLE. GOD
WILL BE WITH THEM
(4) AND WIPE EVERY
TEAR FROM THEIR
EYES. THERE SHALL
BE NO MORE DEATH
OR MOURNING, CRY-
ING OUT OR PAIN,
FOR THE WORLD THAT
WAS HAS PASSED
AWAY." (5) THE ONE SEATED ON THE THRONE
SAID, "SEE, I MAKE ALL THINGS NEW." THEN HE
SAID TO ME, "WRITE THESE WORDS BECAUSE
THEY ARE SURE AND TRUE: (6) IT IS ALREADY
DONE! I AM THE ALPHA AND THE OMEGA, THE BE-
GINNING AND THE END. I MYSELF WILL GIVE
THE THIRSTY TO DRINK WITHOUT COST FROM

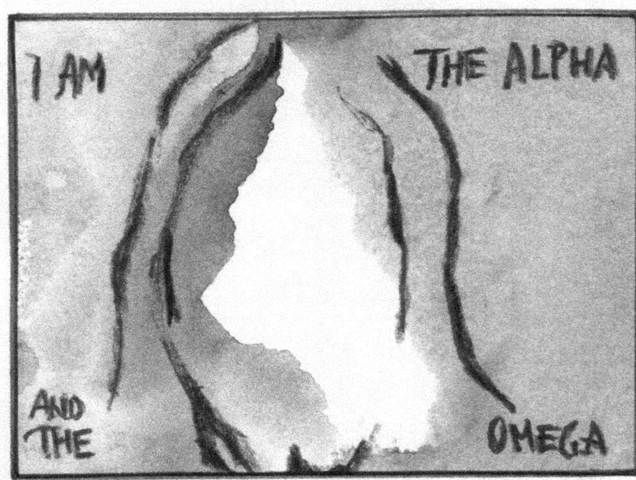

THE FOUNTAIN OF LIVING WATER. (7) THUS
THE WINNER WILL BE REWARDED: FOR HIM
I SHALL BE GOD AND HE WILL BE MY SON.

(8) AS FOR COWARDS, TRAITORS, DEPRAVED,
MURDERERS, ADULTERERS AND SORCERERS,
IDOLATORS AND LIARS, THEIR PLACE IS THE
LAKE OF BURNING SULFUR.

THIS IS THE SECOND DEATH"

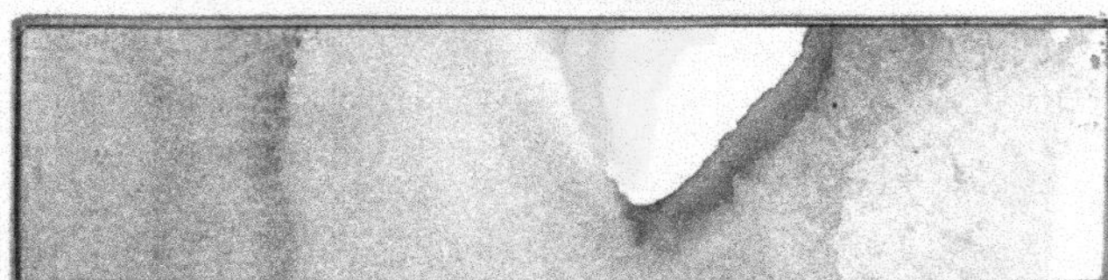

418
CCCCXVIII
DM 09 ©

THE NEW JERUSALEM

9 THEN ONE OF THE SEVEN ANGELS
CAME TO ME, ONE OF THOSE WITH THE SE-
VEN BOWLS FULL OF THE SEVEN LAST
PLAGUES. AND HE SAID, "COME, I AM GO-
ING TO SHOW YOU THE BRIDE, THE WI-
FE OF THE LAMB."

10 HE TOOK ME UP IN A SPIRITUAL VISION

TO A VERY HIGH MOUNTAIN AND HE SHOW-
ED ME THE HOLY CITY OF JERUSALEM, CO-
MING DOWN OUT OF HEAVEN FROM GOD
AND IS ENDOWED WITH THE GLORY OF GOD.

11 IT SHINES LIKE A PRECIOUS JEWEL
THE COLOR OF CRYSTAL-CLEAR JASPER.
12 ITS WALL, LARGE AND HIGH, HAS
TWELVE GATES; STATIONED AT THEM ARE

TWELVE ANGELS.
OVER THE GATES
ARE WRITTEN THE
NAMES OF THE TWELVE
TRIBES OF THE SONS
OF ISRAEL. 13 THREE
GATES FACE THE
EAST; THREE GATES
FACE THE NORTH; THR-
EE GATES FACE THE
SOUTH AND THREE FA-
CE THE WEST. 14 THE
CITY WALL STANDS
ON TWELVE FOUNDATI-
ON STONES ON WHICH
ARE WRITTEN THE NA-
MES OF THE TWELVE
APOSTLES OF THE
LAMB. 15 THE ANGEL
WHO WAS SPEAKING
TO ME HAD A GOLDEN
MEASURING ROD TO
MEASURE THE CITY,
ITS GATES AND ITS
WALL. 16 THE CITY
IS LAID OUT LIKE A
SQUARE: ITS LENGTH
IS THE SAME AS ITS
BREADTH. HE MEASURED IT WITH HIS ROD AND
IT WAS TWELVE THOUSAND FURLONGS; ITS
LENGTH, BREADTH AND HEIGHT ARE EQUAL.

17 THEN HE MEASURED THE WALL; IT WAS
A HUNDRED AND FORTY-FOUR CUBITS HIGH.
18 THE ANGEL USED AN ORDINARY MEA-
SURE WHICH WAS, IN FACT, THAT OF AN AN-
GEL. THE WALL IS MADE OF JASPER AND
THE CITY OF PURE GOLD, CRYSTAL-CLEAR.

19 THE FOUNDATION OF THE WALL ARE ADOR-
NED WITH EVERY
KIND OF PRECIOUS
JEWEL: THE FIRST IS
JASPER, THE SECOND
SAPPHIRE, THE THIRD
TURQUOISE, THE FO-
URTH EMERALD, 20
THE FIFTH AGATE,
THE SIXTH RUBY, THE
SEVENTH CHRYSOLI-
TE, THE EIGHTH BERYL,
THE NINTH TOPAZ,
THE TENTH CHRYS-
OPRAZE, THE ELE-
VENTH HYACINTH
AND THE TWELFTH
AMETHYST. 21
THE TWELVE GATES
ARE TWELVE PEARLS,
EACH GATE MADE
OF A SINGLE PEARL
AND THE SQUARE
OF THE CITY IS
PAVED WITH GOLD
AS PURE AS TRANS-
PARENT CRYSTAL.

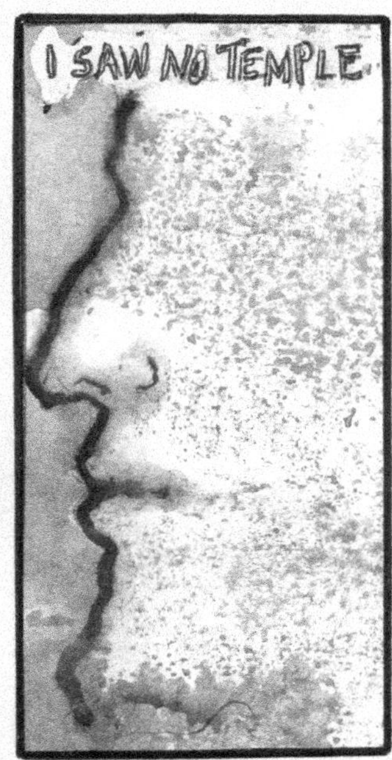

22 I SAW NO TEMPLE
IN THE CITY FOR THE
LORD GOD, MASTER
OF THE UNIVERSE, AND THE LAMB ARE THEM-
SELVES ITS TEMPLE. 23 THE CITY HAS NO
NEED OF THE LIGHT OF THE SUN OR THE MO-
ON, SINCE GOD'S GLORY IS ITS LIGHT AND
THE LAMB IS ITS LAMP. 24 THE NATIONS
WILL WALK IN ITS LIGHT AND THE KINGS OF
THE EARTH WILL BRING THEIR TREASURES

TO IT. 25 ITS GATES WILL NOT BE CLOSED AT SUNSET, FOR
THERE WILL BE NO NIGHT THERE. 26 THERE THE WEALTH
AND THE MOST PRECIOUS THINGS OF THE NATIONS WILL
BE BROUGHT. 27 NOTHING UNCLEAN WILL ENTER IT,
OR ANYONE WHO DOES WHAT IS EVIL AND FALSE
BUT ONLY THOSE WHOSE NAMES ARE WRITTEN
IN THE LAMB'S BOOK OF LIFE.

22 1 THEN HE SHOWED ME THE RIVER
OF LIFE, CLEAR AS CRYSTAL, GUSHING
FROM THE GREAT THRONE OF GOD
AND OF THE LAMB.

2 IN THE MIDDLE OF THE CITY, ON BOTH
SIDES OF THE RIVER ARE THE TREES OF LI-
FE PRODUCING FRUIT TWELVE TIMES, ONCE
EACH TIME OF THE MONTH. THE LEAVES OF
WHICH ARE FOR THE HEALING OF THE NA-
TIONS.
3 NO LONGER WILL THERE BE A CURSE;
THE THRONE OF GOD AND OF THE LAMB WILL
BE IN THE CITY AND GOD'S SERVANTS WILL
LIVE IN HIS PRESENCE. 4 THEY WILL

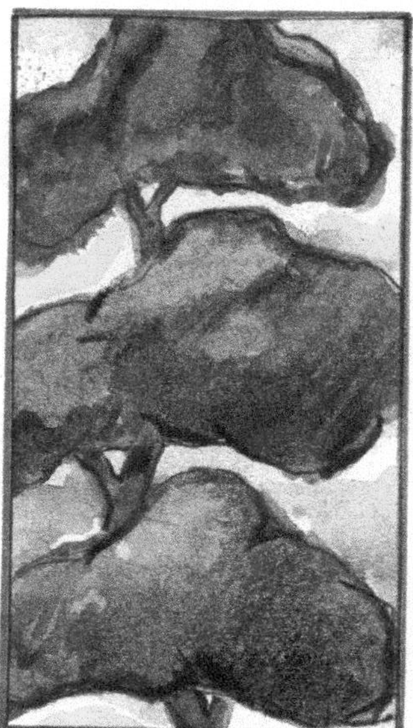

SEE HIS FACE AND
HIS NAME WILL BE
ON THEIR FORE-
HEADS. 5 THERE
WILL BE NO MORE
NIGHT. THEY WILL
NOT NEED THE LIGHT
OF LAMP OR SUN FOR
GOD HIMSELF WILL
BE THEIR LIGHT AND
THEY WILL REIGN
FOREVER.

I AM COMING SOON

6 THEN THE ANGEL SAID
TO ME, "THESE WORDS
ARE SURE AND TRUE; THE
LORD GOD WHO INSPIR-
ES THE PROPHETS HAS
SENT HIS ANGEL TO
SHOW HIS SERVANTS
WHAT MUST HAPPEN
SOON." 7 "I AM CO-
MING SOON! HAPPY
ARE THOSE WHO KEEP THE PROPHETIC WORDS
OF THIS BOOK."
8 I, JOHN, SAW AND HEARD ALL THIS. WHEN I
HAD SEEN AND HEARD THEM I FELL AT THE
FEET OF THE ANGEL WHO HAD SHOWN ME
EVERYTHING, TO WORSHIP HIM.

9 BUT HE SAID, "NO, I AM A FELLOW SERVANT
LIKE YOU AND YOUR BROTHERS, THE PROPHETS,

AND THOSE WHO HEED THE WORDS OF THIS
BOOK. IT IS GOD YOU MUST WORSHIP."

10 HE THEN SAID TO ME, "DO NOT KEEP
SECRET THE PROPHETIC WORDS OF THIS
BOOK BECAUSE THE TIME IS NEAR.

11 LET THE SINNER CONTINUE TO SIN AND
THE DEFILED REMAIN IN HIS DEFILEMENT;
LET THE RIGHTEOUS CONTINUE TO DO WHAT
IS RIGHT AND HE WHO IS HOLY GROW HOLIER."

12 "I AM COMING SOON, BRINGING
WITH ME THE SALARY I WILL PAY TO
EACH ONE ACCORDING TO HIS DEEDS.

13 I AM THE ALPHA AND THE OMEGA, THE
FIRST AND THE LAST, THE BEGINNING
AND THE END". 14

HAPPY ARE THOSE
WHO WASH THEIR
ROBES FOR THEY
WILL HAVE FREE
ACCESS TO THE TREE
OF LIFE AND ENTER
THE CITY THROUGH
THE GATES. 15 OUT-
SIDE ARE THE DOGS,
SORCERERS, THE
IMMORAL, MURD-
ERERS, IDOLATERS
AND ALL WHO
TAKE PLEASURE
IN FALSEHOOD!

16 "I, JESUS, SENT MY ANGEL TO MAKE KNOWN TO
YOU THESE REVELATIONS CONCERNING THE
CHURCHES.
I AM THE SHOOT AND OFFSPRING OF DAVID,
THE RADIANT MORNING STAR."

17 THE SPIRIT AND THE BRIDE SAY,
"COME!" WHO-

EVER HEARS LET
HIM SAY, "COME!"
WHOEVER THIRSTS
LET HIM APPROACH,
AND WHOEVER DESI-
RES, LET HIM FREELY
TAKE THE WATER
OF LIFE. 18 AS
FOR ME, I WARN
EVERYONE WHO HEARS
THE PROPHETIC
WORDS OF THIS BO-
OK: IF ANYONE AD-
DS ANYTHING TO
THEM, GOD WILL
PILE ON HIM THE
PLAGUES DESCRI-
BED IN THIS BOOK.
19 AND IF ANY-
ONE TAKES AWAY
WORDS FROM
THIS BOOK OF
PROPHECY, GOD
WILL TAKE FROM
HIM HIS SHARE
IN THE TREE OF
LIFE AND THE
HOLY CITY DES-
CRIBED IN THIS
BOOK. 20 HE WHO HAS DECLARED ALL
THIS SAYS, "YES, I AM COMING SOON."

AMEN! COME LORD JESUS.

21 MAY THE GRACE OF THE LORD
JESUS BE WITH YOU ALL—

CPSIA information can be obtained
at www.ICGtesting.com
Printed in the USA
LVHW072012260720
661586LV00004B/25